Large Air-Cooled Engine

SERVICE MANUAL ■ 2ND EDITION

PRIMEDIA Business Directories & Books
P.O. Box 12901 ■ Overland Park, KS 66282-2901
Phone: 800-262-1954 Fax: 800-633-6219
www.primediabooks.com

© Copyright 2000 by PRIMEDIA Business Magazines & Media Inc.   Printed in the United States of America.
Library of Congress Catalog Card Number 00-110273

June, 2002

This book can be recycled. Please remove cover.

Cover photo courtesy of:
Briggs & Stratton.

Large Air-Cooled Engine

SERVICE MANUAL ■ 2ND EDITION

Large Air-Cooled Engine Manufacturers:

- Acme
- Briggs & Stratton
- Craftsman
- Honda

- Kawasaki
- Kohler
- Onan
- Robin

- Tecumseh
- Wisconsin
- Wisconsin Robin

CLYMER PUBLICATIONS
PRIMEDIA Business Magazines & Media

Chief Executive Officer Timothy M. Andrews
President Ron Wall

The following product lines are published by PRIMEDIA Business Directories & Books.

More information available at *primediabooks.com*

CONTENTS

GENERAL

ENGINE SERVICE SECTIONS

DUAL DIMENSIONS

This service manual provides specifications in both the Metric (SI) and U.S. Customary systems of measurement. The first specification is give in the the measuring system used during manufacture, while the second specification (given in the parenthesis) is the covereted measurement. For instance, a specification of "0.28 mm (0.011 inch)" would indicate that the equipment was manufactured using the metric system of measurement and U.S. Equivalent of 0.28 mm is 0.011 inch.

ENGINE DESIGN FUNDAMENTALS

ENGINE OPERATING PRINCIPLES

The engines used to power many items of power equipment in use today are basically similar. All are technically known as "Internal Combustion Reciprocating Engines."

The source of power is heat formed by the burning of a combustible mixture, usually petroleum products and air. In a reciprocating engine, this burning takes place in a closed cylinder containing a piston. Expansion resulting from the heat of combustion applies pressure on the piston to turn a shaft by means of a crank and connecting rod.

The fuel-air mixture may be ignited by means of an electric spark (Otto Cycle Engine) or by heat formed from compression of air in the engine cylinder (Diesel Cycle Engine). The complete series of events that must take place in order for the engine to run occurs in two revolutions of the crankshaft (four strokes of the piston in cylinder), which is referred to as a "Four-Stroke Cycle Engine."

Otto Cycle

In a spark ignition engine, a series of five events is required in order for the engine to provide power. This series of events is called the "Cycle" (or "Work Cycle") and is repeated in each cylinder of the engine as long as work is being done. This series of events that comprise the "Cycle" is as follows:

1. The mixture of fuel and air is pushed into the cylinder by atmospheric pressure when the pressure within the engine cylinder is reduced by the piston moving downward in the cylinder.

2. The mixture of fuel and air is compressed by the piston moving upward in the cylinder.

3. The compressed fuel-air mixture is ignited by a timed electric spark.

4. The burning fuel-air mixture expands, forcing the piston downward in the cylinder, thus converting the chemical energy generated by combustion into mechanical power.

5. The gaseous products formed by the burned fuel-air mixture are expelled from the cylinder so that a new "Cycle" can begin.

The above described five events that comprise the work cycle of an engine are commonly referred to as (1) INTAKE;

(2) COMPRESSION; (3) IGNITION; (4) EXPANSION (POWER); and (5) EXHAUST.

Four-stroke Cycle

In a four-stroke cycle engine operating on the Otto Cycle (spark ignition), the five events of the cycle take place in four strokes of the piston, or in two revolutions of the engine crankshaft. Thus, a power stroke occurs only on alternate downward strokes of the piston.

In view "A" of Fig. 1-1, the piston is on the first downward stroke of the cycle. The mechanically operated intake valve has opened the intake port and, as the downward movement of the piston has reduced the air pressure in the cylinder to below atmospheric pressure, air is forced through the carburetor where fuel is mixed with the air, and into the cylinder through the open intake port. The intake valve remains open and fuel-air mixture continues to flow into the cylinder until the piston reaches the bottom of its downward

stroke. As the piston starts on its first upward stroke, the mechanically operated intake valve closes and, because the exhaust valve is closed, the fuel-air mixture is compressed as in view "B."

Just before the piston reaches the top of its first upward stroke, a spark at the spark plug electrode ignites the compressed fuel-air mixture. As the engine crankshaft turns past top center, the burning fuel-air mixture expands rapidly and forces the piston downward on its power stroke as shown in view "C." As the piston reaches the bottom of the power stroke, the mechanically operated exhaust valve starts to open and as the pressure of the burned fuel-air mixture is higher than atmospheric pressure, it starts to flow out the open exhaust port. As the engine crankshaft turns past bottom center, the exhaust valve is almost completely open and remains open during the upward stroke of the piston as shown in view "D." Upward movement of the piston pushes the remaining burned fuel-air mixture out of the exhaust port. Just before the piston reaches the top of its second up-

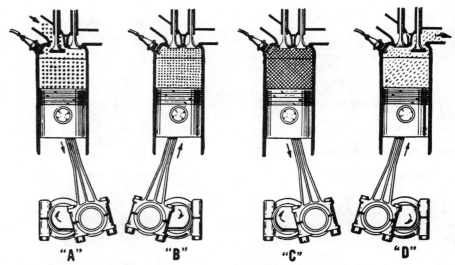

"A"   "B"   "C"   "D"

Fig. 1-1—Schematic diagram of four-stroke cycle engine operating on the Otto (spark ignition) cycle. In view "A," piston is on first downward (intake) stroke and atmospheric pressure is forcing fuel-air mixture from carburetor into cylinder through the open intake valve. In view "B," both valves are closed and piston is on its first upward stroke compressing the fuel-air mixture in cylinder. In view "C," spark across electrodes of spark plug has ignited fuel-air mixture and heat of combustion rapidly expands the burning gaseous mixture forcing the piston on its second downward (expansion or power) stroke. In view "D," exhaust valve is open and piston on its second upward (exhaust) stroke forces the burned mixture from cylinder. A new cycle then starts as in view "A."

ward or exhaust stroke, the intake valve opens and the exhaust valve closes. The cycle is completed as the crankshaft turns past top center and a new cycle begins as the piston starts downward as shown in view "A."

In a four-stroke cycle engine operating on the Diesel Cycle, the sequence of events of the cycle is similar to that described for operation on the Otto Cycle, but with the following exceptions: On the intake stroke, air only is taken into the cylinder. On the compression stroke, the air is highly compressed, which raises the temperature of the air. Just before the piston reaches top dead center, fuel is injected into the cylinder and is ignited by the heated, compressed air. The remainder of the cycle is similar to that of the Otto Cycle.

CARBURETOR FUNDAMENTALS

Function of the carburetor on a spark-ignition engine is to atomize the fuel and mix the atomized fuel in proper proportions with air flowing to the engine intake port or intake manifold. Carburetors used on engines that are to be operated at constant speeds and under even loads are of simple design because they only have to mix fuel and air in a relatively constant ratio. On engines operating at varying speeds and loads, the carburetors must be more complex because different fuel-air mixtures are required to meet the varying demands of the engine.

Requirements

To meet the demands of an engine being operated at varying speeds and loads, the carburetor must mix fuel and air at different mixture ratios. Gasoline-air mixture ratios required for different operating conditions are approximately as follows:

	Fuel	Air
Starting, cold weather	1 lb.	7 lbs.
Accelerating	1 lb.	9 lbs.
Idling (no load)	1 lb.	11 lbs.
Part open throttle	1 lb.	15 lbs.
Full load, open throttle	1 lb.	13 lbs.

Basic Design

Carburetor design is based on the venturi principle, which simply means that a gas or liquid flowing through a necked-down section (venturi) in a passage undergoes an increase in velocity (speed) and a decrease in pressure as compared to the velocity and pressure in full size sections of the passage. The principle is illustrated in Fig. 1-2, which shows air passing through a carburetor venturi. The figures given for air speeds and vacuum are approximate for a typi-

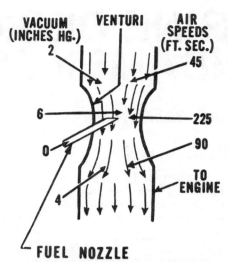

Fig. 1-2—Drawing illustrating the venturi principle upon which carburetor design is based. Figures at left are inches of mercury vacuum and those at right are air speeds in feet per second that are typical of conditions found in a carburetor operating at wide-open throttle. Zero vacuum in fuel nozzle corresponds to atmospheric pressure.

cal wide-open throttle operating condition. Due to low pressure (high vacuum) in the venturi, fuel is forced out through the fuel nozzle by the atmospheric pressure (zero vacuum) on the fuel; as fuel is emitted from the nozzle, it is atomized by the high velocity air flow and mixes with the air.

Carburetor Type

Carburetors used on the engines covered in this manual are of the float type and are either of the downdraft or side draft design. The following paragraphs describe the features and operating principles of the float type carburetor.

THROTTLE VALVE. In order to vary the speed, a valve is installed between the fuel nozzle and engine that limits the volume of combustible mixture available to the combustion chamber. When less mixture is available to the combustion area, there will be less

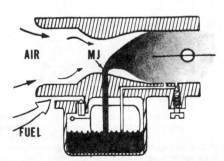

Fig. 1-3—View of carburetor showing disc-type throttle valve completely open for high-speed operation.

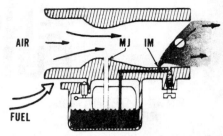

Fig. 1-4—As disc-type throttle valve is moved toward the closed position, vacuum at the main jet (MJ) may not be enough to draw fuel into the passing air and an intermediate jet (IM) is provided.

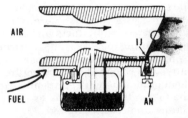

Fig. 1-5—With throttle disc nearly closed, the idle jet (IJ) is used. Usually, an adjustment needle (AN) is provided to adjust the idle mixture fuel-air ratio.

expansion, resulting in less rpm and less power. The disc (butterfly) throttle valve is most commonly used for the carburetors covered in this manual.

A typical disc-type throttle valve is shown in Figs. 1-3, 1-4 and 1-5. When disc is in the open position shown in Fig. 1-3, fuel is drawn from the main jet (MJ) into the passing air. As the throttle disc is turned, the opening of the throttle bore is decreased (Fig. 1-4) and vacuum at the venturi is insufficient to provide correct fuel-air ratio by using only the main jet. Usually an additional intermediate jet (IM) is incorporated to provide fuel at partial throttle opening. When disc is in position shown in Fig. 1-5, the throttle opening is nearly closed and fuel is drawn from an idle jet (IJ). Idle speed adjustment is accomplished by stopping rotation of the valve before throttle bore is completely closed.

VENTURI. As previously explained, a gas or liquid flowing through a necked-down section (venturi) in a passage increases in velocity (speed) and decreases in pressure as shown in Fig. 1-2. When movement of the piston draws air through the carburetor, this change of pressure is what causes the fuel to be drawn into the air as it passes the fuel nozzle. The venturi must be matched to the engine to provide the right amount of pressure drop at the venturi for correct fuel-air mixture. Some adjustment can be accomplished by making the fuel flow less (or more) restricted by changing the jet sizes; however, manufacturer's recommenda-

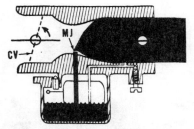

Fig. 1-6—As choke valve (CV) is closed (shown by the broken lines), vacuum is increased at main jet (MJ).

tion of carburetor and jet sizes should be closely followed.

STARTING ENRICHMENT. The ratio of fuel to air must be much richer when starting in cold weather than when running at full open throttle. A choke plate is the most commonly used method of obtaining a rich starting mixture. Fig. 1-6 shows a typical choke plate installation in relation to the carburetor venturi.

At cranking speeds, air flows through the carburetor venturi at a slow speed; thus, the pressure in the venturi does not usually decrease to the extent that atmospheric pressure on the fuel will force enough fuel from the nozzle. If the choke plate is closed, as shown by the broken line in Fig. 1-6, air cannot enter into the carburetor and pressure in the carburetor decreases greatly as the engine is turned at cranking speed. Fuel is then forced from the fuel nozzle. In manufacturing the carburetor choke plate or disc, a small hole or notch is cut in the plate so that some air can flow through the plate when it is in closed position to provide air for the starting fuel-air mixture. In some instances after starting a cold engine, it is advantageous to leave the choke plate in a partly closed position as the restriction of air flow will decrease the air pressure in the carburetor venturi, thus causing more fuel to flow from the nozzle resulting in a richer fuel-air mixture. The choke plate or disc should be in fully open position for normal engine operation.

OPERATING PRINCIPLES. The principle of float type carburetor operation is illustrated in Fig. 1-7. Fuel is delivered at inlet (I) by gravity with fuel positioned above carburetor, or by a fuel lift pump when tank is located below carburetor inlet. Fuel flows into the open inlet valve (V) until fuel level (L) in bowl lifts float against fuel valve needle and closes the valve. As fuel is emitted from the nozzle (N) when engine is running, fuel level will drop, lowering the float and allowing valve to open so that fuel will enter the carburetor to meet the requirements of the engine.

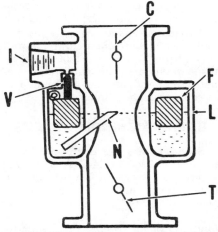

Fig. 1-7—Drawing showing basic float type carburetor design. Fuel must be delivered under pressure either by gravity or by use of fuel pump, to the carburetor fuel inlet (I). Fuel level (L) operates float (F) to open and close inlet valve (V) to control amount of fuel entering carburetor. Also shown are the fuel nozzle (N), throttle (T) and choke.

A cut-away view of a typical float type carburetor is shown in Fig. 1-8. Atmospheric pressure is maintained in fuel bowl through passage (20) which opens into carburetor air horn ahead of the choke plate (21). Fuel level is maintained at just below the level of opening (O) in nozzle (22) by the float (19) actuating the fuel inlet valve needle (8). On most carburetors, float height can be adjusted by bending float tang (5).

When engine is running at slow idle speed (throttle plate nearly closed as indicated by dotted lines in Fig. 1-8), air pressure above the throttle plate is low and atmospheric pressure in fuel bowl

forces fuel up through the nozzle and out through orifice in seat (14) where it mixes with air passing the throttle plate. The idle fuel mixture is adjustable by turning needle (15) in or out as required. Idle speed is adjustable by turning the throttle stop screw (not shown) in or out to control the amount of air passing the throttle plate.

When the throttle plate is opened to increase engine speed, the velocity of air flow through the venturi (18) increases, air pressure at the venturi decreases and fuel will flow from openings (O) in nozzle instead of through the orifice in the idle seat (14). When the engine is running at high speed, pressure in the nozzle (22) is less than at the vent (12) opening in carburetor throat above the venturi. Thus, air will enter vent and travel down the vent into the nozzle and mix with the fuel in the nozzle. This is referred to as air bleeding and is illustrated in Fig. 1-9.

Many different designs of float type carburetors will be found when servicing the different makes and models of engines. Reference should be made to the engine repair section of this manual for adjustment and overhaul specifications. Refer to the carburetor servicing paragraphs in the fundamentals section for service hints.

IGNITION SYSTEM FUNDAMENTALS

The timed spark that ignites the fuel charge in the cylinder may be supplied by either a magneto, a battery ignition system or a solid-state ignition system. To better understand the operation of

Fig. 1-8—Cross-sectional drawing of float type carburetor used on some engines.

O. Orifice
1. Main fuel needle
2. Packing
3. Packing nut
4. Carburetor bowl
5. Float tang
6. Float hinge pin
7. Gasket
8. Inlet valve
9. Fuel inlet
10. Carburetor body
11. Inlet valve seat
12. Vent
13. Throttle plate
14. Idle orifice
15. Idle fuel needle
16. Plug
17. Gasket
18. Venturi
19. Float
20. Fuel bowl vent
21. Choke
22. Fuel nozzle

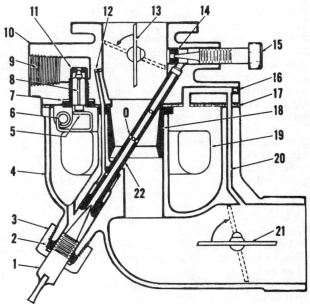

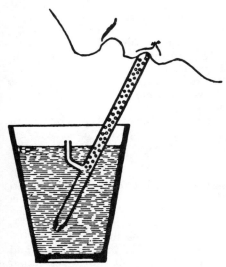

Fig. 1-9—Illustration of air bleed principle explained in text.

the components and the differences and similarities of the two systems, this section will combine the various units, and explain and compare their functions.

Theory

In the modern ignition system, a relatively weak electric current of 6 to 12 volts and 2 to 5 amperes is transformed into a momentary charge of minute amperage and extremely high (10,000-25,000) voltage capable of jumping the spark plug gap in the cylinder and igniting the fuel charge.

To understand the ignition system theory, electricity can be thought of as a stream of electrons flowing through a conductor. The force of the stream can be increased by restricting volume, or the volume increased by reducing the resistance to movement, but the total amount of power cannot be increased except by employing additional outside force. The current has an inertia of motion and resists being stopped once it has started flowing. If the circuit is broken suddenly, the force will tend to pile up temporarily, attempting to convert the speed of flow into energy.

Here is a short list of useful electrical terms and a brief explanation of their meanings:

AMPERE—The unit of measurement used to designate the amount or quantity of flow of an electrical current.

OHM—The unit of measurement used to designate the resistance of a conductor to the flow of current.

VOLT—The unit of measurement used to designate the force or pressure of an electrical current.

WATT—The unit of measurement that designates the ability of an electrical current to perform work or to measure the amount of work performed.

The four terms are directly interrelated: one ampere equaling the flow of current produced by one volt against a resistance of one ohm. One watt designates the work potential of one ampere at one volt in one second.

BATTERY IGNITION SYSTEMS

Some engines are equipped with a battery ignition system. A schematic diagram of a typical battery ignition system for a single cylinder engine is shown in Fig. 1-10.

Ignition Coil

When an electrical current is flowing through a conductor, a magnetic field exists at right angles to the current flow. As long as the conductor is relatively straight, nothing much happens, but if the conductor is coiled around a soft iron core, then the length of the iron core is at approximately right angles to the wire. A path is provided for the magnetic field and the iron core becomes a magnet as long as the current flows.

A second phenomenon of electrical action happens when a magnetic field is interrupted—a pulsation of electrical energy is formed at right angles to the lines of magnetic flow.

In a battery ignition system, these two peculiarities are combined to form an ignition coil as shown in Fig. 1-11. The inner and outer laminations are composed of soft iron and form a continuous path for a magnetic field. Around the inner laminations, but insulated from it, are many coils of fine

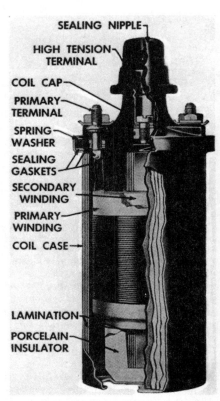

Fig. 1-11—Sectional view of a typical battery ignition coil.

copper wire. Around this coil of fine wire, but insulated from it and the iron core, are several windings of heavier copper wire. These windings are encased in the outer laminations, then in a protective case.

The outer winding of heavier wire is connected to the two screw terminals on the coil case and form the primary circuit of the coil. The inner winding of fine wire is grounded at one end and the other end is connected to the insulated, high tension terminal and forms the secondary circuit.

Primary Circuit

The primary circuit is attached to the power source in both the battery and magneto electrical systems.

In the battery system, the primary circuit consists of the battery, ignition switch, primary windings, contact points, condenser and the necessary connecting wiring as shown at (3—Fig. 1-10). When the ignition switch (2) and contact points (6) are closed, the primary circuit (3), primary windings of coil (4) and the closed contact points (6), the ground connections (G1 at battery and G2 at points) plus the engine casting or frame complete the circuit. As the current flows, a magnetic field is built up in the soft iron laminations of coil (4), which is surrounded by the primary and

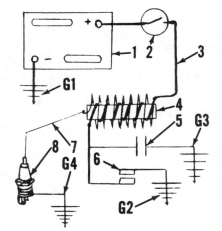

Fig. 1-10—Diagram of a typical battery ignition system. Refer to text for principles of operation.

1. Battery
2. Ignition switch
3. Primary circuit
4. Ignition coil
5. Condenser
6. Contact points
7. Secondary circuit
8. Spark plug
G1-G4. Ground connections

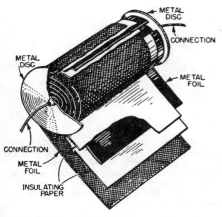

Fig. 1-12—A typical condenser consists of two metal conductors separated by layers of insulating paper and rolled into a tight cylinder.

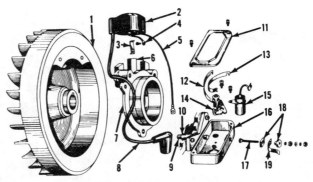

Fig. 1-14—Exploded view of a typical flywheel type magneto used on single cylinder engines in which the breaker points (14) are actuated by a cam on engine camshaft. Push rod (9) rides against cam to open and close points.

1. Flywheel	6. Armature core (laminations)	15. Condenser
2. Ignition coil	7. Crankshaft bearing retainer	16. Breaker box
3. Coil clamps	8. High tension lead	17. Terminal bolt
4. Coil ground lead	9. Push rod	18. Insulators
5. Breaker point lead	10. Bushing	19. Grounding (stop) spring
	11. Breaker box cover	
	12. Point lead strap	
	13. Breaker point spring	
	14. Breaker point assy.	

secondary windings. When the contact points (6) open to break the circuit, the current tries to flow through the path of least resistance, which is the condenser (5) until condenser capacity is reached. Then, the primary current ceases to flow and the magnetic field starts to collapse. This collapse is hastened by the condenser (Fig. 1-12), which tries to discharge its stored energy backward through the primary circuit. When the magnetic field collapses, extremely high voltage is induced in the coil secondary windings. The high voltage flows through the secondary circuit (7—Fig. 1-10) to the spark plug (8) where it jumps the plug gap and is dissipated in the engine frame through ground (G4).

Secondary Circuit

The secondary circuit carries the high voltage current from the coil to the spark plug or plugs. The secondary circuit ground at the spark plug should be of negative polarity. On systems with a separate high-tension coil, the secondary current polarity can be reversed by changing the primary circuit leads at the coil or by reversing the connections. The potential voltage available in the secondary circuit where the system is in good condition may be 18,000 to 25,000 volts. The actual voltage depends on the

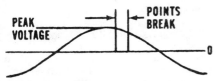

Fig. 1-13—The primary current of a magneto ignition system is an alternating current, thus, voltage varies from zero to a predetermined peak during each positive and negative cycle. To produce an adequate spark to ignite the fuel charge, the contact points must break at or near the voltage peak as shown.

resistance of the secondary circuit and the type and condition of the spark plug plays an important part in establishing the operating resistance. When the secondary current is induced in the coil, current strength continues to build up until a spark is formed across the plug gap, then the energy will be dissipated and voltage will not rise higher.

MAGNETO IGNITION SYSTEMS

In a magneto ignition system, the same principles of magnetism and electricity are involved as discussed in BATTERY IGNITION SYSTEMS section, but the method of application is somewhat different. Instead of stored chemical energy of a battery that produces a constant direct current, the source of energy is a pulsating alternating current induced in the magneto primary windings and derived from permanent magnets. Because of variation in voltage and direction of current flow (see Fig. 1-13), the ignition points must not only be correctly timed with relation to the piston, but also to break at or near peak voltage. The proper position with relation to the position of the permanent magnet is decided by laboratory tests and sometimes becomes a part of the service specifications. This position is referred to as "edge gap."

Two different types of magnetos are used on air-cooled engines and, for discussion in this section of the manual, will be classified as "flywheel type magnetos" and "self-contained unit type magnetos."

Flywheel Type Magneto

The term "flywheel type magneto" is derived from the fact that the engine flywheel carries the permanent mag-

nets and is the magneto rotor (Fig. 1-14). In some similar systems, magneto rotor is mounted on the engine crankshaft as is the flywheel, but is a part separate from the flywheel.

FLYWHEEL MAGNETO OPERATING PRINCIPLES. In Fig. 1-15, a cross-sectional view of a typical engine flywheel (magneto rotor) is shown. The arrows indicate lines of force (flux) of the permanent magnets carried by the flywheel. As indicated by arrows, direction of force of the magnetic field is from the north pole (N) of the left magnet to the south pole (S) of the right magnet.

Figs. 1-16, 1-17, 1-18 and 1-19 illustrate the operational cycle of a flywheel type magneto. In Fig. 1-16, flywheel magnets have moved to a position over the left and center legs of armature (ignition coil) core. As the magnets moved

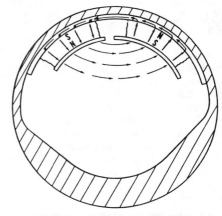

Fig. 1-15—Cross-sectional view of typical engine flywheel used with flywheel magneto type ignition system. The permanent magnets are usually cast into the flywheel. For flywheel type magnetos having the ignition coil and core mounted to outside of flywheel, magnets would be flush with outer diameter of flywheel.

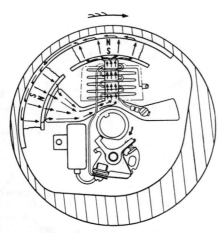

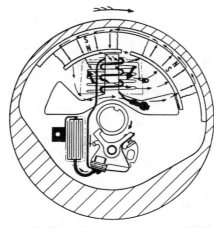

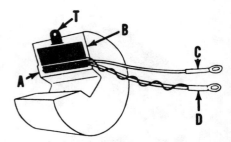

Fig. 1-20—Drawing showing construction of a typical flywheel magneto ignition coil. Primary windings are shown at (A) and secondary windings are shown at (B). Coil primary and secondary ground connection is (D). Primary connection to breaker point and condenser terminal is (C). Coil secondary (high tension) terminal is (T).

Fig. 1-16—View showing flywheel turned to a position so lines of force of the permanent magnets are concentrated in the left and center core legs and are interlocking the coil windings.

Fig. 1-18—The flywheel magnets have now turned slightly past the position shown in Fig. 1-7 and the rate of movement of lines of magnetic force cutting through the coil windings is at the maximum. At this instant, the breaker points are opened by the cam and flow of current in the primary circuit is being absorbed by the condenser, bringing the flow of current to a quick, controlled stop.

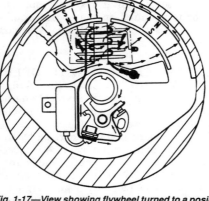

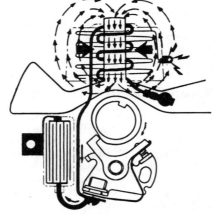

Fig. 1-17—View showing flywheel turned to a position so lines of force of the permanent magnets are being withdrawn from the left and center core legs and are being attracted by the center and right core legs. While this event is happening, the lines of force are cutting up through the coil windings section between the left and center legs and are cutting down through the section between the right and center legs as indicated by the heavy black arrows. As the breaker points are now closed by the cam, a current is induced in the primary ignition circuit as the lines of force cut through the coil windings.

Fig. 1-19—View showing magneto ignition coil, condenser and breaker points at same instant as illustrated in Fig. 1-18; however, arrows illustrate lines of force of the electromagnetic field established by current in primary coil windings rather than the lines of force of permanent magnets. As the current in the primary circuit ceases to flow, the electromagnetic field collapses rapidly, cutting the coil windings as indicated by heavy arrows and inducing a very high voltage in the secondary coil winding resulting in the ignition spark.

into this position, their magnetic field was attracted by the armature core as illustrated in Fig. 1-16 and a potential voltage (emf) was induced in the coil windings. However, this emf was not sufficient to cause current to flow across the spark plug electrode gap in the high tension circuit and the points were open in the primary circuit.

In Fig. 1-17, flywheel magnets have moved to a new position to where their magnetic field is being attracted by the center and right legs of the armature core, and is being withdrawn from the left and center legs. As indicated by heavy black arrows, lines of force are cutting up through the section of coil

windings between the left and center legs of the armature and are cutting down through the coil windings section between the center and right legs. The resulting emf induced in the primary circuit will cause a current to flow through the primary coil windings and breaker points which have now been closed by action of the cam.

At the instant the movement of lines of force cutting through the coil winding section is at the maximum rate, maximum flow of current is obtained in the

primary circuit. At this time, the cam opens the breaker points interrupting the primary circuit and, for an instant, flow of current is absorbed by the condenser as illustrated in Fig. 1-18. An emf is also induced in the secondary coil windings, but the voltage is not sufficient to cause the current to flow across the spark plug gap.

Flow of current in the primary windings created a strong electromagnetic field surrounding the coil windings and up through the center leg of armature core as shown in Fig. 1-19. As the breaker points were opened by the cam, interrupting the primary circuit, the magnetic field starts to collapse cutting through the coil windings as indicated by heavy black arrows. The emf induced in the primary circuit would be sufficient to cause a flow of current across the opening breaker points were it not for the condenser absorbing the flow of current and bringing it to a controlled stop. This allows the electromagnetic field to collapse at such a rapid rate to induce a very high voltage in the coil high tension or secondary windings. This voltage, on the order of 15,000 to 25,000 volts, is sufficient to break down the resistance air gap between the spark plug electrodes and a current will flow across the gap. This creates the ignition spark which ignites the compressed fuel-air mixture in the engine cylinder.

A drawing of an ignition coil typical of the type used on flywheel magneto systems is shown in Fig. 1-20.

Self-Contained Unit Type Magneto

Some engines are equipped with a magneto which is a self-contained unit as shown in Fig. 1-21. This type magneto is driven from the engine timing gears via a gear or coupling. All components of the magneto are enclosed in one housing, and the magneto can be removed from engine as a unit.

Fig. 1-21—Some engines are equipped with a unit type magneto having all components enclosed in a single housing (H). Magneto is removable as a unit after removing retaining nuts (N). Stop button (B) grounds out primary magneto circuit to stop engine. Timing window is (W).

UNIT TYPE MAGNETO OPERATING PRINCIPLES. A schematic diagram of a unit type magneto is shown in Fig. 1-22. Magneto rotor is driven through an impulse coupling (shown at right side of illustration). Function of impulse coupling is to increase rotating speed of the rotor, thereby increasing magneto efficiency, at engine cranking speed.

A typical impulse coupling for a single cylinder engine magneto is shown in Fig. 1-23. At cranking speed, the coupling hub pawl engages a stop pin in magneto housing as engine piston is coming up on compression stroke. This stops the rotation of the coupling hub assembly and magneto rotor. A spring within the coupling shell (see Fig. 1-24) connects the shell and coupling hub; as engine continues to turn, the spring

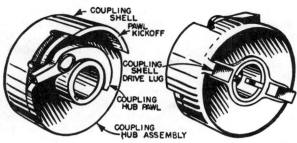

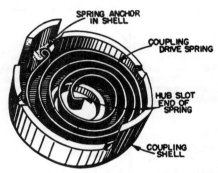

Fig. 1-23—Views of typical impulse coupling for magneto driven by engine shaft with slotted drive connection.

winds up until the pawl kickoff contacts the pawl and disengages it from the stop pin. This occurs at the time an ignition spark is required to ignite the compressed fuel-air mixture in the engine cylinder. As the pawl is released, spring connecting coupling shell and hub unwinds and rapidly spins magneto rotor.

Magneto rotor (see Fig. 1-22) carries permanent magnets. As the rotor turns, the magnetic fields of the magnets alternately are attracted, then withdrawn from laminations. Due to this rapid movement of lines of force, a current will be induced in the primary magneto circuit as the coil windings are cut by lines of force. At the instant maximum current is induced in the primary windings, the breaker points are opened by a cam on the magneto rotor shaft, interrupting the primary circuit. The lines of magnetic force established by the primary current will cut through the secondary windings at a rapid rate to induce a very high voltage in secondary (or high tension) circuit. This voltage will break down the resistance of the spark plug electrode gap and a spark across the electrodes will result.

Fig. 1-24—View showing impulse coupling shell and drive spring removed from coupling hub assembly. Refer to Fig 1-23 for views of assembled unit.

At engine operating speeds, centrifugal force will hold the impulse coupling hub pawl (Fig. 1—23) in a position so it cannot engage the stop pin in the magneto housing, and the magnetic rotor will be driven through the spring (Fig. 1-24) connecting the coupling shell to the coupling hub. The difference in degrees of impulse coupling shell rotation between position of retarded spark at cranking speed and normal running spark is known as impulse coupling lag angle.

SOLID-STATE IGNITION SYSTEMS

Breakerless Magneto System

Solid-state (breakerless) magneto ignition system operates somewhat on the same basic principles as the conventional-type flywheel magneto previously described. The main difference is that the breaker contact points are replaced by a solid-state electronic Gate Controlled Switch (GCS) which has no moving parts. Since in a conventional system the breaker points are closed over a longer period of crankshaft rotation than is the "GCS," a diode has been added to the circuit to provide the same characteristics as closed breaker points.

BREAKERLESS MAGNETO OPERATING PRINCIPLES. The same basic principles as outlined for conventional flywheel type magneto also apply

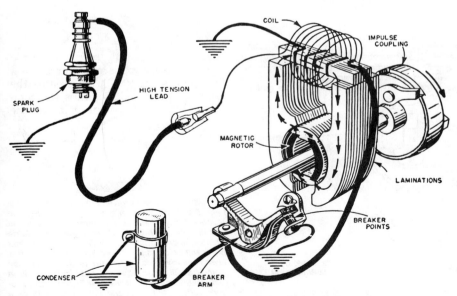

Fig. 1-22—Schematic diagram of typical unit type magneto for single cylinder engine.

to solid-state magneto systems. Therefore, principles of different components (diode and GCS) will complete the operating principles of solid-state magneto.

The diode is represented in wiring diagrams by the symbol shown in Fig. 1-25. The diode is an electronic device

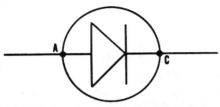

Fig. 1-25—In a diagram of an electrical circuit, the diode is represented by the symbol shown above. The diode will allow current to flow in one direction only, from cathode (C) to anode (A).

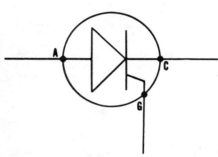

Fig. 1-26—The symbol used for a Gate Controlled Switch (GCS) in an electrical diagram is shown above. The GCS will permit current to flow from cathode (C) to anode (A) when "turned on" by a positive electrical charge at gate (G) terminal.

that will permit passage of electrical current in one direction only. In electrical schematic diagrams, current flow is opposite the direction that the arrow part of the symbol is pointing.

The symbol shown in Fig. 1-26 is used to represent a gate controlled switch (GCS) in wiring diagrams. The GCS acts as a switch to permit passage of current from cathode (C) terminal to anode (A) terminal when in "ON" state and will not permit electric current to flow when in "OFF" state. The GCS can be turned "ON" by a positive surge of electricity at gate (G) terminal and will remain "ON" as long as current remains positive at gate terminal or as long as current is flowing through GCS from cathode (C) terminal to anode (A) terminal.

The basic components and wiring diagram for solid-state breakerless magneto are shown schematically in Fig. 1-27. In Fig. 1-28, magneto rotor (flywheel) is turning and ignition coil magnets have just moved into position so their lines of force are cutting the ignition coil windings and producing a negative surge of current in the primary windings. The diode allows current to flow opposite to the direction of the diode symbol arrow and action is the same as conventional magneto with breaker points closed. As the rotor (flywheel) continues to turn as shown in Fig. 1-29, direction of magnetic flux lines will reverse in the armature center leg. Direction of current will change in the

primary coil circuit and the previously conducting diode will be shut off. At this point, neither diode is conducting. As voltage begins to build up as the rotor continues to turn, condenser acts as a buffer to prevent excessive voltage build up at the GCS before it is triggered.

When rotor reaches the approximate position shown in Fig. 1-30, maximum flux density has been achieved in the center leg or armature. At this time the GCS is triggered. Triggering is accomplished by the triggering coil armature moving into the field of the permanent magnet which induces a positive voltage

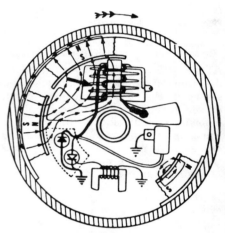

Fig. 1-28—View showing flywheel of breakerless magneto system at position where lines of force of ignition coil magnets are being drawn into left and center legs of magneto armature. The diode acts as a closed set of breaker points in completing the primary ignition circuit at this time.

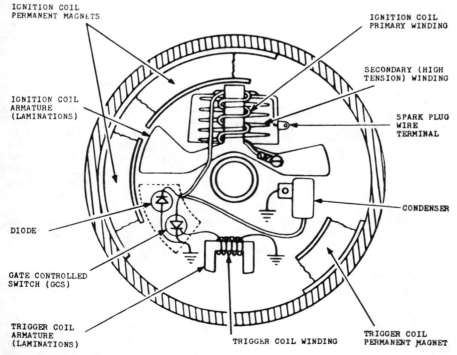

IGNITION COIL PERMANENT MAGNETS

IGNITION COIL PRIMARY WINDING

SECONDARY (HIGH TENSION) WINDING

IGNITION COIL ARMATURE (LAMINATIONS)

SPARK PLUG WIRE TERMINAL

DIODE

CONDENSER

GATE CONTROLLED SWITCH (GCS)

TRIGGER COIL ARMATURE (LAMINATIONS)

TRIGGER COIL WINDING

TRIGGER COIL PERMANENT MAGNET

Fig. 1-27—Schematic diagram of typical breakerless magneto ignition system. Refer to Figs. 1-28, 1-29 and 1-30 for schematic views of operating cycle.

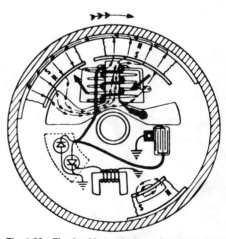

Fig. 1-29—Flywheel is turning to point where magnetic flux lines through armature center leg will reverse direction and current through primary coil circuit will reverse. As current reverses, diode which was previously conducting will shut off and there will be no current flow. When magnetic flux lines have reversed in armature center leg, voltage potential will again build up, but since GCS is in "OFF" state, no current will flow. To prevent excessive voltage build up, the condenser acts as a buffer.

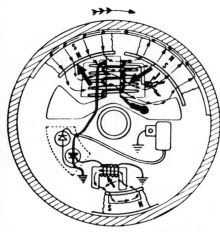

Fig. 1-30—With flywheel in the approximate position shown, maximum voltage potential is present in windings of primary coil. At this time the triggering coil armature has moved into the field of permanent magnet and a positive voltage is induced on the gate of the GCS. The GCS is triggered and primary coil current flows, resulting in the formation of an electromagnetic field around the primary coil which induces a voltage of sufficient potential in the secondary windings to "fire" the spark plug.

on the gate of GCS. Primary coil current flow results in the formation of an electromagnetic field around the primary coil which induces a voltage of sufficient potential in the secondary coil windings to "fire" the spark plug.

When the rotor (flywheel) has moved the magnets past the armature, GCS will cease to conduct and revert to "OFF" state until it is triggered. The condenser will discharge during the time the GCS was conducting.

Capacitor Discharge System

Capacitor discharge (CD) ignition system uses a permanent magnet rotor (flywheel) to induce a current in a coil, but unlike the conventional flywheel magneto and solid-state breakerless magneto described previously, current is stored in a capacitor (condenser). Then, the stored current is discharged

through a transformer coil to create the ignition spark. Refer to Fig. 1-31 for a schematic of a typical capacitor discharge ignition system.

CAPACITOR DISCHARGE OPERATING PRINCIPLES. As the permanent flywheel magnets pass by the input generating coil (1—Fig. 1-31), the current produced charges a capacitor (6). Only half of the generated current passes through the diode (3) to charge the capacitor. Reverse current is blocked by the diode (3) but passes through Zener diode (2) to complete the reverse circuit. Zener diode (2) also limits the maximum voltage of forward current. As the flywheel continues to turn and the magnets pass the trigger coil (4), a small amount of electrical current is generated. This current opens a gate controlled switch (5) allowing the capacitor to discharge through the pulse transformer (7). The rapid voltage rise in transformer primary coil induces a high voltage secondary current which produces the ignition spark when it jumps the spark plug gap.

Spark Plug

In any spark ignition engine, the spark plug (Fig. 1-32) provides the means for igniting the compressed fuel-air mixture in the cylinder. Before an electric charge can move across an air gap, the intervening air must be charged with electricity, or ionized. The spark plug gap becomes more easily ionized if the spark plug ground is of negative polarity. If the spark plug is properly gapped and the system is not shorted, not more than 7,000 volts may be required to initiate a spark. Higher voltage is required as the spark plug warms up, or if compression pressures or the distance of the air gap is increased. Compression pressures are highest at full throttle and relatively slow engine speeds. Therefore, high

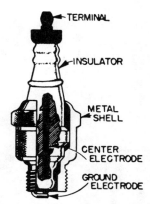

Fig. 1-32—Cross-sectional drawing of spark plug showing construction.

voltage requirements or a lack of available secondary voltage, most often shows up as a miss during maximum acceleration from a slow engine speed. There are many different types and sizes of spark plugs that are designed for a number of specific requirements.

THREAD SIZE. The threaded shell portion of the spark plug and the attaching holes in the cylinder are manufactured to meet certain industry established standards. The diameter is referred to as "Thread Size." Those commonly used are: 10 mm, 14 mm, 18 mm, 7/8 inch and 1/2 inch pipe.

REACH. The length of thread and the thread depth in cylinder head or wall are also standardized throughout the industry. This dimension is measured from gasket seat of plug to cylinder end of thread (Fig. 1-33).

HEAT RANGE. During engine operation, part of the heat generated during combustion is transferred to the spark plug and from the plug to the cooling medium through the shell threads and gasket. The operating temperature of the spark plug plays an important part in engine operation. If too much heat is retained by the plug, the fuel-air mixture may be ignited by contact with the heated surface before the ignition spark occurs. If not enough heat is retained, partially burned combustion products (soot, carbon and oil) may build up on the plug tip resulting in "fouling" or shorting out of the plug. If this happens, the secondary current is dissipated uselessly as it is generated instead of bridging the plug gap as a useful spark and the engine will misfire.

The operating temperature of the plug tip can be controlled, within limits, by altering the length of the path the heat must follow to reach the threads and gasket of the plug (Fig. 1-34). Thus,

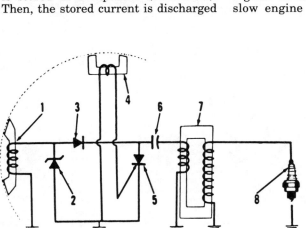

Fig. 1-31—Schematic diagram of typical capacitor discharge ignition system.

1. Generating coil
2. Zener diode
3. Diode
4. Trigger coil
5. Gate controlled switch
6. Capacitor
7. Pulse transformer (coil)
8. Spark plug

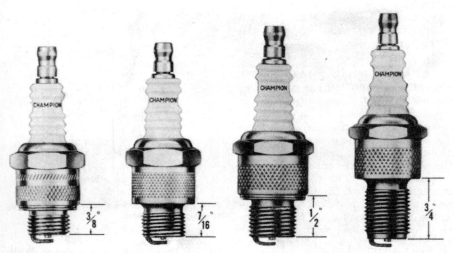

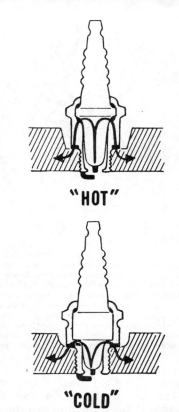

Fig. 1-33—*Views of spark plugs of various "reaches." A 3/8-inch reach spark plug measures 3/8 inch from firing end of shell to gasket surface of shell.*

a plug with a short, stubby insulator around the center electrode will run cooler than one with a long slim insulator. Most plugs in the more popular sizes are available in a number of heat ranges that are interchangeable within the group. The proper heat range is determined by engine design and the type of service. Like most other elements of design, the plug type installed as original equipment is usually a compromise and is either the most suitable plug for average conditions or the best plug to meet the two extremes of service expected. No one spark plug, however, can be ideally suited for long periods of slow-speed operation and still be the best possible type for high-speed operation.

"HOT"

"COLD"

Fig. 1-34—*Spark plug tip temperature is controlled by the length of the path*

SERVICE FUNDAMENTALS

TROUBLESHOOTING

Most performance problems, such as failure to start, failure to run properly or missing out, are caused by malfunction of the ignition system or fuel system. The experienced serviceman generally develops and follows a logical sequence in troubleshooting that will most likely lead him quickly to the source of trouble. One such sequence might be as follows:

FAILS TO START

1. Remove and examine spark plugs. If fuel is reaching the cylinder in proper amount, there should be an odor of gasoline on the plugs if they are cold. Too much fuel can foul the plugs, causing engine not to start. Fouled plugs are wet in appearance and easily detected. The presence of fouled plugs is not a sure indication that the trouble has been located, however. The engine might have started before fouling occurred if the ignition system had been in good shape.

2. With spark plug removed, hold spark plug wire about $1/8$ to $1/4$ inch away from an unpainted part of the cylinder head or cylinder and crank the engine sharply. The resulting spark may not be visible in bright daylight but a distinct snap should be heard as the spark jumps the gap.

If carburetor and ignition were both apparently in good condition when tested in (1) and (2) above, check other elements of the engine such as crossed spark plug wires, improper timing, etc. A systematic search will usually pinpoint the cause of trouble with minimum delay or confusion.

DIAGNOSIS. If the presence of fuel was not apparent when checked as in (1) above and the spark seemed satisfactory when checked as in (2), systematically check the fuel system for the cause of trouble. The following are some of the probable causes:

  a. No fuel in tank
  b. Fuel shut-off valve closed
  c. Fuel tank vent closed or plugged
  d. Carburetor not primed
  e. Choke or starting valve incorrectly used or malfunctioning
  f. Water or dirt in the fuel
  g. Fuel line pinched or kinked
  h. Clogged fuel shut off, fuel line or filter
  i. Carburetor dirty or incorrectly adjusted

  j. Carburetor fuel inlet needle stuck closed
  k. Inlet or exhaust valve stuck open

If the presence of too much fuel was apparent when checked in (1) above and the spark seemed satisfactory when checked as in (2), check the fuel system for the cause of trouble. Some probable causes are as follows:

  a. Choke plate stuck in closed position
  b. Float height set incorrectly
  c. Foreign material stuck in fuel inlet valve preventing needle from seating properly
  d. Worn or damaged fuel inlet valve needle and seat

If ignition trouble was indicated when checked as outlined in (2) above, check the electrical system for causes of trouble. Some probable causes are as follows:

  a. Battery voltage low (battery ignition models)
  b. Ignition breaker points improperly adjusted
  c. Shorted wire or stop switch
  d. Open (broken) wire
  e. Loose or corroded connections
  f. Condenser shorted
  g. Incorrect gap between primary coil and flywheel magnets
  h. Flywheel loose
  i. Flywheel key sheared
  j. Faulty coil
  k. Ignition breaker point contacts pitted, burned or dirty (new ignition points are sometimes coated with protective oil)
  l. Faulty solid-state ignition unit

FAULTY RUNNING ENGINE

The diagnosis of trouble in a running engine depends on experience, knowledge and acute observation. A continuous miss on one cylinder of a two-cylinder engine usually can be isolated by observing the items listed in the previous paragraphs under FAILS TO START.

Faults, such as not enough power or speed, usually can be traced to improper tuning. Make sure that air filter is clean and in good condition and the exhaust pipe and muffler are open (not clogged). Ignition timing and carburetor must be

correctly adjusted. The carburetor jet sizes, clip position in valve needle and idle mixture needle settings listed in the individual service sections in this manual are "normal" settings. Altitude above sea level, rider's weight, driving habits, etc., may require different sizes and settings than those listed. Ignition timing on two-cylinder engines must be the same for each cylinder. In addition to normal engine tuning procedures, check the following: sprocket sizes incorrect; drive chain too tight or too loose; tire pressure too low; brakes dragging; clutch slipping; damaged pistons, rings and/or cylinders; loose cylinder head nuts; leaking head gasket; leaking crankcase seals.

SPECIAL NOTES ON TROUBLESHOOTING

ENGINE OVERHEATS. Probable causes of engine overheating include:

1. Dirt or debris accumulation on or between cooling fins on cylinder and head.

2. Too lean fuel-air adjustment of carburetor.

3. Improper ignition timing. Check breaker point gap and ignition timing.

4. Missing or bent shields or blower housing. (On models with cooling blower, never attempt to operate without all shields and blower housing in place.)

5. Engines being operated under loads in excess of rated engine horsepower or at extremely high ambient (surrounding) air temperatures may overheat.

SPARK PLUG. The appearance of the spark plug will be altered by use, but careful examination of the plug tip can contribute useful information. The accompanying pictures (Figs. 2-1 through

Fig. 2-1—Normal plug appearance. Insulator is light tan to gray in color and electrodes are not burned. Renew plug at regular intervals as recommended by manufacturer.

Fig. 2-2—Appearance of spark plug indicating cold fouling. Cause of cold fouling may be use of a too-cold plug, excessive idling or light loads, carburetor choke out of adjustment, carburetor adjusted too "rich" or air filter dirty or wet.

Fig. 2-3—Appearance of spark plug indicating wet fouling: a wet, black oil film over entire firing end of plug. Cause may be oil getting by worn valve guides, worn oil rings or plugged crankcase breather.

Fig. 2-4—Appearance of spark plug indicating overheating. Check for plugged cooling fins, bent or damaged blower housing or engine being operated without all shields in place. Also can be caused by too lean a fuel air mixture.

2-4) illustrate typical conditions. Listed also are the probable causes and suggested corrective measures.

MAINTENANCE

SPARK PLUG

The recommended type of spark plug, heat range and electrode gap is listed in the appropriate MAINTENANCE section for each engine. Under light loads or low speeds, a spark plug of the same size with a higher (hotter) heat range may be installed. If subjected to heavy loads and high speeds, a colder plug may be necessary.

The spark plug electrode gap should be adjusted on most plugs by bending the ground electrode. Refer to Fig. 2-5.

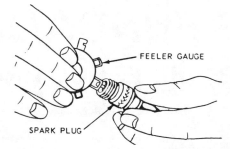

FEELER GAUGE

SPARK PLUG

Fig. 2-5—Be sure to check spark plug electrode gap with proper size feeler gauge and adjust gap to specification recommended by manufacturer.

Spark plugs are usually cleaned by abrasive action commonly referred to as "sand blasting." Actually, ordinary sand is not used. Rather, a special abrasive is used that is nonconductive to electricity even when melted, thus the abrasive cannot short out the plug current. Extreme care should be used in cleaning the plugs after sand blasting; any abrasive particles left on the plug may cause damage to piston rings, piston or cylinder walls.

NOTE: Some engine manufacturers do not recommend cleaning spark plugs with an abrasive cleaner due to the possibility that the abrasive material may not be removed completely from the spark plug following the cleaning procedure.

After plug is cleaned by abrasive, and before gap is set, the electrode surfaces between the grounded and insulated electrodes should be cleaned and returned as nearly as possible to original shape by filing with a point file. Failure to properly dress the electrodes can result in high secondary voltage requirements and misfire of the plugs.

CAUTION: Use special care when filing the electrodes of spark plugs using precious metal electrodes. Precious metal electrodes are usually softer than normal plugs and can be easily damaged by filing. Electrode gap for plugs with precious metal electrodes usually can be set for less gap than other spark plugs.

It is usually necessary to clean or renew spark plugs shortly after overhauling the engine. The oil used to coat engine parts during assembly may foul the plugs quickly. During the break-in period, a higher (hotter) heat range plug may be used to reduce fouling.

CARBURETOR

The bulk of carburetor service consists of cleaning, inspection and adjustment. After considerable service, it may become necessary to overhaul the carburetor and renew worn parts to restore original operating efficiency. Although carburetor condition affects engine operating economy and power, ignition and engine compression also must be considered to determine and correct causes.

Before dismantling carburetor for cleaning and inspection, clean all external surfaces and remove accumulated dirt and grease. If fuel starvation is suspected, all filters in carburetor, shutoff valve and tank should be inspected. Because of inadequate fuel handling methods, rust and other foreign matter may sometimes block or partially block these filters. Under no circumstances should these filters be removed from the fuel system. If filters are removed, the blockage will most likely occur within the carburetor and cleaning will be frequent and more difficult.

Refer to appropriate maintenance section for carburetor exploded or cross sectional views. Disassemble the carburetor and note any discrepancies that may cause a malfunction. Thoroughly clean and inspect each part. Wash jets and passages and blow clear with clean, dry, compressed air.

NOTE: Do not use a drill or wire to clean jets because the possible enlargement of holes will disturb calibration.

Measurement of jets to determine extent of wear is difficult and installation of new parts usually ensures satisfaction. Sizes are usually stamped on each jet.

Inspect float pin and needle valve for wear and renew if necessary. Check metal floats for leaks and dual-type floats for alignment of float sections.

NOTE: Do not attempt to resolder leaky floats.

Check fit of all moving parts. Binding or excessive clearance of all parts should be corrected. Mixture adjustment needles must not be worn or grooved.

When reassembling, be sure float level (or fuel level) is properly adjusted as listed in the CARBURETOR paragraph of the appropriate maintenance section.

Normal adjustment will be limited to replacement of recommended standard-size jets and turning idle mixture and high speed mixture needles (screws). Refer to the appropriate CARBURE-TOR paragraph within the specific maintenance section for further explanation and views of carburetors.

IGNITION AND ELECTRICAL

The fundamentals of ignition and electrical system service are outlined in the following paragraphs. Refer to the appropriate heading for type of system being inspected or overhauled. A simple, easily constructed test lamp is shown in Fig. 2-6. A similar test lamp or ohmmeter can be used to facilitate repair.

BATTERY IGNITION. Repair is usually limited to renewal of breaker points and/or condenser and adjustment of ignition timing. Refer to the appropriate MAINTENANCE section for recommended breaker point gap and ignition timing for each model.

BREAKER POINTS. Using a small screwdriver, separate and inspect condition of contacts. If burned or deeply pitted, points should be renewed. If contacts are clean to grayish in color, disconnect condenser and coil lead wires from breaker point terminal. Connect one lead (C1—Fig. 2-6) to the insulated breaker point terminal and the other (C2) to engine (ground). Light should burn with points closed and go out with points open. If light does not burn, little or no contact is indicated and points should be cleaned or renewed and contact maximum gap should be reset.

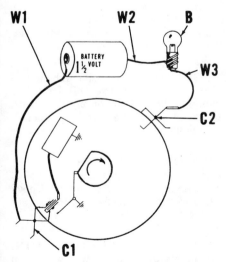

Fig. 2-6—Drawing of a simple test lamp for checking ignition timing and various other complete circuits. Test lamp consists of 1 1/2 volt battery, 1 1/2 volt lamp (B), wires (W1, W2 & W3) and spring clamps (C1 & C2).

NOTE: In some cases, new breaker point contact surfaces may be coated with oil or wax.

If light does not go out when points are opened, breaker arm insulation is defective and points should be renewed.

Adjust breaker point gap as follows unless manufacturer specifies adjusting breaker gap to obtain correct ignition timing. First, turn engine so points are closed to be sure the contact surfaces are in alignment and seat squarely. Then, turn engine so breaker point opening is maximum and adjust breaker gap to manufacturer's specification. Be sure to recheck gap after tightening breaker point base retaining screws.

CONDENSER. To check condition of the condenser without special test equipment, proceed as follows: The condenser case and wire should be visually checked for any obvious damage. Connect one end of the test lamp (C1—Fig. 2-6) to terminal at end of condenser wire and other end to condenser case. If light goes on, condenser is shorted and should be renewed. It is usually a good practice to renew condenser when breaker points are renewed.

IGNITION COIL. If a coil tester is available, condition of coil can be checked. However, if tester is not available, a reasonably satisfactory performance test can be made as follows:

Disconnect high-tension wire from spark plug. Turn engine so cam has allowed breaker points to close. With ignition switch on, open and close points with small screwdriver while holding high-tension lead about 1/8 to 1/4 inch away from engine ground. A bright blue spark should snap across the gap between spark plug wire and ground each time the points are opened. If no spark occurs, or spark is weak and yellow-orange, renewal of the ignition coil is indicated.

Sometimes an ignition coil may perform satisfactorily when cold but fail after engine has run for some time and coil is hot. Check coil when hot if this condition is indicated.

IGNITION TIMING. On some engines, ignition timing is non-adjustable and a certain breaker point gap is specified. On other engines, timing is adjustable by changing the position of the stator plate with a specified breaker point gap or by simply varying the breaker point gap to obtain correct timing. Ignition timing is usually specified either in degrees of engine (crankshaft)

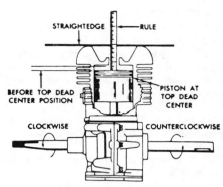

Fig. 2-7—On some engines, it will be necessary to measure piston travel with a rule, dial indicator or special timing gauge when adjusting or checking ignition timing.

rotation or in piston travel before the piston reaches top dead center position.

Some engines may have timing marks or locating pin to locate the crankshaft at proper position for the ignition spark to occur (breaker points begin to open). If not, it will be necessary to measure piston travel (Fig. 2-7) or install a degree wheel on engine crankshaft.

A timing light as shown in Fig. 2-6 is a valuable aid in checking or adjusting engine timing. After disconnecting the ignition coil lead from the breaker point terminal, connect the leads of the timing light as shown. If timing is adjustable by moving the stator plate, be sure the breaker point gap is adjusted as specified. Then, to check timing, slowly turn engine in normal direction of rotation past the point where ignition spark should occur. The timing light should be on, then go out (breaker points open) just as the correct timing location is passed. If not, turn engine to proper timing location and adjust timing by relocating the breaker point base plate or varying the breaker contact gap as specified by appropriate section for each model. Recheck timing to be sure adjustment is correct.

If ignition is equipped with advancing mechanism (manual control or automatic, centrifugal advance), make sure timing is checked when fully advanced. On some models, timing can be checked using an automotive power timing light when engine is running.

Flywheel Magneto

Repair is usually limited to renewal of breaker points and/or condenser and adjustment of ignition timing. Refer to appropriate MAINTENANCE section for recommended breaker point gap and ignition timing for each model.

BREAKER POINTS. The same general service procedure is used as in the preceding paragraph for BATTERY IGNITION. Holes may be provided in the flywheel for adjustment; however, flywheel usually must be removed for renewal of ignition points.

CONDENSER. The same general procedure is used to check condenser as outlined in previous BATTERY IGNITION system. Condenser is usually located under the flywheel.

ARMATURE AIR GAP. To fully concentrate the magnetic field of the flywheel, magnets pass as closely to the armature core as possible without danger of metal-to-metal contact. The clearance between the flywheel magnets and the legs of the armature core is called the armature air gap.

On magnetos where the armature and high-tension coil are located outside of the flywheel rim, adjustment of the armature air gap is made as follows: See Fig. 2-8. Turn the engine so that the flywheel magnets are located directly under the legs of the armature core and check the clearance between the armature core and flywheel magnets. If the measured clearance is not within manufacturer's specifications, loosen the armature mounting screws and place shims of thickness equal to minimum air gap specifications between the magnets and armature core. The magnets will pull the armature core against the shim stock. Tighten the armature core mounting screws, remove the shim stock and turn the engine through several revolutions to be sure the flywheel does not contact the armature core.

Where the armature core is located under or behind the flywheel, the following methods may be used to check and adjust armature air gap: On some engines, slots or openings are provided in the flywheel through which the armature air gap can be checked. Some engine manufacturers provide a cut-away flywheel that can be installed temporarily for checking the armature air gap.

Another method of checking the armature air gap is to remove the flywheel and place a layer of plastic tape equal to the minimum specified air gap over the legs of the armature core. Reinstall flywheel and turn engine through several revolutions and remove flywheel. No evidence of contact between the flywheel magnets and plastic tape should be noticed. Then, cover the legs of the armature core with a layer of tape equal to the maximum specified air gap. Reinstall flywheel and turn engine through several revolutions. Indication of the flywheel magnets contacting the plastic tape should be noticed after the flywheel is again removed. If the magnets contact the first thin layer of tape applied to the armature core legs, or if they do not contact the second thicker layer of tape, armature air gap is not within specifications and should be adjusted.

NOTE: Before loosening armature core mounting screws, scribe a mark on mounting plate against edge of armature core so that adjustment of air gap can be gauged.

MAGNETO EDGE GAP. The point of maximum acceleration of the movement of the flywheel magnetic field through the high-tension coil (and, therefore, the point of maximum current induced in the primary coil windings) occurs when the trailing edge of the flywheel magnet is slightly past the last leg of the armature core. The exact point of maximum primary current is determined by using electrical measuring devices, the distance between the trailing edge of the flywheel magnet and the leg of the armature core at this point is measured and becomes a service specification. This distance, which is stated either in thousandths of an inch or in degrees of flywheel rotation, is called the Edge Gap or "E" Gap.

For maximum strength of the ignition spark, the breaker points should just start to open when the flywheel magnets are at the specified edge gap position. Usually, edge gap is non-adjustable and will be maintained at the proper dimension if the contact breaker points are adjusted to the recommended gap and the correct breaker cam is installed. However, magneto edge gap can change (and thereby reduce spark intensity) due to the following:

a. Flywheel drive key sheared
b. Flywheel drive key worn (loose)
c. Keyway in flywheel or crankshaft worn (oversized)
d. Loose flywheel retaining nut, which also can cause any above listed difficulty
e. Excessive wear on breaker cam
f. Breaker cam loose on crankshaft
g. Excessive wear on breaker point rubbing block so that points cannot be properly adjusted

Unit-Type Magneto

Improper functioning of the carburetor, spark plug or other components often causes difficulties that are thought to be an improperly functioning magneto. Because a brief inspection will often locate other causes for engine malfunction, it is recommended that one be certain the magneto is at fault before opening the magneto housing.

BREAKER POINTS AND CONDENSER. The same general procedure is used to service and check as outlined in previous paragraphs for BATTERY IGNITION system. Usually, complete magneto housing is rotated when adjusting ignition timing.

COIL. The ignition coil can be tested without removing the coil from the housing. The instruction provided with coil tester should have coil test specifications listed.

ROTOR. Usually, service on the magneto rotor is limited to renewal of bushings or bearings if damaged. Check to be sure rotor turns freely and does not drag or have excessive end play.

MAGNETO INSTALLATION. When installing a unit-type magneto on an engine, refer to IGNITION paragraph in appropriate engine repair section for magneto-to-engine timing information.

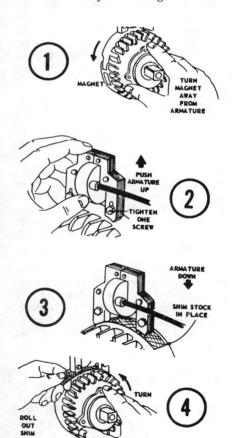

Fig. 2-8—Views showing adjustment of armature air gap when armature is located outside flywheel.

Capacitor Discharge System

This system differs radically from conventional units in that a relatively high-voltage current is fed into a capacitor that discharges through a pulse transformer (ignition coil) to generate the ignition spark. The secondary current is induced by the rapid buildup rather than by collapse of the primary current. The result is a high-energy ignition spark ideally suited to high-speed engine operation.

One development that made the new systems possible was the introduction of semiconductors suitable for ignition system control. Although solid-state technology and the capacitor discharge system are not interdependent, they are uniquely compatible; each has features that are desirable from the standpoint of reliability and performance.

A flywheel magneto is most generally used as the primary current source because of the relatively high voltage obtainable and compact, light-weight parts available. If battery current is used as the power source, it must be amplified or converted to obtain the necessary voltage.

The introduction of the new ignition systems is bringing unfamiliar words into use that might be defined in the following non-technical terms:

Capacitor—The storage capacitor or condenser.

Diode—A device that will allow electrical current to flow in one direction but will block a reverse flow.

Gate-Controlled Switch—A semiconductor that will pass the flow of electrical current in one direction only when a second, small "**Trigger Current**" opens the "**Gate**." Current will not flow in the reverse direction at any time. Properly called "**Gate-controlled Silicon Rectifier**," it is sometimes called "SCR."

Pulse Transformer—Similar in purpose and sometimes in appearance to the ignition coil of a conventional ignition system. Contains the primary and secondary ignition coils and converts the primary pulse current into the secondary ignition current that fires the plug. Cannot be interchanged with regular ignition coil.

Rectifier—Any device that allows the flow of current in one direction only, or converts alternating current to direct current. Diodes are sometimes used in combination to form a **Bridge Rectifier**.

SCR—See **Gate-Controlled Switch**.

Semiconductor—Any of several materials that permit partial or controlled flow of electrical current. Used in the manufacture of diodes, rectifiers, SCRs, thermistors, thyristors, etc.

Silicon Switch—See **Gate-Controlled Switch**.

Solid-State—That branch of electronic technology that deals with the use of semiconductors as control devices. See **Semiconductor**.

Thermistor—A solid-state regulating device that decreases in resistance as its temperature rises. Used for "temperature compensating" a control circuit.

Thyristor—A "safety valve" placed in the circuit that will not pass current in either direction, but is used to provide surge protection for other elements.

Trigger—The timed, small current that controls or opens the "Gate," thus initiating the spark.

Zener Diode—A Zener diode will permit free flow of current in one direction and will also permit current to flow in the opposite direction when the voltage reaches a predetermined level.

Solid-state ignition systems do not require periodic maintenance and normally provide trouble-free operation. Because of differences in solid-state ignition construction, it is impractical to outline a set procedure for solid-state ignition service. In general, a practical method of troubleshooting a suspected faulty solid-state ignition system is to install a known good unit and check for a spark. If ignition system works correctly with the good unit, it can be assumed that the old unit is faulty and should be renewed.

Generating System

FLYWHEEL ALTERNATORS. Alternating current is readily available on engines using a flywheel magneto system by installing an additional armature core (lighting coil) in a position similar to the ignition coil. The principle of this type of system is similar to the flywheel magneto; however, only one winding is necessary. The voltage and amperage can be limited by the resistance (length, diameter, etc.) of the wire used in the lighting coil windings and the alternating current (AC) generated is satisfactory for lighting requirements. However, if a battery is used, the generated alternating current must be changed to direct current (DC), usually via a rectifier.

RECTIFIER. Repair of rectifier is limited to renewal of the unit; however, certain precautions and inspections may be more easily accomplished after a brief description of its operation.

Direct current (DC), like the type available from a battery, has an established negative terminal and a positive terminal. Alternating current, such as generated by a magneto or alternator, changes polarity as the magnetic field of force is broken by the armature core (lighting coil). This simply means that one end of the coil wire is first negative, then, as the flywheel (magnets) move on, the current reverses direction and the same end becomes positive. If the AC current was connected to a battery (DC), the current would first flow into the battery, then, as the AC changed polarity (direction), it would withdraw the same amount.

Electricity in a wire is similar to liquid in a pipe. In a pipe, a check valve can be installed to allow a liquid to flow in only one direction. A rectifier serves as a similar one-way check valve for an electrical system. The changing of AC polarity can be shown on elaborate testing equipment and will appear similar to the drawing in Fig. 2-9. Where the curved line crosses the center line is the exact time the current reverses polarity. Installation of a rectifier stops current flow in one direction so half the current generated (shown below the center line) is lost.

In order to use the current that is normally lost in the previously described simple system, a combination of rectifiers can be used. Normally, they are constructed as one rectifying unit. Fig. 2-10 shows a typical complete system.

Rectifiers must be installed to allow current flow from the alternator into the battery. If the rectifier terminals are

Fig. 2-9—Elaborate testing equipment shows alternating current as a wave. The curved "S" line between the dots is called a cycle.

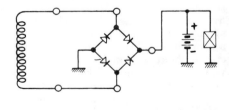

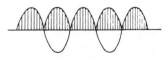

Fig. 2-10—Wiring diagram of full wave rectifier system. The four diodes shown are usually constructed as one unit.

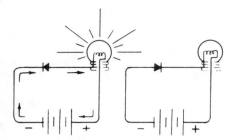

Fig. 2-11—A simple test can be made as shown on a rectifier to show which direction current flow. Wires should be connected to rectifier so that current is allowed to pass as shown by arrows in wiring diagrams.

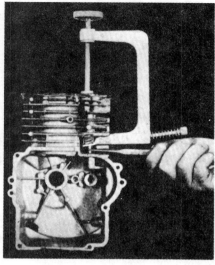

Fig. 2-12—View showing one type of valve spring compressor being used to remove keeper.

reversed, current from the battery will be fed into the lighting coil, and the coil and/or rectifier will be damaged by the resulting short circuit. The rectifier may be damaged if the system is operated without the battery connected or if battery terminals are reversed. Direction of current flow through the rectifier can be easily checked with a battery, light and wire (or ohmmeter) as shown in Fig. 2-11.

If the rectifier will not pass current in either direction using the simple test shown in Fig. 2-11, or if light continues to burn with connections reversed, rectifier may be considered faulty. Paint should not be scraped from rectifier plates and plates should not be discolored (from heat) or bent. The center bolt torque is preset and should NOT be disturbed.

VALVE SERVICE FUNDAMENTALS

When overhauling engines, obtaining proper valve sealing is of primary importance. The following paragraphs cover fundamentals of servicing intake and exhaust valves, valve seats and valve guides.

VALVE TAPPET GAP. Specific settings and procedures for adjusting clearances between valve stem end and tappet are listed in the appropriate individual sections. Valve clearance should not be changed from the clearances listed. When the valves are closed, heat is transferred from the valve to the cylinder head and valves may burn if set too tight. If the valve clearance is too loose, the engine will have decreased power. The "rattle" usually accompanying too much valve clearance is caused by metal parts of the valve system hitting. Although the noise is sometimes not objectionable, the constant pounding will result in increased wear and/or damage.

REMOVING AND INSTALLING VALVES. A valve spring compressor,

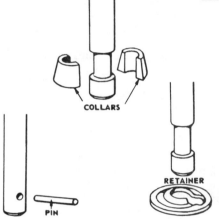

Fig. 2-13—Drawing showing three types of valve spring keepers commonly used.

one type of which is shown in Fig. 2-12, is a valuable aid in removing and installing the engine valves. This tool is used to hold spring compressed while removing or installing pin, collars or retainer from valve stem. Refer to Fig. 2-13 for views showing some of the different methods of retaining valve spring to valve stem.

VALVE REFACING. If valve face (Fig. 2-14) is slightly worn, burned or pitted, valve can usually be refaced, providing proper equipment is available. Many shops will usually renew valves, however, rather than invest in somewhat costly valve refacing tools.

Before attempting to reface a valve, refer to specifications in appropriate engine repair section for valve face angle. On some engines, manufacturer recommends grinding the valve face to an angle of ½ to 1 degree less than that of the valve seat. See Fig. 2-15. Also, nominal valve face angle may be either 30° or 45°.

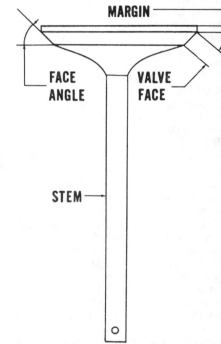

Fig. 2-14—Drawing showing typical four-stroke cycle engine valve. Face angle is usually 30° or 45°. On some engines, valve face is ground to an angle of 1/2 or 1° less than seat angle.

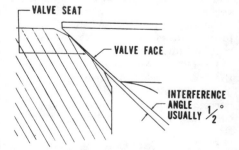

Fig. 2-15—Drawing showing line contact of valve face with valve seat when valve is ground at smaller angle than valve seat, as is specified on some engines.

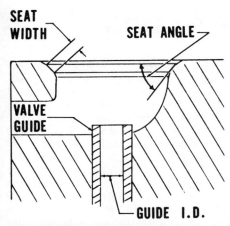

Fig. 2-16—Cross-sectional drawing of typical valve seat and valve guide as used on some engines. Valve guide may be an integral part of cylinder block; on some models, valve guide ID may be reamed out and an oversize valve stem installed. On other models, a service guide may be installed after machining cylinder block guide bore oversize.

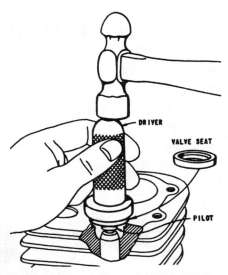

Fig. 2-17—View showing one method used to install valve seat insert. Refer to appropriate engine repair section for manufacturer's recommended method.

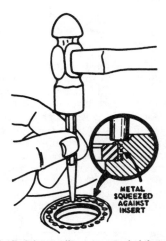

Fig. 2-18—It is usually recommended that on aluminum block engines, metal be peened around valve seat insert after insert is installed.

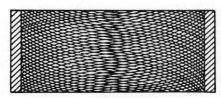

Fig. 2-19—A cross-hatch pattern as shown should be obtained when honing cylinder. Pattern is obtained by moving hone up and down cylinder bore as it is being turned by slow speed electric drill.

After valve is refaced, measure thickness of valve "margin" (Fig. 2-14). If margin is less than manufacturer's minimum specification, or is less than one-half the margin of a new valve, renew the valve. Valves having excessive material removed in refacing operation will not give satisfactory service.

When refacing or renewing a valve, the seat should also be reconditioned. Note that valve seat is renewable on some engines. Refer to following paragraph "REFACING OR RENEWING VALVE SEATS." Then, the valve should be "lapped in" to its seat using a fine valve grinding compound.

REFACING OR RENEWING VALVE SEATS.

Some engines have the valve seat machined directly in the cylinder block casting. The seat can be reconditioned by using a correct angle seat grinding stone or valve seat cutter. When reconditioning valve seat, care should be taken that only enough material is removed to provide a good seating area on valve contact surface. The width of seat should then be measured (Fig. 2-16) and if width exceeds manufacturer's maximum specifications, seat should be narrowed by using a stone or cutter with an angle 15° greater than seat angle and a second stone or cutter with an angle 15° less than seat angle. When narrowing seat, coat seat lightly with Prussion blue and check where seat contacts valve face by inserting valve in guide and rotating valve lightly against seat. Seat should contact approximately the center of valve face. By using only the narrow angle stone or cutter, seat contact will be moved toward outer edge of valve face.

Some engines have renewable valve seats. The seats are retained in cylinder block counterbore by an interference fit; that is, outside diameter of seat is slightly larger than counterbore in block. Refer to appropriate engine repair section in this manual for recommended method of removing old seat and install new seat. Refer to Fig. 2-17 for one method of installing new valve seats.

It sometimes occurs that a valve seat will become loose in counterbore, especially on engines with aluminum cylinder block. Some manufacturers provide oversize valve seat inserts (insert OD larger than standard part) so that if standard size insert fits loosely, counterbore can be cut oversize and a new insert can be tightly installed. After installing valve seat insert in engines of aluminum construction, metal around seat should be peened as shown in Fig. 2-18. Where a loose insert is encountered and an oversize insert is not available, loose insert can usually be tightened by center-punching cylinder block material at three equally spaced points around insert, then peening completely around insert as shown in Fig. 2-18.

OVERSIZE PISTON AND RINGS

Some engine manufacturers have oversize piston and ring sets available for use in repairing engines in which cylinder bore is excessively worn and standard size piston and rings cannot be used. If care and approved procedure are used in oversizing cylinder bore, installation of an oversize piston and ring set should result in a highly satisfactory overhaul.

Cylinder bore may be oversized by using either a boring bar or a hone; however, if a boring bar is used, it is usually recommended cylinder bore be finished with a hone. Refer to Fig. 2-19. After honing is completed, clean cylinder bore thoroughly with warm soapy water, dry and lubricate with engine oil.

Where oversize piston and rings are available, it will be noted in appropriate engine repair section of this manual. Also, the standard bore diameter will be given. Before attempting to rebore or hone the cylinder to oversize, carefully measure the cylinder bore and examine for damage. It may be possible cylinder is excessively worn or damaged and boring or honing to larger oversize will not clean up the cylinder surface.

ENGINE POWER AND TORQUE RATINGS

The following paragraphs discuss terms used in expressing engine horsepower and torque ratings and explain methods for determining different ratings. Some engine repair shops are now equipped with a dynamometer for measuring engine torque and/or horsepower, and the mechanic should be familiar with terms, methods of measurement and how actual power developed by an engine can vary under different conditions.

GLOSSARY OF TERMS

Force– Force is an action against an object that tends to move the object from a state of rest, or to accelerate movement of an object. See Fig. 4-1. For use in calculating torque or horsepower, force is measured in pounds.

Work– When a force moves an object from a state of rest, or accelerates movement of an object, work is done. See Fig. 4-2. Work is measured by multiplying force applied by distance the force moves an object, or:

$$work = force \times distance$$

Thus, if a force of 50 pounds moved an object 50 feet, work done would equal 50 pounds times 50 feet, or 2500 pounds-feet (or as it is usually expressed, 2500 foot-pounds).

Power– Power is the rate at which work is done; thus, if:

$$work = force \times distance$$

then:

$$power = \frac{force \times distance}{time}$$

From the above formula, it is seen that power must increase if time in which work is done decreases.

Horsepower– Horsepower (hp) is a unit of measurement of power. Many years ago, James Watt, a Scotsman noted as inventor of the steam engine, evaluated one horsepower as being equal to doing 33,000 foot-pounds of work in one minute. See Fig. 4-3. This evaluation has been universally accepted since that time. Thus, the formula for determining horsepower is:

$$hp = \frac{pounds \times feet}{33,000 \times minutes}$$

Horsepower ratings are sometimes converted to kilowatt (kW) ratings by using the following formula:

$$kW = hp \times 0.745,699,9$$

When referring to engine horsepower ratings, one usually finds the rating expressed as brake horsepower or rated horsepower, or sometimes as both.

Brake Horsepower– Brake horsepower is the maximum horsepower available from an engine as determined by use of a dynamometer, and is usually stated as maximum observed brake horsepower or as corrected brake horsepower. As will be noted in a later paragraph, observed brake horsepower of a specific engine will vary under different conditions of temperature and atmospheric pressure. Correct brake horsepower is a rating calculated from observed brake horsepower and is a means of comparing engines tested at varying conditions. The method for calculating correct brake horsepower will be explained in a later paragraph.

Rated Horsepower– An engine being operated under a load equal to the maximum horsepower available (brake horsepower) will not have reserve power for overloads and is subject to damage from overheating and rapid wear. Therefore, when an engine is being selected for a particular load, the engine's brake horsepower rating should be in excess of the expected normal operating load. Usually, it is recommended that the engine not be operated in excess of 80% of the engine maximum brake horsepower rating; thus, the "rated horsepower" of an engine is usually equal to 80% of maximum horsepower the engine will develop.

Torque– In many engine specifications, a "torque rating" is given. Engine torque can be defined simply as the turning effect exerted by the engine output shaft when under load.

Torque ratings are sometimes converted to Newton-meters (N•m) by using the following formula:

$$N{\bullet}m = foot\ pounts\ of\ torque \times 1.355818$$

It is possible to calculate engine horsepower being developed by measuring torque being developed and engine output speed. Refer to the following paragraphs.

MEASURING ENGINE TORQUE AND HORSEPOWER

PRONY BRAKE. The prony brake is the most simple means of testing engine performance. Refer to diagram in Fig. 4-4. A torque arm is attached to a brake on wheel mounted on engine output shaft. The torque arm, as the brake

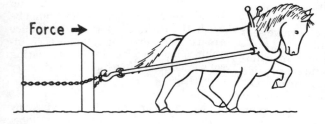

Fig. 4-1–A force, measured in pounds, is defined as an action tending to move an object or to accelerate movement of an object.

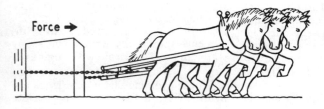

Fig. 4-2–If a force moves an object from a state of rest or accelerates movement of an object, then work is done.

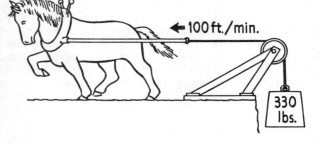

Fig. 4-3–This horse is doing 33,000 foot-pounds of work in one minute, or one horsepower.

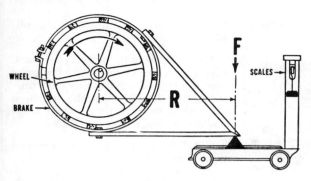

WHEEL

BRAKE

F

SCALES

R

Fig. 4-4—Diagram showing a prony brake on which the torque being developed by an engine can be measured. By also knowing the rpm of the engine output shaft, engine horsepower can be calculated.

is applied, exerts a force (F) on scales. Engine torque is computed by multiplying force (F) times length of torque arm radius (R), or:

$$engine\ torque = F \times R$$

If, for example, torque arm radium (R) is 2 feet and force (F) being exerted by torque arm on scales is 6 pounds, engine torque would be 2 feet × 6 pounds, or 12 foot-pounds.

To calculate engine horsepower being developed by use of the prony brake, we must also count revolutions of engine output shaft for a specific length of time. In formula for calculating horsepower:

$$horsepower = \frac{feet \times pounds}{33,000 \times minutes}$$

Feet in formula will equal circumference transcribed by torque arm radius multiplied by number of engine output shaft revolutions. Thus:

$$feet = 2 \times 3.14 \times R \times revolutions$$

Pounds in formula will equal force (F) of torque arm. If, for example, force (F) is 6 pounds, torque arm radius is 2 feet

and engine output shaft speed is 3300 revolutions per minute, then:

$$hp = \frac{2 \times 3.14 \times 2 \times 3300 \times 6}{33,000 \times minutes}$$

or,

$$hp \times 7.54$$

DYNAMOMETERS. Some commercial dynamometers for testing small engines are now available, although the cost may be prohibitive for all but larger repair shops. Usually, these dynamometers have a hydraulic loading device and scales indicating engine speed and load; horsepower is then calculated by use of a slide rule type instrument. For further information on commercial dynamometers, refer to manufacturers listed in special service tool section of this manual.

HOW ENGINE HORSEPOWER OUTPUT VARIES

Engine efficiency will vary with the amount of air taken into the cylinder on each intake stroke. Thus, air density has a considerable effect on horsepower

output of a specific engine. As air density varies with both temperature and atmospheric pressure, any change in air temperature, barometric pressure, or elevation will cause a variance in observed engine horsepower. As a general rule, engine horsepower will:

A. Decrease approximately 3 percent for each 1000 foot increase above 1000 ft. elevation;

B. Decrease approximately 3 percent for each 1 inch drop in barometric pressure; or

C. Decrease approximately 1 percent for each 10° rise in temperature (Fahrenheit).

Thus, to fairly compare observed horsepower readings, observed readings should be correct to standard temperature and atmospheric pressure conditions of 60° F., and 29.92 inches of mercury. The correction formula specified by the Society of Automotive Engineers is somewhat involved; however for practical purposes, the general rules stated above can be used to approximate corrected brake horsepower of an engine when observed maximum brake horsepower is known.

For example, suppose the engine horsepower of 7.54 as found by use of the prony brake was observed at an altitude of 3000 feet and at a temperature of 100° F. At standard atmospheric pressure and temperature conditions, we could expect an increase of 4 percent due to temperature (100° – 60° × 1 percent per 10°) and an increase of 6 percent due to altitude (3000 ft. – 1000 ft. × 3 percent per 1000 ft.) or a total increase of 10 percent. Thus, corrected maximum horsepower from this engine would be approximately 7.54 + .75, or approximately 8.25 horsepower.

LONG TERM STORAGE

A proper storage procedure can extend the life of an engine by preventing damage when the engine is not used. Exact procedures for storing depend on the type of equipment, length of storage, time of year stored and storage location. To obtain satisfactory results, storage must be coordinated with a regular maintenance program. The following outline lists procedures applicable for extended storage of most small engines.

ENTERING INTO STORAGE

Drain old oil from engine crankcase, gearboxes, chain cases, etc., while oil is warm. Refill with new approved oil specified by engine manufacturer.

Clean and dry all exterior surfaces. Remove all accumulated dirt and repair any damaged surface. Paint exposed surfaces to prevent rust.

Clean all cooling air passages and straighten, repair or renew any part which would interfere with normal air flow. Remove shrouds and deflectors, then inspect and clean all cooling air passages.

Lubricate all moving parts requiring lubrication with approved oil or grease.

Inspect for worn or broken parts. Make necessary adjustments and repair all damage. Tighten all loose hardware.

Fuel should be either drained or treated with an approved stabilizer. All fuel should be drained from tank, fil-

ters, lines, pumps and carburetor unless specifically discouraged by manufacturer. Do not add fuel stabilizer to any fuel containing alcohol. Fuel containing alcohol will separate if permitted to sit for long period of time and internal parts may be extensively damaged by corrosion. Some manufacturers recommend coating inside of tank with a small amount of oil to deter rusting in tank. Filters should be serviced initially and water traps should be serviced regularly while in storage.

Loosen all drive belts and remove pressure from friction drive components. Inspect and note condition of drive belts. If condition is questionable, a new belt should be installed when removing equipment from storage.

Install new filter elements. Some filters can be cleaned and serviced, but most should be installed new at this time.

Remove the spark plug and ground the spark plug wire. Pour a small amount (usually 1 tablespoon) of oil into cylinder of engine through spark plug hole. Crank engine with starter about 12 revolutions to distribute oil, then install spark plug and reconnect spark plug wire.

Install protective caps at ends of all disconnected lines. Seal openings of exhaust, air intake, engine dipstick and crankcase breather tube.

Remove battery and store in a cool, dry place. Do not permit battery to freeze and maintain fully charged, checking approximately every 30 days.

Store the engine in a dry, protected place. If necessary to store outside, cover engine to prevent entrance of water, but don't seal tightly. Sealing may cause condensation and accelerate rusting.

REMOVING FROM STORAGE

Check for obvious damage to covering and equipment. Remove any blocks used during storage.

Charge battery, then install in equipment making sure that battery is properly retained. Clean battery cables and battery posts, then attach cables to battery terminals.

Remove covers from exhaust, air intake, engine dipstick and crankcase breather tube. Remove any protective caps from lines disconnected during disassembly. Be sure ends are clean, then reconnect lines. Check all filters. Install new filters, or clean and service existing filters as required.

Adjust all drive belts and friction drive components to correct tension as recommended by the manufacturer. New belts should be installed if condition is questionable.

Fill fuel tank with correct type of fuel. Check for leaks. Gaskets may dry up or carburetor needle valve may stick during storage. Repair any problems before attempting to start. Drain water traps and check condition of fuel filters.

Check for worn or broken parts and repair before returning to service.

Lubricate all surfaces normally lubricated with oil or grease. Check cooling passages for restrictions such as insect, bird or animal nests. Check oil in all compartments such as engine crankcase, gearboxes, chain cases, etc., for proper level. Evidence of too much oil may indicate water settled below oil. Drain oil if contamination is suspected or if time of storage exceeds recommended time change interval. Fill to proper level with correct type of oil.

SERVICE SHOP TOOL BUYER'S GUIDE

This listing of service shop tools is solely for the convenience of users of the manual and does not imply endorsement or approval by Intertec Publishing Corporation of the tools and equipment listed. The listing is in response to many requests for information on sources for purchasing special tools and equipment. Every attempt has been made to make the listing as complete as possible at time of publication and each entry is made from the latest material available.

Special engine service tools such as drivers, pullers, gages, etc., which are available from the engine manufacturer are not listed in this section of the manual. Where a special service tool is listed in the engine service section of this manual, the tool is available from the central parts or service distributors listed at the end of most engine service sections, or from the manufacturer.

NOTE TO MANUFACTURERS AND NATIONAL SALES DISTRIBUTORS OF ENGINE SERVICE TOOLS AND RELATED SERVICE EQUIPMENT. To obtain either a new listing for your products, or to change or add to an existing listing, write to Intertec Publishing, Book Division, P.O. Box 12901, Overland Park, KS 66212.

ENGINE SERVICE TOOLS

Ammco Tools, Inc.
Wacker Park
North Chicago, Illinois 60064
Valve spring compressor, torque wrenches, cylinder hones, ridge reamers, piston ring compressors, piston ring expanders.

Bloom, Inc.
Highway 939 West
Independence, Iowa 50644
Engine repair stand with crankshaft straightening attachment.

Brush Research Mfg. Co., Inc.
4642 East Floral Drive
Los Angeles, California 90022
Cylinder hones.

E-Z Lok
P.O. Box 2069
Gardena, California 90247
Thread repair insert kits.

Fairchild Fastener Group
3000 W. Lomita Blvd.
Torrance, California 90505
Thread repair insert kits (Keenserts) and installation tools.

Foley-Belsaw Company Outdoor Power Equipment Parts division
6301 Equitable Road
P.O. Box 419593
Kansas City, Missouri 64141
Crankshaft straightener and repair stand, valve refacer, valve seat grinder, parts washer, cylinder hone, ridge reamer, piston ring expander and compressor, flywheel puller, torque wrench.

Frederick Manufacturing Corp.
4840 E. 12th Street
Kansas City, Missouri 64127
Piston groove cleaner, compression tester, piston ring expander and compressor, valve spring compressor, valve seat grinder, valve refacer, cylinder hone, flywheel puller, flywheel wrench, flywheel holder, starter spring rewinder, condenser pliers.

Heli-Coil
Shelter Rock Lane
Danbury, Connecticut 06810
Thread repair kits, thread inserts, installation tools.

Kansas Instruments
1100 Union Street
Council Grove, Kansas 66846
Spray washer cabinets, parts washers, hot tanks, glass bead machines, steel shot machines, bake clean ovens, aluminum head straightening ovens, cylinder boring and honing equipment, head and block surfacing equipment, magnetic crack testing equipment, and valve guide and seat machines.

K-D Tools
3575 Hempland Road
Lancaster, Pennsylvania 17604
Thread repair kits, valve spring compressors, reamers, micrometers, dial indicators, calipers.

Keystone Reamer & Tool Company
South Front Street
P.O. Box 308
Millersburg, Pennsylvania 17061
Valve seat cutter and pilots, reamers, screw extractors, taps and dies.

Ki-Sol Corporation
100 Larkin Williams Ind. Ct.
Fenton, Missouri 63026
Cylinder hone, ridge reamer, ring compressor, ring expander, ring groove cleaner, torque wrenches, valve spring compressor, valve refacing equipment.

K-Line Industries, Inc.
315 Garden Avenue
Holland, Michigan 49424
Cylinder hone, ridge reamer, ring compressor, valve guide tools, valve spring compressor, reamers.

K.O. Lee Company
200 South Harrison
P.O. Box 1416
Aberdeen, South Dakota 57402

Kwik-Way Mfg. company
500 57th Street
Marion, Iowa 52302
Cylinder boring equipment, valve facing equipment, valve seat grinding equipment.

Lisle Corporation
807 East Main
Clarinda, Iowa 51632
Cylinder hones, ridge reamers, ring compressors, valve spring compressors.

Microdot, Inc.
P.O. Box 3001
Fullerton, California 92634
Thread repair insert kits.

Mighty Midget Mfg. Co., Div. of Kansas City Screw Thread company
2908 E. Truman Road
Kansas City, Missouri 64127
Crankshaft straightener.

Neway Manufacturing, Inc.
1013 N. Shiawassee
Corunna, Michigan 48817
Valve seat cutters.

OTC
655 Eisenhower Drive
Owatonna, Minnesota 55060
Valve tools, spark plug tools, piston ring tools, cylinder hones.

Power Lawnmower Parts, Inc.
1920 Lyell Avenue
P.O. Box 60860
Rochester, New York 14606-0860
Flywheel pullers, starter wrench, flywheel holder, gasket cutter tool, gasket scraper tool, crankshaft cleaning tool, ridge reamer, valve spring compressor, valve seat cutters, thread repair kits, valve lifter, piston ring expander.

**Precision Manufacturing
& Sales Co., Inc.**
2140 Range Road
Clearwater, Florida 34625
Cylinder boring equipment, measuring instruments, valve equipment, hones, hand tools, test equipment, threading tools, presses, parts washers, milling machines, lathes, drill presses, glass beading machines, dynos, safety equipment.

Sioux Tools, Inc.
2901 Floyd Blvd.
P.O. Box 507
Sioux City, Iowa 51102
Valve refacing and seat grinding equipment.

Sunnen Product Company
7910 Manchester Avenue
St. Louis, Missouri 63143
Cylinder hones, rod reconditioning, valve guide reconditioning.

TEST EQUIPMENT AND GAGES

AW Dynamometer, Inc.
P.O. Box 428
Colfax, Illinois 61728
Engine test dynamometer.

B.C. Ames Company
131 Lexington
Waltham, Massachusetts 02254
Micrometers, dial gages, calipers.

Dixson, Inc.
287 27 Road
Grand Junction, Colorado 81503
Tachometer, compression gage, timing light.

**Foley-Belsaw Company Outdoor
Power Equipment Parts Division**
6301 Equitable Road
P.O. Box 419593
Kansas City, Missouri 64141
Cylinder gage, amp/volt testers, condenser and coil tester, magneto tester, ignition testers, tachometers, spark testers, compression gages, timing lights and gages, micrometers and calipers, carburetor testers, vacuum gages.

Frederick Manufacturing Corp.
4840 E. 12th Street
Kansas City, Missouri 64127
Ignition tester, tachometer, compression gage

Graham-Lee Electronics, Inc.
4220 Central Avenue N.E.
Minneapolis, Minnesota 55421
Coil and condenser tester.

Kansas Instruments
1100 Union Street
Council Grove, Kansas 66846
Spray washer cabinets, parts washers, hot tanks, glass bead machines, steel shot machines, bake clean ovens, aluminum head straightening ovens, cylinder boring and honing equipment, head and block surfacing equipment, magnetic crack testing equipment, and valve guide and seat machines.

K-D Tools
3575 Hempland Road
Lancaster, Pennsylvania 17604
Diode tester and installation tools, compression gage, timing light, timing gages.

Ki-Sol Corporation
100 Larkin Williams Ind. Ct.
Fenton, Missouri 63026
Micrometers, telescoping gages, compression gages, cylinder gages.

K-Line Industries, Inc.
315 Garden Avenue
Holland, Michigan 49424
Compression gage, leakdown tester, micrometers, dial gages.

**Merc-O-Tronic Instruments
Corporation**
215 Branch Street
Almont, Michigan 48003
Igition analyzers for conventional, solid-state and magneto systems, electric tachometers, electronic tachometer and dwell meter, power timing lights, ohmmeters, compression gages, mechanical timing devices.

OTC
655 Eisenhower Drive
Owatonna, Minnesota 55060
Feeler gages, hydraulic test gages.

Power Lawnmower Parts, Inc.
1920 Lyell Avenue
P.O. Box 60860
Rochester, New York 14606-0860
Compression gage, cylinder gage, magneto tester, compression gage, condenser and coil tester.

**Prestolite Electronic Division
An Allied Company**
4 Seagate
Toledo, Ohio 43691
Magneto test plug.

Simpson Electric Company
853 Dundee Avenue
Elgin, Illinois 60120
Electrical and electronic test equipment.

L.S. Starrett Company
121 Crescent
St. Athol, Massachusetts 01331
Micrometers, dial gages, bore gages, feeler gages.

Stevens Instrument Company
P.O. Box 193
Waukegan, Illinois 60079
Igition analyzers, timing lights, volt-ohm meter, tachometer, spark checkers, CD ignition testers.

Stewart-Warner Corporation
580 Slawin Ct.
Mt. Prospect, Illinois 60056
Compression gage, igntion tachometer, timing light ignition analyzer.

SHOP TOOLS AND EQUIPMENT

**AC Delco Division
General Motors Corp.**
3031 W. Grand Blvd.
P.O. Box 33115
Detroit, Michigan 48232
Spark plug tools.

Black & Decker Mfg. Company
626 Hanover Pike
Hampstead, Maryland 21074
Electric power tools.

**Champion Pneumatic
Machinery Company**
1301 N. Euclid Avenue
Princeton, Illinois 61356
Air compressors.

Champion Spark Plug Company
P.O. Box 910
Toledo, Ohio 43661
Spark plug cleaning and testing equipment, gap tools and wrenches.

Chicago Pneumatic Tool Company
2200 Bleecker St.
Utica, New York 13501
Air impact wrenches, air hammers, air drills and grinders, nut runners, speed ratchets.

Cooper Tools
P.O. Box 728
Apex, North Carolina 27502
Chain type engine hoists and utility slings

E-Z Lok
P.O. Box 2069
Gardena, California 90247
Thread repair insert kits.

Fairchild Fastener Group
3000 W. Lomita Blvd.
Torrance, California 90505
Thread repair insert kits (Keenserts) and installation tools.

Foley-Belsaw Company
Outdoor Power Equipment
Parts Division
6301 Equitable Road
P.O. Box 419593
Kansas City, Missouri 64141
Torque wrenches, parts washers, micrometers and calipers.

Frederick Manufacturing Corp.
4840 E. 12th Street
Kansas City, Missouri 64127
Torque wrenches, gear pullers.

G&H Products, Inc.
P.O. Box 770
St. Paris, Ohio 43027
Equipment lifts.

General Scientific
Equipment Company
525 Spring Garden St.
Philadelphia, Pennsylvania 19122
Safety equipment.

Graymills Corporation
3705 N. Lincoln Avenue
Chicago, Illinois 60613
Parts washing equipment.

Heli-Coil
Shelter Rock Lane
Danbury, Connecticut 06810
Thread repair kits, thread inserts, installation tools.

Ingersoll-Rand
253 E. Washington Avenue
Washington, New Jersey 07882
Air and electric impact wrenches, electric drills and screwdrivers.

Jaw Manufacturing Company
39 Mulberry St.
P.O. Box 213
Reading, Pennsylvania 19603
Files for repair or renewal of damaged threads, rethreader dies, flexible shaft drivers and extensions, screw extractors, impact drivers.

Jenny Division of
Homestead Ind., Inc.
700 Second Avenue
Coraopolis, Pennsylvania 15108
Steam cleaning equipment, pressure washing equipment.

Kansas Instruments
1100 Union Street
Council Grove, Kansas 66846
Spray washer cabinets, parts washers, hot tanks, glass bead machines, steel shot machines, bake clean ovens, aluminum head straightening ovens, cylinder boring and honing equipment, head and block surfacing equipment, magnetic crack testing equipment, and valve guide and seat machines.

K-Line Industries, Inc.
315 Garden Avenue
Holland, Michigan 49424
Pullers, crack detectors, gloves, aprons, eyewear,

Keystone Reamer & Tool Company
South Front Street
P.O. Box 308
Millersburg, Pennsylvania 17061
Adjustable reamers, twist drills, taps, dies.

Microdot, Inc.
P.O. Box 3001
Fullerton, California 92634
Thread repair insert kits.

OTC
655 Eisenhower Drive
Owatonna, Minnesota 55060
Bearing and gear pullers, hydraulic shop presses.

Power Lawnmower Parts, Inc.
1920 Lyell Avenue
P.O. Box 60860
Rochester, New York 14606-0860
Flywheel pullers, starter wrench,

Shure Manufacturing Corp.
1601 S. Hanley Road
St. Louis, Missouri 63144
Steel shop benches, desks, engine overhaul stand.

Sioux Tools, Inc.
2901 Floyd Blvd.
P.O. Box 507
Sioux City, Iowa 51102
Air and electric impact tools, drills, grinders.

Sturtevant Richmont
3203 N. Wolf Rd.
Franklin Park, Illinois 60131
Torque wrenches, torque multipliers, torque analyzers.

MECHANIC'S HAND TOOLS

Channellock, Inc.
1306 South Main St.
P.O. Box 519
Meadville, Pennsylvania 16335

John H. Graham & Company
P.O. Box 739
Oradell, New Jersey 07649

Jaw Manufacturing Company
39 Mulberry St.
P.O. Box 213
Reading, Pennsylvania 19603

K-D Tools
3575 Hempland Road
Lancaster, Pennsylvania 17604

K-Line Industries, Inc.
315 Garden Avenue
Holland, Michigan 49424

OTC
655 Eisenhower Drive
Owatonna, Minnesota 55060

Snap-On Tools
2801 80th Street
Kenosha, Wisconsin 53140

Triangle Corporation-Tool
Division
P.O. Box 1807
Orangeburg, South Carolina 29115

SHOP SUPPLIES
(Chemicals, Metallurgy Products, Seals, Sealers, Common Parts Items, etc.)

Clayton Manufacturing Company
4213 N. Temple City Blvd.
El Monte, California 91731
Steam cleaning compounds and solvents.

E-Z Lok
P.O. Box 2069
Gardena, California 90247
Thread repair insert kits.

Eutectic+Castolin
40-40 172nd Street
Flushing, New York 11358
Specialized repair and maintenance welding alloys.

Fairchild Fastener Group
3000 W. Lomita Blvd.
Torrance, California 90505
Thread repair insert kits (Keenserts) and installation tools.

Foley-Belsaw Company
Outdoor Power Equipment
Parts Division
6301 Equitable Road
P.O. Box 419593
Kansas City, Missouri 64141
Parts washers, cylinder head rethreaders, micrometers, calipers, gasket material, nylon rope, oil and grease products, bolt, nut, washer and spring assortments.

Frederick Manufacturing Corp.
4840 E. 12th Street
Kansas City, Missouri 64127
Thread repair kits.

Graymills Corporation
3705 N. Lincoln Avenue
Chicago, Illinois 60613
Parts cleaning fluids.

Heli-Coil
Shelter Rock Lane
Danbury, Connecticut 06810
Thread repair kits, thread inserts, installation tools.

K-Line Industries, Inc.
315 Garden Avenue
Holland, Michigan 49424
Machining lubricants, solvents, cleaning solutions.

Loctite Corporation
705 North Mountain Road
Newington, Connecticut 06111
Compounds for locking threads, retaining bearings and securing machine parts; sealants and adhesives.

Microdot, Inc.
P.O. Box 3001
Fullerton, California 92634
Thread repair insert kits.

Permatex Industrial
30 Tower Lane
Avon Park South
Avon, Connecticut 06001
Cleaning chemicals, gasket sealers, pipe sealants, adhesives, lubricants, thread locking and forming compounds.

Power Lawnmower Parts, Inc.
1920 Lyell Avenue
P.O. Box 60860
Rochester, New York 14606-0860
Grinding compound paste, gas tank sealer stick, shop aprons, eyewear.

Radiator Specialty company
1900 Wilkinson Blvd.
Charlotte, North Carolina 28208
Cleaning chemicals (Gunk) and solder seal.

ACME

ACME NORTH AMERICA CORP.
5209 W. 73rd St.
Minneapolis, MN 55435

Model	No. Cyls.	Bore	Stroke	Displacement
FE 82 W	1	82 mm (3.23 in.)	79 mm (3.11 in.)	417 cc (25.44 cu. in.)
AL 480 W	1	88 mm (3.46 in.)	79 mm (3.11 in.)	480 cc (29.28 cu. in.)
AL 550 W	1	94 mm (3.70 in.)	79 mm (3.11 in.)	548 cc (33.43 cu. in.)

ENGINE IDENTIFICATION

All models are four-stroke, air-cooled, single cylinder, horizontal crankshaft engines. Valves are located in the cast iron cylinder. Aluminum cylinder head, cast iron cylinder and crankcase are separate assemblies.

Models with the suffix B after the W are gasoline fuel engines and models with the suffix P after the W are kerosene fuel engines.

Engine model and serial numbers are stamped into crankcase just above oil filler cap and cylinder-to-crankcase mating surface (Fig. AC70). Always furnish engine model and serial numbers when ordering parts.

MAINTENANCE

SPARK PLUG. Recommended spark plug for models that use gasoline for fuel is a Champion D16 or equivalent. Recommended spark plug for models using kerosene for fuel is a Champion D21 or equivalent.

Spark plug should be removed, cleaned and inspected at 100-hour intervals. Spark plug electrode gap should be 0.6-0.8 mm (0.024-0.032 in.) for all models.

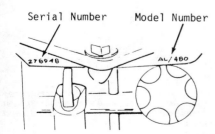

Fig. AC70—View showing location of model and serial numbers on all models.

CARBURETOR. All models are equipped with a float-type carburetor. Refer to Fig. AC71 for exploded view and parts location.

Initial adjustment of idle mixture screw (3) from a lightly seated position is 1¼ turns open. Main fuel mixture is controlled by a fixed main jet (13).

Final adjustments should be made with engine at operating temperature and running. Adjust engine idle speed to 1100 rpm at throttle stop screw (5). Adjust idle mixture screw (3) to obtain smoothest engine idle and smooth acceleration.

When installing new fuel inlet needle and seat, install seat and measure from point (A) to edge of fuel inlet needle seat. Measurement should be 32-34 mm (1.26-1.34 in.). Vary number of fiber washers between fuel inlet seat and carburetor body to obtain correct measurement.

To check float (12) level, carefully remove float bowl (15) and measure distance from carburetor mating surface of bowl to top of fuel level in bowl (Fig. AC72). Measurement should be 32-34 mm (1.26-1.34 in.). If float level is incorrect, fuel inlet needle seat must be shimmed as outlined in previous paragraph.

Float weight is stamped in float. If float is heavier than specified weight, then float must be renewed.

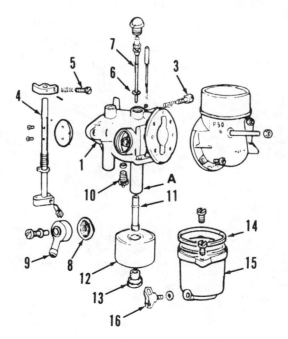

Fig. AC71—Exploded view of carburetor used on all models.

1. Carburetor body
3. Idle mixture screw
4. Throttle shaft
5. Throttle stop screw
6. Gasket
7. Idle jet
8. Screen (filter)
9. Filter housing
10. Fuel inlet meedle valve
11. Nozzle
12. Float
13. Main jet
14. Gasket
15. Float bowl
16. Wing bolt

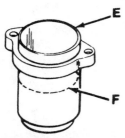

Fig. AC72—Measure distance from fuel level (F) to top of bowl (E). Distance should be 32-34 mm (1.26-1.34 in.).

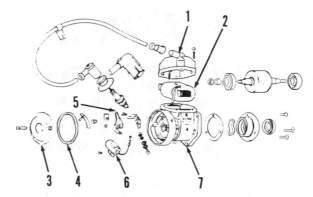

Fig. AC75—Exploded view of the magneto unit used on all models.

1. Cap
2. Coil
3. Cover
4. Seal
5. Points
6. Condenser
7. Housing

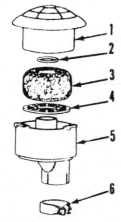

Fig. AC73—Exploded view of a typical oil-bath-type air cleaner.

1. Cover		4. Plate	
2. Gasket		5. Oil reservoir	
3. Element		6. Clamp	

Fuel filter screen (8—Fig. AC71) should be removed and cleaned at 50-hour intervals.

AIR FILTER. All models are equipped with an oil bath-type air filter (Fig. AC73). Air filter element should be removed and cleaned at 8-hour intervals and old oil discarded and new engine oil installed to level indicated on oil reservoir housing (5).

GOVERNOR. All models are equipped with a flyball-type centrifugal governor. Governor assembly is incorporated on the magneto drive shaft. Governor regulates engine speed via external linkage.

When assembling governor, carburetor throttle plate must be at wide-open throttle position when governor assembly is at rest and engine is not running.

IGNITION SYSTEM. Later Model FE 82 engines are equipped with a breakerless, solid-state ignition system and all other models are equipped with the magneto shown in Fig. AC75, which includes a breaker point set, condenser and ignition coil.

On models equipped with a magneto, the point gap should be checked and adjusted at 400-hour intervals. To check point gap, remove cover and use a suitable feeler gauge. Point gap should be 0.4-0.5 mm (0.016-0.020 in.). Install magneto so that breaker points just begin to open when the flywheel is at the 25° mark BTDC. This mark should be located on the flywheel 52.4 mm (2.063 in.) before the piston is at top dead center.

On later Model FE 82 engines with solid-state ignition system, no periodic service is required. Air gap between ignition module and flywheel should be 0.45-0.50 mm (0.018-0.020 in.).

LUBRICATION. Check engine oil level at 8-hour intervals. Maintain oil level at lower edge of fill plug opening.

Change oil at 50-hour intervals. Manufacturer recommends oil with an API service classification SF or SG. Use SAE 40 oil for ambient temperatures above 10° C (50° F); SAE 30 oil for temperatures between 10° C (50° F) and 0°

C (32° F); SAE 20W-20 oil for temperatures between 0° C (32° F) and –10° C (–14° F) and SAE 10W oil for temperatures below –10° C (–14° F).

Crankcase oil capacity is 1.1 L (1.16 qt.) for Models FE 82 W and AL 480 W, and 1.3 L (1.37 qt.) for Model AL 550 W. All models are splash lubricated by an oil dipper located on the bottom of the connecting rod.

VALVE ADJUSTMENT. Valves should be adjusted at 200-hour intervals. Valve stem to tappet clearance for all models should be 0.20 mm (0.008 in.) for intake valve and 0.25 mm (0.010 in.) for exhaust valve. If clearance is not as specified, remove or install shims (7 and 8—Fig. AC76) in shim holder (9) as necessary.

CRANKCASE BREATHER. Crankcase breather must be removed and cleaned at 50-hour intervals. Breather is located on tube mounted on valve chamber cover. Rubber valve must be installed as shown in Fig. AC77 to ensure crankcase vacuum.

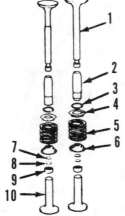

Fig. AC76—View of valve system component parts.

1. Valve		6. Retainer	
2. Guide		7. Shim (valve adjustment)	
3. Seal		8. Shim (valve adjustment)	
4. Seal		9. Shim holder (cap)	
5. Spring		10. Tappet	

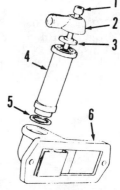

Fig. AC77—Exploded view of the crankcase breather used on all models. Diaphragm (3) must be installed with the flat side facing down toward tube (4).

1. Screw		4. Tube	
2. Cap		5. Seal	
3. Diaphragm		6. Housing	

GENERAL MAINTENANCE.

Check and tighten all loose bolts, nuts or clamps daily. Check for fuel or oil leakage and repair as necessary.

Clean dust, dirt, grease or any foreign material from cylinder head and cylinder block cooling fins at 100-hour intervals. Inspect fins for damage and repair as necessary.

REPAIRS

TIGHTENING TORQUES. Recommended tightening torque specifications are as follows:

Spark plug . . . . 15 N•m
(11 ft.-lbs.)
Cylinder head . . . . 39 N•m
(29 ft.-lbs.)
Cylinder . . . . 22 N•m
(16 ft.-lbs.)
Crankcase cover . . . . 18 N•m
(13 ft.-lbs.)
Flywheel . . . . 176 N•m
(130 ft.lbs.)

CYLINDER HEAD. To remove cylinder head, remove cooling shrouds and loosen head bolts evenly in sequence shown in Fig. AC78 and remove cylinder head.

CAUTION: Never remove cylinder head while engine is hot because cylinder head distortion will result.

Check cylinder head for distortion by placing on a flat surface and using a feeler gauge to determine flatness. If cylinder head is warped more than 0.3-0.5 mm (0.012-0.020 in.), renew cylinder head.

Always install new head gasket and tighten cylinder head bolts to specified torque following sequence shown in Fig. AC78.

CONNECTING ROD. The connecting rod is installed on the connecting rod journal, which is then pressed into the crankshaft halves. The connecting rod bearing is selected together with the connecting rod and crankshaft journal in three classes, each having a tolerance of 0.004 mm (0.00016 in.). Connecting

rod, bearing and crankshaft journal must be renewed as an assembly.

To remove connecting rod, remove all shrouds. Remove the aluminum cylinder head. Remove the cylinder retaining nuts and carefully pull the cast iron cylinder up off the piston assembly. Use a suitable puller (Acme tool 365 111) to remove the flywheel and then the crankcase cover. Remove the crankshaft and connecting rod assembly. Remove the camshaft assembly as required. If the connecting rod must be removed from the crankshaft, remove the piston from the connecting rod. The crankshaft halves must be separated using a suitable puller (Acme tool 365 126). To reassemble the crankshaft, use a suitable jig (Acme tool 365 130) and a press capable of 7 to 8 tons pressure. Press crankshaft together until there is 0.2-0.4 mm (0.0079-0.0157 in.) clearance between connecting rod and crankshaft shoulder. Shims are available to adjust clearance between connecting rod and crankshaft shoulder. The two crankshaft halves must be concentric with the crankshaft connecting rod journal. Maximum off-center allowance is 0.05 mm (0.0020 in.).

Clearance between piston pin and connecting rod pin bore should be 0.02-0.05 mm (0.00079-0.00197 in.). Piston can be installed on connecting rod in either direction.

CYLINDER. The cast iron cylinder can be separated from the cylinder head and crankcase.

Standard cylinder bore diameter is 82.000-82.013 mm (3.23-3.28 in.) for Model FE 82 W; 88.000-88.013 mm (3.46-3.51 in.) for Model AL 480 W and 94.000-94.013 mm (3.70-3.75 in.) for Model Al 550 W. If cylinder bore is 0.06 mm (0.0024 in.) or more out-of-round or tapered, cylinder should be bored to nearest oversize for which piston and rings are available.

CRANKCASE. The aluminum alloy crankcase and crankcase cover can be separated from the cast iron cylinder. The ball bearing main bearings should be a light press fit in the crankcase and crankcase cover bearing bores. Heating crankcase or crankcase cover slightly will aid bearing installation. When installing crankcase cover on crankcase, tighten bolts to the specified torque in a crisscross pattern.

PISTON, PIN AND RINGS. Refer to CONNECTING ROD paragraphs for piston removal and installation procedure.

Standard piston diameter is 81.987-82.000 mm (3.2278-3.2283 in.) for Model FE 82 W; 87.987-88.000 mm (3.4640-3.4646 in.) for Model AL 480 W and 93.987-94.000 mm (3.7003-3.7008 in.) for Model AL 550 W. On all models, pistons are a select fit at the factory.

Piston should be renewed and/or cylinder reconditioned if there is 0.13 mm (0.005 in.) or more clearance between piston and cylinder bore.

Compression ring end gap should be 0.25-0.40 mm (0.010-0.016 in.). Oil control ring end gap should be 0.30-0.50 mm (0.012-0.020 in.). Rings should be installed into piston ring grooves as shown in Fig. AC80. Stagger end gaps equally around piston diameter.

Piston pin should be 0.004-0.012 mm (0.0002-0.0005 in.) interference fit in piston pin bore. It may be necessary to heat piston slightly to aid in pin removal or installation.

CRANKSHAFT. Crankshaft is supported at each end by ball bearing-type main bearings. Crankshaft is a three-piece assembly (Fig. AC79) that must be pressed together using the procedure and special jig described under CONNECTING ROD.

Refer to CONNECTING ROD paragraphs for crankshaft removal and assembly procedure. When installing crankshaft, make certain crankshaft

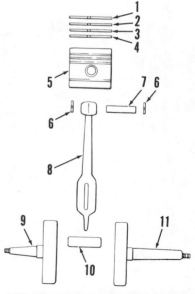

Fig. AC79—Exploded view of crankshaft, connecting rod and piston assembly.

1. Compression ring
2. Compression ring
3. Oil control ring
4. Oil control ring
5. Piston
6. Retaining ring
7. Piston pin
8. Connecting rod
9. Crankshaft half
10. Crankshaft crankpin journal
11. Crankshaft half

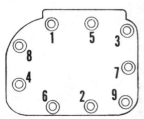

Fig. AC78—Loosen and tighten cylinder head bolts following the sequence shown.

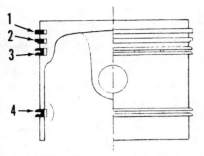

Fig. AC80—Piston rings must be installed so the step on second ring (2) is facing down and the bevel on oil control rings (3 and 4) is facing up.

Fig. AC81—Camshaft axial thrust is controlled by ball (B) and spring (S).

and camshaft gear timing marks are aligned.

CAMSHAFT. The camshaft is supported at each end by renewable bushings. The camshaft gear has helical teeth to reduce noise and improve meshing. Camshaft axial thrust is controlled by a ball tensioned by a spring (Fig. AC 81).

VALVE SYSTEM. Refer to VALVE ADJUSTMENT paragraph in MAINTENANCE section for valve clearance adjustment procedure.

Valve face and seat angles are 45°. Standard valve seat width is 1.2-1.3 mm (0.047-0.051 in.). If seat width is 2 mm (0.079 in.) or more, seat must be narrowed.

If valve face margin is 0.5 mm (0.020 in.) or less, renew valve.

Standard intake valve stem diameter should be 7.9910-8.0000 m (0.3146-0.3150 in.) and standard exhaust valve stem diameter should be 7.9720-7.9870 mm (0.3139-0.3144 in.).

Valve guide inside diameter should be 8.0250-8.0350 mm (0.3159-0.3168 in.) for intake and exhaust guides. If diameter is 8.1000 mm (0.3189 in.) or more, renew valve guide.

Standard valve spring free length is 54 mm (2.126 in.).

ACME

ACME NORTH AMERICA CORP.
5209 W. 73rd St.
Minneapolis, MN 55435

Model	No. Cyls.	Bore	Stroke	Displacement
AT 330	1	80 mm (3.15 in.)	65 mm (2.56 in.)	327 cc (19.95 cu. in.)
VT 88 W	1	88 mm (3.46 in.)	79 mm (3.11 in.)	480 cc (29.28 cu. in.)
VT 94 W	1	94 mm (3.70 in.)	79 mm (3.11 in.)	548 cc (33.43 cu. in.)

ENGINE IDENTIFICATION

All models are four-stroke, air-cooled single cylinder, overhead valve engines. Cylinder and crankcase are cast as a single unit for Model AT 330. Cylinder and crankcase are separate assemblies for all other models.

Models with the suffix "B" after the W are gasoline fuel engines and models with the suffix "P" after the W are kerosene fuel engines.

Engine model number for Model AT 330 is on a plate mounted on cooling shroud on the right-hand side of engine as viewed from flywheel side. The engine serial number is stamped into the engine block approximately 76 mm (3 in.) below the model number plate, just above the oil fill plug (Fig. AC91). Engine model and serial numbers for Models VT 88 W and VT 94 W are stamped into crankcase just above oil filler cap and cylinder-to-crankcase mating surface (Fig. AC92).

Always furnish engine model and serial numbers when ordering parts.

MAINTENANCE

SPARK PLUG. Recommended spark plug for Model AT 330 is Champion L90 for gasoline fuel engines and Champion L86C for kerosene fuel engines. Recommended spark plug for Models VT 88 W and VT 94 W is Champion D16 for gasoline fuel engines and Champion D21 for kerosene fuel engines.

Spark plug should be removed, cleaned and inspected at 100 hour intervals. Spark plug electrode gap for all models should be 0.6-0.8 mm (0.024-0.032 in.).

CARBURETOR. All models are equipped with a float-type carburetor. Refer to Fig. AC93 for an exploded view of the carburetor used on Model AT 330 and to Fig. AC94 for an exploded view of the carburetor used on Models VT 88 W and VT 94 W.

On Model AT 330, initial adjustment of idle mixture screw (3—Fig. AC93)

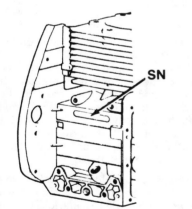

Fig. AC91—On Model AT 330, engine serial number (SN) is stamped into crankcase.

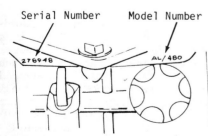

Fig. AC92—On Models VT 88 W and VT 94 W, model and serial numbers are stamped into crankcase as shown.

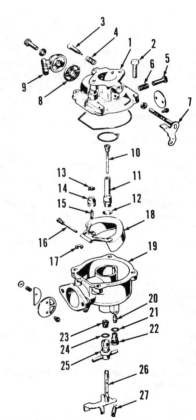

Fig. AC93—Exploded view of the float-type carburetor used on Model AT 330.

1. Carburetor body
2. Screw
3. Idle mixture screw
4. Spring
5. Throttle stop screw
6. Spring
7. Throttle shaft
8. Screen (filter)
9. Filter housing
10. Nozzle
11. Nozzle holder
12. Gasket
13. Gasket
14. Seat
15. Fuel inlet needle
16. Float pin
17. Retainer
18. Float
19. Float bowl
20. Idle jet
21. Gasket
22. Idle jet holder
23. Gasket
24. Gasket
25. Main jet holder
26. Choke shaft
27. Spring

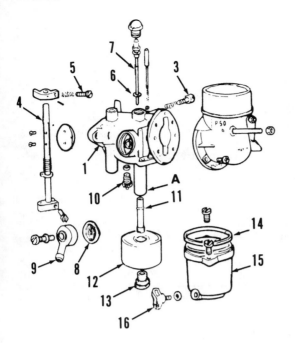

Fig. AC94—Exploded view of float-type carburetor used on Models VT 88 W and VT 94 W.

1. Carburetor body
3. Idle mixture screw
4. Throttle shaft
5. Throttle stop screw
6. Gasket
7. Idle jet
8. Screen (filter)
9. Filter housing
10. Fuel inlet needle valve
11. Nozzle
12. Float
13. Main jet
14. Gasket
15. Float bowl
16. Wing bolt

Fig. AC95—Measure distance from fuel level (F) to top of bowl (E). Distance should be 32-34 mm (1.26-1.34 in.). Refer to text.

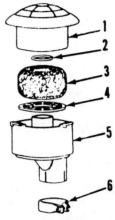

Fig. AC96—Exploded view of the oil bath air filter used on Model AT 330. Filter used on Models VT 88 W and VT 94 W is similar.

1. Cover
2. Gasket
3. Element
4. Plate
5. Oil reservoir
6. Clamp

from a lightly seated position is 1½ turns open. Main fuel mixture is controlled by a fixed main jet (23) that is not adjustable. Final adjustment should be made with engine at operating temperature and running. Adjust engine idle speed to 1100 rpm at throttle stop screw (5). Adjust idle mixture screw (3) so that engine idles smoothly and accelerates without hesitation.

Refer to Fig. AC93 for carburetor disassembly and reassembly. To check float level, invert carburetor body (1) with fuel inlet needle and seat and float (18) installed. Float should be parallel with carburetor body (1) mounting surface.

On Models VT 88 W and VT 94 W, initial adjustment of idle mixture screw (3—Fig. AC94) from a lightly seated position is 1¼ turns open. Main fuel mixture is controlled by a fixed main jet (13) that is not adjustable.

Final adjustments should be made with engine at operating temperature and running. Adjust engine idle speed to 1100 rpm at throttle stop screw (5). Adjust idle mixture screw (3) so that engine idles smoothly and accelerates without hesitation.

When installing new fuel inlet needle and seat, install seat and measure from point (A—Fig. AC94) to edge of fuel inlet needle seat. Measurement should be 33-37 mm (1.30-1.46 in.). Vary number of fiber washers between fuel inlet seat and carburetor body to obtain correct measurement.

To check float level, carefully remove float bowl (15) and measure distance from top of float bowl to the top of fuel level in bowl (Fig. AC95). Measurement should be 32-34 mm (1.26-1.34 in.). If float level is incorrect, fuel inlet needle

seat must be shimmed as outlined in previous paragraph.

Float weight should be 16.5 grams. If float is heavier than recommended weight, float must be renewed.

Fuel filter screen (8—Fig. AC94) should be removed and cleaned at 50 hour intervals.

AIR FILTER. Model AT 330 is equipped with an oil bath type air filter (Fig. AC96). Models VT 88 W and VT 94 W are equipped with a similar oil bath air filter. On all models, air filter element should be removed and cleaned after every 8 hours of operation. Discard oil and refill with new engine oil to level indicated on oil reservoir housing (5).

GOVERNOR. All models are equipped with a flyball type centrifugal governor. On Model AT 330, governor assembly is incorporated on the camshaft gear (Fig. AC97). On Models VT 88 W and VT 94 W, the governor assembly is incorporated on the magneto gear and drive shaft (Fig. AC98). On all models, governor lever should be adjusted to hold carburetor throttle plate in wide open position when engine is not running.

IGNITION SYSTEM. Model AT 330 is equipped with an electronic ignition system (Fig. AC99). Models VT 88 W and VT 94 W are equipped with a self-contained magneto unit (Fig. AC100).

The electronic ignition unit used on Model AT 330 requires no regular maintenance. Air gap between ignition unit and flywheel should be 0.45-0.50 mm (0.018-0.020 in.).

The self-contained magneto unit (Fig. AC100) used on Models VT 88 W and VT 94 W is equipped with a breaker point set, condenser and ignition coil which are located in the magneto unit. Point gap should be checked and adjusted at 400 hour intervals. To check point gap, remove cover (3—Fig. AC100) and use a suitable feeler gauge. Point gap should be 0.4-0.5 mm (0.016-0.020 in.).

Magneto should be installed so the points just begin to open when flywheel is at the 30° BTDC mark. This mark should be located on the flywheel 62.8 mm (2.472 in.) before the piston is at top dead center position.

LUBRICATION. On all models, check engine oil level at 8 hour intervals. Maintain oil level at lower edge of fill plug opening. Change oil at 50 hour intervals. Manufacturer recommends oil with an API service classification SF or SG. Use SAE 30 oil for ambient temperatures above 0° C (32° F); SAE 20W-20 oil for temperatures between 0° C (32° F) and −10° C (−14° F); and SAE 10W oil for temperatures below −10° C (−14° F).

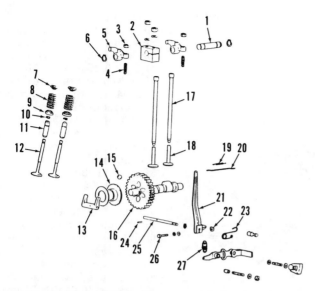

Fig. AC97—Exploded view of Model AT 330 rocker arm, camshaft and governor assemblies. VT series rocker arm assembly is similar.

1. Rocker arm shaft
2. Shaft support
3. Jam nut
4. Adjustment bolt
5. Rocker arm
6. Retaining ring
7. Spring seat
8. Valve spring
9. Retainer
10. Keeper
11. Valve guide
12. Valve
13. Governor fork
14. Governor collar
15. Flyball
16. Camshaft & gear
17. Push rod
18. Valve lifter (tappet)
19. Spring
20. Carburetor-to-governor link
21. Governor lever
22. Clamp nut
23. Spring
24. Pin
25. Governor shaft
26. Clamp bolt
27. Tension spring

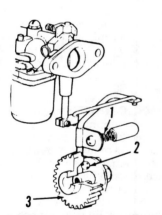

Fig. AC98—View of governor control linkage used on Models VT 88 W and VT 94 W.

1. Spring
2. Flyball
3. Magneto drive gear

Fig. AC99—View showing location of Model AT 330 electronic ignition component parts.

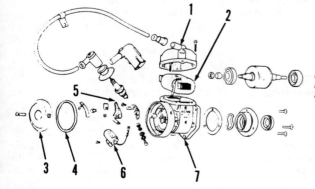

Fig. AC100—Exploded view of the magneto unit used on Models VT 88 W and VT 94 W.

1. Cap
2. Coil
3. Cover
4. Seal
5. Points
6. Condenser
7. Housing

Crankcase oil capacity is 0.75 L (0.8 qt.) for Model AT 330; 1.1 L (1.16 qt.) for Model VT 88 W; and 1.3 L (1.37 qt.) for Model VT 94 W.

VALVE ADJUSTMENT. Valve stem-to-rocker arm clearance should be checked and adjusted at 200 hour intervals. Recommended clearance for Model AT 330 is 0.10 mm (0.004 in.) for the intake valve and 0.15 mm (0.006 in.) for the exhaust valve. Recommended clearance for Models VT 88 W and VT 94 W is 0.05 mm (0.002 in.) for the intake valve and 0.10 mm (0.004 in.) for the exhaust valve. On all models, valve clearance is adjusted with the engine cold and the piston at TDC on compression stroke. Remove the rocker arm cover and loosen jam nut (3—Fig. AC97). Turn adjusting bolt (4) in rocker arm (5) to obtain correct clearance between the rocker arm and the valve stem. When correct clearance is obtained, hold adjustment bolt (4) in position while jam nut (3) is tightened.

CRANKCASE BREATHER. Crankcase breather must be removed and cleaned at 50 hour intervals. On Model AT 330, the breather is part of the valve tappet cover (Fig. AC101). On Models VT 88 W and VT 94 W, the breather is located on the rocker arm cover (Fig. AC102). The flat face of diaphragm (3) must be installed toward rocker arm cover (4).

GENERAL MAINTENANCE. Check and tighten all loose bolts, nuts or clamps daily. Check for fuel or oil leakage and repair as necessary. Clean dust, dirt, grease or any foreign material from cylinder head and cylinder block cooling fins periodically.

REPAIRS

TIGHTENING TORQUES. Recommended tightening torque specifications are as follows:

Cylinder head:
AT 330 . . . . 30 N·m
(22 ft.-lbs.)
VT series . . . . 39 N·m
(29 ft.-lbs.)
Cylinder-to-crankcase
VT series . . . . 22 N·m
(16 ft.-lbs.)
Connecting rod
AT 330 . . . . 19 N·m
(14 ft.-lbs.)
Rocker arm cover . . . . 19 N·m
(14 ft.-lbs.)
Valve adjustment bolt
jam nut . . . . 18 N·m
(13 ft.-lbs.)

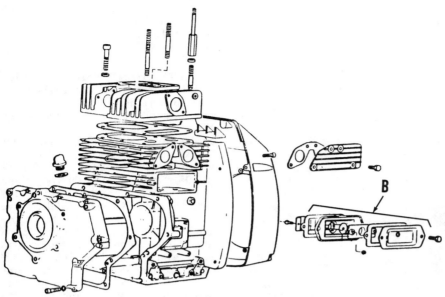

Fig. AC101—Drawing of crankcase breather assembly (B) used on Model AT 330.

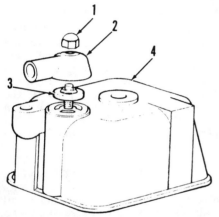

Fig. AC102—View of breather assembly used on Models VT 88 W and VT 94 W.

1. Nut
2. Cap
3. Diaphragm
4. Rocker arm cover

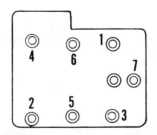

Fig. AC103—Tighten or loosen cylinder head bolts on Model AT 330 following the sequence shown.

Flywheel:
AT 330 . . . . 157 N•m
(116 ft.-lbs.)
VT series . . . . 176 N•m
(130 ft.-lbs.)
Spark plug . . . . 19 N•m
(14 ft.-lbs.)

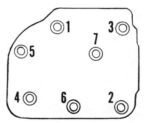

Fig. AC104—Tighten or loosen cylinder head bolts on Models VT 88 W and VT 94 W following the sequence shown.

CYLINDER HEAD AND VALVES.

The cylinder head on all models is an aluminum alloy casting with hardened steel valve seat inserts. To remove the cylinder head on all models, remove all cooling shrouds and the rocker arm cover. Loosen and remove all head bolts in the sequence shown in Fig. AC103 for Model AT 330 or in sequence shown in Fig. AC104 for Models VT 88 W and VT 94 W.

CAUTION: Never remove cylinder head while engine is hot as cylinder head distortion will result.

Check cylinder head for flatness by placing on a flat surface and using a feeler gauge to measure distortion. If cylinder head is warped more than 0.5 mm (0.020 in.), machine the gasket surface as necessary or renew cylinder head.

Always install a new head gasket and tighten cylinder head bolts to specified torque following sequence shown in Fig. AC103 for Model AT 330 or following sequence shown in Fig. AC104 for Models VT 88 W and VT 94 W.

The intake valve guide is cast iron and the exhaust valve guide is bronze. Standard valve guide inside diameter for Model AT 330 is 7.015-7.025 mm (0.2762-0.2766 in.). Maximum allowable inside diameter is 7.097 mm (0.2794 in.). Standard valve guide inside diameter for Models VT 88 W and VT 94 W is 9.025-9.035 mm (0.3553-0.3557 in.). Maximum allowable inside diameter is 9.100 mm (0.3582 in.).

Standard valve stem diameter for Model AT 330 is 6.965-6.987 mm (0.2742-0.2751 in.) for the intake and exhaust valves. Standard valve stem diameter for Models VT 88 W and VT 94 W is 8.965-8.987 mm (0.3530-0.3538 in.) for intake and exhaust valves.

On all models, valve faces and seats should be ground at 45° angle for intake and exhaust. Valve seat width should be 1.2-1.3 mm (0.047-0.051 in.).

Valve spring free length on Model AT 330 should be 35 mm (1.378 in.). If spring free length is 32 mm (1.260 in.) or less, renew spring. Valve spring free length on Models VT 88 W and VT 94 W should be 54 mm (2.126 in.). It should require 45 kg (99 lbs.) force to compress valve spring to 30.4 mm (1.197 in.).

Maximum clearance between rocker arm and rocker arm shaft is 0.15 mm (0.006 in.) on all models. If clearance exceeds specified dimension, renew rocker arm and/or rocker arm shaft.

Model AT 330

CONNECTING ROD. On Model AT 330, the aluminum alloy connecting rod rides directly on the crankpin journal. To remove the connecting rod and piston assembly, remove the cylinder head and crankcase cover. Use care when crankcase cover is removed as governor flyweight balls will fall out of ramps in camshaft gear. Remove connecting rod cap and push connecting rod and piston assembly out of cylinder head end of block. Remove piston pin retaining rings and separate piston from connecting rod. Camshaft and lifters may be removed at this time also.

Clearance between the piston pin and connecting rod pin bore should be 0.000-0.023 mm (0.0000-0.0009 in.). Connecting rod side play on crankpin journal should be 0.15-0.25 mm (0.006-0.010 in.). Connecting rod should be renewed if crankpin bore is worn or out-of-round more than 0.10 mm (0.004 in.).

Piston can be installed on connecting rod either way. However, when installing connecting rod, triangle match marks on connecting rod and cap must be aligned and facing crankcase cover side of engine for clockwise rotation engines or flywheel side of engine for counterclockwise rotation engines. Tighten connecting rod bolts to specified torque. Use heavy grease to retain governor flyweight balls in camshaft ramps or position crankcase in a suitable stand to aid crankcase cover installation. Tighten crankcase cover retaining screws evenly to specified torque.

Models VT 88 W and VT 94 W

On Models VT 88 W and VT 94 W, the connecting rod is installed on the connecting rod journal which is then pressed into the crankshaft halves. The connecting rod bearing is selected together with the connecting rod and crankshaft journal in three classes, each having a tolerance of 0.004 mm (0.00016 in.). Connecting rod, bearing and crankshaft journal must be renewed as an assembly.

To remove connecting rod, remove all shrouds. Remove the cylinder head. Remove the cylinder retaining nuts and carefully pull the cast iron cylinder up off the piston assembly. Use a suitable puller (Acme tool 365111) to remove the flywheel and then the crankcase cover. Remove the crankshaft and connecting rod assembly. If the connecting rod must be removed from the crankshaft, remove the piston from the connecting rod. The crankshaft halves must be separated using a suitable puller (Acme tool 365126). To reassemble the crankshaft, use a suitable jig (Acme tool 365130) and a press. Press the crankshaft together until there is 0.2-0.4 mm (0.008-0.016 in.) clearance between connecting rod and crankshaft shoulder. Shims are available to adjust clearance between connecting rod and crankshaft shoulder. The two crankshaft halves must be concentric with the crankshaft connecting rod journal. Maximum offcenter allowance is 0.05 mm (0.002 in.).

Clearance between the piston pin and connecting rod pin bore should be 0.02-0.05 mm (0.0008-0.0020 in.).

Piston can be installed on connecting rod either way. When installing crankcase cover on crankcase, tighten bolts to the specified torque in a crisscross pattern.

CYLINDER AND CRANKCASE.
On Model AT 330, cylinder and crankcase are an integral casting of aluminum alloy with a high density perlite cylinder sleeve cast as an integral part of the cylinder block. Standard cylinder bore diameter is 80.000-80.013 mm (3.1496-3.1501 in.). On Models VT 88 W and VT 94 W, the cast iron cylinder is a separate casting and can be removed from the crankcase. Standard cylinder bore diameter is 88.000-88.013 mm

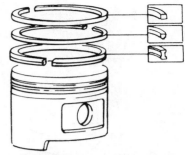

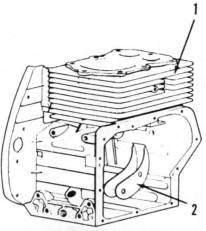

Fig. AC105—View of Model AT 330 cylinder block (1) and oil slinger trough (2). If trough is removed, it must be securely repositioned prior to assembly of engine.

(3.4645-3.4651 in.) for Model VT 88 W and 94.000-94.013 mm (3.7008-3.7013 in.) for Model VT 94 W.

On all models, if the cylinder bore is 0.06 mm (0.0024 in.) or more out-of-round or tapered, cylinder should be bored to nearest oversize for which piston and rings are available.

On all models, crankshaft ball-type main bearings should be a slight press fit in crankcase main bearing bores. Renew bearings if they are loose, rough or damaged.

On Model AT 330, an oil slinger trough (2—Fig. AC105) is installed in the crankcase. If trough is removed, it must be securely repositioned prior to engine reassembly.

PISTON, PIN AND RINGS.
On all models, refer to CONNECTING ROD section for piston removal and installation procedure.

Standard piston diameter is 79.987-80.000 mm (3.1491-3.1496 in.) for Model AT 330; 87.987-88.000 mm (3.4640-3.4645 in.) for Model VT 88 W; and 93.987-94.000 mm (3.7003-3.7008 for Model VT 94 W. On all models, pistons are a select fit at the factory.

Insert piston rings in the cylinder and measure the gap between rings ends using a feeler gauge. On Model AT 330, ring end gap should be 0.30-0.50 mm (0.012-0.019 in.) for compression rings and 0.25-0.50 mm (0.010-0.019 in.) for oil ring. On Models VT 88 W and VT 94 W, ring end gap should be 0.35-0.80 mm (0.014-0.031 in.) for compression rings and 0.25-0.70 mm (0.010-0.027 in.) for oil ring.

On all models, piston pin should be 0.004-0.012 mm (0.0002-0.0005 in.) interference fit in piston pin bore. It will

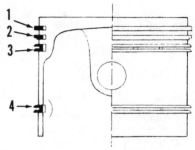

Fig. AC106—On Model AT 330, piston rings should be installed as shown.

Fig. AC107—On models VT 88 W and VT 94 W, piston rings must be installed so the step on the second ring (2) faces down and the bevel on oil control rings (3 and 4) faces up.

be necessary to heat piston slightly to aid in pin removal or installation.

On Model AT 330, refer to Fig. AC106 for correct piston ring installation. On Models VT 88 W and VT 94 W, refer to Fig. AC107 for correct piston ring installation. On all models, stagger ring end gaps equally around piston diameter.

CRANKSHAFT. On all models, the crankshaft is supported at each end by ball bearing-type main bearings. Refer to Fig. AC108 for an exploded view of the crankshaft assembly used on Model AT 330 and to Fig. AC109 for an exploded view of the crankshaft assembly used on Models VT 88 W and VT 94 W. Refer to CONNECTING ROD for crankshaft removal procedure.

On Model AT 330, the crankshaft timing gear (15—Fig. AC108) is a press fit on crankshaft (13). Standard clearance between crankpin journal and connecting rod crankpin bore should be 0.040-0.064 mm (0.0016-0.0025 in.). Standard crankshaft crankpin journal diameter is 29.985-30.000 mm (1.1805-1.811 in.). If crankshaft crankpin journal is worn or out-of-round 0.015 mm (.0006 in.) or more, renew crankshaft. Standard main bearing journal diameter is 30 mm (1.18 in.) and ball-type main bearings should be a slight press fit on crankshaft journal. Renew bearings if they are rough, loose or damaged. Note that crankshaft should be supported on

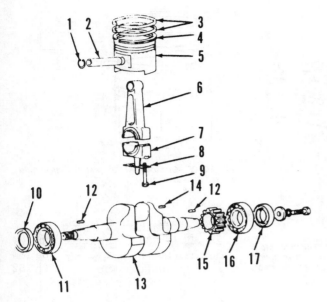

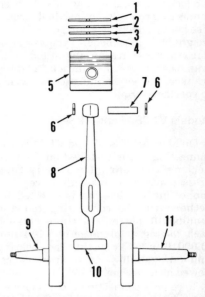

Fig. AC108—Exploded view of crankshaft, connecting rod and piston assembly used on Model AT 330.

1. Retaining ring
2. Piston pin
3. Compression rings
4. Oil control ring
5. Piston
6. Connecting rod
7. Connecting rod cap
8. Lockplate
9. Bolts
10. Seal
11. Main bearing
12. Key
13. Crankshaft
14. Crankshaft gear key
15. Crankshaft gear
16. Main bearing
17. Seal

Fig. AC109—Exploded view of crankshaft, connecting rod and piston assembly used on Models VT 88 W and VT 94 W.

1. Compression ring	7. Piston pin
2. Compression ring	8. Connecting rod
3. Oil control ring	9. Crankshaft half
4. Oil control ring	10. Connecting rod journal
5. Piston	11. Crankshaft half
6. Retaining ring	

counterweights when pressing bearings or crankshaft timing gear onto or off of crankshaft to prevent bending crankshaft. When installing crankshaft, make certain that crankshaft and camshaft gear timing marks are aligned.

On Models VT 88 W and VT 94 W, the crankshaft is a three-piece assembly (Fig. AC109) which must be pressed together using the procedure and special jig described under CONNECTING ROD section. When installing crankshaft, make certain that crankshaft and camshaft gear timing marks are aligned.

CAMSHAFT. On Model AT 330, the camshaft and camshaft gear are an integral casting which rides in bearing bores in crankcase and crankcase cover. A compression release mechanism is mounted on the back side of camshaft gear and governor flyballs are located in ramps machined into face of gear. The spring-loaded compression release

mechanism should snap back against the camshaft when weighted lever is pulled against spring tension and released.

Inspect camshaft journals and lobes and renew camshaft if worn, scored or damaged. Camshaft bearing journal diameters should be 15.973-15.984 mm (0.6289-0.6293 in.). Governor flyball should move smoothly across ramp faces without catching. When installing camshaft, retain governor flyballs in ramps with heavy grease and make certain camshaft and crankshaft gear timing marks are aligned.

On Models VT 88 W and VT 94 W, the camshaft is supported at each end by renewable bushings. The camshaft gear has helical teeth to reduce noise and improve meshing. Camshaft axial thrust is controlled by a ball tensioned by a spring (Fig. AC110). When installing camshaft, make certain that piston is at top dead center when timing marks

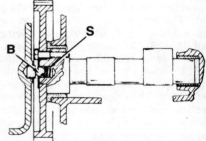

Fig. AC110—Camshaft axial thrust is controlled by ball (B) and spring (S).

on camshaft gear and crankshaft gear are aligned.

ACME
SERVICING ACME ACCESSORIES

REWIND STARTER

Refer to Fig. AC150 for exploded view of rewind starter used on all models so equipped. Rewind spring (5) and spring housing (4) are serviced as an assembly only.

When installing rewind starter assembly on engine, install but do not tighten the six bolts retaining assembly to cooling shroud. Pull cable handle (7) until 150 mm (6 in.) of cable has been pulled from housing and starter dogs (9) have centered assembly. Hold tension on cable while the six bolts are tightened.

ALTERNATOR

A fixed armature type alternator, mounted on the engine crankcase behind the flywheel, is available for some engines. To test alternator output, disconnect rectifier leads (Fig. AC151) and connect to an AC voltmeter with at least a 30 volt capacity. Start engine and refer to the following specifications for voltage output according to engine speed.

2400 rpm	20-22 volts
2800 rpm	23-25 volts
3200 rpm	26-28 volts
3600 rpm	29-30 volts

Rectifier may be checked by connecting an ammeter between positive battery lead and the positive rectifier terminal. Connect a 20 volt DC voltmeter to battery posts and use lights or other battery drain method to lower battery voltage below 13 volts. Start engine and refer to the following specifications for amperage output according to engine speed.

2400 rpm	0.5 amp
2800 rpm	1.5 amp
3200 rpm	2.2 amp
3600 rpm	2.7 amp

If battery charge current is 0 amp with battery voltage 12.5 or less, renew rectifier.

CAUTION: Never operate engine with rectifier disconnected as rectifier will be damaged.

ACME SPECIAL TOOLS

The following special tools are available from Acme Central Parts Distributors or Acme Corporation.

Models ALN 220 W, ALN 290 W, ALN 330 W, AL 290 VW, AL 330 VW, AT 330

Tool Description	Tool Number
Valve spring extractor (except AT 330)	365 110
Ignition coil positioning tool	365 168
Valve guide check tool	365 048
Valve guide puller (except AT 330)	365 109
Electrical tester	365 180
Oil seal installation cone	365 152
Flywheel & timing cover puller	365 113

Models FE 82 W, AL 480 W, AL 550W, VT 88 W, VT 94 W

Tool Description	Tool Number
Flywheel puller	365 111
Timing gear puller	365 104
Crankshaft removal tool	365 126
Crankshaft assembly jig	365 130
Intake guide driver	365 127
Exhaust guide driver	365 128
Seal sleeve (flange side)	365 254
Seal sleeve (flywheel side)	365 153
Electrical tester	365 180
Magneto nut tool	365 135
Valve guide gauge (FE 82 W, AL 480 W, AL 550 W)	365 136
Valve guide gauge (VT 88 W, VT 94 W)	365 137
Oil seal & bearing tool	365 125

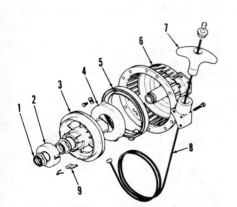

Fig. AC150—Exploded view of rewind starter assembly used on some models.

1. Snap ring
2. Starter dog housing
3. Cable pulley
4. Spring housing
5. Rewind spring
6. Housing
7. Handle
8. Cable
9. Starter dogs

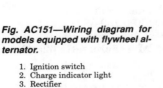

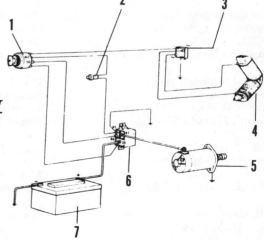

Fig. AC151—Wiring diagram for models equipped with flywheel alternator.

1. Ignition switch
2. Charge indicator light
3. Rectifier
4. Charging coil
5. Starter
6. Solenoid
7. Battery

ACME CENTRAL PARTS DISTRIBUTORS

(Arranged Alphabetically by States)

These franchised firms carry extensive stocks of repair parts. Contact them
for name of the nearest service distributor.

Alyeska Pump & Equipment
Phone: (907) 344-5842
8221 Dimond Hook Drive
Anchorage, Alaska 99507

Construction Equipment
Phone: (907) 563-3822
5400 Homer Drive
Anchorage, Alaska 99518

Fessler Equipment
Phone: (907) 276-5335
2400 Commercial Drive
Anchorage, Alaska 99501

Engine Powered Products
Phone: (602) 258-9396
3040 North 27th Ave.
Phoenix, Arizona 85017

Scotsco Pro Power Products
Phone: (800) 547-3989
8806 Fruitridge Road
Sacramento, California 95826

Webb's Farm Supplies
Phone: (408) 475-1020
5381 Old San Jose Road
Soquel, California 95073

Ace Energy
Phone: (719) 947-3724
60010 East Highway 96
Boone, Colorado 81025

House And Garden
Phone: (203) 322-9676
984 High Ridge Road
Stamford, Connecticut 06905

Mac Equipment, Inc.
Phone: (904) 788-5311
4110 S. Nova Road
Daytona Beach, Florida 32015

Austral International
Phone: (305) 633-0732
3198 N.W. South River Drive
Miami, Florida 33142

Kelly Tractor Co.
Phone: (305) 592-5360
P.O. Box 520775
Miami, Florida 33152

R.B. Grove, Inc.
Phone: (305) 854-5420
261 S.W. 6th Street
Miami, Florida 33130

Diesel Technology
Phone: (813) 425-3039
4325 Highway 60 West
Mulberry, Florida 33860

Elastec
Phone: (618) 382-2525
121 Council Street
Carmi, Illinois 62821

Fauver Co.
Phone: (708) 682-5010
275 Commonwealth Drive
Carol Stream, Illinois 60188

Groban International
Phone: (312) 374-6900
9300 South Drexel Avenue
Chicago, Illinois 60619

Burlington Wholesale
Phone: (219) 546-9010
1533 East 3rd Road
Bremen, Indiana 46506

D & D Enterprises
Phone: (812) 883-6437
955 33rd Avenue S.W.
Cedar Rapids, Iowa 52404

Fauver Co.
Phone: (319) 366-6437
955 33rd Ave. S.W.
Cedar Rapids, Iowa 52404

Buckner Generator & Armature Service
Phone: (504) 868-9138
390 South Van
Houma, Louisiana 70361

Dave's Engine Service
Phone: none
Hwy. 5
Loveville, Maryland 20656

The Engine Room
Phone: (508) 759-3921
57 Onset Ave.
Onset, Massachusetts 02532

Great Plains
Phone: (612) 894-9510
2800 Southcross Drive
Burnsville, Minnesota 55337

Fauver Co.
Phone: (612) 943-1644
10286 West 70th Street
Eden Prairie, Minnesota 55344

Mel's Supply And Repair
Phone: (507) 932-4497
Route 1, Box 185
Utica, Minnesota 55979

Fauver Co.
Phone: (816) 452-4444
3939 N.E. 33rd Terrace, Suite H
Kansas City, Missouri 64117

Phillips Diesel Corporation
Phone: (505) 865-7332
P.O. Box 999
Los Lunas, New Mexico 87301

Amna Pump Corporation
Phone: (718) 784-2004
33-11 Green Point Ave.
Long Island City, New York 11101

Watermill Rental Center
Phone: (516) 726-6664
Montauk Highway
Water Mill, New York 11976

Asheville Opeco./Riverside
Phone: (704) 298-1988
501 Swannanoa River Road
Asheville, North Carolina 28805

Fauver Co.
Phone: (216) 923-8855
895 Hampshire Road, Suite C
Stow, Ohio 44224

Brown Engine & Equipment
Phone: (405) 632-2301
4315 S. Robinson
Oklahoma City, Oklahoma 73109

Pro Power Products
Phone: (503) 777-4726
9162 S.E. 74th Avenue
Portland, Oregon 97206

GD Equipment
Phone: (717) 859-3533
385 West Metzler Road
Ephrata, Pennsylvania 17522

Knox Auto Supply
Phone: (814) 797-1207
Box W, Miller St.
Knox, Pennsylvania 16232

Jerry B. Leach Co.
Phone: (803) 537-2141
447 State Road
Cheraw, South Carolina 29520

SERVICE MANUAL

ACME PARTS DISTRIBUTORS

Ray Wright Pumps
Phone: (713) 487-0665
5514 Sycamor
Pasadena, Texas 77503

Anchor Farms Equipment
Phone: (206) 376-5051
P.O. Box 1271
Eastsound, Washington 98245

Seattle Ship Supply
Phone: (206) 283-7000
1559 West Thurman
C-10 Dock 4
Seattle, Washington 98119

Fauver Co.
Phone: (414) 781-1525
4475-C N. 124th St.
Brookfield, Wisconsin 53005

CANADIAN DISTRIBUTORS

Coast Dieselec, Ltd.
Phone: (604) 533-2601
#111 20120 64th Avenue
Langley, British Columbia V3A 4P7

Premium Pump/Engine/Generator
Phone: (902) 562-6544
Sydport Industrial Park
Sydney, Nova Scotia B1P 6W4

Normand-Michel
Phone: (514) 453-4705
389, 24 'Eme Avenue
Ile Perrot, Quebec J7V 4N1

Provincial Diesel
Phone: (514) 937-9371
730 Rose De Lima
Montreal, Quebec H4C 2L8

United Auto Parts
Phone: (418) 962-6533
335 Laure Boulevard
Sept'lles, Quebec G4R 1X2

BRIGGS & STRATTON ENGINE
IDENTIFICATION INFORMATION

In order to obtain correct service parts for Briggs & Stratton engines it is necessary to correctly identify engine model or series and provide engine serial number.

Briggs & Stratton model or series number also provides information concerning important mechanical features or optional equipment.

Refer to the table below for an explanation of each digit in relation to engine identification or description of mechanical features and options.

As an example, a 401417 series model number is broken down in the following manner:

40 – Designates 40 cubic inch displacement.
1 – Designates design series 1.
4 – Designates horizontal shaft, Flo-Jet carburetor and mechanical governor.
1 – Designates flange mounting with plain bearings.
7 – Designates electric starter, 12 volt gear drive with alternator.

CUBIC INCH DISPLACEMENT	FIRST DIGIT AFTER DISPLACEMENT BASIC DESIGN SERIES	SECOND DIGIT AFTER DISPLACEMENT CRANKSHAFT, CARBURETOR, GOVERNOR	THIRD DIGIT AFTER DISPLACEMENT PTO BEARING, LUBE, REDUCTION GEARS, AUXILIARY DRIVES	FOURTH DIGIT AFTER DISPLACEMENT TYPE OF STARTER
6	0	0 - Horizontal Shaft	0 - Plain Bearing/DU	0 - Without Starter
8	1	Diaphragm Carb.	Non-flange Mount	
9	2	Pneumatic Governor		
10	3	1 - Horizonal Shaft	1 - Plain Bearing	1 - Rope Starter
11	4	Vacu-Jet Carb.	Flange Mount	
12	5	Pneumatic Governor		
13	6	2 - Horizontal	2 - Sleeve Bearing	2 - Rewind Starter
16	7	Pulsa-Jet Carb.	Flange Mount	
17	8	Pneumatic or Mech.	Splash Lube	
18	9	Governor		
19	A to Z	3 - Horizontal Shaft	3 - Ball Bearing	3 - Elec. Starter
22		Flo-Jet Carb.	Flange Mount	3 - 120V Gear Drive
23		Pneumatic Governor	Splash Lube	Starter/Generator
24		4 - Horizontal Shaft	4 - Ball Bearing	4 - Elec.
25		Flo-Jet Carb.	Flange Mount	12V Belt Drive
26		Mech. Governor	Pressure Lube on	
			Horizontal Shaft	
28		5 - Vertical Shaft	5 - Plain Bearing	5 - Elec. Starter
29		Vacu-Jet Carb.	Gear Reduction	12V Gear Drive
30		Pneumatic or	Gear Reduction	
32		Mech. Governor	(6 to 1)	
			CW Rotation	
			Flange Mount	
35		6 - Plain Bearing	6 - Gear Reduction	6 -Alternator Only
40		6 - Vertial Shaft	(6 to 1) CCW Rotation	

(continued)

CUBIC INCH DISPLACEMENT	FIRST DIGIT AFTER DISPLACEMENT	SECOND DIGIT AFTER DISPLACEMENT	THIRD DIGIT AFTER DISPLACEMENT	FOURTH DIGIT AFTER DISPLACEMENT
	BASIC DESIGN SERIES	CRANKSHAFT, CARBURETOR, GOVERNOR	PTO BEARING, LUBE, REDUCTION GEARS, AUXILIARY DRIVES	TYPE OF STARTER
42		7 - Vertical Shaft Flo-Jet Carb. Pneumatic or Mech. Governor	7 - Plain Bearing Pressure Lube on Vertical Shaft	7 - Elec. Starter 12V Gear Drive With Alternator
46		8 - Vertical Shaft Flo-Jet Carb. Mech. Governor	8 - Plain Bearing Auxiliary Drive (PTO) Perpedicular to	8 - Vertical Pull Starter or Side Pull Starter
		9 - Vertical Shaft Pulsa-Jet Carb. Pnuematic or Mech. Governor	9 - Plain Bearing Auxiliary Drive Parallel to Crankshaft	

BRIGGS & STRATTON

BRIGGS & STRATTON CORPORATION
Milwaukee, Wisconsin 53201

SINGLE-CYLINDER OHV ENGINES

Model Series	No. Cyls.	Bore	Stroke	Displacement	Power Rating
287700	1	3.438 in. (87.3 mm)	3.06 in. (77.7 mm)	28.4 cu. in. (465 cc)	14.0 hp (10.4 kW)
28E700, 28N700, 28P700, 28Q700, 28S700, 28U700, 28W700	1	3.438 in. (87.3 mm)	3.06 in. (77.7 mm)	28.4 cu. in. (465 cc)	See text
310700, 311700, 312700	1	3.562 in. (90.6 mm)	3.06 in. (77.7 mm)	31.0 cu. in. (508 cc)	See text

NOTE: Power ratings vary between 14.0 to 16.0 horsepower (10.4-11.9 kW) due to differences in carburetor and camshaft design. Power rating is identified on the blower housing of each model.

Engines in this section are four-stroke, single-cylinder, overhead valve engines with a vertical crankshaft. All engines are constructed of aluminum.

The connecting rod on all models rides directly on the crankpin journal. An oil slinger wheel located on the governor gear provides splash lubrication.

All engines are equipped with a breakerless (Magnetron) ignition system. A float-type carburetor is used on all models.

Refer to BRIGGS & STRATTON ENGINE IDENTIFICATION INFORMATION section for engine identification. Engine model number as well as type and code numbers are necessary when ordering parts.

MAINTENANCE

LUBRICATION. An oil slinger located on the governor gear provides splash lubrication.

Series 31x700 and some 28x700 engines have a pressurized oil filtration system. A gerotor-style pump (Fig. B400) mounted in the engine's sump constantly circulates reservoir oil through the filter, then back into the sump to help keep the oil clean. The pump does not supply pressurized oil to any engine bearings; the engine is still splash lubricated.

A machined tab on the bottom of the camshaft drives the oil pump. Oil pump can be accessed for service from outside bottom of the engine; engine disassembly is not required. Inspect pump components when performing major engine repairs. The pump is serviced as an assembly. Tighten the pump cover screws to 80 in.-lb. (9.0 N·m). Replace filter at every oil change (50 hours).

Engine oil should be changed after first eight hours of operation and after every 50 hours of operation or at least once each operating season. If equipment undergoes severe usage, change oil weekly or after every 25 hours of operation. Drain the oil while the engine is warm. The oil will flow freely and carry away more impurities.

Manufacturer recommends using oil with an API service classification of SH or SJ, or any classification formulated to supercede SH or SJ. Use SAE 30 oil for temperatures above 40° F (4° C); use SAE 10W-30 oil for temperatures between 0° F (−18° C) and 40° F (4° C); below 0° F (−18° C) use petroleum-based SAE 5W-20 or a suitable synthetic oil. Do not use 10W-40 oil.

Crankcase oil capacity is approximately 3 pints (1.4 L).

SPARK PLUG. Replace the spark plug if electrodes are burned away or if the porcelain is cracked or fouled. Recommended spark plug is Champion RC12YC. Specified spark plug electrode gap is 0.030 inch (0.76 mm).

CAUTION: Briggs & Stratton does not recommend using abrasive blasting to clean spark plugs as this may introduce some abrasive material into the engine that could cause extensive damage.

CARBURETOR. The Walbro LMT carburetor is equipped with a fixed

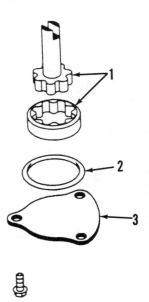

Fig. BS400—An oil pump is used on some models to circulate engine oil through an oil filter.

1. Pump rotors
2. O-ring
3. Cover

main jet and an adjustable idle mixture screw. Carburetor adjustments must be made with the air cleaner installed and engine at operating temperature.

For initial setting of idle mixture screw (12—Fig. B401), turn the screw in (clockwise) until the head of the screw just contacts the spring. Start the engine and place the speed control lever in "SLOW" position. Adjust idle speed screw (11) so engine idles at 1750 rpm. With engine running at idle speed, turn idle mixture screw clockwise until engine speed just starts to drop. Note the screw position. Turn

idle mixture screw counterclockwise until engine speed just starts to drop again. Note the screw position, and turn screw to midpoint between the noted screw positions. Install the limiter cap (13) with the flat facing up. If engine will not accelerate cleanly, slightly enrich mixture by turning idle mixture needle counterclockwise. If necessary, readjust idle speed screw to obtain idle speed specified by equipment manufacturer.

An optional main jet calibrated to compensate for high altitude operation is available.

To disassemble carburetor, remove fuel solenoid (22—Fig. B400) and float bowl (20). Remove the hinge pin (19), float (18) and fuel inlet valve (16). To remove fuel inlet seat (15), thread a 1/4-20 tap or self-tapping screw into the seat and pull it from carburetor body. Remove the main jet (14), then unscrew jet nozzle (1) from the body using a suitable screwdriver. A 5/16-inch diameter pin punch ground flat at the end makes a suitable tool for removing Welch plug (2). Remove limiter cap (13) and idle mixture screw (12). Remove throttle plate (5), shaft (6), seal (4) and bushing (3). Remove choke plate (8) and shaft (9).

Clean fuel passages with commercial carburetor cleaner and compressed air. Inspect components and discard any parts that are damaged or excessively worn. Fuel solenoid operation can be checked using a 9-volt battery. Plunger needle should snap into solenoid body when energized.

When reassembling carburetor, note the following: Do not deform Welch plug (2) during installation; it should be flat. Seal outer edges of plug with fingernail polish or a non-hardening sealer. When installing choke shaft (9), note that small hook in return spring (10) engages the shaft and large hook engages boss on carburetor body. Guide the detent spring (7) into the slot in choke shaft. Install choke plate (8) with single notch on edge towards fuel inlet side of body. Install throttle shaft seal (4) with sealing lip down until flush with top of body. Install throttle plate so numbers are facing outward and toward the idle mixture screw side of body when plate is in closed position. After installing jet nozzle (1), use compressed air to blow out any debris that may have been loosened during installing of the nozzle. Install the main jet (14) after installing the nozzle.

Install fuel inlet seat using B&S driver 19135 or other suitable tool. Press seat in until flush with surface of fuel inlet boss. Float height is not adjustable. If float is not approximately parallel with the body when the carburetor is inverted, replace the float, fuel inlet valve and/or valve seat. Install idle mixture screw (12) with spring and turn in until head of screw just contacts the spring.

Install carburetor with new gasket. Long edge side of gasket should be opposite fuel inlet. Attach governor and choke links. Tighten carburetor mounting nuts to 65 in.-lbs. (7.3 N·m). Adjust carburetor as previously outlined.

REMOTE CONTROL ADJUSTMENT. With throttle control in "Fast" position, hole in governor control lever

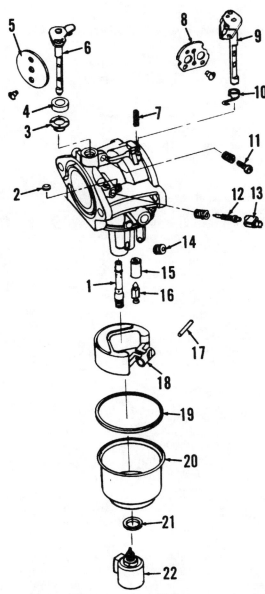

Fig. BS401—Exploded view of Walbro LMT carburetor used on all models.

1. Nozzle	7. Spring	13. Limiter cap	18. Float
2. Welch plug	8. Choke plate	14. Main jet	19. Gasket
3. Bushing	9. Choke shaft	15. Valve seat	20. Float bowl
4. Seal	10. Return spring	16. Fuel inlet valve	21. Gasket
5. Throttle plate	11. Idle speed screw	17. Hinge pin	22. Fuel solenoid
6. Throttle shaft	12. Idle mixture screw		

(3—Fig. B402) must align with hole in control plate (1). If it does not, loosen the throttle cable clamp screw and move the governor control rack (5) until holes are aligned. Tighten cable clamp screw.

FUEL PUMP. A fuel pump is available as optional equipment on some models. Refer to BRIGGS & STRATTON ACCESSORIES section for service information.

GOVERNOR. All engines are equipped with a gear-driven mechanical-type governor attached to the oil pan. The camshaft gear drives the governor. Governor and linkage must operate properly to prevent "hunting" or unsteady operation. The carburetor must be properly adjusted before performing governor adjustments.

To adjust governor linkage, loosen clamp bolt attaching governor lever to governor shaft (Fig. B403). Move governor lever so carburetor throttle plate is in wide-open position and hold in this position. Rotate governor shaft clockwise as far as possible and tighten clamp bolt.

IMPORTANT: Running an engine at a maximum speed other than the speed specified by the equipment manufacturer can be dangerous to the operator, harmful to the equipment and inefficient. Adjust governed engine speed to specification stipulated by equipment manufacturer.

To set maximum no-load speed, start engine and move remote speed control to maximum speed position. Insert a suitable tool between the governor control cover and engine casting and bend governor spring anchor tang to obtain desired maximum no-load speed.

IGNITION SYSTEM. All models are equipped with a Magnetron breakerless ignition system. The system does not require periodic maintenance. Flywheel removal is not necessary except to check or service keyway or crankshaft key.

To check spark, remove spark plug, connect spark plug cable to B&S tester 19051 and ground remaining tester lead on engine cylinder head. Rotate engine at 350 rpm or more. If spark jumps the 0.166 inch (4.2 mm) tester gap, system is functioning properly.

Air gap between armature legs and flywheel magnets should be 0.010-0.014 inch (0.25-0.36 mm). Ignition timing is not adjustable on these models.

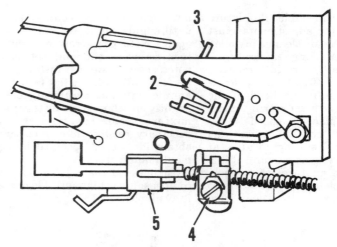

Fig. B402—Refer to text to adjust remote control.

1. Governor control plate hole
2. Stop switch
3. Governor control lever
4. Clamp screw
5. Governor control rack

VALVE ADJUSTMENT. Valve adjustment should be performed with the engine cold, using the following recommended procedure:

Remove spark plug and valve cover. Rotate crankshaft in normal direction (clockwise at flywheel) so piston is at top dead center on compression stroke (both valves closed). Insert a narrow scale into the spark plug hole, then continue to rotate crankshaft so piston is ¼ inch (6.4 mm) down from top dead center. This position places the tappet away from the compression release device on the cam lobe.

Using feeler gauges, measure the clearance between rocker arms and valve stem caps. Refer to table below for specified valve clearance dimensions.

VALVE CLEARANCE

Series 28E700, 28N700, 28P700, 28Q700, 287700

Intake	0.003-0.005 in. (0.08-0.13 mm)
Exhaust	0.005-0.007 in. (0.13-0.18 mm)

Series 28S700, 28U700, 28W700, 310700, 311700, 312700

Intake	0.003-0.005 in. (0.08-0.13 mm)
Exhaust	0.003-0.005 in. (0.08-0.13 mm)

To adjust, loosen set screw inside rocker arm adjusting ball-nut, and adjust ball-nut to obtain proper clearance. While holding ball-nut, tighten rocker arm set screw to 60 in.-lb. (5.7 N·m) for Series 287700 and 28E700-28Q700 engines; 45 in.-lb. (5.0 N·m) for Series

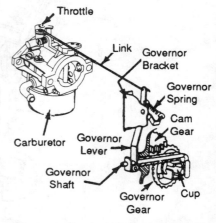

Fig. B403—View of governor assembly typical of all models.

28S700-28W700 and 310700-312700 engines.

Install valve cover with a new gasket. Tighten valve cover screws following the sequence shown in Fig. B404 to 55-60 in.-lb. (6.0-6.8 N·m.)

CRANKCASE BREATHER. A crankcase breather is located on the side of the cylinder block. A vent tube connects the breather to the carburetor air inlet tube. A partial vacuum must exist in crankcase to prevent oil seepage past oil seals, gaskets, breaker point plunger or piston rings. Air can flow out of crankcase through the

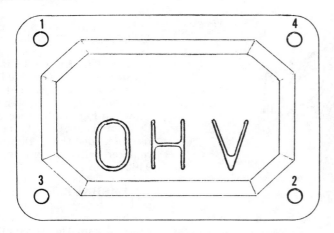

Fig. B404—Tighten valve cover screws in sequence shown.

breather, but a one-way valve blocks return flow, maintaining necessary vacuum.

Make certain the fiber disc valve in the breather is not stuck or binding. The two oil drain holes in the breather housing must be open. Breather mounting holes are offset one way.

CYLINDER HEAD. After 100 to 300 hours of engine operation, the cylinder head should be removed and any carbon or deposits should be removed.

COMPRESSION PRESSURE. Briggs & Stratton does not publish compression pressure specifications.

An alternate method of determining internal engine condition and wear is by using a cylinder leak-down tester. The tester is available commercially or through Briggs & Stratton (part No. 19413). The tester uses compressed air to pressurize the combustion chamber, then gauges the amount of leakage past the piston rings and valves. Instructions are included with the tester.

REPAIRS

TIGHTENING TORQUE. Recommended tightening torque specifications are as follows:

Alternator stator . . . . 18-24 in.-lb.
(2.0-2.7 N·m)
Blower housing . . . . 75-95 in.-lb.
(8.5-10.7 N·m)
Breather screws . . . . . . 20-30 in.-lb.
(2.3-3.4 N·m)
Carburetor mounting
screws . . . . 65-75 in.-lb.
(7.3-8.5 N·m)
Connecting rod . . . . See Text

Crankcase cover . . . . See Text
Cylinder head . . . . 220 in.-lb.
(24.9 N·m)
Electric starter . . . . 130-150 in.-lb.
(14.7-17.0 N·m)
Fan retainer . . . . 130-150 in.-lb.
(14.7-17.0 N·m)
Flywheel nut . . . . 95-105 ft.-lb.
(129-142 N·m)
Fuel pump . . . . 40-50 in.-lb.
(4.5-5.7 N·m)
Governor lever bolt . . . . . . 35-45 in.-lb.
(3.9-5.1 N·m)
Ignition module . . . . 20-28 in.-lb.
(2.3-3.2 N·m)
Intake manifold . . . . 95-105 in.-lb.
(10.7-11.9 N·m)
Oil fill tube . . . . 20-24 in.-lb.
(2.3-2.7 N·m)
Oil filter adapter . . . . . . 110-140 in.-lb.
(12.4-15.8 N·m)
Oil pump cover . . . . 65-95 in.-lb.
(7.3-10.7 N·m)
Rocker arm screw . . . . . . 40-50 in.-lb.
(4.5-5.7 N·m)
Rocker arm stud . . . . 85 in.-lb.
(10.7-11.9 N·m)
Rocker cover . . . . 50-60 in.-lb.
(5.7-6.8 N·m)
Spark plug . . . . 140-200 in.-lb.
15.8-22.6 N·m)
Starter gear cover . . . . . . 20-24 in.-lb.
(2.3-2.7 N·m)
Solenoid ground wire . . . . 40-50 in.-lb.
(4.5-5.7 N·m)

CYLINDER HEAD AND VALVE SYSTEM. Prior to removing cylinder head, relax tension on valve springs by removing spark plug and rotating crankshaft so piston is approximately 1/4 in. (6 mm) down from TDC on power stroke. Remove external parts such as air cleaner, carburetor, intake manifold,

muffler, fuel tank, oil fill tube and blower housing with rewind starter for access to the cylinder head.

When removing cylinder head, note positions of push rods: Exhaust push rod on 28x700 and 31x700 engines is steel, hollow and identified with a band of red paint, intake push rod is aluminum. Remove rocker cover, cylinder head screws, push rods, cylinder head and gasket.

To disassemble valve components, remove rocker arm ball-nuts (9—Fig. B405), and rocker arms (10), studs (11) and push rod guide (12). Remove valve cap (1). Push down on the spring retainer (3) to compress the valve spring until the large end of the slot in the retainer can be slipped off the valve stem. Remove spring retainer, spring and valve. Remove intake valve seal (5) if used.

Inspect valve seats and valves for damage or wear. Valve seats are not replaceable. If valve seats cannot be reconditioned, cylinder head must be replaced.

Valve seat and head dimensions are shown in Fig. B406. If excessive valve stem wear is evident or if valve head wear exceeds dimensions shown in Fig. B406, renew the valve

Valve face angle is 45° for both intake and exhaust; seats should be cut at 46°. Valve lapping is recommended for a good final valve-to-seat seal.

Check valve guides for wear using plug gauge No. 19381. If flat end of gauge can be inserted into guide 1/4 inch (6.35 mm) or more, guide is worn beyond limits. If gauge is not available, valve guide reject dimension is 0.240 inch (6.09 mm) for intake and exhaust. Valve guides are not available for service; replace cylinder head if guides are worn beyond limits.

To reassemble, install push rod guide with "TOP" stamping on guide facing up and toward flywheel side of head. Apply Loctite 270 or equivalent to threads of rocker arm studs. Insert studs through holes in push rod guide and tighten to 85 in.-lb. (9.6 N·m). Lightly coat valve stems with B&S lubricant 93963, Led-Plate or equivalent, then insert valves into guides. Be careful not to get any lubricant on valve seat, valve face or valve stem tip. If a sealing washer is used under the valve seal, place washer over intake valve guide. Lubricate valve stem seal with engine oil and press seal over intake guide. Install valve springs and retainers.

Always install a new cylinder head gasket. Do not apply sealer to head gasket. Apply lubricant to threads of cylinder head bolts. Tighten cylinder head

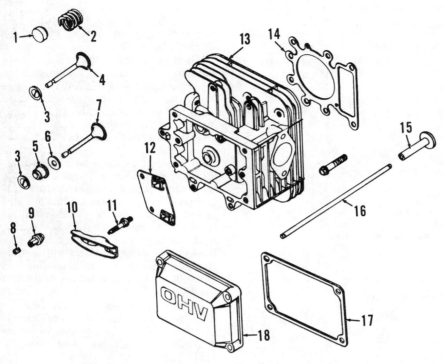

Fig. B405—Exploded view of cylinder head and valve components.

1. Cap	6. Washer	11. Stud	15. Tappet
2. Spring	7. Intake valve	12. Guide plate	16. Push rod
3. Retainer	8. Adjusting screw	13. Cylinder head	17. Gasket
4. Exhaust valve	9. Ball-nut	14. Head gasket	18. Valve cover
5. Seal	10. Rocker arm		

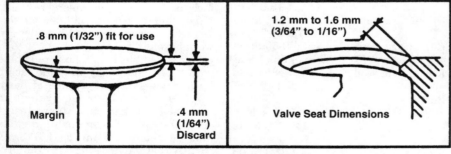

Fig. B406—Valve and valve seat dimensions.

valve clearance as outlined in MAINTENANCE section.

CRANKCASE COVER/OIL PAN. Tighten crankcase cover/oil pan retaining screws evenly to 200 in.-lb. (22.6 N·m) following the fastener sequence shown in Fig. B408. On engines with a Code number of 971120xx or lower, it is recommended that retaining screws be replaced with current style part No. 94624 screws.

CAMSHAFT. The camshaft is supported at both ends in bearing bores machined in crankcase and crankcase cover/oil pan. The camshaft gear is an integral part of camshaft.

Camshaft should be renewed if either journal is worn to a diameter of 0.498 inch (12.66 mm) or less, or if cam lobes are worn or damaged. Refer to the table below for cam lobe reject dimensions.

CAM LOBE REJECT SIZES

Series	Reject Dimension
28S700, 28U700, 28W700, 287700	1.184 in. (30.07 mm)
28E700, 28N700, 28P700, 28Q700	1.221 in. (31.02 mm)
310700, 311700, 312700	1.184 in. (30.07 mm)

Crankcase or crankcase cover/oil pan must be renewed if bearing bores are 0.506 inch (12.85 mm) or larger, or if tool 19164 enters bearing bore ¼ inch (6.4 mm) or more.

Compression release mechanism on camshaft gear holds the exhaust valve slightly open at very low engine rpm as a starting aid. Mechanism should work freely and spring should hold actuator cam against pin. Compression release lobe reject dimension is 0.010 inch (0.25 mm).

When installing the camshaft, align timing marks on camshaft and crankshaft gears as shown in Fig. B409.

PISTON, PIN AND RINGS. Connecting rod and piston are removed from cylinder head end of block as an assembly. To remove, first remove cylinder head as previously outlined. Remove crankcase cover/oil sump and connecting rod cap. Remove any carbon or wear ridge at top of the cylinder to prevent damage to rings or piston during removal. Push the connecting rod and piston out through top of cylinder.

To remove piston pin and connecting rod, rotate piston pin retainer until open end is located in notch in piston pin bore. Grasp end of the retainer with needle nose pliers and pull in and up to

bolts, using the sequence shown in Fig. B407, in 75 in.-lb. (8.5 N·m) increments to final torque of 220 in.-lb. (24.9 N·m).

Insert push rods through push rod guide plate, insuring that they properly seat into valve tappets. Exhaust valve push rod is steel, has a red paint band for identification, and is mounted in the upper position. Make sure valve caps

and valve stem ends are dry, then insert caps onto stems. Install rocker arms. Thread rocker arm ball-nuts onto push rod studs finger-tight, seating rocker arm against push rod and cap. Rotate crankshaft two revolutions (clockwise, viewed from flywheel) to verify proper rocker arm operation. Position the piston ¼ inch (6 mm) down from TDC on power stroke, and adjust

remove the retainer. Push the piston pin out of the piston and rod.

Remove the rings from the piston and thoroughly clean combustion deposits from piston ring grooves and piston crown. Be careful not to damage or enlarge the piston ring grooves.

Reject piston showing visible signs of wear, scoring or scuffing. If, after cleaning carbon from top ring groove, a new top ring has a side clearance of 0.006 inch (0.15 mm) or more, reject the pis-ton. Reject piston or hone piston pin hole to 0.005 inch (0.13 mm) oversize if pin hole is 0.0005 inch (0.013 mm) or more out-of-round, or is worn to a diameter of 0.801 inch (20.34 mm) or more.

If the piston pin is 0.0005 inch (0.013 mm) or more out-of-round, or is worn to a diameter of 0.799 inch (20.30 mm) or smaller, reject pin.

Pistons and rings are available in several oversizes as well as standard. Refer to Fig. B410 for correct installa-tion of piston rings. Assemble connecting rod and piston as shown in Fig. B411. Install piston and rod in engine so notch (N) or arrow is toward flywheel side of engine. Tighten connecting rod cap screws to torque listed in CONNECTING ROD paragraph.

CONNECTING ROD. Connecting rod and piston are removed from cylinder head end of block as an assembly. The aluminum alloy connecting rod rides directly on an induction hardened crankshaft crankpin journal. Rod should be rejected if big end of rod is scored or out-of-round more than 0.0007 inch (0.018 mm) or if piston pin bore is scored or out-of-round more than 0.0005 inch (0.013 mm). Renew connecting rod if either crankpin bore or piston pin bore is worn to, or larger than, sizes given in table.

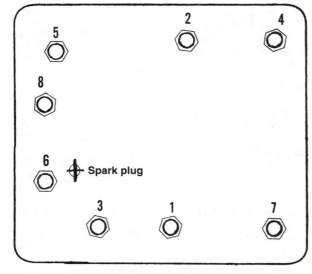

Fig. B407—Tighten cylinder head screws insequence shown. Refer to text.

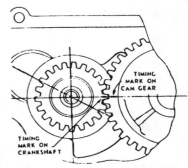

Fig. B409—Align timing marks on cam gear and crankshaft gear.

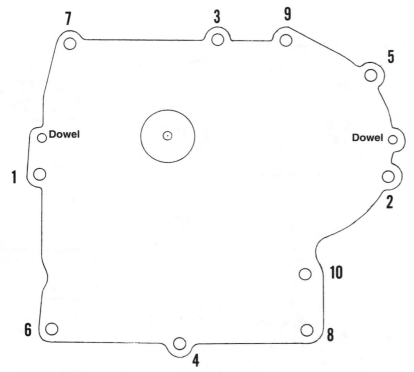

Fig. B408—Tighten crankcase cover/oil sump screws in sequence shown. Refer to text.

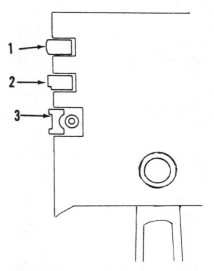

Fig. B410—Refer to illustration above for proper arrangement of piston rings.

1. Top compression ring
2. Middle compression ring
3. Oil control ring

REJECT SIZES FOR CONNECTING ROD

Series	Crankpin Bore	Pin Bore*
310700, 311700, 312700	1.502 in. (38.15 mm)	0.802 in. (20.37 mm)
All other models	1.252 in. (31.8 mm)	0.802 in. (20.37 mm)

*Piston pins that are 0.005 inch (0.13 mm) oversize are available for service. Piston pin bore in rod can be reamed to this size if crankpin bore is within specifications.

Assemble connecting rod to piston as shown in Fig. B411. Install piston and rod in engine so notch (N) or arrow on piston crown is toward flywheel side of engine. Install rod cap with match marks on rod and cap aligned.

Tighten the connecting rod cap screws to torque listed in the table below:

Series	Torque
28x000 with equal size rod bolts	185 in.-lb. (20.9 N·m)
28x000 with two rod bolt sizes—	
Small bolt	130 in.-lb. (14.7 N·m)
Large bolt	260 in.-lb. (29.4 N·m)
310700, 311700, 312700	160 in.-lb. (18.0 N·m)

GOVERNOR. Governor gear and weight unit can be removed when engine is disassembled. The governor weight unit along with the oil slinger rides on the end of the camshaft as shown in Fig. B412.

Remove governor lever, cotter pin and washer from outer end of governor lever shaft. Slide governor lever out of bushing toward inside of engine. Governor gear and weight unit can now be removed. Renew governor lever shaft bushing in crankcase, if necessary, and ream new bushing after installation to 0.2385-0.2390 inch (6.058-6.071 mm). Briggs & Stratton tool 19333 can be used to ream bushing.

Replace governor lever seal if leaking. Use care not to damage seal lip when installing the seal. Wrap the governor lever shaft with thin plastic or cellophane tape before sliding seal over shaft.

CRANKSHAFT AND MAIN BEARINGS. The crankshaft is supported by bearing surfaces that are an integral part of crankcase and crankcase cover/oil sump.

The crankshaft should be renewed or reground if main bearing journals exceed service limits specified in following table.

CRANKSHAFT REJECT SIZES

Series	Magneto End Journal	PTO End Journal
All models	1.376 in. (34.95 mm)	1.376 in. (34.95 mm)

Crankshaft for all models should be renewed or reground if connecting rod crankpin journal diameter exceeds service limit listed in following table.

CRANKSHAFT REJECT SIZES

Series	Crankpin Journal
310700, 311700, 312700	1.497 in. (38.02 mm)
All other models	1.247 in. (31.67 mm)

A connecting rod with undersize big end diameter is available to fit crankshaft that has had crankpin journal reground to 0.020 inch (0.51 mm) undersize.

On models equipped with integral main bearings, crankcase or cover/oil sump must be renewed or reamed to accept service bushings if service limits in following table are exceeded.

MAIN BEARING REJECT SIZES

Model	Magneto End Bearing	PTO End Bearing
310700, 311700, 312700	1.504 in. (38.20 mm)	1.504 in. (38.20 mm)
All other models	1.383 in. (35.13 mm)	1.383 in. (35.13 mm)

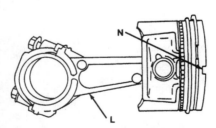

Fig. B411—If piston crown has a notch (N) or arrow, assemble connecting rod and piston as shown while noting relation of long side of rod (L) and notch or arrow on piston crown.

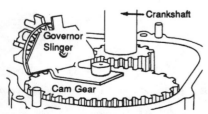

Fig. B412—View of governor weight assembly and oil slinger used on all engines.

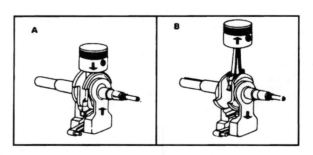

Fig. B413—View showing operating principles of oscillating balancer assembly. Counterweight oscillates in opposite direction of piston.

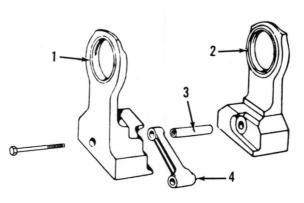

Fig. B414—Exploded view of balancer assembly. Counterweights ride on eccentric journals on crankshaft.

1. Pto side counterweight
2. Magneto side counterweight
3. Dowel pin
4. Link

Install the "DU"-type bushing with oil hole in line with oil hole in crankcase or crankcase cover/sump. If bushing does not have an oil hole, locate split in the bushing so it is not aligned with an oil notch in bearing boss. Stake bushing at oil notches in crankcase or sump. Bushing should be $7/64$ inch (2.8 mm) below face of crankcase bore and $1/8$ inch (3.2 mm) below face of crankcase cover/oil sump.

Crankshaft end play is 0.002-0.023 inch (0.05-0.58 mm) for Series 287700

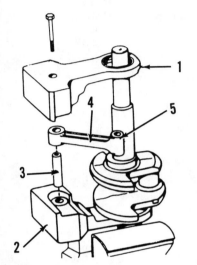

Fig. B415—Assemble balancer on crankshaft as shown. Install link (4) with rounded edge (5) toward pto end of crankshaft.

engines. For all other models, end play is 0.002-0.030 inch (0.05-0.76 mm). At least one 0.015-inch crankcase gasket must be in place when measuring end play. Additional gaskets in several sizes are available to adjust end play as needed. If end play is excessive, replace the crankcase cover/oil sump.

When installing crankshaft, make certain timing marks are aligned (Fig. B409).

CYLINDER. If cylinder bore wear is 0.003 inch (0.08 mm) or more or is 0.0025 inch (0.06 mm) or more out-of-round, cylinder must be replaced or bored to next larger oversize.

Standard cylinder bore diameter is 3.5620-3.5630 inches (90.474-90.500 mm) for 310700, 311700 and 312700 models. Standard cylinder bore diameter is 3.4365-3.4375 inches (87.287-87.313 mm) for all models.

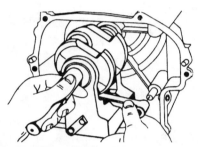

Fig. B416—When installing crankshaft and balancer assembly, place free end of link on anchor pin in crankcase.

OSCILLATING COUNTERBALANCE SYSTEM. All engines are equipped with an oscillating counterbalance system. A balance weight assembly rides on eccentric journals on the crankshaft and moves in opposite direction of piston (Fig. B413).

To disassemble balancer unit, first remove flywheel, oil pan, cam gear, cylinder head, and connecting rod and piston assembly. Carefully pry off crankshaft gear and key. Remove the cap screw holding halves of counterweight together. Separate weights (1 and 2—Fig. B414) and remove link (4) and dowel pin (3). Slide weights from crankshaft.

Inspect the crankshaft eccentrics and counterweight bearings for wear or damage. Eccentric wear limit is 2.202 inches (55.93). Bearing wear limit is 2.212 inches (56.18 mm).

To reassemble, install magneto side weight on magneto end of crankshaft. Place crankshaft (pto end up) in a vise (Fig. B415). Install dowel pin (3) and place link (4) on pin with rounded edge (5) on free end of link facing up. Install pto side weight (1) and cap screw. Tighten cap screw to 115 in.-lbs. (13 N·m). Install key and crankshaft gear with chamfer on inside of gear facing shoulder on crankshaft.

Install crankshaft and balancer assembly in crankcase, sliding free end of link on anchor pin as shown in Fig. B416. Reassemble engine.

BRIGGS & STRATTON

BRIGGS & STRATTON CORPORATION
Milwaukee, Wisconsin 53201

SINGLE-CYLINDER L-HEAD ENGINES

Model Series	No. Cyls.	Bore	Stroke	Displacement	Power Rating
170000, 171000, 176400	1	3.00 in. (76.2 mm)	2.375 in. (60.3 mm)	16.8 cu. in. (275 cc)	7 hp (5.2 kW)
190400, 190700, 191700, 192400, 192700, 193000, 194400, 194700, 195400, 195700, 196400, 196700, 197400, 19A400, 19B400, 19C400, 19E400, 19F400, 19G400	1	3.00 in. (76.2 mm)	2.750 in. (69.85 mm)	19.44 cu. in. (318 cc)	8 hp (6 kW)
220700, 221400, 222400, 226400	1	3.438 in. (87.3 mm)	2.375 in. (60.3 mm)	22.04 cu. in. (361 cc)	10 hp (7.5 kW)
250400, 251000, 252400, 252700, 253400, 253700, 254400, 254700, 255400, 255700, 256400, 256700, 257000, 258700, 259700	1	3.438 in. (87.3 mm)	2.625 in. (66.68 mm)	24.36 cu. in. (399 cc)	11 hp (8.2 kW)
280700, 281700, 282700, 283000, 284700, 28A700, 28B700, 28C700, 28D700	1	3.438 in. (87.3 mm)	3.06 in. (77.7 mm)	28.4 cu. in. (465 cc)	12 hp (9 kW)
285000, 286000, 289700	1	3.438 in. (87.3 mm)	3.06 in. (77.7 mm)	28.4 cu. in. (465 cc)	12.5 hp (9.4 kW)
28M700	1	3.438 in. (87.3 mm)	3.06 in. (77.7 mm)	28.4 cu. in. (465 cc)	13.0 hp (9.7 kW)
28R700	1	3.438 in. (87.3 mm)	3.06 in. (77.7 mm)	28.4 cu. in. (465 cc)	15.5 hp (11.5 kW)
28T700, 28V700	1	3.438 in. (87.3 mm)	3.06 in. (77.7 mm)	28.4 cu. in. (465 cc)	See Note

NOTE: Power ratings vary between 14 to 16 horsepower (10.4-11.9 kW) for these models due to differences in carburetor and camshaft design. Power rating is identified on the blower housing of each engine.

GENERAL INFORMATION

Engines in this section are four-stroke, single-cylinder engines with either a horizontal or vertical crankshaft. The crankshaft may be supported by main bearings that are an integral part of crankcase and crankcase cover/oil pan or by ball bearings pressed on the crankshaft. All engines are constructed of aluminum. Cylinder bore may be either aluminum or a cast iron sleeve that is cast in the aluminum.

The connecting rod on all models rides directly on the crankpin journal. All models are splashed lubricated.

Early models are equipped with a magneto-type ignition system with points and condenser located underneath the flywheel. Later models are equipped with a breakerless (Magnetron) ignition system.

A float-type carburetor is used on all models. A fuel pump is available as optional equipment for some models.

Refer to BRIGGS & STRATTON ENGINE IDENTIFICATION INFORMATION section for engine identification. Engine model number as well as type and code numbers are necessary when ordering parts.

MAINTENANCE

LUBRICATION. An oil dipper attached to the connecting rod provides splash lubrication for horizontal crankshaft engines. An oil slinger wheel on governor gear that is driven by the camshaft gear provides a splash lubrication system for vertical crankshaft engines.

Engine oil should be changed after first eight hours of operation and after every 50 hours of operation or at least once each operating season. If equipment undergoes severe usage, change oil weekly or after every 25 hours of operation. Drain the oil while the engine is warm. The oil will flow freely and carry away more impurities.

Manufacturer recommends using oil with an API service classification of SH or SJ, or any classification formulated to supercede SH or SJ. Use SAE 30 oil for temperatures above 40° F (4° C); use SAE 10W-30 oil for temperatures between 0° F (−18° C) and 40° F (4° C); below 0° F (−18° C) use petroleum based SAE 5W-20 or a suitable synthetic oil. DO NOT use SAE 10W-40 oil.

Crankcase oil capacity for 16.8 and 19.44 cubic inch engines is 2¼ pints (1.1 L) for vertical crankshaft models and 2¾ pints (1.3 L) for horizontal crankshaft models.

Crankcase oil capacity for 22.04, 24.36 and 28.4 cubic inch engines is 3 pints (1.4 L) for vertical crankshaft models and 2½ pints (1.2 L) for horizontal crankshaft models.

SPARK PLUG. The original spark plug may be either 1½ inches or 2 inches long. Recommended spark plug is either Champion or Autolite.

If a Champion spark plug is used and spark plug is 1½ inches long, recommended spark plug is Champion CJ-8 or J-19LM. Install Champion RCJ-8, RJ-12 or RJ-19LM if a resistor-type spark plug is required. If spark plug is 2 inches long, recommended spark plug is Champion J-19LM or J-8C. Install Champion RJ-19LM or RJ-8C if a resistor-type spark plug is required. Engines with Magnetron ignition should be equipped with resistor plugs.

If an Autolite spark plug is used and spark plug is 1½ inches long, recommended spark plug is 235. Install Autolite 245 if a resistor-type spark plug is required. If spark plug is 2 inches long, recommended spark plug is 295. Install Autolite 306 if a resistor-type spark plug is required.

Specified spark plug electrode gap is 0.030 inch (0.76 mm).

CAUTION: Briggs & Stratton does not recommend using abrasive blasting to clean spark plugs as this may introduce some abrasive material into the engine that could cause extensive damage.

AIR CLEANER. Engines may be equipped with cartridge type, dual element or oil foam air cleaner. The air cleaner should be inspected and cleaned after every 25 operating hours or once a season, whichever comes first. Refer to appropriate paragraph for filter type being serviced.

NOTE: When servicing the air filter on Series 280000 engines with a welded two-piece air filter base, inspect the base carefully before reusing. Impact damage or improper service procedures can cause the base to warp or bend between the two metal pieces, allowing unfiltered air to enter the engine. There are two remedies available if damage is evident: Apply a flexible RTV sealant to the filter base at the separated area; or preferably, replace the filter base with newer style one-piece nonmetallic base.

Cartridge Air Cleaner. Thoroughly clean the area surrounding the air cleaner prior to removal. Remove the wing nut and cover, then carefully remove the cartridge to prevent dirt from entering the carburetor.

Clean the cartridge filter element by tapping gently on a flat surface. Do not use cleaning fluids or soap and water to clean the cartridge. Inspect the cartridge for tears or cracks, and replace it if damaged or restricted. Inspect the air cleaner mounting gaskets and replace them if damaged or worn.

Dual Element Air Cleaner. The dual element air cleaner consists of a foam precleaner and a paper cartridge filter element. Carefully remove the filter cover and filter assembly to prevent dirt from entering the carburetor.

Wash the foam precleaner in warm soapy water. Thoroughly dry the element, then saturate the foam with clean engine oil. Squeeze it to remove excess oil. DO NOT apply oil to foam precleaners labeled "DO NOT OIL."

Do not use cleaning fluids or soap and water to clean the paper filter cartridge. Tap the cartridge gently on a flat surface to dislodge debris from surface of the filter. Replace the filter if it is damaged or restricted.

Oil Foam Air Cleaner. Thoroughly clean the area surrounding the air cleaner to prevent dirt from entering the carburetor. Remove the air cleaner cover and withdraw foam filter from air cleaner body.

Clean the foam filter with a solution of warm water and liquid detergent. Squeeze out water and allow to air dry. Soak the foam element in clean engine oil. Squeeze out excess oil.

CARBURETOR. Engines in this section may be equipped with one of three different Flo-Jet carburetors as well as a Walbro carburetor. The Flo-Jet carburetors are identified as Flo-Jet I, Flo-Jet II or Cross-Over Flo-Jet. Refer to appropriate service section for model being serviced.

For engines equipped to run on LPG, refer to LPG FUEL SYSTEM service procedures in SERVICING BRIGGS & STRATTON ACCESSORIES section of this manual.

Flo-Jet I Carburetor. A cross-sectional view of a Flo-Jet I carburetor is shown in Fig. B500. Initial setting of idle mixture screw is one turn out and high-speed needle valve is 1½ turns out. With engine at normal operating temperature and equipment control lever in "SLOW" position, adjust idle speed screw so engine idles at 1750 rpm. With engine running at idle speed, turn idle mixture screw clockwise until engine speed just starts to drop. Note screw position. Turn idle mixture screw counterclockwise until engine speed increases then just starts to drop again and note screw position. Then turn screw to midpoint between the lean and rich screw positions. Adjust high-speed needle valve with control set to "FAST" using same procedure. If engine will not accelerate cleanly, slightly enrich mixture by turning idle mixture needle

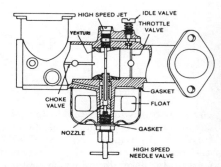

Fig. B500—Cross-sectional view of Flo-Jet I carburetor.

valve counterclockwise. If necessary, readjust idle speed screw.

To disassemble carburetor, remove high-speed jet (6—Fig. B501) and idle mixture screw (7). Remove high-speed needle valve assembly (16) and float bowl (13). Remove pivot pin (19), float (12) and fuel inlet needle (18). Unscrew and remove nozzle (14). Remove choke shaft (1) and plate (3). Drive Welch plug (22) from carburetor body, then extract the venturi (21). On some carburetors there is a choke plate stop pin that must be removed before removing the venturi. Press or drive the pin into the bore.

Clean all parts with aerosol carburetor cleaner, then use compressed air to blow out passages and dry the carburetor. Inspect all parts for wear or damage. Wear between throttle shaft (10) and bushings should not exceed 0.010 inch (0.25 mm). Replacement throttle

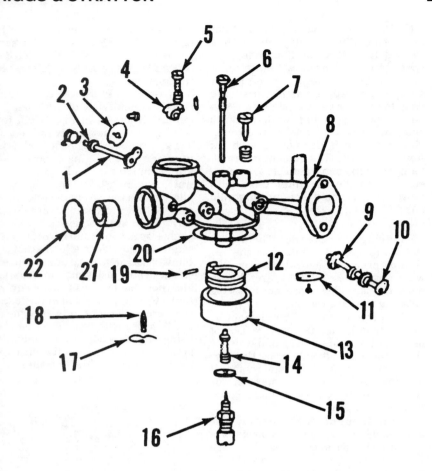

Fig. B501—Exploded view of typical Flo-Jet I carburetor.

1. Choke shaft
2. Seal
3. Choke plate
4. Throttle stop
5. Idle speed stop screw
6. High-speed jet
7. Idle mixture needle
8. Carburetor body
9. Seal
10. Throttle shaft
11. Throttle plate
12. Float
13. Float bowl
14. Nozzle
15. Gasket
16. High-speed mixture screw & packing nut
17. Clip
18. Fuel inlet needle
19. Pin
20. Gasket
21. Venturi
22. Welch plug

shaft bushings are available for some carburetors. Inspect the tip of idle mixture and high-speed mixture needles and replace if tip is bent or grooved. Carburetor assembly must be replaced if the needle seats are damaged. Inspect fuel inlet valve and replace it if tip is grooved. Fuel inlet valve seat may be either threaded or pressed into the carburetor body. Use a 1/4-inch tap or screw extractor to pull pressed-in seat from the carburetor. Install new seat flush with carburetor body.

Note the following special instructions when assembling carburetor. Install the venturi with the groove towards the fuel bowl. Install the nozzle and discharge tube or high-speed mixture screw to hold the venturi in place. Drive in the retaining pin if used. Install choke plate so cutout is down and concave side of dimple is towards intake end of carburetor.

To check float level, invert carburetor body and float assembly. Refer to Fig. B502 for proper float level dimensions. Adjust by bending float lever tang that contacts inlet valve. Be very careful when bending the float lever not to force the fuel inlet needle onto its seat

as the tip of the needle is easily damaged.

Flo-Jet II Carburetor. A cross-sectional view of a Flo-Jet II carburetor is shown in Fig. B503 Initial setting of idle mixture screw is 1¼ turns out and high-speed needle valve is 1½ turns out. With engine at normal operating temperature and equipment control lever in "SLOW" position, adjust idle speed screw so engine idles at 1750 rpm. With engine running at idle speed, turn idle mixture screw clockwise until engine speed just starts to drop. Note screw position. Turn idle mixture screw counterclockwise until engine speed increases then just starts to drop again and note screw position. Then turn screw to midpoint between the lean and rich screw positions. Adjust high-speed needle valve with control set to "FAST" using same procedure. If engine will not accelerate cleanly, slightly enrich mixture by turning idle mixture needle valve counterclockwise. If necessary, readjust idle speed screw.

When disassembling the carburetor, note that the nozzle is angled between the body and cover (Fig. B503). The

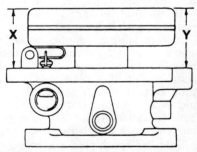

Fig. B502—Float height dimension (Y) must be the same as dimension (X) plus or minus 1/32 inch (0.8 mm).

high-speed needle valve (17—Fig. B504), packing nut (15) and nozzle (13) must be removed before the cover (3) is removed, otherwise, the nozzle will be damaged. Withdraw the float pin (10) and remove float (11) and fuel inlet valve (8). Remove idle mixture needle (4).

Clean all parts with aerosol carburetor cleaner, then use compressed air to blow out passages and dry the carburetor. Inspect all parts for wear or damage. Check upper body for distortion using a 0.002 inch (0.05 mm) feeler

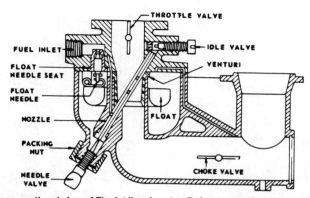

Fig. B503—Cross-sectional view of Flo-Jet II carburetor. Before separating upper and lower body sections, remove packing nut and power needle valve as a unit and use special screwdriver (tool 19062) to remove nozzle.

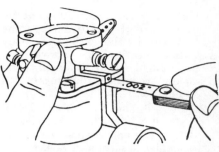

Fig. B505—Check upper body of Flo-Jet II carburetor for distortion as outlined in text.

gauge as shown in Fig. B505. Upper body must be renewed if warped more than 0.002 inch (0.05 mm). Wear between throttle shaft (1—Fig. B504) and bushings should not exceed 0.010 inch (0.25 mm). Replacement throttle shaft bushings are available for some carburetors. Inspect the tip of idle mixture and high-speed mixture needles and replace if tip is bent or grooved. Carburetor assembly must be replaced if the needle seats are damaged. Inspect fuel inlet valve (8) and replace it if tip is grooved. Fuel inlet valve seat may be either threaded or pressed into the carburetor body. Use a screwdriver to remove threaded type seat. Use a 1/4-inch tap or screw extractor to pull pressed-in seat from the carburetor. Install new seat flush with carburetor body.

To check float level, invert carburetor body and float assembly. Refer to Fig. B502 for proper float level dimensions. Adjust by bending float lever tang that contacts inlet valve.

The float, part No. 99333, used in carburetors for 17 and 19-cubic inch engines has been redesigned to allow the float to 'drop' farther in the float bowl during engine operation. This helps prevent the engine from 'running out of gas' while there still appears to be gasoline in the tank. This problem occurs mainly on engines with an engine-mounted tank opposite the carburetor.

Internal fuel leakage can result in the engine flooding and fuel running out of the drain hole in the bottom of carburetor air horn. This internal leakage problem may be caused by corrosion or an improper seal between the tapered seat on the main nozzle and its mating surface inside the lower carburetor body. Three solutions to this problem are:

1. Make a tool by filing or grinding the threads off a new nozzle so it slides easily into and out of the carburetor. Place a light coating of fine-grit lapping compound on the tapered face of the nozzle. Using a screwdriver in the nozzle end slot,

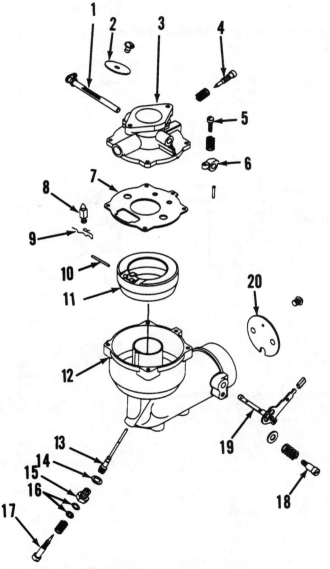

Fig. B504—Exploded view of typical Flo-Jet II carburetor.

1. Throttle shaft	6. Throttle stop	11. Float	16. Packing
2. Throttle plate	7. Gasket	12. Lower body	17. High-speed
3. Upper body	8. Fuel inlet valve	13. Nozzle	mixture needle
4. Idle mixture needle	9. Clip	14. Gasket	18. Shoulder bolt
5. Idle speed stop screw	10. Pin	15. Packing nut	19. Choke shaft
			20. Choke plate

lap the nozzle against the seat. Be very careful not to damage the threads in the carburetor body when rotating the screwdriver. Thoroughly clean all lapping compound from the carburetor. Install a new nozzle.

2. Force a Teflon washer from B&S repair kit No. 391413 over the end of the nozzle and against the nozzle shoulder to serve as a gasket.

3. Replace carburetor lower body and nozzle.

Cross-Over Flo-Jet Carburetor. The Cross-Over Flo-Jet carburetor (Fig. B506) is equipped with an integral diaphragm-type fuel pump.

Initial setting of idle mixture needle (Fig. B507) is one turn out and high-speed mixture needle is 1½ turns out. With engine at normal operating temperature and throttle lever in "SLOW" position, adjust idle speed screw so engine idles at 1750 rpm. With engine running at idle speed, turn idle mixture needle clockwise until engine speed just starts to drop. Note needle position. Turn idle mixture needle counterclockwise until engine speed increases then just starts to drop again and note needle position. Then turn needle to midpoint between the noted lean and rich needle positions. If equipped with high-speed mixture needle, set control to "FAST" and adjust high-speed needle using same procedure. If engine will not accelerate cleanly, slightly enrich low-speed mixture by turning idle mixture needle counterclockwise. If necessary, readjust idle speed screw.

To disassemble carburetor, remove fuel pump cover fasteners and separate fuel pump components (23 through 27—Fig. B506). Remove idle mixture needle (1) and high-speed mixture needle (2). Remove the screw (21) retaining the fuel bowl (18). Remove float pin (14), float (15) and fuel inlet needle valve (16). Unscrew nozzle (19) from carburetor body.

Clean the carburetor with aerosol cleaner, then use compressed air to blow out passages and dry the carburetor. Inspect components and discard any parts that are damaged or excessively worn. Replace the fuel inlet valve needle if the tip is grooved. If fuel inlet valve seat replacement is required, thread a self-tapping screw or a screw extractor into the seat and pull seat from the body. Inspect the tip of idle mixture needle and replace if it is bent or grooved. Check for excessive play between throttle shaft and body. Carburetor must be replaced if throttle shaft bore is excessively worn, as bushings are not available.

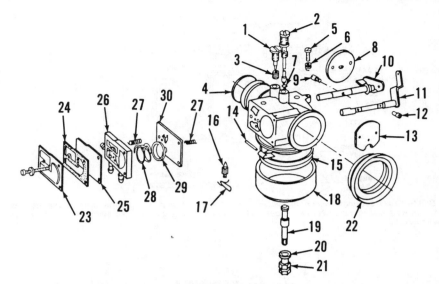

Fig. B506—Exploded view of Cross-Over Flo-Jet carburetor used on some models.

1. Idle mixture needle	9. Screw	16. Fuel inlet valve	23. Fuel pump cover
2. High-speed mixture needle	10. Throttle shaft	17. Clip	24. Diaphragm
3. Spring	11. Choke shaft	18. Fuel bowl	25. Fuel pump body
4. "O" ring	12. Screw	19. Nozzle	27. Spring
5. Idle speed screw	13. Choke plate	20. Washer	28. Spring
6. Spring	14. Pin	21. Screw	29. Spring cup
7. Packing	15. Float	22. Gasket	30. Diaphragm
8. Throttle plate			

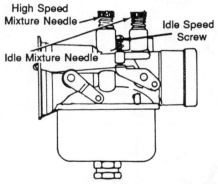

Fig. B507—View of adjustment screws on Cross-Over Flo-jet carburetor.

When reassembling carburetor, note the following: Install throttle plate so indentations on the plate face outward as shown in Fig. B508. Install choke plate so dimple on face of plate faces inward (Fig. B508). Install fuel inlet valve seat so it is flush with carburetor body surface. To check float level, invert carburetor body and float assembly. Float should be parallel to carburetor body as shown in Fig. B502. Adjust float level by bending float lever tang that contacts inlet valve. When assembling fuel pump, install springs (27—Fig. B509) on pegs (P) on pump body and carburetor body.

Walbro Carburetor. The Walbro carburetor may be equipped with a fixed main jet or the adjustable

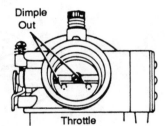

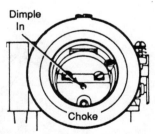

Fig. B508—Install throttle and choke plates on Cross-Over Flo-Jet carburetor so dimples are located as shown above when plates are closed.

high-speed mixture needle shown in Fig. B510.

Initial setting of idle mixture needle (10) is one turn out and high-speed mixture needle (23), if so equipped, is 1½ turns out. With engine at normal operating and equipment control lever in "SLOW" position, adjust idle speed screw (8) so engine idles at 1750 rpm. With engine running at idle speed, turn idle mixture needle clockwise until engine speed just starts to

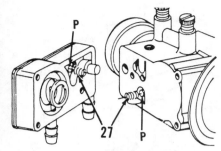

Fig. B509—When assembling fuel pump on Cross-Over Flo-jet carburetor, install springs (27) onto pegs (P) on pump body and carburetor body.

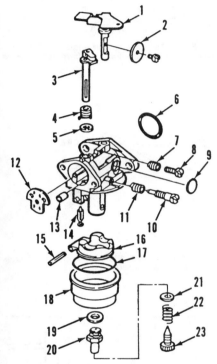

Fig. B510—Exploded view of Walbro-type carburetor.

1. Throttle shaft	13. Air jet
2. Throttle plate	14. Fuel inlet valve
3. Choke shaft	15. Float pin
4. Spring	16. Float
5. Seal	17. Gasket
6. Gasket	18. Fuel bowl
7. Spring	19. Washer
8. Idle speed stop screw	20. Bowl retainer
9. Welch plug	21. "O" ring
10. Idle mixture needle	22. Spring
11. Spring	23. Main fuel
12. Choke plate	mixture needle

INSERT THIS FACE FIRST

GROOVE

INLET NEEDLE TIP SEATS AT THIS POINT

Fig. B511—Install fuel inlet valve seat with grooved side downward.

drop. Note needle position. Turn idle mixture needle counterclockwise until engine speed increases then just starts to drop again and note needle position. Then turn needle to midpoint between the noted lean and rich needle positions. If equipped with high-speed mixture needle, set control to "FAST" and adjust high-speed needle using same procedure. If engine will not accelerate cleanly, slightly enrich low-speed mixture by turning idle mixture needle counterclockwise. If necessary, readjust idle speed screw. If engine does not run properly at high altitude, remove main air jet (13) and adjust mixture for smooth operation.

NOTE: Main air jet (13—Fig. B510) is not removable on carburetors equipped with adjuster needle limiter caps. If limiter caps are removed, new caps MUST be installed on carburetors originally equipped with caps.

To disassemble carburetor, remove bowl retainer (20—Fig. B510) and fuel bowl (18). Remove float pin (15), float (16) and fuel inlet valve needle (14). Remove idle mixture needle (10). A $\frac{5}{32}$-inch punch ground flat at the end makes a suitable tool for removing Welch plug (9).

Clean the carburetor with aerosol cleaner, then use compressed air to blow out passages and dry the carburetor. Inspect components and discard any parts that are damaged or excessively worn. Replace the fuel inlet valve needle if the tip is grooved. Pull the fuel inlet valve seat from carburetor body if seat is worn or damaged. Inspect the tip of idle mixture needle and replace if it is bent or grooved. Check for excessive play between throttle shaft and body. Carburetor must be replaced if throttle shaft bore is excessively worn, as bushings are not available.

Some carburetors are equipped with a replaceable Viton-tipped fuel inlet valve and a non-replaceable brass valve seat. Carburetor body must be replaced if seat is damaged or worn.

On carburetors equipped with a replaceable fuel inlet valve seat, a green-colored seat is used on older style gravity-feed fuel systems and a black-colored seat is used on later style gravity-feed systems. The green-colored seats were prone to leak, and they can be replaced with the newer style black seat. A brown-colored seat is used on engines equipped with a fuel pump.

When reassembling carburetor, note the following: Apply a fuel-resistant sealer such as fingernail polish to outer edge of Welch plug (9—Fig. B510). Do not deform the Welch plug during installation; it should be flat. Install choke and throttle plates so numbers are on outer face when choke or throttle plate is in closed position. If fuel inlet seat is replaceable, install new seat using B&S driver 19057 or a suitable tool so grooved face of seat is down (Fig. B511). Float height is not adjustable. Tighten fuel bowl retaining nut to 50 in.-lbs. (5.6 N•m). Tighten carburetor mounting nuts to 90 in.-lbs. (10.2 N•m).

DUAL-FUEL (GASOLINE AND KEROSENE) SYSTEM. Some engines are equipped to run on both gasoline and kerosene. Dual-fuel engines are equipped with a dual-section fuel tank with double shutoff valves. Recommended operating procedure is to start the engine on gasoline, then switch to kerosene when engine is running. The carburetor may need minor adjustment after either changeover for proper operation. Prior to long-term shutdown, switch back to gasoline to ensure easy cold restart.

A lower compression ratio is required for dual-fuel operation. Some dual-fuel engines are equipped with a special low-compression cylinder head while other engines use two head gaskets. Service procedures for dual-fuel engine components are the same as for gasoline engines.

CHOKE-A-MATIC CARBURETOR CONTROLS. Engines may be equipped with a control unit that operates the carburetor choke, throttle and magneto grounding switch from a single lever (Choke-A-Matic carburetors).

To check operation of Choke-A-Matic controls, move control lever to "CHOKE" position; carburetor choke slide or plate must be completely closed. Move control lever to "STOP" position; magneto grounding switch should be making contact. With control in "RUN," "FAST" or "SLOW" position, carburetor choke should be completely open. On units with remote controls, synchronize movement of remote lever to carburetor control lever by loosening screw (C—Fig. B512) and moving control wire housing (D) as required. Tighten screw to clamp housing securely. Refer to Fig. B513 to check remote control wire movement.

AUTOMATIC CHOKE (THERMOSTAT-TYPE). A thermostat-operated choke is used on some models equipped with Flo-Jet II carburetor. To adjust choke linkage, hold choke shaft so thermostat lever is free. At room temperature, stop screw in thermostat collar should be located midway between thermostat stops. If not, loosen stop

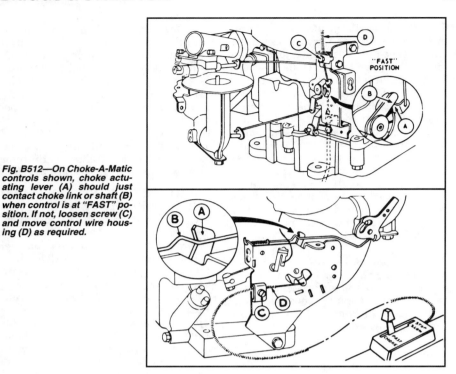

Fig. B512—On Choke-A-Matic controls shown, choke actuating lever (A) should just contact choke link or shaft (B) when control is at "FAST" position. If not, loosen screw (C) and move control wire housing (D) as required.

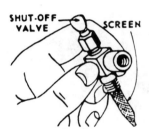

Fig. B515—Turn thermostat shaft counterclockwise until stop screw contacts thermostat stop as shown.

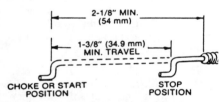

Fig. B513—For proper operation of Choke-A-Matic controls, remove control wire must extend to dimension shown and have a minimum travel of 1-3/8 inches (35 mm).

screw, adjust collar and tighten stop screw. Loosen set screw (S—Fig. B514) on thermostat lever. Slide lever on shaft to ensure free movement of choke unit. Turn thermostat shaft clockwise until stop screw contacts thermostat stop.

While holding shaft in this position, move shaft lever until choke is open exactly $\frac{1}{8}$ inch (3 mm) and tighten lever set screw. Turn thermostat shaft counterclockwise until stop screw contacts thermostat stop as shown in Fig. B515. Manually open choke valve until it stops against top of choke link opening. At this time, choke should be open at least $\frac{3}{32}$ inch (2.4 mm), but not more than $\frac{5}{32}$ inch (4 mm). Hold choke valve in wide-open position and check position of counterweight lever. Lever should be in a horizontal position with free end toward right.

FUEL TANK OUTLET. Some models are equipped with a fuel tank outlet

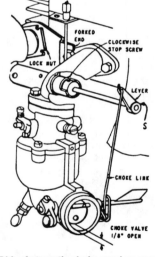

Fig. B514—Automatic choke used on some models equipped with Flo-Jet II carburetor showing unit in "HOT" position.

as shown in Fig. B516. Other models may be equipped with a fuel sediment bowl that is part of the fuel tank outlet shown in Fig. B517.

Clean any debris or dirt from tank outlet screens with a brush. Varnish or other gasoline deposits can be removed using a suitable solvent. Tighten packing nut or remove nut and shutoff valve, then renew packing if leakage occurs around shutoff valve stem.

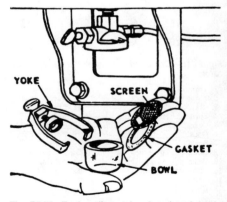

Fig. B516—Fuel tank outlet used on some models includes a filter screen.

Fig. B517—Fuel sediment bowl and tank outlet used on some models.

FUEL PUMP. A fuel pump is available as optional equipment on some models. Refer to BRIGGS & STRATTON ACCESSORIES section for service information.

GOVERNOR. All engines are equipped with a gear-driven mechanical-type governor attached to the crankcase cover or oil pan. The cam-

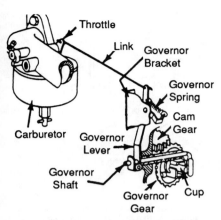

Fig. B518—View of typical governor assembly used on engines with vertical crankshaft.

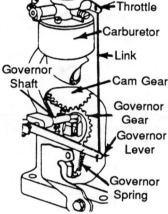

Fig. B519—View of typical governor assembly used on engines with horizontal crankshaft.

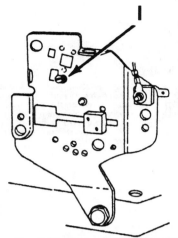

Fig. B520—On engines equipped with a governed idle adjustment screw (I), refer to text for adjustment procedure.

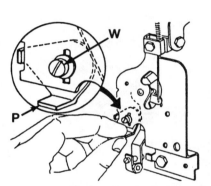

Fig. B521—On models equipped with a governed idle stop (P), refer to GOVERNOR section to adjust governed idle speed.

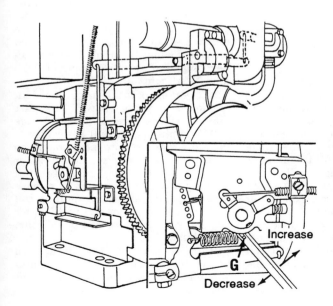

Fig. B522—On Series 253400 and 255400 engines, bend spring anchor tang (G) to adjust governed idle speed.

shaft gear drives the governor. Governor and linkage must operate properly to prevent "hunting" or unsteady operation. The carburetor must be properly adjusted before performing governor adjustments.

To adjust governor linkage, loosen clamp bolt on governor lever shown in Figs. B518 or B519. Move link end of governor lever so carburetor throttle plate is in wide-open position. Using a screwdriver, rotate governor lever shaft clockwise as far as possible and tighten clamp bolt.

On models equipped with governed idle screw (I—Fig. B520), set remote control to idle position, then adjust idle speed screw on carburetor so engine idles at 1550 rpm. Place remote control so engine idles at 1750 rpm, then rotate governed idle screw (I) so screw just contacts remote control lever.

On models equipped with a governed idle stop (P—Fig. B521), set remote control to idle position, then adjust idle speed screw on carburetor so engine idles at 1550 rpm. Loosen governed idle stop screw (W). Place remote control so engine idles at 1750 rpm, then position stop (P) so it contacts remote control lever and tighten screw (W).

On Models 253400 and 255400, set remote control to idle position, then adjust idle speed screw on carburetor so engine idles at 1550 rpm. Bend tang (G—Fig. B522) so engine idles at 1750 rpm.

IMPORTANT: Running an engine at a maximum speed higher than the speed specified by the equipment manufacturer can be dangerous to the operator, harmful to the equipment and inefficient. Adjust governed engine speed to specification stipulated by equipment manufacturer.

To set maximum no-load speed on all models except 253400 and 255400, move remote speed control to maximum speed position. With engine running, bend governor spring anchor tang (T—Fig. B523) to obtain desired maximum no-load speed.

To set maximum no-load speed on Models 253400 and 255400, move remote speed control to maximum speed position. With engine running, turn screw (S—Fig. B524) to obtain desired maximum no-load speed.

Some models are equipped with a top speed screw (T—Fig. B525) that determines maximum no-load speed according to which hole the screw occupies. There may be one, two, three or four numbered holes. If a screw is not installed in one of the numbered holes, the maximum speed determined by adjusting the governor spring anchor tang

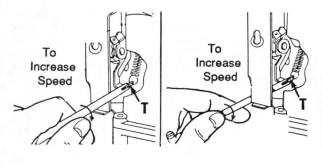

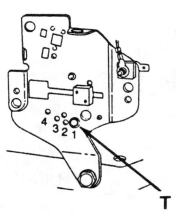

Fig. B523—Insert a suitable tool between cover and engine (left view) or through hole in cover (right view) and bend governor spring anchor tank (T) to adjust maximum governed speed.

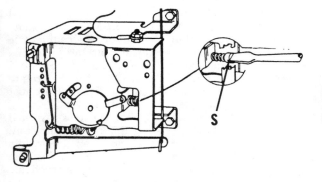

Fig. B524—On Series 253400 and 255400 engines, rotate screw (S) to adjust maximum governed speed.

Fig. B525—Some engines may be equipped with a maximum governed speed limit screw (T). Location of screw in one of the numbered holes determines maximum governed speed. Refer to text.

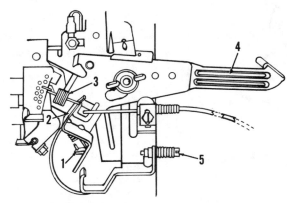

Fig. B526—Drawing of dual-spring governor control linkage used on some 176400, 19x400, 226400 and 250400 series engines. Single-spring linkage is similar. Refer to text for adjustment procedure.

1. Idle speed tang
2. Governor main spring tang
3. Governor main spring
4. Throttle lever
5. High-speed stop screw

will determine maximum no-load engine speed. If a screw is installed in a numbered hole, the maximum speed will be reduced. Installing the top speed screw (T) in a higher numbered hole will reduce top engine speed the most. For instance, installing the screw in hole "2" will reduce engine speed to 3300 rpm while installing the screw in hole "4" will reduce engine speed to 2400 rpm. An accurate tachometer should be used to determine engine speed for specific holes.

On Series 176400, 19A400, 19B400, 19C400, 19E400, 19F400, 19G400, 226400 and 250400 engines with dual-spring governor control (Fig. B526), adjust as follows: Remove the load from engine. Run engine until normal operating temperature is reached. Connect a tachometer to engine. Move the speed control lever (4) to put slack in main governor spring (3). Hold the throttle lever against the idle speed stop screw, and adjust screw to obtain 1750 rpm. While holding throttle lever against idle speed screw, adjust idle mixture screw to midpoint between too lean and too rich. Adjust idle speed stop screw to obtain 1200 rpm. Release the throttle lever, then bend the idle spring tang (1) to obtain idle speed of 1750

rpm. Back out the high-speed stop screw and move the speed control lever handle to 'Fast' position. Determine maximum no-load rpm specification, then bend main governor spring tang (2) until engine speed is 100-150 rpm over maximum no-load speed. Turn high-speed stop screw to bring maximum no-load rpm to specification.

IGNITION SYSTEM. Early models are equipped with a magneto ignition system; later models are equipped with a Magnetron breakerless ignition system. Refer to appropriate section for model being serviced.

Magneto Ignition. All models are equipped with breaker points and condenser located under the flywheel.

One of two different types of ignition points, as shown in Figs. B527 and B528, are used. Breaker point gap is 0.020 inch (0.51 mm) for all models with magneto ignition.

On each type, a plunger that rides against a cam on engine crankshaft actuates the breaker contact arm. The plunger operates in a bore in engine crankcase. The plunger can be removed after removing the breaker points. Renew plunger if worn to a length of 0.870 inch (22.10 mm) or less.

If breaker point plunger bore in crankcase is worn, oil will leak past plunger. Check bore with B&S gauge 19055. If plug gauge will enter bore ¼ inch (6.4 mm) or more, bore should be reamed and a bushing installed. Refer to Fig. B529. To ream bore and install bushing it will be necessary to remove breaker points, armature, ignition coil and crankshaft. Refer to Fig. B530 for steps in reaming bore and installation of bushing.

Plunger must be installed with groove toward top (Fig. B531) to prevent oil contamination in breaker point box.

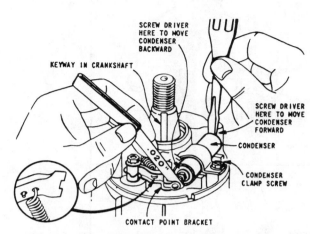

Fig. B527—Drawing showing breaker point adjustment on models with breaker points that are integral with condenser. Move condenser to adjust point gap.

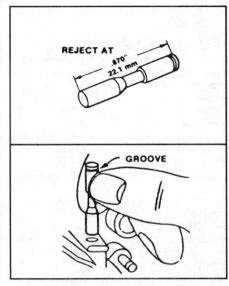

Fig. B531—Insert breaker point plunger into bore with groove toward top.

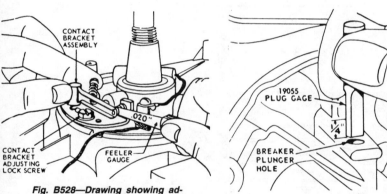

Fig. B528—Drawing showing adjustment of breaker points that are separate from condenser.

Fig. B529—If B&S gauge 19055 can be inserted in plunger bore 1/4 inch (6.4 mm) or more, bore is worn and must be rebushed.

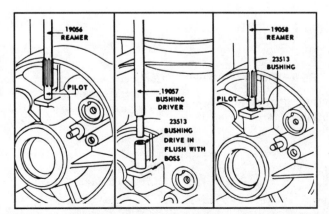

Fig. B530—Views showing reaming plunger bore to accept bushing (left view), installing bushing (center) and finish reaming bore of bushing (right).

To reassemble, set armature-to-flywheel air gap at 0.010-0.014 inch (0.25-0.36 mm) for two-leg armature or 0.012-0.016 inch (0.30-0.41 mm) for three-leg armature. Ignition timing is not adjustable on these models.

Magnetron Ignition. The Magnetron ignition is a self-contained breakerless ignition system. Flywheel removal is not necessary except to check or service keyway or crankshaft key.

To check spark, remove spark plug, connect spark plug cable to B&S tester 19051 and ground remaining tester lead on engine cylinder head. Rotate engine at 350 rpm or more. If spark jumps the 0.166 inch (4.2 mm) tester gap, system is functioning properly.

Armature and module have been manufactured as either one-piece units or as a separable two-piece assembly. The presence of large rivet heads on one side of the armature laminations identifies the two-piece unit. To remove armature and Magnetron module, remove flywheel shroud and armature retaining screws. On one-piece units, disconnect stop switch wire at spade connector. On two-piece units, use a $3/16$ inch (4.8 mm) diameter pin punch to release stop switch wire from module. To remove module on two-piece units, unsolder wires, push module retainer away from laminations and remove module. See Fig. B532.

Solder wires for installation and use RTV sealant to hold ground wires in position.

Armature-to-flywheel air gap should be 0.010-0.014 inch (0.25-0.36 mm) for two-leg armature or 0.012-0.016 inch (0.30-0.41 mm) for three-leg armature.

Ignition timing is not adjustable on these models.

VALVE ADJUSTMENT. To correctly set valve tappet clearance, remove spark plug and, using a suitable measuring tool, rotate crankshaft in normal direction (clockwise at flywheel) so piston is at top dead center on compression stroke. Continue to rotate crankshaft so piston is ¼ inch (6.4 mm) down from top dead center. This position places the tappets away from the compression release device, if used, on the cam lobe.

Exhaust valve tappet clearance (engine cold) for all models is 0.009-0.011 inch (0.23-0.28 mm). Intake valve tappet clearance (engine cold) for all models except Series 253400 and 255400 engines with electric start is 0.005-0.007 inch (0.13-0.18 mm). On Series 253400 and 255400 engines with electric start, intake valve tappet clearance is 0.009-0.011 inch (0.23-0.28 mm). If a Series 253400 or 255400 engine is equipped with a manual starter and an electric starter, intake valve tappet clearance is 0.005-0.007 inch (0.13-0.18 mm).

Valve tappet clearance is adjusted on all models by carefully grinding end of valve stem to increase clearance or by grinding valve seats deeper and/or renewing valve or lifter to decrease clearance.

CRANKCASE BREATHER. A crankcase breather is built into the engine tappet chamber cover. A partial vacuum must exist in crankcase to prevent oil seepage past oil seals, gaskets, breaker point plunger or piston rings. Air can flow out of crankcase through breather, but a one-way valve blocks return flow, maintaining necessary vacuum. Breather mounting holes are offset one way. A vent tube connects breather to carburetor air horn for extra protection against dusty conditions.

CYLINDER HEAD. After 100 to 300 hours of engine operation, the cylinder head should be removed and any carbon or deposits should be removed.

COMPRESSION PRESSURE. Briggs & Stratton does not publish compression pressure specifications.

An alternate method of determining internal engine condition and wear is by using a cylinder leak-down tester. The tester is available commercially or through Briggs & Stratton (part No. 19413). The tester uses compressed air to pressurize the combustion chamber, then gauges the amount of leakage past the piston rings and valves. Instructions are included with the tester.

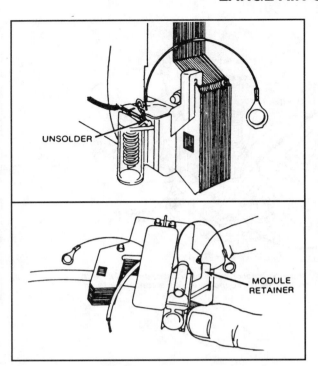

Fig. B532—Wires must be unsoldered to remove Magnetron ignition module.

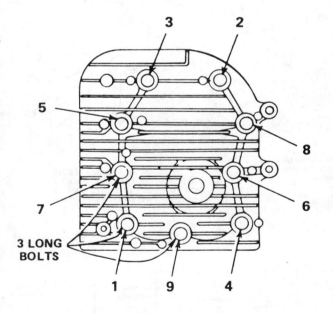

Fig. B533—Tighten cylinder head screws in sequence shown. Note location of three long screws.

REPAIRS

TIGHTENING TORQUE. Recommended tightening torque specifications are as follows:

Alternator stator	18-24 in.-lb.
	(2.0-2.7 N•m)
Blower housing	75-95 in.-lb.
	(8.5-10.7 N•m)
Breather screws	20-30 in.-lb.
	(2.3-3.4 N•m)
Carburetor mounting screws	65-75 in.-lb.
	(7.3-8.5 N•m)
Connecting rod	See Text
Crankcase cover	See Text
Electric starter	130-150 in.-lb.
	(14.7-17.0 N•m)
Fan retainer	130-150 in.-lb.
	(14.7-17.0 N•m)
Flywheel nut:	
170000-250000	65 ft.-lb.
	(88 N•m)
280000	95-105 ft.-lb.
	(129-142 N•m)
Fuel pump	40-50 in.-lb.
	(4.5-5.7 N•m)

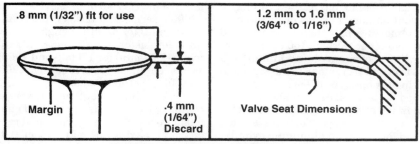

Fig. B534—Valve and valve seat dimensions.

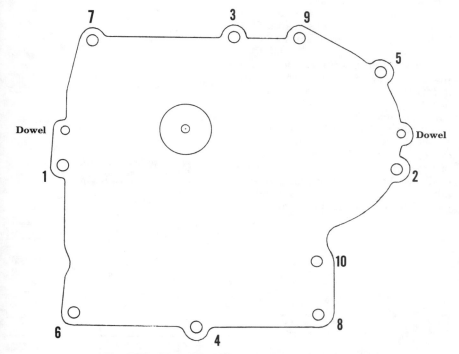

Fig. B535—On 10-bolt crankcase cover/oil pan used on 280000 series engines, it is important to tighten the fasteners in proper sequence to avoid distorting the cover.

cylinder and both valves are closed or seated. Three methods are used to retain the valve spring on the valve stem. Most engines are equipped with a slotted spring retainer that fits in a groove on the valve stem. The valve end will pass through the large end of the slot. Some engines are equipped with a retaining pin that fits in a hole in the end of the valve stem. The third method uses a split key, automotive-type retainer to retain the valve spring. Compress the valve spring using a suitable valve spring compressor tool. Remove the spring retainer, slide the valve out of the block and remove valve spring.

Some intake valves and all exhaust valves have a face angle of 45°. Seats for these valves should be cut at 46°. Some engine models have intake valves with a 30° face angle. Seats for these valves should be cut at 31°.

Renew valve if margin is $\frac{1}{64}$ inch (0.4 mm) or less (Fig. B534). Seat width should be $\frac{3}{64}$ to $\frac{1}{16}$ inch (1.2-1.6 mm).

All models are equipped with renewable valve seat inserts. Use a suitable puller to remove damaged or worn inserts. Chill the new insert in a freezer prior to installation. Use the old seat insert as a spacer between the driver and new insert. Be sure the new insert is bottomed in the cylinder block counterbore. Peen around the new insert to prevent it from loosening.

Valve guides are renewable. Using tool 19204, press in new guide bushing so it is flush with top of guide bore. Valve guide 230655 does not require reaming; however, other valve guides must be finish reamed using B&S reamer 19233 and reamer guide 19234.

Some engines may be equipped with a "Cobalite" exhaust valve and exhaust seat insert as well as a rotocoil on the exhaust valve stem. These components are offered as replacement parts for engines used in severe engine service.

If engine is operated on LP fuel or natural gas, rotocoil should not be used and valve stem and guide should be lubricated with B&S 93963 Valve Guide Lubricant during assembly.

CRANKCASE COVER/OIL PAN. On 170000-250000 series engines, tighten crankcase cover or oil pan fasteners in increments of 70 in.-lb. (7.9 N•m) to final torque of 140 in.-lb. (15.8 N•m). Tighten the fasteners in a criss-cross pattern to avoid distorting the cover. On 10-bolt crankcase cover/oil pan used on 280000 series engines, incrementally tighten the fasteners to 200 in.-lb. (22.6 N•m) using the tightening sequence shown in Fig. B535).

Governor lever bolt . . . . . . 35-45 in.-lb. (3.9-5.1 N•m)
Ignition module . . . . 20-28 in.-lb. (2.3-3.2 N•m)
Intake manifold . . . . 65-75 in.-lb. (7.3-8.5 N•m)
Spark plug . . . . 140-200 in.-lb. (15.8-22.6 N•m)
Starter gear cover . . . . . . 20-24 in.-lb. (2.3-2.7 N•m)
Solenoid ground wire . . . . 40-50 in.-lb. (4.5-5.7 N•m)

CYLINDER HEAD. Remove fan housing and/or cylinder head cover as required to access the cylinder head. Note the location and lengths of cylinder head retaining screws as they are removed so they can be installed in their original positions.

Clean combustion deposits from the cylinder head using a wooden or plastic scraper. Be careful not to nick or otherwise damage the sealing surface for the head gasket.

Always install a new cylinder head gasket. Do not apply sealer to head gasket. Lightly lubricate threads of cylinder head screws with Led-Plate part No. 93963 or graphite grease. Install screws and tighten in steps or increments of 55 in.-lb. (6.2 N•m) following sequence shown in Fig. B533. Final tightening torque is 165 in.-lb. (19 N•m).

VALVE SYSTEM. The valves are located in the cylinder block. To remove the valves, remove cylinder head. Remove components as required to access the crankcase breather. Remove breather/tappet chamber cover. Rotate the flywheel so piston is at top of the

NOTE: On 280000 series engines with Code Number of 971120xx or lower, replace cover/pan bolts with current-style part No. 94624 bolts.

CAMSHAFT. The camshaft is supported at both ends in bearing bores machined in crankcase and crankcase cover or oil pan. The camshaft gear is an integral part of camshaft.

Camshaft should be renewed if either journal is worn to a diameter of 0.498 inch (12.66 mm) or less, or if cam lobes are worn or damaged. Cam lobe wear limit is 0.977 inch (24.82 mm) for 170000 and 190000 series engines and 1.184 inch (30.07 mm) for all other engines.

Crankcase, crankcase cover or oil pan must be renewed if bearing bores are 0.506 inch (12.85 mm) or larger, or if tool 19164 enters bearing bore ¼ inch (6.4 mm) or more.

Compression release mechanism on camshaft gear holds exhaust valve slightly open at very low engine rpm as a starting aid. Mechanism should work freely and spring should hold actuator cam against pin.

When installing camshaft in engines with ball bearing main bearings, align timing marks on camshaft gear and crankshaft counterweight as shown in Fig. B536.

When installing camshaft in engines with integral-type main bearings, align timing marks on camshaft and crankshaft gears as shown in Fig. B537.

If timing mark is not visible on crankshaft gear, align camshaft gear timing mark with second tooth to the left of crankshaft counterweight parting line as shown in Fig. B538.

PISTON, PIN AND RINGS. Connecting rod and piston are removed from cylinder head end of block as an assembly. To remove, first remove cylinder head as previously outlined. Re-

move crankcase cover/oil sump and connecting rod cap. Remove any carbon or wear ridge at top of the cylinder to prevent damage to rings or piston during removal. Push the connecting rod and piston out through top of cylinder.

Cylinder bore may be aluminum or a cast iron sleeve. Pistons are designed to run in only one type of bore. Pistons designed for use in a cast iron bore have a dull finish and are stamped with an "L" on the piston's crown. Some pistons designed for use in an aluminum cylinder bore are chrome plated (shiny finish). Some later-style aluminum-bore pistons are iron-plated and can be identified by their gun metal-blue color. These pistons were first used after Date Code 990101xx. Pistons cannot be interchanged.

Reject piston showing visible signs of wear, scoring and scuffing. After cleaning carbon from top ring groove, insert a new top ring into the groove and measure the side clearance between the ring and ring land with a feeler gauge. Reject the piston if ring side clearance exceeds 0.009 inch (0.23 mm). Reject piston and pin or hone piston pin bore to fit a 0.005 inch (0.13 mm) oversize pin if pin or pin bore exceeds the following service limits. Maximum allowable

pin bore out-of-round is 0.0005 inch (0.013 mm). Wear limit for pin bore ID is 0.673 inch (17.09 mm) for 170000 and 190000 series engines, or 0.801 inch (20.34 mm) for all other engines. Wear limit for piston pin diameter is 0.671 inch (17.04 mm) for 170000 and 190000 series engines, or 0.799 inch (20.30 mm) for all other models.

On aluminum bore engines, reject compression rings having an end gap of 0.035 inch (0.90 mm) or more and reject oil rings having an end gap of 0.045 inch (1.14 mm) or more. On cast iron

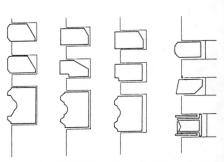

Fig. B539—Refer to above illustration for proper arrangement of piston rings used in engines with aluminum bore.

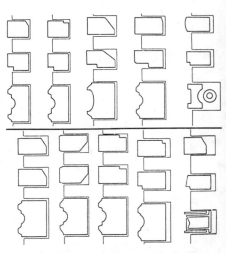

Fig. B540—Refer to above illustration for proper arrangement of piston rings used in engines with cast iron sleeve.

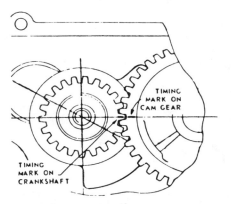

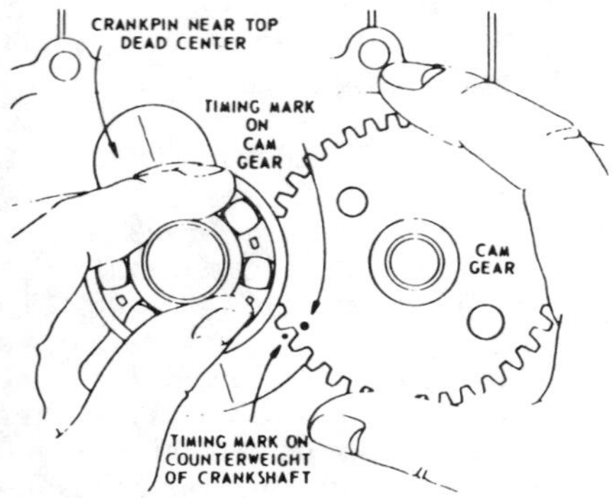

Fig. B537—Align timing marks on cam gear and crankshaft gear on plain bearing models.

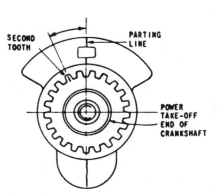

Fig. B538—Location of tooth to align with timing mark on cam gear if mark is not visible on crankshaft gear.

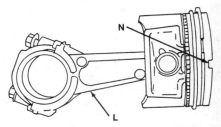

Fig. B541—If piston crown is notched (N), assemble connecting rod and piston as shown while noting relation of long side of rod (L) and notch (N) in piston crown.

Fig. B536—Align timing mark on cam gear with mark on crankshaft counterweight on ball bearing equipped models.

bore engines, reject compression rings having an end gap of 0.030 inch (0.75 mm) or more and reject oil rings having an end gap of 0.035 inch (0.90 mm) or more.

Pistons and rings are available in several oversizes as well as standard.

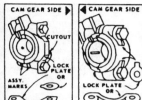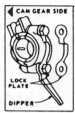

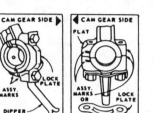

Fig. B542—Install connecting rod in engine as indicated according to type used. Note dipper installation on connecting rod for horizontal crankshaft engine.

Installation instructions are provided with the ring set. Refer to Figs. B539 and B540 for correct installation of piston rings.

A chrome piston ring set is available for slightly worn standard bore cylinders. No honing or cylinder deglazing is required for these rings. The cylinder bore can be a maximum of 0.005 inch (0.13 mm) oversize when using chrome rings.

If piston has a notch (N—Fig. B541) in piston crown, assemble connecting rod and piston as shown in Fig. B541. Install piston and rod in engine so notch (N) is toward flywheel.

CONNECTING ROD. Connecting rod and piston are removed from cylinder head end of block as an assembly. The aluminum alloy connecting rod rides directly on an induction hardened crankshaft crankpin journal. Rod should be rejected if big end of rod is scored or out-of-round more than 0.0007 inch (0.018 mm) or if piston pin bore is scored or out-of-round more than 0.0005 inch (0.013 mm). Renew connecting rod if either crankpin bore or piston pin bore is worn to, or larger than, sizes given in table.

Model Series	Crankpin Bore	Pin Bore*
170000	1.095 in. (27.81 mm)	0.674 in. (17.12 mm)
190000	1.127 in. (28.61 mm)	0.674 in. (17.12 mm)
220000, 250000, 280000	1.252 in. (31.8 mm)	0.802 in. (20.37 mm)

*Piston pins that are 0.005 inch (0.13 mm) oversize are available for service. Piston pin bore in rod can be reamed to this size if crankpin bore is within specifications.

Refer to Fig. B542, locate-type of rod being serviced and note installation instructions. If piston has a notch (N—Fig. B541) in piston crown, install connecting rod in piston as shown in Fig. B541. Install piston and rod in engine so notch (N) is toward flywheel.

Refer to the following table for connecting rod screw tightening torque specifications.

Series	Torque
170000	165 in.-lbs. (18.6 N•m)
190000, 220000, 250000	185 in.-lb. (20.9 N•m)
280000 w/equal size rod bolts	185 in.-lb. (20.9 N•m)
280000 w/two sizes of rod bolts Small bolt	130 in.-lb. (14.7 N•m)
Large bolt	260 in.-lb. (29.4 N•m)

GOVERNOR. Governor gear and weight unit can be removed after crankcase cover or oil pan is removed. Refer to exploded views of engines in Figs. B543, B544, B545 and B546. Gov-

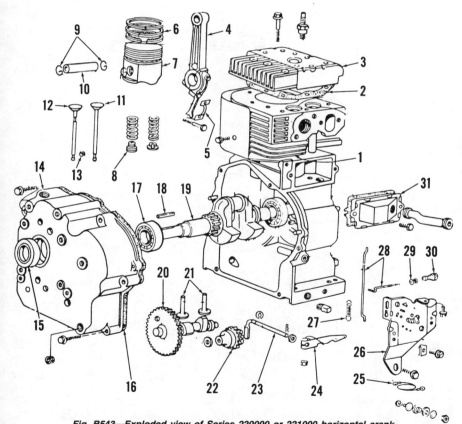

Fig. B543—Exploded view of Series 220000 or 221000 horizontal crankshaft engine assembly. Series 170000, 171000, 176000 and 190000 are similar. Series 222000 is similar, but ball bearings (17) are not used.

1. Cylinder block/ crankcase
2. Head gasket
3. Cylinder head
4. Connecting rod
5. Lock plate
6. Piston rings
7. Piston
8. Rotocoil (exhaust valve)
9. Retainer clips
10. Piston pin
11. Intake valve
12. Exhaust valve
13. Retainers
14. Crankcase cover
15. Oil seal
16. Crankcase gasket
17. Main bearing
18. Key
19. Crankshaft
20. Camshaft
21. Tappet
22. Governor gear
23. Governor crank
24. Governor lever
25. Ground wire
26. Governor control plate
27. Spring
28. Governor rod
29. Spring
30. Nut
31. Breather assy.

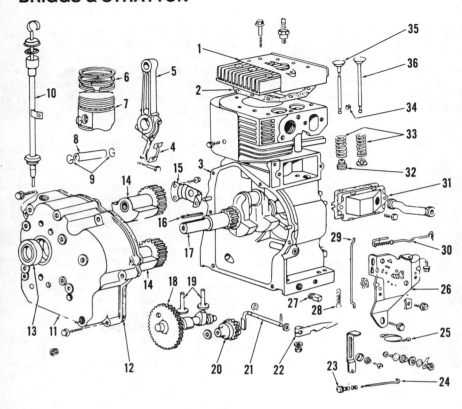

Fig. B544—Exploded view of Series 251000, 252000 or 254000 engine assembly. Series 253000 and 255000 are similar.

1. Cylinder head
2. Head gasket
3. Cylinder block/ crankcase
4. Lock plate
5. Connecting rod
6. Piston rings
7. Piston
8. Piston pin
9. Retainer clips
10. Dipstick
11. Crankcase cover
12. Crankcase gasket
13. Oil seal
14. Counterweight & bearing assy.
15. Retainer
16. Key
17. Crankshaft
18. Camshaft
19. Tappet
20. Governor gear
21. Governor crank
22. Governor lever
23. Governor nut & spring
24. Governor control rod
25. Ground wire
26. Governor control pin
27. Drain plug
28. Spring
29. Governor link
30. Choke link
31. Breather assy.
32. Rotocoil (exhaust valve)
33. Valve springs
34. Retainer
35. Exhaust valve
36. Intake valve

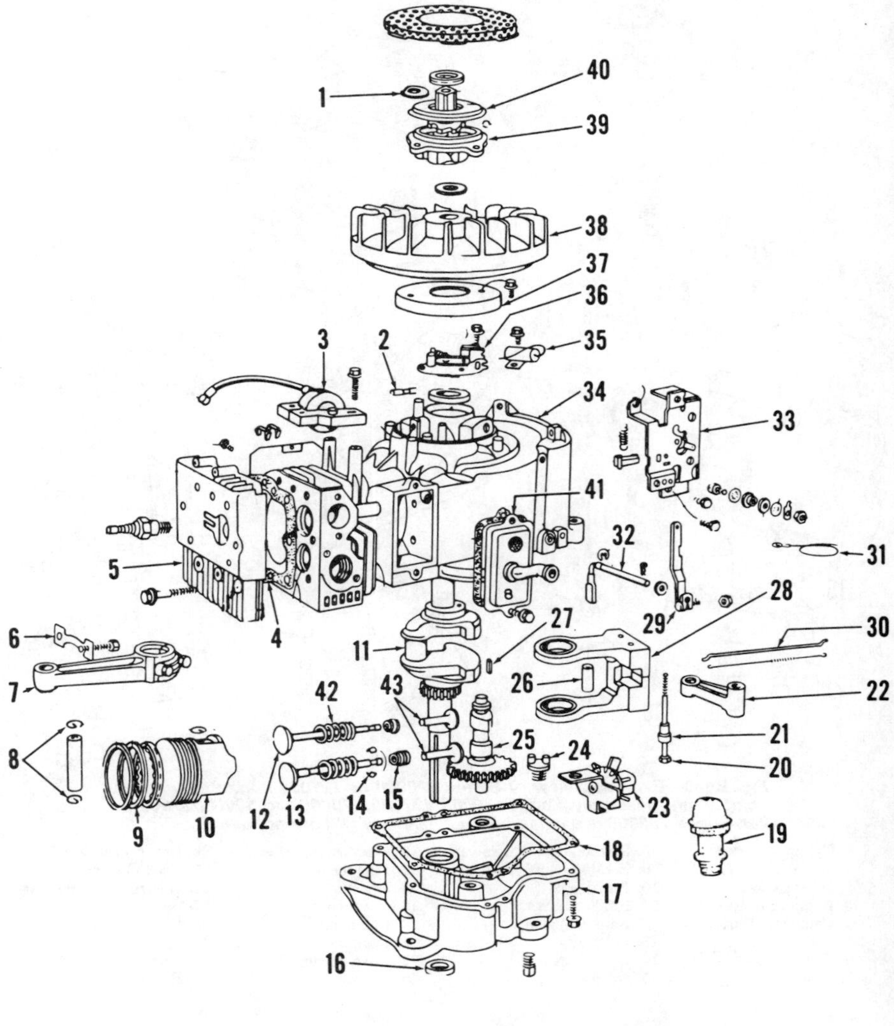

Fig. B545—Exploded view of typical vertical crankshaft engine equipped with Synchro-Balancer. Later models use a solid-state ignition module in place of breaker points and coil assembly.

1. Thrust washer
2. Breaker point plunger
3. Armature assy.
4. Head gasket
5. Cylinder head
6. Lock plate
7. Connecting rod
8. Piston pin & retaining clips
9. Piston rings
10. Piston
11. Crankshaft
12. Intake valve
13. Exhaust valve
14. Retainer
15. Rotocoil (exhaust valve)
16. Oil seal
17. Oil pan
18. Crankcase gasket
19. Oil minder
20. Cap screw (2)
21. Spacer (2)
22. Link
23. Governor & oil slinger
24. Plug
25. Camshaft
26. Dowel pin (2)
27. Key
28. Counterweight assy.
29. Governor lever
30. Governor link
31. Ground wire
32. Governor crank
33. Choke-A-Matic control
34. Cylinder block/ crankcase
35. Condenser
36. Breaker points
37. Cover
38. Flywheel assy.
39. Clutch housing
40. Rewind starter clutch
41. Breather assy.
42. Valve springs
43. Tappet

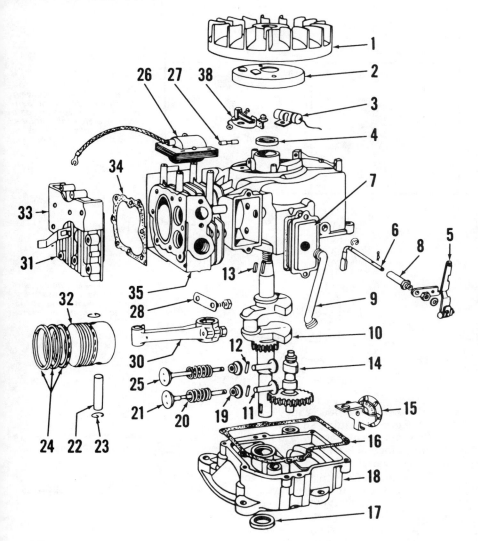

Fig. B546—Exploded view of vertical crankshaft engine not equipped with Synchro-Balancer. Later models are equipped with a solid-state ignition module in place of breaker points and coil assembly.

1. Flywheel	19. Valve spring retainer
2. Cover	20. Valve springs
3. Condenser	21. Exhaust valve
4. Oil seal	22. Piston pin
5. Governor lever	23. Retainer clip
6. Governor crank	24. Piston rings
7. Breather assy.	25. Intake valve
8. Bushing	26. Armature & coil assy.
9. Breather vent tube	27. Breaker point
10. Crankshaft	plunger
11. Tappet	28. Rod bolt lock
12. Valve retaining pins	30. Connecting rod
13. Key	31. Cylinder head
14. Camshaft	32. Piston
15. Governor & oil	33. Air baffle
slinger	34. Head gasket
16. Crankcase gasket	35. Cylinder block/
17. Oil seal	crankcase
18. Oil pan	38. Breaker points

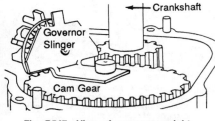

Fig. B547—View of governor weight assembly and oil slinger used on vertical crankshaft models.

ernor weight unit on horizontal crankshaft models rides on a shaft in the crankcase cover. The governor weight unit along with the oil slinger on vertical crankshaft models rides on the end of the camshaft as shown in Fig. B547.

Remove governor lever, cotter pin and washer from outer end of governor lever shaft. Slide governor lever out of bushing toward inside of engine. Gover-nor gear and weight unit can now be removed. Renew governor lever shaft bushing in crankcase, if necessary, and ream new bushing after installation to 0.2385-0.2390 inch (6.058-6.071 mm). Briggs & Stratton tool 19333 can be used to ream bushing.

Replace the governor lever seal if oil leakage past the seal is evident. Use care not to damage the seal lip when installing the new seal. Wrap thin plastic or cellophane tape over the end of the lever shaft to serve as a seal protector.

CRANKSHAFT AND MAIN BEARINGS. The crankshaft may be supported by bearing surfaces that are an integral part of crankcase, crankcase cover or oil pan, or by ball bearings at each end of crankshaft. The ball bearings are a press fit on the crankshaft and fit into machined bores in the crankcase, crankcase cover or oil pan.

The crankshaft used in models with integral bearings should be renewed or reground if main bearing journals exceed service limits specified in following table.

CRANKSHAFT REJECT SIZES

Model	Magneto End Journal	PTO End Journal
170000 and 190000 series	0.997 in.* (25.32 mm)	1.179 in. (29.95 mm)
220000, 250000 and 280000 series	1.376 in. (34.95 mm)	1.376 in. (34.95 mm)

*Models equipped with Synchro-Balancer have a main bearing rejection size for main bearing at magneto side of 1.179 inch (29.95 mm).

Crankshaft for models with ball bearing main bearings should be renewed if new bearings are loose on journals. Bearings should be a press fit.

Crankshaft for all models should be renewed or reground if connecting rod crankpin journal diameter exceeds service limit listed in following table.

CRANKSHAFT REJECT SIZES

Model	Crankpin Journal
170000 series	1.090 in. (27.69 mm)
190000 series	1.122 in. (28.50 mm)
220000, 250000, and 280000 series	1.247 in. (31.67 mm)

A connecting rod with undersize big end diameter is available to fit crankshaft that has had crankpin journal reground to 0.020 inch (0.51 mm) undersize.

On models equipped with integral main bearings, crankcase, crankcase cover or oil pan must be renewed or reamed to accept service bushings if service limits in following table are exceeded.

MAIN BEARING REJECT SIZES

Model	Magneto End Bearing	PTO End Bearing
170000 and 190000 series	1.004 in.* (25.50 mm)	1.185 in. (30.10 mm)
220000, 250000 and 280000 series	1.383 in. (35.13 mm)	1.383 in. (35.13 mm)

*Models equipped with Synchro-Balancer have a main bearing rejection size for main bearing at magneto side of 1.185 inch (30.10 mm).

Install steel-backed aluminum service bushing as follows. Use a suitable tool and, prior to bushing installation, make an indentation in bore of crankcase. Install bushing so oil notches are properly aligned and bushing is flush with bore. Oil hole must be clear after installation. Stake bushing into previously made indentation and finish ream bushing. Do not stake where bushing is split.

When installing "DU"-type bushing, stake bushing at oil notches in crankcase, but locate bushing so bushing split is not aligned with an oil notch. On Series 170000 and 190000 models, bushing should be 3/32 inch (2.4 mm) below face of crankcase bore and 1/32 inch (0.8 mm) below face of crankcase cover or oil pan. On Series 171700, 191700, 192700, 193700, 194700, 195700 and 196700 models, bushing should be 1/64 inch (0.4 mm) below face of crankcase

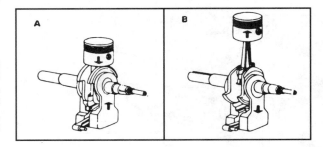

Fig. B548—Drawing showing operating principle of Synchro-Balancer used on some vertical crankshaft engines. Counterweight oscillates in opposite direction of piston.

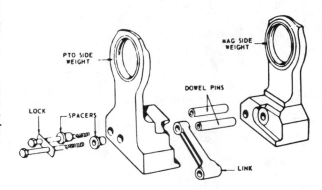

Fig. B549—Exploded view of Synchro-Balancer assembly. Counterweights ride on eccentric journals on crankshaft.

bore. On Series 220000, 250000 and 280000 engines, bushing should be 7/64 inch (2.8 mm) below face of crankcase bore and 1/8 inch (3.2 mm) below face of crankcase cover or oil pan.

Ball bearing mains are a press fit on the crankshaft and must be removed by pressing the crankshaft out of the bearing. Reject ball bearing if worn or rough. Expand new bearing by heating it in oil and install it on crankshaft with seal side toward crankpin journal.

Crankshaft end play is 0.002-0.008 inch (0.05-0.20 mm). At least one 0.015-inch crankcase gasket must be in place when measuring end play. Additional gaskets in several sizes are available to aid in end play adjustment. If end play is excessive, place shims between crankshaft gear and crankcase on plain bearing models, or on flywheel side of crankshaft if equipped with a ball bearing.

When reinstalling crankshaft, make certain timing marks are aligned (Figs. B536 or B537) and, if equipped with counterbalance weights, refer to ROTATING COUNTERBALANCE SYSTEM paragraphs for counterweight alignment procedure.

CYLINDER. If cylinder bore wear is 0.003 inch (0.08 mm) or more or is 0.0025 inch (0.06 mm) or more out-of-round, cylinder must be renewed or bored to next larger oversize.

Standard cylinder bore diameter is 2.9990-3.0000 inches (76.175-76.230

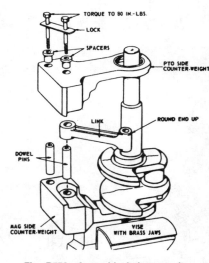

Fig. B550—Assemble balance units on crankshaft as shown. Install link with rounded edge on free end toward pto end of crankshaft.

mm) for Series 170000 and 190000 models. Standard cylinder bore diameter is 3.4365-3.4375 inches (87.287-87.313 mm) for all other models.

Special stones are required to hone aluminum cylinder bore on models so equipped. Follow recommendations and procedures specified by hone manufacturer.

A chrome piston ring set is available for slightly worn standard bore cylin-

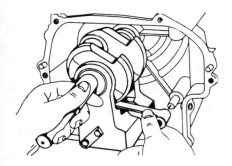

Fig. B551—When installing crankshaft and balancer assembly, place free end of link on anchor pin in crankcase.

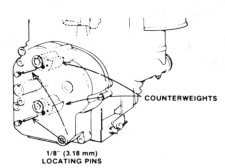

Fig. B553—To properly align counterweights, remove two small screws from crankcase cover and insert 1/8-inch (3.2 mm) diameter locating pins.

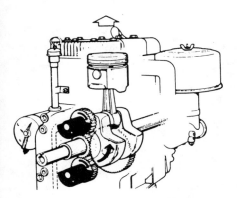

Fig. B552—View of rotating counter-balance system used on some models. A gear on the crankshaft drives the counterweight gears.

ders. No honing or cylinder deglazing is required for these rings. The cylinder bore can be a maximum of 0.005 inch (0.13 mm) oversize when using chrome rings.

SYNCHRO-BALANCER. All vertical crankshaft engines, except Series 220000, 221000 and 222000 models, may be equipped with an oscillating Synchro-Balancer. Balance weight assembly rides on eccentric journals on the crankshaft and move in opposite direction of piston (Fig. B548).

To disassemble balancer unit, first remove flywheel, oil pan, cam gear, cylinder head, and connecting rod and piston assembly. Carefully pry off crankshaft gear and key. Remove the two cap screws holding halves of counterweight together. Separate weights and remove link, dowel pins and spacers. Slide weights from crankshaft (Fig. B549).

To reassemble, install magneto side weight on magneto end of crankshaft. Place crankshaft (pto end up) in a vise (Fig. B550). Install both dowel pins and place link on pin as shown. Note rounded edge on free end of link must be up. Install pto side weight, spacers, lock and cap screws. Tighten cap screws to 80 in.-lbs. (9 N•m) and secure with lock tabs. Install key and crankshaft gear with chamfer on inside of gear facing shoulder on crankshaft.

Install crankshaft and balancer assembly in crankcase, sliding free end of

link on anchor pin as shown in Fig. B551. Reassemble engine

ROTATING COUNTERBALANCE SYSTEM. All horizontal crankshaft engines, except Series 220000, 221000 and 222000 models, may be equipped with two gear-driven counterweights in constant mesh with crankshaft gear. Gears, mounted in crankcase cover, rotate in opposite direction of crankshaft (Fig. B552).

To properly align counterweights when installing cover, remove two small screws from cover and insert $\frac{1}{8}$-inch (3.2 mm) diameter locating pins through holes in cover and into timing holes in counterweights as shown in Fig. B553.

With piston at TDC, install cover assembly. Remove locating pins, coat threads of timing hole screws with sealant and install screws with fiber sealing washers.

NOTE: If counterweights are removed from crankcase cover, exercise care in handling or cleaning to prevent loss of needle bearings.

BRIGGS & STRATTON

BRIGGS & STRATTON CORPORATION
Milwaukee, Wisconsin 53201

Model Series	No. Cyls.	Bore	Stroke	Displacement	Power Rating
19, 19D, 191000, 193000	1	3.00 in. (76.2 mm)	2.625 in. (66.68 mm)	18.56 cu. in. (304 cc)	7.25 hp (5.5 kW)
200000	1	3.00 in. (76.2 mm)	2.875 in. (73.02 mm)	20.32 cu. in. (333 cc)	8 hp (6 kW)
22, 23A, 23C, 23D 231000, 233000	1	3.00 in. (76.2 mm)	3.25 in. (82.55 mm)	22.97 cu. in. (376 cc)	9 hp (6.7 kW)
243000	1	3.0625 in. (77.79 mm)	3.25 in. (82.55 mm)	23.94 cu. in. (392 cc)	10 hp (7.5 kW)
300000, 301000	1	3.4375 in. (87.31 mm)	3.25 in. (82.55 mm)	30.16 cu. in. (494 cc)	12 hp (9 kW)
302000	1	3.4375 in. (87.31 mm)	3.25 in. (82.55 mm)	30.16 cu. in. (494 cc)	13 hp (9.7 kW)
320000	1	3.5625 in. (90.5 mm)	3.25 in. (82.55 mm)	32.4 cu. in. (531 cc)	14 hp (10.4 kW)
325000	1	3.5625 in. (90.5 mm)	3.25 in. (82.55 mm)	32.4 cu. in. (531 cc)	15 hp (11.2 kW)
326000	1	3.5625 in. (90.5 mm)	3.25 in. (82.55 mm)	32.4 cu. in. (531 cc)	16 hp (11.9 kW)

Engines in this section are four-stroke, single-cylinder engines with a horizontal crankshaft. The crankshaft may be supported by main bearings that are integral parts of the crankcase and bearing support plate or by ball bearings pressed on the crankshaft. Cylinder block and bore are a single cast iron casting.

The connecting rod on all models rides directly on the crankpin journal. An oil dipper attached to the connecting rod cap provides splash lubrication for all models.

Early models are equipped with a variety of magneto-type ignition systems with points and condenser either mounted externally or located underneath the flywheel. Later models are equipped with a breakerless (Magnetron) ignition system.

A float-type carburetor is used on all models. A fuel pump is available as optional equipment for some models.

Refer to BRIGGS & STRATTON ENGINE IDENTIFICATION INFORMATION section for engine identification. Engine model number as well as type number and code number are necessary when ordering parts.

MAINTENANCE

LUBRICATION. Engine oil should be changed after first eight hours of operation and after every 50 hours of operation or at least once each operating season. If equipment undergoes severe usage, change oil weekly or after every 25 hours of operation. Drain the oil while the engine is warm. The oil will flow freely and carry away more impurities.

Manufacturer recommends using oil with an API service classification of SH or SJ, or any classification formulated to supercede SH or SJ. Use SAE 30 oil for temperatures above 40° F (4° C); use SAE 10W-30 oil for temperatures between 0°F (−18°C) and 40° F (4° C); below 0° F (−18°C) use petroleum based SAE 5W-20 or a suitable synthetic oil. Do not use SAE 10W-40 oil.

Crankcase oil capacity for 18.56 and 20.32 cubic inch engines is 3 pints (1.4 L). Crankcase oil capacity for all other models is 4 pints (1.9 L).

SPARK PLUG. The original spark plug may be either 1½ inches or 2 inches long. Recommended spark plug is either Champion or Autolite.

If a Champion spark plug is used and spark plug is 1½ inches long, recommended spark plug is Champion J19LM or CJ8. Install Champion RJ19LM or RCJ8 if a resistor-type spark plug is required. If spark plug is 2 inches long, recommended spark plug is J19LM or J8C. Install Champion RJ19LM or RJ8C if a resistor-type spark plug is required. Specified electrode gap is 0.030 inch (0.76 mm).

If an Autolite spark plug is used and spark plug is 1½ inches long, recommended spark plug is 235. Install Autolite 245 if a resistor-type spark plug is required. If spark plug is 2 inches long, recommended spark plug is 295. Install Autolite 306 if a resistor-type spark plug is required. Specified electrode gap is 0.030 inch (0.76 mm).

Series 233000 and 243000 engines set up to run dual-fuel (gasoline/kerosene) must use special spark plug part No. 291835 (Champion J11C) gapped at 0.030 inch (0.76 mm) and a reduced breaker point gap of 0.015 in. (0.38 mm).

CAUTION: Briggs & Stratton does not recommend using abrasive blasting to clean spark plugs as this may introduce some abrasive material into the engine that could cause extensive damage.

CARBURETOR. For engines equipped to run on LPG fuel, refer to LPG FUEL SYSTEMS service procedures in the SERVICING BRIGGS AND STRATTON ACCESSORIES section of this manual. All other engines

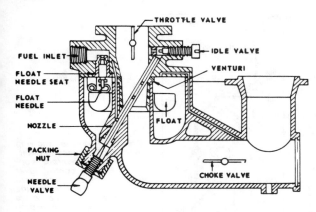

Fig B601—Cross-sectional view of two-piece Flo-Jet II carburetor. Before separating upper and lower body section, loosen packing nut and power needle valve as a unit and use special screwdriver (tool 19062) to remove nozzle.

are equipped with a two-piece Flo-Jet carburetor. Refer to Fig. B601 for a cross-sectional view of carburetor and location of mixture adjustment needles.

Initial setting of idle mixture needle is 1¼ turns out and high-speed needle valve is 1½ turns out. With engine at normal operating temperature and equipment control lever in "SLOW" position, adjust idle speed screw so engine idles at 1750 rpm. With engine running at idle speed, turn idle mixture needle clockwise until engine speed just starts to drop. Note needle position. Turn idle mixture needle counterclockwise until engine speed just starts to drop again. Note needle position, and turn needle to midpoint between the noted positions. Adjust high-speed needle valve with control set to "FAST" using same procedure. If engine will not accelerate cleanly, slightly enrich mixture by turning idle mixture needle valve counterclockwise. If necessary, readjust idle speed screw.

To check float level, invert carburetor body and float assembly. Refer to Fig. B602 for proper float level dimensions. Adjust by bending float lever tang that contacts inlet valve. Check upper body for distortion using a 0.002 inch (0.05 mm) feeler gauge as shown in Fig. B603. Upper body must be renewed if warped more than 0.002 inch (0.05 mm).

The float used in carburetors for 19- and 20-cubic inch engines has been redesigned to allow the float to 'drop' farther into the float bowl during engine operation. This change helps prevent the engine from 'running out of gas' while there still appears to be gasoline in the tank. This problem occurs mainly on engines with an engine-mounted tank opposite the carburetor.

Internal fuel leakage can result in the engine flooding and fuel running out of the drain hole in the bottom of carburetor air horn. This internal leakage problem may be caused by corrosion or an improper seal between the tapered seat on the main nozzle and its mating surface inside the lower carburetor body. Three solutions to this problem are:

1. Make a tool by filing or grinding the threads off a new nozzle so it slides easily into and out of the carburetor. Place a light coating of fine-grit lapping compound on the tapered face of the nozzle. Using a screwdriver in the nozzle end slot, lap the nozzle against the seat. Be very careful not to damage the threads in the carburetor body when rotating the screwdriver. Thoroughly clean all lapping compound from the carburetor. Install a new nozzle.
2. Force a Teflon washer from B&S repair kit No. 391413 over the end of the nozzle and against the nozzle shoulder to serve as a gasket.
3. Replace carburetor lower body and nozzle.

DUAL-FUEL (GASOLINE AND KEROSENE) SYSTEM. Some engines are equipped to run on both gasoline and kerosene. Dual-fuel engines are equipped with a dual-section fuel tank with double shutoff valves. Recommended operating procedure is to start the engine on gasoline, then switch to kerosene when engine is running. The carburetor may need minor adjustment after either changeover for proper operation. Prior to long-term shutdown, switch back to gasoline to ensure easy cold restart.

NOTE: Series 233000 and 243000 dual-fuel engines require a special spark plug (Champion J11C) gapped at 0.030 in. (0.76 mm) and a reduced breaker point gap of 0.015 in. (0.38 mm).

A lower compression ratio is required for dual-fuel operation. Some dual-fuel engines are equipped with a special low-compression cylinder head while other engines use two head gaskets. Service procedures for dual-fuel engine components are the same as for gasoline engines.

AUTOMATIC CHOKE. A thermostat-operated choke is used on some models. To adjust choke linkage, hold choke shaft so thermostat lever is free. At room temperature, stop screw in thermostat collar should be located midway between thermostat stops. If not, loosen stop screw, adjust collar and tighten stop screw. Loosen setscrew (S—Fig. B604) on thermostat lever. Slide lever on shaft to ensure free movement of choke unit. Turn thermostat shaft clockwise until stop screw contacts thermostat stop. While holding shaft in this position, move shaft le-

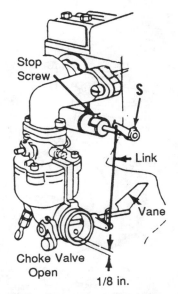

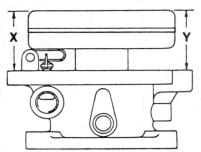

Fig. B602—Dimension (Y) must be the same as dimension (X) plus or minus 1/32 inch (0.8 mm).

Fig. B603—Check upper body of Flo-Jet II carburetor for distortion as outlined in text.

Fig. B604—Typical automatic choke unit in "HOT" position.

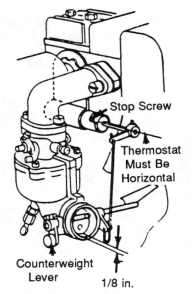

Fig. B605—Turn thermostat shaft counterclockwise until stop screw contacts thermostat stop as shown.

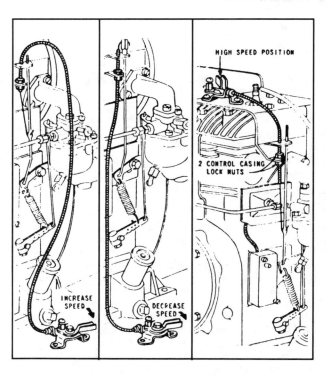

Fig. B607—Views showing method of connecting different remote governor controls. Moving control lever will vary governor spring tension, thus varying engine governed speeds. For views showing remote throttle controls, refer to Fig. B608.

ver until choke is open exactly ⅛ inch (3 mm) and tighten lever setscrew. Turn thermostat shaft counterclockwise until stop screw contacts thermostat stop as shown in Fig. B605. Manually open choke valve until it stops against top of choke link opening. At this time choke should be open at least ³⁄₃₂ inch (2.4 mm), but not more than ⁵⁄₃₂ inch (4 mm). Hold choke valve in wide-open position and check position of counterweight lever. Lever should be in a horizontal position with free end toward the right.

FUEL PUMP. A fuel pump is available as optional equipment on some models. Refer to BRIGGS & STRATTON ACCESSORIES section for service information.

GOVERNOR. All engines are equipped with a gear-driven mechanical-type governor attached to the crankcase cover or oil pan. The camshaft gear drives the governor. Governor and linkage must operate properly to prevent "hunting" or unsteady operation. The carburetor must be properly adjusted before performing governor adjustments.

To adjust governor linkage, loosen clamp bolt nut (N—Fig. B606) on governor lever. Move link end of governor lever so carburetor throttle plate is in wide-open position. Using a screwdriver, rotate governor lever shaft (S) counterclockwise as far as possible and tighten clamp bolt to 35-45 in.-lbs. (4.0-5.1 N•m).

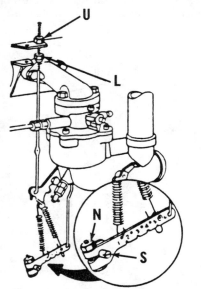

Fig. B606—View showing governor linkage, springs and levers properly installed on 243000, 300000, 301000, 302000, 320000, 325000 and 326000 series engines. Refer to Fig. B609 for remote control hook-up.

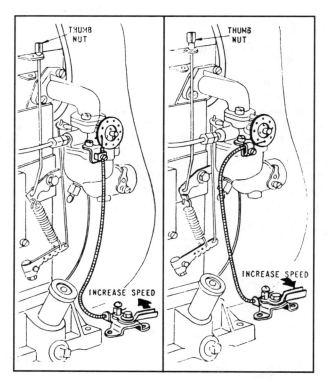

Fig. B608—Views showing methods of connecting remote throttle controls. When control lever is in high-speed position, governor controls speed of engines and governed speed is adjusted by turning thumb nut. Moving control lever to slow speed position moves carburetor throttle shaft stop to decrease engine speed.

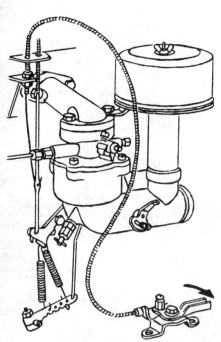

Fig. B609—Remote governor control installation on 243000, 300000, 30100, 302000, 320000, 325000 and 326000 series engines.

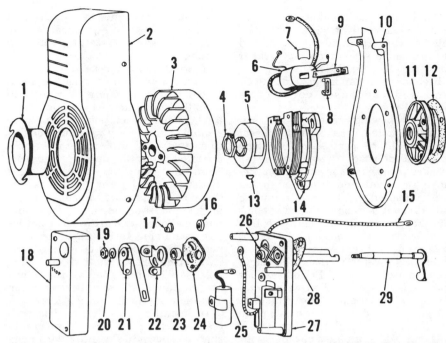

Fig. B611—Exploded view magneto ignition system used on 19, 23 and 23A models and 191000 and 231000 series engines. Flywheel is not keyed to crankshaft and can be installed in any position; however, on crank start models, flywheel should be installed as shown in Fig. B618. Breaker arm (21) is mounted on shaft (29) which is actuated by a cam on engine cam gear. See Fig. B619. Two different methods of attaching magneto rotor (5) to engine crankshaft have been used. Refer to Figs. B614 and B615.

1. Starter pulley	9. Coil core	16. Shaft seal	23. Pivot
2. Blower housing	10. Back plate	17. Eccentric	24. Insulator
3. Flywheel	11. Bearing support	18. Breaker box cover	25. Condenser
4. Rotor clamp	12. Shim gasket	19. Nut	26. Seal retainer
5. Magneto rotor	13. Rotor key	20. Washer	27. Breaker box
6. Ignition coil	14. Armature	21. Breaker point cam	28. Gasket
7. Coil retainer	15. Primary coil lead	22. Breaker point base	29. Shaft
8. Core clip			

Refer to Figs. B606 through B609 for governor control and carburetor linkage hook-up and adjustments.

IGNITION SYSTEM. Early models use a variety of magneto-type ignition systems and late production models use Briggs & Stratton Magnetron ignition system. Refer to appropriate section for model being serviced.

Model 23C Magneto. Refer to Fig. B610 for exploded view of magneto used on 23C series engine. Condenser and breaker points are mounted on crankshaft bearing support plate (17) and are accessible after removing flywheel and magneto cover (7).

Breaker point gap is 0.020 inch (0.51 mm) and condenser capacity is 0.18-0.24 mfd.

Breaker point plunger can be removed from bore in crankshaft bearing support when breaker points are removed. Plunger should be renewed if worn to a length of 0.870 inch (22.10 mm) or less. Plunger bore diameter can be checked using B&S plunger bore gauge 19055. If gauge enters plunger bore ¼ inch (6.4 mm) or more, install service bushing 23513. To install bushing, remove bearing support from engine, then ream bore using B&S reamer 19056, drive bushing in flush with outer end of plunger bore with B&S driver 19057 and use B&S reamer 19058 to finish ream inside of bushing.

When reinstalling flywheel, inspect the soft metal key and renew if damaged in any way.

NOTE: Renew key with correct B&S part. DO NOT substitute a steel key.

After flywheel is installed and retaining nut tightened, check armature air gap and adjust as necessary to 0.022-0.026 inch (0.56-0.66 mm).

Series or Models 19, 23, 23A, 191000 and 231000 Magneto. Refer to Fig. B611 for exploded view of magneto used on these models.

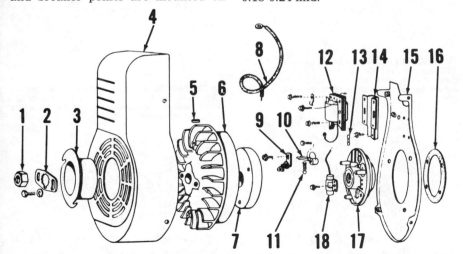

Fig. B610—Exploded view of magneto ignition system used on 23C model engines. Breaker points and condenser are mounted on bearing support (17) and are enclosed by cover (7) and flywheel. Points are actuated by plunger (13) which rides against breaker cam on engine crankshaft.

1. Flywheel nut	6. Flywheel	10. Breaker point arm
2. Nut retainer	7. Breaker cover	11. Breaker spring
3. Start pulley	8. Spark plug wire	12. Coil & armature
4. Blower housing	9. Breaker point base	13. Plunger
5. Flywheel key		

14. Armature support
15. Back plate
16. Shim gasket
17. Bearing support
18. Condenser

Condenser and breaker points are mounted externally in a breaker box located on carburetor side of engine and are accessible after removing breaker box cover (18—Fig. B611).

Breaker point gap is 0.020 inch (0.51 mm) and condenser capacity is 0.18-0.24 mfd.

When renewing breaker points, or if oil leak is noted, breaker shaft oil seal (16) should be renewed. To renew points and/or seal, turn engine so breaker point gap is at maximum. Remove terminal and breaker spring screws. Loosen breaker arm retaining nut (19) so it is flush with end of shaft (29). Tap loosened nut lightly to free breaker arm (21) from taper on shaft, then remove breaker arm, breaker plate (22), pivot (23), insulating plate (24) and eccentric (17). Pry oil seal out and press new oil seal in with metal side out. Place breaker plate on insulating plate with dowel on breaker plate entering hole in insulator. Then install unit with edges of plates parallel with breaker box as shown in Fig. B612. Turn breaker shaft clockwise as far as possible and install breaker arm while holding shaft in this position.

Breaker box can be removed without removing points or condenser. Refer to Fig. B613. Disassembly of unit is evident after removal from engine.

To renew ignition coil, engine flywheel must be removed. Disconnect coil ground and primary wires and pull spark plug wire from hole in back plate. Disengage clips (8—Fig. B611) retaining the coil core (9) to armature (14) and push core from coil. Insert core in new coil with rounded side of core toward spark plug wire. Place coil and core on armature with retainer (7) between coil and armature. Install clips retaining the core. Connect coil ground and primary wires and insert spark plug wire through hole in back plate.

Two types of magnetic rotors have been used. Refer to Fig. B614 for view of rotor retained by setscrew and to Fig.

B615 for rotor retained by clamp ring. If rotor is as shown in Fig. B615, refer to Fig. B616 when installing rotor on crankshaft.

If armature coil has been loosened or removed, rotor timing must be readjusted. With point gap adjusted to 0.020 inch (0.51 mm), connect a static timing light from breaker point terminal to ground (coil primary wire must be disconnected) and turn engine in normal direction of rotation until light goes on. Then turn engine very slowly in same direction until light just goes out (breaker points start to open). Engine model number on magneto rotor should now be aligned with arrow on armature as shown in Fig. B617. If not, loosen armature core retaining cap screws and turn armature in slotted mounting holes so arrow is aligned with appropriate engine model number on rotor. Tighten armature mounting screws.

To install flywheel on models with crank starter, place flywheel on crankshaft as shown in Fig. B618 with magneto timing marks aligned as in previous paragraph. On models not having a crank starter, flywheel can be installed in any position.

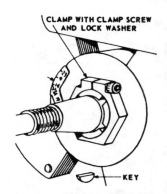

Fig. B615—View showing magneto rotor fastened to crankshaft with clamp. Make certain split in clamp is between two slots in rotor as shown and check clearance between rotor and shoulder on crankshaft as shown in Fig. B616.

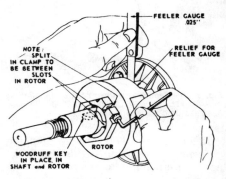

Fig. B616—On models having magneto rotor clamped to crankshaft, position rotor 0.025 inch (6.4 mm) from shoulder on shaft, then tighten clamping screw.

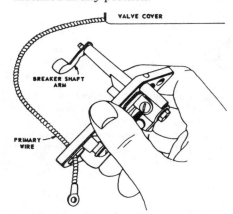

Fig. B613—To remove breaker box on 19, 23 and 23A models and 191000 and 231000 series engines it is not necessary to remove points and condenser as unit can be removed as an assembly.

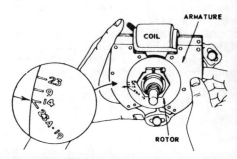

Fig. B617—With engine turned so breaker points are just starting to open, align model number line on rotor with arrow armature by rotating armature in slotted mounting holes.

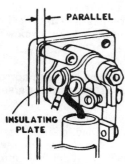

Fig. B612—When installing breaker points on 19, 23 and 23A models and 191000 and 231000 series engines, be sure dowel on breaker point base enters hole in insulator. Place sides of base and insulating plate parallel with edge of breaker box.

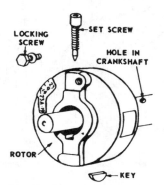

Fig. B614—On some models, magneto rotor is fastened to crankshaft by a set screw that enters hole in shaft. Set screw is locked in place by a second screw. Refer to Fig. B615 also.

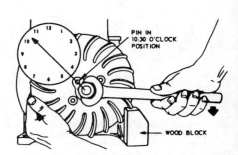

Fig. B618—On 19, 23 and 23A models and 191000 and 231000 series engines equipped with crank starter, mount flywheel with pin in position shown with armature timing marks aligned.

A cam on a centrifugal weight mounted on engine camshaft actuates the breaker points (Fig. B619). When engine is being overhauled, or cam gear is removed, check action of advance spring and centrifugal weight unit by holding cam gear in position shown and pressing weight down. When weight is released, spring should return weight to its original position. If weight does not return to its original position, check weight for binding and renew spring.

Models 19D and 23D Magneto. Refer to Fig. B620 for exploded view of magneto system.

Condenser and breaker points are mounted externally in a breaker box located on carburetor side of engine and are accessible after removing breaker box cover (8—Fig. B620).

Breaker point gap is 0.020 inch (0.51 mm) and condenser capacity is 0.18-0.24 mfd.

Installation of new breaker points is made easier by turning engine so points are open to their widest gap before removing old points. For method of adjusting breaker point gap, refer to Fig. B621.

NOTE: When installing points, apply Permatex or equivalent sealer to retaining screw threads to prevent engine oil from leaking into breaker box.

Breaker points are actuated by a plunger that rides against breaker cam on engine cam gear. Plunger and plunger bushing in crankcase are renewable after removing cam gear and breaker points.

Magneto armature and ignition coil are mounted outside engine flywheel. Adjust armature air gap to 0.022-0.026 inch (0.56-0.66 mm).

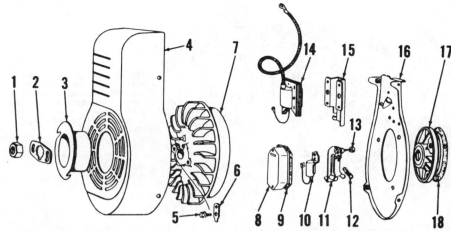

Fig. B620—Exploded view of magneto ignition system used on 19D and 23D models. Magneto rotor (flywheel) to armature is adjustable as shown in Figs. B622 and B623. Adjust breaker points as in Fig. B621.

1. Flywheel nut
2. Nut retainer
3. Starter pulley
4. Blower housing
5. Key cap screw
6. Flywheel key
7. Flywheel
8. Breaker box cover
9. Gasket
10. Condenser
11. Breaker points
12. Breaker spring
13. Locknut
14. Coil & armature assy.
15. Armature mounting bracket
16. Back plate
17. Bearing support
18. Shim gasket

If flywheel has been removed, magneto edge gap (armature timing) must be adjusted. Refer to Figs. B622, B623 and B624. With point gap adjusted to 0.020 inch (0.51 mm) and flywheel loosely installed on crankshaft, install flywheel key leaving retaining cap screw loose. Disconnect magneto primary wire and connect test light across breaker points. Turn flywheel in clockwise direction until breaker points just start to open (timing light goes out). While making sure engine crankshaft does not turn, rotate flywheel back slightly in counterclockwise direction so edge of flywheel insert lines up with edge of armature as shown in Fig. B624. Tighten flywheel key screw, then tighten flywheel retaining nut to 110-118 ft.-lbs. (149-160 N•m) for 19D model and to 138-150 ft.-lbs. (187-203 N•m) for 23D model. Readjust armature air gap as needed.

Series 193000, 200000, 233000, 243000, 300000, 301000, 302000, 320000, 325000 and 326000 Magneto. Refer to Fig. B625 for exploded view of magneto system.

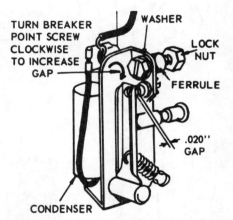

Fig. B621—On all models equipped with this type of breaker points, loosen locknut and turn adjusting screw to obtain 0.020 inch (0.51 mm) gap.

Condenser and breaker points are mounted externally in a breaker box located on carburetor side of engine and are accessible after removing breaker box cover (8—Fig. B625).

Breaker point gap is 0.020 inch (0.51 mm) and condenser capacity is 0.18-0.24 mfd.

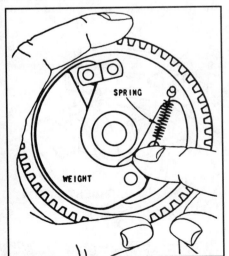

Fig. B619—Check timing advance weight and spring on 19, 23 and 23A models and 191000 and 231000 series engines. Refer to text.

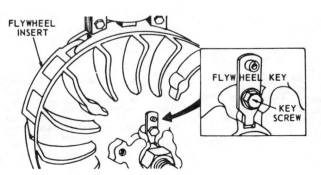

Fig. B622—On 19D and 23D models, magneto timing is adjusted by repositioning flywheel on crankshaft. Flywheel is then locked into proper position by tightening key screw and flywheel retaining nut. Refer also to Figs. B623 and B624.

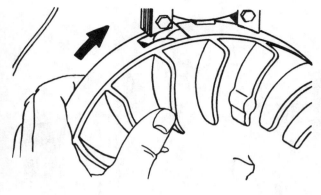

Fig. B623—Turning engine in normal direction of rotation with flywheel and flywheel key loose. Turn engine slowly until breaker points are just starting to open. Refer to text and Figs. B622 and B624.

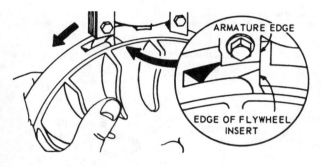

Fig. B624—Turn flywheel counterclockwise on crankshaft until edge of flywheel insert is aligned with edge of armature as shown in insert. Then, tighten flywheel key screw and retaining nut.

NOTE: Series 233000 and 243000 dual-fuel (gasoline/kerosene) engines require a special spark plug (Champion J11C) gapped at 0.030 inch (0.76 mm) and a reduced breaker point gap of 0.015 inch (0.38 mm). Set ignition timing after setting point gap.

Installation of new breaker points is made easier by turning engine so points are open to their widest gap before removing old points. For method of adjusting breaker point gap, refer to Fig. B621.

NOTE: When installing points, apply Permatex or equivalent sealer to retaining screw threads to prevent engine oil from leaking into breaker box.

A plunger that rides against breaker cam on the engine cam gear actuates the breaker points. Plunger and plunger bushing are renewable after removing engine cam gear and breaker points.

Magneto armature and ignition coil are mounted outside engine flywheel. Adjust armature air gap to 0.010-0.014 inch (0.25-0.36 mm) as shown in Fig. B626.

If flywheel has been removed, magneto edge gap (armature timing) must be adjusted. Adjust point gap to 0.020 inch (0.51 mm) and remove armature ignition coil assembly from mounting bracket. Connect a test light across breaker points. Disconnect coil primary wire and slowly turn flywheel in a clockwise direction until light just goes out (breaker points start to open). At this time, arrow on flywheel should be exactly aligned with arrow on armature mounting bracket (Fig. B627). If not, mark the position of bracket. Remove the flywheel, then shift the bracket on

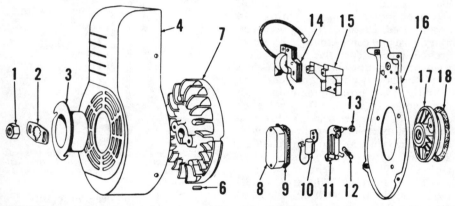

Fig. B625—Exploded view of 193000, 200000, 233000 and 243000 series magneto ignition system. Magneto used on 300000, 301000, 302000, 320000, 325000 and 326000 series is similar. Position of armature is adjustable to time armature with magneto rotor (flywheel) by moving armature mounting bracket (15) on slotted mounting holes. Refer to text and Figs. B627 and B628.

1. Flywheel nut	7. Flywheel	15. Armature mounting Bracket
2. Nut retainer	8. Breaker box cover	16. Back plate
3. Starter pulley	9. Gasket	17. Bearing support
4. Blower housing	10. Condenser	18. Shim gasket
6. Flywheel nut	11. Breaker points	
	12. Breaker spring	
	13. Locknut	
	14. Coil &armature assy.	

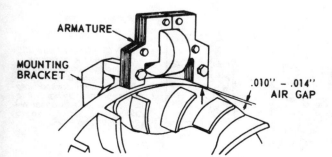

Fig. B626—After mounting bracket is properly installed (Fig. B628), install armature and coil assembly so there is a 0.010-0.014 inch (0.25-0.36 mm) air gap between armature and flywheel.

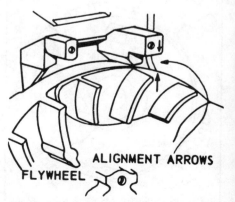

Fig B627—On 193000, 200000, 233000, 243000, 300000, 301000, 302000, 320000, 325000 and 326000 series, time magneto by aligning armature core support so arrow on support is aligned with arrow on flywheel when breaker points are just starting to open. Refer to text for procedure.

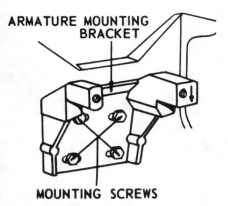

ARMATURE MOUNTING BRACKET

MOUNTING SCREWS

Fig. B628—View with flywheel removed on 193000, 200000, 233000, 243000, 300000, 301000, 302000, 320000, 325000 and 326000 series engines. Magneto is timed by shifting armature mounting bracket on slotted mounting holes. Refer to Fig. B627 also.

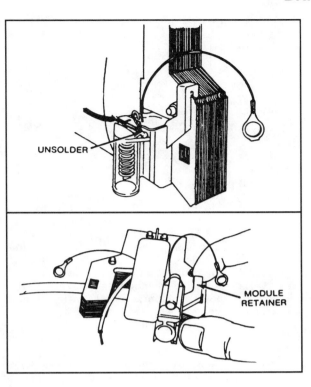

UNSOLDER

MODULE RETAINER

Fig. B629—Wires must be unsoldered to remove Magnetron module.

slotted mounting holes (Fig. B628) to bring arrows into alignment.

Reinstall flywheel, make certain arrows are aligned and tighten flywheel retaining nut to 110-118 ft.-lbs. (149-160 N•m) on 193000 and 200000 series engines and to 138-150 ft.-lbs. (187-203 N•m) on all other models. Readjust armature air gap as needed.

Magnetron Ignition. The Magnetron ignition is a self-contained breakerless ignition system. Flywheel removal is not necessary except to change timing by moving armature bracket or to service crankshaft key or keyway.

To check spark, remove spark plug, connect spark plug cable to B&S tester 19051 and ground remaining tester lead on engine cylinder head. Rotate engine at 350 rpm or more. If spark jumps the 0.166 inch (4.2 mm) tester gap, system is functioning properly.

Armature and module have been manufactured as either one-piece units or as a separable two-piece assembly. The large rivet heads on one side of the armature laminations identifies two-piece units. To remove armature and Magnetron module, remove flywheel shroud and armature retaining screws. On one-piece units, disconnect stop switch wire at spade connector. On two-piece units, use a $\frac{3}{16}$-inch (4.8 mm) diameter pin punch to release stop switch wire from module. To remove module on two-piece units, unsolder wires, push module retainer away from laminations and remove module. See Fig. B629.

Solder wires for installation and use Permatex or equivalent to hold ground wires in position.

To set timing for gasoline fuel operation, install armature bracket so mounting screws are centered in slots (Fig. B630).

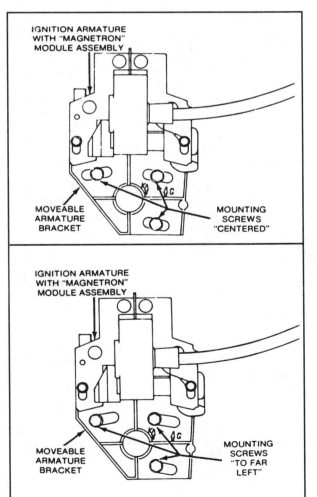

IGNITION ARMATURE WITH "MAGNETRON" MODULE ASSEMBLY

MOVEABLE ARMATURE BRACKET

MOUNTING SCREWS "CENTERED"

IGNITION ARMATURE WITH "MAGNETRON" MODULE ASSEMBLY

MOVEABLE ARMATURE BRACKET

MOUNTING SCREWS "TO FAR LEFT"

Fig. B630—Upper view shows position of armature bracket for gasoline fuels and lower view shows position of armature bracket for kerosene fuels for correct ignition timing.

To set timing for kerosene fuel operation, install armature bracket as far to left as possible (Fig. B630).

Armature-to-flywheel air gap should be 0.010-0.014 inch (0.25-0.36 mm) for two-leg armature or 0.012-0.016 inch (0.30-0.41 mm) for three-leg armature.

VALVE ADJUSTMENT. Valve tappet clearance (cold) for 19, 19D, 191000, 193000 or 200000 series or models is 0.007-0.009 inch (0.18-0.23 mm) for intake valve and 0.014-0.016 inch (0.36-0.41 mm) for exhaust valve.

Valve tappet clearance (cold) for all other models is 0.007-0.009 inch (0.18-0.23 mm) for intake valve and 0.017-0.019 inch (0.43-0.48 mm) for exhaust valve.

To correctly set tappet clearance, remove spark plug and using a suitable measuring tool, rotate crankshaft in normal direction (clockwise at flywheel) so piston is at top dead center on compression stroke. Continue to rotate crankshaft so piston is ¼ inch (6.4 mm) down from top dead center. This position places the tappets away from the compression release device on the cam lobe.

Valve tappet clearance is adjusted on all models by carefully grinding end of valve stem to increase clearance or by grinding valve seats deeper and/or renewing valve or lifter to decrease clearance.

CYLINDER HEAD. After 100 to 300 hours of engine operation, the cylinder head should be removed and any carbon or deposits should be removed.

COMPRESSION PRESSURE. Briggs & Stratton does not publish compression pressure specifications.

An alternate method of determining internal engine condition and wear is by using a cylinder leak-down tester. The tester is available commercially or through Briggs & Stratton (part No. 19413). The tester uses compressed air to pressurize the combustion chamber, then gauges the amount of leakage past the piston rings and valves. Instructions are included with the tester.

REPAIRS

CYLINDER HEAD. When removing cylinder head note location and lengths of cylinder head retaining screws so they can be installed in their original positions.

Always install a new cylinder head gasket. Do not apply sealer to head gasket. Lightly lubricate cylinder head retaining screws with Led-Plate B&S part No. 93963 or graphite grease. Tighten screws in several steps follow-

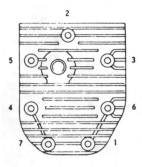 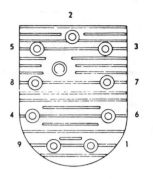

Fig.B631—View of two different cylinder heads used. Tighten cylinder head cap screws in sequence shown to 190 in.-lbs (22 Nm). Refer to text for tightening procedure.

ing the tightening sequence shown in Fig. B631 to 190 in.-lbs. (22 N•m).

VALVE SYSTEM. The intake valve seat is machined directly in the cylinder block. A renewable insert is used as the exhaust valve seat. Valve face and seat angle should be ground at 45°. Renew valve if margin is 1/64 inch (0.4 mm) or less. Seat width should be 3/64 to 1/16 inch (1.2-1.6 mm).

Valve guides are renewable. Check valve guides using valve guide gauge 19151. If gauge enters valve guide 5/16 inch (7.9 mm) or more, guide should be reamed using reamer 19233 and reamer bushing 19234 (part of valve guide repair kit 19232).

Some engines may be equipped with a "Cobalite" exhaust valve and exhaust seat insert as well as a rotocoil on the exhaust valve stem. These components are offered as replacement parts for engines used in severe engine service.

If engine is operated on LP fuel or natural gas, rotocoil should not be used and valve stem and guide should be lubricated with B&S 93963 Valve Guide Lubricant during assembly.

PISTON, PIN AND RINGS. Connecting rod and piston are removed from cylinder head end of block as an assembly.

Reject pistons showing visible signs of wear, scoring or scuffing. If, after cleaning carbon from top ring groove, a new top ring has a side clearance of 0.009 inch (0.23 mm), reject the piston. Reject piston or hone piston pin hole to 0.005 inch (0.13 mm) oversize if pin hole is 0.0005 inch (0.013 mm) or more out-of-round, or if wear exceeds service limit listed in following table.

PISTON PIN BORE REJECTION SIZES

Model Series	Pin Bore
19, 19D, 191000 193000, 200000, 243000	0.673 in. (17.09 mm)

23, 23A, 23C, 23D, 231000, 233000	0.736 in. (18.69 mm)
300000, 301000, 302000, 320000, 325000, 326000	0.801 in. (20.34 mm)

If the piston pin is 0.0005 inch (0.013 mm) or more out-of-round, or if wear exceeds service limit listed in following table, renew piston pin.

PISTON PIN REJECTION SIZES

Model Series	Pin Diameter
19, 19D, 191000 193000, 200000, 243000	0.671 in. (17.04 mm)
23, 23A, 23C, 23D, 231000, 233000	0.734 in. (18.64 mm)
300000, 301000, 302000, 320000, 325000, 326000	0.799 in. (20.30 mm)

Reject compression rings having an end gap of 0.030 inch (0.75 mm) or more and reject oil rings having an end gap of 0.035 inch (0.90 mm) or more.

Pistons and rings are available in several oversizes as well as standard. Refer to Fig. B632 for correct installation of piston rings.

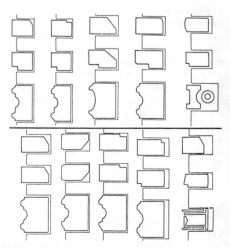

Fig. B632—Refer to above illustration for proper arrangement of piston rings.

A chrome piston ring set is available for slightly worn standard bore cylinders. No honing or cylinder deglazing is required for these rings. The cylinder bore can be a maximum of 0.005 inch (0.13 mm) oversize when using chrome rings.

If piston has a notch (N—Fig. B633) in piston crown, assemble connecting rod and piston as shown in Fig. B633.

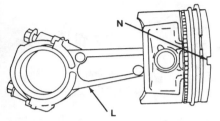

Fig. B633—If piston crown is notched (N), assemble connecting rod and piston as shown while noting relation of long side of rod (L) and notch (N) in piston crown.

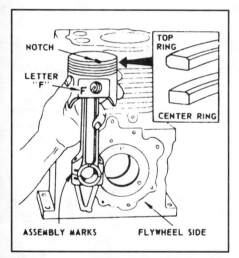

Fig. B634—On 300000, 301000, 302000, 320000, 325000 and 326000 series, assemble piston to connecting rod with notch and stamped letter "F" on piston to same side as assembly marks on rod. Install assembly in cylinder with assembly marks to flywheel side of crankcase.

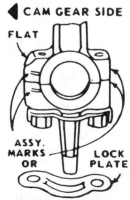

Fig. B635—Drawing of lower end of connecting rod showing clearance flat and assembly mark.

Install piston and rod in engine so notch (N) is toward flywheel.

On Series 300000, 301000, 302000, 320000, 325000 or 326000 engines, notch on piston crown and letter "F" on side of piston must be on the same side as assembly marks on connecting rod (Fig. B634). Install assembly in cylinder with assembly marks toward flywheel side of engine.

On all other models, install piston and connecting rod assembly so flat on connecting rod shoulder is toward camshaft as shown in Fig. B635.

Tighten connecting rod screws on all models to 190 in.-lbs. (22 N•m).

CONNECTING ROD. Connecting rod (55—Fig. B636 and B637 or 30—Fig. B638) and piston are removed from cylinder head end of block as an assembly. The aluminum alloy connecting rod rides directly on an induction hardened crankshaft crankpin journal. Rod should be rejected if big end of rod is scored or out-of-round more than 0.0007 inch (0.018 mm) or if piston pin bore is scored or out-of-round more than 0.0005 inch (0.013 mm). Renew connecting rod if either crankpin bore or piston pin bore is worn to, or larger than, sizes given in table.

REJECT SIZES FOR CONNECTING ROD

Model Series	Crankpin Bore	Pin Bore*
19, 19D, 191000, 193000	1.001 in. (25.43 mm)	0.674 in. (17.12 mm)
200000	1.127 in. (28.61 mm)	0.674 in. (17.12 mm)
23, 23A, 23C, 23D, 231000, 233000	1.189 in. (30.20 mm)	0.736 in. (18.69 mm)
243000	1.314 in. (23.38 mm)	0.674 in. (17.12 mm)
300000, 301000, 302000, 320000, 325000, 326000	1.314 in. (23.38 mm)	0.802 in. (20.37 mm)

*Piston pins that are 0.005 inch (0.13 mm) oversize are available for service. Piston pin bore in rod can be reamed to this size if crankpin bore is within specifications.

Refer to previous section for assembly of connecting rod and piston. Tighten connecting rod screws on all models to 190 in.-lbs. (22 N•m).

CAM GEAR AND CAMSHAFT. On Model 19, 19D, 23, 23A, 23C and 23D engines and Series 191000, 193000, 200000, 233000 and 243000 engines, the timing gear and camshaft lobes are cast as an integral part and are referred to as a "cam gear." Cam gear (31—Fig. B637) turns on a stationary shaft (30) referred to as a "camshaft." Reject camshaft if it is worn to, or less than, a diameter of 0.4968 inch (12.619 mm).

On all remaining models, cam gear and lobes are an integral part referred to as a "cam gear." Camshaft (53—Fig. B638) rotates with cam gear (52). Camshaft rides in a bearing in cylinder block on pto end of engine and journal on cam gear rides in renewable cam bearing (21) on magneto end of engine.

Renew camshaft if worn to 0.6145 inch (15.608 mm) or less and renew cam gear (52) if journal diameter is 0.8105 inch (20.587 mm) or less, or if lobes are worn to a diameter of 1.184 inches (30.07 mm) or less for Series 300000, 301000 and 302000 engines, or 1.215 inches (30.86 mm) or less for Series 320000, 325000 and 326000 engines.

When installing cam gear in Series 300000, 301000, 302000, 320000, 325000 and 326000 engines, cam gear end play should be 0.002-0.008 inch (0.05-0.20 mm) and is controlled by installing different thickness shims (20) between cam gear bearing (21) and crankcase. Shims are available in a variety of thicknesses. Tighten cam gear bearing cap screws to 85 in.-lbs. (10 N•m).

On engines with "Magna-Matic" ignition system, cam gear is equipped with an ignition advance weight (AW—Fig. B637). A tang on the advance weight contacts breaker shaft lever (29—Fig. B611) each camshaft revolution. On all other models, breaker plunger rides against a lobe on cam gear.

On models with "Easy-Spin" starting, intake cam lobe is machined to hold intake valve slightly open during part of compression stroke, thereby relieving compression and making engine easier to start due to increased cranking speed.

NOTE: To check compression on models with "Easy-Spin" starting, engine must be turned backwards.

"Easy-Spin" cam gears can be identified by two holes drilled in web of gear. If part number of older cam gear and "Easy-Spin" cam gear are the same except for an "E" following new part number, gears are interchangeable.

On all models, align timing marks on crankshaft gear and cam gear when reassembling engine.

CRANKSHAFT AND MAIN BEARINGS. Crankshaft is supported

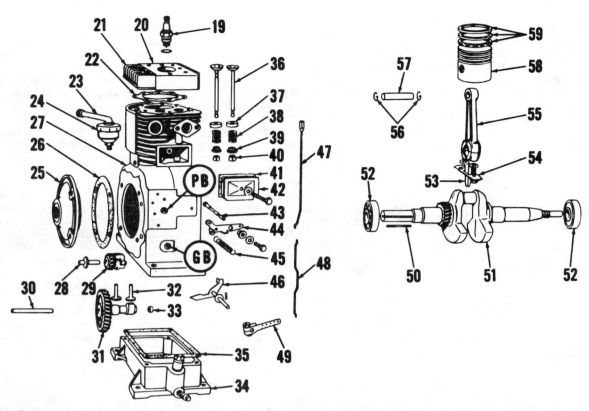

Fig. B636—Exploded view of typical 19D, 23D, 193000, 200000, 233000 and 243000 engines. Breaker plunger bushing (PB) and governor crank bushing (GB) in engine crankcase (27) are renewable. Breaker plunger (43) rides against a lobe on cam gear (31).

19. Gasket plug
20. Air baffle
21. Cylinder head
22. Gasket
23. Breather tube
24. Breather
25. Main bearing plate
26. Gasket

27. Engine crankcase & cylinder block
28. Governor shaft
29. Governor gear & weight unit
30. Camshaft
31. Cam gear
32. Tappets

33. Camshaft plug
34. Engine base
35. Gasket
36. Valves
37. Valve spring washers
38. Valve springs
39. Spring retainers or "Roto-Caps"

40. Keepers
41. Gasket
42. Tappet chamber cover
43. Breaker point plunger
44. Governor control lever
45. Governor spring
46. Governor crank
47. Governor control rod

48. Governor link
49. Governor lever
50. Output drive key
51. Crankshaft
52. Ball bearing (on models so equipped)

53. Oil dipper
54. Rod bolt lock
55. Connecting rod
56. Piston pin retaining rings
57. Piston pin
58. Piston
59. Piston rings

at each end in main bearings that are either an integral part of crankcase and sump or ball bearing mains that are a press fit on crankshaft and fit into machined bores in main bearing support plates.

Crankshaft for models with main bearings as an integral part of main bearing support plates should be renewed if journals are out-of-round 0.0007 inch (0.018 mm) or more. Reject crankshaft on 19, 19D, 191000, 193000 and 200000 series engines if main bearing journals are worn to a diameter of 1.179 inch (29.95 mm) or less. Reject crankshaft on 23, 23A, 23C, 23D, 231000 and 233000 series engines if main bearing journals are worn to a diameter of 1.3759 inch (34.948 mm) or less.

Crankshaft for models with ball bearing main bearings should be renewed if new bearings are loose on journals. Bearings should be a press fit.

Crankshaft for all models should be renewed or reground if connecting rod crankpin journal diameter exceeds service limit listed in following table.

CRANKSHAFT REJECT SIZES

Model Series	Crankpin Journal
19, 19D, 190000, 193000	1.090 in. (27.69 mm)
200000	1.122 in. (28.50 mm)
23, 23A, 23C, 23D, 230000	1.247 in. (31.67 mm)
243000, 300000, 301000, 302000, 320000, 325000, 326000	1.309 in. (33.25 mm)

A connecting rod with undersize big end diameter is available to fit crankshaft that has had crankpin journal reground to 0.020 inch (0.51 mm) undersize.

Crankshaft main bearing support plates should be renewed if integral-type main bearing bores are 0.0007 inch (0.018 mm) or more out-of-round. Renew bearing support plates on 19, 19D, 191000, 193000 and 200000 series engines if main bearing bores are worn to a diameter of 1.185 inch (30.10 mm) or more. Renew bearing support plates on 23, 23A, 23C, 23D, 231000 and 233000 series engines if main bearing bores are worn to a diameter of 1.382 inch (34.10 mm) or less. Service bushings for main bearings are not available.

Ball bearing mains are a press fit on the crankshaft and must be removed by pressing the crankshaft out of the bearing. Reject ball bearing if worn or rough. Expand new bearing by heating it in oil and install it on crankshaft with seal side toward crankpin journal.

Crankshaft end play is 0.002-0.008 inch (0.05-0.20 mm). End play is adjusted by varying thickness of gaskets between flywheel main bearing support plate and crankcase as shown in Fig. B639. Gaskets are available in a variety of thicknesses.

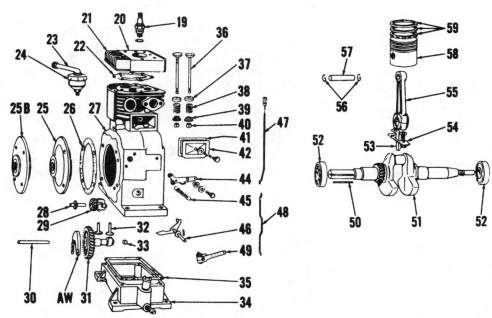

Fig. B637—Exploded view of typical model 19, 23, 23A, 191000 and 231000 engines equipped with "Magna-Matic" ignition system; note ignition advance weight (AW). Refer to B611 for ignition system.

AW. Advance weight
19. Spark plug
20. Air baffle
21. Cylinder head
22. Gasket
23. Breather tube
24. Breather
25. Main bearing plate (plain bushing)

25B. Bearing plate (ball bearing)
26. Gasket
27. Engine crankcase & cylinder block
28. Governor shaft
29. Governor gear & weight unit

30. Camshaft
31. Cam gear
32. Tappets
33. Camshaft plug
34. Engine base
35. Gasket
36. Valves
37. Valve spring washers

38. Valve springs
39. Spring retainers or "Roto-Caps"
40. Keepers
41. Gasket
42. Tappet chamber cover
44. Governor control lever
45. Governor spring

46. Governor crank
47. Governor control rod
48. Governor link
49. Governor lever
50. Output drive key
51. Crankshaft
52. Ball bearings (on models so equipped)

53. Oil dipper
54. Rod bolt lock
55. Connecting rod
56. Piston pin retaining rings
57. Piston pin
58. Piston
59. Piston rings

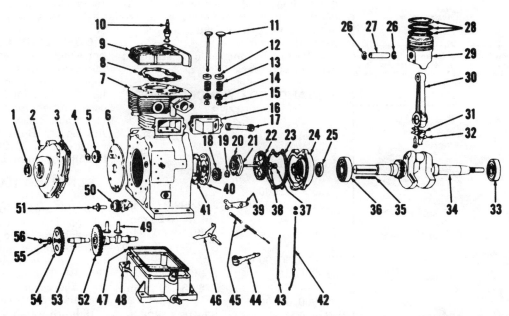

Fig. B638—Exploded view of typical 300000, 301000, 302000, 320000, 325000 and 326000 engines. Balance weights, ball bearings and cover assemblies (2 and 24) are serviced on as assemblies.

1. Oil seal
2. Cover & balance assy. (pto end)
3. Gasket
4. "E" ring
5. Idler gear
6. Bearing support plate
7. Engine crankcase & cylinder block
8. Gasket
9. Cylinder head

10. Spark plug
11. Valves
12. Spring caps
13. Valve springs
14. Spring retainers or "Roto-Caps"
15. Keepers
16. Breather
17. Breather tube
18. Idler gear

19. "E" ring
20. Shim
21. Cam bearing
22. Balancer drive gear
23. Gasket
24. Cover & balance assy. (magneto end)
25. Oil seal
26. Piston pin retaining rings

27. Piston pin
28. Piston rings
29. Piston
30. Connecting rod
31. Oil dipper
32. Rod bolt lock
33. Ball bearing
34. Crankshaft
35. Ball bearing
36. Ball bearing

37. Drive gear bolt
38. Belleville washer
39. Governor control lever
40. Bearing support plate
41. Shim
42. Governor control rod
43. Governor link
44. Governor lever
45. Governor springs
46. Governor crank

47. Gasket
48. Engine base
49. Tappets
50. Governor gear & weight unit
51. Governor shaft
52. Cam gear
53. Camshaft
54. Balancer drive gear
55. Belleville washer
56. Drive gear bolt

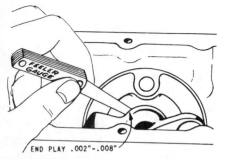

Fig. B639—Crankshaft end play can be checked as shown on models with main bearings that are an integral part of bearing support plates.

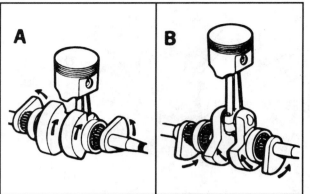

Fig. B642—Synchro-Balance weight rotate in opposite direction of crankshaft counterweights on 300000, 301000, 302000, 320000, 325000 and 326000 series engines.

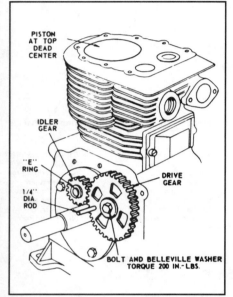

Fig. B640—view showing balancer drive gear (magneto end) being timed. With piston at TDC, insert ¼-inch (6.4 mm) rod through timing hole in crankshaft bearing support plate.

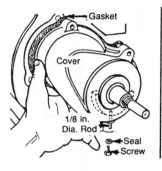

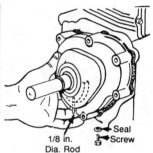

Fig. B643—Insert 1/8-inch (3.2 mm) diameter rod through timing hole in covers and into hole in balance weights when installing cover assemblies. Piston must be at TDC.

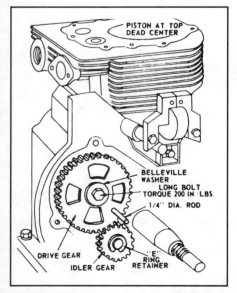

Fig. B641—View showing balancer drive gear on pto end of crankshaft being timed. With piston at TDC, insert ¼-inch (6.4 mm) diameter rod through timing hole in gear and into locating hole in crankshaft bearing support plate.

When reinstalling crankshaft, make certain timing marks are aligned (Fig. B640 or B641).

CYLINDER. If cylinder bore wear is 0.003 inch (0.08 mm) or more or is 0.0025 inch (0.06 mm) or more out-of-round, cylinder must be bored to next larger oversize.

Refer to following table for standard cylinder bore sizes:

STANDARD CYLINDER BORE SIZES

Model Series	Std. Bore Size
19, 19D, 22, 23A, 23C, 23D, 191000, 193000, 200000, 231000, 233000	2.999-3.000 in. (76.18-76.20 mm)
243000	3.0615-3.0625 in. (77.76-77.79 mm)
300000, 301000, 302000	3.4365-3.4375 in. (87.287-87.313 mm)
320000, 325000, 326000	3.5615-3.5625 in. (90.462-90.488 mm)

A chrome piston ring set is available for slightly worn standard bore cylinders. No honing or cylinder deglazing is required for these rings. The cylinder bore can be a maximum of 0.005 inch (0.13 mm) oversize when using chrome rings.

GOVERNOR WEIGHT UNIT. Tangs on governor weights should be square and smooth and weights should operate freely. If not, renew gear and weight assembly (29—Figs. B636 and B637) or (50—Fig. B638). Renew governor shaft if worn or scored.

GOVERNOR CRANK. With governor weight and gear unit removed, remove and inspect governor crank; renew if worn. Governor crank should be a free fit in bushing in engine crankcase with minimum bushing to crank clearance. Renew bushing if new crank fits loosely. Bushing should be finish reamed to 0.2385-0.2390 inch (6.058-6.071 mm) after installation.

SYNCHRO-BALANCER. Series 300000, 301000, 302000, 320000, 325000 and 326000 engines are equipped with rotating balance weights at each end of crankshaft. Balance weights are geared to rotate in opposite direction of crankshaft counterweights (Fig. B642). Balance weights, ball bearings and cover (2 and 24—Fig. B638) are serviced as assemblies only.

Balance weights are driven by idler gears (5 and 18) which are driven by gears (22 and 54). Drive gears (22 and 54) are fastened to the camshaft with a through-bolt (37). To time balance weights, first remove cover and balancer assemblies (2 and 24). Position piston at TDC. Loosen bolts (37 and 56) until drive gears will rotate on cam gear and camshaft. Insert a ¼ inch (6.4

mm) diameter rod through timing hole in each drive gear and into locating holes in main bearing support plates as shown in Figs. B640 and B641. With piston at TDC and ¼ inch (6.4 mm) diameter rods in place, tighten drive gear bolts to a torque of 200 in.-lbs. (23 N•m). Remove ¼-inch (6.4 mm) rods. Remove timing hole screws (Fig. B643) and insert ⅛-inch (3.2 mm) diameter rods through timing holes in cover and into hole in balance weights. Then, with piston at TDC, carefully slide the cover assemblies into position. Tighten cap screws in pto end cover to 200 in.-lbs. (23 N•m) and tighten magneto end cover cap screws to 120 in.-lbs. (14 N•m). Remove ⅛-inch (3.2 mm) rods. Coat threads of timing hole screws with Permatex or equivalent and install screws with fiber sealing washers.

BRIGGS & STRATTON

BRIGGS & STRATTON CORPORATION
Milwaukee, Wisconsin 53201

VANGUARD SINGLE-CYLINDER ENGINES

Model Series	No. Cyls.	Bore	Stroke	Displacement	Power Rating
161400	1	76.2 mm (3.00 in.)	59.3 mm (2.33 in.)	270 cc (16.5 cu.in.)	6.8 kW (9 hp)
185400	1	80.0 mm (3.15 in.)	59.3 mm (2.33 in.)	296 cc (18.0 cu.in.)	6.8 kW (9 hp)
235400	1	89.0 mm (3.50 in.)	63.0 mm (2.48 in.)	391 cc (24.0 cu.in.)	8.2 kW (11.0 hp)
245400	1	89.0 mm (3.50 in.)	63.0 mm (2.48 in.)	391 cc (24.0 cu.in.)	9.7 kW (13.0 hp)
260700, 261700	1	87 mm (3.43 in.)	73 mm (2.86 in.)	435 cc (26.5 cu.in.)	10.5 kW (14 hp)

GENERAL INFORMATION

Metric fasteners are used throughout engine except threaded hole in pto end of crankshaft, flange mounting holes and flywheel puller holes, which are US threads.

The Vanguard models covered in this section are air-cooled, four-stroke, single-cylinder engines. The engine uses an overhead valve system.

Refer to BRIGGS & STRATTON ENGINE IDENTIFICATION INFORMATION section for engine identification. Engine model number, type number and code number are necessary when ordering parts.

NOTE: For service on 28-cubic inch Vanguard engines, refer to SINGLE-CYLINDER OHV ENGINES service section in this manual.

MAINTENANCE

LUBRICATION. Vertical crankshaft engines are lubricated by oil supplied by a rotor-type oil pump located in the bottom of the crankcase. Horizontal crankshaft engines have a splash lubrication system provided by an oil dipper attached to the connecting rod.

Periodically check oil level; do not overfill. Oil dipstick should be screwed in until bottomed for correct oil level reading. Check oil level after first eight hours of operation and every 50 hours thereafter under normal operating conditions. Recommended oil change interval is 25 hours if severe service is encountered.

Series 260700 and 261700 engines may be equipped with a spin-on-type oil filter. If so equipped, manufacturer recommends changing oil filter after every 100 hours of operation. Filter should be changed more frequently if engine is operated in a severe environment.

Manufacturer recommends using oil with an API service classification of SH or SJ, or any classification designed to supercede SH or SJ. Use SAE 30 oil for temperatures above 40° F (4° C), use SAE 10W-30 oil for temperatures between 0° F (–18° C) and 40° F (4° C) and, below 0° F (–18° C), use petroleum based SAE 5W-20 or a suitable synthetic oil. Do not use 10W-40 oil.

Crankcase capacity for Series 161400, 185400, 235400 and 245400 engines is 1.2 liters (2.5 pints). Crankcase capacity for Series 260700 and 261700 engines is 2.1 liters (4.4 pints) if equipped with an oil filter, 1.9 liters (4.0 pints) if not equipped with a filter.

Series 161400 and 185400 engines may be equipped with a low-oil system that uses a float to detect a low oil level in the engine. A switch is connected to the float and, when the oil level is low, a warning light is activated and the engine stops. Unscrew the mounting flange (F—Fig. B701) and remove the float and switch assembly for inspection.

Series 260700 and 261700 engines may be equipped with low oil pressure switch shown in Fig. B702. Switch should be closed at zero pressure and open at 49.0-68.6 kPa (7.1-9.9 psi).

FUEL FILTER. The fuel tank is equipped with a filter at the outlet, and an inline filter may be installed also. Check filters annually and periodically during operating season.

CRANKCASE BREATHER. The engine is equipped with a crankcase breather that provides a vacuum for the crankcase. Vapor from the crankcase is evacuated to the intake manifold. A fiber disk acts as a one-way

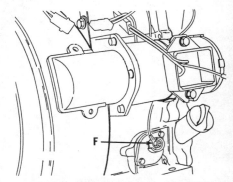

Fig. B701—Unscrew mounting flange on Series 161400 engines to remove low-oil level float assembly.

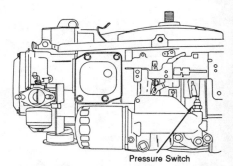

Pressure Switch

Fig. B702—View showing location of oil pressure switch on Series 260700 and 261700 engines.

valve to maintain crankcase vacuum. The breather system must operate properly or excessive oil consumption can result.

The breather valve is located in the top of the rocker arm cover on Series 161400, 185400, 235400 and 245400, or in the side of the crankcase on Series 260700 and 261700 as shown in Fig. B703. The fiber disk valve should be renewed if warped, damaged or excessively worn. It should be possible to insert a 1.27 mm (0.050 in.) wire between disk and breather body (Fig. B703); do not use excessive force when measuring gap. Inspect breather tube for cracks and damage that can cause leakage.

SPARK PLUG. Recommended spark plug is either an Autolite 3924 or Champion RC12YC. Specified spark plug electrode gap is 0.76 mm (0.030 in.). Tighten spark plug to 19 N•m (165 in.-lbs.).

CAUTION: Briggs & Stratton does not recommend using abrasive blasting to clean spark plugs as this may introduce some abrasive material into the engine that could cause extensive damage.

AIR CLEANER. Engines are equipped with a dual-element air cleaner. The air cleaner should be inspected and cleaned after every 25 operating hours or once a season, whichever comes first.

The dual-element air cleaner consists of a foam precleaner and a paper cartridge filter element. Carefully remove the filter cover and filter assembly to prevent dirt from entering the carburetor.

Wash the foam precleaner in warm soapy water. Thoroughly dry the element, then saturate the foam with clean engine oil. Squeeze it to remove excess oil. DO NOT apply oil to foam precleaners labeled "DO NOT OIL."

Do not use cleaning fluids or soap and water to clean the paper filter cartridge. Tap the cartridge gently on a flat sur-

face to dislodge debris from surface of the filter. Replace the filter if it is damaged or restricted.

CARBURETOR. A Mikuni carburetor is used on Series 161400, 185400, 260700 and 261700 engines. A Walbro LMT carburetor is used on Series 235400 and 245000 engines. All carburetors have a fixed high-speed main jet and an adjustable idle mixture screw.

Adjustment. All carburetor adjustments must be made with the air cleaner assembly installed on the engine, and the engine at normal operating temperature. Initial setting of idle mixture screw (11—Fig. B704) is 1¼ turns out from lightly seated position. Move equipment speed control lever to idle position. Hold the carburetor throttle lever against the idle stop and adjust idle speed stop screw to obtain 1300 rpm for Series 185400; 1200 rpm for Series 161400, 260700 and 261700; or 1750 rpm for Series 235400 and 245400.

Turn idle mixture screw clockwise to lean the mixture until engine speed just starts to slow, and note screw position. Turn screw counterclockwise to enrich mixture until engine speed increases then just begins to slow, and note screw position. Then, turn idle mixture screw to midpoint between lean and rich positions. If engine stumbles or hesitates when accelerating, turn idle mixture screw counterclockwise in small increments to enrich the mixture. Install limiter cap on idle mixture screw if carburetor was originally equipped with a cap. Idle mixture pilot jet (15) is not adjustable.

High-speed operation is controlled by fixed main jet (22 or 24—Fig. B705). An optional main jet is available for high altitude operation.

Mikuni Carburetor Overhaul. To disassemble carburetor, remove fuel bowl retaining screw (32—Fig. B705), gasket (31) and fuel bowl (28). Remove the float pivot pin (25) by pushing against round end of pin. Remove the float (26) and fuel inlet needle (20). If equipped with main jet (22), remove the jet prior to removing nozzle (23). Remove throttle and choke shaft assemblies after unscrewing throttle and choke plate retaining screws. Remove idle mixture screw (11), idle mixture jet (15) and air bleeds (17 and 18).

When assembling the carburetor, note the following: Place a small drop of

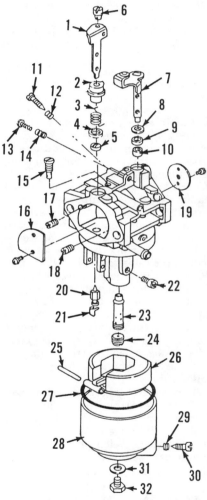

Fig. B705—Exploded view of Mikuni carburetor used on some models.

1. Choke shaft & lever	17. Idle air bleed
2. Bushing	18. Main air bleed
3. Spring	19. Throttle plate
4. Seal	20. Fuel inlet valve
5. Bushing	21. Clip
6. Link retainer	22. Main jet
7. Throttle shaft & lever	23. Main fuel nozzle
8. Washer	24. Main jet
9. Seal	25. Float pin
10. Bushing	26. Float
11. Idle mixture screw	27. Gasket
12. Spring	28. Fuel bowl
13. Idle speed stop screw	29. Spring
14. Spring	30. Drain screw
15. Idle mixture jet	31. Washer
16. Choke plate	32. Screw

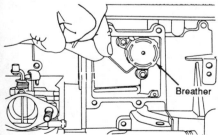

Fig. B703—Crankcase breather for Series 260700 and 261700 engines is located behind cover on side of crankcase.

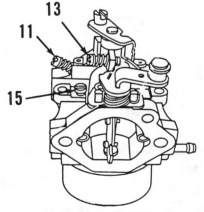

Fig. B704—Idle speed is adjusted by turning screw (13). Idle mixture is adjusted by turning idle mixture screw (11). Idle mixture jet (15) is not adjustable.

hardening sealant, such as Permatex #2 or equivalent, on throttle and choke plate retaining screws. Numbers on choke plate must face out and be on fuel inlet side of carburetor. Install throttle shaft seal with flat side toward carburetor. Numbers on throttle plate must face out and be on fuel inlet side of carburetor. Install the nozzle (23) and then the main jet (22). Be sure groove of fuel inlet valve engages slot in float tab. Float should be parallel with body when carburetor is inverted, as shown in Fig. B706. Float height is not adjustable; replace components necessary so float is parallel.

Walbro Carburetor Overhaul. To disassemble carburetor, remove bowl retainer (22—Fig. B707) and fuel bowl (18). Push the float pin (16) out of the float. Remove the float (15) and fuel inlet needle (13). Remove idle mixture screw (8), idle mixture pilot jet (1), and fuel nozzle and main jet (14). Use a suitable puller screw or a 1/4-20 tap to pull fuel inlet valve seat from carburetor body if renewal is required. A $\frac{5}{32}$-inch punch ground flat at the end makes a suitable tool for removing Welch plug.

Clean the carburetor with aerosol cleaner, then use compressed air to blow out passages and dry the carburetor. Inspect components and discard any parts that are damaged or excessively worn. Replace the fuel inlet valve needle if the tip is grooved. Pull the fuel inlet valve seat from carburetor body if seat is worn or damaged. Press new inlet valve seat into carburetor body until flush with fuel inlet boss. Inspect the tip of idle mixture needle and replace if it is bent or grooved. Check for excessive play between throttle shaft and body. Throttle shaft bushing (12) is available for service.

When assembling the carburetor, note the following: Apply a fuel-resistant sealer such as fingernail polish to outer edge of Welch plug. Do not deform the Welch plug during installation; it should be flat. Float height

is not adjustable. Install throttle plate so numbers on the plate face inward and to the right when throttle plate is in closed position.

NOTE: The throttle plate movement is limited on Series 245400. The throttle plate will not go to the wide-open position.

Installation. On Series 161400, tighten carburetor mounting nuts to 6 N•m (53 in.-lbs.).

On Series 185400 engines, install carburetor using new gaskets. Note that gasket between cylinder head and carburetor spacer has two notches on the inside diameter. Gasket between spacer and carburetor does not have notches. Slide carburetor onto studs. Install spacer between carburetor and cylinder head with arrow on spacer pointing toward cylinder head. Connect governor link in outer hole of throttle shaft lever, and governor link spring in inner hole. Assemble control plate, support bracket and linkage cover. Make sure tab in cover engages slot in control panel. Install air cleaner base and fuel

spray shield. Tighten carburetor stud nuts and screw to 5.1 N•m (45 in.-lb.).

On Series 260700 and 261700 engines, if removed, install spacer between carburetor and manifold so large, irregular opening is toward engine. Tighten carburetor mounting nuts to 14 N•m (124 in.-lbs.).

On Series 235400 and 245400, install carburetor using new gaskets. Connect governor link and link spring to throttle lever, then slide carburetor onto studs. Install choke control bracket on carburetor making sure alignment pin on choke shaft engages hole in control plate. Install air cleaner base and fuel spray shield. Tighten two stud nuts and one screw to 5.1 N •m (45 in.-lb.).

On all engines with remote control, the control wire must travel at least 35 mm (1⅜ in.) for proper operation. See Fig. B708.

On engines with remote control, synchronize movement of remote lever to carburetor control lever by moving remote control lever to "FAST" position. Loosen cable clamp screw shown in Fig. B709 and move cable so holes in governor lever and bracket are aligned. Retighten clamp screw. On Series 161400 equipped with Choke-A-Matic, place control lever in "FAST" position. End of choke link shown in Fig. B710 should just touch choke lever slot end. Bend loop in choke link as needed. With control lever in "CHOKE" position, carburetor choke plate should be closed. Bend loop in choke link as needed.

GOVERNOR. The engine is equipped with a mechanical, flyweight-type governor. To adjust governor linkage, proceed as follows:

On Series 161400, 260700 and 261700 engines, loosen governor lever clamp nut (N—Fig. B711). Rotate governor lever (L) so throttle plate is fully open and hold lever in place. Turn governor shaft (S) **clockwise** as far as possible, then tighten nut (N).

On Series 185400, 235400 and 245400 engines, move throttle control to "FAST" position. Loosen governor lever locknut. Note that nut has left-hand threads; turn clockwise to loosen. Hold the governor lever (L—Fig. B712) so carburetor throttle plate is fully open,

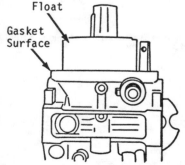

Fig. B706—Float must be parallel with gasket surface when carburetor is inverted. Float height is not adjustable, so components must be renewed if not parallel.

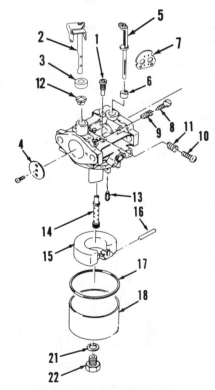

Fig. B707—Exploded view of Walbro LMT carburetor used on Series 235400 and 245400 engines.

1. Idle mixture pilot jet	11. Spring
2. Throttle shaft	12. Bushing
3. Seal	13. Fuel inlet valve
4. Throttle plate	14. Nozzle
5. Choke shaft	15. Float
6. Seal	16. Pin
7. Choke plate	17. Gasket
8. Idle mixture screw	18. Fuel bowl
9. Spring	21. Gasket
10. Idle speed stop screw	22. Screw

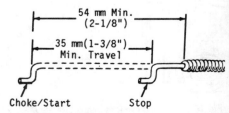

Fig. B708—Control cable wire must be capable of travel shown above for proper operation.

then turn governor shaft (S) **counter-clockwise** to its maximum position. Tighten the locknut and release the throttle.

If internal governor assembly must be serviced, refer to REPAIRS section.

On Series 161400, 260700 and 261700 engines, adjust governed idle speed and maximum no-load speed as follows: Connect tachometer to engine, then start and run engine until normal operating temperature is reached. Set

remote control to "SLOW" position. Insert a ⅛-inch (3.2 mm) diameter pin in alignment holes of governor control lever and bracket as shown in Figs. B713 and B714. Bend tang (T) so engine idle speed is 1400 rpm. Set remote control to "FAST" position. Insert a ⅛-inch (3.2 mm) diameter pin in alignment holes of governor control lever and bracket as shown in Figs. B714 and B715. Bend

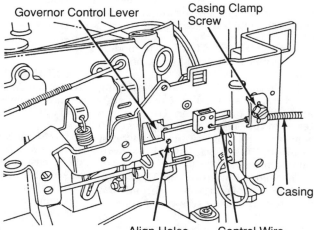

Fig. B709—*Refer to text to adjust remote control on Series 260700 and 261700 engines.*

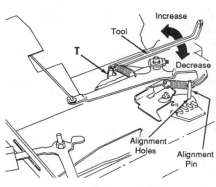

Fig. B713—*To adjust governed idle speed on Series 161400 engines, set remote control to SLOW position. Insert a 3 mm (1/8 in.) diameter pin in alignment holes of governor control lever, then bend tang (T) so engine idle speed is 1400 rpm.*

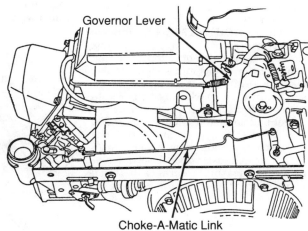

Fig. B710—*On Series 161400 engines equipped with Choke-A-Matic, bend loop in Choke-A-Matic link so end of choke link just touches end of choke lever slot with control in FAST position. Bend loop so carburetor choke plate is closed with control in CHOKE position.*

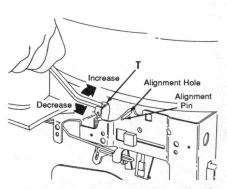

Fig. B714—*To adjust governed idle speed on Series 260700 and 261700 engines, set remote control to SLOW position. Insert a 3 mm (1/8 in.) diameter pin in alignment holes of governor control lever and bracket, then bend tang (T) so engine idle speed is 1400 rpm.*

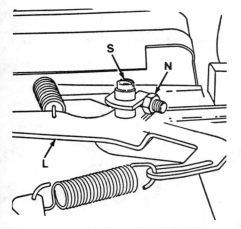

Fig. B711—*On Series 161400, 260700 and 261700 engines, loosen governor lever clamp nut (N). Rotate governor lever (L) so throttle plate is fully open, and hold lever in place. Turn governor shaft (S) clockwise as far as possible, then tighten clamp nut.*

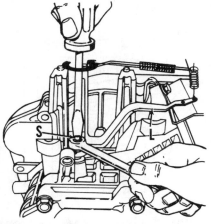

Fig. B712—*On Series 185400, 235400 and 245400 engines, loosen governor lever locknut. Move governor lever (L) to FAST position, and hold lever in place. Turn governor shaft (S) counterclockwise as far as possible, then tighten locknut.*

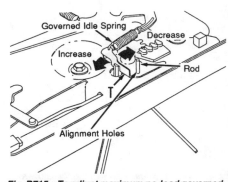

Fig. B715—*To adjust maximum no-load governed speed on Series 161400 engines, set remote control to FAST position. Insert a 3 mm (1/8 in.) diameter pin in alignment holes of governor control lever and bracket, then bend spring tang (T) so engine runs at desired maximum speed.*

spring tang (T—Fig. B715) or rotate screw as shown in Fig. B716 so engine runs at desired maximum no-load speed.

On Series 185400, 235400 and 245400 engine, adjust governed idle speed and maximum no-load speed as follows: Connect tachometer to engine, then start and run engine until normal operating temperature is reached. Remove the limiter cap from idle mixture screw. Move the throttle control to "SLOW" position. Hold carburetor throttle lever (3—Fig. B717) against idle speed stop screw (1), and adjust stop screw to set engine speed to 1300 rpm. Continue to hold throttle lever against idle stop, and adjust idle mixture screw (2) to the midpoint between the too lean and too rich positions. Then, readjust idle speed stop screw to obtain 1200 rpm idle speed. Release the throttle lever, and adjust governed idle screw (4) to set engine speed to 1400 rpm. Move throttle control to "FAST" position. Adjust top speed screw (5) to set top no-load rpm to equipment or engine manufacturer's specification. Turn screw counterclockwise to increase rpm or clockwise to decrease rpm. Shut off the engine, and install limiter cap onto the idle mixture screw.

Some Series 161400, 185400, 235400 and 245400 engines used on generator or welder applications are equipped with an electromagnetic idle-down solenoid device to allow the engine to idle under periods of no-load. Idle-down speed should be 2300 rpm for Series 161400 engines and 2100-2500 rpm for Series 185400, 235400 and 245400 engines, unless the generator or welder manufacturer specifies a different rpm.

To adjust the idle-down solenoid, run the engine until normal operating temperature is reached. Stop the engine. Connect a tachometer to the engine. Disconnect the idle down solenoid wire connector from main harness. Loosen the jam nuts holding solenoid to

bracket. Start the engine and connect a 12-volt DC power supply to the solenoid connector. Adjust the jam nuts to move solenoid in or out until specified idle-down rpm is obtained. Tighten the jam nuts. Disconnect and reconnect 12-volt power supply several times to verify that idle-down rpm is maintained. Readjust if necessary.

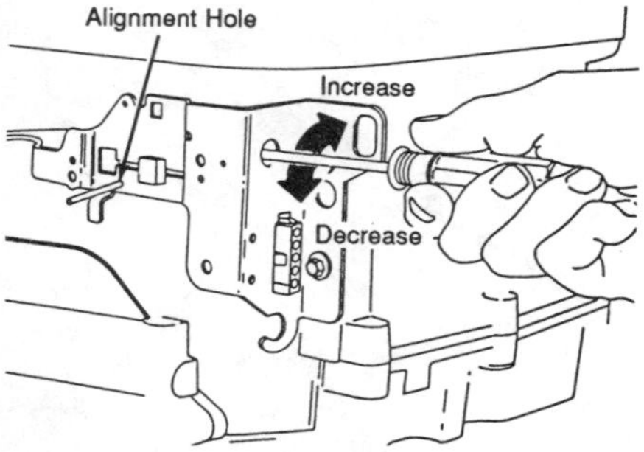

IGNITION SYSTEM. All models are equipped with a Magnetron ignition system.

To check spark, remove spark plug and connect spark plug cable to suitable spark plug tester. Ground the tester to the engine. Spin engine at 350 rpm or more. If spark jumps the 4.2 mm (0.166 in.) tester gap, system is functioning properly.

To remove armature and Magnetron module, remove flywheel shroud and armature retaining screws. Disconnect stop switch wire from module. Position armature so air gap between armature legs and flywheel surface is 0.20-0.30 mm (0.008-0.012 in.) as shown in Fig. B718. Tighten Magnetron fasteners to 5.1 N•m (45 in.-lb.).

VALVE ADJUSTMENT. Remove rocker arm cover. Remove spark plug. Rotate crankshaft so piston is at top dead center on compression stroke. Using a suitable measuring device inserted through spark plug hole, rotate crankshaft clockwise as viewed at flywheel end so piston is 6.35 mm (0.250 in.) below TDC to prevent interference by the compression release mechanism with the exhaust valve. Use a feeler gauge to measure clearance between valve stem or wear button and rocker

arm (Fig. B719). Valve clearance for both intake and exhaust should be 0.08-0.12 mm (0.003-0.005 in.) for Series 161400, 260700 and 261700 engines or 0.05-0.10 mm (0.002-0.004 in.) for Series 185400, 235400 and 245400. Loosen lock screw and turn adjusting nut to obtain desired clearance. Tighten lock screw to 6.2 N•m (55 in.-lbs.). Tighten valve cover screws to 6.2 N•m (55 in.-lbs.).

CYLINDER HEAD. Manufacturer recommends that the cylinder head be removed and cleaned of deposits after every 500 hours of operation.

COMPRESSION PRESSURE. Briggs & Stratton does not publish compression pressure specifications.

An alternate method of determining internal engine condition and wear is by using a cylinder leak-down tester, such as B&S part No. 19413. The tester uses compressed air to pressurize the combustion chamber, then gauges the amount of leakage past the piston, rings and valves. Instructions are included with the tester.

REPAIRS

TIGHTENING TORQUE. Recommended tightening torque specifications are as follows:

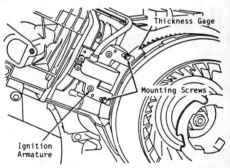

Fig. B718—Adjust air gap between ignition module and flywheel to 0.20-0.30 mm (0.008-0.012 in.)

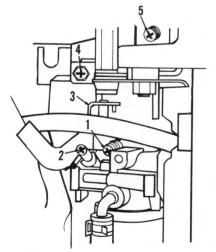

Fig. B716—To adjust maximum no-load governed speed on Series 260700 and 261700 engines, set remote control to FAST position. Insert a 3 mm (1/8 in.) diameter pin in alignment holes of governor control lever and bracket, then rotate screw as shown so engine runs at desired maximum speed.

Fig. B717—View of governor adjustment points for Series 185400, 235400 and 245400 engines. Refer to text for adjustment procedure. Idle mixture screw (2) is equipped with a limiter cap.

1. Idle speed stop screw
2. Idle mixture screw
3. Carburetor throttle lever
4. Governed idle screw
5. Governed top speed screw

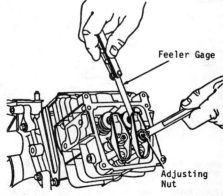

Fig. B719—Use a feeler gauge to measure clearance between valve stem and rocker arm.

Carburetor mounting nuts:
161400 . . . . 6.2 N•m
           (55 in.-lbs.)
185400, 235400, 245400 . . . . 5.1 N•m
           (45 in.-lbs.)
260700, 261700 . . . . 14.0 N•m
           (125 in.-lbs.)

Connecting rod:
161400 . . . . 22.6 N•m
           (200 in.-lbs.)
185400, 235400, 245400 . . . 19.8 N•m
           (175 in.-lb.)
260700, 261700 . . . . 22.6 N•m
           (200 in.-lbs.)

Crankcase cover/oil pan:
161400 . . . . 28.3 N•m
           (250 in.-lb.)
185400, 235400, 245400 . . . 19.8 N•m
           (175 in.-lb.)
260700, 261700 . . . . 28.2 N•m
           (250 in.-lb.)

Cylinder head:
161400 . . . . 18.6 N•m
           (165 in.-lb.)
185400 . . . . 33.9 N•m
           (300 in.-lb.)
235400, 245400 . . . . 47.4 N•m
           (35 ft.-lb.)
260700, 261700 . . . . 25.4 N•m
           (225 in.-lb.)

Flywheel nut:
161400 . . . . 88 N•m
           (65 ft.-lb.)
185400, 235400, 245400 . . . . 81 N•m
           (60 ft.-lb.)
260700, 261700 . . . . 170 N•m
           (125 ft.-lbs.)

Magnetron armature . . . . 5.1 N•m
           (45 in.-lb.)

Oil pump cover . . . . 6.2 N•m
           (55 in.-lbs.)

Rocker arm cover:
161400 . . . . 6.2 N•m
           (55 in.-lbs.)
185400, 235400, 245400 . . . . 5.1 N•m
           (45 in.-lb.)
260700, 261700 . . . . 6.2 N•m
           (55 in.-lbs.)

Rocker arm lock screw/nut:
161400 . . . . 6.2 N•m
           (55 in.-lbs.)
185400 . . . . 3.9 N•m
           (35 in.-lb.)
235400, 245400 . . . . . . 7.8-11.1 N•m
           (70-100 in.-lb.)
260700, 261700 . . . . 6.2 N•m
           (55 in.-lbs.)

Rocker arm stud:
161400 . . . . 15.8 N•m
           (140 in.-lb.)
185400 . . . . 19.8 N•m
           (175 in.-lb.)
235400, 245400 . . . . 9.6 N•m
           (85 in.-lb.)
260700, 261700 . . . . 15.8 N•m
           (140 in.-lb.)

Spark plug . . . . 19 N•m
           (165 in.-lb.)

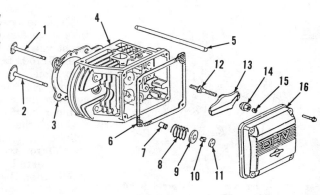

Fig. B720—Exploded view of cylinder head assembly used on Series 260700 and 261700 engines. Series 161400 and 185400 are similar.

1. Exhaust valve
2. Intake valve
3. Head gasket
4. Cylinder head
5. Push rod
6. Gasket
7. Valve seal
8. Valve spring
9. Valve spring retainer
10. Keepers
11. Valve cap
12. Stud
13. Rocker arm
14. Adjusting nut
15. Lock screw
16. Rocker cover

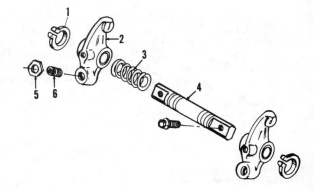

Fig. B721—Exploded view of rocker arm components used on Series 235400 and 245400 engines. Square edges of snap rings should face the rocker arms.

1. Snap ring
2. Rocker arm
3. Spring
4. Rocker arm shaft
5. Jam nut
6. Valve adjusting screw

CYLINDER HEAD AND VALVES. To remove cylinder head, first remove carburetor, muffler, exhaust manifold, blower housing and rocker arm cover. Remove rocker arms and push rods; mark them so they can be installed in their original location.

NOTE: Push rods on Series 260700 and 261700 engines are not interchangeable; upper (exhaust) push rod is hollow.

Unscrew cylinder head bolts and remove cylinder head.

On Series 161400, 185400, 260700 and 261700, the rocker arms (13—Fig. B720) are mounted on studs (12) and retained by nuts (14). Loosen lock screw (15), unscrew nut (14) and remove rocker arm. On Series 235400 and 245400, rocker arms mount on a rocker shaft that is secured to the cylinder head by two bolts (Fig. B721). The rocker arms are retained on the rocker shaft by a snap ring at each end. Either a slotted retainer or a split retainer is used to retain the valve and spring in the cylinder head. Compress the valve spring, remove spring retainer and withdraw valve from the cylinder head. Identify all parts as they are removed so they can be assembled in their original position if reused.

Valve face and seat angles are 45° for intake and exhaust. Specified seat width is 1.09-1.65 mm (0.043-0.065 in.) for intake valve and 1.58-2.16 mm (0.062-0.085 in.) for exhaust valve. Minimum allowable valve margin is 0.38 mm (0.015 in.).

The cylinder head (4—Fig. B720) is equipped with renewable valve guides for Series 161400, 260700 and 261700 engine. Series 185400, 235400 and 245400 engines do not have replaceable valve guides. Cylinder head must be replaced if valve guides are worn beyond specified limit. Maximum allowable inside diameter of guide is 6.10 mm (0.240 in.).

Use B&S tool 19274 to remove and install guides. Guides can be installed either end up. Top of guide should protrude 7.0 mm (0.275 in.) as shown in Fig. B722. Use B&S tools 19345 and 19346 to ream valve guide to correct size.

Rocker arm studs are threaded into cylinder head. When installing studs, tighten to 15.8 N•m (140 in.-lb.) on Series 161400, 260700 and 261700 engines, and 19.8 N•m (175 in.-lb.) on Series 185400. On Series 235400 and 245400 engines, tighten rocker arm shaft bolts to 9.6 N•m (85 in.-lb.).

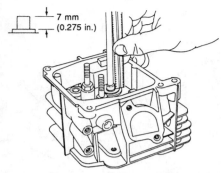

Fig. B722—Valve guides should protrude 7.0 mm (0.275 in.) from surface of valve guide boss.

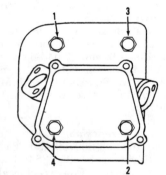

Fig. B723—Tighten cylinder head bolts on Series 161400 engines in sequence shown above.

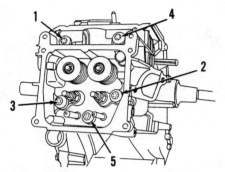

Fig. B724—Tighten cylinder head bolts on Series 185400, 235400 and 245400 engines in sequence shown above.

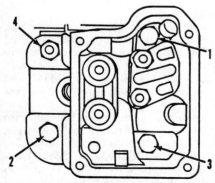

Fig. B725—Tighten cylinder head bolts on Series 260700 and 261700 engines in sequence shown above.

All models use a stem seal on the intake valve. A seal is also used on the exhaust valve on Series 161400, 260700 and 261700. Lubricate all parts with engine oil during assembly.

Note the following when installing cylinder head: Do not apply sealer to cylinder head gasket. Place new head gasket on the locating pins, then install cylinder head and screws. On Series 161400, top two cylinder head screws are inserted through the cylinder shield, then the cylinder head. On Series 260700 and 261700, plain washers are used on cylinder head screws located outside the valve cover and sealing washers are used on screws located inside the valve cover. On all models, tighten cylinder head bolts in three steps using sequence shown in Figs. B723, B724 or B725. Final tightening torque is 18.6 N•m (165 in.-lb.) for Series 161400, 33.9 N•m (300 in.-lb.) for Series 185400, 47.4 N•m (35 ft.-lb.) for Series 235400 and 245400, and 25.4 N•m (225 in.-lbs.) for Series 260700 and 261700.

CAMSHAFT. Camshaft and camshaft gear (22—Fig. B726 or B727) are an integral casting that is equipped with a compression release mechanism. The compression release lobe (L—Fig. B728) extends at cranking speed to hold the exhaust valve open slightly, thereby reducing compression pressure.

To remove camshaft, proceed as follows: Remove engine from equipment and drain crankcase oil. Clean pto end of crankshaft and remove any burrs or rust. Remove rocker arm push rods and mark them so they can be returned to original position. Unscrew fasteners and remove crankcase cover or oil pan. Rotate crankshaft so timing marks shown in Fig. B729 on crankshaft and camshaft gears are aligned (this will position valve tappets out of the way). Remove camshaft and tappets. Mark the tappets so they can be installed in their original guides if reused.

Inspect camshaft bearing journals and cam lobes for wear, scuffing or pitting. Compression release mechanism must operate freely without binding. On Series 185400, 235400 and 245400 engines, compression release lifter pin and pin retainer are replaceable. Compression release lobe height with the weight against the shaft should be 0.56-0.71 mm (0.022-0.028 in.) for Series 161400. Release lobe height for Series 260700 and 261700 before date code 91120900 should be 0.64-0.76 mm (0.025-0.030 in.) or 1.65-1.78 mm (0.065-0.070 in.) for Series 260700 and 261700 after date code 91120800. Re-

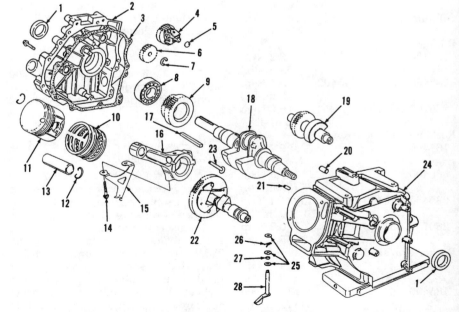

Fig. B726—Exploded view of crankcase and cylinder block assembly typical of Series 161400 engine.

1. Oil seal
2. Crankcase cover
3. Gasket
4. Governor weight assy.
5. Retainer
6. Idler gear
7. Snap ring
8. Ball bearing
9. Crankshaft gear
10. Piston rings
11. piston
12. Snap rings
13. Piston pin
14. Screw
15. Oil dipper
16. Connecting rod
17. Key
18. Crankshaft
19. Balance shaft
20. Dowel pin
21. Dowel pin
22. Camshaft
23. Tappet
24. Crankcase/cylinder block
25. Washers
26. Cotter pin
27. Oil seal
28. Governor shaft

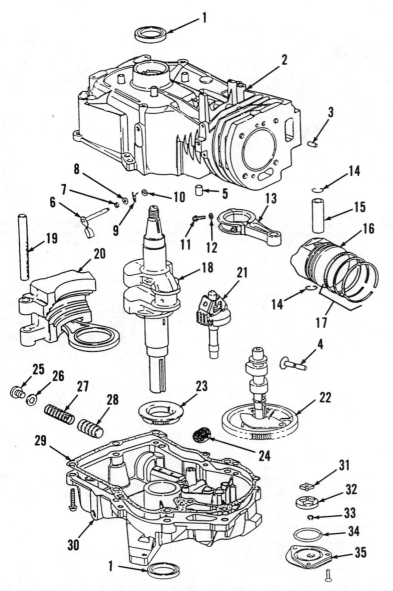

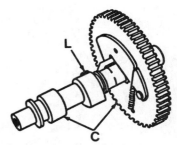

Fig. B728—Lobe (L) on exhaust cam protrudes at cranking speed to slightly open exhaust valve, thereby reducing compression pressure during starting.

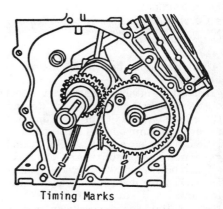

Fig. B729—Install camshaft so timing marks on camshaft and crankshaft gears are aligned.

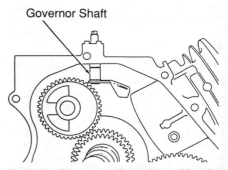

Fig. B730—Governor shaft must be positioned as shown when installing crankcase cover on Series 161400 engines.

Fig. B727—Exploded view of crankcase and cylinder block assembly typical of Series 260700 and 261700 engines.

1. Oil seal	10. Washer	20. Balancer assy.
2. Crankcase/	11. Screw	21. Governor assy.
cylinder block	12. Washer	22. Camshaft
3. Dowel pin	13. Connecting rod	23. Crankshaft gear
4. Tappet	14. Snap rings	24. Oil inlet screen
5. Dowel pin	15. Piston pin	25. Screw
6. Governor shaft	16. Piston	26. Washer
7. Oil seal	17. Piston rings	27. Spring
8. Washer	18. Crankshaft	28. Oil pressure
9. Cotter pin	19. Balancer shaft	relief valve

29. Gasket	32. Oil pump
30. Oil pan	outer rotor
31. Oil pump	33. Snap ring
inner rotor	34. "O" ring
	35. Oil pump cover

new the camshaft if wear exceeds the reject dimensions listed in the following table.

CAMSHAFT REJECT SIZES

Bearing Journals

161400 . . . . 15.82 mm
                              (0.623 in.)

185400 . . . . 14.93 mm
                              (0.5875 in.)

235400, 245400 . . . . 14.93 mm
                              (0.5875 in.)

260700, 261700 . . . . 15.82 mm
                              (0.623 in.)

Cam Lobes

161400 . . . . 30.94 mm
                              (1.218 in.)

235400, 245400 . . . . 32.15 mm
                              (1.2657 in.)

260700, 261700 . . . . 34.93 mm
                              (1.375 in.)

Reverse removal procedure to reassemble components. If camshaft is renewed, tappets should also be renewed. Align the timing marks (Fig. B729) on

crankshaft and camshaft gears as the camshaft is installed. Be sure governor arm is in proper position to contact governor as shown in Fig. B730 or Fig. B731. Install crankcase cover or oil pan as outlined in CRANKCASE COVER/ENGINE SUMP section. Do not force mating of cover or oil pan with crankcase. Reassemble remainder of components.

CRANKCASE COVER/OIL SUMP. The crankcase cover or oil sump controls crankshaft end play. End play should be within specified range when cover or sump is installed with a single, standard gasket. Refer to CRANKSHAFT AND MAIN BEARINGS section for end play specification. Sealant

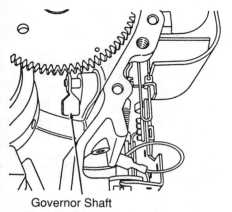

Governor Shaft

Fig. B731—Governor arm must be positioned as shown when installing oil sump on Series 260700 and 261700 engines.

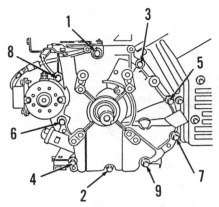

Fig. B732—On Series 161400 engines, tighten crankcase cover fasteners to 28.2 N•m (250 in.-lb.) in the sequence shown above.

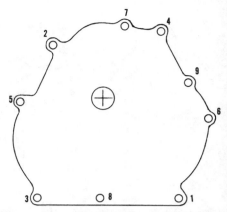

Fig. B734—On Series 235400 and 245400 engines, tighten crankcase cover fasteners to 19.7 N•m (175 in.-lb.) in the sequence shown above.

is not recommended when installing new gasket.

Install a suitable seal protector tool onto crankshaft or wrap tape around the crankshaft end to prevent damage to cover or sump oil seal during installation. Make sure that all shafts and governor components are properly aligned before installing cover or sump. DO NOT force mating of cover or sump to crankcase. Tighten fasteners in three steps in the sequence shown in Fig. B732, Fig. B733, Fig. B734 or Fig. B735. Specified tightening torque is 28.2 N•m (250 in.-lb.) for Series 161400, 260700 and 261700; or 19.7 N•m (175 in.-lb.) for Series 185400, 235400 and 245400.

PISTON, PIN, RINGS AND CONNECTING ROD. To remove piston and rod assembly, drain engine oil and remove engine from equipment. Remove cylinder head as previously outlined. Clean pto end of crankshaft and remove any burrs or rust. Unscrew fasteners and remove crankcase cover or oil pan. Rotate crankshaft so timing marks shown in Fig. B729 on crankshaft and camshaft gears are aligned (this will position valve tappets out of the way). Remove camshaft. Remove carbon or ridge from top of cylinder to prevent ring breakage. Unscrew connecting rod screws and push piston and rod out through top of the cylinder.

Reject piston showing visible signs of wear, scoring or scuffing. After cleaning carbon from ring grooves, insert a new piston ring into each groove and measure the side clearance between the ring and ring land with a feeler gauge. Reject the piston if ring side clearance exceeds 0.10 mm (0.004 in.) for compression rings and 0.20 mm (0.008 in.) for oil control ring on Series 161400, 260700 and 261700 engines; or 0.18 mm (0.007 in.) for compression and oil rings on Series 185400, 235400 and 245400 engines.

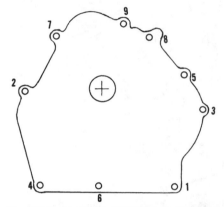

Fig. B733—On Series 185400 engines, tighten crankcase cover fasteners to 19.7 N•m (175 in.-lb.) in the sequence shown above.

Position piston ring squarely into the cylinder approximately 25 mm (1 in.) below top surface of cylinder. Measure ring end gap with a feeler gauge. End gap must not exceed 0.76 mm (0.030 in.) for all models.

Pistons and rings are available in several oversizes as well as standard.

Piston pin is a slip fit in piston and rod. Piston pin and bore reject dimensions are listed in the following table.

PISTON PIN REJECT SIZES

Piston Pin OD

161400	20.32 mm (0.800 in.)
185400	17.96 mm (0.7072 in.)
235400, 245400	20.31 mm (0.7996 in.)
260700, 261700	20.32 mm (0.800 in.)

Pin Bore In Piston

161400	20.35 mm (0.801 in.)
185400	18.04 mm (0.7102 in.)
235400, 245400	20.39 mm (0.8028 in.)

Fig. B735—On Series 260700 and 261700 engines, tighten oil pan fasteners to 28.2 N•m (250 in.-lb.) in the sequence shown above. Remove cover (C) for access to oil pump.

260700, 261700	20.35 mm (0.801 in.)

The connecting rod rides directly on crankpin. A connecting rod with 0.51 mm (0.020 in.) undersize big end diameter is available to accommodate a worn crankpin (machining instructions are included with new rod). Reject sizes for connecting rod are listed in the following table.

CONNECTING ROD REJECT SIZES

Crankpin Bearing ID

161400	36.40 mm (1.433 in.)
185400	34.01 mm (1.339 in.)
235400, 245400	38.06 mm (1.4984 in.)
260700, 261700	41.35 mm (1.627 in.)

Piston Pin Bearing ID

161400	20.35 mm (0.801 in.)
185400	18.04 mm (0.7102 in.)

235400, 245400 . . . . 20.39 mm
(0.8028 in.)
260700, 261700 . . . . 20.35 mm
(0.801 in.)

When assembling piston and connecting rod, be sure notch or arrow in piston crown is on flywheel side of rod (some rods have "MAG" marked on flywheel side of rod). Series 235400 and 245400 pistons can be installed on connecting rod either way, and dot on piston crown can face either direction.

On Series 161400 engines, install compression rings so side marked with a 'T' is toward piston crown. On Series 185400, 235400 and 245400 engines, top compression ring is barrel-faced and can be installed either way. Install middle compression ring so side marked with an 'X' is toward piston crown. On Series 260700 and 261700 engines, refer to Fig. B736 and install top ring so bevel (B) is toward piston crown and install second ring so step (S) is toward piston skirt. Install piston and rod assembly into engine so bolts on angled rod cap are toward camshaft (Fig. B737). Be sure match marks are aligned on rod and rod cap. Install oil dipper on rod cap of Series 161400 engines. Tighten connecting rod cap screws in two steps to torque value listed in TIGHTENING TORQUE

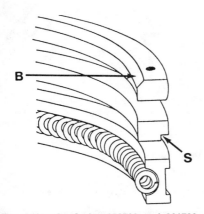

Fig. B736—On Series 260700 and 261700 engines, install top piston ring so bevel (B) is toward piston crown. Install second ring so step (S) is toward piston skirt.

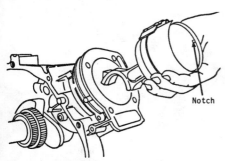

Fig. B737— Install piston and rod assembly into engine so bolts on angled rod cap are toward camshaft.

paragraph. Rotate the crankshaft to make sure the connecting rod is not binding on the crankpin.

Install camshaft as outlined in CAMSHAFT section. Install crankcase cover or oil sump as outlined in CRANCASE COVER/OIL SUMP section. Assemble remainder of components.

GOVERNOR. The governor gear and flyweight assembly is located on the inside of the crankcase cover or oil pan. The plunger in the gear assembly contacts the governor arm and shaft in the crankcase. The governor shaft and arm transfer governor action to the external governor linkage.

To gain access to the governor gear assembly, remove engine from equipment and drain crankcase oil. Clean pto end of crankshaft and remove any burrs or rust. Unscrew fasteners and remove crankcase cover or oil pan. Flyweight assembly must operate freely for proper governor action. On Series 161400 engines, the governor gear is driven by idler gear (6—Fig. B726), which can be removed after detaching snap ring (7).

The governor shaft and arm ride in a bushing in the crankcase. The bushing should be renewed if worn excessively. B&S reamer 19333 will size bushing to desired diameter.

To reassemble, position governor gear assembly in crankcase cover. Be sure governor arm is in proper position to contact governor as shown in Fig. B730 or Fig. B731. Install crankcase cover or oil pan as outlined in CRANKCASE COVER/OIL SUMP paragraph.

CRANKSHAFT AND MAIN BEARINGS. On Series 161400 engines, a ball bearing at the pto end and a replaceable bushing at the magneto end support the crankshaft. On Series 185400, 235400 and 245400 engines, crankshaft is supported by a ball bearing at each end. On Series 260700 and 261700 engines, a non-replaceable bushing at each end supports the crankshaft.

Before removing the crankshaft, remove rust, paint and burrs from pto end of crankshaft to prevent damage to oil seal or bushing. Remove the flywheel, crankcase cover or oil sump and camshaft. Rotate crankshaft so piston is at top dead center and remove connecting rod cap. Rotate crankshaft so it will clear connecting rod, then withdraw crankshaft from crankcase.

Reject crankshaft if journal dimensions are worn beyond the following specifications:

CRANKSHAFT REJECT SIZES

Crankpin Journal
161400 . . . . 36.25 mm
(1.427 in.)
185400 . . . . 33.95 mm
(1.3368 in.)
235400, 245400 . . . . 37.98 mm
(1.4953 in.)
260700, 261700 . . . . 41.20 mm
(1.622 in.)
Magneto Main Journal
161400 . . . . 38.02 mm
(1.497 in.)
185400 . . . . Ball Bearing
235400, 245400 . . . . Ball Bearing
260700, 261700 . . . . 41.20 mm
(1.622 in.)
PTO Main Journal
161400 . . . . Ball Bearing
185400 . . . . Ball Bearing
235400, 245400 . . . . Ball Bearing
260700, 261700 . . . . 41.20 mm
(1.622 in.)

On Series 260700 and 261700 engines, Synchro-Balance pto eccentric reject dimension is 68.05 mm (2.679 in.). On all models, a connecting rod with 0.51 mm (0.020 in.) undersize big end diameter is available to accommodate a worn crankpin (machining instructions are included with new rod).

To replace magneto main bearing bushing on Series 161400, set new bushing against old bushing in bearing bore of crankcase. Make sure that oil holes in bushing and crankcase are aligned (Fig. B738), then press new bushing into place from outside-in. Secure new bushing in the crankcase by punch-staking the oil hole from both ends of bushing. Remove any staking burrs from the ID of the new bushing.

Renew crankcase if bushing ID is 41.35 mm (1.628 in.) or more on Series 260700 and 261700 engines. Renew oil pan on Series 260700 and 261700 engines if bearing bore diameter is 41.35 mm (1.628 in.) or more. A service bushing is not available.

The ball bearing main bearing at pto end of Series 161400 engines is a press

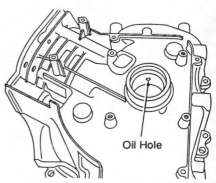

Fig. B738—Oil hole in bushing and crankcase must be open.

fit in crankcase cover. To remove bearing, press bearing toward inside of crankcase cover. Install bearing by pressing toward outside of crankcase cover until bearing is flush with inside face of crankcase cover.

Ball bearing main bearings and gear reduction shaft bearings are all press-fit bearings in their respective cases and slip-fit over the crankshaft and reduction shaft journals. Bearings are removed by pressing from outside toward inside of engine. Governor gear assembly may need to be removed for clearance prior to pressing out main bearing on pto side. Lightly lubricate bearing OD before installing. Press against outer race of the bearing only. Be sure bearing is properly seated in its bore.

CYLINDER. Replace cylinder or rebore to next oversize if cylinder bore wear exceeds 0.08 mm (0.003 in.) or if out-of-round exceeds 0.04 mm (0.0015 in.). Standard cylinder bore diameter is listed in the following table:

CYLINDER BORE ID

Series	Bore Size
161400	76.18-76.20 mm
	(2.999-3.000 in.)
185400	80.00-80.02 mm
	(3.1496-3.1504 in.)
235400, 245400	89.00-89.02 mm
	(3.5039-3.5047 in.)
260700, 261700	87.29-87.31 mm
	(3.4365-3.4375 in.)

IMPORTANT: The cylinder and crankcase must be thoroughly cleaned after refinishing the cylinder bore with a hone. Honing grit is highly abrasive and will cause rapid wear of internal engine components unless it is completely removed.

Wash the cylinder and crankcase using a stiff brush and hot, soapy water. Use a strong detergent capable of breaking down the machining oil while maintaining a good level of suds. Clean until all traces of honing grit are removed. Rinse the cylinder and crankcase with hot, clear water. Dry completely, then apply light coating of engine oil to the cylinder bore.

OIL PUMP. Series 260700 and 261700 engines are equipped with a rotor-type oil pump located in the oil pan and driven by the governor shaft. A relief valve (28—Fig. B727) is located in the side of the oil pan.

Remove engine from equipment for access to oil pump cover (C—Fig. B735). Remove cover, detach snap ring on

shaft (Fig. B739) and extract pump rotors. Mark rotors so they can be reinstalled in their original position. Renew any components that are damaged or excessively worn. Be sure "O" ring (Fig. B739) is installed in cover before installing cover. Tighten oil pump cover screws to 6.2 N•m (55 in.-lb.).

The oil pump filter screen shown in Fig. B740 is removable after removing oil pan. Install screen so hole is away from governor and notch is toward governor.

SYNCHRO-BALANCER. All models are equipped with a balancing system. Series 161400 engines are equipped with a counterweight gear (19—Fig. B726) that rides directly in bores in the crankcase and crankcase cover. Some Series 185400 and all Series 235400 and 245400 engines have a separate rotating counterweight similar to Series 161400 except that the counterweight shaft is supported in ball bearings mounted in the crankcase and crankcase cover. Series 260700 and 261700 engines are equipped with an oscillating weight-type system that is actuated by an eccentric journal on the crankshaft.

Remove crankcase cover for access to counterweight shaft on Series 161400 engines. Renew counterweight if either bearing journal is 15.82 mm (0.623 in.) or less. Renew crankcase or crankcase

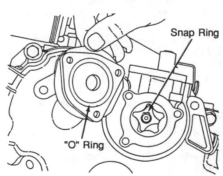

Fig. B739—On Series 260700 and 261700 engines, detach snap ring to remove inner oil pump rotor.

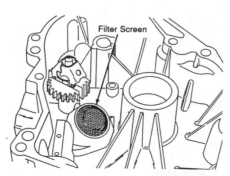

Fig. B740—The oil pump on Series 260700 and 261700 engines is located in the oil sump adjacent to governor assembly.

cover if bearing bore is 15.95 mm (0.628 in.) or more. When installing counterweight, align timing marks on crankshaft gear and cam gear as shown in Fig. B741. Then, install counterweight so timing mark on counterweight gear is aligned with second timing mark on crankshaft gear.

Remove crankcase cover for access to counterweight shaft on Series 185400, 235400 and 245400 engines. Inspect the shaft bearing journals, ball bearings and gear teeth for wear or damage and renew if necessary. When installing counterweight, align timing marks on crankshaft gear and camshaft gear. Install counterweight, aligning timing mark on counterweight gear with second timing mark on crankshaft gear.

To service Synchro-Balancer unit on Series 260700 and 261700 engines, remove oil pan. Rotate crankshaft so timing marks on crankshaft gear and camshaft gear are aligned. Remove crankshaft gear and camshaft, then withdraw balancer unit as shown in Fig. B742. Note reject sizes in following table:

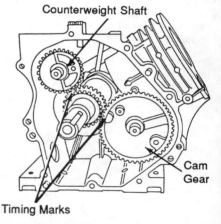

Fig. B741—On Series 161400 engines, timing marks on camshaft gear, crankshaft gear and balancer gear must be aligned during assembly.

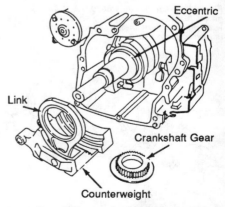

Fig. B742—View of Synchro-Balancer used on Series 260700 and 261700 engines. The balancer link fits around the eccentric on the crankshaft.

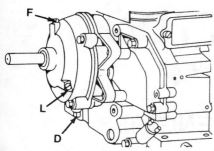

Fig. B743—View of reduction gear unit used on some Series 161400 engines showing location of oil level plug (L), oil fill plug (F) and drain plug (D).

REJECT SIZE

Counterweight shaft....... 12.65 mm
(0.498 in.)

Counterweight
shaft bore .... 12.78 mm
(0.503 in.)

Counterweight link
pin bore................ 15.82 mm
(0.623 in.)

Link pin................. 15.72 mm
(0.619 in.)

Fig. B744—Exploded view of reduction gear unit used on some Series 161400 engines.

1. Gasket
2. Housing
3. Ring gear
4. Gasket
5. Cover

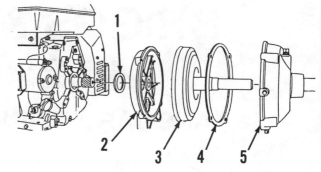

Connector link pin bore .... 15.80 mm
(0.622 in.)

Connector link
eccentric bore .... 68.17 mm
(2.684 in.)

Reassemble Synchro-Balancer unit by reversing disassembly procedure while being sure to align timing marks on crankshaft gear and camshaft gear.

REDUCTION GEAR. Series 161400 engines may be equipped with the reduction gear unit shown in Fig. B743. Maintain oil level even with opening for oil level plug (L). Recommended oil is the same as that used in the crankcase. Fill unit with oil at fill plug (F) opening. Note that fill plug has a vent hole that must be open. Remove drain plug (D) to drain oil.

Refer to Fig. B744 for an exploded view of reduction gear unit. Output shaft end play should be 0.05-0.76 mm (0.002-0.030 in.). Tighten housing (2) screws to 15.8 N•m (140 in.-lb.), and bend ear of lock plate against screw head. Tighten cover (5) screws to 20.9 N•m (185 in.-lb.).

BRIGGS & STRATTON

BRIGGS & STRATTON CORPORATION
Milwaukee, Wisconsin 53201

VANGUARD TWIN-CYLINDER ENGINES

Model Series	No. Cyls.	Bore	Stroke	Displacement	Power Rating
290400, 290700	2	68 mm (2.68 in.)	66 mm (2.60 in.)	480 cc (29.3 cu.in.)	9.4 kW (12.5 hp)
294400, 294700	2	68 mm (2.68 in.)	66 mm (2.60 in.)	480 cc (29.3 cu.in.)	9.4 kW (12.5 hp)
303400, 303700	2	68 mm (2.68 in.)	66 mm (2.60 in.)	480 cc (29.3 cu.in.)	11.9 kW (16 hp)
350400, 350700	2	72 mm (2.83 in.)	70 mm (2.75 in.)	570 cc (34.75 cu.in.)	13.5 kW (18 hp)
351400, 351700	2	72 mm (2.83 in.)	70 mm (2.75 in.)	570 cc (34.75 cu.in.)	14.8 kW (20 hp)
380400, 380700	2	75 mm (2.83 in.)	70 mm (2.97 in.)	627 cc (38.26 cu.in.)	15.6 kW (21 hp)
381400, 381700	2	75 mm (2.97 in.)	70 mm (2.75 in.)	627 cc (38.26 cu.in.)	17.1 kW (23 hp)

NOTE: Metric fasteners are used throughout engine except threaded hole in pto end of crankshaft, flange mounting holes and flywheel puller holes, which are US threads.

The Vanguard models included in this section are air-cooled, four-stroke, twin-cylinder engines. Series 290400, 294400, 303400, 350400, 351400, 380400 and 381400 have a horizontal crankshaft. Series 290700, 294700, 303700, 350700, 351700, 380700 and 381700 have a vertical crankshaft. All models are equipped with an overhead valve system. Number 1 cylinder is nearer flywheel. Cylinder number is marked on cylinder side nearest flywheel.

Refer to BRIGGS & STRATTON ENGINE IDENTIFICATION INFORMATION section for engine identification. Engine model number as well as the type and code numbers are necessary when ordering parts.

MAINTENANCE

LUBRICATION. The engine is lubricated with oil supplied by a rotor-type oil pump attached to the crankcase cover or oil pan.

Periodically check oil level; do not overfill. Oil dipstick should be screwed in until bottomed for correct oil level reading. Change oil after first eight hours of operation and every 50 hours thereafter under normal operating conditions. Recommended oil change interval is 25 hours if severe service is encountered.

The engine may be equipped with a spin-on-type oil filter. If so equipped, manufacturer recommends changing oil filter after every 100 hours of operation. Filter should be changed more frequently if engine is operated in a severe environment.

Manufacturer recommends using oil with an API service classification of SH or SJ or any classification formulated to supercede SH or SJ. Use SAE 30 oil for temperatures above 40° F (4° C), SAE 10W-30 oil for temperatures between 0° F (−18° C) and 40° F (4° C), and below 0° F (−18° C), use petroleum based SAE 5W-20 or a suitable synthetic oil. Do not use 10W-40 oil.

Crankcase capacity is 1.65 liters (3.5 pints) if equipped with an oil filter, 1.42 liters (3 pints) if not equipped with a filter.

A low oil pressure switch may be located on the oil filter housing, if so equipped. Switch should be closed at zero pressure and open at 31 kPa (4.5 psi).

FUEL FILTER. The fuel tank is equipped with a filter at the outlet and an inline filter may be installed. Check filters annually and periodically during operating season.

CRANKCASE BREATHER. The engine is equipped with a crankcase breather that provides a vacuum for the crankcase. Vapor from the crankcase is evacuated to the air cleaner. A fiber disk on early models or a reed valve on later models (Fig. B801) acts as a one-way valve to maintain crankcase vacuum. The breather system must operate properly or excessive oil consumption can result. The breather assembly is located in the valley between the cylinders.

On early models with a fiber disc, it should be possible to insert a 1.0 mm (0.045 in.) wire between disc and breather body; do not use excessive force when measuring gap. Disc should not stick or bind during operation. Renew if distorted or damaged.

On later models with a reed valve, check that the valve seats properly. Do not press against reed valve. Renew if distorted or damaged.

Inspect breather tube for leakage.

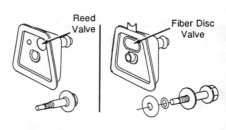

CURRENT STYLE   EARLY STYLE

Fig. B801—Later models are equipped with a reed valve in the breather housing while early models are equipped with a fiber disc.

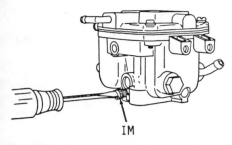

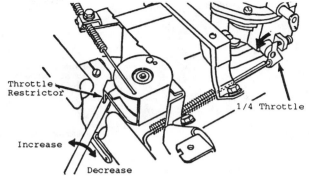

Fig. B804—Bend throttle restrictor tang as outlined in text.

Fig. B802—View showing location of carburetor idle mixture screw on one-barrel carburetor for horizontal crankshaft models.

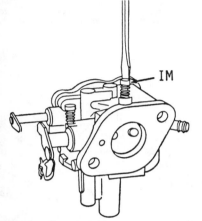

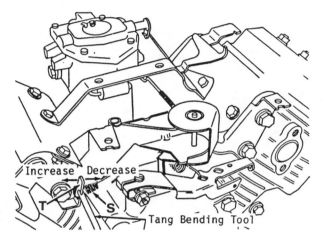

Fig. B805—Adjust governed idle speed as outlined in text.

Fig. B803—View showing location of carburetor idle mixture screw on one-barrel carburetor for vertical crankshaft models.

SPARK PLUG. Recommended spark plug is either an Autolite 3924 or Champion RC12YC. Specified spark plug electrode gap is 0.76 mm (0.030 in.). Tighten spark plug to 20 N•m (180 in.-lb.).

CAUTION: Briggs & Stratton does not recommend using abrasive blasting to clean spark plugs as this may introduce some abrasive material into the engine that could cause extensive damage.

CARBURETOR. Adjustment. Turn idle mixture screw (IM—Figs. B802 or B803) 1¼ turns out from seated position. Remove air cleaner, carburetor cover and valley cover, if so equipped, for access to governor linkage. Place remote speed control in idle position. Bend throttle restrictor tang shown in Fig. B804 so throttle cannot open greater than ¼ open. Run engine until operating temperature is reached. Place remote speed control in idle position. Hold carburetor throttle lever against idle speed adjusting screw and adjust idle speed to 1400 rpm if governed idle spring (S—Fig. B805) is red, or to 1100 rpm if governed idle spring is white. With throttle lever against idle speed adjusting screw, turn idle mix-

ture screw clockwise until a reduction in engine speed is noted and mark screw position. Back out idle mixture screw until engine speed lessens again and mark screw position. Rotate screw so it is halfway between the two marked positions. With throttle lever against idle speed screw, readjust idle speed to 1200 rpm if governed idle spring is red, or to 900 rpm if governed idle spring is white. Release throttle lever. With remote control in governed idle position, bend tab (T—Fig. B805), to obtain 1400 rpm if governed idle spring is red, or to 1100 rpm if governed idle spring is white.

All models are equipped with a fixed high-speed jet. An optional jet for high altitude operation is offered on vertical crankshaft models.

Overhaul. ONE-BARREL HORIZONTAL CRANKSHAFT MODELS. Refer to Fig. B806 or Fig. B807 for an exploded view of carburetor. On Series 350400 engines, mark choke plate so it can be installed in original position and do not lose detent ball when withdrawing choke shaft. Note the following when assembling carburetor: On all engines except Series 350400, apply sealant to Welch plug and install choke plate so hole in plate is toward vent tube (Fig. B808). On all models, install throttle shaft seals with lip facing out.

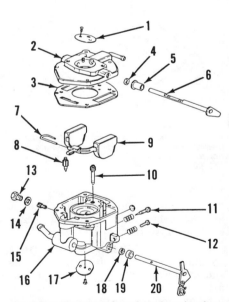

Fig. B806—Exploded view of one-barrel carburetor used on horizontal crankshaft models except Series 350400.

1. Choke plate	11. Idle mixture screw
2. Cover	12. Idle speed screw
3. Gasket	13. Plug
4. Seal	14. Gasket
5. Spacer	15. Main jet
6. Choke shaft	16. Body
7. Float pin	17. Throttle plate
8. Fuel inlet valve	18. Seal
9. Float	19. Spacer
10. Nozzle	20. Throttle shaft

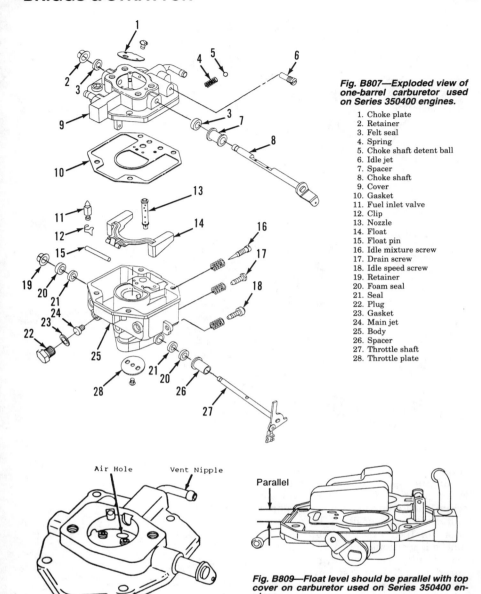

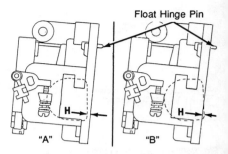

Fig. B810—The one-barrel carburetor used on horizontal crankshaft models, except Series 350400, must be held in a near-vertical position as shown when checking float height (H). Fuel pump carburetor is shown in left drawing "A" and gravity feed carburetor is shown in right drawing "B." See text.

Fig. B807—Exploded view of one-barrel carburetor used on Series 350400 engines.

1. Choke plate
2. Retainer
3. Felt seal
4. Spring
5. Choke shaft detent ball
6. Idle jet
7. Spacer
8. Choke shaft
9. Cover
10. Gasket
11. Fuel inlet valve
12. Clip
13. Nozzle
14. Float
15. Float pin
16. Idle mixture screw
17. Drain screw
18. Idle speed screw
19. Retainer
20. Foam seal
21. Seal
22. Plug
23. Gasket
24. Main jet
25. Body
26. Spacer
27. Throttle shaft
28. Throttle plate

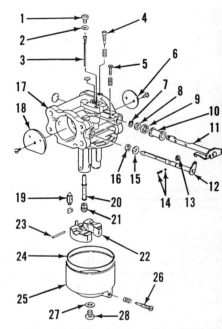

Fig. B811—Exploded view of one-barrel carburetor used on vertical crankshaft models. The idle jet and main jet on Series 350700 engines are located as shown in Figs. B812 and B813.

1. Plug	15. Washer
2. Washer	16. Felt seal
3. Idle jet	17. Body
4. Idle mixture screw	18. Choke plate
5. Idle speed screw	19. Fuel inlet valve
6. Throttle plate	20. Nozzle
7. Clip	21. Main jet
8. Seal	22. Float
9. Foam seal	23. Pin
10. Spacer	24. Gasket
11. Throttle shaft	25. Fuel bowl
12. Choke shaft	26. Drain screw
13. Clip	27. Gasket
14. Choke detent ball	28. Screw

Fig. B808—Install choke plate so hole in plate is toward vent on one-barrel carburetor used on horizontal crankshaft models except Series 350400.

Fig. B809—Float level should be parallel with top cover on carburetor used on Series 350400 engines.

Install throttle plate so flat portion (not sharp edge) of chamfers on plate fit against carburetor bore when plate and shaft are installed in carburetor.

On Series 350400 engine, float should be parallel with top cover as shown in Fig. B809. Bend tang on float arm to adjust float level. To adjust float level on all other horizontal crankshaft engines, note if a fuel pump is used because float level is different for gravity-feed or pressure-feed carburetors. Position carburetor a little past vertical as shown in Fig. B810 and press lightly against float pin so fuel valve just bottoms against seat. On fuel pump equipped engines, float height (H) should be 1.6 mm (1/16 in.). On grav-

ity-feed carburetors, float height (H) should be 2.4 mm (3/32 in.). Measure float height at a point on float just before end radius. Adjust float level by bending float tang. Note that spacer between carburetor and intake manifold has an indexing pin that must fit into intake manifold. Tighten carburetor mounting screws to 7 N•m (62 in.-lb.).

Overhaul. ONE-BARREL VERTI-CAL CRANKSHAFT MODELS. Refer to Fig. B811 for an exploded view of carburetor. On Series 350700, the idle jet is located in side of carburetor as shown in Fig. B812 and the main jet is located in the side of the nozzle stanchion as shown in Fig. B813.

When removing or installing nozzle (Fig. B813) on Series 350700, main jet must be removed. Apply sealant to Welch plug on top of carburetor. Install throttle plate so numbers on plate are

down as shown in Fig. B814. Install throttle shaft seals with lip facing out. Install choke plate so number is out and hole is down as shown in Fig. B815. On Series 350700, install float pin so swaged end is out as shown in Fig. B816. To check float level, invert carburetor body as shown in Fig. B817. Float should be parallel with bowl mating surface. Bend float tang to adjust float level. Note that spacer between carburetor and intake manifold has an index-

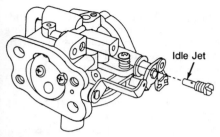

Fig. B812—Idle jet is located on side of carburetor on Series 350700 engines.

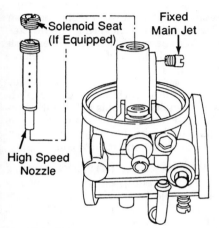

Fig. B813—Main jet is located in side of carburetor nozzle stanchion on Series 350700 engines.

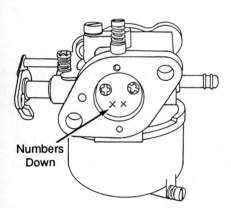

Fig. B814—Install throttle plate so numbers on plate are down.

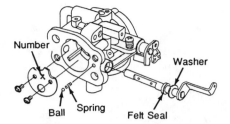

Fig. B815—Install choke plate so number is out and hole is down.

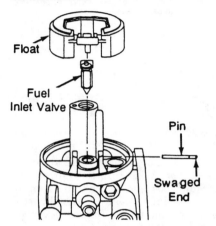

Fig. B816—On Series 350700 engines, install float pin so swaged end is out.

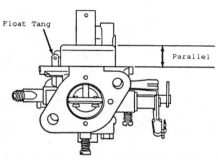

Fig. B817—Float must be level with body surface. Bend float tang to adjust.

SERIES	MAIN JET
351400	#94 (L) #98 (R)
351700	#98 (L) #100 (R)
380400	#110 (L) #114 (R)
380700	#118 (L) #116 (R)

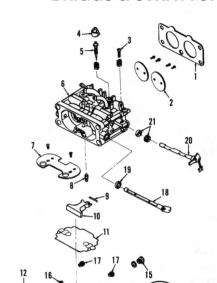

Fig. B818—Exploded view of two-barrel carburetor used on Series 351000 and 380000 engines. Plug (15) is used when not equipped with anti-afterfire solenoid (14).

1. Gasket
2. Throttle plates
3. Idle speed screw
4. Limiter cap
5. Idle mixture screw
6. Body
7. Choke plate
8. Fuel inlet valve
9. Pin
10. Float
11. Gasket
12. Fuel drain screw
13. Fuel bowl
14. Anti-afterfire solenoid
15. Plug
16. Idle jets
17. Main jets
18. Choke shaft
19. Seal
20. Throttle shaft
21. Seal assy.

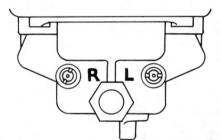

Fig. B819—Fixed main jet location and identification on float bowl of two-barrel carburetor. "R" indicates jet is for No. 2 (right) cylinder and "L" indicates that jet is for No. 1 (left) cylinder. Refer to text.

ing pin that must fit into intake manifold. Tighten carburetor mounting screws to 7 N•m (62 in.-lb.).

Overhaul. TWO-BARREL CARBURETOR. Series 351000 and 380000 engines use a two-venturi (two-barrel) side-draft carburetor (Fig. B818). Service procedures are nearly identical for all carburetors in these two series except for idle mixture screw location and main jet sizes. The "L" and "R" markings (Fig. B819) on the carburetor float bowl identify the cylinders: L is No. 1 cylinder and R is No. 2 cylinder. Note that the fixed main jets (7) are not identical. Jet sizes are as follows:

When servicing the carburetor, note routing of anit-afterfire solenoid wire when removing the solenoid. Remove idle mixture screw limiter caps (4—Fig. B818) by pulling with pliers; discard if damaged. Discard all used gaskets.

Separate the float bowl (13) from upper body (6) for access to internal components. The float hinge pin (9) must be removed and installed from the throttle lever side of the carburetor body. Outer end of pin must be installed flush with support post to prevent interference with the float bowl. Remove the float (10), fuel inlet valve (8), idle jets (16), main jets (17) and idle mixture screws (5). Throttle and choke plates (1 and 7)

have beveled edges and do not have identifying markings. Mark the plates before removing, and reinstall in the same locations and positions.

Clean dirt and gum deposits from the carburetor with a suitable commercial carburetor cleaner. DO NOT soak plastic, neoprene or rubber parts in solvent. Inspect the carburetor carefully and replace damaged components. Throttle and choke shafts ride directly in carburetor body bores without bushings. Shaft-to-bore wear should not exceed 0.25 mm (0.010 in.). Throttle and choke

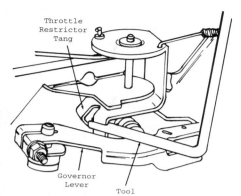

Fig. B820—Adjusting throttle restrictor tang. Refer to text.

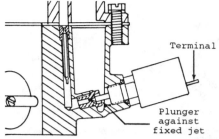

Fig. B821—Drawing of anti-afterfire solenoid used on some carburetors.

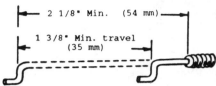

Fig. B822—Remote control wire must extend and travel to dimensions shown above.

shafts are replaceable. Carburetor must be replaced if the shaft bores are excessively worn.

Install new throttle and choke shaft seals (19 and 21) with sealing lip facing outward. Lightly coat the threads of throttle and choke plate screws with Loctite 222 or equivalent. Fuel inlet valve (8) is replaceable, but the seat is not. Carburetor must be replaced if the valve seat is damaged. Float level is not adjustable.

If equipped with anti-afterfire solenoid (14), tighten solenoid to 10 N•m (90 in.-lb.). Route the solenoid wire through the hole in No. 1 cylinder shroud. Carburetor-to-engine and air filter-to-carburetor fasteners should be tightened to 7 N•m (65 in.-lb.).

Adjust carburetor as follows: Initial adjustment for idle mixture screws is ¾ turn out from lightly seated position. DO NOT force screws when seating. Start the engine and run until operating temperature is reached (about five minutes). Connect an accurate tachometer to the engine. Set throttle control in "Slow" position. Hold the throttle lever against idle speed stop screw and adjust idle speed to 1200 rpm. While still holding throttle lever against idle speed screw, slowly close (turn clockwise) No. 1 cylinder idle mixture screw until engine speed begins to decrease from lean mixture, then open the mixture screw exactly ⅜ turn. Check idle speed and readjust to 1200 rpm if necessary. Repeat the mixture screw adjustment for No. 2 cylinder.

Adjust idle speed as follows: If engine has RED governed idle spring, adjust idle speed to 1200 rpm. If engine has WHITE governed idle spring, adjust idle speed to 900 rpm. Release the throttle lever and note idle rpm. If engine has RED governed idle spring, idle speed should be 1750 rpm. If engine has WHITE governed idle spring, idle speed should be 1100 rpm. If necessary, bend governed idle spring tang on throttle

control bracket to bring idle speed to correct rpm. With throttle control still in "Slow" position and engine rpm at governed idle speed, bend throttle restrictor tang to just contact governor lever (Fig. B820).

Move throttle control to "Fast" position; engine should accelerate smoothly. If the engine stumbles, turn the idle mixture screws out (counterclockwise) up to ⅛ turn to enrich the mixture for smooth acceleration. Install limiter caps on idle mixture screws so that cap stop is midway between stops on carburetor body.

ANTI-AFTERFIRE SYSTEM. Some models are equipped with an anti-afterfire system that stops fuel flow through the carburetor when the ignition switch is in off position. A solenoid inserts a plunger into the jet to stop fuel flow. The solenoid is attached to the side of the carburetor on horizontal crankshaft engines or to the bottom

of the fuel bowl on vertical crankshaft engines. Refer to Fig. B821 for drawing of anti-afterfire system. Solenoid can be removed and tested by connecting a 9-volt battery to solenoid. A faulty solenoid will affect engine performance.

CARBURETOR CONTROL MECHANISM. To ensure proper speed control, measure travel of remote control wire with remote control unit installed. Minimum wire travel is 1⅜ inches as shown in Fig. B822.

To adjust speed control cable, move remote control lever to idle position. Carburetor throttle lever should contact idle speed screw. If not, loosen cable housing clamp and reposition cable housing.

Remote choke control should completely close carburetor choke plate when remote control is in "CHOKE" position. If necessary, loosen cable clamp and reposition cable to synchronize carburetor choke and remote control.

MECHANICAL GOVERNOR. Most engines are equipped with a mechanical, flyweight-type governor. To adjust governor linkage, proceed as follows: Remove air cleaner for access to governor linkage. Loosen governor lever clamp nut (N—Fig. B823), rotate governor lever (L) so throttle plate is fully open and hold lever in place. Turn governor shaft (S) counterclockwise as far as possible, then tighten nut (N) to 8 N•m (71 in.-lbs.).

No-load governed top speed is adjusted by bending tang at end of governor spring (G). Normal governed speed is 3600 rpm unless specified otherwise by equipment manufacturer. On remote control engines, governor spring (G) should be attached to oblong hole nearer governor shaft, while governor spring on fixed speed engines should be attached to outer oblong hole on lever.

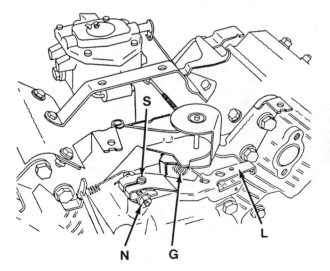

Fig. B823—To adjust governor, loosen governor lever clamp nut (N), rotate governor lever (L) so throttle plate is fully open and hold lever in place. Turn governor shaft (S) counterclockwise and retighten nut.

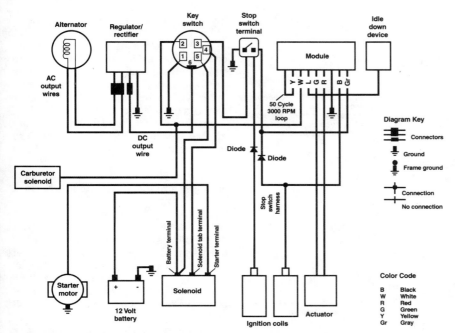

Fig. B824—Wiring diagram for electronic governor control system used on some engines.

The governor flyweight assembly is mounted on the end of the camshaft. Refer to CAMSHAFT and GOVERNOR SHAFT sections if internal service is required.

ELECTRONIC GOVERNOR. Some engines used on welder or generator applications are equipped with an electronic governor system. The system consists of an electronic control module, stop switch harness and a throttle actuator. The wiring diagram for this system is shown in Fig. B824. For applications requiring idle-down, that circuit is incorporated into the control module. The module controls the operational speed of the engine at either 3600 rpm (60 Hz) or 3000 rpm (50 Hz). The presence of an external wire loop on the module, yellow wire on Series 290000-303000 or red wire on Series 350000-380000, indicates 60 Hz operation. Cutting and removing the wire loop converts the module to 50 Hz operation.

System must be tested in the following sequence using an accurate tachometer.

Top governed speed should be 3600 rpm on 60 Hz systems, 3000 rpm on 50 Hz systems. Manually push throttle wide open; governor should limit speed to approximately 4000 rpm. Release the throttle.

On idle-down equipped engines, operate the engine at top governed speed. Disconnect blue wire between module and idle-down device and attach the wire to a good ground (use a jumper wire if necessary). After about five seconds, engine speed should drop to idle

speed (1750 rpm unless otherwise specified). Remove blue wire from ground; engine should return to top governed speed. Reconnect blue wire.

If the above tests indicate inaccurate speed control, use the following static test sequence to determine whether the control module or the actuator is at fault.

Unplug the green and red wires between actuator and control module. Using a separate 12-volt battery and jumper leads, attach battery positive terminal to the RED actuator wire and battery negative terminal to the GREEN actuator wire. Actuator should open throttle fully.

If actuator does not move the throttle lever, actuator is faulty. If actuator opens the throttle, control module is faulty.

When replacing the actuator, tighten the screws attaching the actuator to governor control bracket to 3.4 N•m (30 in.-lb.). The two long screws must not be allowed to turn while tightening the nuts. Hold screw heads with a ¼ inch wrench while tightening nuts. When assembling the actuator and control bracket to the engine, tighten the two 6-mm screws to 10 N•m (70 in.-lb.) and the four 8-mm screws to 17.0 N•m (150 in.-lb.). Prior to connecting governor link from carburetor to actuator, rotate actuator lever to 7 o'clock position, then connect linkage.

IGNITION SYSTEM. All models are equipped with a Magnetron ignition system.

To check spark, remove spark plug and connect spark plug cable to B&S

tester 19051, then ground remaining tester lead to engine. Spin engine at 350 rpm or more. If spark jumps the 4.2 mm (0.166 in.) tester gap, system is functioning properly.

To remove armature and Magnetron module, remove flywheel shroud and armature retaining screws. Disconnect stop switch wire from module.

When installing armature and module, position armature so air gap between armature legs and flywheel surface is 0.20-0.30 mm (0.008-0.012 in.).

Note that rewind starter cup on Series 350400 and 350700 so equipped, is secured by a screw that must be tightened to 48 N•m (35 ft.-lbs.) if removed for access to flywheel.

To prevent cross-fire between the ignition modules, both stop switch wires running from the modules to the common kill terminal each contain a diode. If any of the following conditions occur when attempting to start or stop the engine, the diode in one or both kill wires is likely faulty:

a. Will not start due to no spark from either module.

b. Only runs on one cylinder.

c. Only shuts off one cylinder.

d. Continues to run with ignition turned off.

Individual diodes are not replaceable; replace the kill wire if diode is faulty.

VALVE ADJUSTMENT. Adjust valve clearance with engine cold. Remove rocker arm cover. Remove spark plug. Rotate crankshaft so piston is at top dead center on compression stroke. Using a suitable measuring device inserted through spark plug hole, rotate crankshaft clockwise as viewed at flywheel end so piston is 6.35 mm (0.250 in.) below TDC. Use a feeler gauge to measure clearance between valve stem and rocker arm. Valve clearance should be 0.10-0.16 mm (0.004-0.006 in.). Loosen locknut (Fig. B825) and turn adjusting screw to obtain desired clearance. Tighten lock screw to 7 N•m (60 in.-lb.). Tighten valve cover screws to 3 Nm (25 in.-lb.).

COMPRESSION PRESSURE. Briggs & Stratton does not publish compression pressure specifications. Compression pressure measured at cranking speed should not vary more than 25 percent between cylinders.

An alternate method of determining internal engine condition is by using a cylinder leak-down tester. The tester is available commercially or from Briggs & Stratton (part No. 19413). Tester uses compressed air to pressurize the

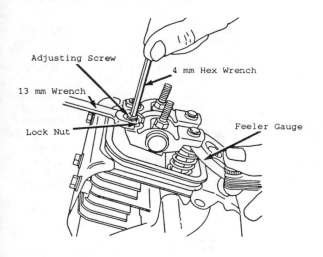

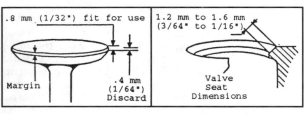

Fig. B825—After loosening locknut, turn rocker arm adjusting screw so valve clearance is 0.10-0.16 mm (0.004-0.006 in.).

Fig. B826—Valve and valve seat dimensions.

combustion chamber, then gauges the amount of leakage past cylinder, piston, rings and valves. Instructions are included with tester.

CYLINDER HEAD. Manufacturer recommends that the cylinder heads be removed and cleaned of deposits after every 500 hours of operation.

REPAIRS

TIGHTENING TORQUE. Recommended tightening torque specifications are as follows:

Alternator stator . . . . 2.0 N•m
(20 in.-lb.)
Carburetor mounting screws . . . 7 N•m
(60 in.-lb.)
Connecting rod . . . . 13 N•m
(115 in.-lb.)
Crankcase cover/oil pan . . . . . . 17 N•m
(150 in.-lb.)
Cylinder head . . . . 19 N•m
(165 in.-lb.)
Exhaust flange . . . . 17.0 N•m
(150 in.-lb.)
Flywheel nut . . . . 175 N•m
(130 ft.-lb.)
Governor lever nut . . . . 8.0 N•m
(70 in.-lb.)
Ignition module . . . . 3.0 N•m
(25 in.-lb.)
Intake manifold . . . . 16 N•m
(140 in.-lb.)
Oil pump . . . . 7 N•m
(60 in.-lb.)
Rewind starter . . . . 7 N•m
(60 in.-lb.)
Rocker arm cover . . . . 3 N•m
(25 in.-lb.)

Rocker arm lock screw . . . . 7 N•m
(60 in.-lb.)
Rocker shaft stud . . . . 16 N•m
(140 in.-lb.)
Rocker stud
(after Code 96040100) . . . . . 11.0 N•m
(100 in.-lb.)
Spark plug . . . . 22.5 N•m
(200 in.-lb.)

CYLINDER HEAD. Cylinder heads are not interchangeable. Cylinder number is cast in area adjacent to valve springs. To remove the cylinder head, first remove carburetor, intake manifold, muffler, exhaust manifold, air baffles and shields. Remove rocker arm cover, rocker arms and push rods.

NOTE: Do not interchange push rods. Push rods for intake valves are aluminum. Identify position and location of push rods when removing; return the push rods to same locations and positions when reinstalling.

Unscrew cylinder head bolts and remove cylinder head and gasket.

Valve face and seat angles are 45°. Specified seat width is 1.2-1.6 mm (0.047-0.063 in.). Minimum allowable valve margin is 0.4 mm (0.016 in.). See Fig. B826.

The cylinder head is equipped with renewable valve guides for both valves. Reject guide if inside diameter is 6.057 mm (0.2385 in.) or more. Use B&S tool 19274 to remove and install guides. Guides can be installed either way. Top of guide should protrude 7 mm (0.275 in.) as shown in Fig. B827. Use B&S

tools 19345 and 19346 to ream valve guide to correct size.

Note the following when reinstalling cylinder head: Do not apply sealer to cylinder head gasket. Sealing washers are used under the heads of the two cylinder head bolts adjacent to the rocker shaft on engines before Code 94050100. Tighten cylinder head bolts using sequence shown in Fig. B828 until final torque reading of 19 N•m (165 in.-lb.) is obtained.

Three styles of rocker arms are used on these engines (Fig. B829). Style 1 rocker arm, used prior to Code 93110100, is stamped steel. Style 2, used between Codes 93110100 and 96040100, is cast aluminum. Style 3, used from Code 96040100, is stamped steel and has its own individual 'saddle' support. Style 3 rocker arm cannot be used on heads designed for Styles 1 or 2. However, Style 3 heads can be installed on earlier engines.

On heads with rocker shaft, the rocker shaft studs are threaded into the cylinder head. Note that rocker shaft stands have offset holes. Hole must be nearer end of shaft as shown in Fig. B830. Tighten studs to 16 N•m (140 in.-lb.) on Style 1 and 2 rocker arm, 11 N•m (100 in.-lb.) on Style 3 arm.

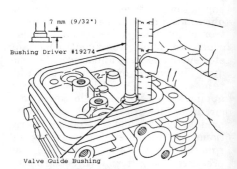

Fig. B827—Install valve guide so standout is 7.0 mm (0.275 in.) as shown above.

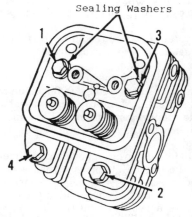

Fig. B828—Follow sequence shown above when tightening cylinder head screws.

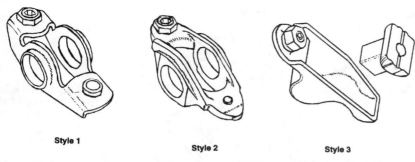

Style 1   Style 2   Style 3

Fig. B829—Three different styles of rockers arms used on V-twin engines. Refer to text for correct application.

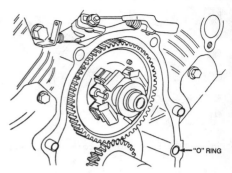

Fig. B832—Be sure "O" ring is in place before installing cover.

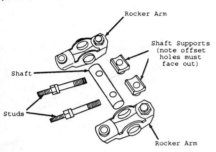

Fig. B830—On heads with rocker shaft, offset hole in shaft supports must be nearer end of rocker shaft.

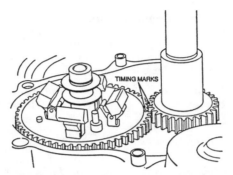

Fig. B831—Timing marks must align after installation of camshaft and crankshaft.

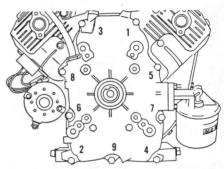

Fig. B833—Follow sequence shown above when tightening crankcase cover or oil pan screws.

CAMSHAFT. Camshaft and camshaft gear are an integral casting. The governor weight assembly and compression release mechanism are attached to the camshaft. Camshaft, governor and compression release are available only as a unit assembly.

To remove camshaft proceed as follows: Remove engine from equipment and drain crankcase oil. Clean pto end of crankshaft and remove any burrs or rust. Remove rocker arm push rods and mark them so they can be returned to original position. Unscrew fasteners and remove crankcase cover or oil pan. Rotate crankshaft so timing marks on crankshaft and camshaft gears are aligned (this will position valve tappets out of the way). Remove camshaft and tappets.

Reject size for camshaft bearing journal at flywheel end is 15.933 mm (0.6273 in.); reject size for bearing journal at pto end is 19.926 mm (0.7845 in.). Reject size for camshaft lobes is 30.25 mm (1.191 in.), except that intake lobe on Series 380000 has a reject size of 31.06 mm (1.223 in.).

Renew crankcase if camshaft bearing bore is 16.08 mm (0.633 in.) or more. Renew crankcase cover or oil pan if camshaft bearing bore is 20.04 mm (0.789 in.) or more.

Be sure compression release and governor components operate freely without binding. Check for loose and excessively worn parts.

Reverse removal procedure to reassemble components. Install camshaft while aligning timing marks (Fig. B831) on crankshaft and camshaft gears. Be sure governor arm is in proper position to contact governor slider on camshaft. Be sure "O" ring (Fig. B832) is in place. Install crankcase cover or oil pan and tighten cover screws to 17 N•m (150 in.-lb.) in sequence shown in Fig. B833. Do not force mating of cover with crankcase. Reassemble remainder of components.

GOVERNOR SHAFT. The governor shaft located in the crankcase cover or oil pan transmits motion from the governor assembly on the camshaft to the governor linkage. The shaft rides in two bushings in the cover. Remove crankcase cover or oil pan for access to shaft and bushings. Upper bushing is renewable, but lower bushing is not. If lower bushing is damaged or excessively worn, renew crankcase cover or oil pan.

When reinstalling crankcase cover or oil pan, be sure governor arm is in proper position to contact governor slider on camshaft. Complete installation as outlined in CAMSHAFT section.

PISTON, PIN, RINGS AND CONNECTING ROD. To remove piston and rod assembly, drain engine oil and remove engine from equipment. Remove cylinder head as previously outlined. Clean pto end of crankshaft and remove any burrs or rust. Unscrew fasteners and remove crankcase cover or oil pan. Rotate crankshaft so timing marks on crankshaft and camshaft gears are aligned (this will position valve tappets out of the way). Remove camshaft. Mark rods and caps so they can be installed in original positions. Unscrew connecting rod screws and remove piston and rod.

Reject size for piston ring end gap is 0.76 mm (0.030 in.) for compression and oil rings. Reject size for piston ring side clearance is 0.10 mm (0.004 in.) for compression rings and 0.20 mm (0.008 in.) for oil ring.

Piston pin is a slip fit in piston and rod. Refer to the following table for piston pin and pin bore reject sizes.

Model Series	Piston Pin	Pin Bore
290000-350000	17.06 mm (0.6718 in.)	17.12 mm (0.674 in.)
380000	17.98 mm (0.7078 in.)	18.06 mm (0.711 in.)

The connecting rod rides directly on crankpin. Reject size for rod big end diameter is 37.122 mm (1.4615 in.) and reject size for small end diameter is 17.107 mm (0.6735 in.). A connecting rod with 0.51 mm (0.020 in.) undersize big end diameter is available to accommodate a worn crankpin (machining instructions are included with new rod).

When assembling piston and rod be sure notch or casting mark on piston crown is toward flywheel and "OUT"

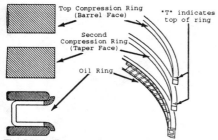

Fig. B834—Drawing showing correct installation of piston rings.

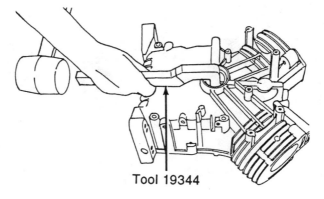

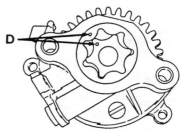

Fig. B836—Install bushing locating pin using B&S tool 19344.

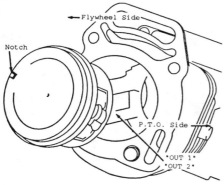

Fig. B835—Install piston and rod so notch or casting mark on piston crown is toward flywheel and "OUT" on rod is toward pto end of crankshaft.

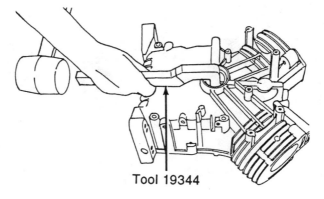

Fig. B837—Install oil pump rotors so dimples (D) are on same side.

side of rod is toward pto end of engine. Install compression rings with "T" side toward piston crown (Fig. B834). Install piston and rod assembly in engine with notch or casting mark on piston crown toward flywheel (Fig. B835). Install rod cap so marks on rod and cap align and tighten rod screws to 13 N•m (115 in.-lb.).

Install camshaft while aligning timing marks (Fig. B831) on crankshaft and camshaft gears. Be sure governor arm is in proper position to contact governor slider on camshaft. Be sure "O" ring (Fig. B832) is in place. Install crankcase cover or oil pan and tighten screws to 17 N•m (150 in.-lb.) in sequence shown in Fig. B833. Do not force mating of cover with crankcase. Reassemble remainder of component.

CYLINDER BLOCK. If cylinder bore wear exceeds 0.076 mm (0.003 in.)

or if out-of-round of bore exceeds 0.038 mm (0.0015 in.), then cylinder should be bored to the next oversize.

Refer to the following table for standard cylinder bore dimensions.

Model Series	Cylinder Bore
290000, 303000	68.00-68.03 mm (2.677-2.678 in.)
350000	72.00-72.03 mm (2.835-2.836 in.)
380000	75.50-75.52 mm (2.9724-2.973 in.)

The crankshaft is supported at the flywheel end by a renewable bushing in the crankcase. Renew bushing if bore is 30.086 mm (1.1845 in.) or more on engines before Code 97050100, 35.12 mm (1.383 in.) on engines after Code 97043000. A locating pin secures the bushing in the block. The pin must be driven out before pressing out bushing. Install new bushing so oil holes are aligned. The new locating pin is tapered at both ends; grind off one tapered end. Install pin, tapered end first, using B&S tool 19344 as shown in Fig. B836 until tool bottoms.

Renew ball bearing in crankcase cover or oil pan if bearing is worn, pitted or turns roughly.

Install oil seal in crankcase so it is flush with outside surface. Install oil seal in crankcase cover or oil pan so seal is 1.6 mm (1/16 in.) below outside surface.

OIL PUMP. The rotor-type oil pump is located in the crankcase cover or oil pan and driven by the camshaft. Re-

move crankcase cover or oil pan for access to pump. Note that rotors are installed so dimples (D—Fig. B837) are on same side. Renew any components that are damaged or excessively worn. Tighten oil pump mounting screws to 7 N•m (60 in.-lb.).

When installing crankcase cover or oil pan, be sure governor arm is in proper position to contact governor slider on camshaft. Be sure "O" ring (Fig. B832) is in place. Install crankcase cover or oil pan and tighten screws to 17 N•m (150 in.-lb.) in sequence shown in Fig. B833. Do not force mating of cover with crankcase.

CRANKSHAFT. The crankshaft (39—Fig. B838 or Fig. B839) is supported at the flywheel end by a bushing in the cylinder block and by a ball bearing at the pto end. Reject crankshaft if worn to 34.92 mm (1.375 in.) or less at pto bearing journal or if worn to 29.95 mm (1.179 in.) or less at flywheel bearing end. Reject crankshaft if crankpin diameter is worn to 36.96 mm (1.455 in.) or less.

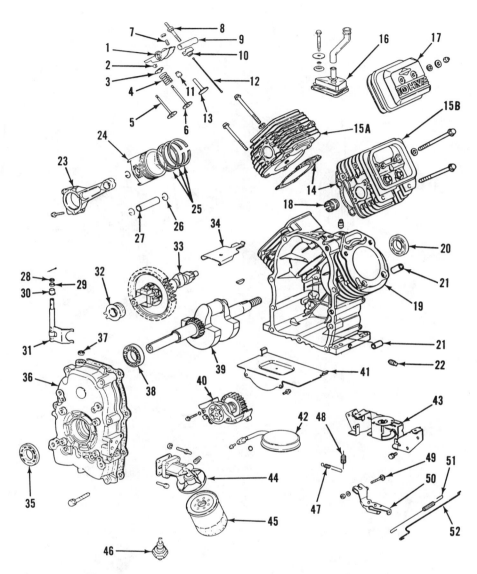

Fig. B838—Exploded view of horizontal crankshaft engine.

1. Rocker arm
2. Retainer
3. Spring retainer
4. Valve spring
5. Intake valve
6. Exhaust valve
7. Adjusting screw
8. Rocker stud
9. Rocker shaft
10. Rocker support
11. Valve seal
12. Push rod
13. Tappet
14. Head gasket
15A. Cylinder head (No. 1)
15B. Cylinder head (No. 2)
16. Breather assy.
17. Rocker arm cover
18. Exhaust port liner
19. Cylinder block
20. Seal
21. Dowel
22. Oil drain plug
23. Connecting rod
24. Piston
25. Piston rings
26. Retaining ring
27. Piston ring
28. Seal
29. Bushing
30. Bushing
31. Governor shaft
32. Slider
33. Camshaft
34. Breather baffle
35. Seal
36. Crankcase cover
37. Washer
38. Bearing
39. Crankshaft
40. Oil pump assy.
41. Windage plate
42. Oil pickup
43. Governor bracket
44. Oil filter adapter
45. Oil filter
46. Oil pressure switch
47. Governed idle spring
48. Governor spring
49. Clamp bolt
50. Governor lever
51. Governor link spring
52. Governor link

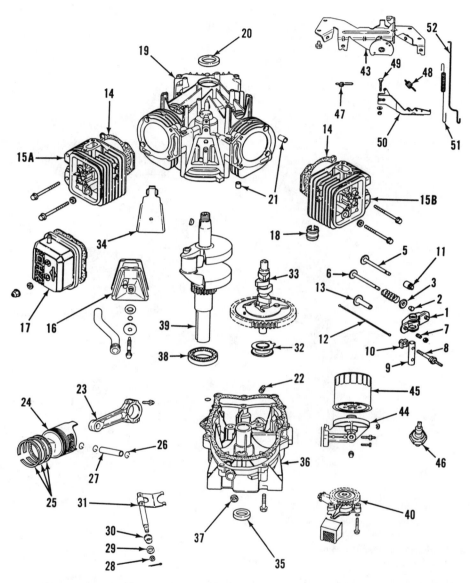

Fig. B839—Exploded view of vertical crankshaft engine. Refer to Fig. B838 for parts identification except: 36. Oil pan.

BRIGGS & STRATTON

BRIGGS & STRATTON CORPORATION
Milwaukee, Wisconsin 53201

Model	No. Cyls.	Bore	Stroke	Displacement	Power Rating
400400	2	3.44 in. (87.3 mm)	2.16 in. (54.8 mm)	40 cu. in. (656 cc)	14 hp (10.4 kW)
400700	2	3.44 in. (87.3 mm)	2.16 in. (54.8 mm)	40 cu. in. (656 cc)	14 hp (10.4 kW)
401400	2	3.44 in. (87.3 mm)	2.16 in. (54.8 mm)	40 cu. in. (656 cc)	16 hp (11.9 kW)
401700	2	3.44 in. (87.3 mm)	2.16 in. (54.8 mm)	40 cu. in. (656 cc)	16 hp (11.9 kW)
402400	2	3.44 in. (87.3 mm)	2.16 in. (54.8 mm)	40 cu. in. (656 cc)	16 hp (11.9 kW)
402700	2	3.44 in. (87.3 mm)	2.16 in. (54.8 mm)	40 cu. in. (656 cc)	16 hp (11.9 kW)
404400	2	3.44 in. (87.3 mm)	2.16 in. (54.8 mm)	40 cu. in. (656 cc)	16 hp (11.9 kW)
404700	2	3.44 in. (87.3 mm)	2.16 in. (54.8 mm)	40 cu. in. (656 cc)	16 hp (11.9 kW)
40A700	2	3.44 in. (87.3 mm)	2.16 in. (54.8 mm)	40 cu. in. (656 cc)	17 hp (12.7 kW)
421400	2	3.44 in. (87.3 mm)	2.28 in. (57.9 mm)	42.33 cu. in. (694 cc)	18 hp. (13.4 kW)
421700	2	3.44 in. (87.3 mm)	2.28 in. (57.9 mm)	42.33 cu. in. (694 cc)	18 hp. (13.4 kW)
422400	2	3.44 in. (87.3 mm)	2.28 in. (57.9 mm)	42.33 cu. in. (694 cc)	18 hp. (13.4 kW)
422700	2	3.44 in. (87.3 mm)	2.28 in. (57.9 mm)	42.33 cu. in. (694 cc)	18 hp. (13.4 kW)
42A700, 42B700, 42C700, 42D700	2	3.44 in. (87.3 mm)	2.28 in. (57.9 mm)	42.33 cu. in. (694 cc)	19 hp (14.1 kW)
42E700	2	3.44 in. (87.3 mm)	2.28 in. (57.9 mm)	42.33 cu. in. (694 cc)	19.5 hp (14.5 kW)
460700	2	3.44 in. (87.3 mm)	2.46 in. (57.9 mm)	45.6 cu. in. (694 cc)	20 hp (14.9 kW)

Engines in this section are four-stroke, two-cylinder, air-cooled engines. The crankshaft is supported at each end either with ball bearings or plain bearings. The plain bearings are either integral with crankcase, crankcase cover or engine base, or renewable DU-type bearings. Cylinder block and crankcase are a single aluminum casting. Some models are equipped with integral cast iron cylinder liners.

Connecting rods for all models ride directly on crankpin journals. Models 402440, 402770, 422440, 422770 and 460700 are pressure lubricated by a rotor-type oil pump. All other models are splash lubricated. Vertical crankshaft models that are splash lubricated are equipped with a gear-driven oil slinger, and horizontal crankshaft models use an oil dipper attached to number one cylinder connecting rod cap.

Early models are equipped with a flywheel magneto ignition with breaker points, condenser and coil mounted externally on engine. Later models are equipped with a Magnetron breakerless ignition.

All models use a float-type carburetor with an integral fuel pump.

Always provide engine model and serial number when ordering parts or special tools.

MAINTENANCE

LUBRICATION. Models 402440, 402770, 422440, 422770 and 460700 are equipped with a pressure lubrication system and an oil filter. Oil is routed from an oil pump driven by the camshaft to the crankshaft. All other models are splash lubricated using a gear-driven oil slinger on vertical crankshaft models or an oil dipper attached to number one connecting rod on horizontal crankshaft models.

Manufacturer recommends using oil with an API service classification of SH or SJ, or any classification formulated to supercede SH or SJ. Use SAE 30 oil for temperatures above 40° F (4° C), SAE 10W-30 oil for temperatures between 0° F (−18° C) and 40° F (4° C), and below 0° F (−18° C), use petroleum-based SAE 5W-20 or a suitable synthetic oil. Do not use SAE 10W-40 oil.

Check oil at regular intervals and maintain at "FULL" mark on dipstick. Dipstick should be pushed or screwed in completely for accurate measurement. DO NOT overfill.

Change oil after first 5 hours of operation. Thereafter, recommended oil change interval is every 25 hours on splash-lubricated models, or every 50 hours on models 402440, 402770, 422440, 422770 and 460700. Decrease oil change interval if usage is severe.

Crankcase oil capacity for early production engines is 3.5 pints (1.65 L). Oil capacity for late production engines is 3 pints (1.42 L). Check oil level with dipstick.

On Models 402440, 402770, 422440, 422770 and 460700, a low oil pressure switch may be located on the oil filter adapter. Switch should be closed at zero pressure and open at 5 psi (34.5 kPa). Switch may be connected to a warning device or into the ignition circuit.

Splash-lubricated models may be equipped with a low oil level warning system called Oil Gard. A sensor is screwed into the engine base and monitors oil level. If the oil level falls below a certain level, the sensor activates a warning device or disables the ignition circuit, depending on the equipment. To check sensor, first disconnect sensor lead. Connect ohmmeter leads to the sensor lead and engine base (ground). Ohmmeter should indicate 50-80 ohms. If not, check condition of connections and sensor wire, and if found satisfactory, renew sensor.

CRANKCASE BREATHER. Crankcase breathers are built into engine valve covers. Horizontal crankshaft models have a breather valve in each cover assembly. Vertical crankshaft models have only one breather in cover of number one cylinder.

Breathers maintain a partial vacuum in the crankcase to prevent oil from being forced out past oil seals and gaskets or past breaker point plunger or piston rings.

Fiber disc of the breather assembly must not be stuck or binding. A 0.045-inch (1.14 mm) wire gauge SHOULD NOT enter space between fiber disc valve and body. Check with gauge at 90° intervals around fiber disc (Fig. B901).

When installing breathers, make certain side of gasket with notches is toward crankshaft.

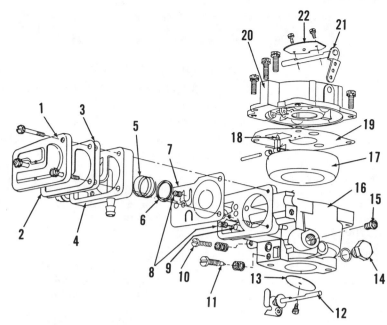

Fig. B902—Exploded view of downdraft Flo-Jet carburetor with integral fuel pump.

1. Diaphragm cover
2. Gasket
3. Damping diaphragm
4. Pump body
5. Pump spring
6. Spring cap
7. Diaphragm
8. Springs
9. Spring boss
10. Idle speed screw
11. Idle mixture screw
12. Throttle shaft
13. Throttle plate
14. Plug
15. Fixed main jet
16. Carburetor lower body
17. Float
18. Fuel inlet valve
19. Carburetor body gasket
20. Carburetor upper body
21. Choke shaft
22. Choke valve

SPARK PLUG. Recommended spark plug for all models is Champion RJ12C or Autolite 308. Electrode gap is 0.030 inch (0.76 mm). Tighten spark plug to 200 in.-lbs. (22.6 N•m).

CAUTION: Briggs & Stratton does not recommend using abrasive blasting to clean spark plugs as this may introduce abrasive material into the engine that could cause extensive damage.

CARBURETOR. A downdraft float-type carburetor is used. The carburetor is equipped with an integral diaphragm-type fuel pump. Refer to Fig. B902 for an exploded view of carburetor and fuel pump.

Adjustment. Initial setting of idle mixture screw (11—Fig. B902) for all models is 1½ turns out. If equipped with a high-speed mixture screw, initial setting is 1½ turns out.

MODELS PRIOR TO TYPE 1100. Run engine until normal operating temperature is reached. To adjust idle mixture screw, place remote speed control in idle position. Hold carburetor throttle lever against idle speed adjusting screw and adjust idle speed to 1200 rpm. With throttle lever against idle speed adjusting screw, turn idle mixture screw clockwise until a reduction in engine speed is noted. Back out idle mixture screw ½ turn. With throttle lever against idle speed screw, readjust idle speed to 900 rpm. Release throttle lever. Move remote speed control to a position where a ⅛-inch diameter pin can be inserted through two holes in governor control plate (Fig. B903). With remote control in governed idle position, bend tab "A," Fig. B904, to obtain 1200 rpm. Remove pin.

If equipped with a high-speed mixture screw, place remote speed control in fast position and adjust high-speed mixture screw for leanest setting that will allow satisfactory acceleration and steady governor operation.

NOTE: Some models are equipped with a fixed main high-speed jet (15—Fig. B902) that appears the same as the adjustable mixture jet, and is located behind a plug in the same posi-

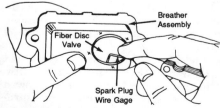

Fig. B901—Clearance between fiber disc valve and crankcase breather housing must be less than 0.045 inch (1.15 mm). A spark plug gauge can be used to check clearance as shown, but do not apply pressure against disc valve.

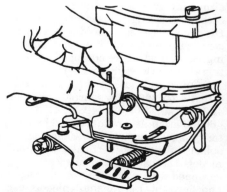

Fig. B903—Insert a 1/8-inch (3.2-mm) diameter pin through the two holes in governor control plate to correctly set governed idle position.

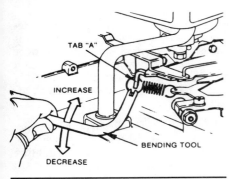

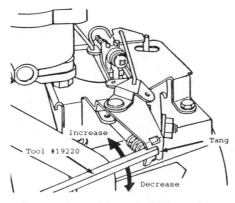

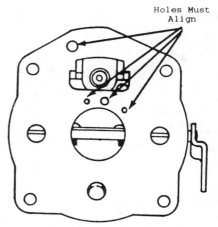

Fig. B908—Holes in body gasket of late models must be properly aligned with holes in upper carburetor body.

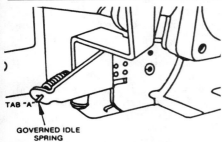

Fig. B906—With remote control in governed idle position, bend tang to obtain 1200 rpm idle speed.

Fig. B904—With governor plate locked with a 1/8-inch (3.2-mm) pin, bend tab "A" to obtain 1200 rpm. Upper view is for a horizontal crankshaft engines and lower view is for vertical crankshaft engines.

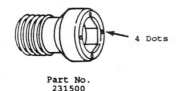

Part No.
231500

Fig. B905—Optional high-speed jet to provide a richer fuel mixture is identified by four dots on the jet face.

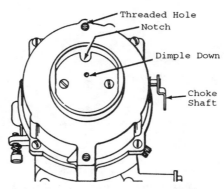

Fig. B907—Install the choke plate so the notch is toward the threaded hole.

tion as the high-speed mixture adjusting screw of other models. The fixed main jet is identified by a smaller hole in the tip. The fixed main jet must be seated fully in the carburetor; backing out main jet screw will result in an overly rich mixture.

An optional high-speed jet for high altitude operation is available. An optional high-speed jet that provides a richer fuel mixture to improve acceleration is also available. The optional richer main jet is identified by four dots on the jet face (Fig. B905). Main jet No. 231500 is available for engines operating with "high shock" starting loads, such as electric pto clutches, to help prevent engine "stumble" when a load is applied suddenly.

MODELS TYPE 1100 AND ABOVE. Run engine until normal operating temperature is reached. To adjust idle mixture screw, place remote speed control in idle position. Hold the throttle lever against idle speed adjusting screw and adjust idle speed to 1200 rpm. With throttle lever against idle speed adjusting screw, turn idle mixture screw

clockwise until a reduction in engine speed is noted and mark screw position. Back out idle mixture screw until engine speed lessens again and mark screw position. Rotate screw so it is halfway between the two marked positions. With throttle lever against idle speed screw, readjust idle speed to 900 rpm. Release throttle lever. With remote control in governed idle position, bend tang (Fig. B906) to obtain 1200 rpm idle speed.

If equipped with a high-speed mixture screw, place remote speed control in fast position and adjust high-speed mixture screw for leanest setting that will allow satisfactory acceleration and steady governor operation.

The fixed main high-speed jet is not adjustable. If throttle response is poor or if engine hesitates when it is accelerated or placed under load due to a lean fuel mixture, a richer jet may be required. The optional richer main jet is identified by four dots on the jet face (Fig. B905). Main jet No. 231500 is available for engines operating with "high shock" starting loads, such as electric pto clutches, to help prevent engine "stumble" when a load is applied suddenly.

An optional jet for high altitude operation is offered.

Carburetors on engines with Code Numbers higher than 981015xx have

been changed to a fixed-jet design on both the high-speed mixture and idle mixture circuits. Idle speed is the only adjustment that can be made on these carburetors. Service procedures are identical to earlier carburetors except for the idle mixture screw. Earlier style air filter bases are not interchangeable with the filter base used on these carburetors.

Overhaul. To disassemble carburetor, remove idle and main fuel mixture screws. Remove anti-afterfire solenoid from carburetor, if so equipped. Remove fuel pump body (4—Fig. B902) and upper carburetor body (20). Remove the float assembly (17) and fuel inlet valve (18). Inlet valve seat is a press fit in upper carburetor body. Use a self-threading screw to remove seat. New seat should be pressed into upper body until flush with body. Remove retaining screws from throttle plate (13) and choke plate (22) and withdraw throttle shaft (12) and choke shaft (21).

If necessary to renew throttle shaft bushings, use a 1/4×20 tap to remove old bushings.

NOTE: If carburetor body has a plug in the side of throttle shaft bore, bushing on the side is not renewable and plug should not be removed.

Press new bushings in using a vise and ream with B&S tool 19056. Align-ream bushings with a 7/32-inch drill if throttle shaft binds.

When assembling the carburetor, note the following: Install the choke plate so the notch is toward the threaded hole in upper body as shown in Fig. B907 and the dimple on the plate faces down. Be sure holes in body gasket are properly aligned with holes in upper carburetor body as shown in Fig. B908 and Fig. B909. Note proper installation of fuel inlet valve clip in Fig.

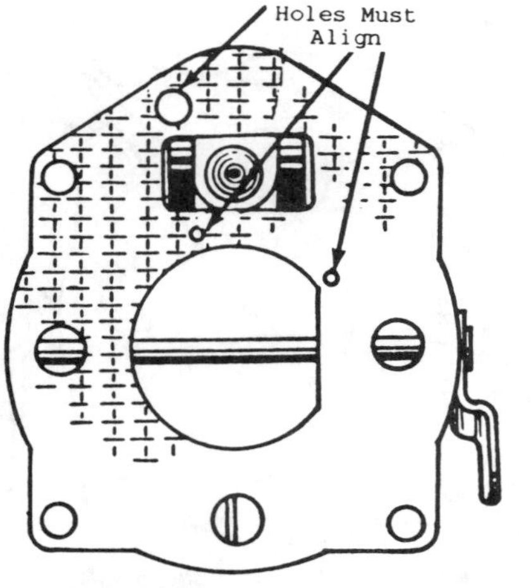

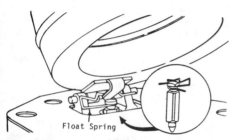

Fig. B909—Holes in body gasket of older models must be properly aligned with holes in upper carburetor body.

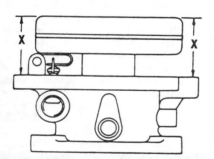

Fig. B910—Install fuel inlet valve clip as shown.

Fig. B911—Check carburetor float setting as shown. Float should be parallel to surface of carburetor body. Bend tang, if necessary, to adjust float level.

B910. To check float level, invert carburetor body and float assembly. Float should be parallel to body as shown in Fig. B911. Adjust float by bending float lever tang that contacts inlet valve. Install throttle plate so that, with throttle closed, dimples will be on opposite side of shaft from idle port, and convex sides of dimples are toward carburetor base surface (see Fig. B912). When installing fixed jet plug or anti-afterfire solenoid, tighten plug or solenoid to 100 in.-lbs. (11.3 N•m). Be sure springs (8—Fig. B902) fit onto spring bosses shown in Fig. B913.

ANTI-AFTERFIRE SYSTEM.
Some models are equipped with an anti-afterfire system that stops fuel

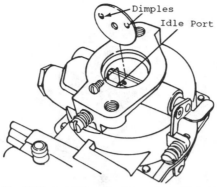

Fig. B912—Install throttle plate so that with throttle closed, dimples will be on opposite side of shaft from idle port, and convex sides of dimples are toward carburetor base surface.

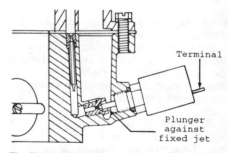

Fig. B913—Fuel pump check valve springs must fit onto spring bosses.

flow through the carburetor when the ignition switch is in off position. Two different systems have been used. Early systems use a vacuum solenoid that blocks vacuum to the fuel bowl, thereby stopping fuel flow through fuel passages. Later systems are found on carburetors with a fixed main fuel jet. A solenoid inserts a plunger into the jet to stop fuel flow.

A view of the vacuum-type anti-afterfire system is shown in Fig. B914. The solenoid is controlled electrically by the ignition switch. The solenoid blocks the fuel bowl vent circuit and allows crankcase vacuum to enter the circuit when the ignition switch is off. Solenoid should "click" if operating properly. All hoses must be clamped tight, without kinks and undamaged. Vacuum block in air cleaner must fit properly.

Refer to Fig. B915 for drawing of anti-afterfire system used on carbure-

Fig. B914—Illustration showing the vacuum-type anti-afterfire system components.

tor with fixed jet. Solenoid can be removed and tested by connecting a 9-volt battery to solenoid. Solenoid plunger should retract when energized and should extend freely when battery is disconnected. A faulty solenoid will affect engine performance.

FUEL PUMP. All parts of the vacuum-diaphragm-type pump are serviced separately. When disassembling pump, take care to prevent damage to pump body (plastic housing) and diaphragm. Inspect diaphragm for punctures, wrinkles or wear. All mounting surfaces must be free of nicks, burrs and debris.

To assemble pump, position diaphragm on carburetor. Place the spring and cup on top of the diaphragm. Install flapper valve springs. Carefully place pump body, remaining diaphragm, gasket and cover plate over carburetor casting and install mounting screws. Tighten screws in a staggered sequence to avoid distortion.

CARBURETOR CONTROL MECHANISM. To assure proper speed control, measure travel of remote control wire with remote control unit installed. Minimum wire travel is $1\frac{3}{8}$ inches (35 mm) as shown in Fig. B916.

To adjust speed control cable on engines with a type number below 1100, move remote control lever to idle position. Carburetor throttle lever should contact idle speed screw. If not, loosen

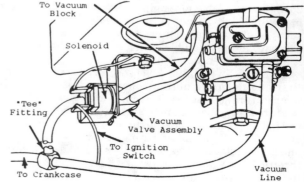

Fig. B915—Carburetors with fixed main jet may be equipped with the anti-afterfire solenoid shown above.

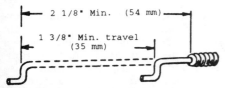

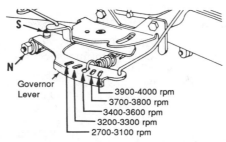

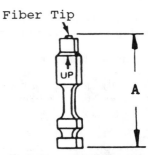

Fiber Tip

Fig. B916—For proper operation, remote control wire must extend to dimension shown above and have minimum travel of 1-3/8 inches (35 mm).

Fig. B918—Governor spring should be installed with end loops as shown. Install loop in appropriate hole in governor lever for engine speed (rpm) desired.

Fig. B920—Breaker-point plunger must be renewed if plunger length (A) is worn to 1.115 inch (28.32 mm) or less.

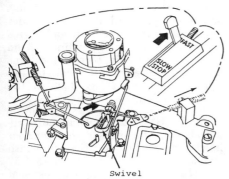

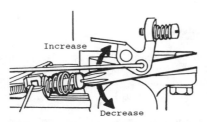

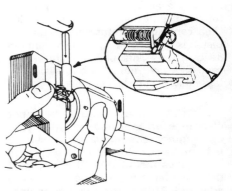

Fig. B917—On engines with type numbers 1100 and above, swivel should be against side of quarter circle when remote control lever is in FAST position.

Fig. B919—Turn top governed speed adjusting screw to obtain desired engine rpm.

Fig. B921—Use a 3/16-inch (5-mm) diameter rod to release wires from Magnetron module. Refer to text.

cable-housing clamp and reposition cable housing.

To adjust speed control cable on engines with type numbers 1100 and above, move remote control lever to FAST position. Swivel shown in Fig. B917 should be against side of quarter circle. If not, loosen cable-housing clamp and reposition cable housing.

Remote choke control should completely close carburetor choke plate when remote control is in "CHOKE" position. If necessary, loosen cable clamp and reposition cable to synchronize carburetor choke and remote control.

GOVERNOR. All models are equipped with a gear-driven mechanical governor. Governor gear and weight assembly is enclosed within the engine and is driven by the camshaft gear.

To adjust governor, loosen nut (N—Fig. B918) securing governor lever to governor shaft (S). Push governor lever counterclockwise until throttle is wide open. Hold lever in this position while rotating governor shaft (S) counterclockwise as far as it will go. Tighten governor lever nut to 100 in.-lbs. (11.3 N•m).

To adjust top governed speed on engines with a type number below 1100, first adjust carburetor and governed idle as outlined in CARBURETOR section. Install governor spring end loop in appropriate hole in governor lever for desired engine rpm as shown in Fig. B918. Check engine top governed speed using an accurate tachometer.

To adjust top governed speed on engines with type numbers 1100 and

above, first adjust carburetor and governed idle as outlined in CARBURETOR section. Turn top governed speed adjusting screw shown in Fig. B919 until desired engine rpm is obtained. Check engine rpm using an accurate tachometer.

IGNITION SYSTEM. Early production engines were equipped with a flywheel-type magneto ignition with points, condenser and coil located externally on engine. Late production engines are equipped with a "Magnetron" breakerless ignition system.

Refer to appropriate paragraph for model being serviced.

Flywheel Magneto Ignition. The flywheel magneto system consists of a permanent magnet cast into flywheel, armature and coil assembly, breaker points and condenser.

Breaker points and condenser are located under or behind intake manifold and are protected by a metal cover that must be sealed around edges and at wire entry location to prevent entry of dirt or moisture.

Breaker point gap should be 0.020 inch (0.52 mm) for all models.

A plunger that rides on the camshaft actuates the breaker points (Fig. B920). The plunger is installed with the smaller diameter end toward breaker points. Renew plunger if length is 1.115 inch (28.32 mm) or less. Renew plunger seal by installing seal on plunger (make certain it is securely attached) and installing seal and plunger assembly into plunger bore. Slide seal over plunger bore. Slide seal over plunger boss until seated against casting at base of boss.

Armature air gap should be 0.010-0.014 inch (0.25-0.36 mm) and is adjusted by loosening armature retaining bolts and moving armature as necessary on slotted holes. Tighten armature retaining bolts.

Magnetron Ignition. "Magnetron" ignition consists of permanent magnets cast in flywheel and a self-contained transistor module mounted on the ignition armature.

To check ignition, attach B&S tester number 19051 to each spark plug lead and ground tester to engine. Spin flywheel at least 350 rpm. If spark jumps the 0.166 inch (4.2 mm) tester gap, ignition system is operating satisfactorily.

Air gap between armature laminations and flywheel magnets should be 0.008-0.012 inch (0.20-0.30 mm) and is adjusted by loosening armature retaining bolts and moving armature as necessary on slotted holes. Tighten armature bolts.

Flywheel does not need to be removed to service Magnetron ignition except to check condition of flywheel key or keyway.

To remove Magnetron module from armature, remove stop switch wire, module primary wire and armature primary wire from module by using a 3/16-inch (5 mm) diameter rod to release spring and retainer (Fig. B921). Remove spring and retainer clip. Unsolder wires. Remove module by pulling out on module retainer while pushing down on module until free of armature laminations.

During installation, use 60/40 rosin core solder and make certain all wires are held firmly against coil body with tape, Permatex No. 2 or equivalent gasket sealer.

VALVE ADJUSTMENT. To correctly set tappet clearance, remove spark plug and insert a suitable measuring tool through spark plug hole. Rotate crankshaft in normal direction (clockwise at flywheel) so piston is at top dead center on compression stroke, then continue to rotate crankshaft so piston is $\frac{1}{4}$ inch (6.4 mm) down from top dead center. This position places the tappets away from the compression release devices on the cam lobes.

NOTE: When adjusting valve tappet clearance on an opposed twin-cylinder engine, recommended procedure is to make sure that the valve springs are always installed on the valves of the cylinder opposite the one being adjusted. This keeps tension against the camshaft for more accurate "operational" clearance settings.

If valve springs are installed, stem end clearance should be 0.007-0.009 inch (0.18-0.23 mm) for exhaust valves and 0.004-0.006 inch (0.10-0.15 mm) for intake valves. Without springs, stem end clearance should be 0.009-0.011 inch (0.23-0.28 mm) for exhaust valves and 0.006-0.008 inch (0.15-0.23 mm) for intake valves. If clearance is less than specified, grind end of stem as necessary. If clearance is excessive, grind the valve seat deeper as necessary or renew the valve.

COMPRESSION PRESSURE. Briggs & Stratton does not publish compression pressure specifications. Compression pressure can be measured at maximum cranking speed and compared; readings should not vary more than 25 percent between cylinders.

An alternate method of determining internal engine condition and wear is by using a cylinder leak-down tester. The tester is available commercially or through Briggs & Stratton (part No. 19413). The tester uses compressed air to pressurize the combustion chamber, then gauges the amount of leakage past the piston rings and valves. Instructions are included with the tester.

CYLINDER HEAD. Combustion deposits should be removed at intervals of 100 to 300 hours, or whenever cylinder head is removed.

REPAIRS

TIGHTENING TORQUE. Recommended tightening torque specifications are as follows:

Carburetor mounting screws	100 in.-lbs. (11.3 N•m)
Connecting rod	190 in.-lbs. (22 N•m)
Crankcase cover: Horizontal crank	225 in.-lbs. (25.4 N•m)
Vertical crank— Aluminum	27 ft.-lbs. (36.7 N•m)
Steel	250 in.-lbs. (28.2 N•m)
Cylinder head	160 in.-lbs. (18 N•m)
Engine base: Horizontal crank	27 ft.-lbs. (36.7 N•m)
Vertical crank	225 in.-lbs. (25.4 N•m)
Flywheel nut	150 ft.-lbs. (204 N•m)
Intake manifold	90 in.-lbs. (10.2 N•m)
Spark plug	200 in.-lbs. (22.6 N•m)

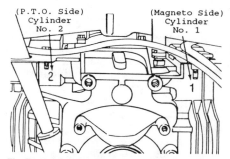

Fig. B922—Cylinder numbers are cast on the tappet chambers on flywheel side of engine. Cylinder heads are also identified (Fig. B923) and must be installed on the corresponding cylinder.

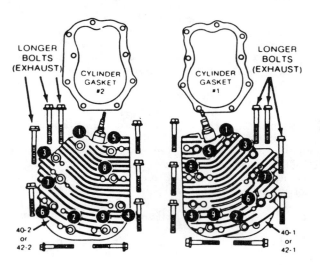

CYLINDER HEADS. When removing cylinder heads, note locations from which different length retaining screws are removed as they must be reinstalled in their original positions. Also note that cylinder heads and cylinders are numbered and heads must be reinstalled on corresponding cylinders. See Figs. B922 and B923.

Always use a new gasket when reinstalling cylinder head. Do not use sealer on gasket. Lubricate cylinder head retaining screw threads with graphite grease. Install cylinder head retaining screws in correct locations and tighten evenly in several steps in sequence shown in Fig. B923 to 160 in.-lbs. (18 N•m).

VALVE SYSTEM. Valves seat in renewable inserts pressed into cylinder head surfaces of block. Valve seat width should be $\frac{3}{64}$ to $\frac{1}{16}$ inch (1.17 to 1.57 mm). Seat angle is 45° for exhaust seat and 30° for intake seat. If seats are loose, check clearance between seat and cylinder block counterbore using a 0.005 inch (0.13 mm) feeler gauge. If feeler gauge cannot be inserted between seat and cylinder block, peen seat as shown in Fig. B924. If feeler gauge can be inserted between seat and cylinder block, renew seat. Use a suitable puller such as B&S tool 19138 to remove valve seat insert. Drive new seat into cylinder block until it bottoms, peen seat as shown in Fig. B924 and grind to correct angle.

Valves should be refaced at a 45° angle for exhaust valves and at a 30° angle for intake valves. Valves should be rejected if margin is less than $\frac{1}{64}$ inch (0.10 mm). See Fig. B925.

Valve guides should be checked for wear using valve guide gauge (B&S tool 19151). If gauge enters guide $\frac{5}{16}$ inch (7.9 mm) or more, guide should be reconditioned or renewed.

Fig. B923—Note locations of various length cylinder head screws. Long screws are used around exhaust valve area. Screws should be tightened in sequence shown to 160 in.-lb. (18 N•m) torque.

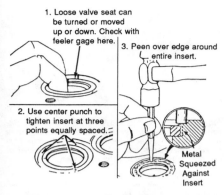

Fig. B924—Loose valve seat inserts can be tightened or renewed as shown. If a 0.005 inch (0.125 mm) feeler gauge can be inserted between seat and seat bore, install an oversize insert or renew cylinder.

1. Loose valve seat can be turned or moved up or down. Check with feeler gage here.
2. Use center punch to tighten insert at three points equally spaced.
3. Peen over edge around entire insert.

Metal Squeezed Against Insert

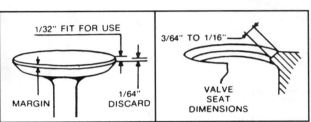

Fig. B925—Drawing showing correct valve face and seat dimensions. Refer to text.

1/32" FIT FOR USE
3/64" TO 1/16"
MARGIN
1/64" DISCARD
VALVE SEAT DIMENSIONS

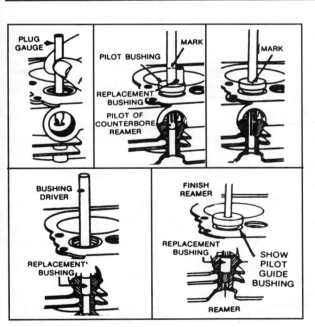

Fig. B926—Drawing showing correct procedure for reconditioning valve guides. Refer to text.

PLUG GAUGE
PILOT BUSHING
MARK
MARK
REPLACEMENT BUSHING
PILOT OF COUNTERBORE REAMER
BUSHING DRIVER
REPLACEMENT BUSHING
FINISH REAMER
REPLACEMENT BUSHING
SHOW PILOT GUIDE BUSHING
REAMER

(.366" O.D.) BRASS	(.367" O.D.) BRASS	(.379"O.D.) BRASS	(.440" O.D.) GRAY	(.441" O.D.) COPPER
USE 231218	USE 231218	USE 230655	USE 261961	USE 261961

Fig. B927—Use correct bushing when renewing valve guide bushings. Refer to adjacent illustration to identify bushing.

To recondition aluminum valve guides, use B&S tool kit 19232. Place reamer 19231 and guide 19234 in worn guide and center with valve seat. Mark reamer 1⁄16 inch (1.57 mm) above top edge of service bushing (Fig. B926). Ream worn guide until mark on reamer is flush with top of guide bushing. DO NOT ream completely through guide. Place service bushing, part 231218, on driver 19204 so grooved end of bushing will enter guide bore first. Press bushing into guide until it bottoms. Finish ream completely through guide using reamer 19233 and guide 19234. Lubricate reamer with kerosene during reaming procedure.

To renew brass or sintered iron guides, use tap 19264 to thread worn guide bushing approximately 1⁄2 inch (12.7 mm) deep. DO NOT thread more than 1 inch (25.4 mm) deep. Install puller washer 19240 on puller screw 19238 and thread screw and washer assembly into worn guide. Center washer on valve seat and tighten puller nut 19239 against washer, continue to tighten while keeping threaded screw from turning until guide has been removed. Use Fig. B927 to identify the guide and find appropriate replacement. Place correct service bushing on driver 19204 so that the two grooves on service bushings 231218 are down. Remaining bushing types can be installed either way. Press bushing in until it bottoms. Finish ream with reamer 19233 and reamer guide 19234. Lubricate reamer with kerosene and ream completely through new service bushing.

When reinstalling valves, note that exhaust valve spring is shorter, has heavier diameter coils and is usually painted red. Intake valve has a stem seal that should be renewed if valve has been removed.

CAMSHAFT. Camshaft and camshaft gear are an integral part that ride on journals at each end of camshaft. Camshaft on pressure lubricated models has an oil passage that extends through the center of the camshaft. Note that camshafts cannot be interchanged between pressure lubricated and splash lubricated models.

To remove camshaft, refer to appropriate paragraph in CRANKSHAFT section for model being serviced.

Camshaft should be renewed if gear teeth or lobes are worn or damaged. Reject camshaft if either bearing journal diameter is 0.623 inch (15.82 mm) or less. Refer to the table below for cam lobe reject dimensions.

CAM LOBE REJECT SIZES

Series	Intake	Exhaust
404000	1.055 in. (26.8 mm)	1.120 in. (28.45 mm)
460700	1.140 in. (28.96 mm)	1.140 in. (28.96 mm)
All other models	1.150 in. (29.21 mm)	1.120 in. (28.45 mm)

Be sure that oil passage in camshaft is open and clean on pressure-lubricated models. When installing the camshaft, be sure that timing marks are aligned as shown in Fig. B928 or Fig. B929.

PISTONS, PINS AND RINGS. Pistons used in engines with cast iron cylinder liners (Series 400400, 400700, 402400, 402440, 402700, 402770,

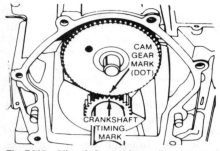

Fig. B928—Align timing marks as shown on models having main bearings as an integral part of crankcase, cover or engine base. Refer to text.

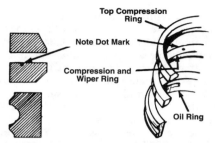

Fig. B930—Drawing of piston rings showing correct installation. Be sure dot mark on second compression ring is toward piston crown.

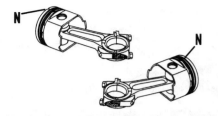

Fig. B932—On Series 460700 engines, install piston and connecting rod assemblies with notches (N) in piston heads facing flywheel, and machined relief area and oil hole on angled end of connecting rods facing the camshaft.

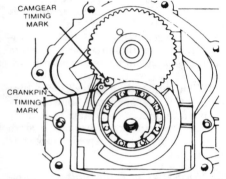

Fig. B929—Align timing marks as shown on models having ball bearing-type main bearings. Refer to text.

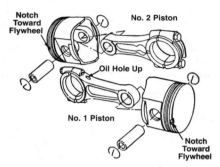

Fig. B931—Install pistons on connecting rods so notches on top of pistons are toward flywheel. Oil hole in No. 1 connecting rod should face toward camshaft, and oil hole in No. 2 connecting rod should face away from camshaft.

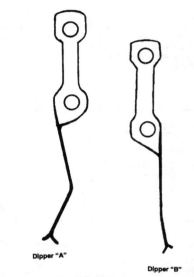

Fig. B933—Different oil dippers used on splash-lubricated, horizontal crankshaft engines. When installing angled-style dipper (A) on Series 421400 and 422400 engines with oil trough, the trough must be removed and discarded.

422400, 422440, 422700, 422770 and 460700) have a shiny finish, and on early models, were marked with an "L" on piston crown. A dull-finish chrome-plated aluminum piston is used in aluminum (Kool-Bore) cylinders. Pistons and piston rings WILL NOT interchange in cast iron and aluminum cylinders.

Pistons for all models should be renewed if they are scored or damaged, or if a 0.009 inch (0.23 mm) feeler gauge can be inserted between a new top ring and ring groove. Refer to the following table for piston ring end gap rejection sizes:

Model Series	Compression Ring	Oil Ring
401400, 401700, 421400, 421700	0.035 in. (0.89 mm)	0.045 in. (1.14 mm)
All Other Models	0.030 in. (0.76 mm)	0.035 in. (0.89 mm)

Pistons and rings are available in several oversizes as well as standard bore size.

Piston pin is a slip fit in both piston and connecting rod bores. If piston pin bore measures 0.802 inch (20.37 mm) or more, piston should be renewed or pin bore reamed for 0.005 inch (0.127 mm) oversize pin. Standard piston pin diam-

eter is 0.8003-0.8005 inch (20.32-20.33 mm) and should be renewed if worn or out-of-round more than 0.0005 inch (0.0127 mm). A 0.005 inch (0.127 mm) oversize pin is available for all models.

Install piston rings on piston as shown in Fig. B930. Arrange piston rings so end gaps are staggered around piston. Install pistons so notch in piston crown is toward flywheel side of engine as shown in Fig. B931 or Fig. B932.

CONNECTING RODS. Connecting rods and pistons are removed from cylinder head end of block as an assembly after first removing cylinder head, crankcase cover or engine base. Identify pistons and connecting rods so they can be reinstalled in original cylinder.

Aluminum alloy connecting rods ride directly on crankpin journals. Connecting rod should be renewed if crankpin bearing bore measures 1.627 inches (41.33 mm) or more, if bearing surfaces are scored or damaged, or if pin bore measures 0.802 inch (20.37 mm) or more. A 0.005 inch (0.127 mm) oversize piston pin is available, as well as a 0.020 inch (0.50 mm) undersize connecting rod.

NOTE: Connecting rods of Series 402440, 402770, 422440, 422770 and 460700 (pressure lubricated) are not interchangeable with other models (splash lubricated).

Connecting rod on all engines except Series 460700 should be assembled to piston so oil hole in No. 1 connecting rod is toward cam gear side of engine and notch on top of piston is toward flywheel with piston and rod assembly installed. Oil hole in No. 2 connecting rod should face away from camshaft. See Fig. B931.

On Series 460700 engines, connecting rods should be assembled to pistons so notches on top of pistons will face the flywheel (Fig. B932) when installed in the engine. Machined relief area and oil hole on angled end of crankshaft rod journal should both be facing the camshaft when the piston and rod assemblies are installed in the engine.

On all engines, make certain match marks on connecting rod and cap are aligned.

NOTE: Splash lubricated, horizontal crankshaft engines operating above 2400 rpm top no-load speeds should have one B&S No. 222480 angled-style oil dipper (A—Fig. B933) mounted on the No. 1 connecting rod. Splash lubricated, horizontal crankshaft engines

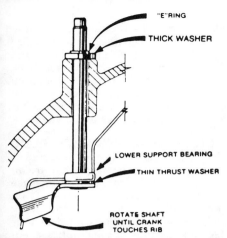

Fig. B934—Cross-sectional view of early governor shaft assembly. To disassemble, remove "E" ring and washer. Carefully guide shaft down past crankshaft.

operating at or below 2400 rpm top no-load speed should have B&S No. 222480 angled-style oil dipper mounted on No. 1 connecting rod and B&S No. 223053 straight-style oil dipper (B—Fig. B933) mounted on No. 2 connecting rod.

IMPORTANT: DO NOT use second oil dipper on No. 2 connecting rod if engine is equipped with low-oil sensor, and remove oil trough from crankcase when installing B&S No. 222480 oil dipper on Series 421400 and 422400 engines.

Install special washers and nuts and tighten to 190 in.-lbs. (22 N•m) for all models.

GOVERNOR. To remove governor shaft, loosen nut and remove governor lever. Remove crankcase cover or engine base. To obtain maximum clearance, rotate crankshaft until timing mark on crankshaft gear is at approximately 10 o'clock position. If equipped with ball bearings, rotate crankshaft to obtain clearance with crankshaft counterweight. On early models (see Fig. B934), remove "E" ring and thick washer on outer end of governor shaft and slide shaft out. On models equipped with two "E" rings (see Fig. B935), detach the two rings and slide out shaft. On models with type numbers 1100 and above (shown in Fig. B936), detach "E" ring and slide out shaft. On all models, it may be necessary to rotate crankshaft to gain clearance for governor shaft removal. DO NOT force shaft against crankshaft when removing.

Later models (Figs. B935 and B936) use a renewable governor shaft bushing. Use suitable tools for removal and installation of bushing. Drive or pull

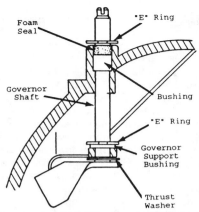

Fig. B935—Drawing of governor shaft assembly used on models below type number 1100 equipped with two "E" rings.

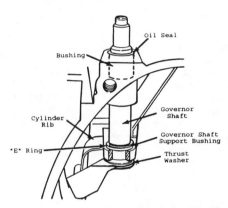

Fig. B936—Drawing of governor shaft assembly used on models with type numbers 1100 and above.

bushing out toward outside of crankcase. Bushing should bottom against shoulder in bore during installation.

After installation, rotate governor shaft so governor arm is against cylinder rib.

Governor gear assembly is available only as a unit assembly. Be sure the assembly rotates and operates freely without binding. Note that there is a thrust washer located between gear assembly and boss. Refer to MAINTENANCE section for governor adjustment.

OIL PUMP. Pressure lubricated engines are equipped with rotor-type oil pump. A slot in the end of the camshaft engages and drives the oil pump shaft on vertical crankshaft engines (Fig. B937). On horizontal crankshaft engines, a separate gear that meshes with the camshaft gear drives the oil pump shaft (Fig. B938).

The oil pump on vertical crankshaft models is accessible by removing pump cover on bottom of sump. On horizontal crankshaft models it is necessary to remove crankcase cover for access to oil pump. Inspect pump components and renew if damaged.

The pump relief valve is located in the oil filter adapter shown in Fig. B939. Remove adapter from crankcase while being careful not to drop spring and ball. Spring length must be 1.091-1.159 inches (27.71-29.44 mm), otherwise reject spring.

CRANKSHAFT. Crankshaft and camshaft used on pressure lubricated engines are dissimilar and not interchangeable with crankshaft and camshaft of splash lubricated engines.

To remove crankshaft from engines with integral-type or DU-type bearings, remove necessary air shrouds. Remove flywheel and front gear cover or sump. Remove connecting rod caps. Remove cam gear making certain valve tappets clear camshaft lobes. Remove crankshaft.

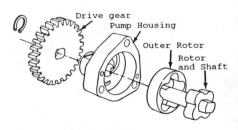

Fig. B938—Exploded view of oil pump used on horizontal crankshaft engines.

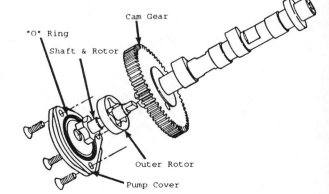

Fig. B937—Exploded view of oil pump used on vertical crankshaft engines.

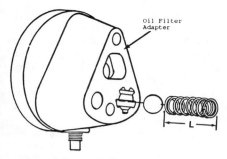

Oil Filter
Adapter

Fig. B939—Relief valve spring length (L) must be 1.091-1.159 inches (27.271-29.44 mm), otherwise reject spring.

When installing the crankshaft, make certain the timing marks are aligned as shown in Fig. B928.

To remove crankshaft from engines with ball bearing main bearing, remove all necessary air shrouds and remove flywheel. Remove front gear cover or sump. Remove connecting rod caps. Compress exhaust and intake valve springs on number two cylinder to provide clearance for camshaft lobes. Remove crankshaft and camshaft together.

When installing the crankshaft, make certain the timing marks are aligned as shown in Fig. B929.

Renew crankshaft if main bearing journal at either end is 1.376 inches (34.95 mm) or less. Renew or regrind crankshaft if crankpin journal diameter is 1.622 inches (41.15 mm) or less. A 0.020 inch (0.51 mm) undersize connecting rod is available.

Crankshaft end play is 0.002-0.026 inch (0.05-0.66 mm) for vertical crankshaft engines and 0.004-0.012 inch (0.10-0.30 mm) for horizontal crankshaft engines. End play should be initially checked with one 0.015 inch (0.4 mm) thick gasket in place. Additional gaskets of 0.005 inch (0.13 mm) and 0.009 inch (0.23 mm) thickness are available if end play is less than minimum specification. If end play is more than maximum specification, metal shims are available for installation between crankshaft gear and cover or sump. Do not use shims on engines with double ball bearings.

CYLINDERS. Cylinder bores may be either aluminum or a cast iron liner that is an integral part of the cylinder block casting. Pistons and piston rings are not interchangeable between the two types. Series 400400, 400700, 402400, 402440, 402700, 402770, 422400, 422440, 422700, 422770 and 460700 engines have cast iron cylinder liners as an integral part of cylinder block casting. Series 401400, 401700, 421400 and 421700 have aluminum cylinder bores (Kool-Bore).

Standard cylinder bore diameter for all models is 3.4365-3.4375 inches (87.287-87.312 mm). Cylinder should be resized if more than 0.003 inch (0.076 mm) oversize or 0.0015 inch (0.038 mm) out-of-round for cast iron bore, or 0.003 inch (0.076 mm) oversize or 0.0025 inch (0.064 mm) out-of-round for aluminum bore. Use a suitable hone such as B&S tool 19205 for aluminum bore or B&S tool 19211 for cast iron bore. Resize to nearest oversize for which piston and rings are available.

CRANKCASE AND MAIN BEARINGS. Crankshaft may be supported at each end in main bearings that are an integral part of crankcase, crankcase cover or engine base. Crankshaft on some models may be supported by DU-type bearings. Some models may use ball bearings in the crankcase, engine base or crankcase cover to support the crankshaft. See Fig. B940 or Fig. B941.

Ball bearing main bearing is a press fit on crankshaft and must be removed by pressing crankshaft out of bearing. Renew ball bearing if worn or rough. Expand new bearing by heating in oil and install with shield side toward crankpin. If ball bearing is loose in crankcase, crankcase cover or engine base bores, renew crankcase, crankcase cover or engine base.

Integral-type main bearings should be reamed out and service bushings installed if bearings are 0.0007 inch (0.018 mm) or more out-of-round or if diameter is 1.383 inches (35.12 mm) or more. Special reamers are available from Briggs & Stratton.

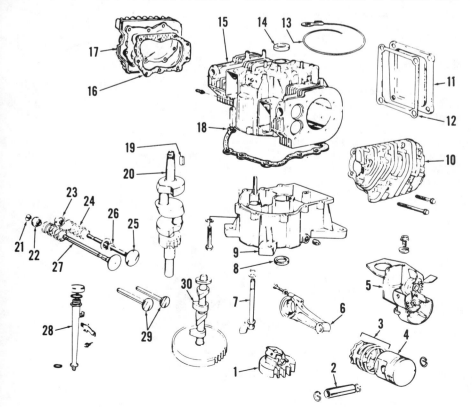

Fig. B940—Exploded view of engine assembly typical of all vertical crankshaft models.

1. Governor gear
2. Piston pin & clips
3. Piston rings
4. Piston
5. Oil slinger assy.
6. Connecting rod
7. Governor shaft assy.
8. Oil seal
9. Engine base
10. Cylinder head
11. Crankcase cover
12. Crankcase gasket
13. Ground wire
14. Oil seal
15. Cylinder/crankcase assy.
16. Head gasket
17. Cylinder head
18. Gasket
19. Key
20. Crankshaft
21. Retainer
22. Rotocoil (exhaust valve)
23. Retainer (intake valve)
24. Valve spring (2)
25. Intake valve
26. Seal & retainer assy.
27. Exhaust valve
28. Oil dipstick
29. Valve tappet (2)
30. Camshaft

Fig. B941—Exploded view of engine typical of all horizontal crankshaft models.

1. Cylinder/crankcase assy.
2. Oil seal
3. Dipstick
4. Piston pin & clips
5. Piston rings
6. Piston
7. Engine base
8. Gasket
9. Valve tappets
10. Exhaust valve
11. Intake valve
12. Valve spring
13. Governor gear assy.
14. Intake valve retainer
15. Rotocoil (exhaust valve)
16. Governor shaft
17. Camshaft
18. Oil seal
19. Crankcase cover
20. Head gasket
21. Cylinder head
22. Elbow connector
23. Fuel line
24. Crankshaft
25. Gasket
26. Key
27. Oil dipper
28. Connecting rods

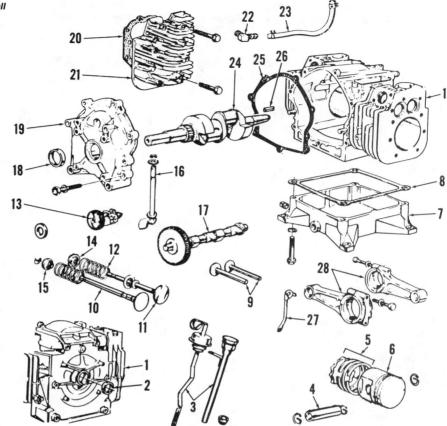

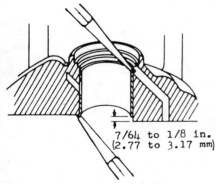

Fig. B942—Press DU-type bushings in until 1/8 inch (3.2 mm) from thrust surface. Make certain the oil holes are aligned. Stake bushing as shown. Refer to text.

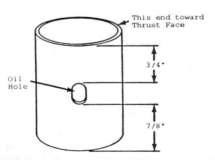

Fig. B943—The pto DU-type bushing on vertical crankshaft models must be installed so oil hole is nearer thrust face of engine base.

DU-type main bearings should be renewed if bearings are 0.0007 inch (0.0178 mm) or more out-of-round or if diameter is 1.383 inches (35.12 mm) or more.

Worn DU-type bearings are pressed out of bores using B&S cylinder support 19227 and driver 19226. Note that pto main bearing of pressure lubricated models has an oil groove in inner diameter. Make certain oil holes in bearings align with oil holes in block and crankcase cover or sump. Press bearings in until they are $\frac{1}{8}$ inch (3.2 mm) below thrust face, except on pto main bearing of vertical crankshaft models discussed in following paragraph. Stake bearings into place. See Fig. B942.

The pto DU bearing on vertical crankshaft models must be installed so oil hole is nearer thrust face of engine base. See Fig. B943. Install bearing so oil hole is aligned and end of bearing is $\frac{1}{32}$ inch (0.8 mm) from thrust face on pressure lubricated models, or $\frac{5}{32}$ inch (4.0 mm) on splash lubricated models. Stake bearing in two places after installation.

NOTE: Models 421400 and 422400 are equipped with an oil trough in the crankcase that encloses the original oil dipper on No. 1 connecting rod. When installing B&S No. 222480 oil dipper (A—Fig. B933) on No. 1 connecting rod on these engines equipped with a trough, the trough MUST BE REMOVED and discarded.

Tighten crankcase cover screws on horizontal crankshaft engines to 225 in.-lbs. (25.4 N•m). Tighten crankcase cover screws on vertical crankshaft engines with an aluminum cover to 27 ft.-lbs. (36.7 N•m), or if equipped with a steel cover, to 250 in.-lbs. (28.2 N•m). Tighten engine base retaining screws on horizontal crankshaft engines to 27 ft.-lbs. (36.7 N•m). Tighten engine base retaining screws on vertical crankshaft engines to 225 in.-lbs. (25.4 N•m).

BRIGGS & STRATTON

BRIGGS & STRATTON CORPORATION
Milwaukee, Wisconsin 53201

INTEK V-TWIN ENGINES

Model Series	No. Cyls.	Bore	Stroke	Displacement	Power Rating
405700	2	2.97 in. (75.4 mm)	2.89 in. (73.4 mm)	40.0 cu. in. (656 cc)	18.0 hp (13.4 kW)
406700	2	2.97 in. (75.4 mm)	2.89 in. (73.4 mm)	40.0 cu. in. (656 cc)	20.0 hp (14.9 kW)
407700	1	2.97 in. (75.4 mm)	2.89 in. (73.4 mm)	40.0 cu. in. (656 cc)	22.0 hp (16.4 kW)
445700	2	3.12 in. (79.25 mm)	2.89 in. (73.4 mm)	44.2 cu. in. (724 cc)	25.0 hp (18.6 kW)

NOTE: U.S. Standard fasteners are used throughout the engine except rocker arm support screw and rocker arm locknut, which are Metric.

The Intek models included in this section are overhead-valve, four-stroke, vertical crankshaft engines having two cylinders mounted in a 90° V configuration. Number one cylinder is the cylinder closest to the flywheel.

Refer to BRIGGS & STRATTON ENGINE IDENTIFICATION section for engine identification. Engine model, type and code numbers are necessary when ordering parts.

MAINTENANCE

LUBRICATION. These engines use a filtered, full-pressure lubrication system. A camshaft-driven, gerotor-type pump mounted in the engine sump supplies the pressurized oil to the system.

Periodically check the oil level; do not overfill. The oil dipstick should be screwed in until bottomed for correct oil level reading. Clean the dipstick and cap before removing.

Change oil and filter after first eight hours of operation and every 50 hours thereafter under normal operating conditions, or more often under severe operating conditions. Drain the oil while the engine is warm. The oil will flow freely and carry away more impurities.

Manufacturer recommends using oil with an API service classification of SH or SJ or any classification formulated to supercede SH or SJ. Use SAE 30 oil for temperatures above 40° F (4° C), SAE 10W-30 oil for temperatures between 0° F (−18° C) and 40° F (4° C), and below 0° F (−18° C), use petroleum based SAE 5W-20 or a suitable synthetic oil. Do not use 10W-40 oil.

Crankcase capacity is 4 pints (1.9 liters) with a new oil filter and 3¾ pints (1.8 liters) without oil filter.

A low-oil pressure switch is located on the oil filter housing. Switch should be closed at zero pressure and open at approximately 4.5 psi (31 kPa).

AIR FILTER. The air filter used on these engines is a dual-element filter consisting of a pleated paper main cartridge and a foam-type pre-cleaner. Recommended service intervals are 25 hours for pre-cleaner and 100 hours for main cartridge for normal operating conditions. Service the filter more often under severe operating conditions.

NOTE: Filter system is a reverse-flow design. Area of filter visible after removing the filter cover is the clean (carburetor) side of the filter. Filter elements must be removed to inspect the atmospheric-air side of the filter. Integrity of the cover seal and blower housing-to-carburetor air box should also be checked when servicing the air filter.

FUEL FILTER. An in-line fuel filter is mounted downstream of the equipment fuel tank. The tank may also be equipped with a separate filter at the fuel outlet fitting. Check filter(s) periodically during the operating season. Annual replacement of the in-line filter is recommended.

CRANKCASE BREATHER. The engine is equipped with a reed valve-style crankcase breather that maintains a partial vacuum in the crankcase during engine operation. The breather is vented to the engine intake.

A mesh-style collector baffle is located below the breather in the breather chamber. It allows oil vapors to collect and drain back into the crankcase, thus minimizing engine oil ingestion through the breather.

Remove the blower housing and flywheel to gain access to the breather for service. Disconnect the breather tube and remove the three screws attaching breather to the crankcase. Check for a positive seal of the reed valve completely around the breather vent hole. Replace the breather if reed valve is faulty. Inspect the breather tube for damage and replace if necessary.

Install the breather with new gasket. Tighten three mounting screws to 55 in.-lb. (6.2 N•m).

SPARK PLUG. Recommended spark plug is Champion RC12YC. If RC12YC is not available, RC14YC is an acceptable substitute. Spark plug electrode gap should be 0.030 inch (0.76 mm). Tighten spark plug to 180 in.-lb. (20 N•m).

NOTE: Briggs & Stratton does not recommend using abrasive blasting to clean spark plugs as this may introduce abrasive grit into the engine, causing serious internal damage.

CARBURETOR. A dual-venturi, single-float bowl, side-draft carburetor is used on all models. Non-adjustable fixed jets are used on the high-speed and idle circuits. The only adjustment is for idle speed rpm. Carburetor is equipped with a fuel shutoff solenoid that stops the flow of fuel through the carburetor when the ignition switch is turned off, thus preventing engine "run-on."

Overhaul. Refer to Fig. BK1 for carburetor exploded view, and carefully disassemble carburetor. Discard all old gaskets, o-rings and seals.

NOTE: Grinding a slot in the sidewall of 14 mm and 16 mm 6-point deep sockets (Fig. BK2) will aid in the safe removal and installation of main jet and solenoid housing (18—Fig. BK1).

Remove screws attaching float bowl (3—Fig. BK1) to carburetor body. Use a 14-mm deep socket to disassemble the fuel solenoid (1) from the main jet housing (18). Remove hinge pin, float (5) and fuel inlet needle (15). Remove emulsion tube body (17). Remove the cover plate (10). Remove choke plate (12), shaft (13) and seal. Remove the nozzle body (21). The sides of the throttle plates (7) are beveled; mark the plates prior to removal so they can be installed in their original position.

Clean the carburetor parts using a suitable commercial carburetor cleaning solvent. DO NOT use wire, drill bits or other metallic items to clean out carburetor passages. Use compressed air to clean out all passages and openings.

Throttle and choke shafts ride directly in machined bores in carburetor body; service bushings are not available. If shaft-to-bore clearance exceeds 0.010 inch (0.25 mm), shafts and/or carburetor must be replaced.

Use new gaskets and seals when assembling carburetor. Install lip-style seals (9) for throttle and choke shafts with lip facing out. Apply a light coat of

Loctite 222 on throttle plate and choke plate screws. Be sure throttle plates are installed in their original positions. Check plates and shaft for freedom of movement in their bores, and adjust if necessary. Main jet and solenoid housing must be assembled so main jet (19) faces AWAY FROM float hinge. Float level is not adjustable.

Tighten fasteners to the torque values listed in the table below.

Carburetor mounting
screws . . . . 65 in.-lb.
(7.4 N•m)
Intake manifold &
blower housing bolts . . . . . . 80 in.-lb.
(9.0 N•m)
Grass screen screws . . . . 20 in.-lb.
(2.2 N•m)

Fuel shutoff solenoid requires a minimum of 9.0 volts DC to operate. When energized (ignition switch in Run position), the solenoid pulls the plunger away from main jet housing, allowing fuel to flow through the carburetor. To test solenoid, apply a known good 12-volt power supply to solenoid terminal and carburetor body; solenoid should audibly click when power is applied.

NOTE: Solenoid testing is recommended with solenoid installed in carburetor. Testing with solenoid removed from carburetor could cause possible plunger over-travel, and a potentially good solenoid could appear faulty by failing to activate.

CARBURETOR CONTROL MECHANISM. To insure proper speed control, measure the travel of remote control wire with the remote control unit installed. Minimum wire travel is 1⅜ inches (35 mm) as shown in Fig. BK3.

To adjust speed control cable, move remote control lever to Idle position. Carburetor throttle lever should contact idle speed stop screw. If not, loosen cable-housing clamp and reposition cable housing.

Remote choke control should completely close carburetor choke plate when remote control is in Choke position. If not, reposition the cable housing as necessary.

GOVERNOR. Engine is equipped with a mechanical flyweight-type governor mounted in the cylinder block and driven by the camshaft gear.

Perform static adjustment of governor as follows: Loosen the governor lever nut (1—Fig. BK4). Rotate the carburetor throttle lever counterclockwise to wide-open throttle position and hold in this position. Rotate governor shaft (2) clockwise as far as possible. Tighten governor lever nut to 130 in.-lb. (14.6 N•m).

Perform running adjustment of governed idle as follows: All running adjustments are made with the air cleaner installed and engine at normal operating temperature. Connect an accurate tachometer to the engine. Move throttle control to Slow and, while holding carburetor throttle lever against idle speed stop screw (6—Fig. BK1), adjust the screw to obtain 1200 rpm idle speed. Release the throttle lever, and bend governed idle tang (6—Fig. BK4) to obtain governed speed of 1750 rpm. With engine running at governed idle speed, bend throttle restrictor tang (3) to just contact governor lever.

Perform running adjustment of top no-load speed as follows: Move throttle control to Fast position. Compare rpm

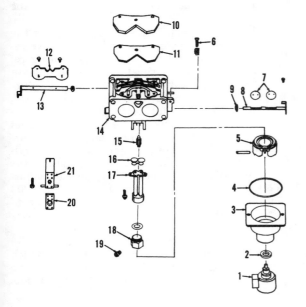

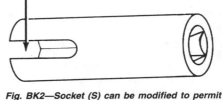

Fig. BK1—Exploded view of 2-barrel carburetor used on V-twin, vertical crankshaft engines.

1. Fuel shutoff solenoid
2. Gasket
3. Float bowl
4. Gasket
5. Float
6. Idle speed adjusting screw
7. Throttle plates
8. Throttle shaft
9. Seal
10. Cover plate
11. Gasket
12. Choke plate
13. Choke shaft
14. Carburetor body
15. Fuel inlet valve
16. Seal
17. Fuel transfer tube
18. Main jet & solenoid housing
19. Main jet
20. Gasket
21. Nozzle

Fig. BK2—Socket (S) can be modified to permit easier removal of carburetor main jet and solenoid housing. Refer to text.

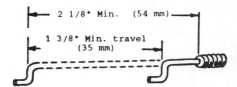

Fig. BK3—Remote control wire must extend and travel to dimensions shown above.

Fig. BK4—View of governor linkage showing adjustment points. Refer to text for adjustment procedure.

1. Clamp nut	4. Control bracket swivel
2. Governor shaft	5. Governor linkage tang
3. Throttle restrictor tang	6. Governed idle tang

with specifications for the equipment. To adjust, bend the governor linkage tang (5—Fig. BK4). If bending tang does not bring rpm to specifications, replace the governor spring and recheck.

IGNITION SYSTEM. All models are equipped with a Magnetron solid-state ignition system.

To check spark, remove spark plug and connect spark plug cable to B&S tester 19368 or other suitable gap-type spark tester. Ground the tester to the engine. Spin flywheel at 350 rpm minimum. If spark jumps the 0.166-inch (4.2-mm) tester gap, system is functioning properly. If spark is weak or nonexistent, remove engine blower housing and disconnect stop switch wire from module. Retest for spark. If the retest produces spark, engine kill circuit is faulty; locate problem and correct it. If retest still produces insufficient spark, replace the Magnetron module.

Air gap between flywheel and armature should be 0.008-0.012 inch (0.20-0.30 mm). Tighten armature screws to 25 in.-lb. (2.8 N•m).

To prevent crossfire between the ignition module, both stop switch wires running from the modules to the common kill terminal each contain a diode. If, when attempting to start or stop the engine, any of the following problems are encountered, the diode in one or both kill wires is likely at fault.

1. Will not start due to no spark from either module.
2. Only runs on one cylinder.
3. Only shuts off one cylinder.
4. Continues to run with ignition turned off.

Test the diodes. If one or both diodes test faulty, replace the kill wire assembly, as individual diodes are not replaceable.

COMPRESSION PRESSURE. Briggs & Stratton does not publish compression pressure specifications. Compression pressure measured at cranking speed should not vary more than 25 percent between cylinders.

An alternate method of determining internal engine condition is by using a cylinder leak-down tester. The tester is available commercially or from Briggs & Stratton (part No. 19413). Tester uses compressed air to pressurize the combustion chamber, then gauges the amount of leakage past cylinder, piston, rings and valves. Instructions are included with tester.

CYLINDER HEAD. Manufacturer recommends that the cylinder heads be removed and cleaned of deposits after every 500 hours of operation.

REPAIRS

TIGHTENING TORQUE. Recommended tightening torque specifications are as follows:

Alternator stator	20 in.-lb.
	(2.2 N•m)
Base/oil sump	200 in.-lb.
	(22.6 N•m)
Blower housing	80 in.-lb.
	(9.0 N•m)
Breather screws	55 in.-lb.
	(6.2 N•m)
Carburetor mounting screws	65 in.-lb.
	(7.4 N•m)
Connecting rod	100 in.-lb.
	(11.2 N•m)
Cylinder back-plate	100 in.-lb.
	(11.2 N•m)
Cylinder head	220 in.-lb.
	(25.0 N•m)
Exhaust manifold	140 in.-lb.
	(16.0 N•m)
Fan retainer	140 in.-lb.
	(16.0 N•m)
Flywheel nut	150 ft.-lb.
	(203 N•m)
Fuel pump	80 in.-lb.
	(9.0 N•m)
Governor control bracket	80 in.-lb.
	(9.0 N•m)
Governor lever nut	130 in.-lb.
	(14.6 N•m)
Ignition module	25 in.-lb.
	(2.8 N•m)
Intake manifold	80 in.-lb.
	(9.0 N•m)
Oil fill tube	20-24 in.-lb.
	(2.3-2.7 N•m)
Oil drain plug	125 in.-lb.
	(14.0 N•m)
Oil pump cover	50 in.-lb.
	(5.6 N•m)
Rocker arm	100 in.-lb.
	(11.2 N•m)
Rocker arm nut	60 in.-lb.
	(6.6 N•m)
Rocker cover	100 in.-lb.
	(11.2 N•m)
Spark plug	180 in.-lb.
	(20.0 N•m)
Starter motor	140 in.-lb.
	(15.8 N•m)
Starter thru-bolts	50 in.-lb.
	(5.6 N•m)
Valley cover	45 in.-lb.
	(5.0 N•m)

CYLINDER HEADS AND VALVE SYSTEM. Cylinder heads are not interchangeable. Cylinder head number is cast between the rocker arm support posts. Number one cylinder is always the cylinder closest to the flywheel.

To remove heads (7 and 11—Fig. BK5), first remove external parts such as chaff screen (1), blower housing (2), air cleaner assembly, carburetor and intake manifold, governor lever (9) and control bracket (10), muffler, cooling shields (8) and spark plugs. Remove rocker covers, rocker arm supports, rocker arms and push rods.

NOTE: Mark and identify valve train components so they can be installed in the same positions as removed. Push rods are not interchangeable: Intake valve push rods are aluminum, exhaust valve push rods are steel.

Remove cylinder head bolts and remove cylinder heads and gaskets. Be careful not to lose the cylinder head alignment dowels when removing the heads.

To remove the valves, compress the valve spring and remove the valve retainer locks (7—Fig. BK6), spring retainer (6), spring (5) and valve. Remove intake valve stem seal (8) and discard.

Thoroughly clean the cylinder head, being careful not to damage the machined surface of the head. Check head for cracks or other damage. Use a surface plate or straightedge to check cylinder head mounting surface for distortion. Replace the head if mounting surface is warped in excess of 0.004 inch (0.10 mm). Resurfacing the cylinder head mounting surface is not recommended.

Valve face and seat angles are 45°. Specified seat width is 0.047-0.063 inch (1.2-1.6 mm). Minimum allowable valve margin is 1/32 inch (0.8 mm). Refer to Fig. BK7.

Fig. BK5—Exploded view of engine components typical of all models.

1. Screen
2. Blower housing
3. Fan
4. Backplate
5. Alternator
6. Push rods
7. Cylinder head #2
8. Air shield
9. Governor lever
10. Control bracket
11. Cylinder head #1
12. Starter motor
13. Ignition module
14. Flywheel

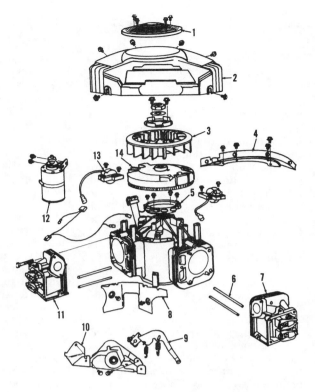

engine cold, using the following recommended procedure:

Remove spark plugs and valve covers. Rotate crankshaft in normal direction (clockwise at flywheel) to locate the number one piston at top dead center (TDC) on compression stroke (both valves closed). Insert a narrow scale into the spark plug hole, then continue to rotate crankshaft so piston is ¼ inch (6.4 mm) down from top dead center. This position places the tappet away from the compression release device on the cam lobe.

Using feeler gauges, measure the clearance between rocker arms and valve stem ends. Valve clearance should be 0.004-0.006 inch (0.10-0.15 mm) for both intake and exhaust.

To adjust, loosen jam nut and turn rocker arm adjusting screw (13—Fig. BK6) to obtain proper clearance. After setting clearance, hold the adjusting screw in place and tighten jam nut to 60 in.-lb. (6.6 N•m). Install the rocker cover with a new gasket, and tighten the screws evenly to 100 in.-lb. (11.2 N•m).

Repeat the procedure for the number two cylinder.

CAMSHAFT. The camshaft gear, compression release mechanism and camshaft (6—Fig. BK9) are serviced as an assembly. Individual parts are not available.

Prior to removing camshaft, engine must be disassembled, including all external components, cylinder heads, valve train, flywheel and starter motor.

Valve seats can be reconditioned using a valve seat cutter. If seats are damage to the point that they cannot be repaired or if valve guides are worn beyond limits of B&S wear gauge tool (Part No. 19381), head must be replaced. Replacement seats and guides are not available, nor are oversize-stem valves. Minimum valve stem diameter is 0.233 inch (5.92 mm). Minimum valve spring free length is 1.320 inch (35.5 mm).

When assembling the heads, lightly lubricate the inner surface and lip of the intake valve stem seal with oil. Use B&S driver (Part No. 19416) or equivalent to fully seat the stem seal over the intake valve guide. Lubricate valve stems with valve guide lubricant prior to installation. Lubricate the contact areas of rocker arms and supports with engine oil. Apply Loctite 242 or equivalent to rocker arm support bolts. Assemble rocker arms (9—Fig. BK6) and supports (10) to the head, and tighten support bolts to 100 in.-lb. (11.2 N•m).

Make sure the cylinder head alignment dowels are positioned in the cylinder block. DO NOT install any sealer to the cylinder head gasket. Install the head with new gasket. Torque the cylinder head bolts evenly to 220 in.-lb. (25.0 N•m) using tightening sequence shown in Fig. BK8.

Install the push rods, making sure the aluminum rod is on intake side and lower rod ends are properly seated in tappet sockets. Using thumb pressure,

compress valve spring with end of rocker arm to allow clearance for locating push rod into socket of rocker arm adjustment screw. Adjust the valve clearance. Install rocker cover with a new gasket, and tighten screws to 100 in.-lb. (11.2 N•m).

VALVE ADJUSTMENT. Valve adjustment should be performed with the

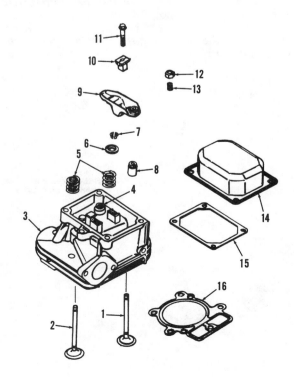

Fig. BK6—Exploded view of cylinder head and components.

1. Intake valve
2. Exhaust valve
3. Cylinder head
4. Valve guides
5. Springs
6. Spring retainer
7. Retainer locks
8. Intake valve seal
9. Rocker arm
10. Rocker arm support
11. Bolt
12. Locknut
13. Adjusting screw
14. Rocker cover
15. Gasket
16. Head gasket

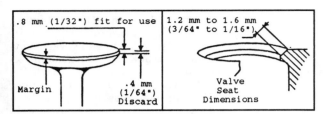

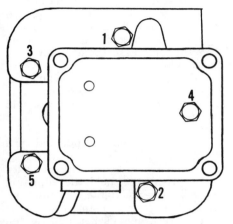

Fig. BK7—Valve and valve seat dimensions.

Fig. BK8—Torque cylinder head bolts to 220 in.-lb. (25.0 N•m) using tightening sequence shown above.

For best results, further engine disassembly should be done with the pto end of crankshaft facing up. Remove the oil pump (8) from engine base/sump, then remove the sump (9). Be careful not to lose the crankcase-to-sump alignment dowels, as they are not pressed-in to either the crankcase or sump.

Remove the governor gear assembly (10) and thrust washer from crankcase. Rotate crankshaft and camshaft to align the timing marks (this will allow camshaft lobes to clear the tappets), then remove the camshaft. Tappets can be removed at this time. Note the tap-

pet locations so they can be installed in their original position.

Inspect all parts for wear and damage. Reject dimensions are listed in the table below.

Camshaft journals . . . . 0.623 in.
(15.82 mm)
Intake lobes. . . . . 1.225 in.
(31.15 mm)
Exhaust lobes . . . . 1.223 in.
(31.06 mm)
Crankcase & sump
bearing bores . . . . 0.6275 in.
(15.93 mm)

Renew parts as necessary if camshaft bearing bores or journals are scored or worn beyond specifications. Make sure that the compression release mechanism operates freely. Check for loose or excessively worn parts.

To install camshaft, first lubricate the camshaft bearings, lobes and tappets with clean engine oil or Lubriplate. Insert tappets into their proper locations. Insert camshaft into crankcase, aligning the timing marks on camshaft and crankshaft gears. Assemble the governor thrust washer, gear assembly and sliding cup onto the crankcase stub shaft. Lubricate the bearing journals in the sump, then install the sump with a new gasket. Torque the sump screws evenly to 200 in.-lb. (22.6 N•m) using the tightening sequence shown in Fig. BK10.

Assemble oil pump components as described in OIL PUMP section.

PISTONS, WRIST PINS, PISTON RINGS AND CONNECTING RODS. To remove pistons and rod, drain crankcase oil and remove engine from equipment. Remove external engine accessories and cylinder heads as instructed in CYLINDER HEAD section. Clean pto end of crankshaft of any rust or burrs. Remove any carbon or ridge from top of cylinder bores to prevent damage to rings or pistons during removal.

Further disassembly of engine should be done with pto end of crankshaft facing up. Remove oil pump assembly. Unscrew sump bolts and remove sump. Rotate crankshaft and camshaft to align timing marks. This allows camshaft lobes to clear the valve tappets. Remove the camshaft. Remove the governor gear assembly from crankcase. Note position of rod cap on the number two connecting rod, then unscrew cap bolts and remove cap. Push the number two piston and connecting rod through top of cylinder. Install the cap loosely on the rod to prevent possible interchanging of caps and rods. Repeat for the number one piston and rod assembly.

If necessary to disassemble pistons from rods, keep each cylinder's piston, wrist pin and connecting rod grouped together. These parts should not be interchanged.

Reject dimensions are listed in the following table.

Ring groove side
clearance (new ring) . . . . 0.005 in.
(0.12 mm)

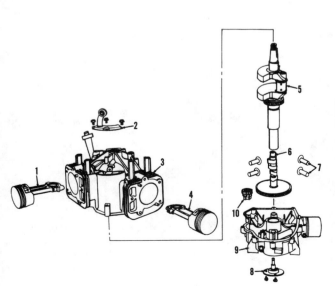

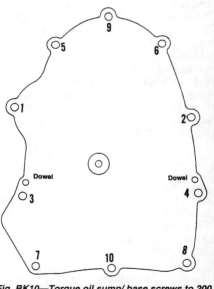

Fig. BK9—Exploded view of crankcase and internal components.

1. Rod & piston #1
2. Breather
3. Cylinder block
4. Rod & piston #2
5. Crankshaft
6. Camshaft
7. Tappets
8. Oil pump assy.
9. Oil sump
10. Governor assy.

Fig. BK10—Torque oil sump/ base screws to 200 in.-lb. (22.6 N•m) using tightening sequence shown above.

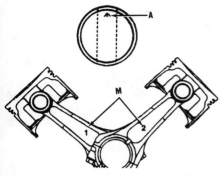

Fig. BK11—Assemble pistons to connecting rods with arrow (A) on piston crown facing opposite direction of cylinder match numbers (M) on connecting rods. Refer to text for proper installation procedure.

Ring end gap	0.030 in. (0.76 mm)
Wrist pin bore, piston or rod	0.6745 in. (17.13 mm)
Wrist pin bore, out-of-round	0.0005 in. (0.01 mm)
Wrist pin	0.6718 in. (17.06 mm)
Wrist pin out-of-round	0.0005 in. (0.01 mm)
Connecting rod crankpin bearing	1.5015 in. (38.13 mm)

A connecting rod with an undersize crankpin bearing is available if crankpin is worn beyond limits.

Lubricate piston rings, wrist pin, crankpin journal and cylinder bores prior to assembly. The pistons are manufactured with an offset piston pin bore. For this reason, the pistons must be installed on the connecting rods with arrow on piston crown facing the opposite direction of cylinder-match number on connecting rod beam (Fig. BK11).

NOTE: One connecting rod part number services both cylinders. The rod has a "1" on one side and a "2" on the other side (Fig. BK11). The rods must be installed with the numbered side that corresponds to the cylinder toward the pto end of the crankshaft.

Use a suitable piston ring expander to install the rings onto the pistons. Assemble the piston rings on the pistons as detailed in Fig. BK12 or Fig. BK13. Lubricate the piston and rings and the connecting rod and cap with engine oil. Install piston and rod assemblies into the cylinders with arrow on piston crown pointing toward the flywheel end of the crankshaft; correct cylinder number on rod beam will then face pto end of crankshaft. Install the number one

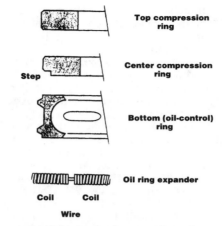

Fig. BK12—Diagram showing installation of piston rings on Series 405700-407700 engines. Top compression ring and bottom oil ring may be installed either side up. Center compression ring must be installed with outer step down toward piston skirt. Oil ring coil expander must have wire fully inserted into coil.

piston and rod assembly first. Repeat the installation procedure for number two piston and rod assembly. Install rod cap on its respective connecting rod, aligning match marks on rod and cap. Torque the rod cap screws to 100 in.-lb. (11.2 N•m). Rotate the crankshaft to check for binding.

Refer to CAMSHAFT section for further assembly instructions.

OIL PUMP. The rotor-type oil pump (8—Fig. BK9) is located in the engine oil sump. A slot in the end of the camshaft engages a tang on the end of pump shaft, providing the drive for the pump.

The oil pump can be accessed externally by removing the circular cover on the sump below the camshaft. After removing the cover (5—Fig. BK14) and "O" ring seal (4), the outer rotor (3), inner rotor (2) and pump shaft (1) can be removed.

Clean pump components and housing, then inspect for scoring, damage or excessive wear. Renew as necessary.

Lubricate the pump components with engine oil prior to assembly. Install pump shaft first, inserting small-diameter shank into the sump. Be sure that flat sides on drive end of pump shaft engage the slot in the end of camshaft. Insert inner and outer rotors. Rotors can be installed either-end up. Install the cover plate with a new O-ring. Torque the plate screws to 50 in.-lb. (5.6 N•m).

GOVERNOR SHAFT AND GEAR. The governor shaft is located in the engine sump, and the governor gear assembly is located inside the crankcase. The camshaft gear drives the governor gear.

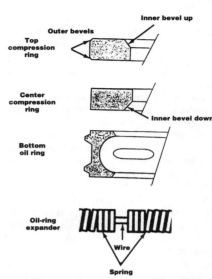

Fig. BK13—Diagram showing installation of piston rings on Series 445700 engines. Identification mark on face of compression rings must face piston crown. Oil control ring may be installed either side up, and must have coil expander wire fully inserted into coil.

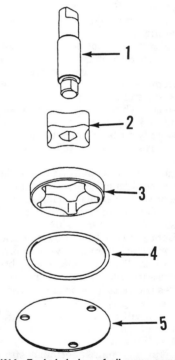

Fig. BK14—Exploded view of oil pump components.

1. Pump shaft
2. Inner rotor
3. Outer rotor
4. O-ring seal
5. Cover plate

To access the governor shaft, drain the engine oil and remove the engine from equipment. Remove the rocker covers, depress the valve springs, and remove the push rods. Note that the aluminum push rod is used on the intake valve. Loosen governor lever nut, lightly spread slotted lever ends, and remove lever from shaft. Remove the oil pump assembly from sump. Remove the sump.

To remove the governor shaft from sump, remove innermost E-ring. Rotate the governor paddle toward the pto bearing, and then slide governor shaft from bushing. Remove and discard the oil seal.

Check the shaft and bushing for indications of wear or damage. If necessary to replace the governor shaft bushing, a bushing removal tool can be improvised as follows: Mount a ¼ inch flat washer having an outside diameter smaller than the bushing diameter on a 1/4-20×3 inch hex-head bolt. Insert the bolt through the bushing from inside the sump. Position a ⅝ inch socket over the bolt threads and against the outer face of the sump. Mount a second 1/4-inch flat washer and a nut onto the bolt. Tighten the nut until bushing is removed.

To install new governor shaft bushing, insert governor shaft into sump to act as bushing pilot (do not install inner E-ring). Lubricate the bushing with oil, then use B&S driver tool number 19129 or other suitable driver to press the bushing over the shaft and into sump bore until the tool bottoms. Make sure the shaft rotates freely, then install inner E-ring and new shaft seal.

Remove governor gear assembly, sliding cup and thrust washer from crankcase stub shaft. A tension ring between gear and cup allows the governor gear assembly to be a snug fit on the stub shaft. Be careful not to lose the tension ring.

Inspect components for freedom of movement, nicks, burrs or other damage or wear. Replace parts as necessary. Stub shaft is integral part of the crankcase and is not serviceable.

Lubricate the thrust washer and governor gear assembly with engine oil, then install onto crankcase stub shaft. Make sure that the lip at base of cup engages the slots at base of governor gear counterweights.

To install the oil sump, be sure that governor gear counterweights are in the collapsed position and governor shaft arm is against bottom of sump. Install the sump with a new gasket.

Tighten sump bolts in 50 in.-lb. (5.6 N•m) increments to final torque of 200 in.-lb. (22.6 N•m) following the sequence shown in BK10.

Lubricate oil pump components with engine oil, and assemble as shown in Fig. BK14. Pump rotors can be installed either way up. Torque pump cover screws to 50 in.-lb. (5.6 N•m).

Install the push rods, making sure that the aluminum push rods are on intake side and ball ends fit into sockets in tappets and rocker arm adjusting screws. Check and adjust valve clearances as outlined in VALVE ADJUSTMENT section. Install rocker covers.

Loosely install the governor lever onto the governor shaft, and follow the governor adjustment procedure in the MAINTENANCE section.

CRANKSHAFT. Both cylinders share a single connecting rod journal. Crankshaft can be removed after first removing all external components, flywheel, cylinder heads, sump, camshaft and connecting rods and pistons. Be sure to remove any rust or burrs from both ends of the crankshaft to avoid damaging the sump and crankcase bearings during removal.

Crankshaft reject sizes are listed in the following table.

Crankpin journal . . . . 1.4965 in.
(38.01 mm)

Main journals—
Magneto end . . . . 1.376 in.
(34.95 mm)
Pto end . . . . 1.623 in.
(41.22 mm)

If crankpin journal is scored, worn beyond specification, or out-of-round more than 0.0005 in. (0.013 mm), journal can be reground to fit a 0.020 inch (0.50 mm) undersize connecting rod. Undersize crankpin finish dimensions (Fig. BK15) are listed in the following table.

Journal
diameter (D) . . . . . . 1.4782-1.4790 in.
(37.54-37.56 mm)
Radius of fillet (R) . . . . 0.170-0.180 in.
(4.32-4.57 mm)
Throw-to-crankshaft
centerline (T) . . . . . 1.4435-1.4465 in.
(33.66-36.74 mm)

Undersize main bearings are not available. If crankshaft main journals are scored or worn beyond specification, renew the crankshaft. Timing gear is replaceable if teeth are damaged or keyway is worn. If timing gear is replaced, the camshaft should also be replaced.

Make sure oil galleries are clean and free of obstructions before installing the crankshaft. Align timing marks on crankshaft and camshaft gears during assembly.

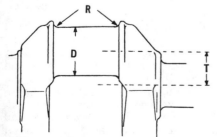

Fig. BK15—Refer to text for crankshaft grinding dimensions.

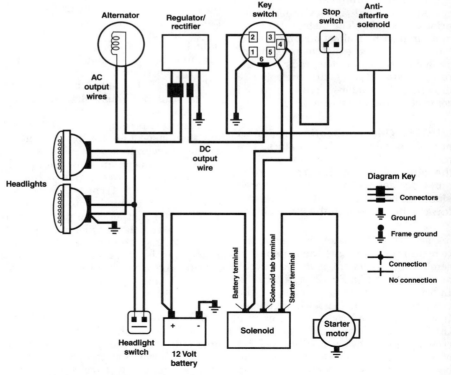

Fig. BK16—Standard 12-volt wiring diagram.

CRANKCASE/CYLINDER BLOCK. Standard cylinder bore size is 2.969-2.970 inches (75.41-75.43 mm) for Series 405700-407700 engines, and 3.1195-3.1205 inches (79.23-79.26 mm) for Series 445700 engines. Cylinders should be bored oversize or cylinder block replaced if any of the following conditions are evident: Cylinder bore is scored, cylinder bore wear or taper exceeds 0.003 inch (0.76 mm), cylinder bore is out-of-round more than 0.0015 inch (0.035 mm). Oversize pistons are available in 0.010, 0.020 and 0.030 inch (0.25, 0.50 and 0.75 mm) oversize dimensions.

Use a straightedge to check the cylinder block for distortion at the head gasket surfaces. If surface is warped more than 0.004 inch (0.10 mm), replace the cylinder block assembly. Resurfacing is not recommended.

Magneto-side main bearing is a replaceable DU-style bushing. Bushing reject dimension is 1.383 inch (35.12 mm). When replacing the bushing, note depth of original bushing prior to removal. Replacement bushing must be installed at same depth. B&S bushing driver number 19226 can be used for both removal and installation of bushing. Be sure that the oil hole in the new bushing is aligned with the oil hole in the cylinder block prior to installation. After installation, stake the bushing on both the inner and outer ends.

Pto-side main bearing is machined as part of the oil sump. Bearing reject dimension is 1.629 inch (41.37 mm). If pto bearing is scored, damaged or worn beyond limits, the sump must be replaced.

OIL SEALS. Oil seals should be installed with lips facing inward. Press in new magneto oil seal until outer face is flush with crankcase face. When installing seal on pto end of crankshaft, seal should be pressed in slightly below face of the seal mount.

WIRING DIAGRAM. Refer to Fig. BK16 for wiring diagram typical of a standard 12-volt electrical system.

BRIGGS & STRATTON
SERVICING BRIGGS & STRATTON ACCESSORIES

REWIND STARTER

Single-Cylinder Models Except Vanguard

To renew broken rewind spring, proceed as follows: Grasp free outer end of spring (S—Fig. BS101) and pull broken end from starter housing. With blower housing removed, bend tangs (T) up and remove starter pulley from housing. Untie knot in rope (R) and remove rope and inner end of broken spring from pulley. Apply a small amount of grease on inner face of pulley. Thread inner end of spring through notch in starter housing, and engage inner end of spring in pulley hub. Place bar in pulley hub, and turn pulley approximately 13½ turns counterclockwise as shown in Fig. BS102. Tie the wrench to the blower housing with wire to hold pulley so hole (H) in pulley is aligned with rope guide (G) in housing as shown in Fig. BS103. Hook a wire in inner end of rope and thread rope through guide and

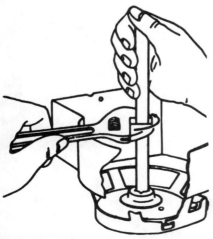

Fig. BS101—View of rewind starter used on single-cylinder engines, except Vanguard models, showing rope (R), spring end (S) and retaining tangs (T).

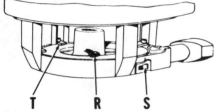

Fig. BS102—Use a square shaft and wrench to wind the rewind starter spring. Refer to text.

hole in pulley; then, tie a knot in rope and release the pulley allowing spring to wind rope into pulley groove.

To renew starter rope only, it is not generally necessary to remove starter pulley and spring. Wind up spring and install new rope as outlined in preceding paragraph.

Two different types of starter clutches have been used; refer to exploded view of early production unit in Fig. BS104 and exploded view of late production unit in Fig. BS105. Outer end of late production ratchet (refer to cut away view in Fig. BS106) is sealed with a felt seal and a retaining plug and a rubber ring is used to seal ratchet to ratchet cover.

To disassemble early type starter clutch unit, refer to Fig. BS104 and proceed as follows: Remove snap ring (3) and lift ratchet (5) and cover (4) from

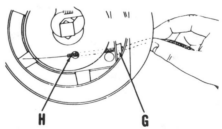

Fig. BS103—Thread rope through guide (G) in housing and hole (H) in starter pulley with wire hooked in end of rope.

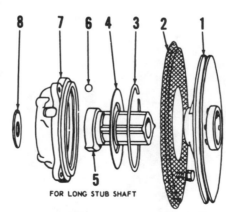

Fig. BS104—Exploded view of early production starter clutch unit; refer to Fig. BS107 for "long stub shaft." A late-style unit (Fig. BS105) should be installed when renewing "long" crankshaft with "short" (late production) shaft.

1. Starter rope pulley
2. Rotating screen
3. Snap ring
4. Ratchet cover
5. Starter ratchet
6. Steel balls
7. Clutch housing (flywheel nut)
8. Spring washer

starter housing (7) and crankshaft. Be careful not to lose steel balls (6). Starter housing (7) is also flywheel retaining nut; to remove housing, first remove screen (2) and using B&S flywheel wrench 19114, unscrew housing from crankshaft in counterclockwise direction. When reinstalling housing, be sure spring washer (8) is placed on crankshaft with cup (hollow) side toward flywheel, then install starter housing and tighten securely. Reinstall rotating screen. Place ratchet on crankshaft and into housing and insert the steel balls. Reinstall cover and retaining snap ring.

To disassemble late starter clutch unit, refer to Fig. BS105 and proceed as follows: Remove rotating screen (2) and starter ratchet cover (4). Lift the ratchet (5) from housing and crank-

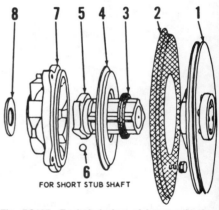

FOR SHORT STUB SHAFT

Fig. BS105—Exploded view of late production sealed starter clutch unit. Some late-style clutches have a polymer thrust washer between ratchet (5) and housing (7). Some factory-installed clutches have a non-metallic composite housing (7) except for threaded nut. All service procedures remain the same.

1. Starter rope pulley
2. Rotating screen
3. Snap ring
4. Ratchet cover
5. Starter ratchet
6. Steel balls
7. Clutch housing (flywheel nut)
8. Spring washer

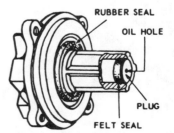

Fig. BS106—Cutaway showing felt seal and plug in end of late production starter ratchet (5—Fig. BS105).

shaft and extract the steel balls (6). If necessary to remove housing (7), hold flywheel and unscrew housing in counterclockwise direction using B&S tool 19114. When installing housing, be sure spring washer (8) is in place on crankshaft with cup (hollow) side toward flywheel. Tighten housing securely. Inspect felt seal and plug in outer end of ratchet. Renew ratchet if seal or plug is damaged, as these parts are not serviced separately. Lubricate the felt with oil and place ratchet on crankshaft. Insert the steel balls and install ratchet cover, rubber seal and rotating screen.

NOTE: Flyball-type starter clutches (Fig. BS104 and Fig. BS105) are used on four styles of crankshaft stub ends. Refer to Fig. BS107.

If renewing early-style crankshaft with long stub end (A—Fig. BS107) with later-style crankshaft (B, C or D), install late-style (Fig. BS105) starter clutch.

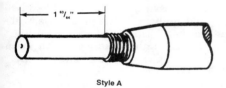

Style A

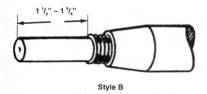

Style B

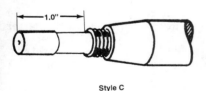

Style C

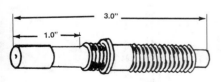

Style D

Fig. BS107—Four different styles of crankshaft starter-clutch stub ends used with B&S-design rewind starter. Clutch stub dimensions are measured from end of crankshaft/stub shaft to machined radius at end of stub shank. Refer to text for proper application.

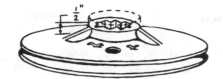

Fig. BS108—When installing late-type starter clutch unit as a replacement for early-type, either install new starter rope pulley or cut hub of old pulley to 1/2 inch (12.7 mm) as shown.

If renewing early starter clutch (Fig. BS104) with late-style unit (Fig. BS105), crankshaft stub end must be shortened to dimension shown for short shaft (Style B—Fig. BS107). Bevel the end of the crankshaft approximately $\frac{1}{16}$ inch (1.6 mm) after it is shortened. If starter rope pulley is not being replaced with new style pulley, the old pulley hub must also be shortened to the $\frac{1}{2}$ inch (12.7-mm) dimension shown in Fig. BS108.

Latest Style C and Style D clutch stub shanks are 1.0 inch (25.4 mm) long and are only to be used with late-style clutch (Fig. BS105). Style C is an integral part of the crankshaft, but has the lower (inner) half of the shank undercut to help prevent debris buildup and subsequent clutch grabbing and starter damage. Style D pilot shaft has a clutch stub identical to Style C, but is a separate shaft that threads into the latest-design crankshafts. Overall length of Style D pilot shaft is 3.0 inch (76 mm).

Replace the clutch-to-flywheel washer if it is cracked or worn. If washer is Belleville design, be sure that high-center inside diameter is toward the clutch.

Prior to inserting clutch over crankshaft stub, thoroughly clean and polish stub shaft and clutch bore. Lightly coat the contact surface of the stub shaft with one to two drops of 10W-30 synthetic engine oil. Insert clutch onto stub shaft with a spinning motion to lubricate the clutch bore. Torque the clutch assembly to the crankshaft. Refer to table below for starter clutch-to-crankshaft tightening torque values.

Series	Torque
170000-250000	65 ft.-lb.
	(88 N•m)
280000	90-100 ft.-lb.
	(122-135 N•m)
400000-420000	150 ft.-lb.
	(203 N•m)

When installing blower housing and starter assembly on horizontal-shaft engines with early-style starter clutch, turn starter ratchet so word "TOP" on ratchet is toward engine cylinder head (Fig. BS109).

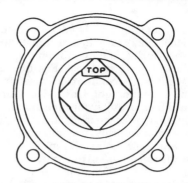

Fig. BS109—When installing blower housing and starter assembly, turn starter ratchet so word "TOP" stamped on outer end of ratchet is toward engine cylinder head.

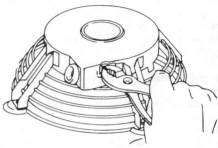

Fig. BS110—Grip outer end of spring with pliers and pull spring out of housing as far as possible. Refer to text.

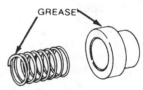

Fig. BS111—Lubricate pulley, spring and adapter with multipurpose grease. Refer to text.

Twin-Cylinder Models Except Vanguard

To remove rewind starter, remove the four nuts and washers from studs in blower housing. Separate starter assembly from blower housing, then separate assembly from blower housing and starter clutch assembly.

To disassemble, remove handle and pin, and allow rope to rewind into housing. Grip end of rope in knot cavity and remove rope. Grip outer end of spring with pliers (Fig. BS110) and pull spring out of housing as far as possible. Turn spring $\frac{1}{4}$ turn and remove from pulley or bend one of the tangs with B&S tool 19229. Remove starter pulley and detach spring.

Clean spring and housing and oil spring sparingly before reinstallation. If pulley was removed, place a small amount of multipurpose grease on pulley, ratchet spring and ratchet spring adapter (Fig. BS111). Place ratchet spring, spring adapter and pulley into rewind housing and bend tang using B&S tool 19229 to bend and adjust tang gap to $\frac{1}{16}$ inch (1.6 mm) minimum.

Fabricate a rewind tool (Fig. BS112) and wind pulley counterclockwise until spring is wound tight. Unwind one turn or until hole in pulley for rope knot and eyelet in blower housing are aligned. Lock spring securely in smaller portion of tapered hole. Reinstall rope.

To disassemble starter clutch unit, refer to Fig. BS105 and proceed as follows: Remove rotating screen (2) and starter ratchet cover (4). Lift the ratchet (5) from housing and crankshaft and extract the steel balls (6). If necessary to remove housing (7), hold flywheel and unscrew housing in counterclockwise direction. When installing housing, be sure spring washer (8) is in place on crankshaft with cup (hollow) side toward flywheel; then, tighten housing securely. Inspect felt seal and plug in outer end of ratchet. Renew ratchet if seal or plug is damaged, as these parts are not serviced separately. Lubricate the felt with oil and place ratchet on crankshaft. Insert the steel balls and install ratchet cover, rubber seal and rotating screen.

Vanguard Models

Refer to Fig. BS113 for exploded view of rewind starter. When installing the starter, position starter on blower housing, then pull out starter rope until dogs engage starter cup. Continue to place tension on rope and tighten starter-mounting screws to 60 in.-lbs. (7 N•m).

To install a new rope, proceed as follows. Rope length should be 70 inches (178 cm). Remove starter and extract old rope from pulley. Allow pulley to unwind then turn pulley counterclockwise until spring is tightly wound. Rotate pulley clockwise until rope hole in pul-

ley is aligned with rope outlet in housing. Pass rope through pulley hole and housing outlet and tie a temporary knot near handle end of rope. Release pulley and allow rope to wind onto pulley. Install rope handle, release temporary knot and allow rope to enter starter.

To disassemble starter, remove rope handle and allow pulley to totally unwind. Remove screw (14—Fig. BS113) and separate retainer (12), dogs (11), springs (10) and brake spring (9) from the pulley. Wear appropriate safety eyewear and gloves before disengaging pulley (7) from starter as spring (6) may uncoil uncontrolled. Place shop towel around pulley and lift pulley out of housing; spring should remain with pulley. Do not attempt to separate spring (6) from cup (5), as they are a unit assembly.

Inspect components for damage and excessive wear. Reverse disassembly procedure to install components. Be sure inner end of rewind spring engages spring retainer adjacent to housing center post. Tighten screw (14) to 70 in.-lbs. (8 N•m). Install rope as previously outlined.

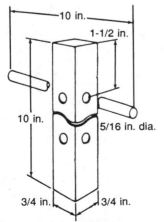

Fig. BS112—Use 3/4-inch square stock to fabricate a spring rewind tool to the dimensions shown.

10 in.

1-1/2 in.

10 in.

5/16 in. dia.

3/4 in.   3/4 in.

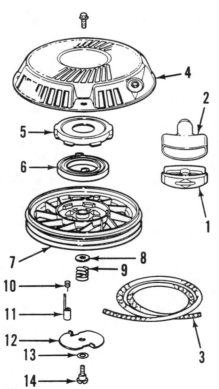

Fig. BS113—Exploded view of rewind starter used on Vanguard models.

1. Insert	8. Washer
2. Rope handle	9. Brake spring
3. Rope	10. Spring
4. Housing	11. Dog
5. Spring cup	12. Retainer
6. Rewind spring	13. Washer
7. Pulley	14. Screw

NOTE: Repeat failure of starter pulley (7—Fig. BS113) could be the result of excess engine compression caused by incorrect valve tappet clearance or a faulty compression-release mechanism.

12-VOLT STARTER-GENERATOR UNITS

The combination starter-generator functions as a cranking motor when the starting switch is closed. When engine is operating and with the starting switch open, unit operates as a generator. A current-voltage regulator controls generator output and circuit voltage for the battery and various operating requirements. On units where voltage regulator is mounted separately from generator unit, do not mount regulator with cover down, as regulator will not function in this position.

To adjust belt tension, apply approximately 30 pounds (13.6 kg) pull on generator adjusting flange and tighten mounting bolts. Belt tension is correct when a pressure of 10 pounds (44.5 N) applied midway between pulleys will deflect belt $\frac{1}{4}$ inch (6.4 mm). See Fig. BS114. On units equipped with two drive belts, always renew belts in pairs. A 50-ampere capacity battery is recommended. Starter-generator units are intended for use in temperatures above 0° F (−18° C). Refer to Fig. BS115 for exploded view of starter-generator. Parts and service on starter-generator are available at authorized Delco-Remy service stations.

GEAR DRIVE STARTERS

Gear drive starters manufactured by Briggs & Stratton, American Bosch or Mitsubishi may be used, either as a 110-volt AC starter or a 12-volt DC starter. Refer to Figs. BS116 and BS117 for exploded views of starter motors. A properly grounded receptacle should be used with power cord connected to 110-volt AC starter motor. A

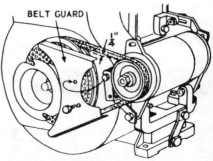

BELT GUARD

Fig. BS114—View showing starter-generator belt adjustment on models so equipped. Refer to text.

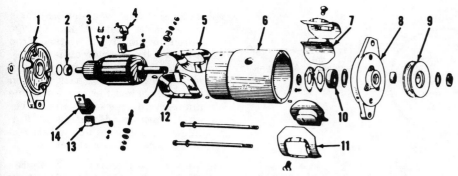

Fig. BS115—Exploded view of Delco-Remy starter-generator used on some models.

1. Commutator end frame
2. Bearing
3. Armature
4. Ground brush holder
5. Field coil (left)
6. Frame
7. Pole shoe
8. Drive end frame
9. Pulley
10. Bearing
11. Field coil insulator
12. Field coil (right)
13. Brush
14. Insulated brush holder

Fig. BS116—Exploded view of 110-volt AC starter motor. A 12-volt DC version is similar. Rectifier and switch unit (8) is used on 110-volt starter motor only.

1. Pinion gear
2. Helix
3. Armature shaft
4. Drive cup
5. Thrust washer
6. Housing
7. End cap
8. Rectifier & switch unit
9. Bolt
10. Nut

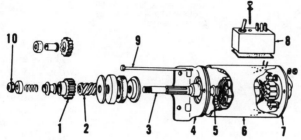

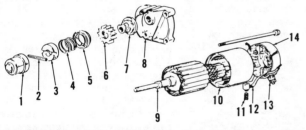

Fig. BS117—Exploded view of 12-volt DC starter motor used on some models.

1. Cap
2. Roll pin
3. Retainer
4. Pinion spring
5. Spring cup
6. Starter gear
7. Clutch assy.
8. Drive end cap assy.
9. Armature
10. Housing
11. Spring
12. Brush assy.
13. Battery wire terminal
14. Commutator end cap assy.

32-ampere hour capacity battery is recommended for use with 12-volt starter motor.

CAUTION: Do not clamp starter motor housing in a vise or strike housing as some motors have ceramic field magnets that may be damaged.

To renew a worn or damaged flywheel ring gear, drill out retaining rivets using a 3/16-inch drill bit. Attach the new ring gear using screws provided with new ring gear.

To check for correct operation of starter motor, remove starter motor from engine and place motor in a vise or other holding fixture. Install a 0-5-amp ammeter in power cord to 110-volt AC starter motor. On 12-volt DC motor, connect a 12-volt battery to motor with a 0-50 amp ammeter in series with positive line from battery to starter motor. Connect a tachometer to drive end of starter motor. Determine manufacturer of starter motor and refer to following table for test specifications (note that some motors are tested using a 6-volt battery). If Briggs & Stratton manufactured the 12-volt starter motor, measure housing length (except on Vanguard models) as shown in Fig. BS118.

12-Volt Starter Motor

Starter Motor	Minimum Rpm	Maximum Amps
B&S		
3 in.	6500	18
3 1/16 in.	6500	18
3 3/8 in.	7000	24
3 5/8 in.	6500	18
3 13/16 in.	6900	19
3 21/32 in.	5000	20
3 3/4 in.	6900	19
4 3/8 in.	6500	20
4 1/2 in.	6500	35
4 9/16 in.	6500	35
Vanguard	6500	35
Bosch		
SME-12A-8*	5000	25
SMH-12A-11	4800	16
1965-23-MO-30-SM	5500	16
Mitsubishi		
MOO1TO2271*, MMO-4FL*, MMO-5ML*	6700	16

*Use 6-volt battery for tests.

On OHV engines with solenoid-style starters, remove heavy-gauge solenoid-to-starter cable prior to testing starter motor as outlined in previous paragraph. If tests indicate starter is good, check for faulty solenoid, ignition switch and related starter circuit wiring.

To test solenoid, connect jumper wires from a separate 12-volt power source to the two small terminals on the solenoid. An audible 'click' should be produced indicating solenoid is functioning. As a further test, connect ohmmeter leads to large terminals on solenoid. When solenoid is activated and 'click' is heard, ohmmeter should indicate continuity. A meter reading of high resistance or infinity indicates faulty solenoid contacts, and solenoid should be replaced.

To test ignition switch, use an ohmmeter to check for continuity at the switch terminals. Terminal positions for Briggs & Stratton 5-terminal and 6-terminal switches are shown in Fig. BS119. Terminal 1 is internally grounded. Note that terminal positions may be different for switches supplied by manufacturers other than Briggs & Stratton. Refer to the Terminals With Continuity table for switch position and

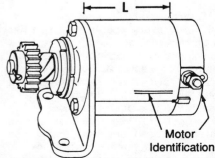

Fig. BS118—On B&S starters, measure length (L) of starter housing to determine correct test specifications. Refer to text.

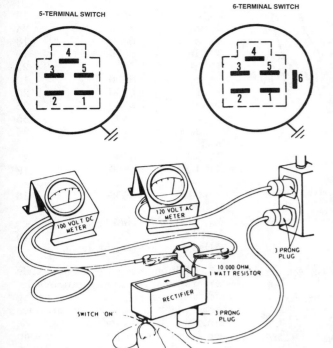

5-TERMINAL SWITCH

6-TERMINAL SWITCH

Fig. BS119—Rear view of both the 5-position and 6-position B&S ignition switches.

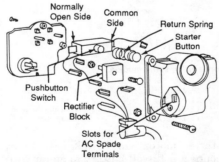

Fig. BS120—View of test connections for 110-volt rectifier. Refer to text for test procedure.

voltmeter should show a reading that is 0-14 volts lower than AC line voltage measured previously. If voltage drop exceeds 14 volts, renew rectifier unit.

To check rectifier in remote control box (Fig. BS121), remove back plate on box and remove rectifier. Use a suitable ohmmeter and check continuity between terminals identified in Fig. BS122. If tests are not as indicated in following table, renew rectifier.

(+) Tester Lead	(−) Tester Lead	Tester Reading
A	B	Infinity
B	A	Continuity
B	C	Infinity
C	B	Continuity
C	D	Continuity
D	C	Infinity
D	A	Continuity
A	D	Infinity

There should be no continuity between any terminal and rectifier case, otherwise, renew rectifier.

Disassembly of starter motor is self-evident after inspection of unit and referral to Figs. BS116, BS117, BS123 and BS124. Mark housing and end caps before disassembly and note position of bolts during disassembly so they can be installed in their original positions during assembly.

On Briggs & Stratton motors, minimum brush length is $\frac{1}{8}$ inch (3.2 mm) and minimum commutator diameter is 1.23 inches (31.24 mm) for 12-volt starter and 1.32 inches (33.53 mm) for 120-volt starter. Lubricate bearings with SAE 20 oil.

If so equipped, be sure to match drive cap keyway to stamped key in housing when sliding armature into motor housing.

Note installation of brushes in Figs. BS125, BS126, BS127 and BS128. If helix (2—Fig. BS116) is separate, splined end must be toward end of armature shaft as shown in Fig. BS129. Some early starters are equipped with shim washers to limit armature shaft end

terminal continuity. Replace the switch if test readings indicate a faulty switch.

Terminals With Continuity

Key Position	5-Terminal Switch	6-Terminal Switch
OFF	1-3	1-3-6
RUN	2-5	2-5-6
START	2-4-5	2-4-5

Replace the switch if test readings indicate a faulty switch.

110-Volt Starter Motor

Starter Motor	Minimum Rpm	Maximum Amps
B&S	6500	2.7
Bosch		
SME-110-C3,		
SME-110-C6		
SME-110-C8	7400	3.5
06026-28-		
M030SM	7400	3
Mitsubishi		
J282188	7800	3.5

If starter motor does not operate satisfactorily, check operation of rectifier in starter control box. If the rectifier and the starter switch are good, disassemble and inspect starter motor.

Two types of rectifiers have been used with 110-volt AC starter motors. Early type is contained in control box (8—Fig. BS116) mounted on motor. Later type has four prongs and can be removed from remote control box. To check rectifier in control box (8—Fig. BS116), remove control box from starter motor. Solder a 10,000-ohm,

1-watt resistor to DC internal terminals of rectifier as shown in Fig. BS120. Connect a 0-100 range DC voltmeter to resistor leads. Measure voltage of AC outlet to be used. With starter switch in "OFF" position, a zero reading should be shown on DC voltmeter. With starter switch in "ON" position, DC

Fig. BS121—Exploded view of control unit for 110-volt AC starter motor used on some engines.

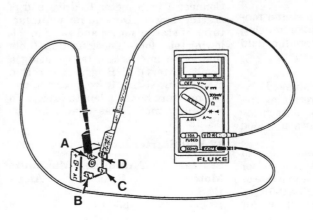

Fig. BS122—Identify terminals on rectifier as shown and refer to text for test procedure. Note that "A" is adjacent to "+" on rectifier case.

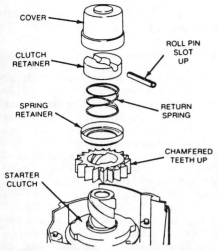

Fig. BS123—Exploded view of starter drive used on some early production starters.

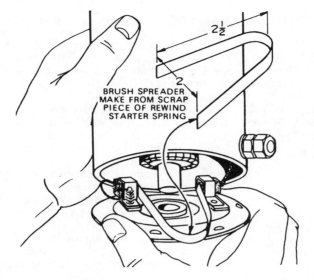

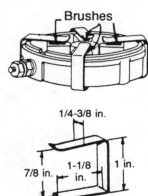

Fig. BS125—Brush retaining tool shown can be fabricated to hold the type of brushes shown when installing motor end cap.

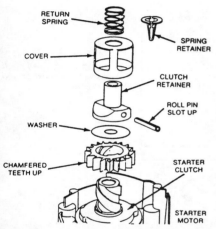

Fig. BS124—Exploded view of starter drive used on some current production starters.

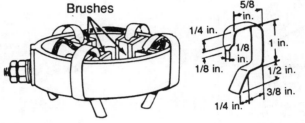

Fig. BS126—To hold brushes shown while assembling starter motor, a brush retainer tool can be fabricated from a piece of rewind starter spring using the dimensions shown.

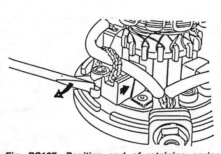

Fig. BS127—Position end of retaining spring against rear of brush as shown to hold brush in guide.

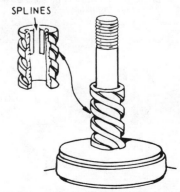

Fig. BS128—To hold brushes shown while assembling starter motor, a brush retainer tool can be fabricated from a piece of rewind starter spring using the dimensions shown.

play to 0.006-0.038 inch (0.15-0.96 mm). Tighten armature shaft nut on models so equipped to 170 in.-lbs. (19 N•m). Tighten through-bolts if 10-24 to 40-45 in.-lbs. (4.5-5.1 N•m), or if ¼-20 to 45-55 in.-lbs. (5.1-6.2 N•m). On models equipped with a retaining pin (Figs. BS123 or BS124), install pin so split is toward end of armature shaft. Note the position of drive components in Figs. BS123 and BS124.

Some electric-start engines have a factory-installed plastic composite flywheel ring gear. This gear requires a different-design starter bendix gear. The compatibility of the ring gear and bendix gear must be maintained to prevent damage. Replacement ring gears are aluminum alloy.

Aluminum ring gears MUST USE Style A bendix gear shown in Fig.BS130.

Style A bendix gear has beveled-edge teeth on one side of the gear. It must be installed with beveled teeth edges toward the ring gear.

Plastic ring gears MUST USE Style B bendix gear. Style B bendix gear has straight-cut teeth with rounded edges on the gaps between the teeth. It must be installed with round-edge gaps toward the ring gear.

Some single-cylinder Series 28xxxx and 31xxxx engines and some Vanguard V-twin engines are equipped with a heavy-duty starter and a steel flywheel ring gear. Refer to Fig. BS131 for exploded view of starter. DO NOT use this starter on engines with aluminum or plastic ring gear, and DO NOT use starter for plastic ring gear engines on engines with steel ring gear.

On engines equipped with a wire ring used as a retainer for the bendix drive (Fig. BS130), ring removal is made eas-

Fig. BS129—Install helix on armature so splines of helix are toward outer end of shaft as shown.

ier by using B&S tool 19436. Tool 19435 is used to install the ring.

ALTERNATOR

Note the configuration, color of stator leads and wire connector to identify the alternator type. Refer to Figs. BS132 through BS163. Identify type to be serviced and refer to appropriate following section.

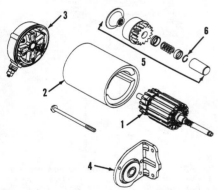

Fig. BS130—Exploded view of starter drive and two different types of drive gears used on later-style starters except those with steel ring gears (see Fig. BS131). Refer to text for starter gear-to-ring gear compatibility.

A. Gear for aluminum ring gear	1. Bendix clutch
B. Gear for plastic ring gear	2. C-ring retainer
	3. Return spring, wave washer & cap

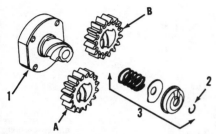

Fig. BS131—Exploded view of 12-volt inertia-drive starter motor and bendix used on single-cylinder Series 28xxxx and 31xxxx engines and two-cylinder Vanguard engines with steel ring gear. Do not use this starter on engines with plastic or aluminum ring gear.

1. Armature	4. Drive end
2. Housing	5. Bendix assy.
3. End cap & brushes	6. C-ring retainer

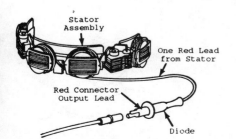

Fig. BS132—Drawing of 3-amp DC alternator used on some models.

3-Amp DC Alternator

The 3-amp DC alternator (Fig. BS132) is regulated only by engine speed and provides 2- to 3-amp charging current to maintain battery state of charge.

To check output, connect an ammeter in series with red lead, start engine and run at 2400 rpm. Ammeter should show 2-amp charging current. Increase engine speed to 3600 rpm. Ammeter should show 3-amp charging current. If charging current is not as specified, stop engine and connect an ohmmeter lead to laminations of stator and connect remaining ohmmeter lead to red stator lead. Ohmmeter should indicate continuity. If not, renew stator. If continuity is indicated, but system fails to

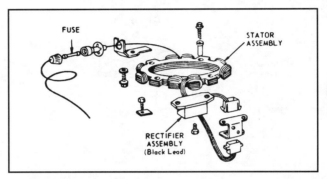

Fig. BS133—Stator and rectifier assemblies used on the 4-amp alternator.

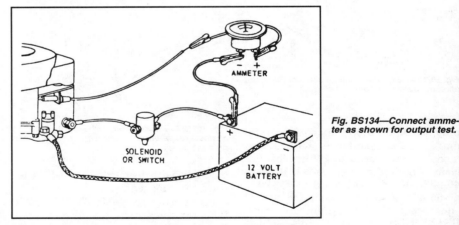

Fig. BS134—Connect ammeter as shown for output test.

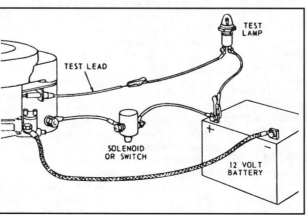

Fig. BS135—Connect a test lamp as shown to test for shorted stator or defective rectifier. Refer to text.

produce charging current, inspect magnets in flywheel.

4-Amp Alternator

Some engines are equipped with the 4-amp alternator shown in Fig. BS133 that is regulated only by engine speed. A solid-state rectifier and 7½-amp fuse are used with this alternator.

If the battery is run down and no output from alternator is suspected, first check the 7½-amp fuse. If the fuse is good, clean and tighten all connections. Disconnect charging lead and connect an ammeter as shown in Fig. BS134. Start the engine and check for alternator output. If ammeter shows no charge, stop engine, remove ammeter and install a test lamp as shown in Fig.

BS135. Test lamp should not light. If it does light, stator or rectifier is defective. Unplug rectifier plug under blower housing. If test lamp does not go out, stator is shorted.

If shorted stator is indicated, use an ohmmeter and check continuity as follows: Touch one test lead to lead inside of fuse holder as shown in Fig. BS136. Touch remaining test lead to each of the four pins in rectifier connector. Unless ohmmeter shows continuity at each of the four pins, stator winding is open and stator must be renewed.

If defective rectifier is indicated, unbolt and remove flywheel blower housing with rectifier. Connect one ohmmeter test lead to blower housing and remaining test lead to the single pin connector in rectifier connector. See Fig. BS137. Check for continuity, then reverse leads and again test for continuity. If tests show no continuity in either direction or continuity in both directions, rectifier is faulty and must be renewed.

5-Amp AC Alternator

The 5-amp alternator shown in Fig. BS138 provides alternating current that is regulated only by engine speed.

To check alternator, connect a voltmeter to black stator lead and check voltage reading with engine running at 3600 rpm. Voltage reading should be at least 14 volts. If not, renew stator.

5-Amp And 9-Amp Regulated Alternator

The 5-amp and 9-amp alternators (Fig. BS139) provide regulated charging current. Charging rate is determined by state of charge in battery. Stator is located under the flywheel and output capacity is determined by the size of magnets cast into the flywheel.

Alternator output is determined by the size of the flywheel magnets. Magnets are $1\frac{1}{16}$ inch $\times \frac{7}{8}$ inch (18 mm $\times$ 22 mm) on 5-amp flywheels and $\frac{15}{16}$ inch $\times 1$ $\frac{1}{16}$ inch (24 mm $\times$ 27 mm) on 16-amp flywheels.

To check stator output, disconnect green connector and connect voltmeter leads to stator lead. With engine running at 3600 rpm, voltmeter should indicate at least 28 VAC for 5-amp systems and 40 VAC for 9-amp systems. If not, renew stator.

To test regulator, the 12-volt battery must have a minimum charge of 5 volts. Connect an ammeter in series with charging circuit positive (red) lead and run engine at normal operating rpm. Test leads must be connected before starting engine and must not be disconnected while engine is running as regulator may be damaged. Ammeter should indicate a charge that will vary according to battery state of charge and capacity of alternator. If no charging current is indicated, check that wires are connected properly and regulator is grounded. Retest and renew regulator if charge current remains unsatisfactory.

7-Amp Alternator

The 7-amp regulated alternator (Fig. BS140) is equipped with a solid state rectifier and regulator. An isolation diode is also used on most models.

If engine will not start using the electric starter motor and starter motor is good, install an ammeter in circuit as shown in Fig. BS141. Start engine manually. Ammeter should indicate charge. If ammeter does not show battery

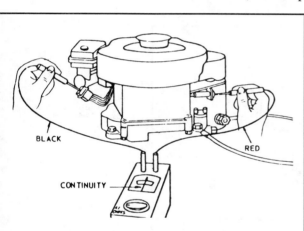

Fig. BS136—Use an ohmmeter to check condition of stator. Refer to text.

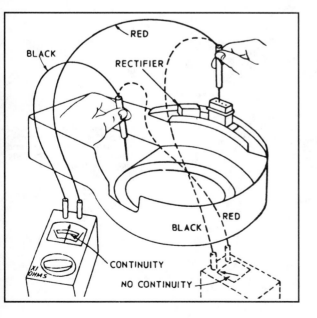

Fig. BS137—If ohmmeter shows continuity in both directions or in neither direction, rectifier is defective.

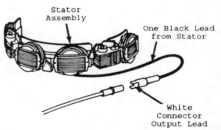

Fig. BS138—Drawing of 5-amp AC alternator used on some models.

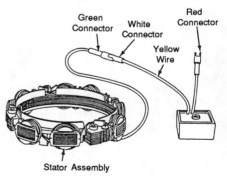

Fig. BS139—Drawing of 5-amp or 9-amp alternator and regulator used on some models.

charging taking place, check for defective wiring and, if necessary, proceed with troubleshooting.

If battery charging occurs with engine running, but battery does not retain charge, then isolation diode may be defective. The isolation diode is used to prevent battery drain if alternator circuit malfunctions. After troubleshooting diode, remainder of circuit should be inspected to find reason for excessive battery drain. To check operation of diode, disconnect white lead of diode from fuse holder and connect a test lamp from the diode white lead to negative terminal of battery. Test lamp should not light. If test lamp lights, diode is defective. Disconnect test lamp and disconnect red lead of diode. Test continuity of diode with ohmmeter by connecting leads of ohmmeter to leads of diode then reverse lead connection. Ohmmeter should show continuity in one direction and an open circuit in the other direction. If readings are incorrect, then diode is defective and must be renewed.

To troubleshoot alternator assembly, proceed as follows: Disconnect white lead of isolation diode from fuse holder and connect a test lamp between positive terminal of battery and fuse holder on engine. Engine must not be started. With connections made, test lamp should not light. If test lamp does light, stator, regulator or rectifier is defective. Unplug rectifier-regulator plug under blower housing. If lamp remains lighted, stator is grounded. If lamp goes out, regulator or rectifier is shorted.

If previous test indicated stator is grounded, check stator leads for defects and repair if necessary. If shorted leads are not found, renew stator. Check stator for an open circuit as follows: Using an ohmmeter, connect positive lead to fuse holder as shown in Fig. BS142 and negative lead to one of the pins in rectifier and regulator connector. Check each of the four pins in connector. Ohmmeter should show continuity at each pin. If not, there is an open in stator and stator must be renewed.

To test rectifier, unplug rectifier and regulator connector plug and remove blower housing from engine. Using an ohmmeter, check for continuity between connector pins connected to black wires and blower housing as shown in Fig. BS143. Be sure good contact is made with metal of blower housing. Reverse ohmmeter leads and check continuity again. Ohmmeter should show a continuity reading for only one direction on each plug. If either pin shows a continuity reading for both directions, or if either pin shows no conti-

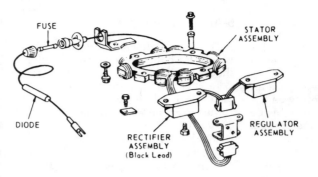

Fig. BS140—Stator, rectifier and regulator assemblies used on 7-amp alternator.

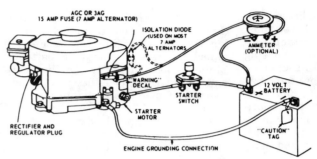

Fig. BS141—Typical wiring diagram for engines equipped with 7-amp alternator system.

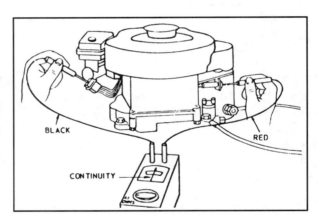

Fig. BS142—Use an ohmmeter to check condition of stator. Refer to text.

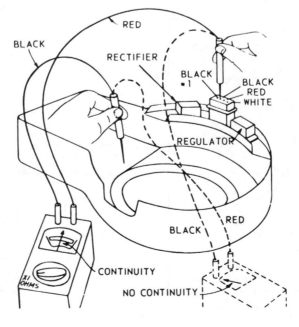

Fig. BS143—Be sure good contact is made between ohmmeter test lead and metal cover when checking rectifier and regulator.

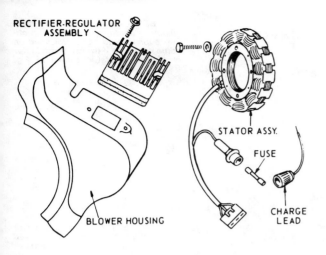

Fig. BS144—Drawing of early 10-amp alternator and rectifier used on some engines.

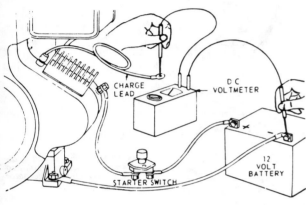

Fig. BS145—A DC voltmeter is used to determine if alternator is functioning. Refer to text.

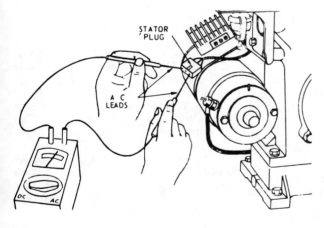

Fig. BS146—An AC voltmeter is used to test stator.

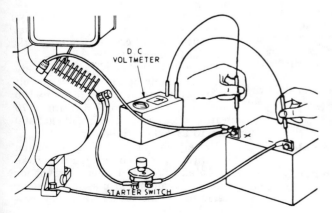

Fig. BS147—A DC voltmeter is used to check battery voltage. Refer to text for rectifier-regulator test.

nuity for either direction, then rectifier must be renewed.

To test regulator unit, repeat procedure used to test rectifier unit except connect ohmmeter lead to pins connected to red wire and white wire. If ohmmeter shows continuity in either direction for red lead pin, regulator is defective and must be renewed. White lead pin should read as an open on ohmmeter in one direction and a weak reading in the other direction. Otherwise, regulator is defective and must be renewed.

Early 10-Amp Alternator

Early engines may be equipped with a 10-amp regulated alternator that uses a solid state rectifier-regulator. The early 10-amp system is identified by a fuse in the system (see Fig. BS144). To check charging system, disconnect charging lead from battery. Connect a DC voltmeter between charging lead and ground as shown in Fig. BS145. Start engine and run at 3600 rpm. A voltmeter reading of 14 volts or above indicates alternator is functioning. If reading is less than 14 volts, stator or rectifier-regulator is defective.

To test stator, disconnect stator plug from rectifier-regulator. Run engine at 3600 rpm and connect AC voltmeter leads to AC terminals in stator plug as shown in Fig. BS146. Voltmeter reading above 20 volts indicates stator is good. A reading less than 20 volts indicates stator is defective.

To test rectifier-regulator, make certain charging lead is connected to battery and stator plug is connected to rectifier-regulator. Check voltage across battery terminals with DC voltmeter (Fig. BS147). If voltmeter reading is 13.8 volts or higher, reduce battery voltage by connecting a 12-volt load lamp across battery terminals. When battery voltage is below 13.5 volts, start engine and operate at 3600 rpm. Voltmeter reading should rise. If battery is fully charged, reading should rise above 13.8 volts. If voltage does not increase or if voltage reading rises above 14.7 volts, rectifier-regulator is defective and must be renewed.

Later 10, 13, 16 and 20-Amp Alternator

The 10, 13, 16, and 20-amp alternators (Fig. BS148) provide regulated charging current. Charging rate is determined by state of charge in battery. Stator is located under the flywheel. The size of the magnets cast into the

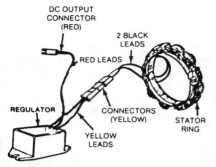

Fig. BS148—Drawing of 10, 13 and 16-amp alternator used on some later models.

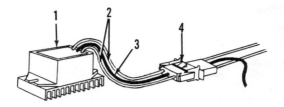

Fig. BS150—Drawing of new-style 20-amp charging system rectifier-regulator and connector used on some Vanguard V-twin engines. Stator is similar to stator shown in Fig. BS148.

1. Rectifier-regulator
2. AC input—yellow
3. DC output—red
4. Connector

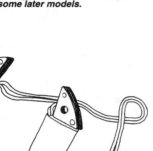

Fig. BS149—Drawing of new-style 10-amp stator used on Series 185400 Vanguard engines. This stator uses the same rectifier-regulator as the system shown in Fig. BS148.

Fig. BS151—Drawing of stator and rectifier assemblies used on early dual-circuit alternator system.

Fig. BS152—Typical wiring diagram for engines equipped with a dual-circuit alternator system.

flywheel determines the output capacity of the system.

Magnets are $\frac{11}{16}$ inch $\times$ $\frac{7}{8}$ inch (18 mm $\times$ 22 mm) on 10-amp flywheels, $\frac{11}{16}$ inch $\times$ $1\frac{1}{16}$ inch (18 mm $\times$ 27 mm) on 13-amp flywheels, $\frac{15}{16}$ inch $\times$ $1\frac{1}{16}$ inch (24 mm $\times$ 27 mm) on 16-amp flywheels and $\frac{29}{32}$ inch $\times$ $1\frac{3}{32}$ inch (23 mm $\times$ 27.5 mm) on 20 amp flywheels.

To check stator output, disconnect yellow wire connector and connect voltmeter leads to pins for stator leads. With engine running at 3600 rpm, voltmeter should indicate at least 20 VAC for 10-amp and 13-amp systems, 30 VAC for 16-amp systems and 26 VAC for 20-amp systems. If not, renew stator.

To test regulator, the 12-volt battery must have a minimum of 5-volt charge. Connect an ammeter in series with charging circuit positive (red) lead and run engine at normal operating rpm. Test leads must be connected before starting engine and must not be disconnected while engine is running as regulator may be damaged. Ammeter should indicate a charge that will vary according to battery state of charge and capacity of alternator. If no charging current is indicated, check that wires are connected properly and regulator is grounded. Retest and renew regulator

if charge current remains unsatisfactory.

Some Series 185400 engines have a 10-amp regulated charging system that uses the stator pictured in Fig. BS149. Service procedures are the same as for other 10-amp systems described previously except for the following caution.

CAUTION: When removing the flywheel, DO NOT install flywheel-puller bolts deeper than thickness of the flywheel, or stator damage may result.

Some Vanguard V-twin engines use a 20-amp regulated charging system (Fig. BS150). The heat-sink fins on the rectifier-regulator base must receive unrestricted flow of cooling air for the system to provide proper output. Test procedures are the same as for the B&S 16-amp regulated system described previously.

Early Dual Circuit Alternator

A dual circuit alternator may be used on some early engines. The early dual circuit system is identified by a

fuse in the system (see Figs. BS151 or BS152). The dual circuit alternator has one circuit to provide charging current to maintain battery state of charge and a separate circuit to provide alternating current for lights. The amount of current produced is regulated only by engine speed.

The charging circuit supplies alternating current through a solid state rectifier that converts the alternating current to direct current to maintain battery state of charge.

The lighting circuit provides alternating current to the lights.

The stator is located under the flywheel. A single ring of magnets cast into the flywheel creates the magnetic field for both circuits.

Current for lights is available only when engine is operating. Twelve-volt lights with a total rating of 60 to 100 watts may be used. With a rating of 70 watts, voltage rises from 8 volts at 2400 rpm to 12 volts at 3600 rpm.

Battery charging current connection is made through a $7\frac{1}{2}$-amp fuse mounted in a fuse holder. Current for lights is available at plastic connector below fuse holder. The $7\frac{1}{2}$-amp fuse pro-

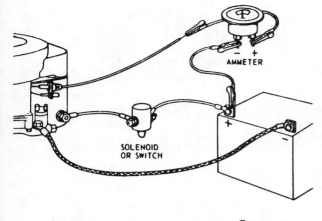

Fig. BS153—Connect ammeter as shown for output test.

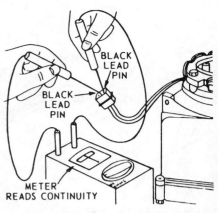

Fig. BS156—Connect an ohmmeter as shown to check charging coils for an open circuit. Meter should show continuity.

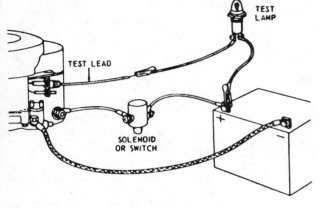

Fig. BS154—Connect a test lamp as shown to test for short in stator or rectifier. Refer to text.

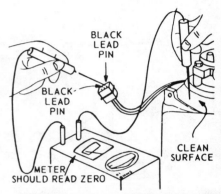

Fig. BS157—Connect an ohmmeter as shown to check charging coils for a grounded circuit. Refer to text.

Fig. BS155—Use an ohmmeter to check charging lead for continuity. Refer to text.

If short cannot be repaired, renew stator. Charging lead should also be checked for continuity as follows: Touch one lead of ohmmeter to lead at fuse holder and other ohmmeter lead to red lead pin in connector as shown in Fig. BS155. If ohmmeter does not show continuity, charging lead is open and stator must be renewed. Charging coils should be checked for continuity as follows: Touch ohmmeter test leads to the two black lead pins as shown in Fig. BS156. If ohmmeter does not show continuity, charging coils are defective and stator must be renewed. Test for grounded charging coils by touching one test lead of ohmmeter to a clean ground surface on the engine and the other test lead to each of the black lead pins as shown in Fig. BS157. If ohmmeter shows continuity, charging coils are grounded and stator must be renewed.

To test rectifier, use an ohmmeter and check for continuity between each of the three lead pin sockets and blower housing. See Fig. BS158. Reverse ohmmeter leads and check continuity again. Ohmmeter should show a continuity reading for one direction only on each lead socket. If any pin socket shows continuity reading in both directions or

tects the 3-amp charging alternator and rectifier from burnout due to reverse polarity battery connections. The 5-amp lighting alternator does not require a fuse.

To check charging alternator output, install an ammeter in circuit as shown in Fig. BS153. Start engine and operate it at 3000 rpm. Ammeter should indicate charging. If not, and fuse is known to be good, test for short in stator or rectifier as follows: Disconnect charging lead from battery and connect a small test lamp between battery positive terminal and fuse cap as shown in Fig.

BS154. DO NOT start engine. Test lamp should not light. If it does light, stator's charging lead is grounded or rectifier is defective. Unplug rectifier plug under blower housing. If test lamp goes out, rectifier is defective. If test lamp does not go out, stator charging lead is grounded.

If test indicates stator charging lead is grounded, remove blower housing, flywheel, starter motor and retaining clamp, then examine length of red lead for damaged insulation or obvious shorts in lead. If bare spots are found, repair with electrical tape and shellac.

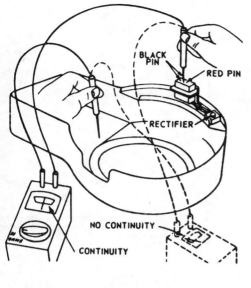

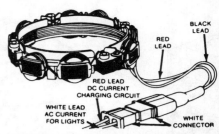

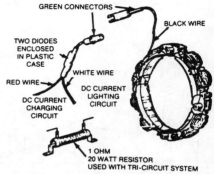

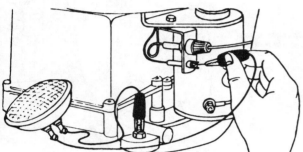

Fig. BS158—If ohmmeter shows continuity in both directions or neither direction, rectifier is defective.

Fig. BS161—Drawing of later dual-circuit alternator used on some models with lights.

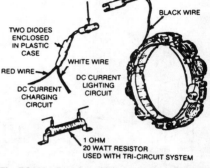

Fig. BS159—A load lamp is used to text AC lighting circuit output.

Fig. BS162—Drawing of tri-circuit alternator used on some models with lights and electric pto clutch.

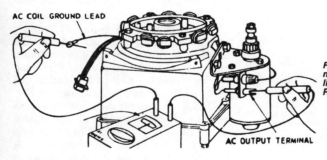

Fig. BS160—Connect an ohmmeter as shown to check AC lighting circuit for continuity. Refer to text.

The stator is located under the flywheel. A single ring of magnets cast into the flywheel creates the magnetic field for both circuits.

To test charging circuit output, connect an ammeter in series with the charging circuit lead (red wire). Start and run engine at 2400 rpm. Ammeter should indicate 2-amp charging current. Increase engine speed to 3600 rpm. Ammeter should indicate 3-amp charging current. If no charging current is indicated, check the diode in the connector. Attach ohmmeter lead to charging circuit connector pin in plug (a bump on the plug identifies the diode). Stick a pin through the red charging circuit wire just behind the plug and connect remaining ohmmeter lead to pin. Note reading then reverse leads. Ohmmeter should indicate continuity in only one position. If not, renew plug assembly. If diode is good, but system still does not show a charge, renew stator.

To test lighting circuit, connect an AC voltmeter in series with stator lighting circuit lead (black wire) and ground. Run engine at 3600 rpm. Voltmeter reading should be at least 14 volts. Renew stator if there is insufficient voltage.

neither direction, rectifier is defective and must be renewed.

To test AC lighting circuit, connect a load lamp to AC output plug and ground as shown in Fig. BS159. Load lamp should light at full brilliance at medium engine speed. If lamp does not light or is very dim at medium speeds, remove blower housing and flywheel. Disconnect ground end of AC coil from retaining clamp screw (Fig. BS160). Connect ohmmeter between ground lead of AC coil and AC output terminal as shown in Fig. BS160. Ohmmeter should show continuity. If not, stator must be renewed. Be sure AC ground lead is not touching a grounded surface, then check continuity from AC output terminal to engine ground. If ohmmeter

indicates continuity, lighting coils are grounded and stator must be renewed.

Later Dual Circuit Alternator

Dual circuit alternator (Fig. BS161) has one circuit to provide charging current to maintain battery state of charge and a separate circuit to provide alternating current for lights. The amount of current produced is regulated only by engine speed.

The charging circuit supplies alternating current through a solid-state rectifier that converts the alternating current to direct current to maintain battery state of charge.

The lighting circuit provides alternating current to the lights.

Tri-Circuit Alternator

The tri-circuit alternator (Fig. BS162) consists of a single ring of magnets cast into the flywheel that provides a magnetic field for the stator located under the flywheel. The stator produces alternating current and has a single output lead. Circuit separation is achieved by the use of a positive (+) diode and a negative (−) diode. The charging lead diode rectifies negative (-) 12 VDC (5 amps at 3600 rpm) for lighting. This same charge lead contains a second diode that rectifies positive (+) 12 VDC (5 amps at 3600 rpm) for battery charging and external loads. Some equipment manufacturers incorporate one or both diodes in wiring harness. Check wiring diagram for models being serviced for diode location.

To test alternator output, connect an AC voltmeter in series between stator output lead and ground. Start and run engine at 3600 rpm. Voltmeter should register 28 volts AC or more. Voltage will vary with engine rpm. If charge current is not indicated, renew stator.

To check diodes, disconnect charge lead from stator output lead. Connect ohmmeter lead to connector pin and connect remaining lead to the white (lighting circuit) wire. Reverse connections. Ohmmeter should indicate continuity in one position only. If not, renew diode. Repeat the procedure on red wire (charging circuit).

Quad Circuit Alternator

The quad circuit alternator (Fig. BS163) provides 8-amp positive (+) DC

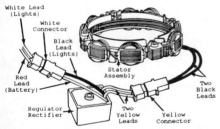

Fig. BS163—Drawing of quad-circuit alternator used on some models.

from the red regulator lead and 8-amp negative (−) DC from the black regulator lead. Note that the black regulator wire changes to a white wire at white connector. Charging rate is determined by state of charge in battery. Stator is located under the flywheel and output capacity is determined by the size of magnets cast into the flywheel.

To check stator output, disconnect yellow connector and connect voltmeter leads to pins for stator leads. With engine running at 3600 rpm, voltmeter should indicate at least 30 VAC. If not, renew stator.

To test regulator output, the 12-volt battery must have a minimum of 5-volt charge. Connect an ammeter in series with charging circuit positive (red) lead and start and run engine at normal operating rpm. Test leads must be connected before starting engine and must not be disconnected while engine is running as regulator may be damaged. Ammeter should indicate a charge that will vary according to battery state of charge and capacity of alternator. If no charging current is indicated, check that wires are connected properly and regulator is grounded. Retest and renew regulator if charge current remains unsatisfactory.

To check lighting circuit of regulator, obtain a 1-ohm, 20-watt resistor. Use a suitable jumper wire and connect to white connector of regulator as shown in Fig. BS164. Connect an ammeter between resistor and battery as shown. Run engine at 3600 rpm just long enough to produce test reading. Ammeter should indicate approximately 8 amp, if not renew regulator.

FUEL PUMP

A diaphragm-type mechanical fuel pump is available on many models as optional equipment. Refer to Fig. BS165 for exploded view of pump.

To disassemble pump, refer to Figs. BS165 and BS166; then, proceed as follows: Remove clamp (1), fuel bowl (2) and screen (4). Remove screws retaining upper body (9) to lower body (16). Pump valves (5) and gaskets (6) can now be removed. Drive pin (14) out to either side of body (16), then press diaphragm (10) against spring (11) as shown in view A, Fig. BS166, and remove lever (13). Diaphragm and spring (11—Fig. BS165) can now be removed.

To reassemble, place diaphragm spring in lower body and place diaphragm on spring, being sure spring en-

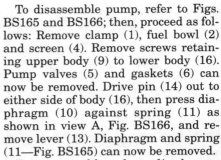

Fig. BS165—Exploded view of diaphragm-type fuel pump used on some engines.

1. Yoke assy.
2. Filter bowl
3. Gasket
4. Filter screen
5. Pump valves
6. Gaskets
7. Elbow fitting
8. Connector
9. Fuel pump head
10. Pump diaphragm
11. Diaphragm spring
12. Gasket
13. Pump lever
14. Lever pin
15. Spring
16. Fuel pump body

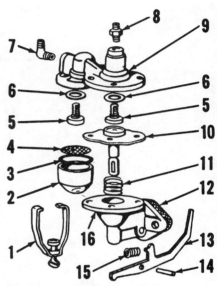

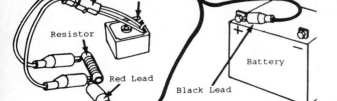

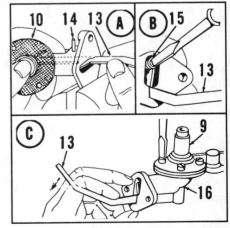

Fig. BS166—Views showing disassembly and assembly of diaphragm-type fuel pump. Refer to text for procedure and to Fig. BS165 for exploded view of pump and parts identification.

Fig. BS164—The regulator lighting circuit can be checked using a 1-ohm, 20-watt resistor connected as shown. Refer to text.

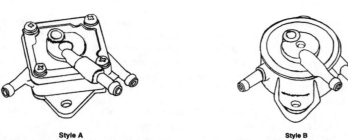

Style A **Style B**

Fig. BS167—Drawing showing vacuum-operated fuel pumps used on some models. Early models appear as Style A, with aluminum square-shaped housing. Later models, Style B, have circular-shaped housings and are made of plastic.

ters cup on bottom side of diaphragm and slot in shaft is at right angle to pump lever. Then, compress diaphragm against the spring as shown in view A, Fig. BS166, and insert hooked end of lever with hole in lower body and drive pin into place. Then, insert lever spring (15) into body and push outer end of spring into place over hook on arm of lever as shown in view B. Hold lever downward as shown in view C while tightening screws holding upper body to lower body. When installing pump on engine, apply a liberal amount of grease on lever (13) at point where it contacts lobe on crankshaft.

Some models use a vacuum-operated fuel pump (Fig. BS167). The pump has a maximum lift of 12 inches (30.5 cm). Vacuum pulses from the engine's crankcase actuate the pump diaphragm.

Pump can be disassembled and cleaned, but no service parts are available. Replace the pump if it is faulty.

BRIGGS & STRATTON SPECIAL TOOLS

The following special tools are available from Briggs & Stratton Central
Parts Distributors.

TOOL KITS

19138—Valve seat insert puller for all models and series so equipped.

19184—Main bearing service kit for Series 170000 and 190000.

19205—Cylinder hone kit for all aluminum bore (Kool-Bore) engines.

19211—Cylinder hone kit for all cast iron cylinder engines.

19228—Main bearing tool kit for all twin-cylinder engines with integral and DU-type main bearings, except Vanguard.

19232—Valve guide puller/reamer kit for Series 170000, 190000, 220000, 250000, 280000, 300000, 320000 and twin-cylinder engines, except Vanguard.

19237—Valve seat cutter kit for most models and series.

19245—Special tap set for cleaning threads in 2-piece Flo-jet carburetors.

19343—Valve seat cutter kit for Vanguard OHV engines.

19407—Ball main bearing service kit for Series 185400-245400 Vanguard single-cylinder engines.

19460—Carburetor socket set for main jet housing on Intek V-twin engines.

PLUG GAUGES

19055—Check breaker plunger bore on Model 23C and Series 170000, 190000 and 220000.

19117—Check main bearing bore on Models 19, 19D, 23, 23A, 23C, 23D and Series 190000, 200000 and 230000.

19151—Check valve guide bores on Models 19, 19D, 23, 23A, 23C, 23D and Series 170000, 190000, 200000, 230000, 240000, 250000, 300000, 320000 and twin-cylinder engines, except Vanguard.

19164—Check camshaft bearings on Series 170000, 190000, 220000 and 250000.

19219—Check integral or DU-type main bearing bore on twin-cylinder engines.

19377—Check magneto-side main bearing bore on Series 161400 Vanguard single-cylinder engine.

19378—Check main bearing bores on Series 26x700 Vanguard single-cylinder engines.

19380—Check main bearing bores on Vanguard.

19381—Check valve guide bores on Vanguard.

19382—Check valve guides on Vanguard V-twins and single-cylinder Series 185400-245400 engines.

19383—Check camshaft bearings on Vanguard single-cylinder Series 161400 and 26x700 engines.

19384—Check camshaft bearings on Vanguard.

19386—Check pto-side main bearing bore on Vanguard V-twins.

REAMERS

19056—Breaker plunger bushing reamer for 170000, 190000, 220000 and 250000.

19058—Finish reamer for breaker plunger bushing for Series 170000, 190000, 220000 and 250000.

19173—Finish reamer for main bearings for Series 170000 and 190000.

19174—Counterbore reamer for main bearings for Series 170000, 171000, 190000 and 191000.

19175—Finish reamer for main bearings for Series 170000, 171000, 190000 and 191000.

19183—Valve guide reamer for bushing installation for Models 19, 19D, 23, 23A, 23C, 23D and Series 170000, 190000, 200000, 220000, 230000, 240000, 251000, 300000 and 320000.

19231—Valve guide bushing reamer for Models 19 and 23 and Series 170000, 190000, 200000, 220000, 230000, 240000, 250000, 300000, 320000 and twin-cylinder engines.

19281—Counterbore reamer for main bearings for Series 170000 and 190000.

19333—Valve guide bushing finish reamer for Series 170000, 190000, 200000, 230000, 240000, 250000, 280000, 300000, 320000 and twin-cylinder engines, except Vanguard.

19346—Valve guide bushing reamer for Vanguard.

19444—Finish reamer for Vanguard V-twin valve guides.

PILOTS

19096—Pilot for main bearing reamer for Series 170000, 171000, 190000 and 191000.

19127—Expansion pilot for valve seat counterbore cutter for Models 19 and 23 and Series 170000, 190000, 200000, 220000, 230000, 240000, 300000, 320000 and twin-cylinder engines.

19130—"T" handle for 19127 pilot.

REAMER GUIDE BUSHING

19192—Guide bushing for valve guide reaming for Models 19 and 23 and Series 170000, 190000, 200000, 220000, 230000, 240000, 251000, 300000 and 320000.

19201—Guide bushing for main bearing reaming for Series 171000 and 191000.

19222—Guide bushing for main bearing reaming for tool kit 19228 for twin-cylinder engines.

19234—Guide bushing for main bearing reaming for tool kit 19232 for twin-cylinder engines.

19282—Guide bushing for main bearing reaming for Series 170000 and 190000.

19301—Guide bushing for main bearing reaming for Series 170000 and 190000.

19345—Guide bushing for valve guide reaming for Vanguard.

PILOT GUIDE BUSHINGS

19168—Pilot guide bushing for main bearing reaming for Series 170000 and 190000.

19169—Pilot guide bushing for main bearing reaming for Series 170000 and 190000.

19220—Pilot guide bushing for main bearing reaming for tool lit 19228 for twin-cylinder engines.

COUNTERBORE CUTTERS

19131—Counterbore valve seat cutter for Models 19, 19D, 23, 23A, 23D and Series 190000, 200000, 230000 and 240000.

CRANKCASE SUPPORT JACK

19123—To support crankcase when removing or installing main bearings on Series 170000 and 190000.

19227—To support crankcase when removing or installing DU-type main bearings on twin-cylinder engines.

CYLINDER BORE GAUGE

19404—Stabilized telescoping gauge measures bores to 3.5 inches (90 mm).

DRIVERS

19057—To install breaker plunger bushing on Series 170000, 190000, 220000 and 250000.

19136—To install valve seat inserts on all engines.

19179—To install main bearing on Series 170000 and 190000.

19344—To install main bearing retaining pin on Vanguard.

19349—To install main bearing on Vanguard.

19367—To install valve guides on Vanguard.

19450—To main bearing on magneto side in Vanguard V-twin after Code 970430xxx.

ELECTRICAL

19359—Shunt used in troubleshooting alternator charging systems.

19464—Digital multimeter recommended for testing.

FLYWHEEL PULLERS

19068—Flywheel removal on Models 19, 19D, 23, 23A, 23C, 23D and Series 190000, 200000, 230000, 240000 300000 and 320000.

19165—Flywheel removal on Series 170000, 190000 and 250000.

19203—Flywheel removal on Models 19 and 23 and Series 190000, 200000, 220000, 230000, 240000, 250000, 280000, 300000, 320000 and twin-cylinder engines.

VALVE SPRING COMPRESSOR

19063—Valve spring compressor for all models and series, except Vanguard.

19347—Valve spring compressor for Vanguard.

PISTON RING COMPRESSOR

19070—Piston ring compressor for Vanguard.

19230—Piston ring compressor for all models and series, except Vanguard.

STARTER MOTOR

19435—C-ring installation tool for late-style bendix drives.

19436—C-ring removal tool for late-style bendix drives.

STARTER WRENCH

19114—All models and series with rewind starter.

19161—All models and series with rewind starter (to be used with ½-inch torque wrench).

19244—To remove, install and torque rewind starter clutches.

BENDING TOOL

19229—Governor tang bending tool, except Vanguard.

19352—Governor tang bending tool for Vanguard.

IGNITION SPARK TESTER

19368—Test ignition spark for all models.

BRIGGS & STRATTON CENTRAL PARTS DISTRIBUTORS

(Arranged Alphabetically by States)
These franchised firms carry extensive stocks of repair parts. Contact them
for name of the nearest service distributor.

Power Equipment Company
Phone (602) 272-3936
#7 North 43rd Avenue
Phoenix, Arizona 85107

Pacific Western Power
Phone (415) 692-3254
1565 Adrain Road
Burlingame, California 94010

Power Equipment Company
Phone (805) 684-6637
1045 Cindy Lane
Carpinteria, California 93013

Pacific Power Equipment Company
Phone (303) 744-7891
1441 W. Bayaud Avenue #4
Denver, Colorado 80223

Central Power Systems of Florida
Phone (813) 253-6035
1114 W. Cass St.
Tampa, Florida 33606

Sedco, Inc.
Phone (770) 925-4706
4305 Steve Reynolds Blvd.
Norcross, Georgia 30093

Small Engine Clinic, Inc.
Phone (808)488-0711
98019 Kam Highway
Aiea, Hawaii 96701

Midwest Engine Warehouse
Phone (630) 833-1200
515 Romans Road
Elmhurst, Illinois 60126

Diamond Engine Sales
Phone (913) 888-8828
15500 W 109th Street
Lenexa, Kansas 66219

Commonwealth Engine, Inc.
Phone (502) 263-7026
11421 Electron Drive
Louisville, Kentucky 40229

Delta Power Equipment Co.
Phone (504) 465-9222
755 E. Airline Highway
Kenner, Louisiana 70062

Atlantic Power
Phone (508) 543-6911
77 Green Street
Foxboro, Massachusetts 02035

Wisconsin Magneto, Inc.
Phone (612) 323-7477
800 McKinley Street
Anoka, Minnesota 55303

Original Equipment, Inc.
Phone (406) 245-3081
905 Second Avenue North
Billings, Montana 59101

Midwest Engine Warehouse of Omaha
Phone (402) 891-1700
10606 S. 144th Street
Omaha, Nebraska 68138

Atlantic Power
Phone (732) 356-8400
650 Howard Avenue
Somerset, New Jersey 08873

Preferred Power, Inc.
Phone (704) 598-1010
6509-A Northpark Blvd.
Charlotte, North Carolina 28216

Central Power Systems
Phone (614) 876-3533
2555 International Street
Columbus, Ohio 43228

Engine Warehouse, Inc.
Phone (405) 364-6868
2701 Venture Drive
Norman, Oklahoma 73069

Brown & Wiser, Inc.
Phone (503) 692-0330
9991 S. W. Avery Street
Tualatin, Oregon 97062

Three Rivers Engine Distributors
Phone (412) 321-4111
1411 Beaver Avenue
Pittsburgh, Pennsylvania 15233

Engine Power Distributors
Phone (901) 345-0300
3250 Millbranch Road
Memphis, Tennessee 38116

Grayson Company, Inc.
Phone (214) 630-3272
1234 Motor Street
Dallas, Texas 75207

Engine Warehouse, Inc.
Phone (713) 937-4000
7415 Empire Central Drive
Houston, Texas 77040

Frank Edwards Company
Phone (801) 281-4660
3653 South 500 West
Salt Lake City, Utah 84115

RBI Corporation
Phone (888) 724-0101
10201 Cedar Ridge Drive
Ashland, Virginia 23005

Wisconsin Magneto, Inc.
Phone (414) 445-2800
4727 N. Teutonia Avenue
Milwaukee, Wisconsin 53209

CANADIAN DISTRIBUTORS

Briggs & Stratton Canada, Inc.
Phone (604) 520-1294
1360 Cliveden Avenue
Delta, British Columbia V3M 6K2

Briggs & Stratton Canada, Inc.
Phone (905) 795-2632
301 Ambassador Drive
Mississauga, Ontario L5T 2J3

CRAFTSMAN

Sears Roebuck & Co.
Chicago, IL 60607

Craftsman engines are manufactured by the Tecumseh Products Company. Except for various parts, Craftsman engines are comparable to Tecumseh models of the same size with the same equipment. Refer to the Tecumseh engine section in this manual for service information. The following cross reference listing may be helpful, but is intended for service information only. The complete Craftsman model number and serial number are necessary when ordering parts.

Craftsman Model Number	Basic Tecumseh Model Number
143.186022	V70
143.186032	V70
143.186042	V70
143.186072	V70
143.196042	V70
143.196052	V70
143.196062	V70
143.196072	V70
143.206022	V70
143.216012	V70
143.216022	V70
143.216072	V70
143.216082	V70
143.216092	V70
143.216132	V80
143.216152	V80
143.216162	V80
143.216172	V80
143.226022	V70
143.226062	V70
143.226072	V70
143.226082	V70
143.226092	V80
143.226102	V80
143.226112	V80
143.226122	V80
143.226142	V70
143.226192	V80
143.226202	V70
143.226212	V70
143.226272	V70
143.226282	V70
143.226292	V80
143.226302	V70
143.226312	V80
143.226342	V70
143.226352	V80
143.236022	VM80
143.236032	VM80
143.236062	VM80
143.236072	VM80
143.236092	V70

Craftsman Model Number	Basic Tecumseh Model Number
143.236122	V70
143.236142	VM80
143.236162	V70
143.236172	V70
143.236222	VM80
143.246022	VM80
143.246032	VM80
143.246052	V70
143.246062	V70
143.246072	V70
143.246082	VM80
143.246092	VM80
143.246102	V70
143.246112	V70
143.246122	VM80
143.246132	V70
143.246142	V70
143.246152	VM80
143.246162	VM80
143.246172	VM80
143.246182	VM80
143.246192	VM80
143.246202	VM80
143.246212	VM80
143.246222	V70
143.246232	VM80
143.246242	V70
143.246252	VM80
143.246262	V70
143.246272	VM80
143.246282	VM80
143.246292	VM80
143.246302	V70
143.246312	V70
143.246322	VM80
143.246332	VM80
143.246342	V70
143.246362	VM100
143.246372	VM80
143.246382	VM100
143.249012	VH100
143.249022	VH100
143.256012	VM80
143.256032	V70
143.256042	VM80
143.256062	VM80
143.256072	VM80
143.256102	V70
143.256112	VM80
143.256132	V70
143.259012	VH100
143.259022	VH100
143.266012	VM80
143.266022	VM80
143.266042	V70
143.266052	V70

Craftsman Model Number	Basic Tecumseh Model Number
143.266092	V70
143.266102	V70
143.266112	V70
143.266122	V70
143.266132	V70
143.266142	VM80
143.266162	VM80
143.266172	VM80
143.266182	VM80
143.266202	VM80
143.266212	VM80
143.266222	VM80
143.266232	VM80
143.266242	VM80
143.266262	VM80
143.266272	V70
143.266282	V70
143.266302	V70
143.266312	VM80
143.266322	VM80
143.266332	V70
143.266342	VM80
143.266352	V70
143.266362	VM80
143.266422	VM80
143.266462	VM100
143.266472	VM100
143.266482	VM80
143.266292	VM100
143.269012	VH100
143.269022	VH100
143.276022	VM100
143.276032	VM80
143.276042	VM80
143.276052	VM100
143.276062	VM80
143.276072	VM80
143.276092	V70
143.276102	V70
143.276112	V70
143.276122	VM80
143.276132	VM100
143.276142	VM80
143.276152	VM80
143.276162	VM80
143.276172	V70
143.276192	V70
143.276212	V70
143.276222	V70
143.276232	VM80
143.276242	VM80
143.276262	VM80
143.276272	VM80
143.276282	V70
143.276292	VM80
143.276302	VM80
143.276322	V70

Craftsman Model Number	Basic Tecumseh Model Number	Craftsman Model Number	Basic Tecumseh Model Number	Craftsman Model Number	Basic Tecumseh Model Number
143.276332	V70	143.296172	VM80	143.326212	V70
143.276342	V70	143.296182	VM80	143.326222	V70
143.276352	VM80	143.296192	VM80	143.326232	V70
143.276362	VM100	143.296202	VM100	143.326242	V70
143.276372	V70	143.296212	VM100	143.326252	V70
143.276382	V70	143.296222	VM80	143.326262	V70
143.276392	V70	143.296232	VM100	143.326272	V70
143.276402	VM100	143.296242	VM80	143.326312	V70
143.276422	V70	143.296252	VM80	143.326322	TVM170
143.276432	VM80	143.296262	VM80	143.326332	TVM195
143.276442	VM80	143.306012	VM80	143.326342	TVM195
143.276452	VM80	143.306022	VM100	143.326372	TVM170
143.276462	VM80	143.306032	VM100	143.336022	TVM220
143.276472	VM80	143.306042	VM100	143.336032	TVM220
143.276482	VM100	143.316012	V70	143.336042	TVM220
143.276012	VM80	143.316022	VM80	143.346012	TVM220
143.279012	VH100	143.316032	V70	143.346022	TVM220
143.286032	V70	143.316042	VM70	143.346032	TVM170
143.286042	VM100	143.316052	VM80	143.346042	TVM195
143.286052	VM100	143.316062	VM80	143.346052	TVM195
143.286062	V70	143.316082	VM80	143.346062	TVM220
143.286072	VM80	143.316092	VM100	143.346072	TVM220
143.286082	VM80	143.316102	VM80	143.346082	TVM170
143.286092	VM80	143.316112	VM80	143.346092 to 143.346132	TVM195
143.286102	VM100	143.316122	VM100	143.346142 to 143.346192	TVM220
143.286112	VM80	143.316132	VM100	143.356012	TVM220
143.286122	VM80	143.316142	VM100	143.356032	TVM195
143.286132	V70	143.316152	VM80	143.356042	TVM220
143.286142	VM80	143.316162	VM100	143.356052	TVM195
143.286152	VM80	143.316172	VM70	143.356072	TVM195
143.286162	VM80	143.316182	VM80	143.356082	TVM220
143.286172	VM80	143.316192	VM100	143.356092	TVM220
143.286182	VM80	143.316202	VM100	143.356102	TVM170
143.286192	VM100	143.316222	VM80	143.356122	TVM195
143.286202	VM80	143.316232	VM80	143.356132	TVM195
143.286212	VM100	143.316242	VM80	143.356142	TVM195
143.286222	V70	143.316252	VM80	143.356152	TVM195
143.286232	VM100	143.316262	VM100	143.356162	TVM220
143.286242	VM100	143.316272	VM100	143.356172	TVM220
143.286252	V70	143.316282	VM100	143.356182	TVM220
143.286262	VM100	143.316292	VM80	143.356192	TVM220
143.286272	VM100	143.316302	VM100	143.356202	TVM220
143.286282	V70	143.316312	VM80	143.356212	TVM220
143.286292	VM100	143.322012	VH100	143.356222	TVM220
143.286312	VM80	143.326012	TVM195	143.356232	TVM220
143.286322	V70	143.326022	TVM195	143.356252	TVM220
143.286332	V70	143.326032	TVM195	143.366012	OVM120
143.286362	VM100	143.326042	TVM195	143.366022	TVM195
143.296012	VM80	143.326052	TVM195	143.366032	TVM220
143.296022	VM100	143.326062	TVM195	143.366042	TVM195
143.296032	VM80	143.326072	TVM195	143.366052	TVM220
143.296042	VM100	143.326082	TVM195	143.366062	TVM220
143.296052	VM80	143.326092	TVM195	143.366072	OVM120
143.296062	VM80	143.326102	TVM195	143.366102	TVM195
143.296072	VM100	143.326112	TVM195	143.366112	TVM220
143.296082	VM80	143.326122	TVM220	143.366122	TVM220
143.296092	VM80	143.326132	TVM220	143.366132	TVM220
143.296102	VM100	143.326142	TVM220	143.366152	TVM195
143.296112	VM100	143.326152	TVM220	143.366172	TVM220
143.296122	VM100	143.326162	TVM220	143.366192	TVM220
143.296132	VM100	143.326172	TVM220	143.366202	OVM120
143.296142	VM80	143.326182	TVM220	143.366212	OVM120
143.296152	VM80	143.326192	V70	143.366222	TVM220
143.296162	VM80	143.326202	V70	143.366232	OVM120

Craftsman Model Number	Basic Tecumseh Model Number	Craftsman Model Number	Basic Tecumseh Model Number	Craftsman Model Number	Basic Tecumseh Model Number
143.376012	OVM120	143.426072	TVXL220	143.579132	HH100
143.376022	TVM220	143.426092	OVXL120	143.582012	HH120
143.376032	OVM120	143.426112	OVXL120	143.582022	HH120
143.376042	TVM195	143.426122	OVXL125	143.582032	HH120
143.376052	TVM220	143.426132	TVXL220	143.582042	HH120
143.376062	TVM195	143.426142	OVXL120	143.582052	HH120
143.376072	OVM120	143.426152	OVXL120	143.582062	HH120
143.376082	OVM120	143.426172	OVXL125	143.582072	HH120
143.376092	TVM220	143.436012	TVXL220	143.582082	HH120
143.386012	OVM120	143.436022	OHV12	143.582092	HH120
143.386022	TVM220	143.436032	OHV125	143.582102	HH120
143.386032	OVM120	143.436042	OHV125	143.582112	HH120
143.386042	TVM220	143.436062	TVXL195	143.582122	HH120
143.386052	TVM195	143.436072	TVXL220	143.582132	HH120
143.386062	TVM220	143.436082	TVXL220	143.582142	HH120
143.386072	TVM220	143.436092	OHV125	143.582172	HH120
143.386082	TVM220	143.436102	OHV125	143.586052	H70
143.386092	OVM120	143.436112	TVXL220	143.586062	H70
143.386102	OVM120	143.436122	TVXL220	143.586112	H70
143.386122	TVM195	143.436132	OHV125	143.586122	H70
143.386132	TVM195	143.436142	OHV12	143.586132	H70
143.386142	TVM220	143.436152	OHV125	143.586142	H70
143.386152	OVM120	143.436172	TVXL195	143.586162	H70
143.386162	OVM120	143.558012	HH80	143.586252	H70
143.386172	TVM220	143.558022	HH80	143.588012	HH80
143.386182	TVM220	143.558032	HH80	143.588032	HH80
143.396012	OVXL120	143.558052	HH80	143.589012	HH100
143.396022	TVXL220	143.559012	HH100	143.589022	HH100
143.396032	OVXL120	143.559022	HH100	143.589032	HH100
143.396042	TVXL220	143.559032	HH100	143.589042	HH100
143.396052	TVXL220	143.559042	HH100	143.589052	HH100
143.396062	OVXL120	143.560212	HH120	143.589072	HH100
143.396072	OVXL120	143.562022	HH120	143.592012	HH120
143.396082	TVXL220	143.562032	HH120	143.592022	HH120
143.396092	OVM120	143.568032	HH80	143.592032	HH120
143.396112	OVXL120	143.569022	HH100	143.592052	HH120
143.396122	TVXL220	143.569032	HH100	143.592062	HH120
143.396132	OVXL120	143.569042	HH100	143.592072	HH120
143.406012	OVXL120	143.569052	HH100	143.592082	HH120
143.406022	TVXL220	143.569082	HH100	143.596012	H70
143.406032	TVXL220	143.572012	HH120	143.596022	H70
143.404042	TVXL220	143.572022	HH120	143.596052	H70
143.406052	OVXL120	143.572032	HH120	143.598012	HH80
143.406062	OVXL120	143.572042	HH120	143.599012	HH100
143.406072	OVXL120	143.572052	HH120	143.599022	HH100
143.406092	TVXL195	143.572062	HH120	143.599042	HH100
143.406102	TVXL220	143.572092	HH120	143.599052	HH100
143.406122	TVXL220	143.572102	HH120	143.599062	HH100
143.406132	OVXL120	143.578012	HH80	143.602012	HH120
143.406142	OVXL120	143.578022	HH80	143.602022	HH120
143.406152	OVXL120	143.578052	HH80	143.602032	HH120
143.406162	OVXL125	143.578062	HH80	143.602052	HH120
143.406172	TVXL195	143.578072	HH80	143.602062	HH120
143.416012	OVXL120	143.579012	HH100	143.602072	HH120
143.416022	TVXL195	143.579022	HH100	143.602082	HH120
143.416032	TVXL220	143.579032	HH100	143.602092	HH120
143.416042	OVXL125	143.579042	HH100	143.602102	HH120
143.416072	TVXL220	143.579052	HH100	143.602112	HH120
143.416082	OVXL125	143.579062	HH100	143.602122	HH120
143.426022	TVXL195	143.579072	HH100	143.606012	H70
143.426032	TVXL195	143.579082	HH100	143.606022	H70
143.426042	TVXL220	143.579092	HH100	143.606032	H70
143.426052	TVXL220	143.579102	HH100	143.606042	H70
143.426062	TVXL220	143.579112	HH100	143.606052	H70

Craftsman Model Number	Basic Tecumseh Model Number	Craftsman Model Number	Basic Tecumseh Model Number	Craftsman Model Number	Basic Tecumseh Model Number
143.606102	H70	143.640022	HH160	143.666032	HM80
143.608012	HH80	143.640032	HH160	143.666042	H70
143.608022	HH80	143.640042	0H160	143.666052	H70
143.608032	HH80	143.640052	HH160	143.666062	H70
143.609022	HH100	143.642012	HH120	143.666072	H70
143.609032	HH100	143.642022	HH120	143.666082	HM80
143.609042	HH100	143.642032	HH120	143.666092	HM80
143.609052	HH100	143.642042	HH120	143.666152	HM80
143.609072	HH100	143.646012	H70	143.666162	HM80
143.612012	HH120	143.646022	H70	143.666222	H70
143.612022	HH120	143.646032	H70	143.666232	HM80
143.616012	H70	143.646042	HM80	143.666252	H70
143.616122	H70	143.646052	HM80	143.666282	H70
143.619012	HH100	143.646062	H70	143.666302	H70
143.622012	HH120	143.646072	H70	143.666312	H70
143.622022	HH120	143.646082	H70	143.666322	HM80
143.622032	HH120	143.646092	H70	143.666332	HM100
143.622042	HH120	143.646102	H70	143.666342	H70
143.622052	HH120	143.646122	H70	143.666352	HM80
143.622062	HH120	143.646132	H70	143.666362	HM100
143.622072	HH120	143.646142	HM80	143.666382	H70
143.622082	HH120	143.646152	H70	143.669012	HH100
143.622092	HH120	143.646162	HM80	143.670012	0H140
143.622102	HH120	143.646172	H70	143.670022	OH160
143.626012	H70	143.646182	H70	143.670032	OH160
143.626032	H70	143.646202	H70	143.670042	OH140
143.626052	H70	143.646212	HM80	143.670052	OH160
143.626062	H70	143.646222	HM80	143.670062	OH160
143.626082	H70	143.646232	HM80	143.670072	OH160
143.626092	H70	143.649012	HH100	143.670082	OH140
143.626102	H70	143.649022	HH100	143.670092	OH140
143.626122	H70	143.650012	HH160	143.672012	HH120
143.626142	H70	143.650022	HH140	143.672022	HH120
143.626152	H70	143.650032	HH160	143.672032	HH120
143.626172	H70	143.652012	HH120	143.672042	HH120
143.626192	H70	143.652022	HH120	143.672052	HH120
143.626212	H70	143.652032	HH120	143.672062	HH120
143.626282	HM80	143.652042	HH120	143.672072	HH120
143.626292	H70	143.652052	HH120	143.676012	HM80
143.626312	H70	143.652062	HH120	143.676022	HM80
143.626322	H70	143.652072	HH120	143.676032	H70
143.628012	HH80	143.656062	H70	143.676042	HM80
143.628022	HH80	143.656072	HM80	143.676052	HM80
143.629012	HH100	143.656082	HM80	143.676062	HM100
143.629022	HH100	143.656102	H70	143.676072	HM100
143.629032	HH100	143.656122	H70	143.676082	HM100
143.629042	HH100	143.656132	H70	143.676092	HM100
143.629052	HH100	143.656152	H70	143.676102	H70
143.629062	HH100	143.656192	H70	143.676122	H70
143.629072	HH100	143.656212	HM80	143.676142	HM80
143.630012	HH160	143.656222	HM80	143.676152	HM100
143.630022	HH160	143.656232	H70	143.676162	HM100
143.632012	HH120	143.656242	HM80	143.676172	H70
143.632022	HH120	143.656262	H70	143.676182	HM80
143.632032	HH120	143.656272	H70	143.676192	H70
143.632042	HH120	143.656282	HM80	143.676202	HM80
143.636012	H80	143.659012	HH100	143.676212	HM100
143.636022	H80	143.659022	HH100	143.676222	HM80
143.636032	H70	143.659032	HH100	143.676252	HM80
143.636042	HM80	143.660012	HH160	143.676262	HM100
143.636062	H70	143.660022	HH160	143.679012	HH100
143.636072	HM80	143.662012	HH120	143.679022	HH100
143.639012	HH100	143.666012	H70	143.679032	HH100
143.640012	HH160	143.666022	H70	143.680012	OH140

Craftsman Model Number	Basic Tecumseh Model Number	Craftsman Model Number	Basic Tecumseh Model Number	Craftsman Model Number	Basic Tecumseh Model Number
143.680022	OH140	143.716252	H70	143.766102	HM80
143.680032	OH160	143.716262	HM100	143.766112	HM80
143.686012	HM70	143.716312	H70	143.766122	HM100
143.686022	HM70	143.716322	H70	143.766132	H70
143.686032	HM80	143.716332	HM100	143.766142	HM100
143.686042	HM80	143.716342	HM70	143.766152	HM80
143.686052	HM80	143.716362	H70	143.770012	OH140
143.686062	H70	143.716372	HM100	143.770022	OH180
143.686082	HM80	143.716382	HM100	143.776012	HM80
143.686092	HM80	143.716392	HM80	143.776022	H70
143.686102	HM100	143.716432	HM100	143.776042	HM80
143.686132	H70	143.726022	HM100	143.776052	HM100
143.686142	HM80	143.726032	HM80	143.776062	HM100
143.686152	HM100	143.726042	H70	143.776072	H70
143.686172	HM100	143.726052	H70	143.780012	HH120
143.696032	HM80	143.726102	HM100	143.786012	HM80
143.696052	H70	143.726152	HM80	143.786022	HM80
143.696062	HM80	143.726182	H70	143.786032	HM80
143.696072	HM100	143.726192	H70	143.786042	HM100
143.696092	HM80	143.726202	H70	143.786052	HM80
143.696102	H70	143.726212	H70	143.786062	HM100
143.696112	HM100	143.726232	HM100	143.786072	HM100
143.696132	HM80	143.726252	H70	143.786092	HM80
143.700012	OH180	143.726282	H70	143.786102	H70
143.706032	HM80	143.726292	HM100	143.786112	HM80
143.706042	HM80	143.726312	HM100	143.786122	HM100
143.706052	HM80	143.726322	HM100	143.786132	H70
143.706072	HM80	143.730012	OH160	143.786142	H70
143.706082	HM80	143.730022	OH140	143.786152	H70
143.706092	H70	143.736042	HM80	143.786172	HM80
143.706112	H70	143.736082	HM80	143.786182	HM100
143.706122	HM80	143.736092	H70	143.786192	HM100
143.706132	HM100	143.736102	HM100	143.786202	HM100
143.706152	HM100	143.736122	HM80	143.790012	OH180
143.706162	HM80	143.736132	HM80	143.796012	HM80
143.706172	H70	143.736142	HM100	143.796022	HM80
143.706182	H70	143.740012	OH140	143.796032	HM80
143.706222	HM80	143.740022	OH160	143.796042	HM80
143.706232	HM100	143.742032	HM80	143.796052	HM100
143.710012	OH160	143.746022	HM80	143.796062	HM100
143.710022	OH140	143.746072	HM100	143.796072	HM100
143.712012	HH120	143.746082	HM80	143.796082	HM80
143.712022	HH120	143.746092	HM80	143.796092	HM80
143.712032	HH120	143.746102	HM100	143.796102	HM100
143.712042	HH120	143.756042	H70	143.796112	OH120
143.716012	HM70	143.756052	H70	143.796122	H70
143.716022	HM80	143.756062	HM100	143.796132	HM80
143.716052	HM70	143.756082	HM80	143.796142	H70
143.716062	HM70	143.756102	HM80	143.796152	HM80
143.716072	HM80	143.756112	HM100	143.796162	HM100
143.716082	HM80	143.756132	H70	143.796172	HM100
143.716092	HM100	143.756152	HM100	143.796182	H70
143.716102	HM100	143.756162	H70	143.796192	HM80
143.716112	H70	143.756172	HM100	143.796202	HM80
143.716122	H70	143.756182	HM80	143.800012	OH180
143.716132	H70	143.756192	HM80	143.806012	HM80
143.716142	H70	143.756202	HM100	143.806022	HM80
143.716152	HM80	143.756212	HM80	143.806032	HM80
143.716172	HM80	143.756222	H70	143.806042	HM100
143.716182	HM80	143.760012	HH120	143.806052	HM100
143.716192	HM80	143.766012	HM80	143.806062	OH120
143.716202	H70	143.766072	HM80	143.806072	HM80
143.716212	HM100	143.766082	HM80	143.806082	HM80
143.716222	HM80	143.766092	HM100	143.806092	HM100

Craftsman Model Number	Basic Tecumseh Model Number	Craftsman Model Number	Basic Tecumseh Model Number	Craftsman Model Number	Basic Tecumseh Model Number
143.806102	HM80	143.836082	HM80	143.951600	OHV165
143.806112	H70	143.941000	TVXL220	143.951602	OHV165
143.806122	H70	143.941001	HM100	143.958000	TVM195
143.806132	HM100	143.941002	TVXL220	143.958001	HM80
143.806142	H70	143.941003	HM100	143.958003	HM80
143.806152	HM80	143.941004	TVXL220	143.958005	HM80
143.806162	HM100	143.941005	HM100	143.958007	HM80
143.806172	HM100	143.941006	TVXL220	143.959001	HM90
143.806182	HM80	143.941007	HM100	143.959003	HM90
143.816012	HM100	143.941008	TVXL220	143.959005	HM90
143.816022	HM80	143.941009	HM100	143.961000	TVM220
143.816032	HM100	143.941200	OHV125	143.961001	HM100
143.816042	OH120	143.941201	OH120	143.961003	HM100
143.816052	HM80	143.941202	OHV12	143.961005	HM100
143.816072	H70	143.948000	TVXL195	143.961007	HM100
143.826012	HM80	143.948001	HM80	143.961201	OH120
143.826022	HM100	143.948003	HM80	143.961300	OHV13
143.826032	HM80	143.948005	HM80	143.968000	TVM195
143.826052	HM100	143.948007	HM80	143.968001	HM80
143.826072	HM80	143.948009	HM80	143.968003	HM80
143.826082	HM100	143.951000	TVM220	143.968005	HM80
143.826102	HM80	143.951001	HM100	143.969001	HM90
143.826122	HM80	143.951002	TVM220	143.969003	HM90
143.836012	HM80	143.951003	HM100	143.969005	HM90
143.836022	HM80	143.951004	TVM220	143.969007	HM90
143.836032	HM100	143.951005	HM100	143.971001	HM100
143.836042	HM100	143.951006	TVM220	143.971201	OH120
143.836052	OH120	143.951008	TVM220	143.975071	H850
		143.951010	TVM220	143.978001	HM80

HONDA

AMERICAN HONDA MOTOR CO., INC.
4475 River Green Parkway
Duluth, GA 30136

Model	No. Cylinders	Bore	Stroke	Displacement	Power Rating
G300	1	76 mm (3.0 in.)	60 mm (2.4 in.)	272 cc (16.6 cu. in.)	5.2 kW (7 hp)
G400	1	86 mm (3.4 in.)	70 mm (2.8 in.)	406 cc (28.1 cu. in.)	7.5 kW (10 hp)
GV400	1	86 mm (3.4 in.)	70 mm (2.8 in.)	406 cc (28.1 cu. in.)	14.8 kW (11 hp)

ENGINE IDENTIFICATION

Model G300 engine develops 5.2 kW (7 hp) at 3600 rpm, Model G400 engine develops 7.5 kW (10 hp) at 3600 rpm and Model GV400 develops 14.8 kW (11 hp) at 3600 rpm. All models are single cylinder, four-stroke gasoline engines. Valves are located in the cylinder block. Models G300 and G400 are horizontal crankshaft engines and Model GV400 is a vertical crankshaft engine. Models G300 and G400 are splash lubricated and Model GV400 is equipped with a trochoid oil pump.

Engine model number decal is located on engine cooling shroud just above or beside rewind starter. On Models G300 and G400, engine serial number is stamped into crankcase as shown in Fig. HN50. On Model GV400, engine serial number is located in a similar location. Always furnish engine model and serial numbers when ordering parts.

MAINTENANCE

SPARK PLUG. Recommended spark plug for Models G300 and G400 is a Champion L92YC or equivalent. Recommended spark plug for Model GV400 is a Champion CJ8 or equivalent. On all models, spark plug should be removed and cleaned after each 100 hours of operation.

CAUTION: Caution should be exercised if abrasive-type spark plug cleaner is used. Inadequate cleaning procedure may allow the abrasive cleaner to be deposited in engine cylinder causing rapid wear and part failure.

Electrode gap should be 0.6-0.7 mm (0.024-0.028 in.) for all models not equipped with CDI ignition. Electrode gap for models equipped with CDI ignition should be 0.9-1.0 mm (0.035-0.039 in.).

CARBURETOR. All models are equipped with a float-type side draft carburetor (Fig. HN51). Idle fuel mixture is controlled by adjusting the pilot jet. High-speed fuel mixture is controlled by a fixed main jet. Engine idle speed should be 1400 rpm for Models G300 and G400 and 1700 rpm for Model GV400. On all models, maximum engine speed (unloaded) should be 3700-4000 rpm. Standard main jet size for Model G300 engine is a number 88 jet, standard main jet size for Model G400 is a number 92 jet and standard main

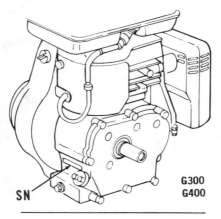

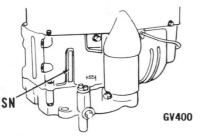

Fig. HN50—Engine serial number (SN) is stamped into crankcase as shown.

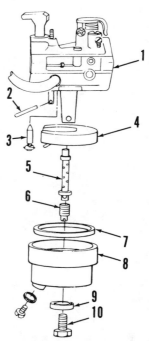

Fig. HN51—Exploded view of carburetor used on all models.

1. Carburetor throttle body
2. Float pin
3. Fuel inlet needle
4. Float
5. Main nozzle
6. Main jet
7. Gasket
8. Float bowl
9. Gasket
10. Bolt

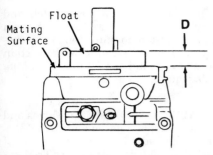

Fig. HN52—To measure float height, invert carburetor body and measure from carburetor mating surface to edge of float. Refer to text for dimension (D) for model being serviced.

jet size for Model GV400 is a number 105 jet.

Initial pilot jet adjustment is 1½ turns open from a lightly seated position. After engine reaches operating temperature, adjust pilot jet to obtain highest engine rpm, then adjust throttle stop screw so engine idles at 1400 rpm for Models G300 and G400 and 1700 rpm for Model GV400.

Float height should be 8.2 mm (0.32 in.) for Model G300, 8.6 mm (0.34 in.) for Model G400 and 7.1-10.1 mm (0.28-0.40 in.) for Model GV400. To measure float height, invert carburetor throttle body and float assembly, and measure from

top of float to mating surface of carburetor throttle body to float bowl (Fig. HN52). If dimension is not as specified, renew float.

FUEL FILTER. A fuel filter screen is located in sediment bowl below fuel shut-off valve (Fig. HN53). To remove sediment bowl (6), shut off fuel, unscrew threaded ring nut (7) and remove ring nut, sediment bowl (6) and gasket (5). Make certain gasket (5) is in place before reassembly. To clean filter (2), drain fuel tank (1) and remove fuel shut-off valve (4) from fuel tank.

AIR FILTER. Engines may be equipped with one of four different types of air cleaners (filter): single element (dry) type, dual element type, foam (semi-dry) type or an oil bath type. On all models, air filter should be removed and serviced after every 20 hours of operation. Refer to appropriate following service information for type being serviced:

Dry Type Air Filter. To remove element, loosen the two wing nuts and remove air filter cover. Remove element and separate foam element from paper element. Direct low-pressure air from inside filter elements toward the foreign material. Reassemble elements and reinstall.

Dual Element Type Air Filter. Remove wing nut, cover and elements. Separate foam outer element from pa-

per element. Wash foam element in warm, soapy water and thoroughly rinse in clean water. Allow element to air dry. Dip foam element into clean engine oil and gently squeeze out excess oil.

Direct low-pressure air from inside paper element toward the outside to remove all loose dirt and foreign material. Reassemble elements and reinstall.

Foam (Semi-Dry) Type Air Filter. Remove air cleaner cover and element. Clean element in nonflammable solvent and squeeze dry. Soak element in new engine oil and gently squeeze out excess oil. Reinstall element and cover.

Oil Bath Type Air Filter. Remove air cleaner assembly and separate cover, element and housing. Clean element in nonflammable solvent and air dry. Drain old oil from housing and thoroughly clean housing. Fill housing to oil level mark with new engine oil and reassemble air cleaner.

GOVERNOR. On all models, the internal centrifugal flyweight governor assembly is located inside crankcase. Governor flyweights are mounted on camshaft gear.

To adjust governor, first stop engine and make certain all linkage is in good condition and tension spring (2—Fig. HN54) is not stretched or damaged. Spring (4) must pull governor lever (3) toward throttle pivot (6).

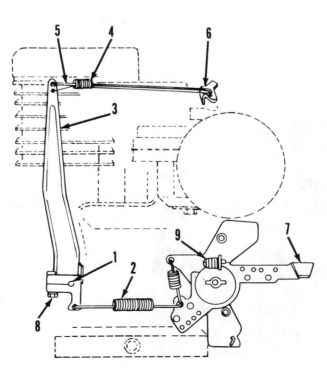

Fig. HN54—View of external governor linkage similar to linkage used on all models.

1. Governor shaft
2. Tension spring
3. Governor lever
4. Spring
5. Carburetor-to-governor lever rod
6. Throttle pivot
7. Throttle lever
8. Clamp bolt
9. Maximum speed screw

Fig. HN53—View of fuel filter and sediment bowl used on Model G300. Models G400 and GV400 are similar.

1. Fuel tank
2. Filter
3. Seal
4. Fuel shut-off valve
5. Gasket
6. Sediment bowl
7. Threaded ring nut

Loosen clamp bolt (8) and turn governor shaft counterclockwise as far as possible while moving governor lever so throttle valve is in wide-open position. Tighten retaining bolt. Start and run engine until it reaches operating temperature. Adjust throttle stop screw to obtain 3700-4000 rpm.

IGNITION SYSTEM. Engines may be equipped with breaker-point ignition system or a capacitor discharge ignition (CDI) system. Refer to the appropriate following service information for type being serviced:

Breaker-Point Ignition System. Breaker-point set and ignition coil are located behind the flywheel on all models. Breaker points should be inspected and gap checked at 300-hour intervals. Initial breaker-point gap should be 0.3-0.4 mm (0.012-0.016 in.). Point gap must be varied to obtain 20° BTDC timing setting.

NOTE: Timing tool 07974-8830001 is available from Honda Motor Company to allow timing adjustment with flywheel removed.

To check ignition timing, connect positive ohmmeter lead to engine stop switch wire and connect remaining lead to engine ground. Rotate flywheel until ohmmeter just breaks continuity. At this point, "F" mark on flywheel should align with index mark on crankcase (Fig. HN55). Remove flywheel and vary point gap to obtain correct timing setting if timing tool is not being used.

To check ignition coil, connect positive ohmmeter lead to spark plug wire and remaining lead to coil laminations. Ohmmeter should register 6600 ohms on standard coil or 8500 ohms on coils

with separate primary coil. Connect positive ohmmeter lead to the coil black lead and remaining lead to coil laminations. Ohmmeter should register 1.46 ohms.

When installing ignition coil, make certain coil is positioned correctly on locating pins.

CDI Ignition System. The capacitor discharge ignition (CDI) system consists of the flywheel magnets, exciter coil (located under flywheel) and CDI unit. CDI system does not require regular maintenance.

To test exciter coil on all models, connect an ohmmeter lead to the red and black coil lead wires. Ohmmeter should register 240 ohms. Ohmmeter should register infinity when one ohmmeter lead is connected to either the red or the black coil lead wire and the remaining ohmmeter lead to the ground. Connect one ohmmeter lead to the blue coil lead wire and the remaining ohmmeter lead to the black coil lead wire. Ohmmeter should register 1400 ohms. Ohmmeter should register infinity when one ohmmeter lead is connected to the blue coil lead and remaining ohmmeter lead is connected to the ground. If ohmmeter readings are not as specified, renew exciter coil.

NOTE: Exciter coil must be installed and timed according to timing number on CDI unit. Refer to Fig. HN56.

Determine CDI unit timing number (Fig. HN56) and position coil so its inner edge aligns with scale position indicated by the CDI unit timing number (Fig. HN57). Distance between scale ridges indicates 2°. Tighten exciter coil mounting cap screws and recheck alignment. Reinstall flywheel and cooling shrouds.

If timing, ignition stop switch and exciter coil check satisfactory, but an ignition system malfunction is still suspected, renew CDI unit. Make certain ground terminal on CDI unit is making an adequate connection.

VALVE ADJUSTMENT. Valves and seats should be refaced and stem clearance adjusted after every 300 hours of operation. Refer to VALVE SYSTEM under REPAIRS section for service procedures and specifications.

CYLINDER HEAD AND COMBUSTION CHAMBER. Cylinder head, combustion chamber and piston should be cleaned and carbon and other deposits removed after every 300 hours of operation. Standard engine cylinder compression should be 586 kPa (85 psi) with engine cranking at 500-600 rpm.

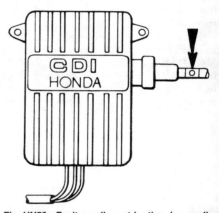

Fig. HN56—Exciter coil must be timed according to timing number located on CDI unit.

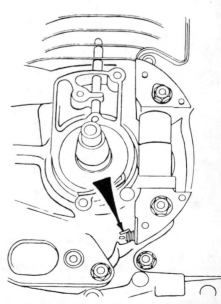

Fig. HN57—Distance between scale ridges indicate 2° ignition timing positions.

"F" Mark on Flywheel

Timing (Index) Mark

Fig. HN55—"F" mark on flywheel should align with timing mark on crankcase when points just begin to open. Honda timing tool 07974-8830001 is available to adjust timing with flywheel removed.

Refer to REPAIRS section for service procedure.

LUBRICATION. Engine oil should be checked prior to each operating interval. Oil level should be maintained between reference marks on dipstick with dipstick just touching first threads. Do not screw dipstick in to check oil level.

Manufacturer recommends SAE 10W-40 oil with an API service classification of SF or SG.

Oil should be changed after the first 20 hours of operation and after every 100 hours of operation thereafter. Crankcase oil capacity is 1.2 L (1.27 qt.) for all models.

GENERAL MAINTENANCE. Check and tighten all loose bolts, nuts and clamps prior to each operating interval. Check for fuel and oil leakage and repair if necessary.

Clean dust, dirt, grease and any foreign material from cylinder head and cylinder block cooling fins after every 100 hours of operation. Inspect fins for damage and repair if necessary.

REPAIRS

TIGHTENING TORQUES. Recommended tightening torque specifications are as follows:

Spark plug . . . . 10-15 N•m
(7-11 ft.-lbs.)
Flywheel nut . . . . 79-88 N•m
(58-65 ft.-lbs.)
Cylinder head:
G300 . . . . 23-26 N•m
(17-19 ft.-lbs.)
G400 . . . . 42-46 N•m
(31-34 ft.-lbs.)
GV400 . . . . 42-54 N•m
(31-40 ft.-lbs.)
Tappet cover:
G300 & G400 . . . . 8-12 N•m
(6-9 ft.-lbs.)
Crankcase cover:
G300 & G400 . . . . 20-23 N•m
(15-17 ft.-lbs.)
Oil pan, GV400 . . . . 20-27 N•m
(15-20 ft.-lbs.)
Connecting rod:
G300 . . . . 12-15 N•m
(9-11 ft.-lbs.)
G400 & GV400 . . . . 22-26 N•m
(16-19 ft.-lbs.)

CYLINDER HEAD. To remove cylinder head, all cooling shrouds, gasoline tank and supports must be removed. Clean engine to prevent entrance of foreign material. Loosen cylinder head bolts in ¼-turn increments following sequence shown in Fig. HN58 for Models G300 and G400 or following se-

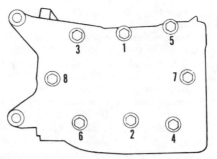

Fig. HN58—Cylinder head bolts should be loosened and tightened following the sequence shown for Models G300 and G400.

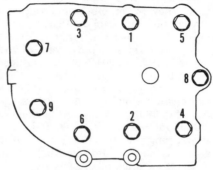

Fig. HN59—Cylinder head bolts should be loosened and tightened following the sequence shown for Model GV400.

quence shown in Fig. HN59 for Model GV400. Remove spark plug on all models and clean carbon and other deposits from cylinder head.

Reinstall cylinder head with a new gasket. Tighten cylinder head bolts to specified torque following sequence shown in Fig. HN58 for Models G300 and G400, or following sequence shown in Fig. HN59 for Model GV400.

CONNECTING ROD AND BEARING. On all models, connecting rod is equipped with renewable-type connecting rod bearing inserts. Piston and connecting rod are removed as an assembly after cylinder head has been removed and crankcase cover or oil pan has been separated from crankcase. Remove the two connecting rod bolts, lockplate, oil dipper plate (Models G300 and G400 only) and connecting rod cap. Push piston and connecting rod assembly out through the top of cylinder block. Remove snap rings and piston pin to separate piston from connecting rod.

Standard diameter for piston pin bore in connecting rod small end is 16 mm (0.630 in.) for Models G300 and G400. If diameter is 16.08 mm (0.633 in.) or larger, renew connecting rod. Standard diameter for piston pin bore in connecting rod small end is 19.005-19.020 mm (0.7482-0.7488 in.) for

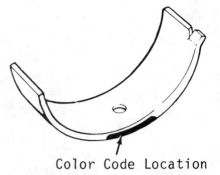

Color Code Location

Fig. HN60—On Model G400, connecting rod bearing inserts are color coded and should be matched to the connecting rod and crankshaft identification numbers. Refer to text.

Connecting Rod Identification Number Location

Fig. HN61—View showing location of the connecting rod identification number stamped into connecting rod according to connecting rod bearing bore size on Model G400. Refer to text.

Model GV400. If diameter is 19.08 mm (0.751 in.) or larger, renew connecting rod.

Standard connecting rod side clearance at the crankpin journal is 0.1-0.8 mm (0.004-0.032 in.) for Models G300 and G400. If side play is 1.0 mm (0.039 in.) or more, renew connecting rod and/or crankshaft. Standard connecting rod side clearance at the crankpin journal is 0.2-0.7 mm (0.008-0.028 in.) for Model GV400. If side clearance is 1.0 mm (0.039 in.) or more, renew connecting rod and/or crankshaft.

On Model G400, connecting rod bearing inserts are color coded (Fig. HN60) and connecting rod and crankshaft are stamped with an identification number (Figs. HN61 and HN62) which identify different connecting rod bearing bore sizes or crankshaft connecting rod journal sizes. Bearing inserts, connecting rod and crankshaft must be matched by

Crankshaft Identification
Number Location

Fig. HN62—View showing location of crankshaft identification number stamped into crankshaft to identify connecting rod journal size on Model G400. Refer to text.

referring to CRANKSHAFT, MAIN BEARINGS AND SEALS.

On all models, assemble piston to connecting rod with the arrow mark on top of piston toward ribbed side of connecting rod. Install piston pin retaining rings with gaps opposite notch in piston pin bore of piston. Align connecting rod and cap match marks and install connecting rod so ribbed side is toward crankcase cover or oil pan. Arrow stamped on piston top should be toward valve side of engine after installation. Install connecting rod cap, oil dipper (Models G300 and G400 only) and lockplate. Tighten connecting rod bolts to specified torque.

PISTON, PIN AND RINGS. On all models, piston and connecting rod are removed as an assembly. Refer to CONNECTING ROD AND BEARING for removal and installation procedure.

After separating piston and connecting rod, carefully remove rings and clean carbon and other deposits from piston surface and ring lands.

CAUTION: Exercise extreme care when cleaning ring lands. Do not damage squared edges or widen ring grooves. If ring lands are damaged, piston must be renewed.

Measure piston diameter on piston thrust surface 90° from piston pin. Standard piston diameter is 75.95-75.98 mm (2.990-2.991 in.) for Model G300. If diameter is 75.85 mm (2.986 in.) or less, renew piston. Standard piston diameter is 85.95-85.98 mm (3.383-3.385 in.) for Models G400 and GV400. If diameter is 85.85 mm (3.380 in.) or less, renew piston.

On all models, before installing rings, install piston in cylinder bore and use a suitable feeler gauge to measure clearance between piston and cylinder bore. Standard clearance is 0.05 mm (0.002 in.). If clearance exceeds 0.25 mm (0.010

in.), renew piston and/or recondition cylinder bore.

Standard piston pin bore diameter in piston is 16.002-16.008 mm (0.6300-0.6302 in.) for Model G300. If piston pin bore diameter is 16.046 mm (0.6317 in.) or more, renew piston. Standard piston pin bore diameter in piston is 19.002-19.008 mm (0.7480-0.7483 in.) for Models G400 and GV400. If piston pin bore diameter is 19.046 mm (0.7498 in.) or more, renew piston.

Standard piston pin outside diameter is 15.994-16.000 mm (0.6297-0.6299 in.) for Model G300. If piston pin outside diameter is 15.97 mm (0.6290 in.) or less, renew piston pin. Standard piston pin outside diameter is 18.994-19.000 mm (0.7478-0.7480 in.) for Models G400 and GV400. If piston pin outside diameter is 18.97 mm (0.7468 in.) or less, renew pin.

Standard piston ring to piston groove side clearance for all models is 0.02-0.06 mm (0.0008-0.0024 in.) for top ring and 0.01-0.05 mm (0.0004-0.0020 in.) for second ring and oil control ring. If clearance exceeds 0.15 mm (0.006 in.) for any ring, renew ring and/or piston.

Standard ring end gap for Models G300 and GV400 is 0.2-0.4 mm (0.008-0.016 in.) for all rings. If ring end gap exceeds 0.6 mm (0.024 in.), renew ring and/or recondition cylinder bore. Standard ring end gap for Model G400 is 0.2-0.4 mm (0.008-0.016 in.) for top ring and second ring, and 0.2-0.3 mm (0.008-0.012 in.) for oil control ring. If ring end gap of top and second ring exceeds 0.6 mm (0.024 in.) or if ring end gap of oil control ring exceeds 0.5 mm (0.020 in.), renew ring and/or recondition cylinder bore.

Install marked piston rings with marked side toward top of piston and stagger ring end gaps equally around circumference of piston.

CYLINDER AND CRANKCASE. Cylinder and crankcase are an integral casting. Standard cylinder bore diameter is 76.00-76.02 mm (2.9921-2.9929 in.) for Model G300. If cylinder bore diameter is 76.10 mm (2.996 in.) or larger, recondition cylinder bore. Standard cylinder bore diameter is 86.00-86.02 mm (3.3858-3.3866 in.) for Models G400 and GV400. If cylinder bore diameter is 86.10 mm (3.390 in.) or larger, recondition cylinder bore.

CRANKSHAFT, MAIN BEARINGS AND SEALS. On all models, crankshaft is supported by ball bearing-type main bearings at each end. To remove crankshaft, remove all cooling shrouds, flywheel, cylinder head and crankcase cover or oil pan. Remove pis-

ton and connecting rod assembly. Carefully remove crankshaft and camshaft. Remove engine balancer assembly as equipped. Remove main bearings and crankshaft oil seals as necessary.

Crankshaft connecting rod journal diameter for Model G300 should be 29.943-29.959 mm (1.1789-1.1795 in.). If journal diameter is 29.85 mm (1.1750 in.) or less, renew or recondition crankshaft.

Crankshaft connecting rod journal diameter for Model G400 should be 36.943-36.959 mm (1.4544-1.4551 in.). However, crankshaft journal diameter will vary according to the identification number (0, 1, 2 or 3) stamped into crankshaft as shown in Fig. HN62. Connecting rod is also stamped with an identification number as shown in Fig. HN61, and bearings are color coded as shown in Fig. HN60. Connecting rod and bearings are a select fit according to the chart shown in Fig. HN63.

Crankshaft connecting rod journal diameter for Model GV400 with white identification color on crankshaft should be 36.951-36.958 mm (1.4548-1.4550 in.). Crankshaft connecting rod journal diameter for Model GV400 with

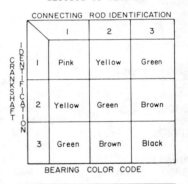

**Engine Serial Number
1200001 to 1286491**

| | | CONNECTING ROD IDENTIFICATION | | |
		1	2	3
C R A N K S H A F T I D E N T I F I C A T I O N	1	Pink	Yellow	Green
	2	Yellow	Green	Brown
	3	Green	Brown	Black
		BEARING COLOR CODE		

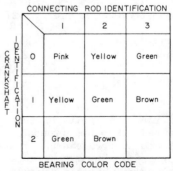

**Engine Serial Number
1286492 And Above**

| | | CONNECTING ROD IDENTIFICATION | | |
		1	2	3
C R A N K S H A F T I D E N T I F I C A T I O N	0	Pink	Yellow	Green
	1	Yellow	Green	Brown
	2	Green	Brown	
		BEARING COLOR CODE		

Fig. HN63—On Model G400, crankshaft, connecting rod and bearings are identified by number and color. Select correct crankshaft, connecting rod and bearing combinations according to the chart.

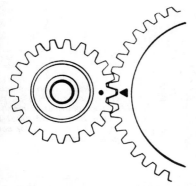

Fig. HN64—When installing crankshaft and camshaft gears, timing marks must be aligned as shown. On Model GV400 equipped with a timing chain, align timing marks so they are pointing directly toward each other with chain installed.

red identification color on crankshaft should be 36.943-36.951 mm (1.4544-1.4548 in.). If journal diameter for either crankshaft is 36.85 mm (1.451 in.) or less, renew or recondition crankshaft.

On all models, main bearings are a light press fit on crankshaft and in bearing bores of crankcase and crankcase cover or oil pan. It may be necessary to slightly heat crankcase and crankcase cover or oil pan to install bearings. If main bearings are rough, loose, or fit loosely on crankshaft journals or in crankcase and crankcase cover or oil pan, renew bearings.

If crankcase oil seals have been removed, use a suitable seal driver to install new seals. Seals should be pressed in evenly until they are slightly below flush with seal bores.

Make certain crankshaft gear and camshaft gear timing marks are aligned as shown in Fig. HN64 during crankshaft installation. If equipped with an engine balancer assembly, refer to ENGINE BALANCER for assembly and timing procedure.

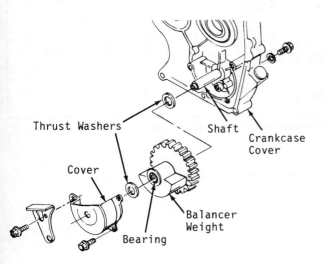

Thrust Washers

Shaft

Crankcase Cover

Cover

Balancer Weight

Bearing

CAMSHAFT. On all models, camshaft is supported at each end by bearings that are an integral part of the crankcase and crankcase cover or oil pan. Refer to CRANKSHAFT, MAIN BEARINGS AND SEALS for camshaft removal procedure.

Camshaft lobe height on Models G300 and G400 should be 38.6 mm (1.52 in.). Camshaft lobe height on Model GV400 should be 38.5-38.7 mm (1.516-1.524 in.). On all models, if lobe height is 38.3 mm (1.51 in.) or less, renew camshaft.

Camshaft bearing journal diameter on Models G300 and G400 with crankshaft-type pto and all GV400 models should be 17.766-17.784 mm (0.6994-0.7000 in.). If journal diameter is 17.716 mm (0.6875 in.) or less, renew camshaft.

Camshaft bearing journal diameter on Models G300 and G400 with camshaft-type pto should be 25.0 mm (0.984 in.). If journal diameter is 24.950 mm (0.982 in.) or less, renew camshaft.

Make certain camshaft gear and crankshaft gear timing marks are aligned as shown in Fig. HN64 during installation. If engine is equipped with an engine balancer assembly, refer to ENGINE BALANCER for assembly and timing procedure.

ENGINE BALANCER. Models G300 and G400 can be equipped with an engine balancer as shown in Fig. HN65.

Engine balancer (Fig. HN65) is mounted on a stub shaft located in crankcase cover and is driven by an auxiliary gear pressed onto crankshaft. Bearing is pressed into balancer counterweight to a depth of 1.0 mm (0.4 in.) using bearing driver 07945-8910000 available from Honda Motor Corporation (Fig. HN66). To install engine balancer weight and crankcase cover, position piston at TDC. Remove the 8 mm plug from crankcase cover and se-

Fig. HN65—Exploded view of the engine balancer used on so equipped G300 and G400 models.

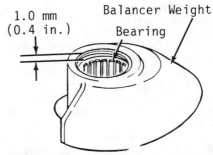

1.0 mm (0.4 in.)

Balancer Weight

Bearing

Fig. HN66—Balancer bearing is pressed into engine balancer weight to a depth of 1.0 mm (0.4 in.) using special driver (part 07945-8910000) available from Honda Motor Corporation.

cure balancer by inserting locating dowel rod as shown in Fig. HN67. Remove dowel rod after crankcase cover or oil pan bolts are tightened to specified torque and install the 8 mm plug.

GOVERNOR. The internal centrifugal flyweight governor is located on camshaft gear. Refer to GOVERNOR under MAINTENANCE section for external governor adjustments.

To remove governor assembly, remove external linkage, metal cooling shrouds and crankcase cover or oil pan. The governor flyweight assembly is located on the camshaft gear.

When reassembling, make certain governor sliding sleeve and internal governor linkage are correctly positioned.

OIL PUMP. Model GV400 is equipped with a trochoid-type oil pump located inside crankcase. Oil pump rotors may be removed and checked without disassembling the engine. Remove oil pump cover and withdraw outer and inner rotors. Remove "O" ring. Make certain oil passages are clear and pump body is thoroughly clean. Inner-to-outer rotor clearance should be 0.18 mm (0.007 in.). If clearance is 0.30 mm (0.010 in.) or more, renew rotors. Oil pump body-to-outer rotor clearance should be 0.15-0.20 mm (0.006-0.008 in.). If clearance is 0.26 mm (0.010 in.) or more, renew outer rotor and/or oil pump body. Oil pump body inside diameter should be 29 mm (1.14 in.). If diameter is 29.21 mm (1.150 in.) or more, renew oil pump body.

Reverse disassembly procedure for reassembly.

VALVE SYSTEM. Clearance between valve stem and valve tappet (cold) for Models G300 and G400 should be 0.06-0.12 mm (0.002-0.005 in.) for intake valve and 0.09-0.15 mm (0.004-0.006 in.) for exhaust valve. Clearance between valve stem and valve tappet (cold) for Model GV400 should be 0.08-0.15 mm (0.0031-0.0063 in.) for intake valve and 0.11-0.19 mm (0.0043-0.0075 in.) for exhaust valve.

On all models, valve clearance is adjusted by removing valve and grinding off end of stem to increase clearance or by grinding valve seat deeper to reduce clearance.

Valve face and seat angle should be 45° and standard valve seat width is 1.06 mm (0.0417 in.) for the intake valve and 1.414 mm (0.0557 in.) for the exhaust valve. On all models, if intake seat width is 2.5 mm (0.10 in.) or more, or if exhaust seat width is 2.0 mm (0.08 in.) or more, valve seats must be narrowed.

On all models, valve spring free length should be 42.7 mm (1.68 in.). If spring free length is 41.0 mm (1.61 in.) or less, renew spring.

Standard valve stem diameter for all models should be 6.955-6.970 mm (0.2738-0.2744 in.) for intake valve and 6.910-6.925 mm (0.2720-0.2726 in.) for exhaust valve. If intake valve stem is 6.91 mm (0.272 in.) or less, or if exhaust valve stem is 6.89 mm (0.271 in.) or less, renew valve.

Standard valve guide inside diameter is 7.000-7.015 mm (0.2756-0.2762 in.) for all models. If inside diameter of guide exceeds 7.07 mm (0.278 in.), guides must be renewed.

To remove and install valve guides, use the following procedure and refer to the sequence of illustrations in Fig. HN68. Cover tappet opening to prevent fragments from entering crankcase and use a suitable driver (Honda part 07942-8230000) to drive valve guide down into valve chamber slightly (A). Use a suitable cold chisel to fracture guide adjacent to guide bore (B). Drive remaining piece of guide into valve chamber (C) and remove from chamber. Place new guide on driver and start guide into guide bore (D). Alternate between driving guide into bore and measuring guide depth below cylinder head surface (E). Depth "X" in sequence (F) is 32 mm (1.3 in.) for intake valve guide and 30 mm (1.2 in.) for exhaust valve guide. Finish ream intake and exhaust valve guides using reamer 07984-6890100 available from Honda Motor Corporation.

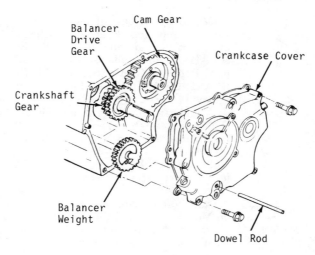

Fig. HN67—When installing crankcase cover or oil pan and balance gear assembly, a guide dowel rod must be used. Refer to text for complete procedure.

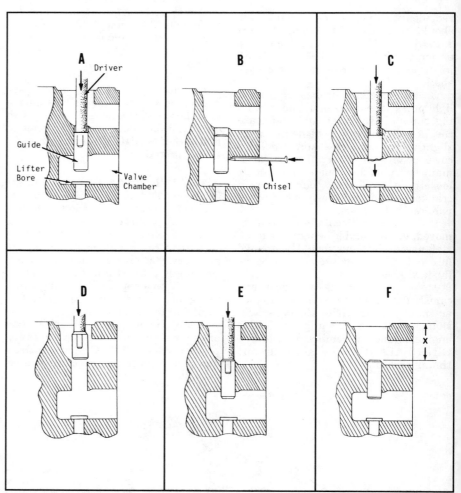

Fig. HN68—View showing valve guide removal and installation sequence. Refer to text.

HONDA

AMERICAN HONDA MOTOR CO., INC.
4475 River Green Parkway
Duluth, GA 30136

Model	No. Cyls.	Bore	Stroke	Displacement	Power Rating
GX270	1	77 mm (3.03 in.)	58 mm (2.28 in.)	270 cc (16.5 cu. in.)	6.7 kW (9 hp)
GX340	1	82 mm (3.23 in.)	64 mm (2.52 in.)	337 cc (20.6 cu. in.)	8.2 kW (11 hp)
GX390	1	88 mm (3.46 in.)	64 mm (2.52 in.)	389 cc (23.7 cu. in.)	9.7 kW (13 hp)
GXV270	1	77 mm (3.03 in.)	58 mm (2.28 in.)	270 cc (16.5 cu. in.)	6.7 kW (9 hp)
GXV340	1	82 mm (3.23 in.)	64 mm (2.52 in.)	337 cc (20.6 cu. in.)	8.2 kW (11 hp)
GXV390	1	88 mm (3.46 in.)	64 mm (2.52 in.)	389 cc (23.7 cu. in.)	9.7 kW (13 hp)

All models are four-stroke, overhead valve, single-cylinder, air-cooled engines. Models GXV270, GXV340 and GXV390 are vertical crankshaft engines. All other models are horizontal crankshaft engines with the cylinder inclined 25°.

Engine model number is cast into side of crankcase (Fig. HN101). Unless noted, procedures and specifications apply to all "K" variations, i.e. Model GX340K1.

Engine serial number is stamped into crankcase (Fig. HN102). Always furnish engine model and serial number when ordering parts.

MAINTENANCE

LUBRICATION. Check engine oil level prior to operating engine. Maintain oil level at top of reference marks (R—Fig. HN103) when checked with plug not screwed in, but just touching first threads.

Change oil after the first 20 hours of engine operation and every 100 hours thereafter.

Engine oil should meet or exceed latest API service classification. Use SAE 30 oil for temperatures above 90° F (32° C); use SAE 10W-30 oil for temperatures between 0° F (-18° C) and 90° F (32° C); below 0° F (-18° C) use SAE 5W-30.

Crankcase capacity for all models is 1.1 L (1.16 qt.).

Some engines are equipped with a low-oil warning system. If engine oil is low, an indicator lamp will light and the engine will stop or not run. Refer to OIL WARNING SYSTEM in REPAIRS section.

The reduction gear unit on Model GX270 engines may be lubricated by oil from the engine or by a separate oil supply. If there is no oil dipstick attached to the oil fill cap, then the unit is lubricated by oil from the engine. Check oil level similar to checking engine oil by unscrewing the oil fill plug. Maintain oil level at top of notch on gauge when checked with plug not screwed in, but just touching first threads. Fill with same oil recommended for engine. Capacity is 0.3 L (0.32 qt.).

AIR CLEANER. Engine may be equipped with either a dry type, semi-dry type or oil bath air filter that should be cleaned and inspected after every 50 hours of operation. Refer to appropriate paragraph for type being serviced.

Dry Type Air Cleaner. Remove foam and paper air filter elements from air filter housing. Foam element should be washed in a mild detergent and water solution, rinsed in clean water and allowed to air dry. Soak foam element in clean engine oil. Squeeze out excess oil.

Paper element can be cleaned by directing stream of low-pressure com-

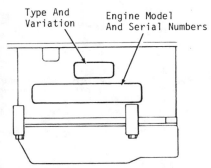

Fig. HN101—Engine model information is stamped on the crankcase of vertical crankshaft engines as shown.

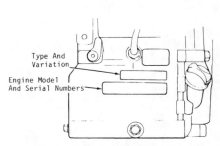

Fig. HN102—Engine model information is stamped on the crankcase of horizontal crankshaft engines as shown.

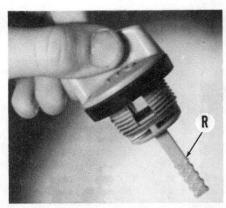

Fig. HN103—Do not screw in oil plug and gauge when checking oil level. Maintain oil level at top edge of reference marks (R) on dipstick.

pressed air from inside filter toward the outside. Renew the element if it can not be cleaned satisfactorily or if it is damaged in any way. Reinstall elements.

Semi-Dry Type Air Cleaner. Remove element and clean in solvent. Wring out excess solvent and allow element to air dry. Dip element in clean engine oil and wring out excess oil. Reinstall element.

Oil Bath Type Air Cleaner. Remove elements and clean in suitable solvent. Foam element should be washed in mild detergent and water solution and allowed to air dry. Discard the oil and clean the oil reservoir with solvent. Refill oil reservoir with 60 mL (1.3 pt.) of clean engine oil. Soak foam element in clean engine oil and wring out excess oil. Reassemble air cleaner.

SPARK PLUG. The spark plug should be removed, cleaned and inspected after every 100 hours of use.

Recommended spark plug is a NGK BPR6ES or ND W20EPR-U. Spark plug electrode gap should be 0.7-0.8 mm (0.028-0.031 in.) for all models.

When installing spark plug, manufacturer recommends installing spark plug finger-tight, then for a new plug, tighten an additional ½ turn. For a used plug, tighten an additional ¼ turn.

CARBURETOR. All models are equipped with a Keihin float-type carburetor with a fixed main fuel jet and an adjustable low-speed fuel mixture needle.

Adjustment. Carburetor adjustment settings and jet sizes are different on some models due to external or internal venting of carburetor as well as emissions requirements on later engines. Engines with type designation "QXC" or QXE" (see Figs. HN101 and HN102) have an internally vented carburetor. Note initial adjustment setting for idle mixture screw (P—Fig. HN104) in following table (turns out from a lightly seated position):

Non-compliant Engines

Model	Except Type QXC or QXE	Type QXC or QXE
GX270	2⅞ turns	2 turns
GXV270	2¼ turns	....
GX340	2½ turns	3 turns
GXV340	2½ turns	....
GX390	2¼ turns	2¼ turns
GXV390	2½ turns	....

For final adjustment engine must be at normal operating temperature and running. Operate engine at idle speed and adjust idle mixture screw (P) to obtain a smooth idle and satisfactory acceleration. Adjust idle speed by turning idle speed screw (T). Note that recommended idle speed may be 1250-1550

rpm, depending on application and equipment manufacturer's recommendation.

NOTE: Limiter cap (1—Fig. HN105) on idle mixture screw must be removed to set initial position of mixture screw, however, removing limiter cap damages the mixture screw. Refer to carburetor overhaul paragraphs.

Emission-compliant Engines

Model	Except Type QXC	Type QXC
GX240K1	1⅞ turns*	1½ turns
GX270	2⅛ turns	2¾ turns
GX340K1	1½ turns	1½ turns
GX390K1	1⅞ turns	1½ turns

*External vent with oil bath or semi-dry air cleaner require 1⅝ turns.

If equipped with remote control, adjust effective throttle cable length by loosening jam nuts and turning cable adjuster, if so equipped. The choke should be fully closed when remote control lever is in "CHOKE" position, and engine should stop when throttle lever is in "STOP" position.

For final adjustment engine must be at normal operating temperature and running. Operate engine at idle speed and adjust idle mixture screw (LS) to obtain a smooth idle and satisfactory acceleration. Adjust idle speed by turning throttle stop screw (TS) to obtain desired idle speed.

Overhaul. Refer to Fig. HN105 for an exploded view of carburetor. Note that throttle shaft and throttle plate are not available separately from body and should not be removed.

Use a suitable carburetor cleaning solvent to clean all parts and fuel passages. Be sure the solvent used will not damage plastic parts of carburetor.

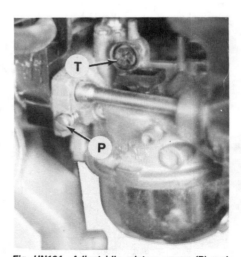

Fig. HN104—Adjust idle mixture screw (P) and idle speed screw (T) as outlined in text.

To check float level, remove float bowl and invert carburetor. Measure from top edge of float to fuel bowl mating edge of carburetor body. Measurement should be 13.2 mm (0.52 in.). Float height is not adjustable. If fuel inlet valve (11) and seat are in good condition, renew float (18) if float height is incorrect.

Refer to following table for standard main jet size. Optional jet sizes are available.

Model	Except Type QXC or QXE	Type QXC or QXE
GX270	#88	#95
GXV270	#85	....
GX340	#98	#108
GX340K1	#92	#98
GXV340	#88	....
GX390	#105	#115
GX390K1	#92	#100
GXV390	#95	....

On emissions engines, rotation of the idle mixture screw (2—Fig. HN105) is restricted by a limiter cap (1) attached to the mixture screw.

NOTE: Detaching the limiter cap from the idle mixture screw will break the mixture screw. A new mixture screw must be installed.

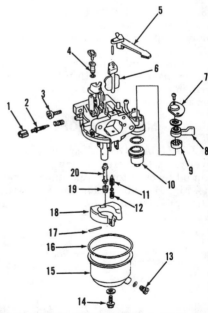

Fig. HN105—Exploded view of typical carburetor. Idle mixture screw limiter cap (12) is used only on emissions-compliant engines.

1. Limiter cap	11. Fuel inlet valve
2. Idle mixture jet	12. Spring
3. Idle speed screw	13. Fuel drain screw
4. Pilot jet	14. Screw
5. Choke lever	15. Float bowl
6. Choke plate	16. Gasket
7. Fuel shutoff valve	17. Float pin
8. Fuel shutoff valve	18. Float
9. Fuel strainer	19. Main jet
10. Strainer cup	20. Main nozzle

To install the idle mixture screw on emissions-compliant engines, install mixture screw and position screw at initial setting. Apply Loctite 638 on limiter cap, then install cap on end of mixture screw so mixture screw cannot rotate counterclockwise with cap in place. Do not rotate mixture screw while installing limiter cap.

GOVERNOR. A mechanical flyweight type governor is located inside engine crankcase. To adjust external linkage, stop engine and make certain all linkage is in good condition and tension spring (5—Fig. HN106 or HN107) is not stretched or damaged. Spring (2) on horizontal crankshaft models must pull governor lever (3) and throttle pivot toward each other. On all models, loosen clamp bolt (7) and move governor lever (3) so throttle is completely open. Hold governor lever in this position and rotate governor shaft (6) in the same direction until it stops. Tighten clamp bolt.

Start engine and operate at an idle until operating temperature has been reached. Attach a tachometer to engine. Open throttle so engine is operating at maximum speed and adjust throttle stop screw (8) so engine runs at 3850 rpm for horizontal crankshaft engine or 3550 rpm for vertical crankshaft engine.

IGNITION SYSTEM. The breakerless ignition system requires no regular maintenance. Ignition coil unit is mounted outside the flywheel. Air gap between flywheel and coil should be 0.2-0.6 mm (0.008-0.024 in.).

To check ignition coil primary side, connect one ohmmeter lead to primary (black) coil lead and touch iron coil laminations with remaining lead. Ohmmeter should indicate 0.8-1.0 ohm.

To check ignition coil secondary side, remove the spark plug cap and connect one ohmmeter lead to the spark plug lead wire and remaining lead to the iron core laminations. Ohmmeter should indicate 5.9k-7.1k ohms. If ohmmeter readings are not as specified, renew ignition coil.

VALVE ADJUSTMENT. Valve-to-rocker arm clearance should be checked and adjusted after every 300 hours of operation.

To adjust valve clearance, first remove rocker arm cover. Rotate crankshaft so piston is at top dead center (TDC) on compression stroke (both valves closed). Insert a feeler gauge between rocker arm (3—Fig. HN108) and end of valve stem. Loosen rocker arm jam nut (1) and turn adjusting nut (2) to obtain desired clearance. Specified clearance is 0.13-0.17 mm (0.005-0.007 in.) for intake and 0.18-0.22 mm (0.007-0.009 in.) for exhaust. Tighten jam nut and recheck clearance. Install rocker arm cover.

CYLINDER HEAD. Manufacturer recommends removal of combustion deposits from cylinder head combustion chamber, valves and valve seats after every 300 hours of operation.

COMPRESSION PRESSURE. Compression pressure measured at cranking speed of 600 rpm should be 588-833 kPa (85-121 psi).

REPAIRS

TIGHTENING TORQUE. Recommended tightening torque specifications are as follows:

Connecting rod . . . . 14 N•m
(124 in.-lb.)

Crankcase cover/oil
pan . . . . 24 N•m
(212 in.-lb.)

Cylinder head . . . . 35 N•m
(26 ft.-lb.)

Flywheel nut . . . . 115 N•m
(85 ft.-lb.)

Rocker arm jam nut . . . . 10 N•m
(88 in.-lb.)

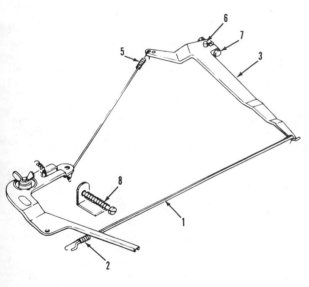

Fig. HN106—External governor linkage on horizontal crankshaft engines is constructed as shown.

1. Governor-to-carburetor rod
2. Spring
3. Governor lever
5. Tension spring
6. Governor shaft
7. Clamp bolt
8. Throttle stop screw

Fig. HN107—View of external governor linkage used on vertical crankshaft engines.

1. Governor-to-carburetor rod
3. Governor lever
4. Choke rod
5. Tension spring (behind plate)
6. Governor shaft
7. Clamp bolt
8. Throttle stop screw

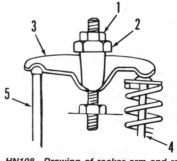

Fig. HN108—Drawing of rocker arm and related valve actuating components.

1. Jam nut
2. Adjustment nut
3. Rocker arm
4. Valve stem
5. Push rod

Rocker arm pivot
stud . . . . 24 N•m
(212 in.-lb.)

CYLINDER HEAD. To remove cylinder head, remove cooling shroud, disconnect and remove carburetor linkage and carburetor. Remove muffler. Remove rocker arm cover and the four cylinder head retaining screws. Remove cylinder head.

Remove carbon deposits from combustion chamber being careful not to damage gasket sealing surface. Inspect cylinder head for cracks, nicks or other damage. Place cylinder head on a flat surface and check entire sealing surface for distortion using a feeler gauge. Distortion service limit is 0.10 mm (0.004 in.).

Before installing cylinder head on vertical crankshaft models, be sure breather disc located between block and cylinder head is installed so raised side is towards head. On all models, tighten cylinder head retaining screws in a crossing pattern evenly to 35 N•m (26 ft.-lb.). Adjust valves as outlined in VALVE ADJUSTMENT paragraph.

VALVE SYSTEM. Remove cylinder head as previously outlined. Remove rocker arms, compress valve springs and remove valve retainers. Note exhaust valve is equipped with a valve rotator on valve stem and that exhaust valve spring retainer has a recess to accept valve rotator. Remove valves and springs. Remove push rod guide plate if necessary.

Valve face and seat angles are 45°. Standard valve seat width is 1.1 mm (0.043 in.). Narrow the seat if seat width is 2.0 mm (0.079) or more.

NOTE: On engines running on LPG or propane fuel, standard valve seat width is 2.2 mm (0.087 in.). Narrow the seat if seat width is 3.0 mm (0.118) or more.

Standard valve spring free length is 39.0 mm (1.54 in.). Renew valve spring if free length is 37.5 mm (1.48 in.) or less.

Standard valve guide inside diameter is 6.60 mm (0.260 in.). Renew guide if inside diameter is 6.66 mm (0.262 in.) or more.

Valve stem-to-guide clearance for Models GX270, GXV270, GXV340 and GXV390 should be 0.010-0.037 mm (0.0004-0.0015 in.) for intake valve and 0.050-0.077 mm (0.002-0.003 in.) for exhaust valve. Renew valve guide and/or valve if clearance is 0.10 mm (0.004 in.) or more for intake valve, or 0.12 mm (0.005 in.) or more for exhaust valve.

Valve stem-to-guide clearance for Models GX340 and GX390 should be 0.010-0.040 mm (0.0004-0.0016 in.) for intake valve and 0.050-0.080 mm (0.0020-0.0031 in.) for exhaust valve. Renew valve guide and/or valve if clearance is 0.11 mm (0.0043 in.) or more for intake valve, or 0.13 mm (0.0051 in.) or more for exhaust valve.

To renew valve guide, heat entire cylinder head to 150° C (300° F). DO NOT heat head above recommended temperature as valve seats may loosen. On horizontal crankshaft engines, use valve guide driver 07742-0010200 to remove and install guides. On vertical crankshaft engines, use valve guide driver 07942-6570100 to remove and install guides. Drive in the intake valve guide so the top of the guide stands 9.0 mm (0.35 in.) above the cylinder head boss (D—Fig. HN109). On horizontal crankshaft engines, drive in the exhaust valve guide so the clip is bottomed in the head. On vertical crankshaft engines, drive in the exhaust valve guide so it stands 7.0 mm (0.28 in.) above the cylinder head boss (D). Ream new valve guides after installation.

When assembling valve system components in head, note that the exhaust valve spring retainer has a recess that fits the valve rotator.

PISTON, PIN AND RINGS. Remove piston and connecting rod as an assembly. To remove piston and connecting rod, remove cylinder head and crankcase cover or oil pan. Remove carbon or ridge from top of cylinder before removing the piston. Remove connecting rod cap screws and cap. Push connecting rod and piston assembly out of cylinder. Camshaft can also be removed if required. Remove piston pin retaining rings and separate piston from connecting rod.

Standard piston diameter and reject size measured 10 mm (0.4 in.) above lower edge of skirt and 90 degrees from piston pin is listed in the following table:

Model	Piston Diameter
GX270, GXV270	76.985 mm
	(3.0301 in.)
Reject size	76.85 mm
	(3.026 in.)
GX340, GXV340	81.985 mm
	(3.2277 in.)
Reject size	81.85 mm
	(3.222 in.)
GX390, GXV390	87.985 mm
	(3.4640 in.)
Reject size	87.85 mm
	(3.459 in.)

Oversize pistons are available for some models.

Standard clearance between piston pin and pin bore in piston is 0.002-0.014 mm (0.0001-0.0006 in.) for all models. If clearance is 0.08 mm (0.0031 in.) or greater, renew piston and/or pin.

Standard piston pin bore diameter is 18.002 mm (0.7087 in.) for Models GX270 and GXV270 and 20.002 mm (0.7875 in.) for remaining models. Reject piston of Models GX270 and GXV270 if piston pin bore diameter is 18.042 mm (0.7103 in.) or more. Reject piston of remaining models if piston pin bore diameter is 20.042 mm (0.7890 in.) or more.

Standard piston pin diameter is 18.000 mm (0.7087 in.) for Models GX270 and GXV270 and 20.000 mm (0.7874 in.) for remaining models. Reject piston pin of Models GX270 and GXV270 if diameter is 17.95 mm (0.707 in.) or less. Reject piston pin of remaining models if piston pin diameter is 19.95 mm (0.785 in.) or less.

Compression ring side clearance should be 0.015-0.045 mm (0.0006-0.0018 in.) for Models GX270 and GXV270 and 0.030-0.060 mm (0.0012-0.0024 in.) for remaining models. Maximum allowable compression ring side clearance for all models is 0.15 mm (0.006 in.). Ring end gap for compression rings on all models should be 0.2-0.4 mm (0.008-0.016 in.). If ring end gap for any ring is 1.0 mm (0.039 in.) or more, renew ring and/or cylinder. Oversize piston rings are available for some models.

Install marked piston rings with marked side toward piston crown and stagger ring end gaps equally around piston. Install chrome plated piston ring in top piston ring groove.

When reassembling piston on connecting rod, long side (LS—Fig. HN110) of connecting rod and arrowhead on piston crown (Fig. HN111) must be on the same side.

When reinstalling piston and connecting rod assembly in cylinder, position piston so arrowhead on piston crown is on push rod side of engine. Align connecting rod cap and connecting rod match marks (AM—Fig.

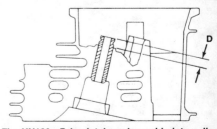

Fig. HN109—Drive intake valve guide into cylinder head so the top of the guide stands 9.0 mm (0.35 in.) above the cylinder head boss (D).

HN110). Note that oil dipper (5—Fig. HN111) on models with a horizontal crankshaft must be toward camshaft. Install connecting rod screws and tighten to 14 N•m (124 in.-lb.).

CONNECTING ROD. The aluminum alloy connecting rod rides directly on crankpin journal on all models. Connecting rod cap for all horizontal crankshaft models is equipped with an oil dipper (Fig. HN111). There is no dipper on vertical crankshaft models (Fig. HN112). Refer to previous PISTON, PIN AND RINGS paragraphs for removal and installation procedure.

Standard piston pin bore diameter in connecting rod is 18.005 mm (0.7088

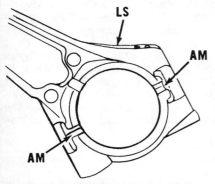

in.) for Models GX270 and GXV270 and 20.005 mm (0.7876 in.) for remaining models. Renew connecting rod if diameter is 18.07 mm (0.711 in.) or more for Models GX270 and GXV270, or 20.07 mm (0.790 in.) for remaining models.

Standard connecting rod bearing bore-to-crankpin clearance is 0.040-0.066 mm (0.0016-0.0026 in.) for all models. Renew connecting rod and/or crankshaft if clearance is 0.12 mm (0.005 in.) or more. Standard big end diameter is 33.025 mm (1.3002 in.) for Models GX270 and GXV270, and 36.025 mm (1.4183 in.) for remaining models. Maximum allowable standard big end diameter is 33.07 mm (1.302 in.) for Models GX270 and GXV270, and 36.07 mm (1.420 in.) for remaining models. An undersize connecting rod is available for some models.

Connecting rod side play on crankpin should be 0.1-0.7 mm (0.004-0.028 in.) for all models. Renew connecting rod if side play is 1.0 mm (0.039 in.) or more.

When reassembling piston on connecting rod, long side (LS—Fig. HN110) of connecting rod and arrowhead on piston crown (Fig. HN111) must be on the same side.

When reinstalling piston and connecting rod assembly in cylinder, position piston so arrowhead on piston crown is on push rod side of engine. Align connecting rod cap and connecting rod match marks (AM—Fig. HN110). Note that oil dipper (5—Fig. HN111) on models with a horizontal crankshaft must be towards camshaft.

Install connecting rod screws and tighten to 14 N•m (124 in.-lb.).

CAMSHAFT. The camshaft is accessible after removing crankcase cover or oil pan. Camshaft and camshaft gear are an integral casting equipped with a compression release mechanism (Fig. HN113).

Standard camshaft bearing journal diameter is 15.984 mm (0.6293 in.). Renew camshaft if journal diameter is 15.92 mm (0.627 in.) or less. Refer to following table for camshaft lobe height specifications:

GX270

Intake lobe	31.52-31.92 mm (1.241-1.257 in.)
Wear limit	31.35 mm (1.234 in.)
Exhaust lobe	31.56-31.96 mm (1.242-1.258 in.)
Wear limit	31.35 mm (1.234 in.)

GXV270, GXV340

Intake lobe	33.00 mm (1.299 in.)
Wear limit	32.75 mm (1.289 in.)
Exhaust lobe	32.60 mm (1.283 in.)
Wear limit	32.35 mm (1.274 in.)

GX340

Intake lobe	31.85-32.25 mm (1.254-1.270 in.)
Wear limit	32.10 mm (1.264 in.)
Exhaust lobe	31.57-31.97 mm (1.243-1.259 in.)
Wear limit	31.80 mm (1.252 in.)

GX390

Intake lobe	32.40-32.80 mm (1.276-1.291 in.)

Fig. HN110—View of connecting rod used on vertical crankshaft models. Rod cap used on horizontal crankshaft models is equipped with an oil dipper as shown in Fig. HN111.

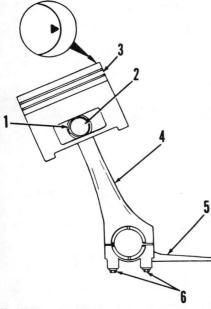

Fig. HN111—Drawing of piston and connecting rod assembly used on horizontal crankshaft models. Note location of oil dipper on connecting rod cap.

1. Retaining ring
2. Piston pin
3. Piston
4. Connecting rod
5. Rod cap & dipper
6. Screws

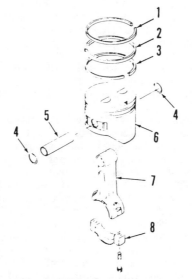

Fig. HN112—Exploded view of piston and connecting rod assembly used on vertical crankshaft models.

1. Top compression ring (chrome plated)
2. Second compression ring
3. Oil control ring
4. Retaining ring
5. Piston pin
6. Piston
7. Connecting rod
8. Connecting rod cap

Fig. HN113—All models are equipped with a compression release mechanism (C) that is located on the camshaft gear.

Wear limit . . . . 32.25 mm
(1.270 in.)
Exhaust lobe . . . . 31.89-32.29 mm
(1.256-1.271 in.)
Wear limit . . . . 31.75 mm
(1.250 in.)

GXV390

Intake lobe . . . . 32.60 mm
(1.283 in.)
Wear limit . . . . 32.35 mm
(1.274 in.)
Exhaust lobe . . . . 32.09 mm
(1.263 in.)
Wear limit . . . . 31.84 mm
(1.254 in.)

The camshaft rides directly in bearing bores in crankcase and crankcase cover or oil pan. Camshaft bearing bore diameter in crankcase and crankcase cover or oil pan should be 16.0 mm (0.63 in.). Renew crankcase, crankcase cover or oil pan if bearing diameter is 16.05 mm (0.632 in.) or more.

Inspect compression release mechanism for damage. Spring must pull weight tightly against camshaft so decompressor lobe holds exhaust valve slightly open. Weight overcomes spring tension at 1000 rpm and moves decompressor lobe away from cam lobe to release exhaust valve.

When installing camshaft, refer to ENGINE BALANCER section for correct timing procedure.

GOVERNOR. A centrifugal flyweight type governor (Fig. HN114) controls engine rpm via external linkage. Governor is located in crankcase cover on Models GX270, GX340 and GX390 and in oil pan on Models GXV270, GXV340 and GXV390. Refer to GOVERNOR paragraphs in MAINTENANCE section for adjustment procedure.

To remove governor assembly, remove crankcase cover or oil pan. Remove governor sleeve (1), thrust washer

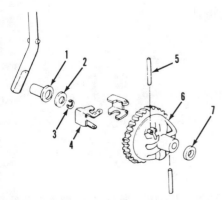

Fig. HN114—Exploded view of typical governor flyweight assembly used on all models.

(2) and retaining clip (3), then remove governor weight assembly from shaft.

Reinstall governor assembly by reversing removal procedure. Adjust external linkage as outlined under GOVERNOR in MAINTENANCE section.

CRANKSHAFT, MAIN BEARINGS AND SEALS. The crankshaft is supported at each end in ball bearing type main bearings. To remove crankshaft, refer to previous paragraphs and remove piston and camshaft.

Standard crankpin journal diameter is 32.985 mm (1.2986 in) for Models GX270 and GXV270. If crankpin diameter is 32.92 mm (1.296 in.) or less, renew crankshaft. Standard crankpin diameter for all other models is 35.985 mm (1.4167 in.). If crankpin diameter is 35.93 mm (1.414 in.) or less, renew crankshaft. On some models an undersize connecting rod is available to fit a reground crankshaft.

On some models the timing gear is a press fit on the crankshaft. Prior to removal of timing gear, mark position of gear on crankshaft using the timing mark on the gear as a reference point. Transfer marks to new timing gear so it can be installed in same position as old gear.

Ball bearing type main bearings are a press fit on crankshaft journals and in bearing bores of crankcase and cover. Renew bearings if loose, rough or fits loosely on crankshaft or in bearing bores.

Press seals into seal bores until outer edge of seal is flush with seal bore.

When installing crankshaft, refer to ENGINE BALANCER section for correct timing procedure.

OIL PUMP. Vertical crankshaft engines are equipped with a rotor type oil pump located in the oil pan and driven by the camshaft.

Remove oil pump cover on outside of oil pan for access to oil pump components. Make certain oil passages are clear and pump body is not damaged. Inner-to-outer rotor clearance should be 0.18 mm (0.007 in.). If clearance is 0.30 mm (0.012 in.) or more, renew rotor and/or outer rotor. Oil pump body-to-outer rotor clearance should be 0.15-0.20 mm (0.006-0.008 in.). If clearance is 0.26 mm (0.010 in.) or more, renew outer rotor and/or oil pan. Oil pump body inside diameter should be 29 mm (1.14 in.). If diameter is 29.21 mm (1.150 in.) or more, renew oil pan. Outer rotor thickness should be 7.48 mm (0.294 in.). If outer rotor thickness is 7.45 mm (0.293 in.) or less, renew outer rotor. Pump body depth should be

7.50 mm (0.295 in.). If pump body depth is 7.56 (0.298 in.) or more, renew oil pan.

Reassemble oil pump by reversing disassembly procedure. Tighten oil pump cover screws to 8-12 N•m (71-106 in.-lb.).

ENGINE BALANCER. Horizontal crankshaft models are equipped with a single engine crankshaft balancer shaft, while vertical crankshaft models are equipped with double engine balancer shafts. When installing balancer shaft in horizontal crankshaft engine, align timing marks as shown in Fig. HN115. When installing balancer shafts in vertical crankshaft engine, align timing marks as shown in Fig. HN116.

OIL WARNING SYSTEM. Models **GX270, GX340 And GX390.** These models are equipped with a low oil level switch and module that grounds the ignition system and lights a warning lamp if the oil level is low. To test switch, run engine then disconnect yellow switch wire. Grounding the yellow wire to the engine should cause the warning light to flash and the engine

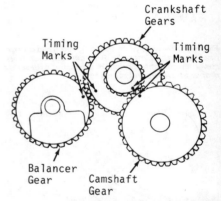

Fig. HN115—Drawing showing correct alignment of timing marks on balancer, camshaft and crankshaft gears of horizontal crankshaft models.

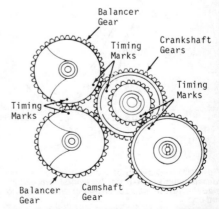

Fig. HN116—Drawing showing correct alignment of timing marks on balancer, camshaft and crankshaft gears of vertical crankshaft models.

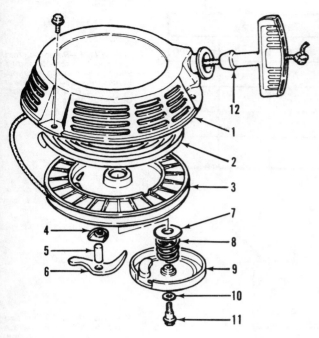

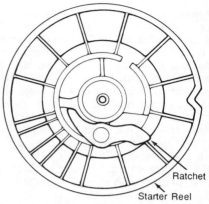

Fig. HN117—Exploded view of single-pawl rewind starter used on some models.

1. Starter housing
2. Rewind spring
3. Pulley
4. Guide plate
5. Pin
6. Pawl
7. Washer
8. Friction spring
9. Cover
10. Washer
11. Screw
12. Rope handle

Fig. HN119—Install pawl on pulley in direction shown.

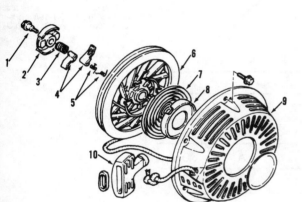

Fig. HN118—Exploded view of dual-pawl rewind starter used on some models.

1. Screw
2. Cover
3. Friction spring
4. Pawls
5. Springs
6. Pulley
7. Rewind spring
8. Spring cup
9. Starter housing
10. Rope handle

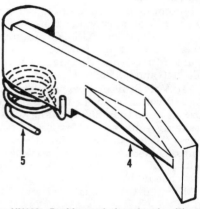

Fig. HN120—Position end of pawl spring (5) so it forces pawl (4) inward.

should stop. Stop engine. With oil level correct and both switch leads disconnected, use an ohmmeter or continuity tester and check continuity between switch leads. Tester should indicate no continuity.

The oil level switch is connected to a module that contains the oil warning lamp. To check lamp, connect a 6-volt battery to yellow and black leads of module with positive battery terminal connected to black module lead. If lamp does not light, renew module or replace with a good unit.

Models GXV270, GXV340 and GXV390. Vertical crankshaft models may be equipped with a float type switch in the oil pan that grounds the ignition system and activates a buzzer if the oil level is low. The oil pan must be removed from the engine so the oil level switch can be removed for testing. Connect an ohmmeter or continuity tester and check continuity between switch leads. With switch in normal position, there should be continuity. With switch

inverted, there should be no continuity. When switch is progressively inserted in a fluid, resistance should increase from zero to infinity.

REWIND STARTER. The engine may be equipped with the rewind starter shown in Fig. HN117 or HN118. To disassemble starter remove rope handle and allow rope to wind into starter. Unscrew center retaining screw. Wear appropriate safety eyewear and gloves before disengaging pulley from starter as spring may uncoil uncontrolled. Place shop towel around pulley and lift pulley out of housing. Use caution when detaching rewind spring from pulley or housing.

On both types of starter, wrap rope around pulley in counterclockwise direction viewed from flywheel side of pulley. Apply light coating of grease to sliding surfaces of rewind spring, pawls and friction spring.

On single-pawl starter (Fig. HN117), install rewind spring (2) on pulley (3) in

a counterclockwise direction from outer end and install pawl in direction shown in Fig. HN119. Rotate pulley three revolutions counterclockwise to place tension on rewind spring. Tighten center screw (11—Fig. HN117) to 8-12 N•m (71-106 in.-lb.).

On dual-pawl starter (Fig. HN118), install rewind spring (7) in spring cup (8) in a clockwise direction from outer end. Install spring cup with rewind spring on pulley so outer end of spring engages notch on pulley. Install pawl spring (5) so end of spring forces pawl (4) inward as shown in Fig. HN120. Rotate pulley five revolutions counterclockwise to place tension on rewind spring.

ELECTRIC STARTER. All engines may be equipped with a 12 volt DC starter. Engines running on LPG or propane fuel may be equipped with a 110 volt AC starter.

12 Volt Starter. Test specifications for electric starter on Model GX270 are: Under load at more than 393 rpm and with a cranking voltage of 9.7 volts DC, the current draw should be less than 80 amps. Under no load with a cranking voltage of 11.5 volts DC, the current draw should be less than 31 amps.

Test specifications for electric starter on Models GX340 and GX390 are: Under load at more than 325 rpm and with a cranking voltage of 9.9 volts DC, the current draw should be less than 103 amps. Under no load with a cranking voltage of 11.5 volts DC, the current draw should be less than 31 amps.

Test specifications for electric starter on Models GXV270, GXV340 and GXV390 are: Under load at more than 270 rpm and with a cranking voltage of 8.5 volts DC, the current draw should be less than 165 amps. Under no load with a cranking voltage of 11.5 volts DC, the current draw should be less than 20 amps.

Minimum brush length is 3.5 mm (0.14 in.) for starter used on Models GX270, GX340 and GX390. Minimum brush length is 8.5 mm (0.34 in.) for starter used on Models GXV270, GXV340 and GXV390.

110 Volt Starter. Test specifications for 110 volt electric starter are: Under load at more than 800 rpm and with a cranking voltage of 117 volts AC, the current draw should be less than 4.5 amps. Under no load with a cranking voltage of 117 volts AC, the current draw should be less than 2.5 amps.

Minimum brush length is 5 mm (0.20 in.).

A rectifier is contained in the starter switch box. To check rectifier, remove rectifier and use an ohmmeter or continuity tester to check continuity between each pair of adjacent terminals (do not test terminals that are diagonally opposite). Tester should indicate continuity with leads connected to a pair of terminals and infinity when leads are reversed. If not, renew rectifier or replace with a good unit.

CHARGING SYSTEM. The engine may be equipped with a charging system that provides alternating or direct current.

Models GXV270, GXV340 and GXV390. These models may be equipped with a charging system that includes a charge coil under the flywheel that supplies current to a rectifier mounted on the blower housing. The charge coil can be tested without removing the flywheel. Disconnect coil leads and connect ohmmeter leads to coil leads. Ohmmeter should indicate 3.0-4.0 ohms, otherwise, renew rectifier or replace with a good unit. To test rectifier, remove rectifier from engine and connect an ohmmeter to leads while referring to test specifications in Fig. HN121. Note that readings on ohmmeter may not match specified readings

		–Tester Lead			
		Green	Green	Red	Housing
+Tester Lead	Green		A	A	B
	Green	A		A	B
	Red	B	B		C
	Housing	A	A	A	

Fig. HN121—Refer to text and table to test rectifier on 1 and 3 amp charging systems. Values indicated in table are: A. Infinity; B. 0.1-20k ohms; C. 0.5-50k ohms.

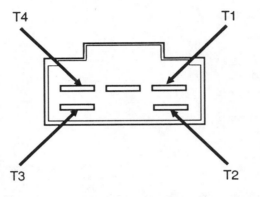

Fig. HN122—Refer to text and table to test rectifier on 10 amp charging systems. Values indicated in table are: A. Infinity; B. 0.1-50k ohms; C. 1-200k ohms; D. 0.5-100k ohms.

		–Tester Lead			
		T1	T2	T3	T4
+Tester Lead	T1		A	A	D
	T2	B		A	C
	T3	B	A		C
	T4	A	A	A	

exactly, but ohmmeter should indicate continuity or infinity as noted on table.

Models GX270, GX340 and GX390. These models may be equipped with a 1, 3, 10 or 18 amp direct current charging system as well as a lighting coil that provides alternating current. The 1 and 3 amp charging system consists of one charge coil and a rectifier (coil has one lead). Two charge coils and a regulator-rectifier are used for the 10 amp system (coils are connected and lead has two terminals). Four charge coils and a regulator-rectifier are used for the 18 amp system. The coils are located underneath the flywheel. The rectifier for 1 and 3 amp systems is located in the control switch box. The lighting coil is located underneath the flywheel and has two leads. A blade-type fuse located in the control switch box protects the system. A 5-amp fuse is used in the 1 amp system while a 15-amp fuse is used in the 3 and 10 amp systems. A

25-amp fuse is used on the 18 amp systems. A circuit breaker is also used on 1 and 3-amp systems.

To test charge coil of 1 or 3 amp system, connect an ohmmeter between charge coil lead and ground other test lead to coil core. Ohmmeter should indicate 3.0-4.0 ohms for 1 amp charge coil and 0.62-0.93 ohm for 3 amp charge coil, otherwise, renew charge coil or replace with a good unit. To test charge coils of 10 amp system, connect an ohmmeter to two terminals of coil lead. Ohmmeter should indicate 0.16-0.24 ohm, otherwise, renew charge coil or replace with a good unit. To test charge coils of 18 amp system, connect an ohmmeter to two terminals of coil lead. Ohmmeter should indicate 0.12-0.16 ohm, otherwise, renew charge coil assembly or replace with a good unit.

To test rectifier of 1 or 3 amp system, detach rectifier from wire lead. Using an ohmmeter, alternately connect tester leads to terminals of rectifier.

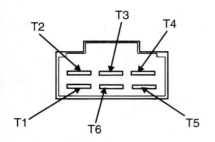

		–Tester Lead					
		T1	T2	T3	T4	T5	T6
+ Tester Lead	T1		A	B	C	D	A
	T2						A
	T3				A	A	A
	T4	B	A	G		B	A
	T5	D	A	B	C		A
	T6	E	A	H	F	E	

Ohmmeter should indicate continuity with leads connected to terminals and infinity when leads are reversed. If not, renew rectifier or replace with a good unit.

To test regulator-rectifier of 10 amp system, disconnect wire lead from unit and connect an ohmmeter to terminals while referring to test specifications in Fig. HN122. Note that readings on ohmmeter may not match specified readings exactly, but ohmmeter should indicate continuity or infinity as noted on table.

To test regulator-rectifier of 18 amp system, disconnect wire lead from unit and connect an ohmmeter to terminals while referring to test specifications in Fig. HN123. Note that readings on ohmmeter may not match specified readings exactly, but ohmmeter should indicate continuity or infinity as noted on table.

REDUCTION GEAR. Models GX270, GX340 and GX390 may be equipped with a reduction gear unit that attaches to the crankcase cover. Power is transferred via gears or a chain, while the unit on Model GX270 may also contain a plate-type automatic clutch.

The reduction gear unit on all models not equipped with an automatic clutch is lubricated by oil from the engine. The reduction gear unit with an automatic clutch has a separate oil supply. Oil level is checked similar to checking engine oil by unscrewing the oil fill plug. Maintain oil level at top of notch on gauge when checked with plug not screwed in, but just touching first threads. Fill with same oil recommended for engine. Capacity is 300 mL (0.6 pt.).

Overhaul of unit is apparent after inspection of unit. On units without automatic clutch, tighten input gear or sprocket retaining screw to 24 N•m (212 in.-lb.) and cover screws to 24 N•m (212 in.-lb.). On units with an automatic clutch, wear limit thickness for friction plates is 3.0 mm (0.118 in.) and maximum allowable warpage of steel plates is 0.10 mm (0.004 in.). When assembling clutch pack in clutch drum, alternately install fiber and steel plates with a fiber plate first and a steel plate last.

HONDA

AMERICAN HONDA MOTOR CO., INC.
4475 River Green Parkway
Duluth, GA 30136

Model	No. Cyls.	Bore	Stroke	Displacement	Power Rating
GX610	2	77 mm (3.0 in.)	66 mm (2.6 in.)	615 cc (37.7 cu. in.)	13.4 kW (18 hp)
GX620	2	77 mm (3.0 in.)	66 mm (2.6 in.)	615 cc (37.7 cu. in.)	14.9 kW (20 hp)

Both models are four-stroke, overhead-valve, twin-cylinder, air-cooled engines equipped with a horizontal crankshaft.

Engine identification numbers are cast into side of crankcase above oil drain plug. Always furnish engine model and serial number when ordering parts.

Number 1 cylinder is on the right when engine is viewed at flywheel end. Numbers 1 or 2 are cast into cylinder heads and cylinders for identification.

MAINTENANCE

LUBRICATION. Lubrication System. Both models are equipped with a pressure lubrication system and an oil filter. A gear-driven oil pump forces the lubricating oil through the oil filter to the main bearing in the crankcase cover. Some of the oil passes through drilled passages in the crankshaft to lubricate the connecting rod bearings and the main bearing at the flywheel end of the crankshaft. Oil spraying from the connecting rods lubricates and cools the undersides of the pistons. An oil passage from the crankcase cover main bearing directs oil to an orifice in the crankcase cover that sprays oil onto the timing gears. Oil in the passage travels into the hollow camshaft, which has oil holes so oil can spray onto the governor and decompression assemblies and the exhaust valve lifters. Oil also flows from the crankcase cover oil passage into a passage in the cylinder, then into the holes of one of the cylinder bolts in each cylinder head. Oil flows from under the cylinder bolt to lubricate the valve actuating assembly. Return oil passages direct the oil back to the crankcase.

Maintenance. Gasoline Engines. Check engine oil level prior to operating engine. Maintain oil level between reference marks on dipstick. Drain oil by removing drain plug in engine base.

Add oil by pouring oil through oil fill hole in rocker arm cover on cylinder head.

Change oil after the first 20 hours of engine operation and every 100 hours or 6 months thereafter. Replace the oil filter annually or after every 200 hours of operation.

Engine oil should meet or exceed latest API service classification. Use SAE 30 oil for temperatures above 50° F (10° C); use SAE 10W-30 oil for temperatures between 0° F (-18° C) and 90° F (32° C); below 0° F (-18° C) use SAE 5W-30.

Crankcase capacity for both models is 1.2 L (1.27 qt.) not including oil filter.

Crankcase capacity is 1.5 L (1.32 qt.) including oil filter.

Propane Engines. Check engine oil level prior to operating engine. Maintain oil level between reference marks on dipstick. Drain oil by removing drain plug in engine base. Add oil by pouring oil through oil fill hole in rocker arm cover on cylinder head.

Change oil after the first 20 hours of engine operation and every 50 hours or 3 months thereafter. Replace the oil filter annually or after every 200 hours of operation.

Engine oil must be designed for use in engines that run on LPG (propane) and meet or exceed latest API service classification. SAE 30 is recommended for most operating temperatures. Mobil 1 5W-30 may be used for temperatures below 0° F (-18° C), but do not use above 0° F (-18° C). Do not use multi-grade, mineral-based oil.

Crankcase capacity for both models is 1.2 L (1.27 qt.) not including oil filter.

Crankcase capacity is 1.5 L (1.32 qt.) including oil filter.

Warning System. Some engines are equipped with a low-oil warning system or low-oil pressure warning system. If engine oil level or oil pressure is low, an indicator lamp will light and the engine will stop or not run. Refer to OIL WARNING SYSTEM in REPAIRS section.

Oil Pressure. Normal oil pressure is 200 kPa (28.4 psi). Oil pressure can be measured by connecting a suitable gauge to the oil pressure switch hole adjacent to the oil filter, or the plug hole if not equipped with an oil pressure switch. When reinstalling the switch or plug, apply a suitable sealer to the threads. Tighten the oil pressure switch to 8.5 N•m (75 in.-lb.). Tighten the plug to 9 N•m (80 in.-lb.).

AIR CLEANER. The engine is equipped with a paper type air filter and a foam element. Clean the air cleaner elements after every 50 hours of operation. Renew the paper element annually or after every 300 hours of operation. Service more frequently if engine is operated in severe conditions.

Clean foam element by washing in soapy water. Allow to dry, then apply clean engine oil. Squeeze out excess oil.

The paper element should be renewed rather than cleaned. Tap the element to dislodge dirt. Do not attempt to brush dirt off element. Do not wash or direct high pressure air at filter.

SPARK PLUG. The spark plug should be removed, cleaned and inspected after every 100 hours of use.

Recommended spark plug is a NGK BPR6ES or ND W20EPR-U. Spark plug electrode gap should be 0.7-0.8 mm (0.028-0.031 in.).

When installing spark plug, manufacturer recommends installing spark plug finger-tight, then for a new plug, tighten an additional ½ turn. For a used plug, tighten an additional ¼ turn.

FUEL FILTER. The engine is equipped with a fuel filter attached to the side of the engine. Inspect the filter after every 100 hours of operation. Renew filter annually or after 300 hours of operation. Install filter so arrow on filter points in direction of fuel flow.

CARBURETOR. Gasoline Engines. Both models are equipped with a float type carburetor with a fixed main fuel jet and an adjustable low-speed fuel mixture needle. The engines are designed to comply with emissions regulations. Emissions-compliant engines may be identified by the presence of a limiter cap on the low speed mixture screw that limits rotation of the mixture screw.

The carburetor is equipped with a fuel shutoff solenoid (18—Fig. HN201) that uses a plunger to stop fuel flow through the main jet when the engine is stopped. The spring-loaded plunger should retract when the solenoid is energized.

Adjustment. Limiter cap (1—Fig. HN 201) on idle mixture screw must be removed to set initial position of mixture screw, however, removing limiter cap damages the mixture screw. Initial setting of idle mixture screw is 1¾ turns out on Model GX610 and 1¼ turns out on Model GX620. Refer to overhaul section to install limiter cap.

Engine must be at normal operating temperature and running for final adjustment. Operate engine at idle speed and adjust idle mixture screw to obtain a smooth idle and satisfactory acceleration. Adjust idle speed by turning idle speed screw (4). Standard idle speed is 1,250-1,550 rpm.

Overhaul. Refer to Fig. HN201 for an exploded view of carburetor. Note that throttle and choke shaft and plate assemblies are not available separately from body and should not be removed.

Use a suitable carburetor cleaning solvent to clean all parts and fuel passages. Be sure that the cleaning solvent used will not damage plastic parts of carburetor.

To check float level, remove fuel bowl and invert carburetor. Measure from top edge of float to fuel bowl mating edge of carburetor body. Measurement should be 14.0 mm (0.55 in.). Float height is not adjustable. If fuel inlet valve and seat are in good condition, renew float if float height is incorrect.

Standard main jet size is #88 for Model GX610 and #95 for Model GX620. Optional jet sizes are available.

A limiter cap (1) attached to the idle mixture screw (2) restricts the rotation of the mixture screw.

NOTE: Detaching the limiter cap from the idle mixture screw will break the mixture screw. A new mixture screw must be installed.

To install the idle mixture screw, install mixture screw and position screw at initial setting. Apply Loctite 638 on limiter cap, then install cap on end of mixture screw so mixture screw cannot rotate counterclockwise with cap in place. Do not rotate mixture screw while installing limiter cap.

When installing carburetor, install the insulator between the carburetor and intake manifold so the straight side is up as shown in Fig. HN202. Also install gaskets on both sides of insulator so the straight side is up as shown in Fig. HN202.

To test fuel shutoff solenoid (18—Fig. HN201), disconnect electrical connector and remove solenoid. Connect a 12-volt battery to solenoid so positive terminal of battery is connected to solenoid electrical connector. Connect battery negative terminal to solenoid housing. Solenoid plunger should retract so plunger length is 10.2 mm (0.40 in.) or less. With battery disconnected from solenoid, plunger length should be 13.4 mm (0.53 in.) or more.

Propane Engines. Carburetor on propane-fueled engines is available only as a unit assembly. Individual carburetor components are not available.

When installing carburetor, install the insulator between the carburetor and intake manifold so the straight side is up as shown in Fig. HN202. Also install gaskets on both sides of insulator so the straight side is up as shown in Fig. HN202.

GOVERNOR. The engine is equipped with a mechanical flyball-type governor mounted on the camshaft.

To adjust external governor linkage, stop engine and loosen adjustment screw (S—Fig. HN203). Move throttle control lever (T) to wide open throttle position. Push governor lever (L) toward carburetor, then tighten adjustment screw (S).

Maximum governed speed is determined according to application. Standard maximum governed engine speed is 3,700-4,000 rpm. Adjust maximum governed speed by turning adjustment screw (W).

Note that the hole (H) nearest the end of governor lever (L) is attachment point for governor spring of engines with 3,000 rpm maximum governed speed.

IGNITION SYSTEM. The breakerless ignition system requires no regular maintenance. Ignition coils are mounted outside the flywheel. Air gap between flywheel and coil should be 0.2-0.6 mm (0.008-0.024 in.). Note that spark plug wires on ignition coils are

Fig. HN201—Exploded view of typical carburetor.

1. Limiter cap	10. Main jet
2. Idle mixture screw	11. Gasket
3. Spring	12. Float
4. Idle speed screw	13. Gasket
5. Spring	14. Fuel bowl
6. Body	15. Drain screw
7. Float pin	16. Gasket
8. Inlet fuel valve	17. Gasket
9. Main nozzle	18. Fuel shutoff solenoid

UP

UP

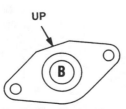

Fig. HN202—Install carburetor gasket (A) and insulator (B) with straight side positioned up as shown.

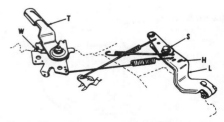

Fig. HN203—Refer to text for governor adjustment procedure.

not equal length. Ignition coil for number 1 cylinder has a shorter spark plug wire than ignition coil for number 2 cylinder.

To check ignition coil primary side, connect one ohmmeter lead to primary (black) coil lead and touch iron coil laminations with remaining lead. Ohmmeter should indicate 0.8-1.0 ohm.

To check ignition coil secondary side, remove the spark plug cap and connect one ohmmeter lead to the spark plug lead wire and remaining lead to the iron core laminations. Ohmmeter should indicate 5.9k-7.1k ohms. If ohmmeter readings are not as specified, renew ignition coil.

When installing ignition coils, be sure wires are properly located and retained to prevent contact with moving parts.

An engine stop diode unit is located behind the fan cover adjacent to the electric starter motor. The diode unit contains a pair of diodes that are in series with the ignition coil primary circuit. To test the diode unit, disconnect the unit wires. Connect an ohmmeter lead to the black/red wire terminal, then alternately connect the remaining ohmmeter lead to each of the black wires. Check the ohmmeter reading. Reverse the ohmmeter leads and recheck the resistance between the black/red wire terminal and the black wires. The ohmmeter should indicate infinity or continuity for one reading, then an opposite reading when the leads are reversed. Some ohmmeters have a diode check provision that may be used as well.

Fig. HN204—Loosen locknut (N) and turn adjusting screw (S) to obtain desired clearance (G) specified in text.

VALVE ADJUSTMENT. Adjust valve clearance with engine cold. Remove rocker arm cover. Remove rewind starter or screen. Rotate crankshaft so T mark on cooling fan aligns with T mark for cylinder being adjusted. The T mark indicates top dead center. The T reference mark for each cylinder is located on the fan cover beneath each respective cylinder. Be sure the piston is at top dead center on compression stroke (both valves closed).

Valve clearance should be 0.13-0.17 mm (0.005-0.007 in.) for intake valve and 0.18-0.22 mm (0.007-0.009 in.) for exhaust valve. Loosen locknut (N—Fig. HN204) and turn adjusting screw (S) to obtain desired clearance. Tighten locknut to 9 N•m (80 in.-lb.). Install rewind starter or screen and rocker arm covers.

CRANKCASE BREATHER. The engine is equipped with a disc-type crankcase breather. The breather is mounted on the crankcase above and behind the flywheel. The breather hose extends from the breather to the air cleaner elbow. Maintenance is not normally required other than periodically checking breather hose.

COMPRESSION PRESSURE. Compression pressure measured at cranking speed should be 600-800 kPa (87-114 psi).

REPAIRS

TIGHTENING TORQUE. Recommended tightening torque specifications are as follows:

Connecting rod . . . . 17 N•m
 (150 in.-lb.)
Crankcase cover . . . . 27 N•m
 (20 ft.-lb.)
Cylinder head . . . . 30 N•m
 (22 ft.-lb.)
Flywheel nut . . . . 200 N•m
 (147 ft.-lb.)
Rocker arm locknut . . . . 9 N•m
 (80 in.-lb.)

CYLINDER HEAD. To remove a cylinder head, proceed as follows: Mark any electrical connectors so they can be properly reconnected during assembly. Remove muffler and air cleaner assembly. Remove upper fan housing cover. Remove speed control assembly, carburetor and intake manifold. Remove fan housing and, if so equipped, remove the electrical control box. Remove starter motor. Remove shrouds on each cylinder. Remove rocker arm covers.

Rotate crankshaft so piston under cylinder head being removed is at TDC on compression stroke. Unscrew cylinder head retaining bolts in two steps using a crossing pattern and remove cylinder head. Repeat procedure for remaining cylinder head.

If removed, mark push rods so they can be returned to their original positions.

Remove carbon deposits from combustion chamber being careful not to damage gasket sealing surface. Inspect cylinder head for cracks, nicks or other damage. Place cylinder head on a flat surface and check entire sealing surface for distortion using a feeler gauge. Distortion service limit is 0.10 mm (0.004 in.).

When reinstalling cylinder head, position piston at TDC on compression stroke. Be sure push rods are properly positioned in lifters. Be sure to install hollow dowel pins in two lower bolt holes in each cylinder before installing head gasket and cylinder head. Install longest cylinder head bolt in hole above rocker arm shaft. Tighten cylinder head screws in three steps to a final torque of 30 N•m (22 ft.-lb.). Install intake manifold gasket as shown in Fig. HN205.

VALVE SYSTEM. Remove cylinder head as previously outlined. Remove rocker arm shaft (13—Fig. HN206) and rocker arms (12). Compress valve springs and remove valve retainers. Remove valves and springs. Note that a valve seal (4) is located on intake valve

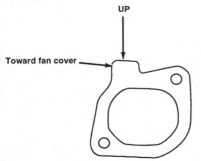

Fig. HN205—Install intake manifold gasket with tab positioned up as shown.

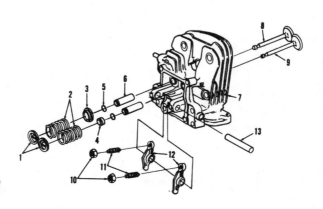

Fig. HN206—Exploded view of cylinder head.

1. Valve retainers
2. Valve springs
3. Spring seat
4. Oil seal
5. "O" rings
6. Valve guides
7. Cylinder head
8. Exhaust valve
9. Intake valve
10. Locknuts
11. Adjusters
12. Rocker arms
13. Rocker arm shaft

Fig. HN207—Exploded view of engine.

1. Oil seal
2. Plug
3. Oil pressure switch
4. Crankcase cover
5. Gasket
6. Thrust washer
7. Camshaft
8. Valve lifter
9. Bearing
10. Thrust washer
11. Crankshaft
12. Connecting rod bearing insert
13. Rod cap
14. Dowel pin
15. Dowel pin
16. "O" rings
17. Oil level switch
18. Spacers
19. Flange nut
20. Crankcase
21. Main bearing
22. Oil seal
23. Connecting rod bearing insert
24. Piston
25. Rod bolt

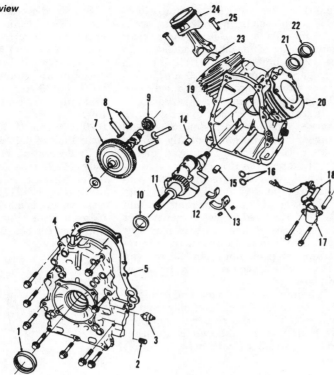

the head. Ream new valve guides after installation.

Standard rocker arm shaft diameter is 11.98 mm (0.472 in.). Renew rocker shaft if shaft diameter is less than 11.93 mm (0.470 in.). Standard rocker arm inside diameter is 12.018 mm (0.4731 in.). Renew rocker arm if inside diameter exceeds 12.04 mm (0.474 in.). Specified clearance between shaft and rocker arm is 0.016-0.052 mm (0.0006-0.0020 in.) with a maximum allowable clearance of 0.11 mm (0.004 in.).

CAMSHAFT. To remove camshaft, drain engine oil. Position engine with pto up so lifters will not fall out when removing camshaft. Remove the crankcase cover (4—Fig. HN207). Withdraw camshaft (7) while noting thrust washer (6) on end of camshaft. Remove and mark lifters (8) so they can be installed in their original positions.

Camshaft and camshaft gear are an integral casting equipped with a compression release mechanism. Governor flyballs are located in camshaft gear (see GOVERNOR).

Standard camshaft bearing journal diameter is 16.974 mm (0.6683 in.). Renew camshaft if journal diameter is 16.9 mm (0.67 in.) or less.

Standard camshaft lobe height for intake and exhaust valves is 29.70-29.80 mm (1.169-1.177 in.). Minimum allowable lobe height is 29.5 mm (1.16 in.).

Camshaft rides in a ball bearing in the crankcase, and directly in the crankcase cover. Renew crankcase cover if camshaft bearing diameter in cover exceeds 17.06 mm (0.672 in.). When installing ball bearing in crankcase, position bearing so sealed side is toward outside of crankcase.

The camshaft is equipped with a compression reduction device to aid starting. The lever and weight mechanism on the camshaft gear moves a pin (3—Fig. HN208) inside each exhaust cam lobe. During starting the pin protrudes above the cam lobe and forces

and a spring seat (3) is situated under exhaust valve spring. Intake valve diameter is 31.5 mm (1.24 in.) and exhaust valve diameter is 27.5 mm (1.08 in.).

NOTE: Valves for gasoline-fueled and propane-fueled engines are not the same. Do not interchange.

Valve face and seat angles are 45°. Standard valve seat width is 1.1 mm (0.043 in.). Narrow the seat if seat width is 2.0 mm (0.079) or more.

NOTE: On engines running on LPG or propane fuel, standard valve seat width is 2.2 mm (0.087 in.). Narrow the seat if seat width is 3.0 mm (0.118) or more.

Standard valve spring free length is 39.0 mm (1.54 in.). Renew valve spring

if free length is 37.5 mm (1.48 in.) or less.

Standard valve guide inside diameter is 6.60 mm (0.260 in.). Renew guide if inside diameter is 6.66 mm (0.262 in.) or more.

Specified valve stem-to-guide clearance is 0.010-0.040 mm (0.0004-0.0016 in.) for intake valve and 0.050-0.080 mm (0.0020-0.0031 in.) for exhaust valve. Renew valve guide and/or valve if clearance is 0.10 mm (0.004 in.) or more for intake valve, or 0.12 mm (0.005 in.) or more for exhaust valve.

To renew valve guide, heat entire cylinder head to 150° C (300° F). DO NOT heat head above recommended temperature as valve seats may loosen. Use valve guide driver 07942-6570100 to remove and install guides. Drive in the valve guide so the clip is bottomed in

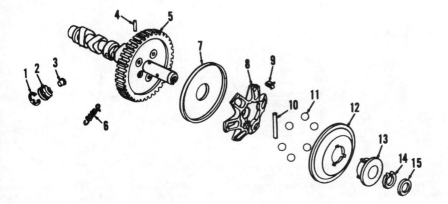

Fig. HN208—Exploded view of camshaft and governor assembly.

1. Clip
2. Retainer
3. Compression release pin
4. Pin
5. Camshaft
6. Compression release spring
7. Plate
8. Governor flyball holder
9. Plate
10. Pin
11. Flyball
12. Plate
13. Slider
14. Snap ring
15. Thrust washer

the exhaust valve to stay open longer thereby reducing compression. At running speed the pin remains below the surface of the cam lobe.

Inspect the mechanism for freedom of movement. Detach clip (1) and remove retainer (2) for access to pin (3). Pin should extend 0.85-1.05 mm (0.033-0.041 in.) above camshaft during starting. Various pin lengths are available to obtain correct pin height.

When installing camshaft, align timing marks on camshaft and crankshaft gears. Refer to Fig. HN209 and align projection (P) on camshaft gear with punch mark (M) on crankshaft gear.

Carefully install the crankcase cover. Do not use excessive force when installing cover, or oil pump gear may be damaged. Tighten retaining screws in a crossing pattern to 20 N•m (27 ft.-lb.).

PISTON, PIN AND RINGS. Remove piston and connecting rod as an assembly. To remove piston and connecting rod, remove cylinder head, crankcase cover and camshaft. Remove carbon and ridge (if present) from top of cylinder prior to removing piston. Unscrew connecting rod cap retaining nuts and remove rod cap. Push connecting rod and piston assembly out of cylinder. Remove piston pin retaining rings and separate piston from connecting rod.

Measure piston diameter 10 mm (0.4 in.) above lower edge of skirt and 90 degrees from piston pin. Standard piston diameter is 76.985 mm (3.0301 in.). Piston reject size is 76.85 mm (3.026 in.). Oversize pistons are available.

Standard clearance between piston pin and pin bore in piston is 0.002-0.004 mm (0.0001-0.0006 in.). If clearance is 0.08 mm (0.0031 in.) or greater, renew piston and/or pin.

Standard piston pin bore diameter is 18.002 mm (0.7087 in.). Reject piston if piston pin bore diameter is greater than 18.042 mm (0.7103 in.).

Compression ring side clearance should be 0.030-0.060 mm (0.0012-0.0024 in.). Maximum allowable compression ring side clearance is 0.15 mm (0.006 in.). Ring end gap for compression rings on all models should be 0.2-0.4 mm (0.008-0.016 in.). If ring end gap for any ring is 1.0 mm (0.039 in.) or more, renew ring and/or cylinder. Oversize piston rings are available.

Install marked piston rings with marked side toward piston crown and stagger ring end gaps equally around piston. Install chrome plated piston ring in top piston ring groove.

When reassembling piston on connecting rod, "1" or "2" mark (Fig. HN210) on side of connecting rod and FW or arrowhead on piston crown must be on opposite sides as shown in Fig. HN210. When installing piston pin retaining rings, do not align the end gap of the ring with the cutout in the piston pin bore.

When installing piston and connecting rod assembly in cylinder, install piston and rod in correct cylinder bore by matching number on connecting rod (Fig. HN210) with cylinder number.

NOTE: Cylinder identification number is cast in the side of cylinder.

Position piston so arrowhead or FW on piston crown is toward flywheel side of engine. Align number on connecting rod cap and connecting rod (Fig. HN211). Install connecting rod cap retaining nuts and tighten to 17 N•m (150 in.-lb.).

CONNECTING ROD. The connecting rod is equipped with an insert type bearing in the big end. Refer to previous PISTON, PIN AND RINGS paragraphs for removal and installation procedure. Measure rod side clearance with a feeler gauge before removing connecting rods.

Standard piston pin bore diameter in connecting rod is 18.006 mm (0.7089 in.). Renew connecting rod if diameter is 18.07 mm (0.711 in.).

Standard crankshaft crankpin diameter is 39.976 mm (1.5739 in.). Renew crankshaft if crankpin diameter is less than 39.92 mm (1.572 in.).

Specified clearance between crankpin and connecting rod bearing is 0.020-0.036 mm (0.0008-0.0014 in.). Maximum clearance is 0.05 mm (0.002 in.). Specified rod side clearance is 0.20-0.22 mm (0.008-0.009 in.) with a wear limit of 0.4 mm (0.016 in.).

To determine correct bearing size, note code letter size mark (Fig. HN212) on crankshaft and code number size mark (Fig. HN211) on connecting rod. Bearing size is marked on edge of insert using a color (Fig. HN213). To determine correct bearing, refer to chart in Fig. HN214.

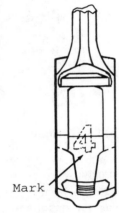

Fig. HN211—Install rod cap on rod so number mark on side matches number mark on rod.

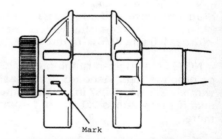

Fig. HN212—Drawing showing location of bearing identification mark on crankshaft. Refer to text.

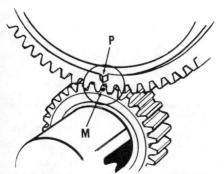

Fig. HN209—When installing camshaft, align timing projection (P) on camshaft gear and timing mark (M) on crankshaft gear.

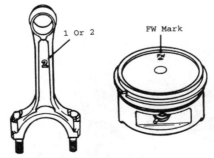

Fig. HN210—When installing piston on connecting rod, "1" or "2" mark on side of connecting rod and FW or arrowhead on piston crown must be on opposite sides as shown.

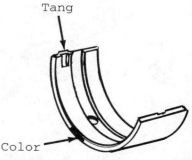

Fig. HN213—Connecting rod bearing color identification mark is located on edge of bearing insert.

Con Rod Mark \ Crankpin Mark	A	B	C	D
1	Red	Pink	Yellow	Green
2	Pink	Yellow	Green	Brown
3	Yellow	Green	Brown	Black
4	Green	Brown	Black	Blue

Fig. HN214—Refer to table and text to determine correct bearing size.

When installing bearing insert in rod or rod cap, be sure tang (Fig. HN213) on insert fits properly in notch in rod or cap.

CRANKSHAFT, MAIN BEARINGS AND SEALS.

The crankshaft is supported at each end in removable plain bearing-type main bearings.

To remove crankshaft, remove fan cover hood. Disconnect, mark and remove as needed any electrical wiring that prevents removal of fan cover. On models so equipped, remove electrical control box. Disconnect fuel hoses and remove fuel pump. Remove fan cover. Remove electric starter motor. Remove ignition coils, then remove flywheel. Refer to previous paragraphs and remove pistons and connecting rods. Remove crankshaft.

Crankshaft timing gear is not removable from crankshaft.

Specified crankshaft main bearing diameter is 37.985 mm (1.4955 in.). Renew crankshaft if diameter is less than 37.93 mm (1.493 in.). Specified main bearing inside diameter is 38.034 mm (1.4974 in.). Minimum allowable bearing inside diameter is 38.05 mm (1.498 in.).

To renew main bearings, proceed as follows. Use special driver tool 07749-0010000 and driver attachment 07PPF-ZJ10110 to press out main bearing. Do not attempt to drive bearing by striking tool. Measure bore at both ends in crankcase cover or crankcase. Measure diameter at several points, then calculate average for both ends. Use smaller average. Main bearings are color coded according to size with a color applied to the edge of the bearing as shown in Fig. HN215. Refer to the following table and select the correct bearing:

COVER/CRANKCASE BEARING BORE	BEARING COLOR	PART NUMBER
42.026-42.038 mm (1.6545-1.6550 in.)	Blue	13321-ZJ1-000
42.013-42.025 mm (1.6540-1.6545 in.)	Black	13322-ZJ1-000
42.000-42.012 mm (1.6535-1.6540 in.)	Brown	13323-ZJ1-000

Press new bearings into crankcase cover or crankcase using removal tools plus pilot 07PPF-ZJ10120. Lubricate outer surface of bearing with engine oil prior to installation. Position bearing so tang on outer surface aligns with notch in crankcase cover or crankcase. Press bearing into crankcase cover until bearing is 1.2-1.5 mm (0.05-0.06 in.) below inside surface of cover. Press bearing into crankcase so bearing is flush with inside surface of crankcase.

GOVERNOR.

Internal governor components include a flyball assembly mounted on the end of the camshaft as shown in Fig. HN208. Movement of governor flyballs (11) forces the slider (13) against the governor fork in the crankcase cover. The governor fork shaft extends through the crankcase cover to operate the external governor linkage.

Remove the crankcase cover for access to the internal governor components. Detach snap ring (14) to remove governor components. After assembly, be sure slider (13) moves smoothly.

OIL PUMP.

The engine is equipped with a rotor-type oil pump located in the crankcase cover. The crankshaft timing gear drives the oil pump.

Remove crankcase cover for access to oil pump components. Unscrew oil pump base retaining screws to remove oil pump (3—Fig. HN216). After remov-

Fig. HN215—Main bearing color identification mark is located on edge of bearing.

Color

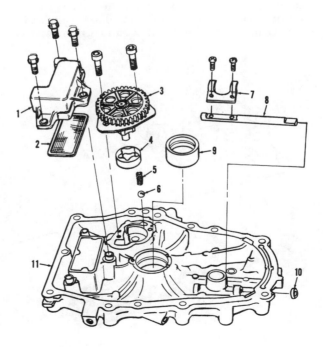

Fig. HN216—Exploded view of crankcase cover.

1. Oil filter cover
2. Oil filter screen
3. Oil pump
4. Oil pump outer rotor
5. Oil pressure relief spring
6. Oil pressure relief ball
7. Governor fork
8. Governor shaft
9. Main bearing
10. Oil seal
11. Crankcase cover

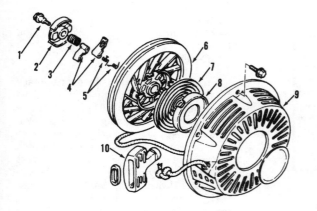

leads. Tester should indicate no continuity.

FUEL PUMP. Gasoline-fueled engines are equipped with a diaphragm-type fuel pump. Fuel pump must be serviced as a unit assembly.

REWIND STARTER. The engine may be equipped with the rewind starter shown in Fig. HN217. To disassemble starter remove rope handle and allow rope to wind into starter. Unscrew center retaining screw. Wear appropriate safety eyewear and gloves before disengaging pulley from starter as spring may uncoil uncontrolled. Place shop towel around pulley and lift pulley out of housing. Use caution when detaching rewind spring from pulley or housing.

When assembling starter, wrap rope around pulley in counterclockwise direction viewed from flywheel side of pulley. Apply light grease to sliding surfaces of rewind spring, pawls and friction spring. Install rewind spring (7) in spring cup (8) in a clockwise direction from outer end. Install spring cup with rewind spring on pulley so outer end of spring engages notch on pulley. Install pawl spring (5) so end of spring forces pawl (4) inward as shown in Fig. HN218. Rotate pulley five revolutions counterclockwise to place tension on rewind spring.

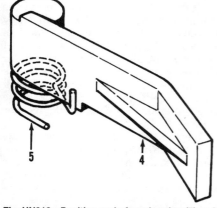

Fig. HN218—Position end of pawl spring (5) so it forces pawl (4) inward.

or more, renew oil pump body and/or outer rotor. Crankcase cover-to-outer rotor clearance should be 0.15-0.21 mm (0.006-0.008 in.). If clearance is 0.30 mm (0.012 in.) or more, renew outer rotor and/or crankcase cover.

Reassemble oil pump by reversing disassembly procedure. Be sure to lubricate oil pump prior to assembly. Align pins on oil pump base with holes in crankcase cover. Reinstall oil filter screen and cover.

OIL WARNING SYSTEM. The engine is equipped with a low oil level switch and module (17—Fig. HN207) that grounds the ignition system and lights a warning lamp if the oil level is low. To test the switch, run the engine and disconnect yellow switch wire. Grounding the yellow wire to the engine should cause the warning light to flash and the engine should stop. Stop engine. With oil level correct and the yellow and the green switch leads disconnected, use an ohmmeter or continuity tester and check continuity between yellow and green switch

ing pump, oil pressure relief spring (5) and ball (6) will be loose. Remove oil filter cover (1) and screen (2). Clean screen and make certain oil passages are clear.

Inspect pump housing in crankcase cover for damage. Inner-to-outer rotor clearance should be 0.14 mm (0.0055 in.). If clearance is 0.30 mm (0.012 in.)

ELECTRIC STARTER AND SOLENOID. Test specifications for electric starter motor are: Under load at more than 250 rpm and with a cranking voltage of 9.6 volts DC, the current draw should be less than 200 amps. Under no load with a cranking voltage of 11.5 volts DC, the current draw should be less than 30 amps.

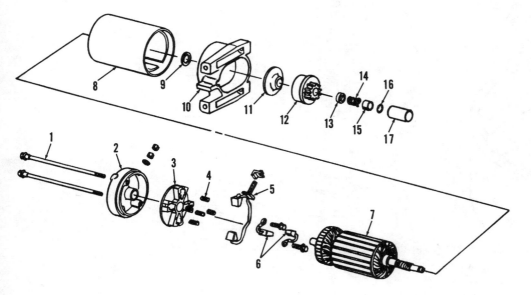

		–Tester Lead			
		Green	Green	White	Housing
+Tester Lead	Green		A	A	B
	Green	A		A	B
	White	B	B		B
	Housing	A	A	A	

Fig. HN220—Refer to text and above table to test rectifier on 3 amp charging systems. Values indicated in table are: A. Infinity; B. Continuity.

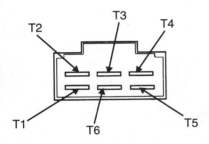

		–Tester Lead					
		T1	T2	T3	T4	T5	T6
+Tester Lead	T1		A	B	C	D	A
	T2						A
	T3				A	A	A
	T4	B	A	G		B	A
	T5	D	A	B	C		A
	T6	E	A	H	F	E	

Fig. HN221—Refer to text and above table to test rectifier on 20 amp charging systems. Values indicated in table are:

A. Infinity
B. 2k-230k ohms

C. 90-40k ohms
D. 4k-400k ohms

E. 100k ohms
F. 2k-400k ohms

G. 1k-600k ohms
H. 2k-600k ohms

If starter does not operate, check wiring, starter solenoid and battery before removing starter for inspection.

Refer to Fig. HN219 for an exploded view of starter. Individual components are not available; starter is available only as a unit assembly. Mark end cap, frame and drive housing before disassembly so they can be reassembled in original positions.

Minimum brush length is 7.5 mm (0.30 in.). Lightly lubricate bores of drive hub (11) and drive gear (12) with SAE 10 oil before assembly. Tighten through-bolts (1) to 7 N•m (62 in.-lb.).

When connecting wires to solenoid, attach black wire to lowest solenoid terminal and black/white wire to middle terminal. When tightening eyelet type terminal on white, upper wire, position eyelet so it is approximately 15° down from horizontal.

CHARGING SYSTEM. The engine may be equipped with a charging system that provides direct current.

The engine may be equipped with a 3 or 20 amp direct current charging system. The charging system consists of one charge coil and a rectifier for the 3 amp system (coil has one lead), or three charge coils and a regulator-rectifier for the 20 amp system. The coils are located underneath the flywheel.

The rectifier for 3 amp systems is located on the control switch box. Both systems are protected by a 25-amp, blade type fuse.

To test charge coil of 3 amp system, connect an ohmmeter between gray charge coil leads. Ohmmeter should indicate 0.23-0.31 ohms, otherwise, renew charge coil or replace with a good unit. To test charge coils of 20 amp system, connect an ohmmeter to two gray wire terminals. Ohmmeter should indicate 0.17-0.23 ohm, otherwise, renew charge coil assembly or replace with a good unit.

To test regulator-rectifier of 3 amp system, disconnect wire leads from unit and connect an ohmmeter to terminals while referring to test specifications in Fig. HN220.

To test regulator-rectifier of 20 amp system, disconnect wire lead from unit and connect an ohmmeter to terminals while referring to test specifications in Fig. HN221. Note that readings on ohmmeter may not match specified readings exactly, but ohmmeter should indicate continuity or infinity as noted on table.

WIRING DIAGRAMS. Refer to Fig. HN222 and HN223 for wiring diagrams of typical electrical systems.

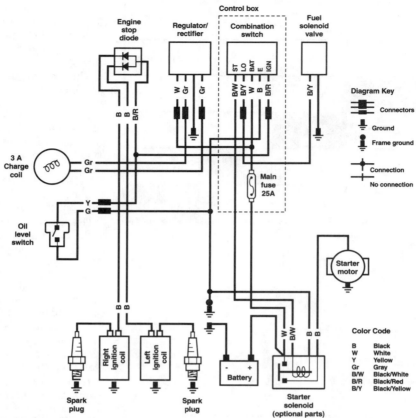

Fig. HN222—Wiring diagram for engines equipped with 3-amp charging system.

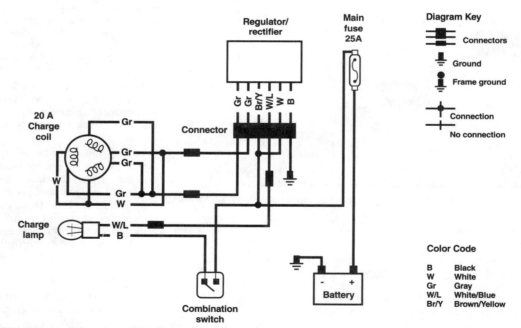

Fig. HN223—Wiring diagram for engines equipped with 20-amp charging system.

HONDA

AMERICAN HONDA MOTOR CO., INC.
4475 River Green Parkway
Duluth, GA 30136

Model	No. Cyls.	Bore	Stroke	Displacement	Power Rating
GXV610	2	77 mm (3.0 in.)	66 mm (2.6 in.)	615 cc (37.7 cu. in.)	13.4 kW (18 hp)
GXV620	2	77 mm (3.0 in.)	66 mm (2.6 in.)	615 cc (37.7 cu. in.)	14.9 kW (20 hp)

Both models are four-stroke, overhead-valve, twin-cylinder, air-cooled engines equipped with a vertical crankshaft.

Engine identification numbers are cast into side of crankcase above oil drain plug. Always furnish engine model and serial number when ordering parts.

Number 1 cylinder on the right when engine is viewed at flywheel end. Numbers 1 or 2 are cast into cylinder heads and cylinders for identification.

MAINTENANCE

LUBRICATION. Lubrication System. Both models are equipped with a pressure lubrication system and an oil filter. A gear-driven oil pump forces the lubricating oil through the oil filter to the main bearing in the oil pan. Some of the oil passes into the crankshaft to lubricate the connecting rod bearings and the main bearing at the flywheel end of the crankshaft. Oil spraying from the connecting rods lubricates and cools the undersides of the pistons. An oil passage from the oil pan main bearing directs oil to an orifice in the oil pan that sprays oil onto the timing gears. Oil in the passage travels into the hollow camshaft, which has oil holes so oil can spray onto the governor and decompression assemblies and the exhaust valve lifters. Oil also flows from the oil pan oil passage into a passage in the cylinder, then into the holes of one of the cylinder bolts in each cylinder head. Oil flows from under the cylinder bolt to lubricate the valve actuating assembly. Return oil passages direct the oil back to the crankcase.

Maintenance. Gasoline Engines. Check engine oil level prior to operating engine. Maintain oil level between reference marks on dipstick. Drain oil by removing drain plug in engine base. Add oil by pouring oil through oil fill hole in rocker arm cover on cylinder head.

Change oil after the first 20 hours of engine operation and every 100 hours or 6 months thereafter. Replace the oil filter annually or after every 200 hours of operation.

Engine oil should meet or exceed latest API service classification. Use SAE 30 oil for temperatures above 50°F (10° C); use SAE 10W-30 oil for temperatures between 0° F (-18° C) and 90° F (32° C); below 0° F (-18° C) use SAE 5W-30.

Oil pan capacity for both models is 1.8 L (1.9 qt.) not including oil filter.

Oil pan capacity is 2.1 L (2.23 qt.) including oil filter.

Propane Engines. Check engine oil level prior to operating engine. Maintain oil level between reference marks on dipstick. Drain oil by removing drain plug in engine base. Add oil by pouring oil through oil fill hole in rocker arm cover on cylinder head.

Change oil after the first 20 hours of engine operation and every 50 hours or 3 months thereafter. Replace the oil filter annually or after every 200 hours of operation.

Engine oil must be designed for use in engines that run on LPG (propane) and meet or exceed latest API service classification. SAE 30 is recommended for most operating temperatures. Mobil 1 5W-30 may be used for temperatures below 0° F (-18° C), but do not use above 0° F (-18° C). Do not use multi-grade, mineral-based oil.

Oil pan capacity for both models is 1.8 L (1.9 qt.) not including oil filter.

Oil pan capacity is 2.1 L (2.23 qt.) including oil filter.

Warning System. Some engines are equipped with a low-oil warning system or low-oil pressure warning system. If engine oil level or oil pressure is low, an indicator lamp will light and the engine will stop or not run. Refer to OIL WARNING SYSTEM in REPAIRS section.

Oil Pressure. Normal oil pressure is 200 kPa (28.4 psi). Oil pressure can be measured by connecting a suitable gauge to the oil pressure switch hole adjacent to the oil filter, or the plug hole if not equipped with an oil pressure switch. When reinstalling the switch or plug, apply a suitable sealer to the threads. Tighten the oil pressure switch to 8.5 N•m (75 in.-lb.). Tighten the plug to 9 N•m (80 in.-lb.).

AIR CLEANER. The engine is equipped with a paper-type air filter and a foam element. Clean the air cleaner elements after every 50 hours of operation. Renew the paper element annually or after every 300 hours of operation. Service more frequently if engine is operated in severe conditions.

Clean foam element by washing in soapy water. Allow to dry, then apply clean engine oil. Squeeze out excess oil.

The paper element should be renewed rather than cleaned. Tap the element to dislodge dirt. Do not attempt to brush dirt off element. Do not wash or direct high pressure air at filter.

SPARK PLUG. The spark plug should be removed, cleaned and inspected after every 100 hours of use.

Recommended spark plug is a NGK BPR5ES or ND W16EPR-U. Spark plug electrode gap should be 0.7-0.8 mm (0.028-0.031 in.).

When installing spark plug, manufacturer recommends installing spark plug finger-tight, then for a new plug, tighten an additional ½ turn. For a used plug, tighten an additional ¼ turn.

FUEL FILTER. The engine is equipped with a fuel filter attached to the side of the engine. Inspect the filter after every 100 hours of operation. Renew filter annually or after 300 hours of operation. Install filter so arrow on filter points in direction of fuel flow.

CARBURETOR. Gasoline Engines. Both models are equipped with a float-type carburetor with a fixed main fuel jet and an adjustable low-speed fuel mixture needle. The engines are designed to comply with emissions regulations. Emissions-compliant engines may be identified by the presence of a limiter cap on the low speed mixture screw that limits rotation of the mixture screw.

The carburetor is equipped with a fuel shutoff solenoid (18—Fig. HN301) that uses a plunger to stop fuel flow through the main jet when the engine is stopped. The spring-loaded plunger should retract when the solenoid is energized.

Adjustment. Limiter cap (1—Fig. HN301) on idle mixture screw must be removed to set initial position of mixture screw, however, removing limiter cap damages the mixture screw. Initial setting of idle mixture screw is 1¾ turns out on Model GXV610 and 1¼ turns out on Model GXV620. Refer to overhaul section to install limiter cap.

Engine must be at normal operating temperature and running for final adjustment. Operate engine at idle speed and adjust idle mixture screw to obtain a smooth idle and satisfactory accelera-tion. Adjust idle speed by turning idle speed screw. Standard idle speed is 1,250-1,550 rpm.

Overhaul. Refer to Fig. HN301 for an exploded view of carburetor. Note that throttle and choke shaft and plate assemblies are not available separately from body and should not be removed.

Clean all parts and fuel passages using carburetor cleaning solvent and compressed air. Be sure that the cleaning solvent used will not damage plastic parts of carburetor.

To check float level, remove fuel bowl and invert carburetor. Measure from top edge of float to fuel bowl mating edge of carburetor body. Measurement should be 14.0 mm (0.55 in.). Float height is not adjustable. If fuel inlet valve and seat are in good condition, renew float if float height is incorrect.

Standard main jet size is #88 for Model GXV610 and #95 for Model GXV620. Optional jet sizes are available.

A limiter cap (1) attached to the idle mixture screw (2) restricts the rotation of the mixture screw.

NOTE: Detaching the limiter cap from the idle mixture screw will break the mixture screw. A new mixture screw must be installed.

To install the idle mixture screw, install mixture screw and position screw at initial setting. Apply Loctite 638 on limiter cap, then install cap on end of mixture screw so mixture screw cannot rotate counterclockwise with cap in place. Do not rotate mixture screw while installing limiter cap.

When installing carburetor, install the insulator between the carburetor and intake manifold so the straight side is up as shown in Fig. HN302. Also install gaskets on both sides of insulator so the straight side is up as shown in Fig. HN302.

To test fuel shutoff solenoid (18—Fig. HN301), disconnect electrical connector and remove solenoid. Connect a 12-volt battery to solenoid so positive terminal of battery is connected to solenoid electrical connector. Connect battery negative terminal to solenoid housing. Solenoid plunger should retract so plunger length is 10.2 mm (0.40 in.) or less. With battery disconnected from solenoid, plunger length should be 13.4 mm (0.53 in.) or more.

Propane Engines. Carburetor on propane-fueled engines is available only as a unit assembly. Individual carburetor components are not available.

When installing carburetor, install the insulator between the carburetor and intake manifold so the straight side is up as shown in Fig. HN302. Also install gaskets on both sides of insulator so the straight side is up as shown in Fig. HN302.

GOVERNOR. The engine is equipped with a mechanical flyball-type governor mounted on the camshaft.

To adjust external governor linkage, stop engine and loosen adjustment screw (S—Fig. HN303). Move throttle control lever to wide open throttle position. Push governor lever (L) toward carburetor, then tighten adjustment screw (S).

Maximum governed speed is determined according to application. Standard maximum governed engine speed is 3,250-3,550 rpm. Adjust maximum governed speed by turning adjustment screw (W).

Note that the hole (H) nearest the end of governor lever (L) is attachment point for governor spring of engines with 3,000 rpm maximum governed speed.

IGNITION SYSTEM. The breakerless ignition system requires no regular maintenance. Ignition coils are

Fig. HN301—Exploded view of typical carburetor.

1. Limiter cap	10. Main jet
2. Idle mixture screw	11. Gasket
3. Spring	12. Float
4. Idle speed screw	13. Gasket
5. Spring	14. Fuel bowl
6. Body	15. Drain screw
7. Float pin	16. Gasket
8. Inlet fuel valve	17. Gasket
9. Main nozzle	18. Fuel shutoff solenoid

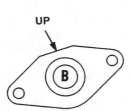

Fig. HN302—Install carburetor gasket (A) and insulator (B) with straight side positioned up as shown.

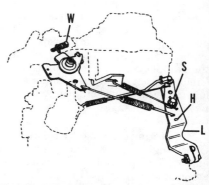

Fig. HN303—Refer to text for governor adjustment procedure.

mounted outside the flywheel. Air gap between flywheel and coil should be 0.2-0.6 mm (0.008-0.024 in.). Note that spark plug wires on ignition coils are not equal lengths. Ignition coil for number 1 cylinder has a shorter spark plug wire than ignition coil for number 2 cylinder.

To check ignition coil primary side, connect one ohmmeter lead to primary (black) coil lead and touch iron coil laminations with remaining lead. Ohmmeter should indicate 0.8-1.0 ohm.

To check ignition coil secondary side, remove the spark plug cap and connect one ohmmeter lead to the spark plug lead wire and remaining lead to the iron core laminations. Ohmmeter should indicate 5.9k-7.1k ohms. If ohmmeter readings are not as specified, renew ignition coil.

When installing ignition coils, be sure wires are properly located and retained to prevent contact with moving parts.

An engine stop diode unit is located behind the fan cover adjacent to the electric starter motor. The diode unit contains a pair of diodes that are in series with the ignition coil primary circuit. To test the diode unit, disconnect the unit wires. Connect an ohmmeter lead to the black/red wire terminal, then alternately connect the remaining ohmmeter lead to each of the black wires. Check the ohmmeter reading. Reverse the ohmmeter leads and recheck the resistance between the black/red wire terminal and the black wires. The ohmmeter should indicate infinity or continuity for one reading, then an opposite reading when the leads are reversed. Some ohmmeters have a diode check provision that may be used as well.

VALVE ADJUSTMENT. Adjust valve clearance with engine cold. Remove rocker arm cover.

NOTE: With cover removed, rocker arm shaft can slide down out of shaft support and rocker arms. Prevent downward movement of shaft by screwing a flange screw or screw and washer into upper end of shaft. Be sure to remove screw before installing rocker arm cover.

Remove rewind starter or screen. Rotate crankshaft so T mark on cooling fan aligns with T mark for cylinder being adjusted. The T mark indicates top dead center. The T reference mark for each cylinder is located on the fan cover beneath each respective cylinder. Be sure the piston is at top dead center on

compression stroke (both valves closed).

Valve clearance should be 0.13-0.17 mm (0.005-0.007 in.) for intake valve and 0.18-0.22 mm (0.007-0.009 in.) for exhaust valve. Loosen locknut (N—Fig. HN304) and turn adjusting screw (S) to obtain desired clearance. Tighten locknut to 9 N•m (80 in.-lb.). Install rewind starter or screen and rocker arm covers.

CRANKCASE BREATHER. The engine is equipped with a disc-type crankcase breather. The breather is mounted on the crankcase above and behind the flywheel. The breather hose extends from the breather to the air cleaner elbow. Maintenance is not normally required other than periodically checking breather hose.

COMPRESSION PRESSURE. Compression pressure measured at cranking speed should be 600-800 kPa (87-114 psi).

REPAIRS

TIGHTENING TORQUE. Recommended tightening torque specifications are as follows:

Connecting rod	17 N•m
	(150 in.-lb.)
Oil pan	27 N•m
	(20 ft.-lb.)
Cylinder head	30 N•m
	(22 ft.-lb.)
Flywheel nut	200 N•m
	(147 ft.-lb.)
Rocker arm locknut	9 N•m
	(80 in.-lb.)

CYLINDER HEAD. To remove a cylinder head, proceed as follows: Mark any electrical connectors so they can be properly reconnected during assembly. Remove muffler. Remove cover above air cleaner, then remove air cleaner assembly. Remove speed control assembly, carburetor and intake manifold. Remove fan housing and, if so equipped, remove the electrical control box. Remove starter motor. Remove shrouds on each cylinder. Remove rocker arm covers.

Rotate crankshaft so piston under cylinder head being removed is at TDC on compression stroke. Unscrew cylinder head retaining bolts in two steps using a crossing pattern and remove cylinder head. Repeat procedure for remaining cylinder head.

If removed, mark push rods so they can be returned to their original positions.

Remove carbon deposits from combustion chamber being careful not to damage gasket sealing surface. Inspect cylinder head for cracks, nicks or other damage. Place cylinder head on a flat surface and check entire sealing surface for distortion using a feeler gauge. Distortion service limit is 0.10 mm (0.004 in.).

When installing cylinder head, position piston at TDC on compression stroke. Be sure push rods are properly positioned in lifters. Be sure to install hollow dowel pins in two larger bolt holes in each cylinder before installing head gasket and cylinder head. Install longest cylinder head bolt in hole above rocker arm cover. Tighten cylinder head screws in three steps to a final torque of 30 N•m (22 ft.-lb.). Install intake manifold gasket as shown in Fig. HN305.

VALVE SYSTEM. Remove cylinder head as previously outlined. Remove rocker arm shaft (13—Fig. HN306) and rocker arms (12). Compress the valve springs and remove valve retainers. Remove valves and springs. Note that a valve seal (4) is located on intake valve and a spring seat (3) is situated under exhaust valve spring. Intake valve diameter is 31.5 mm (1.24 in.) and exhaust valve diameter is 27.5 mm (1.08 in.).

NOTE: Valves for gasoline-fueled and propane-fueled engines are not the same. Do not interchange.

Valve face and seat angles are 45°. Standard valve seat width is 1.1 mm

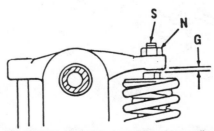

Fig. HN304—Loosen locknut (N) and turn adjusting screw (S) to obtain desired clearance (G) specified in text.

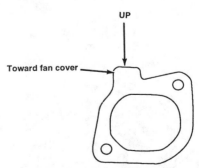

Fig. HN305—Install intake manifold gasket with tab positioned up as shown.

(0.043 in.). Narrow the seat if seat width is 2.0 mm (0.079) or more.

NOTE: On engines running on LPG or propane fuel, standard valve seat width is 2.2 mm (0.087 in.). Narrow the seat if seat width is 3.0 mm (0.118) or more.

Standard valve spring free length is 39.0 mm (1.54 in.). Renew valve spring if free length is 37.5 mm (1.48 in.) or less.

Standard valve guide inside diameter is 6.60 mm (0.260 in.). Renew guide if inside diameter is 6.66 mm (0.262 in.) or more.

Specified valve stem-to-guide clearance is 0.010-0.040 mm (0.0004-0.0016 in.) for intake valve and 0.050-0.080 mm (0.0020-0.0031 in.) for exhaust valve. Renew valve guide and/or valve if clearance is 0.10 mm (0.004 in.) or more

for intake valve, or 0.12 mm (0.005 in.) or more for exhaust valve.

To renew valve guide, heat entire cylinder head to 150° C (300° F). DO NOT heat head above recommended temperature as valve seats may loosen. Use valve guide driver 07942-6570100 to remove and install guides. Drive in the valve guide so the clip is bottomed in the head. Ream new valve guides after installation.

Standard rocker arm shaft diameter is 11.98 mm (0.472 in.). Renew rocker shaft if shaft diameter is less than 11.93 mm (0.470 in.). Standard rocker arm inside diameter is 12.018 mm (0.4731 in.). Renew rocker arm if inside diameter exceeds 12.04 mm (0.474 in.). Specified clearance between shaft and rocker arm is 0.016-0.052 mm (0.0006-0.0020 in.) with a maximum allowable clearance of 0.11 mm (0.004 in.).

CAMSHAFT. To remove camshaft, drain engine oil and remove cylinder heads as previously outlined. Mark and remove push rods. Position engine with pto up so lifters will not fall out when removing camshaft. Remove the oil pan (4—Fig. HN307). Withdraw camshaft (7) while noting thrust washer (6) on end of camshaft. Remove and mark lifters so they can be installed in their original positions.

Camshaft and camshaft gear are an integral casting equipped with a compression release mechanism. Governor flyballs are located in camshaft gear (see GOVERNOR).

Standard camshaft bearing journal diameter is 16.974 mm (0.6683 in.). Renew camshaft if journal diameter is 16.9 mm (0.67 in.) or less.

Standard camshaft lobe height for intake and exhaust valves is 29.70-29.80 mm (1.169-1.177 in.). Minimum allowable lobe height is 29.5 mm (1.16 in.).

Camshaft rides in a ball bearing in the crankcase, and directly in the oil pan. Renew oil pan if camshaft bearing diameter in oil pan exceeds 17.06 mm (0.672 in.). When installing ball bearing in crankcase, position bearing so sealed side is toward outside of crankcase.

The camshaft is equipped with a compression reduction device to aid starting. The lever and weight mechanism on the camshaft gear moves a pin (3—Fig. HN308) inside each exhaust cam lobe. During starting, the pin protrudes above the cam lobe and forces the exhaust valve to stay open longer

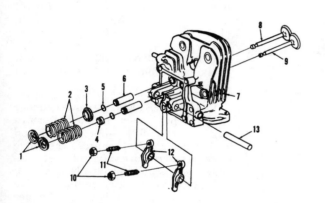

Fig. HN306—Exploded view of cylinder head.

1. Valve retainers
2. Valve springs
3. Spring seat
4. Oil seal
5. "O" rings
6. Valve guides
7. Cylinder head
8. Exhaust valve
9. Intake valve
10. Locknuts
11. Adjusters
12. Rocker arms
13. Rocker arm shaft

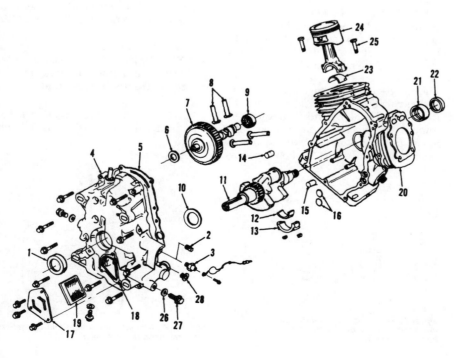

Fig. HN307—Exploded view of engine.

1. Oil seal
2. Plug
3. Oil pressure switch
4. Oil pan
5. Gasket
6. Thrust washer
7. Camshaft
8. Valve lifter
9. Bearing
10. Thrust washer
11. Crankshaft
12. Connecting rod bearing insert
13. Rod cap
14. Dowel pin
15. Dowel pin
16. "O" rings
17. Cover
18. "O" ring
19. Oil filter screen
20. Crankcase
21. Main bearing
22. Oil seal
23. Connecting rod bearing insert
24. Piston
25. Rod bolt
26. Washer
27. Oil drain screw
28. Screw

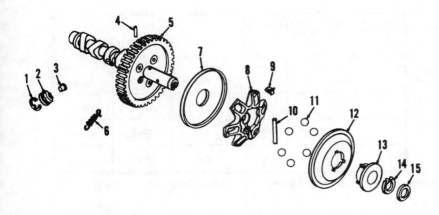

Fig. HN308—Exploded view of camshaft and governor assembly.

1. Clip
2. Retainer
3. Compression release pin
4. Pin
5. Camshaft
6. Compression release spring
7. Plate
8. Governor flyball holder
9. Plate
10. Pin
11. Flyball
12. Plate
13. Slider
14. Snap ring
15. Thrust washer

thereby reducing compression. At running speed the pin remains below the surface of the cam lobe. Inspect mechanism for freedom of movement.

Detach clip (1) and remove retainer (2) for access to pin (3). Pin should extend 0.85-1.05 mm (0.033-0.041 in.) above camshaft during starting. Various pin lengths are available to obtain correct pin height.

When installing camshaft, align timing marks on camshaft and crankshaft gears. Refer to Fig. HN309 and align projection (P) on camshaft gear with punch mark (M) on crankshaft gear.

Carefully install oil pan. Do not use excessive force when installing oil pan, or oil pump gear may be damaged. Be sure oil control shaft (1—Fig. HN316) does not drop out during installation. Tighten retaining screws in a crossing pattern to 20 N•m (27 ft.-lb.).

PISTON, PIN AND RINGS. Remove piston and connecting rod as an assembly. To remove piston and connecting rod, remove cylinder head, oil pan and camshaft. Remove carbon and ridge (if present) from top of cylinder prior to removing the piston. Unscrew connecting rod cap retaining nuts and remove rod cap. Push connecting rod and piston assembly out of cylinder. Remove piston pin retaining rings and separate piston from connecting rod.

Measure piston diameter 10 mm (0.4 in.) above lower edge of skirt and 90° from piston pin. Standard piston diameter is 76.985 mm (3.0301 in.). Piston reject size is 76.85 mm (3.026 in.). Oversize pistons are available.

Standard clearance between piston pin and pin bore in piston is 0.002-0.004 mm (0.0001-0.0006 in.). If clearance is 0.08 mm (0.0031 in.) or greater, renew piston and/or pin.

Standard piston pin bore diameter is 18.002 mm (0.7087 in.). Reject piston if piston pin bore diameter is greater than 18.042 mm (0.7103 in.).

Compression ring side clearance should be 0.030-0.060 mm (0.0012-0.0024 in.). Maximum allowable compression ring side clearance is 0.15 mm (0.006 in.). Ring end gap for compression rings on all models should be 0.2-0.4 mm (0.008-0.016 in.). If ring end gap for any ring is 1.0 mm (0.039 in.) or more, renew ring and/or cylinder. Oversize piston rings are available.

Install marked piston rings with marked side toward piston crown and stagger ring end gaps equally around piston. Install chrome plated piston ring in top piston ring groove.

When reassembling piston on connecting rod, "1" or "2" mark (Fig. HN310) on side of connecting rod and FW or arrowhead on piston crown must

be on opposite sides as shown in Fig. HN310. When installing piston pin retaining rings, do not align the end gap of the ring with the cutout in the piston pin bore.

When reinstalling piston and connecting rod assembly in cylinder, install piston and rod in correct cylinder bore by matching number on connecting rod (Fig. HN310) with cylinder number.

NOTE: Cylinder identification number is cast in the side of cylinder.

Position piston so arrowhead or FW on piston crown is toward flywheel side of engine. Align number on connecting rod cap and connecting rod (Fig. HN311). Install connecting rod cap retaining nuts and tighten to 17 N•m (150 in.-lb.).

CONNECTING ROD. The connecting rod is equipped with an insert-type bearing in the big end. Refer to previous PISTON, PIN AND RINGS paragraphs for removal and installation procedure. Measure rod side clearance with a feeler gauge before removing connecting rods.

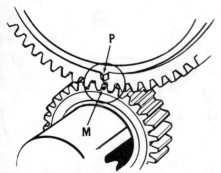

Fig. HN309—When installing camshaft, align timing projection (P) on camshaft gear and timing mark (M) on crankshaft gear.

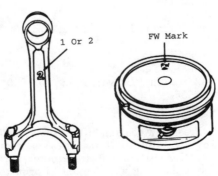

Fig. HN310—When installing piston on connecting rod, "1" or "2" mark on side of connecting rod and FW or arrowhead on piston crown must be on opposite sides as shown.

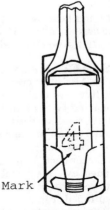

Fig. HN311—Install rod cap on rod so number mark on side matches number mark on rod.

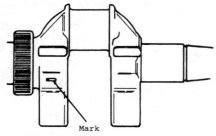

Fig. HN312—Drawing showing location of bearing identification mark on crankshaft. Refer to text.

Con Rod Mark	Crankpin Mark			
	A	B	C	D
1	Red	Pink	Yellow	Green
2	Pink	Yellow	Green	Brown
3	Yellow	Green	Brown	Black
4	Green	Brown	Black	Blue

Fig. HN314—Refer to table and text to determine correct bearing size.

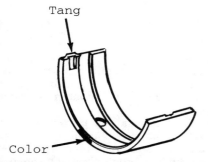

Fig. HN313—Connecting rod bearing color identification mark is located on edge of bearing insert.

Standard piston pin bore diameter in connecting rod is 18.006 mm (0.7089 in.). Renew connecting rod if diameter is 18.07 mm (0.711 in.).

Standard crankshaft crankpin diameter is 39.976 mm (1.5739 in.). Renew crankshaft if crankpin diameter is less than 39.92 mm (1.572 in.).

Specified clearance between crankpin and connecting rod bearing is 0.020-0.036 mm (0.0008-0.0014 in.). Maximum clearance is 0.05 mm (0.002 in.). Specified rod side clearance is 0.20-0.22 mm (0.008-0.009 in.) with a wear limit of 0.4 mm (0.016 in.).

To determine correct bearing size, note code letter size mark (Fig. HN312) on crankshaft and code number size mark (Fig. HN311) on connecting rod. Bearing size is marked on edge of insert using a color (Fig. HN313). To determine correct bearing, refer to chart in Fig. HN314.

When installing bearing insert in rod or rod cap, be sure tang (Fig. HN313) on insert fits properly in notch in rod or cap.

CRANKSHAFT, MAIN BEARINGS AND SEALS. The crankshaft is supported at flywheel end in a removable plain bearing-type main bearing. The crankshaft rides directly in main bearing bore in oil pan at pto end.

To remove crankshaft, remove fan cover hood. Disconnect, mark and remove as needed any electrical wiring that prevents removal of fan cover. On models so equipped, remove electrical control box. Disconnect fuel hoses and remove fuel pump. Remove fan cover.

Remove electric starter motor. Remove ignition coils, then remove flywheel. Refer to previous paragraphs and remove pistons and connecting rods. Remove crankshaft.

Crankshaft timing gear is not removable from crankshaft.

Specified crankshaft main bearing diameter is 37.985 mm (1.4955 in.). Renew crankshaft if diameter is less than 37.93 mm (1.493 in.). Specified main bearing inside diameter is 38.034 mm (1.4974 in.). Minimum allowable bearing inside diameter is 38.05 mm (1.498 in.). Renew oil pan if bearing bore is damaged or excessively worn.

To renew main bearing in crankcase, proceed as follows. Use special driver tool 07749-0010000 and driver attachment 07PPF-ZJ10110 to press out main bearing. Do not attempt to drive bearing by striking tool. Measure bearing bore at both ends at several points, then calculate average for both ends. Use smaller average. Main bearings are color coded according to size with a color applied to the edge of the bearing as shown in Fig. HN315. Refer to the following table and select the correct bearing:

CRANKCASE

BEARING BORE	BEARING COLOR	PART NUMBER
42.026-42.038 mm (1.6545-1.6550 in.)	Blue	13321-ZJ1-000
42.013-42.025 mm (1.6540-1.6545 in.)	Black	13322-ZJ1-000
42.000-42.012 mm (1.6535-1.6540 in.)	Brown	13323-ZJ1-000

Press new bearing into crankcase using removal tools plus pilot 07PPF-ZJ10120. Lubricate outer surface of bearing with engine oil prior to installation. Position bearing so tang on outer surface aligns with notch in crankcase. Press bearing into crankcase so bearing is flush with inside surface of crankcase.

GOVERNOR. Internal governor components include a flyball assembly mounted on the end of the camshaft as shown in Fig. HN308. Movement of governor flyballs (11) forces the slider (13) against the governor fork in the oil pan. The governor fork shaft extends through the oil pan to operate the external governor linkage.

Remove the oil pan for access to the internal governor components. Detach snap ring (14) to remove governor components. After assembly, be sure slider (13) moves smoothly.

OIL PUMP. The engine is equipped with a rotor-type oil pump located in the oil pan. The crankshaft timing gears drives the oil pump.

Remove oil pan for access to oil pump components. Unscrew oil pump base retaining screws to remove oil pump (3—Fig. HN316). After removing pump, oil pressure relief spring (5) and ball (6) will be loose. Make certain oil passages are clear.

Inspect pump housing in oil pan for damage. Inner-to-outer rotor clearance should be 0.14 mm (0.0055 in.). If clearance is 0.30 mm (0.012 in.) or more, renew oil pump body and/or outer rotor. Place outer rotor (4) in oil pan. Oil

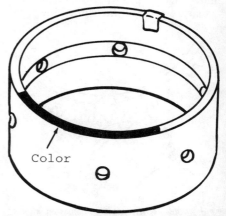

Fig. HN315—Main bearing color identification mark is located on edge of bearing.

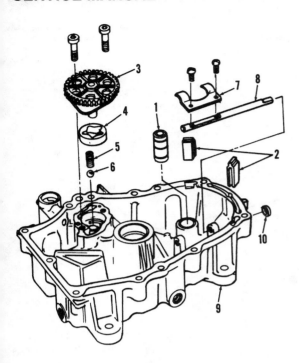

1. Oil control shaft
2. Oil return insert
3. Oil pump
4. Oil pump outer rotor
5. Oil pressure relief spring
6. Oil pressure relief ball
7. Governor fork
8. Governor shaft
9. Oil pan
10. Oil seal

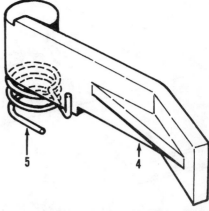

**Fig. HN318—Position end of pawl spring (5) so it
forces pawl (4) inward.**

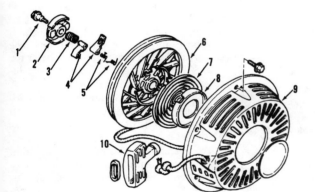

**Fig. HN317—Exploded view
of rewind starter used on
some models.**

1. Screw
2. Cover
3. Friction spring
4. Pawls
5. Springs
6. Pulley
7. Rewind spring
8. Spring cup
9. Starter housing
10. Rope handle

When assembling starter, wrap rope around pulley in counterclockwise direction viewed from flywheel side of pulley. Apply light grease to sliding surfaces of rewind spring, pawls and friction spring. Install rewind spring (7) in spring cup (8) in a clockwise direction from outer end. Install spring cup with rewind spring on pulley so outer end of spring engages notch on pulley. Install pawl spring (5) so end of spring forces pawl (4) inward as shown in Fig. HN318. Rotate pulley five revolutions counterclockwise to place tension on rewind spring.

ELECTRIC STARTER AND SOLENOID. Test specifications for electric starter motor are: Under load at more than 250 rpm and with a cranking voltage of 9.6 volts DC, the current draw should be less than 200 amps. Under no load with a cranking voltage of 11.5 volts DC, the current draw should be less than 30 amps.

If starter does not operate, check wiring, starter solenoid and battery before removing starter for inspection.

Refer to Fig. HN319 for an exploded view of starter. Individual components are not available; starter is available only as a unit assembly. Mark the end cap, frame and drive housing before disassembly so they can be reassembled in original positions.

Minimum brush length is 7.5 mm (0.30 in.). Lightly lubricate bores of drive hub (11) and drive gear (12) with SAE 10 oil before assembly. Tighten through-bolts (1) to 7 N•m (62 in.-lb.).

When connecting wires to solenoid, attach black wire to lowest solenoid terminal and black/white wire to middle terminal. When tightening eyelet type terminal on white, upper wire, position eyelet so it is approximately 15° down from horizontal.

pan-to-outer rotor clearance should be 0.15-0.21 mm (0.006-0.008 in.). If clearance is 0.30 mm (0.012 in.) or more, renew outer rotor and/or oil pan. Depth of outer rotor below surface of oil pan should be 0.04-0.11 mm (0.002-0.004 in.). If depth exceeds 0.13 mm (0.005 in.), renew outer rotor and/or oil pan.

Reassemble oil pump by reversing disassembly procedure. Be sure to lubricate oil pump prior to assembly. Align pins on oil pump base with holes in oil pan. Reinstall oil filter screen and oil pan.

OIL WARNING SYSTEM. The engine is equipped with a low oil level switch (3—Fig. HN307) that grounds the ignition system and lights a warning lamp if the oil level is low. To test switch, disconnect switch wire. With oil level correct, use an ohmmeter or conti-

nuity tester and check continuity between switch wire terminal and switch body. Tester should indicate no continuity.

FUEL PUMP. Gasoline-fueled engines are equipped with a diaphragm-type fuel pump. Fuel pump must be serviced as a unit assembly.

REWIND STARTER. The engine may be equipped with the rewind starter shown in Fig. HN317. To disassemble starter, remove rope handle and allow rope to wind into starter. Unscrew center retaining screw. Wear appropriate safety eyewear and gloves before disengaging pulley from starter as spring may uncoil uncontrolled. Place shop towel around pulley and lift pulley out of housing. Use caution when detaching rewind spring from pulley or housing.

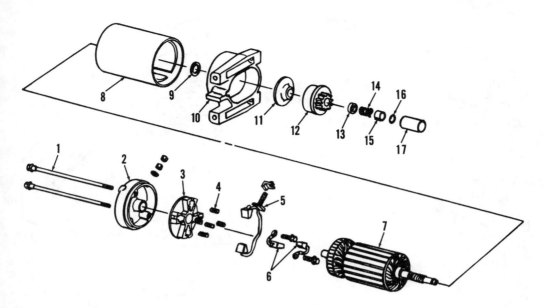

Fig. HN319—Exploded view of electric starter motor.

1. Through-bolt
2. End cap
3. Brush holder
4. Spring
5. Positive brush assy.
6. Negative brushes
7. Armature
8. Frame
9. Washer
10. Drive housing
11. Drive hub
12. Drive gear
13. Spring holder
14. Spring
15. Pinion stop
16. Retaining ring
17. Cover

		−Tester Lead			
		Green	Green	White	Housing
+Tester Lead	Green		A	A	B
	Green	A		A	B
	White	B	B		B
	Housing	A	A	A	

Fig. HN320—Refer to text and above table to test rectifier on 3-amp charging systems. Values indicated in table are: A. Infinity; B. Continuity.

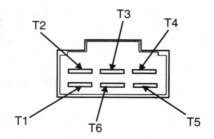

Fig. HN321—Refer to text and table below to test rectifier on 20-amp charging systems. Values indicated in table are:

A. Infinity
B. 2k-230k ohms
C. 90-40k ohms
D. 4k-400k ohms
E. 100k ohms
F. 2k-400k ohms
G. 1k-600k ohms
H. 2k-600k ohms

		−Tester Lead					
		T1	T2	T3	T4	T5	T6
+ Tester Lead	T1		A	B	C	D	A
	T2						A
	T3				A	A	A
	T4	B	A	G		B	A
	T5	D	A	B	C		A
	T6	E	A	H	F	E	

CHARGING SYSTEM. The engine may be equipped with a charging system that provides direct current.

The engine may be equipped with a 3 or 20 amp direct current charging system. The charging system consists of one charge coil and a rectifier for the 3 amp system (coil has one lead) or three charge coils and a regulator-rectifier for the 20 amp system. The coils are located underneath the flywheel.

The rectifier for 3 amp systems is located on the control switch box. Both systems are protected by a 25-amp, blade type fuse.

To test charge coil of 3 amp system, connect an ohmmeter between gray charge coil leads. Ohmmeter should indicate 0.23-0.31 ohms, otherwise, renew charge coil or replace with a good unit. To test charge coils of 20 amp system, connect an ohmmeter to two gray wire terminals. Ohmmeter should indicate 0.17-0.23 ohm, otherwise, renew charge coil assembly or replace with a good unit.

To test regulator-rectifier of 3 amp system, disconnect wire leads from unit and connect an ohmmeter to terminals while referring to test specifications in Fig. HN320.

To test regulator-rectifier of 20 amp system, disconnect wire lead from unit and connect an ohmmeter to terminals while referring to test specifications in Fig. HN321. Note that readings on ohmmeter may not match specified readings exactly, but ohmmeter should indicate continuity or infinity as noted on table.

WIRING DIAGRAMS. Refer to Fig. HN322 and HN323 for wiring diagrams of typical electrical systems.

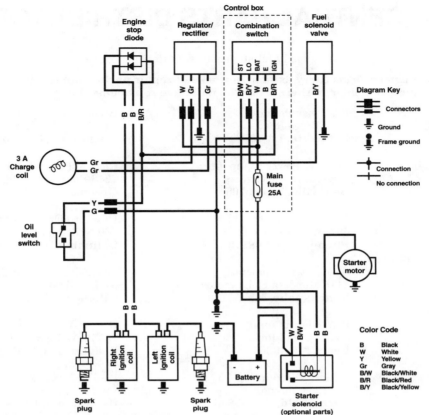

Fig. HN322—Wiring diagram for engines equipped with 3-amp charging system.

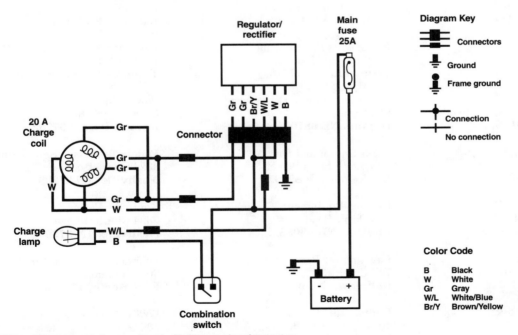

Fig. HN323—Wiring diagram for engines equipped with 20-amp charging system.

HONDA CENTRAL PARTS DISTRIBUTORS

(Arranged Alphabetically by States)

**These franchised firms carry extensive stocks of repair parts. Contact them
for name of dealer in their area who will have replacement parts.**

Bama Power Products, Inc.
708 Newport Ave.
Clanton, AL 35045

Totem Equipment & Supply, Inc.
2536 Commercial Drive
Anchorage, AK 99501

Southwest Engine Distributor
808 S. Edward Dr.
Tempe, AZ 85281

Northcoast Power Prod., Inc.
4592 E. Second St.
Benicia, CA 94510

Trimmer of Fresno, Inc.
2531 East McKinley
Fresno, CA 93703

Tru-Cut, Inc.
3221 San Fernando Rd.
Los Angeles, CA 90065

Bliss Power Lawn Equipment Co.
101 Commerce Circle
Sacramento, CA 95815

Pacific Turf
7163 Engineer Rd.
San Diego, CA 92111

Small Engines Unlimited
4699 Nautilus Court S., Suite 404
Boulder, CO 80301

Eastern Equipment, Inc.
84 Platt Road
Shelton, CT 06484

Blalock Machinery & Equip.
5112 Blalock Industrial
College Park, GA 30349

Roberts Supply, Inc.
4203 Metric Dr.
Winter Park, GA 30349

Paradise Power Products
411 E. Kawii St.
Hilo, HI 96720

Power Equipment Company
645 S. Route 83
Elmhurst, IL 60126

Iowa Power Products
520 Broods Rd.
Iowa Falls, IA 50126

R.W. Distributors
1701 Ridge Road
Lafayette, LA 70503

Pump & Power Equip. Corp.
6784 Mid Cities Ave.
Beltsville, MD 20705

Plymouth Air Cooled Equip.
587 W. Ann Arbor Trail
Plymouth, MI 48170

Specialty Equipment Co.
1415 Mendota Heights Road
Minneapolis, MN 55120

R.W. Distributors, Inc.
365 Fox Hall Road
Pearl, MS 39208

Modern Distributing Co., Inc.
440 East Tampa
Springfield, MO 65805

C.K. Power Products Corp.
9290 W. Florissant Ave.
St. Louis, MO 63136

Power Plus Distributing
8342 Huffine Lane
Bozeman, MT 59715

Anderson Industrial Engines Co.
2123 South 56th Street
Omaha, NE 68106

Jacks Equipment Dist.
708 South Main Street
Las Vegas, NV 89101

Eastern Equipment
453 Derry Road
Chester, NH 03036

Lawnmower Parts, Inc.
717 Creek Rd.
Bellmawr, NJ 08031

Bunton Turf Products
4054 Quaker Bridge Rd.
Trenton, NJ 08619

Southwest Engine Distributors
2031 Candelaria N.E.
Albuquerque, NM 87107

A.J. Vel, Ltd.
7 Hemlock Street
Latham, NY 12110

Brooks Gravely Company, Inc.
2425 Brighton Henrietta Town Line
Rochester, NY 14623

Central Power & Equipment Co.
2643 Randleman Rd.
Greensboro, NC 27406

Hayward Distributing Co.
460 Neilston St.
Columbus, OH 43215

Smith Distributing Co.
6415 S. Western Ave.
Oklahoma City, OK 73139

Oregon-Wash. Small Engine Dist.
1355 S.W. Farmington Rd.
Beaverton, OR 97005

Paul B. Moyer & Sons, Inc.
190 S. Clinton Street
Doylestown, PA 18901

PALCO, Inc.
Rt. 30 West
Latrobe, PA 15650

Laubrach Saw Equipment Corp.
Route 22 West
Thompsontown, PA 17094

Power House
3448 Sturgis Rd.
Rapid City, SD 57702

Middle Tennessee Equipment
3324 Charlotte Ave.
Nashville, TN 37209

Kentucky Power Equipment
3324 Charlotte Ave.
Nashville, TN 37209

Pearson Equipment Co., Inc.
3001 Ramona
Fort Worth, TX 77506

Wyatt Power Equipment
109 Gum Springs Rd.
Longview, TX 75602

Langston Power & Equip., Inc.
4412 Ave. A
Lubbock, TX 79404

Power Products Plus
921 W. Pasadena Frwy. #C
Pasadena, TX 77506

Small Engines Unlimited
7018 South 4 West
Midvale, UT 84047

Tidewater Power Equipment Co.
820 Poplar Hall Drive
Norfolk, VA 23502

Oregon-Wash. Small Engine
3420 "C" St. N.E. #402
Auburn, WA 98002

Norwest Engine Distributor
North 1403 Greene #6
Spokane, WA 99202

Palco, Inc.
#2 Wall St. Box 33
Winfield, WV 25213

Clymar, Inc.
N55 W13787 Oak Lane
Menomonee Falls, WI 53051

KAWASAKI

KAWASAKI MOTORS
5080 36th Street, S.E.
Grand Rapids, Michigan 49512

Model	No. Cyls.	Bore	Stroke	Displacement	Power Rating
FC290V	1	78 mm (3.07 in.)	60 mm (2.36 in.)	286 cc (17.4 cu. in.)	6.7 kW (9 hp)
FC400V	1	87 mm (3.43 in.)	68 mm (2.68 in.)	404 cc (24.6 cu. in.)	9.7 kW (13 hp)
FC401V	1	89 mm (3.50 in.)	68 mm (2.68 in.)	423 cc (25.8 cu. in.)	9.7 kW (13 hp)
FC420V	1	89 mm (3.50 in.)	68 mm (2.68 in.)	423 cc (25.8 cu. in.)	10.5 kW (14 hp)
FC540V	1	89 mm (3.50 in.)	86 mm (3.38 in.)	535 cc (32.6 cu. in.)	12.8 kW (17 hp)

All models are four-stroke, overhead-valve, single-cylinder, air-cooled engines with a vertical crankshaft. Splash lubrication is used on Model FC290V, while an oil pump provides pressure lubrication on Models FC400V, FC401V, FC420V and FC540V. Engine serial number plate is located on the flywheel blower housing.

MAINTENANCE

LUBRICATION. Check engine oil level prior to operation. Maintain oil level between reference marks on dipstick with dipstick just touching first threads. Do not screw dipstick in to check oil level (Fig. KW201).

Engine oil should meet or exceed latest API service classification. Use oil of suitable viscosity for the expected air temperature range during the period between oil changes. Refer to temperature/viscosity chart shown in Fig. KW202.

On models without an oil filter, change engine oil after every 50 hours of operation or yearly, whichever comes first. On models equipped with an oil filter, change oil and filter after every 100 hours of operation or yearly, whichever comes first. Drain oil while engine is warm. Crankcase oil capacity for FC290V is approximately 1.1 L (2.3 pt.). Crankcase oil capacity for FC400V, FC401V and FC420V is approximately 1.3 L (2.75 pt.) with filter. Crankcase oil capacity for FC540V is approximately 1.6 L (3.4 pt.) with filter. Check oil level using dipstick after running engine momentarily.

Models FC400V, FC401V, FC420V and FC540V may be equipped with an oil pressure sensor located on the oil filter adapter, if equipped with an oil filter, or on the oil passage cover if not equipped with an oil filter. Switch should be closed at zero pressure and open at 29.4 kpa (4.3 psi). Switch is connected to a warning device.

AIR FILTER. Remove and clean the air filter element after every 25 hours of operation, or more often if operating in extremely dusty conditions. Renew paper element (5—Figs. KW203 and KW204) after every 300 hours of operation. Renew either filter element anytime it is damaged.

To remove filter elements (4 and 5), remove the retaining knob or wing bolts (1) and washers (2). Remove the filter cover (3), foam precleaner element and paper element. Clean foam element in a solution of warm water and liquid detergent, then squeeze out excess water and allow to air dry. DO NOT wash paper element. Apply light coat of engine oil to foam element and squeeze out excess oil. Clean paper element by tapping gently to remove dust. DO NOT use compressed air to clean element. Inspect paper element for holes or other damage. Reinstall by reversing removal procedure.

CRANKCASE BREATHER. Crankcase pressure is vented to the cylinder head. A reed valve is located on the top of the cylinder on Model FC290V or in the rocker arm chamber on all other models. Renew reed valve if tip of reed stands up more than 0.2 mm (0.008 in.) on Model FC290V or 2.0 mm (0.080 in.) on all other models, or if reed is damaged or worn excessively.

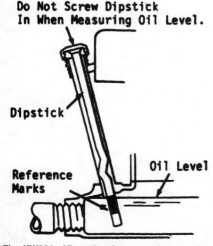

Do Not Screw Dipstick In When Measuring Oil Level.

Dipstick

Reference Marks

Oil Level

Fig. KW201—View showing procedure to check crankcase oil level. Refer to text.

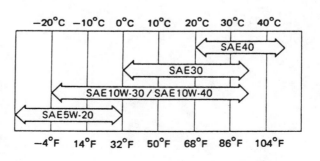

Fig. KW202—Engine oil viscosity should be based on expected air temperature as indicated in chart above.

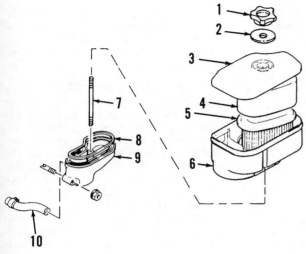

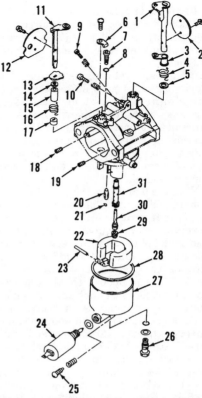

Fig. KW203—Exploded view of air filter assembly used on Model FC290V.

1. Knob
2. Washer
3. Cover
4. Foam element
5. Paper element
6. Housing
7. Stud
8. Gasket
9. Base
10. Breather hose

SPARK PLUG.

Recommended spark plug is NGK BPR5ES or Champion RN11YC.

Remove, clean and set spark plug after every 100 hours of operation. Specified spark plug gap is 0.7-0.8 mm (0.028-0.031 in.).

CARBURETOR.

All models are equipped with a float-type side draft carburetor. Check carburetor whenever poor or erratic performance is noted.

Recommended engine idle speed is 1450-1650 rpm. Adjust idle speed by turning idle speed screw (10—Fig. KW205) clockwise to increase idle speed or counterclockwise to decrease idle speed.

Adjust throttle control as follows: Place engine throttle lever in fast position. Insert a 15/64 inch drill bit through the hole (H—Fig. KW206) in speed control lever (7) and bracket (8). Loosen throttle cable housing clamp screw (10), pull cable housing tight and retighten cable clamp screw. Rotate choke lever screw (9) on back side of bracket so there is a gap between screw and choke control lever, then turn the screw back in until it just touches the lever. Remove drill bit. With throttle control lever in choke position, carburetor choke plate should be closed, if not, repeat procedure.

Initial adjustment of pilot air screw (7—Fig. KW205) is 1½ turns open from a lightly seated position. Make final adjustment with engine at operating temperature and running. Adjust pilot screw to obtain maximum engine idle speed, then turn pilot screw out (counterclockwise) an additional ¼ turn. Adjust idle speed screw (10) so engine idles at 1450-1650 rpm.

Main fuel mixture is controlled by a fixed main jet (29). Different size main jets are available for high altitude operation.

Fig. KW204—Exploded view of air filter assembly used on Models FC400V, FC401V, FC420V and FC540V.

1. Wing bolt
2. Washer
3. Cover
4. Foam element
5. Paper element
6. Housing
7. "O" ring

Fig. KW205—Exploded view of typical float-type carburetor used on all models. Fuel shut-off solenoid (24) is not used on some engines.

1. Throttle shaft
2. Throttle plate
3. Ring
4. Spring
5. Seal
6. Retainer plate
7. Pilot jet
8. "O" ring
9. Pilot screw
10. Idle speed screw
11. Choke shaft
12. Choke plate
13. Plate
14. Seal
15. Ring
16. Spring
17. Ring
18. Pilot air jet
19. Main air jet
20. Fuel inlet needle
21. Clip
22. Float
23. Pin
24. Fuel shut-off solenoid
25. Drain screw
26. Special bolt
27. Float bowl
28. Gasket
29. Main jet
30. Bleed pipe
31. Main nozzle

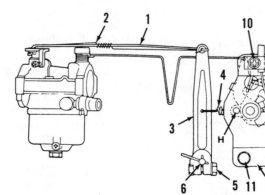

Fig. KW206—View of external governor linkage used on all models.

1. Governor-to-carburetor rod
2. Spring
3. Governor lever
4. Tension spring
5. Clamp bolt
6. Governor shaft
7. Speed control lever
8. Control plate
9. Choke setting screw
10. Clamp bolt
11. Screws

Remove the float bowl (27—Fig. KW205) for access to internal components. Note that pilot jet (7) is pressed into carburetor body on some FC540V engines.

Clean carburetor parts (except plastic components) using suitable carburetor cleaner. Do not clean jets or passages with drill bits or wire as enlargement of passages could affect calibration of carburetor. Rinse parts in warm water to neutralize corrosive action of carburetor cleaner and dry with compressed air.

When assembling the carburetor, note the following. Place a small drop of nonhardening sealant such as Permatex #2 or equivalent on throttle and choke plate retaining screws. Float should be parallel with body when carburetor is inverted as shown in Fig. KW207. If equipped with white plastic float, float height is not adjustable; replace any components that are damaged or excessively worn and adversely affect the float position. On models with an adjustable float, bend float tab to adjust float height. On Models FC290V and FC540V, measure float drop (D—Fig. KW208). Float drop should be 10.5-12.5 mm (0.413-0.492 in.). Bend tab on back of float arm to adjust float drop.

GOVERNOR. A gear-driven, flyweight-type governor is located inside engine crankcase. Before adjusting governor linkage, make certain all linkage is in good condition and that tension spring (4—Fig. KW206) is not stretched.

To adjust external linkage, place engine throttle control in "FAST" position.

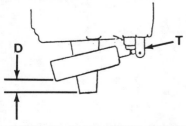

Fig. KW207—Float height (H) should be parallel with fuel bowl mounting surface of carburetor body. If float height is adjustable, bend float tab (T) to adjust float height.

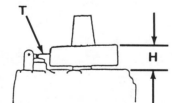

Fig. KW208—On Models FC290V and FC540V, float drop (D) should be 10.5-12.5 mm (0.413-0.492 in.). Bend tab on back of float arm to adjust float drop.

Spring (2) around governor-to-carburetor rod must pull governor lever (3) and throttle lever toward each other. Loosen governor lever clamp bolt (5) and turn governor shaft (6) clockwise as far as possible. Tighten clamp bolt nut.

Maximum no-load engine speed should be 3275-3425 rpm unless specified otherwise by equipment manufacturer. Adjust maximum no-load engine speed as follows: Run engine until normal operating temperature is reached. Align holes in speed control lever (7) and bracket (8) and insert a $\frac{15}{64}$ inch drill bit through hole (H). Run engine under no load and determine engine speed using an accurate tachometer. If engine speed is not 3275-3425 rpm, loosen bracket retaining screws (11) and reposition bracket to obtain desired engine speed. Retighten screws and recheck engine speed. Check choke operation as outlined in CARBURETOR section.

IGNITION SYSTEM. All models are equipped with an electronic ignition system and regular maintenance is not required. Ignition timing is not adjustable. Ignition coil is located outside flywheel. Air gap between ignition coil and flywheel should be 0.30 mm (0.012 in.).

To test ignition coil, remove cooling shrouds and disconnect spark plug cable and primary lead wire (Fig. KW209). Connect ohmmeter test leads between coil core (ground) and high tension (spark plug) terminal. Secondary coil resistance should be 10.9k-16.3k ohms. Remove the test lead connected to high tension terminal and connect lead to coil primary terminal. Primary coil resistance should be 0.48-0.72 ohms. If readings vary significantly from specifications, renew ignition coil.

To test control unit, refer to Fig. KW210 and disconnect all electrical leads. Connect positive ohmmeter lead to terminal (T) and negative ohmmeter lead to the ground lead or control unit case (G) according to model being ser-

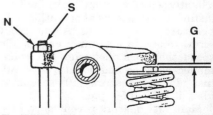

Fig. KW209—View of ignition coil showing location of primary terminal, spark plug lead and iron core.

viced. Ohmmeter reading should be 400-600 ohms. Reverse leads. Ohmmeter reading should be 60-100 ohms. If ohmmeter readings are not as specified, renew control unit.

VALVE ADJUSTMENT. Clearance between valve stem ends and rocker arms should be checked and adjusted after every 300 hours of operation. Engine must be cold for valve adjustment. Rotate crankshaft so piston is at top dead center on compression stroke. Remove rocker arm cover. Valve clearance gap (G—Fig. KW211) for both valves should be 0.15 mm (0.006 in.). Loosen nut (N) and turn adjusting screw (S) to obtain desired clearance. Tighten nut to 20 N•m (177 in.-lb.) and recheck adjustment.

CYLINDER HEAD AND COMBUSTION CHAMBER. Standard compression reading should be 483 kPa (71 psi).

NOTE: When checking compression pressure, spark plug high tension lead must be grounded or electronic ignition could be damaged.

Excessive carbon build-up on piston and cylinder head are indicated by higher than standard compression reading. A leaking cylinder head gasket, worn piston rings and cylinder bore, or poorly seated valves are indicated by lower than standard compression reading.

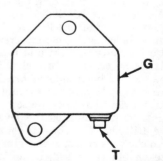

Fig. KW210—All models are equipped with the ignition control unit shown. Refer to text for test procedure.

Fig. KW211—Valve clearance gap (G) is adjusted by loosening nut (N) and rotating adjusting screw (S). Valve clearance should be 0.15 mm (0.006 in.).

REPAIRS

TIGHTENING TORQUE. Recommended tightening torque specifications are as follows:

Connecting rod . . . . 20 N•m
(177 in.-lb.)

Crankshaft
(pto end) . . . . 38 N•m
(28 ft.-lb.)

Cylinder head:
FC290V . . . . 24 N•m
(212 in.-lb.)

All other models. . . . . 52 N•m
(38 ft.-lb.)

Flywheel:
FC290V . . . . 86 N•m
(63 ft.-lb.)

FC540V . . . . 172 N•m
(126 ft.-lb.)

All other models . . . . 137 N•m
(101 ft.-lb.)

Oil drain plug . . . . 23 N•m
(204 in.-lb.)

Oil pan . . . . 26 N•m
(19 ft.-lb.)

CYLINDER HEAD. To remove cylinder head, remove cylinder head shroud and blower housing. Remove carburetor and muffler. Remove rocker arm cover, loosen cylinder head mounting bolts evenly and remove cylinder head and gasket.

Remove carbon deposits from combustion chamber being careful not to damage gasket sealing surface. Inspect cylinder head for cracks, nicks or other damage. Place cylinder head on a flat surface and check entire sealing surface for distortion using a feeler gauge. Renew cylinder head if sealing surface is warped more than 0.05 mm (0.002 in.).

To reinstall cylinder head, reverse removal procedure. Surfaces of cylinder head gasket are coated with a sealant and do not require additional sealant. Push rods should be installed in their original positions. Tighten cylinder head screws in sequence shown in Fig. KW212 to initial torque of 18 N•m (159 in.-lb.) on Model FC290V and 32 N•m (24 ft.-lb.) on all other models. On Model FC290V, tighten screws 3 N.m (27 in.-lb.) at a time following sequence in Fig. KW212. On all other models, tighten screws 7 N•m (5 ft.-lb.) at a time following sequence in Fig. KW212. Final torque is 24 N•m (18 ft.-lb.) on Model FC290V and 52 N•m (38 ft.-lb.) on all other models. Adjust valve clearance as outlined in MAINTENANCE section.

VALVE SYSTEM. Remove cylinder head as outlined above. Remove rocker arm shaft (21—Fig. KW213) and rocker arms (6 and 7). Compress valve springs using a suitable valve spring compressor, and remove collet halves (8). Remove the retainers (9), springs (10) and valves (19 and 20). Remove the valve stem seals (11) from top of valve guides.

NOTE: Removal of valve stem seal will damage the seal. Renew seals whenever they are removed.

Check all parts for wear or damage. Refer to the following specifications:
Rocker arm shaft OD—
Wear limit . . . . 12.94 mm
(0.509 in.)

Rocker arm ID—
Wear limit . . . . 13.07 mm
(0.515 in.)

Valve spring free length—
Minimum allowable:
FC290V . . . . 31.00 mm
(1.220 in.)

All other models . . . . 37.50 mm
(1.476 in.)

Valve guide ID—
Wear limit . . . . 7.07 mm
(0.278 in.)

Renew valves if stem is warped more than 0.03 mm (0.001 in.) or if valve margin is less than 0.60 mm (0.020 in.). Valve stem ends should be ground square. Valve face and seat angles are 45° for intake and exhaust.

Valve seating surface should be 0.80 mm (0.031 in.) for Model FC290V, 1.10-1.46 mm (0.039-0.057 in.) for all other models. Seats can be narrowed using a 30° stone or cutter. Lap valves into the seats to ensure proper contact. Seats should contact center of valve face.

Valve guides (14) can be renewed using suitable valve guide driver. Press guides into cylinder head until snap ring (13) just contacts cylinder head. Ream new guides with a 7 mm valve guide reamer. Valve guide finished inside diameter should be 7.000-7.015 mm (0.2756-0.2762 in.).

CONNECTING ROD. Connecting rod (16—Fig. KW214 or Fig. KW215) and piston are removed as an assembly

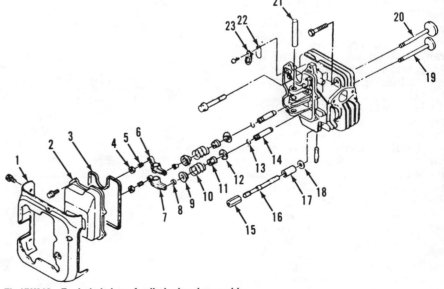

Fig.KW213—Exploded view of cylinder head assembly.

1. Shroud	7. Rocker arm, exhaust	13. Snap ring
2. Rocker arm cover	8. Retainer	14. Valve guide
3. Gasket	9. Retainer	15. Nut
4. Locknut	10. Valve spring	16. Stud
5. Adjusting screw	11. Seal	17. Bushing
6. Rocker arm, intake	12. Plate	18. Washer
		19. Exhaust valve
		20. Intake valve
		21. Rocker arm shaft
		22. Breather valve
		23. Retainer plate

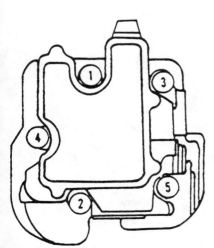

Fig. KW212—Tighten cylinder head bolts in sequence shown.

Fig. KW214—Exploded view of

Fig. KW214—Exploded view of FC400V, FC401V, FC420V and FC540V engines. Model FC290V is similar, but bushing (12) is not renewable. Refer to Fig. KW215 for Model FC290V.

1. Check valve
2. Cylinder block & crankcase
3. Oil seal
4. Counterweight support shaft
5. "O" ring
6. Governor shaft
7. Washer
8. Main bearing
9. Spacer
10. Link rod
11. Bushing
12. Bushing
13. Balancer counterweight
14. Rod cap
15. Crankshaft
16. Connecting rod
17. Piston pin
18. Snap ring
19. Piston
20. Piston rings
21. Compression release mechanism
22. Camshaft assy.
23. Valve tappets
24. Spacer
25. Gear
26. Shims
27. Governor flyweight assy.
28. Gear
29. Oil pump housing
30. Oil pressure relief valve
31. Oil pump rotors
32. Oil pan
33. Oil seal

connecting rod in cylinder so arrow on top of piston is toward flywheel side of engine. Tighten connecting rod cap bolts to 20 N•m (180 in.-lb.).

PISTON, PIN AND RINGS. Piston and connecting rod are removed as an assembly after removing cylinder head and oil pan. Refer to CONNECTING ROD section for removal and installation procedure.

After separating piston and connecting rod, carefully remove piston rings and clean carbon and other deposits from piston surface and piston ring lands.

CAUTION: Exercise extreme care when cleaning piston rings lands. Do not damage squared edges or widen piston ring grooves. If piston ring lands are damaged, renew the piston.

Maximum inside diameter of pin bore in piston is 19.031 mm (0.7493 in.) Model FC290V and 22.037 mm (0.8676 in.) for all other models. Piston pin out-

after removing cylinder head and oil pan. Remove carbon and ring ridge (if present) from top of cylinder before removing piston. Remove connecting rod bolts and connecting rod cap, then push connecting rod and piston out through top of cylinder. Remove retaining rings (18) and push piston pin (17) out of piston to separate piston from connecting rod.

Connecting rod rides directly on crankshaft journal. Maximum allowable inside diameter for connecting rod big end bearing surface is 35.567 mm (1.4003 in.) for Model FC290V and 41.068 mm (1.6169 in.) for all other models. Maximum connecting rod-to-crankpin clearance is 0.14 mm (0.006 in.). A connecting rod is available with 0.50 mm (0.020 in.) undersize big end for use with undersize crankshaft crankpin. Refer to CRANKSHAFT AND BALANCER section.

Maximum inside diameter of connecting rod small end is 19.059 mm (0.7540 in.) for Model FC290V, and 22.059 mm (0.8685 in.) for all other models. Maximum allowable connecting rod-to-piston pin clearance is 0.08 mm (0.003 in.).

When reassembling, install piston on connecting rod so arrow on top of piston is toward the "MADE IN JAPAN" side of connecting rod. Install piston and

Fig. KW215—Exploded view of Model FC290V. Refer to Fig. KW214 for parts identification except for the following:

34. Governor drive gear
35. Oil slinger
36. Bushing
37. Compression release spring
38. Shim

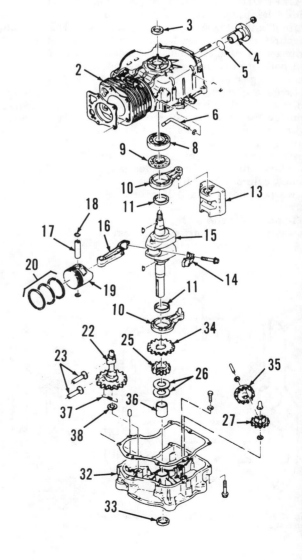

side diameter wear limit is 18.981 mm (0.7473 in.) for Model FC290V, and 21.977 mm (0.8652 in.) for all other models. Maximum piston-to-pin clearance is 0.05 mm (0.0020 in.) for Model FC290V, and 0.06 mm (0.0024 in.) for all other models.

To check piston ring grooves for wear, insert a new ring in ring groove and use a feeler gauge to measure ring side clearance in groove. On Model FC290V, renew piston if side clearance exceeds 0.16 mm (0.006 in.) for top ring, 0.14 mm (0.005 in.) for second ring or 0.19 mm (0.007 in.) for oil ring. On all other models, renew piston if side clearance exceeds 0.17 mm (0.007 in.) for top ring, 0.15 mm (0.006 in.) for second ring or 0.20 mm (0.008 in.) for oil ring.

Insert each ring squarely in cylinder bore about 25 mm (1 in.) below top of cylinder and measure ring end gap. On Model FC290V, maximum allowable end gap is 0.70 mm (0.028 in.) for compression rings and 1.20 mm (0.047 in.) for oil control ring. On Models FC420V and FC540V, maximum allowable end gap is 0.90 mm (0.035 in.) for compression rings and 1.30 mm (0.051 in.) for oil control ring. If piston ring gap is greater than specified, check cylinder bore for wear.

During assembly, install piston on connecting rod so arrow on top of piston is toward "MADE IN JAPAN" side of connecting rod. Use NEW snap rings

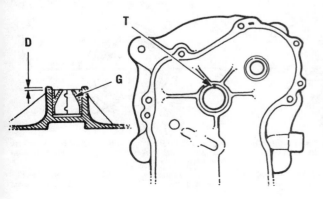

Fig. KW216—Cross-sectional view of piston showing correct installation of piston rings. Refer to text.

1. Top ring
2. Second ring
3. Spacer
4. Side rails

(18—Fig. KW214 or Fig. KW215) to retain piston pin in piston. Install oil ring spacer (3—Fig. KW216) first, then install side rails (4). Position side rail end gaps 180° apart. Install the second ring (2) and first ring (1) on piston with "R", "N" or "NPR" mark on ring facing up. Stagger piston ring end gaps 180° apart, but do not align with side rail end gaps. Lubricate piston and cylinder with engine oil. Use a suitable ring compressor to compress rings when installing piston in cylinder. Be sure that arrow on top of piston faces flywheel side of engine.

CYLINDER, CRANKCASE, MAIN BEARINGS AND SEALS. Cylinder and crankcase are an integral casting. Standard cylinder bore diameter is 77.98-78.00 mm (3.070-3.071 in.) for Model FC290V, and 88.90-89.00 mm (3.500-3.504 in.) for all other models. Cylinder bore wear limit is 78.067 mm (3.0735 in.) for Model FC290V, and 89.076 mm (3.5069 in.) for all other models. Cylinder can be bored or honed to fit an oversize piston. Oversize pistons are available.

The main bearing on pto side is a renewable bushing in the oil pan on Model FC290V, while an integral bushing is a part of the oil pan on all other models. Main bearing on flywheel side of all models is a ball bearing.

On Model FC290V, maximum outside diameter of bushing in oil pan is 30.125 mm (1.1860 in.). If bushing renewal is required, use a suitable tool and press out old bushing. Install new bushing so grooves (G—Fig. KW217) point toward inside of oil pan and split (T) in bushing is located as shown in Fig. KW217. Bearing on flywheel side should be a press fit on crankshaft and in bearing bore of crankcase.

On Models FC400V, FC401V, FC420V and FC540V, maximum inside diameter for integral bearing bore in oil pan is 35.069 mm (1.3807 in.) for FC400V, FC401V and FC420V, and 38.056 mm (1.4983 in.) for FC540V. Bearing on flywheel side should be a

Fig. KW217—Install new bushing on FC290V engine so grooves (G) point toward inside of oil pan and split (T) in bushing is located as shown. Bushing depth (D) must be 1 mm (0.030 in.) below surface.

press fit on crankshaft and in bearing bore of crankcase.

Renew crankshaft seals (3 and 33—Fig. KW214 or Fig. KW215) if worn or damaged. Install seals with open side facing inside of engine and press in until flush with crankcase or oil pan. Pack seals with lithium-base grease prior to crankshaft installation.

When installing oil pan, tighten retaining screws to 26 N•m (19 ft.-lb.). On all models, tighten mounting screws in sequence shown in Fig. KW218 or KW219.

CRANKSHAFT AND BALANCER. The crankshaft is supported on flywheel side by a ball-type main bearing, and on pto side by a plain-type bearing in the oil pan. A reciprocating balancer is used on all models.

To remove crankshaft, remove shrouds, fan housing, flywheel, cylinder head and oil pan. Rotate crankshaft until timing marks on camshaft gear and crankshaft gear are aligned, then re-

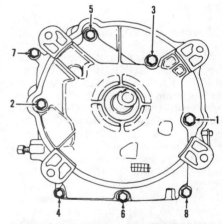

Fig. KW218—Oil pan screws on FC290V engines must be tightened evenly to specified torque following sequence shown.

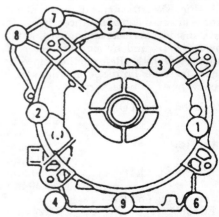

Fig. KW219—Oil pan screws on FC400V, FC401V, FC420V and FC540V engines must be tightened evenly to specified torque following sequence shown.

move camshaft and gear. Remove valve tappets (23—Fig. KW214); identify tappets so they can be reinstalled in original position. Remove connecting rod and piston. Unbolt and remove counterweight support shaft (4). Remove crankshaft and balancer assembly from crankcase.

To disassemble balancer, remove collar (9), gear (25), spacer (24) and link rods (10) from crankshaft (15) and balancer (13) wrist pins.

Clean and inspect all parts for wear or damage. Refer to following table for crankshaft main journal minimum diameter:

FC290V
Pto end . . . . 29.922 mm
(1.1780 in.)
Flywheel end... . . . . 29.940 mm
(1.1787 in.)
FC540V
Pto end . . . . 37.904 mm
(1.4923 in.)
Flywheel end. . . . . 34.945 mm
(1.3758 in.)
All other models
Pto end . . . . 34.919 mm
(1.3747 in.)
Flywheel end. . . . . 34.945 mm
(1.3758 in.)

Main journals cannot be resized. Refer to CYLINDER, CRANKCASE, MAIN BEARINGS AND SEALS section for main bearing dimensions. Measure crankshaft runout at the main journals. Renew crankshaft if runout exceeds 0.05 mm (0.002 in.). Crankshaft cannot be straightened.

Crankpin journal minimum diameter is 35.428 mm (1.3948 in.) for Model FC290V and 40.928 mm (1.6113 in.) for all other models. Crankpin can be reground to accept undersize connecting rod. Refer to CONNECTING ROD section.

Measure outside diameter of crankshaft balancer link rod journals (A—Fig. KW220), inside diameter of big end and small end of balancer link rods (B), inside diameter of support shaft bushing (D) and outside diameter of support shaft (E). Refer to the following table for wear limit specifications and renew parts as necessary.

Link rod journal OD—
FC290V . . . . 46.953 mm
(1.8485 in.)
FC540V . . . . 57.941 mm
(2.2811 in.)
All other models . . . . 53.950 mm
(2.1240 in.)
Link rod big end ID—
FC290V . . . . 7.121 mm
(1.8552 in.)
FC540V . . . . 58.153 mm
(2.2895 in.)

All other models . . . . 54.121 mm
(2.1307 in.)
Link rod small end ID—
All models . . . . 12.06 mm
(0.475 in.)
Support shaft bushing ID—
All models . . . . 26.097 mm
(1.0274 in.)
Support shaft OD—
All models . . . . 25.927 mm
(1.0208 in.)

Balancer link rod bushing (11—Fig. KW214 and KW215) is renewable on all models. When installing new link rod bushing, press bushing into link rod from side opposite oil grooves (G—Fig. KW221). Position seam (S) of bushing 90° from centerline (C) of link rod. Install bushing so depth (D) below machined surface of rod is 1.0 mm (0.040 in.).

Support shaft bushing (D) is renewable on all models except Model FC290V. When installing new support shaft bushing, make sure that oil hole in bushing is aligned with oil passage in balancer.

To assemble crankshaft and balancer, install balance weight (W—Fig. KW220) with oil hole (O) toward flywheel side of crankshaft. Install link rods (B) with oil grooves facing away from crank webs. Install spacer (24—Fig. KW214) on Models FC400V, FC401V, FC420V and FC540V with chamfered face toward link rod. On Model FC290V, install governor gear (34—Fig. KW215) with chamfered face toward link rod. On all models, install spacer (9—Fig. KW214 or KW215) so conical face is out. On all models, install

balancer assembly with the crankshaft into the crankcase, being careful not to damage crankshaft oil seal. Align balancer weight with hole in crankcase and insert support shaft (4). Install connecting rod and piston. Rotate crankshaft until piston is at top dead center.

Install valve tappets in their original bores. Align timing marks on crankshaft gear and camshaft gear and install camshaft. Install oil pan with original shims (26), then use a dial indicator to measure crankshaft end play. Add or remove shims as necessary to obtain specified end play of 0.09-0.22 mm (0.004-0.009 in.).

CAMSHAFT AND BEARINGS. Camshaft is supported at each end in bearings that are integral part of crankcase or oil pan. Refer to CRANKSHAFT AND BALANCER section for camshaft and valve tappet removal. Mark tappets so they can be installed in their original guides if reused.

Camshaft minimum lobe height for intake and exhaust lobes is 27.08 mm (1.066 in.) for FC290V engine, 37.10 mm (1.461 in.) for FC540V engine or 36.75 mm (1.446 in.) for all other model engines.

Bearing journal minimum diameter for FC290V engine is 13.922 mm (0.5481 in.) for pto end of camshaft and 15.921 mm (0.6268 in.) for flywheel end. Bearing journal minimum diameter for FC400V, FC401V and FC420V engines is 20.912 mm (0.8233 in.) for pto end of camshaft and 19.912 mm (0.7839 in.) for flywheel end. Bearing journal minimum diameter for FC540V engine is 20.91 mm (0.823 in.) for both ends of camshaft.

Camshaft bearing bore maximum inside diameter for FC290V engine is 14.054 mm (0.5533 in.) for oil pan bearing and 16.055 mm (0.6321 in.) for crankcase bearing. Camshaft bearing

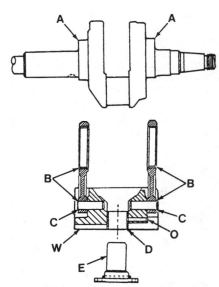

Fig. KW220—View of crankshaft and engine balancer wear check points. Refer to text.

A. Crankshaft journals
B. Link rod bearings
C. Wrist pins
D. Support shaft bushing
E. Support shaft

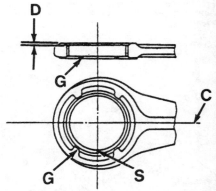

Fig. KW221—Bushing in big end of balancer link rod is renewable. Refer to text for special installation instructions.

C. Link rod centerline
D. Bushing depth
G. Oil grooves
S. Bushing seam

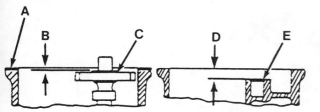

Fig. KW222—Refer to text to determine shim thickness to adjust camshaft end play on all FC290V engines and FC540 engines prior to serial number 014455.

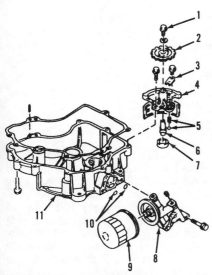

Fig. KW223—Exploded view of engine oil pump assembly used on all models except FC290V.

1. Cap screw
2. Drive gear
3. Retainer plate
4. Pump housing
5. Pressure relief valve assy.
6. Pump inner rotor
7. Pump outer rotor
8. Filter base
9. Oil filter
10. "O" rings
11. Oil pan

bore maximum inside diameter for FC400V, FC401V and FC420V engine is 21.076 mm (0.8298 in.) for oil pan bearing and 20.076 mm (0.790 in.) for crankcase bearing. Camshaft bearing bore maximum inside diameter for FC540V engine is 21.076 mm (0.8298 in.) for both crankcase and oil pan bearings.

Camshaft end play must be adjusted on all FC290V engines and FC540V engines prior to serial number 014455

whenever camshaft, oil pan or crankcase is renewed. Correct end play is 0.20 mm (0.008 in.). Adjust end play by changing the thickness of shim located between oil pan and camshaft. To calculate correct shim thickness, position camshaft and oil pan gasket on crankcase as shown in Fig. KW222. Measure distance (B) from gasket (A) to thrust face (C) on camshaft. Measure distance (D) from oil pan face to top of camshaft bearing boss (E). For FC290V engine, subtract measurement (B) from measurement (D). For FC540V engine, add measurement (B) to measurement (D). For either engine, subtract 0.20 mm (0.008 in.) from the result of the above calculation to determine required shim thickness. Install shim (38—Fig. KW215) on camshaft thrust face (C—Fig. KW222).

When installing camshaft and tappets, be sure that tappets are installed in their original position. If camshaft is renewed, tappets should also be renewed. Make sure that timing marks on camshaft gear and crankshaft gear are aligned.

GOVERNOR. The internal centrifugal flyweight governor (27—Figs. KW214 and KW215) is mounted in the oil pan. On Model FC290V, the governor is gear driven by gear (34—Fig. KW215) on the crankshaft, while the governor on all other models is driven by the camshaft gear. The governor gear on Model FC290V also drives the oil slinger gear (25—Fig. KW215).

To remove governor assembly, remove oil pan from crankcase. Use two screwdrivers to snap governor gear and

flyweight assembly off governor stub shaft. Governor unit will be damaged when removed and must be renewed if removed. Be sure to install thrust washer between gear and oil pan. Install governor by pushing down until it snaps onto the locating groove.

If removed, install governor shaft and arm in side of crankcase and attach cotter pin.

Refer to MAINTENANCE section for external governor linkage adjustment.

OIL PUMP AND RELIEF VALVE. All models except FC290V are equipped with an oil pump. Model FC290V is equipped with an oil slinger gear.

The trochoid-type oil pump (Fig. KW223) used on Models FC400V, FC401V, FC420V and FC540V is mounted in the oil pan (11).

To remove oil pump, first separate oil pan from cylinder block. Remove pump drive gear (2). Remove pump housing mounting cap screws and withdraw pump housing (4) and inner rotor shaft (6) together from oil pan. Remove retainer plate (3) and relief valve ball and spring (5).

Inspect seating of relief valve ball. Measure relief valve spring free length. Renew spring if free length is less than 19.00 mm (0.748 in.).

Measure diameter of outer rotor shaft (6); wear limit is 12.63 mm (0.497 in.). Measure inside diameter of rotor shaft bearing surface in pump housing; wear limit is 12.76 mm (0.502 in.).

To reinstall pump, reverse removal procedure. Lubricate parts with engine oil.

ELECTRIC STARTER. Place alignment marks on pinion housing, frame and end cover before disassembly so they can be reinstalled in original position. Renew brushes if length is less than 8.5 mm (0.33 in.) on Model FC290V, 6 mm (0.24 in.) on Models FC400V, FC401V and FC420V, or 10.5 mm (0.41 in.) on Model FC540V.

KAWASAKI

KAWASAKI MOTORS
5080 36th Street, S.E.
Grand Rapids, Michigan 49512

Model	No. Cyls.	Bore	Stroke	Displacement	Power Rating
FE250D	1	76 mm (2.99 in.)	55 mm (2.16 in.)	249 cc (15.2 cu. in.)	5.2 kW (7 hp)
FE290D	1	78 mm (3.07 in.)	60 mm (2.36 in.)	286 cc (17.4 cu. in.)	6.7 kW (9 hp)

All models are four-stroke, single-cylinder, air-cooled engines with a vertical crankshaft. Splash lubrication is used on Model FE250D. Lubrication on Model FE290D is provided by an oil pump. Engine serial number plate is located on the flywheel blower housing.

MAINTENANCE

LUBRICATION. Engine oil level should be checked prior to each operating interval. Oil should be maintained between reference marks on dipstick with dipstick just touching first threads. Do not screw dipstick in to check oil level.

Manufacturer recommends using oil with an API service classification of SF or SG. Use oil of suitable viscosity for the expected air temperature range during the period between oil changes. Refer to temperature/viscosity chart shown in Fig. KW301.

Fig. KW301—Engine oil viscosity should be based on expected air temperature as indicated in chart above.

Oil and oil filter, if so equipped, should be changed after first 20 hours of operation. On models without an oil filter, engine oil should be changed after every 50 hours of operation. On models equipped with an oil filter, oil should be changed after every 100 hours of operation and oil filter should be changed after every 200 hours of operation. Oil should be drained while engine is warm.

Model FE290D may be equipped with an oil level sensor that disables the ignition if oil level is low.

AIR FILTER. The air filter element should be removed and cleaned after every 50 hours of operation, or more often if operating in extremely dusty conditions. Paper element should be renewed after every 300 hours of operation, or at any other time if it is very dirty or damaged in any way.

Clean foam element in solution of warm water and liquid detergent, then squeeze out water and allow to air dry. DO NOT wash paper element. Apply light coat of engine oil to foam element and squeeze out excess oil. Clean paper element by tapping gently to remove dust. DO NOT use compressed air to clean element. Inspect paper element for holes or other damage. Reinstall by reversing removal procedure.

CRANKCASE BREATHER. Crankcase pressure is vented to the cylinder head. A reed valve is located on the top of the cylinder head in the rocker arm chamber. Renew reed valve if tip of reed stands up more than 0.2 mm (0.008 inch) or if reed is damaged or worn excessively.

SPARK PLUG. Recommended spark plug is NGK BPR5ES. Spark plug should be removed, cleaned and electrode gap set after every 100 hours of operation. Specified spark plug gap is 0.7-0.8 mm (0.028-0.032 in.). Renew spark plug if electrode is severely burned or damaged. Tighten spark plug to 27 N·m (20 ft.-lbs.).

CARBURETOR. All models are equipped with a float-type side draft carburetor. Idle mixture is adjustable and high-speed mixture is determined by a fixed main jet.

Initial setting for idle mixture screw (2—Fig. KW302) is two turns out from a lightly seated position. Make final adjustment with engine at operating temperature and running. Adjust idle mixture screw to obtain maximum engine idle speed, then turn screw out (counterclockwise) an additional ¼ turn. Adjust throttle stop screw (1) so engine idles at 1200 rpm.

Disassembly of carburetor is self-evident upon examination of unit and reference to Fig. KW302.

Clean carburetor parts (except plastic components) using suitable carburetor cleaner. Do not clean jets or passages with drill bits or wire as enlargement of passages could affect calibration of carburetor. Rinse parts in warm water to neutralize corrosive action of carburetor cleaner and dry with compressed air.

When assembling the carburetor, note the following. Place a small drop of nonhardening sealant, such as Permatex #2 or equivalent, on throttle and choke plate retaining screws. Float height is not adjustable; replace any components that are damaged or excessively worn and adversely affect float position.

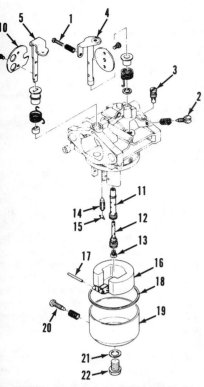

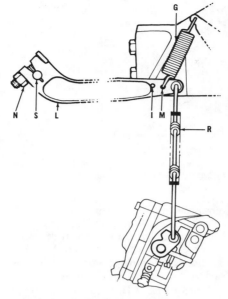

Fig. KW302—Exploded view of typical float-type carburetor used on all models.

1. Throttle stop screw	14. Fuel inlet needle
2. Idle mixture screw	15. Clip
3. Pilot jet	16. Float pin
4. Throttle plate shaft	18. Gasket
5. Choke plate shaft	19. Float bowl
6. Choke plate	20. Drain screw
11. Main nozzle	21. Washer
12. Bleed pipe	22. Plug
13. Main jet	

GOVERNOR.

A gear-driven fly-weight-type governor is located inside engine crankcase. Before adjusting governor linkage, make certain all linkage is in good condition and that governor spring (G—Fig. KW303) is not stretched.

Note that governor spring should be attached to inner hole (I) on Model FE250D and middle hole (M) on Model FE290D.

To adjust external linkage, place engine throttle control in "FAST" position. Spring (R) around governor-to-carburetor rod must pull governor lever (L) and throttle lever toward each other. Move governor lever (L) so throttle is in wide open position. Loosen governor lever clamp bolt nut (N) and turn governor shaft (S) counterclockwise as far as possible. Tighten clamp bolt nut. Governed idle speed should be 1300 rpm and is adjusted by turning governed idle speed screw. Maximum no-load engine speed should be 4000 rpm and is adjusted by turning high-speed governed speed screw.

Fig. KW303—View of external governor linkage used on all models.

R. Throttle rod spring	
L. Governor lever	I. Inner governor
G. Governor spring	lever hole (FE250D)
N. Clamp nut	M. Middle governor
S. Governor shaft	lever hole (FE290D)

IGNITION SYSTEM.

The engine is equipped with a transistor ignition system that does not require regular maintenance. Ignition timing is not adjustable. Ignition coil is located outside flywheel. Air gap between ignition coil and flywheel should be 0.30 mm (0.012 in.).

To test ignition coil, remove cooling shrouds and disconnect spark plug cable and primary lead wire. Connect ohmmeter test leads between coil core (ground) and high-tension (spark plug) lead. Secondary coil resistance should be 7.2k-8.8k ohms on Model FE250D and 6.0k-10.0k ohms on Model FE290D. Remove test lead connected to high-tension lead and connect tester lead to coil

		+Tester Lead		
		Black	Brown	Yellow
−Tester Lead	Black		B	D
	Brown	A		B
	Yellow	C	C	

Fig. KW304—Connect ohmmeter leads to ignition control unit leads as indicated in chart and note desired readings in legend.

Model FE250D	Model FE290D
A. 1k-10k ohms	A. 0.1k-2k ohms
B. 5k-20k ohms	B. 1k-10k ohms
C. 50k-200k ohms	C. 10k ohms-infinity
D. 10k-30k ohms	D. 5k-20k ohms

primary terminal. Primary coil resistance should be 0.8-1.0 ohm on Model FE250D and 0.67-1.10 ohms on Model FE290D. If readings vary significantly from specifications, renew ignition coil.

To test control unit, disconnect leads to control unit and connect an ohmmeter to control unit leads as shown in chart shown in Fig. KW304. Renew or replace with a good control unit if ohmmeter readings are not as specified in chart.

VALVE ADJUSTMENT.

Clearance between valve stem ends and rocker arms should be checked and adjusted after every 300 hours of operation. Engine must be cold for valve adjustment. Rotate crankshaft so piston is at top dead center on compression stroke. Remove rocker arm cover. Valve clearance gap (G—Fig. KW305 or KW306) for both valves should be 0.12 mm (0.005 in.). Loosen nut (N) and turn adjusting screw or nut (A) to obtain desired clearance. Tighten nut (N) and recheck adjustment.

CYLINDER HEAD AND COMBUSTION CHAMBER.

Standard compression reading should be 483 kPa (71 psi).

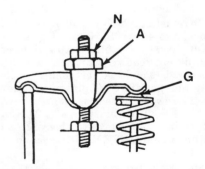

Fig. KW305—On Model FE250D, valve clearance gap (G) between valve stem and rocker arm is adjusted by loosening nut (N) and rotating adjusting pivot nut (A). Valve clearance should be 0.12 mm (0.005 in.).

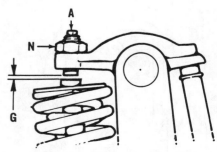

Fig. KW306—On Model FE290D, valve clearance gap (G) between valve stem and rocker arm is adjusted by loosening nut (N) and rotating adjusting screw (A). Valve clearance should be 0.12 mm (0.005 in.).

REPAIRS

TIGHTENING TORQUES. Recommended tightening torques are as follows:

Connecting rod . . . . 20 N•m
(177 in.-lbs.)
Crankcase cover:
  FE250D . . . . 23 N•m
(204 in.-lbs.)
  FE290D . . . . 26 N•m
(19 ft.-lbs.)
Cylinder head . . . . 24 N•m
(212 in.-lbs.)
Flywheel . . . . 86 N•m
(63 ft.-lbs.)
Oil drain plug . . . . 20 N•m
(177 in.-lbs.)

CYLINDER HEAD. To remove cylinder head, remove cylinder head shroud and blower housing. Remove carburetor and muffler. Remove rocker arm cover, loosen cylinder head mounting bolts evenly and remove cylinder head and gasket.

Remove carbon deposits from combustion chamber, being careful not to damage gasket sealing surface. Inspect cylinder head for cracks, nicks or other damage. Place cylinder head on a flat surface and check entire sealing surface for distortion using a feeler gauge. Renew cylinder head if sealing surface is warped more than 0.05 mm (0.002 in.).

To reinstall cylinder head, reverse removal procedure. Surfaces of cylinder head gasket are coated with a sealant and do not require additional sealant. Push rods should be installed in their original positions. Tighten cylinder head screws in steps in sequence shown in Fig. KW307 to final torque of 24 N•m (18 ft.-lbs.). Adjust valve clearance as outlined in MAINTENANCE section.

VALVE SYSTEM. Valves on Model FE250D are actuated by rocker arms

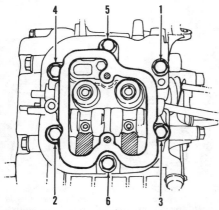

Fig. KW307—Tighten cylinder head bolts in sequence shown.

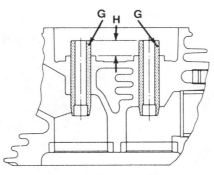

Fig. KW308—On Model FE250D, valve guide height (H) should be 8.50 mm (0.335 in.).

mounted on a stud threaded into the cylinder head. Valves on Model FE290D are actuated by rocker arms that rotate on a rocker shaft mounted on the cylinder head. Refer to appropriate following section for service information.

Model FE250D. Check all parts for wear or damage. Valve face and seat angles are 45° for intake and exhaust. Valve seat width should be 0.50-1.10 mm (0.020-0.043 in.). A seat width of 0.80 mm (0.031 in.) is desirable. Seats can be narrowed using a 30° stone or cutter.

Minimum allowable valve guide inside diameter is 7.065 mm (0.278 in.). Minimum allowable valve stem diameter is 6.065 mm (0.2388 in.) for both valves. Renew valves if stem is warped more than 0.03 mm (0.001 in.) or if valve margin is less than 0.60 mm (0.020 in.).

Valve guides can be renewed using suitable valve guide driver. Press or drive guide out towards rocker arm side of head. Press or drive guide into cylinder head so height (H—Fig. KW308) above head surface is 8.50 mm (0.335 in.). Ream new guides with a 6 mm valve guide reamer. Valve guide finished inside diameter should be 6.000-6.015 mm (0.2362-0.2368 in.).

Minimum valve spring free length is 32.75 mm (1.289 in.). The valve spring dampening coils are coils wound closer together at one end than the other. The end with closer coils should be installed against cylinder head.

Model FE290D. On Model FE290D, the rocker arm shaft is located by an "E" ring attached to the center of the shaft between the center rocker shaft pedestals. To remove rocker shaft, detach "E" ring and withdraw rocker shaft from exhaust side of cylinder head.

Check all parts for wear or damage. Valve face and seat angles are 45° for intake and exhaust. Valve seat width should be 0.50-1.10 mm (0.020-0.043 in.). A seat width of 0.80 mm (0.031 in.) is desirable. Seats can be narrowed using a 30° stone or cutter.

Minimum allowable valve guide inside diameter is 7.065 mm (0.278 in.). Minimum allowable valve stem diameter is 6.930 mm (0.2728 in.) for intake valve and 6.915 mm (0.2722 in.) for exhaust valve. Renew valves if stem is warped more than 0.03 mm (0.001 in.) or if valve margin is less than 0.60 mm (0.020 in.).

Valve guides can be renewed using suitable valve guide driver. Press or drive guide out toward rocker arm side of head. Press or drive guide in toward combustion chamber side of head. Guides should be pressed into cylinder head until snap ring just seats against cylinder head. Ream new guides with a 7 mm valve guide reamer. Valve guide finished inside diameter should be 7.000-7.015 mm (0.2756-0.2762 in.).

Maximum allowable rocker arm shaft outside diameter is 11.949 mm (0.4704 in.). Minimum allowable rocker arm inside diameter is 12.074 mm (0.4754 in.). Minimum valve spring free length is 32.75 mm (1.289 in.).

CAMSHAFT. Camshaft is supported at each end in bearings that are an integral part of crankcase or oil pan.

To remove camshaft, remove rocker cover, rocker arms and push rods. Mark rocker arms and push rods so they can be returned to original position. Remove crankcase cover. Invert engine so tappets will not interfere with camshaft removal, then remove camshaft. If tappets are removed, mark them so they can be installed in their original guides.

Camshaft minimum lobe height for intake and exhaust lobes is 31.04 mm (1.222 in.) for FE290D engine and 32.70 mm (1.287 in.) for FE250D engine.

Bearing journal minimum diameter for both ends is 19.927 mm (0.7845 in.) for Model FE250D and 22.927 mm (0.9026 in.) for Model FE290D.

Camshaft bearing bore maximum inside diameter for both ends is 20.063 mm (0.7899 in.) for Model FE250D and 23.063 mm (0.9080 in.) for Model FE290D.

Camshaft end play must be adjusted on Model FE250D whenever camshaft, crankcase or oil pan is renewed. Correct end play is 0.20 mm (0.008 in.). End play is adjusted by changing the thickness of shim located between oil pan and camshaft. To calculate correct shim thickness, position camshaft and gasket (K—Fig. KW309) on crankcase (C) and measure distance (A) from gasket to thrust face (G) on camshaft. Measure distance (B) from face of crankcase cover (R) to top of camshaft bearing boss (S). Subtract measurement (A) from measurement (B), then subtract 0.20 mm (0.008 in.) from the result of this

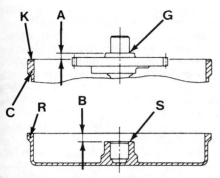

Fig. KW309—On Model FE250D, determine camshaft end play by measuring at points shown as outlined in text.

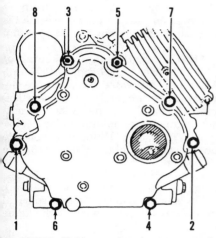

Fig. KW310—Tighten crankcase cover screws in sequence shown.

calculation to determine required shim thickness. Install shim on camshaft thrust face (G—Fig. KW309).

When reinstalling camshaft and tappets, be sure that tappets are installed in their original position. If camshaft is renewed, tappets should also be renewed. Make sure that timing marks on camshaft gear and crankshaft gear are aligned. When installing crankcase cover, be sure drive tang on end of oil pump shaft is properly aligned with slot in camshaft. Do not force crankcase cover on crankcase. Light tapping only should be required if all components are properly aligned. Tighten crankcase cover screws in sequence shown in Fig. KW310 to 23 N·m (204 in.-lbs.) on Model FE250D and to 26 N·m (19 ft.-lbs.) on Model FE290D.

PISTON, PIN AND RINGS. Piston and connecting rod are removed as an assembly after removing cylinder head, crankcase cover and camshaft.

Maximum inside diameter of pin bore in piston is 18.033 mm (0.7100 in.) for Model FE250D and 19.033 mm (0.7493 in.) for Model FE290D. Minimum piston

pin outside diameter is 17.975 mm (0.7077 in.) for Model FE250D and 18.975 mm (0.7470 in.) for Model FE290D.

To check piston ring grooves for wear, insert a new ring in ring groove and use a feeler gauge to measure ring side clearance in groove. On Model FE290D, renew piston if side clearance exceeds 0.16 mm (0.006 in.) for top ring or 0.14 mm (0.005 in.) for second ring. On Model FE250D, renew piston if side clearance exceeds 0.15 mm (0.006 in.) for top ring or 0.12 mm (0.005 in.) for second ring.

Insert each ring squarely in cylinder bore about 25 mm (1 in.) below top of cylinder and measure ring end gap. On Model FE290D, maximum allowable end gap is 1.20 mm (0.047 in.) for compression rings. On Model FE250D, maximum allowable end gap is 1.00 mm (0.039 in.) for compression rings. If piston ring gap is greater than specified, check cylinder bore for wear.

During reassembly, install piston on connecting rod so arrow on top of piston is on opposite side of "MADE IN JAPAN" side of connecting rod. Position oil control ring side rail end gaps 180° apart. Install second ring and first ring on piston with marks on ring toward piston crown. Stagger piston ring end gaps 180° apart, but do not align with oil control ring side rail end gaps. Arrow on top of piston must be toward flywheel side of engine. Tighten connecting rod screws to 20 N·m (177 in.-lbs.). Install cylinder head and camshaft as previously outlined.

CONNECTING ROD. Connecting rod and piston are removed as an assembly as outlined in previous section.

Connecting rod rides directly on crankshaft journal. Maximum allowable inside diameter for connecting rod big end bearing surface is 34.067 mm (1.3412 in.) for Model FE250D and 35.567 mm (1.4003 in.) for Model FE290D. An undersize connecting rod is available for use with undersize crankshaft crankpin. Refer to CRANKSHAFT AND BALANCER section.

Maximum inside diameter of connecting rod small end is 18.051 mm (0.7107 in.) for Model FE250D and 19.051 mm (0.7500 in.) for Model FE290D.

Install connecting rod as outlined in previous section.

CRANKSHAFT AND BALANCER. On Model FE250D, both ends of the crankshaft are supported by ball bearings. The crankshaft on Model FE290D is supported on flywheel side by a plain-type bearing and on pto side

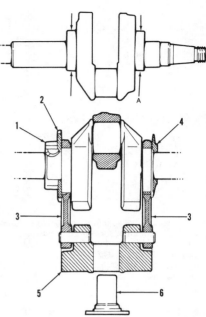

Fig. KW311—Drawing showing arrangement of balancer components.

1. Crankshaft gear
2. Governor drive gear
3. Balancer link rod
4. Spacer
5. Weight
6. Support shaft

by a ball-type main bearing in the crankcase cover. A reciprocating balancer is used on all models.

To remove crankshaft, remove piston and connecting rod and camshaft as previously outlined. Unscrew and remove counterweight support shaft (6—Fig. KW311) in side of crankcase. Remove crankshaft and balancer assembly from crankcase.

To disassemble balancer, remove spacer (4), crankshaft gear (1), governor drive gear (2) and link rods (3) from crankshaft (15) and balancer (5) wrist pins.

Clean and inspect all parts for wear or damage. Crankshaft main journal minimum diameter for both ends is 29.930 mm (1.1783 in.). Main journals cannot be resized. Refer to CYLINDER, CRANKCASE, MAIN BEARINGS AND SEALS section for main bearing dimensions. Measure crankshaft runout at the main journals. Crankshaft should be renewed if runout exceeds 0.05 mm (0.002 in.). Crankshaft cannot be straightened.

Crankpin journal minimum diameter is 33.944 mm (1.3364 in.) for Model FE250D and 35.444 mm (1.3954 in.) for Model FE290D. Crankpin can be reground to accept undersize connecting rod.

Measure outside diameter of crankshaft balancer link rod journals (A—Fig. KW311), inside diameter of big end and small end of balancer link rods (3), inside diameter of support shaft bush-

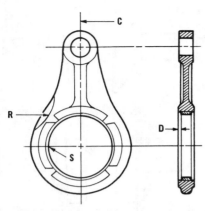

Fig. KW312—Install bushing in big end of balancer link rod so seam (S) is toward depression (R) on rod and 90° from centerline (C). Bushing depth (D) should be 1.00 mm (0.040 in.).

C. Link rod centerline
D. Bushing depth
G. Oil grooves
S. Bushing seam

ing in weight (5) and outside diameter of support shaft (6). Refer to the following table for wear limit specifications and renew parts as necessary.

Link rod journal OD . . . . . 46.924 mm (1.8474 in.)

Link rod big end ID—
FE250D . . . . 47.106 mm (1.8546 in.)
FE290D . . . . 47.126 mm (1.8554 in.)

Link rod small end ID—
FE250D . . . . 12.057 mm (0.4747 in.)
FE290D . . . . 12.064 mm (0.4750 in.)

Support shaft bushing ID . 26.118 mm (1.0283 in.)

Support shaft OD . . . . . . 25.907 mm (1.0200 in.)

Balancer link rod bushing is renewable on all models. When installing new link rod bushing, position seam (S—Fig. KW312) of bushing 90° from centerline (C) of link rod on same side as depression (R) in rod. Install bushing so depth (D) below machined surface of rod is 1.00 mm (0.040 in.).

Support shaft bushing in weight (5—Fig. KW311) is renewable. When installing new support shaft bushing, make sure that oil hole in bushing is aligned with oil passage in balancer.

Assemble and install crankshaft and balancer by reversing removal and disassembly procedure while noting the following: Install governor drive gear (2—Fig. KW311) and spacer (4) on crankshaft with chamfer toward crankpin. Install valve tappets in their original bores. Align timing marks on crankshaft gear and camshaft gear and install camshaft. Install original shims on crankshaft. Install crankcase cover and tighten screws in sequence shown

in Fig. KW310 to 23 N·m (204 in.-lbs.) on Model FE250D and to 26 N·m (19 ft.-lbs.) on Model FE290D. Measure crankshaft end play. Add or remove shims as necessary to obtain end play of 0.05-0.17 mm (0.002-0.007 in.) on Model FE250D or 0.35 mm (0.014 in.) on Model FE290D.

CYLINDER, CRANKCASE, MAIN BEARINGS AND SEALS. Cylinder and crankcase are an integral casting. Standard cylinder bore diameter is 75.990-76.000 mm (2.9917-2.9921 in.) for Model FE250D and 77.980-78.000 mm (3.0700-3.0709 in.) for Model FE290D. Cylinder bore wear limit is 76.070 mm (2.9949 in.) for Model FE250D and 78.067 mm (3.0735 in.) for Model FE290D. Maximum allowable cylinder bore out-of-round is 0.056 mm (0.0022 in.). Cylinder can be bored or honed to fit oversize pistons.

The flywheel end of the crankshaft on Model FE290D rides in an integral bushing in the crankcase. Renew crankcase if bearing bore exceeds 30.075 mm (1.1840 in.).

Renew crankshaft seals if worn or damaged. Install seals with lip facing inside of engine. Press in oil seal in crankcase until flush with surface. Press in oil seal in crankcase cover until 4.0 mm (0.16 in.) below surface.

When installing crankcase cover, be sure drive tang on end of oil pump shaft is properly aligned with slot in camshaft. Do not force crankcase cover on crankcase. Light tapping only should be required if all components are properly aligned. Tighten crankcase cover screws in sequence shown in Fig. KW310 to 23 N·m (204 in.-lbs.) on Model FE250D and to 26 N·m (19 ft.-lbs.) on Model FE290D.

GOVERNOR. The internal centrifugal flyweight governor is mounted in the

crankcase cover. The governor is gear driven by a gear on the crankshaft.

To remove governor assembly, separate crankcase cover from crankcase. Use two screwdrivers to snap governor gear and flyweight assembly off governor stub shaft. Governor unit will be damaged when removed and must be renewed if removed. Install governor by pushing down until it snaps onto the locating groove.

Refer to MAINTENANCE section for external governor linkage adjustment.

OIL PUMP AND RELIEF VALVE. Model FE290D is equipped with an oil pump.

The trochoid-type oil pump is mounted on the crankcase cover and is accessible after removing the oil pump cover.

Minimum allowable diameter of pump shaft is 12.627 mm (0.4971 in.). Maximum allowable tip clearance between inner rotor and outer rotor is 0.30 mm (0.012 in.). Minimum allowable outside diameter of outer rotor is 40.467 mm (1.5932 in.). Minimum allowable outer rotor thickness is 9.920 mm (0.3905 in.).

Renew relief valve spring if free length is less than 19.00 mm (0.748 in.).

To reinstall pump, reverse removal procedure. Lubricate parts with engine oil.

REWIND STARTER. Refer to Fig. KW313 for exploded view of rewind starter. To disassemble the rewind starter, release spring tension by pulling rope handle until about 30 cm (12 in.) of rope extends from unit. Use thumb pressure to prevent pulley from rewinding and place rope in notch in outer rim of pulley. Release thumb pressure slightly and allow spring mechanism to slowly unwind. Unscrew center screw (2), and remove components (3

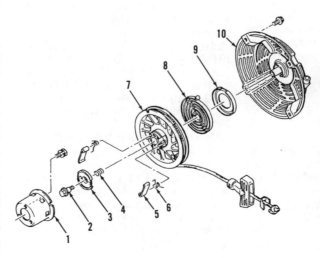

Fig. KW313—Exploded view of rewind starter used on some engines.

1. Starter cup
2. Center screw
3. Retainer
4. Spring
5. Pawl
6. Spring
7. Pulley
8. Rewind spring
9. Spring cup
10. Starter housing

through 6). Slowly remove pulley from support shaft in housing.

CAUTION: Take extreme care that rewind spring cup remains in recess of pulley. Do not remove spring unless new spring is to be installed.

Using a new rope of same length and diameter as original, place rope in handle and tie a figure eight knot about 25 mm (1 in.) from end. Pull knot into top of handle. Install other end of rope through guide bushing of housing and through hole in pulley groove. Pull rope out through opening in pulley, tie a knot at end of rope and pull knot against pulley. Wind rope 2½ turns counterclockwise on pulley, then lock rope in notch of pulley. Install pulley on support shaft and rotate pulley counterclockwise until inner end of rewind spring is engaged. Assemble remainder of components. Hook a loop of rope into pulley notch and preload rewind spring by turning pulley four full turns counterclockwise. Remove rope from notch and allow pulley to slowly turn clockwise as rope winds on pulley and handle returns to guide bushing on housing. Check operation of starter.

ELECTRIC STARTER. Place alignment marks on pinion housing, frame and end cover before disassembly so they can be reinstalled in original position. Renew brushes if length is less than 6 mm (0.24 in.). Minimum commutator diameter is 27.0 mm (1.06 in.).

KAWASAKI

KAWASAKI MOTORS
5080 36th Street, S.E.
Grand Rapids, Michigan 49512

Model	No. Cyls.	Bore	Stroke	Displacement	Power Rating
FH500V	2	68 mm (2.68 in.)	68 mm (2.68 in.)	494 cc (30.1 cu. in.)	12.8 kW (17 hp)

Model FH500V is a four-stroke, over-head-valve, twin-cylinder, air-cooled engine equipped with a vertical crankshaft. An oil pump provides pressure lubrication to the engine.

Engine serial number plate is located on the flywheel blower housing.

Number 1 cylinder is on the left when engine is viewed at flywheel end.

MAINTENANCE

LUBRICATION. Check engine oil level prior to operation. Maintain oil level between reference marks on dipstick with dipstick just touching first threads. Do not screw dipstick in to check oil level (Fig. KW401).

Engine oil should meet or exceed latest API service classification. Use oil of suitable viscosity for the expected air temperature range during the period between oil changes. Refer to temperature/viscosity chart shown in Fig. KW402.

Change oil and filter after first eight hours of operation and every 100 hours of operation thereafter or yearly, whichever comes first. Drain oil while engine is warm. Crankcase oil capacity is approximately 1.7 L (3.6 pt.) with filter. Check oil level using dipstick after running engine momentarily.

The engine may be equipped with an oil pressure warning switch located above the oil filter. Switch should be closed at zero pressure and open at 98 kpa (14.2 psi).

AIR FILTER. Remove and clean the foam air filter element after every 25 hours of operation. Remove and clean the paper filter element after every 50 hours of operation. Clean elements more frequently if engine is operated in a dirty environment. Renew paper element after every 200 hours of operation. Renew either filter element anytime it is damaged.

Clean foam element in solution of warm water and liquid detergent, then squeeze out excess water and allow to air dry. DO NOT wash paper element. Apply light coat of engine oil to foam element and squeeze out excess oil. Clean paper element by tapping gently to remove dust. DO NOT use compressed air to clean element. Inspect paper element for holes or other damage.

CRANKCASE BREATHER. The engine is equipped with a closed breather system. Crankcase pressure is vented through a separator and filter on the crankcase, then routed through the cylinder head and a hose to the air cleaner. The separator and filter are located behind a cover located on the flywheel side of the crankcase between the cylinders. Filter element catches solid particles, but does not require normal maintenance other than replacement when plugged.

SPARK PLUG. Recommended spark plug is Champion RCJ8Y.

Remove, clean and set spark plug after every 100 hours of operation. Specified spark plug gap is 1.0 mm (0.040 in.).

CARBURETOR. Adjustment. To comply with emissions requirements, the idle mixture screw is equipped with a limiter cap (2—Fig. KW403). The position of the idle mixture screw (3) is established at the factory to obtain best performance while complying with emissions requirements. The limiter cap prevents movement of the idle mixture screw to positions that will adversely affect engine operation. Adjust idle mixture by turning limiter cap so engine idles at highest speed with engine at normal operating speed. If engine does not idle properly due to improper idle mixture, remove limiter cap and set idle mixture screw at initial setting of 2¼ turns out. Replace limiter cap on idle mixture screw, then readjust idle mixture with engine running.

Idle speed is governed. To adjust idle speed, run engine until it reaches normal operating temperature. Stop engine and remove air cleaner assembly for access to carburetor. Run engine and hold carburetor throttle lever against idle speed screw (1—Fig. KW403). Adjust idle speed screw so engine idles at 1,450 rpm. Release throttle, then adjust governed idle speed by rotating screw (S—Fig. KW404). Ad-

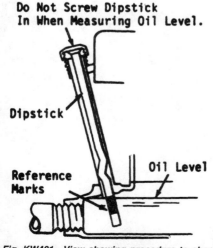

Do Not Screw Dipstick In When Measuring Oil Level.

Dipstick

Oil Level

Reference Marks

Fig. KW401—View showing procedure to check crankcase oil level. Refer to text.

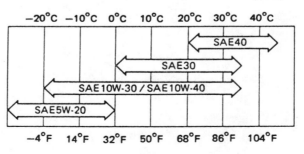

Fig. KW402—Engine oil viscosity should be based on expected air temperature as indicated in chart above.

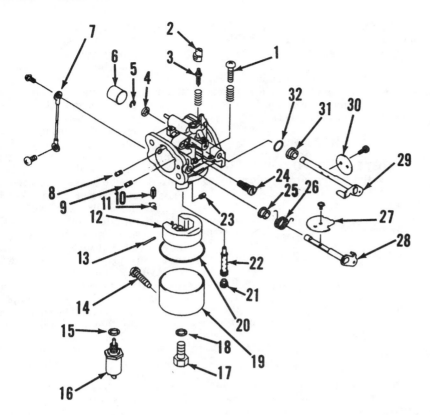

Fig. KW403—Exploded view of carburetor. Fuel shutoff solenoid (16) and ground wire (7) are used on engines

1. Idle speed screw
2. Limiter cap
3. Idle mixture screw
4. Washer
5. Clip
6. Cap
7. Ground wire
8. Pilot air jet
9. Main air jet
10. Fuel inlet valve
11. Clip
12. Float
13. Pin
14. Drain screw
15. Gasket
16. Fuel shutoff solenoid
17. Screw
18. Gasket
19. Float bowl
20. Gasket
21. Valve seat
22. Main nozzle
23. Main jet
24. Pilot jet
25. Collar
26. Spring
27. Choke plate
28. Choke shaft
29. Throttle shaft
30. Throttle plate
31. Collar
32. Seal

ust governed idle speed screw so engine idles at 1,550 rpm. Stop engine and install air cleaner. Refer to GOVERNOR section for high speed adjustment.

Main fuel mixture is controlled by a fixed main jet (23—Fig. KW403). Standard main jet size is #125. Additional main jets are available for high altitude operation.

On engines equipped with an electric starter, the carburetor is equipped with a fuel shutoff solenoid (16—Fig. KW403). The solenoid uses a plunger to stop fuel flow through valve seat (21) when ignition switch is in OFF position. The spring-loaded plunger should retract when the solenoid is energized.

Overhaul. Refer to Fig. KW403 for an exploded view of carburetor. Do not attempt to remove any passage balls. When removing idle mixture screw limiter cap, do not move idle mixture screw. After removing cap, screw in idle mixture screw until lightly seated while counting number of turns. When reassembling carburetor, reinstall idle mixture screw in original position based on number of turns, then install limiter cap. If original position is unknown or engine operated poorly at idle due to incorrect idle mixture, set idle mixture screw at initial setting of 2¼ turns out and perform idle mixture adjustment after assembly.

When assembling carburetor, install throttle plate so numbers on plate are toward outside of carburetor. Install throttle shaft seals with lip facing out. Install choke plate so number is out and hole is down. Install float pin so large end is toward intake manifold end of carburetor. To check float level, invert carburetor body. Float should be parallel with bowl mating surface. Bend float tang to adjust float level. Note that spacer between carburetor and intake manifold has an indexing pin that must fit into intake manifold. Tighten carburetor retaining nuts to 6.9 N•m (61 in.-lb.).

GOVERNOR. The engine is equipped with a mechanical flyball-type governor mounted on the camshaft.

To adjust external linkage, place engine throttle control in "FAST" position. Spring (R—Fig. KW405) around governor-to-carburetor rod must pull governor lever (L) and throttle lever toward each other. Move governor lever (L) so throttle is in wide open position. Loosen

governor lever clamp bolt nut (N) and turn governor shaft (S) counterclockwise as far as possible. Tighten clamp bolt nut. Governor shaft (S) must protrude approximately 7 mm (0.028 in.) from side of governor lever (L).

Refer to CARBURETOR section for governed idle speed adjustment procedure. Maximum no-load engine speed should be 3600 rpm. To adjust maximum engine speed, loosen control panel (KW404) retaining screws. Note that right retaining screw on control panel

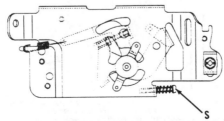

Fig. KW404—Rotate governed idle speed screw (S) so engine idles at 1,550 rpm. See text.

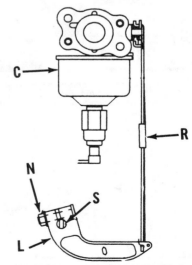

Fig. KW405—Drawing showing governor external linkage. Refer to text for governor adjustment.

fits in a slotted hole. Move right side of panel up or down as required to obtain desired engine speed.

IGNITION SYSTEM. The engine is equipped with an electronic ignition system that does not require regular maintenance. Ignition timing is not adjustable. The ignition coil assembly is located outside flywheel. Air gap between ignition coil and flywheel should be 0.25-0.40 mm (0.010-0.016 in.).

To test ignition coil and ignitor, disconnect spark plug cable and stop switch wire. Refer to Fig. KW406 and connect ohmmeter test leads as noted in table. If readings vary significantly from specifications noted in table, renew ignition coil.

VALVE ADJUSTMENT. Check and adjust clearance between valve stem ends and rocker arms after every 300 hours of operation. Engine must be cold for valve adjustment. Remove rocker arm cover. Rotate flywheel clockwise so forward projection (A—Fig. KW407) on flywheel aligns with leg (B) on ignition coil of cylinder being adjusted. Be sure both valves are closed. If not, rotate flywheel one revolution clockwise. Valve clearance gap (G—Fig. KW408) for both valves should be 0.05-0.10 mm (0.002-0.004 in.). Loosen setscrew (S) and turn pivot nut (A) to obtain desired clearance. Tighten setscrew (S) and recheck adjustment.

		+ Tester Lead	
	A	B	C
A		9kΩ	10kΩ
B	∞		∞
C	10kΩ	20kΩ	

(left side label: −Tester Lead)

Fig. KW406—Connect an ohmmeter to ignition coil at: A. Coil leg; B. Stop switch terminal; C. Spark plug cap. Renew ignition coil if it fails tests.

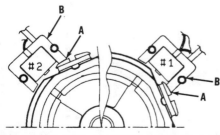

Fig. KW407—Piston is at TDC when ignition coil leg (B) is aligned with projection (A) on flywheel.

CYLINDER HEAD AND COMBUSTION CHAMBER. Standard compression reading should be 390 kPa (57 psi).

Manufacturer recommends removing each cylinder head and cleaning combustion chamber in cylinder head after every 300 hours of operation.

REPAIRS

TIGHTENING TORQUE. Recommended tightening torque values are as follows:

Connecting rod . . . . 5.9 N•m
(52 in.-lb.)
Cylinder head. . . . . 25 N•m
(221 in.-lb.)
Flywheel . . . . 56 N•m
(41 ft.-lb.)
Intake manifold. . . . . 6.9 N•m
(61 in.-lb.)
Muffler . . . . 6.9 N•m
(61 in.-lb.)
Oil pan . . . . 25 N•m
(221 ft.-lb.)

CYLINDER HEAD. To remove a cylinder head, proceed as follows: Mark any electrical connectors so they can be properly reconnected during assembly. Remove muffler. Remove air cleaner assembly. Remove fan housing. Remove carburetor and intake manifold. Remove rocker arm covers and spark plugs. Rotate flywheel clockwise so forward projection (A—Fig. KW407) on flywheel aligns with leg (B) on ignition coil of cylinder head being removed. Both valves should be closed. If not, rotate flywheel one revolution. Loosen cylinder head screws in ¼ turn increments in the sequence shown in Fig. KW409. Remove cylinder head. If removing push rods, mark push rods so they can be installed in original position.

Remove carbon deposits from combustion chamber being careful not to damage gasket sealing surface. Inspect cylinder head for cracks, nicks or other damage. Place cylinder head on a flat surface and check entire sealing surface for distortion using a feeler gauge. Renew cylinder head if sealing surface is warped more than 0.05 mm (0.002 in.).

Be sure that the mating surfaces of the cylinder head and cylinder are clean before installing the cylinder head. Always install a new head gasket. Note that head gasket is coated with a sealant, and care must be taken not to damage the sealing surfaces.

Each cylinder must be at TDC on compression stroke when installing cylinder head. Rotate flywheel clockwise so forward projection (A—Fig. KW407) on flywheel aligns with leg (B) on ignition coil of cylinder head being removed. If cylinder is on compression stroke, push rods will be equal height. If not, rotate flywheel one revolution. Tighten cylinder head screws in sequence shown in Fig. KW409. Tighten screws in steps to a final torque of 25 N•m (221 in.-lb.).

Note that intake manifold gaskets are asymmetrical and must be properly aligned with intake passage and screw holes. Tighten intake manifold screws to 6.9 N•m (61 in.-lb.). Tighten muffler retaining nuts to 6.9 N•m (61 in.-lb.).

VALVE SYSTEM. Valves are actuated by rocker arms mounted on studs (12—Fig. KW410) threaded into the cylinder head. Valve guides are not renewable. An oil seal (3) is located at the top of each valve guide. Both valves are equipped with wear caps (10).

Valve face and seat angles are 45° for intake and exhaust. Valve seat width should be 0.6-0.9 mm (0.024-0.036 in.). Minimum allowable valve head thickness (margin) is 0.35 mm (0.014 in). Minimum allowable valve stem diameter is 5.950 mm (0.2342 in.) for intake valve and 5.930 mm (0.2335 in.) for ex-

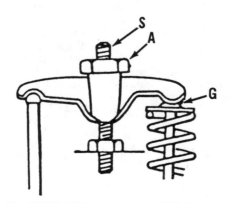

Fig. KW408—Valve clearance gap (G) between valve stem and rocker arm is adjusted by loosening setscrew (S) and rotating adjusting pivot nut (A). Valve clearance should be 0.05-0.10 mm (0.002-0.004 in.).

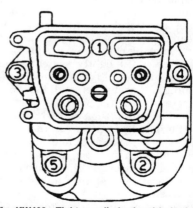

Fig. KW409—Tighten cylinder head bolts in sequence shown.

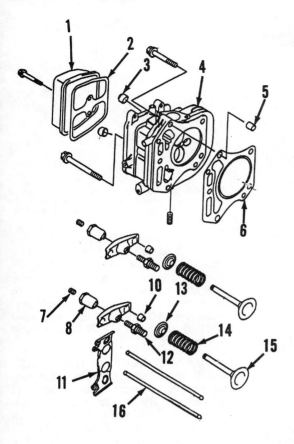

Fig. KW410—Exploded view of cylinder head assembly.

1. Rocker arm cover
2. Gasket
3. Oil seal
4. Cylinder head
5. Dowel pin
6. Head gasket
7. Setscrew
8. Pivot nut
9. Rocker arm
10. Wear cap
11. Push rod guide plate
12. Rocker arm stud
13. Valve spring retainer
14. Valve spring
15. Valve
16. Push rod

should be applied only to the shaded area (A) indicated in Fig. KW412. Be careful not to get sealant into the oil return hole (3). Tighten oil pan screws evenly following the tightening sequence shown in Fig. KW413. Tighten the screws in several steps to final torque of 25 N•m (19 ft.-lb.).

CAMSHAFT. To remove camshaft, drain engine oil and remove cylinder heads as previously outlined. Mark and remove push rods. Position engine with pto up so lifters will not fall out when removing camshaft. Remove the oil pan (23—Fig. KW414). Withdraw camshaft (8) while noting thrust washer (16) on end of camshaft. Remove and mark valve lifters (6) so they can be installed in their original positions.

Camshaft and camshaft gear are an integral casting equipped with a compression release mechanism. Governor flyballs are located in camshaft gear (see GOVERNOR).

Camshaft minimum lobe height for intake and exhaust lobes is 29.131 mm (1.1469 in.). Bearing journal minimum diameter is 15.985 mm (0.6293 in.).

Camshaft bearing bore maximum inside diameter is 16.136 mm (0.6353 in.).

The camshaft is equipped with a compression reduction device to aid starting. The lever and weight mechanism

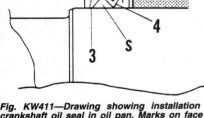

Fig. KW411—Drawing showing installation of crankshaft oil seal in oil pan. Marks on face of seal (2) face out. Pack high-temperature grease in space (S) between seal lips.

1. Oil pump flange
2. Seal face
3. Dust lip
4. Seal lip

pan. It may be necessary to gently tap the oil pan with a plastic mallet to loosen the oil pan gasket sealant.

Clean the old gasket material from the oil pan and crankcase mating surfaces. When replacing crankshaft oil seal, install the seal with the marks on face of seal (2—Fig. KW411) facing outward. Press in new seal until it is flush with flange surface of oil pan (1). Pack high-temperature grease into the space (S) between the dust lip (3) and seal lip (4).

When replacing the governor shaft oil seal, install the seal after the governor shaft is inserted into the oil pan. Marks on face of seal must face outward.

Apply a smooth coat of silicone sealant to the mating surfaces of the oil pan (1—Fig. KW412) and the crankcase side of the new gasket (2). Sealant

haust valve. Valve stem runout should not exceed 0.05 mm (0.020 in.).

Maximum allowable valve guide inside diameter is 6.08 mm (0.239 in.). Renew cylinder head if valve guide is excessively worn.

Specified valve spring free length is 26.7 mm (1.05 in.). Maximum push rod runout is 0.5 mm (0.020 in.).

OIL PAN/CRANKCASE COVER. To remove the oil pan/crankcase cover, first drain the engine oil. Remove the exhaust pipe and muffler and the governor control panel. Remove mounting bolts from oil pan, and withdraw oil

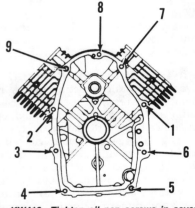

Fig. KW413—Tighten oil pan screws in several steps following sequence indicated in above drawing.

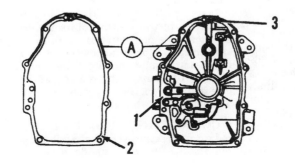

Fig. KW412—Apply silicone sealant to oil pan (1) and gasket (2) in area indicated by dark shading (A). Avoid getting sealant in oil drain hole (3).

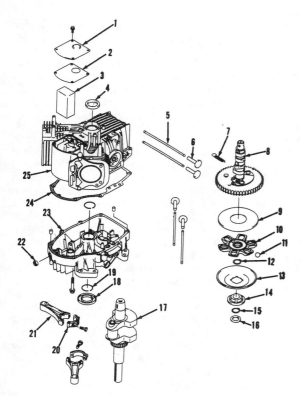

1. Cover
2. Gasket
3. Breather element
4. Seal
5. Push rod
6. Valve lifter
7. Spring
8. Camshaft
9. Plate
10. Flyball holder
11. Flyball
12. Snap ring
13. Plate
14. Slider
15. Snap ring
16. Thrust washer
17. Crankshaft
18. Seal
19. Ring
20. Rod cap
21. Connecting rod
22. Seal
23. Oil pan
24. Gasket
25. Crankcase

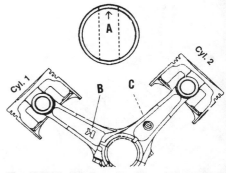

Fig. KW415—Drawing showing relationship of pistons and connecting rods as viewed from pto end. Arrow (A) on piston must point toward flywheel.

on the camshaft gear moves a pin inside each exhaust cam lobe. During starting the pin protrudes above the cam lobe and forces the exhaust valve to stay open longer thereby reducing compression. At running speed the pin remains below the surface of the cam lobe. Inspect mechanism for proper operation.

When installing camshaft, be sure timing marks on camshaft gear and crankshaft gear are aligned. Install thrust washer onto end of camshaft.

PISTON, PIN AND RINGS. Remove piston and connecting rod as an assembly. To remove piston and connecting rod, remove cylinder head, oil pan and camshaft. Remove carbon and ring ridge (if present) from top of cylinder before removing piston. Mark rod and rod cap so cap can be reinstalled in original position during assembly. Unscrew connecting rod cap retaining screws and remove rod cap. Push connecting rod and piston assembly out of cylinder. Remove piston pin retaining rings and separate piston from connecting rod.

Measure piston diameter 12.5 mm (0.5 in.) above lower edge of skirt and 90° from piston pin. Renew piston if piston diameter is less than 67.79 mm (2.669 in.). Oversize pistons are available.

Piston pin bore diameter service limit is 16.08 mm (0.633 in.). Service limit for piston pin is 15.96 mm (0.628 in.).

Maximum allowable compression ring side clearance for top compression ring is 0.15 mm (0.006 in.). Maximum

allowable side clearance for second compression ring is 0.12 mm (0.005 in.). Service limit for thickness of both compression rings is 1.40 mm (0.055 in.). Maximum allowable ring end gap is 0.70 mm (0.028 in.) for top compression ring, 0.78 mm (0.031 in.) for second compression ring and 1.05 mm (0.041 in.) for oil control ring. Oversize piston rings are available.

When reassembling piston on connecting rod, note arrow on piston crown and "K" on side of connecting rod. When assembling piston and rod for number one cylinder, arrow on piston and K on side of rod (B) must be on opposite sides. See Fig. KW415. Arrow on piston and K on side of rod (C) must be on same side for number two cylinder. Use new snap rings to retain piston pin in piston. Do not align the end gap of the snap ring with the cutout in the piston pin bore.

Install marked piston rings with marked side toward piston crown and stagger ring end gaps equally around piston. Install chrome plated piston ring in top piston ring groove.

Install piston and rod in cylinder so arrow on piston crown points toward flywheel side of engine. Be sure to install rod cap in original position according to marks made during disassembly. Apply oil to connecting rod screws before installation, then tighten screws to 5.9 N•m (52 in.-lb.).

CONNECTING ROD. Connecting rod rides directly on crankshaft journal. Maximum allowable inside diameter

for connecting rod big end bearing surface is 35.055 mm (1.3801 in.). Maximum inside diameter of connecting rod small end is 16.05 mm (0.632 in.). Renew connecting rod if rod is twisted or bent more than 0.15 mm (0.006 in.) measured 100 mm (3.94 in.) from small end. Big end width service limit is 18.80 mm (0.740 in.).

CRANKSHAFT, MAIN BEARINGS AND SEALS. The crankshaft is supported at both ends in integral bushings in the crankcase and oil pan. Maximum inside diameter for both bearing bores is 35.15 mm (1.384 in.). Bushings in crankcase and oil pan are not renewable.

Crankshaft main journal minimum diameter is 34.90 mm (1.374 in.) for pto end and 34.93 mm (1.375 in.) for flywheel end.

Crankpin journal minimum diameter is 34.94 mm (1.376 in.). Maximum allowable crankpin width is 39.50 mm (1.555 in.).

Install main bearing seals so they are flush with surface of crankcase or oil pan.

GOVERNOR. Internal governor components include a flyball assembly mounted on the end of the camshaft as shown in Fig. KW414. Movement of governor flyballs (11) forces the slider (14) against the governor fork in the oil pan. The governor fork shaft extends through the oil pan to operate the external governor linkage.

Remove the oil pan (23) for access to the internal governor components. Detach snap ring (15) to remove governor components. After assembly, be sure slider (14) moves smoothly. Install new oil seal (22) after governor shaft is inserted in the oil pan.

OIL PUMP. The engine is equipped with a rotor-type oil pump located in the oil pan. The crankshaft timing gear drives the oil pump.

Remove oil pan (9—Fig. KW416) for access to oil pump components. Remove

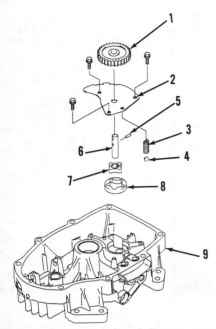

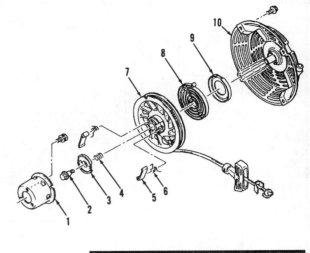

Fig. KW417—Exploded view of typical rewind starter.

1. Starter cup
2. Center screw
3. Retainer
4. Spring
5. Pawl
6. Spring
7. Pulley
8. Rewind spring
9. Spring cup
10. Starter housing

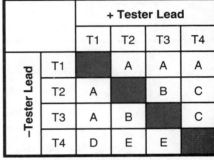

Fig. KW416—Exploded view of oil pump assembly.

1. Gear
2. Base
3. Pressure relief spring
4. Pressure relief valve ball
5. Pin
6. Shaft
7. Inner rotor
8. Outer rotor
9. Oil pan

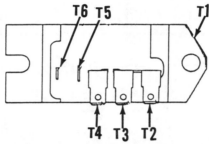

Fig. KW418—Note identification of regulator terminals and mounting base for purpose of testing and refer to Fig. KW419 or KW420 for test specifications. Terminals T5 and T6 are not found on some regulators.

		+ Tester Lead			
		T1	T2	T3	T4
−Tester Lead	T1		A	A	A
	T2	A		B	C
	T3	A	B		C
	T4	D	E	E	

Fig. KW419—Refer to test specifications in table when checking a regulator with three terminals.

A. Infinity
B. Zero ohms
C. 500 ohms - infinity
D. 7.8k ohms - infinity
E. 800 ohms - infinity

the screws from oil pump base (2) and withdraw oil pump components from the oil pan. After removing pump base, oil pressure relief spring (3) and ball (4) will be loose.

Make certain oil passages are clear. Inspect pump housing in oil pan for damage. Maximum allowable inner-to-outer rotor clearance is 0.2 mm (0.008 in.). If clearance is excessive, renew rotors. Minimum allowable outside diameter of outer rotor (8) is 40.470 mm (1.5933 in.). Minimum allowable width of outer rotor is 9.830 mm (0.3870 in.). Renew rotors as a set.

Maximum allowable inside diameter in oil pan is 40.801 mm (1.6063 in.). Maximum allowable depth in oil pan is 10.230 mm (0.4028 in.). Minimum allowable oil pump shaft diameter is 10.923 mm (0.4300 in.). Maximum allowable oil pump shaft bore in oil pan is 11.072 mm (0.4359 in.). Minimum pressure relief spring free length is 19.50 mm (0.768 in.).

Reassemble oil pump by reversing disassembly procedure. Be sure to lubricate oil pump prior to assembly. When installing pump base, align 6 mm hole in oil pump base with hole for pressure relief valve in oil pan.

ELECTRIC STARTER AND SOLENOID. If starter does not operate, check wiring, starter solenoid and battery before removing starter for inspection.

Before disassembling starter, mark end cap, frame and drive housing so they can be reassembled in original positions.

Minimum brush length is 6.4 mm (0.25 in.). Lightly lubricate bores of drive hub and drive gear with SAE 10 oil before assembly.

REWIND STARTER. Refer to Fig. KW417 for exploded view of typical rewind starter. To disassemble the rewind starter, release spring tension by pulling rope handle until about 30 cm (12 in.) of rope extends from unit. Use thumb pressure to prevent pulley from rewinding and place rope in notch in outer rim of pulley. Release thumb pressure slightly and allow spring mechanism to slowly unwind. Unscrew center screw (2), and remove components (3 through 6). Carefully remove pulley from support shaft in housing.

CAUTION: Take extreme care that rewind spring cup remains in recess of pulley. Do not remove spring unless new spring is to be installed.

Using a new rope of same length and diameter as original, place rope in handle and tie a figure eight knot about 25 mm (1 in.) from end. Pull knot into top of handle. Install other end of rope

through guide bushing of housing and through hole in pulley groove. Pull rope out through opening in pulley, tie a knot at end of rope and pull knot against pulley.

Wind the rope two turns counterclockwise on pulley, then lock rope in notch of pulley. Install pulley on support shaft and rotate pulley counterclockwise until inner end of rewind spring is engaged. Assemble remainder of components. Hook a loop of rope into pulley notch and preload rewind spring by turning pulley counterclockwise. Remove rope from notch and allow pulley to slowly turn clockwise as rope winds on pulley and handle returns to guide bushing on housing. Check operation of starter.

CHARGING SYSTEM. The engine may be equipped with a charging system that provides direct current. The regulator may be equipped with three or five terminals. Test the regulator using an ohmmeter. Note number of terminals on regulator (Fig. KW418), then refer to Fig. KW419 or Fig. KW420 for test specifications.

Refer to Fig. KW421 for engine wiring diagram.

207

		+ Tester Lead					
		T1	T2	T3	T4	T5	T6
− Tester Lead	T1		A	A	A	B	C
	T2	A		D	E	A	A
	T3	A	D		E	A	A
	T4	F	G	G		H	H
	T5	I	A	A	A		J
	T6	K	A	A	A	L	

Fig. KW420—Refer to test specifications in table when checking a regulator with five terminals.

- A. Infinity
- B. 19 - 3k ohms
- C. 3k ohms - infinity
- D. Zero ohms
- E. 500 ohms - infinity
- F. 7.5k ohms - infinity
- G. 925 ohms - infinity
- H. 10k ohms - infinity
- I. 330 - 14k ohms
- J. 1.2k ohms - infinity
- K. 14k ohms - infinity
- L. 110 ohms - infinity

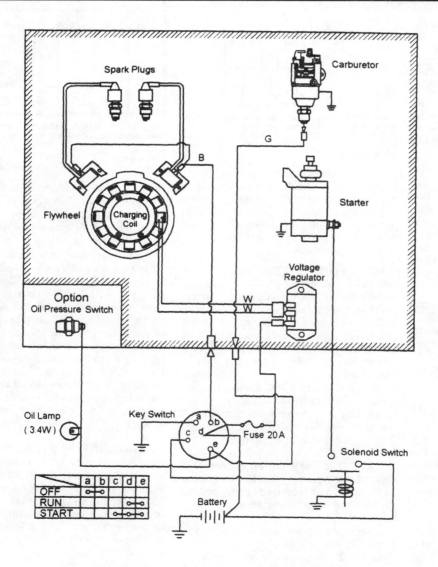

Fig. KW421—Engine wiring diagram.

KAWASAKI CENTRAL PARTS DISTRIBUTORS

(Arranged Alphabetically by States)

These franchised firms carry extensive stocks of repair parts. Contact them for name of dealer in their area who will have replacement parts.

Artesco, Inc.
2949 E. Washington Street
Phoenix, AZ 85034

Bee Tee Equipment Sales
21075 Alexander Crt., Unit H
Hayward, CA 94540

T M C Power Equipment Inc.
2051 Saturn Street
Monterey Park, CA 91754

Colorado Outdoor Power Equip.
1441 W. Bayaud, Suite 1 A
Denver, CO 80223

Engine Power Supply
3685 Old Winter Garden Road
Orlando, FL 32805

Power Systems Div. E. C Dist.
4499 Market Street
Boise, ID 83705

Remco Power Equipment Company
2100 West 16th Street
Broadview, IL 60135

Strietters II Distributors
1333 Street Road #2 West
La Porte, IN 46350

A-1 Distributors Ltd.
2600 Hyw. 75 North
Sioux City, IA 51102

Parrish Implement Co., Inc.
913 E. Liberty
Louisville, KY 40204

Gulf Engine & Equipment
2306 Engineers Road
Belle Chasse, LA 70037

C V Foster Equipment Co.
2502 Hartford Road
Baltimore, MD 21218

D & S Sales
197 Main Street
Agawan, MA 01001

Plymouth Air Cooled Equip. Inc.
587 W. Ann Arbor Trail
Plymouth, MI 48170

Fowler Electric Co.
2208 W. 94 Street
Bloomington, MN 55431

Pro Engine Sales
Route 206 S of Ross Corner
Augusta, NJ 07822

Arbordale Power Products
480 Dodge Road
Getzville, NY 14068

Dixie Sales Co. Inc.
335 North Greene
Greensboro, NC 27402

Power Equipment Company
4050 W. Main Avenue
Fargo, ND 58103

Hayward Distributing Co.
460 Neilston Street
Columbus, OH 43215

Brown Engine & Equipment
4315 S. Robinson
Oklahoma City, OK 73109

E C Distributing Company
2122 Northwest Upshur
Portland, OR 97210

Stull Company
701 4th Avenue
Corapolis, PA 15108

Sullivan Brothers Inc.
Creek Road & Langoma Ave.
Elverson, PA 19520

Trinity Metro Distributors Inc.
100 Lewisville W. Shop Ctr.
Lewisville, TX 75067

M & M Distributing
7476 Harwin
Houston, TX 77036

Industrial Energy Equipment
145 North Highway 89
N. Salt Lake City, UT 84054

Northwest Motor Parts
2930 6th Avenue
Seattle, WA 98124

Morley Murphy
700 Morley Road
Green Bay, WI 54303

Morley-Murphy
8500 W. Bradley Road
Milwaukee, WI 53224

CANADA

Oliver Industrial Supply Ltd.
236 36th Street
Lethbridge, ALB T1J 4B2

Coast Dieselec Ltd.
101 11471 Blacksmith Place
Richmond, BC V7A 4T7

Coast Dieselec Ltd.
10 1235 Shawson Drive
Mississauga, ONT L4W 1C4

Oliver Agricultural Supply
140 East 4th Avenue
Regina, SASK S4P 3B2

KOHLER

KOHLER COMPANY
Kohler, Wisconsin 53044

Model	No. Cyls.	Bore	Stroke	Displacement	Power Rating
M8	1	2.94 in. (74.6 mm)	2.75 in. (69.9 mm)	18.64 cu. in. (305 cc)	8 hp (6.0 kW)
M10	1	3.25 in. (82.5 mm)	2.88 in. (73.0 mm)	23.85 cu. in. (392 cc)	10 hp (7.5 kW)
M12	1	3.38 in. (85.7 mm)	3.25 in. (82.5 mm)	29.07 cu. in. (476 cc)	12 hp (8.9 kW)
M14	1	3.50 in. (88.9 mm)	3.25 in. (82.5 mm)	31.27 cu. in. (512 cc)	14 hp (10.4 kW)
M16	1	3.75 in. (95.2 mm)	3.25 in. (82.5 mm)	35.90 cu. in. (588 cc)	16 hp (11.9 kW)

ENGINE IDENTIFICATION

All models are four-stroke, single cylinder, horizontal crankshaft-type engines. All engines are equipped with ball bearing mains at each end of crankshaft and are splash lubricated. A side draft carburetor is used on all engines. Engine model, specification and serial numbers are located on a tag on carburetor side of the rewind starter and cooling fan housing. Always furnish engine model, specification and serial number when ordering parts.

An automotive diaphragm-type fuel pump is used on some models. This pump is equipped with a priming lever. A fuel pump repair kit is available.

MAINTENANCE

SPARK PLUG. Recommended spark plug for Model M8 is a Champion RJ12C or RJ19LM. Recommended spark plug for Models M10, M12, M14 and M16 is a Champion RH10C. Recommended electrode gap is 0.025 inch (0.64 mm) for all models.

CARBURETOR. All models are equipped with a Kohler side-draft carburetor. For initial adjustment, open idle mixture screw (7—Fig. KO100) 1¼ turns from a lightly seated position on Model M8. For Models M10 and M12, open idle mixture screw (7) 2½ turns and main mixture screw (1) 1½ turns from a lightly seated position. For Models M14 and M16, open idle and main mixture screws 2½ turns from a lightly seated position.

Make final adjustments on all models with engine at operating temperature and running. Place engine under load and adjust main mixture screw (1) to leanest mixture that will allow satisfactory acceleration and steady governor

operation. If engine misses and backfires under load, mixture is too lean. If engine shows a sooty exhaust and is sluggish under load, mixture is too rich. Adjust idle speed stop screw (5) to maintain an idle speed of 1200 rpm. Then, adjust idle mixture screw (7) for smoothest idle operation.

Main and idle mixture adjustments have some effect on each other. Recheck engine operation and readjust mixture

screws as necessary for smoothest operation.

To check float level, invert carburetor body and float assembly. There should be ¹¹⁄₆₄ inch (4 mm) clearance between machined surface of body casting and free end of float as shown in upper view of Fig. KO101. Adjust as necessary by bending float lever tang that contacts inlet valve. Turn carburetor over and

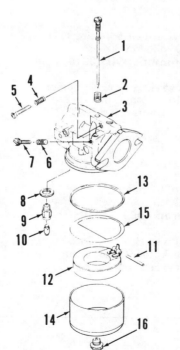

Fig. KO100—Exploded view of Kohler side draft carburetor.

1. Main mixture screw	9. Inlet valve seat
2. Spring	10. Inlet valve
3. Carburetor body	11. Float pin
4. Spring	12. Float
5. Idle speed stop screw	13. Gasket
6. Spring	14. Float bowl
7. Idle mixture screw	15. Baffle gasket
8. Sealing washer	16. Bowl retainer

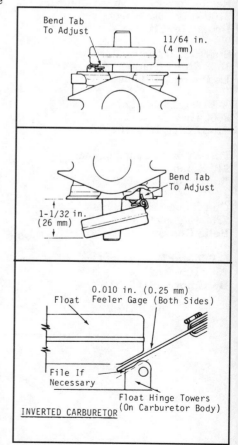

Fig. KO101—View showing float adjustment procedure. Refer to text.

measure float drop. Float drop should be 1 1/32 inches (26 mm) between the machined surface of body and the bottom of the free end of float, as shown in middle view of Fig. KO101. Bend the float tab to adjust. Float-to-float hinge tower clearance should be 0.010 inch (0.25 mm) as shown in lower view of Fig. KO101. File float hinge tower as needed to obtain recommended clearance.

NOTE: Carburetors on engines used on rough or sloping ground may require installation of manufacturer-supplied bowl-vent baffle kit to prevent raw fuel from splashing into carburetor bowl vent.

AIR FILTER. All models are equipped with a foam-type precleaner and a paper air filter element. Foam precleaner should be serviced after every 25 hours of operation and paper element should be cleaned after every 100 hours of operation and renewed after every 300 hours of operation.

To service foam precleaner, remove precleaner and wash in a solution of warm water and detergent. Rinse thoroughly with clean water until all traces of detergent are eliminated. Squeeze out water and allow foam element to air dry. Saturate foam element in clean engine oil and squeeze out excess oil.

To clean the paper element, remove the foam precleaner and paper element. Remove the foam precleaner element from the paper element and gently tap paper element to dislodge dirt. Do not wash the paper element or use compressed air to clean.

GOVERNOR. All models are equipped with a gear-driven, flyweight governor that is located inside engine crankcase. Maximum recommended governed engine speed is 3600 rpm. Recommended idle speed of 1200 rpm is controlled by adjustment of throttle stop screw on carburetor.

For initial adjustment of governor linkage, loosen governor lever clamp bolt nut and pull governor lever away from carburetor as far as it will go. Then, turn governor shaft counterclockwise as far as it will go while holding governor lever. Tighten clamp bolt nut. On Model M8, make certain there is at least 1/16 inch (1.6 mm) clearance between governor lever and cross shaft bushing nut (Fig. KO102). On Models M10, M12, M14 and M16, make certain there is at least 1/16 inch (1.6 mm) clearance between governor lever and upper left cam gear cover bolt (Fig. KO103).

High speed setting depends on engine application. Maximum allowable speed is 3600 rpm. Maximum speed is adjusted by loosening jam nut on high-speed adjusting screw and turning screw until desired speed is obtained. Governor sensitivity is adjusted by repositioning governor spring in the holes in governor lever (Fig. KO104). Standard spring position on Model M8 is the third hole from the cross shaft. Standard spring position on Models M10, M12, M14 and M16 is the sixth hole from the cross shaft. To increase sensitivity, move spring toward cross shaft and to decrease sensitivity, move spring away from cross shaft.

IGNITION SYSTEM. All models are equipped with an electronic magneto ignition system consisting of a magnet cast into the flywheel, an electronic magneto ignition module mounted on the engine bearing plate outside of flywheel and an ignition switch that grounds ignition module to stop engine.

Air gap between flywheel and ignition module should be 0.012-0.016 inch (0.30-0.41 mm).

Ignition system is considered satisfactory if system will produce a spark that will jump a test plug gap of 0.035 inch (0.89 mm). To test the primary side of ignition module using an ohmmeter, connect the positive ohmmeter lead to ignition module laminations (A—Fig. KO105) and the negative ohmmeter lead to kill terminal (B). Ohmmeter reading should be 1.0-1.3 ohms. To test the secondary side of ignition module using an ohmmeter, connect the positive ohmmeter lead to ignition module lamination (A) and the negative ohmmeter lead to high-tension lead (C). Ohmmeter reading should be 7,900-10,850 ohms. If ohmmeter readings are not as specified, renew ignition module.

VALVE ADJUSTMENT. Valve stem-to-tappet clearance should be checked after every 500 hours of operation. To check clearance, remove air cleaner, carburetor and crankcase breather assembly. Rotate crankshaft until piston is at top dead center on compression stroke. Use a feeler gauge to measure clearance between end of valve stem and tappet.

Valve stem-to-tappet clearance (engine cold) for Model M8 should be 0.006-0.008 inch (0.15-0.20 mm) for intake valve and 0.017-0.019 inch (0.43-0.48 mm) for exhaust valve. If clearance is too small, remove the valve and grind the end of the valve stem to obtain correct clearance. If clearance is too large, grind the valve seat or face to reduce clearance or renew the valve.

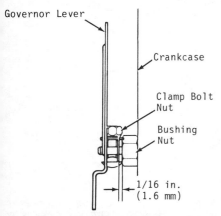

Fig. KO102—View of Model M8 governor linkage. Refer to text for adjustment procedure.

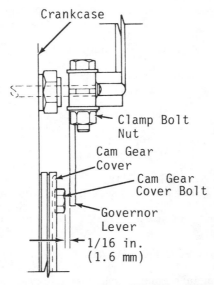

Fig. KO103—View of Models M10, M12 and M16 governor linkage. Refer to text for adjustment procedure.

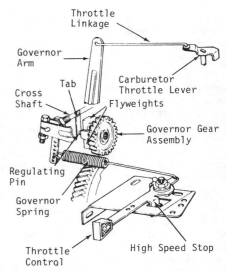

Fig. KO104—View showing typical governor linkage arrangement used on most models.

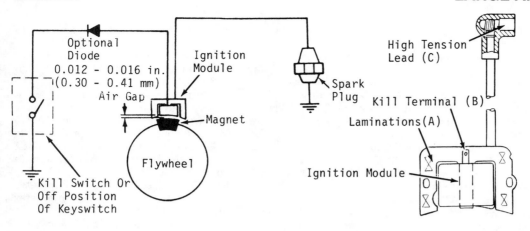

Fig. KO105—Typical wiring diagram for all models.

Valve stem-to-tappet clearance (engine cold) for Models M10, M12, M14 and M16 should be 0.008-0.010 inch (0.20-0.25 mm) for intake valve and 0.017-0.019 inch (0.43-0.48 mm) for exhaust valve. On these models, clearance is adjusted by turning the adjusting screw on the tappet.

CYLINDER HEAD AND COMBUSTION CHAMBER. Cylinder head should be removed and carbon deposits cleaned after every 500 hours of operation. Refer to CYLINDER HEAD under REPAIR section for cylinder head removal procedure.

LUBRICATION. Engine oil should be checked daily and oil level maintained between the "F" and "L" marks on dipstick. Push dipstick all the way down in tube to obtain reading.

Manufacturer recommends using oil having an API service rating of SG or SH, or any oil formulated to supercede the SG or SH rating. Use SAE 30 oil for ambient temperatures above 32° F (0° C) and SAE 5W-20, 5W-30, or 10W-30 oil for temperatures below 32° F (0° C). Manufacturer specifies that SAE 10W-40 oil should not be used.

Oil should be changed after the first 5 hours of operation and at 25-hour intervals thereafter. Depending on oil pan design, the crankcase oil capacity is usually 1 quart (0.95 L) for Model M8 and 2 quarts (1.9 L) for Models M10, M12, M14 and M16. A deep-design oil pan will increase the engine's oil capacity. Always check the dipstick level prior to starting the engine, making sure that oil is at "Full" mark on dipstick. Do not overfill.

On Models equipped with OIL SENTRY system, the Oil Sentry float switch should be removed, and switch magnet should be cleaned of any metal particles, every 500 hours of operation. Upon installation of switch, manufacturer recommends using GE SILMATE No.

1473 RTV silicone (or equivalent) to properly seal the float switch.

GENERAL MAINTENANCE. Check and tighten all loose bolts, nuts and clamps daily. Check for fuel and oil leakage and repair as necessary. Clean cooling fins and external surfaces at 50-hour intervals.

REPAIR

TIGHTENING TORQUE. Recommended tightening torque specifications are as follows:

Spark plug . . . . 18-22 ft.-lbs. (24-29 N•m)

Cylinder head:
Model M8 . . . . 15-20 ft.-lbs. (20-27 N•m)

Models M10, M12,
M14, M16 . . . . 25-30 ft.-lbs. (34-40 N•m)

Flywheel:
Model M8 . . . . 85-90 ft.-lbs. (115-122 N•m)

Models M10,
M12, M14,
M16 (plastic fan) . . . . . . 35-40 ft.-lbs. (48-54 N•m)

Models M10, M12,
M14, M16 (iron fins) . . . 22-27 ft.-lbs. (29-37 N•m)

Connecting rod:
Model M8 (New) . . . . 12 ft.-lbs. (16 N•m)

Model M8 (Used) . . . . 8 ft.-lbs. (11 N•m)

Models M10, M12,
M14, M16 (New) . . . . 22 ft.-lbs. (29 N•m)

Models M10, M12,
M14, M16 (Used) . . . . 17 ft.-lbs. (23 N•m)

Engine base . . . . 7 ft.-lbs. (10 N•m)

CYLINDER HEAD. To remove cylinder head, first remove all necessary metal shrouds. Clean engine to prevent entrance of foreign material and remove cylinder head retaining bolts.

Always use a new head gasket when installing cylinder head. Make certain that threaded holes in cylinder block are free of dirt, oil or water. Lightly lubricate cylinder head bolts with oil before installation. Tighten cylinder head bolts evenly and in graduated steps using the sequence shown in Fig. KO106 for the model being serviced. Tighten bolts to specified torque.

CONNECTING ROD. The aluminum alloy connecting rod rides directly

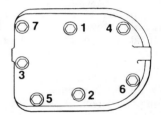

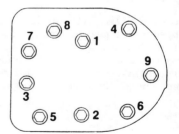

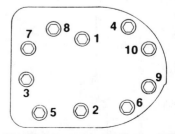

Fig. KO106—Cylinder head bolts must be tightened in the sequence shown. Upper view is for Model M8, middle is for Models M10, M12 and M14, and lower view is for Model M16.

on the crankpin journal. Model M8 engines are equipped with a narrow connecting rod for engines equipped with style "D" piston or a wider connecting rod for engines equipped with style "A" piston. Refer to following PISTON, PIN AND RINGS and upper view of Fig. KO107. Connecting rod and piston are removed as an assembly after cylinder head and engine base have been removed. Remove the two connecting rod cap nuts and connecting rod cap and push piston and rod assembly out top of cylinder. Remove snap rings retaining piston pin and push pin out of piston and connecting rod.

Inside diameter for piston pin hole in connecting rod should be 0.6255-0.6258 inch (15.888-15.895 mm) for Model M8, 0.8596-0.8599 inch (21.834-21.842 mm) for Model M10 and 0.8757-0.8760 inch (22.243-22.250 mm) for Models M12, M14 and M16. Piston pin-to-connecting rod running clearance should be 0.0006-0.0011 inch (0.015-0.028 mm) for Model M8 and 0.0003-0.0008 inch (0.008-0.020 mm) for Models M10, M12, M14 and M16.

Connecting rod side play on crankpin should be 0.005-0.016 inch (0.13-0.41 mm) for Model M8 and 0.007-0.016 inch (0.18-0.41 mm) for Models M10, M12, M14 and M16.

Connecting rod-to-crankpin running clearance should be 0.001-0.002 inch (0.025-0.50 mm) for all models. If running clearance is 0.0025 inch (0.064 mm) or greater, renew connecting rod and/or recondition crankshaft journal. A 0.010-inch (0.25-mm) undersize connecting rod is available. Undersize connecting rod is identified by a drilled hole in connecting rod just above crankpin bearing end as shown in lower view of Fig. KO107.

Reinstall connecting rod and piston assembly with match marks on connecting rod and cap and the word "FLY" stamped on piston top toward flywheel side of engine. Tighten connecting rod nuts to specified torque.

PISTON, PIN AND RINGS. The aluminum alloy piston is fitted with two compression rings and one oil control ring. Piston pin outside diameter should be 0.6247-0.6249 inch (15.867-15.873 mm) for Model M8 and 0.8752-0.8754 inch (22.230-22.235 mm) for Models M10, M12, M14 and M16. Model M8 can be equipped with either a style "A" or "C" piston (Fig. KO108), Models M10, M12 and M14 will be equipped with style "A" piston and Model M16 can be equipped with either style "C" or "D" piston. Refer to the following paragraphs for style "A," "C" and "D" piston specifications.

On all models, piston must be installed on connecting rod so the match marks on connecting rod and cap and the word "FLY" stamped on piston top are toward flywheel side of engine after installation.

Style "A" Piston. Diameter of piston is measured just below oil control ring groove as shown in upper view of Fig. KO108.

Piston diameter should be 2.9281-2.9297 inches (74.374-74.414 mm) for Model M8, 3.2413-3.2432 inches (82.329-82.377 mm) for Model M10, 3.365-3.368 inches (85.47-85.55 mm) for Model M12 and 3.4925-3.4941 inches (88.710-88.754 mm) For Model M14. If piston diameter is 2.925 inches (74.295 mm) or less for Model M8, 3.238 inches (82.245 mm) or less for Model M10, 3.363 inches (85.420 mm) or less for Model M12 or 3.491 inches (88.671 mm) or less for Model M14, renew piston.

Piston-to-cylinder clearance for Models M8, M10, M12 and M14 should be 0.007-0.010 inch (0.18-0.25 mm). Piston ring side clearance for Models M8, M10, M12 and M14 should not exceed 0.006 inch (0.15 mm). Piston ring end gap for new rings should be 0.007-0.017 inch (0.18-0.37 mm) for Model M8 and 0.010-0.020 inch (0.25-0.51 mm) for Models M10, M12 and M14. Piston ring end gap (maximum) for used rings is 0.027 inch (0.69 mm) for Model M8 and 0.030 inch (0.76 mm) for Models M10, M12 and M14. If

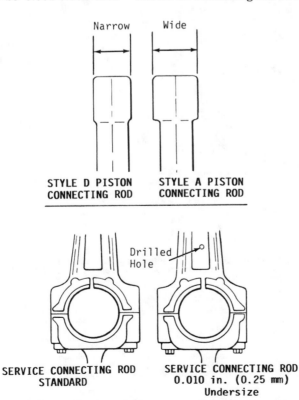

Fig. KO107—Style "D" piston must be mounted on narrow connecting rod. Style "A" piston must be mounted on wide connecting rod. Lower view shows location of drilled hole used to identify connecting rod used on 0.010 inch (0.25 mm) undersize crankpin journal.

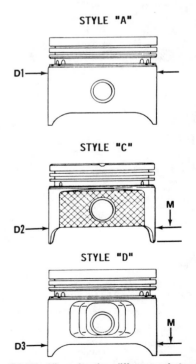

Fig. KO108—View showing differences between style "A", "C" and "D" pistons. Measure diameter of piston at location identified by (D1, D2 or D3). Dimension (M) is 1/2 inch (12.7 mm). Refer to text.

dimensions are not as specified, renew piston and/or rings.

Piston rings must be installed correctly. Ring installation instructions are usually included with new ring sets. Refer to Fig. KO109 (top view) for the location and arrangement of piston rings. Top compression ring and center compression ring must be installed with "pip" mark on ring facing up. Installing the rings upside down will result in poor engine performance and excessive oil consumption.

Styles "C" and "D" Pistons. Diameter of piston is measured ½ inch (12.7 mm) up from bottom of skirt as shown in middle and lower view of Fig. KO108. Piston diameter should be 2.9329-2.9336 inches (74.496-74.513 mm) for Model M8 and 3.7455-3.7465 inches (95.136-95.161 mm) for Model M16. If piston diameter is 2.9312 inches (74.453 mm) or less for Model M8, or 3.7435 inches (95.085 mm) or less for Model M16, renew piston. Piston-to-cylinder clearance should be 0.0034-0.0051 inch (0.086-0.130 mm) for Model M8 and 0.0030-0.0050 inch (0.076-0.127 mm) for Model M16.

Piston ring side clearance should not exceed 0.006 inch (0.15 mm) for Models M8 and M16. Piston ring end gap for new rings should be 0.010-0.023 inch (0.25-0.58 mm) for Model M8 and

0.010-0.020 inch (0.25-0.51 mm) for Model M16. Piston ring end gap (maximum) for used rings is 0.032 inch (0.81 mm) for Model M8 and 0.030 inch (0.76 mm) for Model M16. If dimensions are not as specified, renew piston and/or rings.

Piston rings must be installed correctly. Ring installation instructions are usually included with new ring sets. Refer to Fig. KO109 (center or bottom view) for the location and arrangement of piston rings. Top compression ring and center compression ring must be installed with "pip" mark on ring facing up. Installing the rings upside down will result in poor engine performance and excessive oil consumption.

CYLINDER AND CRANKCASE. Cylinder and crankcase are integral castings. Cylinder bore diameter

should be 2.9370-2.9380 inches (74.600-74.625 mm) for Model M8, 3.2505-3.2515 inches (82.563-82.588 mm) for Model M10, 3.3745-3.3755 inches (85.712-85.738 mm) for Model M12, 3.4995-3.5005 inches (88.887-88.913 mm) for Model M14 and 3.7495-3.7505 inches (95.237-95.263 mm) for Model M16. Recondition the cylinder bore if bore diameter exceeds the following wear limits: 2.941 inches (74.679 mm) or more for Model M8; 3.254 inches (82.652 mm) or more for Model M10; 3.378 inches (85.801 mm) or more for Model M12; 3.503 inches (88.976 mm) or more for Model M14; 3.753 inches (95.326 mm) or more for Model M16.

If cylinder bore is out-of-round more than 0.005 inch (0.13 mm), recondition cylinder bore. If cylinder bore taper exceeds 0.003 inch (0.08 mm) for Model

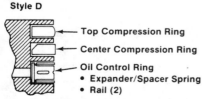

Fig. KO109—Cross-sectional drawing showing correct installation of piston rings. Install the top and center compression rings with "pip" mark on ring facing up.

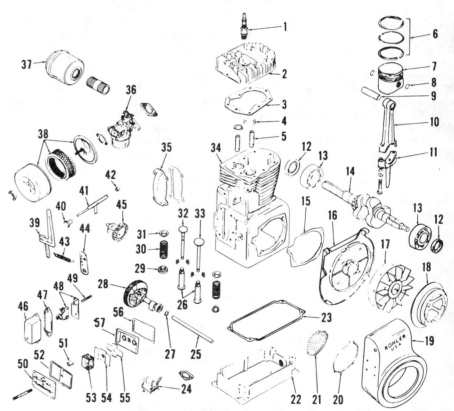

Fig. KO110—Exploded view of engine similar to Magnum series engine. Shroud (19) has been replaced with a new design. Cooling fins may be cast with flywheel (17) on some models or be a bolt-on plastic assembly on others.

1. Spark plug
2. Cylinder head
3. Head gasket
4. Valve seat insert
5. Valve guide
6. Piston rings
7. Piston
8. Retaining ring
9. Piston ring
10. Connecting rod
11. Rod cop
12. Oil seal
13. Ball bearing
14. Crankshaft
15. Gasket
16. Bearing plate

17. Flywheel
18. Pulley
19. Shroud
20. Screen retainer
21. Screen
22. Oil pan
23. Gasket
24. Fuel pump
25. Camshaft pin
26. Valve tappets
27. Shim washer
28. Camshaft
29. Valve rotator
30. Valve spring
31. Spring retainer

32. Exhaust valve
33. Intake valve
34. Cylinder block
35. Camshaft cover
36. Carburetor
37. Muffler
38. Air cleaner assy.
39. Governor lever
40. Bushing
41. Governor shaft
42. Needle bearing
43. Governor spring
44. Speed lever
45. Governor gear
    & weight unit

46. Breaker cover
    (not used on
    M series)
47. Gasket
48. Breaker assy.
    (not used on
    M series)
49. Push rod
50. Breather cover
51. Breather seal
52. Gasket
53. Filter
54. Baffle
55. Reed
56. Gasket
57. Breather plate

M8 or 0.002 inch (0.05 mm) for Models M10, M12, M14 or M16, recondition cylinder bore.

CRANKSHAFT, MAIN BEAR-INGS AND SEALS. The crankshaft is supported at each end by a ball bearing-type main bearing. Renew bearings (13—Fig. KO110) if excessively rough or loose. Crankshaft end play should be 0.002-0.023 inch (0.05-0.58 mm) for Model M8 and 0.003-0.020 inch (0.08-0.51 mm) for Models M10, M12, M14 and M16.

Standard crankpin journal diameter is 1.1855-1.1860 inches (30.112-30.124 mm) for Model M8, 1.5745-1.5749 inches (39.99-40.00 mm) for Models M10, M12, M14 and M16. If crankpin journal is out-of-round 0.0005 inch (0.013 mm) or more, recondition crankpin journal. If crankpin journal taper is 0.001 inch (0.025 mm) or more, recondition crankpin journal.

Main bearings should be a light press fit on crankshaft journals and in crankcase and bearing plate bores. If not, renew bearings and/or crankshaft or crankcase and bearing plate.

Front oil seal should be pressed into bearing plate seal bore so seal is 1/32 inch (0.8 mm) below seal bore surface. Rear oil seal should be pressed into crankcase bearing bore so seal is 1/8 inch (3 mm) below seal bore surface.

When installing crankshaft, align timing marks on crankshaft and camshaft gears as shown in Fig. KO111.

NOTE: On models equipped with dynamic balancer, refer to following DYNAMIC BALANCER for installation and timing of balancer gears.

CAMSHAFT. The hollow camshaft and integral camshaft gear turn on a pin that is a slip fit in flywheel side of crankcase and a drive fit in closed side of crankcase. Remove and install pin from open side (bearing plate side) of crankcase. Drive camshaft pin into pto side of crankcase until pin is 0.275-0.285 inch (6.99-7.24 mm) from

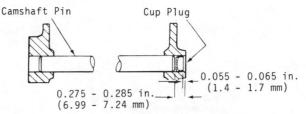

Fig. KO112—View showing dimensions for camshaft pin installations.

machined bearing plate gasket surface (Fig. KO112). Apply chemical locking compound on cup plug and install into bore in bearing plate mounting surface to a depth of 0.055-0.065 inch (1.4-1.7 mm) (Fig. KO112). Camshaft end play should be 0.005-0.010 inch (0.127-0.254 mm) and is controlled by use of 0.005 and 0.010 inch thick spacer washers between camshaft and cylinder block at bearing plate side of crankcase.

All models are equipped with automatic compression release mechanism. The automatic compression release mechanism holds exhaust valve slightly open during first part of compression stroke, reducing compression pressure and allowing easier cranking of engine. At engine speeds above 650 rpm, compression release mechanism is inactive. To check cylinder compression, engine must be cranked at 650 rpm or higher to overcome compression release action. A reading can also be obtained by rotating flywheel in reverse direction with throttle in wide-open position. Compression reading should be 110-120 psi (758-827 kPa) for an engine in top mechanical condition. When compression reading falls below 100 psi (689 kPa), engine should be disassembled as needed and worn or damaged component or components renewed.

VALVE SYSTEM. Valve tappet gap (cold) should be 0.006-0.008 inch (0.15-0.20 mm) for intake valve and 0.017-0.019 inch (0.43-0.48 mm) for exhaust valve on Model M8. For all other models, valve tappet gap should be 0.008-0.010 inch (0.20-0.25 mm) for intake valve and 0.017-0.019 inch (0.43-0.48 mm) for exhaust valve.

Correct valve tappet gap is obtained on Model M8 by grinding ends of valve stem to increase clearance or by grinding seat or face of valve to decrease clearance. Models M10, M12, M14 and M16 are equipped with adjustable tappets.

Valve face and seat should be ground at a 45° angle for intake and exhaust valves. Standard seat width should be 1/32 to 1/16 inch (0.794-1.588 mm).

Renewable valve guides are used on all models. Intake valve stem-to-guide clearance should be 0.001-0.0025 inch (0.025-0.064 mm) and exhaust valve

stem-to-guide clearance should be 0.0025-0.004 inch (0.064-0.102 mm) on all models. Ream valve guides after installation to obtain correct inside diameter of 0.312-0.313 inch (7.93-7.95 mm). Diameter of intake valve stem should be 0.3103 inch (7.88 mm) for all models. Exhaust valve stem on all models is slightly tapered. Exhaust valve stem diameter should be 0.3074 inch (7.81 mm) at upper valve stem area that enters valve guide.

DYNAMIC BALANCER. Some models may be equipped with a dynamic balancer system (Fig. KO113). Balancer gears, equipped with renewable needle bearings, rotate on stub shafts that are pressed into bosses on the pto side of the crankcase. Snap rings secure gears on the stub shafts and shim spacers are used to control gear end play. Two or three balancer gears may be used. Balancer gears are driven by the crankshaft gear in opposite direction of crankshaft rotation.

To renew stub shafts, press oil shafts out and discard. Press new shaft in until it is 1.087-1.097 inches (27.61-27.86 mm) above stub shaft boss and use the 3/8-inch (9.52 mm) spacer between block and gear (Fig. KO114).

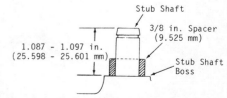

Fig. KO113—View showing dynamic balancer system with two balancer gears used on some models.

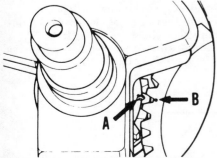

Fig. KO111—Crankshaft gear and camshaft gear timing marks (A&B) must be aligned as shown during installation.

Fig. KO114—View showing balancer gear stub shaft installation. Refer to text.

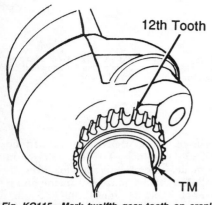

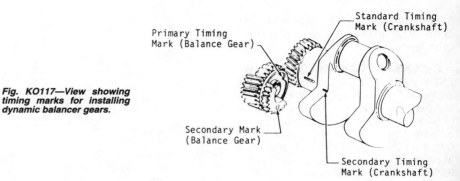

Fig. KO117—View showing timing marks for installing dynamic balancer gears.

Fig. KO115—Mark twelfth gear tooth on crankshaft gear counterclockwise from primary timing mark (TM) on gear.

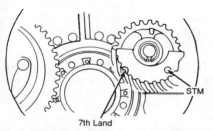

Fig. KO116—Mark seventh land on top balancer gear from secondary timing mark (STM) on gear.

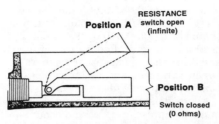

Fig. KO118—Testing Oil Sentry switch. Switch is shown installed in oil pan. Testing is easier with switch removed unless oil pan has been removed from engine.

To install top balancer gear and bearing assembly, first place one 0.010-inch shim on stub shaft, install top gear assembly on shaft making certain timing marks are facing flywheel side of crankcase. In the following order, install one 0.005-inch shim, one 0.010-inch shim and one 0.020-inch shim on stub shaft and retain with snap ring. Using a feeler gauge, check gear end play. Correct end play of balancer gear is 0.005-0.010 inch (0.13-0.25 mm). Add or remove shims in 0.005-inch increments as necessary to obtain correct end play.

NOTE: Always install the 0.020-inch shim next to snap ring.

To install remaining balancer gear(s) and crankshaft, proceed as follows: Note the timing mark (A—Fig. KO111) on the side of crankshaft gear. Looking at the crankshaft from the pto end, mark the twelfth tooth on the crankshaft gear (Fig. KO115) counterclockwise from timing mark. Note the secondary timing mark on the top balance gear (Fig. KO116) and mark the seventh land clockwise from the timing mark. Install the crankshaft so the previously marked tooth on the crankshaft and land on balancer gear are engaged, but do not engage the camshaft gear. Rotate the camshaft so the crankshaft and camshaft gear timing marks (Fig. KO111) are aligned, then insert the crankshaft fully into main bearing.

Place ⅜-inch spacer and 0.010-inch shim on the bottom balance gear stub shaft, then rotate the crankshaft so the crankpin is approximately 15° past bottom dead center. Align the secondary timing mark on bottom balance gear with secondary timing mark on crankshaft counterweight (Fig. KO117) and install the balancer gear on the shaft. If correctly installed, the secondary timing mark on the bottom balance gear will be aligned with standard timing mark on the crankshaft after the gear is fully on stub shaft. Install one 0.020-inch shim on gear, then install the snap ring with round side toward gear. Add 0.005-inch shims as necessary so gear end play is 0.005-0.010 inch (0.13-0.25 mm). Make certain that the 0.020-inch shim is against the snap ring.

Place ⅜-inch spacer and 0.010-inch shim on third balance gear stub shaft. Rotate the crankshaft so the crankpin is 90° from top dead center and toward camshaft side of engine. Install the third balance gear so that, when it is seated on shaft, the flat surface is parallel with flat surfaces on other balance gears. Install one 0.020-inch shim on gear, then install snap ring with round side toward gear. Add 0.005-inch shims as necessary so gear end play is 0.005-0.010 inch (0.13-0.25 mm). Make certain that the 0.020-inch shim is against the snap ring.

OIL SENSOR. When removing or installing Oil Sentry float switch, tilt the engine whenever possible to allow for a vertical work position. If tilting is not possible, and the switch becomes stuck during installation or removal, carefully use smooth screw/unscrew movements to release it. Seal the threads of the float-switch with GE Silmate No. 1473 RTV silicon sealant or equivalent.

To test the switch, use an analog-type ohmmeter set on the R×10,000 scale. Connect ohmmeter test leads to the float switch leads and observe the resistance readings as shown in Fig. KO118. There should be infinite resistance (no continuity) with switch in position A (switch open). There should be zero resistance (continuity) with switch in position B (switch closed). If switch fails this test, install a new switch.

Note that color of switch wire leads identifies the type of switch: Black leads—shutdown style; white leads—warning light style.

KOHLER

KOHLER COMPANY
Kohler, Wisconsin 53044

Model	No. Cyls.	Bore	Stroke	Displacement	Power Rating
MV14	2	3.12 in. (79.2 mm)	2.75 in. (69.85 mm)	42.18 cu. in. (691 cc)	14 hp (10.4 kW)
MV16	2	3.12 in. (79.2 mm)	2.75 in. (69.85 mm)	42.18 cu. in. (691 cc)	16 hp (11.9 kW)
MV17	2	3.12 in. (79.2 mm)	2.75 in. (69.85 mm)	42.18 cu. in. (691 cc)	17 hp (12.6 kW)
M18, MV18	2	3.12 in. (79.2 mm)	2.75 in. (69.85 mm)	42.18 cu. in. (691 cc)	18 hp (13.4 kW)
M20, MV20	2	3.12 in. (79.2 mm)	3.06 in. (78.0 mm)	46.98 cu. in. (769.8 cc)	20 hp (14.9 kW)

ENGINE IDENTIFICATION

All models are four-stroke, twin-cylinder, air-cooled engines. Models M18 and M20 are horizontal crankshaft engines. Models MV14, MV16, MV17, MV18 and MV20 are vertical crankshaft engines. All models are pressure lubricated and equipped with an oil filter.

Engine identification and serial numbers are located on a decal (or decals) located as shown in Fig. KO120 for Models M18 and M20, or as shown in Fig. KO121 for Models MV16, MV18 and MV20. Refer to Fig. KO122 to de-

termine engine features and date of manufacture.

MAINTENANCE

SPARK PLUG. Recommended spark plug for all models is Champion RV17YC or equivalent. Recommended spark plug electrode gap is 0.035 inch (0.9 mm).

CARBURETOR. Early Models M18 and M20 are equipped with a Kohler adjustable jet, float-type side draft car-

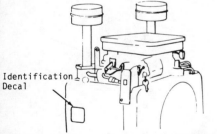

Fig. KO120—View showing location of decal for identification of engine model and serial numbers on Models M18 and M20.

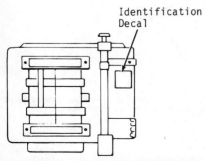

Fig. KO121—View showing location of decal for identification of engine model and serial numbers on Models MV16, MV18 and MV20.

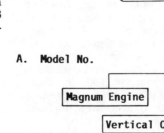

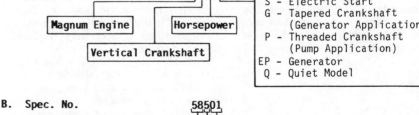

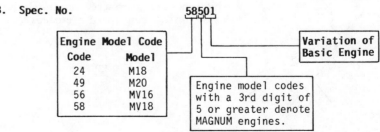

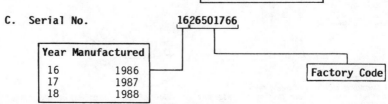

Fig. KO122—Engine model and serial number interpretation.

buretor. Model M18 after serial number 1629500986, Model M20 after serial number 1619504206 and all Models MV14, MV16, MV17, MV18 and MV20 are equipped with a float-type side draft carburetor manufactured by Walbro to meet Kohler specifications. Refer to the appropriate service information for type carburetor being serviced.

Kohler Adjustable Jet Carburetor. Initial adjustment for main mixture needle (MN—Fig. KO123) should be 2½ turns open from a lightly seated position. Initial adjustment for idle mixture needle (IN) should be 1 turn open from a lightly seated position.

Final adjustments should be made with engine running at normal operating temperature. Place engine under load with throttle in wide-open position. Slowly turn main mixture needle (MN) out (counterclockwise) until engine rpm decreases and note position of needle. Slowly turn main mixture needle in (clockwise) until engine speed again decreases and note needle position. Adjust main mixture needle to a position midway between the two noted positions. Remove load from engine and place throttle in idle position. Adjust idle mixture needle (IN) using the same procedure used to adjust main mixture needle. Adjust throttle stop screw (TS) so engine idles at 1125-1275 rpm.

Models M18 and M20 may be equipped with an electrically operated automatic choke. The bimetal spring closes the choke plate when ambient air is cold. Electric current from the rectifier-regulator heats the spring when the engine is running thereby opening the choke. When the ignition switch is held in the start position for five seconds, the choke should close, then open when the starter is disengaged. The choke is adjusted by turning the cover on the choke (rotate counterclockwise for leaner setting). To install and adjust unit, ambient temperature must be 70-75° F (21-24° C). Retaining screws should be slightly loose. Hold choke unit against carburetor and turn the choke unit clockwise until choke plate is 4-6° closed from open position. Hold the choke unit and tighten retaining screws.

The carburetor may be equipped with a fuel shut-off solenoid that uses a plunger to stop fuel flow through a fuel passage when the engine is stopped. The spring-loaded plunger should retract when the solenoid is energized, allowing fuel flow.

Walbro Carburetor. Initial adjustment of idle mixture needle (IN—Fig. KO124) should be 1¼ turns out from a lightly seated position for Models M18 and M20, and 1 turn out for Models MV14, MV16, MV17, MV18 and MV20.

On models equipped with adjustable high speed mixture screw, initial setting of mixture screw is 1¼ turns out from a lightly seated position on Models MV16 and MV18, and 1 turn out on Model MV20. Some models are equipped with a fixed, nonadjustable main jet.

Final adjustments on all models must be performed with engine running at normal operating temperature. Adjust idle speed by turning idle speed screw (TS) to obtain an idle speed of 1200 rpm. Run engine at idle speed and turn idle mixture screw (IN) counterclockwise until engine speed decreases and note screw position. Turn screw clockwise until engine speed decreases again and note screw position. Turn screw so it is halfway between the two noted positions. If necessary, readjust idle speed screw.

If equipped with adjustable high speed screw, proceed as follows: Run engine at full speed under load and turn high speed mixture screw counterclockwise until engine speed decreases and note screw position. Turn screw clockwise until engine speed decreases again and mark screw position. Turn screw so it is halfway between the two noted positions.

On models equipped with fixed main jet, a high altitude jet is available.

AIR FILTER. Three types of air filter assemblies have been used: Square type (Fig. KO125), Dome type (Fig. KO126) and an Anti-Icing type (Fig. KO127). For service information, refer to the appropriate following paragraphs for type being serviced.

NOTE: If a significant amount of oil is coming into the air cleaner past the crankcase breather on a Magnum vertical shaft engine, Serial Number

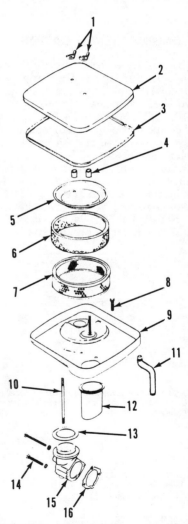

Fig. KO125—Exploded view of the square type air filter assembly used on some models.

1. Wing nuts	9. Base
2. Cover	10. Stud
3. Gasket	11. Breather hose
4. Seals	12. Intake tube
5. Element cover	13. Gasket
6. Foam precleaner	14. Bolts
7. Paper element	15. Intake elbow
8. Screw	16. Gasket

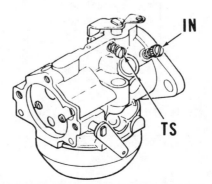

Fig. KO123—View showing location of main mixture needle (MN), idle mixture needle (IN) and throttle stop screw (TS) on Kohler adjustable carburetor.

Fig. KO124—View showing location of idle mixture needle (IN) and throttle stop screw (TS) on Walbro fixed jet carburetor.

2513703355 or lower, replace the crankcase breather with new design.

Square Type Air Filter. Optional foam precleaner element (6—Fig. KO125) should be removed and cleaned after every 25 hours of normal use. Clean foam precleaner in a suitable solvent, rinse and air dry. Soak element in clean engine oil and squeeze out excess oil before reinstalling.

Paper element (7) should be removed and cleaned after every 100 hours of normal use. Paper element can be cleaned using low pressure compressed air. Renew element if it cannot be properly cleaned or if it is damaged.

Dome Type Air Filter. Optional foam precleaner element (5—Fig. KO126) should be removed and cleaned after every 25 hours of normal use. Clean foam precleaner in a suitable solvent, rinse and air dry. Soak element in clean engine oil and squeeze out excess oil before reinstalling.

Paper element (6) should be removed and cleaned after every 100 hours of normal use. Paper element can be cleaned using very low pressure compressed air.

Anti-Icing Air Filter. Optional foam precleaner element (7—Fig. KO127) should be removed and cleaned after every 25 hours of normal use. Clean foam precleaner in a suitable solvent, rinse and air dry. Soak element in clean engine oil and squeeze out excess oil before reinstalling.

Paper element (8) should be removed and cleaned after every 100 hours of normal use. Paper element can be cleaned using very low pressure compressed air. Renew element if it cannot be properly cleaned or if it is damaged.

When installing air filter cover (2), refer to Fig. KO128 and install cover as shown in the left view when ambient temperature is below 45° F (10° C).

GOVERNOR. All models are equipped with a centrifugal flyweight mechanical governor. Governor gear and flyweight mechanism is located inside engine crankcase and is driven by the camshaft gear. For an exploded view of the governor assembly and external linkage, refer to Fig. KO129 for Models M18 and M20, and to Fig. KO130 for Models MV14, MV16, MV17, MV18 and MV20.

On Models M18 and M20, make initial adjustment of governor linkage whenever governor lever is loosened or removed from cross shaft. Make certain throttle linkage is connected to governor lever and throttle lever on carburetor. Loosen governor lever clamp bolt nut (1—Fig. KO129). Pull governor lever (10) away from carburetor as far as possible to fully open carburetor throttle plate. Rotate the governor shaft (2) clockwise as far as possible and tighten clamp nut (1) to 4-5 ft.-lbs. (5-6 N•m). Maximum engine speed with no load is 3600 rpm and is controlled by the high speed stop screw.

Governor sensitivity is adjusted by changing the position of spring (4) in the holes in governor lever (10) and speed control lever (5). Standard spring position is the fifth hole from the cross shaft in governor lever and in the sixth hole from the hex head cap screw in the speed control lever. Always mark spring location prior to spring removal. To increase governor sensitivity, increase spring tension by moving spring in governor lever toward cross shaft. To decrease sensitivity and allow broader speed control, decrease spring tension by moving spring in governor lever away from cross shaft.

On Models MV14, MV16, MV17, MV18 and MV20, make initial adjustment of governor linkage whenever the governor lever is loosened or removed from cross shaft. Make certain the governor linkage is connected to governor lever and throttle lever on intake manifold. Throttle linkage is connected to throttle lever on the intake manifold and throttle lever on carburetor as shown in Fig. KO130. Loosen governor lever clamp bolt nut (7). Pull the governor lever (5) down and away from the carburetor as far as possible to fully open the carburetor throttle plate. Turn

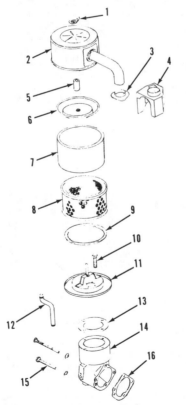

Fig. KO126—Exploded view of dome type air filter assembly used on some models.

1. Wing nut	
2. Cover	8. Base
3. Seal	9. Breather hose
4. Element cover	10. Gasket
5. Foam precleaner	11. Intake elbow
6. Paper element	12. Bolts
7. Screw	13. Gasket

Fig. KO127—Exploded view of the anti-icing air filter assembly used on some models.

1. Wing nut	9. Base seal
2. Cover	10. Screw
3. Heater plate	11. Base
4. Heater cover	12. Breather hose
5. Seal	13. Gasket
6. Element cover	14. Intake elbow
7. Foam precleaner	15. Bolts
8. Paper element	16. Gasket

Heater Cover

Below 45°F (10°C)   Above 45°F (10°C)

Fig. KO128—Cover (2) should be installed on air filter as shown according to ambient temperature.

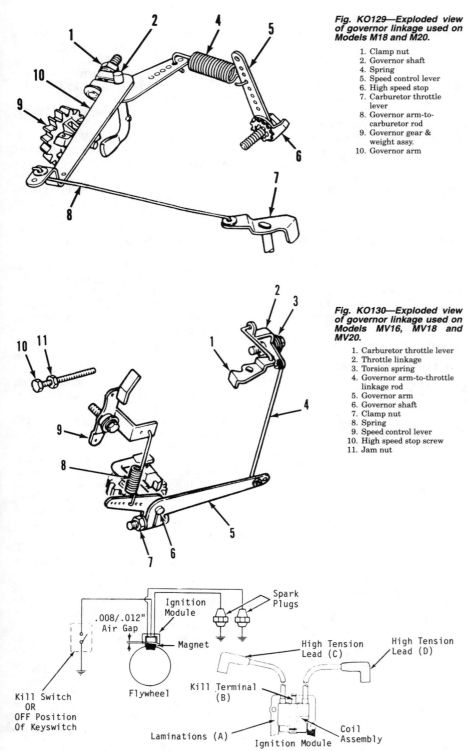

Fig. KO131—Schematic of the electronic magneto ignition system used on all models.

allow broader speed control, decrease spring tension by moving spring in governor lever away from cross shaft.

IGNITION SYSTEM. All models are equipped with an electronic magneto ignition system, which consists of a magnet assembly permanently affixed to the flywheel, an electronic magneto ignition module mounted on number one cylinder and a kill switch that stops the engine by grounding the ignition module.

Electronic magneto ignition module should be installed so a 0.008-0.012 inch (0.21-0.31 mm) air gap is between the module and flywheel.

To test the ignition module, attach ohmmeter negative test lead to kill switch terminal (B—Fig. KO131) and positive test lead to coil lamination (A). Ohmmeter should register 5-1000 ohms. If resistance is 0 ohms or infinite, primary circuit is shorted or open and module should be renewed. Reverse the positions of ohmmeter test leads to check primary resistance. Ohmmeter should register a minimum of 30,000 ohms. To check secondary resistance, attach ohmmeter test leads to terminal end of each spark plug cable. Ohmmeter should register 22,000-42,000 ohms. If ohmmeter readings vary considerably from specified values, renew ignition module.

VALVE ADJUSTMENT. Valve stem-to-tappet clearance should be checked after every 500 hours of operation. To check clearance, remove breather/valve cover assemblies from each cylinder. Rotate flywheel to position piston for No. 1 cylinder at top dead center of compression stroke. Use a feeler gauge to measure clearance between valve stem ends and tappets. Rotate flywheel one complete turn (360°) to position piston for No. 2 cylinder at top dead center and measure valve clearance for No. 2 cylinder.

On all models, valve-to-tappet clearance with engine cold should be 0.003-0.006 inch (0.08-0.15 mm) for intake valves. Recommended exhaust valve-to-tappet clearance is determined by engine serial number as follows: 0.016-0.019 inch (0.41-0.48 mm) before serial number 1816500656; 0.011-0.014 inch (0.30-0.35 mm) after serial number 1816500646 but before 1917809296; 0.013-0.016 inch (0.33-0.41 mm) after serial number 1917809296.

If clearance is too small, remove valves and grind valve stem end to increase clearance. If clearance is too large, grind the valve seat or install a new valve to decrease clearance.

the governor shaft (6) clockwise as far as possible and tighten clamp bolt nut (7) to 4-5 ft.-lbs. (5-6 N•m). Maximum engine speed with no load is 3750 rpm and is controlled by high-speed stop screw (10).

Changing the position of spring (8) in speed control lever (9) or the governor lever (5) controls governor sensitivity.

Standard spring position is the third hole from the cross shaft in governor lever and the second hole from the pivot point in the speed control lever. Always mark spring location prior to removal. To increase governor sensitivity, increase governor spring tension by moving spring in governor lever toward cross shaft. To decrease sensitivity and

CYLINDER HEAD. Cylinder heads should be removed and carbon and other deposits removed from cylinder heads and combustion chambers at 250 hour intervals if leaded gasoline is used or at 500 hour intervals if unleaded gasoline is used. Clean combustion deposits using a wooden or plastic scraper. Install new head gaskets and tighten cylinder head bolts to 15-20 ft.-lbs. (20-27 N•m) as outlined under CYLINDER HEAD in the REPAIRS section.

LUBRICATION. All models are equipped with a pressure lubrication system. Refer to OIL PUMP in the REPAIRS section for oil pump service information.

Most engines are equipped with an oil filter. Some engines may experience oil seepage past the oil filter adapter (or block-off plate) gasket. An adapter leak kit is available from the manufacturer to correct this problem.

NOTE: On engines equipped with an oil filter, it is recommended that the filter be pre-filled with oil prior to installation to assure adequate lubrication to critical components during initial engine restart.

Periodically check oil level; do not overfill. Oil dipstick should be screwed in until bottomed for correct oil level reading. If engine is equipped with an oil filter, change oil after the first 5 hours of operation and every 50 hours thereafter. If not equipped with an oil filter, change oil after every 25 hours of operation. Oil in all engines used in heavy-duty operation should be changed after every 25 hours of operation.

Oil capacity for Models M18 and M20 is 3 pints (1.4 L) without a filter or 3.5 pints (1.7 L) with a filter. Oil capacity for Models MV14, MV16, MV17, MV18 and MV20 is 3.5 pints (1.7 L) without a filter or 4 pints (1.9 L) with a filter.

Manufacturer recommends using oil with an API service rating of SG or SH, or any rating formulated to supercede SG or SH. Use SAE 30 oil for temperatures above 32° F (0° C); use SAE 5W-20, 5W-30, or 10W-30 for temperatures between 0°F (−18° C) and 32° F (0° C); below 0° F (−18° C) use only SAE 5W-20 or 5W-30.

DO NOT use SAE 10W-40 oil.

NOTE: On M18 and M20 engines equipped with Oil Sentry pressure switch, an oil switch bypass kit can be installed to help eliminate engine backfiring during hot engine restart due to warm oil causing insufficient oil

pressure. The bypass kit (part No. 82 755 25) is available from the engine manufacturer.

REPAIRS

TIGHTENING TORQUES. Recommended tightening torque specifications are as follows:

Spark plug . . . . 10-15 ft.-lbs.
(13-20 N•m)
Main fuel jet:
  Fixed type. . . . . 12-16 in.-lbs.
(1.4-1.8 N•m)
Carburetor fuel
  bowl nut. . . . . 45-55 in.-lbs.
(5.1-6.2 N•m)
Connecting rod:
  New nuts . . . . 140 in.-lbs.
(15.8 N•m)
  Used nuts . . . . 100 in.-lbs.
(11.3 N•m)
Cylinder barrel . . . . See Text
Cylinder head . . . . 15-20 ft.-lbs.
(20-27 N•m)
Flywheel. . . . . 40 ft.-lbs.
(54 N•m)
Oil filter bypass
  cover . . . . 125 in.-lbs.
(14 N•m)
Closure plate . . . . 150 in.-lbs.
(17 N•m)
Crankcase screws:
  $\frac{5}{16}$ in . . . . 200 in.-lbs.
(22.6 N•m)
  $\frac{3}{8}$ in . . . . 260 in.-lbs.
(29.4 N•m)

CARBURETOR. Kohler Adjustable Jet Carburetor. To disassemble carburetor, refer to Fig. KO132 and remove the float bowl retaining plug (16) and float bowl (15). Remove float pin (14), float assembly (13) and fuel inlet needle (10). Remove fuel inlet needle seat (9) and gasket (8). Remove idle mixture needle (5) and spring (6). Remove main fuel needle (1) and spring (2).

If throttle or choke shaft bores in carburetor are worn, a bushing kit is available for repair. Follow directions provided with kit carefully and use a suitable drill press to drill out shaft bores for bushing renewal.

Clean carburetor in carburetor cleaner only after all rubber and fiber washers and seals have been removed. Rinse and blow out all passages with compressed air. Do not use wire or a drill bit to clean fuel passages as calibration of carburetor could be affected if passages are enlarged.

To adjust float level, invert carburetor throttle body so the float tab rests on the fuel inlet needle. Float height (H—Fig. KO133) should be $\frac{11}{64}$ inch (4.4 mm) from the carburetor mating sur-

face to the float. Carefully bend float height tab to adjust.

After float level is adjusted, turn carburetor throttle body over and check the float drop. Float drop should be limited to $1\frac{1}{32}$ inches (26.2 mm) between the carburetor mating surface and the edge of the float (Fig. KO134). Carefully bend the float drop limiting tab to adjust.

Invert the carburetor throttle body and use a feeler gauge to measure clearance between the float and the float hinge towers. Clearance should be at least 0.010 inch (0.25 mm) as shown in Fig. KO135. If necessary, file the float tower to obtain the recommended clearance.

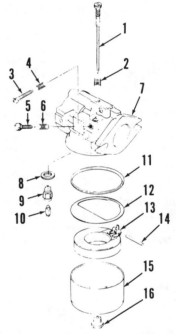

Fig. KO132—Exploded view of Kohler adjustable jet carburetor.

1. Main mixture needle
2. Spring
3. Throttle stop screw
4. Spring
5. Idle mixture needle
6. Spring
7. Carburetor body
8. Gasket
9. Inlet needle seat
10. Fuel inlet needle
11. Gasket
12. Baffle gasket
13. Float
14. Float pin
15. Float bowl
16. Plug & gasket

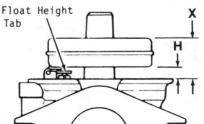

Fig. KO133—View of correct procedure to determine float height. Refer to text for specifications for model being serviced.

Walbro Carburetor. To disassemble carburetor, refer to Fig. KO136 and remove the bowl retaining plug (20) and float bowl (19). Remove float pin (17), float assembly (18) and fuel inlet needle (16). Do not attempt to remove the fuel inlet seat as it is not a serviceable item. Remove idle mixture needle (7), spring (8), throttle stop screw (10), spring (9) and the main fuel jet (14).

To clean the bowl vent channel and the off-idle ports, use a small punch to pierce and remove the Welch plugs (11 and 12). Use care not to damage carburetor body during this procedure. Throttle and choke shaft may be removed as required. Use care not to lose the choke detent ball and spring (5) as the choke shaft (13) is removed.

Clean the carburetor in a suitable carburetor cleaner only after all rubber and fiber washers and seals have been removed. Rinse and blow out all passages with compressed air. Do not use wire or a drill bit to clean passages as calibration of carburetor could be affected if passages are enlarged.

To reassemble, reverse the disassembly procedure. When installing Welch plugs, apply a suitable sealant to outer edge of plugs and allow to dry. Install main fuel jet and tighten to 12-18 in.-lbs. (1.4-2.0 N•m).

To adjust float level, invert carburetor throttle body so that float tab rests on the fuel inlet needle. Float height (X—Fig. KO133) should be 0.690-0.720 inch (17.53-18.29 mm) from the carburetor body mating surface to the float.

Carefully bend float height tab to adjust.

NOTE: If muffler is covered by a sheet metal heat shield on vertical-shaft engines, make certain that heat shield does not contact carburetor bowl. Bend the shield, if necessary, to prevent it from rubbing a hole in the bowl.

CYLINDER HEAD. To remove cylinder heads, remove blower housing and cylinder head air baffles. Remove cylinder head bolts and remove cylinder heads and head gaskets. Note that cylinders are identified by a number 1 or number 2 mark stamped near the valve spring chamber. Mark cylinder heads with a corresponding number so they can be reinstalled in original location.

Clean carbon and other combustion deposits from cylinder heads, then check heads for distortion or other damage. If head is warped more than 0.003 inch (0.076 mm), both the head and head bolts should be renewed.

NOTE: Lightly lubricate the cylinder head bolt threads with clean engine oil prior to assembly.

To install cylinder heads, reverse the removal procedure using new head gaskets. Tighten head bolts in two steps to specified final torque of 15-20 ft.-lbs. (20-27 N•m) following the sequence shown in Fig. KO137.

CONNECTING ROD. To remove connecting rods, first mark the cylinder heads and crankcase halves as No. 1 side and No. 2 side as shown in Fig KO138. Drain engine oil and remove oil filter. Remove mufflers, exhaust elbows, air cleaner, intake manifold and carburetor. Disconnect and remove all wiring, regulator, kill switch and solenoid. Remove blower housing and all cooling shrouds. Remove breather and valve tappet chamber covers. Remove fuel pump, ignition module and module bracket. Remove flywheel using a suitable puller. Remove starter motor.

Remove cylinder heads, then remove cylinder retaining nuts and pull cylinder barrels off piston and connecting rod assemblies. Mark pistons and connecting rods as No. 1 and No. 2, then remove piston pin retaining rings, piston pins and pistons.

Remove crankcase closure plate, oil pressure relief valve and oil filter adapter. Scribe a line across the camshaft bore plug and the No. 1 crankcase side. This line is used to align the plug during assembly. Wrap a rubber band or tape around valve tappet stems in No. 2 crankcase side to prevent tappets from falling out when crankcase is split. Remove crankcase retaining nuts and screws. With No. 2 crankcase half facing upward, insert a screwdriver into splitting notch provided in the crankcase halves and carefully pry crankcase halves apart.

Remove camshaft and camshaft bore plug from No. 1 crankcase half. Mark tappet locations, then remove tappets. Remove crankshaft, connecting rods,

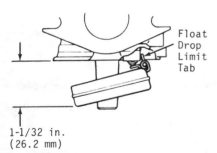

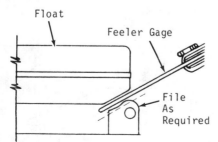

Fig. KO134—Float drop should be limited to 1-1/32 in. (26.2 mm).

1-1/32 in. (26.2 mm)

Float Drop Limit Tab

Float

Feeler Gage

File As Required

Fig. KO135—Check clearance between float tower and float as shown. Refer to text for specifications for model being serviced.

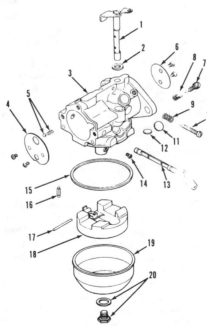

Fig. KO136—Exploded view of Walbro fixed jet carburetor.

1. Throttle shaft	11. Welch plug
2. Dust seal	12. Welch plug
3. Carburetor body	13. Choke shaft
4. Choke plate	14. Main jet
5. Choke detent ball & spring	15. Gasket
6. Throttle plate	16. Fuel inlet needle
7. Idle mixture needle	17. Float pin
8. Spring	18. Float
9. Spring	19. Float bowl
10. Throttle stop screw	20. Plug & gasket

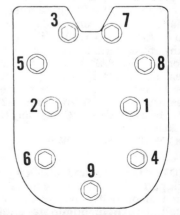

Fig. KO137—Cylinder head bolts should be loosened and tightened following the sequence shown.

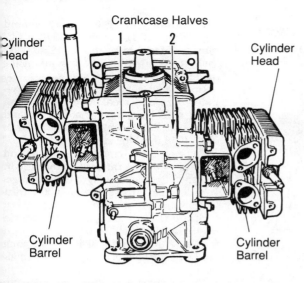

Fig. KO138—Prior to disassembly, identify engine side to ensure correct reassembly. No. 1 side of engine has cylinder closest to flywheel end of crankshaft.

front oil seal and bearings as an assembly. Mark connecting rods and rod caps as No. 1 and No. 2, then remove from crankshaft.

The aluminum alloy Posi-Lock connecting rods ride directly on the crankpin journal. Standard connecting rod-to-crankpin journal clearance is 0.0012-0.0024 inch (0.031-0.061 mm). If clearance exceeds 0.003 inch (0.075 mm), renew connecting rod and/or recondition crankshaft. A connecting rod with 0.010 inch (0.25 mm) undersize big end bore is available. The 0.010 inch (0.25 mm) undersize connecting rod is identified by a drilled hole in the connecting rod just above the big end bore (Fig. KO139). Standard connecting rod-to-piston pin clearance is 0.0006-0.0011 inch (0.015-0.028 mm) for all models. Standard connecting rod side play on crankpin is 0.005-0.016 inch (0.13-0.41 mm).

Reinstall connecting rods by reversing the removal procedure. Number one connecting rod should be installed on the crankshaft journal closest to the flywheel end of crankshaft, and number two connecting rod should be installed on crankshaft journal closest to the pto end of crankshaft.

On Model M20, install the connecting rods with the shanks angled down and away from the camshaft (Fig. KO140).

Make certain that match marks on connecting rods and caps are aligned (Fig. KO140). Lubricate connecting rod bolt threads with clean engine oil, then tighten rod cap nuts to 140 in.-lbs. (15.8 N•m). for new connecting rods or 100 in.-lbs. (11.3 N•m) for used connecting rods.

When installing crankshaft assembly, be sure that locating tab of sleeve bearing on pto end of shaft is positioned in notch in crankcase and that oil hole in bearing on flywheel end of shaft is aligned with oil passage in crankcase.

Make certain that camshaft gear timing mark is aligned with crankshaft timing mark.

Prior to joining crankcase halves or installing closure plate (horizontal crankshaft), oil pan (vertical crankshaft) or cylinders, apply silicone type sealant as shown in Figs. KO141, KO142, KO143 and KO144.

NOTE: The closure plate gasket included in some gasket sets is only used on earlier horizontal twin-cylinder engines, NEVER ON ANY VERTICAL TWIN-CYLINDER ENGINES.

Tighten crankcase fasteners as follows: Tighten fasteners (1 through 6—Fig. KO141) in sequence shown to torque of 100 in.-lbs. (11.3 N•m), and tighten remaining fasteners (any sequence) to torque of 100 in.-lbs. (11.3 N•m). Then tighten crankcase fasteners (1 through 4) to 260 in.-lbs. (29.4 N•m), and tighten remaining fasteners (any sequence) to 200 in.-lbs. (22.6 N•m).

Tighten oil pan or closure plate fasteners to 150 in.-lbs. (17 N•m) following the sequence shown in Fig. KO142 or Fig. KO143. Tighten cylinder barrel nuts first to 100 in.-lbs. (11.3 N•m), then to final torque of 200 in.-lbs. (22.6 N•m) following sequence shown in Fig. KO144.

Be sure that cam plug scribe mark is aligned with mark on crankcase half. Stake cam plug in place using the previous stake marks.

PISTON, PIN AND RINGS. The aluminum alloy piston is fitted with

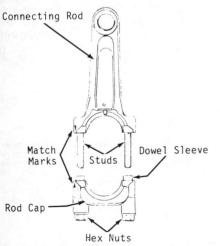

Fig. KO139—Connecting rods are available in 0.010 inch (0.25 mm) undersize for reconditioned crankshaft. Undersize connecting rod can be identified by the hole just above crankpin bearing bore.

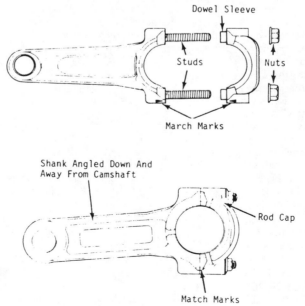

Fig. KO140—Align match marks on connecting rod and cap prior to installation. Connecting rods used on Model M20 (lower view) must be installed wih shank angled away from camshaft (top of crankcase).

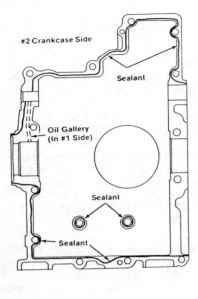

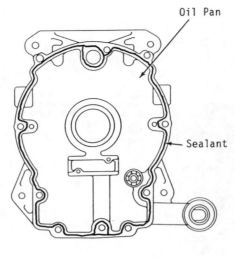

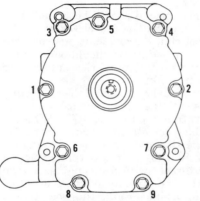

Fig. KO142—Prior to installing oil pan (vertical crankshaft), apply a silicone type sealant around all mating surfaces. Tighten oil pan fasteners to specified torque following sequence shown.

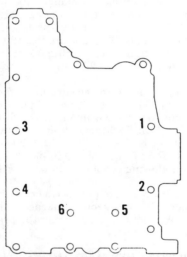

Fig. KO141—Prior to assembling crankcase, apply a silicone type sealant to No. 2 crankcase half as shown. Refer to text for fastener tightening sequence.

Piston-to-cylinder clearance should be 0.0030-0.0047 inch (0.0076-0.117 mm) for Model M20 and 0.0035-0.0052 inch (0.089-0.132 mm) for all other models.

Insert each compression ring into cylinder bore and measure ring end gap using a feeler gauge. Piston ring end gap should be 0.010-0.023 inch (0.25-0.58 mm) for all models.

Position new rings on piston and measure side clearance of piston ring in piston ring groove using a feeler gauge. If side clearance exceeds 0.006 inch (0.15 mm), renew piston.

Standard piston pin diameter is 0.7499-0.7501 inch (19.048-19.053 mm) for Model M20 and 0.6247-0.6249 inch (15.867-15.872 mm) for all other models.

Piston rings should be installed on piston with side of ring marked "PIP" facing upward (Fig. KO145).

NOTE: In some replacement ring sets, the second or intermediate ring envelope showed an incorrect installation illustration: It instructs the installer to mount the ring with the "PIP" mark facing down. Always install both compression rings with the identifying "PIP" mark facing the top, or dome, of the piston.

Ring end gaps should be spaced equally around piston diameter. Lubricate piston, rings and cylinder with engine oil prior to assembly.

Use a suitable ring compressor to install pistons in cylinder barrels. Be sure that arrow stamped on piston crown points toward flywheel side of engine. Install piston pin using new retaining rings. Complete the installation by reversing the removal procedure.

CYLINDER. Cylinders can be removed from crankcase as separate assemblies. Number one cylinder is the

two compression rings and one oil control ring. To remove pistons, remove mufflers, exhaust elbows, air cleaner, intake manifold and carburetor. Disconnect and remove all wiring, regulator, kill switch and solenoid. Remove blower housing and all cooling shrouds. Remove breather and valve tappet chamber covers. Remove fuel pump, ignition module and module bracket and starter motor. Unbolt and remove cylinder heads and cylinder barrels. Remove piston pin retainers, piston pins and pistons from connecting rods.

Remove piston rings from piston and clean ring grooves. Check piston for scoring, scuffing and excessive wear and renew as necessary.

Standard piston diameter is 3.1208-3.1215 inches (79.268-79.286 mm) for Model M20 and 3.1203-3.1210

inches (79.256-79.273 mm) for all other models. Piston diameter is measured ½ inch (13 mm) above lower edge of skirt, perpendicular to piston pin. If skirt diameter is 3.1186 inches (79.212 mm) or less on Model M20 or 3.1181 inches (79.200 mm) or less on all other models, renew piston.

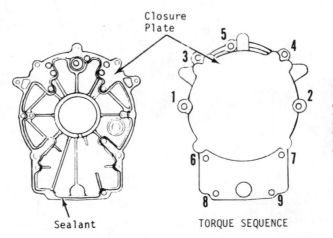

Fig. KO143—Prior to installation of closure plate (horizontal crankshaft), apply a silicone type sealant as shown. Tighten retaining bolts and nuts to specified torque following sequence shown.

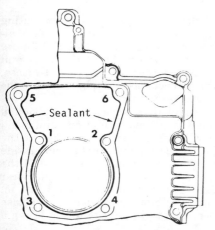

Fig. KO144—Prior to cylinder barrel installation, apply a silicone type sealant as shown. Tighten retaining nuts to specified torque following sequence shown.

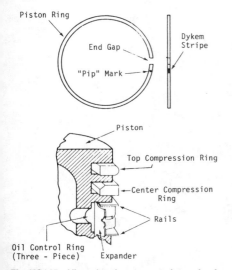

Fig. KO145—View showing correct piston ring installation.

cylinder closest to the flywheel and number two cylinder is the cylinder closest to the pto side of crankcase.

Standard cylinder bore diameter is 3.1245-3.1255 inches (79.362-79.388 mm) for all models. If cylinder bore diameter is 3.128 inches (79.451 mm) or larger, cylinder must be bored to nearest oversize for which piston and rings are available, or renewed.

If cylinder is out-of-round 0.002 inch (0.05 mm) or more, cylinder should be bored oversize, or renewed.

CRANKSHAFT, MAIN BEARINGS AND SEALS. The crankshaft is supported at each end in a sleeve type bearing. To remove crankshaft assembly, refer to CONNECTING ROD section.

Crankshaft end play is controlled by a thrust washer located at flywheel side of crankshaft on most models (Fig.

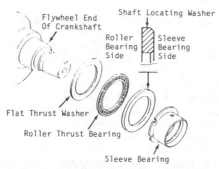

Fig. KO146—Some models are equipped with a crankshaft thrust bearing as shown. Refer to text.

KO146). Thrust washers are available in three sizes: 0.121, 0.130 and 0.139 inch. The 0.130 inch thick washer is considered standard. Crankshaft end play should be 0.002-0.014 inch (0.05-0.35 mm).

Some models may be equipped with a roller thrust bearing (Fig. KO146). Install the 0.039 inch thrust washer, the bearing, then the 0.156 inch shaft locating washer with the chamfered side of washer toward sleeve bearing as shown in Fig. KO146.

Standard crankshaft main bearing journal diameter is 1.7488-1.7510 inches (44.420-44.475 mm) for all models. If journal diameter is 1.7407 inches (44.214 mm) or less, renew crankshaft.

Crankshaft main bearing-to-crankshaft journal clearance should be 0.005 inch (0.125 mm) for all models. If clearance exceeds 0.006 inch (0.15 mm), renew bearing and/or crankshaft.

Inside diameter of new main bearing after installation should be 1.7439-1.7461 inches (44.295-44.351 mm) for all models.

Crankshaft crankpin diameter on Model M20 should be 1.4993-1.4998 inches (38.073-38.095 mm); recondition crankshaft if crankpin diameter is 1.4988 (38.069 mm) or less. Crankpin diameter for all other models should be 1.3733-1.3738 inches (34.882-34.895 mm); recondition crankshaft if crankpin diameter is 1.3728 inches (34.869 mm) or less.

On all models, if crankpin journal is 0.0005 inch (0.013 mm) or more out-of-round, or if journal has 0.001 inch (0.025 mm) or more taper, recondition or renew crankshaft.

When installing crankshaft, make certain that timing marks on crankshaft and camshaft are aligned as shown in Fig. KO147. Make certain the locating tab of main bearing on pto end of shaft engages notch in crankcase and that oil hole in main bearing on flywheel end of shaft is aligned with oil passage in crankcase. Crankshaft oil seals should be installed so they are ¹⁄₃₂ inch (0.79 mm) below flush with seal

bores. Refer to CONNECTING ROD section for remainder of assembly procedure.

NOTE: When installing the pto-side closure plate on splined-crankshaft engines below serial No. 1830500016, the correct alignment pins must be used to insure proper crankshaft run-out tolerances. Manufacture recommended and supplied pins are two inches long and 0.4979-0.4985 in. (12.65-12.66 mm) diameter for Hobart Welder applications or 0.4345-0.4355 in. (11.04-11.06 mm) diameter of all other splined applications. Splines must be lubricated every 500 hours of operation with Led-Plate antiseize compound or Dow Corning G-N Metal Assembly Paste or equivalent.

CAMSHAFT. The camshaft is supported at each end in bearings that are an integral part of the crankcase castings. To remove camshaft, split crankcase halves as outlined in CONNECTING ROD section. Be sure to identify tappets so they can be reinstalled in their original positions if reused.

Clearance between camshaft journals and bearing bores should be 0.0010-0.0025 inch (0.025-0.064 mm) for all models. Camshaft end play should be 0.003-0.013 inch (0.08-0.33 mm) and is controlled by shims installed between crankcase and camshaft at gear side of camshaft.

When replacing the camshaft on engines prior to Serial No. 1917809296, a separate 30 degree valve kit must be installed. The valve kit includes new valve and valve seat. Valve seat installation instructions are included with the kit.

When installing camshaft, make certain that crankshaft timing mark and camshaft timing mark are aligned as shown in Fig. KO147.

Fig. KO147—When installing crankshaft and camshaft, align timing marks as shown.

GOVERNOR. The mechanical governor (4—Fig. KO148 or Fig. KO149) is located in the crankcase. If governor gear is damaged or broken, crankcase halves must be split as outlined in CONNECTING ROD to remove the gear pieces. If governor gear is complete but governor must be removed, considerable time can be saved by only removing the No.2 cylinder barrel (with piston and pin), then carefully "fishing" the gear out of the cylinder opening using the jaws of a mechanical finger. Gear can be reinserted by using tag wire and mechanical fingers, and rocking the crankshaft so the camshaft

teeth will "walk" the governor gear back into place.

Engines with serial number 18063 and later have a thrust washer behind the gear; do not lose this washer. Older engines prior to this serial number should be upgraded to the new style governor gear with thrust washer when replacing the original gear.

A 0.002 in. (0.05 mm) press fit holds the governor shaft (7—Fig. KO148 or Fig. KO149) in position in its crankcase bore. A retainer is installed as a secondary stop. Shaft retention and fit are unaffected by normal engine operation; however, abnormal thermal expansion

of the crankcase due to overheating from obstructed cooling surfaces can allow the stub shaft to loosen. If failure occurs in which the crankcase is still usable but the press-fit is slightly loose, the governor stub shaft can be pinned to the crankcase as follows:

Insure that governor shaft bore in crankcase is clean and dry, and use a new shaft. Apply Loctite 609 to the larger OD of governor shaft and inside the bore in the crankcase. Install the governor shaft, with small diameter facing inward, to a depth of 0.285 in. (7.1 mm) from outer edge of crankcase bore. Allow the Loctite to set. Using a

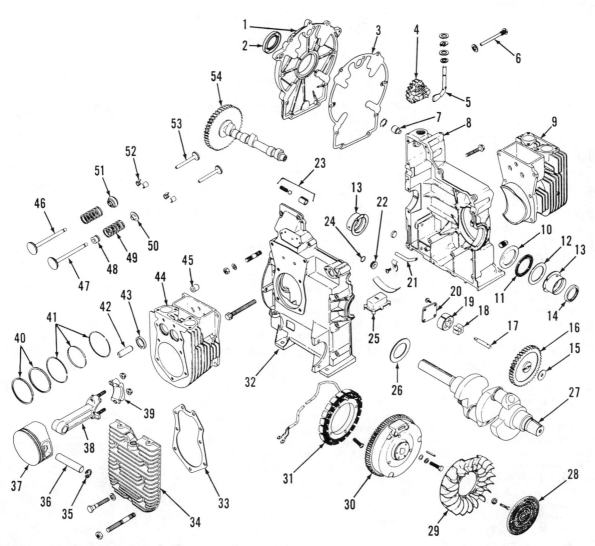

Fig. KO148—Exploded view of Kohler twin-cylinder, horizontal crankshaft engine.

1. Closure plate	10. Thrust washer	19. Outer rotor	28. Screen	37. Piston	46. Exhaust valve
2. Oil seal	11. Thrust bearing	20. Pump cover	29. Fan	38. Connecting rod	47. Intake valve
3. Gasket	12. Thrust washer	21. Oil pickup tube	30. Flywheel	39. Rod cap	48. Valve seal
4. Governor assy.	13. Main bearing	22. Camshaft bore plug	31. Stator	40. Compression rings	49. Spring
5. Governor cross shaft	14. Oil seal	23. Oil pressure relief valve	32. Crankcase half	41. Oil ring	50. Spring retainer
6. Governor stop pin	15. Spacer	24. "O" ring	33. Head gasket	42. Valve guide	51. Valve rotator
7. Governor stub shaft	16. Oil pump gear	25. Oil pickup screen	34. Cylinder head	43. Valve seat insert	52. Split retainer
8. Crankcase half	17. Oil pump shaft	26. Thrust washer	35. Retaining ring	44. Cylinder barrel	53. Tappet
9. Cylinder barrel	18. Inner rotor	27. Crankshaft	36. Piston pin	45. Alignment bushing	54. Camshaft

Fig. KO149—Exploded view of Kohler twin-cylinder, vertical crankshaft engine.

1. Oil seal
2. Oil pan
4. Governor assy.
5. Governor cross shaft
6. Governor stop pin
7. Governor stub shaft
8. Crankcase half
9. Cylinder barrel
13. Main bearing
14. Oil seal
15. Spacer
16. Oil pump gear
17. Oil pump shaft
18. Inner rotor
19. Outer rotor
20. Pump cover
23. Oil pressure relief valve
26. Thrust washer
27. Crankshaft
28. Screen
30. Flywheel
31. Stator
32. Crankcase half
33. Head gasket
34. Cylinder head
35. Retaining ring
36. Piston pin
37. Piston
38. Connecting rod
39. Rod cap
40. Compression rings
41. Oil ring
42. Valve seat insert
43. Valve guide
44. Cylinder barrel
46. Exhaust valve
47. Intake valve
48. Valve seal
49. Spring
50. Spring retainer
51. Valve rotator
52. Split retainer
53. Tappet
54. Camshaft

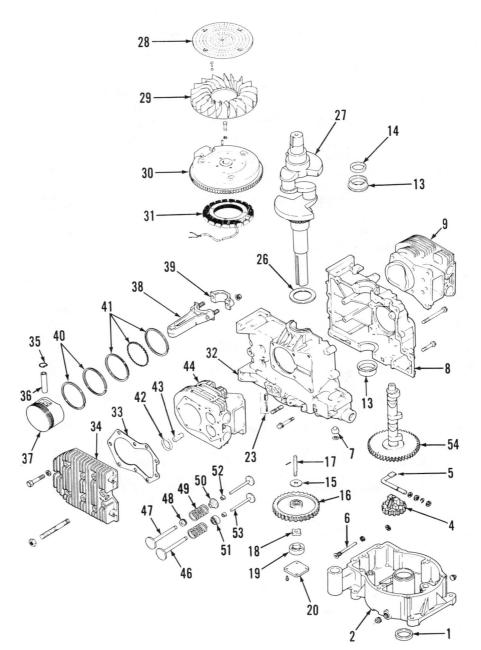

$\frac{3}{32}$ or $\frac{1}{8}$ inch cobalt or carbide tipped drill bit, carefully drill through the curved outer boss area of the crankcase casting and about halfway into the case-hardened governor shaft. Do not allow the drill bit to walk or wander, elongating the hole. Install a $\frac{3}{4}$ to $\frac{7}{8}$ inch long roll pin into the drilled hole. Any portion of roll pin that is exposed may be trimmed. Install new governor shaft retainer against the shaft inside the crankcase recess.

VALVE SYSTEM. Refer to VALVE ADJUSTMENT under MAINTENANCE section for valve clearance and adjustment information.

To remove valves, remove breather/valve cover assemblies and cylinder heads. Compress the valve springs and remove valve spring retainers.

All models have renewable hardened alloy exhaust valve seats. Exhaust valve face and seat angles are 45° for early models, and 30° for later models (serial numbers 1917809296 and higher). Valve face and seat angles are 30° for all replacement exhaust valves and seats. Intake valve face and seat angles are 45° for all models.

Standard seat width for all valves is 0.037-0.045 inch (0.94-1.14 mm). See Fig. KO148. To renew valve seats, use a

suitable puller (Tool No. NU-11726 or NU-11913) to remove the valve seats from cylinder barrel. Be sure new seat is bottomed in cylinder barrel counterbore.

Valve stem-to-guide clearance should be 0.0025-0.0045 inch (0.064-0.114 mm) for the intake valve and 0.0045-0.0065 inch (0.114-0.165 mm) for the exhaust valve on all models. If intake valve stem diameter is 0.3103 inch (7.882 mm) or less, renew valve. If exhaust valve stem diameter is 0.3088 inch (7.843 mm) or less, renew valve.

Standard inside diameter for intake and exhaust valve guides is 0.3125 inch (7.94 mm). If intake valve guide inside

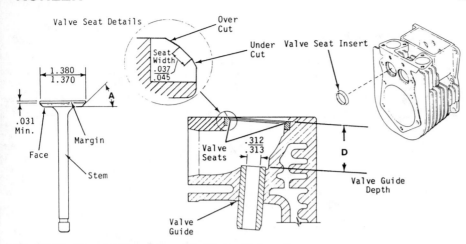

Fig. KO150—View showing valve specifications and information.

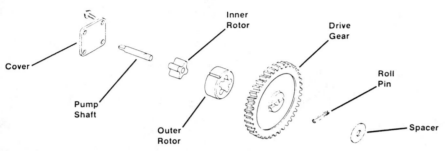

Fig. KO151—Exploded view of the rotor type oil pump used on all models.

diameter is worn 0.005 inch (0.13 mm) or more, or if exhaust valve guide inside diameter is worn 0.007 inch (0.18 mm) or more, renew guides.

Use a suitable puller to remove old valve guide, and install new valve guide using a suitable valve guide driver. Guide should be installed so end sur-

face of guide is 1.125 inches (28.57 mm) below top edge of valve seat on Models M18, MV16 and MV18, or 1.390 inches (35.31 mm) on Models M20 and MV20. See Fig. KO150.

Install new intake valve seals on intake valve guides. Lubricate valve stems with Dow Corning G-N Metal Assembly Paste or Led-Plate antiseize compound or equivalent. Position valves in cylinder barrel and check valve clearance as outlined in MAINTENANCE section. Install valve springs with close coils facing away from spring retainers. Complete installation by reversing the removal procedure.

OIL PUMP. All models are equipped with a rotor type oil pump driven by the crankshaft (Fig. KO151). Oil pump assembly is located behind closure plate (horizontal crankshaft) or oil pan (vertical crankshaft) on pto side of engine. Oil pump rotors, cover and pressure relief valve on all models can be serviced without splitting the crankcase.

Oil pump shaft-to-crankcase clearance should be 0.0010-0.0025 inch (0.025-0.064 mm). Oil pump drive gear end play should be 0.010-0.029 inch (0.25-0.74 mm).

Free length of oil pressure relief valve spring should be 0.992 inch (25.20 mm).

Oil pump cover (Fig. KO149) outer side is marked "OUT" and is retained by self-tapping screws.

KOHLER

KOHLER COMPANY
Kohler, Wisconsin 53044

Model	No. Cyls.	Bore	Stroke	Displacement	Power Rating
CH11, CV11	1	87 mm (3.43 in.)	67 mm (2.64 in.)	398 cc (24.3 cu. in.)	8.2 kW (11 hp)
CH12.5, CV12.5	1	87 mm (3.43 in.)	67 mm (2.64 in.)	398 cc (24.3 cu. in.)	9.33 kW (12.5 hp)
CH14, CV14	1	87 mm (3.43 in.)	67 mm (2.64 in.)	398 cc (24.3 cu. in.)	10.5 kW (14 hp)
CH15, CV15	1	90 mm (3.55 in.)	67 mm (2.64 in.)	426 cc (26.0 cu. in.)	11.2 kW (15 hp)
CV16	1	90 mm (3.55 in.)	67 mm (2.64 in.)	398 cc (26.0 cu. in.)	11.9 kW (16 hp)

NOTE: Metric fasteners are used throughout engine.

The Kohler engines covered in this section are four-stroke, air-cooled, single-cylinder engines using an overhead valve system. Engine identification numbers are located on a decal affixed to flywheel fan shroud. Refer to preceding Kohler section for engine identification information.

MAINTENANCE

LUBRICATION. Periodically check oil level; do not overfill. To check oil level, seat the dipstick cap on the oil fill tube. Remove the dipstick and check oil level on dipstick. Oil level should be up to, but not over, the "F" mark on dipstick.

Manufacturer recommends using oil with an API service rating of SG or SH, or any rating formulated to supercede SG or SH. Use SAE 10W-30 oil for temperatures above 0° F (−18° C). When operating in temperatures below 32° F (0° C), SAE 5W-20, 5W-30 or 10W-30 oil may be used, except 10W-30 oil should not be used below 0° F (−18° C). Do not use SAE 10W-40 oil in any temperature.

In overhauled or new engines or short blocks, use SAE 10W-30 oil for first 5 hours of operation, then change oil according to ambient temperature requirements. Recommended oil change interval after 5-hour break-in is every 100 hours of operation. Oil should be drained while engine is warm.

It is recommended that a new oil filter be installed at each oil change. Apply a light coating of clean engine oil to filter gasket. Install oil filter until the rubber gasket contacts the filter adapter plate, then tighten an additional ½ turn.

Crankcase oil capacity is approximately 2.1 quarts (2.0 L) with oil filter.

The engine may be equipped with a low-oil sensor. The sensor circuit may be designed to stop engine or trigger a warning device if oil level is low.

AIR FILTER. The engine is equipped with a foam precleaner element and paper-type air filter. Service the precleaner after every 25 hours of operation and the air filter after every 100 hours of operation. Service more frequently if engine is operated in severe conditions.

Clean precleaner element by washing in soapy water. Allow to dry then apply clean engine oil. Squeeze out excess oil.

The air filter should be renewed rather than cleaned. Do not wash or direct pressurized air at filter.

After performing air cleaner maintenance on horizontal-shaft engines, insure that inner air cleaner cover (Fig. KO200A) is properly installed so that the baffle on the back of the inner air filter cover does not interfere with the spit-back tray on the air cleaner base. Interference at this point can prevent the air filter cover from sealing properly. Note that spit-back tray is standard equipment on horizontal-shaft engines beginning with serial No. 2512100014; earlier horizontal-shaft engines will benefit by being upgraded with this spit-back control tray.

NOTE: Vertical-shaft engines prior to serial No. 2813402183: It is recommended that a short stud seat, part No. 230046, be installed over the air filter stud above the air filter element wing nut (Fig. KO200B) to prevent the wing nut from loosening during engine operation. Engines after this serial number are equipped with this seal from the factory. Insure that the seal is in place prior to installing air cleaner cover.

FUEL FILTER. If so equipped, periodically inspect fuel filter. If dirty or damaged, renew filter.

CRANKCASE BREATHER. A breather valve is attached to the top of

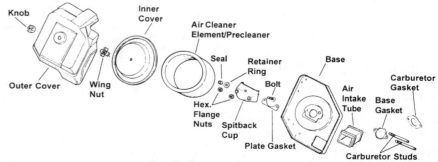

Fig. KO200A—Exploded view of air filter components on CH engines with spitback tray on air filter base. Inner cover must not interfere with spitback tray, or cover will not seal.

the cylinder head under the rocker cover. A tube connects valve cover to the air cleaner base to allow crankcase vapors to be burned by the engine. Inspect and clean breather valve as needed to prevent or remove restrictions.

SPARK PLUG. Recommended spark plug is Champion RC12YC or equivalent. Specified electrode gap is 1.0 mm (0.040 in.). Tighten spark plug to 38-43 N•m (28-32 ft.-lbs.).

NOTE: Manufacturer does not recommend spark plug cleaning using abrasive grit as grit may enter engine.

CARBURETOR. Initial setting of idle mixture screw (Fig. KO201) is $1\frac{1}{4}$ turns out on Models CH11 and CH12.5, $1\frac{3}{4}$ turns out on Model CH14, and one turn out on all CV models. Initial setting of high-speed mixture screw is $1\frac{1}{2}$ turns out on Models CH11 and CH12.5, and $1\frac{1}{4}$ turns out on Model CH14 (there is no high-speed mixture screw on CV models). Final adjustment of mixture screws should be made with engine at normal operating temperature. Adjust idle speed screw so engine idles at 1500 rpm on CH models and at 1200 rpm on CV models, or at speed specified by equipment manufacturer. Turn the idle mixture screw counterclockwise until engine rpm decreases and note screw position. Turn screw clockwise until engine rpm decreases again and note

screw position. Turn screw to midpoint between the two noted positions. Reset idle speed screw if necessary to obtain desired idle speed.

To adjust high-speed mixture screw (Fig. KO201) on CH models, run engine at maximum speed under load. Slowly rotate high-speed mixture screw in until engine speed decreases, then turn screw out $\frac{1}{4}$ turn.

A fixed main jet controls the high-speed mixture on CV models. No optional jets are offered, although a high altitude kit may be available for non-EPA/CARB compliant engines.

To disassemble carburetor, refer to Fig. KO202. The edges of throttle and choke plates (3 and 8) are beveled and must be reinstalled in their original positions. Mark choke and throttle plates before removal to ensure correct assembly. Use a suitably sized screw to pull out the fuel inlet seat if seat is to be renewed. Do not reinstall a seat that has been removed. Use a sharp punch to pierce Welch plug and pry plug from carburetor body. Be careful to prevent punch from contacting and damaging carburetor body.

Clean all parts in suitable carburetor cleaner and blow out all passages with compressed air. Be careful not to enlarge any fuel passages or jets as calibration of carburetor may be altered.

Press new fuel inlet seat into carburetor body so seat is bottomed. Apply Loctite 609 to throttle plate retaining screw. Be sure throttle plate is properly seated against carburetor bore before tightening screw. Be sure choke shaft properly engages detent spring on carburetor. Locking tabs on choke plate must straddle choke shaft. Use a suitable sealant on Welch plug.

On CV-16 engines with self-relieving choke, the original design choke lever housing has a cavity on the underside that allows the lever to pivot around

the stop pin. In dirty or dusty operation, the cavity can accumulate dirt hindering both movement and travel of the choke lever. Periodically remove choke housing and clean cavity, or replace housing with manufacturer's upgraded choke repair kit (part No. 12 757 32) which has an exposed cavity, preventing dirt buildup.

IGNITION. The engine is equipped with a breakerless, electronic magneto ignition system. The electronic ignition module is mounted outside the flywheel. The ignition switch grounds the module to stop the engine. There is no periodic maintenance or adjustment required with this ignition system.

Air gap between module and flywheel should be 0.20-0.30 mm (0.008-0.012 in.). Loosen module retaining screws and position module to obtain desired gap. Tighten screws to 4 N•m (35 in.-lbs.) for used engines or to 6.2 N•m

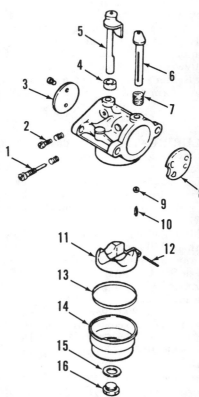

Fig. KO202—Exploded view of float-type carburetor used on all engines. A high-speed mixture screw is located in bottom of fuel bowl in place of retaining screw (16) on CH models. Some engines may be equipped with an electric fuel shut-off solenoid located in bottom of fuel bowl in place of retaining screw (16).

1. Idle mixture screw
2. Idle speed screw
3. Throttle plate
4. Throttle shaft dust seal
5. Throttle shaft
6. Choke shaft
7. Return spring
8. Choke plate
9. Fuel inlet valve seat
10. Fule inlet valve
11. Float
12. Float shaft
13. Gasket
14. Fuel bowl
15. Gasket
16. Retaining screw

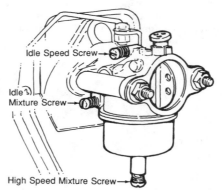

Fig. KO201—View of carburetor showing adjustment points. High-speed mixture screw is not used on CV models. Some models may be equipped with a fuel shutoff solenoid valve on bottom of fuel bowl.

Fig. KO200B—Exploded view of air filter components on CV engines showing position of short seal over inner wing nut. Seal prevents wing nut from loosening.

Air Cleaner Cover w/Knob
Foam Precleaner
Short Seal
Wing Nut
Air Cleaner Element w/Seals
Long Seal
Screw (2)
Stud
Gasket
Air Cleaner Base

(55 in.-lbs.) on a new engine cylinder block.

If ignition module fails to produce a spark, check for faulty kill switch or grounded wires. Measure resistance of ignition module secondary using suitable ohmmeter. Connect one test lead to spark plug terminal of high-tension wire and other test lead to module core laminations. Resistance should be 7900-10,850 ohms. If resistance is low or infinite, renew module.

GOVERNOR. A flyweight-type governor is located in the crankcase. The governor gear is driven by the camshaft gear. Refer to REPAIRS section for overhaul information.

To adjust governor linkage, proceed as follows: Loosen governor lever clamp nut (N—Fig. KO203) and push the governor lever so throttle is wide open. Turn the governor shaft (S) counterclockwise as far as possible and tighten clamp nut.

The engine should never run at speeds exceeding 3750 rpm. Maximum high-speed setting depends on engine application. Use a tachometer to check engine speed.

To adjust high idle speed setting on CV models, first loosen throttle control cable clamp (Fig. KO204A). Move the equipment speed control lever to "Fast" position. Align the hole in throttle lever with hole in speed control bracket by inserting a pencil or drill bit through the

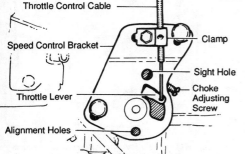

Fig. KO203—View of governor external linkage. Refer to text for adjustment procedure.

holes. Pull up on throttle control cable shield to remove slack and tighten cable clamp.

Start the engine and allow it to reach operating temperature. Align hole in throttle lever with hole in speed control bracket as previously outlined. Loosen speed control bracket mounting screws and move bracket up (toward flywheel) to decrease high idle speed or down (toward pto) to increase high idle speed. When desired speed is obtained, tighten control bracket screws to 10.7 N•m (95 in.-lbs.) on a new short block or to 7.3 N•m (65 in.-lbs.) on all other engines.

On CH models, governor spring end should be located in following specified hole from end of governor lever for specified high idle speed: outer hole for 3800 rpm, second hole for 3600 rpm, third hole for 3400 rpm, fifth hole for 3200, sixth hole for 3000 rpm. Note that throttle end of governor spring is attached to third hole from top of throttle lever for 3800 rpm and first hole for all other speeds.

Governor sensitivity is adjusted by positioning governor spring in different holes in governor lever arm. On CV models, it is recommended that spring be installed in the hole closest to governor shaft if high idle speed is 3600 rpm or less. If high idle speed is greater than 3600 rpm, use the second hole that is farthest from governor cross shaft. On CH models, governor sensitivity is adjusted by reattaching governor spring to another hole in governor arm. Move spring to an outer hole on arm to decrease governor sensitivity.

On vertical-shaft engines with governed idle control (Fig. KO204B), if idle speed adjustment is necessary, manually move the governor lever so throttle shaft (5—Fig. KO202) is tight against idle speed stop screw (2). Check idle speed with a tachometer and adjust idle speed stop screw to obtain 900-1000 rpm. Release governor lever and allow engine to return to governed idle speed. If idle speed is not within equipment manufacturer's specification, turn gov-

erned idle speed adjusting screw (Fig. KO204B) clockwise to increase idle speed or counterclockwise to decrease speed.

VALVE CLEARANCE. All models are equipped with hydraulic valve lifters that automatically maintain proper valve clearance. No periodic adjustment is required.

REPAIRS

TIGHTENING TORQUE. Recommended tightening torque values are as follows:

Air cleaner base	9.9 N•m (88 in.-lb.)
Charging stator	4.0 N•m (35 in.-lb.)
Connecting rod	(See Text)
Crankcase cover/oil pan	24.4 N•m (216 in.-lb.)
Cylinder head	40.7 N•m (30 ft.-lb.)
Rocker arm pedestal	9.9 N•m (88 in.-lb.)
Flywheel	66 N•m (49 ft.-lb.)
Fuel pump*	7.3/9.0 N•m (65/80 in.-lb.)
Governor lever	9.9 N•m (88 in.-lb.)
Ignition module*	4.0/6.2 N•m (35/55 in.-lb.)
Muffler	24.4 N•m (216 in.-lb.)
Oil drain plug	8.0 N•m (70 in.-lb.)
Oil Sentry switch	8.0 N•m (70 in.-lb.)
Oil pump cover*	4.0/6.2 N•m (35/55 in.-lb.)

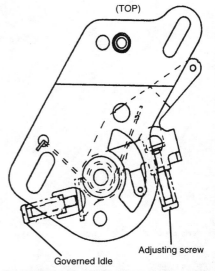

(TOP)

Adjusting screw

Governed Idle

Fig. KO204B—View of throttle control on engines with governed idle. Refer to text for adjustment procedure.

Fig. KO204A—View of typical speed control linkage on CV models. Refer to text for adjustment procedure.

Throttle Control Cable

Speed Control Bracket

Clamp

Sight Hole

Choke Adjusting Screw

Throttle Lever

Alignment Holes

Spark plug. . . . . 38.0-43.4 N•m
(28-32 ft. in.-lb.)
Speed control bracket* . . 7.3/10.7 N•m
(65/95 in.-lb.)
Starter drive pinion . . . . . . 15.3 N•m
(135 in.-lb.)
Valve cover*. . . . . 7.3/10.7 N•m
(65/95 in.-lb.)

*When installing self-tapping fasteners into new unthreaded holes, use higher torque value; use lower torque value for installation into previously tapped holes and weld nuts.

FUEL PUMP. Some engines may be equipped with a mechanically operated diaphragm-type fuel pump. An eccentric on engine camshaft actuates the fuel pump. Individual components are not available; pump must be renewed as a unit assembly.

When installing fuel pump assembly, make certain that fuel pump lever is positioned to the right side of camshaft. Damage to fuel pump and engine may result if lever is positioned on left side of camshaft. Tighten fuel pump mounting screws to 9.0 N•m (80 in.-lbs.) for first-time installation on new short block. On all other engines, tighten mounting screws to 7.3 N•m (65 in.-lbs.).

When repairing an engine with oil leaking around fuel pump mounting pad, or if fuel pump body is cracked, visually inspect mounting pad face. If mounting face has machined surface, a spacer must be installed between fuel pump gasket and mounting pad face to

prevent recurring damage. The spacer is furnished in the manufacturer's replacement fuel pump kit.

CYLINDER HEAD. To remove cylinder head, remove air cleaner assembly and base. Detach speed control linkage and fuel line. Unbolt and remove carburetor and muffler. Remove recoil starter, blower housing and cylinder head air baffles and shields. Remove rocker arm cover. Rotate crankshaft so piston is at top dead center on compression stroke. Push rods and rocker arms should be marked so they can be reinstalled in their original position. Unscrew cylinder head bolts and remove cylinder head and gasket.

To disassemble, remove spark plug. Remove breather retainer (14—Fig. KO205) and reed (15). Push the rocker shaft (13) out the breather side of rocker arm bridge (12) and remove the rocker arms (11). Use a valve spring compressor tool to compress valve springs. Remove the split retainers (2), release the spring tension and remove valves from cylinder head.

Clean combustion deposits from cylinder head and inspect for cracks or other damage. Check cylinder head surface for flatness; renew head if warped more than 0.076 mm (0.003 in.).

To assemble cylinder head components, reverse disassembly procedure. Be sure rocker pedestal (12) is installed with small counterbored hole toward exhaust port side of cylinder head. Tighten rocker pedestal mounting

screws to 9.9 N•m (88 in.-lbs.). Install a new stem seal (6) on intake valve; do not reuse old seal.

NOTE: New cylinder head bolts should always be installed. The rust-preventative coating on the bolts affects torque retention, and most of the coating wears off the threads once bolts are installed and tightened. Attempting to reuse bolts results in loss of torque retention, and will likely cause short term head gasket failure.

Reverse removal procedure to reinstall head. Tighten cylinder head screws in increments of 14 N•m (10 ft.-lbs.) following sequence shown in Fig. KO206 until final torque of 41 N•m (30 ft.-lbs.) is reached. Install push rods in their original position, compress valve springs and snap push rods underneath rocker arms.

Silicone sealant is used as a gasket between valve cover and cylinder head. GE Silmate-type RTV-1473 or RTV-108 sealant (or equivalent) is recommended. The use of a silicone removing solvent is recommended to remove old silicone gasket, as scraping the mating surfaces may damage them and could cause leaks. Apply a 1.6 mm (1/16 in.) bead of sealant to gasket surface of cylinder head. Follow tightening sequence shown in Fig. KO207 and tighten valve cover screws to 10.7 N•m (95 in.-lbs.) if a new cylinder head is installed, or to 7.3 N•m (65 in.-lbs.) if original head is installed.

VALVE SYSTEM. Clean valve heads and stems with a wire brush. Inspect each valve for warped or burned head, pitting or worn stem and renew as required.

Valve face and seat angles are 45° for intake and exhaust. Renew valve if valve margin is less than 1.5 mm (0.060 in.) after grinding valve face.

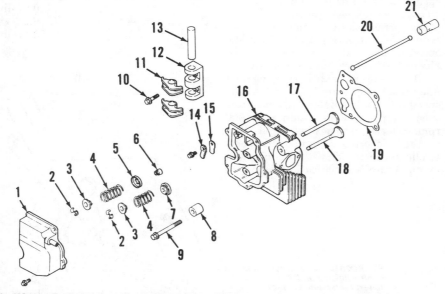

Fig. KO205—Exploded view of cylinder head and valve components. Exhaust valve rotator (7) is used on early production CV model engines before S.N. 1933593554.

1. Valve cover	
2. Split retainer	7. Valve rotator (exhaust)
3. Spring retainer	8. Spacer
4. Valve spring	9. Head bolt
5. Spring seat	10. Screw
6. Valve seal (intake)	11. Rocker arm

12. Rocker bridge	17. Intake valve
13. Rocker shaft	18. Exhaust valve
14. Retainer plate	19. Head gasket
15. Breather reed	20. Push rod
16. Cylinder head	21. Valve lifter

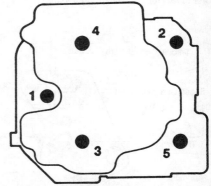

Fig. KO206—Follow sequence shown when tightening cylinder head bolts. Refer to text.

Specified valve stem-to-guide clearance is 0.038-0.076 mm (0.0015-0.0030 in.) for intake valve and 0.050-0.088 mm (0.0020-0.0035 in.) for exhaust valve. Specified new valve stem diameter is 6.982-7.000 mm (0.2749-0.2756 in.) for intake and 6.970-6.988 mm (0.2744-0.2751 in.) for exhaust. Specified new valve guide inside diameter for either valve is 7.033-7.058 mm (0.2769-0.2779 in.). Maximum allowable valve guide inside diameter is 7.134 mm (0.2809 in.) for intake guide and 7.159 mm (0.2819 in.) for exhaust

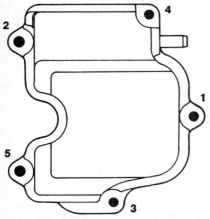

Fig. KO207—Follow sequence shown when tightening valve cover mounting screws. Refer to text.

guide. Valve guides are not renewable; however, guides can be reamed to accept valves with 0.25 mm oversize stem.

On late production CV engines, starting with serial number 1933503554, the exhaust valve rotator (7—Fig. KO205) has been eliminated and a new spring seat with different length valve spring is used in its place. Free length of the new valve spring is 55.8 mm (2.197 in.), and spring is color coded green for identification. Free length of early production exhaust valve spring is 48.69 mm (1.917 in.).

Note that three different styles of rocker arms and pivots (Fig. KO208) are used. Engines with serial No. 2617200734 and higher use the latest Style "C." If rocker arm replacement is required due to valve train wear, Style "B" can be upgraded to Style "C" with engine manufacturer's retrofit kit. Engines with Style "A" components can only be upgraded to Style "C" by installing a complete new cylinder head.

CAMSHAFT AND HYDRAULIC LIFTERS. To remove camshaft, first rotate crankshaft so piston is at top dead center on compression stroke. Remove the rocker cover, compress the valve springs and disengage the push rods from rocker arms. Remove push rods while marking them so they can be

returned to original position. Remove crankcase cover or oil pan mounting screws, then pry cover or oil pan from crankcase at prying lugs located on cover or oil pan. Rotate crankshaft so timing marks on crankshaft and camshaft gears are aligned. Remove camshaft from crankcase. Identify the valve lifters as either intake or exhaust so they can be returned to original position, then remove lifters from crankcase.

The camshaft is equipped with a compression reduction device to aid starting. The lever and weight mechanism on the camshaft gear moves a pin inside the exhaust cam lobe. During starting the pin protrudes above the cam lobe and forces the exhaust valve to stay open longer thereby reducing compression. At running speeds the pin remains below the surface of the cam lobe. Inspect mechanism for proper operation.

Inspect camshaft and lifters for scoring, pitting and excessive wear. Minimum cam lobe height is 8.96 mm (0.353 in.) for intake lobe and 9.14 mm (0.360 in.) for exhaust lobe. If camshaft is renewed, new valve lifters should also be installed.

If the hydraulic valve lifters are noisy after engine has run for several minutes and reached operating temperature, it is probably an indication that contamination is preventing the lifter check ball from seating or there is internal wear in the lifter. Individual parts are not available for the hydraulic lifters. Lifters should be renewed if faulty.

Current production engines are equipped with new style "quick-purge" lifters that reduce the lifter pump-up time and resultant noisy operation during engine start-up. The new style lifters, part No. 25 351 01, are available for service replacement on all engines.

Lubricate lifter bores with oil and install hydraulic lifters in their original position. The exhaust lifter bore is closest to crankcase gasket surface.

Install camshaft, aligning timing marks (Fig. KO209) on crankshaft and camshaft gears as shown. Camshaft end play is adjusted with shims (19—Fig. KO210 or KO211), which are installed between camshaft and crankcase cover or oil pan. To determine camshaft end play, install camshaft with original thickness shim in crankcase. Attach end play checking tool KO-1031 to crankcase and use a feeler gauge to measure clearance between the shim and checking tool. Camshaft end play should be 0.076-0.127 mm (0.003-0.005 in.). Install different thickness shim as necessary to obtain desired end play.

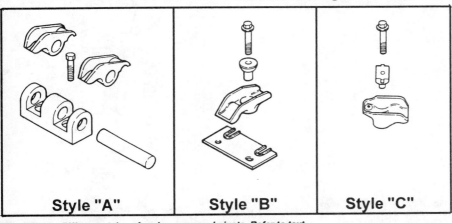

Style "A"   Style "B"   Style "C"

Fig. KO208—Different styles of rocker arms and pivots. Refer to text.

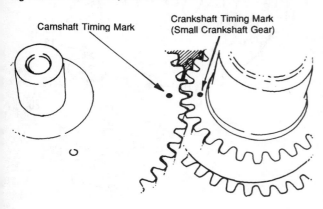

Camshaft Timing Mark   Crankshaft Timing Mark (Small Crankshaft Gear)

Fig. KO209—Align timing mark on small crankshaft gear with timing mark on camshaft gear.

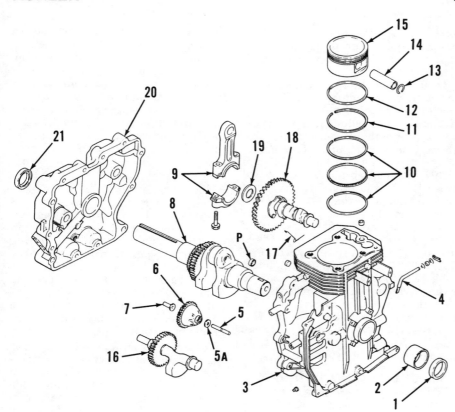

Fig. KO210—Exploded view of crankcase/cylinder block assembly of CH models.

1. Oil seal
2. Main bearing
3. Crankcase/cylinder block
4. Governor cross shaft
5. Governor gear shaft
5A. Thrust washer
6. Governor gear assy.
7. Governor pin
8. Crankshaft
9. Connecting rod
10. Oil control ring
11. Second compression ring
12. Top compression ring
13. Snap ring
14. Piston pin
15. Piston
16. Balance shaft & gear assy.
17. Compression release spring
18. Camshaft & gear assy.
19. Shim
20. Crankcase cover
21. Oil seal

No gasket is used with crankcase cover or oil pan. Apply a 1.6 mm (1/16 in.) bead of silicone gasket sealant (GE Silmate RTV-108, RTV-1473 or equivalent) around crankcase cover or oil pan mating surface as shown in Fig. KO212. Tighten crankcase cover or oil pan screws to 24.4 N•m (216 in.-lbs.) using sequence shown in Fig. KO213.

After completing assembly of engine, rotate crankshaft slowly and check for compression. If there is compression, valves are seating and engine may be started.

PISTON, PIN AND RINGS. The piston and connecting rod are removed as an assembly. Remove cylinder head and camshaft as previously outlined. Remove balance shaft from crankcase. Remove carbon deposits and ring ridge (if present) from top of cylinder before removing piston and rod assembly. Remove connecting rod cap and push connecting rod and piston out of cylinder. Remove piston pin retaining rings and separate piston and rod.

To determine piston clearance in cylinder, measure piston skirt diameter at a point 6 mm (0.24 in.) from bottom of skirt and perpendicular to piston pin bore. Measure cylinder bore inside diameter at point of greatest wear, approximately 63 mm (2.5 in.) below top

Fig. KO211—Exploded view of crankcase/cylinder block assembly of CV models.

1. Oil seal
2. Main bearing
3. Crankcase/cylinder block
4. Governor cross shaft
5. Governor gear shaft
5A. Thrust washer
6. Governor gear assy.
7. Governor pin
8. Crankshaft
9. Connecting rod
10. Oil control ring
11. Second compression ring
12. Top compression ring
13. Snap ring
14. Piston pin
15. Piston
16. Balance shaft & gear assy.
17. Compression release spring
18. Camshaft & gear assy.
19. Shim
20. Oil pan
21. Oil seal

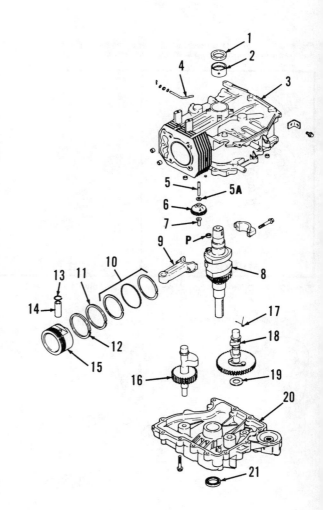

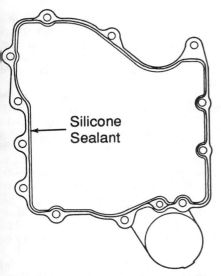

Fig. KO212—Apply silicone sealant in a 1.6 mm (1/16 in) bead around crankcase cover mating surface as shown.

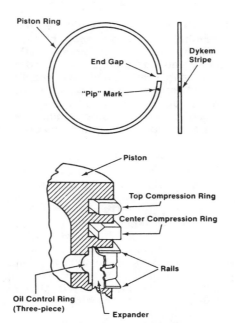

Fig. KO214—Cross-sectional view of piston showing correct installation of piston rings. Refer to text for details.

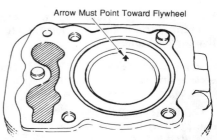

Fig. KO215—Piston must be installed with arrow pointing toward flywheel side of engine.

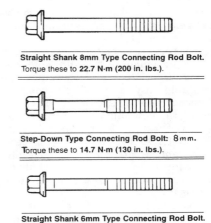

Straight Shank 8mm Type Connecting Rod Bolt. Torque these to 22.7 N·m (200 in. lbs.).

Step-Down Type Connecting Rod Bolt: 8mm. Torque these to 14.7 N·m (130 in. lbs.).

Straight Shank 6mm Type Connecting Rod Bolt. Torque these to 11.3 N·m (100 in. lbs.).

Fig. KO216—Different styles of connecting rod bolts. Refer to text.

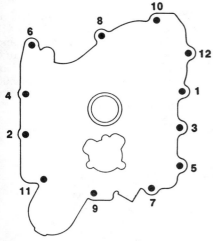

Fig. KO213—Follow sequence shown when tightening crankcase cover or oil pan mounting screws.

of cylinder and perpendicular to piston pin. The difference between the two measurements is piston clearance in bore, which should be 0.041-0.044 mm (0.0016-0.0017 in.).

Piston and rings are available in standard size and oversizes of 0.25 and 0.50 mm (0.010 and 0.020 in.). Standard piston skirt diameter is 86.941-86.959 mm (3.4229-3.4236 in.), and wear limit is 86.814 mm (3.418 in.).

Specified piston pin bore is 19.006-19.012 mm (0.7483-0.7485 in.), and wear limit is 19.025 mm (0.749 in.). Specified piston pin diameter 18.995-19.000 mm (0.7478-0.7480 in.), and wear limit is 18.994 mm (0.7478 in.). Piston-to-piston pin clearance should be 0.006-0.017 mm (0.0002-0.0007 in.).

Insert new rings in piston ring grooves and measure ring side clear-ance using a feeler gauge. Piston ring side clearance should be 0.040-0.105 mm (0.0016-0.0041 in.) for top compres-sion ring; 0.040-0.072 mm (0.0016-0.0028 in.) for second compres-sion ring; 0.551-0.675 mm (0.0217-0.0266 in.) for oil control ring. Renew piston if side clearance is exces-sive.

Specified piston ring end gap for com-pression rings is 0.30-0.50 mm (0.012-0.020 in.). Maximum allowable ring end gap in a used cylinder is 0.77 mm (0.030 in.).

When assembling piston rings on pis-ton, install oil control ring expander (Fig. KO214) first and then the side rails. Install compression rings so side marked with "pip" mark is toward pis-ton crown and stripe on face of ring is to the left of end gap. Second compression ring has a bevel on inside of ring and has a pink stripe on face of ring. Top compression ring has a barrel face and has a blue stripe on face of ring. Stagger ring end gaps evenly around the piston.

Lubricate piston and cylinder with oil, then use suitable ring compressor tool to install piston and rod. Be sure that arrow on piston crown is toward flywheel side of crankcase as shown in Fig. KO215. Refer to CONNECTING ROD section for connecting rod tighten-ing torque. Install balance shaft, cam-shaft and cylinder head as outlined in appropriate sections.

CONNECTING ROD. Piston and connecting rod are removed as an as-sembly as outlined in PISTON, PIN AND RINGS section. Remove piston pin retaining rings and separate piston and rod.

Renew connecting rod if bearing sur-faces are scored or excessively worn. Specified connecting rod small end di-ameter is 19.015-19.023 mm (0.7486-0.7489 in.), and wear limit is 19.036 mm (0.7495 in.). Specified con-necting rod-to-piston pin running clear-ance is 0.015-0.028 mm (0.0006-0.0011 in.).

Specified connecting rod-to-crankpin bearing clearance is 0.030-0.055 mm (0.0011-0.0022 in.), and maximum al-lowable clearance is 0.07 mm (0.0025 in.). A connecting rod with 0.25 mm (0.010 in.) undersize big end is avail-able. The undersized rod can be identi-fied by the drilled hole located in lower end of the rod.

Specified rod side clearance on crankpin is 0.18-0.41 mm (0.007-0.016 in.).

To reinstall connecting rod and pis-ton assembly, reverse the removal pro-cedure. Be sure that arrow mark on top of piston is toward flywheel side of crankcase (Fig. KO215).

NOTE: Three different style con-necting rod bolts are used (Fig. KO216). Each style bolt has a different

tightening torque. Refer to Fig. KO216 to identify rod bolts and their respective torque values.

Refer to PISTON, PIN AND RINGS section and reverse removal procedure to install remainder of components.

GOVERNOR. The engine is equipped with a flyweight mechanism mounted on governor gear (6—Figs. KO210 or KO211). Remove crankcase cover or oil pan (20) for access to governor gear. Inspect gear assembly for excess wear and damage. The governor gear is held onto governor shaft (5) by molded tabs on the gear. When gear is removed, the tabs are damaged and replacement of governor gear will be required. Gear and flyweight are available only as a unit assembly. If governor gear shaft (5) requires renewal, tap new shaft into crankcase so it protrudes 32.64-32.84 mm (1.285-1.293 in.) above crankcase boss. Remove cotter pin to remove governor lever shaft (4). Inspect shaft oil seal in crankcase bore and renew if necessary.

No gasket is used with crankcase cover or oil pan. Apply a 1.6 mm (1/16 in.) bead of silicone gasket sealant (GE Silmate RTV-108, RTV-1473 or equivalent) around crankcase cover or oil pan mating surface as shown in Fig. KO212. Tighten crankcase cover or oil pan screws to 24.4 N•m (216 in.-lbs.) using sequence shown in Fig. KO213. Adjust governor as previously outlined in MAINTENANCE section.

CRANKSHAFT. To remove crankshaft, remove starter and flywheel. Remove crankcase cover or oil pan, piston, connecting rod and camshaft as previously outlined. Remove balance shaft. Remove crankshaft from crankcase. The crankshaft rides in a renewable bushing (2—Fig. KO210 or KO211) in the crankcase and in an integral bearing in the crankcase cover or oil pan.

NOTE: When replacing a vertical-shaft crankshaft, short block, or engine, insure that the threads on PTO bolt removed from old crankshaft are compatible with threads in new crankshaft. Some equipment manufacturers have requested "inch" threads instead of metric. Some engine Spec Numbers could have either thread.

Specified main journal diameter at flywheel end is 44.913-44.935 mm (1.7682-1.7691 in.), and wear limit is 44.84 mm (1.765 in.). Bearing inside diameter at flywheel end is 44.965-45.003 mm (1.7703-1.7718 in.), and wear limit is 45.016 mm (1.7723 in.). Crankshaft-to-bearing running clearance should be 0.03-0.09 mm (0.0012-0.0035 in.). When renewing main bearing, make certain that oil hole in bearing aligns with oil passage in crankcase.

Specified main journal diameter at pto end is 41.915-41.935 mm (1.6502-1.6510 in.), and wear limit is 41.86 mm (1.648 in.). Crankshaft-to-oil pan bore running clearance should be 0.03-0.09 mm (0.0012-0.0035 in.).

Maximum allowable main journal taper is 0.020 mm (0.0008 in.) and maximum allowable out-of-round is 0.025 mm (0.0010 in.). Main journals cannot be machined undersize.

Specified standard crankpin diameter is 38.958-38.970 mm (1.5338-1.5343 in.). Minimum allowable crankpin diameter is 38.94 mm (1.533 in.). Maximum allowable crankpin taper is 0.012 mm (0.0005 in.) and maximum allowable out-of-round is 0.025 mm (0.0010 in.). Crankpin can be ground to accept a connecting rod that is 0.25 mm (0.010 in.) undersize. Plug (P—Fig. KO210 or KO211) should be removed after machining operation so oil passages can be cleaned thoroughly. Use a suitable screw-type puller to extract plug. Be sure new plug does not leak.

Maximum allowable crankshaft runout is 0.15 mm (0.006 in.) measured at

pto end of crankshaft with crankshaft supported in engine. Maximum allowable crankshaft runout is 0.10 mm (0.004 in.) measured at any point on crankshaft with crankshaft supported in V-blocks.

To install crankshaft, reverse the removal procedure. Install balance shaft aligning timing marks on large crankshaft gear and balance shaft gear as shown in Fig. KO217. Install camshaft aligning timing marks on small crankshaft gear and camshaft gear as shown in Fig. KO209. No gasket is used with crankcase cover or oil pan. Apply a 1.6 mm (1/16 in.) bead of silicone gasket sealant (GE Silmate RTV-108, RTV-1473 or equivalent) around crankcase cover or oil pan mating surface as shown in Fig. KO212. Tighten crankcase cover or oil pan screws to 24.4 N•m (216 in.-lbs.) using sequence shown in Fig. KO213. Tighten flywheel retaining nut to 66 N•m (49 ft.-lbs.).

CYLINDER/CRANKCASE. Cylinder bore standard diameter is 87.000-87.025 (3.4252-3.4262 in.), and wear limit is 87.063 mm (3.4277 in.). Maximum bore out-of-round is 0.12 mm (0.005 in.). Maximum bore taper is 0.05 mm (0.002 in.). Cylinder can be bored to accept an oversize piston.

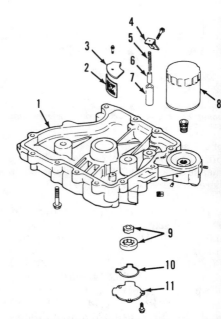

Fig. KO218—Gerotor-type engine oil pump is mounted in crankcase cover on CH models or in oil pan on CV models. Oil pickup screen (2) and cover (3) are used on CV models. Not shown is oil pickup tube assembly used on CH models.

1. Crankcase cover/oil pan
2. Oil pick-up screen
3. Cover
4. Relief valve bracket
5. Relief valve spring
6. Relief valve piston
7. Relief valve body
8. Oil filter
9. Inner & outer rotors
10. "O" ring
11. Pump cover

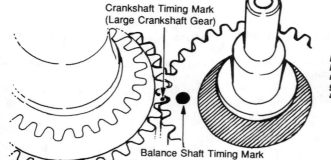

Fig. KO217—When assembling engine, align timing mark on large crankshaft gear with timing mark on balance shaft gear.

Install crankshaft oil seals in crankcase and oil pan using seal driver KO-1036. Force seal into crankcase or oil pan until tool bottoms.

OIL PUMP. A gerotor-type oil pump is located in crankcase cover of CH models or oil pan of CV models. The oil pump is driven by the engine balance shaft. Oil pump rotors (9—Fig. KO218) can be removed for inspection after removing pump cover (11) from bottom of crankcase cover or oil pan. The crankcase cover or oil pan must be removed for access to oil pick-up or oil pressure regulator valve (5 through 7).

Check oil pump rotors and oil pan cavity for scoring or excessive wear. Pressure relief valve body (7) and piston (6) must be free of scratches or burrs. Relief valve spring (5) free length should be approximately 25.20 mm (0.992 in.).

Lubricate the oil pump cavity and pump rotors with engine oil during assembly. Install new "O" ring (10) in groove in crankcase cover or oil pan. Install pump cover (11) and tighten mounting screws to 6.2 N•m (55 in.-lbs.) on a new crankcase cover or oil pan or 4.0 N•m (35 in.-lbs.) on a used crankcase cover or oil pan.

No gasket is used with crankcase cover or oil pan. Apply a 1.6 mm ($\frac{1}{16}$ in.) bead of silicone gasket sealant (GE Silmate RTV-108, RTV-1473 or equivalent) around crankcase cover or oil pan mating surface as shown in Fig. KO212. Tighten crankcase cover or oil pan screws to 24.4 N•m (216 in.-lbs.) using sequence shown in Fig. KO213.

OIL SENSOR. Some engines are equipped with an Oil Sentry oil pressure monitor. The system uses a pressure switch installed in one of the main oil galleries of the crankcase cover or oil pan, or on the oil filter adapter. The pressure switch is designed to break contact as oil pressure increases to normal pressure, and to make contact when oil pressure decreases within the range of 20-35 kPa (3-5 psi). When switch contacts close, either the engine will stop or a "Low Oil" warning light will be activated, depending on engine application.

To check sensor pressure switch, a regulated supply of compressed air and a continuity tester are required. With zero pressure applied to switch, tester should indicate continuity across switch terminal and ground. When pressure is increased through range of 20-35 kPa (3-5 psi), switch should open and tester should indicate no continuity. If switch fails test, install new switch.

KOHLER

KOHLER COMPANY
Kohler, Wisconsin 53044

Model	No. Cyls.	Bore	Stroke	Displacement	Power Rating
CV17	2	73 mm (2.87 in.)	67 mm (2.64 in.)	561 cc (34.2 cu. in.)	12.7 kW (17 hp)
CH18, CV18	2	77 mm (3.03 in.)	67 mm (2.64 in.)	624 cc (38.1 cu. in.)	13.4 kW (18 hp)
CH20, CV20	2	77 mm (3.03 in.)	67 mm (2.64 in.)	624 cc (38.1 cu. in.)	14.9 kW (20 hp)
CH22, CV22	2	77 mm (3.03 in.)	67 mm (2.64 in.)	624 cc (38.1 cu. in.)	16.4 kW (22 hp)
CH22 Pro, CV22 Pro	2	80 mm (3.15 in.)	67 mm (2.64 in.)	674 cc (41.1 cu. in.)	16.4 kW (22 hp)
CH25, CV25	2	83 mm (3.27 in.)	67 mm (2.64 in.)	725 cc (44.0 cu. in.)	18.6 kW (25 hp)
CH26 (EFI)	2	83 mm (3.27 in.)	67 mm (2.64 in.)	725 cc (44.0 cu. in.)	19.4 kW (26 hp)

NOTE: Metric fasteners are used throughout the engine.

Engines in this section are four-stroke, two-cylinder, air-cooled engines using an overhead valve system. Engine identification information is provided on a decal located on the side of the blower housing.

MAINTENANCE

LUBRICATION. All models are equipped with a pressure lubrication system and an oil filter. Oil is routed from a gear-driven oil pump to the crankshaft, camshaft and connecting rod.

Check oil level at regular intervals, and maintain oil level at full mark on dipstick. Dipstick should be pushed in completely for accurate measurement. DO NOT overfill.

Manufacturer recommends using oil with an API service rating of SG or SH, or any rating formulated to supercede SG or SH. Use SAE 10W-30 oil for temperatures above 0° F (−18° C). When operating in temperatures below 32° F (0° C), SAE 5W-20, 5W-30 oil or 10W-30 oil may be used. Do not use SAE 10W-40 oil in any temperature.

In overhauled or new short blocks, use SAE 10W-30 oil for the first five hours of operation, then change oil according to ambient temperature requirements. Recommended oil change interval after 5-hour break-in is every 100 hours of operation.

Always drain the dirty oil while the engine is warm. The oil will flow freely and carry away more impurities.

It is recommended that a new oil filter be installed at each oil change. When installing new oil filter, lubricate the filter gasket with clean oil prior to installation. Thread the filter on the filter adapter until gasket contacts the adapter, then hand-tighten filter an additional ½ turn.

Crankcase oil capacity is approximately 2.0 liters (2.1 qt.).

The engine may be equipped with a low oil pressure switch located on the breather cover between the cylinders. Switch should be closed at zero pressure and open at 21-34 kPa (3-5 psi). Switch may be connected to a warning device or into the ignition circuit.

AIR CLEANER. The engine is equipped with a foam precleaner element and paper-type air filter. Service the precleaner after every 25 hours of operation and the air filter after every 100 hours of operation. Service more frequently if engine is operated in severe conditions.

Clean precleaner element by washing in soapy water. Allow to dry, then apply clean engine oil. Squeeze out excess oil.

The air filter should be renewed rather than cleaned. Do not wash or direct pressurized air at filter.

To prevent water from entering air cleaner by way of the knob in center of the air filter cover, make certain that the knob base and knob seal are not damaged. If necessary, replace knob and knob seal.

CRANKCASE BREATHER. The crankcase breather assembly is located on the top of the crankcase between the cylinders. Under the breather cover and baffles are a reed valve and filter. Periodic maintenance is not required. Inspect and clean breather components as needed. Apply a suitable silicone sealant to breather cover and tighten retaining screws in a crossing pattern to 8.6 N•m (65 in.-lbs.).

SPARK PLUG. Recommended spark plug is Champion RC12YC. Electrode gap is 0.75 mm (0.030 inch). Tighten spark plug to 24.4-29.8 N•m (18-22 ft.-lbs.).

Inductive spark plugs (Champion QC12YC or equivalent) should be used in place of RC12YC resistor plugs to prevent radio frequency interference (RFI) on engines or systems with hour meters. This RFI may randomly reset the hour meter back to zero hours.

CAUTION: Kohler does not recommend using abrasive blasting to clean spark plugs because this may introduce abrasive material into the engine that could cause extensive damage.

CARBURETOR. Horizontal Crankshaft Engines. If engine uses LPG fuel, refer to LPG FUEL SYSTEM in SERVICING KOHLER ACCESSORIES section of this manual.

For gasoline carburetor, idle mixture and speed are adjustable by turning screws shown in Fig. KO301. A fixed main jet (MJ) controls the high-speed mixture. Initial setting of idle mixture screw (IN) is 1½ turns out from a lightly seated position. Unless equipment manufacturer states otherwise, idle speed should be 1200 rpm.

To adjust idle mixture, run engine until normal operating temperature is reached. Make certain that the choke plate is fully open. Rotate idle mixture screw (IN) clockwise until engine speed slows, then turn screw counterclockwise ¾ turn. Turn idle speed adjusting screw (IS) to adjust idle speed if necessary.

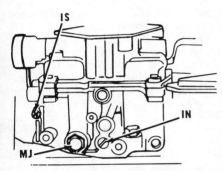

Fig. KO301—View showing location of idle speed adjustment screw (IS), idle mixture adjustment screw (IN) and fixed main jet (MJ) for carburetor used on horizontal-crankshaft engines.

Main jet kits may be available for some engines to lean the high-speed mixture for operation at high altitudes.

The carburetor may be equipped with a fuel shutoff solenoid (13—Fig. KO302) that uses a plunger to stop fuel flow through the main jet when the engine is stopped. When the solenoid is energized, the spring-loaded plunger should retract, allowing fuel to flow through the main jet.

If carburetor overhaul is evident after inspection, refer to Fig. KO302. Separate the carburetor upper body (1) from the lower body (9) for access to internal components. Thoroughly clean all components using carburetor cleaner and compressed air.

The "O" ring-type gasket (3) should be discarded if removed from carburetor body. Choke and throttle shaft assemblies are available only as factory-assembled unit assemblies with carburetor body and should not be removed. The choke plate is spring-loaded. Remove the cap from the end of the choke shaft to inspect spring. Be sure the choke operates properly without sticking or binding.

To check float height, hold carburetor so float is hanging down as shown in Fig. KO303. Float arm must press lightly against fuel inlet valve without compressing spring in valve. Float height should be 22 mm (0.86 in.) measured from bottom of float to air horn casting. Adjust float height by carefully bending float arm tang.

CARBURETOR. Vertical Crankshaft Engines. If engine uses LPG fuel, refer to LPG FUEL SYSTEM in SERVICING KOHLER ACCESSORIES section of this manual.

For gasoline carburetor, idle mixture and speed are adjustable by turning screws shown in Fig. KO304. A fixed main jet controls the high-speed mixture. Initial setting of idle mixture screw is 2¼ turns out from a lightly seated position. Unless equipment manufacturer states otherwise, idle speed should be 1200 rpm.

To adjust idle mixture, run engine until normal operating temperature is reached. Make certain that the choke plate is fully open. Rotate idle mixture screw clockwise until engine speed slows, then turn screw counterclockwise ¾ to 1 turn. Turn idle speed adjusting screw to adjust idle speed if necessary.

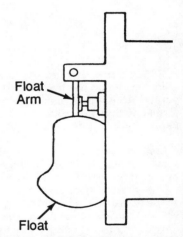

Fig. KO303—On downdraft carburetor, measure float height with carburetor body in a near-vertical position so the float arm is just resting against fuel inlet valve without compressing the valve spring.

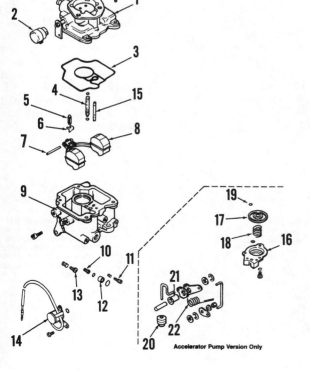

Fig. KO302—Exploded view of down draft carburetor used on horizontal-crankshaft engines.

1. Upper body
2. Automatic choke
3. Gasket
4. Slow speed jet
5. Inlet needle valve
6. Clip
7. Float pin
8. Float
9. Lower body
10. Main jet
11. Idle fuel needle
12. Solenoid seat
13. Shutoff solenoid
14. Idle speed adjustment screw
15. Jet (accelerator pump carb. only)
16. Accelerator pump cover
17. Diaphragm
18. Diaphragm spring
19. O-ring
20. Rubber boot
21. Bushing
22. Return spring

Accelerator Pump Version Only

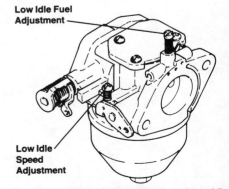

Fig. KO304—View showing location of low idle fuel adjustment screw and low idle speed adjustment screw for carburetor used on vertical-crankshaft engines.

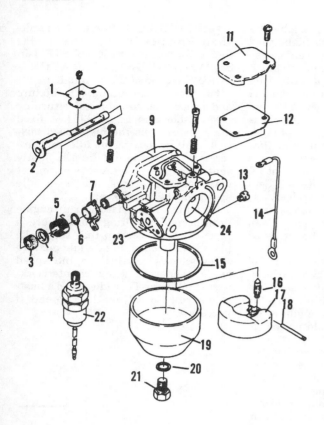

Fig. KO305—Exploded view of side draft carburetor used on vertical-crankshaft engines.

1. Choke plate
2. Choke shaft
3. Dust filter
4. Collar
5. Return spring
6. Ring
7. Choke lever
8. Idle speed adjustment screw
9. Carburetor body
10. Low idle speed needle
11. Cover
12. Gasket
13. Main jet
14. Ground lead (solenoid only)
15. Gasket
16. Inlet needle valve
17. Float
18. Float pin
19. Fuel bowl
20. Gasket
21. Screw
22. Shutoff solenoid
23. Throttle shaft
24. Throttle plate

let valve without compressing spring in valve. Float height should be 16.5 mm (0.65 in.) measured from bottom of float to carburetor casting. The float is not adjustable. If float height is not to specification, replace the float, float pin and fuel inlet valve.

Reassemble the carburetor using new gaskets. Tighten fuel bowl retaining screw or solenoid to 5.1-6.2 N•m (45-55 in.-lb.).

GOVERNOR. A flyweight-type governor is located in the crankcase cover. The camshaft gear drives the governor gear. Refer to REPAIRS section for overhaul information.

To adjust governor linkage, proceed as follows: Loosen the governor lever clamp nut (N—Fig. KO307) and push the governor lever so throttle is wide open. Rotate the governor shaft (S) counterclockwise as far as possible and tighten clamp nut (N).

The engine should never run at speeds exceeding 3750 rpm. Adjust top idle speed as recommended by equipment manufacturer. Two different governor springs may be used based on engine maximum speed above or below 3400 rpm. Governor sensitivity is adjusted by reattaching the governor spring to another hole in governor arm. Move spring to an outer hole on arm to decrease governor sensitivity.

Two different styles of throttle and choke control systems are used: a single-cable (Fig. KO308) and a dual-cable (Fig. KO309). Both systems have provisions for the cable(s) pulling from either the left or right side. A kit, part No. 24 755 12, is available from the manufacturer to provide improved speed regulation on some applications.

On engines equipped with an air cleaner system designed for commercial mowers, the governor linkage will appear as in Fig. KO310. Governor adjustment is the same as for standard equipment. If the governor spring has been disconnected, reconnect as fol-

NOTE: Some carburetors may have a limiter cap on the idle fuel adjusting screw. Adjustment can only be performed within the limits allowed by the cap.

Main jet kits may be available for some engines to lean the high-speed mixture for operation at high altitudes.

The carburetor may be equipped with a fuel shutoff solenoid (22—Fig. KO305) that uses a plunger to stop fuel flow through the main jet when the engine is stopped. When the solenoid is energized, the spring-loaded plunger should retract, allowing fuel to flow through the main jet.

If carburetor overhaul is evident after inspection, refer to Fig. KO305. Re-

move the fuel bowl nut (21) or fuel solenoid (22) and separate the fuel bowl (19) from the carburetor body (9). Remove the float (17) and fuel inlet needle (16). Remove passage cover (11), idle mixture needle (10) and main jet (13). It is not necessary to remove the choke assembly (1 through 7) or throttle (23 and 24) unless excessive wear is evident. To remove choke or throttle assembly, remove set screws from choke plate or throttle plate and withdraw the shafts.

Clean all components using carburetor cleaner and compressed air. Replace parts that are worn or damaged.

To check float height, hold carburetor so float arm is resting on the fuel inlet valve as shown in Fig. KO306. Float arm must press lightly against fuel in-

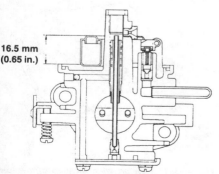

16.5 mm (0.65 in.)

Fig. KO306—On side draft carburetor, measure float height with carburetor body inverted so float arm rests against fuel inlet valve.

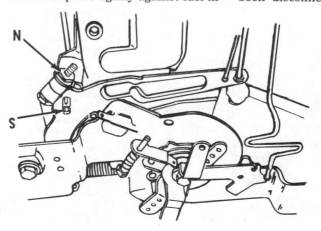

Fig. KO307—To adjust governor, loosen governor lever clamp nut (N) and push governor lever so throttle is wide open. Rotate governor shaft (S) counterclockwise as far as possible and tighten nut (N).

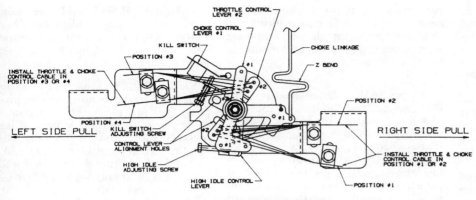

SINGLE-CABLE CONTROL SYSTEM
COMMAND V-TWIN

Fig. KO308—Typical throttle control using single-cable operation. Cable can mount and pull from either side.

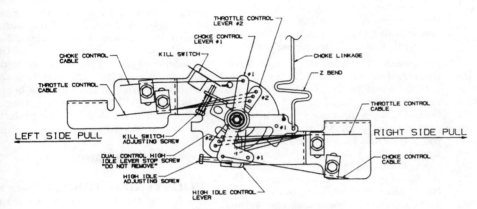

DUAL-CABLE CONTROL SYSTEM
COMMAND V-TWIN

Fig. KO309—Typical throttle control using dual-cable operation. Cables can mount and pull from either side.

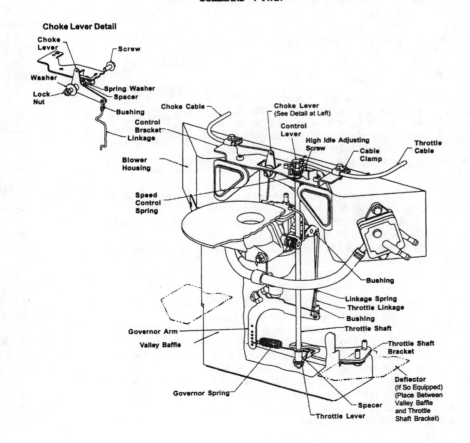

Fig. KO310—View of governor linkage typical of engines equipped with the commercial mower air cleaner system.

gine when installed. Hook the long end of the spring through the throttle lever and short end through appropriate hole in the governor arm.

IGNITION. The engine is equipped with a breakerless, electronic magneto ignition system. Two electronic ignition modules are mounted outside the flywheel. The ignition switch grounds the modules to stop the engine. There is no periodic maintenance or adjustment required for the ignition system.

The air gap between the flywheel and each ignition module is 0.25-0.33 mm (0.010-0.013 in.) for 22 and 25 horsepower engines with part No. 24 584 11 ignition module. Air gap for all other models, is 0.20-0.30 mm (0.008-0.012 in.). Loosen module retaining screws to adjust air gap. Tighten module retaining screws to 4 N•m (35 in.-lbs.).

SPARK-ADVANCE MODULE. Ignition systems on 22 and 25 horsepower engines are equipped with a spark-advance module (SAM). A faulty module can cause the engine to run rough, lose power, accelerate poorly, backfire or stall. The SAM can be tested using Kohler tester part No. 25 761 21. If the tester is not available, test the SAM as follows:

The engine must be cold (ambient temperature) for the first portion of the test. Use a marking pen or piece of narrow tape to make a line near the edge of the flywheel screen. Connect a timing light to No. 1 cylinder. Run the engine at idle and use the timing light to locate the timing line on the flywheel screen. Mark the blower housing to correspond to the screen line. Stop the engine. Connect the timing light to No. 2 cylinder and repeat the procedure to locate the timing line. Accelerate the engine to full throttle and observe the timing lines. The SAM is performing properly if the following results are observed: The blower housing marks corresponding to the respective cylinders are 90° apart; the timing lines advance 5-15° or 16-19 mm (⅝-¾ in.), and hold steady after acceleration to full speed. Check the wires and connections from the SAM to ignition modules if either of these conditions is not met. If the wires and connections are good, replace the SAM.

If the cold engine tests do not indicate a problem, run the engine until hot and repeat the test procedure. The test results should be the same as those obtained with the engine cold. If not, a heat-related diode breakdown is indicated and the SAM must be replaced.

NOTE: Make sure that SAM leads attach securely to the modules. If lead terminals are loose or slide easily on-and-off the male spade terminals, lightly pinch the female lead terminals with pliers until a snug connection is obtained.

If the SAM tests satisfactory both cold and hot, test the ignition modules as follows: Remove the blower housing and inspect ignition wiring, terminals and connections. Clean and repair if necessary. Disconnect brown and yellow leads from both ignition modules. If a dark coating is observed on the terminals, thoroughly clean them with an electrical contact solvent. Check between the ignition modules and mounting bosses for graphite washers. Remove and discard all graphite washers. Install the modules and adjust the flywheel-to-module air gap setting.

Disconnect yellow and brown leads from ignition module for No. 2 cylinder. Test for spark at the No. 1 cylinder using tester part No. 24 455 02 or equivalent. Ignition module is performing properly if a spark is produced. Connect the yellow and brown leads to the ignition module for No. 2 cylinder and disconnect the leads from the module for the No. 1 cylinder. Test for spark at the No. 2 cylinder. If a module does not produce a spark, disconnect the yellow lead from it and connect an ohmmeter between the narrow terminal and the module laminations. Resistance should be 900-1100 ohms. Replace the module if resistance is considerably lower than specification.

NOTE: If a module is found faulty on engines before serial No. 2726520717, check the vendor part number on the opposite module. Modules with MA-2, MA-2A or MA-2B part numbers should also be replaced.

After ignition system is tested and repaired, use a silicone dielectric compound such as Fel-Pro Lubri-Sel or GE/Novaguard G661 and apply an overlapping bridge bead of compound around the base of each pair of terminal connectors to prevent arcing. DO NOT put any compound inside the connectors or on the terminal contact surfaces.

Other problem areas that may cause ignition-related malfunctions are: Battery voltage below 7 volts, faulty key switch, loose wire connections or shorted wiring, sheared flywheel key, engine improperly grounded, unit interlock switches faulty, poorly connected spark plug cable leads, and weak flywheel magnets.

VALVE ADJUSTMENT. The engine is equipped with hydraulic valve lifters that automatically maintain proper valve clearance. No periodic adjustment is required.

FUEL PUMP. Most engines are equipped with a nonserviceable pulse-type fuel pump that is activated by crankcase pressure. Minimum fuel delivery rate must be 7.5 L/hr. (2.0 gal./hr.) with a pressure of 2.0 kPa (0.3 psi) and a fuel lift of 46 cm (18 in.) for horizontal-shaft engines and 61 cm (24 in.) for vertical-shaft engines.

Some horizontal-shaft 18-25 horsepower engines beginning with serial No. 2625400007 use a mechanical fuel pump activated by the intake rocker arm of the No. 2 cylinder. Pulse pump equipped engines above serial No. 2520800007 can be converted to the mechanical-type pump with the addition of a retrofit kit available from the engine manufacturer. Engines below serial No. 252080007 may require a rocker arm upgrade kit to upgrade to the mechanical pump.

REPAIRS

TIGHTENING TORQUE. Recommended tightening torque values are as follows:

Blower housing
M5 Fastners . . . . 4.0 N•m
(35 in.-lb.)
M6 Fastners . . . . 6.8 N•m
(60 in.-lb.)
Carburetor. . . . . 9.9 N•m
(88 in.-lb.)
Charging stator. . . . . 4.0 N•m
(35 in.-lb.)
Connecting rod . . . . See Text
Cylinder head . . . . See Text
Exhaust manifold . . . . 24.3 N•m
(215 in.-lb.)
Flywheel . . . . 66.4 N•m
(49 ft.-lbs.)
Flywheel fan . . . . 9.9 N•m
(88 in.-lb.)
Governor control lever . . . . . . 9.9 N•m
(88 in.-lb.)
Ignition module. . . . . 4.0-6.2 N•m
(35-55 in.-lb.)
Intake manifold. . . . . 9.9 N•m
(88 in.-lb.)
Oil cooler . . . . 40.6 N•m
(30 ft.-lb.)
Oil drain plug . . . . 13.5 N•m
(10 ft.-lb.)
Oil pan/closure plate. . . . . . . 24.3 N•m
(215 in.-lb.)
Rectifier-regulator. . . . . 4.0 N•m
(35 in.-lb.)
Spark plug. . . . . 24.4-29.8 N•m
(18-22 ft.-lbs.)

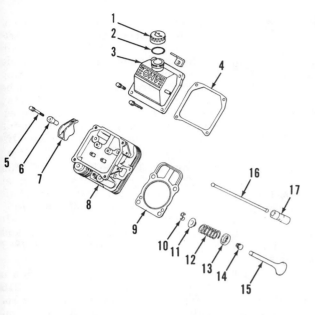

Fig. KO311—Exploded view of cylinder head assembly. Seal (14) is used only on the intake valve.

1. Oil fill cap
2. O-ring
3. Rocker arm cover
4. Gasket
5. Screw
6. Pivot ball
7. Rocker arm
8. Cylinder head
9. Gasket
10. Split retainer
11. Spring retainer
12. Valve spring
13. Spring seat
14. Seal
15. Valve
16. Push rod
17. Hydraulic lifter

studs with engine oil prior to installation.

On all models, tighten the bolts or nuts in sequence shown in Fig. KO313. Tighten the head bolts in two steps, first to 22.6 N•m (200 in.-lb.), then to final torque of 41.8 N•m (370 in.-lb.). Tighten the stud nuts in two steps, first to 16.9 N•m (150 in.-lb.), then to final torque of 33.9 N•m (300-in.-lb.).

Tighten rocker arm nuts 14 N•m (125 in.-lb.). Tighten intake manifold screws to 9.9 N•m (88 in.-lb.). Tighten exhaust manifold nuts to 24.8 N•m (215 in.-lb.).

To help eliminate oil leakage at the valve cover, flat-style valve cover gaskets are no longer serviced. Reusing valve covers originally sealed with silicone sealer only is not recommended. New design valve covers utilize an O-ring for sealing. The new style valve covers require that the fasteners be tightened incrementally to 7.9 N•m (70 in.-lb.) in the sequence shown in Fig. KO314.

VALVE SYSTEM. Intake and exhaust valve face and valve seat angles are 45°. Valve seat inserts are factory press-fitted into the cylinder head, and are not replaceable. Renew the cylinder head if the seats cannot be properly refaced or if the inserts are cracked, warped or loose. Renew valve if valve margin is less than 1.5 mm (0.060 in.) after grinding valve face.

Specified valve stem-to-guide clearance is 0.038-0.076 mm (0.0015-0.0030 in.) for intake valve and 0.050-0.088 mm (0.0020-0.0035 in.) for exhaust valve. Specified new valve stem diameter is 6.982-7.000 mm (0.2749-0.2756 in.) for intake and 6.970-6.988 mm (0.2744-0.2751 in.) for exhaust. Specified new valve guide inside diameter for both valves is 7.038-7.058 mm

Starter motor . . . . 15.3 N•m (135 in.-lbs.)
Speed control bracket . . . 7.3-10.7 N•m (65-95 in.-lb.)
Valve cover . . . . 3.4 N•m (30 in.-lb.)

CYLINDER HEAD. To remove a cylinder head, proceed as follows: Remove muffler and air cleaner assembly.

NOTE: When removing exhaust system from cylinder heads, check to see if there are port liners (sleeves) located in the cylinder head exhaust ports. All heads with port liners must have the liners positioned in the exhaust ports prior to reinstalling the exhaust manifolds.

Remove fuel pump with bracket, fuel line and breather tube. Detach speed control bracket. Remove carburetor, disconnect interfering wires and remove blower housing and air baffles. Disconnect interfering wires and remove intake manifold. Remove rocker arm cover. Remove and mark push rods so they can be returned to their original position. Note that cylinder head is identified by a number embossed on the head that matches the cylinder number marked on the crankcase. Remove retaining screws or nuts and lift cylinder

head from cylinder block. If removed, mark rocker arms and pivot balls so they can be returned to their original positions.

Clean deposits from cylinder head and inspect for cracks or other damage. Check cylinder head for distortion using a straightedge and feeler gauges. Maximum allowable cylinder head distortion is 0.076 mm (0.003 in.).

Reverse disassembly procedure to install cylinder head. If intake valve was removed, a new oil seal (14—Fig. KO311) must be installed.

NOTE: New cylinder head bolts or nuts should always be installed. Attempting to reuse bolts or nuts results in loss of torque retention, and will likely cause short term head gasket failure.

On Command 25 and 26 horsepower engines that have cylinder heads mounted with bolts, the head gaskets and bolts must be Style 1, not Style 2 (Fig. KO312). Some engines have cylinder heads mounted with studs and nuts. The nuts are Grade 10 and have a gold color. The stud nuts must not be interchanged with hose used on the starter and exhaust studs (silver color). Lightly lubricate threads of the bolts or

Fig. KO314—Valve cover fastener torque sequence for new design valve cover with O-ring seal.

STYLE 1   STYLE 2

Fig. KO312—Comparison of correct (style 1) and incorrect (style 2) head gaskets and head bolts used on some Command 25 and 26 horsepower engines.

Fig. KO313—Tighten cylinder head retaining screws to 40.7 N•m (30 ft.-lb.) in the sequence shown.

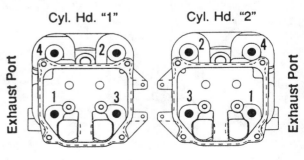

(0.2771-0.2779 in.). Maximum allowable valve guide inside diameter is 7.134 mm (0.2809 in.) for intake and 7.159 mm (0.2819 in.) for exhaust. Valve guides are not renewable; however, guides can be reamed to accept valves with 0.25 mm oversize stem.

Command V-twin engines were originally built with hollow push rods. Engines built since late 1993 have solid push rods. A push rod kit part No. 24 755 13 is available to convert earlier engines if needed.

HYDRAULIC LIFTERS. The engine is equipped with hydraulic lifters that use pressurized oil to maintain proper valve clearance.

If the hydraulic lifters are noisy after the engine has run for several minutes and reached operating temperature, it is probably an indication that contamination is preventing the lifter check ball from seating or there is excessive

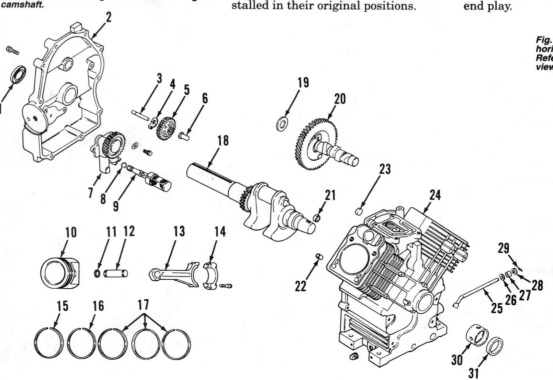

Fig. KO315—Align timing marks (TM) on camshaft and crankshaft gears when installing the camshaft.

internal wear. Lifter must be serviced as a unit assembly.

To remove hydraulic lifters, remove cylinder head as previously outlined and use a suitable tool such as Kohler tool No. KO1044 to extract lifters. Mark lifter so it can be installed in its original position. Intake valve lifters are on flywheel side of engine. Specified lifter clearance in crankcase lifter bore is 0.0124-0.0501 mm (0.0005-0.0.0020 in.).

Priming the hydraulic lifters prior to installation is not necessary, as there is no significant difference in pump-up time between primed and unprimed lifters. To reduce lifter pump-up time and resultant noisy lifters, "quick-purge" service replacement lifters part No. 25 351 01 are available for installation in all engines.

Lubricate lifter bores with oil and install hydraulic lifters in their original positions.

CAMSHAFT. To remove camshaft, rotate crankshaft so piston is at top dead center and drain engine oil. Remove rocker arm cover, unscrew rocker arm nut and separate push rods from rocker arms. Remove push rods while marking them so they can be returned to original position. Unscrew and remove crankcase cover (prying lugs are located on cover). Position engine so lifters cannot fall out, then withdraw camshaft while noting any shims. Remove and mark lifters so they can be installed in their original positions.

The camshaft is equipped with a compression reduction device to aid starting. The lever and weight mechanism on the camshaft gear moves a pin inside the exhaust cam lobe. During starting the pin protrudes above the cam lobe and forces the exhaust valve to stay open longer, thereby reducing compression. At running speed the pin remains below the surface of the cam lobe. Inspect mechanism for proper operation.

Minimum cam lobe height is 8.07 mm (0.318 in.) for intake and exhaust valves. Minimum allowable camshaft journal diameter is 19.959 mm (0.7858 in.). Maximum allowable camshaft bearing bore diameter in crankcase and crankcase cover is 20.038 mm (0.7889 in.).

Before installing camshaft, rotate governor cross shaft (25—Fig. KO316 or Fig. KO317) clockwise so lower end of shaft contacts crankcase. Align the timing marks (TM—Fig. KO315) on crankshaft and camshaft gears as the camshaft is installed. Check and adjust the camshaft end play as follows: Install the camshaft with original thickness shim (19—Fig. KO316 or Fig. KO317) between camshaft and crankcase cover. Attach camshaft end play checking tool KO-1031 to crankcase and use a feeler gauge to measure clearance between the shim and checking tool. The measured clearance is the camshaft end play. Specified end play is 0.076-0.127 mm (0.003-0.005 in.). Install required shim to obtain desired end play.

Fig. KO316—Exploded view of horizontal-crankshaft engine. Refer to Fig. KO311 for exploded view of cylinder head assembly.

1. Oil seal
2. Crankcase cover
3. Governor gear shaft
4. Lock tab
5. Governor gear & flyweight assy.
6. Governor pin
7. Oil pump
8. O-ring
9. Oil pickup
10. Piston
11. Retainer
12. Piston pin
13. Connecting rod
14. Rod cap
15. Top compression ring
16. Second compression ring
17. Oil control ring
18. Crankshaft
19. Shim
20. Camshaft
21. Plug
22. Dowel pin
23. Plug
24. Cylinder block/ crankcase
25. Governor cross shaft
26. Washer
27. Seal
28. Washer
29. Hitch pin
30. Bushing
31. Oil seal

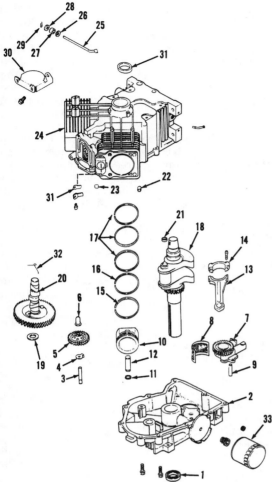

Fig. KO317—Exploded view of vertical-crankshaft engine. Refer to Fig. KO311 for exploded view of cylinder head.

1. Oil seal
2. Crankcase cover/oil pan
3. Governor gear shaft
4. Lock tab
5. Governor gear & flyweight assy.
6. Governor pin
7. Oil pump
8. Screen
9. Oil pickup
10. Piston
11. Retainer
12. Piston pin
13. Connecting rod
14. Rod cap
15. Top compression ring
16. Second compression ring
17. Oil control ring
18. Crankshaft
19. Shim
20. Camshaft
21. Plug
22. Dowel
23. Plug
24. Cylinder block/crankcase
25. Governor cross shaft
26. Washer
27. Seal
28. Washer
29. Hitch pin
30. Cover
31. Breather reed
32. Spring (automatic compression release)
33. Oil filter

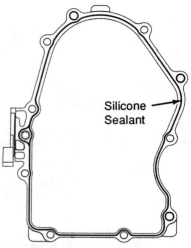

Fig. KO318—Apply RTV sealant in a 1/6 mm (1/16 in.) bead around crankcase cover/oil pan mounting surface as shown.

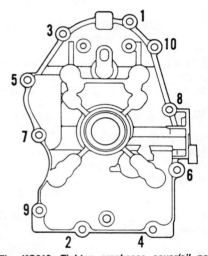

Fig. KO319—Tighten crankcase cover/oil pan screws in sequence shown.

NOTE: After completing assembly of engine, rotate crankshaft slowly by hand to allow the valve springs to seat the valves and bleed any excess oil out of the hydraulic lifters. If the crankshaft turns through two complete revolutions and compression is noted for both cylinders, the valves are seating and engine may be started.

CRANKCASE COVER/OIL PAN.

A gasket (not sealant) is used between the crankcase and oil pan for CV25 engines. For all other engines, RTV sealant is used instead of a gasket to seal the crankcase cover or oil pan.

For all engines except CV25, apply a 1.6 mm ($\frac{1}{16}$ in.) bead of RTV gasket sealant (GE Silmate RTV-108, RTV-1473 or equivalent) around crankcase cover mating surface as shown in Fig. KO318.

On all engines, tighten crankcase cover screws in sequence shown in Fig. KO319 to a torque of 24.4 N•m (216 in.-lb.).

PISTON, PIN AND RINGS.

The piston and connecting rod are removed as an assembly. Remove cylinder head and camshaft as previously outlined. Remove connecting rod cap and push connecting rod and piston out of cylinder. Mark piston and connecting rod so they can be reinstalled in original cylinder. Remove piston pin retaining rings, remove piston pin and separate piston and rod.

To determine piston clearance in cylinder, measure piston skirt diameter at a point 6 mm (0.24 in.) from bottom of skirt and perpendicular to piston pin bore. Measure cylinder bore inside diameter at point of greatest wear, approximately 63.5 mm (2.5 in.) below top of cylinder and perpendicular to piston pin. The difference between the two measurements is piston clearance in bore. Refer to the following tables for piston and cylinder specifications:

PISTON SKIRT DIAMETER

Model	Piston O.D.
CV17	
New	72.966-72.984 mm
	(2.8727-2.8734 in.)
Wear limit	72.839 mm
	(2.8677 in.)

CH18, CH20, CH22

New	76.967-76.985 mm
	(3.0302-3.0309 in.)
Wear limit	76.840 mm
	(3.0252 in.)

CV18, CV20, CV22 (624 cc)

New	76.967-76.985 mm
	(3.0302-3.0309 in.)
Wear limit	76.840 mm
	(3.0252 in.)

CV22 (674 cc)

New	79.963-79.979 mm
	(3.1481-3.1488 in.)
Wear limit	79.831 mm
	(3.1430 in.)

CV25

New	82.956-82.974 mm
	(3.2660-3.2667 in.)
Wear limit	82.841 mm
	(3.2615 in.)

CH25
New . . . . 82.986 mm
(3.3194 in.)
Wear limit . . . . 82.841 mm
(3.3136 in.)

PISTON-TO-CYLINDER CLEARANCE

MODEL	CLEARANCE
CV17	0.022-0.065 mm
	(0.0009-0.0026 in.)
CV18, CV20,	
CV22 (624 cc)	0.035-0.078 mm
	(0.0014-0.0031 in.)
CV22 (674 cc)	0.021-0.062 mm
	(0.0008-0.0024 in.)
CV	250.030-0.067 mm
	(0.0012-0.0026 in.)
CH18, CH20,	
CH22	0.015-0.058 mm
	(0.0006-0.0023 in.)
CH25	0.020-0.045 mm
	(0.0008-0.0018 in.)

CYLINDER BORE DIAMETER

MODEL	CYLINDER I.D.
CV17	
New	73.006-73.031 mm
	(2.8742-2.8752)
Wear limit	73.070 mm
	(2.8767 in.)
CH18, CH20, CH22	
New	77.000-77.025 mm
	(3.0315-3.0325 in.)
Wear limit	77.063 mm
	(77.063 in.)
CV18, CV20,	
CV22 (624 cc)	
New	77.000-77.025 mm
	(3.0315-3.0325 in.)
Wear limit	77.063 mm
	(77.063 in.)
CV22 (674 cc)	
New	80.000-80.025 mm
	(3.1496-3.1506 in.)
Wear limit	80.065 mm
	(3.1522 in.)
CV25 (nickel-silicon	
plated bore)	
New	82.977-83.023 mm
	(3.2686-3.2668 in.)
Wear limit	83.0511 mm
	(3.2697 in.)
CV25 (cast iron liner)	
New	83.006-83.031 mm
	(3.2679-3.2689 in.)
Wear limit	83.071 mm
	(3.2705 in.)

CYLINDER WEAR LIMIT

MODEL	WEAR LIMIT
CV17	
Out-of-round	0.13 mm
	(0.0051 in.)

CH18-25, CV20-25
Out-of round . . . . 0.12 mm
(0.0047 in.)
All Models
Taper . . . . 0.05 mm
(0.0020 in.)

Piston and ring sets are available in standard size and oversizes of 0.08, 0.25 and 0.50 mm (0.003, 0.010 and 0.020 in.).

NOTE: Oversize piston and ring sets are not available for CH25 and CV25 engines with nickel-silicon plated POWER-BORE cylinders.

Specified piston pin bore is 17.006-17.012 mm (0.6695-0.6698 in.) with a wear limit of 17.025 mm (0.6703 in.). Specified piston pin diameter is 16.995-17.000 mm (0.6691-0.6693 in.) with a wear limit of 16.994 mm (0.6691 in.). Piston pin-to-piston bore clearance should be 0.006-0.017 mm (0.0002-0.0007 in.).

Check the piston ring side clearance in the ring groove to determine ring groove wear. Insert a new ring in the corresponding piston ring groove, and use a feeler gauge to measure clearance between side of the ring and the groove. Renew piston if side clearance is excessive. Refer to the following table for piston ring-to-groove side clearance specifications.

PISTON RING SIDE CLEARANCE

MODEL	CLEARANCE
CV17	
Top Ring	0.040-0.085 mm
	(0.0016-0.0033 in.)
Middle Ring	0.030-0.080 mm
	(0.0012-0.0031 in.)
Oil Control Ring	0.046-0.201 mm
	(0.0018-0.0079 in.)
CH18, CH20, CH22	
Top Ring	0.040-0.080 mm
	(0.0016-0.0031 in.)
Middle Ring	0.040-0.072 mm
	(0.0016-0.0028 in.)
Oil Control Ring	0.060-0.202 mm
	(0.0024-0.0080 in.)
CV18, CV20,	
CV22 (624 cc)	
Top Ring	0.040-0.080 mm
	(0.0016-0.0031 in.)
Middle Ring	0.040-0.080 mm
	(0.0016-0.0031 in.)
Oil Control Ring	0.060-0.202 mm
	(0.0024-0.0080 in.)
CV22 (674 cc)	
Top Ring	0.030-0.076 mm
	(0.0012-0.0030 in.)
Middle Ring	0.030-0.076 mm
	(0.0012-0.0030 in.)

Oil Control Ring	0.046-0.196 mm
	(0.0018-0.0077 in.)
CH25, CV25	
Top Ring	0.025-0.048 mm
	(0.0010-0.0019 in.)
Middle Ring	0.015-0.037 mm
	(0.0006-0.0015 in.)
Oil Control Ring	0.026-0.176 mm
	(0.0010-0.0070 in.)

Before installing rings on piston, position compression rings (one at a time) in running area of cylinder and measure ring end gap using a feeler gauge. Refer to the following table for piston ring end gap specifications.

PISTON RING END GAP

MODEL	END GAP
CV17	
Top Ring	0.180-0.380 mm
	(0.0071-0.0150 in.)
Middle Ring	0.180-0.440 mm
	(0.0071-0.0173 in.)
CH18, CH20, CH22, CV18,	
CV20, CV22 (624 cc)	
Standard	0.25-0.45 mm
	(0.0098-0.0177 in.)
Maximum	0.77 mm
	(0030 in.)
CV22 (674 cc)	
Standard	0.18-0.46 mm
	(0.0071-0.0181 in.)
Maximum	0.80 mm
	(0.0315 in.)
CH25, CV25	
Standard	0.25-0.56 mm
	(0.0100-0.0224 in.)
Maximum	0.94 mm
	(0.037 in.)

Assemble piston and rod for No. 1 cylinder so long side of rod is on same side as "FLY" on piston crown (see Fig. KO320). Assemble piston and rod for No. 2 cylinder so that longer side of rod is on opposite side of "FLY" on piston crown.

DO NOT reuse old piston rings. When installing piston rings on piston, install compression rings so "pip" or other mark identifying top of ring is towards piston crown and stripe on face of ring is to the left of end gap (see Fig. KO321). Second compression ring has a white stripe on face of ring. Top compression ring has a blue stripe on face of ring. Stagger ring end gaps evenly around piston.

Install piston and rod assembly in cylinder as instructed in CONNECTING ROD section.

CONNECTING ROD. The piston and connecting rod are removed as an assembly. Refer to PISTON, PIN AND RINGS section for removal procedure.

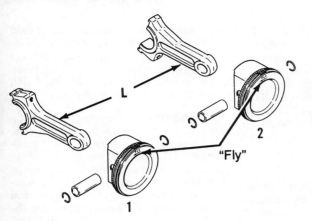

Fig. KO320—Note relationship of longer side of connecting rod (L) and "FLY" on piston crown when assembling piston and connecting rod.

The connecting rod rides directly on the crankpin. Renew connecting rod if bearing surfaces are scored or excessively worn. Specified connecting rod small end diameter is 17.015-17.023 mm (0.6699-0.6702 in.) with a wear limit of 17.036 mm (0.6707 in.). Piston pin-to-connecting rod clearance should be 0.015-0.028 mm (0.0006-0.0011 in.).

Specified connecting rod-to-crankpin clearance is 0.030-0.055 mm (0.0012-0.0022 in.) with a maximum allowable clearance of 0.07 mm (0.0025 in.). A connecting rod with a 0.25 mm

(0.010 in.) undersize big end is available. If crankshaft must be reground to accept an undersize connecting rod, refer to CRANKSHAFT section for machining information.

Specified rod side clearance on crankpin is 0.26-0.63 mm (0.010-0.025 in.).

Assemble piston and rod for No. 1 cylinder so long side of rod is on same side as "FLY" on piston crown (see Fig. KO320). Assemble piston and rod for No. 2 cylinder so that longer side of rod is on opposite side of "FLY" on piston crown.

Install piston and rod assembly in cylinder so arrow under "FLY" stamped on piston crown points toward flywheel side of engine. Install rod cap so chamfers on cap and rod are matched. Three different style connecting rod bolts are used (Fig. KO322). Each style bolt has a different tightening torque. Refer to Fig. KO322 to identify rod bolts and their respective torque values.

GOVERNOR. The engine is equipped with a flyweight mechanism

mounted on governor gear (5—Fig. KO316 or Fig. KO317). Remove crankcase cover for access to governor gear. Inspect gear assembly for excess wear and damage. The governor gear is held on governor shaft (3) by molded tabs on the gear. When gear is removed, the tabs are damaged and replacement of governor gear will be required. Gear and flyweight are available only as a unit assembly.

Specified governor shaft diameter is 5.990-6.000 mm (0.2358-0.2362 in.) with a wear limit of 5.977 mm (0.2353 in.). Clearance between governor gear bore and shaft should be 0.015-0.140 mm (0.0006-0.0055 in.).

OIL PUMP. The oil pump (7—Fig. KO316 or Fig. KO317) is attached to the inside of the crankcase cover. Unscrew and remove pump. Inspect gear for excessive wear and damage. Drive out pin to remove relief valve and spring. Specified spring free length is approximately 47.4 mm (1.87 in.). Inspect relief valve piston for nicks, burrs and other damage. Oil pump must be serviced as a unit assembly.

Tighten oil pump mounting screws to 10.7 N•m (95 in.-lb.) if installing pump on a new crankcase cover or to 6.7 N•m (60 in.-lbs.) if installing pump on a used crankcase cover. Check pump operation by rotating drive gear. If pump binds, loosen screws, relocate pump and recheck operation.

OIL COOLER AND REMOTE OIL FILTER. Some Command V-twin engines use an oil cooler and/or a remote-mounted oil filter (Fig. KO323). Make sure the cooler passages and filter adapter, fittings and hoses are clean and free-flowing. Clean and inspect all components for damage, including the

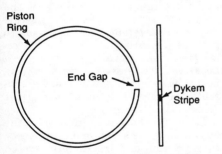

Fig. KO321—Colored stripe on face of ring should be left of gap when viewed from top.

Straight Shank 8mm Type Connecting Rod Bolt.
Torque these to **22.7 N•m (200 in. lbs.).**

Step-Down Type Connecting Rod Bolt: 8mm.
Torque these to **14.7 N•m (130 in. lbs.).**

Straight Shank 6mm Type Connecting Rod Bolt.
Torque these to **11.3 N•m (100 in. lbs.).**

Fig. KO322—Connecting rod bolt styles and their respective torque values.

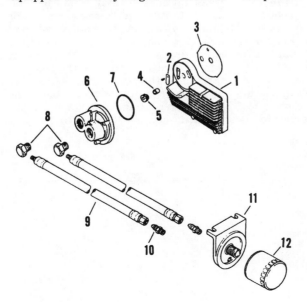

Fig. KO323—Exploded view of oil cooler and remote oil filter option used on some engines.

1. Oil cooler
2. Oil cooler relief valve
3. Gasket
4. Dowel
5. Adapter nipple
6. Remote filter adapter
7. O-ring
8. Fittings
9. Oil hose
10. Nipple
11. Oil filter base
12. Oil filter

oil cooler fins. Renew leaking or damaged components.

CRANKSHAFT. To remove crankshaft, remove flywheel, piston and rod assemblies as previously outlined, then withdraw crankshaft. Crankshaft rides in a renewable bushing in the crankcase and in an integral bearing in the crankcase cover.

Specified main journal diameter at both ends is 40.913-40.935 mm (1.6107-1.6116 in.) with a wear limit of 40.84 mm (1.608 in.). Maximum allowable main journal taper is 0.022 mm (0.0009 in.) and maximum allowable out-of-round is 0.025 mm (0.0010 in.). Main bearing journals cannot be machined undersize.

Specified inside diameter of the crankcase main bearing bushing is 40.965-41.003 mm (1.6128-1.6143 in.) with a maximum diameter of 41.016 mm (1.6148 in.). Clearance between crankshaft journal and main bearing at flywheel end should be 0.030-0.090 mm (0.0012-0.0035 in.). When renewing main bearing bushing in crankcase, be sure oil hole in bushing is aligned with oil hole in crankcase.

Specified inside diameter of the crankcase cover main bearing bushing is 40.974-40.987 mm (1.6131-1.6136 in.). Clearance between crankshaft journal and main bearing at pto end should be 0.039-0.074 mm (0.0015-0.0029 in.). The crankcase cover must be renewed if bearing bore diameter is excessively worn or damaged.

Specified standard crankpin diameter is 35.955-35.973 mm (1.4155-1.4162 in.) with a wear limit of 35.94 mm (1.415 in.). Maximum allowable crankpin taper is 0.018 mm (0.0007 in.) and maximum allowable out-of-round is 0.025 mm (0.0010 in.). Crankpin can be ground to accept a 0.25 mm (0.010 in.) undersize rod. Plug (21—Fig. KO316 or Fig. KO317) should be removed after machining operation so oil passages can be cleaned thoroughly. Use a suitable screw-type puller to extract plug. Be sure new plug does not leak.

Maximum allowable crankshaft runout is 0.15 mm (0.006 in.) measured at pto end of crankshaft with crankshaft supported in engine. Maximum allowable crankshaft runout is 0.10 mm (0.004 in.) measured at any point on crankshaft with crankshaft supported in V-blocks.

NOTE: Use Adapter Alignment Kit part No. 25 761 19 to correctly remount and realign the pto adapter on short blocks and engines equipped with a splined crankshaft. Kit consists of four alignment pins, RTV sealant and installation instructions. Failure to properly align PTO adapter will result in excessive crankshaft runout and damage to the engine and equipment.

To install crankshaft, reverse removal procedure.

Some engines equipped with Warner CVX-model electric clutches can exhibit severe main bearing erosion and pitting if the clutch develops shorted windings. If a faulty clutch is transferred to a new or reconditioned engine or short block, the bearings will be damaged again in as few as 30 hours of operation. If a bearing failure is experienced, the electric clutch must be tested for proper operation prior to use. Test the clutch as follows:

Disconnect the clutch leads from the equipment harness. Zero an ohmmeter on the R×1 scale. Measure the resistance across the clutch leads. Resistance should read 2-4 ohms. Test the resistance from each lead terminal to the clutch housing. Infinity (no continuity or an open circuit) should be indicated. Connect a 14-gauge or larger jumper wire from the positive terminal of a fully charged battery to one of the clutch leads. Connect another jumper wire of the same gauge to the negative terminal of the battery. Touch the other end of the negative jumper cable to the engine crankshaft, and listen for the clutch to engage. Reverse the battery leads and repeat the test. Clutch should NOT engage with leads connected in either direction. If resistance readings are other than indicated or if clutch engages during the above test, the clutch is faulty and must be replaced.

OIL SENSOR. Some engines may be equipped with an Oil Sentry oil pressure monitor. The system uses a pressure switch installed on the breather cover between the cylinders. The switch is designed to break contact as oil pressure increases to normal pressure and to make contact when oil pressure decreases within the range of 20.7-34.5 kPa (3-5 psi). Switch may be connected to a warning device or into the ignition circuit so the engine will stop.

To check the sensor switch, a regulated supply of compressed air and a continuity tester are required. With zero pressure applied to switch, tester should indicate continuity across switch terminal and ground. When pressure is increased through range of 20.7-34.5 kPa (3-5 psi), switch should open and tester should indicate no continuity. If switch fails test, install a new switch.

GRASS SCREEN. Some late production CH18-20 engines with the 7-post cooling fan grass screen have had retainers added to three of the seven fan retaining posts to provide more positive retention of the screen. To prevent fracturing the posts when removing the retainers, insert a hook-type tool next to the mounting posts and carefully pull outward to separate the retainers. Then unsnap the screen from the posts.

To install the screen, first snap the screen onto the seven mounting posts, then position and install retainers on three nonadjacent posts.

NOTE: Retainers should not be reinstalled on posts that have had retainers previously installed.

To install the retainers, place a 6 mm (¼ in.) socket over each retainer and tap lightly to lock in place on the posts.

KOHLER

KOHLER COMPANY
Kohler, Wisconsin 53044

Model	No. Cyls.	Bore	Stroke	Displacement	Power Rating
TH14	2	73 mm (2.87 in.)	62 mm (2.44 in.)	520 cc (31.7 cu. in.)	10.5 kW (14 hp)
TH16	2	73 mm (2.87 in.)	62 mm (2.44 in.)	520 cc (31.7 cu. in.)	11.9 kW (16 hp)
TH18	2	75 mm (2.95 in.)	65 mm (2.56 in.)	574 cc (35.0 cu. in.)	13.4 kW (18 hp)

ENGINE IDENTIFICATION

All models are four-stroke, air-cooled, horizontal-crankshaft, twin-cylinder engines. They are overhead cam engines, with the camshafts driven by a cog-toothed timing belt located behind the flywheel. The upper crankcase, cylinders, heads and intake manifold are cast in one piece. All models have a full-pressure, filtered lubrication system, a fixed-jet side draft carburetor, and electronic capacitive discharge ignition system. No. 1 cylinder is the cylinder closest to the flywheel.

Engine model, specification and serial numbers are usually located on a decal on the No. 2 cylinder side of the blower housing, just below the crankshaft centerline. Always furnish engine identification numbers when ordering parts.

Metric fasteners are used throughout, except that the crankshaft pto pilot hole is usually 3/8-24 inch thread.

MAINTENANCE

SPARK PLUG. Recommended spark plug is Champion RC12YC or equivalent. Electrode gap is 0.75 mm (0.030 inch). Tighten spark plug to 24.4-29.8 N•m (18-22 ft.-lbs.).

CAUTION: Kohler does not recommend using abrasive blasting to clean spark plugs because this may introduce abrasive material into the engine that could cause extensive damage.

LUBRICATION. Check oil level at regular intervals, and maintain oil level at full mark on dipstick. Clean dipstick/cap area before removing the dipstick. Push the dipstick in until seated in the dipstick tube, then remove it to check oil level. DO NOT overfill.

When changing oil, always drain the dirty oil while the engine is still warm from operation, and tilt the engine slightly toward the oil drain. Tighten drain plug to 13.6 N•m (10 ft.-lb.).

Manufacturer recommends using oil with an API service rating of SG or SH, or any rating formulated to supercede SG or SH. Use SAE 10W-30 oil for temperatures above 0° F (–18° C). When operating in temperatures below 32° F (0° C), SAE 5W-20, 5W-30 oil or 10W-30 oil may be used. Do not use SAE 10W-40 oil in any temperature.

In overhauled or new short blocks, use SAE 10W-30 oil for the first five hours of operation, then change oil according to ambient temperature requirements. Recommended oil change interval after 5-hour break-in is every 100 hours of operation.

It is recommended that a new oil filter be installed at each oil change. When installing new oil filter, lubricate the filter gasket with clean oil prior to installation. Thread the filter on the filter adapter until gasket contacts the adapter, then hand-tighten filter an additional ½ turn.

Crankcase oil capacity is approximately 1.4 liters (1.5 qt.).

Some engines are equipped with a low oil pressure warning system. If oil pressure falls below a predetermined value due to problems such as low oil level or clogged oil passages, the oil sensor will either shut down the engine or activate a warning signal, depending on the system.

AIR CLEANER. These engines are equipped with a high-density paper air cleaner element. Most engines are also equipped with an oiled-foam precleaner wrapped around the paper air filter. Standard air filters are shown in Fig. KO400. Inspect the air filter and filter mount components daily.

NOTE: Operating the engine with damaged or loose air filter components could allow the engine to ingest unfiltered air, resulting in rapid wear of internal components.

Service the precleaner after every 25 hours of operation and the air filter after every 100 hours of operation. Service more frequently if engine is operated in severe conditions.

Clean precleaner element by washing in soapy water. Allow to dry, then apply clean engine oil. Squeeze out excess oil.

The paper air filter should be renewed rather than cleaned. Do not wash or direct pressurized air at filter.

Be sure the air filter cover knob is secure prior to operating the engine.

CRANKCASE BREATHER. The crankcase breather assembly is located in the 'vee' between the two cylinders. Refer to REPAIRS section for service.

FUEL PUMP. The fuel pump is integral with the No. 1 cylinder valve cover, and is operated by its own lobe on the No. 1 camshaft. Fuel pump outlet pressure should not exceed 13.8 kPa (2 psi).

The fuel pump is not serviceable. If it becomes inoperative, the fuel pump/valve cover assembly must be replaced. Tighten pump/cover fasteners to 5.6 N•m (50 in.-lb.).

CARBURETOR. The carburetors used on these engines have fixed idle mixture and high-speed circuits. The only adjustment to the carburetor is for the low idle speed (Fig. KO401). Refer to the equipment manufacturer's specifications for correct idle speed. For unspecified applications, basic low idle speed is 1200 rpm. Turn idle speed adjustment screw clockwise to increase speed, counterclockwise to decrease speed.

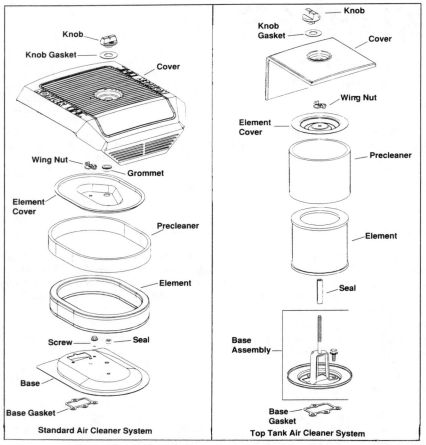

Fig. KO400—Exploded view of air cleaner components. Standard system is shown in left view and top tank system is shown in right view.

ing correct repair parts, note the part number of the carburetor is stamped on the top choke flange of the carburetor body.

To check float height, hold carburetor upside-down so float arm is resting on the fuel inlet valve as shown in Fig. KO404. Float arm must press lightly against fuel inlet valve without compressing the spring in valve. Float height should be 16.5 mm (0.65 in.) measured from bottom of float to carburetor body flange. Float is not adjustable. If float height is not to specification, replace the float, float pin and fuel inlet valve.

Reassemble the carburetor using new gaskets. Tighten fuel bowl retaining screw or solenoid to 5.1-6.2 N•m (45-55 in.-lb.).

To service engines with LP-gas carburetors, refer to SERVICING KOHLER ACCESSORIES section, LPG FUEL SYSTEMS.

GOVERNOR. A camshaft-mounted, centrifugal-flyball mechanical governor is used on all engines (Fig. KO405).

To adjust governor linkage, first make sure that all throttle and governor linkages are in good operating condition. Loosen the governor lever cross-shaft hex nut. Move the governor lever so carburetor is in wide-open throttle position. While holding governor lever, insert a pin into the hole in top of governor cross-shaft. Rotate the cross-shaft counterclockwise to its stop, then tighten hex nut to 9.9 N•m (88 in.-lb.).

Governor sensitivity determines how quickly the governor reacts when a load

To overhaul carburetor, carefully disassemble only those components shown in Fig. KO402.

NOTE: Slow jet nozzle (2—Fig. KO403) and high-speed emulsion tube (11) are non-serviceable parts of the carburetor body. No attempt should be made to remove these components, or carburetor may be permanently damaged.

Clean the carburetor with a good-quality commercial carburetor solvent and compressed air. Inspect all components for wear or damage and renew if necessary. To help insure obtain-

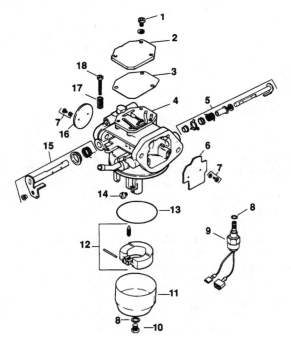

Fig. KO401—Idle speed screw (S) is only adjustment available for the carburetor.

Fig. KO402—Exploded view of carburetor typical of all models. Optional fuel shutoff solenoid (9) is installed in place of bowl screw (10).

1. Screw
2. Passage cover
3. Gasket
4. Carburetor body
5. Choke shaft assy.
6. Choke plate
7. Setscrew
8. Gasket
9. Shutoff solenoid
10. Bowl retaining screw
11. Fuel bowl
12. Float & fuel inlet needle
13. Gasket
14. Main jet
15. Throttle shaft assy.
16. Throttle plate
17. Spring
18. Idle speed screw

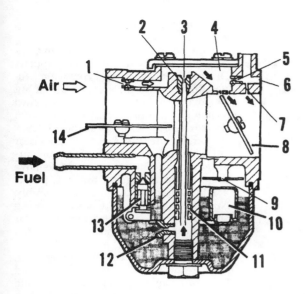

Fig. KO403—Cross-sectional view of carburetor.

1. Slow air bleed jet
2. Slow jet
3. Transfer port
4. Idle progression chamber
5. Idle limiter jet
6. Idle port passage
7. Idle port
8. Throttle plate
9. Bowl vent
10. Float
11. Emulsion tube
12. Main jet
13. Fuel inlet needle
14. Choke plate

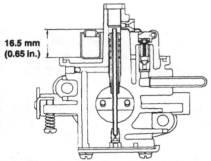

Fig. KO404—Float height is measured with carburetor body inverted. Refer to text.

is applied to the engine. The governor setting is too sensitive if speed surging occurs with a change in engine load. The governor setting is not sensitive enough if a large drop in speed occurs when a load is applied to the engine. Governor sensitivity is adjusted by repositioning the governor spring in the holes in the governor pivot lever (Fig. KO406). Move end of governor spring away from governor lever pivot point to decrease sensitivity. Move the spring closer to the governor lever pivot point to increase sensitivity.

Constant-speed governor linkage with fixed-throttle positioning is shown in Fig. KO407. Reposition the flange nuts on the constant speed rod to adjust engine speed setting. Governor sensitivity adjustment is the same as for the variable-speed governor. Move the governor spring end away from the governor lever pivot point to increase sensitivity, or closer to the pivot point to decrease sensitivity.

IGNITION. The electronic CD (capacitive discharge) ignition system con-

sists of a magnet permanently fastened to the flywheel and two ignition modules (one for each cylinder). An ignition switch stops the engine by grounding the primary circuit of each module.

WARNING: Touching electrical wires or components while the engine is running can produce harmful electrical shock.

Inspect the engine wiring prior to testing the ignition system. Faulty wiring or poor connections can cause ignition problems. Misfire under load, hard starting or low power may be caused by excessive resistance in the engine stop circuit. Isolate the engine from the stop circuit by disconnecting any auxiliary stop switch wires or safety interlock switches connected to the stop circuit, then test run the engine to determine if the stop circuit is the problem source. Make certain the safety interlock

switches are properly connected after completion of testing.

Test the system for spark using Tester No. 24 455 02. Connect the tester ground clip to a good engine ground, not to the spark plug. Make sure the spark plug lead on the cylinder not being tested is properly attached to its spark plug. Alternately connect the spark plug leads to the tester, then crank engine and observe spark. If tests show spark but the engine runs poorly, replace the spark plugs. If only one side is not firing, check connections and wiring on that side. If wiring and connections are satisfactory, replace the module and retest. If neither side indicates spark, check for faulty ignition switch or shorted stop lead.

Air gap between ignition modules and flywheel should be set to 0.20-0.30 mm (0.008-0.012 in.).

BATTERY CHARGING SYSTEM. Refer to SERVICING KOHLER ACCESSORIES section.

VALVE ADJUSTMENT. Refer to REPAIRS section.

REPAIRS

TIGHTENING TORQUE. Recommended torque values are as follows:

Blower housing
M5 fasteners . . . . 4.0 N•m (35 in.-lb.)

M6 fasteners
(into crankcase) . . . . 7.3 N•m (65 in.-lb.)

M6 fasteners
(into sheet metal). . . . . 4.0 N•m (35 in.-lb.)

Carburetor stud nuts . . . . . . 9.9 N•m (88 in.-lb.)

Charging stator . . . . 4.0 N•m (35 in.-lb.)

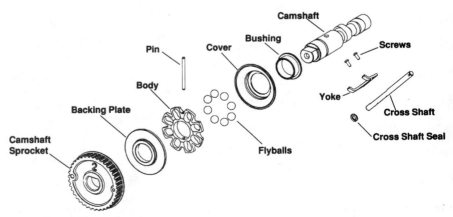

Fig. KO405—Exploded view of governor components.

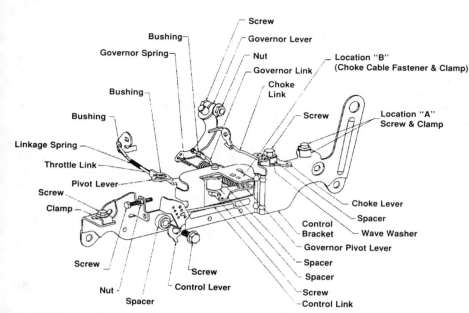

Fig. KO406—Standard throttle control plate and governor linkage assembly.

Screw
Governor Lever
Nut
Governor Link
Choke Link
Bushing
Governor Spring
Bushing
Bushing
Linkage Spring
Throttle Link
Pivot Lever
Screw
Clamp
Screw
Nut
Spacer
Screw
Control Lever
Location "B"
(Choke Cable Fastener & Clamp)
Screw
Location "A"
Screw & Clamp
Choke Lever
Spacer
Wave Washer
Control Bracket
Governor Pivot Lever
Spacer
Spacer
Screw
Control Link

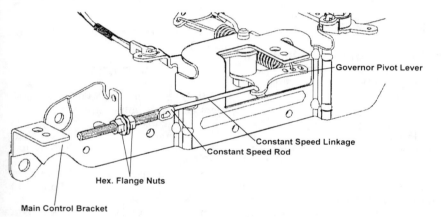

Fig. KO407—Constant-speed governor linkage and control plate assembly.

Governor Pivot Lever
Constant Speed Linkage
Constant Speed Rod
Hex. Flange Nuts
Main Control Bracket

Connecting rod	11.3 N•m (100 in.-lb.)
Crankcase breather	
Breather cover	5.6 N•m (50 in.-lb.)
Breather retainer	4.0 N•m (35 in.-lb.)
Reed retainer	4.0 N•m (35 in.-lb.)
Crankcase halves	24.4 N•m (216 in.-lb.)
Flywheel	66.4 N•m (49 ft.-lb.)
Flywheel fan	9.9 N•m (88 in.-lb.)
Ignition module	4.0-6.2 N•m (35-55 in.-lb.)
Oil pickup screen	4.0 N•m (35 in.-lb.)
Oil pump cover	7.3 N•m (65 in.-lb.)
Oil pump drive gear	9.9 N•m (88 in.-lb.)
Oil pressure relief plug	11.3 N•m (100 in.-lb.)
Oil sentry switch (max.)	3.4 N•m (30 in.-lb.)
Rectifier/regulator	4.0 N•m (35 in.-lb.)
Rocker arm cover	5.6 N•m (50 in.-lb.)
Rocker arm shaft	4.0 N•m (35 in.-lb.)
Spark plug	24.4-29.8 Nm (18-22 ft.-lb.)
Starter motor	7.9 N•m (70 in.-lb.)
Throttle control bracket	9.9 N•m (88 in.-lb.)
Timing belt idler	7.3 N•m (65 in.-lb.)

DISASSEMBLY SEQUENCE. The following disassembly sequence is suggested for complete engine disassembly. Sequence may be altered for special op-

tions or accessories. Refer to Fig. KO408.

Shut off fuel supply and remove engine-mounted fuel tank (if equipped). Drain crankcase oil and remove oil filter. Remove the air cleaner assembly. Remove exhaust system and discard gaskets. Disconnect breather hose from the carburetor. Loosen governor lever nut and slide the lever off governor cross shaft. Remove the nuts from carburetor mounting studs, then remove the carburetor, control bracket, governor lever and linkage as an assembly. Note the position of governor spring ends in the holes in governor levers for proper assembly. Remove grass screen or rewind starter. If the rectifier/regulator is mounted on the blower housing, remove the screw securing the ground lead. Remove blower housing and side shrouds, noting locations of different length screws. If equipped with electric starter motor, disconnect leads and remove the solenoid.

NOTE: The starter through-bolts are also the mounting bolts. Tape the end caps to the frame to prevent them from separating when the bolts are loosened.

Loosen the electric starter motor mounting bolts just enough to remove the starter. Do not completely remove the bolts from the starter. Remove side baffles from the cylinders. Turn the flywheel magnet away from the modules, and disconnect the white "kill" leads. Remove the ignition modules and spark plugs.

NOTE: Use a proper tool, such as a ring gear lock or strap wrench, to hold the flywheel when loosening or tightening the flywheel screw. Do not use a pry bar or wedge to hold the flywheel, as the flywheel could be damaged.

Turn flywheel retaining screw counterclockwise to remove it. Use a flywheel puller to remove the flywheel from the crankshaft taper. Note the location of tension spring on crankshaft behind flywheel. The spring must be installed in same position during assembly. Also note stator wiring and harness routing for proper assembly. Remove flywheel key from the crankshaft. Remove the stator. Remove the timing belt idler pulley, then slip the timing belt off the pulleys.

Remove the valve covers and dipstick. Rotate camshafts to relieve spring tension from rocker arms. On No. 1 cylinder, remove C-clip that retains the camshaft. Withdraw the cam-

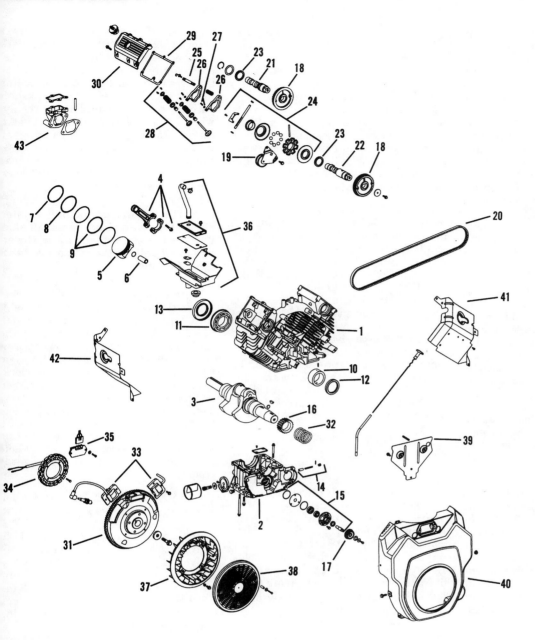

Fig. KO408—Exploded view of engine typical of all models.

1. Crankcase/cylinder assy.
2. Lower crankcase/oil pan
3. Crankshaft
4. Connecting rod
5. Piston
6. Wrist pin
7. Top compression ring
8. Middle compression ring
9. Oil control ring
10. Sleeve-type main bearing
11. Ball-type main bearing
12. Oil seal
13. Oil seal
14. Oil pressure relief valve assy.
15. Oil pump assy.
16. Timing belt drive sprocket
17. Oil pump drive sprocket
18. Camshaft drive sprockets
19. Belt idler assy.
20. Timing belt
21. No. 1 camshaft
22. No. 2 camshaft
23. Camshaft oil seals
24. Governor assy.
25. Rocker arm shaft
26. Rocker arms
27. Adjusting screw
28. Valve components
29. Gasket
30. Valve cover
31. Flywheel
32. Tension spring
33. Ignition modules
34. Charging stator
35. Rectifier-regulator
36. Crankcase breather assy.
37. Cooling fan
38. Fan screen
39. Valley baffle
40. Blower housing
41. Side shield
42. Side shield
43. Air filter elbow

haft and remove thrust washer from ocker box. Remove two screws securing rocker arm shaft, then remove shaft nd rocker arms as an assembly. On No. 2 cylinder, rotate the camshaft until the coiled spring pin is visible in the governor body. Use a punch to drive the pin down about 16 mm (⅝ in.). Rotate he camshaft 180°, and pull the pin out f the camshaft. Hold the governor alves together while removing the amshaft, then remove the governor assembly. Remove two screws from ocker arm shaft, then lift rocker arm nd shaft off rocker box. Remove overnor yoke and cross shaft.

Remove the rectifier/regulator. Remove the valley baffle and engine wire harness. Remove the crankcase breather. Note that the grommet located beneath the breather housing fits snugly and will cause some resistance when removing the breather housing. Remove the Oil Sentry switch if equipped. Remove the oil filter adapter nipple.

To separate crankcase halves, remove the two screws from the flywheel side of the crankcase. On engines without an engine-mounted gas tank, use the two carburetor stud nuts as jam nuts and remove the air filter mounting stud from top of the intake manifold. Turn the crankcase upside-down and remove remaining crankcase screws. Note that pto side has two M8x115 screws and all others are M8x40. Separate crankcase halves by carefully prying between the tabs located on both corners of pto side. Remove connecting rod cap screws.

NOTE: Connecting rod and cap match marks face flywheel side on No. 1 cylinder and pto side on No. 2 cylinder. Number the rod caps to correspond to their respective cylinder. DO NOT mix the connecting rods and caps.

Remove piston and connecting rod assemblies from cylinders. Mark the pistons and rods to match the previously numbered rod caps. Lift the crankshaft out of the crankcase.

To remove oil pump components, place lower crankcase half on workbench with mount feet down. Using a flywheel holding tool or equivalent, block oil pump sprocket from turning while removing the retaining screw from the sprocket. Remove the sprocket from pump shaft using a small puller if necessary. Remove oil pump cover. Note the position of components inside the oil pump, then remove the components. To remove oil pressure relief valve components, remove Allen-head pipe plug from lower crankcase half. Drive the retaining pin from the relief valve, then remove relief valve piston and spring.

To remove valves and valve springs, install valve blocking tools from tool kit No. 28 761 02 into the cylinder. Install the lower crankcase half and secure with two M8x40 bolts. Turn the crankcase upright. Compress the valve springs, and remove the valve keepers and springs. Identify the location of components for assembly in original locations. Turn the crankcase upside-down. Remove the lower crankcase half and valve blocking tools. Pull the valves from the cylinder heads using a long magnet or suction cup end of valve lapping tool.

CAMSHAFTS. These engines have two camshafts, one mounted within each cylinder head. Camshafts are not interchangeable. The camshaft for No. 1 cylinder has three lobes—one for each valve rocker arm and one to operate the fuel pump. Camshaft for No. 2 cylinder serves as the mount and drive for the governor assembly. The camshafts ride in bearing bores machined directly into the cylinder block casting. Camshaft specifications are as follows:

End play
No. 1 cylinder . . . . 0.0-0.7 mm
    (0.0-0.0275 in.)
No. 2 cylinder . . . . 0.0-1.3 mm
    (0.0-0.051 in.)
Running clearance . . 0.025-0.105 mm
    (0.001-0.004 in.)
Bearing bore ID
Front . . . . 32.000-32.025 mm
    (1.2598-1.2608 in.)
Wear limit . . . . 32.04 mm
    (1.2614 in.)
Rear . . . . 24.800-24.825 mm
    (0.9764-0.9774 in.)
Wear limit . . . . 24.84 mm
    (0.9779 in.)
Camshaft bearing
journal OD
Front . . . . 31.920-31.975 mm
    (1.2567-1.2589 in.)
Wear limit . . . . 31.91 mm

    (1.2562 in.)
Rear . . . . 24.720-24.775 mm
    (0.9732-0.9754 in.)
Wear limit . . . . 24.71 mm
    (0.9728 in.)
Replace camshafts if wear exceeds specified limits, or if lobes are badly worn. When replacing a camshaft, always replace its corresponding rocker arms to prevent premature lobe wear on the new camshaft. Replace the cylinder block if camshaft bearing bores are worn beyond specified limits.

CAMSHAFT DRIVE SYSTEM. Refer to Fig. KO409. A toothed timing belt drives the camshafts from the crankshaft. The flywheel and charging stator must be removed for access to the timing belt. Refer to the DISASSEMBLY SEQUENCE for procedure.

Inspect the belt and replace if it is cracked, split or missing teeth. Inspect the camshaft sprockets and replace if damaged or excessively worn. Note that both camshafts use the same part number sprocket. The sprocket is mounted on the No. 1 camshaft with the side marked number "1" facing outward. On the No. 2 camshaft, the sprocket is reversed so the number "2" on its face is facing outward.

Install the timing belt as follows: The use of Timing Tool Set part No. 28 761 01 is recommended when installing the timing belt to ensure correct camshaft timing. Install the flywheel key in the crankshaft. Rotate camshafts until sprocket numbers are at the top and the four timing holes in sprockets are horizontal (Fig. KO409). Insert pins of timing tool set into sprocket timing holes. Rotate crankshaft to set engine at TDC of No. 1 cylinder. The third tooth to the left of keyway will be at 12 o'clock and

keyway will be at approximately 2 o'clock (Fig. KO410). The timing mark on sprocket should line up with vertical boss on upper crankcase casting. Slide the crankshaft holding tool of timing tool set over flywheel end of crankshaft with the tool's keyway slot over the flywheel key and the mounting tab toward the crankcase. Secure the mounting tab to the stator lower mounting boss. Route the timing belt around the sprockets as shown in Fig. KO409, leaving idler assembly loose.

NOTE: Engine crankshaft rotates clockwise viewed from camshaft side. If belt is marked with an arrow, the arrow must point in the clockwise direction of rotation.

Install top screw into idler bracket finger tight. Install square drive of ³⁄₈ inch torque wrench in square slot in idler bracket. Apply leverage to the idler bracket so that the lower screw can be installed. Apply 3.4-4.5 N•m (30-40 in.-lb.) torque in a counterclockwise direction to the idler bracket, then tighten the idler bracket lower screw. Tighten idler bracket screws to 7.3 N•m (65 in.-lb.). Remove the timing tools. Install the stator and tighten mounting screws to 4.0 N•m (35 in.-lb.). Make sure the stator wiring is routed away from the belt.

VALVE SERVICE. Refer to the following table for valve system specifications.
Valve seat angle 44.5
Valve face angle 45
Valve margin (min.)
Intake . . . . 1.10 mm
    (0.043 in.)
Exhaust . . . . 1.13 mm
    (0.045 in.)
Valve stem OD
Intake . . . . 5.982-6.000 mm
    (0.2355-0.2362 in.)

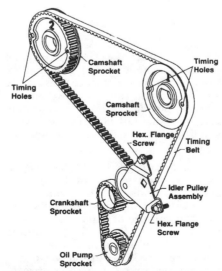

Fig. KO409—A single timing belt drives both camshafts and the oil pump.

Timing Mark

Fig. KO410—Crankshaft sprocket with timing mark.

Exhaust. . . . . 5.970-5.988 mm
(0.2350-0.2357 in.)
Valve guide ID . . . . . . 6.038-6.058 mm
(0.2377-0.2385 in.)
Wear limit. . . . . 6.19 mm
(0.2413 in.)

To check valve stem-to-guide clearance, thoroughly clean valve guide and measure guide inside diameter. Measure valve stem outside diameter at the guide contact area. The difference between the two measurements is the stem-to-guide clearance. Maximum allowable clearance is 0.038-0.076 mm (0.0015-0.0030 in.) for intake and 0.050-0.088 mm (0.0020-0.0035 in.) for exhaust.

Valve guides are not replaceable. If guide is excessively worn, ream the guide 0.25 mm (0.010 in.) oversize and install new valve with oversize stem. Replace the crankcase assembly if guide inside diameter is worn beyond 6.44 mm (0.2513 in.).

Hardened steel alloy intake and exhaust valve seat inserts are factory installed and are not replaceable. If seat face is worn, reface the insert to proper specification. Lap new or refaced valves to their seats.

NOTE: Thoroughly clean the upper crankcase and valve with warm soapy water to remove all lapping compound. After drying parts, apply light coat of engine oil to prevent rust.

VALVE ADJUSTMENT. Remove the valve covers for access to the rocker arms. Rotate flywheel clockwise to set No. 1 piston at TDC on compression stroke. Measure clearance between rocker arms and valve stems for No. 1 cylinder using a feeler gauge. Clearance for intake valve should be 0.013-0.064 mm (0.0005-0.0025 in.) and exhaust valve clearance should be 0.076-0.127 mm (0.003-0.005 in.). To adjust clearance, loosen rocker arm locknut and adjusting screw (11—Fig. KO411). Insert proper thickness feeler gauge between rocker arm and valve stem. Turn the adjusting screw until a slight drag is felt as the feeler gauge is withdrawn. Tighten the adjusting screw locknut and recheck clearance.

Rotate the flywheel 270° (¾ turn) clockwise to set the No. 2 piston at TDC on compression stroke. Repeat the clearance setting procedure for valves on No. 2 cylinder.

Install new valve cover gasket. Tighten valve cover fasteners to 5.6 N•m (50 in.-lb.) in the sequence shown in Fig. KO412.

CYLINDERS. The upper crankcase casting includes non-serviceable cylinder liners. The cylinders cannot be bored, and oversize pistons and rings are not available. If either cylinder bore is scored, tapered, out-of-round or worn beyond specified limit, the upper crankcase/cylinder assembly must be replaced.

Refer to the following table for cylinder bore specifications.

Cylinder ID
TH14, TH16 . . . . . 73.006-73.031 mm
(2.8742-2.8752 in.)
Wear limit . . . . 73.07 mm
(2.8767 in.)
TH18 . . . . 75.025-75.050 mm
(2.9537-2.9547 in.)
Wear limit . . . . 75.09 mm
(2.9563 in.)
Out-of-round, max. . . . . 0.13 mm
(0.005 in.)
Taper, max. . . . . 0.13 mm
(0.005 in.)
Piston-to-bore clearance
TH14, TH16 . . . . 0.022-0.065 mm
(0.0009-0.0026 in.)
TH18 . . . . 0.041-0.084 mm
(0.0016-0.0033 in.)

To determine piston-to-bore clearance, use a micrometer to measure piston skirt diameter at a point 6 mm (¼ in.) above bottom of skirt, perpendicular to piston pin (Fig. KO413). Using an inside micrometer, telescoping gauge or bore gauge, measure cylinder bore approximately 63 mm (2.5 in.) below the top of bore, perpendicular to piston pin. The difference between the two measurements is the piston-to-bore clearance.

Use new ring sets when installing the pistons. Do not reuse old rings. Cylinders must be deglazed before installing pistons with new rings. Use only a ball hone, not a flat-stone type hone, to deglaze and renew the crosshatch in the cylinders. Do not allow the hone balls to contact the combustion chamber area.

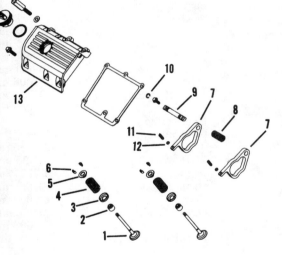

Fig. KO411—Exploded view of valve train components.

1. Valve
2. Oil seal
3. Valve spring seat
4. Valve spring
5. Valve spring retainer
6. Valve spring keepers
7. Rocker arm
8. Spacer
9. Rocker arm shaft
10. Retaining clip
11. Adjusting screw
12. Locknut
13. Rocker cover

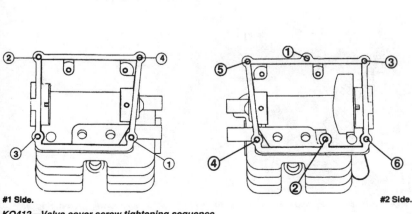

#1 Side.   #2 Side.

Fig. KO412—Valve cover screw tightening sequence.

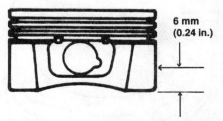

6 mm
(0.24 in.)

Fig. KO413—Measure piston skirt diameter 6 mm (0.24 in.) above bottom of skirt at right angle to piston pin.

Thoroughly clean the cylinders using a stiff brush with warm soapy water after the honing is completed. Rinse with warm running water. Repeat washing and rinsing until all traces of honing grit are removed. Do not attempt to clean the cylinder with any type of solvent, as it will not remove the fine metal particles from the crosshatch grooves. Dry the cylinder walls, then lubricate with clean engine oil to prevent rust.

PISTONS, PINS AND RINGS. Pistons may be reused if within specified wear limits. The original piston pin can be reused also, but new piston pin retainers must be installed. Do not reuse old piston rings. If reusing old pistons, thoroughly clean combustion deposits from ring grooves being careful not to damage the ring lands.

Prior to installing new rings on the pistons, position the top and middle compression rings (one at a time) into their intended cylinders and measure ring end gap as shown in Fig. KO414. Specified end gap for top ring is 0.180-0.380 mm (0.0071-0.0150 in.) for all models. Specified end gap for middle ring is 0.180-0.440 mm (0.0071-0.0173 in.) for TH14 and TH16, and 0.180-0.450 mm (0.0071-0.0178 in.) for TH18. If end gap is too large, check cylinder bore for excessive wear. If end gap is less than specified, check to make sure the correct ring is being installed.

Carefully follow instructions included with the ring set when installing the rings. Use a ring expander tool to install the compression rings. Install bottom (oil control ring) first followed by the middle, then top compression rings. Refer to Fig. KO415 for correct piston ring installation. Install oil ring expander and then the oil-wiper rails in

lower ring groove. Note that one rail is positioned below the expander and the other rail is positioned above the expander. Make sure the ends of the expander do not overlap. Install the lower compression ring in middle groove, making sure the "PIP" marked side faces top of the piston. Install the top compression ring with either side up.

After installing new compression rings on piston, measure the ring side clearance by installing a feeler gauge between ring and piston groove (Fig. KO416). Side clearance for top ring should be 0.040-0.085 mm (0.0016-0.0033 in.) for all models. Side clearance for middle ring should be 0.030-0.080 mm (0.0012-0.0031 in.) for TH14 and TH16, and 0.030-0.076 mm (0.0012-0.0030 in.) for TH18. Replace piston if side clearance exceeds specifications.

Stagger ring end gaps at approximately 120° intervals. Oil ring rails should also be staggered. Lubricate pistons, rings and cylinders with clean engine oil prior to assembling pistons into cylinders.

CONNECTING RODS. Inspect connecting rod crankpin and wrist pin bearing surfaces for wear or damage. Check the connecting rod-to-crankpin running clearance with Plastigage, following instructions provided with the Plastigage. Refer to the following table for connecting rod dimensions and clearances.

Connecting rod-to-crankpin running clearance
New . . . . 0.030-0.056 mm
(0.0012-0.0022 in.)

Wear limit . . . . 0.07 mm
(0.0028 in.)
Connecting rod-to-
crankpin side
clearance . . . . 0.250-0.740 mm
(0.0098-0.0291 in.)
Wrist pin bearing bore ID
New . . . . 17.015-17.023 mm
(0.6699-0.6702 in.)
Wear limit . . . . 17.04 mm
(0.6708 in.)

Service replacement connecting rods are available in standard and 0.25 mm (0.010 in.) undersize crankpin dimensions. Undersized rod can be identified by the hole drilled in the lower end of the rod beam.

CRANKSHAFT. Inspect crankshaft for wear or damage. Measure the wear surfaces and compare with the specifications listed in the table below.

Sleeve bearing ID
New . . . . 45.071-45.111 mm
(1.7744-1.7760 in.)
Wear limit . . . . 45.120 mm
(1.7764 in.)
Crankshaft journal-
to-sleeve
clearance . . . . 0.030-0.090 mm
(0.0012-0.0035 in.)
Flywheel-end main
bearing journal
OD, new . . . . 45.021-45.041 mm
(1.7725-1.7735 in.)
OD, wear limit . . . . 44.95 mm
(1.7696 in.)
Taper, max. . . . . 0.020 mm
(0.0008 in.)
Out-of-round, max. . . . . . . 0.020 mm
(0.0008 in.)
Connecting rod journal
OD, new . . . . 31.948-31.966 mm
(1.2578-1.2585 in.)
OD, wear limit . . . . 31.93 mm
(1.2571 in.)
Taper, max. . . . . 0.020 mm
(0.0008 in.)
Out-of-round, max. . . . . 0.020 mm
(0.0008 in.)
Crankshaft end play . . . Not adjustable

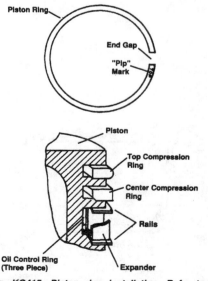

Fig. KO414—Measuring piston ring end gap. Refer to text.

Fig. KO415—Piston ring installation. Refer to text.

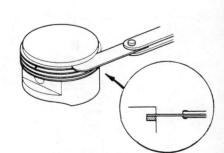

Fig. KO416—Measuring piston ring side clearance. Refer to text.

Crankshaft total indicated runout
  Pto end, crankshaft
    in engine . . . . 0.015 mm
                          (0.0006 in.)
  Entire crankshaft,
    in V-blocks . . . . 0.010 mm
                          (0.0004 in.)

The following procedure is recommended to disassemble the crankshaft: Remove the belt drive sprocket. The sprocket has a low interference fit on the crankshaft. If it will not slide off with minimum effort, heat the sprocket slightly with a propane torch until it expands and loosens, then remove it. Remove sprocket key from crankshaft. Remove the oil seals and discard them. Remove the sleeve bearing from flywheel end of crankshaft. Check the ball bearing on pto end of crankshaft for roughness or looseness. If bearing turns easily and noiselessly, it can be reused. Use appropriate puller or press to remove the ball bearing if renewal is necessary.

NOTE: On TH18 engines, remove the snap ring from crankshaft shoulder prior to removing the bearing. Do not discard the snap ring unless replacing.

Connecting rod journal and flywheel-end main journal can be reground 0.25 mm (0.010 in.) undersize. If crankpin is reground, make sure that the fillet blends smoothly with the reground crankpin (Fig. KO417).

IMPORTANT: After crankshaft journals are reground, the plug located in the end of the crankpin oil passage must be removed in order to clean grinding deposits from oil passages. Failure to remove the plug and clean the passages will result in serious engine damage.

To remove the oil passage plug, drill a 3/16 inch hole through the plug. Place a flat washer over the face of the plug

bore. Thread a 1-inch long self-tapping screw into the plug through the washer (Fig. KO418). Tighten the screw until it pulls the plug from the crankshaft. Thoroughly clean the oil passages and the plug bore before installing a new plug. Tap the plug into the bore until it seats at bottom of the bore (Fig. KO419).

When pressing ball bearing onto crankshaft, support the counterweight gap to prevent rod journal stress. Press ball bearing flush to shoulder (Fig. KO419). Note that TH18 engines have a snap ring that locks the ball bearing to the crankshaft. Be sure to install the snap ring after the bearing is pressed onto the crankshaft.

Lubricate the flywheel-end main bearing sleeve and crankshaft journal with engine oil, then position the sleeve onto the crankshaft.

CRANKCASE OIL SEALS. Lubricate the oil seal lips with engine oil prior to installation. It is recommended that the oil seals be installed after the crankshaft is assembled into the crankcase. Flywheel-end seal and pto-end seal are not interchangeable. Use a suitable seal driver to install the seals to depths shown in Fig. KO420.

Camshaft oil seals are interchangeable. Camshaft seals and governor cross-shaft oil seal should be installed prior to installing the shafts. Install seals to depths shown in Fig. KO421 and Fig. KO422.

Oil pump shaft seal should be pressed into the oil pump cover to the depth shown in Fig. KO423.

OIL PUMP. The oil pump is located in the lower crankcase/oil pan. To ser-

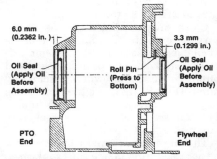

Fig. KO420—Cross-sectional view of crankcase showing installation of crankshaft oil seals and locator pin for main bearing sleeve.

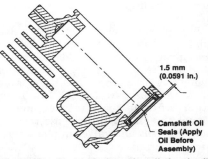

Fig. KO421—Camshaft oil seal installation detail.

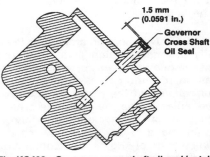

Fig. KO422—Governor cross-shaft oil seal installation detail.

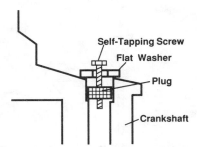

Fig. KO418—Removing crankpin cup plug. Refer to text.

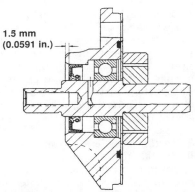

Fig. KO423—Cross-sectional view of oil pump showing oil seal installation detail.

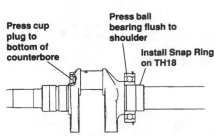

Fig. KO419—Cross-sectional view of crankshaft showing installation of oil gallery plug and ball bearing.

Fig. KO417—Check crankshaft journal fillets after regrinding.

vice oil pump without completely disassembling the engine, remove blower housing, flywheel and timing belt. Remove retaining screw from oil pump sprocket, and pull the sprocket off the pump shaft. Remove the oil pump cover. Note position of components as they are removed from oil pan.

Clean, inspect and renew as necessary. A complete oil pump assembly is available for service replacement. Always install new pump shaft oil seal and pump cover O-ring when assembling pump (Fig. KO423). Tighten oil pump cover fasteners to 7.3 N•m (65 in.-lb.). Tighten screw attaching sprocket to pump shaft to 9.9 N•m (88 in.-lb.).

The oil pressure relief valve can only be accessed from inside the crankcase.

ASSEMBLY SEQUENCE. After all components and subassemblies have been reconditioned or renewed, recommended engine assembly sequence is as follows:

Install valve seals. Lubricate valve guides and stems with engine oil. Turn the upper crankcase upside-down. Install intake and exhaust valves into their correct guides. Position valve blocking tools part No. 28 761 02 or other suitable tools into cylinders. Mount the oil pan with two screws to hold the tools and valves in place, then turn the crankcase upright. Assemble valve retainers, springs, spring caps and valve keepers onto valve stems. Turn the crankcase over and remove the oil pan and holding tools.

NOTE: Numbers on crankcase identify cylinders. Match piston and rod assemblies to their correct cylinders as noted during disassembly. Proper orientation of the piston and rod assemblies inside the engine is critical to prevent internal damage. Pistons must have "FLY" mark toward flywheel side of engine, and connecting rod and cap match marks must face toward outside of engine.

Lubricate cylinder bores, pistons and rings with engine oil. Mount the rod caps on their correct rods and tighten cap screws finger tight. Stagger piston ring end gaps 120° apart. Compress piston rings and correctly align piston in cylinder, then install connecting rods and pistons into the crankcase. Push pistons to top of cylinders, then remove rod caps.

To install crankshaft assembly, turn rod journal up (away from cylinders) and carefully set crankshaft with bearings into upper crankcase. Note that alignment hole in flywheel-end bearing sleeve must fit over its roll pin locator,

and oil hole in the sleeve must align with groove in crankshaft journal. The large snap ring on ball bearing outer race must fit into groove in crankcase.

Lubricate crankshaft journals, connecting rod bearings and rod caps with engine oil. Position the connecting rods onto the journals, match the rod caps to the connecting rods. Tighten the rod bolts in several steps to final torque of 11.3 N•m (100 in.-lb.). Turn the crankshaft by hand as the bolts are tightened to check for free rotation.

Install oil pump relief valve assembly in the lower crankcase half (Fig. KO424). Apply Teflon-base pipe sealant to threads of relief valve pipe plug, and tighten plug to 11.3 N•m (100 in.-lb.). Install oil pump assembly with a new O-ring into crankcase. Tighten oil pump cover screws to 7.3 N•m (65 in.-lb.). Install oil pump drive sprocket on pump shaft, and tighten mounting screw to 9.9 N•m (88 in.-lb.).

Carefully clean old sealant from sealing surfaces of crankcase halves. Crankcase joint does not use a gasket. Apply a 1.5 mm ($\frac{1}{16}$ in.) bead of high-temperature RTV gasket making compound to sealing surface of lower crankcase/oil pan as shown in Fig. KO425. Invert the oil pan, align pto-side bearing groove with snap ring on ball bearing, and carefully place oil pan onto inverted upper crankcase. Loosely install crankcase fasteners.

NOTE: Flywheel-end bearing positions 1 and 2 (Fig. KO425) use 70 mm long bolts, pto-end bearing positions 3 and 4 use 115 mm long bolts, side positions 5 through 12 use remaining eight 40 mm long bolts.

Position a straightedge across pto-side crankcase faces. The face surfaces must be in alignment prior to tightening crankcase fasteners. Tighten the crankcase fasteners in several steps to final torque of 24.4 N•m (216 in.-lb.) in the sequence shown in Fig. KO425.

Install crankshaft oil seals as instructed in CRANKCASE OIL SEALS in this section. After seals are installed, install the key and timing belt sprocket onto the crankshaft. The sprocket can be heated with a light bulb or on a hot plate to make installation easier. Make sure the sprocket timing mark (Fig. KO410) faces outward. Install flywheel key into crankshaft keyway. Make certain the key is properly seated and that flat top of key is parallel with crankshaft centerline, NOT the flywheel mount taper.

Turn the engine upright. Assemble the crankcase breather as shown in Fig. KO426. Tighten the reed retainer screw to 4.0 N•m (35 in.-lb.). If breather cover gasket does not have imprinted sealant bead, apply 1.5 mm ($\frac{1}{16}$ in.) bead of RTV sealant to both side of cover gasket as

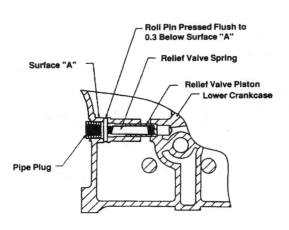

Fig. KO424—Oil pump relief valve assembly.

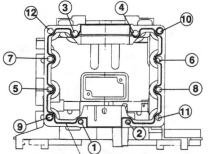

Apply 1.5 mm (1/16") Sealant Bead of RTV Silicone Rubber or Equivalent

Fig. KO425—Crankcase sealant pattern and fastener tightening sequence.

shown in Fig. KO427. Assemble the gasket to breather housing with large hole opposite breather reed, and assemble breather cover over gasket with cover hole opposite large hole in gasket. Tighten cover mounting screws to 5.6 N•m (50 in.-lb.)

Lightly lubricate breather grommet, then insert grommet into crankcase hole between cylinders. Press nipple on bottom of breather assembly into grommet. Tighten breather mounting screws to 4.0 N•m (35 in.-lb.)

NOTE: Engines equipped with top-mounted fuel tank have a wire retaining clip under breather screw on No. 1 cylinder.

Oil filter adapter does not use a gasket. Apply a 1.5 mm (1/16 in.) bead of RTV sealant to mounting face of adapter as shown in Fig. KO428. Install adapter to crankcase, and tighten adapter nipple to 40.7 N•m (30 ft.-lbs.).

If equipped with Oil Sentry switch, apply Teflon-base pipe sealant to switch threads. Install switch into oil filter adapter.

IMPORTANT: To prevent obstruction of oil passage, do not use Teflon tape and do not apply thread sealant to end of switch. Tightening torque for switch must not exceed 3.4 N•m (30 in.-lb.).

Install valley baffle, rectifier/regulator and stator, routing wiring as follows: Stator wiring harness must run vertically between valley baffle and intake manifold. Ground wire terminal mounts between valley baffle and head of baffle lower mounting screw. Oil Sentry wire runs under bottom fin of No. 2 cylinder, between cylinder and rocker box oil drain tube. On engines with top-mounted fuel tanks, rectifier/regulator mounts to the valley baffle, and terminal connector feeds through slot in baffle. Tighten valley baffle bolt to

7.3 N•m (65 in.-lb.) and breather-to-baffle bolt to 4.0 N•m (35 in.-lb.).

Assemble rocker arms with spring spacer and E-clips to No. 1 rocker shaft. Install the rocker assembly into the No. 1 cylinder rocker chamber. Tighten mounting screws to 4.0 N•m (35 in.-lb.). Position thrust washer inside the chamber, then slide No. 1 camshaft through the seal, thrust washer and rocker arms. Install C-clip into camshaft groove against thrust washer.

Insert governor cross-shaft into bushing from inside No. 2 cylinder valve chamber. Secure governor yoke to cross-shaft with two Allen-head screws.

NOTE: Outside curves of yoke fingers must face flywheel side of engine and lower edge of yoke must rest on shaft spacer.

Lubricate rocker arm shaft, and assemble to rocker arms with spring spacer and E-clips. Install rocker assembly in No. 2 valve chamber, and tighten mounting screws to 4.0 N•m (35 in.-lb.). Position governor assembly inside valve chamber, then slide camshaft through the oil seal, governor and rocker arms. While holding governor, rotate camshaft until camshaft hole lines up with hole in governor body. Drive roll pin in until flush with governor body.

To install camshaft timing belt, temporarily remove stator and follow instructions in CAMSHAFT DRIVE SYSTEM in this REPAIRS section.

NOTE: Timing belt routing diagram with belt torque specification is shown inside engine blower housing, facing the No. 2 camshaft sprocket.

Install stator and tighten mounting screws to 4.0 N•m (35 in.-lb.).

WARNING: Using improper procedures to install the flywheel can crack or damage the flywheel and/or crank-

shaft. **This not only causes extensive engine damage, but can also cause personal injury, since broken fragments can be thrown from the engine. Observe and use proper precautions and procedures when installing the flywheel.**

Be sure the crankshaft taper and flywheel hub are clean, dry, undamaged and free of lubricants or solvents. An oil film between the flywheel and crankshaft can cause overstressing of the flywheel when the flywheel bolt is tightened. Install tension spring, flywheel, rewind starter drive cup (if equipped), washer and bolt. Use a strap wrench or other suitable flywheel holding tool to secure the flywheel when tightening mounting bolt. Do not use a pry bar, wedge or other similar tool to hold the flywheel as damage to the flywheel could result. Tighten flywheel bolt to 66.4 N•m (49 ft.-lb.).

Install ignition modules. Module for No. 1 cylinder should have "kill" terminal facing outward towards blower housing. Module for No. 2 cylinder should have "kill" terminal facing inward towards cylinder. Air gap between modules and flywheel magnet should be 0.20-0.30 mm (0.008-0.012 in.). To adjust, insert a nonmagnetic feeler gauge or shim of proper thickness between magnet and module. Loosen module screws and allow magnet to pull module against the gauge. Tighten module screws to 4.0-6.2 N•m (35-55

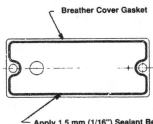

Apply 1.5 mm (1/16") Sealant Bead of RTV Silicone Rubber or Equivalent on Both Sides

Fig. KO427—Sealant pattern for crankcase breather cover gasket. Apply sealant to both sides of gasket.

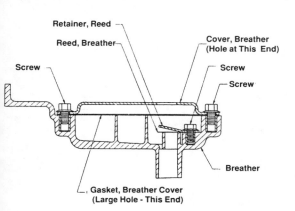

Fig. KO426—Cross-sectional view of crankcase breather components.

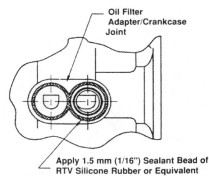

Apply 1.5 mm (1/16") Sealant Bead of RTV Silicone Rubber or Equivalent

Fig. KO428—Sealant pattern for oil filter adapter-to-crankcase joint.

in.-lb.), rotate flywheel and remove the gauge. Make sure modules do not contact the magnet or flywheel.

Adjust valve clearance as previously outlined in VALVE ADJUSTMENT paragraphs. Install valve covers with new gaskets. It may be necessary to lightly press the No. 1 valve cover against the engine to overcome fuel pump spring pressure while installing fasteners. If equipped with top-mounted fuel tank, the top two fasteners on No. 1 valve cover and top three fasteners on No. 2 valve cover are the fuel tank mounting studs for the tank.

Install spark plugs and tighten to 24.4-29.8 N•m (18-22 ft.-lb.). Install sheet metal cylinder side baffles, but do not tighten fasteners at this time. The baffle for No. 1 cylinder requires two fasteners that also mount the starter solenoid if equipped. Securely fasten engine harness connector to No. 1 baffle. Do not install screws in exhaust-side baffle at this time.

Install electric starter motor if equipped. Tighten bottom through-bolt first, then top bolt. Tighten through-bolts in steps to 7.9 N•m (70 in.-lb.).

Install blower housing in position over flywheel. The two shorter M6×16 bolts fit through the upper holes in housing into the cylinder side shields. The four longer M6x19 bolts fit through lower holes in housing into the lower crankcase.

If engine is not equipped with a rewind starter, install grass screen to flywheel. If engine is equipped with a rewind starter, assemble the starter to blower housing. Pull on the starter rope to make sure the starter pawls engage the drive cup, then securely tighten starter mounting screws.

On engines with oval air filter and remote fuel tank, apply Loctite thread locking compound to bottom threads of air filter stud. Install the stud into post in center of intake manifold, then remove jam nuts from stud.

Assemble carburetor linkages to throttle control plate as shown in Fig. KO406. While holding the governor lever, control plate and carburetor assembly over the engine, connect fuel shutoff solenoid leads. Slide end of governor lever onto governor cross-shaft. Using new gaskets, slide carburetor and air filter elbow onto intake manifold studs. Install flange nuts and tighten to 9.9 N•m (88 in.-lb.). Mount throttle control plate to cylinder head posts. At this time, install and tighten all blower housing, cylinder side baffle and throttle plate fasteners. Tighten four upper blower housing fasteners to 4.0 N•m (35 in.-lb.). Tighten remaining fasteners for blower housing, cylinder side baffles and throttle control plate to 7.3 N•m (65 in.-lb.). Connect fuel line from fuel pump to carburetor.

Set static governor adjustment as follows: Insert a pin through hole in end of governor shaft and rotate shaft counterclockwise as far as it will go and hold in this position. Push governor lever toward carburetor control bracket, and tighten governor lever nut.

Feed crankcase breather hose through control bracket, and insert lower end into hole in breather. Make sure that flanges on lower end of hose snap into correct position around breather hole. Failure to properly fit lower end of hose will cause erratic engine performance and rapid internal engine wear. Attach upper end of hose to air filter elbow.

Install air filter assembly using new base plate gasket, seals and air filter elements. On oval-style filter, be sure that element cover grommet correctly aligns with drain hole in base plate. Misalignment will allow the engine to ingest unfiltered air. On engines with top-mounted fuel tank, do not install outer cover until fuel tank has been mounted.

Install top-mounted fuel tank if so equipped. Install exhaust components.

Be sure oil drain plug(s) are securely installed. Prefill oil filter to bottom of center hole threads with clean engine oil, and wipe a thin film of oil onto oil filter gasket. Install oil filter hand tight, ½ turn past point where filter gasket contacts filter base. Fill crankcase with oil. Crankcase capacity is 1.4 L (1.5 qt.) with oil filter. After initial engine run, check oil level and refill as needed.

NOTE: An Adapter Alignment Kit Part No. 25 761 19 is available to correctly mount and align the pto adapter on engines and short blocks equipped with a splined-pto shaft. Failure to properly align pto adapter will result in excessive crankshaft runout tolerances and possible damage to engine and equipment.

KOHLER

SERVICING KOHLER ACCESSORIES

REWIND STARTERS

When servicing rewind starter, refer to the Fig. KA100 and Fig. KO102 to identify the starter used on your engine, then refer to the appropriate paragraph for service procedure.

Eaton

OVERHAUL. Exploded view of clockwise starter is shown in Fig. KA100. To disassemble starter, first release tension of rewind spring as follows: Hold starter assembly with pulley facing up. Pull starter rope until notch in pulley is aligned with rope hole in cover. Use thumb pressure to prevent pulley from rotating. Engage rope in notch of pulley and slowly release thumb pressure to allow spring to unwind until all tension is released.

When removing rope pulley, use extreme care to keep starter spring confined in housing. Replace starter spring if it is cracked, distorted or broken. If starter spring is to be renewed, carefully remove it from housing, noting direction of rotation of spring before removing. Check pawl, brake, spring, retainer and hub for wear and renew as necessary. If starter rope is worn or frayed, remove from pulley, noting direction it is wrapped on pulley. Renew rope and install pulley in housing, aligning notch in pulley assembly with rope outlet in housing. Align notch in pulley hub with hook in end of spring. Use a wire bent to form a hook to aid in positioning spring in hub.

After securing pulley assembly in housing, engage rope in notch and rotate pulley at least two full turns in same direction it is pulled to properly preload starter spring. Pull rope to fully extended position. Rope will fully rewind when handle is released if spring is properly preloaded.

Before installing starter on engine, check teeth in starter driven hub (165—Fig. KA101) for wear and renew hub if necessary.

Command And Later Magnum Models

OVERHAUL. Command models may be equipped with the rewind starter shown in Fig. KA102. To disassemble starter, remove rope handle and allow rope to wind into starter. Remove retaining screw from center of starter, and separate starter components. To disengage rewind spring from starter housing, rotate pulley two turns clockwise. Wear appropriate safety eyewear and gloves to prevent injury should rewind spring uncoil uncontrolled. The rewind spring is contained in cup (9) and manufacturer recommends installation of a new spring and cup if spring uncoils from cup.

Assemble starter before installing rope. Lubricate rewind spring before installation. Apply a small amount of grease on brake spring (4) ends. Apply Loctite 271 to threads of center screw (1) and tighten to 7.4-8.5 N•m (65-75 in.-lbs.). Use following procedure to install rope. With starter assembled except for rope, rotate pulley six turns counterclockwise and stop when rope hole on pulley is aligned with rope outlet on starter housing. Hold pulley so it cannot rotate and insert rope through rope outlet and attach rope end to pulley. Attach rope handle and release pulley. Check starter operation.

12-VOLT GEAR DRIVE STARTERS

Four types of gear drive starters are used on Kohler engines. Refer to Figs. KA103, KA104, KA106, KA107, KA108, KA109 and KA110 for exploded views of starter motors and drives.

TWO-BRUSH COMPACT-TYPE. To disassemble starting motor, clamp mounting bracket in a vise. Remove through-bolts (H—Fig. KA103) and slide commutator end plate (J) and frame assembly (A) off armature. Clamp steel armature core in a vise and remove Bendix drive (E), drive end plate (F), thrust washer (D) and spacer (C) from armature (B).

Renew brushes if unevenly worn or worn to a length of $\frac{5}{16}$ inch (7.9 mm) or less. To renew ground brush (K), drill out rivet, then rivet new brush lead to end plate. Field brush (P) is soldered to field coil lead.

Reassemble by reversing disassembly procedure. Lubricate bushings with a light coat of SAE 10 oil. Inspect Bendix drive pinion and splined sleeve for damage. If Bendix is in good condition, wipe clean and install completely dry. Tighten Bendix drive retaining nut to a torque of 130-150 in.-lbs. (15-18 N•m). Tighten through-bolts (H) to a torque of 40-55 in.-lbs. (4-7 N•m).

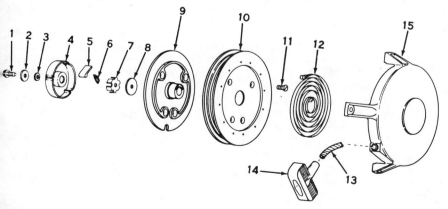

Fig. KA100—Exploded view of Eaton rewind starter used on some models.

1. Retainer screw	5. Pawl	9. Pulley hub
2. Brake washer	6. Spring	10. Pulley
3. Spacer	7. Brake	11. Screw
4. Retainer	8. Thrust washer	12. Recoil spring

13. Rope	
14. Handle	
15. Starter housing	

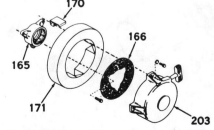

Fig. KA101—View showing rewind starter and starter hub.

165. Starter hub	
166. Screen	171. Air director
167. Bracket	203. Rewind starter

Fig. KA102—Exploded view of rewind starter used on Command and later Magnum models.

1. Screw
2. Washer
3. Pawl retainer
4. Brake spring
5. Washer
6. Pawls
7. Pawl springs
8. Pulley
9. Rewind spring & cup
10. Rope
11. Starter housing

PERMANENT MAGNET-TYPE.

To disassemble starting motor, clamp mounting bracket in a vise and remove through-bolts (19—Fig. KA104).

CAUTION: Do not clamp frame (11) in a vise or strike frame as it has ceramic field magnets that may be damaged.

Carefully slide the end cap (10) and frame (11) off armature. Clamp steel armature core in a vise and remove nut (18), spacer (17), anti-drift spring (16), drive assembly (15), end plate (14) and thrust washer (13) from armature (12).

The two input brushes are part of terminal stud (6). Remaining two brushes (9) are secured with cap screws. When reassembling, lubricate bushings with American Bosch lubricant LU3001 or equivalent. Do not lubricate starter drive. Use rubber band or clip shown in Fig. KA105 to hold brushes in position until started in the commutator. Cut and remove rubber band after assembly. Tighten through-bolts to 80-95 in.-lbs. (8-10 N•m). Apply Loctite to threads of nut (18) and tighten to 135 in.-lbs. (15.2 N•m).

Fig. KA103—Exploded view of two-brush compact gear drive starting motor.

A. Frame & field coil assy.
B. Armature
C. Spacer
D. Thrust washer
E. Bendix drive assy.
F. Drive end plate
G. Lockwasher
H. Through-bolt
J. Commutator end plate
K. Ground brush
L. Terminal nuts
M. Lockwashers
N. Flat washer
O. Insulating washer
P. Field brush

FOUR-BRUSH BENDIX DRIVE-TYPE.

To disassemble starter motor, remove screws securing drive end plate (K—Fig. KA106) to frame (I). Carefully withdraw armature and drive assembly from frame assembly. Clamp the steel armature core in a vise and remove Bendix drive retaining nut. Remove drive assembly (A), end plate (K) and thrust washer from armature (J). Remove the cover (H). Remove screws securing end plate (E) to frame. Pull the field brushes (C) from brush holders, then remove the end plate assembly.

The two ground brush leads are secured to the end plate (E), and the two field brush leads are soldered to field coils. Renew brush set if excessively worn.

Inspect bushing (L) in end plate (K), and renew bushing if necessary. When assembling, lubricate bushings with light coat of SAE 10 oil. Lightly lubri-

Fig. KA104—Exploded view of permanent magnet-type starting motor.

1. Terminal nut
2. Lockwasher
3. Insulating washer
4. Terminal insulator
5. Flat washer
6. Terminal stud & input brushes
7. Brush springs (4)
8. Brush holders
9. Brushes
10. Commutator end cap
11. Frame & magnets
12. Armature
13. Thrust washer
14. Drive end plate
15. Drive assy.
16. Anti-drift spring
17. Spacer
18. Nut
19. Through-bolt

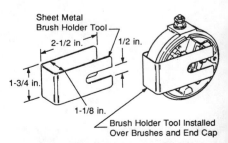

Sheet Metal Brush Holder Tool

2-1/2 in. 1/2 in.

1-3/4 in.

1-1/8 in.

Brush Holder Tool Installed Over Brushes and End Cap

Fig. KA105—A brush retaining clip can be fabricated as shown to hold brushes in end cap during starter assembly.

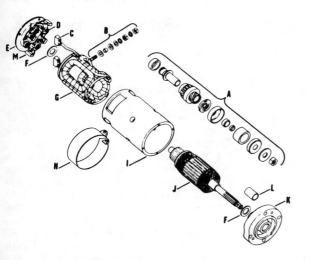

Fig. KA106—Exploded view of four-brush starting motor with Bendix drive.

A. Bendix drive assy.
B. Terminal stud
C. Field brushes
D. Brush springs
E. Commutator end plate
F. Thrust washers
G. Field coils
H. Cover
I. Frame
J. Armature
K. Drive end plate
L. Bushing
M. Ground brushes

cate Bendix drive splines with Kohler Drive Lube part No. 52 357 01 or equivalent.

Note that starter can be installed with Bendix in engaged or disengaged

position. Do not attempt to disengage Bendix if it is in the engaged position.

Fig. KA107 shows the late-style inertia-drive (Bendix) permanent magnet four-brush starter motor. This motor comes in two styles as identified in Fig. KA107. Repair procedures are similar to those for early-style motor shown in Fig. KA106. To access retaining ring on the style "B" Bendix, extend drive pinion fully. Grasp the dust cover tip with

pliers, then pull dust cover free. The retaining ring and Bendix assembly can now be removed. A stop nut retains the style "A" Bendix.

SOLENOID-SHIFT STARTERS

Manufacturer recommends a minimum 500-hour or annual (whichever occurs first) maintenance schedule for solenoid-shift starters. The starter should be disassembled, cleaned, inspected and lubricated as necessary. Drive splines should be lightly lubricated with Kohler Bendix Drive Lubricant part No. 52 357 01 or equivalent. Solenoid shift lever and shaft should be lubricated with Shifter Shaft Lubricant part No. 52 357 02 or equivalent.

If starter will not engage the flywheel and crank the engine, the problem could be caused by an accumulation of dirt or debris in the solenoid and/or starter. This is especially true for vertical-shaft and/or high-hour usage engines.

NOTE: Engine cranking speed must be 200 rpm minimum for proper starting.

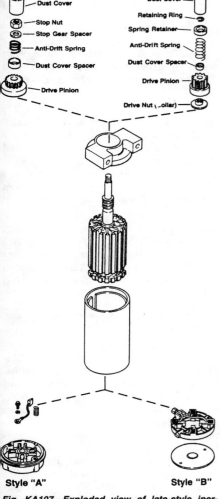

Fig. KA107—Exploded view of late-style inertia-drive permanent magnet four-brush starter motor showing both styles of brush end plates and Bendix drives.

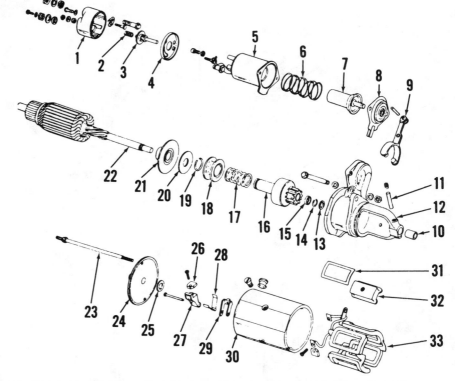

Fig. KA108—Exploded view of four-brush starting motor with solenoid shift engagement.

1. Switch cover	10. Bushing	18. Shift collar	26. Brushes (4)
2. Spring	11. Lubrication wick	19. Snap ring	27. Insulated brush holder
3. Contact disc	12. Drive housing	20. Brake washer	28. Brush spring
4. Gasket	13. Thrust washer	21. Center bearing	29. Ground brush
5. Coil assy.	14. Snap ring	22. Armature	30. Frame
6. Return spring	15. Retainer	23. Through-bolt	31. Field coil insulator
7. Plunger	16. Drive unit	24. End plate	32. Pole shoe
8. Seal	17. Spring	25. Thrust washer	33. Field coil assy.
9. Shift lever			

KOHLER ACCESSORIES

Fig. KA109—Exploded view of permanent magnet-type starter with solenoid shift engagement.

1. Clip
2. Solenoid
3. Spring
4. Plunger
5. Shift lever
6. Commutator end cap
7. Terminal stud & input brushes
7A. Brush
8. Brush springs (4)
9. Frame & magnets
10. Armature
11. Through-bolts
12. Drive assy.
13. Seal
14. Retainer
15. Thrust washer
16. Dust cover
17. Drive housing

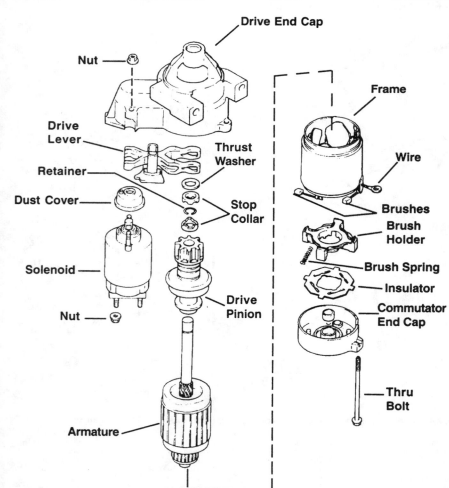

Fig. KA110—Exploded view of late-style Nippendenso solenoid shift-type starter motor.

LARGE AIR-COOLED ENGINES

SOLENOID SHIFT-TYPE (K-Series). Refer to Fig. KA108 for exploded view of starting motor. To disassemble, unbolt and remove solenoid switch assembly (items 1 through 6). Remove through-bolts (23), end plate (24) and frame (30) with brushes (26), brush holders (27 and 29) and field coil assembly (33). Remove screws retaining center bearing (21) to drive housing (12), remove shift lever pivot bolt, raise shift lever (9) and carefully withdraw armature and drive assembly. Drive unit (16) and center bearing (21) can be removed from armature (22) after snap ring (14) and retainer (15) are removed. Drive out shift lever pin and separate plunger (7), seal (8) and shift lever (9) from drive housing. Any further disassembly is obvious after examination of unit. Refer to Fig. KA108. Renew brushes (26), center bearing (21) and bushings in end plate (24) and drive housing (12) as needed.

SOLENOID SHIFT-TYPE (Magnum And Command Series). Refer to Fig. KA109 for an exploded view of starter.

CAUTION: Do not clamp frame (9) in a vise or strike frame as it has ceramic field magnets that may be damaged.

To disassemble starter, detach clip (1) then unscrew and remove solenoid. Mark frame (9), end cap (6) and drive housing (17) so they can be assembled in original position. Unscrew through-bolts and separate starter components. Detach retainer (14) from armature to remove drive unit (12) from shaft.

The two input brushes are part of terminal stud (7). Remaining two brushes (7A) are secured with cap screws. Renew brushes as needed. The clip shown in Fig. KA105 can be fabricated to hold brushes in end cap during assembly.

SOLENOID SHIFT-TYPE (Nippendenso). An exploded view of starter is shown in Fig. KA110. To disassemble, remove solenoid nuts and solenoid. Remove two through-bolts and commutator end cap. Remove insulator and brush springs from brush holder, then slide brushes from holder and remove holder. Slide the farm off armature. Remove armature and drive lever assembly from drive end cap, then separate drive lever from armature. Be careful not to lose the drive end cap thrust washer when removing the lever and armature. Pry the two-piece stop collar off the armature shaft retainer. Remove the retainer and discard it.

Clean, inspect and renew starter components as necessary. If brushes require replacement, Brush Kit part No. 52 221 01 contains the needed brushes, springs, and instructions to replace the frame-fastened brushes. Solenoid is not serviceable and must be replaced if faulty.

To assemble starter, slide the drive pinion onto the armature shaft. Insert the rear stop collar on the armature shaft. Place a NEW retaining ring into armature shaft groove. Insert the front stop collar on the armature shaft, and using two pair of pliers, mash the two collars together by applying an even force over the retainer. Make sure the drive end cap thrust washer is installed between the stop collar and end cap. Complete assembly in reverse order of disassembly.

FLYWHEEL ALTERNATORS

3-AMP ALTERNATOR. The 3-amp alternator consists of a permanent magnet ring with five or six magnets on flywheel rim and a stator assembly attached to crankcase. A diode is located in the charging output lead. See Fig. KA111.

To avoid damage to the charging system, the following precautions must be observed:

1. Negative post of battery must be connected to engine ground and correct battery polarity must be observed at all times.
2. Prevent alternator leads (AC) from touching or shorting.
3. Remove battery or disconnect battery cables when recharging battery with battery charger.

4. Do not operate engine for any length of time without a battery in system.
5. Disconnect plug before electric welding is done on equipment powered by, and in common ground with, the engine.

Troubleshooting. Defective conditions and possible causes are as follows:

1. No output. Could be caused by:
   A. Faulty windings in stator.
   B. Defective diode.
   C. Broken lead wire.
2. No lighting. Could be caused by:
   A. Shorted stator wiring.
   B. Broken lead.

If "no output" condition is the trouble, run following tests:

1. Connect ammeter in series with charging lead. Start engine and run at 2400 rpm. Ammeter should register 2-amp charge. Run engine at 3600 rpm. Ammeter should register 3-amp charge.
2. Disconnect battery charge lead from battery, measure resistance of lead to ground with an ohmmeter. Reverse ohmmeter leads and take another reading. One reading should be about mid-scale with meter set at R×1. If both readings are high, diode or stator is open.
3. Expose diode connections on battery charge lead. Check resistance on stator side to ground. Reading should be 1 ohm. If zero ohms, winding is shorted. If infinity ohms, stator winding is open or lead wire is broken.

If "no lighting" condition is the trouble, use an AC voltmeter and measure open circuit voltage from lighting lead to ground with engine running at 3000 rpm. If 15 volts, wiring may be shorted.

Check resistance of lighting lead to ground. If 0.5 ohms, stator is good, zero ohms indicates shorted stator and a reading of infinity indicates stator is open or lead is broken.

3/6 AMP ALTERNATOR. The 3/6-amp alternator consists of a permanent magnet ring with six magnets on flywheel rim and a stator assembly attached to crankcase. Two diodes are located in battery charging lead and auxiliary load lead. See Fig. KA112.

To avoid damage to the charging system, the following precautions must be observed:

1. Negative post of battery must be connected to engine ground and correct battery polarity must be observed at all times.
2. Prevent alternator leads (AC) from touching or shorting.

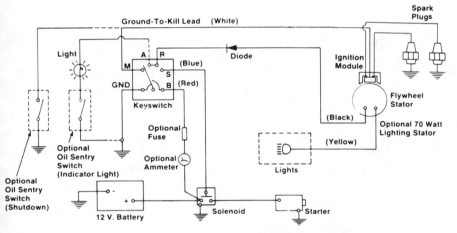

Fig. KA111—Typical electrical wiring diagram for engines equipped with 3-amp unregulated charging system.

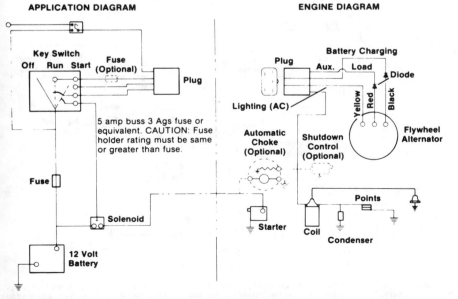

Fig. KA112—Typical electrical wiring diagram for engines equipped with 3/6-amp alternator.

3. Remove battery or disconnect battery cables when recharging battery with battery charger.

4. Do not operate engine for any length of time without a battery in system.

5. Disconnect plug before electric welding is done on equipment powered by, and in common ground with, the engine.

Troubleshooting. Defective conditions and possible causes are as follows:

1. No output. Could be caused by:
   A. Faulty windings in stator.
   B. Defective diode.
   C. Broken lead wire.
2. No lighting. Could be caused by:
   A. Shorted stator wiring.
   B. Broken lead.

If "no output" condition is the trouble, run following tests:

1. Disconnect auxiliary load lead and measure voltage from lead to ground with engine running at 3000 rpm. If 17 volts or more, stator is good.
2. Disconnect battery-charging lead from battery. Measure voltage from charging lead to ground with engine running at 3000 rpm. If 17 volts or more, stator is good.
3. Disconnect battery charge lead from battery and auxiliary load lead from switch. Measure resistance of both leads to ground. Reverse ohmmeter leads and take another reading. One reading should be about mid-scale with meter set at R×1. If both readings are low, diode is shorted. If both readings are high, diode or stator is open.
4. Expose diode connections on battery charge lead and auxiliary load lead. Check resistance on stator side of diodes to ground. Reading should be 0.5 ohm. If zero ohms, winding is shorted. If infinity ohms, stator winding is open or lead wire is broken.

If "no lighting" condition is the trouble, disconnect lighting lead and measure open circuit voltage with an AC voltmeter from lighting lead to ground with engine running at 3000 rpm. If 22 volts or more, stator is good. If less than 22 volts, wiring may be shorted.

Check resistance of lighting lead to ground. If 0.5 ohms, stator is good, zero ohms indicates shorted stator and a reading of infinity indicates stator is open or lead is broken.

10-, 15-, 20-, 25-AMP ALTERNATOR. Some engines may be equipped with a 10-, 15-, 20- or 25-amp alternator. Alternator output is controlled by a solid state rectifier-regulator. See Figs. KA113, KA114, KA115, KA116 and KA117 for wiring diagrams typical of most models.

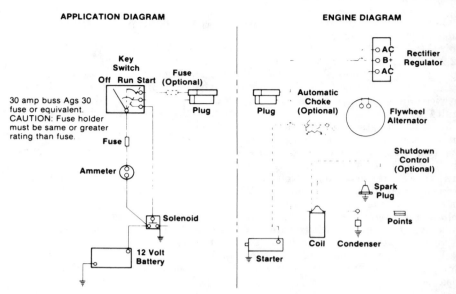

Fig. KA113—Typical electrical wiring diagram for engines equipped with 15-amp alternator and breaker point ignition.

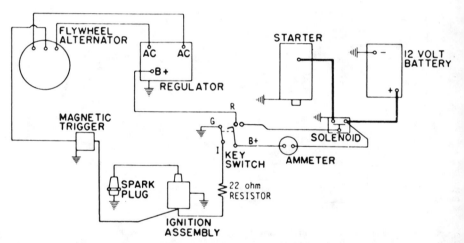

Fig. KA114—Typical electrical wiring diagram for engines equipped with early 15-amp flywheel alternator and breakerless ignition system. The 10-amp alternator is similar.

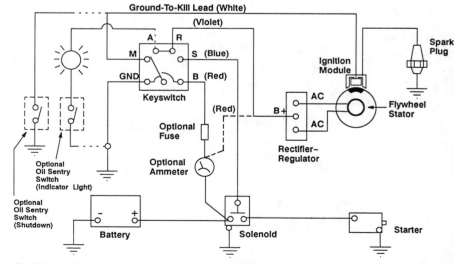

Fig. KA115—Typical electrical wiring diagram for later engines equipped with 15-amp and 25-amp flywheel alternator. Note that B+ wire (dashed line) from rectifier-regulator on 25-amp system is routed to ammeter rather than key switch.

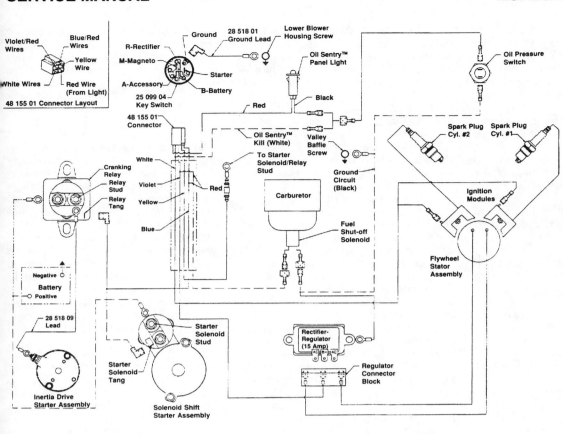

Fig. KA116—Typical wiring diagram for overhead cam engines equipped with 15-amp regulated charging system and engine-mounted control panel.

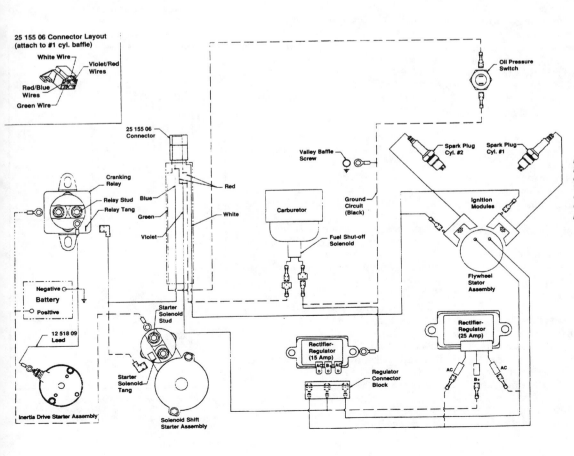

Fig. KA117—Typical wiring diagram for overhead cam engines equipped with 15/25-amp regulated charging system without engine-mounted control panel.

Rectifier-regulator for 15-, 20- and 25-amp charging systems can be tested with Tester part No. 25 761 20. Instructions are included with the tester. If tester is not available, or if servicing a 10-amp system, use the test procedure that follows:

To avoid damage to charging system, the following precautions must be observed:

1. Negative post of battery must be connected to engine ground and correct battery polarity must be observed at all times.
2. Rectifier-regulator must be connected in common ground with engine and battery.
3. Disconnect leads at rectifier-regulator if electric welding is to be done on equipment in common ground with engine.
4. Remove battery or disconnect battery cables when recharging battery with battery charger.
5. Do not operate engine with battery disconnected.
6. Prevent possible grounding of AC leads.

Operation. Alternating current (AC) produced by the alternator is changed to direct current (DC) in the rectifier-regulator. The rectifier-regulator electronically "senses" the counter-voltage created by the battery, and controls or limits the charging rate accordingly. No adjustments are possible on alternator charging system. Faulty components must be renewed. Note that rectifier-regulators used on 10-amp and early 15-amp systems are similar in appearance (Fig. KA118), but units are not interchangeable.

Refer to the following troubleshooting paragraph to help locate possible defective parts.

Troubleshooting. Defective conditions and possible causes are as follows:

1. No output. Could be caused by:
   A. Faulty windings in stator.
   B. Defective diode(s) in rectifier.
   C. Rectifier-regulator not properly grounded.
   D. Battery fully discharged or less than 4 volts.
2. Full charge-no regulation. Could be caused by:
   A. Defective rectifier-regulator.
   B. Defective battery.

If "no output" condition is the trouble, disconnect B+ cable from rectifier-regulator. Connect a DC voltmeter between B+ terminal on rectifier-regulator and engine ground. Start engine and operate at 3600 rpm. Voltage should be above 13.8 volts. If reading is above zero volts but less than 13.8 volts, check for defective recti-

fier-regulator. If reading is zero volts, check for defective rectifier-regulator or defective stator by disconnecting AC leads from rectifier-regulator and connecting an AC voltmeter to the two AC leads.

Check AC voltage with engine running at 3600 rpm. If reading is less than 20 volts (10-amp alternator) or 28 volts (15-amp alternator), stator is defective. If reading is more than 20 volts (10-amp alternator) or 28 volts (15-amp alternator), rectifier-regulator is defective.

If "full charge-no regulation" is the condition, use a DC voltmeter and check B+ to ground with engine operating at 3600 rpm. If reading is over 14.7 volts, rectifier-regulator is defective. If reading is under 14.7 volts but over 14.0 volts, alternator and rectifier-regulator are satisfactory and battery is probably defective (unable to hold a charge).

If a 25-amp regulator failure is encountered on a Command twin-cylinder engine with a serial number beginning with '25' or lower, the engine might need to be upgraded to allow more cooling air over the regulator fins. Regulator kits available for service include all necessary components and instructions to properly complete this upgrade.

30-AMP ALTERNATOR. A 30-amp flywheel alternator, consisting of a permanent field magnet ring (on flywheel) and an alternator stator (on bearing plate on single-cylinder engines or gear cover on two-cylinder engines), is used on some models. Alternator output is controlled by a solid-state rectifier-regulator.

To avoid damage to charging system, the following precautions must be observed:

1. Negative post of battery must be connected to engine ground and correct battery polarity must be observed at all times.
2. Rectifier-regulator must be connected in common ground with engine and battery.
3. Disconnect wire from rectifier-regulator terminal marked "BATT. NEG" if electric welding is to be done on equipment in common ground with engine.
4. Remove battery or disconnect battery cables when recharging battery with battery charger.
5. Do not operate engine with battery disconnected.
6. Prevent possible grounding of AC leads.

Operation. Two black wires carry alternating current (AC) produced by alternator to a full wave bridge rectifier where it is changed to direct current

(DC). Two red stator wires serve to complete a circuit from regulator to secondary winding in the stator. A zener diode is used to sense battery voltage and control a silicone controller rectifier (SCR). The SCR functions as a switch to allow current to flow in the secondary winding in stator when battery voltage exceeds a specific level.

An increase in battery voltage increases the current flow in secondary winding in stator. This increased current flow in secondary winding brings about a corresponding decrease in AC current in primary winding, thus controlling output.

When battery voltage decreases, zener diode shuts off the SCR and no current flows to secondary winding. Maximum AC current is produced in primary winding at this time.

Troubleshooting. Refer to Figs. KA119 or KA120 for wiring diagram. Defective conditions and possible causes are as follows:

1. No output. Could be caused by:
   A. Faulty windings in stator.
   B. Defective diode(s) in rectifier.
2. No charge (when normal load is applied to battery). Could be caused by:
   A. Faulty secondary winding in stator.
3. Full charge-no regulation. Could be caused by:
   A. Faulty secondary winding in stator.

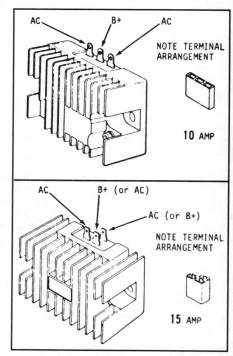

Fig. KA118—View of rectifier-regulators used on 10-amp and early 15-amp alternators. Although similar in appearance, units must not be interchanged.

B. Defective regulator.

If "no output" is the trouble, check stator windings by disconnecting all four stator wires from rectifier-regulator. Check resistance on R×1 scale of ohmmeter. Connect ohmmeter leads to the two red stator wires. About 2.0 ohms should be indicated. Connect ohmmeter leads to the two black stator wires. Approximately 0.1 ohm should be indicated. If readings are not within specified values, renew stator. If ohmmeter readings are correct, stator is good and trouble is in rectifier-regulator. Renew rectifier-regulator.

If "no charge when normal load is applied to battery" is the trouble, check stator secondary winding by disconnecting red wire from "REG" terminal on rectifier-regulator. Operate engine at 3600 rpm. Alternator should now charge at full output. If full output of at least 30 amps is not attained, renew stator.

If "full charge-no regulation" is the trouble, check stator secondary winding by removing both red wires from rectifier-regulator and connecting ends of these two wires together. Operate engine at 3600 rpm. A maximum 4-amp charge should be noted. If not, stator secondary winding is faulty. Renew stator. If maximum 4-amp charge is indicated, stator is good and trouble is in rectifier-regulator. Renew rectifier-regulator.

BRAKING STATOR. Some CV11-16 engines are equipped with a braking stator for safety purposes. The stator rapidly stops the engine when the seat safety switch is activated. The stator is designed to 'short-circuit' upon activation, creating an increased magnetic drag on the flywheel.

The 15-amp stator shown in Fig. KA121 has a short pigtail lead attached to each of the AC-lead terminals. When the seat safety switch is activated, it completes a circuit through these pigtail leads, shorting the AC windings. Refer to the equipment manufacturer's instructions to test the seat switch circuit.

The 3-amp/70 watt stator (Fig. KA122) has a third wire that connects to the seat safety switch circuit.

Troubleshooting. Faulty conditions and possible causes are as follows:
1. No charge to battery. Could be caused by:
   A. Faulty windings in stator.
   B. Faulty diode in stator.
2. No lights. Could be caused by:
   A. Faulty lights.
   B. Loose connections or shorts in wiring.
   C. Stator winding shorted.
3. No lights or battery charging. Could be caused by:
   A. Braking lead is shorted.
   B. Stator is shorted.
   C. Stator or lighting lead is open.

If no charge to battery is the trouble, run engine at 3400 rpm and measure voltage across battery terminals with a DC voltmeter. If voltage is 12.5 volts or higher, charging system is satisfactory. If voltage is less than 12.5 volts, stator or diode is probably defective.

Disconnect charging lead (black) from wiring harness. Run engine at 3400 rpm and measure voltage from charging lead to ground with a DC voltmeter. If voltage is 5 volts or more, stator winding is satisfactory. If voltage is less than 5 volts, test stator for open or shorted circuit as follows:

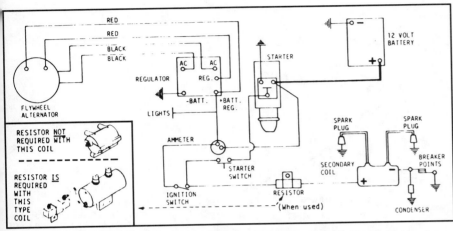

Fig. KA119—Typical electrical wiring diagram for two-cylinder engines equipped with 30-amp alternator charging systems. The 30-amp alternator on single-cylinder engines is similar.

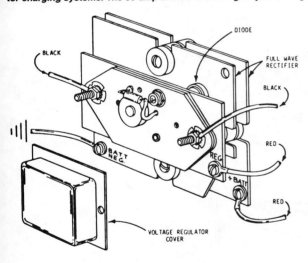

Fig. KA120—Rectifier-regulator used with 30- amp flywheel alternator, showing wire connections. Refer also to Fig. KA119.

Fig. KA121—Typical 15-amp braking stator for single-cylinder Command vertical-shaft engines.

With charging lead disconnected from wiring harness and engine stopped, measure resistance from charging lead to ground with an ohmmeter. Reverse the meter test lead connections and measure resistance again. In one test, the resistance should be infinity (open circuit). In the other test, very low resistance should be measured. If resistance is low in both directions, the diode is shorted. If resistance is infinity in both directions, the diode or stator winding is open.

If no lighting is the problem, disconnect the lighting lead (yellow) from the wiring harness. Run the engine at 3400 rpm and measure voltage from lighting lead to ground with an AC voltmeter. If voltage is 13 volts or more, stator is satisfactory. Check for loose connections or shorts in wiring harness. If voltage is less than 13 volts, test stator with an ohmmeter as follows:

With lighting lead (yellow) disconnected from the wiring harness and engine stopped, measure resistance from the lighting lead to ground with an ohmmeter. If resistance is approximately 0.15 ohms, stator winding is satisfactory. If resistance is 0 ohms, stator winding is shorted. Replace the stator. If resistance is infinity, stator or lighting lead is open. Replace the stator.

If no lights and no charge to battery are the problem, perform braking system test as follows: Disconnect braking lead (green) from the wiring harness. Run engine at 3400 rpm and measure voltage from braking lead to ground with an AC voltmeter. If voltage is 35 volts or more, stator is satisfactory. Check the unit that grounds the braking lead for short circuit. If voltage is less than 35 volts, test stator as follows:

With braking lead disconnected and engine stopped, measure resistance from braking lead to ground using an ohmmeter. If resistance is approximately 0.2-0.4 ohms, stator is satisfactory. If resistance is 0 ohms, stator is shorted. If resistance is infinity, stator or lighting lead is open. Replace stator.

CLUTCH

Some models are equipped with either a dry disc clutch (Fig. KA123) or a wet-type clutch (Fig. KA124). Both clutches are lever operated. Refer to the following paragraphs for adjustment procedure.

Dry Disc-Type Clutch. A firm pressure should be required to engage overcenter linkage. If clutch is slipping, remove nameplate (Fig. KA123) and locate adjustment lock by turning flywheel. Release clutch, back out

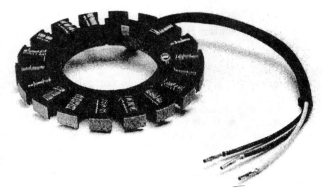

Fig. KA122—Typical 3-amp/70-watt braking stator for single-cylinder Command vertical-shaft engines.

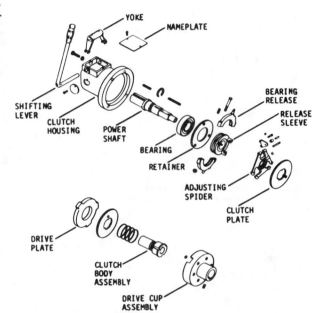

Fig. KA123—Exploded view of dry disc-type clutch used on some models.

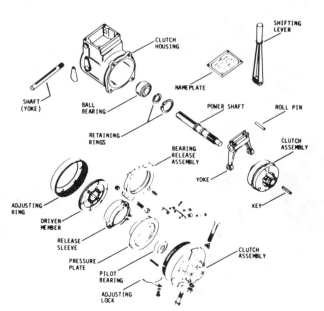

Fig. KA124—Exploded view of wet-type clutch used on some models.

adjusting lock screw, then turn adjusting spider clockwise until approximately a 20-pound (9 kg) pull is required to snap clutch overcenter. Tighten adjusting lock screw. Lubricate clutch bearing collar through inspection cover opening after every 50 operating hours.

Wet-Type Clutch. To adjust wet-type clutch, remove nameplate and use a screwdriver to turn adjusting ring (Fig. KA124) in clockwise direction until a pull of 40-50 pounds (18-23 kg) at hand grip lever is required to snap clutch overcenter.

NOTE: Do not pry adjusting lock away from adjusting ring as spring-type lock prevents adjusting ring from backing off during operation.

Change oil after each 100 hours of normal operation. Fill housing to level plug opening with nondetergent oil. Use SAE 30 oil in temperatures above 50° F (10° C), SAE 20 oil in temperatures from 50° F (10° C) to freezing and SAE 10 oil in temperatures below freezing.

REDUCTION DRIVE (GEAR-TYPE)

The 6:1 ratio reduction gear unit (Fig. KA125) is used on some models. To remove unit, first drain lubricating oil,

and then unbolt cover from housing. Remove cover and reduction gear. Unbolt and remove gear housing from engine. Separate reduction gear, shaft and thrust washer from cover. Renew oil seals and needle bearings (bronze bushings on early units) as necessary.

When reassembling, wrap tape around gear on crankshaft to protect oil seal and install gear housing. Use new copper washers on two cap screws on inside of housing. Wrap tape on shaft to prevent keyway from damaging cover oil seal and install thrust washer, shaft and reduction gear in cover. Install cover and gear assembly using new gaskets as required to provide a shaft end play of 0.001-0.006 inch (0.025-0.152 mm). Different thickness gaskets are available. Fill unit to oil check plug opening with same grade oil as used in engine.

FILTER-MINDER

A "Filter-Minder" kit part No. 25 755 18 is available from the engine manufacturer to provide a remote-mounted gauge to monitor vacuum inside the air filter. The Filter-Minder alerts the engine operator to the need to service or replace the air filter. With the exception of overhead camshaft (OHC) engines with top-mounted fuel tank, the kit can be mounted on all Command and OHC engines and most K-series and Magnum engines with dry-element air fil-

ters. Periodically inspect gauge housing, hose and fittings for loose connections and air leaks.

LIQUEFIED-PETROLEUM GAS (LPG) FUEL SYSTEMS

IMPORTANT: Proper service and repair of LPG fuel systems requires qualified technicians and special equipment. Many states require special licensing or certification for LPG repair shops and/or technicians. Check state and local regulations before attempting any adjustment, service or repair of the LPG system or components. Faulty repairs by unqualified personnel can have very serious consequences. The information in this section is for exclusive use of qualified LPG service providers.

WARNING: LPG is extremely flammable and is heavier than air. It tends to settle in low areas where a spark or flame could ignite the gas. Do not start and operate the engine or service the fuel system in a poorly ventilated area where leaking gas could accumulate and endanger the safety of persons in the area.

CH18-25 and TH14-18 series LPG engines having serial numbers beginning with "27" use a fuel system produced by Kohler. All other LPG engines use a fuel system produced by an aftermarket source.

OPERATION. A typical vapor withdrawal LPG fuel system is shown in Fig. KA126. This type system provides a relatively low-volume fuel delivery, and is typically limited to use on smaller engines.

The liquefied petroleum gas is stored in the fuel tank under high pressure. A vapor space is maintained in the top portion of the tank to allow room for fuel vaporization within the tank. The vaporized fuel flows from the tank to a dry gas filter. The filtered fuel then flows to the primary regulator (Fig. KA127) where the fuel pressure is reduced from as high as 1380 kPa (200 psi) from the tank to approximately 29 kPa (4 psi). The vacuum safety lock-off stops fuel flow when the engine stops. On some applications, an electric lock-off solenoid is used in place of the vacuum lock-off. The secondary regulator (Fig. KA128), activated by intake manifold vacuum, further reduces the fuel pressure to a value just slightly above 0 kPa (0 psi). It controls the flow of low-pressure LPG to the engine, and also stops fuel flow when the engine

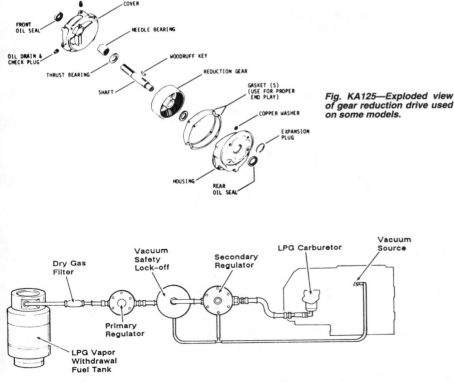

Fig. KA125—Exploded view of gear reduction drive used on some models.

Fig. KA126—Components of typical vapor withdrawal-type LPG fuel system.

stops. The LPG carburetor (Fig. KA129) mixes the vaporized fuel with air in the correct ratio for efficient combustion.

Some LPG systems use a two-stage regulator (Fig. KA130) that combines the primary and secondary regulators into one unit. It may even include the safety lock-off, thereby necessitating only one component in-line between the fuel tank and engine.

The liquid withdrawal fuel system (Fig. KA131) is capable of delivering a higher volume of fuel than the vapor withdrawal system, and it is typically used on larger displacement engines. This system draws liquid fuel from the tank through an in-line vaporizer. The vaporizer absorbs heat from the engine's cooling air and transfers it to the fuel, changing the liquefied petroleum fuel to a vapor or gas. The gas then flows to the remainder of the fuel system in the same manner as the vapor withdrawal system described above.

NOTE: LPG tanks should be marked to denote either vapor or liquid withdrawal. Always make sure your system has the correct tank.

Aftermarket LPG System

Troubleshooting. When a problem occurs, check the following obvious causes first:
1. Correct type fuel tank.
2. Tank shutoff valve open.
3. Sufficient fuel in tank.
4. Loose or kinked lines or hoses.
5. Loose or clogged air filter.

If these items check satisfactory, use the following recommended test procedures to isolate the problem.

CAUTION: Use suitable hand and eye protective wear when servicing the LPG system. Escaping gas is extremely cold and can cause frost bite upon contact to exposed skin. Shut off the fuel tank valve. Run the engine until out of fuel, then slowly loosen the high-pressure fuel line fitting to bleed any remaining pressure from the system before disconnecting any fuel lines.

Primary Regulator Test. Refer to Fig. KA132. Disconnect the fuel inlet line from the vacuum lock-off and install a U-tube water manometer. Apply 345-690 kPa (50-100 psi) air pressure to inlet side of primary regulator. Positive side of manometer tube should indicate a 7 to 11-inch water column.

To adjust regulator, remove bonnet cap and turn adjusting screw clockwise

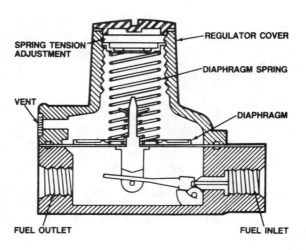

Fig. KA127—Typical LPG primary regulator.

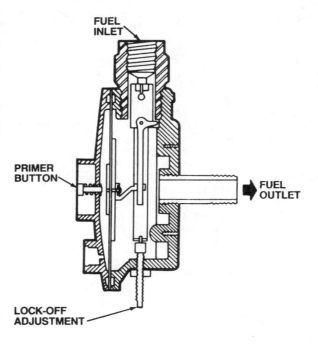

Fig. KA128—Typical LPG secondary regulator.

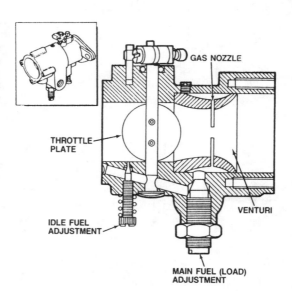

Fig. KA129—Typical LPG carburetor.

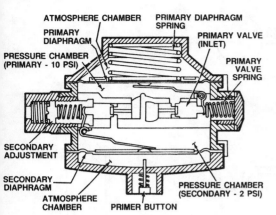

Fig. KA130—Typical LPG 2-stage regulator.

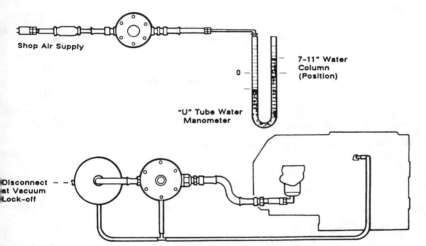

Fig. KA131—Typical liquid withdrawal-type LPG system.

Fig. KA132—Test connections for LPG primary regulator.

connected end of fuel line with air and vacuum applied, and should stop when vacuum is released. If leakage is indicated at the secondary regulator, turn regulator adjusting screw (if equipped) in until leakage stops. If leakage does not stop when turning the adjusting screw or if regulator is not equipped with an adjusting screw, renew the regulator.

CH18-25 and TH14-18 Kohler LPG System

The Kohler LPG system used on CH18-25 and TH14-18 engines is the liquid withdrawal type (Fig. KA131). The system uses two lock-offs: A combination vaporizer and electric lock-off and a two-stage regulator with integral vacuum lock-off.

TROUBLESHOOTING. If the engine is hard to start, runs roughly, stalls or lacks power, use the following guide to troubleshoot the engine.

Engine cranks but will not start. Could be caused by:
1. Fuel tank empty or shutoff valve on tank closed.
2. Lock-off valve not opening electrically, preventing fuel flow to vaporizer.
3. Fuel filter located inside lock-off is blocked.
4. Restricted or blocked fuel line.
5. Vacuum line between carburetor and regulator broken or leaking.
6. Loose carburetor or intake manifold mounting.
7. Faulty regulator.
   A. Primary valve not opening.
   B. Diaphragm spring adjustment incorrect.
   C. Idle adjustment screw incorrectly set.
   D. Air vent blocked.

Hard to start, runs roughly or stalls at idle speed. Could be caused by:
1. LPG fuel tank low.
2. Vacuum line between carburetor and regulator leaking.
3. Carburetor idle speed set too low.
4. Carburetor idle circuit restricted.
5. Restricted air cleaner.
6. Restricted lock-off filter.
7. Faulty regulator.

Irregular or inconsistent idle. Could be caused by:
1. Improper adjustment of regulator, idle adjustment screw, throttle opening or governor.
2. Loose or leaking vacuum line.
3. Loose carburetor mounting.
4. Faulty diaphragm within regulator.

to increase outlet pressure or counterclockwise to decrease pressure. If adjustments do not solve the problem, renew the regulator.

NOTE: Cleanliness and security of LPG fittings is critical. Recommended thread sealant is Loctite Thread Sealant with Teflon or Perm-Lok H-D sealant with Teflon. Do not use Teflon tape. Make certain that sealant does not enter the fuel system.

Vacuum Lock-off Test. Refer to Fig. KA133. Disconnect lock-off outlet line from inlet of secondary regulator. Leave the fuel line connected between primary regulator and lock-off. Disconnect

lock-off vacuum line from first downstream fitting. Apply 345-690 kPa (50-100 psi) air pressure to primary regulator inlet. Apply vacuum to lock-off vacuum hose; low-pressure air should flow from lock-off outlet. Release vacuum from vacuum line; low pressure air flow should stop. If either test did not give the result indicated, lock-off is faulty.

Secondary Regulator Test. Refer to Fig. KA134. Connect fuel line to secondary regulator. Disconnect fuel line from carburetor inlet. Apply shop air pressure to primary regulator inlet, and apply vacuum to line feeding both lock-off and secondary regulator. Low-pressure air should flow from dis-

5. Debris in regulator.

6. Debris in carburetor.

Engine stalls during operation.
Could be caused by:

1. Fuel tank empty.
2. Faulty lock-off or blocked filter.
3. Improper governor setting.
4. Damaged diaphragm within regulator.
5. Leaking vacuum line.
6. Restricted fuel line.

Low power. Could be caused by:

1. Air cleaner or exhaust system restricted.
2. Low fuel.
3. Lock-off filter or fuel line restricted.
4. Leaking vacuum line.
5. Air leakage in intake system.
6. Faulty regulator.
7. Improper ignition timing.

High fuel consumption. Could be caused by:

1. Fuel leak. Check lines, connections and system components for leaks with soapy water.
2. Incorrectly set regulator.
3. Air cleaner restricted.
4. Choke plate in carburetor not opening fully.

COMBINATION VAPORIZER/ ELECTRIC LOCK-OFF. The vaporizer absorbs heat from the engine cooling air and transfers it to the fuel, changing the liquid petroleum gas to a vapor or gas. Make sure that the outer surface of the vaporizer is kept clean and free of dirt or debris, and that the cooling air path from engine is unobstructed. No internal servicing of the vaporizer is required. Renew the vaporizer if it is faulty.

To test the electric lock-off (Fig. KA135), remove it from the system. Connect one of the electrical leads to positive terminal of a 12-volt DC power supply. Touch the second lead to the negative terminal. An audible "click" should be heard; indicating the lock-off is opening. While the lock-off is open, attempt to blow low-pressure compressed air through it to check for flow. Air should flow unrestricted. If flow is restricted, check the fuel filter element mounted inside the lock-off.

NOTE: Cleaning of the filter element is NOT recommended. Element should be replaced every 500 operating hours or sooner if restricted or clogged.

TWO-STAGE REGULATOR. The regulator (Fig. KA136) combines the functions of the primary regulator, the

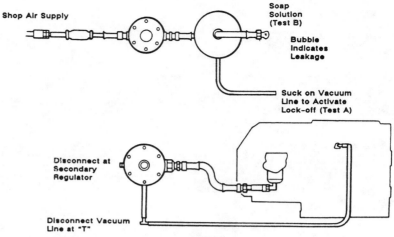

Fig. KA133—Test connections for LPG vacuum lock-off.

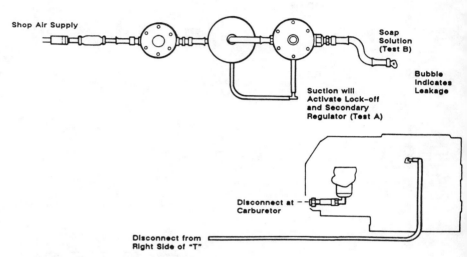

Fig. KA134—Test connections for LPG secondary regulator.

Fig. KA135—LPG electric lock-off with integral fuel filter.

Filter Element

secondary regulator and the vacuum lock-off.

The primary regulator (Fig. KA137) reduces the high-pressure fuel flow from the tank and vaporizer to approximately 28 kPa (4 psi). Fuel flowing from the vaporizer enters the regulator inlet at approximately 76 kPa (11 psi). The fuel flows past the primary valve (1) into the primary chamber (3). As the pressure within the primary chamber approaches 28 kPa (4 psi), the primary diaphragm (4) overcomes the tension of the diaphragm spring (5) and moves upward. The primary lever spring (8) then moves the primary valve lever (7), closing the primary valve and shutting off fuel flow. As the engine consumes fuel and the pressure drops below 28 kPa (4 psi), diaphragm spring tension will overcome the fuel pressure and move the diaphragm downward, re-

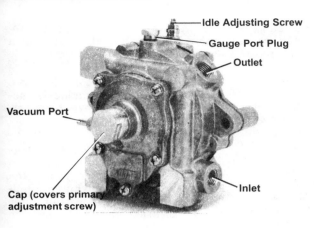

Fig. KA136—Two-stage LPG regulator with integral vacuum lock-off.

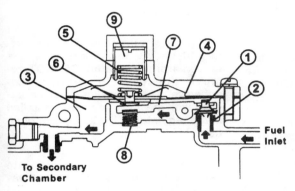

Fig. KA137—Fuel regulation through the primary chamber of 2-stage LPG regulator.

1. Primary valve
2. Primary valve seat
3. Primary chamber
4. Primary diaphragm
5. Primary diaphragm spring
6. Contact button
7. Primary valve lever
8. Primary lever spring
9. Primary pressure adjustment screw

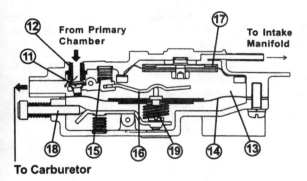

Fig. KA138—Fuel regulation through the secondary chamber of 2-stage LPG reg-

11. Secondary valve
12. Secondary valve seat
13. Secondary chamber
14. Secondary diaphragm
15. Secondary diaphragm spring
16. Secondary valve lever
17. Vacuum lock-off diaphragm
18. Idle adjust screw
19. Balance spring

opening the primary valve and admitting more fuel. This cycle maintains a relatively constant pressure of 28 kPa (4 psi) in the primary chamber.

The secondary regulator (Fig. KA138) further reduces the 28 kPa (4 psi) primary chamber fuel pressure to less than 3.5 kPa (0.5 psi) to provide the correct fuel flow to the carburetor. Fuel flows from the primary chamber past the secondary valve (11) into the secondary chamber (13). When the pressure reaches approximately 3.5 kPa (0.5 psi), the secondary diaphragm is forced downward, closing the secondary valve and stopping fuel flow.

When the engine is running, fuel is being drawn from the secondary chamber, reducing the downward force on the secondary diaphragm. Atmospheric pressure raises the diaphragm, thereby lifting the secondary valve lever (16) and opening the secondary valve. Fuel flows into the secondary chamber and to the carburetor.

A very low fuel flow is required when the engine is idling. The idle adjusting screw (18—Fig. KA138) and the balance spring (19) are used to apply just enough pressure on the diaphragm to maintain sufficient fuel flow for idle operation.

The vacuum lock-off (17—Fig. KA138) is also located in the secondary chamber. When the engine is running, manifold vacuum draws the lock-off diaphragm away from the secondary valve lever to allow operation of the secondary valve and permit fuel flow. When the engine and manifold vacuum

stop, a spring located behind the center pin of the lock-off diaphragm pushes the center pin against the end of secondary valve lever, thereby closing the valve and stopping fuel flow.

REGULATOR MAINTENANCE.
After 500 operating hours or annually, whichever occurs first, drain fuel-residue deposits from the secondary regulator as follows: Turn fuel tank valve off, then run the engine until out of fuel. Disconnect and ground the spark plug leads. Remove ⅛ inch pipe plug from bottom of regulator and allow any deposits to drain. Apply a Teflon-based thread sealant to plug threads. DO NOT use Teflon tape. Install and tighten plug.

After 1500 operating hours, complete disassembly, cleaning and resetting of the regulator is recommended. Note that primary chamber components should be kept separate from secondary components, as they are not interchangeable.

SERVICE PRIMARY CHAMBER.
Purge fuel from the system as follows: Shut off fuel tank valve while the engine is idling and in "neutral." When the engine dies the system is purged. Turn off the ignition key. Disconnect tank supply hose.

Remove the regulator from the system. Remove tamper-proof caps covering the primary adjustment screw (9—Fig. KA137) and idle adjustment screw (18—Fig. KA138). Remove primary pressure adjustment screw (9) and spring (5). Remove fasteners from primary diaphragm cover, and carefully lift cover from regulator body. Remove the diaphragm (4). Discard the diaphragm if it is damaged.

Position a straightedge across machined housing surface and measure gap between end of primary valve lever (7—Fig. KA137) and the straightedge. Gap should measure 2.7-3.7 mm (0.105-0.145 in.). Record the dimension. Remove screws securing the primary lever guide to the housing, the lift out primary lever and valve assembly. If the measured gap between the lever and straightedge was beyond the specifications or if valve or seat damage is evident, install primary valve repair kit. DO NOT attempt to bend or reuse the lever.

Remove primary lever spring (8—Fig. KA137) and shims if used. If shims are used, same thickness of shims must be installed when assembling regulator. Remove valve seat using a 10 mm socket.

Thoroughly clean regulator components with a petroleum-based solvent.

Inspect parts and renew any that are damaged or excessively worn. A diaphragm repair kit and a primary valve repair kit are available for service.

Assemble primary regulator as follows: Install valve seat into housing with one shim/sealing washer, and tighten to 2.9-4.8 N•m (26-43 in.-lb.). Install original quantity of shims (if used) into the housing, followed by the lever spring. Assemble valve lever into housing, making sure that valve is centered over the valve seat and that lever spring fits into recess at end of lever. Tighten lever screws to 2.9 N•m (26 in.-lb.). Place a straightedge across machined surface of housing and measure gap between valve lever and straightedge. Gap should be 2.7-3.7 mm (0.120-0.145 in.). If necessary, install shim/sealing washers under valve seat to obtain correct gap. Note that valve seat needs at least one shim/washer between seat and housing to seal properly.

To check the valve and seat for leakage, immerse the regulator housing in a petroleum-based solvent (not soap and water) and pressurize fuel inlet with regulated air pressure of 300-310 kPa (43-45 psi). If leakage is noted, carefully rotate the valve with pliers and retest. When no leakage is indicated, remove regulator from liquid and blow dry.

Position primary diaphragm with "solid" head of center rivet down against tang in end of valve lever, and gasket facing upward. Install cover and tighten fasteners in a criss-cross pattern to 4.8 N•m (43 in.-lb.). Install primary lever spring and spring adjustment screw. Turn screw in 1½ turns. Refer to TEST AND ADJUST REGULATOR paragraphs for final adjustment procedure.

SERVICE SECONDARY CHAMBER AND VACUUM LOCK-OFF. Remove fasteners from secondary chamber cover, and carefully lift cover from regulator housing. Remove diaphragm (14—Fig. KA138). Position a straightedge across machined surface of housing and note position of secondary valve lever (16). Top edge of lever should be even with to 0.5 mm (0.020 in.) above bottom edge of straightedge. Remove valve lever and seat assembly. If valve lever height was incorrect and/or valve or seat damage is evident, replace the lever, valve and seat. Remove secondary valve seat using an 8 mm socket.

Remove vacuum lock-off diaphragm retaining ring, diaphragm and spring. Thoroughly clean regulator components with petroleum-based solvent.

Inspect all parts for wear or damage and replace if necessary. A diaphragm repair kit and a secondary valve repair kit are available for service.

To assemble, install valve seat and tighten to 4.8 N•m (43 in.-lb.). Position lock-off diaphragm and spring in housing with spring down into the recess. Install diaphragm retaining ring with rounded edge of retaining ring ID down against diaphragm. Tighten retaining ring fasteners to 4.8 N•m (43 in.-lb.). Test the diaphragm for leakage by applying 28 kPa (4 psi) regulated air pressure to vacuum fitting on housing. Apply soapy water around the diaphragm area. No bubbles should form.

Install secondary lever and spring assembly. Tighten lever fasteners to 2.9 N•m (26 in.-lb.). Place a straightedge across machined surface of the housing and check secondary lever height. Top edge of lever should be even with to 0.5 mm (0.020 in.) above bottom edge of straightedge (Fig. KA139). The lever can be adjusted slightly if necessary. Remove lever from housing and carefully bend it at top and bottom of flat angled arm (T and B—Fig. KA139). Note that valve end of lever must remain parallel to housing surface after making adjustment.

Test secondary valve for leakage as follows: Seal regulator inlet port with pipe plug. Apply sufficient vacuum at vacuum fitting to draw lock-off diaphragm away from lever. Apply 28 kPa (4 psi) regulated air pressure to primary chamber gauge port (Fig. KA136), then check valve and seat area for leakage using a petroleum-based solvent. Do not use soapy water. If leakage is ev-

ident, relieve pressure and carefully rotate valve slightly and retest until a leak-proof position is obtained.

NOTE: If original valve and lever are being used, remove the adhesive securing the valve to the lever before attempting to rotate the valve.

After valve is properly seated, thoroughly dry the area being careful not to disturb the valve position. Secure the lever to the valve by applying epoxy adhesive as shown in Fig. KA140. After epoxy has dried, repeat the leakage test. There must not be any leakage past the secondary valve.

NOTE: For purposes of clarity, Fig. KA140 shows secondary lever removed from regulator. DO NOT remove the lever to apply epoxy adhesive. The adhesive must be applied with the lever and valve installed in the regulator in the leak-proof position.

Install secondary diaphragm into regulator housing with the diaphragm's protruding stud positioned down into the recess of the secondary lever. Install secondary chamber cover and tighten fasteners in a criss-cross pattern to 4.8 N•m (43 in.-lb.).

TEST AND ADJUST REGULATOR. Install a 0-175 kPa (0-25 psi) air pressure gauge into the primary chamber gauge port (C—Fig. KA141). Apply 300-310 kPa (43-45 psi) regulated air pressure to regulator inlet (A), then test

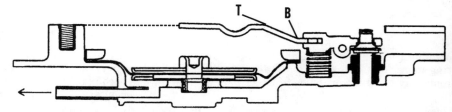

Fig. KA139—Cross-sectional view of 2-stage LPG regulator showing correct secondary lever height and bending points (T & B) for secondary lever alignment. Refer to text for lever adjustment procedure.

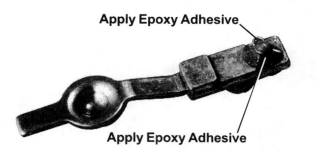

Apply Epoxy Adhesive

Apply Epoxy Adhesive

Fig. KA140—Secondary lever is attached to secondary valve with epoxy adhesive. Refer to text for proper procedure.

Fig. KA141—Check 2-stage LPG regulator for leakage at points A-D. Refer to text for procedure.

Fig. KA142—View of carburetor used on CH18-25 and TH14-18 series LPG engines.

the engine for 5-10 minutes. With throttle control in slow idle position, turn idle adjusting screw counterclockwise until engine speed begins to drop from lean operation. Turn screw clockwise just enough to restore smooth idle speed.

Install new tamper-resistant caps on the primary and idle adjusting screws.

LPG Carburetor

The carburetor (Fig. KA142) has factory preset high-speed and low-idle mixture settings. The only carburetor adjustment is the idle-speed adjusting screw. The carburetor is designed to deliver the correct fuel-air mixture under all operating conditions and at all altitudes. High altitude modifications are neither necessary nor available.

IDLE SPEED ADJUSTMENT. Start and run engine until normal operating temperature is reached. Move throttle control to "idle" position. Use an accurate tachometer to check engine RPM. Adjust idle speed screw to obtain idle speed specified by the equipment manufacturer. Idle speed for unspecified applications should be 1125-1275 RPM.

CLEAN CARBURETOR. Purge fuel from the system by shutting off fuel tank supply valve while engine is idling. When engine dies, system is purged. Turn the ignition key OFF after engine stops.

Remove air cleaner and disconnect fuel line, vacuum and breather hoses, and throttle and choke linkages. Remove carburetor mounting nuts and lift carburetor off intake manifold.

Remove fuel transfer chamber cover (Fig. KA142). Remove rear plug to access fixed main jet for cleaning. Do not attempt to remove the main jet, as carburetor damage will result. Clean all passages with carburetor cleaning solvent and compressed air. Do not use wire or metal objects to clean carburetor body or fuel passages.

Inspect carburetor body for any signs of damage. Inspect throttle and choke shafts and bushings for wear and freedom of motion. Choke and throttle components are not available individually. Renew the carburetor if excessive wear is evident.

Assemble carburetor using new gaskets. Tighten carburetor mounting nuts to 9.9 N•m (88 in.-lb.). Start and run engine until operating temperature is reached. Check idle speed and governed top speed. Adjust as required.

for leakage at inlet fitting (A), primary cover sealing surface (B), primary chamber test port (C) and primary pressure adjusting screw (D). Note that minor leakage at the adjusting screw is acceptable at this time. Correct any leakage noted at points A, B and C before proceeding.

Slowly turn primary adjusting screw clockwise until primary chamber pressure gauge indicates 31-38 kPa (4.5-5.5 psi). If 38 kPa (5.5 psi) is accidentally exceeded, turn adjustment screw counterclockwise and apply vacuum at lock-off vacuum fitting to relieve primary chamber pressure. Repeat the adjustment procedure.

When adjustment is complete, install the adjusting screw cap and tighten it to 17 N•m (150 in.-lb.). Test for leakage as previously described.

Apply vacuum to lock-off port fitting while leaving test gauge and air pressure supply still connected. Turn idle screw clockwise until primary chamber pressure drops to 28 kPa (4 psi) or less. Then turn idle screw counterclockwise and stop when primary chamber pressure reaches 35 kPa (5 psi). Disconnect the vacuum hose and observe pressure test gauge. Primary chamber pressure should be 31-38 kPa (4.5-5.5 psi). If pressure exceeds this figure, internal

leakage is occurring. Locate and correct leakage before proceeding.

Turn off regulated air supply and remove the pressure gauge from the test port. Apply Teflon-based thread sealant to threads of test port plug. Install plug and tighten to 9.3 N•m (82 in.-lb.). Turn the air supply on and check the plug for leakage with soapy water. When no leakage is evident, disconnect the air supply.

Apply 10.5-13.5 kPa (1.5-2.0 psi) regulated air pressure into regulator outlet. Check for leakage along secondary cover sealing surface with soapy water. When no leakage is indicated, disconnect the air supply.

Install the regulator into the fuel system, but leave the vacuum line disconnected and do not connect the fuel supply hose to the fuel tank at this time. Apply 300-310 kPa (43-45 psi) regulated air pressure to the supply line tank valve fitting. Apply vacuum to lock-off chamber fitting on regulator. Turn the ignition switch to "ON" position. Check for leakage at all fuel line connections with soapy water. Correct any leakage.

Disconnect the air supply and vacuum test line. Connect the system vacuum line to the regulator. Connect fuel supply line to fuel tank. Start and run

KOHLER CENTRAL PARTS DISTRIBUTORS

(Arranged Alphabetically by States)
**These franchised firms carry extensive stocks of repair parts. Contact them
for name of dealer in their area who will have replacement parts.**

Auto Electric & Carburetor Company
Phone: (205) 323-7155
2625 4th Avenue South
Birmingham, Alabama 35233

Loftin Equipment Company
Phone: (602) 272-9466
12 N. 45th Avenue
Phoenix, Arizona 85043

H.G. Makelim Company
Phone: (714) 978-0071
1520 South Harris Ct.
Anaheim, California 92806

H.G. Makelim Company
Phone: (650) 873-4757
219 Shaw Road
S. San Francisco, California 94080

Spitzer Industrial Products Company
Phone: (303) 287-3414
6601 N. Washington Street
Thornton, Colorado 80229

Gardner, Inc.
Phone: (904) 262-1661
5200 Sunbeam Road
Jacksonville, Florida 32257

Small Engine Clinic
Phone: (808) 488-0711
98019 Kam Hwy.
Aiea, Hawaii 96701

E.C. Power Systems
Phone: (208) 342-6541
4499 Market Street
Boise, Idaho 83705

Medart, Inc.
Phone: (314) 422-3100
2644 S. 96th Street
Edwardsville, Kansas 66111

Engines Southwest
Phone: (318) 222-3871
1255 N Hearne Street
Shreveport, Louisiana 71162

W.J. Connell Company
Phone: (508) 543-3600
65 Green Street
Foxboro, Massachusetts 02035

Central Power Distributors, Inc.
Phone: (612) 576-0901
1101 McKinley Street
Anoka, Minnesota 55303

Medart, Inc. - St. Louis
Phone: (314) 343-0505
100 Larkin Williams Ct.
Fenton, Missouri 63026

Original Equipment, Inc.
Phone: (406) 245-3081
905 Second Avenue, North
Billings, Montana 59103

Gardner, Inc. - New Jersey
Phone: (609) 860-8060
106 Melrich Road
Cranbury, New Jersey 08512

Gardner, Inc. - Ohio
Phone: (614) 488-7951
1150 Chesapeake Avenue
Columbus, Ohio 43212

E.C. Power Systems
Phone: (503) 224-3623
1835 NW 21st Avenue
Portland, Oregon 97296

Pitt Auto Electric Company
Phone: (412) 766-9112
2900 Stayton Street
Pittsburgh, Pennsylvania 15212

Medart, Inc. -Memphis
Phone: (314) 343-0505
4365 Old Lamar
Memphis, Tennessee 38118

Waukesha-Pearce Industries, Inc.
Phone: (713) 551-0463
12320 South Main Street
Houston, Texas 77235

E.C. Power Systems
Phone: (801) 886-1424
Unit A, 3683 W 2270 South
Salt Lake City, Utah 84120

Chesapeake Engine Distributors
Phone: (804) 550-2231
10241 Sycamore Drive
Ashland, Virginia 23005

E.C. Power Systems
Phone: (253) 872-7011
6414 S. 196th Street
Kent, Washington 98032

Central Power Distributors, Inc.
Phone: (414) 250-1977
N90 W14635 Commerce Dr.
Menomonee Falls, Wisconsin 53051

Kohler Company
Engine Division
Phone: (414) 457-4441
Kohler, Wisconsin 53044

CANADIAN DISTRIBUTORS

Lotus Equipment Sales, Ltd.
Phone: (403) 253-0822
Bay 120, 5726 Burleigh Cres. SE
Calgary, Alberta T2H 1Z8

Yetman's Ltd.
Phone: (204) 586-8046
949 Jarvis Avenue
Winnipeg, Manitoba R2X 0A1

CPT Canada Power Technologies, Ltd.
Phone: (905) 890-6900
161 Watline Avenue
Mississauga, Ontario L4Z 1P2

ONAN

ONAN CORPORATION
1400 73rd Avenue, N.E.
Minneapolis, Minnesota 55432

Model	No. Cyls.	Bore	Stroke	Displacement	Power Rating
BF	2	3.125 in. (79.38 mm)	2.625 in. (66.68 mm)	40.3 cu. in. (660 cc)	16 hp (11.9 kW)
BG	2	3.250 in. (82.55 mm)	3 in. (76.2 mm)	49.8 cu. in. (815.7 cc)	18 hp (13.4 kW)
B43M, B43E	2	3.250 in. (82.55 mm)	2.620 in. (66.55 mm)	43.3 cu. in. (712.4 cc)	16 hp (11.9 kW)
B43G	2	3.250 in. (82.55 mm)	2.620 in. (66.55 mm)	43.3 cu. in. (712.4 cc)	18 hp (13.4 kW)
B48G	2	3.250 in. (82.55 mm)	2.875 in. (73.03 mm)	47.7 cu. in. (781.7 cc)	20 hp (14.9 kW)
B48M	2	3.250 in. (82.55 mm)	2.875 in. (73.03 mm)	47.7 cu. in. (781.7 cc)	18 hp (13.4 kW)

Engines in this section are four-stroke, twin-cylinder opposed, horizontal crankshaft-type in which crankshaft is supported at each end in precision sleeve-type bearings.

Connecting rods ride directly on crankshaft journals and all except early BF engines are pressure lubricated by a gear-type oil pump driven by crankshaft gear. Early BF engines were splash lubricated.

McGRAW-EDISON

Onan

B 48 G G A 020 / 1 D

MODEL AND SPEC NO.

SERIAL NO.

B 48 G G A 020 / 1 D

1 2 3 4 5 6   7 8

Fig. O19—Typical model, specification and serial number plate on Onan engine showing digit interpretation.

1. Identification of basic engine series
2. Displacement (in cubic inches)
3. Engine duty cycle
4. Fuel required
5. Cooling system designation
6. Power rating (in Bhp)
7. Designated optional equipment
8. Production modifications

All models use a battery ignition system consisting of points, condenser, coil, battery and spark plug. Timing is adjustable only by varying point gap.

All models use a single, down draft, float-type carburetor and may have a vacuum-operated fuel pump attached to carburetor or mounted separately, according to model and application.

Refer to model and specification number (Fig. O19) for engine model identification and interpretation.

Always give model, specification and serial numbers when ordering parts.

MAINTENANCE

SPARK PLUG. Recommended spark plug for Models BF, BG, B43E, B43M and B48M is Champion RH18Y or equivalent. Recommended spark plug for Models B43G and B48G is Champion RS14YC or equivalent. Electrode gap for all models using gasoline fuel is 0.025 inch (0.635 mm). Electrode gap for all models using vapor (butane, LP or natural gas) fuel is 0.018 inch (0.457 mm).

CARBURETOR. According to model and application, all engines use a single, down draft, float-type carburetor manufactured by Marvel Schebler, Walbro or Nikki. Exploded view of each carburetor is shown in either Fig. O20, Fig. O20A or Fig. O20B. Refer to appropriate figure for model being serviced.

For initial adjustment of Marvel Schebler carburetor, refer to Fig. O20. Open idle mixture screw 1 turn and main fuel mixture screw 1¼ turns.

For initial adjustment of Walbro carburetor, refer to Fig. O20A. Open idle mixture screw 1⅛ turns. If equipped with optional main fuel adjustment, open main fuel mixture screw 1½ turns.

For initial adjustment of Nikki carburetor, refer to Fig. O20B. Later models may be equipped with a limiter cap on the idle fuel adjustment screw. On models so equipped, remove cap for initial setting of idle mixture screw and turn screw 1¼ turns out. After adjustment,

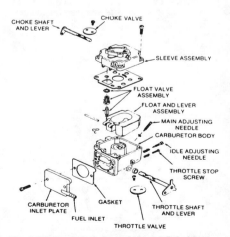

Fig. O20—Exploded view of Marvel Schebler carburetor showing component parts and their relative positions.

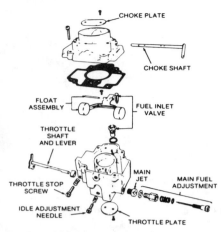

Fig. O20A—Exploded view of Walbro carburetor showing component parts and their relative positions.

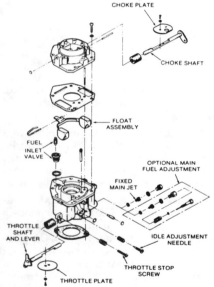

Fig. O20B—Exploded view of Nikki carburetor showing component parts and their relative positions.

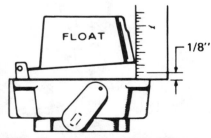

Fig. O21—Float valve setting for Marvel Schebler carburetor. Measure between inverted float and surface of gasket.

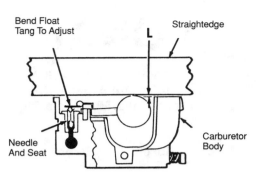

Fig. O22—Float level (L) on Walbro carburetor should be 0.00-0.04 inch (0.0-1.0 mm). Push down float arm tang so fuel inlet valve just contacts seat.

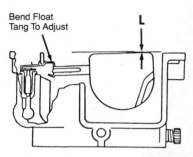

Fig. O23—Float level (L) on Nikki carburetor without idle mixture screw limiter cap should be 0.000-0.056 inch (0.00-1.42 mm). Push down float arm tang so fuel inlet valve just contacts seat.

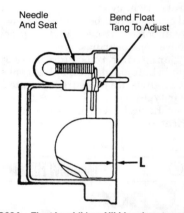

Fig. O23A—Float level (L) on Nikki carburetor with idle mixture screw limiter cap should be 0.023-0.079 inch (0.58-2.00 mm).

install limiter cap so it is at midpoint of travel. On models not equipped with a limiter cap, open idle mixture screw 3/4 turn. If equipped with optional main fuel adjustment screw, open main fuel adjustment screw 1½ turns.

Make final adjustment to all models with engine at operating temperature and running. Place engine under load and adjust main fuel mixture screw to leanest mixture that will allow satisfactory acceleration and steady governor operation.

Run engine at idle speed, no load, and adjust idle mixture screw for smoothest idle operation. As each adjustment affects the other, adjustment procedure may have to be repeated.

To check float level of Walbro or Nikki carburetor, refer to Figs. O22, O23 or O23A and position carburetor as shown. Float level (L–Fig. O22) on Walbro carburetor should be 0.00-0.004 inch (0.0-1.0 mm). Float level (L–Fig. O23) on Nikki carburetor without idle mixture screw limiter cap should be 0.000-0.056 inch (0.00-1.42 mm) Float level (L–Fig. O23A) on Nikki carburetor with idle mixture screw limiter cap should be 0.023-0.079 inch (0.58-2.00 mm) mm). Float level (L—Fig. O23) on Nikki carburetor without idle mixture screw limiter cap should be 0.000-0.056 inch (0.00-1.42 mm). Float level (L—Fig. O23A) on Nikki carburetor with idle mixture screw limiter cap should be 0.023-0.079 inch (0.58-2.00 mm).

To check float drop, measure from surface of carburetor body to uppermost point on float. Float drop should be 0.20 inch (5.1 mm) on Walbro carburetor, 0.231 inch (5.87 mm) on Nikki carburetor without idle mixture screw limiter cap and 0.291 inch (7.40 mm) on Nikki carburetor with idle mixture screw limiter cap.

All models use a pulsating diaphragm fuel pump. Refer to **SERVICING ONAN ACCESSORIES** section for service information.

GOVERNOR. All models use a flyball weight governor located under timing gear on camshaft gear. Various linkage arrangements allow for either fixed speed operation or variable speed operation.

FIXED SPEED. Fixed speed linkage is used on electric generators and welders, or any application that requires a single, constant speed under varying load conditions. Fig. O24 shows typical linkage arrangement.

Governor link length should be adjusted so stop on throttle shaft almost touches stop on side of carburetor with engine stopped and governor spring under tension.

Sensitivity is adjusted by varying tension of governor spring and changing

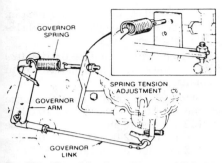

Fig. O24—View of fixed-speed governor linkage.

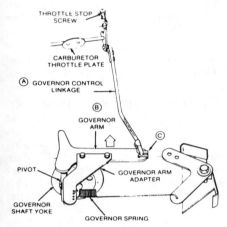

Fig. O25—View of front pull variable speed governor linkage.

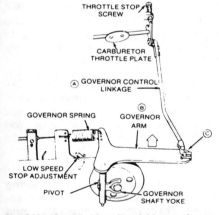

Fig. O26—View of side pull variable speed governor linkage.

location of governor spring on governor arm.

Engine speed should be set to manufacturer's specifications and output of generators should be checked with a frequency meter.

VARIABLE SPEED. Variable speed linkage is used where it is necessary to maintain a wide range of engine speeds under varying load conditions. Moving a control lever determines engine speed and governor maintains this speed under varying loads.

Front pull (Fig. O25) and side pull (Fig. O26) linkage arrangements are used and service procedures are similar.

For correct governor link installation on either front- or side-pull system, disconnect linkage (A) from hole (C) and push linkage and governor arm (B) toward carburetor as far as they will go. While held in this position, insert end of linkage into nearest hole in governor arm. If between two holes, insert in next hole out.

Normal factory setting is in third hole from pivot for side-pull linkage and second hole from pivot for front-pull linkage.

Sensitivity is increased by connecting governor spring closer to pivot and decreased by connecting governor spring further from pivot.

Engine speed should be set to manufacturer's specifications and speed should be checked after linkage adjustments.

IGNITION. A battery-type ignition system is used on all models. Breaker point box is non-movable and only means of changing timing is to vary point gap slightly. See Fig. O27. Static timing should be checked if point gap is changed or new points are installed. Use a continuity test light across breaker points to check timing and remove air intake hose from blower housing for access to timing marks. Refer to ignition specifications as follows:

Initial Model	Point Gap	Static Timing BTDC
BF	0.025 in. (0.635 mm)	21°
BF*	0.025 in. (0.635 mm)	21°
BF**	0.025 in. (0.635 mm)	26°
BG, B43M, B48M	0.021 in. (0.533 mm)	21°
B48G	0.020 in. (0.508 mm)	20°
B48G*	0.016 in. (0.406 mm)	16°

*Specification letter "C" and after.
**"Power Drawer" models.

LUBRICATION. Early Model BF is splash lubricated and all other models are pressure lubricated by a gear-type pump driven by crankshaft gear. Internal pump parts are not serviced separately so entire pump must be renewed if worn or damaged. Clearance between pump gear and crankshaft gear should be 0.002-0.005 inch (0.05-0.13 mm) and

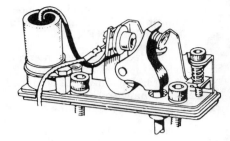

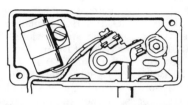

Fig. O27—Two different-type point boxes are used according to model and application. Upper illustration shows top-adjust point models and lower illustration shows side-adjust point model.

normal operating pressure should be 30 psi (207 kPa). Oil pressure is regulated by an oil pressure relief valve (Fig. O28) located in engine block near timing gear cover. Spring (3) free length should be 1.00 inch (25.4 mm) and valve (4) diameter should be 0.3365-0.3380 inch (8.55-8.59 mm).

Oils approved by manufacturer must meet requirements of API service classification SF or SG.

Use SAE 5W-30 oil in below freezing temperatures and SAE 20W-40 oil in above freezing temperatures.

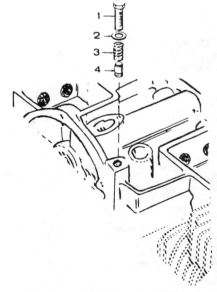

Fig. O28—View showing location of oil pressure relief valve and spring.

1. Cap screw
2. Sealing washer
3. Spring
4. Valve

Check oil level with engine stopped and maintain at "FULL" mark on dipstick. **DO NOT OVERFILL.**

Recommended oil change intervals for models without oil filter is every 25 hours of normal operation. If equipped with a filter, change oil at 50-hour intervals and filter every 100 hours.

Crankcase capacity without filter is 3.5 pints (1.66 L) for BG model, 4 pints (1.86 L) for BF model, 1.5 quarts (1.4 L) for B43E, B43G and B48G models. If filter is changed, add an additional 0.5 pint (0.24 L) for BF and BG models and an additional 0.5 quart (0.47 L) for B43E, B43G and B48G models. Oil filter is screw-on type and gasket should be lightly lubricated before installation. Screw filter on until gasket contacts, then turn an additional ½ turn. Do not overtighten.

REPAIRS

TIGHTENING TORQUES. Recommended tightening torques are as follows:

Cylinder heads—
  BF, BG . . . . 14-16 ft.-lbs.
  (19-22 N•m)
  B43E*, B43G*, B48G*,
  B43M*, B48M* . . . . . . 16-18 ft.-lbs.
  (22-24 N•m)
*If graphoil gasket is used, tighten to 14-16 ft.-lbs. (19-22 N•m) torque.

Rear bearing plate . . . . . 25-27 ft.-lbs.
  (34-37 N•m)
Connecting rod—
  BG, BF . . . . 14-16 ft.-lbs.
  (19-22 N•m)
  All others . . . . 12-14 ft.-lbs.
  (16-19 N•m)
Flywheel . . . . 35-40 ft.-lbs.
  (48-54 N•m)
Oil Base . . . . 18-23 ft.-lbs.
  (24-31 N•m)
Timing cover . . . . 8-10 ft.-lbs.
  (11-13 N•m)
Oil pump . . . . 7-9 ft.-lbs.
  (10-12 N•m)

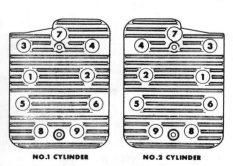

NO.1 CYLINDER **NO.2 CYLINDER**

Fig. O29—Torque sequence shown is for all models even though spark plug may be in different location in head.

CYLINDER HEADS. It is recommended that cylinder heads be removed and carbon cleaned at 200-hour intervals.

CAUTION: Cylinder heads should not be unbolted from block when hot due to danger of head warping.

When installing cylinder heads, torque bolts in sequence shown in Fig. O29 in gradual, even steps until correct torque for model being serviced is obtained. Note spark plug location on some models varies, but torque sequence is the same.

CONNECTING RODS. Connecting rod and piston are removed from cylinder head surface end of block after removing cylinder head and oil base. Connecting rods ride directly on crankshaft journal on all models and standard journal diameter should be 1.6252-1.6260 inches (41.28-41.30 mm). Connecting rods are available for 0.005, 0.010, 0.020, 0.030 and 0.040 inch (0.127, 0.254, 0.508, 0.762 and 1.016 mm) undersize crankshafts as well as standard.

Connecting rod to crankshaft journal running clearance should be 0.002-0.0033 inch (0.0508-0.838 mm) and side play should be 0.002-0.016 inch (0.0508-0.406 mm).

When reinstalling connecting rods, make certain rods are installed with rod bolts offset toward outside of block and tighten to specified torque.

PISTON, PIN AND RINGS. Aluminum pistons are fitted with two compression rings and one oil control ring. Pistons in BF models should be renewed if top compression ring has 0.008 inch (0.2032 mm) or more side clearance and pistons in all other models should be renewed if 0.004 inch (0.1016 mm) or more side clearance is present.

Pistons and rings are available in 0.005, 0.010, 0.020, 0.030 and 0.040 inch (0.127, 0.254, 0.508, 0.762 and 1.016 mm) oversize as well as standard.

Recommended piston to cylinder wall clearance for BF engines, when measured 0.10 inch (2.54 mm) below oil control ring 90° from pin, should be 0.001-0.003 inch (0.0254-0.0762 mm).

Recommended piston to cylinder wall clearance for B43M and B48M engines, when measured 0.35 inch (8.89 mm) below oil control ring 90° from pin, should be 0.0033-0.0053 inch (0.0838-0.1346 mm).

Recommended piston to cylinder wall clearance for B43E, B43G and B48G engines, when measured 0.35 inch (8.89

mm) below oil control ring 90° from pin, should be 0.0044-0.0064 inch (0.1118-0.1626 mm).

Ring end gap should be 0.010-0.020 inch (0.254-0.508 mm) clearance in standard bore.

Piston pin to piston bore clearance should be 0.0002-0.0004 inch (0.0051-0.0102 mm) and pin to rod clearance should be 0.0002-0.0007 inch (0.0051-0.0178 mm) for all models.

Standard cylinder bore of BF engine is 3.1245-3.1255 inches (79.36-79.39 mm) and standard cylinder bore for all other models is 3.249-3.250 inches (82.53-82.55 mm).

Cylinders should be bored oversize if taper exceeds 0.005 inch (0.127 mm) or if 0.003 inch (0.0762 mm) out-of-round.

CRANKSHAFT, BEARINGS AND SEALS. Crankshaft is supported at each end by precision-type sleeve bearings located in cylinder block housing and rear bearing plate (Fig. O30). Main bearing journal standard diameter should be 1.9992-2.000 inches (50.7797-50.800 mm) and bearing operating clearance should be 0.0025-0.0038 inch (0.0635-0.0965 mm). Main bearings are available for a variety of undersize crankshafts as well as standard.

Oil holes in bearing and bore **MUST** be aligned when bearings are installed and bearings should be pressed into bores so inside edge of bearing is 1/16- to 3/32-inch (1.6 to 2.4 mm) back from inside end of bore to allow clearance for radius of crankshaft (Fig. O31). Oil grooves in thrust washers must face crankshaft. The two alignment notches on thrust washers must fit over lock pins. Thrust washers must be in good condition or excessive crankshaft end play will result.

NOTE: Replacement front bearing and thrust washer is a one-piece assembly. Do not install a separate thrust washer.

Recommended crankshaft end play should be 0.006-0.012 inch (0.15-0.30 mm) and is adjusted by varying thrust washer thickness or placing shim between thrust washer and rear bearing plate. Shims are available in a variety of thicknesses. See Fig. O31.

It is recommended rear bearing plate and front timing gear cover be removed for seal renewal. Rear seal is pressed in until flush with seal bore. Timing cover seal should be driven in until it is 1 1/32 inch (26.29 mm) from mounting face to cover.

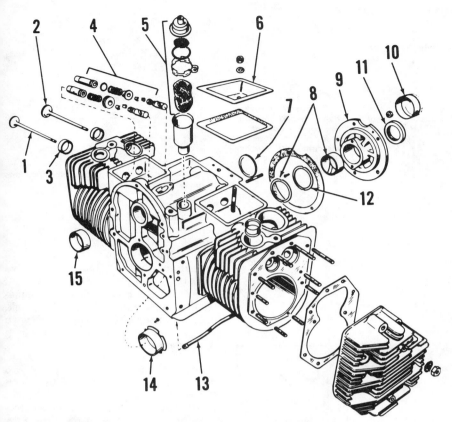

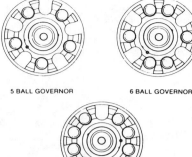

Fig. O32—Flyballs must be arranged in pockets as shown, according to total number used to obtain governor sensitivity desired. Refer to text.

Fig. O30—Exploded view of cylinder and crankcase assembly typical of all models.

1. Exhaust valve
2. Intake valve
3. Seat insert (2)
4. Guide, spring, tappet group
5. Crankcase breather group
6. Valve compartment cover
*7. Camshaft expansion plug
8. Two-piece main bearing
9. Rear main bearing plate
*10. Timing control cover
11. Crankshaft seal
12. Crankshaft thrust shim
13. Oil tube
14. One-piece main bearing
15. Camshaft bearing (2)
*Plug is installed on engine without timing control.

CAMSHAFT, BEARINGS AND GOVERNOR. Camshaft is supported at each end in precision-type sleeve bearings. Make certain oil holes in bearings are aligned with oil holes in block (Fig. O31), press front bearing in flush with outer surface of block and press rear bearing in until flush with bottom of counterbore. Camshaft to bearing clearance should be 0.0015-0.0030 inch (0.0381-0.0762 mm).

Camshaft end play should be 0.003 inch (0.0762 mm) and is adjusted by varying thickness of shims located between camshaft timing gear and engine block.

Camshaft timing gear is a press fit on end of camshaft and designed to accommodate 5, 8 or 10 flyballs arranged as shown in Fig. O32. Number of flyballs is varied to alter governor sensitivity. Fewer flyballs are used on engines with variable speed applications and greater number of flyballs are used for continuous speed application. Flyballs must be arranged in "pockets" as shown according to total number used. Make certain timing mark on cam gear aligns with timing mark on crankshaft gear when reinstalling.

Center pin (Fig. O33) should extend ¾ inch (19 mm) from end of camshaft to allow ⁷/₃₂ inch (5.6 mm) in-and-out movement of governor cup. If distance is incorrect, remove pin and press new pin in to correct depth.

Always make certain governor shaft pivot ball is in timing cover by measuring as shown in Fig. O34 inset and check length of roll pin that engages bushed hole in governor cup. This pin must extend ²⁵/₃₂ inch (19.844 mm) from timing cover mating surface.

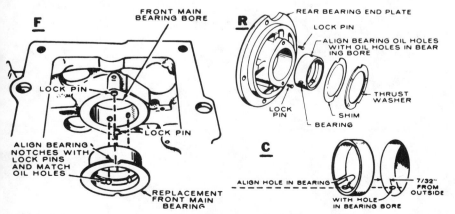

Fig. O31—Alignment of precision main crankshaft bearing at rear (view R). Note shim used for end play adjustment. View C shows placement of camshaft bearings.

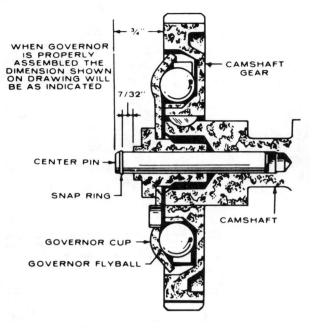

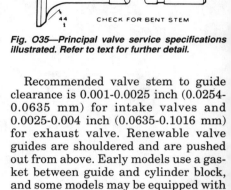

WHEN GOVERNOR IS PROPERLY ASSEMBLED THE DIMENSION SHOWN ON DRAWING WILL BE AS INDICATED

CAMSHAFT GEAR

CENTER PIN

SNAP RING

CAMSHAFT

GOVERNOR CUP

GOVERNOR FLYBALL

Fig. O33—Cross-sectional view of camshaft gear and governor assembly showing correct dimensions for center pin extension from camshaft. Further detail in text.

VALVE
SEAT
INTERFERENCE ANGLE
1/32" MINIMUM
REFER TO SPECIFICATIONS FOR CORRECT DIAMETER
CHECK FOR BENT STEM

Fig. O35—Principal valve service specifications illustrated. Refer to text for further detail.

Recommended valve stem to guide clearance is 0.001-0.0025 inch (0.0254-0.0635 mm) for intake valves and 0.0025-0.004 inch (0.0635-0.1016 mm) for exhaust valve. Renewable valve guides are shouldered and are pushed out from above. Early models use a gasket between guide and cylinder block, and some models may be equipped with valve stem seal on intake valve, which must be renewed if valve is removed.

Recommended valve tappet gap (cold) for B43E model is 0.003 inch (0.0762 mm) for intake valves and 0.010 inch (0.254 mm) for exhaust valves. Recommended valve tappet gap (cold) for all remaining models is 0.008 inch (0.2032 mm) for intake valves and 0.013 inch (0.3302 mm) for exhaust valves.

Adjustment is made by turning tappet adjusting screw as required (Fig. O36). Valves of each cylinder must be adjusted with cylinder at "top dead center" on compression stroke. At this position, both valves will be fully closed.

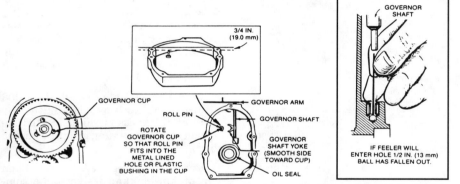

Fig. O34—View of governor shaft, timing cover and governor cup showing assembly details. Refer to text.

VALVE SYSTEM. Valve seats are renewable insert-type and are available in a variety of oversizes as well as standard. Seats are ground at a 45° angle and seat width should be $\frac{1}{32}$ to $\frac{3}{64}$ inch (0.794-1.191 mm).

Valves should be ground at a 44° angle to provide an interference angle of 1° (Fig. O35). Stellite valves and seats are available and rotocaps are available for exhaust valves.

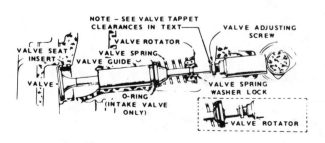

Fig. O36—Typical valve train on all models. Refer to text.

ONAN

ONAN CORPORATION
1400 73rd Avenue N.E.
Minneapolis, Minnesota 55432

Model	No. Cyls.	Bore	Stroke	Displacement	Power Rating
N52M	2	3.563 in. (90.50 mm)	2.64 in. (67.1 mm)	52.2 cu. in. (856 cc)	19.9 hp. (14.9 kW)
NH	2	3.563 in. (90.50 mm)	3 in. (76.2 mm)	60 cu. in. (980 cc)	25 hp. (18.6 kW)
NHA	2	3.563 in. (90.50 mm)	3 in. (76.2 mm)	60 cu. in. (980 cc)	18 hp. (13.4 kW)
NHB	2	3.563 in. (90.50 mm)	3 in. (76.2 mm)	60 cu. in. (980 cc)	20 hp. (14.9 kW)
NHC	2	3.563 in. (90.50 mm)	3 in. (76.2 mm)	60 cu. in. (980 cc)	25 hp. (18.6 kW)
T-260G	2	3.563 in. (90.50 mm)	3 in. (76.2 mm)	60 cu. in. (980 cc)	24 hp. (17.9 kW)

Engines in this section are four-stroke, twin-opposed-cylinder engines with a horizontal crankshaft. The crankshaft is supported at each end in precision sleeve type bearings.

Engines may be equipped with aluminum connecting rods that ride directly on crankshaft or with iron connecting rods that are equipped with renewable precision insert-type bearings. All mod-els are pressure lubricated by a gear-type oil pump. Oil is routed through a "spin-on" oil filter with a bypass.

Most models are equipped with a battery ignition system. However, a magneto system is available for manual start models.

Side draft or down draft carburetor may be used according to model or application and fuel is supplied by either a mechanically operated or vacuum operated fuel pump.

Refer to Figs. O38 or O38A for interpretation of engine specification and model numbers. Always give specification, model and serial numbers when ordering parts.

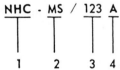

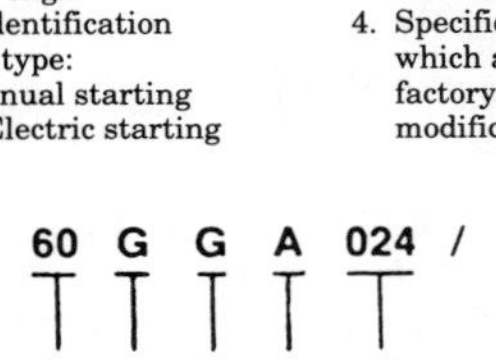

Fig. O38—Interpretation of engine model and specification number as an aid to identification of various engines.

1. General engine model identification
2. Specific type:
   S—Manual starting
   MS—Electric starting
3. Optional equipment identification
4. Specification letter, which advances with factory production modifications

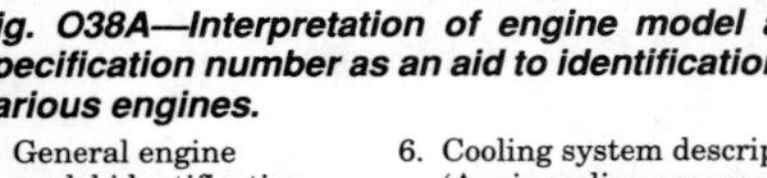

Fig. O38A—Interpretation of engine model and specification number as an aid to identification of various engines.

1. General engine model identification
2. Number of cylinders
3. Cubic inch displacement
4. Engine duty cycle (M=medium duty)
5. Fuel required (G=gasoline)
6. Cooling system description (A=air cooling pressure)
7. Bhp rating
8. Optional equipment identification
9. Specification letter, which advances with factory production modifications

MAINTENANCE

SPARK PLUG. Recommended spark plug for NH models, with specification letter A through C, is Onan part number 167-0240 for non-resistor plug and 167-0247 for a resistor-type plug or Champion RN5C. Recommended spark plug for all other models is Onan part number 167-0291 or Champion RS14YC. Electrode gap for all models using vapor (butane, LP or natural gas) fuel is 0.018 inch (0.4572 mm) and gap for models using gasoline for fuel is 0.025 inch (0.635 mm).

CARBURETOR. According to model and application, engine may be equipped with either a side draft or a downdraft carburetor. Refer to appropriate paragraph for model being serviced.

SIDE DRAFT CARBURETOR. Side draft carburetor is used on some NH and NHC model engines. Refer to Fig. O39 for exploded view of carburetor and location of mixture adjustment screws.

For initial carburetor adjustment, open idle mixture screw and main fuel mixture screw 1 to 1½ turns. Make final adjustments with engine at normal operating temperature and running. Place engine under load and adjust main fuel mixture screw for leanest setting that will allow satisfactory acceleration and steady governor operation. Set engine at idle speed, no load and adjust idle mixture screw for smoothest idle operation.

As each adjustment affects the other, adjustment procedure may have to be repeated.

To check float level, refer to Fig. O39A. Invert carburetor throttle body and float assembly. With gasket installed, float level (D) should be ¹⁄₁₆-³⁄₁₆ inch (1.6-4.8 mm) between gasket and free end of float. Bend float lever tang to adjust float level.

DOWNDRAFT CARBURETORS. Engine may be equipped with one of the downdraft carburetors shown in Figs. O40, O41 or O42. Refer to following paragraphs for service information.

Fig. O40. Initial setting of idle mixture screw is one turn out. Initial setting of main fuel screw is 1-1½ turns out.

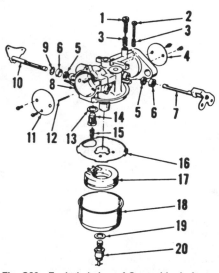

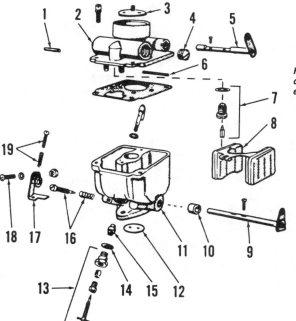

Fig. O40—Exploded view of down-draft carburetor used on some models.

1. Choke stop pin
2. Cover assy.
3. Choke valve
4. Gas inlet plug
5. Choke shaft
6. Float pin
7. Inlet valve assy.
8. Float
9. Throttle shaft
10. Shaft bushing
11. Body assy.
12. Throttle plate
13. Main fuel valve
14. Gasket
15. Main jet*
16. Idle mixture adjustment screw
17. Idle stop lever
18. Clamp screw
19. Stop screw & spring

*Either 13 or 15 is used.

Fig. O39—Exploded view of Onan side draft carburetor used on NH and NHC model engines.

1. Idle mixture needle	11. Choke plate
2. Throttle stop screw	12. Float pin
3. Springs (2)	13. Washer
4. Throttle plate	14. Inlet valve seat
5. Shaft seal (2)	15. Inlet valve needle
6. Seal retainer (2)	16. Body gasket
7. Throttle shaft	17. Float
8. Body	18. Float bowl
9. Washer	19. Washer
10. Choke shaft	20. Main fuel valve

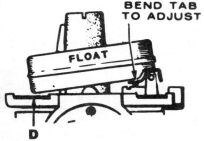

Fig. O39A—To check float level on side draft carburetor, invert carburetor throttle body and float assembly. With gasket installed, float level (D) should be 1/16-3/16 inch (1.6-4.8 mm) between gasket and free end of float.

Make final adjustments with engine running at normal temperature. To adjust idle mixture screw, turn adjusting screw to find the lean drop-off point and the rich drop-off point. Then, set adjusting screw midway between the two extremes. When correctly set, engine should idle smoothly. To adjust main fuel mixture screw, run engine under load and turn adjusting screw so engine accelerates cleanly with steady governor operation.

To check float height, refer to Fig. O40A. Invert carburetor throttle body and float assembly. Float height (A) should be 1/4 inch (6.4 mm) as measured from gasket to closest edge of float. Adjust float by bending float arm tang that contacts fuel valve.

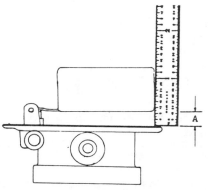

Fig. O40A—Float height (A) should be 1/4 inch (6.4 mm) as measured from gasket to closest edge of float. Adjust float by bending float arm tang that contacts fuel valve.

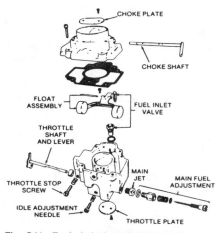

Fig. O41—Exploded view of Walbro LUA downdraft carburetor used on some models.

Walbro LUA. Refer to Fig. O41 for exploded view of Walbro LUA downdraft carburetor. Initial setting of idle mixture screw is indicated in following table:

	Turns Out
N52M & NHC (Spec. A-C):	
LUA 2	1½-1¾
LUA 5	1⅜-1⅝
LUA 9	1⅛-1⅜
NHC (Spec. E)	1⅜-1⅝
T-260G	1¼

Initial setting of main fuel adjustment screw is indicated in following table:

	Turns Out
N52M & NHC (Spec. A-C):	
LUA 2	1-1¼
LUA 5	1½-1¾
LUA 9	1⅛-1⅜
NHC (Spec. E)	1¼-1½
T-260G	1½

Make final adjustments with engine running at normal temperature. To adjust idle mixture screw, turn adjusting screw to find the lean drop-off point and the rich drop-off point. Set adjusting screw midway between the two extremes, then turn screw out ⅛ turn. When correctly set, engine should idle smoothly. To adjust main fuel mixture screw, run engine under load and turn adjusting screw so engine accelerates cleanly with steady governor operation.

Float level (L—Fig. O41A) should be 0.00-0.04 inch (0.0-1.0 mm). To check

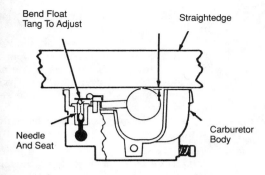

Fig. O41A—Float level (L) for Walbro carburetor should be 0.00-0.04 inch (0.0-1.0 mm). Push down float arm tang so fuel inlet valve just contacts seat.

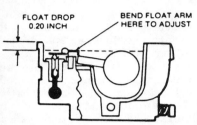

Fig. O41B—Float drop for Walbro carburetor should be 0.20 inch (0.5 mm).

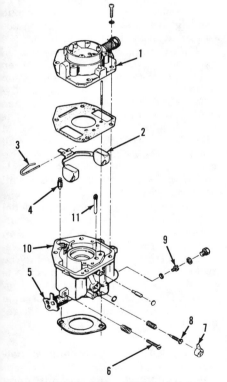

Fig. O42—Exploded view of Nikki carburetor.

1. Air horn
2. Float
3. Pivot pin
4. Needle valve
5. Throttle shaft
6. Throttle stop screw
7. Cap
8. Idle adjustment needle
9. Main jet
10. Carburetor body
11. Main nozzle

float drop, measure from surface of carburetor body to uppermost point on float. Float drop should be 0.20 inch (5.1 mm) measured as shown in Fig. O41B.

Nikki. Note that idle mixture screw was originally equipped with a limiter

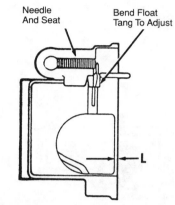

Fig. O42A—Position carburetor as shown when measuring float level (L). Float level should be 0.023-0.079 inch (0.58-2.00 mm).

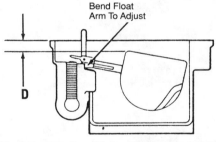

Fig. O43—Float drop (D) should be 0.291 inch (7.40 mm).

cap (Fig. O42). Remove cap for initial setting of idle mixture screw. Initial adjustment of idle mixture screw is 1½ turns out. Run engine until normal operating temperature is reached. Adjust idle mixture screw so engine idles at maximum speed and will accelerate cleanly. Install limiter cap so it is at midpoint of travel. High-speed mixture is determined by a fixed main jet. An optional main jet may be installed for engine operation above 5000 feet.

Carburetor overhaul is evident after inspection of unit and referral to Fig. O42. Use care when cleaning carburetor as caustic solvents may damage non-metallic parts. To check float level, position carburetor as shown in Fig. O42A so float arm is just touching fuel inlet valve. Bend tang as required so float

level (L) is 0.023-0.079 inch (0.58-2.00 mm). Float drop (D—Fig. O43) should be 0.291 inch (7.40 mm). Bend float arm to obtain correct float drop.

Various mechanical, electrical and pulse-type fuel pumps are used according to model and application. Refer to **SERVICING ONAN ACCESSORIES** section for service information.

GOVERNOR. All models use a flyball weight governor located under timing gear cover on camshaft gear. Various linkage arrangements allow for either fixed speed operation or variable speed operation.

FIXED SPEED. Fixed speed linkage is used on electric generators and welders or any application that requires a single constant speed under varying load conditions. Fig. O44 shows typical linkage arrangement.

Engines with fixed speed governors start at wide-open throttle and engine speed is preset at factory to 2400 rpm unless specially ordered with different specified speed.

With engine stopped, adjust length of linkage connecting throttle arm to governor arm so stop on carburetor throttle lever is 1/32 inch (0.794 mm) from stop boss. This allows immediate governor control at engine start and synchronizes travel of governor arm and throttle shaft.

Engine speed is determined by governor spring tension. Increasing spring tension results in higher engine speeds and decreasing spring tension results in lower engine speeds. Adjust spring tension as necessary by turning nut on spring adjusting stud. See Fig. O44.

Governor sensitivity is determined by location of governor spring at governor spring bracket. Refer to Fig. O44 for adjustment.

VARIABLE SPEED. Variable speed linkage is used where it is necessary to maintain a wide range of different engine speeds under varying load conditions. Moving a control lever determines engine speed and governor maintains this speed under varying loads.

To adjust variable speed governor linkage adjust throttle stop screw on carburetor so engine idles at 1100 rpm, then adjust governor spring tension so engine idles at 1500 rpm when manual control lever is at minimum speed position (Fig. O45) or "Bowden" cable control know (Fig. O46) is at first notch (low speed) position.

Adjust sensitivity with engine running at minimum speed to obtain smoothest engine operation by moving governor spring outward on extension arm to decrease sensitivity or inward to

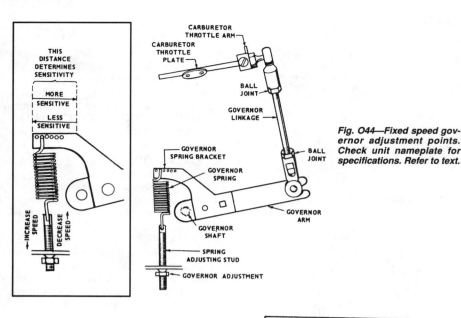

Fig. O44—Fixed speed governor adjustment points. Check unit nameplate for specifications. Refer to text.

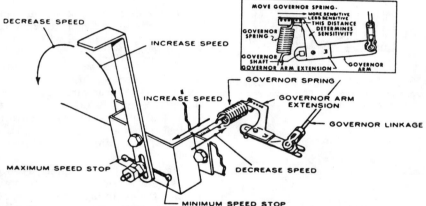

Fig. O45—Variable speed governor linkage adjustment points and procedure. Refer to text.

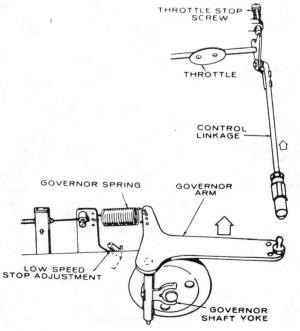

Fig. O46—View of variable speed governor linkage when "Bowden" cable is used. Refer to text for adjustment procedure.

increase sensitivity. Refer to Figs. O45 or O46.

Maximum full load speed should not exceed 3000 rpm for continuous operation. To adjust, apply full load to engine and move control lever knob to maximum speed position and adjust set screw in bracket slot to stop lever travel or turn knob until desired speed is attained.

IGNITION SYSTEM. Most models are equipped with battery ignition system; however, a magneto system is available for manual start models. Refer to appropriate paragraph for model being serviced.

BATTERY IGNITION. **Breaker-Point Ignition.** Breaker points are located in a nonmovable breaker box (Fig. O47) and timing is adjusted by varying point gap slightly. Static timing should be checked if point gap is changed or new points are installed.

Remove air intake hose from blower housing on pressure cooled engines or remove sheet metal plug in air shroud over right cylinder of "Vacu-Flo" engines to gain access to timing marks.

Static ignition timing can be checked by connecting a test light across ignition points and rotating engine in direction of normal rotation (clockwise at flywheel) until light comes on and then goes out. Initial point gap setting is 0.020 inch (0.51 mm) on Models N52M and NH, and 0.016 inch (0.41 mm) on all other models. Adjust point gap so ignition timing is 25° BTDC on Models N52M and NH, and 20° BTDC on all other models.

Breakerless Ignition. Later Model T-260G engines are equipped with a battery-type ignition system that uses an electronic, breakerless triggering system. The trigger ring is attached to the crankshaft and the ignition module is located on the crankcase (see Fig. O47A). The spark plugs fire at the same time. Regular maintenance is not required.

CAUTION: Due to presence of battery in circuit, improper test connections or incorrect wiring connections can damage ignition module.

Ignition timing is 20° BTDC, but is not adjustable. To check ignition timing, remove spark plugs. Using a voltmeter, connect the positive tester lead to negative terminal (larger diameter) on ignition coil and ground the negative tester lead to the engine. Turn ignition switch on and turn flywheel clockwise slowly by hand. When voltmeter reading changes from 1-1.5 volts to battery volt-

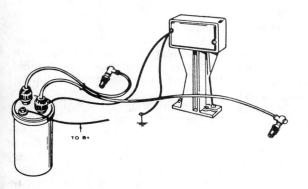

Fig. O47—View of external wiring of engines with battery ignition. Breaker box is nonadjustable and timing is set by varying point gap slightly.

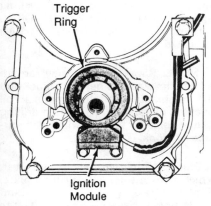

Fig. O47A—View of trigger ring and ignition module used on later Model T-260G.

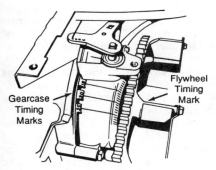

Fig. O47B—View of timing marks on T-260G.

age, a bolt on the rotating screen should be positioned between timing marks on blower housing shown in Fig. O47B. Note that flywheel must be rotated in complete revolutions to obtain required meter fluctuation; back-and-forth flywheel movement will not trigger ignition.

To test ignition module, follow procedure in previous paragraph to check ignition timing. If voltmeter does not indicate fluctuation between 1-1.5 volts and battery voltage, ignition module is faulty. Renew module and recheck ignition system.

To check ignition coil primary windings, connect ohmmeter leads to negative and positive terminals on coil.

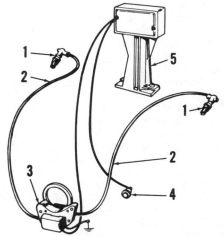

Fig. O48—Magneto ignition used on NH model. Stop button (4) grounds breaker points to halt engine.

1. Spark plugs
2. Plug leads
3. Magneto coil
4. Stop button
5. Breaker box & stand

Ohmmeter should indicate 2.90-3.60 ohms. To check ignition coil secondary windings, disconnect spark plug wires from ignition coil. Connect ohmmeter leads to the two spark plug wire receptacles on the ignition coil. Ohmmeter should indicate 14.5k-19.8k ohms. If ohmmeter readings are not as specified, renew ignition coil.

MAGNETO IGNITION. Magneto ignition system is used on manual start models and a stop button wired across breaker points is used to ground primary circuit to stop engine (Fig. O48).

To prevent engine recoil starter damage during starting, spark is retarded to

3° ATDC and advance mechanism shown in Fig. O49 automatically advances timing to 22° BTDC for normal operation.

Initial point gap is 0.020 inch (0.508 mm) and running timing should be checked using a timing light. Timing should be 22° BTDC at 1500 rpm and is adjusted by varying point gap.

If spark advance does not respond when engine is over 1500 rpm, or if advance is sluggish, remove cup-shaped cover (9—Fig. O49) at rear of camshaft on engine block and check advance mechanism condition. Clean assembly thoroughly and renew worn parts as necessary.

LUBRICATION. All models are pressure lubricated by a gear-type pump driven by crankshaft gear. Internal pump parts are not serviced separately so entire pump must be renewed if worn or damaged. Clearance between pump gear and crankshaft gear should be 0.002-0.005 inch (0.05-0.13 mm) and normal operating pressure should be 30 psi (207 kPa).

Oil pressure is regulated by an oil pressure relief valve located on top of engine block near timing gear cover. Relief valve spring free length should be $2^5/_{16}$ inches (58.7 mm) on Model N52M and 1.00 inch (25.4 mm) on all other models. Relief valve diameter should be 0.3365-3380 inch (8.547-8.585 mm) on early models and 0.3105-0.3125 inch (2.142-2.156 mm) on later models.

Oils approved by manufacturer must meet requirements of API service classification SF or SG.

Use SAE 5W-30 oil in below freezing temperatures and SAE 20W-40 oil in above freezing temperatures.

Check oil level with engine stopped and maintain at "FULL" mark on dipstick. **DO NOT** overfill.

Recommended oil change interval for T-260G models is every 50 hours of normal operation and change filter at 100-hour intervals. T-260G model oil capacity is 2.5 quarts (2.4 L) without filter change and 3 quarts (2.8 L) with filter change.

Recommended oil change interval for all other models is every 100 hours of

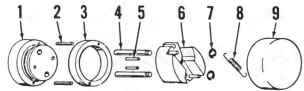

Fig. O49—Exploded view of spark advance (timing control) used on NH model engine.

1. Camshaft
2. Cam roll pin
3. Control cam
4. Groove pin
5. Roll pin
6. Weights (2)
7. Retainers (2)
8. Control spring
9. Cover

normal operation and change filter at 200-hour intervals. Oil capacity is 3.5 quarts (3.3 L) without filter change and 4 quarts (3.8 L) with filter change.

Oil filter is screw-on-type and gasket should be lightly lubricated before installation. Screw filter on until gasket contacts, then turn an additional ½ turn. Do not overtighten.

REPAIRS

TIGHTENING TORQUES. Recommended tightening torques are as follows:

Connecting rod:

Nodular iron rod . . . . . . 27-29 ft.-lbs.
(37-39 N·m)

Aluminum rod . . . . 14-16 ft.-lbs.
(19-22 N·m)

Exhaust manifold . . . . . . 20-23 ft.-lbs.
(27-31 N·m)

Flywheel . . . . 50-55 ft.-lbs.
(68-74 N·m)

Gearcase cover . . . . 96-120 in.-lbs.
(10.8-13.6 N·m)

Intake manifold . . . . 20-23 ft.-lbs.
(27.2-31.3 N·m)

Oil pump . . . . 84-108 in.-lbs.
(9.5-12.2 N·m)

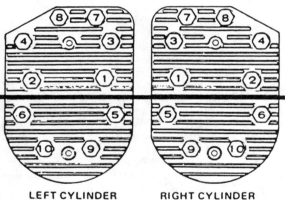

LEFT CYLINDER   **RIGHT CYLINDER**

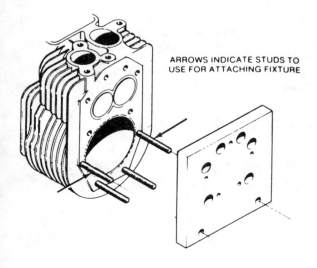

ARROWS INDICATE STUDS TO USE FOR ATTACHING FIXTURE

Rear bearing plate . . . . . . 25-28 ft.-lbs.
(34-38 N·m)

Other ⅜-inch
cylinder block nuts . . . . . 18-23 ft.-lbs.
(24-31 N·m)

CYLINDER HEADS. It is recommended cylinder heads be removed and carbon cleaned at 200-hour intervals (400 hours if using unleaded fuel).

CAUTION: Cylinder heads should not be unbolted from block when hot due to danger of head warping.

Cylinder heads are retained to block by studs and nuts. Late model engines use compression washers between nuts and hardened flat washers on top six studs and these should be installed on early models during service.

Onan recommends testing the top six original equipment studs on each cylinder to make certain they are not pulling out of threads in cylinder block.

To test studs, remove nuts and compression washers from top six studs (Fig. O50) leaving hardened flat washers in place. Reinstall nuts and tighten to 30 ft.-lbs. (40 N.m) torque. Studs with weak threads will pull out of head be-

Fig. O50—View of cylinder heads showing correct torque sequence and location of the six studs to be checked, above solid line, as outlined in text.

Fig. O51—Special drilling fixture is required to drill out damaged threads in stud holes. Fixture part number is 420-398.

fore 30 ft.-lbs. (40 N·m) torque is reached.

A special stepped renewal stud, part number 520-0912 and a drilling fixture, part number 420-0398, are available from Onan to service damaged stud hole threads.

To install stepped renewal stud, remove cylinder head and gasket. Examine head and block surface. If head or block is warped or has a depression of more than 0.005 inch (0.127 mm), it may be resurfaced with a maximum total of 0.010 inch (0.254 mm) of material removed. Remove studs from holes with damaged threads and install drilling fixture (Fig. O51) securing it in position with nuts and flat washers on studs indicated.

NOTE: Some engines may require adding flat washers between block and fixture plate to clear sheet metal scroll backing plate. If so, be certain drilling fixture remains parallel with head surface of block.

Place bushing with small hole in it, which is furnished with drilling plate, in plate hole over stud hole with damaged threads. Use a ²⁷⁄₆₄-inch drill bit to drill damaged threads out of block. Holes at side of block should be drilled through to the fourth cooling fin and holes at top of block should penetrate into corresponding intake or exhaust valve port. Manifolds should be removed during drilling procedure. Remove small bushing and install bushing with larger hole and lock in place. Use a ½-13 tap to thread hole for new stepped stud. Repeat process for any other hole with damaged threads. Remove any ridge around holes with a flat file or a 45° chamfer tool. When using chamfer tool, chamfer depth should be ¹⁄₃₂-¹⁄₁₆ inch (0.794-1.588 mm). Apply Loctite 242 to stepped stud threads and install in holes making certain entire stepped portion is below gasket surface of cylinder block.

NOTE: Stepped studs installed in holes corresponding with exhaust ports must have ³⁄₁₆-¹⁄₄ inch (4.763-6.350 mm) cut off large end of stud so it does not extend into exhaust port.

Remove any metal particles from engine ports and place new graphoil-type gasket on cylinder head and install gasket and head on studs at the same time to avoid damaging gasket.

NOTE: Graphoil-type gaskets become soft and gummy at temperatures above 100° F (38° C). Avoid installation

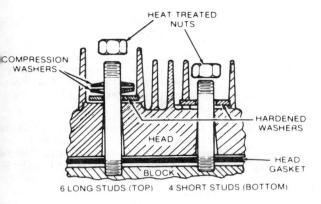

Fig. O52—View showing correctly installed compression washers. Compression washers are installed on top six (long) studs only. Hardened flat washers are installed on all studs.

HEAT TREATED NUTS

COMPRESSION WASHERS

HARDENED WASHERS

HEAD

HEAD GASKET

BLOCK

6 LONG STUDS (TOP)   4 SHORT STUDS (BOTTOM)

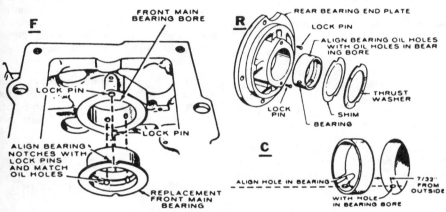

F

FRONT MAIN BEARING BORE

LOCK PIN

LOCK PIN

ALIGN BEARING NOTCHES WITH LOCK PINS AND MATCH OIL HOLES

REPLACEMENT FRONT MAIN BEARING

R

REAR BEARING END PLATE

LOCK PIN

ALIGN BEARING OIL HOLES WITH OIL HOLES IN BEARING BORE

THRUST WASHER

LOCK PIN

SHIM

BEARING

C

ALIGN HOLE IN BEARING

WITH HOLE IN BEARING BORE

7/32" FROM OUTSIDE

Fig. O53—Alignment of precision main and camshaft bearings. One-piece bearing is used at front (view F), two-piece bearing at rear (view R). Note shim use for end play adjustment. View C shows placement of camshaft bearings.

or removal if engine temperature exceeds this.

Install hardened flat washers on all studs, two compression washers on each of the top six long studs (Fig. O52) so outside edges of compression washers are in contact with each other. Install nuts and tighten in several even steps until top six studs reach 12 ft.-lbs. (16 N•m) torque and the bottom studs reach 15 ft.-lbs. (20 N•m) torque.

Tighten in sequence shown in Fig. O50 and recheck all nuts after initial torque has been reached.

CAUTION: Too much torque will flatten compression washers and could result in engine damage.

Recheck torque before engine has a total of 50 hours operation.

CONNECTING ROD. Connecting rod and piston are removed from cylinder head surface end of block after removing cylinder head and oil base.

Engine may be equipped with an aluminum connecting rod that rides directly on crankpin or with an iron connecting rod that is equipped with renewable insert bearings and a renewable piston pin bushing.

Standard crankpin journal diameter is 1.6252-1.6260 inches (41.280-41.300 mm) for all models. Connecting rod or bearing inserts are available in a variety of sizes for undersize crankshafts as well as standard.

Connecting rod to crankshaft journal running clearance for aluminum rods is 0.002-0.003 inch (0.05-0.08 mm) and running clearance for bearings in iron rod should be 0.0005-0.0028 inch (0.013-0.071 mm).

Piston and rod assembly should be installed so rod bolts are offset toward outside of cylinder block. If rod has an oil hole, hole must be toward camshaft. Tighten connecting rod cap screws to 27-29 ft.-lbs. (37-39 N•m) on iron rod and to 14-16 ft.-lbs. (19-22 N•m) on aluminum rod.

PISTON, PIN AND RINGS. Model N52M with specification letter "A" and NH, NHA, NHB and NHC models with specification letters "A" through "C" use a strut-type piston. On all models, measure piston diameter at a point 0.10 inch (2.54 mm) below oil control ring and perpendicular to piston pin. Piston clearance in bore for strut-type piston

should be 0.0015-0.0035 inch (0.038-0.089 mm). Piston clearance on all other models should be 0.0070-0.0090 inch (0.178-0.229 mm).

Top ring side clearance should be 0.002-0.008 inch (0.05-0.20 mm). Piston ring end gap should be 0.010-0.020 inch (0.25-0.50 mm).

Piston pin to piston pin bore clearance is 0.0001-0.0005 inch (0.0025-0.0127 mm) for all models and pin to rod clearance is 0.0002-0.0008 inch (0.005-0.020 mm) for aluminum rod and 0.00005-0.00055 inch (0.0013-0.0014 mm) for bushing in nodular iron rod.

Standard piston pin diameter is 0.7500-0.7502 inch (19.05-19.06 mm) for all models and pins are available in 0.002 inch (0.0508 mm) oversize for aluminum rod.

Standard cylinder bore diameter for all models is 3.5625-3.5635 inches (90.49-90.51 mm) and cylinders should be bored to nearest oversize for which piston and rings are available if cylinder is scored or out-of-round more than 0.003 inch (0.076 mm), or if taper exceeds 0.005 inch (0.127 mm). Pistons and rings are available in a variety of oversizes as well as standard.

CRANKSHAFT, BEARINGS AND SEALS. Crankshaft is supported at each end by precision-type sleeve bearings located in cylinder block housing and rear bearing plate. Main bearing journal standard diameter should be 1.9992-2.000 inches (50.7797-50.800 mm) and bearing operating clearance should be 0.0025-0.0038 inch (0.0635-0.0965 mm) for T-260G model and 0.0015-0.0043 inch (0.0381-0.1092 mm) for all other models. Main bearings are available for a variety of undersize crankshafts as well as standard.

Oil holes in bearing and bore **MUST** be aligned when bearings are installed and rear bearing should be pressed into bearing plate until flush, or recessed into bearing plate 1/64 inch (0.40 mm). Make certain bearing notches are aligned with lock pins (Fig. O53) during installation.

Apply Loctite Bearing Mount to front bearing and press bearing in until flush with block. Make certain bearing notches are aligned with lock pins (Fig. O53) during installation.

NOTE: Replacement front bearing and thrust washer is a one-piece assembly. Do not install a separate thrust washer.

Rear thrust washer is installed with oil grooves toward crankshaft. Measure crankshaft end play as shown in Fig.

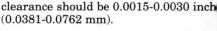

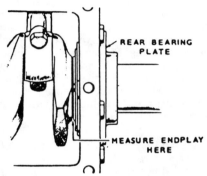

Use heavy fiber or cup grease in space between seals to improve seal.

GEAR COVER

OIL SEAL

MOUNTING FACE OF GEAR COVER

*New style thin open-face seal dimension is 1-7/64"

$1\frac{1}{32}$"

THIS SURFACE SHOULD BE CLEANED OF ALL OLD SEALING COMPOUND BEFORE INSTALLING SEAL.

GEAR COVER OIL SEAL

REAR BEARING PLATE

SHOULDER

THIS SURFACE SHOULD BE CLEANED OF ALL OLD SEALING COMPOUND BEFORE INSTALLING SEAL.

DRIVE OR PRESS OIL SEAL TO SHOULDER OF THE PLATE BORE

REAR BEARING PLATE OIL SEAL

Fig. O53A—View showing correct seal installation procedure. Fill cavity between lips of seal with heavy grease to improve sealing efficiency.

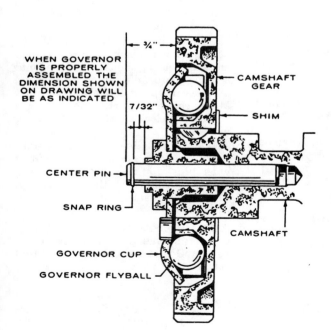

REAR BEARING PLATE

MEASURE ENDPLAY HERE

Fig. O54—View of crankshaft end play measurement procedure. Refer to text.

O54 and add or remove shims or renew thrust washer (Fig. O53) as necessary to obtain 0.005-0.009 inch (0.13-0.23 mm) end play.

It is recommended that rear bearing plate and front timing gear cover be removed for seal installation. Rear seal is pressed in until flush with seal bore. Timing cover seal should be driven in until it is $1\frac{1}{32}$ inch (26.19 mm) from mounting face of cover for old-style seal and $1\frac{7}{64}$ inch (28.18 mm) from mounting face of cover for new-style, thin, open-faced seal. See Fig. O53A.

CAMSHAFT, BEARINGS AND GOVERNOR. Camshaft is supported at each end in precision-type sleeve bearings. Make certain oil holes in bearings are aligned with oil holes in block (Fig. O53), press front bearing in flush with outer surface of block and press rear bearing in until flush with bottom of counterbore. Camshaft to bearing

clearance should be 0.0015-0.0030 inch (0.0381-0.0762 mm).

Camshaft end play should be 0.003 inch (0.076 mm) and is adjusted by varying thickness of shim located between camshaft timing gear and engine block. See Fig. O55.

Camshaft timing gear is a press fit on end of camshaft and is designed to accommodate 5, 6 or 8 flyballs arranged as shown in Fig. O56. Number of flyballs is varied to alter governor sensitivity. Fewer flyballs are used on engines with variable speed applications and greater number of flyballs are used for continuous (fixed) speed application. Flyballs must be arranged in "pockets" as shown according to total number used. Note correct installation of ball spacer, if so equipped, in Fig. O56A.

Center pin (Fig. O55) should extend $\frac{3}{4}$ inch (19 mm) from end of camshaft to allow $\frac{7}{32}$ inch (5.6 mm) in-and-out movement of governor cup. If distance

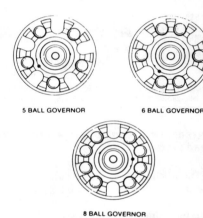

5 BALL GOVERNOR   6 BALL GOVERNOR

8 BALL GOVERNOR

Fig. O56—View showing correct spacing of governor flyballs according to total number of balls used.

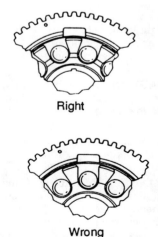

Right

Wrong

Fig. O56A—On models so equipped, governor ball spacer must be installed as shown. Otherwise, a flyball may be displaced causing governor malfunction.

WHEN GOVERNOR IS PROPERLY ASSEMBLED THE DIMENSION SHOWN ON DRAWING WILL BE AS INDICATED

$\frac{3}{4}$"

$\frac{7}{32}$"

CAMSHAFT GEAR

SHIM

CENTER PIN

SNAP RING

CAMSHAFT

GOVERNOR CUP

GOVERNOR FLYBALL

Fig. O55—Cross-sectional view of camshaft gear and governor assembly showing correct dimensions for center pin extension from camshaft. Note shim placement for adjusting end play in camshaft. Refer to text.

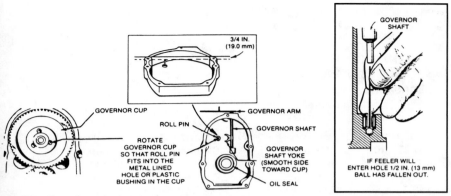

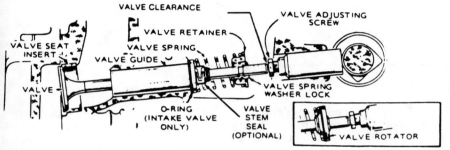

Fig. O57—View of governor shaft, timing gear cover and governor cup showing assembly details. Refer to text.

Fig. O58—Valve train typical of NH and T-260G engines, Refer to text.

Make certain timing mark on camshaft gear is aligned with timing mark on crankshaft gear during installation.

VALVE SYSTEM. Valve seats are renewable insert-type and are available in a variety of oversizes as well as standard. Seats are ground at a 45° angle and seat width should be $\frac{1}{32}$ to $\frac{3}{64}$ inch (0.794 to 1.191 mm).

Valves should be ground at a 44° angle to provide an interference angle of 1°.

Recommended valve stem to guide clearance is 0.001-0.0025 inch (0.0254-0.0635 mm) for intake valves and 0.0025-0.004 inch (0.0635-0.1016 mm) for exhaust valves. Renewable shouldered valve guides are pushed out from head surface end of block. An "O" ring is installed on intake valve guide of some models and a valve stem seal is also available for intake valve. See Fig. O58.

Valve tappet gap (cold) for intake valve should be 0.005 inch (0.13 mm). Exhaust valve tappet gap (cold) should be 0.012 inch (0.33 mm) on engines running on gasoline and 0.014 inch (0.36 mm) on engines running on gaseous fuels.

Adjust tappet gap by turning tappet adjusting screw (Fig. O58). Perform adjustment with piston at top dead center on compression stroke. At this position both valves are fully closed.

is incorrect, remove pin and press new pin in to correct depth.

Always make certain governor shaft pivot ball is in timing cover by measuring as shown in Fig. O57 inset and check length of roll pin that engages bushed hole in governor cup. This pin must extend to within ¾ inch (19 mm) of timing gear cover mating surface.

ONAN

ONAN CORPORATION
1400 73rd Avenue N.E.
Minneapolis, Minnesota 55432

Model	No. Cyls.	Bore	Stroke	Displacement	Power Rating
P216, P216V	2	3.250 in. (82.55 mm)	2.625 in. (66.68 mm)	43.6 cu. in. (715 cc)	16 hp. (11.9 kW)
P218, P218V	2	3.250 in. (82.55 mm)	2.875 in. (73.03 mm)	47.7 cu. in. (782 cc)	18 hp. (13.4 kW)
P220, P220V	2	3.250 in. (82.55 mm)	2.875 in. (73.03 mm)	47.7 cu. in. (782 cc)	20 hp. (14.9 kW)
P224	2	3.560 in. (90.42 mm)	3.000 in. (76.20 mm)	59.7 cu. in. (978 cc)	24 hp. (18 kW)

Engines in this section are four-stroke, twin-opposed-cylinder engines. Models P216, P218, P220 and P224 are equipped with a horizontal crankshaft and Models P216V, P218V and P220V are equipped with a vertical crankshaft.

Refer to Fig. O200 for explanation of engine model and specification identification numbers.

MAINTENANCE

LUBRICATION. All models are equipped with a pressure lubrication system and an oil filter. Oil is routed from an oil pump located behind the gear cover and driven by the crankshaft gear.

Manufacturer recommends oil with an API service classification of SF or SG. Use SAE 30 oil for ambient temperatures above 32° F (0° C); use SAE 10W-30 oil for temperatures between 0° F (–18° C) and 80° F (27° C); below 20° F (–7° C), use SAE 5W-20.

Check oil at regular intervals and maintain at "FULL" mark on dipstick. DO NOT overfill.

On all models, engine oil and oil filter, if so equipped, should be changed after

Fig. O200—Typical model and specification number showing digit interpretation.

1. Basic engine series
2. Number of cylinders
3. Power rating (Bhp)
4. Crankshaft direction (G—horizontal, V—vertical)
5. Engine duty cycle
6. Designated optional equipment
7. Production specification letter

first 25 hours of operation. If engine is not equipped with an oil filter, oil should be changed after every 25 hours of operation. If engine is equipped with a standard capacity oil pan and an oil filter, engine oil should be changed after every 50 hours of operation and oil filter should be changed after every 100 hours of operation. If engine is equipped with a high-capacity oil pan and an oil filter, engine oil and oil filter should be changed after every 100 hours of operation. Change oil and filter more frequently if engine undergoes severe operation.

On Models P216V, P218V and P220V, crankcase capacity is 2.0 quarts (1.9 L) if oil filter is changed with oil refill, 1.7 quarts (1.6 L) if oil filter is not changed.

On Models P216, P218, P220 and P224, crankcase capacity varies according to size of oil pan installed. Crankcase capacity for standard oil pan is 1.8 quarts (1.7 L) if oil filter is changed with oil refill, 1.5 quarts (1.4 L) if oil filter is not changed. Crankcase capacity for medium capacity oil pan is 2.5 quarts (2.4 L) if oil filter is changed with oil refill, 2.2 quarts (2.1 L) if oil filter is not changed. Crankcase capacity for high-capacity oil pan is 3.0 quarts (2.9 L) if oil filter is changed with oil refill, 2.7 quarts (2.6 L) if oil filter is not changed.

Normal oil pressure should be 20 psi (138 kPa) on Models P216, P218 and P220, 25 psi (172.5 kPa) on Models P216V, P218V and P220V, and 30 psi (207 kPa) on Model P224. If engine oil pressure is less than 8 psi (55.2 kPa) at engine speed of 1500 rpm, cause for low oil pressure should be determined.

The engine may be equipped with a low oil pressure switch located on the oil filter adapter. Switch may be connected to a warning device or into the ignition circuit.

CRANKCASE BREATHER. The engine is equipped with a crankcase breather that provides a vacuum for the crankcase. Model P224 is equipped with the breather unit shown in Fig. O201. Disassemble and clean breather after every 200 hours of normal operation. Wash components, including filter, in a suitable solvent. Valve balls must move freely; otherwise, renew unit.

Early Models P216, P218 and P220 are equipped with the crankcase breather shown in Fig. O202. Disassemble and clean breather after every 200 hours of normal operation. Wash components, including filter, in a suitable sol-

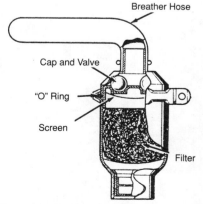

Fig. O201—View of crankcase breather used on Model P224.

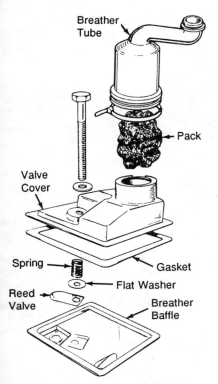

Fig. O202—View of crankcase breather used on early Models P216, P218 and P220.

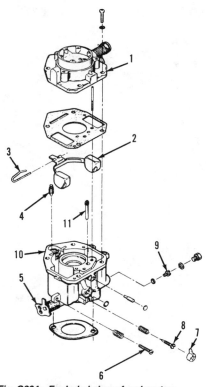

Fig. O204—Exploded view of carburetor.

1. Air horn
2. Float
3. Pivot pin
4. Needle valve
5. Throttle shaft
6. Throttle stop screw
7. Cap
8. Idle adjustment needle
9. Main jet
10. Carburetor body
11. Main nozzle

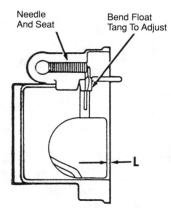

Fig. O205—Position carburetor as shown when measuring float level (L). Float level should be 0.023-0.079 inch (0.58-2.00 mm).

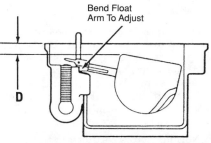

Fig. O206—Float drop (D) should be 0.291 inch (7.40 mm).

vent. Renew reed valve if cracked, creased or otherwise damaged.

The crankcase breather on all other models does not require periodic maintenance, but it should be renewed if it malfunctions.

SPARK PLUG. Recommended spark plug for all models is Champion RS14YC or equivalent. Electrode gap should be 0.025 inch (0.64 mm).

CARBURETOR. All models are equipped with a downdraft float-type carburetor. Note that idle mixture screw was originally equipped with a limiter

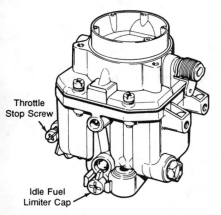

Fig. O203—View showing location of throttle stop screw and idle mixture screw on carburetor. Limiter cap must be removed to perform initial adjustment of idle mixture screw.

cap (Fig. O203). Remove cap for initial setting of idle mixture screw. Initial adjustment of idle mixture screw is 1½ turns out on Model P224 and 1¼ turns out on all other models. Run engine until normal operating temperature is reached. Back out governor idle screw or bend governor idle tab (see GOVERNOR section) so idle speed is determined by throttle stop screw (Fig. O203) on carburetor. Rotate throttle stop screw so engine idle speed is 1000 rpm. Adjust idle mixture screw so engine idles at maximum speed and will accelerate cleanly, then readjust throttle stop screw so engine idles at 1000 rpm. Adjust governed idle speed as outlined in GOVERNOR section. Install limiter cap so it is at midpoint of travel. High-speed mixture is determined by a fixed main jet. An optional main jet may be installed for engine operation above 5000 feet.

Carburetor overhaul is evident after inspection of unit and referral to Fig. O204. Use care when cleaning carburetor as caustic solvents may damage non-metallic parts. To check float level, position carburetor as shown in Fig. O205 so float arm is just touching fuel inlet valve. Bend tang as required so

float level (L) is 0.023-0.079 inch (0.58-2.00 mm). Float drop (D—Fig. O206) should be 0.291 inch (7.40 mm). Bend float arm to obtain correct float drop.

GOVERNOR. All models are equipped with a flyball weight governor located under timing gear on camshaft gear. Refer to following paragraphs for governor linkage adjustment.

Models P216, P218, P220 and P224. These models may be equipped with a front pull (Fig. O207) or side pull

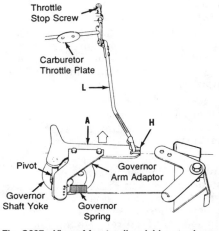

Fig. O207—View of front pull variable speed governor linkage used on Models P216, P218, P220 and P224.

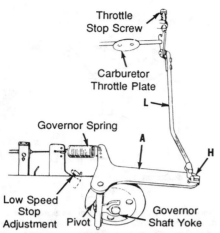

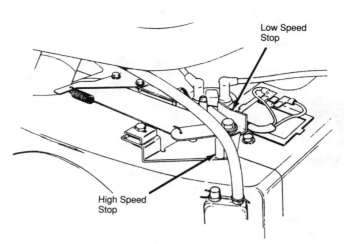

Fig. O209—Low and high governed engine speeds are adjusted by bending stops on front pull governor linkage.

Fig. O208—View of side pull variable speed governor linkage used on Models P216, P218, P220 and P224.

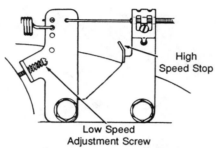

Fig. O210—On side pull governor linkage, rotate adjustment screw to obtain desired low governed engine speed or bend high speed stop to adjust high governed engine speed.

(Fig. O208) linkage arrangement. Service procedures are similar. Disconnect link (L) from hole (H) and push link and governor arm (A) toward carburetor as far as possible. While held in this position, insert end of linkage into nearest hole in governor arm. Insert rod end in next outer hole if between two holes.

Normal factory setting is in third hole from pivot for side pull linkage and second hole from pivot for front pull linkage.

Sensitivity is increased by connecting governor spring closer to pivot and decreased by connecting governor spring farther from pivot.

Engine governed speed is adjusted by rotating adjustment screw or bending stop tab shown in Figs. O209 or O210. Governed idle speed should be set at 1100 rpm unless otherwise specified by equipment manufacturer. Maximum governed speed should be set to equipment manufacturer's specifications.

Models P216V, P218V And P220V. Governor linkage is shown in Fig. O211. Upper end of governor control rod should engage middle hole on governor arm. Ends of governor spring should be connected to second hole from outside of governor control arm and third hole from pivot on governor arm.

Sensitivity is increased by connecting governor spring closer to pivot and decreased by connecting governor spring farther from pivot.

Engine governed speed is adjusted by rotating adjustment screw or bending stop tab shown in Fig. O212. Governed idle speed should be set at 1100 rpm unless otherwise specified by equipment manufacturer. Maximum governed speed should be set to equipment manufacturer's specifications.

IGNITION SYSTEM. All engines are equipped with a battery-type ignition system that uses an electronic, breakerless triggering system. The trigger ring is attached to the crankshaft and the ignition module is located on the crankcase (see Fig. O213). The spark plugs fire at the same time. Refer to Fig.

O214 for wiring diagram. Regular maintenance is not required.

CAUTION: Due to presence of battery in circuit, improper test connections or incorrect wiring connections can damage ignition module.

Ignition timing is 20° BTDC, but is not adjustable. To check ignition timing, remove spark plugs. Using a voltmeter, connect the positive tester lead to negative terminal (larger diameter) on ignition coil and ground the negative tester lead to the engine. Turn ignition switch on and turn flywheel clockwise slowly by hand. When voltmeter reading changes from 1-1.5 volts to battery voltage, a bolt on the rotating screen should be positioned between timing marks on blower housing shown in Fig. O215. Note that flywheel must be rotated in complete revolutions to obtain required

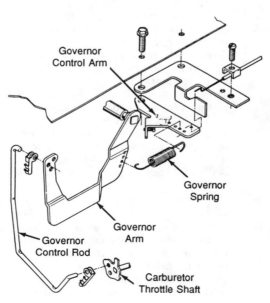

Fig. O211—View of variable speed governor linkage used on Models P216V, P218V and P220V.

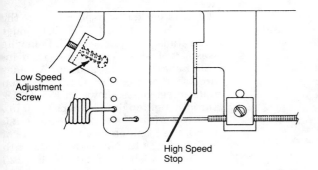

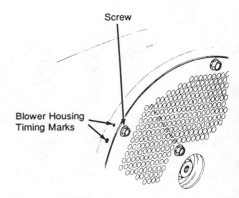

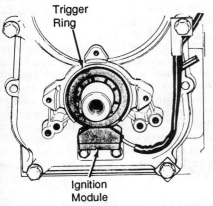

Fig. O212—On Models P216V, P218V and P220V, rotate adjustment screw to obtain desired low governed engine speed or bend high speed stop to adjust high governed engine speed.

Fig. O213—View of trigger ring and ignition module.

Fig. O215—Ignition timing is correct if screen bolt aligns with timing marks when following ignition timing checking procedure in text.

meter fluctuation; back-and-forth flywheel movement will not trigger ignition.

To test ignition module, follow procedure in previous paragraph to check ignition timing. If voltmeter does not indicate fluctuation between 1-1.5 volts and battery voltage, ignition module is faulty. Renew module and recheck ignition system.

To check ignition coil primary windings, connect ohmmeter leads to negative and positive terminals on coil. Ohmmeter should indicate 2.90-3.60 ohms. To check ignition coil secondary windings, disconnect spark plug wires from ignition coil. Connect ohmmeter leads to the two spark plug wire receptacles on the ignition coil. Ohmmeter should indicate 14.5k-19.8k ohms. If ohmmeter readings are not as specified, renew ignition coil.

VALVE ADJUSTMENT. Specified valve tappet clearance (cold) is 0.005 inch (0.13 mm) for intake valve and 0.013 inch (0.33 mm) for exhaust valve. Piston must be at top dead center for cylinder requiring valve adjustment. Rotate screw on tappet shown in Fig. O216 to adjust valve stem-to-tappet clearance.

REPAIRS

TIGHTENING TORQUES. Recommended tightening torques are as follows:

Connecting rod:
    P224 . . . . 27-29 ft.-lbs.
                    (37-39 N•m)
    All other models . . . . 144-168 in.-lbs.
                    (16.3-19 N•m)
Exhaust manifold . . . . 108-132 in.-lbs.
                    (12.2-14.9 N•m)
Flywheel . . . . 50-55 ft.-lbs.
                    (68-74 N•m)

Gearcase cover:
    P216, P218,
    P220, P224 . . . . 96-120 in.-lbs.
                    (10.8-13.6 N•m)
    P216V, P218V,
    P220V . . . . 120-144 in.-lbs.
                    (13.6-16.3 N•m)

Intake manifold:
    P224 . . . . 20-23 ft.-lbs.
                    (27.2-31.3 N•m)
    All other models . . . . . 96-120 in.-lbs.
                    (10.8-13.6 N•m)

Oil base:
    P216, P218,
    P220, P224 . . . . 18-23 ft.-lbs.
                    (24.5-31.3 N•m)
    P216V, P218V, P220V . . . . 27-29.-lbs.
                    (36.7-39.4 N•m)

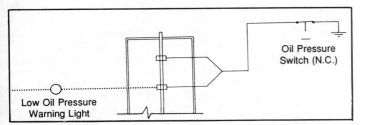

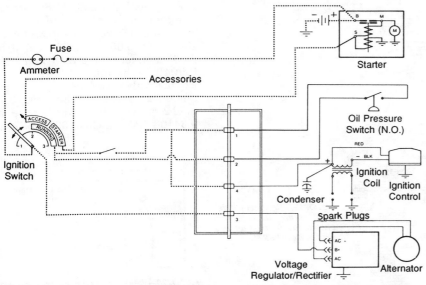

Fig. O214—Typical wiring diagram. Circuit shown in inset is for an oil pressure switch connected to a warning device.

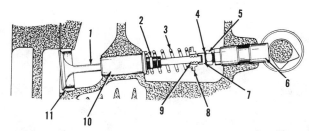

Fig. O216—Cross-sectional view of intake valve assembly. Valve cap is not used on Model P224.

1. Valve
2. Valve stem seal
3. Valve spring
4. Tappet gap
5. Tappet adjusting screw
6. Tappet
7. Valve cap
8. Valve retainer
9. Valve keepers
10. Valve guide
11. Seat insert

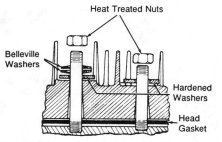

Fig. O217—View of cylinder head fasteners used on Model P224. Note position of Belleville washers on long studs. Hardened washers are used on all studs.

Oil base cover—
P216V, P218V, P220V:
  Inner screws . . . . 19-21 ft.-lbs.
    (25.8-28.6 N•m)
  Outer screws . . . . . . 108-132 in.-lbs.
    (12.2-14.9 N•m)

Oil pump . . . . 84-108 in.-lbs.
    (9.5-12.2 N•m)
Rear bearing plate:
  P216, P218,
  P220, P224 . . . . 25-27 ft.-lbs.
    (34-36.7 N•m)

CYLINDER HEADS. The cylinder heads are accessible after removing shrouds.

CAUTION: Cylinder heads should not be detached from block when hot due to possibility of head warping.

The cylinder head on Model P224 is secured by studs and nuts. When installing the head gasket and cylinder head, position the gasket on the cylinder head, then install head and gasket simultaneously. Attempting to install

the head gasket by itself may tear the gasket on the studs. Upper six cylinder head studs are equipped with Belleville washers. Install flat washer, then install Belleville washers so concave sides are together (see Fig. O217). Tighten nuts in sequence shown in Fig. O218. Initially tighten nuts in steps to 60 in.-lbs. (6.8 N•m) and 120 in.-lbs. (13.5 N•m), then tighten to a final torque of 168 in.-lbs. (19 N•m) on studs with Belleville washers or 204 in.-lbs. (23 N•m) on studs without Belleville washers.

On all models except Model P224, note type of head gasket before installation. Use the following assembly procedure to prevent damage to head gasket. Insert cylinder head screws in cylinder head then place gasket on cylinder head around screws. Install head with gasket on block. Tighten nuts in sequence shown in Fig. O219. Initially tighten nuts in steps to 60 in.-lbs. (6.8 N•m) and 120 in.-lbs. (13.5 N•m), then tighten to a final torque of 192-216 in.-lbs. (21.7-24.4 N•m) if head gasket is asbestos, or 168-192 in.-lbs. (19-21.7 N•m) if gasket is Graphoil.

VALVE SYSTEM. Intake valve on all models is equipped with a stem seal that must be renewed whenever valve is removed. All valves except on Model P224 are equipped with valve caps (see Fig. O216). The exhaust valve on Model P224 is equipped with a valve rotator.

Valve seats are renewable insert-type and are available in a variety of oversizes as well as standard. Seats are ground at a 45° angle. Seat width should be 0.031-0.047 inch (0.79-1.19 mm).

Valves should be ground at a 44° angle to provide an interference angle of one degree (Fig. O220). Minimum valve margin is 0.030 inch (0.8 mm).

On Model P224, valve stem clearance should be 0.0010-0.0025 inch (0.025-0.064 mm) for intake valve and 0.0025-0.0040 inch (0.064-0.102 mm) for exhaust valve. Specified valve stem diameter is 0.3425-0.3430 inch (8.700-8.712 mm) for intake valve and 0.3410-0.3420 inch (8.661-8.687 mm)

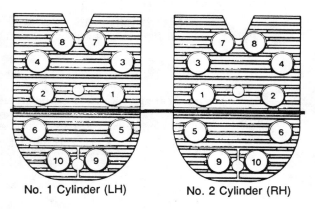

No. 1 Cylinder (LH)   No. 2 Cylinder (RH)

Fig. O218—Tighten cylinder head nuts on Model P224 in sequence shown. Six long studs are located above solid line.

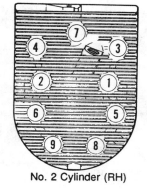

No. 1 Cylinder (LH)   No. 2 Cylinder (RH)

Fig. O219—Tighten cylinder head screws in sequence shown above on all models except Model P224.

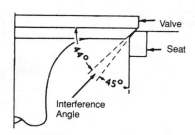

Fig. O220—Valve seat and valve face are ground to obtain a one-degree interference angle. See text.

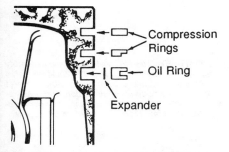

Fig. O221—Install piston rings in piston grooves as shown.

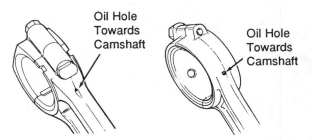

Fig. O222—Install connecting rod so oil hole is toward camshaft. Connecting rod on right is used on Model P224. Connecting rod on left is used on all other models.

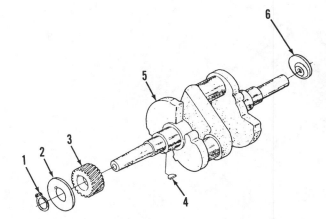

Fig. O223—Exploded view of crankshaft used on all models. Some models may be equipped with balancer weight (6).

1. Snap ring
2. Washer
3. Crankshaft gear
4. Key
5. Crankshaft
6. Balancer weight

for exhaust valve. Specified valve guide diameter for both valves is 0.3440-0.3460 inch (8.738-8.788 mm).

On all models except Model P224, valve stem clearance should be 0.0010-0.0025 inch (0.025-0.064 mm) for intake valve and 0.0020-0.0035 inch (0.051-0.089 mm) for exhaust valve. Specified valve stem diameter is 0.2795-0.2800 inch (7.099-7.112 mm) for intake valve and 0.2780-0.2785 inch (7.061-7.074 mm) for exhaust valve. Specified valve guide diameter is 0.2810-0.2820 inch (7.137-7.163 mm) for intake valve guide and 0.2805-0.2815 inch (7.125-7.150 mm) for exhaust valve guide.

Valve guides are renewable. Intake valve guide is equipped with a gasket. Drive out old guide toward camshaft. Valve guide is tapered; small end must be toward valve seat. Use a suitable puller to install new valve guide so guide extends $\frac{11}{32}$ inch (8.7 mm) above surface at valve spring end of guide.

PISTON, PIN AND RINGS. Piston and connecting rod are removed from cylinder head end of block as an assembly after removing cylinder head and oil base.

Specified piston ring end gap is 0.010-0.020 inch (0.25-0.51 mm). Piston should be renewed if top compression ring side clearance exceeds 0.008 inch (0.20 mm). Specified piston ring groove width is 0.0800-0.0810 inch (2.032-2.057 mm) for compression rings and 0.1880-0.1890 inch (4.775-4.801 mm) for oil control ring.

Piston pin-to-piston bore clearance should be 0.00004-0.00064 inch (0.0010-0.0163 mm). Specified pin bore in piston is 0.7502-0.7506 inch (19.055-19.065 mm) for Model P224 and 0.6877-0.6882 inch (17.468-17.480 mm) for all other models. Specified piston pin diameter is 0.7500-0.7502 inch (19.050-19.055 mm) for Model P224 and 0.6875-0.6877 inch (17.463-17.468 mm) for all other models.

Piston clearance in bore should be 0.0070-0.0090 inch (0.178-0.229 mm) for Model P224 and 0.0033-0.0053 inch (0.084-0.135 mm) for all other models. When determining piston clearance, measure piston diameter at a point that is perpendicular to piston pin bore and 1.187 inches (30.15 mm) from piston crown.

Some Model P224 engines are equipped from factory with pistons that are 0.005 inch (0.13 mm) oversize. A letter "E" is stamped after the serial number on the cylinder block and ID plate.

Install piston rings as shown in Fig. O221. When installing piston and connecting rod, oil hole (Fig. O222) in rod must be toward camshaft. Tighten connecting rod nuts to an initial torque of 60 in.-lbs. (6.8 N•m) and then to a final torque of 27-29 ft.-lbs. (37-39 N•m) on Model P224 and 144-168 in.-lbs. (16.3-19 N•m) on all other models.

CONNECTING ROD. Connecting rod and piston are removed from cylinder head end of block as an assembly after removing cylinder head and oil base.

Connecting rods on Model P224 are equipped with renewable bearing inserts and a renewable piston pin bushing. Connecting rod big end diameter without bearing inserts installed should be 1.7505-1.7510 inches (44.463-44.475 mm). Specified small end bushing inner diameter is 0.7504-0.7508 inch (19.060-19.070 mm).

On all models except Model P224, connecting rods ride directly on crankshaft journal. Specified connecting rod big end diameter is 1.6280-1.6285 inch (41.351-41.364 mm). Specified small end diameter is 0.6879-0.6882 inch (17.473-17.480 mm).

On all models, connecting rod-to-crankpin clearance should be 0.0020-0.0033 inch (0.051-0.084 mm). Connecting rod side play should be 0.002-0.016 inch (0.05-0.41 mm). Undersize connecting rod bearings are available for Model P224 and undersize connecting rods are available for all other models to fit a reground crankshaft crankpin.

When installing piston and connecting rod, oil hole (Fig. O222) in rod must be toward camshaft. Tighten connecting rod nuts to an initial torque of 60 in.-lbs. (6.8 N•m) and then to a final torque of 27-29 ft.-lbs. (37-39 N•m) on Model P224 and 144-168 in.-lbs. (16.3-19 N•m) on all other models.

CRANKSHAFT, BEARINGS AND SEALS. The crankshaft (Fig. O223) is supported at each end by precision-type sleeve bearings located in cylinder block (Figs. O224 or O225) and rear bearing plate or oil base (Fig. O226). Refer to following sections for service specifications.

Models P216, P218, P220 And P224. Specified crankshaft main bearing journal diameter is 1.9992-2.0000 inches (50.780-50.800 mm) for both main bearings. Main bearing journals can be reground to fit undersize main bearings.

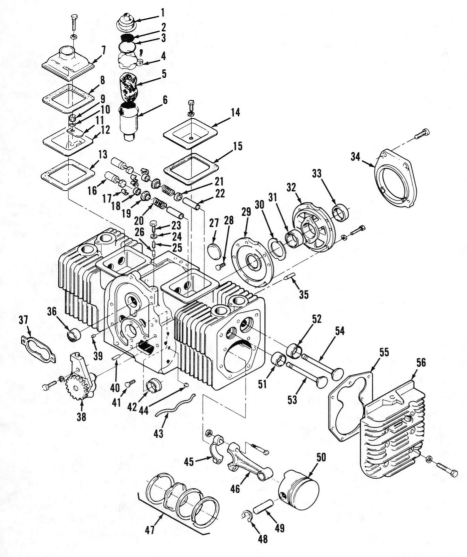

Fig. O224—Exploded view of crankcase assembly used on Models P216, P218 and P220. Model P224 is similar. Crankcase breather components (1 through 6) are used on early models and breather components (7 through 13) are used on later models. Adapter plate (34) is not used on all models.

1. Valve cap
2. Screen
3. "O" ring
4. Clamp
5. Baffle
6. Breather tube
7. Breather cover
8. Gasket
9. Spring
10. Washer
11. Breather valve
12. Baffle
13. Gasket
14. Valve cover
15. Gasket
16. Tappet
17. Valve retainers
18. Valve cap
19. Valve spring retainer
20. Valve spring
21. Intake valve seal
22. Valve guide
23. Screw
24. Washer
25. Oil pressure relief valve spring
26. Oil pressure relief valve
27. Welch plug
28. Drive pin
29. Gasket
30. Shim
31. Main bearing
32. Rear bearing plate
33. Oil seal
34. Adapter plate
35. Socket screw
36. Camshaft bearing
37. Oil pump gasket
38. Oil pump
39. Plug (early models)
40. Dowel
41. Drive pin
42. Main bearing
43. Oil tube
44. Plug
45. Rod cap
46. Connecting rod
47. Piston rings
48. Retainer ring
49. Piston pin
50. Piston
51. Exhaust valve seat
52. Intake valve seat
53. Exhaust valve
54. Intake valve
55. Head gasket
56. Cylinder head

Specified crankpin diameter is 1.6252-1.6260 inches (41.280-41.300 mm). Crankpin can be reground to fit undersize rod bearings on Model P224 or to accept an undersize connecting rod on all other models.

The new front main bearing is supplied with a cloth that is used to wipe the outside of the bearing and the bearing bore in the cylinder block. Main bearing should be chilled and cylinder block should be heated to 200° F (93° C) to ease bearing installation. Apply Loctite to outer bearing surface before installation. When installing front main bearing in cylinder block, make certain bearing notches are aligned with lock pins as shown in Fig. O227.

Install bearing in rear bearing plate so bearing is 0.000-0.015 inch (0.38 mm) from surface and oil holes are aligned. A thrust washer is located between the crankshaft and the rear bearing plate (see Fig. O228). Install thrust washer so notches align with lock pins and grooves on thrust washer are toward crankshaft.

Crankshaft end play should be 0.006-0.012 inch (0.15-0.30 mm) and is adjusted by installing shims between thrust washer and oil base as shown in Fig. O228. Be sure shims and thrust washer are properly aligned with lock pins during assembly.

To remove crankshaft oil seals, the timing gear cover and rear bearing plate

must be removed. Force out oil seals from inside. Install oil seal in timing gear cover so seal is 0.645 inch (16.38 mm) below face of bore as shown in Fig. O229. Drive oil seal into rear bearing plate until bottomed in bearing plate.

Models P216V, P218V And P220V. Specified crankshaft main bearing journal diameter is 1.9992-2.0000 inches (50.780-50.800 mm) for top main bearing and 1.9972-1.9980 inches (50.729-50.750 mm) for bottom main bearing. Main bearing journals can be reground to fit undersize main bearings.

Specified crankpin diameter is 1.6252-1.6260 inches (41.280-41.300 mm). Crankpin can be reground to accept an undersize connecting rod.

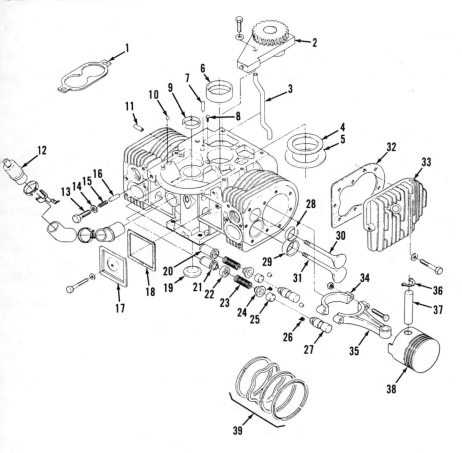

Fig. O225—Exploded view of crankcase assembly used on Models P216V, P218V and P220V. Refer to Fig. O226 for exploded view of oil base assembly.

1. Oil pump gasket
2. Oil pump
3. Oil tube
4. Shim
5. Thrust washer
6. Main bearing
7. Dowel
8. Drive pin
9. Camshaft bearing
10. Plug
11. Fuel pump vacuum tube
12. Breather valve
13. Screw
14. Washer
15. Spring
16. Oil passage plug
17. Valve cover
18. Gasket
19. Welch plug
20. Exhaust valve guide
21. Intake valve guide
22. Intake valve seal
23. Valve spring
24. Valve spring retainer
25. Valve cap
26. Valve retainers
27. Tappet
28. Exhaust valve seat
29. Intake valve seat
30. Exhaust valve
31. Intake valve
32. Head gasket
33. Cylinder head
34. Rod cap
35. Connecting rod
36. Retainer ring
37. Piston pin
38. Piston
39. Piston rings

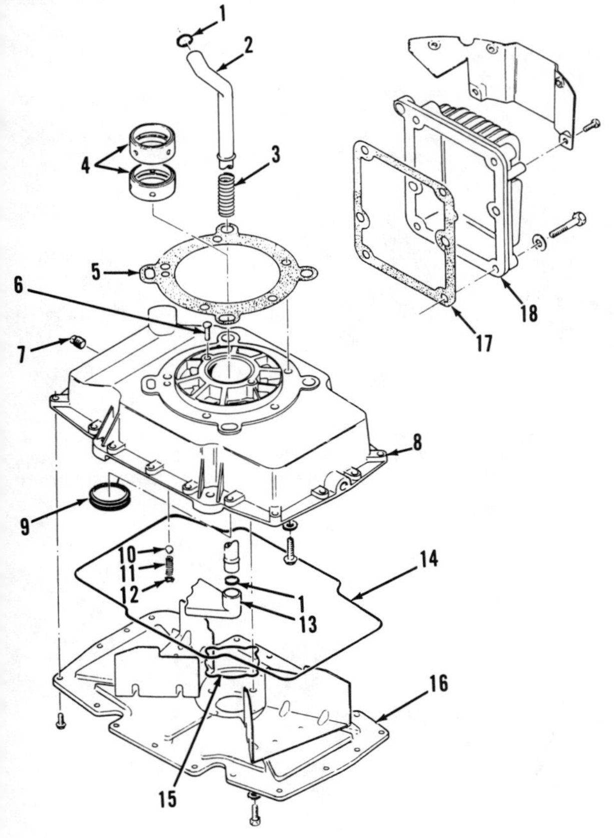

The new top main bearing is supplied with a cloth that is used to wipe the outside of the bearing and the bearing bore in the cylinder block. Main bearing should be chilled and cylinder block should be heated to 200° F (93° C) to ease bearing installation. Apply Loctite to outer bearing surface before installation. When installing top main bearing in cylinder block, make certain bearing notches are aligned with lock pins as shown in Fig. O227.

Fig. O226—Exploded view of crankcase assembly used on Models P216V, P218V and P220V.

1. "O" ring
2. Oil pickup tube
3. Spring
4. Main bearings
5. Gasket
6. Drive pin
7. Plug
8. Oil base
9. Oil seal
10. Oil pressure relief valve
11. Oil pressure relief valve spring
12. Retainer
13. Oil pickup
14. Gasket
15. Gasket
16. Cover
17. Gasket
18. Oil cooler

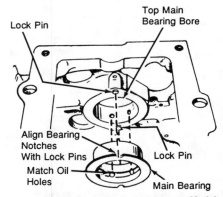

Fig. O227—Align top main bearing on Models P216V, P218V and P220V in cylinder block as shown. Illustration also applies to front main bearing on Models P216, P218, P220 and P224.

NOTE: Replacement top main bearing is flanged. The original bearing includes a sleeve bearing and thrust washer. Do not install a thrust washer with new replacement bearing.

Two bearing inserts are located in the oil base. Lubricate outside surface of bearings and drive bearings into oil

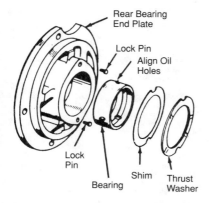

Fig. O228—Align thrust washer and shim with lock pins on rear bearing plate of Models P216, P218, P220 and P224. Oil grooves on thrust washer must be toward crankshaft.

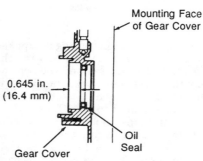

Fig. O229—Install oil seal in timing gear cover as shown.

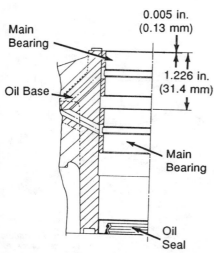

Fig. O230—Install lower main bearings in oil base of Models P216V, P218V and P220V as shown.

base until located as shown in Fig. O230. Be sure oil holes are aligned. A thrust washer is located between the crankshaft and the oil base. Install thrust washer so notches align with lock pins shown in Fig. O231 and grooves on thrust washer are toward crankshaft.

Crankshaft end play should be 0.006-0.012 inch (0.15-0.30 mm) and is adjusted by installing shims between thrust washer and oil base as shown in Fig. O231. Be sure shims and thrust washer are properly aligned with lock pins during assembly.

To remove crankshaft oil seals, the timing gear cover and oil base must be removed. Force out oil seals from inside. Install oil seal in timing gear cover so seal is 0.645 inch (16.38 mm) below face of bore as shown in Fig. O229. Install oil seal in oil base so it is flush with surface as shown in Fig. O230.

CAMSHAFT, BEARINGS AND GOVERNOR. The camshaft (Fig. O232) is supported at each end in precision-type sleeve bearings. Apply Loctite Bearing Mount to bearing before installation. Make certain oil holes in bearing and block are aligned. Press front or top bearing in flush with outer surface of block. Press rear or bottom bearing in so it is 0.50 inch (12.7 mm) from outer surface of block as shown in Fig. O233. Camshaft-to-bearing clearance should be 0.0015-0.0030 inch (0.038-0.076 mm).

Camshaft end play should be 0.011-0.048 inch (0.28-1.22 mm). Camshaft

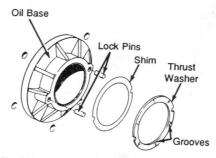

Fig. O231—Align thrust washer and shim with lock pins on oil base of Models P216V, P218V and P220V. Oil grooves on thrust washer must be toward crankshaft.

Fig. O232—Exploded view of camshaft used on all models. Number of governor balls (4) may be five or ten depending on engine model and application.

end play is adjusted by varying thickness of shim located between camshaft timing gear and cylinder block.

Camshaft lobe height wear limit for exhaust valve is 1.1570 inches (29.388 mm). Wear limit for intake valve lobe is 1.1370 inches (28.880 mm) on Models P216, P216V, P218 and P218V, and 1.1670 inches (29.642 mm) on all other models.

Camshaft timing gear is a press fit on end of camshaft and is designed to accommodate five or ten flyballs arranged as shown in Fig. O234. Number of flyballs is varied to alter governor sensitivity. Fewer flyballs are used on engines with variable speed applications and greater number of flyballs are used for continuous speed applications. Flyballs must be arranged in "pockets" as shown according to total number used.

When installing camshaft, align timing marks on camshaft gear and crankshaft gear as shown in Fig. O235.

Center pin (Fig. O236) should extend ¾ inch (19 mm) from end of camshaft to allow ⁷⁄₃₂ inch (5.6 mm) in-and-out movement of governor cup. If distance

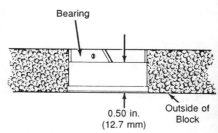

Fig. O233—Press lower camshaft bearing on Models P216V, P218V and P220V in cylinder block as shown. Illustration also applies to rear camshaft bearing on Models P216, P218, P220 and P224.

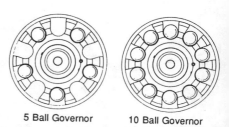

5 Ball Governor   10 Ball Governor

Fig. O234—Flyballs must be arranged as shown, according to total number used to obtain desired governor sensitivity.

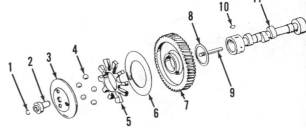

is incorrect, remove pin and press new pin in to correct depth.

Always make certain governor shaft pivot ball is in timing cover by measuring as shown in Fig. O237 inset and check length of roll pin that engages bushed hole in governor cup. This pin must extend ¾ inch (19.05 mm) from timing cover mating surface.

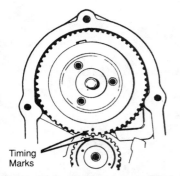

Fig. O235—Timing marks on camshaft and crankshaft gears must be aligned during assembly.

OIL PUMP. Oil pump is a unit assembly; separate components are not available.

Oil pressure is regulated by an oil pressure relief valve that is located in cylinder block (Fig. O238) on Models P216, P218, P220 and P224, and in oil base (Fig. O239) on Models P216V, P218V and P220V. Relief valve spring free length should be 1.00 inch (25.4 mm) on all models. Relief valve spring pressure should be 2.4-2.8 pounds (10.6-12.5 N) at spring length of 0.5 inch (12.7 mm). Relief valve diameter on Models P216, P218, P220 and P224 should be 0.3105-0.3125 inch (2.142-2.156 mm). Minimum relief ball diameter on Models P216V, P218V and P220V is 0.3125 inch (2.156 mm).

Relief valve spring on Models P216V, P218V and P220V is secured by a retaining ring (12—Fig. O226). Install retaining ring with outside edge out and press ring into bore so depth (D—Fig. O239) is 0.12-0.14 inch (3.0-3.6 mm).

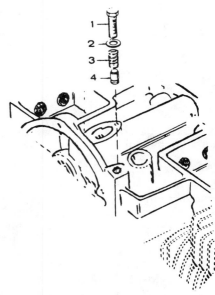

Fig. O238—View showing location of oil pressure relief valve and spring used on Models P216, P218, P220 and P224.

1. Cap screw
2. Sealing washer
3. Spring
4. Valve

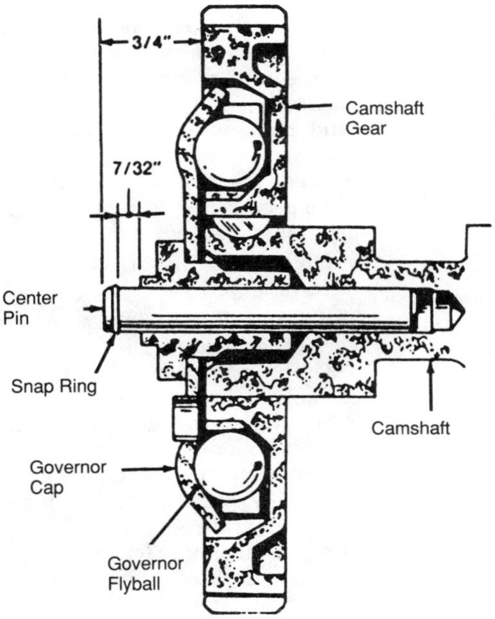

Fig. O236—Cross-sectional view of camshaft gear and governor assembly showing correct dimensions for center pin extension from camshaft. Refer to text.

Fig. O237—View of governor shaft, timing cover and governor cup showing assembly details. Refer to text.

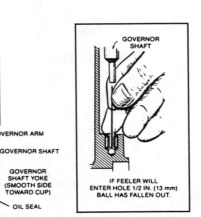

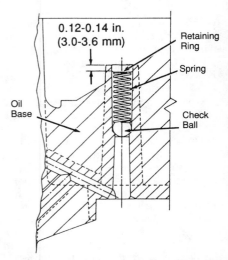

Fig. O239—Drawing of oil pressure relief valve used on Models P216V, P218V and P220V.

ONAN

ONAN CORPORATION
1400 73rd Avenue N.E.
Minneapolis, Minnesota 55432

Model	No. Cyls.	Bore	Stroke	Displacement	Power Rating
E125V	1	84.2 mm (3.31 in.)	70 mm (2.76 in.)	389 cc (23.7 cu. in.)	9.4 kW (12.5 hp)
E140V	1	84.2 mm (3.31 in.)	70 mm (2.76 in.)	389 cc (23.7 cu. in.)	10.5 kW (14 hp)

NOTE: Metric fasteners are used throughout engine.

The Onan engines covered in this section are four-stroke, air-cooled, single-cylinder engines using an overhead valve system. All models are equipped with a vertical crankshaft. The engine is pressure lubricated by an oil pump located in the oil pan.

MAINTENANCE

LUBRICATION. All models are equipped with a pressure lubrication system, an oil filter is optional. Oil is routed from an oil pump located in the oil pan and driven by a balancer shaft.

Manufacturer recommends using oil with an API service classification of SF or SG. Use SAE 30 oil for ambient temperatures above 32° F (0° C); use SAE 10W-30 oil for temperatures between 0° F (−18° C) and 80° F (27° C); below 20° F (−7° C) use SAE 5W-20.

Check oil at regular intervals and maintain at "FULL" mark on dipstick. DO NOT overfill.

On all models, engine oil should be changed after first 25 hours of operation and oil filter, if so equipped, should be changed after first 50 hours of operation. Thereafter, if engine is not equipped with an oil filter, engine oil should be changed after every 50 hours of operation. If engine is equipped with an oil filter, engine oil and filter should be changed after every 100 hours of operation. Change oil and filter more frequently if engine undergoes severe operation.

Crankcase capacity is 1.54 liters (1.65 qt.) if oil filter is changed with oil refill, 1.4 liters (1.5 qt.) if oil filter is not changed.

Normal oil pressure should be 97 kPa (14 psi) at 3350 rpm. If engine oil pressure is less than 26.4 kPa (4 psi) at engine speed of 3350 rpm, cause for low oil pressure should be determined.

AIR FILTER. The engine is equipped with a foam precleaner element and paper-type air filter. Service the unit after every 25 hours of operation. Renew the air filter after every 200 hours of operation. Service more frequently if engine is operated in severe conditions.

Clean precleaner element by washing in soapy water. Allow to dry then apply clean engine oil. Squeeze out excess oil.

The air filter should be renewed rather than cleaned. Tap element to dislodge dirt or debris. Do not wash or direct pressurized air at filter.

FUEL FILTER. If so equipped, inspect fuel filter after 200 hours of operation. If dirty or damaged, renew filter.

CRANKCASE BREATHER. A reed-type breather valve is attached to the top of the cylinder head under the rocker cover. Inspect and clean breather valve as needed to prevent or remove restrictions.

SPARK PLUG. Recommended spark plug is Champion RL95YC or equivalent. Specified electrode gap is 0.9 mm (0.035 in.). Tighten spark plug to 23-24 N·m (17-18 ft.-lbs.).

CARBURETOR. Initial setting of idle mixture screw (I—Fig. O301) is 2½ turns out. Final adjustment of idle mixture screw should be made with engine at normal operating temperature. Adjust idle speed screw so engine idles at 1500 rpm or at speed specified by

equipment manufacturer. Turn idle mixture screw counterclockwise until engine rpm decreases and note screw position. Turn screw clockwise until engine rpm decreases again and note screw position. Turn screw to midpoint between the two noted positions. Reset idle speed screw if necessary to obtain desired idle speed.

High-speed mixture is controlled by a fixed main jet.

Refer to Fig. O302 for an exploded view of carburetor. Disassembly and reassembly is evident after inspection of carburetor and referral to Fig. O302. When removing or installing nozzle (10), main jet (6) must be removed. If a cleaning solvent is used to clean carburetor, be sure it will not damage plastic parts of carburetor or soak only metal parts in cleaner. Float level is not adjustable. Tighten carburetor mounting screws to 10.8-16.3 N·m (96-144 in.-lbs.).

CARBURETOR CONTROLS. Before adjusting carburetor control linkage, refer to GOVERNOR section and, if required, adjust governor linkage. To

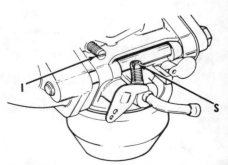

Fig. O301—Refer to text for adjustment of carburetor idle speed screw (S) and idle mixture screw (I).

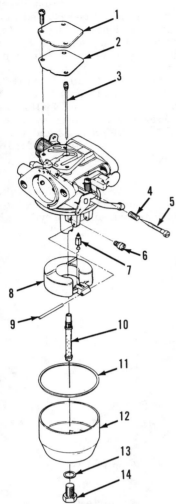

Fig. O302—Exploded view of carburetor.

1. Cover
2. Gasket
3. Slow jet
4. Spring
5. Idle mixture screw
6. Main jet
7. Fuel inlet valve
8. Float
9. Float pin
10. Nozzle
11. Gasket
12. Fuel bowl
13. Washer
14. Screw

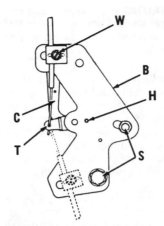

Fig. O304—View of carburetor control bracket used on Specification "B" and "C" engines.

adjust carburetor control linkage, loosen throttle cable clamp screw (W—Figs. O303 or O304) and place equipment throttle lever in fast position. Move throttle control lever (T) to wide open position and insert a rod through hole (H) in control bracket (B) and control lever (T). Pull cable housing tight and retighten cable clamp screw (W). With rod still in hole (H), loosen choke rod swivel screw (on back side of bracket) and move choke rod so carburetor choke plate is wide open. On Specification "A" engines, move choke lever (C) so it is 0.25-0.51 mm (0.010-0.030 inch) from control lever (T) and tighten swivel screw. On Specification "B" and "C" engines, tighten swivel screw after verifying that choke plate is wide open. Remove rod and check operation.

GOVERNOR. To adjust governor linkage, proceed as follows: Loosen governor lever clamp bolt (B—Fig. O305) and push governor lever (G) so throttle is wide open. Turn governor shaft (S)

clockwise as far as possible and tighten clamp bolt (B).

Maximum governed speed is determined by equipment manufacturer. Carburetor controls must be adjusted as outlined in previous section. To adjust high idle speed setting, move the equipment speed control lever to "Fast" position. Align the hole in throttle lever (T—Figs. O303 or O304) with hole (H) in speed control bracket (B) by inserting a suitable rod through the holes. Start engine and allow to reach operating temperature. Loosen speed control bracket mounting screws (S) and move bracket to adjust engine speed. When desired speed is obtained, tighten control bracket screws.

IGNITION SYSTEM. The breakerless ignition system requires no regular maintenance. Ignition coil unit is mounted outside the flywheel. Air gap between flywheel and coil should be 0.5 mm (0.020 in.).

To check ignition coil primary side, connect one ohmmeter lead to primary coil lead and touch iron coil laminations with remaining lead. Ohmmeter should indicate 1.0 ohm.

To check ignition coil secondary side, connect one ohmmeter lead to the spark plug lead wire and remaining lead to the iron core laminations. Ohmmeter should indicate 9.5k ohms. If ohmmeter readings are not as specified, renew ignition coil.

VALVE ADJUSTMENT. Clearance (G—Fig. O306) between valve stem ends and rocker arms should be checked and adjusted after every 100 hours of operation. To check clearance, turn crankshaft until piston is at top dead center on compression stroke. Remove rocker cover and measure clearance using a feeler gauge. Specified clearance with engine cold is 0.08 mm (0.003 in.) for intake and exhaust. To adjust, loosen locknut (N) and turn rocker arm adjusting screw (S) as necessary.

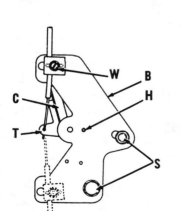

Fig. O303—View of carburetor control bracket used on Specification "A" engines.

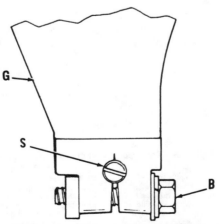

Fig. O305—View of governor lever used on later models. Early models are similar.

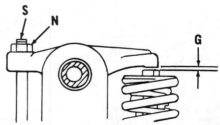

Fig. O306—To adjust valve clearance for either valve, loosen locknut (N) and turn rocker arm adjusting screw (S) so clearance (G) is 0.08 mm (0.003 in.) with engine cold.

COMPRESSION PRESSURE. Compression pressure measured at cranking speed should be 483 kPa (70 psi).

REPAIRS

NOTE: End play of balancer shafts and camshaft is adjusted at factory and cannot be measured in field. Note factory-installed shims when balancer shafts and camshaft are involved in disassembly and reinstall original shims during reassembly.

TIGHTENING TORQUES. Recommended tightening torques are as follows:

Carburetor . . . . 10.8-16.3 N•m
(96-144 in.-lbs.)
Connecting rod . . . . . . 24.5-27.2 N•m
(18-20 ft.-lbs.)
Exhaust manifold . . . . . 10.8-20.3 N•m
(96-180 in.-lbs.)
Flywheel . . . . 122-138 N•m
(90-102 ft.-lbs.)
Intake manifold . . . . . . 10.8-16.3 N•m
(96-144 in.-lbs.)
Oil pan . . . . 16.3-21.8 N•m
(144-192 in.-lbs.)
Spark plug . . . . 23-24 N•m
(17-18 ft.-lbs.)

CYLINDER HEAD. To remove cylinder head, remove intake and exhaust manifold assemblies. Remove rocker arm cover, then unscrew rocker arm assembly mounting screw and remove rocker assembly. Remove and mark push rods so they can be installed in their original position.

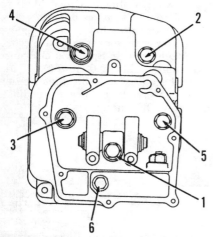

Fig. O307—Tighten cylinder head screws in sequence shown. Note length of screws as listed below:

1. 125 mm		4. 66 mm	
2. 66 mm		5. 86 mm	
3. 86 mm		6. 50 mm	

CAUTION: Cylinder head retaining screws should not be unscrewed when engine is hot due to possibility of head warping.

Loosen cylinder head retaining screws evenly and remove cylinder head and gasket. Note that cylinder head retaining screws are of different lengths.

Remove carbon deposits from combustion chamber being careful not to damage gasket sealing surface. Inspect cylinder head for cracks, nicks or other damage.

To reinstall cylinder head, reverse removal procedure. Surfaces of cylinder head gasket are coated with a sealant and do not require additional sealant. Push rods should be installed in their original positions. Note lengths of cylinder head retaining screws in Fig. O308. Tighten cylinder head screws in sequence shown in Fig. O307 in steps to final torque of 42.2-50.3 N•m (31-37 ft.-lbs.) for screws 1 through 5 in Fig. O307, and to 16.3-21.7 N•m (144-192 in.-lbs.) for screw 6. After all screws are tightened, retorque screws 2 and 4. Adjust valve clearance as outlined in MAINTENANCE section.

VALVE SYSTEM. Remove cylinder head as outlined above. Refer to Fig. O308 for exploded view of cylinder head

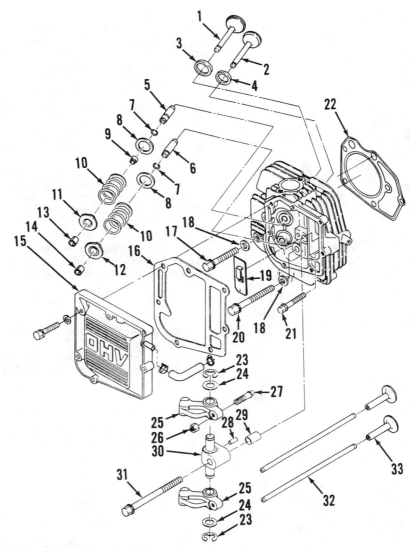

Fig. O308—Exploded view of cylinder head assembly.

1. Intake valve				
2. Exhaust valve				
3. Intake valve seat	10. Valve spring	18. Washer	26. Locknut
4. Exhaust valve seat	11. Intake valve spring retainer	19. Breather assy.	27. Adjuster screw
5. Intake valve guide	12. Exhaust valve spring retainer	20. Screw	28. Dowel
6. Exhaust valve guide	13. Intake valve retainers	21. Screw	29. Sleeve
7. Retainer	14. Exhaust valve retainers	22. Head gasket	30. Rocker arm shaft
8. Washer	15. Rocker arm cover	23. "E" ring	31. Screw
9. Intake valve seal	16. Gasket	24. Washer	32. Push rod
	17. Screw	25. Rocker arm	33. Tappet

and valve system. Specified rocker arm inside diameter is 12.000-12.018 mm (0.4724-0.4731 in.). Specified rocker shaft diameter is 11.973-11.984 mm (0.4714-0.4718 in.). Rocker arm-to-shaft clearance is 0.016-0.045 mm (0.0006-0.0018 in.) with a maximum allowable clearance of 0.15 mm (0.006 in.).

When disassembling valve components, note that intake and exhaust valve retainers and valve spring retainers are dissimilar.

NOTE: Removal of valve stem seal will damage the seal. Renew seals whenever they are removed.

Valve face and seat angles are 45°. Standard valve seat width is 1.1 mm (0.043 in.). Narrow seat if seat width is 1.7 mm (0.067 in.) or more.

Standard valve spring free length is 45.5-45.8 mm (1.79-1.80 in.). Renew valve spring if free length is 45.0 mm (1.77 in.) or less.

Standard valve guide inside diameter is 7.000-7.015 mm (0.2756-0.2762 in.) for intake and 8.000-8.015 mm (0.3150-0.3156 in.) for exhaust. Specified valve stem diameter is 6.960-6.975 mm (0.2740-0.2746 in.) for intake valve and 7.960-7.975 mm (0.3134-0.3140 in.) for exhaust valve. Valve stem-to-guide clearance should be 0.025-0.055 mm (0.0010-0.0022 in.) for intake valve and 0.040-0.075 mm (0.0016-0.0030 in.) for

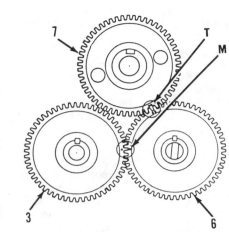

Fig. O310—View of timing marks on crankshaft and balancer shaft gears. Note that twin timing marks (T) appear on crankshaft gear (7) and thick balancer gear (6), while single timing marks (M) appear on balancer gears (3) and (6).

exhaust valve. Renew valve guide and/or guide if clearance is 0.10 mm (0.004 in.) or more for either valve.

To renew valve guide, press or drive guide out towards rocker arm side of head. Press or drive in valve guide so clip (7—Fig. O308) is bottomed against head.

BALANCER SHAFTS. The engine is equipped with a pair of balancer shafts that are gear-driven off the crankshaft gear. Ends of the balancer shafts are supported by ball bearings in the crankcase and oil pan. Remove the oil pan for access to the balancer shafts.

NOTE: Thickness of shims (4—Fig. O309) was determined at factory. Reinstall original shims.

Balancer shafts and gears on early models can be separated. Shaft and gear on later models are one piece. The oil

pump rotor is driven by a slot in the end of the shaft (5) with the thicker drive gear (6).

Align timing marks shown in Fig. O310 when installing balancer shafts. There are two sets of timing marks on thicker balancer gear (6). Twin timing marks (T) must align with twin timing marks on crankshaft gear (7). Single timing mark (M) must align with single timing mark on thinner balancer gear (3).

When installing oil pan, be sure end of balancer shaft mates with oil pump rotor shaft. Tighten oil pan retaining screws to 16.3-21.8 N•m (144-192 in.-lbs.).

PISTON, PIN AND RINGS. Piston and connecting rod are removed as an assembly. To remove piston and connecting rod, remove cylinder head and oil pan. Remove balancer shafts. Remove connecting rod cap screws and cap. Push connecting rod and piston assembly out of cylinder. Mark piston so it can be reinstalled on connecting rod in same position. Detach piston pin retaining rings (2—Fig. O311), remove piston pin and separate piston from connecting rod.

Measure piston diameter at a point 23 mm (0.91 in.) above lower edge of skirt and perpendicular to piston pin. Specified standard piston diameter is 84.150-84.170 mm (3.3130-3.3138 in.) with a wear limit of 84.05 mm (3.3090 in.). Specified diameter for 0.25 mm oversize piston is 84.400-84.420 mm (3.3228-3.3236 in.) with a wear limit of 84.30 mm (3.3189 in.). Specified diameter for 0.50 mm oversize piston is 84.650-84.670 mm (3.3327-3.3334 in.) with a wear limit of 84.55 mm (3.3287 in.).

Specified piston pin diameter is 20.000-20.005 mm (0.7874-0.7876 in.).

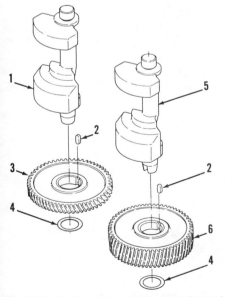

Fig. O309—Exploded view of balancer shafts used on Specification "A" engines. Balancer shafts and gears are one piece on Specification "B" and "C" engines. Note that balancer shaft (5) with thick gear (6) drives oil pump rotor shaft.

1. Balancer shaft	4. Shim
2. Key	5. Balancer shaft
3. Gear (thin)	6. Gear (thick)

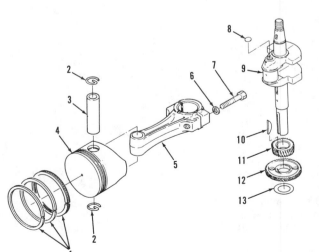

Fig. O311—Exploded view of piston, rod and crankshaft assemblies.

1. Piston rings
2. Retaining ring
3. Piston pin
4. Piston
5. Connecting rod
6. Washer
7. Screw
8. Plug
9. Crankshaft
10. Key
11. Small crankshaft gear
12. Large crankshaft gear
13. Shim

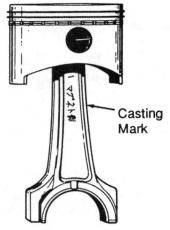

Casting
Mark

Fig. O312—Install piston and rod in engine so casting mark on side of connecting rod is toward flywheel.

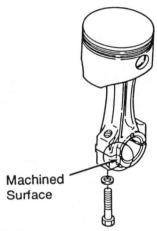

Machined
Surface

Fig. O313—Install rod cap on rod so machined surfaces are aligned.

Reject piston pin if diameter is less than 19.96 mm (0.7858 in.). Specified piston pin bore diameter in piston is 19.995-20.003 mm (0.7872-7875 in.). Reject piston if piston pin bore diameter is more than 20.040 mm (0.7890 in.).

Compression ring side clearance should be 0.020-0.060 mm (0.0008-0.0024 in.). Maximum allowable compression ring side clearance is 0.10 mm (0.004 in.). Ring end gap for compression rings should be 0.35-0.55 mm (0.014-0.022 in.). If compression ring end gap exceeds 0.9 mm (0.033 in.), renew ring and/or cylinder. Maximum allowable end gap for oil control piston ring rails is 0.9 mm (0.033 in.).

Before assembling piston and connecting rod, heat piston to 212° F (100° C) to ease insertion of piston pin. Install piston on connecting rod so previously made mark on piston crown is properly aligned with connecting rod. Install compression piston rings on piston so marked side is toward piston crown.

Stagger piston ring end gaps around piston. Install piston and rod in engine so casting mark (Fig. O312) on side of connecting rod is toward flywheel. Mate connecting rod cap with rod while being sure machined surfaces (Fig. O313) are aligned. Tighten connecting rod screws to 24.5-27.2 N•m (18-20 ft.-lbs.). Install balancer shafts and cylinder head as previously outlined.

CONNECTING ROD. The aluminum alloy connecting rod rides directly on crankpin journal. Refer to previous PISTON, PIN AND RINGS paragraphs for removal and installation procedure.

Specified piston pin bore diameter in connecting rod is 20.015-20.025 mm (0.7880-0.7884 in.). Renew connecting rod if diameter is 20.070 mm (0.7902 in.) or more.

Specified connecting rod-to-crankpin clearance is 0.015-0.050 mm (0.0006-0.0020 in.). Renew connecting rod and/or regrind crankshaft if clearance is 0.10 mm (0.004 in.) or more. Standard big end diameter is 33.500-33.525 mm (1.3189-1.3199 in.). Connecting rods that are 0.25 and 0.50 mm undersize are available.

Connecting rod side play on crankpin should be 0.4-1.1 mm (0.016-0.043 in.).

Renew connecting rod if side play is 1.5 mm (0.059 in.) or more.

Install connecting rod as outlined in previous section.

GOVERNOR. A centrifugal flyweight-type governor (7—Figs. O314 or O315) controls engine rpm via external linkage. Governor is located in oil pan. Refer to GOVERNOR paragraphs in MAINTENANCE section for adjustment procedure.

To remove governor assembly, remove oil pan. Remove governor sleeve (4) and retaining clip (5), then remove governor weight assembly from shaft. Flyweight assembly must operate freely without binding.

When installing oil pan, be sure end of balancer shaft mates with oil pump rotor shaft. Tighten oil pan retaining screws to 16.3-21.8 N•m (144-192 in.-lbs.). Adjust external linkage as outlined under GOVERNOR in MAINTENANCE section.

CRANKSHAFT. The crankshaft is supported at ends by ball bearings in the crankcase and oil pan. To remove crankshaft, remove flywheel, then remove piston and connecting rod assembly as previously outlined. Due to arrangement of gears on crankshaft and

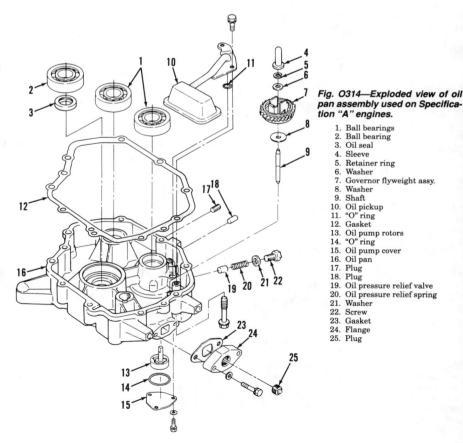

Fig. O314—Exploded view of oil pan assembly used on Specification "A" engines.

1. Ball bearings
2. Ball bearing
3. Oil seal
4. Sleeve
5. Retainer ring
6. Washer
7. Governor flyweight assy.
8. Washer
9. Shaft
10. Oil pickup
11. "O" ring
12. Gasket
13. Oil pump rotors
14. "O" ring
15. Oil pump cover
16. Oil pan
17. Plug
18. Plug
19. Oil pressure relief valve
20. Oil pressure relief spring
21. Washer
22. Screw
23. Gasket
24. Flange
25. Plug

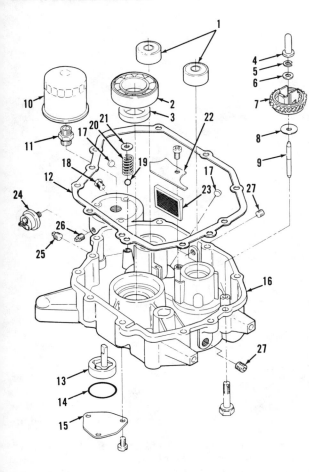

Fig. O315—Exploded view of oil pan assembly used on Specification "B" and "C" engines.

1. Ball bearings
2. Ball bearing
3. Oil seal
4. Sleeve
5. Retainer ring
6. Washer
7. Governor flyweight assy.
8. Washer
9. Shaft
10. Oil filter
11. Adapter
12. Gasket
13. Oil pump rotors
14. "O" ring
15. Oil pump cover
16. Oil pan
17. Plug
18. Plug
19. Oil pressure relief ball
20. Oil pressure relief spring
21. Washer
22. Cover
23. Oil screen
24. Oil pressure switch
25. Plug
26. Plug
27. Plug

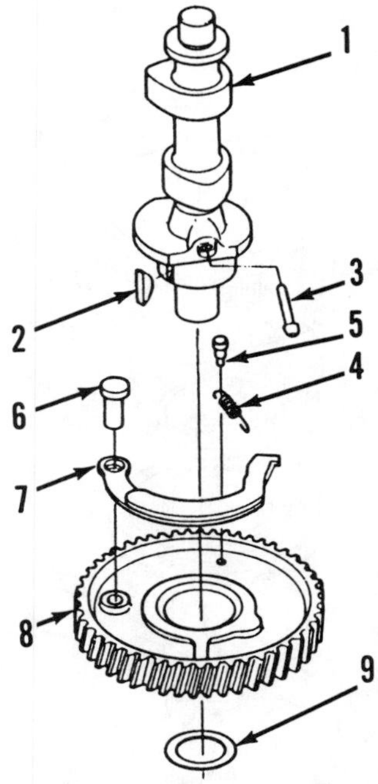

Fig. O317—Exploded view of camshaft assembly.

1. Camshaft
2. Key
3. Pin
4. Spring
5. Pin
6. Pin
7. Compression relief lever
8. Camshaft gear
9. Shim

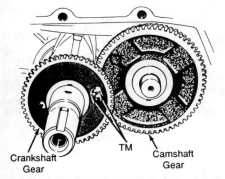

Crankshaft Gear   TM   Camshaft Gear

Fig. O316—Look through hole in large crankshaft gear to align timing marks (TM) on small crankshaft gear and camshaft gear.

camshaft, the camshaft must be removed along with crankshaft.

Standard crankpin journal diameter is 33.475-33.485 mm (1.3179-1.3183 in). Specified connecting rod-to-crankpin clearance is 0.015-0.050 mm (0.0006-0.0020 in.). Renew connecting rod and/or regrind crankshaft if clearance is 0.10 mm (0.004 in.) or more. Connecting rods that are 0.25 and 0.50 mm undersize are available. Plug (8—Fig. O311) is available separately so oil passages can be cleaned in crankshaft.

Timing marks (TM—Fig. O316) on crankshaft and camshaft gears must be

aligned before installing crankshaft and camshaft in crankcase. Note hole in large crankshaft gear that allows viewing of timing marks.

Maximum crankshaft end play is 0.1 mm (0.004 in.). Adjust crankshaft end play by changing thickness of shim (13—Fig. 311).

CAMSHAFT. The camshaft is supported at ends by ball bearings in the crankcase and oil pan. Due to arrangement of gears on camshaft and crankshaft, the crankshaft must be removed along with the crankshaft. Remove crankshaft as outlined in CRANKSHAFT section.

NOTE: Thickness of shim (9—Fig. O317) was determined at factory. Reinstall original shim.

Specified camshaft lobe height for both valves is 34.685-34.715 mm (1.3656-1.3667 in.). Renew camshaft if either lobe height is less than 34.50 mm (1.358 in.).

The camshaft is equipped with a compression release mechanism. The compression release pin (3—Fig. O317) extends at cranking speed to hold the exhaust valve open slightly, thereby re-

ducing compression pressure. Check mechanism for sticking and binding.

Install camshaft and crankshaft as outlined in CRANKSHAFT section.

OIL PUMP. A gerotor-type oil pump is located in the oil pan. The oil pump is driven by one of the engine balance shafts. Oil pump rotors (13—Figs. O314 or O315) can be removed for inspection after removing pump cover (15) from bottom of oil pan. The oil pan must be removed for access to oil pick-up. The oil pressure relief valve (19—Fig. O314) and spring (20) on Specification "A" engines is located in side of oil pan. On Specification "B" and "C" engines, the oil pan must be removed for access to oil pressure relief valve ball (19—Fig. O315) and spring (20).

Check oil pump rotors and oil pan cavity for scoring or excessive wear. Inner-to-outer rotor clearance should be 0.150 mm (0.0059 in.) or less. If clearance exceeds 0.200 mm (0.079 in.), renew rotors. Oil pump body-to-outer rotor clearance should be 0.130-0.223 mm (0.0051-0.0088 in.). If clearance exceeds 0.250 mm (0.0098 in.), renew rotors and/or oil pan. Specified clearance between rotor and pump cover is 0.020-0.060 mm (0.0008-0.0024 in.) with a wear limit of 0.250 mm (0.0098 in.).

Reassemble oil pump by reversing disassembly procedure.

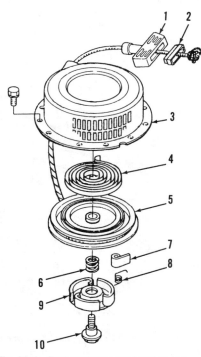

Fig. O318—Exploded view of rewind starter.

1. Rope handle	6. Brake spring
2. Insert	7. Pawl
3. Starter housing	8. Spring
4. Rewind spring	9. Retainer
5. Pulley	10. Screw

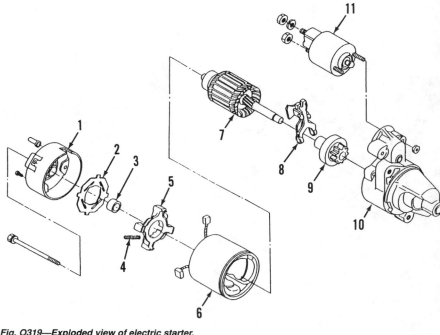

Fig. O319—Exploded view of electric starter.

1. End cap	4. Brush spring	7. Armature
2. Insulator plate	5. Brush holder	8. Yoke
3. Bushing	6. Frame	9. Drive pinion
		10. Drive housing
		11. Solenoid

REWIND STARTER. To disassemble starter, remove rope handle and allow rope to wind into starter. Unscrew center screw (10—Fig. O318) and remove retainer (9) and pawl assembly. Wear appropriate safety eyewear and gloves before disengaging pulley from starter as spring may uncoil uncontrolled. Place rags around pulley and lift pulley out of housing; spring should remain with pulley. If spring must be removed from pulley, position pulley so spring side is down and against floor, then tap pulley to dislodge spring.

Reassemble starter by reversing disassembly procedure while noting the following. Lightly grease sides of rewind spring and pulley. Wind rope around pulley in counterclockwise direction as viewed from pawl side of pulley. Preload rewind spring by turning pulley before passing rope through outlet and attaching rope handle. Check starter operation before installing on engine. With rope pulled to full length, it should be possible to rotate rope pulley at least one-half turn counterclockwise, otherwise, reduce preload on rewind spring. When rope handle is released, it should retract into outlet on housing and fit snugly, otherwise, increase preload on rewind spring.

ELECTRIC STARTER. Refer to Fig. O319 for an exploded view of starter. To disassemble starter, unscrew retaining nuts and remove solenoid. Mark end cap (1), frame (6) and drive housing (10) so they can be assembled in original position. Unscrew through bolts and separate starter components.

Minimum allowable commutator diameter is 27.00 mm (1.063 in.). Specified armature shaft-to-bushing clearance is 0.020-0.070 mm (0.0008-0.0028 in.) with a maximum allowable clearance of 0.20 mm (0.008 in.).

Assemble starter by reversing disassembly procedure. Align marks on end cap (1), frame (6) and drive housing (10) during assembly.

ALTERNATOR. The engine may be equipped with a 2.5-amp alternator or a 20-amp alternator with regulator-rectifier. The alternator stator is located under the flywheel.

To check stator coil for 2.5-amp alternator, disconnect leads to stator coil and connect ohmmeter to coil leads. Ohmmeter should indicate 0.33 ohms, otherwise, renew stator coil.

To check stator of 20-amp alternator, disconnect stator leads and connect an AC voltmeter to leads. With engine running at 1800 rpm, voltmeter should indicate approximately 29 volts. With engine running at 3600 rpm, voltmeter should indicate approximately 57 volts. Stop engine and connect an ohmmeter to stator leads. Ohmmeter should indicate 0.10-0.19 ohm. Check for continuity between each stator lead and engine ground. Ohmmeter should read infinity.

To test regulator-rectifier of 20-amp alternator, battery must be in good condition and fully charged. Connect a DC voltmeter to battery and check battery voltage with engine running. If voltage is greater than 14.7 volts, replace regulator-rectifier with a new or good unit. If voltage is less than 13.6 volts, check circuit for possible cause, and if none is found, and stator is good, replace regulator-rectifier with a new or good unit.

ONAN
SERVICING ONAN ACCESSORIES
(Except "E" Series)

NOTE: The following sections cover only components used on standard-type applications. Electrical components not covered here should be taken to an experienced electric motor-generator repair shop.

REWIND STARTER

Engines of LK series and larger, when so equipped, are fitted with manual "Readi-Pull" starter shown in exploded view in Fig. OA101. For convenience, direction of starter rope pull may be adjusted to suit special cases by loosening clamps that hold starter cover (5) in position on its mounting ring (20), then turning cover (5) so rope (2) exits in desired direction.

Mounting ring (20) must be firmly attached to engine blower housing, which must be as rigid as possible. If blower housing is damaged, or if mounting holes for starter are misshaped or worn, it may be necessary to renew entire blower housing. See Fig. OA102 for a cross section of starter mounting ring attachment to blower housing.

To attach starter to earlier production engines, refer to Fig. OA103, and use a pair of 10-penny (3 inch) common nails passed through holes in cover to insert into recesses in heads of special screws that retain ratchet wheel to engine fly-

wheel. In later production (after specification "D"), spiral pin (12A—Fig. OA101) is centered upon and engages drilled head screws (17) that secure ratchet wheel (22) and rope sheave hub bearing (16) for alignment during assembly.

Common repairs to manual starter can be made with minimum disassembly. Mounting ring (20) is left in place and only cover assembly (5) need be removed after its four clamps (19) are released. To renew starter rope (2), remove cover (5) from mounting ring (20), release clamp (15) to remove old rope from sheave (10). Then rotate sheave (10) in normal direction of crankshaft rotation to tighten spring (8) all the way. Align rope hole in sheave with rope slot in cover, secure new rope by its clamp (15) and, when sheave (10) is released, spring (8) will recoil and wind rope on sheave. If renewal of recoil spring (8) is required, sheave (10) must be lifted out of cover (5). Remove starter rope (2) from sheave. Starting at outer end, wrap new spring (8) into a coil small enough to fit into recess in cover with loop at inner end of spring engaging roll pin (7) in cover. It may be necessary to secure wound-up spring with a temporary restraint, such as a wire, while doing so. Then, reinstall rope sheave (10) so tab on sheave fits into loop at

outer end of recoil spring. Install thrust washer (9) and spring washer (6A) if starter is so equipped.

Whenever starter is disassembled for any service, it is advisable to add a small amount of grease to factory-packed sheave hub bearing (16) and to clean and lubricate pawls (11) and ratchet arms (13) at pivot and contact points. If ratchet arms (13) require renewal due to wear, pawls (11) must first be removed.

ELECTRIC STARTER

Engines may be equipped with electric starter motors that use either a Bendix (Figs. OA104 and OA105) or

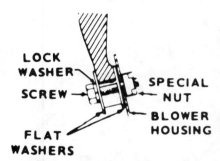

Fig. OA102—Cross-section of mounting ring bolt to show housing attachment detail.

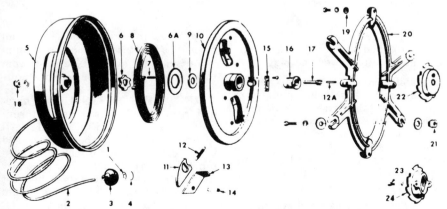

Fig. OA101—Exploded view of "Readi-Pull" manual starter that is installed on LK and larger engines.

1. Rope retainer	7. Roll pin	12A. Spiral pin	18. Flexlock nut
2. Starter rope	8. Recoil spring	13. Ratchet arm (2)	19. Washer
3. Starter grip	9. Thrust washer	14. Pivot roll pin (2)	20. Mounting ring
4. Grip plug	10. Rope sheave	15. Rope clamp	21. Speed grip nut
5. Cover	11. Pawl (2)	16. Hub bearing	22. Ratchet wheel (late)
6. Anti-backlash cog	12. Pawl spring	17. Recessed screw	23. Special cap screw
6A. Spring washer			24. Ratchet wheel (early)

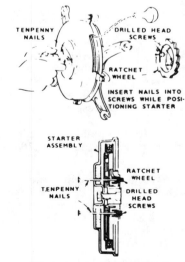

Fig. OA103—Technique for mounting older-style starter to ratchet wheel on engine flywheel. Refer to text.

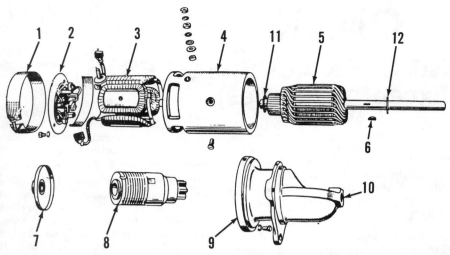

Fig. OA104—Exploded view of electric starter motor equipped with Bendix drive used on some models.

1. Cover band
2. End plate & brush assy.
3. Field coils
4. Frame
5. Armature
6. Key
7. Intermediate bearing
8. Bendix drive
9. Drive housing
10. Bushing
11. Spacer
12. Thrust washer

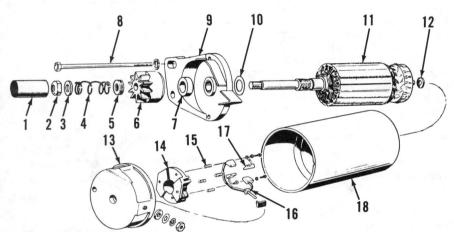

Fig. OA105—Exploded view of electric starter motor equipped with Bendix drive used on some models.

1. Cover
2. Nut
3. Washer
4. Anti-drift spring
5. Spacer
6. Bendix drive
7. Seal
8. Through bolt
9. Drive housing
10. Thrust washer
11. Armature
12. Washer
13. End cap
14. Brush holder
15. Brush spring
16. Brush & terminal stud
17. Brush
18. Frame

lever-type (Fig. OA106) engagement system. The pinion shift lever on early models is exposed (Fig. OA107), but on later models, the shift lever is enclosed (Fig. OA106). Disassembly and reassembly is conventional and procedure is obvious after examination of units and reference to Figs. OA104, OA105 and OA106.

On NH and NHC engines after Specification "A" and on "P" series engines, renew brushes if worn to less than 0.45 inch (11.5 mm). On all other engines, renew brushes if worn to less than 0.3 inch (7.6 mm).

Armature shaft end play on starter motors shown in Figs. OA104 and OA106 should be 0.004-0.020 inch (0.10-

0.51 mm). Install spacers (11) as required to obtain desired end play.

On shift-lever-type starters, energize solenoid or push solenoid plunger or shift lever to full engaged position and measure clearance between end of drive pinion and stop as shown in Fig. OA107. Clearance should be 0.02-0.06 inch (0.51-1.5 mm) and is adjusted by installing required number of fiber gaskets (19—Fig. OA106).

On Bendix-type starter shown in Fig. OA104, starter pinion to ring gear clearance (Fig. OA108) should be $\frac{1}{16}$-$\frac{1}{8}$ inch (1.6-3.2 mm). Install thickness of thrust washer (12—Fig. OA104) required for desired clearance, then recheck armature end play.

FLYWHEEL ALTERNATOR

Systems With Mechanical Regulator

The flywheel-mounted permanent magnet rotor provides a rotating magnetic field to induce AC voltage in the fixed stator coil (Fig. OA109). Current is then routed through a two-step mechanical regulator to a full-wave rectifier that converts this regulated alternating current to direct current for battery charging. Later models are equipped with a fuse between negative (-) side of rectifier and ground to protect rectifier from accidental reversal of battery polarity. See schematic in Fig. OA110. Maintenance is limited to keeping components clean and ensuring wiring connections are secure.

TESTING. Check alternator output by connecting an ammeter in series between positive (+) red terminal of rectifier and ignition switch. Refer to Fig. OA110. At 1800 engine rpm, a discharged battery should cause about 8 amps to register on a meter so connected. As battery charge builds up, current should decrease. Regulator will switch from high charge to low charge at about 14½ volts with low charge current of about 2 amps. Switch from low charge to high charge occurs at about 13 volts. If output is inadequate, test as follows:

Check rotor magnetism with a piece of steel. Attraction should be strong.

Check stator for grounds after disconnecting by grounding each of the three leads through a 12-volt test lamp. If grounding is indicated by lighted test lamp, renew stator assembly.

To check stator for shorts or open circuits, use an ohmmeter of proper scale connected across open leads to check for correct resistance values. Identify leads by reference to schematic.

From lead 7 to lead 8 . . . . . . 0.25 ohm
From lead 8 to lead 9 . . . . . . 0.95 ohm
From lead 9 to lead 7 . . . . . . 1.10 ohm

Variance by over 25 percent from these values calls for renewal of stator.

RECTIFIER TESTS. Use an ohmmeter connected across a pair of terminals as shown in Fig. OA111. All rectifier leads should be disconnected when testing. Check directional resistance through each of the four diodes by comparing resistance reading when test leads are reversed. One reading should be much higher than the other.

If a 12-volt test lamp is used instead of an ohmmeter, bulb should light, but dimly. Full bright or no light indicates diode being tested is defective.

Voltage regulator may be checked for high charge rate by installing a jumper

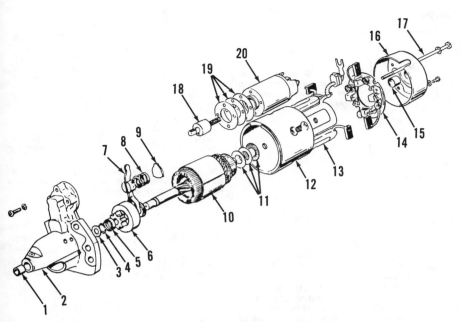

Fig. OA106—Exploded view of lever-type electric starter motor used on some models.

1. Bushing
2. Drive housing
3. Thrust washer
4. Snap ring
5. Retainer
6. Drive unit
7. Shift lever
8. Spring
9. Spring retainer
10. Armature
11. Spacers
12. Frame
13. Field coil assy.
14. Brush plate assy.
15. Bushing
16. End cap
17. Through bolt
18. Plunger
19. Fiber gaskets
20. Solenoid

lead across regulator terminals (B and C—Fig. OA110). With engine running, battery charge rate should be about 8 amps. If charge rate is low, alternator or its wiring is defective.

If charge rate is correct (near 8 amps), defective regulator or its power circuit is indicated. To check, use a 12-volt test lamp to check input at regulator terminal (A). If lamp lights, showing adequate input, regulator is defective and should be renewed.

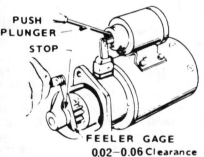

Fig. OA107—On starters equipped with a shift lever, measure clearance between starter pinion and pinion stop as shown.

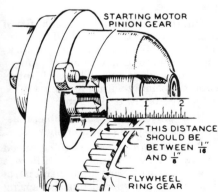

Fig. OA108—Check starter pinion-to-ring gear clearance as shown and as outlined in text.

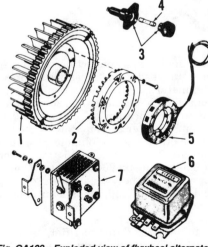

Fig. OA109—Exploded view of flywheel alternator system that uses a mechanical regulator (6).

1. Flywheel
2. Rotor
3. Fuse holder
4. Fuse
5. Stator & leads
6. Regulator
7. Rectifier assy.

NOTE: Due to mechanical design of regulator, it is sensitive to vibration. Be sure to mount it on bulkhead or firewall separate from engine for protection from shock and pulsating motion.

Engine should not be run with battery disconnected; however, this alternator system will not be damaged if battery terminal should be accidentally separated from binding post.

Systems With Solid-State Regulator/Rectifier

Later models may be equipped with a flywheel alternator that uses a solid-state regulator-rectifier. The regulator and rectifier are separate on early versions (Figs. OA112 and OA113), but a one-piece regulator-rectifier is used on later versions (Figs. OA114 and OA115). Refer to following paragraphs for service information.

Separate Regulator and Rectifier (Fig. OA112). To check stator output, disconnect stator lead and connect an AC voltmeter to stator leads and ground with engine running. Note desired voltage readings in following table:

Engine Rpm	Red to Ground	Either Black to Ground	Black to Black
500	35	8.5	17
1000	60	15	30
2000	115	29	58
3000	160	40	80
3600	185	46	92

To check stator using an ohmmeter, proceed as follows: Connect ohmmeter leads to red wire and engine ground. Ohmmeter should indicate approximately 2.0 ohms. Connect one ohmmeter lead to engine ground and remaining ohmmeter lead alternately to each black stator wire. Ohmmeter should read approximately 0.1 ohm. Resistance between black stator leads should be 0.5-0.7 ohm. Resistance between red lead and one of the black leads should be 1.8-2.2 ohms and resistance between red lead and remaining black lead should be 1.3-1.5 ohms.

To check rectifier, connect an ohmmeter to black and white wire leads, then reverse ohmmeter leads (diode test procedure). Ohmmeter should indicate low resistance with one connection and infinity with test wires reversed. Repeat test by connecting an ohmmeter to white wire again and remaining black wire. Renew rectifier if test indicates a faulty diode.

To check regulator, connect a DC voltmeter to battery and check battery voltage with engine running. If voltage is

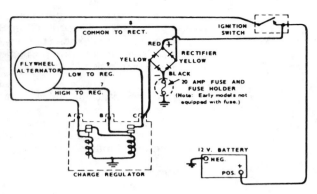

Fig. OA110—Schematic of flywheel alternator system that uses a mechanical regulator.

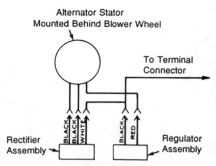

Fig. OA113—Wiring schematic for 20-amp flywheel alternator system that is equipped with separate regulator and rectifier.

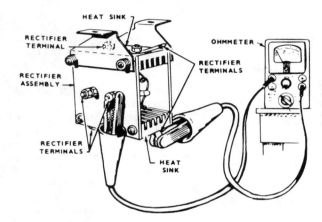

Fig. OA111—Test each of four diodes in rectifier using voltmeter-ohmmeter as shown. Refer to text.

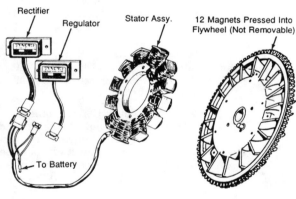

Fig. OA112—View of 20-amp flywheel alternator system that is equipped with separate regulator and rectifier. Refer to Fig. OA113 for wiring schematic.

with a new or good unit. If voltage is less than 13.6 volts, check circuit for possible cause, and if none is found, and stator is good, replace regulator-rectifier with a new or good unit.

FUEL PUMPS

ELECTRIC FUEL PUMP. Some engines may be furnished with a Bendix electric fuel pump, code R-8 or after.

Maintenance is generally limited to simple disassembly and cleaning of removable components, not electrical overhaul.

Refer to Fig. OA117 for sequence of disassembly, beginning with cover (1) by turning 5/8-inch hex to release cover from bayonet lugs after fuel lines have been disconnected. Wash parts in solvent and blow dry using compressed air. Renew damaged or deteriorated parts, especially gasket (2) or filter element (4). Use needlenose pliers to remove retainer (5) and withdraw remainder of parts (6 through 10) from plunger tube (11). Clean and dry each item and inspect carefully for wear or damage. Plunger (10) calls for special attention. Clean rough spots very gently using crocus cloth if necessary. Clean bore of plunger tube (11) thoroughly and blow dry. For best results, use a swab on a stick to remove stubborn deposits from inside tube.

During reassembly, check fit of plunger (10) in tube (11). Full, free, in-and-out motion with no binding or sticking is required. If movement of plunger does not produce an audible click, interrupter assembly within housing (12) is defective. Renew entire pump.

If all parts appear serviceable, reassemble pump parts in order shown.

Pump output pressure can be raised or lowered by selection of a different plunger return spring (9). Consult parts department for special purpose spring or other renewable electric fuel pump parts.

greater than 14.8 volts, replace regulator with a new or good unit. If voltage is less than 14.2 volts, check circuit for possible cause, and if none is found, replace regulator with a new or good unit.

One-Piece Regulator and Rectifier (Figs. OA114, OA115 and OA116). This system produces either 15-, 20- or 35-amp current. Test procedure is same for both systems.

To check stator, disconnect stator leads and connect an AC voltmeter to leads. With engine running at 1800 rpm, voltmeter should indicate approximately 20-30 volts. With engine running at 3600 rpm, voltmeter should indicate approximately 50-60 volts.

Stop engine and connect an ohmmeter to stator leads. On "P" series engines, ohmmeter should indicate 0.06-0.10 ohms for 35-amp stator and 20-amp stator on Specification "A" engine, or 0.1-0.2 ohm on later 20-amp stator systems. On all other engines, ohmmeter should indicate 0.1-0.2 ohm on 15-amp stator or 0.3-0.5 ohm on 20-amp stator. Check for continuity between each stator lead and engine ground. Ohmmeter should read infinity.

To test regulator-rectifier, battery must be in good condition and fully charged. Connect a DC voltmeter to battery and check battery voltage with engine running. If voltage is greater than 14.7 volts, replace regulator-rectifier

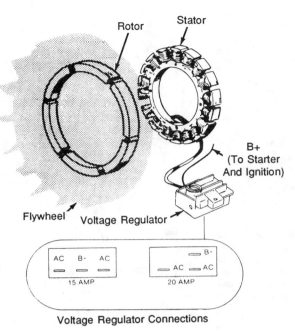

Fig. OA114—View of 15-amp and 20-amp flywheel alternator system that is equipped with a one-piece regulator and rectifier, but not used on "P" series engines. Refer to Fig. OA116 for wiring schematic.

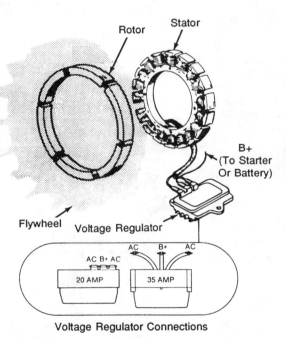

Fig. OA115—View of 20-amp and 35-amp flywheel alternator system used on "P" series engines. Refer to Fig. OA116 for wiring schematic.

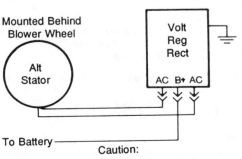

Fig. OA116—Wiring schematic for 15-, 20- and 35-amp flywheel alternator systems that are equipped with a one-piece regulator and rectifier.

NOTE: Seal at center of pump case mounting bracket retains a dry gas in pump electrical system. Be sure this seal is not damaged during disassembly for servicing.

MECHANICAL FUEL PUMP. A mechanical fuel pump (Fig. OA118) is used on some models. Pump operation may be checked by disconnecting fuel line at carburetor and slowly cranking engine by hand. Fuel should discharge from line.

CAUTION. Make certain engine is cool and there is nothing present to ignite discharged fuel.

To recondition pump, scribe a locating mark across upper and lower pump bodies and remove retaining screws. Noting location for reassembly, remove upper pump body, valve plate screw and washer, valve retainer, valves, valve springs and valve gasket. To remove lower diaphragm, hold mounting bracket and press down on diaphragm to compress spring. Turn bracket 90° to unhook diaphragm. Clean all parts thoroughly.

To reassemble, hold pump cover with diaphragm surface up. Place valve gasket and assembled valve springs and valves in cavity. Assemble valve retainer and lock in position by inserting and tightening valve retainer screw. To reassemble lower diaphragm section, hold mounting bracket and press down on diaphragm to compress spring. Turn bracket 90° to hook diaphragm. Assemble pump upper and lower bodies, but do not tighten screws. Push pump lever to its limit of travel, hold in this position and tighten the four screws. This prevents stretching diaphragm. Reinstall pump.

PULSATING DIAPHRAGM FUEL PUMP. A pulsating diaphragm-type fuel pump (Fig. OA119) is used on some models. Pump may be mounted directly to side of carburetor or at a remote mounting location.

Pump relies on a combination of crankcase pressure and spring pressure for correct operation.

Refer to Fig. OA119 for disassembly and reassembly noting air bleed hole (10) must be open for correct pump operation.

GASEOUS FUEL SYSTEMS

GASEOUS FUEL OPERATION. This section is concerned only with exclusive operation on gaseous (vapor-type) fuels such as natural gas, methane, butane, propane or mixtures

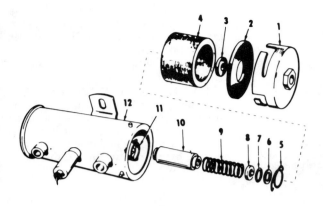

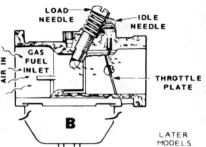

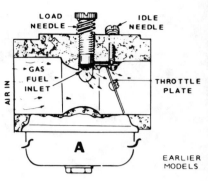

Fig. OA117—Exploded view of electric fuel pump used on some engines.

1. Cover
2. Cover gasket
3. Magnet
4. Filter element
5. Retainer spring
6. Washer
7. "O" ring
8. Cup valve
9. Plunger spring
10. Plunger
11. Plunger tube
12. Pump housing

Fig. OA120—Cross-section of carburetor designed for gaseous fuel only. A—Early style. B—Late style.

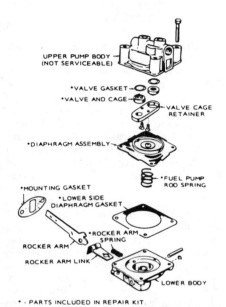

Fig. OA118—Exploded view of mechanical-type fuel pump used on some models. Refer to text for assembly information.

such as LPG. See CCK engine section for dual-fuel (gas-gasoline) operations.

Refer to Figs. OA120 or OA121 for cross-sectional view of carburetors that may be used on engines operating on gaseous fuel. Note location of adjustment screws. Adjustment of vapor fuel carburetors is essentially the same as for gasoline fueled models. Note that

idle adjustment has only a limited effect on engine performance of these engines as they normally operate at rated rpm. If carburetor is entirely out of adjustment, to such extent that the engine will not start or run, proceed as follows:

To adjust carburetor shown in Fig. OA120, turn idle adjustment and main adjustment needles inward until lightly seated. Then open idle needle from one to two turns and crank engine while opening main adjustment needle a little at a time until engine starts. As with gasoline carburetors, final adjustment is made to provide a smooth running engine at both idle speed and rated rpm.

To adjust carburetor shown in Fig. OA121, turn idle adjustment screw 2½-3½ turns out from a lightly seated position. Set main fuel adjustment knob to position shown in Fig. OA121. Run engine and adjust carburetor as needed to obtain best engine operation. Note that this carburetor was designed for use on a variety of engines, including large engines. At maximum engine speed the throttle plate should be open no more than 20° from vertical. Adjusting the throttle stop screw for excessive throttle opening may cause governor malfunction.

GASEOUS FUELS. It should be noted operation on gaseous fuels sometimes involves changes in types of fuel available for use and not all gaseous fuels have the same power potential.

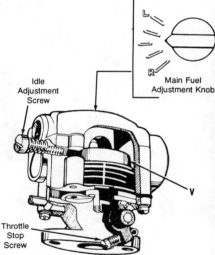

Fig. OA121—Some engines powered by gaseous fuel may be equipped with carburetor shown. Main fuel adjustment knob is located on top of carburetor. A spring-loaded valve (V) shuts off fuel and air when vacuum is zero in manifold (engine stopped).

Rating of these fuels is based on their heat output measured in Btu's per cubic foot of volume.

Butane. Butane develops about 3200 Btu/cu. ft. and is rated on a par with gasoline as a fuel. It is generally compounded with other gases for regulator use.

Propane. This gas, rated at about 2500 Btu/cu. ft., will also perform near the level of gasoline. It is also frequently

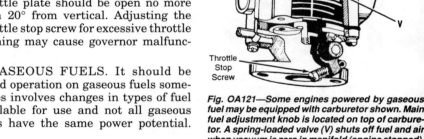

Fig. OA119—Exploded view of pulsating diaphragm fuel pump used on some models. Hole (10) must be open before reassembly.

1. Pump cover
2. Gasket
3. Reed valve
4. Valve body
5. Gasket
6. Diaphragm
7. Pump plate
8. Spring
9. Pump base
10. Air bleed hole

mixed with other gases to suit special circumstances of its use.

LPG. Liquefied Petroleum Gas (sometimes called "bottled gas") is specially compounded to meet requirements for energy (heat) output and for performance reliability in different climates. LPG is a variable proportion of butane, propane and other hydrocarbons, generally "tailor-made" for a particular requirement. As with butane and propane gases, no derating of engine is required for its use.

Natural Gas. The principal component of natural gas is methane (sometimes called marsh gas) that has a heat output of about 500 Btu/cu. ft. As delivered to users, natural gas will contain 80-95 percent methane with propane and ethane making up the difference. Heat values, based on such compounding, will range from 900 to 1200 Btu/cu. ft.

For comparison purposes, available gaseous fuels are rated by a percentage figure against pump grade regular gasoline:

FUEL COMPARISON TABLE

Gaseous Fuel	Gasoline
LPG (Butane, Propane)	98-100%
1100 Btu gas*	80-95%
850 Btu gas*	80-85%
600 Btu gas*	70-75%
450 Btu gas*	50-60%

*Check supplier for Btu rating of fuel gas used.

GAS REGULATOR. Engines that operate on gaseous fuels require a pressure regulator be installed in supply line to carburetor. Regulators used are highly sensitive demand-types, opening only when fuel is called for by vacuum at carburetor inlet. Ease of starting is dependent upon rapid cranking for high vacuum at intake manifold. Reduced or disconnected engine load during cranking helps. If manual instead of electric

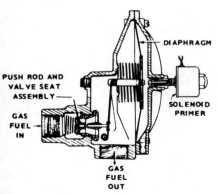

Fig. OA122—Cross-section of Algas regulator used on early vapor (butane, LP or natural gas) fuel systems. Note installation of optional solenoid-controlled primer. Refer to text for primer adjustment.

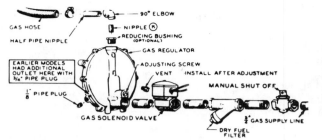

Fig. OA123—Garretson regulator with installation fittings shown in normal arrangement. Gas solenoid valve shown is optional, but may be required by safety code in some areas. Refer to text.

cranking is employed, gas used should have a rating of 800 Btu/cu. ft. or higher. Supply line to regulator should be shut off when engine is being serviced to prevent accidental starting if engine is turned over as part of test procedures. Factory furnished flexible tubing (hose) between carburetor and regulator should never be replaced by a rigid fuel line. Engine vibration must not be transmitted to regulator. Typical regulators used are shown in Figs. OA122 and OA123.

REGULATOR TESTING. For a quick operational check of regulator response, blow into vent hole in regulator cover. Hissing sound will indicate release of gas and that diaphragm is reacting to open regulator valve.

For proper operation of a gaseous fuel system, required pressure tests should be made using a "U-tube" water manometer having a minimum working range of 14 inches. A commercial model manometer, as shown in Fig. OA124, is recommended; however, a length of clear plastic tubing of about 3/8-inch inside diameter, formed into a "U" shape comparable to that shown in the figure, may be attached to a board and will serve to make pressure measurements. Pour water (add coloring if hard to see) in open end of tube so that it rises into each leg of the "U" for 7 or 8 inches, or to ZERO level if commercial (scaled) manometer is used. It should be kept in mind that pressure is read as the **difference** in fluid level in tube legs. Space between levels, high and low, measured in inches, is pressure of gas in inches of water. For conversion purposes, 1.73 inches of water is equal to one ounce of gas pressure. One inch of water lift or displacement is equal to 0.58 ounce of pressure. When testing or adjusting systems, be sure to identify unit of measure used on gas bottle gauges or in utility gas mains and convert where necessary.

To test regulator for leaking, proceed as follows:

Refer to Fig. OA123. Turn off gas supply valve.

Remove 1/8-inch pipe plug and connect manometer as shown in Fig.

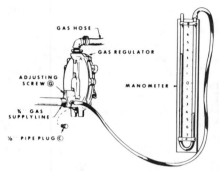

Fig. OA124—Typical connection of water column manometer to regulator. Note pressure is read as difference between tube levels expressed in inches of water. See text.

OA124. Detach carburetor gas hose from regulator outlet.

Open supply valve (plug valve shown in Fig. OA123) and quickly cover open regulator outlet with your hand. Observe manometer while alternately covering and uncovering regulator outlet. Pressure reading will be constant if regulator valve is closing properly. If manometer reading drops slightly or fluctuates each time hand is removed from outlet, turn adjustment screw (G—Fig. OA124), located just above inlet line, inward a little at a time, until reading is constant when outlet is repeatedly covered and uncovered.

If regulator does not respond to this lock-off screw adjustment and leaking persists, remove and carefully disassemble regulator body. A repair kit furnished with parts for renewal of both valve and diaphragm of regulator is available.

When regulator tests satisfactorily, close supply valve, remove manometer, bleed air from supply line and replace test-hole pip plug. Reconnect carburetor and test run engine.

IMPORTANT NOTE: Many test and leak detection procedures in general use for servicing gaseous fueled equipment specify a "soap bubble" test. Do not use to test closing of these highly sensitive demand-type regulators. Soap bubble tension alone over regulator outlet is enough to block and shut off this regulator and such a test will prove inaccurate.

REGULATOR ADJUSTMENT. Algas regulator (Fig. OA122) is nonadjustable. It operates with an inlet pressure ranging from 6 ounces to 5 psi. It is no longer furnished on production engines. The Algas regulator features an optional solenoid primer as shown in Fig. OA122 to assist in starting. Its function is to hold regulator open during cranking. One electrical lead connects to starter solenoid switch on starter side and the other lead is grounded. Adjustment, for rapid start of a cold engine, should be performed when engine is hot and regulator, fuel line and carburetor are charged with gas. To adjust, loosen lock nut that secures primer stem to regulator cover and turn primer body inward (clockwise) for richer mixture. Primer is correctly set when slightly rough running and somewhat dark exhaust occur briefly when restarting the hot engine.

When a cold engine must be started and a solenoid primer is known to be out of adjustment, make coarse preliminary adjustment as follows:

Remove carburetor hose from regulator outlet and apply temporary battery voltage across solenoid primer leads.

Then, slowly turn primer body inward (clockwise) until valve opens and gas flow can be heard.

Reconnect primer leads in normal fashion and connect gas hose to regulator. If engine starts in three seconds or less, adjustment is correct. If engine is slow to start, repeat procedure until cold engine with no gas in hose or carburetor can be rapidly started.

If engine cannot be started properly, test primer. To do so, remove primer from regulator cover and connect battery across solenoid leads while observing if primer plunger extends when power switch is on. If plunger is inoperative, check for mechanical interference or sticking in primer body and perform a continuity check to determine if there

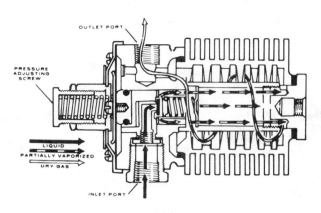

Fig. OA126—Cross-section view of vaporizer-regulator used on LP gas systems. Note change of liquid to dry vapor as it is warmed in passing from inlet to outlet. Adjust high-pressure (primary) regulator as discussed in text.

is an open circuit in windings or solenoid. Renew if defective.

Garretson regulator is shown in Fig. OA123. As a demand-type regulator, it performs no metering function in regard to gas flow; it is only open or closed. Maximum allowable inlet pressure is 8 ounces and minimum is 2 ounces. If supply line pressure exceeds 8 ounces (13.8 inches), a primary regulator should be installed in supply line to reduce working pressure. It is generally recognized that a two-stage regulator is advisable in most gas systems. An appliance-type primary regulator installed ahead of secondary (final) regulator is excellent insurance against unsafe increase of pressure, regardless of fluctuations in pressure from gas supply or source. Such primary regulators should be set to deliver controlled pressure at the same level as operating pressure of secondary regulator. Secondary regulator should be adjusted so it will close off gas flow to carburetor at supply line pressure when there is no demand. This prevents gas leaks (seepage) when engine is not running and provides maximum regulator sensitivity. Factory setting is for operation between 2 and 4 ounces (3½ to 7 inches) of pressure. If pressure in gas supply line is from 4 to 8 ounces, readjust at lockout screw as in Fig. OA125. Test of regulator shut-off by use of manometer is previously covered under REGULATOR TESTING.

PRIMARY REGULATORS. When gas source pressures range from 6 ounces to 4 pounds, a pressure-reducing primary regulator is available. Engine Model LK uses part number 148P33 that has a maximum gas flow capacity of 190 cubic feet per hour (cfh). CCK series and Models JB and NH use part number 148P23 that delivers 330 cfh. For Model JC, use number 148P34, which has a capacity of 680 cfh. These regulators deliver an outlet pressure of 11 inches (water column). These engine models, equipped with Garretson regulators in gas line to carburetor, accept

an inlet pressure of 2 to 8 ounces (3.5-13.8-inch water column).

LPG VAPORIZER. A vaporizer, sometimes referred to as a converter (converts liquid to vapor), must be used in a system designed for LPG fuel. Its function is to offset cooling by expansion of liquid petroleum gas as it vaporizes from its liquid state. Vaporizer is normally installed in the path of the warm air flow off an air-cooled engine's cooling system to provide warming effect needed.

Fig. OA126 shows a cross section of a typical vaporizer with vaporization process illustrated. Note unit also contains an adjustable pressure regulator for control of outlet gas pressure.

Adjustment procedure proposed by manufacturer recommends vaporizer-regulator be removed from LPG line and fitted to a compressed air source at its inlet port. Seventy-five pounds air pressure is adequate. Fit a pressure gauge of sufficient range to regulator outlet port and back knurled pressure adjusting screw out nearly all the way. Turn on air pressure and slowly screw adjuster down until test gauge reads 7 psi. If pressure rises after being set to specification, regulator valve or diaphragm is leaking and overhaul will be necessary.

NOTES ON GASEOUS FUEL OPERATION. Vibration and dirt contamination are major problems in vapor fuel systems. Use of flexible lines that will not transmit engine vibration or shock to regulators or controls is essential. Fuel filters and strainers, as installed or recommended by manufacturer, must be used and maintained.

Local safety codes that pertain to dispersal of exhaust fumes and engine heat, venting of regulators and fuel storage areas, and location of fuel tanks and service lines in relation to structures must be observed.

Many local codes require an electric shut-off valve in fuel line (see Fig. OA123), which is usually a solenoid-op-

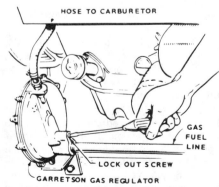

Fig. OA125—Adjustment of regulator shut-off of Garretson regulator. Regulator should be set to close gas valve when there is no demand (vacuum) from carburetor. Refer to text.

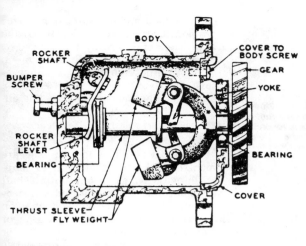

Fig. OA127—Cross-section view of Hoof governor used on older four-cylinder gasoline models (early JC). Refer to text for description of parts functions.

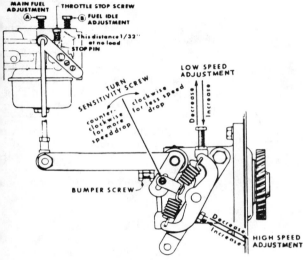

Fig. OA128—View of external linkage and adjustments for Hoof governor. Refer to text.

erated gate valve connected so it will shut off the gas supply when engine is halted. Some safety codes will accept the final regulator as an adequate shut-off valve.

Ensign regulator, though no longer furnished by manufacturer, may still be encountered on older production series engines. If a problem develops, contact local factory branch for advice.

Fire safety and electrical installation codes, NEC and local, must be meticulously observed.

Keep in mind that, when fitting gaseous system fuel line pipe assemblies, strainers or regulators, high-grade, non-drying pipe joint compound should be used on the threads. Gaseous fuels have a severe drying effect and using oil-base paint or other unsatisfactory substitutes as thread sealants must be avoided or dangerous leaks may result.

HOOF GOVERNOR

The Hoof governor is flyweight-operated cam gear driven to control engine rpm at all points of engine speed range.

Pressure, generated by centrifugal force of revolving flyweights, is exerted against thrust sleeve and bearing, shown in Fig. OA127, to impart rotary motion to governor rocker shaft through rocker shaft lever. Governor mechanism is liberally lubricated from engine crankcase and severe wear of parts is unusual. If erratic governor performance is traced to its speed sensor (flyweight mechanism), refer to Fig. OA127 and proceed as follows:

Disconnect linkages.

Unbolt governor body flange and remove governor from engine.

Entire shaft assembly with gear and front cover can be removed after backing out the one cover to body screw.

At this point, any abnormal condition should be apparent when all sludge and contaminated oil is flushed away. Further disassembly is not likely to be needed. Flyweights, pivots and limiting stops should be checked. If necessary, remove retainers and flyweight pins to disassemble governor completely. Thrust bearing and washers can be removed from thrust sleeve after removal of lock ring. After flyweight assembly

and thrust sleeve are removed from shaft and shaft is withdrawn, shaft ball bearing can be pressed from cover. Necessary renewal parts should be ordered from governor manufacturer. Check nameplate for information that may required to order parts.

ADJUSTMENTS. All preliminary adjustments should be made to fuel system. Be sure 1/32-inch (0.8 mm) gap is set between stop pin and throttle stop screw as low speed-no load setting. See Fig. OA128. Be sure governor bumper screw does not restrict governor action.

Set low speed limits first, then high speed to specifications using most accurate means available to measure engine rpm. Refer to nameplate of electric generator sets for correct speed settings. Increase or decrease spring tension at adjustment points shown in Fig. OA128 to set low and high speeds correctly.

Operate engine through entire speed range with and without load to determine need for sensitivity adjustment. Proper sensitivity adjustment should result in constant stable engine speed over a complete range of load condition with no hunting or stumbling as load varies. Deviation from rated speed should not exceed 50 rpm. When making sensitivity adjustment, note condition of adjustment screw. If serration on screw body that engage matching serration in lever slot, are badly worn so as not to hold adjustment, renewal of parts is in order. As in all governor adjustments, movement of sensitivity adjuster away from its pivot control point will decrease sensitivity.

AIR COOLING SYSTEMS

PRESSURE COOLING. Most widely used conventional cooling system on Onan air-cooled models is referred to as pressure cooling. In this system, free air is drawn by flywheel rotation into engine sheet metal housing through flywheel grille opening and is forced through cylinder cooling fins and out through a rear or side aperture.

Larger "J" series engines may be equipped with a thermostatically controlled shutter (Vernatherm) that allows engine compartment air to reach 120° F (49° C) before opening and becomes wide-open at 140° F (60° C) for full ventilation of enclosure. Opening temperature of sensing element is not adjustable. To determine if this operating element is in working order, remove two screws that retain it to mounting bracket (note slotted holes to adjust position) and test it by application of heat. Opening should begin at 120° F (49° C) and plunger should be fully extended at 140° F (60° C). Total movement should

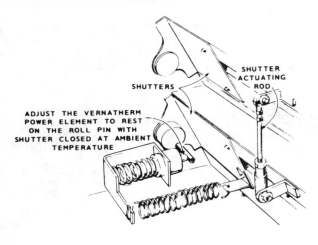

Fig. OA129—View of thermostatically controlled power shutter for pressure cooled engines. Note adjustment. Refer to text for details.

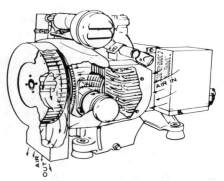

Fig. OA130—Typical cooling air flow in Vacu-Flo system used for closed compartment installation.

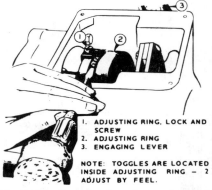

Fig. OA131—Procedure for adjustment of Rockford clutch.

1. Ring lock & screw
2. Adjuster ring
3. Clutch lever

be at least $\frac{13}{64}$ inch (5.16 mm). Reinstall so plunger, when fully withdrawn into element body, just touches roll pin as in Fig. OA129 with shutter completely closed at ambient (free air) temperature.

If shutter operation is unsatisfactory, check for a weak shutter return (closing) spring and examine nylon shutter bearings for dirt or damage. Clean and renew as necessary.

VACU-FLO COOLING. This system is designed for cooling industrial power plants that are installed in a closed compartment. Note in Fig. OA130 that flow of coolant air is drawn through engine shroud and cooling fins and forced out by flywheel blower through a vent or outside duct. Flow is in reverse direction from that of pressure-cooled engines. IMPORTANT: If flywheel or flywheel blower is renewed, be sure new part is correct for engine cooling system, whether pressure or Vacu-Flo.

Air volume requirement for proper cooling of these engines, expressed in cubic feet per minute, is specified for each engine in factory-furnished operator's manual. Dependent upon engine size, this may range from 300 to 1600

cfm. Duct and vent sizes are detailed for each model and type of cooling system.

HIGH-TEMPERATURE CUT-OFF. Some larger engine models were equipped with a high-temperature safety switch for protection from overheating. Switch is normally closed, but

opens to halt engine if compartment air temperature rises to 240° F (116° C) due to problem in cooling system caused by blockage or shutter failure to open. When engine compartment temperature drops to about 190° F (88° C), switch will automatically close and engine can be restarted.

CLUTCH

When optional Rockford clutches are furnished with these engines, an adaptor flange is fitted to engine output shaft for mounting clutch unit and a variety of housings are used dependent upon application and model of engine or clutch used. Refer to Fig. OA131 for guidance in adjustment and proceed as follows:

Remove plate from top of housing and rotate engine manually until lock screw (1—Fig. OA131) is at top of ring (2) as shown. Loosen lock screw and turn adjusting ring clockwise (as facing through clutch toward engine) until toggles cannot be locked over center. Then, turn ring in reverse direction until toggles can just be locked over center by a very firm pull on operating lever. If a new clutch plate has been installed, slip under load to knock off "fuzz" and readjust. Lubricate according to instructions on unit plate.

REDUCTION GEAR

A typical reduction gear unit is shown in Fig. OA132. Ratio of 1:4 is common in industrial applications. Lubrication calls for use of SAE 50 motor oil or SAE 90 gear oil. Refer to instructions printed on gearcase for guidance. In most cases, a total of six plugs are fitted into case for lubricant fill or level check. Plug openings to be used are de-

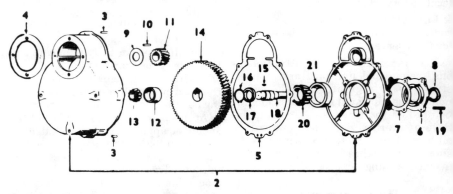

Fig. OA132—Exploded view of typical reduction gear set. See text for service details.

2. Housing & cover	7. Shims	12. Bearing cup	17. Bearing space
3. Dowel pins (2)	8. Oil seal	13. Bearing cone	18. Shaft
4. Gasket (engine)	9. Pinion washer	14. Driven gear	19. Key
5. Cover gasket	10. Pinion key	15. Gear key	20. Bearing cone
6. Bearing retainer	11. Pinion gear	16. Snap ring	21. Bearing cup

termined by positioning of gear box in relation to horizontal or vertical. It is recommended that square plug heads be cut off those plugs not to be used to fill, check or drain so as to eliminate chance of error by overfill or underfill.

All parts shown are available for renewal if needed in overhaul.

NOTE: In some installations, no shaft seal is fitted between engine crankcase and reduction gear housing. In these cases, with a common oil supply, engine oil lubricates gears and bearings of reduction gear unit and gear oil is not used. Be sure to check nameplate or operator's manual.

ONAN SPECIAL TOOLS

Following special tool list indicates Onan part number, tool name,
use and application. Refer to list of ONAN CENTRAL WAREHOUSE DIS-
TRIBUTORS as a source for these tools.

VALVE TOOLS

420-0270-VALVE SEAT
   DRIVER . . . . J Series

420-0274-CUTTER
   BLADE . . . . For 420-031
      Seat Remover

420-0310-VALVE SEAT
   STAKER . . . . . . (For Exhaust
      Valve) NH, NHA,
      NHB, NB,
      N52, T-260G

420-0311-VALVE SEAT
   REMOVER . . . . . . J Series, NH,
      HNA, NHB, NHC,
      NB, N52, T-260G

420-0349-SEAT CUTTER . All Series

420-0351-CUTTER
   BLADE . . . . For 420-0349
      Seat Cutter

420-0461-VALVE SEAT
   STAKER . . . . (For Intake
      Valve) BF, BG,
      B43, B48, P Series

420-0462-VALVE SEAT
   STAKER . . . . (For Exhaust
      Valve) BF, BG,
      B43, B48, P Series

420-0537-VALVE GUIDE
   DRIVER . . . . BF, BG, B43,
      B48, CCK, CCKA,
      CCKB, LK, LKB,
      NB, NH, NHA,
      NHB, NHC, N52,
      T-260G, J Series, P Series

420-0538-VALVE SEAT
   DRIVER . . . . NH, NHA,
      NHB, NB,
      N52, T-260G

OIL SEAL GUIDES AND DRIVERS

420-0387-BEARING
   PLATE . . . . BF, BG, B43,
      B48, CCK, CCKA,
      CCKB, LK, LKB,
      NB, NH, NHA,
      NHB, NHC, N52,
      T-260G, P Series

420-0456-BEARING
   PLATE . . . . J Series

420-0539-GEAR COVER . . . BF, BG,
      B43, B48, CCK,
      CCKA, CCKB,
      NB, NH, NHA,
      NHB, NHC, N52,
      T-260G, P Series

PULLERS

420-0533-FLYWHEEL
   PULLER . . . . BF, BG,
      B43, B48, CCK,
      CCKA, CCKB, LK,
      LKB, NB, NH,
      NHA, NHB, NHC,
      N52, T-260G,
      J Series, P Series

WRENCHES

420-0169-CARBURETOR
   ADJUSTING WRENCH . . . . BF,
      BG, B43, B48,
      CCK, CCKA, CCKB

420-0294-CARBURETOR AD-
   JUSTING WRENCH . . . . CCK,
      CCKA, CCKB, NB,
      NH, NHA, NHB,
      NHC, N52, J Series

ONAN CENTRAL PARTS DISTRIBUTORS

(Arranged Alphabetically by States)
**These firms carry extensive stocks of repair parts. Contact them for the name
of dealers in their area who will have replacement parts.**

Cummins Alabama, Inc.
Phone: (205) 841-0421
2200 Pinson Highway
Birmingham, Alabama 35201

Cummins Alabama, Inc.
Phone: (334) 456-2236
1924 N. Beltline Highway
Mobile, Alabama 36607

Cummins Alabama, Inc.
Phone: (334) 263-2594
2325 West Fairview Ave.
P.O. Box 9271
Montgomery, Alabama 36108

Cummins Northwest, Inc.
Phone: (907) 279-7594
2618 Commercial Drive
Anchorage, Alaska 99501

Cummins Southwest, Inc.
Phone: (602) 252-8021
2222 N. 23rd Drive
P.O. Box 6688 (85005)
Phoenix, Arizona 85009

Cummins Southwest, Inc.
Phone: (520) 887-7440
1912 W. Prince Road
Tucson, Arizona 85705

Cummins Mid-South, Inc.
Phone: (501) 569-5600
6600 Interstate 30
Little Rock, Arkansas 72209

Cummins West
Phone: (800) 595-5050
4801 West End Road
Arcata, California 95524

Cummins West, Inc.
Phone: (805) 325-9404
4801 East Brundage Lane
Bakersfield, California 93307

Cummins Cal-Pacific
Phone: (619) 593-3093
310 North Johnson Avenue
El Cajon, California 92020

Cummins West
Phone: (800) 595-5050
5355 N. Golden State Blvd., #110
Fresno, California 93722

Cummins Cal Pacific, Inc.
Phone: (949) 253-6000
1939 Deere Avenue, Suite A
Irvine, California 92606

Cummins Cal-Pacific
Phone: (323) 869-7442
1105 South Greenwood
Montbello, California 90640

Cummins West
Phone: (800) 595-5050
20247 Charlanne Drive
Redding, California 96002

Cummins Cal-Pacific
Phone: (909) 877-0433
3061 South Riverside
Rialto, California 92377

Cummins West, Inc.
Phone: (510) 351-6101
14775 Wicks Blvd.
San Leandro, California 94577

Cummins Cal-Pacific
Phone: (805) 644-7281
3958 Transport Street
Ventura, California 93003

Cummins West, Inc.
Phone: (916) 371-0630
2661 Evergreen Avenue
West Sacramento, California 95691

Cummins Rocky Mountain, Inc.
Phone: (303) 286-7697
5100 East 58th Avenue
Commerce City, Colorado 80022

Cummins Rocky Mountain, Inc.
Phone: (970) 259-7470
13595 County Road 213
Durango, Colorado 81301

Cummins Rocky Mountain, Inc.
Phone: (970) 242-5776
2380 U.S. Hwy. 6 & 50
Grand Junction, Colorado 81501

Cummins Metropower
Phone: (860) 529-7474
914 Cromwell
Rocky Hill, Connecticut 06067

Cummins Southeastern Power, Inc.
Phone: (941) 337-1211
2671 Edison Avenue
Ft. Myers, Florida 33916

Cummins Southeastern Power, Inc.
Phone: (305) 821-4200
9900 N.W. 77th Court
Hialeah Gardens, Florida 33016

Cummins Southeastern Power, Inc.
Phone: (904) 355-3437
2060 West 21st Street
Jacksonville, Florida 32209

Cummins Southeastern Power, Inc.
Phone: (352) 861-1122
321 S.W. 52nd Avenue
Ocala, Florida 34474

Cummins Southeastern Power, Inc.
Phone: (407) 298-2080
4820 Orange Blossom Trail
Orlando, Florida 32810

Cummins Southeastern Power, Inc.
Phone: (813) 626-1101
5910 East Hillsborough Ave.
Tampa, Florida 33680

Cummins South, Inc.
Phone: (912) 888-6210
1915 W. Oakridge Drive
Albany, Georgia 31707

Cummins South, Inc.
Phone: (706) 722-8825
1255 New Savanah Road
Augusta, Georgia 30901

Cummins Onan South Power Systems
Phone: (404) 763-0233
5125 Highway 85
College Park, Georgia 30349

Cummins South, Inc.
Phone: (912) 232-5565
8 Interchange Court
Savannah, Georgia 31401

Cummins Hawaii
Phone: (808) 682-8110
91-30 Kalaeloa Blvd
Kapolei, Hawaii 96707

GenPlus
Phone: (208) 336-5000
2851 Federal Way
Boise, Idaho 83705

GenPlus
Phone: (208) 234-1661
14299 Highway 3 West
Pocatello, Idaho 83201

Cummins Mid-States Power, Inc.
Phone: (309) 452-4454
U.S. 51N & I-55
P.O. Box 348
Bloomington-Normal, Illinois 61761

Gateway Industrial Power
Phone: (618) 394-0123
One Extra Mile Drive
Caseyville, Illinois 62234

Cummins/Onan
Phone: (708) 563-7070
8745 West 82nd Place
Justice, Illinois 60458

Cummins Great Plains Diesel
Phone: (309) 787-4300
7820 42nd St. West
Rock Island, Illinois 61204

Onan-Indiana
Phone: (219) 262-4611
23900 County Road 6
Elkhart, Indiana 46514

Cummins Cumberland
Phone: (812) 867-4400
7901 Highway 41 North
Evansville, Indiana 47711

Mid-States Power & Refrigeration
Phone: (317) 240-1967
4301 W. Morris St.
Indianapolis, Indiana 46241

Cummins Great Plains Diesel
Phone: (319) 366-7537
625 33rd Avenue S.W.
Cedar Rapids, Iowa 52406

Midwestern Power Products
Phone: (515) 264-1650
5194 NE 17th St.
Des Moines, Iowa 50313

Cummins Mid-America, Inc.
Phone: (913) 462-3945
1880 S. Range
Colby, Kansas 67701

Cummins Mid-America, Inc.
Phone: (316) 275-2277
2008 West Mary
Garden City, Kansas 67846

Cummins Mid-America, Inc.
Phone: (316) 838-0875
5101 North Broadway
Wichita, Kansas 67219

Cummins Cumberland
Phone: (606) 436-5718
Highway 15 South
Hazard, Kentucky 41701

Cummins Cumberland
Phone: (502) 491-4263
9820 Bluegrass Parkway
Louisville, Kentucky 40299

Cummins Mid-South, Inc.
Phone: (504) 631-0576
Highway 90E, P.O. Box 1229
Amelia, Louisiana 70340

Cummins Mid-South, Inc.
Phone: (504) 468-3535
110 E. Airline Highway
Kenner, Louisiana 70062

Cummins Northeast, Inc.
Phone: (207) 883-8155
10 Gibson Road
Scarborough, Maine 04074

Cummins Power Systems
Phone: (410) 590-8700
1907 Park 100 Drive
Glen Burnie, Maryland 21061

Cummins Northeast, Inc.
Phone: (781) 329-1750
100 Allied Drive
Dedham, Massachusetts 02026

Cummins Northeast, Inc.
Phone: (413) 737-2659
177 Rocus St.
Springfield, Massachusetts 01104

Standby Power, Inc.
Phone: (616) 281-2211
7580 Expressway Drive, S.W.
Grand Rapids, Michigan 49548

Standby Power, Inc.
Phone: (313) 538-0200
12130 Dixie
Redford, Michigan 48239

Standby Power, Inc.
Phone: (517) 249-1122
3850 Carver
Saginaw, Michigan 48503

Cummins North Central
Phone: (651) 636-1000
2690 Cleveland Ave. N.
St. Paul, Minnesota 55113

Cummins North Central
Phone: (218) 628-3641
3115 Truck Center Drive
Duluth, Minnesota 55807

Cummins Mid-South, Inc.
Phone: (601) 932-7016
P.O. Box 54224 (39208)
Jackson, Mississippi 39218

Cummins Mid-America, Inc.
Phone: (417) 623-1661
3507 East 20th Street
Joplin, Missouri 64801

Cummins Mid-America, Inc.
Phone: (816) 414-8200
8201 NE Parvin Road
Kansas City, Missouri 64161

Cummins Mid-America, Inc.
Phone: (417) 862-0777
3637 East Kearney
Springfield, Missouri 65803

Cummins Power, Inc.
Phone: (406) 245-4194
5151 Midland Road
Billings, Montana 59101

Cummins Power, Inc.
Phone: (406) 452-8561
415 Vaughn Road
Great Falls, Montana 59404

Cummins Northwest, Inc.
Phone: (406) 728-1300
4950 North Reserve Street
Missoula, Montana 59802

Cummins Great Plains Diesel
Phone: (308) 234-1994
515 Central Avenue
Kearney, Nebraska 68847

Cummins Great Plains Diesel
Phone: (402) 551-7678
5515 Center Street
Omaha, Nebraska 68106

GenPlus
Phone: (702) 738-6405
5370 East Idaho Street
Elko, Nevada 89801

GenPlus
Phone: (702) 399-2339
2750 Losee Road (89030)
P.O. Box 3997
North Las Vegas, Nevada 89036

GenPlus
Phone: (702) 331-4983
150 Glendale Avenue
Sparks, Nevada 89431

Cummins Metropower, Inc.
Phone: (201) 491-0100
41-85 Deramus Ave.
Newark, New Jersey 07105

Cummins Southwest, Inc.
Phone: (505) 247-2441
1921 Broadway Northeast
Albuquerque, New Mexico 87102

Cummins Southwest, Inc.
Phone: (505) 327-7331
1101 N. Troy King Road
Farmington, New Mexico 87401

Cummins Northeast
Phone (518) 459-1710
101 Railroad Ave.
Albany, New York 12205

Cummins Metropower, Inc.
Phone: (718) 892-2400
890 Zerega Avenue
Bronx, New York 10473

Cummins Northeast
Phone (315) 437-2751
6193 Eastern Ave.
Syracuse, New York 13211

Cummins Northeast
Phone (716) 631-3211
480 Lawrence Bell Drive
Williamsville, New York 14221

Cummins Atlantic
Phone: (704) 588-1240
11101 Nations Ford Road
Charlotte, North Carolina 28224

Cummins Atlantic
Phone: (704) 596-7690
3700 North I-85
Charlotte, North Carolina 28206

Cummins Atlantic
Phone: (336) 275-4531
513 Preddy Blvd.
Greensboro, North Carolina 27406

Cummins Atlantic, Inc.
Phone: (919) 237-9111
1514 Cargill Avenue
Wilson, North Carolina 27894

Cummins North Central
Phone: (701) 852-3585
1501 20th Avenue S.E.
Minot, North Dakota 58701

Cummins North Central
Phone: (701) 282-2466
4050 West Main Avenue
Fargo, North Dakota 58103

Cummins North Central
Phone: (701) 775-8197
4728 Gateway Drive
Grand Forks, North Dakota 58201

Cummins Interstate Power
Phone: (513) 563-6670
10470 Evendale Drive
Cincinnati, Ohio 45241

Cummins Interstate Power
Phone: (440) 439-6800
7585 Northfield Road
Cleveland, Ohio 44146

Cummins Interstate Power
Phone: (440) 771-1000
4000 Lyman Drive
Hilliard, Ohio 43026

Cummins Interstate Power
Phone: (330) 534-1935
7145 Masury Road
Hubbard, Ohio 44425

Cummins Interstate Power
Phone: (419) 893-8711
801 Illinois Avenue
Maumee, Ohio 43537

Cummins Interstate Power
Phone: (330) 878-5511
777 S. Wooster Ave.
Strasburg, Ohio 44680

Southern Plains Power, Inc.
Phone: (405) 946-4481
5800 W. Reno
Oklahoma City, Oklahoma 73127

Southern Plains Power, Inc.
Phone: (918) 234-3240
16525 East Skelly Drive
Tulsa, Oklahoma 74116

Cummins Northwest, Inc.
Phone: (541) 389-1900
3500 North Highway 97
Bend, Oregon 97701

Cummins Northwest, Inc.
Phone: (541) 687-0000
91201 Coburg Industrial Parkway
P.O. Box 10887
Coburg, Oregon 97401

Cummins Northwest, Inc.
Phone: (541) 779-0151
4045 Crater Lake Highway
Medford, Oregon 97504

Cummins Northwest, Inc.
Phone: (541) 276-2561
223 S.W. 23rd St.
Pendleton, Oregon 97801

Cummins Northwest, Inc.
Phone: (503) 289-0900
4711 N. Basin Avenue
Portland, Oregon 97217

Cummins Power System
Phone: (215) 785-6005
2727 Ford Rd.
Bristol, Pennsylvania 19007

Cummins Power System
Phone: (717) 564-1344
1549 Bobali Drive
Harrisburg, Pennsylvania 17104

Cummins Power System
Phone: (412) 820-8300
3 Alpha Drive
Pittsburgh, Pennsylvania 15238

Cummins Atlantic, Inc.
Phone: (803) 799-2410
1233 Bluff Road
Columbia, South Carolina 29201

Cummins Atlantic, Inc.
Phone: (843) 851-9819
231 Farmington Road
Summerville, South Carolina 29483

Cummins Great Plains Diesel
Phone: (605) 336-1715
701 East 54th Street North
Sioux Falls, South Dakota 57104

Cummins South
Phone: (423) 629-1447
1509 East 26th St.
Chattanooga, Tennessee 37407

Cummins Cumberland, Inc.
Phone: (423) 523-0446
1211 Ault Road
Knoxville, Tennessee 37914

Cummins Mid-South, Inc.
Phone: (901) 345-7424
1784 East Brooks Road
Memphis, Tennessee 38116

Cummins Cumberland, Inc.
Phone: (615) 366-4341
706 Spence Lane
Nashville, Tennessee 37217

Southern Plains Power
Phone: (806) 373-3793
5224 Interstate 40
Expressway East
P.O. Box 31570
Amarillo, Texas 79120

Southern Plains Power
Phone: (817) 640-6801
600 N. Watson Road
Arlington, Texas 76004

Southern Plains Power
Phone: (512) 289-0700
1302 Corn Products Road
P.O. Box 48
Corpus Christi, Texas 78403

Southern Plains Power
Phone: (214) 631-6400
3707 Irving Boulevard
Dallas, Texas 75247

Cummins Southwest, Inc.
Phone: (915) 852-4200
14333 Gateway West
El Paso, Texas 79927

Southern Plains Power
Phone: (817) 624-2107
3250 North Freeway
Fort Worth, Texas 76111

Southern Plains Power
Phone: (713) 675-7421
4750 Homestead Road
Houston, Texas 77251

Southern Plains Power
Phone: (713) 956-0020
1155 West Loop North
Houston, Texas 77055

Southern Plains Power
Phone: (214) 321-5555
2615 Big Town Road
Mesquite, Texas 75150

Southern Plains Power
Phone: (512) 655-5420
6226 Pan Am Expressway
North San Antonio, Texas 78218

Southern Plains Power
Phone: (915) 332-9121
1210 South Grandview
P.O. Box 633
Odessa, Texas 79760

GenPlus
Phone: (801) 355-6500
1033 South 400 W.
P.O. Box 25428 (84125)
Salt Lake City, Utah 84101

GenPlus
Phone: (801) 789-5732
1435 East 355 South
P.O. Box 903
Vernal, Utah 84078

Cummins Atlantic
Phone: (757) 458-4848
3729 Holland Blvd.
Chesapeake, Virginia 23323

Cummins Atlantic
Phone: (540) 966-3169
2987 Simmons Drive
Cloverdale, Virginia 24077(

Cummins Atlantic
Phone: (804) 232-7891
3900 Deepwater Terminal Road
Richmond, Virginia 23234

Cummins Northwest, Inc.
Phone: (360) 748-8841
326 NW Maryland
Chehalis, Washington 98532

Cummins Northwest, Inc.
Phone: (425) 235-3400
811 Southwest Grady Way
Renton, Washington 98055

Cummins Northwest, Inc.
Phone: (509) 455-4411
11134 W. Westbow Blvd.
Spokane, Washington 99204

Cummins Northwest, Inc.
Phone: (253) 922-2191
3701 Pacific Highway E
Tacoma, Washington 98424

Cummins Northwest, Inc.
Phone: (509) 248-9033
1905 East Central Avenue
Yakima, Washington 98901

Cummins Cumberland, Inc.
Phone: (304) 367-0196
145 Middletown Road
Fairmont, West Virginia 26554

Cummins Cumberland, Inc.
Phone: (304) 744-6373
3100 MacCorkle Ave., S.W.
South Charleston, West Virginia 25303

Cummins Great Lakes
Phone: (920) 337-9750
875 Lawrence Drive
Depere, Wisconsin 54115

Cummins Rocky Mountain
Phone: (307) 682-9611
2700 Highway 14 & 16
North Gillette, Wyoming 82717

GenPlus
Phone: (307) 362-5168
2000 Foothill Blvd.
Rock Springs, Wyoming 82901

CANADA

Cummins Alberta
Phone: (800) 461-3801
4887 35th St. SE
Calgary, Alberta T2B 3H6

Cummins Alberta
Phone: (403) 455-2151
11751-181 Street
Edmonton, Alberta T5S 2K5

Cummins Alberta
Phone: (604) 882-5000
18452-96th Avenue
Surrey, British Columbia V4N 3O8

Pryme Power Division
Cummins Mid-Canada Ltd.
Phone: (204) 632-5470
489 Oak Point Road
Winnipeg, Manitoba R3C 3R1

Cummins Eastern
Phone: (506) 451-1929
P.O. Box 1178 Station A
Fredericton, New Brunswick E3B 5C8

Cummins Eastern
Phone: (709) 747-0176
122 Clyde Avenue
Mount Pearl, Newfoundland A1N 4S3

Cummins Eastern
Phone: (902) 468-7938
50 Simmonds Drive
Dartmouth, Nova Scotia B3B 1R3

Cummins Mid-Canada
Phone: (807) 548-1941
P.O. Box 8
Kenora, Ontario P9N 3X1

Cummins Ontario, Inc.
Phone: (905) 795-0050
7175 Pacific Circle
Mississauga, Ontario L5T 2A5

Cummins Ontario, Inc.
Phone: (613) 736-1146
3189 Swanson Crescent
Ottawa, Ontario K1G 3W5

Onan Eastern Canada
Phone: (514) 631-5000
580 Lepine
Dorval, Quebec H9P 1G2

Onan Eastern Canada
Phone: (418) 653-6411
5185 Rue John Molson
Quebec City, Quebec G1X 3X4

Cummins Eastern
Phone: (819) 825-0993
1025 rue L'Echo
Val D'Or, Quebec J9P 4P6

Pryme Power Division
Cummins Mid-Canada Ltd.
Phone: (306) 933-4022
3001 Faithful Avenue
Saskatoon, Saskatchewan S7K 4R4

ROBIN
(WISCONSIN ROBIN)

Robin America, Inc.
940 Lively Boulevard
Wood Dale, Illinois 60191

Model	No. Cyls.	Bore	Stroke	Displacement	Power Rating
EY21W	2	75 mm (2.95 in.)	70 mm (2.76 in.)	618 cc (37.7 cu. in.)	12.5 kW (16.8 hp)
EY25W	1	72 mm (2.83 in.)	62 mm (2.44 in.)	251 cc (15.4 cu. in.)	4.9 kW (6.5 hp)
EY27W	1	74 mm (2.91 in.)	62 mm (2.44 in.)	265 cc (16.3 cu. in.)	5.6 kW (7.5 hp)
EY35, W1-340	1	78 mm (3.07 in.)	70 mm (2.76 in.)	334 cc (20.4 cu. in.)	6.7 kW (9 hp)
EY40, W1-390	1	84 mm (3.30 in.)	70 mm (2.76 in.)	388 cc (23.7 cu. in.)	8.2 kW (11 hp)
EY44W	1	90 mm (3.54 in.)	68 mm (2.68 in.)	432 cc (26.4 cu. in.)	7.8 kW (10.5 hp)

All models are four-stroke, air-cooled gasoline engines with a horizontal crankshaft. Model EY21W has two cylinders while all other models are single-cylinder engines. All models are splash-lubricated by an oil dipper attached to the connecting rod cap.

The crankshaft on Model EY21W is supported by a ball bearing at the front end and a roller bearing at the rear. The crankshaft on all other models is supported by ball bearings at both ends. The connecting rod of Model EY44W is equipped with renewable insert type bearings, while the connecting rod of all other models rides directly on the crankpin.

Later models with EY prefix do not have W suffix in model designation, for instance, Model EY27W designation was changed to Model EY25 in later versions. The engine model and specification numbers are located on the nameplate on flywheel shroud. The serial number is stamped on the crankcase. Always furnish engine model, specification and serial numbers when ordering parts.

MAINTENANCE

LUBRICATION. Oil dippers attached to connecting rod cap provide splash lubrication on all models. Oil dippers on single-cylinder models pick up oil directly from crankcase. Oil dipper on two-cylinder models picks up oil from a trough located directly under the crankpins. A small capacity oil pump located inside the crankcase supplies oil to the trough to maintain a constant oil level.

Check engine oil level daily and maintain oil level at full mark on dipstick.

Engine oil should meet or exceed latest API service classification.

For single-cylinder models, use SAE 30 oil when temperature is above 40° F (4° C), SAE 20 oil when temperature is between 15° F (-9° C) and 40° F(4° C), and SAE 10W-30 oil when temperature is below 15° F (-9° C).

For two-cylinder models, use SAE 30 oil when temperature is above 60° F (16° C), SAE 10W-30 oil when temperature is between 0° F (-18° C) and 60° F (16° C), and SAE 5W-20 oil when temperature is below 0° F (-18° C).

Oil should be changed after every 50 hours of operation. Crankcase capacity is 0.76 liter (1.6 pt.) for EY25W and EY27W models, 1.14 liters (2.4 pt.) for Model EY44W, 2.48 liters (5.25 pt.) for Model EY21W, and 1.2 liters (2.5 pt.) for Models EY35, EY40, W1-340 and W1-390.

SPARK PLUG. Recommended spark plug is a Champion L86 or equivalent for single-cylinder models and Champion J8 or equivalent for two-cylinder models. Specified spark plug electrode gap is 0.6 mm (0.024 in.).

CARBURETOR. All models are equipped with a Mikuni float type carburetor. A side draft style carburetor (Fig. R501) is used on single-cylinder models and a downdraft style carburetor (Fig. R502) is used on two-cylinder models.

For initial carburetor adjustment, open idle mixture screw 1 5/8 turns on Model EY25W, 1 1/2 turns on Models EY27W, EY40 and W1-390, 1 3/4 turns on Model EY44W, 1 1/4 turns on Model EY21W, and one turn on Models EY35 and W1-340.

Main fuel mixture is controlled by a fixed main jet.

Make final adjustment with engine at normal operating temperature and running. Run engine with no load at idle speed of 1000 rpm for Model EY21W, 1200 rpm for Model EY44W, 1250 rpm for Models EY25W and EY27W, and 1150 rpm for Models EY35, EY40, W1-340 and W1-390. Adjust idle mixture screw to obtain smoothest idle speed and acceleration.

To check float level on Models EY25W, EY27W and EY44W, position carburetor as shown in Fig. R503. Measure distance between body flange and free end of float. Distance should be 23.11-24.89 mm (0.910-0.980 in.) on Models EY25W and EY27W and 21.39-23.39 mm (0.842-0.921 in.) on Model EY44W. Adjust float by bending float lever tang that contacts fuel inlet valve.

To check float level on Model EY21W, refer to Fig. R504 and note that float setting will be within specified range if distance from top of float lever to bot-

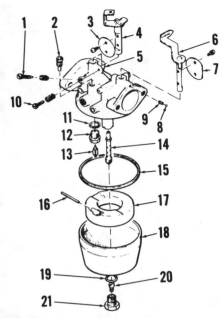

Fig. R501—Exploded view of typical Mikuni float-type carburetor used on all models except Model EY21W. Main jet (20) is located on nozzle stanchion of carburetor body on some models.

1. Idle mixture screw
2. Idle jet
3. Throttle plate
4. Throttle shaft
5. Body
6. Choke shaft
7. Choke plate
8. Choke detent ball
9. Detent spring
10. Idle speed screw
11. Gasket
12. Fuel inlet valve seat
13. Fuel inlet valve
14. Main nozzle
15. Gasket
16. Float pin
17. Float
18. Fuel bowl
19. Gasket
20. Main fuel jet
21. Jet holder

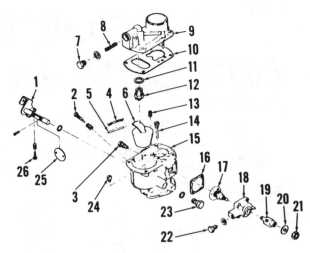

Fig. R502—Exploded view of Mikuni float-type carburetor used on Model EY21W.

1. Throttle shaft
2. Idle mixture screw
3. Idle jet
4. Float pin retainer
5. Float pin
6. Float
7. Plug
8. Fuel screen
9. Upper body
10. Gasket
11. Gasket
12. Fuel inlet valve
13. Idle air jet
14. Main nozzle
15. Lower body
16. Gasket
17. Starting valve
18. Valve housing
19. Starting lever
20. Washer
21. Nut
22. Plug
23. Starting jet
24. Main fuel jet
25. Throttle plate
26. Idle speed screw

tom of float is 30.56 mm (1¹³⁄₆₄ in.) as shown. If necessary, bend float lever to obtain correct setting. Float lever must be parallel with float in area where fuel inlet valve contacts float lever.

Float level on Models EY35, EY40, W1-340 and W1-390 is not adjustable.

Mikuni downdraft carburetor used on Model EY21W has a special starting fuel valve instead of a choke. Fuel from the fuel bowl in lower body (15—Fig. R502) is metered through the starting jet (23) and is mixed with air from inside vent. Mixture then flows into the starting valve assembly where additional air from the main air intake maintains a correct air-fuel ratio for easy starting.

GOVERNOR. The mechanical flyweight governor used on all models is mounted on and operated by the camshaft gear (Fig. R505 and R506). Engine speed is controlled by tension on the governor spring.

Before attempting to adjust governed speed on single-cylinder models, synchronize governor linkage by loosening clamp nut (16—Fig. R505) and turning governor lever (15) counterclockwise until carburetor throttle plate is in wide-open position. Insert a screw-

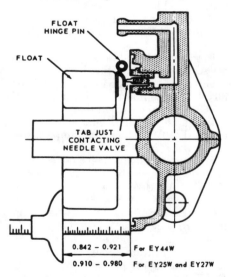

VIEW LOOKING DOWN
Carburetor Setting on Manifold Flange

FLOAT HINGE PIN

FLOAT

TAB JUST CONTACTING NEEDLE VALVE

0.842 – 0.921 For EY44W
0.910 – 0.980 For EY25W and EY27W

Fig. R503—With fuel bowl removed, stand carburetor on manifold flange and measure float setting as shown for all models except Model EY21W.

driver in slot in end of governor lever shaft (1) and rotate shaft counterclockwise as far as possible. Tighten governor clamp nut.

No governor linkage adjustment is possible on two-cylinder models, as a slotted hole in the governor lever link (Fig. R506) fits on flat sides of governor shaft end.

To adjust all models for a particular loaded rpm, loosen the wing nut (9—Fig. R505) or lock knob (Fig. R506). Start the engine and adjust the stop screw at control lever to obtain correct no-load speed. If engine is to operate at

Fig. R504—Float setting on Model EY21W will be correct if distance from top of float lever to bottom of float is 30.56 mm (1-13/64 in.). Refer to text.

a fixed speed, tighten the wing nut or lock knob. For variable speed operation, do not tighten the wing nut or lock knob.

For the following loaded engine speeds, adjust to the following no-load speeds:

MODEL EY21W

Loaded Rpm	No-load Rpm
1800	2000
2000	2200
2200	2390
2400	2580
2600	2770
2800	2960
3000	3150
3200	3350
3400	3730
3600	3920

MODEL EY25W

Loaded Rpm	No-load Rpm
1800	2330
2000	2445

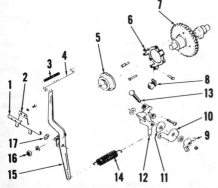

Fig. R505—Exploded view of typical mechanical governor and linkage used on all models except Model EY21W.

1. Governor lever shaft
2. Yoke
3. Link spring
4. Carburetor link
5. Thrust sleeve
6. Governor plate
7. Camshaft assy.
8. Flyweights (3 used)
9. Wing nut
10. Stop plate
11. Wave washer
12. Control lever
13. Speed stop screw
14. Governor spring
15. Governor lever
16. Clamp nut
17. Retaining spring

Loaded Rpm	No-load Rpm
2200	2595
2400	2745
2600	2900
2800	3065
3000	3230
3200	3400
3400	3580
3600	3765

MODEL EY27W

Loaded Rpm	No-load Rpm
1800	2210
2000	2375
2200	2500
2400	2660
2600	2850
2800	3020
3000	3210
3200	3385
3400	3590
3600	3760

MODELS EY35 & W1-340

Loaded Rpm	No-load Rpm
2000	2270
2200	2460
2400	2650
2600	2850
2800	3035
3000	3225
3200	3415
3400	3605
3600	3795

Governor spring is attached to outermost hole on speed control lever (12—Fig. R505) and middle hole on governor lever (15).

MODELS EY40 & W1-390

Loaded Rpm	No-load Rpm
2000	2250
2200	2445
2400	2640
2600	2835
2800	3030
3000	3225
3200	3420
3400	3615
3600	3810

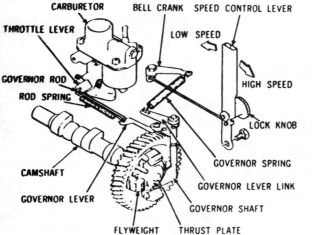

Fig. R506—View showing mechanical governor and linkage used on Model EY21W.

Governor spring is attached to outermost hole on speed control lever (12—Fig. R505) and innermost hole on governor lever (15).

MODEL EY44W

Loaded Rpm	No-load Rpm
1800	2200
2000	2365
2200	2510
2400	2675
2600	2850
2800	3025
3000	3250
3200	3420
3400	3605
3600	3770

IGNITION SYSTEM. Single-cylinder engines are equipped with a magneto type-ignition system, while two-cylinder engines are equipped with a battery type ignition system. Models EY35, EY40, W1-340 and W1-390 may be equipped with a magneto-type ignition systems that has a breakerless, solid-state trigger system.

MAGNETO IGNITION. **Models With Breaker Points.** The breaker points and condenser are located beneath the flywheel. Initial point gap setting is 0.35 mm (0.014 in.). See Fig. R507.

To check and adjust ignition timing, disconnect lead from shut-off switch. Connect one lead of a continuity light to disconnected lead and ground remaining lead from light to engine. Slowly turn flywheel in normal direction of rotation until light goes out. Immediately stop turning flywheel and check location of timing marks. Timing marks should be aligned as shown in Fig. R508. If timing mark (M) on flywheel is below timing mark (D) on crankcase, breaker point gap is too wide. If mark (M) is above mark (D), breaker point gap is too narrow. Carefully measure distance necessary to align the two marks, then remove flywheel and breaker point cover. Changing gap 0.025 mm (0.001 in.) will change timing mark (M) position approximately 3.2 mm (1/8 in.). Reassemble and tighten flywheel nut to 60-64 N•m (44-47 ft.-lb.) on Models EY25W and EY27W, 92-98 N•m (68-72 ft.-lb.) on Model EY44W, or 80-100 N•m (59-74 ft.-lb.) on Models EY35, EY40, W1-340 and W1-390.

Breakerless Ignition System. Some EY35, EY40, W1-340 and W1-390 models may be equipped with a breakerless magneto ignition system (see Fig. R509 for wiring schematic). No adjustment or maintenance is required.

To check exciter coil, connect an ohmmeter to exciter coil lead and engine ground. Ohmmeter should indicate

0.78-1.16 ohms if engine is not equipped with an alternator, 1.76-2.64 if engine is equipped with 3.3 amp alternator, or 3.6-5.4 ohms if engine is equipped with 12.5 amp alternator.

To check the pulser coil, connect an ohmmeter to pulser coil lead and engine ground. Ohmmeter should indicate 52.8-79.2 ohms.

To check ignition module, connect an ohmmeter or circuit tester as indicated in chart in Fig. R510 to module leads. Do not use a tester that uses high voltage as module may be damaged.

BATTERY IGNITION. A 12-volt battery ignition system is standard on Model EY21W engines. Breaker points and condenser are located in ignition timer on top of engine (Fig. R511).

A pinion on engine camshaft drives the ignition timer. Two-lobe breaker cam rotates at half crankshaft speed and is equipped with a centrifugal spark advance mechanism. Initial point gap is 0.35 mm (0.014 in.).

Static timing is 8° BTDC. The centrifugal advance mechanism starts at 600 rpm and continues to 18° BTDC at 2000 rpm and over.

To check and adjust ignition timing, first make certain that points are properly adjusted. Disconnect primary wire connector at ignition timer and connect one lead of continuity light to wire leading from timer. Connect remaining light lead to ground on engine (Fig. R511). Slowly rotate crankshaft in normal direction of engine rotation until timing hole (8° BTDC static timing mark) in dust plate is aligned with timing pointer on blower housing as shown in Fig. R512. Continuity light should just go out when timing marks are aligned. If light goes out before or after timing marks line up, align timing marks and loosen timer advance arm screw (Fig. R511). Rotate timer body slowly until breaker points are just beginning to open and light just goes out. Tighten clamp screw. Slowly rotate crankshaft in normal direction of rotation and recheck to make certain continuity light goes out just as timing marks are aligned.

VALVE ADJUSTMENT. Valve tappet gap (cold) should be 0.13-0.17 mm (0.005-0.007 in.) on Models EY35, EY40, W1-340 and W1-390, and 0.16-0.20 mm (0.006-0.008 in.) on all other models. To check tappet gap, remove the breather plate from side of the crankcase. Rotate flywheel until piston is at top dead center on the compression stroke. Insert proper size feeler gauge between valve stem and tappet.

To increase clearance, grind off end of valve stem. To reduce clearance, grind the valve seat deeper or renew valve and/or valve tappet.

REPAIRS

TIGHTENING TORQUE. Recommended tightening torque specifications are as follows:

Camshaft nut:
  EY21W . . . . 50-61 N•m
      (37-45 ft.-lb.)
Connecting rod:
  EY25W, EY27W . . . . 20-24 N•m
      (15-18 ft.-lb.)
  All other models . . . . 25-30 N•m
      (18-22 ft.-lb.)
Crankcase cover:
  EY21W . . . . 13-16 N•m
      (115-142 in.-lb.)
  All other models . . . . 17-19 N•m
      (150-168 in.-lb.)

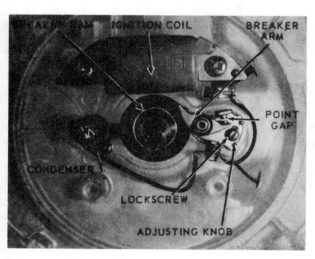

Fig. R507—View showing flywheel magneto used on Models EY25W and EY27W. Magneto on Models EY44W and Models EY35, EY40, W1-340 and W1-390 equipped with breaker points is similar. Flywheel and breaker cover are removed.

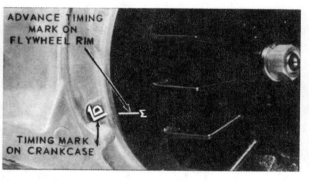

Fig. R508—View showing 23° BTDC timing mark (M) on flywheel aligned with timing mark (D) on crankcase. On Models EY35, EY40, W1-340 and W1-390, the crankcase timing mark is identified by a "M." Refer to text for timing procedure.

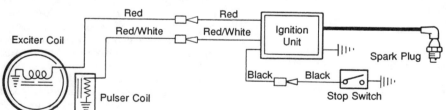

Fig. R509—Wiring schematic of breakerless ignition system used on some Model EY35, EY40, W1-340 and W1-390 engines.

Connect (−) Terminal of Tester	Connect (+) Terminal of Tester			
	Red	Red/White	Black	Core
Red		ON	ON	ON
Red/White	OFF		ON	ON
Black	OFF	OFF		OFF
Core	OFF	ON	ON	ON

Fig. R510—The ignition module on Models EY35, EY40, W1-340 and W1-390 may be tested using an ohmmeter or circuit tester connected as indicated in chart.

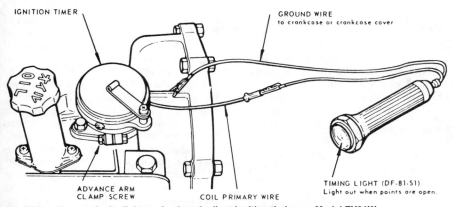

Fig. R511—Use continuity light to check and adjust ignition timing on Model EY21W.

Cylinder:
EY21W............... 31-35 N•m
(23-26 ft.-lb.)
EY44W............... 34-39 N•m
(25-29 ft.-lb.)
Cylinder head:
EY21W............... 45-49 N•m
(33-36 ft.-lb.)
EY25W, EY27W........ 34-37 N•m
(25-27 ft.-lb.)
EY44W............... 49-50 N•m
(36-37 ft.-lb.)
EY35, EY40,
W1-340, W1-390 ...... 34-42 N•m
(25-31 ft.-lb.)
Engine base:
EY21W............... 30-37 N•m
(22-27 ft.-lb.)
Flywheel nut:
EY21W............... 60-70 N•m
(81-95 ft.-lb.)
EY25W, EY27W........ 60-64 N•m
(81-95 ft.-lb.)
EY44W............... 92-98 N•m
(68-72 ft.-lb.)
EY35, EY40,
W1-340, W1-390 ..... 80-100 N•m
(59-74 ft.-lb.)
Main bearing housing:
EY21W............... 13-16 N•m
(115-142 in.-lb.)
Spark plug:
EY21W............... 30-39 N•m
(22-29 ft.-lb.)

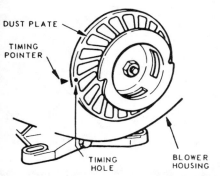

Fig. R512—View showing timing hole (8° BTDC static timing mark) in dust plate aligned with timing pointer on blower housing.

EY25W, EY27W........ 33-37 N•m
(24-27 ft.-lb.)
EY44W............... 24-30 N•m
(18-22 ft.-lb.)
EY35, EY40,
W1-340, W1-390 ...... 26-30 N•m
(19-22 ft.-lb.)

CYLINDER HEAD. On Model EY21W, note locations of cylinder head screws during removal so they can be returned to original location.

Clean carbon deposits from the combustion chamber being careful not to damage the gasket sealing area. Inspect the head for cracks or other damage. Check the cylinder head for distortion using a straightedge and feeler gauge. On all models, renew cylinder head if gasket surface is warped in excess of 0.15 mm (0.006 in.).

Always use a new head gasket when installing cylinder head. Tighten cylinder head screws or nuts evenly and in stages until reaching final specified torque.

VALVE SYSTEM. To remove valves, first remove cylinder head and breather/tappet chamber cover. Disengage the spring retainers from the valve springs. Remove the valves and springs from the crankcase.

On all models, valve face and seat angles should be 45°. Standard seat width is 1.2-1.6 mm (0.047-0.062 in.).

Valve stem diameter dimensions are listed in the table below.

Valve Stem O.D
EY21W—
Intake .... (7.93-7.95 mm)
(0.3118-0.3128 in.)
Exhaust............ 7.89-7.91 mm
(0.3106-0.3114 in.)
EY25W, EY27W—
Intake & exhaust.... (6.93-6.96 mm)
(0.273-0.274 in.)
EY44W—
Intake .... (7.95-7.98 mm)
(0.310-0.311 in.)

Exhaust............ 7.87-7.90 mm
(0.310-0.311 in.)
EY35, EY40, W1-340,
W1-390—
Intake .... (7.945-7.970 mm)
(0.3128-0.3138 in.)
Exhaust............ 7.91-7.93 mm
(0.3114-0.3122 in.)
Valve guide inside diameter specifications are listed in the table below.

Valve Guide I.D.
EY21W—
Intake & exhaust.... (8.00-8.04 mm)
(0.3150-0.3165 in.)

EY25W, EY27W—
Intake & exhaust.... (7.00-7.04 mm)
(0.2755-0.2770 in.)

EY44W—
Intake & exhaust.... (8.00-8.03 mm)
(0.315-0.316 in.)

EY35, EY40, W1-340,
W1-390—
Intake & exhaust.. (8.000-8.036 mm)
(0.3150-0.3164 in.)
Refer to the table below for valve stem-to-guide clearance specifications.

Valve Stem-to-Guide Clearance
EY21W—
Intake .... (0.056-0.119 mm)
(0.0022-0.0047 in.)
Exhaust.......... 0.091-0.150 mm
(0.0036-0.0059 in.)
EY25W, EY27W—
Intake & exhaust .. (0.038-0.101 mm)
(0.0015-0.0040 in.)
EY44W—
Intake .... (0.025-0.076 mm)
(0.0010-0.0030 in.)
Exhaust.......... 0.101-0.152 mm
(0.0040-0.0060 in.)
EY35, EY40, W1-340,
W1-390—
Intake .... (0.030-0.091 mm)
(0.0012-0.0036 in.)
Exhaust.......... 0.070-0.126 mm
(0.0028-0.0050 in.)

Valve guides are renewable on Models EY25W, EY27W, EY35, EY40, W1-340 and W1-390. On all other models, cylinder head must be renewed if guides are worn excessively.

Valve spring free length should be 34.50-36.00 mm (1.358-1.417 in.) on Models EY25W and EY27W, and 44.45-46.00 mm (1.750-1.811 in.) on all other models.

PISTON, PIN AND RINGS. On Models EY21W and EY44W, piston can be serviced by removing cylinder. On all other models, piston and connecting rod must be serviced as a unit after removing cylinder head and crankcase cover. Be sure to remove carbon and ring ridge (if present) from top of cylinder before removing the piston.

The piston of Model EY44W is equipped with four piston rings (Fig. R513) while the piston on all other models is equipped with three rings (Figs. R514 and R515).

Specified ring end gap is 0.05-0.30 mm (0.002-0.012 in.) for Model EY21W, 0.05-0.25 mm (0.002-0.010 in.) for Model EY25W, 0.20-0.40 mm (0.008-0.016 in.) for Models EY27W, EY35, EY40, W1-340 and W1-390.

Insert each ring into its piston ring groove and measure side clearance between the ring and ring land with a feeler gauge. Renew piston rings and/or piston if ring side clearance exceeds 0.15 mm (0.006 in.).

Refer to following table for specified piston clearance:

Model	Piston Clearance
EY21W	0.048-0.108 mm
	(0.0019-0.0042 in.)
EY25W	0.060-0.099 mm
	(0.0024-0.0039 in.)
EY27W	0.072-0.111 mm
	(0.0028-0.0044 in.)
EY35, W1-340	0.048-0.108 mm
	(0.0019-0.0042 in.)
EY40, W1-390	0.048-0.111 mm
	(0.0019-0.0044 in.)
EY44W	0.155-0.177 mm
	(0.0061-0.0070 in.)

Measure piston diameter at bottom of skirt perpendicular to piston pin. Standard piston diameter specifications are listed in the table below.

Standard Piston Diameter

EY21W	74.92-74.95 mm
	(2.9496-2.9508 in.)
EY25W	71.920-71.940 mm
	(2.8315-2.83230 in.)
EY27W	73.908-73.928 mm
	(2.9098-2.9105 in.)
EY35, W1-340	77.911-77.951 mm
	(3.0674-3.0689 in.)
EY40, W1-390	83.911-83.951 mm
	(3.3035-3.3052 in.)
EY44W	89.87-89.89 mm
	(3.538-3.539 in.)

Standard and oversize piston and rings are available for service.

Refer to following table for specified piston pin diameter:

Model	Piston Pin Diameter
EY21W	17.986-17.994 mm
	(0.7081-0.7084 in.)
EY25W, EY27W	15.987-15.995 mm
	(0.6294-0.6297 in.)
EY35, EY40, EY44W, W1-340, W1-390	19.991-20.000 mm
	(0.7870-0.7874 in.)

Piston pin clearance in piston should be 0.011 mm (0.0004 in.) tight to 0.011 mm (0.0004 in.) loose. Maximum clearance is 0.060 mm (0.0024 in.) loose.

On Model EY21W, install piston so "V1" on piston crown is towards cooling blower end of engine. Make certain match marks (cast dots) on connecting rods and caps are together. Note location of deep relief on rod and oil dipper as shown in Fig. R516. Tighten connecting rod cap screws to 25-30 N•m (18-22 ft.-lb.).

On Models EY25W and EY27W, make certain match marks (cast ribs) on rod and cap are together as shown in Fig. R517. Install the piston and rod so oil dipper offset is towards flywheel if engine is level during operation or towards crankcase cover if engine is tilted towards the pto end. Use a new lockplate and tighten connecting rod cap screws to 20-24 N•m (15-18 ft.-lb.).

On Model EY44W, make certain match marks (cast ribs) on rod and cap are together as shown in Fig. R518. Install the piston and rod so the oil dipper offset is towards flywheel if engine is level during operation or towards crankcase cover if engine is tilted towards the pto end. Use a new lockplate and tighten connecting rod cap screws to 25-30 N•m (18-22 ft.-lb.).

On Models EY35, EY40, W1-340 and W1-390, make certain match marks (cast ribs) on rod and cap are together as shown in Fig. R519. On early models with single-prong oil dipper, install the piston and rod so the oil dipper offset is towards crankcase cover. On later models, the oil dipper has two prongs and piston may be installed in either direction. Use a new lockplate and tighten

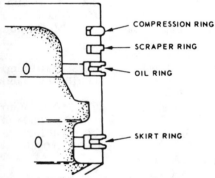

Fig. R513—Install piston rings as shown on Model EY44W.

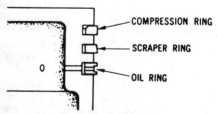

Fig. R514—Install piston rings as shown on Models EY21W, EY25W and EY27W.

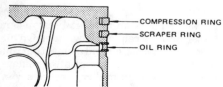

Fig. R515—Piston rings on Models EY35, EY40, W1-340 and W1-390 should be installed on piston as shown.

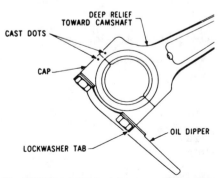

Fig. R516—Install connecting rods and rod caps with cast dot (match marks) together on Model EY21W.

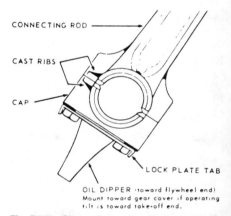

Fig. R517—Connecting rod and cap must be installed with cast ribs (match marks) together on Models EY25W and EY27W.

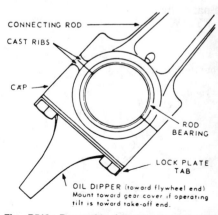

Fig. R518—Renewable insert-type connecting rod bearings are used on Model EY44W. Cast ribs (match marks) on connecting rod and cap must be installed together.

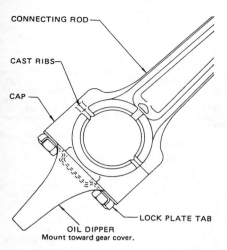

CONNECTING ROD

CAST RIBS

CAP

OIL DIPPER
Mount toward gear cover.

LOCK PLATE TAB

Fig. R519—On Models EY35, EY40, W1-340 and W1-390, install rod cap on rod so ribs are adjacent. If equipped with single-prong oil dipper, install piston and rod so oil dipper offset is toward crankcase cover.

connecting rod cap screws to 25-30 N•m (18-22 ft.-lb.).

CONNECTING ROD. Refer to appropriate following section to service connecting rod.

Model EY21W. Connecting rods ride directly on the crankpin. Specified connecting rod clearance on crankpin is 0.05-0.10 mm (0.002-0.004 in.) with a maximum clearance of 0.2 mm (0.008 in.). Specified rod side clearance is 0.20-0.50 mm (0.008-0.020 in.) with a maximum clearance of 1.0 mm (0.039 in.).

Specified piston pin clearance in rod is 0.026-0.046 mm (0.0010-0.0018 in.) with a maximum clearance of 0.120 mm (0.0047 in.).

An undersize connecting rod is available to fit a reground crankshaft.

Models EY25W And EY27W. Connecting rod rides directly on the crankpin. Specified connecting rod clearance on crankpin is 0.040-0.066 mm (0.0016-0.0026 in.) with a maximum clearance of 0.2 mm (0.008 in.). Specified rod side clearance is 0.10-0.30 mm (0.004-0.012 in.) with a maximum clearance of 1.0 mm (0.039 in.).

Specified piston pin clearance in rod is 0.021-0.040 mm (0.0008-0.0016 in.) with a maximum clearance of 0.12 mm (0.005 in.).

An undersize connecting rod is available to fit a reground crankshaft.

Model EY44W. Connecting rod is fitted with renewable insert-type bearings. Specified connecting rod clearance on crankpin is 0.040-0.107 mm (0.0016-0.0042 in.) with a maximum clearance of 0.2 mm (0.008 in.). Specified rod side clearance is 0.20-0.50 mm (0.008-0.020 in.) with a maximum clearance of 1.0 mm (0.039 in.).

Specified piston pin clearance in rod is 0.025-0.047 mm (0.0010-0.0018 in.) with a maximum clearance of 0.12 mm (0.005 in.).

An undersize connecting rod bearing is available to fit a reground crankshaft.

Models EY35, EY40, W1-340 And W1-390. Connecting rod rides directly on the crankpin. Specified connecting rod clearance on crankpin is 0.070-0.102 mm (0.0028-0.0040 in.). Specified rod side clearance is 0.10-0.40 mm (0.004-0.016 in.) with a maximum clearance of 1.0 mm (0.039 in.).

Specified piston pin clearance in rod is 0.020-0.042 mm (0.0008-0.0016 in.) with a maximum clearance of 0.12 mm (0.005 in.).

An undersize connecting rod is available to fit a reground crankshaft.

Install connecting rod as outlined in PISTON, PIN AND RINGS section.

CYLINDER. The cylinder is removable on Models EY21W and EY44W. On all other models, the cylinder and crankcase are one piece.

If cylinder bore is scored, or out-of-round more than 0.08 mm (0.003 in.), or tapered more than 0.15 mm (0.006 in.), the cylinder should be bored to next larger oversize for which piston and rings are available.

Refer to following table for standard cylinder bore diameter:

Model	Standard Cylinder Bore Diameter
EY21W	75.001-75.030 mm
	(2.9528-2.9539 in.)
EY25W	72.000-72.019 mm
	(2.8346-2.8354 in.)
EY27W	74.000-74.019 mm
	(2.9134-2.9141 in.)
EY35, W1-340	78.000-78.019 mm
	(3.0701-3.0716 in.)
EY40, W1-390	84.000-84.019 mm
	(3.3071-3.3078 in.)
EY44W	90.035-90.057 mm
	(3.5447-3.5455 in.)

When installing cylinder on Models EY21W and EY44W, tighten the cylinder retaining nuts to 31-35 N•m (23-26 ft.-lb.) on Model EY21W and 34-39 N•m (25-29 ft.-lb.) on Model EY44W.

CRANKSHAFT AND MAIN BEARINGS. The crankshaft on Models EY25W, EY27W, EY35, EY40, EY44W, W1-340 and W1-390 is supported at each end by ball bearings (see Figs. R520 and R521).

The crankshaft on Model EY21W is supported by a ball bearing (15—Fig. R522) at the front and by a roller bearing (58) at the rear.

On all models, ball bearings are a press fit on the crankshaft and should

be renewed if any indication of roughness, noise or excessive wear is found.

Refer to following table for specified crankpin journal diameter:

Model	Crankpin Journal Diameter
EY21W	35.00-35.15 mm
	(1.378-1.384 in.)
EY25W, EY27W	27.947-27.960 mm
	(1.1002-1.1008 in.)
EY44W	34.920-34.934 mm
	(1.3748-1.3754 in.)
EY35, EY40, W1-340, W1-390	33.920-33.930 mm
	(1.3354-1.3358 in.)

Renew or regrind the crankshaft if crankpin is scored or worn more than 0.150 mm (0.0059 in.) on all models. Be sure timing marks on the crankshaft and camshaft gears are aligned during installation as shown in Fig. R523.

Crankshaft end play for Model EY21W should be 0.05-0.25 mm (0.002-0.010 in.). End play is controlled by the condition of front main ball bearing (15—Fig. R522). If end play is excessive, renew front bearing.

Crankshaft end play on Models EY25W and EY27W should be 0.0-0.2 mm (0.000-0.008 in.). End play is controlled by an adjusting collar (28—Fig. R520). With crankcase cover removed, proceed as follows to determine correct length of adjusting collar: Refer to Fig. R524 and measure distance (A) between machined surface of crankcase face and end of crankshaft gear. Measure distance (B) between machined surface of crankcase cover and end of main bearing. Compressed thickness of gasket (C) is 0.15 mm (0.006 in.). Select adjusting collar that is 0.0-0.2 mm (0.000-0.008 in.) less in length than total of A, B and C. Install adjusting collar on crankshaft with recessed side toward crankshaft gear. After assembly, check crankshaft end play.

Crankshaft end play on Model EY44W and Models EY35, EY40, W1-340 and W1-390 with a balancer is controlled by an adjusting collar (34—Fig. R521). With crankcase cover removed, proceed as follows to determine correct length of adjusting collar: Refer to Fig. R525 and measure distance (A) between machined surface of crankcase face and face of balancer drive gear. Measure distance (B) between machined surface of crankcase cover and end of main bearing. Compressed thickness of gasket (C) is 0.20 mm (0.008 in.). Select adjusting collar that is 0.0-0.2 mm (0.000-0.008 in.) less in length than total of B plus C, minus distance A. Install adjusting collar on crankshaft with recessed side toward

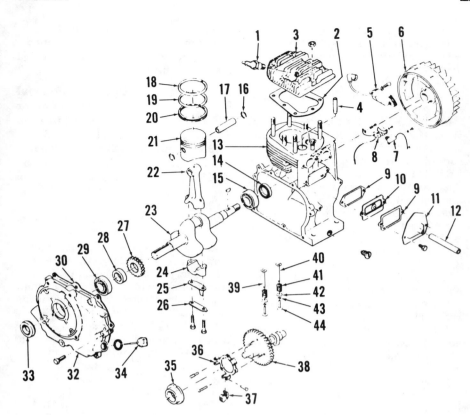

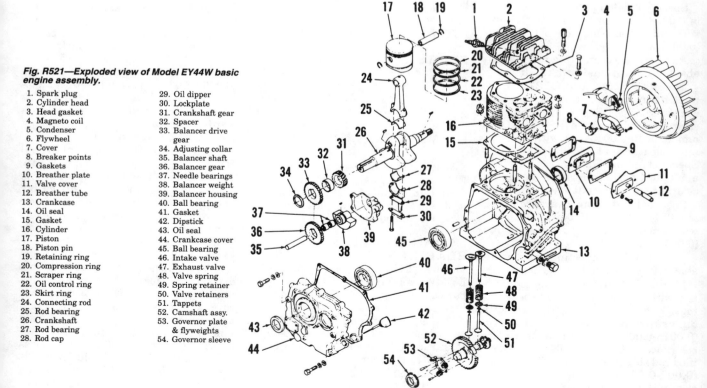

Fig. R520—Exploded view of Model EY25W and EY27W basic engine assembly. Models EY35, EY40, W1-340 and W1-390 are similar. Balancer (35 through 39—Fig. R521 may be used on some EY35, EY40, W1-340 and W1-390 engines. On Models EY35, EY40, W1-340 and W1-390, component (28) is a spacer. A shim used to adjust crankshaft end play is located between spacer (28) and bearing (29).

1. Spark plug
2. Head gasket
3. Cylinder head
4. Valve guides
5. Magneto coil
6. Flywheel
7. Condenser
8. Breaker points
9. Gaskets
10. Breather plate
11. Valve cover
12. Breather tube
13. Crankcase
14. Oil seal
15. Ball bearing
16. Ball bearing
17. Piston pin
18. Compression ring
19. Scraper ring
20. Oil control ring
21. Piston
22. Connecting rod
23. Crankshaft
24. Rod cap
25. Oil dipper
26. Lockplate
27. Crankshaft gear
28. Adjusting collar/ spacer
29. Ball bearing
30. Gasket
32. Crankcase cover
33. Oil seal
34. Dipstick
35. Governor sleeve
36. Governor plate
37. Flyweights
38. Camshaft assy.
39. Intake valve
40. Exhaust valve
41. Valve spring
42. Spring retainer
43. Valve retainers
44. Tappets

Fig. R521—Exploded view of Model EY44W basic engine assembly.

1. Spark plug
2. Cylinder head
3. Head gasket
4. Magneto coil
5. Condenser
6. Flywheel
7. Cover
8. Breaker points
9. Gaskets
10. Breather plate
11. Valve cover
12. Breather tube
13. Crankcase
14. Oil seal
15. Gasket
16. Cylinder
17. Piston
18. Piston pin
19. Retaining ring
20. Compression ring
21. Scraper ring
22. Oil control ring
23. Skirt ring
24. Connecting rod
25. Rod bearing
26. Crankshaft
27. Rod bearing
28. Rod cap
29. Oil dipper
30. Lockplate
31. Crankshaft gear
32. Spacer
33. Balancer drive gear
34. Adjusting collar
35. Balancer shaft
36. Balancer gear
37. Needle bearings
38. Balancer weight
39. Balancer housing
40. Ball bearing
41. Gasket
42. Dipstick
43. Oil seal
44. Crankcase cover
45. Ball bearing
46. Intake valve
47. Exhaust valve
48. Valve spring
49. Spring retainer
50. Valve retainers
51. Tappets
52. Camshaft assy.
53. Governor plate & flyweights
54. Governor sleeve

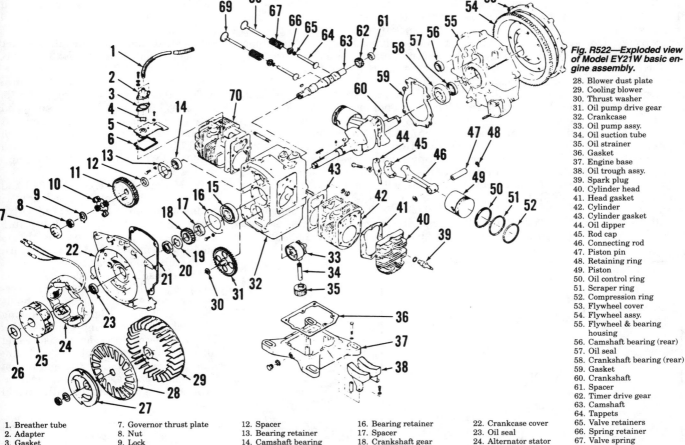

Fig. R522—Exploded view of Model EY21W basic engine assembly.

28. Blower dust plate
29. Cooling blower
30. Thrust washer
31. Oil pump drive gear
32. Crankcase
33. Oil pump assy.
34. Oil suction tube
35. Oil strainer
36. Gasket
37. Engine base
38. Oil trough assy.
39. Spark plug
40. Cylinder head
41. Head gasket
42. Cylinder
43. Cylinder gasket
44. Oil dipper
45. Rod cap
46. Connecting rod
47. Piston pin
48. Retaining ring
49. Piston
50. Oil control ring
51. Scraper ring
52. Compression ring
53. Flywheel cover
54. Flywheel assy.
55. Flywheel & bearing housing
56. Camshaft bearing (rear)
57. Oil seal
58. Crankshaft bearing (rear)
59. Gasket
60. Crankshaft
61. Spacer
62. Timer drive gear
63. Camshaft
64. Tappets
65. Valve retainers
66. Spring retainer
67. Valve spring
68. Exhaust valve
69. Intake valve
70. Cylinder & head assy.

1. Breather tube	7. Governor thrust plate
2. Adapter	8. Nut
3. Gasket	9. Lock
4. Breather valve	10. Governor plate & flyweights
5. Valve cover	11. Camshaft gear
6. Gasket	

12. Spacer	16. Bearing retainer
13. Bearing retainer	17. Spacer
14. Camshaft bearing (front)	18. Crankshaft gear
15. Crankshaft bearing (front)	19. Lock
	20. Nut
	21. Gasket

22. Crankcase cover	
23. Oil seal	
24. Alternator stator	
25. Rotor	
26. Spacer	
27. Pulley	

balancer drive gear. After assembly, check crankshaft end play.

Crankshaft end play on Models EY35, EY40, W1-340 and W1-390 not equipped with a balancer should be 0.0-0.2 mm (0.001-0.008 in.). End play is controlled by a shim located between spacer (28—Fig. R520) and bearing (29). With crankcase cover removed, proceed as follows to determine correct thickness of shim: Refer to Fig. R526 and measure distance (A) between machined surface of crankcase face and

end of crankshaft spacer. Measure distance (B) between machined surface of crankcase cover and end of main bearing. Compressed thickness of gasket (C) is 0.20 mm (0.008 in.). Select shim that is 0.0-0.2 mm (0.000-0.008 in.) less in length that total of A, B and C. Install shim on crankshaft with recessed side toward spacer. After assembly, check crankshaft end play.

CAMSHAFT. Model EY21W. The camshaft on Model EY21W rides in ball bearings at both ends. To remove camshaft, remove blower housing, pulley (27—Fig. R522), dust plate (28), blower (29), spacer (26), rotor (25), stator (24) and crankcase cover (22). Release the valve springs and move the tappets away from camshaft. Unbolt and remove fuel pump and ignition timer. Re-

Fig. R523—View of typical timing marks on crankshaft and camshaft gears on single-cylinder models.

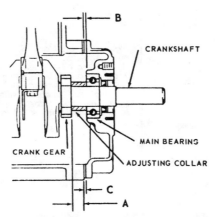

Fig. R524—On Models EY25W and EY27W, crankshaft end play is controlled by an adjusting collar. Refer to text for adjustment procedure.

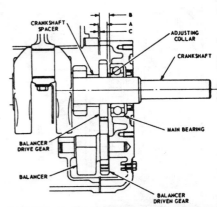

Fig. R525—On Model EY44W and Models EY35, EY40, W1-340 and W1-390 with a balancer, crankshaft end play is controlled by an adjusting collar. Refer to text for adjustment procedure.

move governor sleeve (7), nut (8) and lock (9). Use a suitable puller to remove camshaft gear (11), Woodruff key and spacer (12). Unbolt retainer (13) and withdraw camshaft assembly.

Check camshaft bearings (14 and 56) for excessive wear or other damage and renew as needed. If the valve tappets are removed they must be reinstalled in their original positions.

When installing the camshaft, make certain the punch-marked tooth on crankshaft gear is between the two punch-marked teeth on camshaft gear. Tighten camshaft gear retaining nut (8) to 50-61 N•m (37-45 ft.-lb.) and secure with lock tab.

All Models Except EY21W. On all models except EY21W, the camshaft rides directly in bores in crankcase and crankcase cover. When removing camshaft, position the engine so the valve tappets will not fall out. If the tappets are removed, they should be marked so they can be returned to their original positions.

Specified camshaft journal diameter for both ends on Models EY25W and EY27W without gear reduction is 14.957-14.968 mm (0.5888-0.5893 in.). On Models EY25W and EY27W equipped with gear reduction, specified camshaft journal diameter is 29.988-29.997 mm (1.1806-1.1810 in.) at pto end and 19.988-19.997 mm (0.7869-0.7873 in.) at flywheel end.

Specified camshaft journal diameter on Model EY44W is 34.986-34.997 mm (1.3773-1.3778 in.) at gear end and 24.988-24.997 mm (0.9838-0.9841 in.) at flywheel end.

Specified camshaft journal diameter for both ends on Models EY35, EY40, W1-340 and W1-390 without gear reduction is 16.973-16.984 mm (0.6682-0.6687 in.). On Models EY35, EY40, W1-340 and W1-390 equipped with gear reduction, specified camshaft journal diameter is 34.986-34.997 mm (1.3774-1.3778 in.) at pto end and 24.988-24.997 mm (0.9838-0.9841 in.) at flywheel end.

On Models EY35, EY40, W1-340 and W1-390, specified intake lobe height is 35.90-36.10 mm (1.413-1.421 in.) with a wear limit of 35.75 mm (1.407 in.). Specified exhaust lobe height is 35.40-35.60 mm (1.394-1.402 in.) with a wear limit of 35.25 mm (1.388 in.).

The camshaft on Model EY44W is equipped with an automatic compression release. At cranking speed it holds the exhaust valve slightly open during the first part of the compression stroke. This reduces compression pressure and allows easier cranking of engine. As engine rpm increases, centrifugal action overcomes compression release mechanism and engine operates with normal compression.

BALANCER. Model EY44W and some Model EY35, EY40, W1-340 and W1-390 engines are equipped with an engine balancer. The balancer is driven by a gear on the crankshaft and rotates in opposite direction of crankshaft. Balancer components are not serviced separately. However, unit can be disassembled for cleaning and inspection. Refer to Fig. R521 for exploded view.

When installing crankcase cover on models equipped with balancer, time

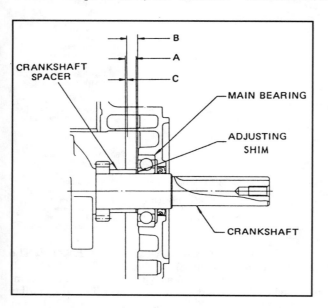

Fig. R526—On Models EY35, EY40, W1-340 and W1-390 not equipped with a balancer, crankshaft end play is controlled by a shim. Refer to text for adjustment procedure.

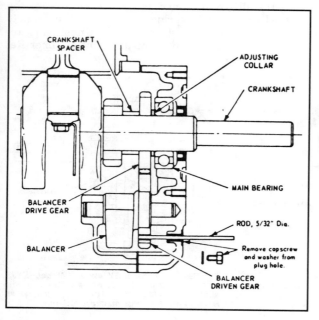

Fig. R527—On Model EY44W and Models EY35, EY40, W1-340 and W1-390 with a balancer, the balancer driven gear is held in position by a 5/32-inch rod when installing crankcase cover for proper balancer timing. Refer to text.

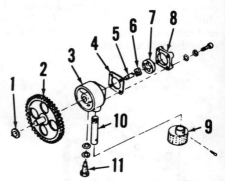

Fig. R528—Exploded view of oil pump used on Model EY21W. Shaft (5), rotor (6), stator (7) and housing (8) are serviced only as an assembly.

1. Thrust washer
2. Pump drive gear
3. Adapter
4. Gasket
5. Shaft
6. Rotor
7. Stator
8. Housing
9. Oil strainer
10. Oil intake pipe
11. Lockscrew

the balancer driven gear (36) to the drive gear (33) by rotating crankshaft until piston is at top dead center. Refer to Fig. R527, remove cap screw and washer from crankcase cover and insert a $\frac{5}{32}$ inch rod through hole in crankcase cover and into hole in driven gear. Carefully install crankcase cover and balancer assembly allowing balancer gears to mesh. Tighten crankcase cover screws to 17-19 N•m (150-168 in.-lb.) and remove timing rod. Install cap screw and washer.

OIL PUMP. Model EY21W is equipped with an oil pump that transfers oil from sump to oil trough. To remove oil pump, remove blower housing, blower and crankcase cover. Withdraw oil pump gear and shaft (2—Fig. R528) with thrust washer (1). Unbolt and remove engine base, loosen pump adapter lockscrew (11) and remove oil pump assembly from inside crankcase. Remove the four screws and separate pump from adapter (3). Shaft (5), rotor (6), stator (7) and housing (8) are serviced only as an assembly.

When assembling the pump, use a new gasket (4) and make certain the shaft (5), rotor (6) and stator (7) turn freely when screws are tightened securely.

ROBIN
(WISCONSIN ROBIN)

Robin America, Inc.
940 Lively Boulevard
Wood Dale, Illinois 60191

Model	No. Cyls.	Bore	Stroke	Displacement	Power Rating
EY28, W1-280	1	75 mm (2.95 in.)	62 mm (2.44 in.)	273 cc (16.66 cu. in.)	5.6 kW (7.5 hp)

Model EY28 or W1-280 is a four-stroke, air-cooled, single-cylinder gasoline engine with a horizontal crankshaft. The engine is splash-lubricated. The engine model and specification numbers are located on the nameplate on flywheel shroud. The serial number is stamped on the crankcase base. Always furnish engine model, specification and serial numbers when ordering parts.

MAINTENANCE

LUBRICATION. Check engine oil level daily and maintain oil level at full mark on dipstick.

Engine oil should meet or exceed latest API service classification. Use SAE 30 oil when temperature is above 40° F (4° C), SAE 20 oil when temperature is between 15° F (-9° C) and 40° F (4° C), and SAE 10W-30 oil when temperature is below 15°e F (-9° C).

Oil should be changed after every 50 hours of operation. Crankcase capacity is 0.85 liter (1.5 pt.).

SPARK PLUG. Recommended spark plug is a NGK B6HS or equivalent. Specified spark plug electrode gap is 0.6-0.7 mm (0.024-0.028 in.). Tighten spark plug to 23-27 N•m (17-20 ft.-lb.).

CARBURETOR. The engine is equipped with a Mikuni float type carburetor. Refer to Fig. R601 for exploded view of carburetor. Carburetor has a fixed high-speed jet.

Initial adjustment of low speed mixture screw (8) is 1¼ turns open from a lightly seated position. Make final carburetor adjustment with engine at normal operating temperature and running. Adjust low speed mixture screw to obtain smoothest idle operation and acceleration.

Adjust idle speed screw to obtain an idle speed of 1200 rpm at normal operating temperature.

Remove the fuel bowl (17—Fig. R601) for access to internal components. Remove the float (16), fuel inlet valve (11), main jet (14) and nozzle (13). Unscrew idle mixture screw (8).

Clean all parts and fuel passages with carburetor cleaning solvent and compressed air. Replace parts that are worn or damaged.

To check or adjust float level, remove fuel bowl and place carburetor body on end (on manifold flange) so float pin is in vertical position. Position the float so the float arm just contacts fuel inlet valve.

NOTE: Needle valve (11—Fig. R601) is spring-loaded. Float tab should just contact needle valve pin but should not compress spring.

Measure float setting as shown in Fig. R602. Dimension "A" should be 13.0-15.0 mm (0.51-0.59 in.). Carefully

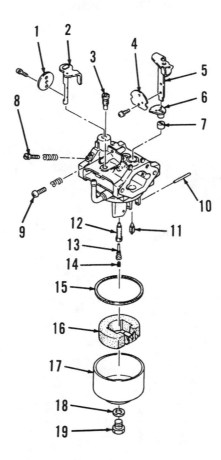

Fig. R601—Exploded view of carburetor.

1. Throttle plate
2. Throttle shaft
3. Idle mixture jet
4. Choke plate
5. Choke shaft
6. Detent plate
7. Bushing
8. Idle mixture screw
9. Idle speed screw
10. Pin
11. Fuel inlet valve
12. Main nozzle
13. Nozzle
14. Main jet
15. Gasket
16. Float
17. Fuel bowl
18. Gasket
19. Plug

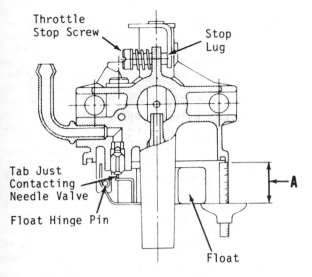

Fig. R602—Float setting (A) should be 13.0-15.0 mm (0.51-0.59 in.).

bend tab on float arm to obtain correct setting.

GOVERNOR. The engine is equipped with a centrifugal flyweight type governor. To adjust external governor linkage, loosen clamp screw on governor lever (see Fig. R603). Move governor lever so throttle valve in carburetor is wide open. Hold lever in this position and rotate governor shaft clockwise as far as possible. Tighten clamp screw.

Changing the attaching point of the governor spring in the holes in the speed control lever (Fig. R604) will vary the engine speed. Two different governor springs are used to obtain desired engine operating range. Refer to Fig.

R605 and note differences between spring used to obtain governed engine speeds below 3400 rpm and spring used for governed engine speeds of 3400 rpm and above. Fine tuning the governed engine speed by varying the governor spring tension is possible by turning adjusting screw on speed control bracket shown in Fig. R604.

IGNITION SYSTEM. The engine is equipped with a breakerless, solid-state ignition system. There is no scheduled maintenance. Specified air gap between ignition coil and flywheel is 0.3-0.5 mm (0.012-0.020 in.).

VALVE ADJUSTMENT. Valve tappet gap (cold) should be 0.08-0.12 mm (0.003-0.005 in.). To check tappet gap, remove breather cover. Rotate flywheel to position piston at top dead center on compression stroke (both valves closed). Measure clearance between end of valve and tappet stem with a feeler gauge.

To increase clearance, grind off end of valve stem. To reduce clearance, grind

the valve seat deeper or renew the valve and/or valve tappet.

REPAIRS

TIGHTENING TORQUE. Recommended tightening torque specifications are as follows:

Connecting rod........... 17-20 N•m
(150-177 in.-lb.)
Crankcase cover .... 17-19 N•m
(150-168 in.-lb.)
Cylinder head .... 22-26 N•m
(16-19 ft.-lb.)
Flywheel nut .... 60-65 N•m
(44-48 ft.-lb.)
Spark plug.............. 23-27 N•m
(17-20 ft.-lb.)

CYLINDER HEAD. Remove the cylinder head and discard the head gasket. Clean combustion deposits from the combustion chamber being careful not to damage the gasket sealing area.

Inspect the head for damage. Check the head gasket sealing surface for distortion. On all models, renew cylinder head if gasket surface is warped in excess of 0.15 mm (0.006 in.).

Always use a new head gasket when installing cylinder head. Tighten cylinder head bolts or nuts evenly and in stages until reaching final torque of 22-26 N•m (16-19 ft.-lb.).

VALVE SYSTEM. To remove valves, first remove the cylinder head, intake manifold, muffler and breather cover. Disengage the valve retainer (26—Fig. R606) from valve stem and withdraw the valve and valve spring.

On all models, valve face and seat angles should be 45°. Standard seat width is 1.2-1.5 mm (0.047-0.059 in.). Maximum allowable seat width is 2.5 mm (0.098 in.).

Valve stem-to-guide clearance should be 0.025-0.062 mm (0.0010-0.0024 in.) for intake valve and 0.056-0.100 mm

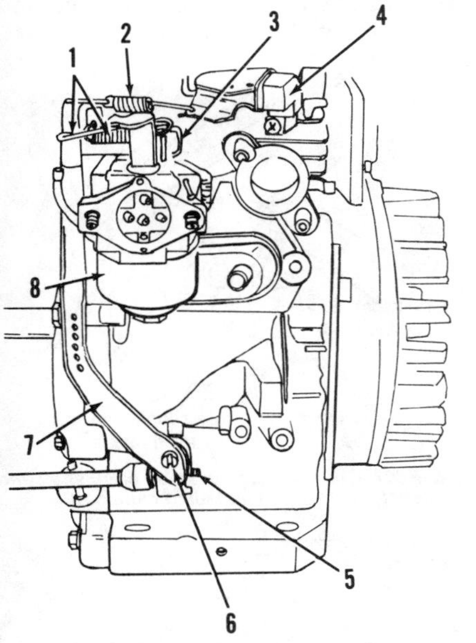

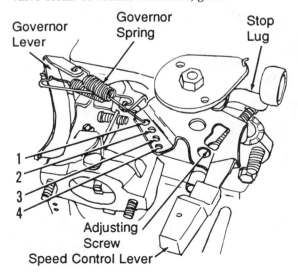

Fig. R604—Changing governor spring location in holes in speed control lever will vary engine speed.

Fig. R603—View of governor linkage.

1. Control rod & spring
2. Governor spring
3. Throttle lever
4. Speed control lever
5. Clamp screw
6. Governor shaft
7. Governor lever
8. Carburetor

(0.0022-0.0039 in.) for exhaust valve. Maximum allowable valve stem-to-guide clearance for both valves is 0.300 mm (0.0118 in.).

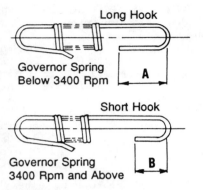

Fig R605—Two different governor springs are used according to engine operating speed.

Specified intake valve stem diameter is 6.460-6.475 mm (0.2543-0.2549 in.). Specified exhaust valve stem diameter is 6.422-6.444 mm (0.2528-0.2537 in.). Wear limit for either valve is 6.35 mm (0.250 in.).

Valve guides are renewable. Specified valve guide inside diameter for both valves is 6.500-6.522 mm (0.2559-0.2568 in.) with a wear limit of 6.650 mm (0.2618 in.).

Specified valve spring length is 37.0 mm (1.46 in.) with a minimum spring length of 35.5 mm (1.40 in.).

CAMSHAFT. The camshaft (27—Fig. R606) rides in bores in crankcase and crankcase cover.

When removing camshaft, rotate the flywheel to place the piston at top dead center on the compression stroke to relieve valve spring tension on the cam lobes. Position engine so the valve tappets (28) will not fall out. If valve tappets are removed, they should be marked so they can be returned to their original positions. Remove any rust or burrs from pto end of crankshaft. Remove the crankcase cover (12), and withdraw the camshaft.

Specified camshaft journal diameter is 14.973-14.984 mm (0.5895-0.5899 in.) at gear end with a wear limit of 14.95 mm (0.5886 in.). Specified camshaft journal diameter at flywheel end is 24.967-24.980 mm (0.9830-0.9835 in.) with a wear limit of 24.95 mm (0.9823 in.). Specified lobe height is 30.70-30.90 mm (1.209-1.216 in.) with a wear limit of 30.55 mm (1.203 in.).

When installing camshaft, align timing marks (Fig. R607) on camshaft and crankshaft gears.

PISTON, PIN AND RINGS. To remove piston and rod assembly, drain engine oil and remove engine from equipment. Remove cylinder head. Remove carbon and ridge (if present) from top of cylinder before removing the piston. Clean pto end of crankshaft and remove any burrs or rust. Unscrew fasteners and remove crankcase cover. Unscrew connecting rod screws and push piston and rod out through top of cylinder.

All models are equipped with one compression ring, one scraper ring and one oil control ring. Install rings as shown in Fig. R608. Stagger ring end gaps at 90° intervals around piston.

Standard and oversize piston and rings are available for service.

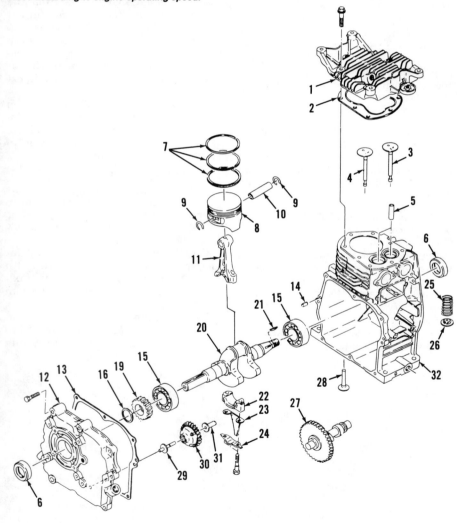

Fig. R606—Exploded view of engine.

1. Cylinder head	9. Snap ring	19. Gear
2. Head gasket	10. Piston pin	20. Crankshaft
3. Exhaust valve	11. Connecting rod	21. Key
4. Intake valve	12. Crankcase cover	22. Rod cap
5. Valve guide	13. Gasket	23. Oil dipper
6. Oil seal	14. Dowel pin	24. Lock plate
7. Piston rings	15. Ball bearing	25. Valve spring
8. Piston	16. Shim	26. Valve retainer

27. Camshaft
28. Tappet
29. Governor shaft
30. Governor flyweight & gear assy.
31. Thrust sleeve
32. Crankcase

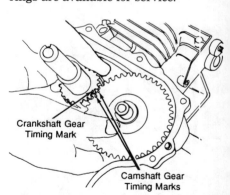

Fig. R607—Align timing marks on crankshaft and camshaft gears when installing camshaft.

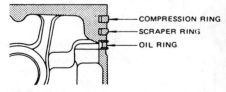

Fig. R608—Install piston rings as shown.

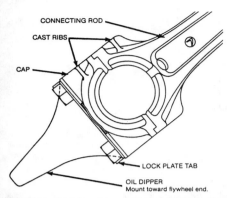

Fig. R609—Install rod cap on rod so ribs are adjacent. Install piston and rod so oil dipper offset is toward flywheel.

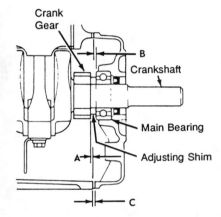

Fig. R610—View showing location of measuring points to determine correct shim thickness for obtaining correct crankshaft end play. Refer to text.

Piston ring end gap for the top two rings should be 0.10-0.30 mm (0.004-0.012 in.); maximum allowable gap is 1.5 mm (0.059 in.).

Specified piston ring side clearance is listed in table below:

Top ring. . . . . 0.050-0.090 mm
(0.0020-0.0035 in.)
Second ring. . . . . 0.030-0.070 mm
(0.0012-0.0028 in.)
Oil ring . . . . 0.010-0.065 mm
(0.0004-0.0025 in.)

Insert each ring into its piston ring groove and measure side clearance between the ring and ring land with a feeler gauge. Renew piston rings and/or piston if ring side clearance exceeds 0.15 mm (0.006 in.).

Specified piston-to-cylinder clearance is 0.030-0.069 mm (0.0012-0.0027 in.) with a maximum clearance of 0.25 mm (0.010 in.).

Specified piston diameter is 74.950-74.970 mm (2.9508-2.9516 in.) with a wear limit of 74.88 mm (2.948

in.). Measure at piston diameter on skirt perpendicular to pin hole.

Specified piston pin diameter is 15.992-16.000 mm (0.6296-0.6299 in.); minimum allowable diameter is 15.960 mm (0.6283 in.). Specified piston bore diameter for pin is 15.991-16.002 mm (0.6296-0.6230 in.); maximum allowable diameter is 16.035 mm (0.6313 in.). Piston pin should be 0.009 mm (0.00035 in.) interference fit to a 0.010 mm (0.00039 in.) loose fit in piston pin bore. Piston pin looseness must not exceed 0.06 mm (0.0023 in.).

When installing piston and connecting rod assembly, make certain match marks (cast ribs) on connecting rod and cap are adjacent to each other as shown in Fig. R609. Install piston and rod so oil dipper offset is towards flywheel. Use a new lock plate and tighten connecting rod cap screws to 17-20 N•m (150-177 in.-lb.).

CONNECTING ROD. Connecting rod and piston are removed as a unit as outlined in previous section. Connecting rod rides directly on crankpin.

Connecting rod-to-crankpin clearance should be 0.020-0.046 mm (0.0008-0.0018 in.). If clearance exceeds 0.20 mm (0.008 in.), renew rod and/or crankshaft.

Connecting rod side clearance for all models should be 0.1-0.3 mm (0.004-0.012 in.). If side clearance exceeds 1.0 mm (0.039 in.), renew connecting rod and/or crankshaft.

Specified connecting rod big end diameter is 28.000-28.013 mm (1.1024-1.1029 in.) with a wear limit of 28.100 mm (1.1063 in.).

Connecting rod-to-piston pin clearance for all models should be 0.010-0.029 mm (0.0004-0.0011 in.). If clearance exceeds 0.12 mm (0.005 in.), renew piston pin and/or connecting rod. Specified connecting rod small end diameter is 16.010-16.021 mm (0.6303-0.6307 in.) with a wear limit of 16.080 mm (0.6331 in.).

Install connecting rod as outlined in PISTON, PIN AND RINGS section.

GOVERNOR. The governor assembly is located in the crankcase cover. The camshaft gear drives the governor gear. Flyweight and gear assembly snaps onto governor shaft (29—Fig. R606). Governor assembly must be separated from shaft before thrust sleeve (31) can be removed or installed in flyweights. Flyweights and gear are serviced only as a unit. Components must move freely without binding.

CRANKSHAFT. The crankshaft is supported by a ball bearing at both ends. Renew bearings if rough, noisy, excessively worn or otherwise damaged.

Specified crankpin diameter is 27.967-27.980 mm (1.1011-1.1016 in.) with a wear limit of 27.86 mm (1.097 in.). Specified main bearing journal diameter at both ends is 29.988-29.997 mm (1.1806-1.1810 in.) with a wear limit of 29.95 mm (1.179 in.).

Connecting rod-to-crankpin clearance should be 0.020-0.046 mm (0.0008-0.0018 in.). If clearance exceeds 0.20 mm (0.008 in.), renew rod and/or crankshaft. Maximum allowable crankpin taper and out-of-round is 0.005 mm (0.0002 in.).

Install crankshaft seals with lips toward ball bearings.

Crankshaft end play should be 0.00-0.20 mm (0.000-0.008 in.). End play is controlled by a shim (16—Fig. R606) located between crankshaft gear and main bearing. Shims are available in several thicknesses, but only one shim is installed.

To determine the correct thickness of adjusting shim with crankcase cover removed, measure distance (A—Fig. R610) between machined surface of crankcase face and end of crankshaft gear. Measure distance (B) between machined surface of crankcase cover and end of main bearing. The compressed thickness of gasket (C) is 0.22 mm (0.0087 in.). Select shim that is 0.00-0.20 mm (0.000-0.008 in.) less than the total of A, B and C. After assembly, crankshaft end play should be checked with a dial indicator.

When reassembling engine, make certain the timing marks (Fig. R607) on crankshaft and camshaft gears are aligned.

CYLINDER. If cylinder bore is scored, or out-of-round more than 0.01 mm (0.0004 in.), or tapered more than 0.015 mm (0.0006 in.), the cylinder should be bored to next larger oversize for which piston and rings are available.

Specified standard bore diameter is 75.000-75.019 mm (2.9528-2.9535 in.) with a wear limit of 75.15 mm (2.959 in.).

WIRING DIAGRAM. Wiring schematic for engines with rewind starter is shown in Fig. R611. Wiring schematic for engines equipped with an electric starter is included in the Robin ACCESSORIES section of this manual.

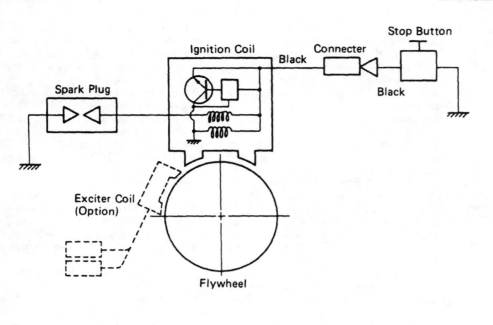

Fig. R611—Wiring schematic for models with rewind starter.

ROBIN
(WISCONSIN ROBIN)

Robin America, Inc.
940 Lively Boulevard
Wood Dale, Illinois 60191

Model	No. Cyls.	Bore	Stroke	Displacement	Power Rating
EY45V, W1-450V	1	90 mm (3.54 in.)	70 mm (2.76 in.)	445 cc (27.17 cu. in.)	9 kW (12 hp)

Models EY45V and W1-450V are four-stroke, air-cooled, single-cylinder gasoline engines with a vertical crankshaft. The engine is pressure-lubricated by an oil pump located in the oil pan. The engine model and specification numbers are located on the name plate on flywheel shroud. The serial number is stamped on the crankcase base. Always furnish engine model, specification and serial numbers when ordering parts.

MAINTENANCE

LUBRICATION. Check engine oil level daily and maintain oil level at full mark on dipstick.

Engine oil should meet or exceed latest API service classification. Use SAE 30 oil when temperature is above 40° F (4° C), SAE 20 oil when temperature is between 15degree F (-9° C) and 40° F (4° C), and SAE 10W-30 oil when temperature is below 15° F (-9° C).

Oil should be changed after every 50 hours of operation. Crankcase capacity is 1.3 liters (2.7 pt.).

SPARK PLUG. Recommended spark plug is a NGK BM6A or equivalent. Specified spark plug electrode gap is 0.6-0.7 mm (0.024-0.028 in.). Tighten spark plug to 12-16 N•m (106-142 in.-lb.).

CARBURETOR. A Mikuni float type carburetor is used. Refer to Fig. R701 for exploded view of carburetor. Carburetor has a fixed high-speed jet.

Initial adjustment of low speed mixture screw (8) is 1½ turns open from a lightly seated position. Make final carburetor adjustment with engine at normal operating temperature and running. Adjust low speed mixture screw to obtain smoothest idle operation and acceleration.

Adjust idle speed screw to obtain an idle speed of 1200 rpm at normal operating temperature.

Remove the fuel bowl (17—Fig. R701) for access to internal components. Remove the float (16), fuel inlet valve (11), main jet (14) and nozzle (13). Unscrew idle mixture screw (8).

Clean all parts and fuel passages with carburetor cleaning solvent and compressed air. Replace parts that are worn or damaged.

To check or adjust float level, remove fuel bowl and place carburetor body on end (on manifold flange) so float pin is in vertical position. Position the float so float arm just contacts fuel inlet valve.

NOTE: Needle valve (11—Fig. R701) is spring-loaded. Float tab should just contact needle valve pin but should not compress spring.

Float should be parallel with fuel bowl mating surface as shown in Fig. R702. Carefully bend tab on float arm to obtain correct setting.

Refer to Fig. R703 for correct installation of gaskets used with carburetor and intake manifold.

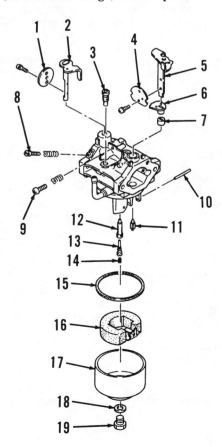

Fig. R701—Exploded view of carburetor.

1. Throttle plate
2. Throttle shaft
3. Idle mixture jet
4. Choke plate
5. Choke shaft
6. Detent plate
7. Bushing
8. Idle mixture screw
9. Idle speed screw
10. Pin
11. Fuel inlet valve
12. Main nozzle
13. Nozzle
14. Main jet
15. Gasket
16. Float
17. Fuel bowl
18. Gasket
19. Plug

GOVERNOR. The engine is equipped with a centrifugal flyweight type governor. To adjust external governor linkage, loosen clamp screw (R—Fig. R704) on governor lever (L). Move governor lever so throttle valve in carburetor is wide open. Hold lever in this position and rotate governor shaft (S) clockwise as far as possible. Tighten clamp screw. Run engine under no load and rotate speed control lever (D) until it contacts speed adjusting screw. Rotate screw so desired no-load engine speed is obtained; this also establishes choke operating point. Governor sensitivity is adjusted by relocating governor spring end (E) in holes in governor lever (L).

IGNITION SYSTEM. The engine is equipped with a breakerless, solid-state ignition system. There is no scheduled maintenance. Specified air gap between ignition coil and flywheel is 0.5 mm (0.020 in.).

VALVE ADJUSTMENT. Valve tappet gap (cold) should be 0.08-0.12 mm (0.003-0.005 in.) for intake and ex-

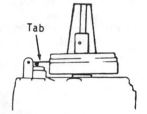

Tab

Fig. R702—Float should be parallel with fuel bowl mating surface.

haust. To check tappet gap, remove breather cover. Rotate flywheel to position piston at top dead center on compression stroke (both valves closed). Measure clearance between end of valve and tappet stem with a feeler gauge.

To increase clearance, grind off end of valve stem. To reduce clearance, grind the valve seat deeper or renew the valve and/or valve tappet.

REPAIRS

TIGHTENING TORQUE. Recommended tightening torque specifications are as follows:

Connecting rod . . . . 25-30 N•m
(18.4-22 ft.-lb.)
Cylinder head . . . . 34-39 N•m
(25-29 ft-lb.)
Flywheel nut . . . . 80-100 N•m
(59-74 ft-lb.)
Oil pan . . . . 17-19 N•m
(150-168 in.-lb.)
Spark plug . . . . 12-16 N•m
(106-142 in.-lb.)

CYLINDER HEAD. Remove the cylinder head and discard the head gasket. Clean combustion deposits from the combustion chamber being careful not to damage the gasket sealing area.

Inspect the head for damage. Check the cylinder head for distortion using a straightedge and feeler gauge. On all models, renew cylinder head if gasket surface is warped in excess of 0.15 mm (0.006 in.).

Always use a new head gasket when installing cylinder head. Tighten cylin-

der head bolts or nuts evenly and in stages until reaching final torque of 34-39 N•m (25-29 ft-lb.).

VALVE SYSTEM. To remove valves, first remove the cylinder head, intake manifold, muffler and breather cover. Disengage the valve retainer from valve stem and withdraw the valve and valve spring.

On all models, valve face and seat angles should be 45°. Standard seat width is 1.2-1.5 mm (0.047-0.059 in.). Maximum allowable seat width is 2.5 mm (0.098 in.).

Valve stem-to-guide clearance should be 0.030-0.091 mm (0.0012-0.0036 in.) for intake valve and 0.070-0.126 mm (0.0028-0.0050 in.) for exhaust valve. Maximum allowable valve stem-to-guide clearance for both valves is 0.300 mm (0.0118 in.).

Specified valve stem diameter is 7.945-7.970 mm (0.3128-0.3138 in.) for intake valve and 7.904-7.930 mm (0.3112-0.3122 in.) for exhaust valve. Wear limit for either valve is 7.85 mm (0.309 in.).

Valve guides are renewable. Specified valve guide inside diameter for both valves is 7.964-8.000 mm (0.3135-0.3150 in.) with a wear limit of 8.150 mm (0.3209 in.).

Specified valve spring length is 46.0 mm (1.81 in.) with a minimum spring length of 44.5 mm (1.75 in.).

PISTON, PIN AND RINGS. To remove piston and rod assembly, drain engine oil and remove engine from equipment. Remove cylinder head. Remove carbon and ridge (if present) from top of cylinder before removing the piston. Clean pto end of crankshaft and remove any burrs or rust. Unscrew fasteners and remove oil pan. Remove the balancer shafts. Unscrew connecting rod screws and push the piston and rod out through top of the cylinder.

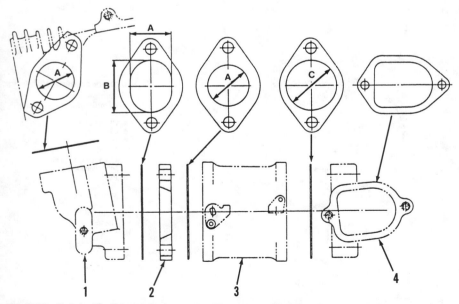

Fig. R703—Note inside diameter and corresponding correct location of carburetor and intake manifold gaskets.

A. 32 mm (1.26 in.)
B. 41 mm (1.61 in.)

C. 39 mm (1.53 in.)
1. Intake manifold

2. Insulator
3. Carburetor

4. Elbow

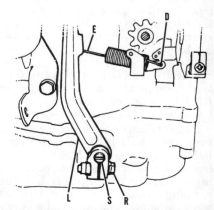

Fig. R704—View of governor linkage. Refer to text for adjustment.

Standard and oversize piston and rings are available for service.

Piston ring end gap for the top two rings should be 0.10-0.30 mm (0.004-0.012 in.); maximum allowable gap is 1.5 mm (0.059 in.).

Specified piston ring side clearance is listed below:

Top ring. . . . . 0.110-0.150 mm
(0.0043-0.0059 in.)
Second ring. . . . . 0.060-0.100 mm
(0.0024-0.0039 in.)
Oil ring . . . . 0.010-0.050 mm
(0.0004-0.0020 in.)

Insert each ring into its piston ring groove and measure side clearance between the ring and ring land with a feeler gauge. Renew piston rings and/or piston if ring side clearance exceeds 0.15 mm (0.006 in.).

Specified piston-to-cylinder clearance is 0.011-0.053 mm (0.0004-0.0021 in.) with a maximum clearance of 0.28 mm (0.011 in.).

Specified piston diameter is 89.950-89.970 mm (3.5413-3.5421 in.) with a wear limit of 89.87 mm (3.538 in.). Measure piston diameter on skirt perpendicular to pin hole.

Specified piston pin diameter is 19.991-20.000 mm (0.7870-0.7874 in.); minimum allowable diameter is 19.965 mm (0.7860 in.). Specified piston bore diameter for pin is 19.989-20.002 mm (0.7870-0.7875 in.); maximum allowable diameter is 19.960 mm (0.7858 in.). Piston pin clearance in piston should be 0.011 mm (0.0004 in.).

The piston is equipped with one compression ring, one scraper ring and one oil control ring. Install rings as shown in Fig. R705. Stagger ring end gaps at 90° intervals around piston.

Install piston and rod so "MAG" on side of rod (see Fig. R706) is towards flywheel. Align match marks (cast ribs) on connecting rod and cap as shown in Fig.

R706. Tighten connecting rod cap screws to 25-30 N•m (18.4-22 ft.-lb.).

When installing oil pan, be sure the drive pin in end of camshaft is properly aligned with slot in oil pump shaft. Do not force the oil pan onto the crankcase. Light tapping only should be required if all components are properly aligned.

CONNECTING ROD. Connecting rod and piston are removed as a unit as outlined in previous section. Connecting rod rides directly on crankpin.

Connecting rod-to-crankpin clearance should be 0.050-0.082 mm (0.0020-0.0032 in.). If clearance exceeds 0.20 mm (0.008 in.), renew rod and/or crankshaft.

Connecting rod side clearance should be 0.1-0.3 mm (0.004-0.012 in.). If side clearance exceeds 1.0 mm (0.039 in.), renew connecting rod and/or crankshaft.

GOVERNOR. The governor flyweight assembly is mounted on the camshaft gear and is not available separately from camshaft. Components must move freely without binding. When installing thrust sleeve (V—Fig. R707) on camshaft (C), be sure sleeve flange properly engages slots in flyweights (F).

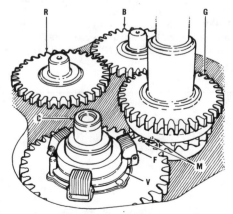

Fig. R706—Install rod cap on rod so ribs are adjacent. Install piston and rod so "MAG" on rod is toward flywheel.

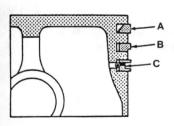

Fig. R705—Install piston rings as shown. Note that bevel on top compression ring (A) and slot in oil control ring (C) is toward piston crown. Bevel in second compression ring (B) is toward piston skirt.

A. Top compression ring
B. Second compression ring
C. Oil control ring
D. Expander

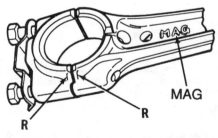

Fig. R707—Align timing marks (M) on crankshaft and camshaft gears when installing camshaft. Timing marks on large crankshaft gear (G) and balancer gear (B) must be aligned, as well as timing marks on balancer gears (B and R).

CRANKSHAFT. The crankshaft is supported by a ball bearing at both ends. Renew bearings if rough, noisy, excessively worn or otherwise damaged.

Specified crankpin diameter is 37.934-37.950 mm (1.4935-1.4941 in.) with a wear limit of 37.85 mm (1.490 in.). Specified main bearing journal diameter at flywheel end is 34.986-35.000 mm (1.3774-1.3780 in.) with a wear limit of 34.95 mm (1.376 in.). Specified main bearing journal diameter at pto end is 34.997-35.000 mm (1.3778-1.3780 in.) with a wear limit of 34.95 mm (1.376 in.).

Connecting rod-to-crankpin clearance should be 0.050-0.082 mm (0.0020-0.0032 in.). If clearance exceeds 0.20 mm (0.008 in.), renew rod and/or crankshaft. Maximum allowable crankpin taper and out-of-round is 0.005 mm (0.0002 in.).

Install crankshaft seals with lips toward ball bearings.

Crankshaft end play should be 0.00-0.25 mm (0.000-0.009 in.). End play is controlled by a shim (16—Fig. R708) located between crankshaft gear and main bearing. Shims are available in several thicknesses, but only one shim is installed.

To determine shim thickness, measure from inner race of bearing (D—Fig. R709) to machined surface on oil pan and add compressed thickness (C) of gasket, which is 0.22 mm (0.0087 in.). From total, subtract distance from thrust surface (B) of large crankshaft gear to surface of crankcase machined surface (A). Calculation establishes end play without shim. Select shim so crankshaft end play is 0.00-0.25 mm (0.000-0.009 in.).

When reassembling engine, make certain timing marks (M—Fig. R707) on crankshaft and camshaft gears are aligned. Align timing marks on large crankshaft gear (G) and balancer gear (B).

When installing oil pan, be sure drive pin in end of camshaft is properly aligned with slot in oil pump shaft. Do not force oil pan on crankcase. Light tapping only should be required if all components are properly aligned.

CAMSHAFT. The camshaft drives the oil pump and rides in bores in crankcase and oil pan.

When removing camshaft, position engine so tappets will not fall out. If valve tappets are removed, they should be marked so they can be returned to their original positions.

Specified camshaft journal diameter at both ends is 19.967-19.980 mm (0.7861-0.7866 in.) with a wear limit of

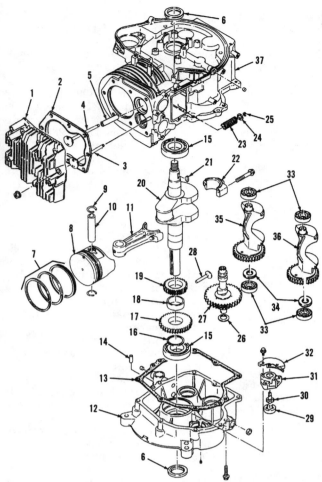

Fig. R708—Exploded view of engine.

1. Cylinder head
2. Head gasket
3. Exhaust valve
4. Intake valve
5. Valve guide
6. Oil seal
7. Piston rings
8. Piston
9. Snap ring
10. Piston pin
11. Connecting rod
12. Oil pan
13. Gasket
14. Dowel pin
15. Ball bearing
16. Shim
17. Crankshaft gear (large)
18. Spacer
19. Crankshaft gear (small)
20. Crankshaft
21. Key
22. Rod cap
23. Valve spring
24. Valve spring retainer
25. Valve retainer
26. Shim
27. Camshaft
28. Tappet
29. Outer rotor
30. Inner rotor
31. Oil pump housing
32. Cover
33. Ball bearings
34. Washers
35. Balancer shaft
36. Balancer shaft
37. Crankcase

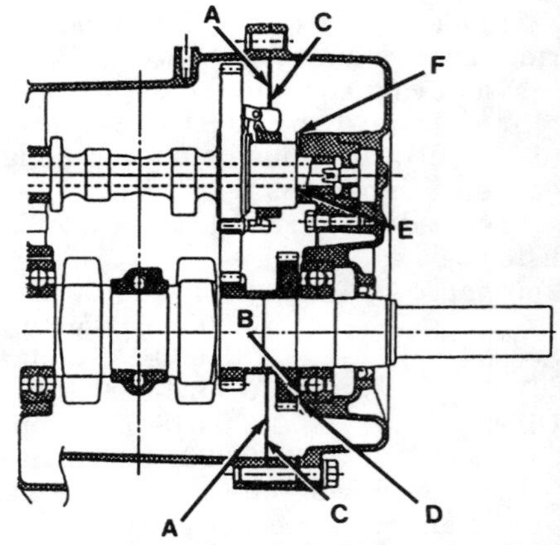

Fig. R709—View showing location of measuring points to determine correct shim thickness for obtaining correct camshaft and crankshaft end play. Refer to text.

When installing oil pan, be sure drive pin in end of camshaft is properly aligned with slot in oil pump shaft. Do not force oil pan on crankcase. Light tapping only should be required if all components are properly aligned.

BALANCER SHAFTS. The engine is equipped with two balancer shafts that ride in ball bearings in the crankcase and oil pan. During installation, align timing mark on balancer gear (B—Fig. R707) with timing mark on crankshaft gear (G). Align timing marks on balancer gears (B) and (R).

OIL PUMP. An oil pump located in the oil pan provides pressure lubrication for the engine. A pin located in the end of the camshaft drives the oil pump.

The oil pan must be removed for access to oil pump components (29 through 32—Fig. R708). Renew the pump as an assembly if damage or excessive wear is evident.

When installing oil pan, be sure drive pin in end of camshaft is properly aligned with slot in oil pump shaft. Do not force the oil pan onto the crankcase. Light tapping only should be required if all components are properly aligned.

19.75 mm (0.7776 in.). Specified intake lobe height is 35.90-36.10 mm (1.413-1.421 in.) with a wear limit of 35.75 mm (1.407 in.). Specified exhaust lobe height is 35.40-35.60 mm (1.394-1.402 in.) with a wear limit of 35.25 mm (1.388 in.).

When installing camshaft, align timing marks (M—Fig. R707) on camshaft and crankshaft gears.

Camshaft end play should be 0.00-0.25 mm (0.000-0.009 in.) and is controlled by a shim (26—Fig. R708).

Shims are available in several thicknesses, but only one shim is installed.

To determine required shim thickness, measure from thrust surface (F—Fig. R709) on oil pan to machined surface on oil pan. Add compressed thickness (C) of gasket, which is 0.22 mm (0.0087 in.), to the measured dimension. From total, subtract distance from camshaft thrust surface (E) to surface of crankcase machined surface (A). Calculation establishes end play without shim. Select shim so camshaft end play is 0.00-0.25 mm (0.000-0.009 in.).

ROBIN
(WISCONSIN ROBIN)

Robin America, Inc.
940 Lively Boulevard
Wood Dale, Illinois 60191

Model	Bore	Stroke	Displacement	Rated Power
EH25, WO1-250	75 mm (2.95 in.)	57 mm (2.24 in.)	252 cc (15.4 cu. in.)	6.3 kW (8.5 hp)

All models are air-cooled, four-stroke, single-cylinder engines. All models utilize an overhead valve system and are equipped with a horizontal crankshaft.

Engine model and specification numbers are indicated on the nameplate attached to the flywheel shroud. The engine serial number is stamped on the crankcase base.

MAINTENANCE

LUBRICATION. The engine may be equipped with an oil sensor unit that grounds the ignition if oil level in sump is low. See OIL SENSOR paragraph.

Check engine oil level daily and maintain oil level at full mark on dipstick.

Engine oil should meet or exceed latest API service classification. Use SAE 30 oil when temperature is above 50° F (10° C), SAE 20 oil when temperature is between 32° F (0° C) and 60° F (15° C), SAE 10W oil when temperature is between 5° F (-15° C) and 32degree F (0° F) and SAE 5W for temperatures below 5degree F (-15° C). SAE 10W-30 oil is acceptable for use when temperature is between 5° F (-15° C) and 95° F (35° C).

Change oil after initial 20 hours of operation and then every 50 hours of operation thereafter. Crankcase capacity is 1.0 liter (2.2 pt.).

AIR FILTER. Clean the air filter element weekly or after every 50 hours of operation, whichever occurs first. Clean the foam element using warm water and soap. Dry the filter, then apply light oil. Squeeze excess oil from filter while noting if filter is completely coated with oil. Clean filter more frequently if extremely dirty or dusty conditions exist.

FUEL FILTER. On models so equipped, the fuel filter should be cleaned monthly or after every 100 hours of operation, whichever occurs first. The filter may be located in the fuel line or the fuel shutoff valve.

CRANKCASE BREATHER. All models are equipped with a breather to maintain a vacuum in the crankcase. Renew breather plate if reed is cracked or otherwise damaged.

SPARK PLUG. Recommended spark plug for all models is NGK B6HS or Champion L86C. Electrode gap should be 0.6-0.7 mm (0.024-0.028 inch). Tighten a new spark plug to 11.8-14.7 N•m (104-130 in.-lb.). Tighten a used spark plug to 22.6-26.5 N•m (17-19 ft.-lb.).

CARBURETOR. Refer to Fig. R751 for an exploded view of carburetor. The carburetor is equipped with an adjustable idle mixture screw (3) and a fixed main jet (21).

Initial setting of idle mixture screw (3) is 1½ turns open from a lightly seated position. Make final adjustment of idle mixture screw with engine at normal operating temperature. Adjust idle mixture screw so engine idles smoothly and accelerates without hesitation. Adjust idle speed screw (6) so engine idle speed is 1200 rpm.

Before removing carburetor from the engine, carefully note the position of governor linkage and springs to insure correct assembly. Remove air cleaner assembly from the carburetor. Disconnect fuel line from carburetor. Discon-

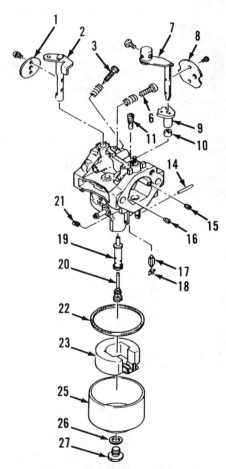

Fig. R751—Exploded view of carburetor.

1. Throttle plate
2. Throttle shaft
3. Idle mixture screw
6. Idle speed screw
7. Choke shaft
8. Choke plate
9. Bushing
10. Seal
11. Idle mixture jet
12. "O" ring
13. Fuel pump
14. Pin
15. Air jet
16. Air jet
17. Fuel inlet valve
18. Clip
19. Main nozzle
20. Nozzle
21. Main jet
22. Gasket
23. Float
24. Cap
25. Fuel bowl
26. Gasket
27. Screw

nect governor springs. Pull carburetor away from engine and disconnect governor link rod.

To disassemble carburetor, refer to Fig. R751 and remove float bowl (25). Remove float pin (14), float (23) and fuel inlet valve (17). Unscrew main jet (21) before removing nozzle (20). Remove idle mixture screw (3) and idle jet (11). Throttle plate (1) and choke plate (8) are retained by screws. Throttle shaft (2) and choke shaft (7) can be withdrawn after throttle and choke plates are removed.

Metal parts may be cleaned in carburetor cleaner. Direct compressed air through orifices and passageways in the opposite direction of normal fuel flow. Do not use wires or drill bits to clean orifices as enlargement of the orifice could affect the calibration of the carburetor.

Inspect carburetor and renew any damaged or excessively worn components. Renew float if it is dented, contains fuel or if wear is evident in area of pivot pin or float tab. Renew fuel inlet valve (17—Fig. R751) if tip is grooved or otherwise damaged. Carburetor body must be renewed if fuel inlet valve seat is faulty.

To check or adjust float level, install fuel inlet valve and float. Invert carburetor and note position of float in relation to carburetor body. Float should be parallel to gasket surface of carburetor as shown in Fig. R752. Bend tab of float to adjust float level.

To reassemble carburetor, reverse the disassembly procedure.

GOVERNOR. All models are equipped with a centrifugal flyweight type governor. Governor assembly is located in the crankcase cover. To adjust governor linkage, loosen governor lever clamp bolt (B—Fig. R753) so that governor lever (L) can be moved independently from governor shaft (S). Move governor lever (L) so carburetor throttle plate is fully open. Turn governor shaft (S) as far clockwise as possible and tighten clamp bolt.

IGNITION. A solid-state ignition system is used on all models. A one-piece ignition module/coil is mounted outside the flywheel. Air gap between ignition coil legs and flywheel should be 0.3-0.5 mm (0.012-0.020 in.). Adjust air gap by loosening ignition coil mounting screws and relocating coil. Ignition timing is not adjustable.

VALVE ADJUSTMENT. Engine must be cold when adjusting valve clearance. Rotate crankshaft so piston is at top dead center on compression stroke. To determine piston position, note if the crankshaft or the camshaft is the pto shaft. If crankshaft is pto shaft, piston is at top dead center when keyway on pto (crankshaft) is straight up. See Fig. R754. If camshaft is pto shaft, piston is at top dead center when keyway on pto (camshaft) is 45° from vertical. See Fig. R754. Both valves will

be closed (rocker arms loose) on compression stroke.

To check clearance, remove the rocker cover. Use a feeler gauge to measure clearance between rocker arm and valve stem. Specified clearance is 0.085-0.115 mm (0.0034-0.0045 inch). To adjust clearance, loosen nut (N—Fig. R755) and turn adjusting screw (S). Tighten nut and recheck clearance.

CYLINDER HEAD. Manufacturer recommends removal of carbon from cylinder head combustion chamber after 500-600 hours of operation.

REPAIRS

TIGHTENING TORQUE. Recommended tightening torque specifications are as follows:
Connecting rod . . . . 22-27 N•m
(16-20 ft.-lb.)
Crankcase cover . . . . 17-19 N•m
(150-168 in.-lb.)
Cylinder head . . . . 34-41 N•m
(25-30 ft.-lb.)
Flywheel nut . . . . 59-63 N•m
(44-46 ft.-lb.)
Spark plug:
New . . . . 11.8-14.7 N•m
(104-130 in.-lb.)
Used . . . . 22.6-26.5 N•m
(17-19 ft.-lb.)

CYLINDER HEAD. To remove cylinder head (15—Fig. R756), remove interfering air baffles and shroud.

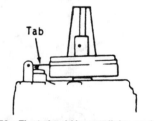

Fig. R752—Float should be parallel to gasket surface of carburetor. Bend tab to adjust float level.

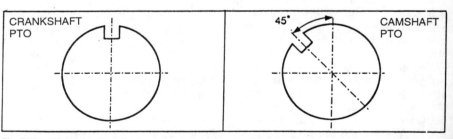

Fig. R754—Piston is at top dead center when keyway in pto shaft, either crankshaft or camshaft, is positioned as shown.

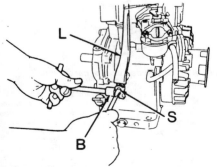

Fig. R753—With governor lever (L) in wide open throttle position, turn governor shaft (S) clockwise as far as possible and tighten clamp bolt (B).

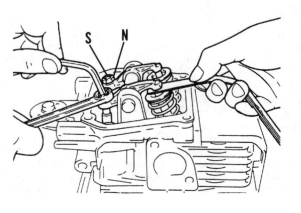

Fig. R755—To adjust valve clearance, loosen nut (N) and turn adjusting screw (S). Clearance should be 0.085-0.115 mm (0.0034-0.0045 inch).

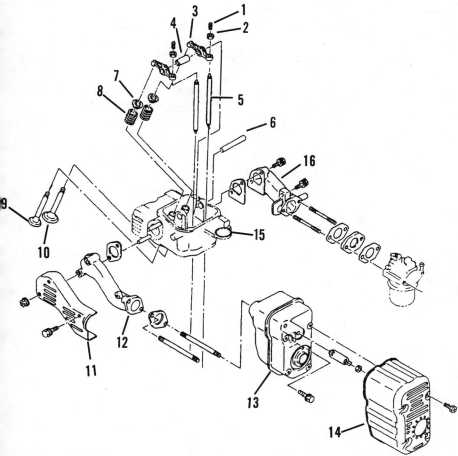

Fig. R756—Exploded view of cylinder head. Renewable valve guides are not shown.

1. Adjusting screw	5. Push rod	9. Exhaust valve	13. Muffler
2. Nut	6. Rocker arm shaft	10. Intake valve	14. Cover
3. Rocker arm	7. Valve retainer	11. Cover	15. Cylinder head
4. Spacer	8. Valve spring	12. Exhaust manifold	16. Intake manifold

Remove fuel tank on models so equipped. Disconnect throttle linkage and fuel line and remove the carburetor and intake manifold (16). Remove muffler and exhaust manifold (12). Remove spark plug and rotate crankshaft so piston is at top dead center on compression. Remove rocker arm cover. Mark push rods so they can be returned to original position. Unscrew cylinder head bolts and remove cylinder head.

Clean combustion deposits from the combustion chamber being careful not to damage the gasket sealing area. Inspect the head for cracks or other damage. Check the cylinder head for distortion using a straightedge and feeler gauge. On all models, renew cylinder head if gasket surface is warped in excess of 0.10 mm (0.004 in.).

Always use a new head gasket when installing the cylinder head. Tighten cylinder head screws to 34-41 N•m (25-30 ft.-lb.).

VALVE SYSTEM. Valve face and seat angles are 45°. Valve seat width should be 0.7-1.0 mm (0.028-0.039 in.); maximum allowable seat width is 2.0 mm (0.079 in.).

Valve stem-to-guide clearance should be 0.050-0.087 mm (0.0020-0.0034 in.) for intake valve and 0.056-0.100 mm (0.0022-0.0039 in.) for exhaust valve. Maximum allowable valve stem-to-guide clearance for both valves is 0.300 mm (0.0118 in.).

Specified intake valve stem diameter is 6.535-6.550 mm (0.2573-0.2579 in.). Specified exhaust valve stem diameter is 6.522-6.544 mm (0.2568-0.2576 in.). Wear limit for either valve is 6.45 mm (0.2539 in.).

Specified valve guide inside diameter for both valves is 6.600-6.622 mm (0.2598-0.2607 in.) with a wear limit of 6.750 mm (0.2657 in.). Valve guides are renewable.

Specified valve spring free length is 35.5 mm (1.40 in.).

Rocker arm clearance on shaft should be 0.012-0.038 mm (0.0005-0.0015 in.). Specified rocker shaft diameter is 11.986-11.994 mm (0.4719-0.4722 in.)

with a wear limit of 11.920 mm (0.4693 in.). Specified rocker arm bore is 12.006-12.024 mm (0.4727-0.4734 in.) with a wear limit of 12.070 mm (0.4752 in.).

CAMSHAFT AND TAPPETS. Standard engines are equipped with a conventional camshaft that is referred to as the "D" type camshaft, while some engines may be equipped with a camshaft that serves as the pto shaft and is referred to as the "B" type camshaft. See Fig. R757.

To remove camshaft, proceed as follows: Remove rocker arm cover and disengage push rods from rocker arms. Drain oil. Remove crankcase cover. Position engine so tappets cannot fall out, or hold the tappets in their bores. Withdraw camshaft. If tappets are to be removed, mark them so they can be returned to original bores.

Camshaft lobe height for both valves should be 29.60-29.80 mm (1.165-1.173 in.). Minimum allowable lobe height is 29.45 mm (1.159 in.). Specified camshaft bearing journal diameter is 24.967-24.980 mm (0.9830-0.9835 in.) at inner end and 14.973-14.984 mm (0.5895-0.5899 in.) at gear end. Service limit is 24.95 mm (0.982 in.) at inner end and 14.95 mm (0.589 in.) at gear end.

Specified outside diameter of tappets is 8.960-8.975 mm (0.3528-0.3533 in.). Tappet clearance in bore should be 0.025-0.055 mm (0.0010-0.0022 in.).

The camshaft is equipped with a compression release device. Release lever (10—Fig. R758) extends above the camshaft exhaust lobe at slow engine speed (starting) thereby holding the exhaust valve open and reducing compression pressure. At running speed, the weight on the release lever moves the lever below the camshaft lobe. Release lever should move freely without binding.

Install camshaft by reversing removal procedure. Align timing marks

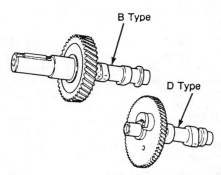

Fig. R757—"D" type camshaft is used when crankshaft is output shaft (pto), while "B" type camshaft is used when camshaft is output shaft.

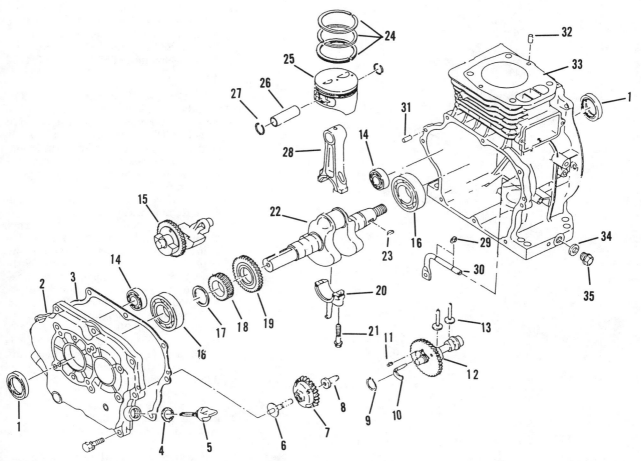

Fig. R758—Exploded view of engine internal components. Governor shaft (6) is attached to crankcase cover (2) and not available separately.

1. Seal	7. Governor assy.	12. Camshaft	18. Gear	24. Piston rings	30. Governor shaft
2. Crankcase cover	8. Sleeve	13. Tappet	19. Balancer drive gear	25. Piston	31. Dowel pin
3. Gasket	9. Snap ring	14. Ball bearing	20. Rod cap	26. Piston pin	32. Dowel pin
4. Gasket	10. Compression	15. Balancer	21. Screw	27. Snap ring	33. Crankcase
5. Oil dipstick/fill plug	release arm	16. Ball bearing	22. Crankshaft	28. Connecting rod	34. Washer
6. Shaft	11. Pin	17. Shim	23. Key	29. Retaining rings	35. Drain plug

(Fig. R759) on crankshaft and camshaft gears.

Camshaft on engines that use the camshaft as the pto ("B" type camshaft) are equipped with a shim at the gear end of the camshaft to adjust camshaft end play. Camshaft end play should be 0.00-0.20 mm (0.000-0.008 in.). Shims are available in several thicknesses, but only one shim is installed.

To determine shim thickness on "B" type camshaft, measure distance (A2—Fig. R760) from thrust surface on crankcase cover to machined surface on crankcase cover. Add the compressed thickness (3) of gasket, which is 0.3 mm (0.012 in.), to the measurement. From this total, subtract distance (B2) from camshaft thrust surface to surface of crankcase machined surface. Calculation establishes end play without shim. Select shim to obtain specified camshaft end play.

Tighten crankcase cover screws to 17-19 N•m (150-168 in.-lb.).

BALANCER SHAFTS. The engine is equipped with a balancer shaft that is supported at both ends by ball bearings. A gear on the crankshaft drives the balancer shaft.

During installation be sure the timing marks on the balancer shaft gear and crankshaft gear are aligned as shown in Fig. R759.

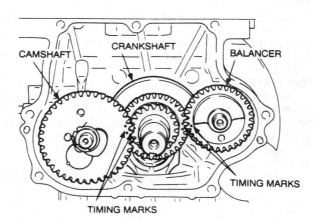

Fig. R759—View of timing marks on crankshaft, camshaft and balancer gears.

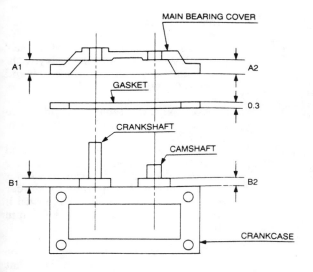

Fig. R760—View showing location of measuring points to determine correct shim thickness for obtaining correct camshaft and crankshaft end play. Refer to text.

PISTON, PIN AND RINGS. To remove piston and rod assembly, drain engine oil and remove engine from equipment. Remove cylinder head. Remove carbon and ridge (if present) from upper end of cylinder before removing the piston. Clean pto end of crankshaft and remove any burrs or rust. Unscrew fasteners and remove crankcase cover. Remove camshaft and balancer shaft. Unscrew connecting rod screws and push piston and rod out through the top of cylinder.

Standard and oversize pistons are available for service.

Specified piston-to-cylinder clearance is 0.025-0.064 mm(0.0010-0.0025 in.) with a maximum clearance of 0.250 mm (0.0098 in.).

Specified piston diameter is 74.960-74.980 mm (2.9512-2.9520 in.) with a wear limit of 74.87 mm (2.948 in.).

Specified piston pin diameter is 17.992-18.000 mm (0.7083-0.7087 in.); minimum allowable diameter is 17.960 mm (0.7071 in.). Specified piston bore diameter for pin is 17.991-18.002 mm (0.7083-0.7087 in.); maximum allowable diameter is 18.035 mm (0.7100 in.).

Specified piston ring end gap for the compression rings is 0.10-0.30 mm (0.004-0.012 in.); maximum allowable gap is 1.5 mm (0.059 in.). Specified piston ring end gap for the oil control ring is 0.10-0.30 mm (0.004-0.012 in.); maximum allowable gap is 1.5 mm (0.059 in.).

Specified piston ring side clearance is listed below:

Top ring............0.050-0.090 mm
(0.0020-0.0035 in.)
Second ring.........0.030-0.070 mm
(0.0012-0.0028 in.)
Oil ring............0.010-0.065 mm
(0.0004-0.0026 in.)

Insert each ring into its piston ring groove and measure side clearance between the ring and ring land with a feeler gauge. Renew piston rings and/or piston if ring side clearance exceeds 0.15 mm (0.006 in.).

Assemble piston and connecting rod so "MAG" on side of rod is on same side as arrow or triangle on piston crown as shown in Fig. R761.

Install rings as shown in Fig. R762. Side of piston ring marked "N" or with a punch mark should be towards piston crown. Stagger ring end gaps at 90° intervals around piston.

Lubricate piston and cylinder wall with engine oil. Install piston and rod in engine so arrow or triangle mark on piston crown is toward flywheel.

Align match marks (cast ribs) on connecting rod and cap as shown in Fig.

R763. Tighten crankcase cover screws to 17-19 N•m (150-168 in.-lb.)

CONNECTING ROD. Connecting rod and piston are removed as a unit as outlined in previous section. Connecting rod rides directly on crankpin.

Connecting rod-to-crankpin clearance should be 0.025-0.057 mm (0.0010-0.0022 in.). If clearance exceeds 0.20 mm (0.008 in.), renew rod and/or crankshaft. Specified connecting rod big end diameter is 34.000-34.016 mm (1.3386-1.3392 in.) with a wear limit of 34.100 mm (1.3425 in.). Oversize connecting rods are not available.

Connecting rod side clearance should be 0.1-0.7 mm (0.004-0.028 in.). If side clearance exceeds 1.0 mm (0.039 in.), renew connecting rod and/or crankshaft.

Piston pin clearance in connecting rod should be 0.010-0.029 mm (0.0004-0.0011 in.); maximum allowable clearance is 0.120 mm (0.0047 in.). Specified connecting rod small end diameter is 18.010-18.021 mm (0.7090-0.7095 in.).

GOVERNOR. The governor gear and flyweight assembly rides on a stud (6—Fig. R758) located in the crankcase cover. Components must move freely without binding. Governor gear and flyweight are serviced as an assembly.

CRANKSHAFT. The crankshaft is supported by ball bearings at both ends. Renew bearings if excessively worn or otherwise damaged.

Specified crankpin diameter is 33.959-33.975 mm (1.3370-1.3376 in.) with a wear limit of 33.85 mm (1.333 in.).

Specified main bearing journal diameter at flywheel end on all models is

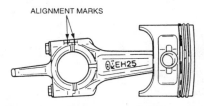

Fig. R763—Install rod cap so alignment marks on rod and cap are on same side.

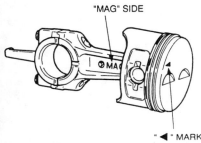

Fig. R761—"MAG" mark on side of rod and arrow on piston crown must be on same side. Arrow must point toward flywheel when piston is installed.

Fig. R762—Install piston rings as shown.

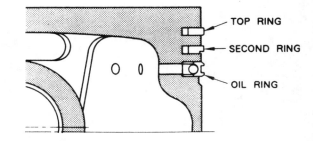

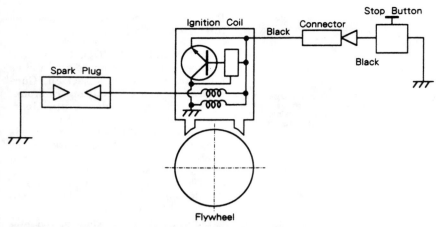

Fig. R764—Standard wiring schematic for engines with recoil starter.

29.991-30.000 mm (1.1807-1.1811 in.). For models that use crankshaft as the pto, specified main bearing journal diameter at pto end is 29.988-29.997 mm (1.1806-1.1810 in.). For models that use camshaft as the pto, specified main bearing journal diameter at pto end is 27.988-27.997 mm (1.1019-1.1022 in.).

Connecting rod-to-crankpin clearance should be 0.025-0.057 mm (0.0010-0.0022 in.). If clearance exceeds 0.20 mm (0.008 in.), renew rod and/or crankshaft.

Crankshaft end play should be 0.00-0.20 mm (0.000-0.008 in.). End play is controlled by a shim (17—Fig. R758) located between crankshaft gear and main bearing. Several thicknesses are available, but only one shim is installed.

To determine shim thickness, measure distance (A1—Fig. R760) from inner race of bearing to machined surface on crankcase cover. Add compressed thickness of gasket (3), which is 0.3 mm (0.012 in.), to the measurement. From this total, subtract distance (B1) from thrust surface of crankshaft gear to surface of crankcase machined surface. Calculation establishes end play without shim. Select shim so crankshaft end play is 0.00-0.20 mm (0.000-0.008 in.).

CYLINDER. Standard cylinder bore diameter is 75.000-75.019 mm (2.9528-2.9535 in.).

Measure the cylinder bore at top and bottom, and parallel and perpendicular to the crankshaft to determine cylinder taper (wear) and out-of-round. Cylinder should be bored oversize or renewed if taper or out-of-round exceeds 0.1 mm (0.004 in.).

OIL SENSOR. The engine may be equipped with an oil sensor unit that grounds the ignition if oil level in sump is low. The oil sensor probe is located in the crankcase cover. The oil sensor module is attached to the side of the crankcase.

WIRING DIAGRAM. Wiring schematic for engines with rewind starter is shown in Fig. R764. Wiring schematic for engines equipped with an electric starter is included in the Robin ACCESSORIES section of this manual.

ROBIN (WISCONSIN ROBIN)

Robin America, Inc.
940 Lively Boulevard
Wood Dale, Illinois 60191

Model	No. Cyls.	Bore	Stroke	Displacement	Power Rating
EH30, EH30V	1	78 mm (3.07 in.)	61 mm (2.40 in.)	291 cc (17.8 cu. in.)	6.7 kW (9 hp)
EH34, EH34V	1	84 mm (3.31 in.)	61 mm (2.40 in.)	338 cc (20.6 cu. in.)	8.2 kW (11 hp)
EH43V	1	89 mm (3.50 in.)	69 mm (2.71 in.)	429 cc (26.2 cu. in.)	10.4 kW (14 hp)
WO1-300, WO1-300V	1	78 mm (3.07 in.)	61 mm (2.40 in.)	291 cc (17.8 cu. in.)	6.7 kW (9 hp)
WO1-340, WO1-340V	1	84 mm (3.31 in.)	61 mm (2.40 in.)	338 cc (20.6 cu. in.)	8.2 kW (11 hp)
WO1-430V	1	89 mm (3.50 in.)	69 mm (2.71 in.)	429 cc (26.2 cu. in.)	10.4 kW (14 hp)

All models are air-cooled, four-stroke, single-cylinder engines. All models utilize an overhead valve system. Models EH30, EH34, WO1-300 and WO1-340 are equipped with a horizontal crankshaft, while Models EH30V, EH34V, EH43V, WO1-300V, WO1-340V and WO1-430V are equipped with a vertical crankshaft.

The crankshaft on Models EH43V and WO1-430V is supported by a ball bearing at flywheel end and a bushing at pto end. The crankshaft on all other models is supported by ball bearings at both ends.

Model EH30, EH34, WO1-300 and WO1-340 engines are lubricated by splash lubrication. Models EH30V, EH34V, WO1-300V and WO1-340V are equipped with an oil pump in the oil pan that provides oil for splash lubrication of the engine. Models EH43V and WO1-430V are equipped with an oil pump in the oil pan that provides pressurized oil to the crankshaft.

Engine model and specification numbers are indicated on the nameplate attached to the flywheel shroud. The engine serial number is stamped on the crankcase base.

MAINTENANCE

LUBRICATION. Models EH30, EH34, WO1-300 and WO1-340 may be equipped with an oil sensor unit that grounds the ignition if oil level in sump is low. See OIL SENSOR paragraph.

Models EH43V and WO1-430V may be equipped with an oil pressure switch that grounds the ignition if oil pressure is low. Models EH30V, EH34V, EH43V, WO1-300V, WO1-340V and WO1-430V may be equipped with a spin-on type oil filter.

Oil should be changed after first 20 hours of operation and after every 50 hours of operation thereafter.

Engine oil should meet or exceed latest API service classification. Use SAE 30 oil when temperature is above 50° F (10° C), SAE 20W oil when temperature is between 50° F (10° C) and 32° F (0° C), SAE 10W oil when temperature is between 32° F (0° C) and 5° F (-15° C), and SAE 5W oil when temperature is below 5° F (-15° C).

Crankcase capacity is 1.2 liters (2.5 pt.) for Models EH30, EH34, WO1-300 and WO1-340, 1.1 liters (2.3 pt.) for Models EH30V, EH34V, WO1-300V and WO1-340V, and 1.3 liters (2.7 pt.) for Models EH43V and WO1-430V.

AIR FILTER. The air filter element should be cleaned weekly or after every 50 hours of operation, whichever occurs first. The foam element may be cleaned using warm water and soap. Dry the filter, then apply light oil. Squeeze excess oil from filter while noting if filter is completely coated with oil. Clean filter more frequently if extremely dirty or dusty conditions exist.

FUEL FILTER. On models so equipped, the fuel filter should be cleaned weekly or after every 100 hours of operation, whichever occurs first. The filter may be located in the fuel line or the fuel shutoff valve.

CRANKCASE BREATHER. All models are equipped with a breather to maintain a vacuum in the crankcase. Renew breather plate if reed is cracked or otherwise damaged. On Models EH30, EH34, WO1-300 and WO1-340, install breather plate so reed is towards crankcase cover.

SPARK PLUG. Recommended spark plug for all models is NGK BP6ES or Champion N9Y. Electrode gap should be 0.6-0.7 mm (0.024-0.028 inch). Tighten a new spark plug to 11.8-14.7 N•m (104-130 in.-lb.). Tighten a used spark plug to 22.6-26.5 N•m (17-19 ft.-lb.).

CARBURETOR. Refer to Fig. R801 for an exploded view of carburetor. The carburetor is equipped with an adjustable idle mixture screw (5) and a fixed main jet (21).

Initial setting of idle mixture screw (5) is 1 turn open from a lightly seated position for Models EH30 and WO1-300, 2 turns open for Models EH30V, WO1-300V and WO1-340V, ¾ turn open for Models EH34 and WO1-340 and 1½ turns open for Models EH43V and WO1-430V. Adjust idle mixture screw with engine at normal operating temperature so engine idles smoothly and accelerates without hesi-

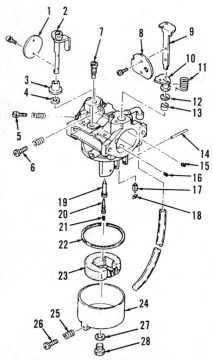

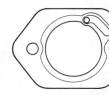

Fig. R801—Exploded view of carburetor used on Models EH43V and WO1-430V. Other models are similar.

1. Throttle plate
2. Throttle shaft
3. Spacer
4. Seal
5. Idle mixture screw
6. Idle speed screw
7. Idle mixture jet
8. Choke plate
9. Choke shaft
10. Collar
11. Spring
12. Seal
13. Bushing
14. Float pin

15. Air jet
16. Air jet
17. Fuel inlet valve
18. Clip
19. Main nozzle
20. Nozzle
21. Main jet
22. Gasket
23. Float
24. Fuel bowl
25. Spring
26. Drain screw
27. Gasket
28. Screw

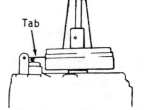

Fig. R802—Float should be parallel to gasket surface of carburetor. Bend tab to adjust float level.

tation. Adjust idle speed screw (6) so engine idle speed is 1200 rpm.

Remove the fuel bowl (24—Fig. R801) for access to internal components. Remove the float (23), fuel inlet valve (17), main jet (21) and nozzle (20). Unscrew idle mixture screw (5).

Clean all parts and fuel passages with carburetor cleaning solvent and compressed air. Replace parts that are worn or damaged.

To check or adjust float level, remove fuel bowl and invert carburetor. Float should be parallel to gasket surface of carburetor as shown in Fig. R802. Care-

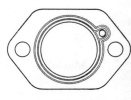

Fig. R803—Note design of gasket between carburetor and air cleaner base and install as shown. Lips on gasket must be towards air cleaner base.

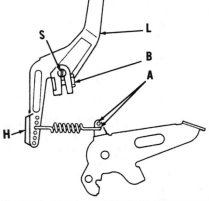

Fig. R804—Loosen clamp bolt (B), then with governor lever (L) in wide open throttle position, turn governor shaft (S) counterclockwise as far as possible. Governor spring is attached to holes (H) in governor lever and holes (A) in speed control lever. Spring location shown applies to engine operating at 3600 rpm and used on generator running at 60 hertz. Refer to Fig. R805 for governor linkage on vertical crankshaft engines.

fully bend the tab on float to adjust float level.

Refer to Fig. R803 and note configuration of gasket between carburetor and air cleaner base. Lips on gasket must be towards air cleaner base.

GOVERNOR. All models are equipped with a centrifugal flyweight type governor. Governor assembly is located in the crankcase cover or oil pan. To adjust governor, loosen governor lever clamp bolt (B—Fig. R804) and move governor lever (L) so carburetor throttle plate is fully open. Turn governor shaft (S) as far counterclockwise as possible and tighten clamp bolt.

On Models EH30, EH34, WO1-300 and WO1-340, governed speed is determined by location of governor spring ends in holes of governor lever and speed control lever as shown in Fig. R804. On Models EH30V, EH34V, EH43V, WO1-300V, WO1-340V and

WO1-430V, the location of governor spring ends in holes of governor lever and the adjustment of screw (Fig. R805) determines the governed speed. Governed speed may vary depending on engine application.

IGNITION. A solid-state ignition system is used on all models. A one-piece ignition module/coil is mounted outside the flywheel. Ignition timing is not adjustable. Air gap between coil legs and flywheel should be 0.3-0.5 mm (0.012-0.020 in.). Adjust air gap by loosening ignition coil mounting screws and relocating coil.

VALVE ADJUSTMENT. Engine must be cold when adjusting valve clearance. Rotate crankshaft so piston is at top dead center on compression stroke (Fig. R806). Both valves will be closed (rocker arms loose) on the compression stroke.

To check clearance, remove the rocker cover. Use a feeler gauge to measure clearance between rocker arm and valve stem. Specified clearance is 0.085-0.115 mm (0.0034-0.0045 inch) for intake and exhaust.

To adjust clearance, loosen nut (N—Fig. R807) and turn adjusting screw (S). Tighten nut and recheck clearance.

CYLINDER HEAD. Manufacturer recommends removal of carbon from cylinder head combustion chamber after 500-600 hours of operation.

REPAIRS

TIGHTENING TORQUE. Recommended tightening torque specifications are as follows:
Connecting rod . . . . 22-27 N•m
(16-20 ft.-lb.)

Crankcase cover/
oil pan . . . . 17-19 N•m
(150-168 in.-lb.)

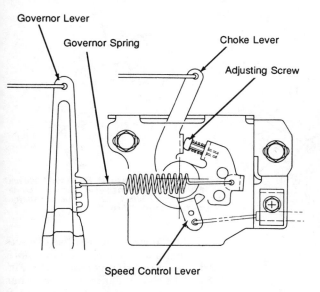

Governor Lever

Governor Spring

Choke Lever

Adjusting Screw

Speed Control Lever

Fig. R805—View of governor linkage used on vertical crankshaft engines. Location of governor spring ends in holes of governor lever and adjustment of screw determine governed speed.

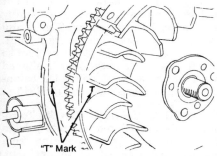

"T" Mark

Fig. R806—The piston is at top dead center when "T" marks on flywheel and crankcase are aligned.

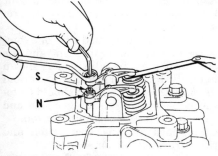

S

N

Fig. R807—To adjust valve clearance, loosen nut (N) and turn adjusting screw (S). Clearance should be 0.085-0.115 mm (0.0034-0.0045 inch).

Cylinder head	34-41 N•m
	(25-30 ft.-lb.)
Flywheel nut	84-93 N•m
	(62-68 ft.-lb.)
Spark plug:	
New	11.8-14.7 N•m
	(104-130 in.-lb.)
Used	22.6-26.5 N•m
	(17-19 ft.-lb.)

CYLINDER HEAD. To remove cylinder head, remove interfering air baffles and shroud. If required, remove fuel tank on models so equipped. On all models, disconnect throttle linkage and fuel line and remove carburetor. Remove muffler. Remove spark plug and rotate crankshaft so piston is at top dead center on compression (Fig. R806). Remove rocker arm cover. Mark push rods so they can be returned to original position. Unscrew cylinder head bolts and remove the cylinder head.

Clean carbon deposits from the combustion chamber being careful not to damage the gasket sealing area. Inspect the head for cracks or other damage. Check the cylinder head for distortion using a straightedge and feeler gauge. On all models, renew cylinder head if gasket surface is warped in excess of 0.10 mm (0.004 in.).

Always use a new head gasket when installing cylinder head. Tighten cylinder head screws evenly to 34-41 N•m (25-30 ft.-lb.).

VALVE SYSTEM. Valve face and seat angles are 45°. Valve seat width should be 0.7-1.0 mm (0.028-0.039 in.); maximum allowable seat width is 2.0 mm (0.079 in.).

Valve stem-to-guide clearance should be 0.050-0.087 mm (0.0020-0.0034 in.) for intake valve and 0.056-0.100 mm (0.0022-0.0039 in.) for exhaust valve. Maximum allowable valve stem-to-guide clearance for both valves is 0.300 mm (0.0118 in.).

Specified intake valve stem diameter is 6.535-6.550 mm (0.2573-0.2579 in.). Specified exhaust valve stem diameter is 6.522-6.544 mm (0.2568-0.2576 in.). Wear limit for either valve is 6.45 mm (0.2539 in.).

Specified valve guide inside diameter for both valves is 6.600-6.622 mm (0.2598-0.2607 in.) with a wear limit of 6.750 mm (0.2657 in.). Valve guides (7—Fig. R808) are renewable.

Models EH30V, EH34V, EH43V, WO1-300V, WO1-340V and WO1-430V are equipped with seals (6) for both valves while Models EH30, EH34, WO1-300 and WO1-340 are equipped with a seal for only the intake valve.

Specified valve spring free length is 39.5 mm (1.55 in.).

Rocker arm clearance on shaft should be 0.012-0.038 mm (0.0005-0.0015 in.). Specified rocker shaft diameter is 11.986-11.994 mm (0.4719-0.4722 in.) with a wear limit of 11.920 mm (0.4693 in.). Specified rocker arm bore is 12.006-12.024 mm (0.4727-0.4734 in.) with a wear limit of 12.070 mm (0.4752 in.).

CAMSHAFT AND TAPPETS. On Models EH30, EH34, WO1-300 and WO1-340, standard engines are equipped with a conventional camshaft which is referred to as the "D" type camshaft, while some engines may be equipped with camshaft that serves as the pto shaft and is referred to as the "B" type camshaft. See Fig. R809.

To remove camshaft, proceed as follows: Remove rocker arm cover and disengage push rods from rocker arms. Drain oil. Remove crankcase cover or oil pan. Position the engine so tappets cannot fall out or hold tappets in bores. Withdraw camshaft. If tappets are to be removed, mark them so they can be returned to original bores.

Camshaft lobe height for both valves should be 36.100-36.300 mm (1.4212-1.4291 in.). Minimum allowable lobe height is 35.950 mm (1.4154 in.). Specified camshaft bearing journal diameter is 19.967-19.980 mm (0.7861-0.7866 inch) for both ends, with a wear limit of 19.950 mm (0.7854 in.).

Specified outside diameter of tappets is 8.960-8.975 mm (0.3528-0.3533 in.). Tappet clearance in bore should be 0.025-0.055 mm inch (0.0010-0.0022).

The camshaft is equipped with a compression release device. Release lever (30—Fig. R810 or R811) extends above the camshaft exhaust lobe at slow engine speed (starting) thereby holding the exhaust valve open and reducing compression pressure. At running speed, the weight on the release lever moves the lever below the camshaft lobe. Release lever should move freely without binding.

Install camshaft by reversing removal procedure. Align timing marks (Fig. R812) on crankshaft and camshaft gears.

Camshaft end play on Models EH30, EH34, WO1-300 and WO1-340 should be 0.00-0.20 mm (0.000-0.008 in.) if

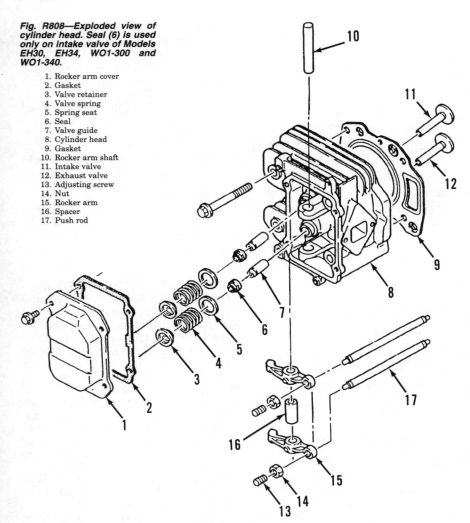

Fig. R808—Exploded view of cylinder head. Seal (6) is used only on intake valve of Models EH30, EH34, WO1-300 and WO1-340.

1. Rocker arm cover
2. Gasket
3. Valve retainer
4. Valve spring
5. Spring seat
6. Seal
7. Valve guide
8. Cylinder head
9. Gasket
10. Rocker arm shaft
11. Intake valve
12. Exhaust valve
13. Adjusting screw
14. Nut
15. Rocker arm
16. Spacer
17. Push rod

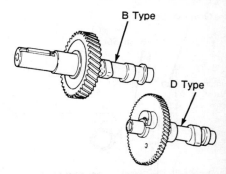

Fig. R809—On Models EH30, EH34, WO1-300 and WO1-340, "D" type camshaft is used when crankshaft is output shaft, while "B" type camshaft is used when camshaft is output shaft.

equipped with "B" type camshaft or 0.13-0.29 mm (0.005-0.011 in.) if equipped with "D" type camshaft (see Fig. R809). Camshaft end play on Models EH30V, EH34V, WO1-300V and WO1-340V should be 0.13-0.29 mm (0.005-0.011 in.). Camshaft end play on Models EH43V and WO1-430V should be 0.13-0.38 mm (0.005-0.015 in.). Camshaft end play is controlled by a shim (31—Fig. R810 or Fig. R811). Shims are available in several thicknesses, but only one shim is installed.

To determine shim thickness, measure from thrust surface (F—Fig. R813) on crankcase cover or oil pan to machined surface on crankcase cover or oil pan. Then, add the compressed thickness (C) of gasket, which is 0.26 mm (0.010 in.), to the measurement. From this total, subtract distance from camshaft thrust surface (E) to surface of crankcase machined surface (A). Calculation establishes end play without shim. Select shim to obtain specified camshaft end play.

When installing oil pan on Models EH30V, EH34V, EH43V, WO1-300V,

WO1-340V and WO1-430V, be sure drive pin in end of camshaft is properly aligned with slot in oil pump shaft. Do not force the oil pan onto crankcase. Light tapping only should be required if all components are properly aligned.

Tighten crankcase cover or oil pan screws to 17-19 N•m (150-168 in.-lb.).

BALANCER SHAFTS. The engine is equipped with two balancer shafts that are supported at both ends by ball bearings.

On Models EH30, EH34, WO1-300 and WO1-340, both balancer shaft gears contact the crankshaft drive gear as shown in Fig. R814. Note that the balancer shaft gear on the right has one timing mark on the gear face while the balancer shaft gear on the left has two timing marks. During installation be sure the balancer shafts are installed as shown in Fig. R814 and the timing marks are aligned with the correct timing marks on the drive gear on the crankshaft.

On Models EH30V, EH34V, EH43V, WO1-300V, WO1-340V and WO1-430V,

the left balancer shaft gear has two sets of timing marks, a single timing mark and a set of two timing marks. See Fig. R815. The right balancer shaft gear has a single timing mark. Install the left balancer shaft and align the two timing marks on the balancer shaft gear and on the drive gear on the crankshaft. Then install the right balancer shaft so the timing mark on the gear is aligned with the timing mark on the left balancer shaft gear as shown in Fig. R815.

PISTON, PIN AND RINGS. To remove piston and rod assembly, drain engine oil and remove engine from equipment. Remove cylinder head. Clean pto end of crankshaft and remove any burrs or rust. Unscrew fasteners and remove crankcase cover or oil pan. Remove camshaft and balancer shafts. Unscrew connecting rod screws and remove piston and rod.

The piston is equipped with one compression ring, one scraper ring and one oil control ring. Install rings as shown in Fig. R816. Side of piston ring marked "N" or with a punch mark should be towards piston crown. Stagger ring end gaps at 90° intervals around piston.

Standard and oversize piston and rings are available for service.

Piston ring end gap for the top compression ring on all models should be 0.20-0.40 mm (0.008-0.016 in.); maximum allowable gap is 1.5 mm (0.059 in.). Piston ring end gap for the second compression (scraper) ring should be 0.20-0.40 mm (0.008-0.016 in.). Piston ring end gap for the oil control ring should be 0.10-0.30 mm (0.004-0.012 in.); maximum allowable gap is 1.5 mm (0.059 in.).

Specified piston ring side clearance is listed below:

Top ring	0.050-0.090 mm
	(0.0020-0.0035 in.)
Second ring	0.030-0.070 mm
	(0.0012-0.0028 in.)
Oil ring	0.010-0.065 mm
	(0.0004-0.0026 in.)

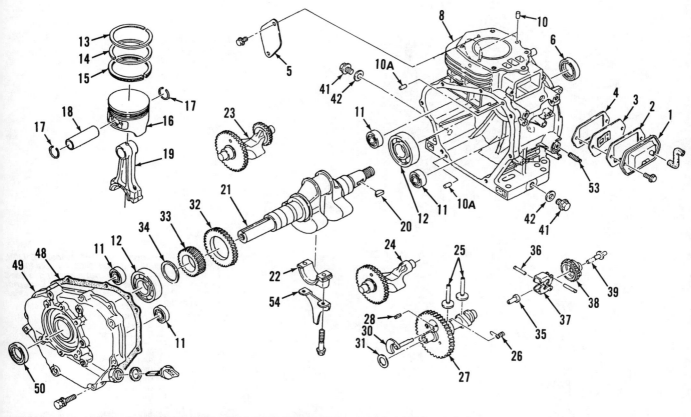

Fig. R810—Exploded view of Models EH30, EH34, WO1-300 and WO1-340. Governor shaft (39) is attached to crankcase cover (49) and not available separately.

1. Breather cover	10A. Dowel pin	23. Balancer	31. Shim	39. Shaft
2. Gasket	11. Ball bearing	24. Balancer	32. Balancer drive gear	41. Drain plug
3. Breather plate	12. Bearing	25. Tappet	33. Gear	42. Washer
4. Gasket	13. Top compression ring	26. Spring	34. Shim	48. Gasket
5. Cover	14. Second compression	27. Camshaft	35. Sleeve	49. Crankcase cover
6. Seal	ring	28. Pin	36. Pin	50. Seal
8. Crankcase	15. Oil ring	30. Compression release	37. Flyweight	53. Stud
10. Dowel pin	16. Piston	arm	38. Governor gear	54. Oil slinger
	17. Snap ring	21. Crankshaft		
	18. Piston pin	22. Rod cap		
	19. Connecting rod			
	20. Key			

Insert each ring into its piston ring groove and measure side clearance between the ring and ring land with a feeler gauge. Renew piston rings and/or piston if ring side clearance exceeds 0.15 mm (0.006 in.).

Specified piston-to-cylinder clearance is 0.025-0.064 mm (0.0010-0.0025 in.) with a maximum clearance of 0.250 mm (0.0098 in.).

Piston diameter specifications are listed in the table below. Measure piston diameter on skirt perpendicular to pin hole.

Model   Piston Diameter
EH30, EH30V, WO1-300,
  WO1-300V . . . . . (77.960-77.980 mm)
                                (3.0693-3.0701 in.)
  Wear limit . . . . (77.87 mm)
                                (3.066 in.)

EH34, EH34V, WO1-340,
  WO1-340V . . . . . (83.960-83.980 mm)
                                (3.3055-3.3063 in.)
  Wear limit . . . . (83.87 mm)
                                (3.302 in.)

EH43V,
  WO1-430V . . . . . (88.960-88.980 mm)
                                (3.5024-3.5031 in.)
  Wear limit . . . . (88.87 mm)
                                (3.499 in.)

Piston pin specifications are listed in the table below.
Piston pin—
  Diameter . . . . (20.991-21.000 mm)
                                (0.8264-0.8268 in.)
  Wear limit . . . . (20.960 mm)
                                (0.8252 in.)

Pin bore in piston—
  Diameter . . . . (20.995-21.008 mm)
                                (0.8266-0.8271 in.)
  Wear limit . . . . (21.035 mm)
                                (0.8281 in.)

Pin-to-bore clearance should be 0.005 mm (0.0002 in.) tight to 0.017 mm (0.0007 in.) loose. Maximum allowable piston pin clearance in piston is 0.060 mm (0.0024 in.).

Assemble piston and connecting rod on Models EH30V, EH34V, EH43V, WO1-300V, WO1-340V and WO1-430V so "DF" on side of rod is on same side as "DF" on piston crown as shown in Fig. R817. Install piston and rod in engine so "DF" marks are towards flywheel.

Assemble piston and connecting rod on Models EH30, EH34, WO1-300 and WO1-340 with "D" type camshaft (see Fig. R809) so "DF" on side of rod is on same side as "DF" on piston crown as shown in Fig. R817. Install piston and rod in engine so "DF" marks are towards flywheel.

Assemble piston and connecting rod on Models EH30, EH34, WO1-300 and WO1-340 with "B" type camshaft (see Fig. R809) so "BF" on side of rod is on same side as "BF" on piston crown. See Fig. R817. Install piston and rod in engine so "BF" marks are towards flywheel.

Align match marks (cast ribs) on connecting rod and cap as shown in Fig. R818. On Models EH30, EH34, WO1-300 and WO1-340, install oil dipper so offset is towards flywheel. On all

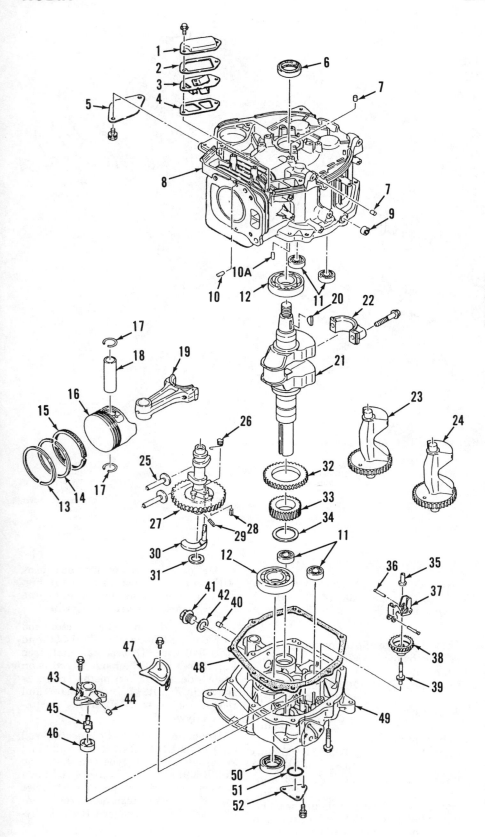

Fig. R811—Exploded view of Models EH30V, EH34V, WO1-300V and WO1-340V. Models EH43V and WO1-430V are similar, but a bushing is used in place of lower main ball bearing (12). Governor shaft (39) is attached to oil pan (49) and not available separately.

1. Breather cover
2. Gasket
3. Breather plate
4. Gasket
5. Cover
6. Seal
7. Plug
8. Crankcase
9. Governor shaft seal
10. Dowel pin
10A. Dowel pin
11. Ball bearing
12. Bearing
13. Top compression ring
14. Second compression ring
15. Oil ring
16. Piston
17. Snap ring
18. Piston pin
19. Connecting rod
20. Key
21. Crankshaft
22. Rod cap
23. Balancer
24. Balancer
25. Tappet
26. Spring
27. Camshaft
28. Pin
29. Pin
30. Compression release arm
31. Shim
32. Balancer drive gear
33. Gear
34. Shim
35. Sleeve
36. Pin
37. Flyweight
38. Governor gear
39. Shaft
40. Plug
41. Drain plug
42. Washer
43. Oil pump housing
44. Plug
45. Inner rotor
46. Outer rotor
47. Cover
48. Gasket
49. Oil pan
50. Seal
51. "O" ring
52. Cover

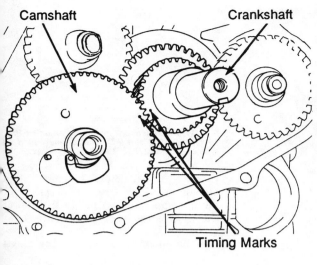

Fig. R812—View of timing marks on crankshaft and camshaft gears on Models EH30, EH34, WO1-300 and WO1-340. Other models are similar.

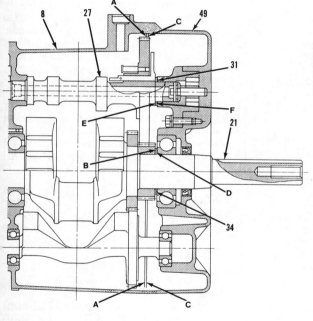

Fig. R813—View showing location of measuring points to determine correct shim thickness for obtaining correct camshaft and crankshaft end play. Refer to text.

8. Crankcase
21. Crankshaft
27. Camshaft
31. Shim
34. Shim
49. Crankcase cover or oil pan

models, tighten connecting rod cap screws to 22-27 N•m (16-20 ft.-lb.).

When installing oil pan on Models EH30V, EH34V, EH43V, WO1-300V, WO1-340V and WO1-430V, be sure drive pin in end of camshaft is properly aligned with slot in oil pump shaft. Do not force the oil pan onto crankcase. Light tapping only should be required if all components are properly aligned.

Tighten crankcase cover or oil pan screws to 17-19 N•m (150-168 in.-lb.)

CONNECTING ROD. Connecting rod and piston are removed as a unit as outlined in previous section. Connecting rod rides directly on crankpin.

Connecting rod-to-crankpin clearance should be 0.030-0.060 mm (0.0012-0.0024 in.). If clearance exceeds 0.20 mm (0.008 in.), renew rod and/or crankshaft. Specified connecting rod big end diameter is 38.000-38.016 mm (1.4961-1.4967 in.) with a wear limit of 38.100 mm (1.5000 in.). Oversize connecting rods are not available.

Connecting rod side clearance should be 0.1-0.3 mm (0.004-0.012 in.). If side clearance exceeds 1.0 mm (0.039 in.), renew connecting rod and/or crankshaft.

Piston pin clearance in connecting rod should be 0.010-0.032 mm (0.0004-0.0012 in.); maximum allowable clearance is 0.120 mm (0.0047 in.). Specified connecting rod small end diameter is 21.010-21.023 mm (0.8272-0.8277 in.).

GOVERNOR. The governor gear and flyweight assembly rides on a stud (39—Fig. R810 or Fig. R811) located in the crankcase or oil pan. Components must move freely without binding.

Governor sleeve (35) is available separately for service. All other components of governor are serviced as an assembly.

CRANKSHAFT. The crankshaft on Models EH43V and WO1-430V is supported by a ball bearing at flywheel end and by a bushing in the oil pan at pto end. The crankshaft on all other models is supported by ball bearings at both ends. Renew bearings if excessively worn or otherwise damaged.

Specified crankpin diameter is 37.956-37.970 mm (1.4943-1.4949 in.) with a wear limit of 37.85 mm (1.490 in.). Specified main bearing journal diameter at flywheel end on all models is 34.986-34.997 mm (1.3774-1.3778 in.). Specified main bearing journal diameter at pto end on Models EH43V and WO1-430V is 34.984-35.000 mm (1.3773-1.3780 in.). Specified main bearing journal diameter at pto end on

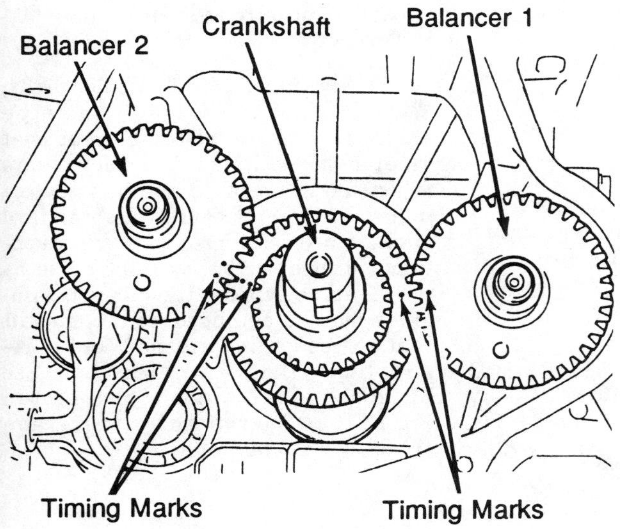

Fig. R814—View showing balancer gear timing marks on Models EH30, EH34, WO1-300 and WO1-340.

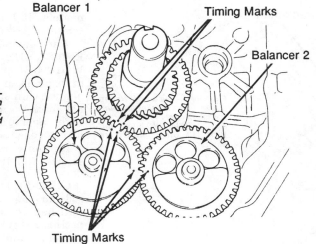

Fig. R815—View showing balancer gear timing marks on Models EH30V, EH34V, EH43V, WO1-300V, WO1-340V and WO1-430V.

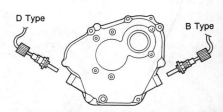

Fig. R819—Oil sensor location on Models EH30, EH34, WO1-300 and WO1-340 is determined by type of camshaft (Fig. R809) used. See text.

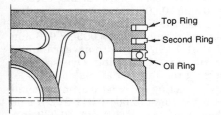

Fig. R816—Install piston rings as shown.

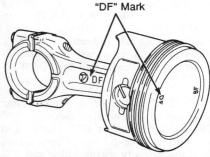

Fig. R817—Except as noted in text, "DF" marks on rod and piston should be on same side.

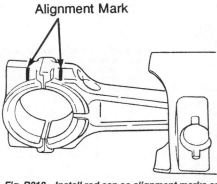

Fig. R818—Install rod cap so alignment marks on rod and cap are on same side.

all models except Models EH43V and WO1-430V is 34.986-34.997 mm (1.3774-1.3778 in.).

Main bearing bushing in oil pan on Models EH43V and WO1-430V is renewable.

Connecting rod-to-crankpin clearance should be 0.030-0.060 mm (0.0012-0.0024 in.). If clearance exceeds 0.20 mm (0.008 in.), renew rod and/or crankshaft.

Crankshaft end play should be 0.00-0.20 mm (0.000-0.008 in.). End play is controlled by a shim (34—Fig. R810 or R811) located between crankshaft gear and main bearing. Shims are available in several thicknesses, but only one shim is installed.

To determine shim thickness, measure from inner race of bearing (D—Fig. R813) to machined surface on crankcase cover or oil pan. Add the compressed thickness (C) of gasket, which is 0.26 mm (0.010 in.), to the measurement. From this total, subtract distance from thrust surface (B) of large crankshaft gear to surface of crankcase machined surface (A). Calculation establishes end play without shim. Select shim so crankshaft end play is 0.00-0.20 mm (0.000-0.008 in.).

When installing oil pan on Models EH30V, EH34V, EH43V, WO1-300V, WO1-340V and WO1-430V, be sure drive pin in end of camshaft is properly aligned with slot in oil pump shaft. Do not force the oil pan onto crankcase. Light tapping only should be required if all components are properly aligned.

Tighten crankcase cover or oil pan screws to 17-19 N•m (150-168 in.-lb.).

OIL PUMP. On Models EH30V, EH34V, EH43V, WO1-300V, WO1-340V and WO1-430V, an oil pump (43—Fig. R811) located in the oil pan provides

pressure lubrication to the engine. The oil pan must be removed for access to oil pump components. A pin in the end of the camshaft drives the oil pump.

Renew the oil pump housing and rotors if damage or excessive wear is evident.

When installing oil pan, be sure drive pin in end of camshaft is properly aligned with slot in oil pump shaft. Do not force the oil pan onto crankcase. Light tapping only should be required if all components are properly aligned.

Tighten crankcase cover or oil pan screws to 17-19 N•m (150-168 in.-lb.)

CYLINDER. Measure the cylinder bore at the top and bottom, and parallel and perpendicular to crankshaft to determine cylinder wear and out-of-round dimensions. Standard cylinder bore diameter is listed in the table below.

Model	Cylinder Bore Diameter
EH30, EH30V, WO1-300, WO1-300V	(78.000-78.019 mm) (3.0709-3.0716 in.)
EH34, EH34V, WO1-340, WO1-340V	(84.000-84.022 mm) (3.3071-3.3079 in.)
EH43V, WO1-430V	(89.000-890.22 mm) (3.5040-3.5048 in.)

Cylinder should be bored for oversize piston or renewed if cylinder taper (wear) or out-of-round is 0.1 mm (0.004 in.) or more.

OIL SENSOR. Models EH30, EH34, WO1-300 and WO1-340 may be equipped with an oil sensor unit that grounds the ignition if oil level in sump is low. Location of oil sensor is determined by type of camshaft. Standard engines are equipped with a conventional camshaft that is referred to as the "D" type camshaft, while some engines may be equipped with camshaft that serves as the pto shaft and is referred to as the "B" type camshaft. See Fig. R809. Note location of oil sensor in Fig. R819 as determined by type of camshaft used in engine.

ROBIN
(WISCONSIN ROBIN)
SERVICING ROBIN ACCESSORIES

REWIND STARTER

Models EH25 and EY28

OVERHAUL. Refer to Fig. RA100 for an exploded view of starter used on Models EH25 and EY28. To disassemble starter, remove the rope handle and allow rope to wind into starter. Unscrew the retaining screw (2). Wear appropriate safety eyewear and gloves before disengaging the pulley (5) from the starter housing as the rewind spring may uncoil uncontrolled. Place a shop cloth around the pulley and lift it out of the housing. Use caution when detaching the rewind spring (8) from the pulley or housing. If spring must be removed from the starter housing, position the housing so spring side is down and against floor, then tap housing to dislodge the spring.

Apply light grease to the pulley shaft and the sliding surfaces of rewind spring, pawls (6) and friction springs (7). Wrap the starter rope around the pulley in counterclockwise direction viewed from flywheel side of pulley. Install the rewind spring (8—Fig. RA100) in spring cavity in the pulley in a coun-terclockwise direction from outer end. Install the pulley in the starter housing so inner end of spring engages the tab on starter housing, and route rope through rope outlet in housing. Attach the rope handle. Install snap ring (4) on shaft. Install the friction springs (7), pawls (6), ratchet guide (3) and screw (2).

To place tension on starter rope, pull the rope out of the housing until the notch in the pulley is aligned with rope outlet. Use thumb pressure against the pulley to prevent pulley rotation. Pull the rope back into the housing while positioning the rope in pulley notch. Turn the rope pulley two turns counterclockwise, disengage rope from notch and allow the rope to wind onto the pulley. Check starter operation.

Models EY21W, EY25W, EY27W And EY44W

OVERHAUL. To disassemble the rewind starter, refer to Fig. RA101 and release spring tension as follows: Pull the rope handle until about 18 inches (457 mm) of rope extends from the starter housing. Use thumb pressure against ratchet retainer to prevent the reel from rewinding, and place rope in notch in outer rim of reel. Release thumb pressure slightly and allow the spring mechanism to slowly unwind. Twist loop of return spring and slip loop through slot in ratchet retainer.

Refer to Fig. RA102 and remove nut, lockwasher, plain washer and ratchet retainer. The reel will completely unwind as these parts are removed. Remove the compression spring, three ratchets and spring retainer washer. Slip your fingers into two of the cavity openings in reel hub (Fig. RA103) and carefully lift reel from support shaft in housing.

CAUTION: Take extreme care that the rewind spring remains in recess of housing. Do not remove spring unless new spring is to be installed.

If the rewind spring escapes from the starter housing, form a 4½ inch (114 mm) wire ring and twist ends together securely. Starting with the outside loop, wind spring inside the ring in a counterclockwise direction.

NOTE: New rewind springs are secured in a similar wire ring for ease in assembly.

Place the spring assembly over the recess in starter housing so hook in outer loop of spring is positioned over the tension tab in housing. Carefully press the spring from the wire ring and into the recess of housing.

Using a new rope of same length and diameter as original, place rope in han-

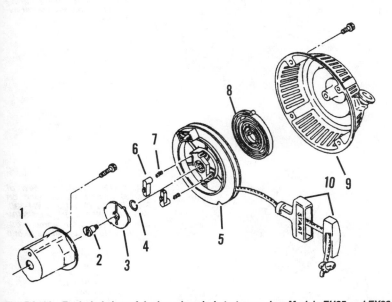

Fig. RA100—Exploded view of dual-pawl rewind starter used on Models EH25 and EY28.

1. Drive cup	4. Snap ring	
2. Screw	5. Pulley	7. Spring	9. Starter housing
3. Ratchet guide	6. Pawl	8. Rewind spring	10. Rope handle

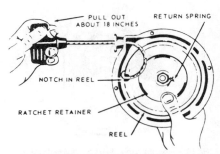

Fig. RA101—View showing method of releasing spring tension on rewind starter assembly.

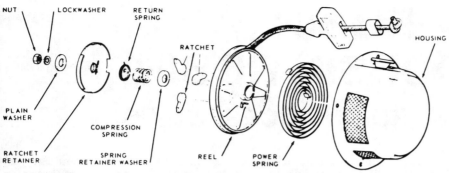

Fig. RA102—Exploded view of rewind starter assembly used on Models EY21W, EY25W, EY27W and EY44W.

dle and tie a figure eight knot about 1½ inches (38 mm) from end. Pull the knot into the top of handle. Install other end of rope through the guide bushing of housing and through the hole in reel groove. Pull the rope out through cavity opening and tie a slip knot about 2½ inches (64 mm) from end. Place a slip knot around center bushing as shown in Fig. RA104 and pull the knot tight. Stuff end of rope into the reel cavity. Spread a film of light grease on the rewind spring and support shaft.

Wind the rope ¼ turn counterclockwise in the reel and place rope in notch on reel. Install the reel on the support shaft and rotate reel counterclockwise until the tang on reel engages the hook on inner loop of power spring. Place the outer flange of the starter housing in a vise and use finger pressure to keep reel in housing. Hook a loop of rope in the reel notch and preload the rewind spring by turning the reel 7 full turns counterclockwise. Remove the rope from notch in pulley and allow the reel to slowly turn clockwise as the rope winds on the reel and the handle returns to the guide bushing on the housing.

Install the spring retainer washer (Fig. RA102), cup-side up, and place the compression spring into cupped washer.

Install the return spring with bent end hooked into hole of reel hub. Place the three ratchets in position so they fit the contour of the recesses. Mount the ratchet retainer so loop end of return spring extends through the slot. Rotate the retainer slightly clockwise until ends of slots just begin to engage the three ratchets. Press down on the retainer, install the flat washer, lockwasher and nut.

Models EH30V, EH34V, EH43V, EY35, EY40, W1-280, W1-340, W1-390, W1-450V, WO1-300V, WO1-340V and WO1-450V

OVERHAUL. To disassemble the rewind starter, refer to Fig. RA105 and release spring tension as follows: Pull the rope handle until about 14 inches (356 mm) of rope extends from the starter housing. Use thumb pressure to prevent the reel from rewinding, and place the starter rope in notch in outer rim of reel. Release thumb pressure slightly and allow spring mechanism to slowly unwind.

Remove clip or nut (2—Fig. RA106), and remove components (3 through 7). Slowly remove reel from support shaft in housing.

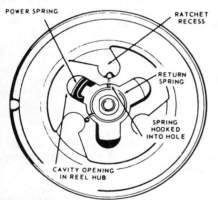

Fig. RA103—Use fingers in reel hub cavities to lift reel from support shaft.

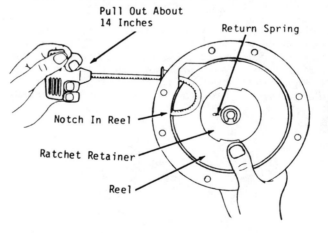

Fig. RA105—View showing method of releasing spring tension on rewind starter assembly.

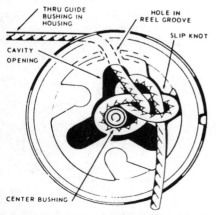

Fig. RA104—Install rope through guide bushing end hole in reel groove, then tie slip knot around center bushing.

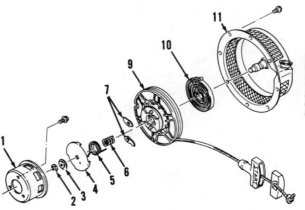

Fig. RA106—Exploded view of typical rewind starter used on Models W1-280, W1-340, W1-390, W1-450V, WO1-300V, WO1-340V and WO1-450V. On some models, a nut is used in place of clip (2).

1. Starter cup
2. Clip
3. Thrust washer
4. Ratchet retainer
5. Return spring
6. Compression spring
7. Ratchet
9. Reel
10. Rewind spring
11. Housing

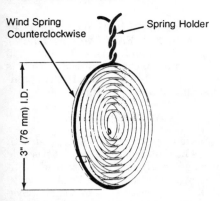

Fig. RA107—Illustration showing fabricated spring holder used to hold rewind spring.

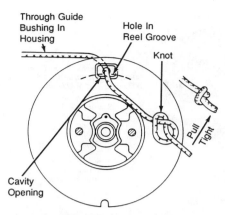

Fig. RA109—Install rope through guide bushing and hole in reel groove, then tie knot as shown.

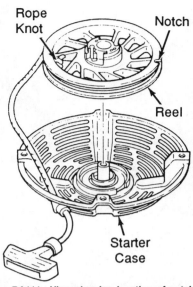

Fig. RA111—View showing location of notch in pulley rim and end of rope in hole of reel.

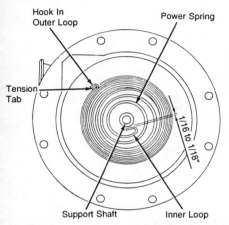

Fig. RA108—Reel must be installed with hook in outer loop of rewind spring engaged on tension tab and inner loop of spring spaced as shown from support shaft.

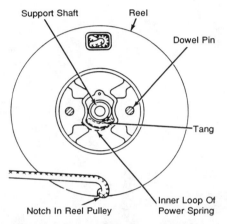

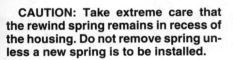

Fig. RA110—When installing reel in housing, engage inner loop of rewind spring on tang of reel. Refer to text.

and looped end toward outside, then mount the ratchet retainer so the loop end of return spring extends through slot. Rotate the retainer slightly clockwise until ends of slots just begin to engage the ratchets. Press down on the retainer, install the washer and clip.

Models EH30, EH34, WO1-300 and WO1-340

OVERHAUL. To disassemble the rewind starter, refer to Fig. RA111 and release spring tension as follows: Pull the rope handle until about 14 inches (356 mm) of rope extends from the starter housing. Use thumb pressure to prevent the reel from rewinding and place rope in notch (Fig. RA111) in outer rim of reel. Release thumb pressure slightly and allow the spring mechanism to slowly unwind.

Unscrew the center screw (2—Fig. RA112), and remove components (3 through 6). Slowly remove the reel from the support shaft in starter housing.

CAUTION: Take extreme care that the rewind spring cup remains in the recess of reel. Do not remove spring unless a new spring is to be installed.

If the rewind spring escapes from the spring cup, install the rewind spring and cup in reel so the spring ends are positioned as shown in Fig. RA113. Using a new rope of same length and diameter as original, place the rope in the handle and tie a figure eight knot about 1 inch (25 mm) from the end. Pull the knot into the top of the handle. Install other end of the rope through the guide

CAUTION: Take extreme care that the rewind spring remains in recess of the housing. Do not remove spring unless a new spring is to be installed.

If the rewind spring escapes from the housing, form a wire ring of same circumference as recess in housing and twist ends together securely. Starting with the outside loop, wind the spring inside the ring in counterclockwise direction as shown in Fig. RA107.

NOTE: New rewind springs are secured in a similar wire ring for ease in assembly.

Place the new spring assembly over recess in housing so the hook in outer loop of spring is positioned over the tension tab in the housing. Carefully press the spring from the wire ring and into recess of housing. See Fig. RA108.

Using a new rope of same length and diameter as original, place rope in handle and tie a figure eight knot about 1 inch (25 mm) from the end. Pull the knot into top of handle. Install the other

end of the rope through the guide bushing of housing and through the hole in the reel groove. Pull the rope out through cavity opening and tie a knot about 1 inch (25 mm) from the end. Tie the knot as illustrated in Fig. RA109 and stuff knot into the cavity opening. Wind the rope 2½ turns counterclockwise on reel, then lock the rope in the notch of reel. Install the reel on the support shaft and rotate reel counterclockwise until tang on the reel engages the hook on inner loop of rewind spring (see Fig. RA110).

Place the outer flange of the housing in a vise and use finger pressure to keep the reel in the housing. Hook a loop of rope into the reel notch and preload the rewind spring by turning reel four full turns counterclockwise. Remove the rope from the notch and allow the reel to slowly turn clockwise as the rope winds on the reel and the handle returns to the guide bushing on housing. Refer to Fig. RA106 and install components (2 through 7).

Install the return spring (5) with bent end hooked into hole of reel hub

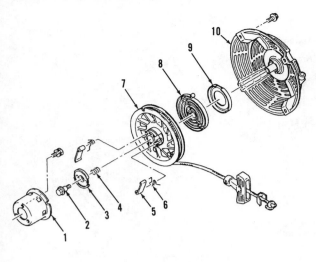

Service specifications for starter shown in Fig. RA117 are as follows. Minimum brush length is 9.0 mm (0.35 in.). Minimum commutator diameter is 29.00 mm (1.142 in.). Brush spring tension should be 1.4-1.8 kg (3-4 lbs.).

ALTERNATORS

Some engines may be equipped with a flywheel alternator. To avoid possible damage to alternator system, the following precautions must be observed:
1. Observe correct system polarity. System is for negative ground only.
2. Connect booster battery properly (positive to positive and negative to negative.)

Fig. RA112—Exploded view of rewind starter used on Models WO1-300 and WO1-340.

1. Starter cup
2. Center screw
3. Retainer
4. Spring
5. Pawl
6. Spring
7. Reel
8. Rewind spring
9. Spring cup
10. Starter housing

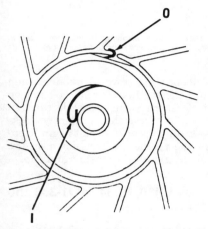

Fig. RA113—Note position of inner end (I) and outer end (O) of rewind spring in reel.

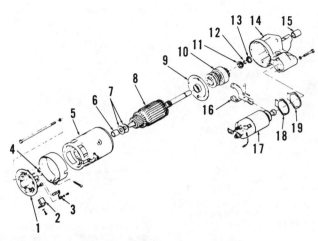

Fig. RA114—Exploded view of starter motor used on Model EY21W.

1. End cover & brush holder assy.
2. Negative brush (2 used)
3. Positive brush (2 used)
4. Brush spring
5. Frame & coil assy.
6. Bushing
7. Thrust washer
8. Armature
9. Center bearing
10. Drive assy.
11. Pinion stop collar
12. Snap ring
13. Thrust washer
14. Drive end housing
15. Bushing
16. Shift lever
17. Solenoid
18. Gasket
19. Dust plate

bushing of the housing and through the hole in reel groove. Pull the rope out through the opening in the reel. Tie a knot at end of rope and pull the knot against the reel as shown in Fig. RA111. Wind the rope 2½ turns counterclockwise on the reel, then lock the rope in notch of reel. Install the reel on the support shaft and rotate the reel counterclockwise until inner end of rewind spring is engaged. Assemble remainder of components.

Hook a loop of rope into the reel notch and preload the rewind spring by turning the reel four full turns counterclockwise. Remove the rope from the notch and allow the reel to slowly turn clockwise as the rope winds on the reel and the handle returns to the guide bushing on the starter housing. Check operation of starter.

12-VOLT STARTER MOTORS

Refer to Figs. RA114, RA115, RA116, RA117 and RA118 for exploded views of 12-volt starter motors used on some Robin engines. Parts are available from Robin distributors or service centers.

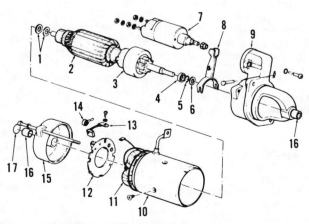

Fig. RA115—Exploded view of starter motor used on Model EY44W.

1. Thrust washers
2. Armature
3. Drive assy.
4. Pinion stopper
5. Snap ring
6. Thrust washer
7. Solenoid
8. Shift lever
9. Drive end housing
10. Frame
11. Field coils
12. Brush plate
13. Brush
14. Brush spring
15. End cap
16. Bushings
17. Expansion plug

Fig. RA116—Exploded view of starter motor used on Models W1-340 and W1-390.

1. Snap ring
2. Pinion stopper
3. Return spring
4. Drive assy.
5. Drive end housing
6. Thrust washers
7. Armature
8. Frame
9. Thrust washers
10. Pole magnets
11. Field coils
12. Brush spring
13. Brush plate
14. Brush
15. End cap
16. Through bolt

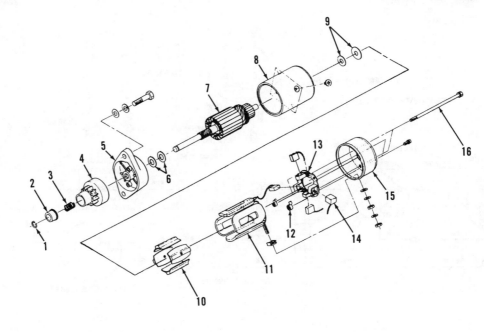

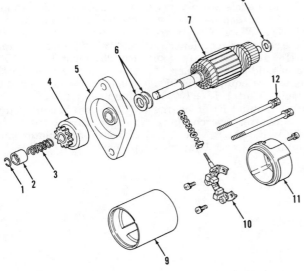

Fig. RA117—Exploded view of starter motor used on Models W1-450V, WO1-300, WO1-300V, WO1-340, WO1-340V and WO1-430V.

1. Snap ring
2. Pinion stopper
3. Return spring
4. Drive assy.
5. Drive end housing
6. Thrust washers
7. Armature
8. Thrust washer
9. Frame
10. Brush plate
11. End cap
12. Through-bolt

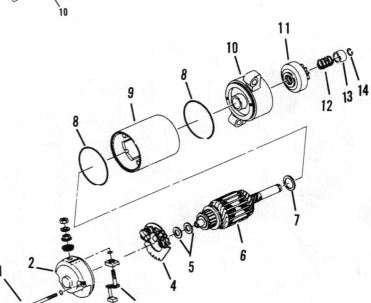

Fig. RA118—Exploded view of starter motor used on Model EH25 engines.

1. Through-bolt
2. End cap
3. Brush assy.
4. Brush holder
5. Thrust washers
6. Armature
7. Thrust washer
8. "O" ring
9. Frame
10. Drive end housing
11. Drive assy.
12. Spring
13. Pinion stop nut
14. Snap ring

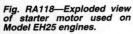

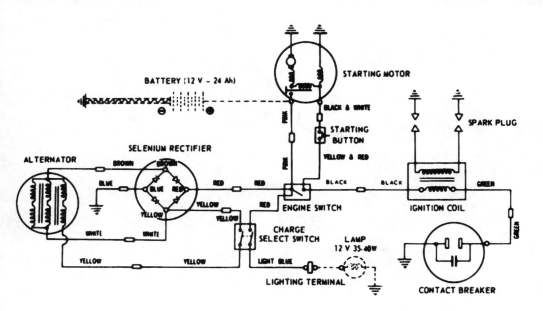

Fig. RA119—Typical wiring diagram of Model EY21W electrical system.

3. Do not attempt to polarize alternator.

4. Do not ground any wires from stator or modules that terminate at connectors.

5. Do not operate engine with battery disconnected.

6. Disconnect battery cables when charging battery with a battery charger.

Refer to Figs. RA119, RA121, RA122, RA123, RA124, RA125, RA126, RA127, RA128, RA129 and RA130 for wiring schematics. On all models, the alternator stator is located behind the flywheel. Models EY21W and EY44W are equipped with a selenium rectifier (Fig. RA120) while other models are equipped with a solid-state rectifier.

Some systems are equipped with a charge switch. Model EY21W is equipped with a manual Hi-Lo charge switch to prevent battery overcharging. On Model EY44W, if battery overcharging is indicated, disconnect light blue wire marked 1.5A from rectifier and connect light blue wire marked 1.0A. The charge switch on Models W1-340 and W1-390 with 12.5 amp system (Fig. RA125) must be in "ON" position to charge battery and in "OFF" position when engine is stopped to prevent discharge of battery.

If system is equipped with a regulator, be sure battery is sufficiently charged or regulator may not function properly.

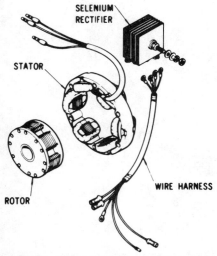

Fig. RA120—Alternator stator and rotor and selenium rectifier used on Model EY21W.

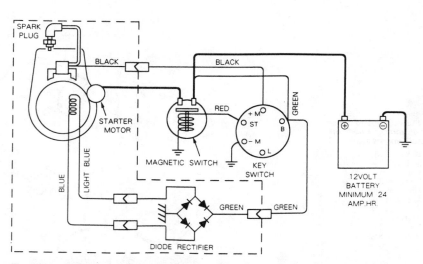

Fig. RA121—Wiring diagram for Model EH25 engine with electric starter.

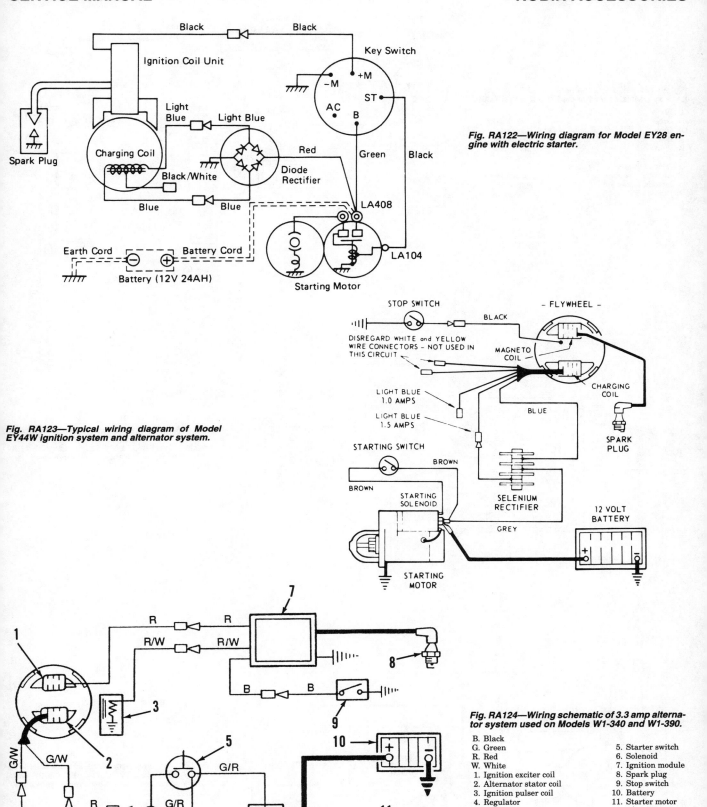

Fig. RA122—Wiring diagram for Model EY28 engine with electric starter.

Fig. RA123—Typical wiring diagram of Model EY44W ignition system and alternator system.

Fig. RA124—Wiring schematic of 3.3 amp alternator system used on Models W1-340 and W1-390.

B. Black
G. Green
R. Red
W. White
1. Ignition exciter coil
2. Alternator stator coil
3. Ignition pulser coil
4. Regulator
5. Starter switch
6. Solenoid
7. Ignition module
8. Spark plug
9. Stop switch
10. Battery
11. Starter motor

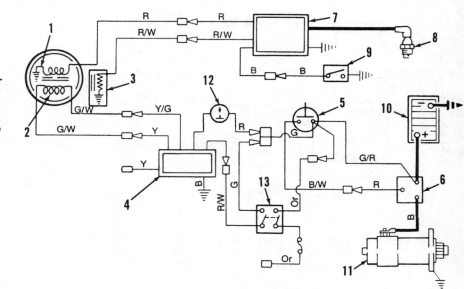

Fig. RA125—Wiring schematic of 12.5 amp alternator system used on Models W1-340 and W1-390.

- B. Black
- G. Green
- Or. Orange
- R. Red
- W. White
- Y. Yellow
- 1. Ignition exciter coil
- 2. Alternator stator coil
- 3. Ignition pulser coil
- 4. Regulator
- 5. Starter switch
- 6. Solenoid
- 7. Ignition module
- 8. Spark plug
- 9. Stop switch
- 10. Battery
- 11. Starter motor
- 12. Ammeter
- 13. Charge switch

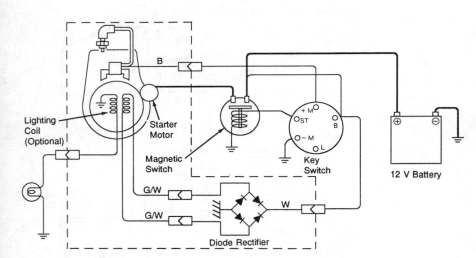

Fig. RA126—Wiring schematic for Models EH30, EH30V, EH34, EH34V, EH43V, W1-450V, WO1-300, WO1-300V, WO1-340, WO1-340V and WO1-430V equipped with an alternator system and key switch.

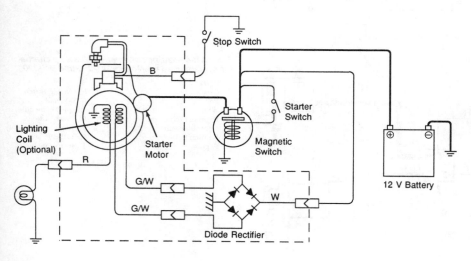

Fig. RA127—Wiring schematic for Models W1-450V, WO1-300, WO1-300V, WO1-340, WO1-340V and WO1-430V equipped with an alternator system and starter switch.

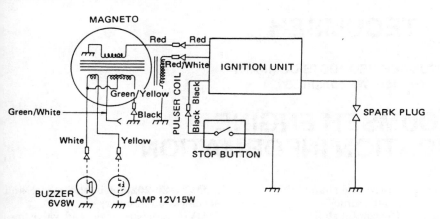

Fig. RA128—Wiring schematic for Models EY35 and EY40 with rewind starter and lighting coil.

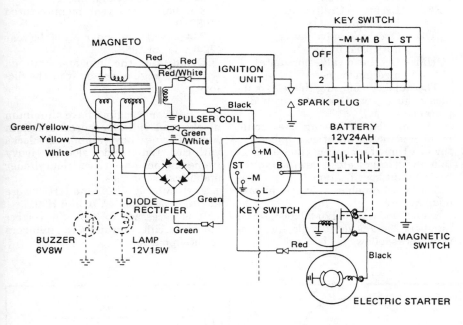

Fig. RA129—Wiring schematic for Models EY35 and EY40 with solid-state ignition and electric starter.

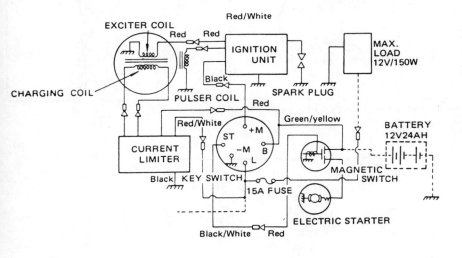

Fig. RA130—Wiring schematic for Models EY35 and EY40 with solid-state ignition and 150W alternator system.

TECUMSEH

TECUMSEH PRODUCTS COMPANY
Grafton, Wisconsin 53024

TECUMSEH ENGINE
IDENTIFICATION INFORMATION

In order to obtain correct service parts it is necessary to locate and correctly identify engine model, specification and serial numbers.

Model and serial numbers can be stamped into blower housing at cylinder head end or on a nameplate or tag located on the side of the blower housing. Refer to Fig. T1.

Letters at the beginning of the model number indicates the basic engine type.

　　V – Vertical shaft
　VM – Vertical shaft, medium frame
　LAV – Lightweight aluminum, vertical shaft
　VH – Vertical shaft, heavy duty (cast iron)
　TVS – Tecumseh vertical styled
　TNT – Toro N' Tecumseh
　ECV – Exclusive Craftsman vertical
　OVM – Overhead valve, vertical medium frame
OVRM – Overhead valve vertical rotary mower
　　H – Horizontal shaft

　HS – Horizontal shaft, small frame
　HM – Horizontal shaft, small frame
HHM – Horizontal shaft heavy duty, medium frame
　HH – Horizontal shaft heavy duty (cast iron)
ECH – Exclusive Craftsman horizontal
　OH – Overhead valve heavy duty (cast iron)
OHM – Overhead valve horizontal medium frame

The number following the letters indicate horsepower or cubic inch displacement.

The number following the model number is the specification number and the last three numbers of the specification number indicate a variation to the basic engine specification.

The serial number indicates the production date.

Using Model OVM120-202008, serial number 8234C as an example, interpretation is as follows:

OVM120-202008 is the model and specification number;

OVM indicates overhead valve medium frame;

120 indicates 12 horsepower;

202008 is the specification number required for correct parts identification;

8234C is the serial number;

8 indicates the year manufactured (1988);

234 indicates calendar day of the year (234th day of 1988);

C indicates the line and shift on which the engine was built at the factory.

Small frame engines have aluminum blocks and cylinder bores. Medium frame engines have aluminum blocks with cast iron cylinder sleeves. Heavy frame engines have caset iron cylinder and block assemblies.

Early Models VH70 and HH70 were identified as Models V70 and H70.

It is necessary to have the correct model, specification and serial numbers to obtain parts.

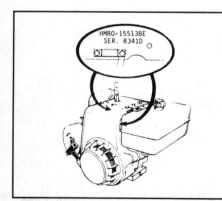
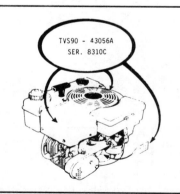
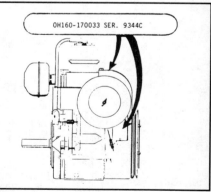

Fig. T1—View showing locations of engine model, specification and serial numbers on a variety of engines.

TECUMSEH

TECUMSEH PRODUCTS COMPANY
Grafton, Wisconsin 53204

Model	No. Cyls.	Bore	Stroke	Displacement	Power Rating
H70, HSK70	1	2.75 in. (69.9 mm)	2.531 in. (64.3 mm)	15 cu. in. (246.8 cc)	7 hp (5.2 kW)
HM70*	1	2.94 in. (74.6 mm)	2.531 in. (64.3 mm)	17.16 cu. in. (281 cc)	7 hp (5.2 kW)
HM70	1	3.125 in. (79.38 mm)	2.531 in. (64.3 mm)	19.4 cu. in. (318 cc)	8 hp (6.0 kW)
HMXL70	1	3.125 in. (79.38 mm)	2.531 in. (64.3 mm)	19.4 cu. in. (318 cc)	8 hp (6.0 kW)
V70, VM70	1	2.75 in. (69.9 mm)	2.531 in. (64.3 mm)	15 cu. in. (246.8 cc)	7 hp (5.2 kW)
TVM170	1	2.94 in. (74.6 mm)	2.531 in. (64.3 mm)	17.16 cu. in. (281 cc)	7 hp (5.2 kW)
H80	1	3.062 in. (77.8 mm)	2.531 in. (64.3 mm)	18.65 cu. in. (305.7 cc)	8 hp (6 kW)
HM80*	1	3.062 in. (77.8 mm)	2.531 in. (64.3 mm)	18.65 cu. in. (305.7 cc)	8 hp (6 kW)
HM80, HMSK80	1	3.125 in. (79.38 mm)	2.531 in. (64.3 mm)	19.4 cu. in. (318 cc)	8 hp (6 kW)
HHM80	1	3.125 in. (79.38 mm)	2.531 in. (64.3 mm)	19.4 cu. in. (318 cc)	8 hp (6 kW)
V80	1	3.062 in. (77.8 mm)	2.531 in. (64.3 mm)	18.65 cu. in. (305.7 cc)	8 hp (6 kW)
VM80*	1	3.062 in. (77.8 mm)	2.531 in. (64.3 mm)	18.65 cu. in. (305.7 cc)	8 hp (6 kW)
VM80	1	3.125 in. (79.38 mm)	2.531 in. (64.3 mm)	19.4 cu. in. (318 cc)	8 hp (6 kW)
TVM195, TVXL195	1	3.125 in. (79.38 mm)	2.531 in. (64.3 mm)	19.4 cu. in. (318 cc)	8 hp (6 kW)
HM100	1	3.187 in. (80.95 mm)	2.531 in. (64.3 mm)	20.2 cu. in. (330.9 cc)	10 hp (7.5 kW)
HM100**, HMSK100	1	3.313 in. (84.15 mm)	2.531 in. (64.3 mm)	21.82 cu. in. (357.6 cc)	10 hp (7.5 kW)
VM100	1	3.187 in. (80.95 mm)	2.531 in. (64.3 mm)	20.2 cu. in. (330.9 cc)	10 hp (7.5 kW)
TVM220, TVXL220	1	3.313 in. (84.15 mm)	2.531 in. (64.3 mm)	21.82 cu. in. (357.6 cc)	10 hp (7.5 kW)

*HM70, HM80 or VM80 models prior to type letter E.
HM70, HM80 or VM80 models type letter E and after.
Early HM100 models.
**Later HM100 models.

All models are small or medium frame aluminum block, four-stroke, single-cylinder engines, except Model HHM80. Small frame engines have an aluminum block and cylinder bore. Medium frame engines have aluminum blocks with a cast iron cylinder sleeve liner that is an integral part of the cylinder casting, except Model HHM80, which has a cast iron cylinder block. Refer to the TECUMSEH ENGINE IDENTIFICATION INFORMATION section to correctly identify engine to be serviced.

The connecting rod for all models rides directly on the crankshaft crankpin journal. Lubrication for all horizontal crankshaft engines is provided by splash lubrication. An oil dipper is either bolted to the connecting rod cap or is an integral part of the connecting rod cap casting. A positive displacement plunger-type oil pump that is operated by an eccentric on the camshaft provides lubrication for all vertical crankshaft engines.

MAINTENANCE

LUBRICATION. Vertical crankshaft models are equipped with a positive displacement barrel and plunger-type oil pump located in the oil pan/sump. An eccentric on the camshaft drives the pump. Oil from the pump lubricates the upper main bearing and the connecting rod journal.

All horizontal crankshaft models are splash lubricated. On some models, the dipper is an integral part of the connecting rod cap, while on other models the dipper is retained on the connecting rod by the connecting rod bolts.

Manufacturer recommends using oil with an API service classification of SF through SJ.

Use an SAE 30 oil for temperatures above 32° F (0° C) and SAE 5W-20 or 5W-30 oil for temperatures below 32° F (0° C).

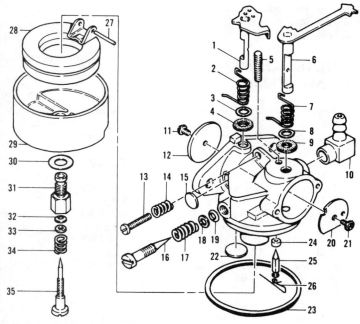

Fig. T501—Exploded view of Tecumseh carburetor.

1. Throttle shaft	10. Fuel inlet fitting	19. "O" ring	28. Float
2. Spring	11. Screw	20. Choke plate	29. Fuel bowl
3. Washer	12. Throttle plate	21. Screw	30. Washer
4. Felt washer	13. Idle speed screw	22. Welch plug	31. Fuel bowl nut
5. Spring	14. Spring	23. Gasket	32. "O" ring
6. Choke shaft	15. Welch plug	24. Fuel inlet valve seat	33. Washer
7. Spring	16. Idle mixture screw	25. Fuel inlet valve	34. Spring
8. Washer	17. Spring	26. Clip	35. High-speed
9. Felt washer	18. Washer	27. Float pin	mixture screw

Check oil level after every 5 hours of operation or before initial start up of engine. As equipped, maintain oil level at edge of filler hole or at "FULL" mark on dipstick.

Oil should be changed after 25 hours of normal operation, more frequently if operation is severe.

SPARK PLUG. Recommended spark plug for early models is Champion J8C or equivalent. Recommended spark plug for later models or models that require a resistor type plug is a Champion RJ17LM. Engines that require a hotter plug may be equipped with a Champion RJ19LM. Electrode gap should be 0.030 inch (0.76 mm).

CARBURETOR. Engine may be equipped with a Tecumseh or Walbro float type carburetor. Later engines may be equipped with a Tecumseh low-emission carburetor. These carburetors are identified by a fixed idle jet on the side of the carburetor. Refer to appropriate following section for carburetor service information.

Tecumseh Carburetor. Refer to Fig. T501 for an exploded view of Tecumseh carburetor and location of fuel mixture screws.

For initial carburetor adjustment on all models, open idle mixture screw (16) and main fuel mixture screw (35) 1½ turns from a lightly seated position.

Make final adjustments with engine at normal operating temperature and running. Place engine under load and adjust main fuel mixture screw (35) for leanest mixture that will allow satisfactory acceleration and steady governor operation. Set engine at idle speed (no load) and adjust idle mixture screw (16) to obtain smoothest idle operation.

As each adjustment affects the other, adjustment procedure may have to be repeated.

When overhauling carburetor, refer to Fig. T501 for exploded view of carburetor.

Make note of the position of the choke parts before disassembly so they can be reassembled in their original positions. The choke may operate in either direction depending on application. Compressed air can be used to dislodge the inlet valve seat (1—Fig. T502), but extreme care must be exercised. Cover the carburetor so the seat will not be ejected uncontrolled.

Remove the Welch plugs (2—Fig. T502) by piercing the plug with a thin-blade screwdriver or sharp punch, then prying out the plug. Insert the screwdriver into the plug only far enough to pierce the plug, otherwise, underlying metal may be damaged.

The fuel inlet fitting (10—Fig. T501) on the side of the carburetor can be removed by simultaneously twisting and pulling. Note the fitting's position before removal so it can be reinstalled in its original position.

Do not attempt to remove the nozzle (3—Fig. T502) as it is pressed into position and movement will affect carburetor operation. Do not remove or loosen any other cup or ball plugs.

When assembling the carburetor, install the Welch plugs with the concave side toward the carburetor (Fig. T503). Do not indent the plug; the plug should

Fig. T502—Compressed air may be used to remove Viton fuel inlet seat (1). Cover the carburetor so the seat will not be ejected uncontrolled. Do not attempt to remove integral main nozzle (3).

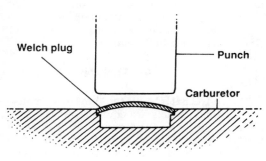

Fig. T503—Install Welch plug with concave side toward body, then use a punch to seat plug. Do not indent the plug; the plug should be flat after installation.

be flat after installation. The installation tool should have a diameter that is the same or larger than the plug.

When reinstalling Viton inlet valve seat (24—Fig. T501), grooved side of seat must be installed in bore first so inlet valve will seat against smooth side (Fig. T504). Some later models have a Viton tipped inlet needle and a brass seat.

Install throttle plate (12—Fig. T501) with the two stamped lines facing out and at 12 and 3 o'clock positions. The 12 o'clock line should be parallel with throttle shaft and facing toward top of carburetor.

Install choke plate (20) with flat side toward bottom of carburetor.

Fuel fitting (10) is pressed into body. When installing fuel inlet fitting, start fitting into bore, then apply a light coat of Loctite 271 sealant on shank and press fitting into place.

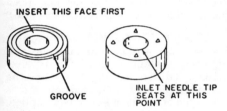

Fig. T504—Viton fuel inlet valve seat used on some Tecumseh carburetors must be installed correctly to operate properly. An all-metal needle valve is used with seat shown.

Fig. T505—Wire clip on the fuel inlet valve must be positioned around the float tab. The long end of the wire clip must point toward the choke end of the carburetor.

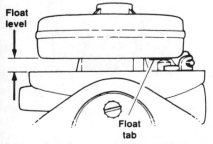

Fig. T506—Float height should be measured as shown. Bend adjusting tab to adjust height.

The wire clip on the fuel inlet valve must be positioned around the float tab as shown in Fig. T505. The long end of the wire clip must point toward the choke end of the carburetor.

To check float height, invert the carburetor throttle body and float assembly. Float level setting (Fig. T506) should be $\frac{7}{32}$ inch (5.6 mm) measured between free end of float and rim on carburetor body. Adjust the float by carefully bending the float lever tab that contacts inlet valve.

The fuel bowl retaining nut may have one or two holes (Fig. T507) adjacent to the hex. If a replacement nut is re-

Fig. T507—Fuel bowl retaining nut has drilled fuel passages. Be sure replacement nut is same as defective nut.

quired, the new nut must have the same number of holes as the original nut.

Walbro Carburetor. Refer to Fig. T508 for an exploded view of the Walbro float type carburetor and location of fuel mixture adjustment screws.

For initial carburetor adjustment on Models VM80, HHM80 and HM80, open idle mixture screw (10) 1¾ turns and main mixture screw (31) 2 turns from a lightly seated position.

For initial carburetor adjustment on all remaining models, open idle mixture screw (10) and main mixture screw (31) one turn from a lightly seated position.

Make final adjustments with engine at normal operating temperature and running. Place engine under load and adjust main fuel mixture screw (31) for leanest mixture that will allow satisfactory acceleration and steady governor operation. Set engine at idle speed (no load) and adjust idle mixture screw (10) to obtain smoothest idle operation. As each adjustment affects the other, adjustment procedure may have to be repeated.

When overhauling carburetor, refer to Fig. T508 for exploded view of carbu-

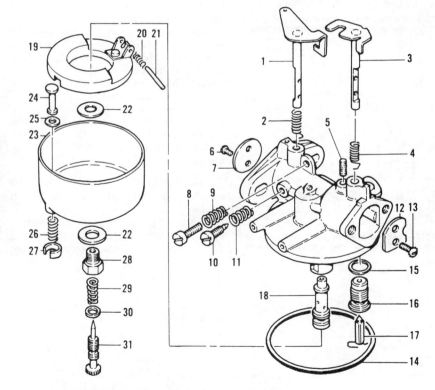

Fig. T508—Exploded view of Walbro carburetor.

1. Throttle shaft	9. Spring	17. Fuel inlet valve	25. Washer
2. Spring	10. Idle mixture screw	18. Nozzle	26. Spring
3. Choke shaft	11. Spring	19. Float	27. Retainer
4. Spring	12. Choke plate	20. Spring	28. Fuel bowl nut
5. Spring	13. Screw	21. Float pin	29. Spring
6. Screw	14. Gasket	22. Gasket	30. "O" ring
7. Throttle plate	15. Gasket	23. Fuel bowl	31. High-speed
8. Idle speed screw	16. Fuel inlet valve seat	24. Drain valve stem	mixture screw

retor. If the nozzle does not have a groove (Fig. T509) cut in the threaded portion, discard it. A service replacement nozzle has a groove. A nozzle with a groove can be reused. See Fig. T509.

Be sure to install gasket (15—Fig. T508) under the fuel inlet valve seat (16). Tighten the valve seat to 40-50 in.-lb. (4.5-5.6 N•m).

Install the choke plate so the straight edge is toward the fuel bowl side of the carburetor (Fig. T510). The numbered or lettered side of the choke plate should be on the inside when the choke plate is closed. Install the throttle plate so the numbers or letters face out when the throttle plate is closed (Fig. T511).

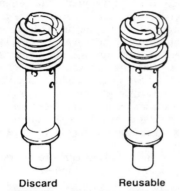

Fig. T509—Discard a nozzle that does not have a circumferential groove in the threaded portion.

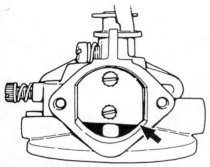

Fig. T510—Install the choke plate so the straight edge is toward the fuel bowl side of the carburetor.

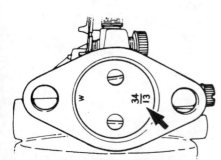

Fig. T511—Install the throttle plate so the numbers or letters face out when the throttle plate is closed.

The spring clip on the fuel inlet valve must fit around the tab on the float as shown in Fig. T512.

To check float height, invert the carburetor throttle body and float assembly (Fig. T506). Float level should be $\frac{1}{8}$ inch (3.2 mm) for horizontal crankshaft engines and 3/32 inch (2.4 mm) for vertical crankshaft engines. Adjust float height by carefully bending the float lever tab.

Float drop (travel) for all models should be $\frac{9}{16}$ inch (14.3 mm) and is adjusted by carefully bending limiting tab on float.

The ends of spring (Fig. T512) must point toward the choke end of the carburetor when the float is installed. The spring fits around the float pin. The short spring end must be pushed against spring tension so it fits in the gasket groove of the carburetor body as shown in Fig. T513. The fuel bowl gasket fits over the spring end.

Tecumseh Low-Emission Carburetor. Some later engines are equipped with a low-emission carburetor that enables the engine to comply with CARB (California Air Resources Board) and EPA emission requirements. The carburetor is equipped with a fixed main jet (31—Fig. T514) and a fixed idle jet (17) that is covered by a cap (16).

When servicing carburetor, refer to service procedures for Tecumseh float-type carburetors while also noting the following: Upper "O" ring (18) may remain in carburetor body when the nozzle (19) is removed. If the upper "O" ring remains in the body, it can be removed using a wire with a small hook on the end. Before inserting nozzle in carburetor body, place both "O" rings on nozzle.

GOVERNOR. A mechanical flyweight type governor is used on all models.

To adjust governor lever position on vertical crankshaft models, refer to Fig. T515. Loosen clamp screw on governor

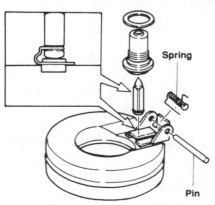

Fig. T512—The spring clip on the fuel inlet valve must fit around the tab on the float as shown.

lever and rotate governor lever shaft counterclockwise as far as possible. Move governor lever to left until throttle is fully open, then tighten clamp screw.

On horizontal crankshaft models, loosen clamp screw on lever and rotate governor lever shaft clockwise as far as possible. See Fig. T516. Move governor lever clockwise until throttle is wide open, then tighten clamp screw.

On Snow King engines equipped with a loop (L—Fig. T517) in speed control link, open or close link to adjust engine speed.

On some engines, the governed idle speed is adjusted by bending tab (T—Fig. T518) rather than by adjusting the idle speed screw on carburetor.

On some TVM170, TVM195 and TVM200 engines, a governor override system is used. Linkage is shown in Fig. T519. On these engines, high speed setting is adjusted by turning top screw (H) of override lever and low idle speed is adjusted by turning bottom screw (L).

IGNITION SYSTEM. Engines may be equipped with either a magneto type ignition system or a solid-state electronic ignition system. Note that the type of ignition system used determines the type of flywheel key to be installed. Refer to the appropriate service information for type of ignition being serviced.

Magneto Ignition System. Tecumseh flywheel type magnetos are used on some H70, V70, HM70, VM70, H80, V80, HHM80, HM80, VM80, HM100 and VM100 models. The round shape of the coil identifies this ignition system. The stamping "GRAY KEY" in the coil identifies the correct flywheel key to be used.

Breaker points are located behind the flywheel. Breaker-point gap should be adjusted to 0.020 inch (0.51 mm).

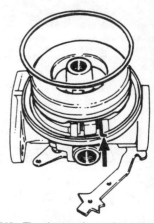

Fig. T513—The short spring end must be pushed against spring tension so it fits in the gasket groove of the carburetor body as shown. Position the fuel bowl gasket over the spring end.

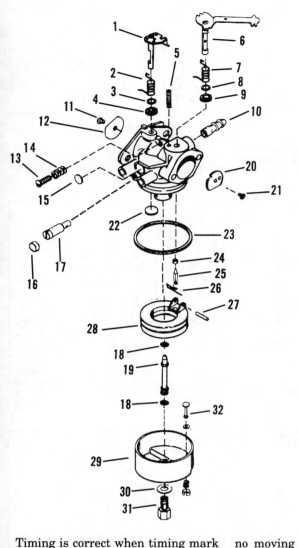

Fig. T514—Exploded view of Tecumseh float type carburetor used on emissions-compliant engines.

1. Throttle shaft
2. Spring
3. Washer
4. Felt washer
5. Spring
6. Choke shaft
7. Spring
8. Washer
9. Felt washer
10. Fuel inlet fitting
11. Screw
12. Throttle plate
13. Idle speed screw
14. Spring
15. Welch plug
16. Cap
17. Idle mixture jet
18. "O" ring
19. Main nozzle
20. Choke plate
21. Screw
22. Welch plug
23. Gasket
24. Fuel inlet valve seat
25. Fuel inlet valve
26. Clip
27. Float pin
28. Float
29. Fuel bowl
30. Washer
31. Main jet
32. Drain valve

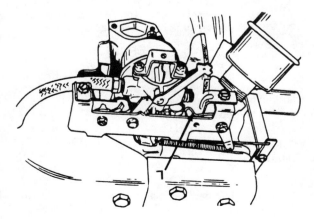

Fig. T515—When adjusting governor linkage on Models V70, VM70, V80, VM80, VM100, TVM170, TVM195 or TVM220, loosen clamp screw and rotate governor lever shaft and lever counterclockwise as far as possible.

Fig. T516—On Models H70, HM70, HMXL70, H80, HHM80, HM80 and HM100, rotate governor lever shaft and lever clockwise when adjusting linkage.

Timing is correct when timing mark on magneto base plate is in line with mark on bearing plate as shown in Fig. T520. If timing marks are defaced, points should start to open when piston is 0.085-0.095 inch (2.16-2.41 mm) BTDC.

Coil edge gap at flywheel should be 0.0125 inch (0.32 mm) on all models. To adjust the air gap, turn the flywheel magnet into position under the coil core. Loosen retaining screws and place shim stock or feeler gauge of specified thickness between the coil and magnet. Press the coil against the gauge and tighten screws.

Original magneto ignition coil must be installed using the gray flywheel key. The original magneto ignition coil is no longer available and if ordered, the solid state module and key assembly will be substituted. Make certain the gray flywheel key is used with the magneto (round) ignition coil (Fig. T521).

Solid-State Ignition System. Tecumseh solid-state ignition module has

no moving parts except the flywheel. The square-shaped module (Fig. T522) identifies this system. The stamping "GOLD KEY" in the module identifies the correct flywheel key to be used.

Test all solid-state ignition systems by holding the high-tension lead ⅛ inch (3.2 mm) from spark plug (Fig. T523). Crank the engine and check for a good blue spark. If no spark is present, check

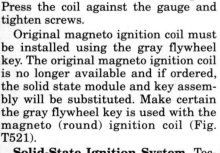

high-tension lead and coil lead for loose connections or faulty insulation.

Check the air gap between flywheel and ignition unit as shown in Fig. T524. Air gap should be 0.0125 inch (0.32 mm). To adjust air gap, loosen the two retaining screws and move ignition unit as necessary, then tighten retaining screws.

Some ignition modules are equipped with charging (alternator) coils. To test ignition charging (alternator) coil, remove coil lead from ignition terminal and connect an ohmmeter as shown in Fig. T525. If series resistance is below 400 ohms, renew stator and coil assem-

Fig. T517—On some Snow King engines, open or close loop (L) in speed control link to adjust engine speed.

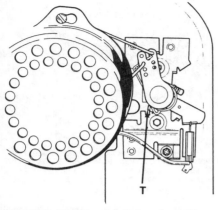

Fig. T518—On horizontal shaft engines with governed idle speed, bend tab (T) to adjust idle speed.

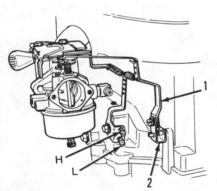

Fig. T519—Drawing of governor external linkage typical of engines equipped with governor override system. Refer to text for adjustment procedure.

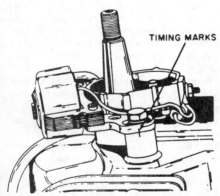

Fig. T520—On Models H70, HM70, V70, VM70, H80, HHM80, HM80, V80, VM80, HM100 and VM100 equipped with magneto ignition, adjust breaker-point gap to 0.020 inch (0.51 mm) and align timing marks as shown.

bly (Fig. T526). If resistance is above 400 ohms, renew ignition unit.

VALVE ADJUSTMENT. Valve tappet gap (cold) on all models should be 0.010 inch (0.25 mm) with piston at TDC on compression stroke. The check valve tappet gap, remove the breather cover from the valve tappet chamber.

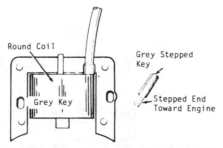

Fig. T521—View showing round breaker-point ignition coil that uses a gray flywheel key. Refer to text.

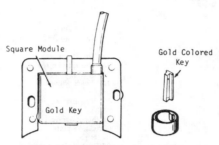

Fig. T522—View showing square solid-state ignition module that uses a gold flywheel key. Refer to text.

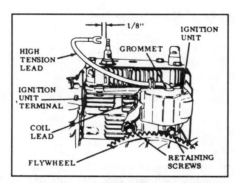

Fig. T523—View of solid-state ignition unit used on some models equipped with a flywheel alternator. System should produce a good blue spark that is 1/8 inch (3.2 mm) long at cranking speed.

Measure the clearance between valve stem and tappet with a feeler gauge.

To increase clearance, remove the valve and grind end of valve stem. To reduce clearance, grind the valve seat deeper or renew valve and/or valve tappet. Refer also to VALVE SYSTEM paragraphs in REPAIRS section.

REPAIRS

TIGHTENING TORQUE. Recommended tightening torque specifications are as follows:

Ball bearing retainer nut:
All models so
  equipped .... 15-22 in.-lb.
                    (1.7-3 N•m)
Carburetor .... 70 in.-lb.
                    (7.9 N•m)
Connecting rod screws ..... 210 in.-lb.
                    (23.7 N•m)

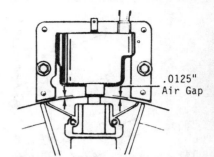

Fig. T524—Air gap between flywheel and ignition coil or module should be 0.0125 inch (0.32 mm).

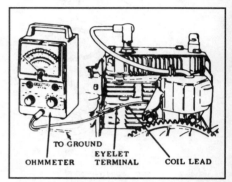

Fig. T525—View showing an ohmmeter connected for resistance test of ignition charging (alternator) coil.

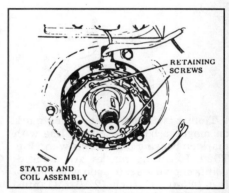

Fig. T526—Ignition charging (alternator) coil and stator are serviced only as an assembly.

Crankcase cover ...... 115-125 in.-lb.
                    (13.0-14.1 N•m)
Cylinder head............ 200 in.-lb.
                    (22.6 N•m)
Flywheel nut:
  Light frame .... 37 ft.-lb.
                    (50 N•m)

  Medium frame
  (Internal coil)............ 40 ft.-lb.
                    (54 N•m)

  Medium frame
  (External coil) .... 58 ft.-lb.
                    (78.5 N•m)
Ignition module .... 45 in.-lb.
                    (5.0 N•m)
Recoil starter .... 50 in.-lb.
                    (5.6 N•m)

CYLINDER HEAD. When removing cylinder head, note the location of washers and different length cap screws to aid in assembly.

Clean carbon from the combustion chamber being careful not to scratch or nick the sealing surface for the head gasket. Inspect the head for damage or distortion. If head is warped in excess of 0.005 inch (0.13 mm), replace the head. Slight distortion can be corrected by placing a sheet of 400 grit sandpaper on a flat surface and lapping the head gasket surface in a circular motion. Apply honing oil on the sandpaper to make it easier to slide the head on the sandpaper.

Always install a new head gasket. Tighten the cylinder head screws evenly following the sequence shown in Fig. T527 or Fig. T528. On all models, tighten the screws in 50 in.-lb. (5.6 N•m) increments to final torque of 200 in.-lbs. (22.6 N•m).

VALVE SYSTEM. To remove the valves, remove the cylinder head and valve tappet chamber cover. Remove the valve spring retainer, then withdraw the valve and spring. Identify all parts so they can be installed in their original position.

Valve seats are machined directly into cylinder block assembly. Valve seat angle is 45° for intake and exhaust. Standard valve seat width is 0.042-0.052 inch (1.07-1.32 mm).

Valve face angle should be 45° for intake and exhaust. Valve margin should not be less than 1/32 inch (0.79 mm). See Fig. T529. Valves are available with 0.03125 inch (0.793 mm) oversize stem for use with oversize valve guide bore.

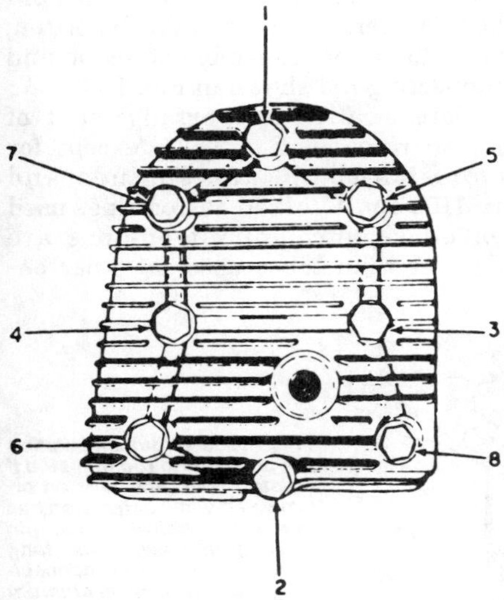

Valve guides are not renewable. If guides are excessively worn, ream to 0.3432-0.3442 inch (8.72-8.74 mm) and install a valve with 0.03125 inch (0.793 mm) oversize valve stem. Drill the upper and lower valve spring caps as necessary to fit oversize valve stem.

Lubricate the valve stems and guides with engine oil during assembly. If the valve spring has dampening coils (spring coils that are closer together at one end), they always go toward the cylinder block (stationary) surface.

OIL PUMP. Vertical crankshaft models are equipped with a positive displacement barrel and plunger type oil pump (Figs. T530 and T531) driven by an eccentric on the camshaft. Oil from the pump lubricates the upper main bearing and the connecting rod journal.

When installing early type pump (Fig. T530), chamfered side of drive collar must be against thrust bearing surface on camshaft gear. When installing late type pump, place side of drive collar with large flat surface shown in Fig. T531 away from camshaft gear.

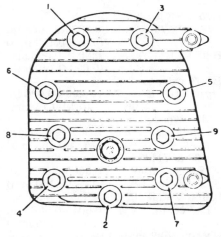

Fig. T528—On HHM80, HM80, VM80, HM100, VM100, TVM170, TVM195, TVXL195, TVM220 and TVXL220 models, tighten cylinder head cap screws evenly to 200 in.-lbs. (22.6 N•m) following tightening sequence shown.

CAMSHAFT. The camshaft and camshaft gear are an integral part that rides on journals at each end of camshaft.

The camshaft may be equipped with a compression release mechanism. The compression release raises the exhaust valve for easier starting. Two designs have been used. Some engines are equipped with a camshaft equipped with a compression release mechanism (Fig. T532) that uses a flyweight, spring and actuating pin to raise the exhaust valve lifter. The other compression release design uses a camshaft machined with a slight bump on the base of the exhaust camshaft lobe to raise the exhaust valve lifter.

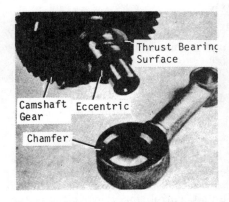

Fig. T530—View of early type oil pump used on V70, VM70 and VM80 models. Chamfered face of drive collar should be towards camshaft gear.

Fig. T531—Install late type oil pump so large flat surface on drive collar is away from camshaft gear.

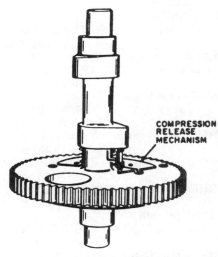

Fig. T532—View of Insta-matic Ezee-Start compression release camshaft assembly used on all models.

Fig. T527—On H70, V70, H80 and V80 models, tighten cylinder head cap screws evenly to 200 in.-lbs. (22.6 N•m) following tightening sequence shown.

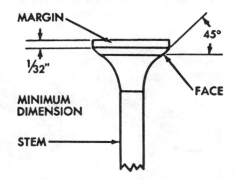

Fig. T529—Valve face angle should be 45° Minimum valve head margin is 1/32 inch (0.79 mm).

A camshaft equipped with a compression release mechanism is easier to remove and install if the crankshaft is rotated three teeth past the aligned timing mark position. This position allows the compression release mechanism to clear the exhaust valve lifter.

Remove the crankcase cover/oil pan to access the camshaft. Mark the valve lifters according to position during removal so they can be reinstalled in their original positions. Some models use lifters of different length. Install short lifter at intake position and longer lifter at exhaust position.

Compression release mechanism parts should work freely with no binding or sticking. Parts are not serviced separately from the camshaft assembly.

Camshaft journal diameter should be 0.6230-0.6235 inch (15.82-15.84 mm) and journal to bearing running clearance should be 0.003 inch (0.08 mm). Renew camshaft if gear teeth are worn or if journal or lobe surfaces are worn or damaged.

Make certain timing marks on camshaft gear and crankshaft gear are aligned during assembly.

PISTON, PIN AND RINGS. The engine is fitted with an aluminum piston that has two compression rings and an oil control ring. Remove the piston and connecting rod as an assembly from cylinder head end of engine. Remove carbon or ridge (if present) from top of cylinder before removing the piston.

Measure piston skirt diameter at bottom edge of skirt at a right angle to piston pin for all models. Refer to following list of standard piston diameter sizes:

PISTON DIAMETER

H70, HSK70,
V70, VM70 . . . . 2.7450-2.7455 in.
(69.723-69.736 mm)
HM70 prior to
type letter E . . . . . . 2.9325-2.9335 in.
(74.486-74.511 mm)
HM70 type letter
E or after. . . . . 3.1195-3.1205 in.
(79.235-79.261 mm)
HMXL70 . . . . 3.1195-3.1205 in.
(79.235-79.261 mm)
H80, V80, VM80 . . . . 3.0575-3.0585 in.
(77.660-77.686 mm)
HHM80 . . . . 3.1195-3.1205 in.
(79.235-79.261 mm)
HM80 prior to
type letter E . . . . . . 3.0575-3.0585 in.
(77.660-77.686 mm)
HM80 type letter
E or after. . . . . 3.1195-3.1205 in.
(79.235-79.261 mm)

HMSK80 . . . . 3.1195-3.1205 in.
(79.235-79.261 mm)
VM80 . . . . 3.1195-3.1205 in.
(79.235-79.261 mm)
HM100 (early models),
VM100 . . . . 3.1817-3.1842 in.
(80.815-80.879 mm)
HM100
(late models)* . . . . . 3.3090-3.3105 in.
(84.049-84.087 mm)
TVM170 . . . . 2.9325-2.9335 in.
(74.486-74.511 mm)
TVM195, TVXL195. . 3.1195-3.1205 in.
(79.235-79.261 mm)
TVM220 prior to
type letter G . . . . . . 3.3090-3.3105 in.
(84.049-84.087 mm)
TVM220 type letter
G or after. . . . . 3.3098-3.3108 in.
(84.069-84.094 mm)
TVXL220. . . . . 3.3098-3.3108 in.
(84.069-84.094 mm)

*Piston diameter on some late HM100 engines may be 3.3098-3.3108 in. (84.069-84.094 mm).

Refer to the following table for specified piston-to-cylinder wall clearance:

PISTON-TO-CYLINDER CLEARANCE

H70, HSK70,
V70, VM70 . . . . 0.0030-0.0048 in.
(0.076-0.123 mm)
H80, V80 . . . . 0.0035-0.0055 in.
(0.089-0.140 mm)
HM70 prior to
type letter E . . . . . . 0.004-0.006 in.
(0.10-0.15 mm)
HM70 type letter
E or after. . . . . 0.0045-0.0065 in.
(0.114-0.165 mm)
HM80 & VM80
(18.65 cu. in.) . . . . . 0.0035-0.0055 in.
(0.089-0.140 mm)
HM80 & VM80
(19.4 cu. in.) . . . . . . 0.0045-0.0065 in.
(0.114-0.165 mm)
HM100 (20.2 cu. In.)
VM100. . . . . 0.0045-0.0065 in.
(0.114-0.165 mm)
HM100 (21.82 cu. In.)*,
TVM220 . . . . 0.0015-0.0040 in.
(0.038-0.102 mm)

TVM170 prior to
type letter E . . . . 0.004-0.006 in.
(0.10-0.15 mm)
TVM170 type
letter E . . . . 0.0030-0.0048 in.
(0.076-0.123 mm)
HMSK100,
TVXL220. . . . . 0.0012-0.0032 in.
(0.030-0.081 mm)
TVM170 type
letter F or after. . . . 0.0045-0.0065 in.
(0.114-0.165 mm)
TVM220 prior to
type letter G . . . . . . 0.0015-0.0040 in.
0.038-0.102 mm)
TVM220 type
letter G or after . . . 0.0012-0.0032 in.
(0.030-0.081 mm)

*If HM100 piston diameter is 3.3098-3.3108 in. (84.069-84.094 mm), piston clearance should be 0.0012-0.0032 in. (0.030-0.081 mm).

Clean carbon from top of piston and piston ring grooves. Be careful not to damage the ring lands or enlarge the ring grooves during cleaning.

Insert a new piston ring in top groove and measure side clearance using a feeler gauge. Side clearance of top ring in piston groove should be 0.002-0.003 inch (0.05-0.08 mm) on Models H70, V70 and VM70 with breaker-point ignition. Ring side clearance should be 0.0015-0.0035 inch (0.038-0.089 mm) on Models HM100, HMSK100, TVM220 and TVXL220 with solid-state ignition. Ring side clearance should be 0.002-0.005 inch (0.05-0.13 mm) for all other models.

If piston crown has an arrow, install piston on connecting rod so arrow on piston crown will point toward carburetor side of engine after installation. If an arrow is located below the piston pin bore or there is no arrow on the piston, note the proper assembly of piston and connecting rod shown in Fig. T533.

Note location and arrangement of piston rings in Fig. T534, except for emission-compliant engines and HM100 and TVM220. Piston rings used on emission-compliant engines are thinner than those used on other en-

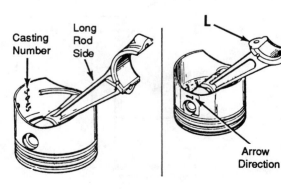

Fig. T533—Note installation of connecting rod in piston if piston does not have an arrow (left view) or if piston has an arrow below piston pin hole (right view). Install long screw in hole (L) if connecting rod screws have different lengths.

gines and must not be used on pistons of non-emission compliant engines. Install second compression ring on emission-compliant engine so notch is toward piston skirt.

Stagger ring end gaps equally around circumference of piston during installation, however, on models with a "trenched" cylinder (see Fig. T535), position ring end gaps so they are not in trenched area. This will lessen the possibility of the ring ends snagging during installation of piston.

Standard and oversize piston and rings are available for service.

CONNECTING ROD. Piston and connecting rod are removed as an assembly from cylinder head end of engine. Connecting rod rides directly on the crankpin journal of crankshaft. On horizontal crankshaft models, an oil dipper is an integral part of connecting rod cap or a separate oil dipper is attached to the rod by the connecting rod bolts.

Standard connecting rod big end diameter may be either 1.3760-1.3765 inch (34.950-34.963 mm) or 1.1880-1.1885 inch (30.175-30.188 mm). Check unworn portion of crankpin to determine original specification.

Connecting rod-to-crankpin journal running clearance should be 0.002 inch (0.05 mm) for all models.

Connecting rods are equipped with match marks that must be aligned and face the pto end of the crankshaft after installation. See Fig. T536. If equipped with connecting rod screws with different lengths, long screw must be installed in hole (L—Fig. T533) nearer piston pin bore.

GOVERNOR. Governor weight and gear assembly rides on a renewable

shaft that is pressed into the engine crankcase or crankcase cover. The camshaft gear drives the governor assembly.

If renewal of governor shaft is necessary, press governor shaft in until shaft end is located as shown in Fig. T537 or Fig. T538.

Adjust external linkage as outlined in MAINTENANCE section.

CRANKSHAFT AND MAIN BEARINGS. On vertical crankshaft engines, crankshaft main journals ride directly in aluminum alloy bearings in crankcase and oil pan (engine base). On horizontal crankshaft engines, crankshaft main journals ride in two renewable steel-backed bronze bushings or a renewable sleeve bushing at flywheel end and a ball bearing or bushing at pto end.

Refer to following table for main bearing bushing inner diameters:

Main Bearing Diameter

H70, HSK70
   Both bearings . . . . . 1.0005-1.0010 in.
      (25.413-25.425 mm)
HM70 — Early Models
   Cylinder bearing. . . 1.0005-1.0010 in.
      (25.413-25.425 mm)
Pto bearing . . . . 1.1890-1.1895 in.
      (30.201-30.213 mm)

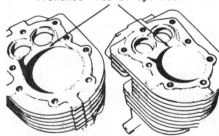

Trenched Area of Cylinder

Fig. T535—Cylinder block on Models HHM80, HM80, HM100 and TVM220 has been "trenched" to improve fuel flow and power.

HM70 — Later Models
   Both bearings . . . . . 1.3765-1.3770 in.
      (34.963-34.976 mm)
HMXL70
   Both bearings . . . . . 1.3765-1.3770 in.
      (34.963-34.976 mm)
H80, HMSK80
   Cylinder bearing. . . 1.0005-1.0010 in.
      (25.413-25.425 mm)
   Pto bearing . . . . 1.1890-1.1895 in.
      (30.201-30.213 mm)
HHM80
   Cylinder bearing. . . 1.0005-1.0010 in.
      (25.413-25.425 mm)
   Pto bearing . . . . 1.1890-1.1895 in.
      (30.201-30.213 mm)
HM80, HM100 — Early Models:
   Cylinder bearing. . . 1.0005-1.0010 in.
      (25.413-25.425 mm)
   Pto bearing . . . . 1.1890-1.1895 in.
      (30.201-30.213 mm)
HM80, HM100 — Later Models:
   Both bearings . . . . . 1.3765-1.3770 in.
      (34.963-34.976 mm)
HMSK100
   Both bearings . . . . . 1.3765-1.3770 in.
      (34.963-34.976 mm)
V70, VM70
   Both bearings. . . . 1.0005-1.0010 inch
      (25.413-25.425 mm)

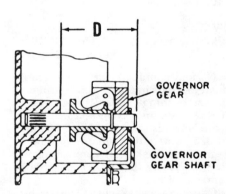

Fig. T537—Correct installation of governor shaft, gear and weight assembly on Models H70, HM70, HMXL70, H80, HHM80, HM80 and HM100. Dimension (D) should be 1-3/8 inches (34.92 mm) on all models.

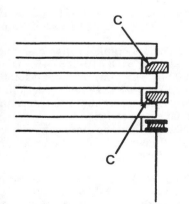

Fig. T534—Chamfer (C) on top piston ring must be up. If second ring on Models HM100 and TVM220 has a chamfer (C), chamfer must be down. On all other engines, chamfer, if so equipped, on second ring must be up. If outside diameter of ring is notched, notch must be down.

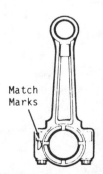

Match Marks

Fig. T536—Match marks on connecting rod and cap must be aligned and face pto end of crankshaft after installation. Connecting rod used on horizontal crankshaft engines is equipped with an oil dipper on connecting rod cap.

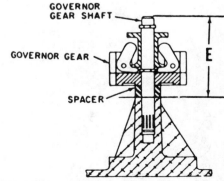

GOVERNOR GEAR SHAFT

GOVERNOR GEAR

SPACER

Fig. T538—Governor gear and shaft installation on Models V70, VM70, V80, VM80, VM100, TVM170, TVM195, TVXL195, TVM220 and TVXL220. Dimension (E) should be 1-19/32 inches (40.48 mm).

V80, VM80, VM100
Cylinder bearing... 1.0005-1.0010 in.
(25.413-25.425 mm)
Pto bearing . . . . . . 1.1890-1.1895 in.
(30.201-30.213 mm)
TVM170 — Early Models:
Cylinder bearing... 1.0005-1.0010 in.
(25.413-25.425 mm)
Pto bearing . . . . . . 1.1890-1.1895 in.
(30.201-30.213 mm)
TVM170 — Later Models:
Both bearings . . . . . 1.3765-1.3770 in.
(34.963-34.976 mm)
TVM195 — Early Models:
Cylinder bearing... 1.0005-1.0010 in.
(25.413-25.425 mm)
Pto bearing . . . . . . 1.1890-1.1895 in.
(30.201-30.213 mm)
TVM195 — Later Models:
Both bearings . . . . . 1.3765-1.3770 in.
(34.963-34.976 mm)
TVXL195
Both bearings . . . . . 1.3765-1.3770 in.
(34.963-34.976 mm)
TVM220 — Early Models:
Cylinder bearing... 1.0005-1.0010 in.
(25.413-25.425 mm)
Pto bearing . . . . . . 1.1890-1.1895 in.
(30.201-30.213 mm)
TVM220 — Later Models:
Both bearings . . . . . 1.3765-1.3770 in.
(34.963-34.976 mm)
TVXL220
Both bearings . . . . . 1.3765-1.3770 in.
(34.963-34.976 mm)

Normal running clearance of crankshaft journals in aluminum bearings or bronze bushings is 0.0015-0.0025 inch (0.038-0.064 mm). Renew crankshaft if main journals are more than 0.001 inch (0.025 mm) out-of-round. Renew or regrind crankshaft if connecting rod journal is more than 0.0005 inch (0.013 mm) out-of-round.

Check crankshaft gear for wear, broken teeth or loose fit on crankshaft. If crankshaft gear is damaged, remove gear from crankshaft with an arbor

press. Renew gear pin and press new gear on shaft making certain timing mark is facing pto end of shaft.

On models equipped with a ball bearing at pto end of shaft, refer to Figs. T539 and Fig. T540 before removing crankcase cover. Loosen the locknuts and rotate protruding ends of lock pins counterclockwise to release bearing and remove cover. Ball bearing will remain on crankshaft. When assembling, turn the lock pins clockwise until flats on pins face each other, then tighten locknuts to 15-22 in.-lbs. (2-3 N•m).

Crankshaft end play for all models should be 0.005-0.027 inch (0.13-0.69 mm). End play is controlled by varying thickness of thrust washers between crankshaft and cylinder block or crankcase cover.

Bronze or aluminum bushing-type main bearings are renewable. Replacement bearings must be reamed to final size. Finish reamers are available from Tecumseh.

Refer to following list for specified crankshaft main bearing journal diameters:

Main Bearing Journal Diameter

H70, HSK70, V70, VM70
Both ends . . . . . . 0.9985-0.9990 inch
(25.362-25.375 mm)
HM70—Early Models
Magneto end . . . . . 0.9985-0.9990 in.
(25.362-25.375 mm)
Pto end . . . . 1.1870-1.1875 in.
(30.150-30.162 mm)
HM70—Later Models
Both ends . . . . . . 1.3745-1.3750 in.
(34.912-34.925 mm)
HMXL70
Both ends . . . . . . 1.3745-1.3750 in.
(34.912-34.925 mm)
H80, HMSK80
Magneto end . . . . . 0.9985-0.9990 in.
(25.362-25.375 mm)
Pto end . . . . 1.1870-1.1875 in.
(30.150-30.162 mm)
HHM80
Magneto end . . . . . 0.9985-0.9990 in.
(25.362-25.375 mm)

Pto end . . . . 1.1870-1.1875 in.
(30.150-30.162 mm)
HM80, HM100—Early Models
Magneto end . . . . . 0.9985-0.9990 in.
(25.362-25.375 mm)
Pto end . . . . 1.1870-1.1875 in.
(30.150-30.162 mm)
HM80, HM100—Later Models
Both ends . . . . . . 1.3745-1.3750 in.
(34.912-34.925 mm)
HMSK100
Both ends . . . . . . 1.3745-1.3750 in.
(34.912-34.925 mm)
V80, VM80, VM100
Magneto end . . . . . 0.9985-0.9990 in.
(25.362-25.375 mm)
Pto end . . . . 1.1870-1.1875 in.
(30.150-30.162 mm)
TVM170—Early Models
Magneto end . . . . . 0.9985-0.9990 in.
(25.362-25.375 mm)
Pto end . . . . 1.1870-1.1875 in.
(30.150-30.162 mm)
TVM170—Later Models
Both ends . . . . . . 1.3745-1.3750 in.
(34.912-34.925 mm)
TVM195—Early Models
Magneto end . . . . . 0.9985-0.9990 in.
(25.362-25.375 mm)
Pto end . . . . 1.1870-1.1875 in.
(30.150-30.162 mm)
TVM195—Later Models
Both ends . . . . . . 1.3745-1.3750 in.
(34.912-34.925 mm)
TVXL195
Both ends . . . . . . 1.3745-1.3750 in.
(34.912-34.925 mm)
TVM220—Early Models
Magneto end . . . . . 0.9985-0.9990 in.
(25.362-25.375 mm)
Pto end . . . . 1.1870-1.1875 in.
(30.150-30.162 mm)
TVM220—Later Models
Both ends . . . . . . 1.3745-1.3750 in.
(34.912-34.925 mm)
TVXL220
Both ends . . . . . . 1.3745-1.3750 in.
(34.912-34.925 mm)

Crankshaft crankpin diameter may be either 1.3740-1.3745 inch (34.900-34.912 mm) or 1.1860-1.1865 inch (30.124-30.137 mm). Check unworn portion of crankpin to determine original specification.

Make certain the timing marks on camshaft gear and crankshaft gear are aligned during assembly.

CYLINDER. If cylinder is scored or excessively worn, or if taper or out-of-round exceeds 0.004 inch (0.10 mm), bore cylinder to next oversize for which piston and rings are available. Refer to table below for list of standard bore diameters:

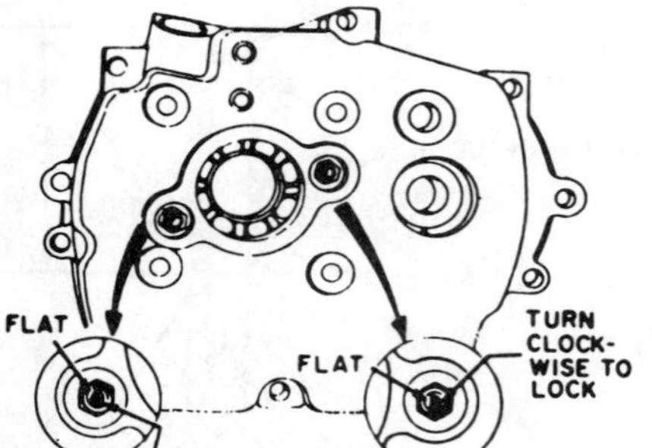

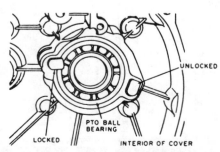

Fig. T539—View showing bearing locks on HM70, HM80 and HM100 models equipped with ball bearing main bearings. Locks must be released before removing crankcase cover. Refer to Fig. T542 for interior view of cover and locks.

Fig. T540—Interior view of crankcase cover and ball bearing locks used on HM70, HM80 and HM100 models.

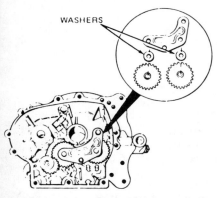

Fig. T541—View showing Dyna-Static balancer gears installed in models so equipped. Note location of washers between gears retaining bracket.

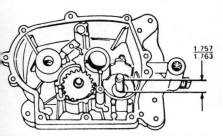

Fig. T542—On VM80 and VM100 models, press balancer gear shafts into cover or oil pan so height between boss on crankcase cover or oil pan and step on shafts is 1.757-1.763 inches (44.63-44.78 mm).

STANDARD CYLINDER BORE

H70, HSK70,
  V70, VM70 . . . . 2.750-2.751 in.
          (69.85-69.88 mm)

HM70, HMXL70
  TVM170 . . . . 2.9375-2.9385 in.
          (74.612-74.638 mm)

H80, V80, VM80 . . . . . 3.062-3.063 in.
          (77.77-77.80 mm)

HHM80, HMSK80 . . . . 3.125-3.126 in.
          (79.38-79.40 mm)

HM80 prior to
  type letter E . . . . 3.062-3.063 in.
          (77.77-77.80 mm)

HM80 with type
  letter E or after. . . . . . 3.125-3.126 in.
          (79.38-79.40 mm)

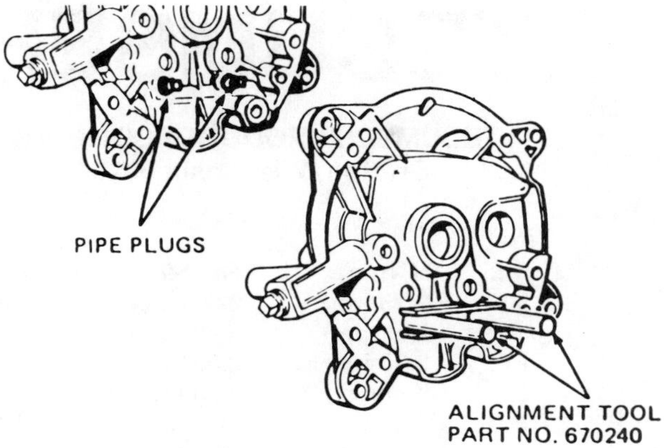

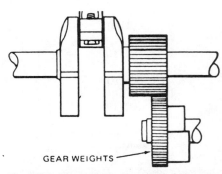

Fig. T543—To time engine balancer gears, remove pipe plugs and insert Tecumseh alignment tool 670240 through oil pan and into slots in balancer gears. Refer also to Fig. T544.

VM80, TVM195,
  TVXL195 . . . . 3.125-3.126 in.
          (79.38-79.40 mm)

HM100 —
  Early production . . . . . 3.187-3.188 in.
          (80.95-80.98 mm)
  Late production . . . . . 3.312-3.313 in.
          (84.12-84.15 mm)

HMSK100 . . . . 3.312-3.313 in.
          (84.12-84.15 mm)

VM100 . . . . 3.187-3.188 in.
          (80.95-80.98 mm)

TVM170 . . . . 2.9375-2.9385 in.
          (74.612-74.638 mm)

TVM220, TVXL220. . . . 3.312-3.313 in.
          (84.12-84.15 mm)

DYNA-STATIC BALANCER. The Dyna-Static engine balancer used on medium frame models consists of counterweighted gears driven by the crankshaft gear to counteract unbalance caused by the counterweights on the crankshaft.

Counterweight gears are held in position on shafts by a bracket bolted to crankcase or oil pan (Fig. T541).

Renewable balancer gear shafts are pressed into crankcase cover or oil pan. Press shafts into cover or oil pan so height between boss on crankcase cover or oil pan and step on shafts is 1.757-1.763 inches (44.63-44.78 mm) as shown in Fig. T542.

Balancer gears are equipped with renewable caged needle bearings. Using Tecumseh tool 670210, press new bear-

Fig. T544—View showing correct balancer gear timing to crankshaft gear on VM80 and VM100 models. With piston at TDC, weights should be directly opposite.

ings into gears until cage is flush to 0.015 inch (0.38 mm) below edge of bore.

When reassembling engine, balancer gears must be timed with crankshaft for correct operation. Refer to Fig. T543 and remove pipe plugs. Insert Tecumseh alignment tool 670240 through crankcase cover or engine base and into timing slots in balancer gears. Rotate the flywheel until the piston is at TDC on compression stroke, and install cover and gear assembly while tools retain gears in correct position. See Fig. T543.

When correctly assembled, piston should be at TDC and weights on balancer gear should be directly opposite. See Fig. T544.

TECUMSEH

TECUMSEH PRODUCTS COMPANY
Grafton, Wisconsin 53204

Model	No. Cyls.	Bore	Stroke	Displacement	Power Rating
HH70	1	2.75 in. (69.9 mm)	2.531 in. (64.3 mm)	15 cu. in. (246.8 cc)	7 hp (5.2 kW)
VH70	1	2.75 in. (69.9 mm)	2.531 in. (64.3 mm)	15 cu. in. (246.8 cc)	7 hp (5.2 kW)
HH80*	1	3.00 in. (76.2 mm)	2.75 in. (69.9 mm)	19.4 cu. in. (318 cc)	8 hp (6 kW)
HH80**	1	3.31 in. (84.2 mm)	2.75 in. (69.9 mm)	23.75 cu. in. (389 cc)	8 hp (6 kW)
VH80	1	3.31 in. (84.2 mm)	2.75 in. (69.9 mm)	23.75 cu. in. (389 cc)	8 hp (6 kW)
HH100	1	3.31 in. (84.2 mm)	2.75 in. (69.9 mm)	23.75 cu. in. (389 cc)	10 hp (7.5 kW)
VH100	1	3.31 in. (84.2 mm)	2.75 in. (69.9 mm)	23.75 cu. in. (389 cc)	10 hp (7.5 kW)
HH120	1	3.50 in. (88.9 mm)	2.88 in. (72.9 mm)	27.66 cu. in. (453 cc)	12 hp (9 kW)

*Prior to type letter B.
**Type letter B and after.

All models are heavy frame, cast iron, four-stroke, single-cylinder engines. Refer to the TECUMSEH ENGINE IDENTIFICATION INFORMATION section to correctly identify engine to be serviced.

The connecting rod for all models rides directly on the crankshaft crankpin journal. Lubrication for all horizontal crankshaft engines is provided by splash lubrication. An oil dipper is either bolted to the connecting rod cap or is an integral part of the connecting rod cap casting. Lubrication for vertical crankshaft engines may be provided by splash lubrication or by a positive displacement plunger-type oil pump that is operated by an eccentric on the camshaft.

MAINTENANCE

LUBRICATION. Vertical crankshaft models may be equipped with a positive displacement barrel and plunger-type oil pump driven by an eccentric on the camshaft. Oil from the pump lubricates the upper main bearing and the connecting rod journal. Some vertical crankshaft engines are splash lubricated by an oil slinger attached to the crankshaft.

All horizontal crankshaft models are splash lubricated. On some models, the dipper is an integral part of connecting rod cap and, on other models, the dipper is retained on connecting rod by the connecting rod bolts.

Manufacturer recommends oil with an API service classification of SJ.

Use an SAE 30 oil for temperatures above 32° F (0° C) and SAE 5W-20 or 5W-30 oil for temperatures below 32° F (0° C).

Check oil level after every 5 hours of operation or before initial start up of engine. As equipped, maintain oil level at edge of filler hole or at "FULL" mark on dipstick.

Oil should be changed after 25 hours of normal operation, more frequently if operation is severe.

SPARK PLUG. Recommended spark plug for all models is Champion J8C, RJ17LM or equivalent. Electrode gap should be 0.030 inch (0.76 mm)

CARBURETOR. Engine may be equipped with a Tecumseh or Walbro float-type carburetor. Refer to appropriate following section for carburetor service information.

Tecumseh Carburetor. Refer to Fig. T601 for an exploded view of Tecumseh carburetor and location of fuel mixture screws.

For initial carburetor adjustment on Model VH70, open idle mixture screw (13) one turn and main fuel mixture screw (34) 1¼ turns from a lightly seated position.

For initial carburetor adjustment on all other models, open idle mixture screw (13) 1¼ turns and main fuel mixture screw (34) 1¾ turns from a lightly seated position.

Make final adjustments with engine at normal operating temperature and running. Place engine under load and adjust main fuel mixture screw (34) for leanest mixture that will allow satisfactory acceleration and steady governor operation. Set engine at idle speed (no load) and adjust idle mixture screw (13) to obtain smoothest idle operation.

As each adjustment affects the other, adjustment procedure may have to be repeated.

To check float height, invert carburetor throttle body and float assembly. Float setting should be ⁷⁄₃₂ inch (5.6 mm) measured between free end of float and rim on carburetor body. Adjust float

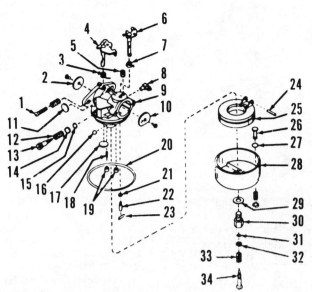

Fig. T601—Exploded view of Tecumseh carburetor.

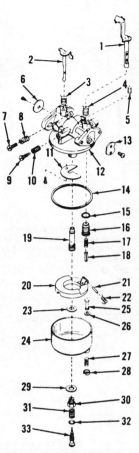

1. Idle speed screw
2. Throttle plate
3. Return spring
4. Throttle shaft
5. Choke stop spring
6. Choke shaft
7. Return spring
8. Fuel inlet spring
9. Carburetor body
10. Choke plate
11. Welch plug
12. Spring
13. Idle mixture screw
14. Washer
15. "O" ring
16. Ball plug
17. Welch plug
18. Pin
19. Cup plugs
20. Gasket
21. Fuel inlet valve seat
22. Fuel inlet valve
23. Clip
24. Pin
25. Float
26. Drain stem
27. Gasket
28. Fuel bowl
29. Gasket
30. Bowl retainer
31. "O" ring
32. Washer
33. Spring
34. Main fuel screw

Fig. T604—Exploded view of Walbro carburetor.

1. Choke shaft
2. Throttle shaft
3. Throttle return spring
4. Choke return spring
5. Choke stop spring
6. Throttle plate
7. Idle speed screw
8. Spring
9. Idle mixture screw
10. Spring
11. Baffle
12. Carburetor body
13. Choke plate
14. Gasket
15. Gasket
16. Fuel inlet valve seat
17. Spring
18. Fuel inlet valve
19. Main nozzle
20. Float
21. Pin
22. Spring
23. Gasket
24. Fuel bowl
25. Drain stem
26. Gasket
27. Spring
28. Retainer
29. Gasket
30. Bowl retainer
31. Spring
32. "O" ring
33. Main mixture screw

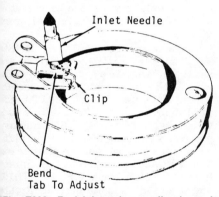

Fig. T602—Fuel inlet valve needle shown is equipped with a resilient tip and a clip. Bend tab on float arm to adjust float level.

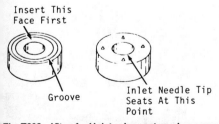

Fig. T603—Viton fuel inlet valve seat used on some Tecumseh carburetors must be installed correctly to operate properly. An all-metal needle valve is used with seat shown.

by carefully bending float lever tab that contacts inlet valve (Fig. T602).

Refer to Fig. T601 for exploded view of carburetor during disassembly. When reinstalling Viton inlet valve seat, grooved side of seat must be installed in bore first so inlet valve will seat against smooth side (Fig. T603). Some later models have a Viton tipped inlet needle (Fig. T602) and a brass seat.

Install throttle plate (2—Fig. T601) with the two stamped lines facing out and at 12 and 3 o'clock positions. The 12 o'clock line should be parallel with throttle shaft and facing toward top of carburetor.

Install choke plate (10) with float side toward bottom of carburetor.

Fuel fitting (8) is pressed into body. When installing fuel inlet fitting, start fitting into bore, then apply a light coat of Loctite 262 on shank and press fitting into place.

Walbro Carburetor. Refer to Fig. T604 for an exploded view of the Walbro float-type carburetor and location of fuel mixture adjustment screws.

For initial carburetor adjustment, open idle mixture screw (9) 1¼ turns from a lightly seated position and open main mixture screw (33) 1½ turns.

Make final adjustments with engine at normal operating temperature and running. Place engine under load and adjust main fuel mixture screw (33) for leanest mixture that will allow satisfactory acceleration and steady governor operation. Set engine at idle speed (no load) and adjust idle mixture screw (9) to obtain smoothest idle operation.

As each adjustment affects the other, adjustment procedure may have to be repeated.

When overhauling carburetor, do not remove main nozzle (19) unless necessary as original type nozzle must be discarded and a service nozzle must be installed. Service nozzle may be reused. Refer to Fig. T605 to identify nozzle type.

To check float height, invert carburetor throttle body and float assembly (Fig. T606). Note if fuel inlet valve has a metal tip (early design) or Viton tip (later design). If fuel inlet valve has a metal tip, float setting (dimension H) should be ⅛ inch (3.2 mm) for all engines. If fuel inlet valve has a Viton tip, float setting (dimension H) should be 9/64 inch (3.6 mm) for horizontal crank-

383

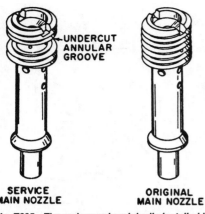

Fig. T605—The main nozzle originally installed is drilled after installation through hole in body. Main nozzles available for service are grooved so alignment is not necessary.

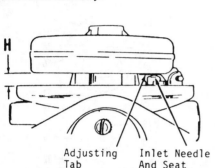

Fig. T606—Float height (H) on Walbro carburetor should be measured as shown. Bend adjusting tab to adjust height.

shaft engines with a fuel pump, 5/64 inch (1.9 mm) for horizontal crankshaft engines without a fuel pump, and 3/32 inch (2.4 mm) for all vertical crankshaft engines. Adjust float height by carefully bending float lever tab.

Float drop (travel) for all models should be 9/16 inch (14.3 mm) and is adjusted by carefully bending limiting tab on float.

GOVERNOR. A mechanical flyweight-type governor is used on all models.

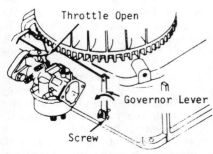

Fig. T607—When adjusting governor linkage on Model VH70, loosen clamp screw and rotate governor lever shaft and lever counterclockwise as far as possible.

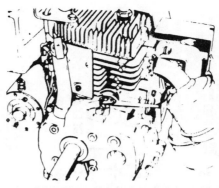

Fig. T608—On Model HH70, rotate governor lever shaft and lever clockwise when adjusting linkage.

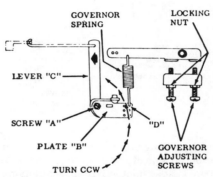

Fig. T609—External governor linkage on VH80 and VH100 models. Refer to text for adjustment procedure.

To adjust governor lever position on vertical crankshaft models, refer to Fig. T607. Loosen clamp screw on governor lever. Rotate governor lever shaft counterclockwise as far as possible. Move governor lever to left until throttle is fully open, then tighten clamp screw.

On horizontal crankshaft models, loosen clamp screw on lever and rotate

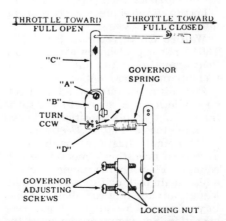

Fig. T610—External governor linkage on HH80, HH100 and HH120 models. Refer to text for adjustment procedure.

governor lever shaft clockwise as far as possible. See Fig. T608. Move governor lever clockwise until throttle is wide open, then tighten clamp screw.

For external linkage adjustments, refer to Figs. T609 and T610. Loosen screw (A), turn plate (B) counterclockwise as far as possible and move lever (C) to left until throttle is fully open. Tighten screw (A). Governor spring must be hooked in hole (D) as shown. Adjusting screws on bracket shown in Figs. T609 and T610 are used to adjust fixed or variable speed settings.

IGNITION SYSTEM. Engines may be equipped with either a magneto-type ignition system or a solid-state electronic ignition system. Refer to the appropriate service information for type of ignition being serviced.

Magneto Ignition System. Tecumseh flywheel-type magnetos are used on some models. On Models HH70 and VH70, breaker points are located behind the flywheel. Breaker-point gap should be adjusted to 0.020 inch (0.51 mm). Timing is correct when timing mark on magneto base plate is in line with mark on bearing plate as shown in Fig. T611. If timing marks are defaced, points should start to open when piston is 0.085-0.095 inch (2.16-2.41 mm) BTDC.

Breaker points on Models HH80, VH80, HH100, VH100 and HH120 are located in crankcase cover as shown in Fig. T612. Timing should be correct when points are adjusted to 0.020 inch (0.51 mm). To check timing with a continuity light, refer to Fig. T613. Remove pop rivets securing identification plate on blower housing. Remove plate to expose a 1¼-inch hole. Connect continuity light to terminal screw (78—Fig. T612) and a suitable engine ground. Rotate engine clockwise until piston is on compression stroke and timing mark is just

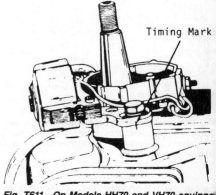

Fig. T611—On Models HH70 and VH70 equipped with magneto ignition, adjust breaker-point gap to 0.020 inch (0.51 mm) and align timing marks as shown.

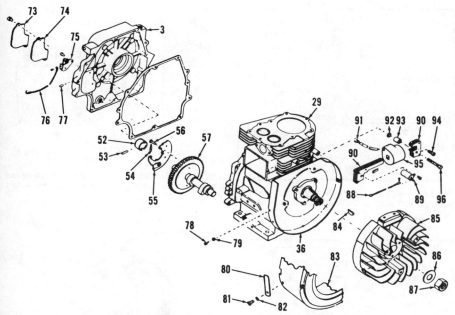

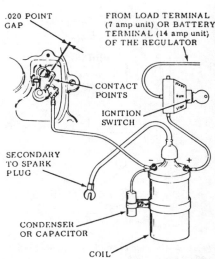

Fig. T614—Typical battery ignition wiring diagram for so equipped HH80, HH100 and HH120 model engines.

Fig. T612—Exploded view of magneto ignition components used on HH80, HH100 and HH120 models. Timing advance and breaker points used on engines equipped with battery ignition are identical.

3. Crankcase cover		88. Condenser wire
29. Cylinder block	57. Camshaft assy.	80. Ground switch	89. Condenser
36. Blower air baffle	73. Breaker box cover	81. Screw	90. Armature core
52. Breaker point cam	74. Gasket	82. Washer	91. High-tension lead
53. Push rod	75. Breaker points	83. Blower housing	92. Washer
54. Spring	76. Ignition wire	84. Flywheel key	93. Spacer
55. Timing advance	77. Pin	85. Flywheel	94. Screw
weight	78. Screw	86. Washer	95. Coil
56. Rivet	79. Clip	87. Nut	96. Screw

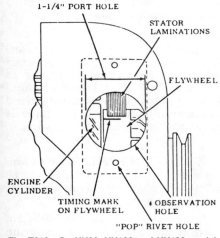

Fig. T613—On HH80, HH100 and HH120 models, remove identification plate to view timing mark on flywheel through the 1-3/4 inch (45 mm) hole in blower housing.

below stator laminations as shown in Fig. T613. At this time, points should be ready to open and continuity light should be on. Rotate flywheel until mark just passes under edge of laminations. Points should open and light should be out. If not, adjust points slightly until light goes out. Points are actuated by push rod (53—Fig. T612) that rides against cam (52). Breaker cam is driven by a tang on advance weight (55). When cranking, spring (54)

holds advance weight in retarded position (TDC). At operating speeds, centrifugal force overcomes spring pressure and weight moves cam to advance ignition so spark occurs when piston is at 0.095 inch (2.14 mm) BTDC.

Air gap between flywheel and stator laminations should be 0.0125 inch (0.32 mm) on all models. To adjust air gap, turn flywheel magnet into position under coil core. Loosen retaining screws and place shim stock or feeler gauge of specified thickness between coil and magnet. Press coil against gauge and tighten screws.

Battery Ignition System. Models HH80, HH100 and HH120 may be equipped with a battery ignition system. Coil and condenser are externally mounted and points are located in crankcase cover. See Fig. T614. Breaker-point gap should be adjusted to 0.020 inch (0.51 mm). To check timing, disconnect primary wire between coil and points and follow the same procedure as described in MAGNETO IGNITION paragraphs.

Solid-State Ignition System (Without Alternator). Tecumseh solid-state ignition system shown in Fig. T615 may be used on some models not equipped with a flywheel alternator. This system does not use ignition breaker points. The only moving part of

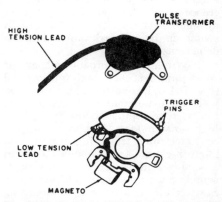

Fig. T615—View of solid-state ignition system used on some models not equipped with a flywheel alternator.

the system is the rotating flywheel with charging magnets. As flywheel magnet passes position (1A—Fig. T616), a low voltage alternating current is induced into input coil (2). Current passes through rectifier (3) converting this current to direct current. It then travels to capacitor (4) where it is stored. Flywheel rotates approximately 180° to position (1B). As it passes trigger coil (5), it induces a very small electric charge into coil. This charge passes through resistor (6) and turns on SCR (silicon controlled rectifier) switch (7). With SCR switch closed, low voltage current stored in capacitor (4) travels to pulse transformer (8). Voltage is stepped up instantaneously and current is discharged across electrodes of spark plug (9), producing a spark before top dead center.

Some units are equipped with a second trigger coil and resistor set to turn SCR switch on at a lower rpm. This second trigger pin is closer to the fly-

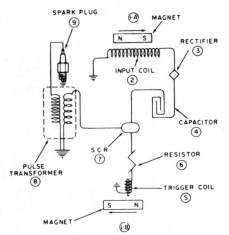

Fig. T616—Diagram of solid-state ignition system used on some models.

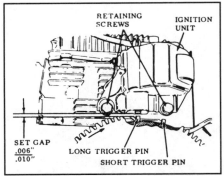

Fig. T618—Adjust air gap between long trigger pin and ignition unit to 0.006-0.010 inch (0.15-0.25 mm).

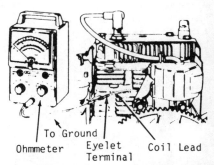

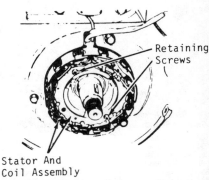

Fig. T620—View showing an ohmmeter connected for resistance test of ignition charging (alternator) coil.

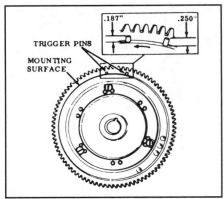

Fig. T619—Remove flywheel and drive trigger pins in or out as necessary until long pin is extended 0.250 inch (6.35 mm) and short pin is extended 0.187 inch (4.76 mm) above mounting surface.

wheel and produces a spark at TDC for easier starting. As engine rpm increases, first (shorter) trigger pin picks up small electric charge and turns SCR switch on, firing spark plug before top dead center.

If system fails to produce a spark at spark plug, first check high-tension lead (Fig. T615). If condition of high-tension lead is questionable, or if insulation is faulty, renew pulse transformer and high-tension lead. Magneto charging coil, electronic triggering system and mounting plate are available only as an assembly. If necessary to renew this assembly, place unit in position on engine. Start retaining screws, turn mounting plate counterclockwise as far as possible, then tighten retaining screws to 60-84 in.-lbs. (7-10 N•m).

Solid-State Ignition System (With Alternator). Tecumseh solid-state ignition system used on some models equipped with a flywheel alternator does not use breaker points. The only moving part of system is rotating flywheel with charging magnets and trigger pins. Other components of system are ignition charging (alternator) coil

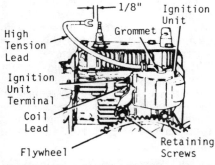

Fig. T617—View of solid-state ignition unit used on some models equipped with a flywheel alternator. System should produce a good blue spark that is 1/8-inch (3.2 mm) long at cranking speed.

and stator assembly, spark plug and ignition unit.

The long trigger pin induces a small charge of current to close SCR (silicon controlled rectifier) switch at engine cranking speed and produces a spark at top dead center for starting. As engine rpm increases, first (shorter) trigger pin induces current that produces a spark when piston is 0.095 inch (2.41 mm) BTDC.

Test solid-state ignition system by holding high-tension lead 1/8 inch (3.2 mm) from spark plug (Fig. T617). Crank engine and check for a good blue spark. If no spark is present, check high-tension lead and coil lead for loose connections or faulty insulation. Check air gap between trigger pin and ignition unit as shown in Fig. T618. Air gap should be 0.006-0.010 inch (0.15-0.25 mm). To adjust air gap, loosen the two retaining screws and move ignition unit as necessary, then tighten retaining screws.

NOTE: Long trigger pin should extend 0.250 inch (6.35 mm) and short trigger pin should extend 0.187 inch (4.76 mm), measured as shown in Fig.

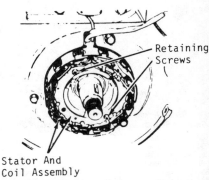

Fig. T621—Ignition charging (alternator) coil and stator serviced only as an assembly.

T619. If not, remove flywheel and drive pins in or out as required.

To test ignition charging (alternator) coil, remove coil lead from ignition terminal and connect an ohmmeter as shown in Fig. T620. If series resistance is below 400 ohms, renew stator and coil assembly (Fig. T621). If resistance is above 400 ohms, renew ignition unit.

VALVE ADJUSTMENT. Valve tappet gap (cold) on all models should be 0.010 inch (0.25 mm) with piston at TDC on compression stroke.

To increase clearance, grind off end of valve stem. To reduce clearance, grind valve seat deeper or renew valve and/or valve tappet. Refer also to VALVE SYSTEM paragraphs in REPAIRS section.

REPAIRS

TIGHTENING TORQUES. Recommended tightening torque specifications are as follows:
Ball bearing retainer nut:
　All models so equipped . 15-22 in.-lbs.
　　　　　　　　　　　(1.7-3 N•m)

Bearing retainer cap:
　HH80, VH80, HH100,
　VH100, HH120 . . . . . . 65-110 in.-lbs.
　　　　　　　　　　　(7.3-12 N•m)

Connecting rod:
HH70, VH70 . . . . 120 in.-lbs.
(13 N•m)
HH80, VH80, HH100,
VH100, HH120 . . . . 110 in.-lbs.
(12 N•m)
Crankcase cover . . . . . . 65-110 in.-lbs.
(7.3-12 N•m)
Cylinder head:
HH70, VH70 . . . . 170 in.-lbs.
(19 N•m)
HH80, VH80, HH100,
VH100, HH120 . . . . 200 in.-lbs.
(22.6 N•m)
Flywheel nut . . . . 50-55 ft.-lbs.
(68-75 N•m)

CYLINDER HEAD. When removing cylinder head, note location of different length cap screws to aid in reassembly. Always install new head gasket and tighten cap screws evenly following sequence shown in Figs. T622, T623 and T624. Tighten cylinder head screws to 200 in.-lbs. (22.6 N•m).

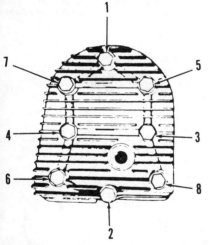

Fig. T622—On Models HH70 and VH70, tighten cylinder head cap screws evenly to 170 in.-lbs. (19 N•m) following sequence shown.

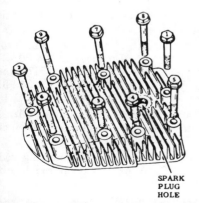

Fig. T623—Follow sequence shown when tightening cylinder head cap screws on early Models HH80, HH100 and HH120. Tighten screws to 200 in.-lbs. (23 N•m). Note length and type of screws.

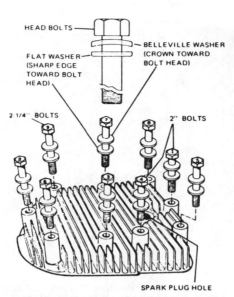

Fig. T624—Flat washers and Belleville washers are used on cylinder head cap screws on late HH80, HH100 and HH120 and all VH80 and VH100 engines. Tighten cap screws to 200 in.-lbs. (23 N•m) following sequence shown.

VALVE SYSTEM. Valve seats are machined directly into cylinder block assembly. Seats are ground at a 45° angle and should not exceed $\frac{3}{64}$ inch (1.19 mm) in width.

Valve face angle should be 45°. Valve margin should not be less than $\frac{1}{32}$ inch (0.79 mm). See Fig. T625. Valves are available with $\frac{1}{32}$ inch (0.79 mm) oversize stem for use with oversize valve guide bore.

Valve guides are not renewable. If guides are excessively worn, ream to 0.3432-0.3442 inch (8.72-8.74 mm) and install a valve with $\frac{1}{32}$ inch (0.794 mm) oversize valve stem. Drill upper and lower valve spring caps as necessary to fit oversize valve stem.

OIL PUMP. Some vertical crankshaft models are equipped with a positive displacement barrel and plunger-type oil pump (Figs. T626 and T627) driven by an eccentric on the camshaft. Oil from the pump lubricates the

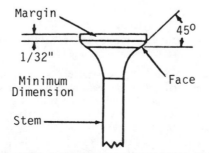

Fig. T625—Valve face angle should be 45°. Minimum valve head margin is 1/32 inch (0.79 mm).

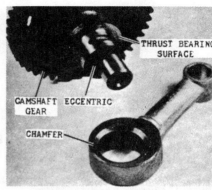

Fig. T626—View of early-type oil pump used on some vertical crankshaft models. Chamfered face of drive collar should be toward camshaft gear.

Fig. T627—Install late-type oil pump so large flat surface on drive collar is away from camshaft gear.

upper main bearing and the connecting rod journal.

When installing early type pump (Fig. T626), chamfered side of drive collar must be against thrust bearing surface on camshaft gear. When installing late type pump, place side of drive collar with large flat surface shown in Fig. T627 away from camshaft gear.

All other models are splash lubricated using an oil slinger or oil dipper. Refer to CRANKSHAFT and CONNECTING ROD sections.

CAMSHAFT. The camshaft and camshaft gear are an integral part that rides on journals at each end of camshaft.

Some engines have a camshaft equipped with a compression release mechanism (Fig. T628). A camshaft equipped with a compression release mechanism is easier to remove and install if the crankshaft is rotated three teeth past aligned position that allows compression release mechanism to clear exhaust valve lifter. Compression release mechanism parts should work freely with no binding or sticking. Parts are not serviced separately from camshaft assembly.

Valve lifters should be identified before removal so they can be reinstalled in their original positions. Some models use lifters of different length. Short lifter is installed at intake position and longer lifter is installed at exhaust position.

Camshaft journal diameter should be 0.6235-0.6240 inch (15.837-15.850 mm) and journal to bearing running clear-

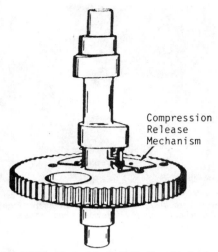

Fig. T628—View of Insta-Matic Ezee-Start compression release camshaft assembly used on some models.

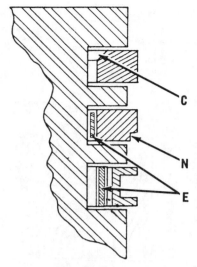

Fig. T629—View showing typical location and arrangement of piston rings. Note location of chamfer (C) on top ring, notch (N) on second ring and expander rings (E).

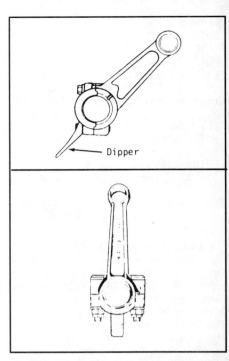

Fig. T630—View of connecting rods equipped with an oil dipper used on most horizontal crankshaft engines.

Fig. T631—Connecting rods used on VH80 and VH100 have two oil holes.

ance should be 0.003 inch (0.08 mm). Renew camshaft if gear teeth are worn or if journal or lobe surfaces are worn or damaged.

Make certain timing marks on camshaft gear and crankshaft gear are aligned during assembly. On some models there is a single chamfered tooth on crankshaft gear instead of a timing mark.

PISTON, PIN AND RINGS. The engine is fitted with an aluminum piston that has two compression rings and an oil control ring. Piston and connecting rod are removed as an assembly from cylinder head end of engine.

Measure piston skirt diameter at bottom edge of skirt at a right angle to piston pin for all models.

Piston Diameter

HH70, VH70 . . . . . . 2.7450-2.7455 in.
(69.723-69.736 mm)
HH80 prior to
type letter B. . . . . 2.9325-2.9335 in.
(74.486-74.511 mm)
HH80 with type
letter B or after . . . . 3.308-3.310 in.
(84.023-84.074 mm)
VH80, HH100,
VH100 . . . . 3.308-3.310 in.
(84.023-84.074 mm)
HH120 . . . . 3.4950-3.4970 in.
(88.773-88.824 mm)

Measure piston skirt-to-cylinder wall clearance at bottom edge of skirt at a right angle to piston pin for all models. Refer to following list for specified piston clearance:

Piston Clearance

HH70, VH70 . . . . . . 0.0045-0.0060 in.
(0.114-0.152 mm)

HH80 prior to
type letter B . . . . 0.004-0.006 in.
(0.10-0.15 mm)
HH80 with type
letter B or after. . . . . 0.002-0.005 in.
(0.05-0.13 mm)
VH80, HH100,
VH100 . . . . 0.002-0.005 in.
(0.05-0.13 mm)
HH120 . . . . 0.003-0.006 in.
(0.08-0.15 mm)

Side clearance of top ring in piston groove should be 0.002-0.005 inch (0.05-0.13 mm) for all other models.

Standard piston pin diameter is 0.6252-0.6256 inch (15.880-15.890 mm) for Models HH70 and VH70 and 0.6873-0.6875 inch (17.457-17.462 mm) for all other models.

Piston pin clearance should be 0.0001-0.0008 inch (0.0025-0.0203 mm) in connecting rod and 0.0002-0.0005 inch (0.0051-0.0127 mm) in piston. Piston pin is available only as an assembly with piston.

If piston crown has an arrow, install piston on connecting rod so arrow on piston crown will point toward carburetor side of engine after installation.

Note location and arrangement of piston rings in Fig. T629.

Piston and rings are available in standard size and oversizes.

CONNECTING ROD. Piston and connecting rod are removed as an assembly from cylinder head end of engine. Connecting rod rides directly on crankpin journal of crankshaft.

On horizontal crankshaft models, an oil dipper is an integral part of connecting rod cap or a separate oil dipper is

attached to the rod by the connecting rod bolts. See Fig. T630.

Standard crankpin journal diameter is 1.1865-1.1870 inches (30.124-30.137 mm) for Models HH70 and VH70 and 1.3750-1.3755 inches (34.925-34.938 mm) for all other models.

Connecting rod-to-crankpin journal running clearance should be 0.002 inch (0.05 mm) for all models.

If installing a new connecting rod, wipe off any oxidation on rod before installation.

Connecting rods are equipped with match marks that must be aligned and face pto end of crankshaft after installation. See Figs. T631 and T632.

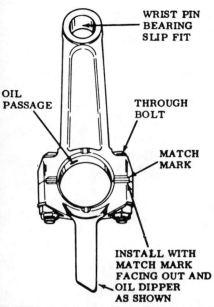

Fig. T632—Note location of match marks and oil hole when assembling and installing connecting rod on Models HH80, HH100 and HH120.

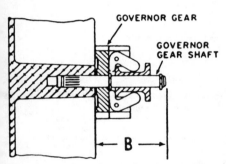

Fig. T633—View showing installation of governor shaft and governor gear, and weight assembly on HH80, HH100 and HH120 models. Dimension (B) should be 1 inch (25.4 mm).

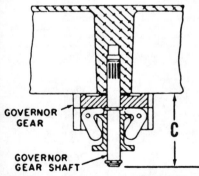

Fig. T634—Governor gear and shaft installation on VH80 and VH100 models. Dimension (C) should be 1 inch (25.4 mm).

Connecting rod is available in standard size as well as undersizes.

GOVERNOR. Governor weight and gear assembly is driven by camshaft gear and rides on a renewable shaft that

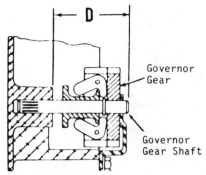

Fig. T635—Correct installation of governor shaft, gear and weight assembly on Model HH70. Dimension (D) should be 1-17/64 inches (32.15 mm).

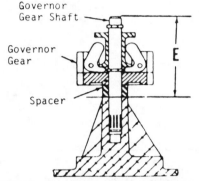

Fig. T636—Governor gear and shaft installation on Model VH70. Dimension (E) should be 1-19/32 inches (40.48 mm).

is pressed into engine crankcase or crankcase cover.

If renewal of governor shaft is necessary, press governor shaft in until shaft end is located as shown in Figs. T633, T634, T635 or T636.

Adjust external linkage as outlined in MAINTENANCE section.

CRANKSHAFT AND MAIN BEARINGS. Crankshaft main journals ride in two renewable steel-backed bronze bushings. On some horizontal crankshaft engines, the crankshaft is supported in a renewable sleeve bushing at flywheel end and a ball bearing or bushing at pto end. Models HH80, VH80, HH100, VH100 and HH120 are equipped with tapered roller bearings at each end of crankshaft.

Standard main bearing bore diameter for bushing-type main bearings on Models HH70 and VH70 is 1.0005-1.0010 inches (25.413-25.425 mm) for each bearing.

Normal running clearance of crankshaft journals in bronze bushings is 0.0015-0.0025 inch (0.038-0.064 mm). Renew crankshaft if main journals are more than 0.001 inch (0.025 mm) out-of-round or renew or regrind crankshaft if

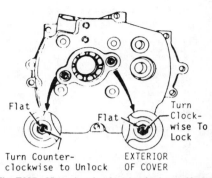

Fig. T637—View showing bearing locks on Model HH70 equipped with ball bearing main bearings. Locks must be released before removing crankcase cover. Refer to Fig. T638 for interior view of cover and locks.

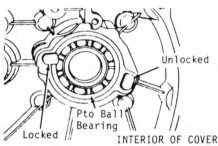

Fig. T638—Interior view of crankcase cover and ball bearing locks used on Model HH70.

connecting rod journal is more than 0.0005 inch (0.013 mm) out-of-round.

Check crankshaft gear for wear, broken teeth or loose fit on crankshaft. If crankshaft gear is damaged, remove gear from crankshaft with an arbor press. Renew gear pin and press new gear on shaft making certain timing mark is facing pto end of shaft.

On models equipped with a ball bearing at pto end of shaft, refer to Figs. T637 and T638 before removing crankcase cover. Loosen locknuts and rotate protruding ends of lock pins counterclockwise to release bearing and remove cover. Ball bearing will remain on crankshaft. When reassembling, turn lock pins clockwise until flats on pins face each other, then tighten locknuts to 15-22 in.-lbs. (2-3 N·m).

Crankshaft end play for all models except those with tapered roller main bearings should be 0.005-0.027 inch (0.13-0.69 mm) and is controlled by varying thickness of thrust washers between crankshaft and cylinder block or crankcase cover.

Crankshaft main bearing preload of all models with tapered roller bearing main bearings should be 0.001-0.007 inch (0.025-0.18 mm) and is controlled by varying thickness of shim gasket (32—Fig. T639 or T640). On Model VH100 equipped with an oil pump,

Fig. T639—Exploded view of VH80 and VH100 vertical crankshaft engine.

1. Governor arm bushing
2. Oil seal
3. Oil pan (engine base)
7. Governor arm
8. Thrust spool
9. Snap ring
10. Governor gear & weight assy.
11. Governor shaft
12. Bearing cup
13. Gasket
14. Piston & pin assy.
15. Top compression ring
16. Second compression ring
17. Ring expander
18. Oil control ring
19. Retaining ring
20. Spark plug
21. Cylinder head
22. Head gasket
23. Exhaust valve
24. Intake valve
25. Pin
26. Exhaust valve spring
27. Intake valve spring
28. Spring cap
29. Cylinder block
30. Bearing cone
31. Bearing cup
32. Shim gasket
33. Steel washer (0.010 in.)
34. Oil seal
35. Bearing retainer cap
36. Blower air baffle
38. Gasket
39. Breather
40. Breather tube
42. Rod cap
43. Locknut
44. Washer
45. Crankshaft gear pin
46. Crankshaft
47. Connecting rod
48. Rod bolt
49. Crankshaft gear
50. Valve lifters
51. Bearing cone
57. Camshaft assy.
58. "O" ring
59. Oil slinger

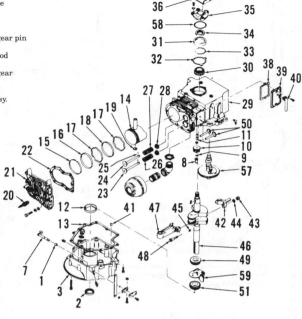

Fig. T640—Exploded view of HH80, HH100 and HH120 horizontal crankshaft engine.

1. Governor arm bushing
2. Oil seal
3. Crankcase cover
4. Dipstick
5. Gasket
6. Oil filler tube
7. Governor arm
8. Thrust spool
9. Snap ring
10. Governor gear & weight assy.
11. Governor shaft
12. Bearing cup
13. Gasket
14. Piston & pin assy.
15. Top compression ring
16. Second compression ring
17. Ring expander
18. Oil control ring
19. Retaining ring
20. Spark plug
21. Cylinder head
22. Head gasket
23. Exhaust valve
24. Intake valve
25. Pin
26. Exhaust valve spring
27. Intake valve spring
28. Spring cap
29. Cylinder block
30. Bearing cone
31. Bearing cup
32. Shim gasket
33. Steel washer (0.010 in.)
34. Oil seal
35. Bearing retainer cap
36. Blower air baffle
38. Gasket
39. Breather
40. Breather tube
41. Dowel pin
42. Rod cap
43. Locknut
44. Washer
45. Crankshaft gear pin
46. Crankshaft
47. Connecting rod
48. Rod bolt
49. Crankshaft gear
50. Valve lifters
51. Bearing cone
52. Breaker cam
53. Push rod
54. Spring
55. Timing advance weight
56. Rivet
57. Camshaft assy.
58. "O" ring

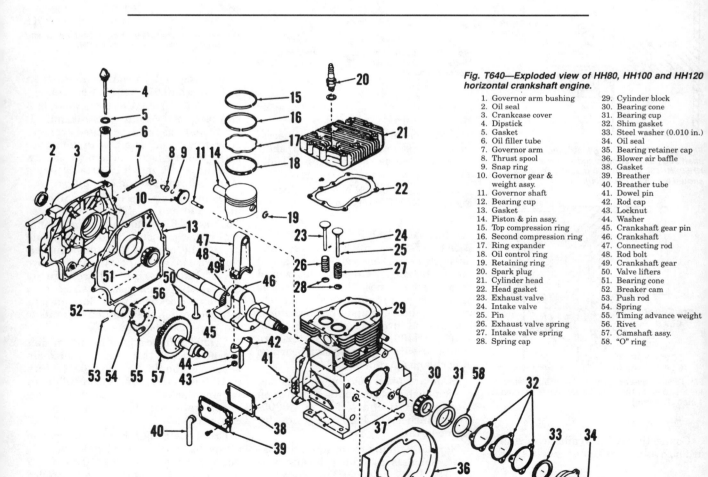

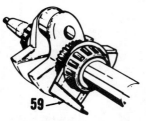

Fig. T641—Oil slinger (59) on VH80 and VH100 models must be installed on crankshaft as shown.

crankshaft main bearing preload should be 0.002-0.007 inch (0.05-0.18 mm).

Tapered roller bearings are a press fit on crankshaft and must be renewed if removed. Heat bearings in hot oil to aid in installation.

Bronze bushing-type main bearings are renewable and finish reamers are available from Tecumseh.

Standard crankshaft main bearing journal diameter for both ends is 0.9985-0.9990 inch (25.362-25.375 mm) for Models HH70 and VH70 and 1.1865-1.1870 inches (30.137-30.150 mm) for all other models. Standard crankshaft connecting rod journal diameter should be 1.3750-1.3755 inches (34.925-34.938 mm) for Models HH80, VH80, HH100 and HH120, and 1.1865-1.1870 inch (30.137-30.150 mm) for all other models.

Connecting rod is available in standard size as well as undersizes.

On Models VH80 and VH100, an oil slinger (59—Fig. T641) is installed on the crankshaft between gear and lower bearing. The oil slinger directs oil upward to lubricate the engine. A tang in the slinger hub must be inserted in a slot on the crankshaft gear.

Make certain timing marks on camshaft gear and crankshaft gear are aligned during assembly.

CYLINDER. If cylinder is scored or excessively worn, or if taper or out-of-round exceeds 0.004 inch (0.10 mm), cylinder should be bored to next oversize for which piston and rings are available. Refer to following list of standard bore diameters:

	Std. Bore Diameter
HH70, VH70	2.750-2.751 in. (69.85-69.88 mm)
HH80 prior to type letter B	2.9375-2.9385 in. (74.61-74.64 mm)

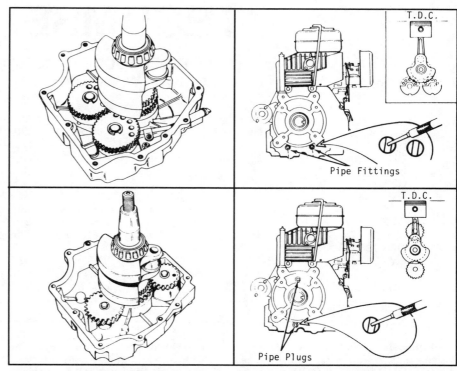

Fig. T642—View showing locations of pipe fittings and plugs that must be removed for access to correctly time balancer gears. Refer to text.

HH80 with type letter B or after	3.312-3.313 in. (84.12-84.15 mm)
VH80, HH100, VH100	3.312-3.313 in. (84.12-84.15 mm)
HH120	3.500-3.501 in. (88.90-88.92 mm)

DYNA-STATIC BALANCER. The Dyna-Static engine balancer used on some models consists of counterweighted gears driven by the crankshaft gear to counteract unbalance caused by the counterweights on the crankshaft.

Snap rings are used to retain counterweight gears on shafts that are pressed into crankcase cover.

Renewable balancer gear shafts are pressed into crankcase cover. Press shafts into cover so height between boss on crankcase cover and step on shafts is 1.7135-1.7185 inches (43.523-43.650 mm) as shown in Fig. T643.

Balancer gears are equipped with renewable caged needle bearings. Using Tecumseh tool 670210, press new bearings into gears until cage is flush to 0.015 inch (0.38 mm) below edge of bore.

MEASURE FROM COVER BOSS TO RING GROOVE OUTER EDGE

Fig. T643—On Models HH80, HH100 and HH120, press balancer gear shafts into cover so height between boss on crankcase cover and step on shafts is 1.7135-1.7185 inches (43.523-43.650 mm).

When reassembling engine, balancer gears must be timed with crankshaft for correct operation. Refer to Fig. T642 and remove pipe plugs. Insert Tecumseh alignment tool 670239 through crankcase cover and into timing slots in balancer gears. Rotate engine until piston is at TDC on compression stroke and install cover and gear assembly while tools retain gears in correct position.

When correctly assembled, piston should be at TDC and weights on balancer gear should be directly opposite. See appropriate inset in Fig. T642.

TECUMSEH

TECUMSEH PRODUCTS COMPANY
Grafton, Wisconsin 53204

Model	No. Cyls.	Bore	Stroke	Displacement	Power Rating
OHM120, OHSK120	1	3.31 in. (84.2 mm)	2.53 in. (64.3 mm)	21.82 cu. in. (357 cc)	12 hp (8.9 kW)
OHV12, OVM120	1	3.31 in. (84.2 mm)	2.53 in. (64.3 mm)	21.82 cu. in. (357 cc)	12 hp (8.9 kW)
OVXL120	1	3.31 in. (84.2 mm)	2.53 in. (64.3 mm)	21.82 cu. in. (357 cc)	12 hp (8.9 kW)
OHV125, OVXL125, OVXL/C125	1	3.31 in. (84.2 mm)	2.53 in. (64.3 mm)	21.82 cu. in. (357 cc)	12.5 hp (9.3 kW)
OHV13	1	3.31 in. (84.2 mm)	2.53 in. (64.3 mm)	21.82 cu. in. (357 cc)	13 hp (9.7 kW)

All models are four-stroke, overhead valve, single-cylinder gasoline engines. Models OHM120 and OHSK120 are equipped with a horizontal crankshaft, while all other models are equipped with a vertical crankshaft. The aluminum alloy cylinder and crankcase assembly is equipped with a cast iron cylinder sleeve that is an integral part of the cylinder. Splash lubrication is used for all horizontal crankshaft engines. A positive displacement, plunger-type oil pump that is operated by an eccentric on the camshaft provides pressure lubrication on all vertical crankshaft engines.

Engine model number, serial number and specification number are stamped into the cooling shroud just above the rocker arm cover (Fig. T700). Always furnish correct engine model, serial and specification numbers when ordering parts.

MAINTENANCE

LUBRICATION. Vertical crankshaft models are equipped with a positive displacement, plunger-type oil pump that is located in the bottom of the oil pan. An eccentric on the camshaft works the oil pump plunger back and forth in the barrel to force oil up the center of the camshaft. The pressurized oil lubricates the top main bearing and top camshaft bearing. Oil is sprayed out of a hole between the camshaft and main bearings to lubricate the connecting rod and other internal parts.

All horizontal crankshaft models are splash lubricated by a dipper on the connecting rod cap.

Oil level should be checked before initial start-up and at five-hour intervals. Maintain oil level at "FULL" mark on dipstick.

Recommended oil change interval is every 25 hours of normal operation. Oil should be drained when engine is warm. Manufacturer recommends using oil with API service classification SJ. Use SAE 30 oil for temperatures above 32° F (0° C) and SAE 5W-20 or 10W-30 for temperatures below 32° F (0° C).

SPARK PLUG. Recommended spark plug is a Champion RN4C or equivalent. Recommended electrode gap is 0.030 in. (0.76 mm). Tighten spark plug to 21 ft.-lb. (28 N•m).

CARBURETOR. All models are equipped with a float type carburetor. Some models are equipped with a carburetor with both an idle and a high-speed fuel mixture adjustment screw. However, some models are equipped with just an idle speed fuel mixture screw; the high-speed mixture is controlled by a fixed main jet. Other than adjustment, service procedure is similar for either type carburetor.

Initial adjustment of idle mixture screw (2—Fig. T701) for all models is one turn open from a lightly seated position. Initial adjustment of high-speed adjustment screw (3), if so equipped, is 1½ turns open from a lightly seated position.

Make final adjustments on all models with engine at normal operating temperature. On models with high speed adjustment screw, set engine speed at full throttle and turn adjusting screw to find the lean drop-off point and the rich drop-off point. Then, set adjusting screw midway between the two extremes. When correctly set, engine

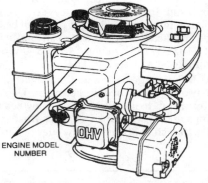

Fig. T700—Engine model number, serial number and specification number are stamped into the cooling shroud.

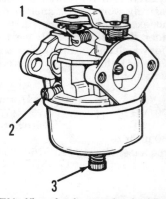

Fig. T701—View of carburetor showing idle speed screw (1), idle mixture adjusting screw (2) and high-speed fuel mixture adjusting screw (3). Some models may not be equipped with adjustable high-speed mixture screw (3).

should accelerate smoothly and run under load with steady governor operation. On all models, turn idle speed adjustment screw (1) to obtain desired idle speed as specified by the equipment manufacturer. Adjust idle mixture adjustment screw (2) to obtain smoothest idle operation using the same procedure as outlined for high-speed adjustment screw.

Because each adjustment affects the other, readjustment may be necessary.

To clean the carburetor, disassemble and clean all metallic parts with solvent or carburetor cleaner. To clean internal passages, remove Welch plugs from the carburetor body to expose drilled passages. Use a small, sharp pointed chisel to pierce the Welch plug and pry the plug out of carburetor body. When installing new plugs, use a flat punch equal or greater in size than the plug and just flatten the plug. Do not drive the center of plug below surface of carburetor body.

NOTE: Do not remove main nozzle tube in the carburetor body. Tube is installed to a predetermined depth, and altering its position in the carburetor body will affect metering characteristics of the carburetor.

Use compressed air and solvent to clean drilled passages and jets. Do not use drill bits or wire to clean jets or passages as carburetor calibration may be affected if openings are enlarged.

There are two different types of bowl nuts (33—Fig. T702) used on carburetors equipped with adjustable main jets. One type has one fuel inlet port at the bottom of the nut, and the other type has two fuel inlet ports at the bottom of the nut (Fig. T703). The difference between the nuts has to do with calibration changes of the carburetor, depending on engine application. If it is necessary to replace the bowl nut, make certain the correct type nut is installed. DO NOT interchange bowl nuts. Fuel inlet port(s) and idle fuel transfer port, located in annular groove at top of nut, must be open and free of any debris to ensure proper fuel flow to high and low speed circuits.

When reassembling carburetor, it is important that throttle plate is installed with line on the plate facing outward and positioned at the 3 o'clock position. Choke plate must be installed with cutout section facing downward. Be sure that throttle and choke plates open and close without binding.

Fuel inlet needle (23—Fig. T702) and seat (22) are renewable. If needle tip or seat is worn or deformed, new needle

and seat should be installed. Make certain when installing new seat that grooved side of seat is installed in bore first so the inlet needle will seat against the smooth side of seat (Fig. T704).

Assemble float, inlet needle and needle clip as shown in Fig. T705. To prevent binding, the long end of clip should face choke end of carburetor body.

To check float height, invert carburetor body and use float setting tool 670253A as shown in Fig. T706. Float height is correct if float does not touch

step portion of tool (1) and contacts step (2) as tool is pulled toward float hinge pin as shown. If tool is not available, measure the distance from top of main nozzle boss to surface of float. Distance should be 0.275-0.315 inch (7.0-8.0 mm). If adjustment is required, bend the float tab that contacts the fuel inlet needle, being careful not to force the inlet needle onto its seat.

GOVERNOR. All models are equipped with a mechanical flyweight type governor located inside the crankcase.

To adjust external governor linkage, stop engine and loosen the screw securing the governor lever (1—Fig. T707 or Fig. T708) and governor clamp (2). Push governor lever to fully open the carburetor throttle. On vertical crankshaft models, turn the governor

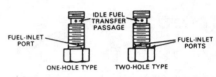

Fig. T703—Two different types of fuel bowl retaining nuts are used on adjustable main jet type carburetors. Different type nuts must not be interchanged. Refer to text.

Fig. T704—Fuel inlet needle seat must be installed with grooved side against carburetor body. Refer to text.

Fig. T702—Exploded view of carburetor. Some models are not equipped with high speed mixture adjusting screw (37), choke spring (5) or drain pin (27).

1. Choke shaft	20. Welch plug
2. Choke return spring	21. Bowl gasket
3. Washer	22. Inlet valve seat
4. Dust seal	23. Fuel inlet valve
5. Choke stop spring	24. Clip
6. Throttle shaft	25. Float pin
7. Throttle return spring	26. Float
8. Washer	27. Drain stem
9. Dust seal	28. Gasket
10. Throttle plate	29. Fuel bowl
11. Idle speed screw	30. Spring
12. Spring	31. Retainer
13. Welch plug	32. Washer
14. Idle mixture needle	33. Bowl retainer
15. Spring	34. "O" ring
16. Washer	35. Washer
17. "O" ring	36. Spring
18. Carburetor body	37. High speed
19. Choke plate	mixture screw

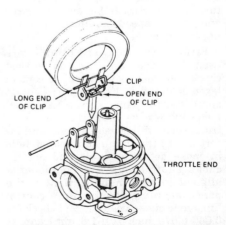

Fig. T705—View of carburetor float assembly showing correct installation of fuel inlet needle clip.

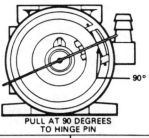

PULL AT 90 DEGREES
TO HINGE PIN

1 NO HIGHER THAN HERE

2 CAN TOUCH HERE WITHOUT GAP

Fig. T706—Float height can be adjusted using float setting tool 670253A.

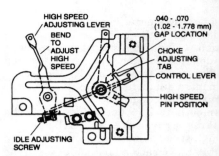

Fig. T709—Drawing of typical speed control plate used on engines equipped with remote control linkage.

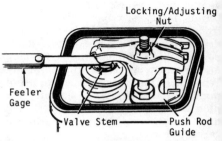

Fig. T710—Use a feeler gauge to correctly set valve clearance.

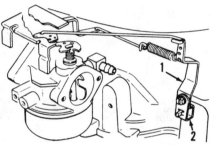

Fig. T707—Drawing of governor external linkage typical of standard engines without governor override system. Refer to text for adjustment procedure.

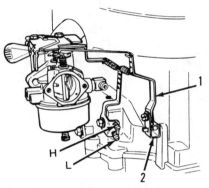

Fig. T708—Drawing of governor external linkage typical of engines equipped with governor override system. Refer to text for adjustment procedure.

clamp counterclockwise as far as it will go. On horizontal crankshaft models, rotate the governor lever shaft clockwise as far as possible. While holding clamp and lever in this position, tighten screw.

On 1985 and later production OVM120 and OVXL120 engines, a governor override system is used. Linkage is shown in Fig. T708. On these engines, the high speed setting is adjusted by turning top screw (H) of override lever and low idle speed is adjusted by turning bottom screw (L).

Various types of speed controls are used. A typical panel used on vertical crankshaft models with remote control lever is shown in Fig. T709. To adjust speed control panel, loosen the panel mounting screws. Move the speed control lever to full speed position and insert a wire through hole in panel, hole in choke actuating lever, and hole in choke shaft arm. With components aligned in this manner, tighten the panel mounting screws. Move control linkage to choke position, and check for 0.040-0.070 inch (1.0-1.8 mm) gap at control lever as shown in Fig. T709. Bend the choke adjusting tab if neces-

sary. Engine idle speed can be set by turning the idle speed adjusting screw. Maximum governed speed is adjusted by bending the high speed adjusting lever. Bend the lever away from panel to increase speed and the opposite direction to decrease speed.

IGNITION SYSTEM. A solid-state ignition system is used on all models. Ignition system has no moving parts and is considered satisfactory if a spark will jump a ⅛ inch (3.2-mm) air gap when engine is cranked at 125 rpm.

Ignition module is mounted outside of the flywheel. Air gap setting between ignition module and flywheel magnets is 0.0125 inch (0.32 mm). To set air gap, loosen the module mounting screws, move the module as necessary and retighten screws.

VALVE ADJUSTMENT. Clearance between the rocker arms and valve stem ends should be checked and adjusted with the engine cold. Specified clearance is 0.002 inch (0.05 mm) for in-

take valve and 0.004 inch (0.10 mm) for exhaust valve.

To adjust valves, remove rocker arm cover and rotate crankshaft to position piston at top dead center (TDC) of compression stroke. Both valves should be closed and the push rods loose at this point. Use a feeler gauge to measure clearance between rocker arm and valve stem as shown in Fig. T710. Turn rocker arm locking/adjusting nut to obtain specified clearance.

REPAIRS

TIGHTENING TORQUE. Recommended tightening torque values are as follows:

Alternator coil	90 in.-lb.
	(10.1 N•m)
Connecting rod bolts	210 in.-lb.
	(23.7 N•m)
Crankcase cover/ oil pan	125 in.-lb.
	(14.1 N•m)
Cylinder head bolts	230 in.-lb.
	(26.0 N•m)
Flywheel nut	58 ft.-lb.
	(78 N•m)
Intake pipe	95 in.-lb.
	(10.7 N•m)
Rocker arm studs	190 in.-lb.
	(21.5 N•m)
Rocker cover	18 in.-lb.
	(2.0 N•m)
Spark plug	250 in.-lb.
	(28.2 N•m)

CYLINDER HEAD. Always allow engine to cool completely before loosening cylinder head bolts. To remove cylinder head, first remove muffler, carburetor and intake pipe, blower housing and cylinder head cover. Position the piston at top dead center of compression stroke. Remove rocker arm cover, rocker arm adjusting nuts (1—Fig. T711), bearing (2) and rocker arms (3). Depress valve spring caps (14) and remove split retainers (13), caps, springs (15), spring seats (16) and "O" rings. Note that a white Teflon "O" ring (17) is used on exhaust valve guide and a black rubber "O" ring (18) is used on intake valve guide. Remove rocker arm studs (4), push rod guide (5) and rocker arm housing retaining screw (10) and withdraw rocker arm housing (7). Remove cylinder head mounting bolts and remove cylinder head (22) and valves. Remove valves from cylinder head.

Thoroughly clean cylinder head and inspect for cracks or other damage. Position cylinder head on a flat plate and use a feeler gauge to check flatness of head gasket sealing surface. Renew cylinder head if necessary.

Use a new head gasket when installing cylinder head. Install Belleville washer on cylinder head bolt with crown up toward bolt head, then install flat washer (Fig. T712). The two 1⅜ inch (34.9 mm) long head bolts go in positions marked "1" and "5" in Fig. T713. Tighten head bolts in 60 in.-lb. (6.8 N•m) increments following sequence shown in Fig. T713 until specified torque is obtained.

When installing valve guide seals, be sure that white Teflon "O" ring (17—Fig. T711) is installed on exhaust valve guide (guide is bronze in color) and black "O" ring (18) is installed on intake valve guide (guide is silver in color). Switching the position of "O"

rings may result in improper sealing and possible engine damage. Be sure to install new "O" rings on push rod tube (9) and underneath push rod guide (5) and retaining screw (10).

To install valve springs, valves must be raised and held on their seats. One way to do this is to insert a piece of rubber fuel line through intake and exhaust ports and wedge each end of the hose on opposite sides of the valve stem. Install valve springs with dampening coils (coils closer together) toward cylinder head. Place spring retainer on spring, use suitable tool to compress valve spring, and install split retainer.

NOTE: Any time rocker arm housing assembly is removed from engine, new rocker arm locking/adjusting nuts and rocker arm cover screws should be installed.

Tighten rocker arm studs (4) to 190 in.-lb. (21.5 N•m). Install rocker arms and adjust valve clearance as outlined in MAINTENANCE section.

VALVE SYSTEM. Valve seats are machined directly in the cylinder head. Seats should be cut at a 46° angle and valve faces cut or ground at a 45° angle. Valve seat width should be ³⁄₆₄ inch (1.2 mm). The recommended procedure to cut the valve seats is as follows: First, use a 60° cutter to narrow seat from bottom toward the center. Second, use a 30° cutter to narrow seat from top toward the center. Then, use 46° cutter to cut seat to desired width.

Clean all combustion deposits from valves. Renew valves that are burned, excessively pitted, warped or if valve head margin after grinding is less than ¹⁄₃₂ inch (0.8 mm). Valves should be

lapped to their seats using fine lapping compound. Thoroughly clean the cylinder head and valves after lapping is completed.

Valve spring free length should be 1.980 inches (50.29 mm). It is recommended that valve springs be renewed when engine is overhauled. The valve spring dampening coils are coils wound closer together at one end than the other. The end with closer coils should be installed against the cylinder head.

Standard valve guide inside diameter is 0.312-0.313 inch (7.93-7.95 mm). Guides can be reamed to 0.343-0.344 inch (8.71-8.74 mm) for use with oversize valve stems.

To renew valve guides, submerge cylinder head in a large pan of oil. Heat on a hot plate to temperature of 375°–400° F (190°-205° C) for about 20 minutes. Remove cylinder head from the oil and use an arbor press and ½ inch (13-mm) driver to push the valve guides out top side of cylinder head. Make certain that the driver does not contact and damage head as guide is removed.

To install new guides, place replacement guides in a freezer or on ice for minimum of 30 minutes prior to installation. Heat head in a pan of oil as previously outlined. Install locating snap rings on new guides, then press guides into cylinder head from the top until snap rings contact surface of head. Make certain that silver colored guide

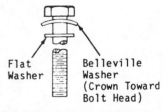

Fig. T712—Belleville washer is installed on head bolt with crown toward bolt head, then install flat washer with sharp edge toward bolt head.

Fig. T711—Exploded view of cylinder head assembly.

1. Adjusting nut
2. Rocker arm bearing
3. Rocker arm
4. Rocker arm stud
5. Push rod guide
6. "O" ring
7. Rocker arm housing
8. "O" ring
9. Push rod tube
10. Cap screw
11. Washer
12. "O" ring
13. Split retainers
14. Spring cap
15. Valve springs
16. Spring seats
17. "O" ring (white)
18. "O" ring (black)
19. Snap rings
20. Valve guide (intake)
21. Valve guide (exhaust)
22. Cylinder head
23. Head bolt
24. Belleville washer
25. Flat washer

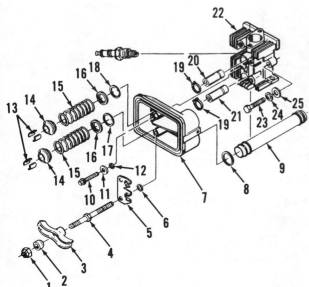

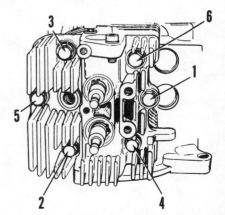

Fig. T713—Cylinder head bolts should be loosened and tightened following the sequence shown. The two 1-3/8 inch (34.9 mm) long bolts are installed in positions "1" and "5."

is installed in intake side and brass colored guide is installed in exhaust side. Allow the cylinder head to cool, then reface both valve seats to ensure that they are concentric with valve guides.

OIL PUMP. Models with a vertical crankshaft are equipped with a positive displacement oil pump (33—Fig. T714). Oil pump is located in the oil pan and is driven by an eccentric on the camshaft.

When installing the oil pump, be sure that the chamfered side of pump faces the camshaft, and the plunger ball seats in recess in oil pan.

CAMSHAFT. Camshaft and camshaft gear are an integral part which can be removed from engine after removing the rocker arms, push rods and oil pan or crankcase cover. Identify position of tappets as they are removed so they can be installed in their original position if reused.

Camshaft bearings are an integral part of crankcase and oil pan or crankcase cover. Camshaft journal diameter should be 0.6235-0.6240 inch (15.84-15.85 mm). Camshaft bearing inside diameter should be 0.6245-0.6255 inch (15.86-15.89 mm). Clearance between the camshaft jour-

nal and camshaft bearing should not exceed 0.003 inch (0.08 mm). Inspect camshaft lobes for pitting, scratches or excessive wear and renew as necessary. Tappets should be renewed whenever a new camshaft is installed.

Camshaft is equipped with a compression release mechanism (Fig. T715) to aid starting. Compression release mechanism parts should work freely with no binding or sticking. Parts are not serviced separately from camshaft.

When installing the camshaft, be sure that timing marks on camshaft

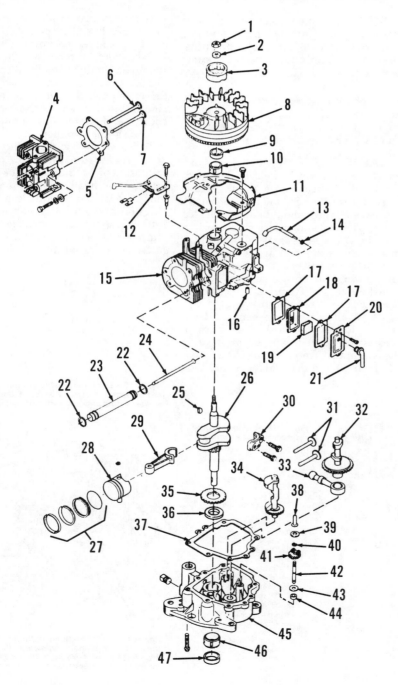

Fig. T714—Exploded view of OVM120 and OVMXL120 engines. Other vertical and horizontal crankshaft models are similar. Push rod tubes (23) and bushings (10 and 46) are not used on all models. Oil pump (33) and spacer (44) are not used on horizontal crankshaft engines.

1. Nut
2. Lockwasher
3. Starter cup
4. Cylinder head
5. Gasket
6. Intake valve
7. Exhaust valve
8. Flywheel
9. Oil seal
10. Bushing
11. Baffle
12. Ignition module
13. Governor shaft
14. Washer
15. Cylinder block
16. Dowel pin
17. Gasket
18. Breather
19. Breather element
20. Cover
21. Breather tube
22. "O" ring
23. Push rod tube
24. Push rod
25. Key
26. Crankshaft
27. Piston rings
28. Piston
29. Connecting rod
30. Rod cap
31. Tappets
32. Camshaft
33. Oil pump
34. Balancer
35. Gear
36. Shim
37. Gasket
38. Thrust spool
39. Washer
40. Snap ring
41. Governor gear & weight assy.
42. Governor shaft
43. Washer
44. Spacer
45. Oil pan
46. Bushing
47. Oil seal

gear and crankshaft gear are aligned as shown in Fig. T716.

PISTON, PIN AND RINGS. Piston and connecting rod are removed as an assembly. Refer to CONNECTING ROD section for removal procedure.

Standard piston skirt diameter, measured at bottom of skirt 90 degrees from piston pin bore, is 3.309-3.311 inches (84.05-84.09 mm) for all models. Specified clearance between piston skirt and cylinder wall is 0.0012-0.0032 inch (0.031-0.081 mm). Oversize pistons are available. Oversize piston size should be stamped on top of piston.

To check piston ring grooves for wear, clean carbon from ring grooves and install new rings in grooves. Use a feeler gauge to measure side clearance between ring land and ring. Specified side clearance is 0.0015-0.0035 inch (0.038-0.089 mm) for compression rings and 0.001-0.004 inch (0.025-0.102 mm)

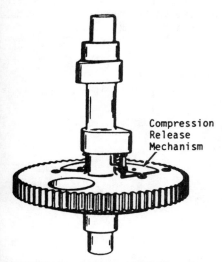

Fig. T715—Camshaft is equipped with a compression release mechanism.

Compression Release Mechanism

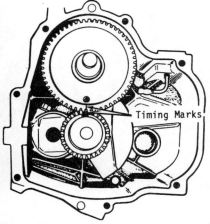

Timing Marks

Fig. T716—Camshaft and crankshaft timing marks must be aligned after installation for proper valve timing.

for oil control ring. Renew piston if ring side clearance is excessive.

Ring end gap should be 0.010-0.020 inch (0.25-0.51 mm) for all rings.

Rings must be installed on piston as shown in Fig. T717. Stagger ring end gaps around piston. Lubricate piston and cylinder with engine oil prior to installing piston. Be sure that arrow on top of piston points toward push rod side of engine and match marks on connecting rod and cap are toward open side of crankcase after installation.

CONNECTING ROD. Piston and connecting rod are removed as an assembly as follows: Remove all cooling shrouds. Remove rocker arm cover and cylinder head as previously outlined. Drain oil and remove oil pan or crankcase cover. Remove connecting rod cap. Remove carbon or ring ridge (if present) from top of cylinder before removing piston. Push the connecting rod and piston out top of cylinder.

Connecting rod rides directly on crankshaft crankpin. Inside diameter of connecting rod bearing bore at crankshaft end should be 1.3775-1.3780 inches (34.989-35.001 mm).

Piston must be assembled on connecting rod so arrow on top of piston will be pointing towards push rod side of engine. Connecting rods are equipped with match marks that must be aligned and face the pto end of crankshaft after installation. See Fig. T718. If equipped with connecting rod screws with different lengths, long screw must be installed in the hole nearer piston pin hole as shown in Fig. T718.

GOVERNOR. Governor weight and gear assembly is driven by camshaft gear and rides on a renewable shaft that is pressed into engine crankcase or crankcase cover.

Governor gear, flyweights and shaft are serviced only as an assembly. If governor gear shaft is renewed, new shaft should be pressed into oil pan or crank-

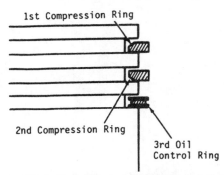

1st Compression Ring
2nd Compression Ring
3rd Oil Control Ring

Fig. T717—Piston rings must be installed on piston so chamfered edge of top ring is facing up and chamfered edge of second ring is facing down.

case cover boss until exposed shaft length is 1 3/32 inches (27.8 mm) on Models OHM120 and OHSK120 and 1 23/64 inches (34.5 mm) on all other models.

Adjust external linkage as outlined in MAINTENANCE section.

CRANKSHAFT, MAIN BEARINGS AND SEALS. To remove crankshaft, first remove all shrouds. Remove flywheel. Remove connecting rod and piston as previously outlined. Remove the balancer gear and shaft assembly. Remove the balancer drive gear from crankshaft. Position engine so tappets fall away from camshaft, then withdraw camshaft from cylinder block and remove crankshaft.

On engines equipped with a vertical crankshaft, crankshaft is supported at each end in renewable bushing type main bearings. On Models OHM120 and OHSK120, the bushing in the crankcase cover is renewable but the bushing in the crankcase is not renewable. On other models, main bearings are integral part of crankcase and oil pan or crankcase cover. On all models, main bearing inside diameter should be 1.3765-1.3770 inches (34.963-34.976 mm).

Standard crankshaft main journal diameter is 1.3745-1.3750 inches (34.912-34.925 mm) for each end. Standard crankpin journal diameter is 1.3740-1.3745 inches (34.900-34.912 mm).

Crankshaft end play should be 0.001-0.004 inch (0.025-0.10 mm) and is controlled by varying thickness of thrust washers between crankshaft and oil pan or crankcase cover.

When renewing crankshaft oil seals, note if old seal is raised or flush with outer surface of crankcase and oil pan or crankcase cover and install new seal to same dimension. Attempting to in-

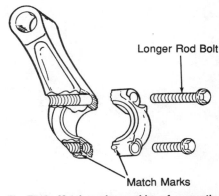

Longer Rod Bolt

Match Marks

Fig. T718—Match marks on sides of connecting rod and cap must be aligned. Install rod and piston so match marks are towards pto end of crankshaft. On models with connecting rod cap screws of different lengths, long screw must be installed in the hole nearer piston pin.

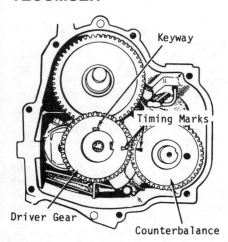

Fig. T719—Counterbalance gear and drive gear timing marks must be aligned after installation.

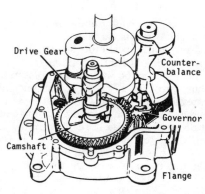

Fig. T720—View of relative position of camshaft, crankshaft and counterbalance shaft in oil pan or crankcase cover.

stall seal too far into casting bore may damage seal or engine. Use suitable installing tool to install new seal until it is lightly seated in casting bore.

When installing crankshaft, align timing mark on crankshaft gear with timing mark on camshaft gear to en-sure correct valve timing. See Fig. T716. With piston at top dead center, install counterbalance gear assembly and crankshaft balancer drive gear with timing marks (arrow) on gears facing each other as shown in Fig. T719. Install oil pump and oil pan or crankcase cover. Apply Loctite 242 to threads of oil pan or crankcase cover cap screws and tighten to 125 in.-lb. (14.1 N•m).

CYLINDER AND CRANKCASE. A cast iron liner is permanently cast into the aluminum alloy cylinder and crankcase assembly. Standard piston bore inside diameter is 3.312-3.313 inches (84.125-84.150 mm). If cylinder taper or out-of-round exceeds 0.004 inch (0.10 mm), cylinder should be renewed or bored to nearest oversize for which piston and rings are available.

ULTRA-BALANCE SYSTEM. All models are equipped with Tecumseh's Ultra-Balance system that consists of a single counterbalance shaft driven by a gear on the crankshaft (Fig. T720).

To correctly time the balancer shaft and the crankshaft during installation, position the piston at top dead center and insert the counterbalance shaft into its boss in the crankcase with arrow on counterbalance gear pointing toward crankshaft. Slide the drive gear onto the crankshaft, making certain the drive gear is secured in its keyway and that the arrow on the drive gear is aligned with the arrow on counterbalance shaft gear (Fig. T719).

TECUMSEH

TECUMSEH PRODUCTS COMPANY
Grafton, Wisconsin 53204

Model	No. Cyls.	Bore	Stroke	Displacement	Power Rating
HH140	1	3.312 in. (84.12 mm)	2.750 in. (69.85 mm)	23.7 cu. in. (388 cc)	14 hp (10.4 kW)
HH150	1	3.500 in. (88.9 mm)	2.875 in. (73.02 mm)	27.66 cu. in. (453 cc)	15 hp (11.2 kW)
HH160	1	3.500 in. (88.9 mm)	2.875 in. (73.02 mm)	27.66 cu. in. (453 cc)	16 hp (11.9 kW)
OH120	1	3.125 in. (79.38 mm)	2.750 in. (69.85 mm)	21.1 cu. in. (346 cc)	12 hp (8.9 kW)
OH140	1	3.312 in. (84.12 mm)	2.750 in. (69.85 mm)	23.7 cu. in. (388 cc)	14 hp (10.4 kW)
OH150	1	3.500 in. (88.9 mm)	2.875 in. (73.02 mm)	27.66 cu. in. (453 cc)	15 hp (11.2 kW)
OH160	1	3.500 in. (88.9 mm)	2.875 in. (73.02 mm)	27.66 cu. in. (453 cc)	16 hp (11.9 kW)
OH180	1	3.625 in. (92.08 mm)	2.875 in. (73.02 mm)	30 cu. in. (492 cc)	18 hp (13.4 kW)

Engines in this section are single-cylinder, four-stroke, horizontal crankshaft models. The crankshaft is supported at both ends in tapered roller bearings. Intake and exhaust valves are located in cylinder head. Cylinder and crankcase are a single cast iron unit.

The connecting rod rides directly on crankpin journal. All models are splash lubricated by an oil dipper attached to the connecting rod cap.

All models are equipped with a solid-state ignition system and an alternator.

Refer to TECUMSEH ENGINE IDENTIFICATION INFORMATION section for engine identification. Model, serial and specification numbers may be required when ordering parts.

MAINTENANCE

LUBRICATION. All models are splash lubricated. The oil dipper is an integral part of connecting rod cap.

Manufacturer recommends oil with an API service classification of SJ.

Use SAE 30 oil for temperatures above 32° F (0° C) and SAE 5W-20 or 5W-30 oil for temperatures below 32° F (0° C).

Check oil level after every 5 hours of operation or before initial start up of engine. As equipped, maintain oil level at edge of filler hole or at "FULL" mark on dipstick.

Oil should be changed after 25 hours of normal operation, more frequently if operation is severe.

SPARK PLUG. Recommended spark plug of Model OH180 is a Champion N4C, RN4C or equivalent. Recommended spark plug for all other models is Champion L82C, RL82C or equivalent. Electrode gap should be 0.030 inch (0.76 mm) for all models.

BREATHER. A breather valve is located in the rocker cover to maintain vacuum in the engine. The rocker cover must be installed so the trough (see Fig. T801) is opposite the carburetor side of the engine. Breather is sealed and must be serviced as an assembly.

CARBURETOR. The engine may be equipped with a Walbro LMH or WHG float-type carburetor. Refer to appropriate following section for carburetor service information.

Walbro LMH. Some models are equipped with a carburetor with both an idle and a high-speed fuel mixture adjustment screw. However, some models are equipped with just an idle speed fuel mixture screw; the high-speed mixture is controlled by a fixed main jet.

Initial adjustment of idle mixture screw (9—Fig. T802) for all models is one turn open from a lightly seated position. Initial adjustment of high-speed mixture screw (27), if so equipped, is one turn open.

Make final adjustments with engine at normal operating temperature and running. Place engine under load and adjust high-speed mixture screw for leanest mixture that will allow satisfactory acceleration and steady governor operation. Adjust idle speed screw so engine idles at 1200 rpm, or equipment manufacturer's desired idle speed, and adjust idle mixture screw to obtain smoothest idle operation.

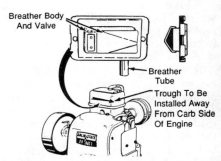

Fig. T801—Install rocker arm cover so trough is opposite the carburetor side of the engine.

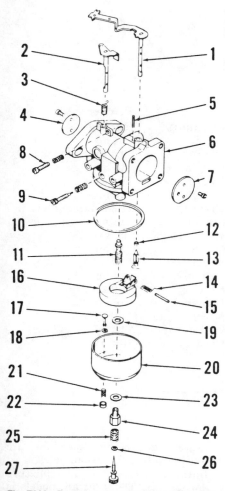

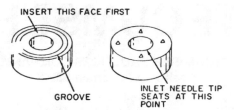

Fig. T803—Fuel inlet needle seat must be installed with grooved side against carburetor body. Refer to text.

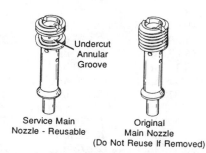

Fig. T804—Service replacement main nozzle is identified by undercut annular groove adjacent to threads. Do not reinstall original-type main nozzle.

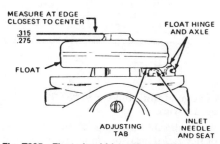

Fig. T805—Float should be measured as shown. Bend adjusting tab to adjust float setting.

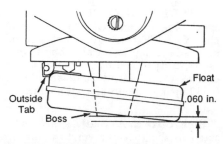

Fig. T806—Bend float tab so float drop is within 0.060 inch (1.52 mm) of nozzle boss as shown.

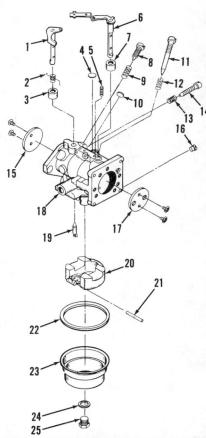

Fig. T807—Exploded view of Walbro WHG carburetor. Carburetor may be equipped with either high-speed mixture adjusting screw (11) or fixed main jet (16).

Fig. T802—Exploded view of Walbro LMH carburetor.

1. Choke shaft	15. Float shaft
2. Throttle shaft	16. Float
3. Throttle return spring	17. Drain stem
4. Throttle plate	18. Gasket
5. Choke stop spring	19. Gasket
6. Carburetor body	20. Bowl
7. Choke plate	21. Spring
8. Idle speed stop screw	22. Retainer
9. Idle mixture needle	23. Gasket
10. Bowl gasket	24. Bowl retainer
11. Main nozzle	25. Spring
12. Inlet valve seat	26. "O" ring
13. Inlet valve	27. Main fuel
14. Float spring	adjusting needle

1. Throttle shaft	13. Spring
2. Throttle return spring	14. Idle speed screw
3. Dust seal	15. Throttle plate
4. Welch plug	16. Main jet
5. Choke stop spring	17. Choke plate
6. Choke shaft	18. Carburetor body
7. Dust seal	19. Fuel inlet valve
8. Idle mixture screw	20. Float
9. Spring	21. Float pin
10. Welch plug	22. Bowl gasket
11. High-speed	23. Fuel bowl
mixture screw	24. Washer
12. Spring	25. Bowl retainer screw

As each adjustment affects the other, adjustment procedure may have to be repeated.

A Viton seat (12—Fig. T802) is used with fuel inlet valve (13). The renewable seat must be installed grooved side first in bore so inlet valve will seat at smooth side. See Fig. T803.

If main nozzle (11—Fig. T802) is removed and is original type (Fig. T804), obtain and install a new service nozzle. The service nozzle is identified by an undercut annular groove in the threaded area, as shown in Fig. T804.

Install choke and throttle plates so numbers are out when plate is in closed position and numbers are toward idle mixture screw for choke plate and on fuel inlet side for throttle plate.

To check float setting, hold carburetor and float assembly in inverted position. A distance of 0.275-0.315 inch (7.0-8.0 mm) should exist between float and center boss measured as shown in Fig. T805. Carefully bend adjusting tab on float to adjust float setting. With carburetor upright, outer end of float should be even with nozzle boss, within 0.060 inch (1.52 mm), as shown by float drop in Fig. T806.

Walbro WHG. Some models are equipped with a carburetor with both an idle and a high-speed fuel mixture adjustment screw. However, some models are equipped with just an idle speed fuel mixture screw; the high-speed mixture is controlled by a fixed main jet.

Initial adjustment of idle mixture screw (8—Fig. T807) for all models is one turn open from a lightly seated position. Initial adjustment of high-speed mixture screw (11), if so equipped, is 1-1/4 turns open.

Make final adjustments with engine at normal operating temperature and running. Place engine under load and adjust high-speed mixture screw for leanest mixture that will allow satisfactory acceleration and steady governor operation. Adjust idle speed screw so

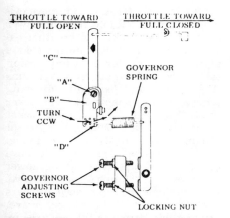

Fig. T808—Typical external governor linkage. Refer to text for adjustment procedure.

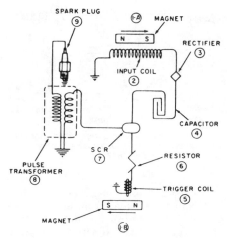

Fig. T810—Operational diagram of solid-state ignition system used on some models.

Start retaining screws, turn mounting plate counterclockwise as far as possible, then tighten retaining screws to 60-84 in.-lbs. (7-10 N·m).

Solid-State Ignition System (With Alternator). Tecumseh solid-state ignition system used on some models equipped with a flywheel alternator does not use breaker points. The only moving part of system is rotating flywheel with charging magnets and trigger pins. Other components of system are ignition charging (alternator) coil and stator assembly, spark plug and ignition unit.

The long trigger pin induces a small charge of current to close SCR (silicon controlled rectifier) switch at engine cranking speed and produces a spark at top dead center for starting. As engine rpm increases, first (shorter) trigger pin induces current that produces a spark when piston is 0.095 inch (2.41 mm) BTDC.

Test solid-state ignition system by holding high-tension lead ⅛ inch (3.2 mm) from spark plug (Fig. T811). Crank engine and check for a good blue spark. If no spark is present, check high-tension lead and coil lead for loose connections or faulty insulation. Check air gap between trigger pin and ignition unit as

engine idles at 1200 rpm, or equipment manufacturer's desired idle speed, and adjust idle mixture screw to obtain smoothest idle operation.

As each adjustment affects the other, adjustment procedure may have to be repeated.

GOVERNOR. A mechanical flyweight-type governor is used on all models.

To adjust external governor linkage, refer to Fig. T808. Loosen screw (A), turn plate (B) counterclockwise as far as possible and move governor lever (C) to left until throttle is in wide-open position. Tighten screw (A). Governor spring must be hooked in hole (D) as shown. Adjusting screws on bracket are used to adjust fixed or variable speed settings. Engine high-idle speed should not exceed 3600 rpm.

IGNITION SYSTEM. All engines are equipped with a solid-state ignition system. Some models are also equipped with an alternator charging system. Refer to the appropriate service information for type of ignition being serviced.

Solid-State Ignition (Without Alternator). The Tecumseh solid-state ignition system shown in Fig. T809 may be used on some models not equipped with a flywheel alternator. This system does not use ignition breaker points. The only moving part of the system is the rotating flywheel with charging magnets. As flywheel magnet passes position (1A—Fig. T810), a low voltage alternating current is induced into input coil (2). Current passes through rectifier (3) converting this current to direct current. It then travels to capacitor (4) where it is stored. Flywheel rotates approximately 180° to position (1B). As it passes trigger coil (5), it induces a very small electric charge into coil. This charge passes through resistor (6) and turns on SCR (silicon controlled rectifier) switch (7). With SCR switch closed, low voltage current stored in capacitor (4) travels to pulse transformer (8). Voltage is stepped up instantaneously and current is discharged across electrodes of spark plug (9), producing a spark before top dead center.

Some units are equipped with a second trigger coil and resistor set to turn SCR switch on at a lower rpm. This second trigger pin is closer to the flywheel and produces a spark at top dead center for easier starting. As engine rpm increases, first (shorter) trigger pin picks up small electric charge and turns SCR switch on, firing spark plug before top dead center.

If system fails to produce a spark at spark plug, first check high-tension lead (Fig. T809). If condition of high-tension lead is questionable or if insulation is faulty, renew pulse transformer and high-tension lead. Magneto charging coil, electronic triggering system and mounting plate are available only as an assembly. If necessary to renew this assembly, place unit in position on engine.

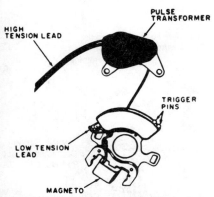

Fig. T809—View of solid-state ignition system used on models not equipped with flywheel alternator.

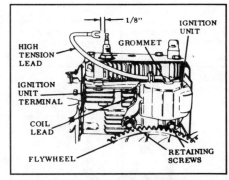

Fig. T811—View of solid-state ignition unit used on models equipped with flywheel alternator. System should produce a good blue spark ⅛ inch (3.2 mm) long at cranking speed.

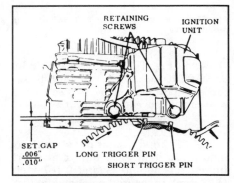

Fig. T812—Adjust air gap between long trigger pin and ignition unit to 0.006-0.010 inch (0.15-0.25 mm).

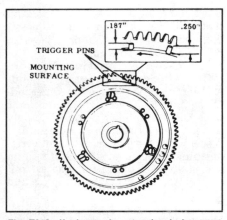

Fig. T813—If trigger pin extension is incorrect, remove flywheel and drive pins in or out, as necessary, until long pin is extended 0.250 inch (6.35 mm) and short pin is extended 0.187 inch (4.75 mm) above mounting surface.

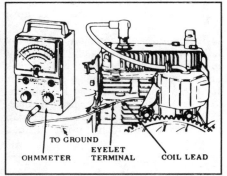

Fig. T814—View showing ohmmeter connected for resistance test of ignition generator coil.

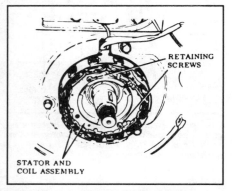

Fig. T815—Ignition generator coil and stator is serviced only as an assembly.

shown in Fig. T812. Air gap should be 0.006-0.010 inch (0.15-0.25 mm). To adjust air gap, loosen the two retaining screws and move ignition unit as necessary, then tighten retaining screws.

NOTE: Long trigger pin should extend 0.250 inch (6.35 mm) and short trigger pin should extend 0.187 inch (4.76 mm), measured as shown in Fig. T813. If not, remove flywheel and drive pins in or out as required.

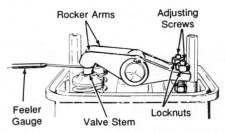

Fig. T816—Use a feeler gauge when adjusting valve tappet gap. Refer to text for adjustment procedure. See also Fig. T817.

To test ignition charging (alternator) coil, remove coil lead from ignition terminal and connect an ohmmeter as shown in Fig. T814. If series resistance is below 400 ohms, renew stator and coil assembly (Fig. T815). If resistance is above 400 ohms, renew ignition unit.

VALVE ADJUSTMENT. Clearance between rocker arms and valve stem ends should be checked and adjusted with engine cold. Specified clearance is 0.005 inch (0.13 mm) for intake valve and 0.010 inch (0.25 mm) for exhaust valve.

To adjust valves, remove rocker arm cover and rotate crankshaft to position piston at top dead center (TDC) of compression stroke. Both valves should be closed and the push rods loose at this point. Use a feeler gauge to measure clearance between rocker arm and valve stem. Loosen locknut and turn rocker arm adjusting screw shown in Fig. T816 to obtain specified clearance.

REPAIRS

TIGHTENING TORQUES. Recommended tightening torque specifications are as follows:

Bearing retainer	60-108 in.-lbs. (7-12 N•m)
Carburetor to inlet pipe	48-60 in.-lbs. (5-7 N•m)
Connecting rod	84-108 in.-lbs. (10-12 N•m)
Crankcase cover	60-108 in.-lbs. (7-12 N•m)
Cylinder head	15-20 ft.-lbs. (20-27 N•m)
Flywheel nut	50-55 ft.-lbs. (68-75 N•m)
Inlet pipe to head	60-96 in.-lbs. (7-11 N•m)
Rocker arm shaft screw	15-18 ft.-lbs. (20-24 N•m)
Rocker housing to head	84-96 in.-lbs. (10-11 N•m)
Spark plug	18-23 ft.-lbs. (24-31 N•m)
Stator	60-84 in.-lbs. (7-10 N•m)

CYLINDER HEAD. To remove cylinder head, unbolt and remove blower housing, valve cover and breather assembly. Turn crankshaft until piston is at top dead center on compression stroke, loosen locknuts on rocker arms (Fig. T816) and back off adjusting screws. Remove snap rings from rocker shaft (Fig. T817) and remove rocker arms. Using valve spring compressor (Tecumseh tool 670237) as shown in Fig. T818, remove valve retainers. Remove upper spring cap, valve spring, lower spring cap and "O" ring from each valve. Remove the three cap screws, washers and "O" rings from inside rocker arm housing and carefully lift off housing. Push rods and push rod tubes can now be withdrawn. Unbolt and remove carburetor and inlet pipe assembly from cylinder head. Remove cylinder head cap screws and lift off cylinder head, taking care not to drop intake and exhaust valves.

Always use a new head gasket when reinstalling cylinder head and make certain Belleville washers and flat washers are properly installed (Fig. T819). Note location of the two short cap

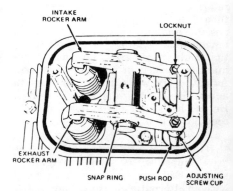

Fig. T817—View showing rocker arms used on all models. Slotted adjusting screws were used on early production engines. Later engines have adjusting nut on screw below rocker arm.

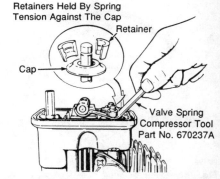

Fig. T818—Use Tecumseh tool 670237 to compress valve springs while removing retainers.

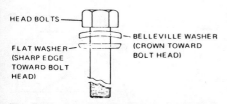

Fig. T819—Install Belleville washer and flat washer on cylinder head cap screws as shown.

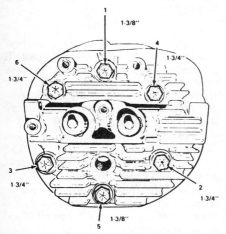

Fig. T820—Tighten cylinder head cap screws evenly to 15-20 ft.-lbs. (20-27 N•m) using tightening sequence shown. Note location of different length cap screws.

screws (Fig. T820) for correct installation. Tighten cylinder head cap screws in three steps to 15-20 ft.-lbs. (20-27 N•m) torque following sequence shown in Fig. T820. Place new "O" rings on push rod tubes and install push rods and tubes. Install rocker arm housing using new "O" rings on the three mounting cap screws, then tighten cap screws to 84-96 in.-lbs. (10-11 N•m). Install new "O" ring, lower spring cap, valve spring and upper spring cap on each valve. Use a valve spring compressor (Tecumseh tool 670237) to compress valve springs and install retainers. Install rocker arms and secure them with snap rings. Adjust valve gap as outlined in VALVE ADJUSTMENT section. Install remainder of components. Run engine for 30 minutes, then stop and allow to cool until cylinder head is cool to the touch. Retorque the cylinder head screws (except number "1" screw) in the same sequence shown in Fig. T820 to specified torque.

VALVE SYSTEM. Seats are machined directly into cylinder head surface. Seats should be ground at a 46° angle and seat width should be 0.042-0.052 inch (1.07-1.32 mm).

Valves should be ground at a 45° angle. Valve should be renewed if margin is 0.060 inch (1.52 mm) or less.

Valves are available with 0.030 inch (0.79 mm) oversize stems for installation in guides that are badly worn. Guides must be reamed to proper dimension.

Standard valve guide inside diameter should be 0.312-0.313 inch (7.92-7.95 mm) for all models. Guides may be reamed to 0.343-0.344 inch (8.71-8.74 mm) for use with 0.030 inch (0.79 mm) oversize valve stems.

To renew valve guides, remove and submerge head in a large pan of oil. Heat on a hot plate until oil begins to smoke, about 15-20 minutes. Remove head from pan and place head on an arbor press with valve seats facing up. Use a drift punch ½ inch (12.7 mm) in diameter to press guides out.

CAUTION: Be sure to center punch. DO NOT allow punch to contact head when pressing guides out.

To install new guides, place guides in freezer or on ice for 30 minutes prior to installation. Submerge head in pan of oil. Heat on hot plate until oil begins to smoke, about 15-20 minutes. Remove head and place gasket surface down on a 6 × 12 inch (15 × 30 cm) piece of wood. Using snap rings to locate both guides, insert silver color guide in intake side and brass colored guide in exhaust side. It may be necessary to use a rubber or rawhide mallet to fully seat snap rings. DO NOT use a metal hammer or guide damage may result. Allow head to cool and reface both valve seats.

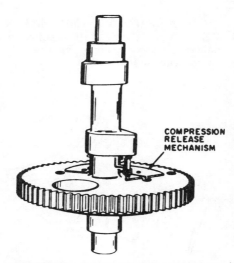

Fig. T821—View of Insta-Matic Ezee-Start compression release camshaft assembly used on all models.

CAMSHAFT. The camshaft and camshaft gear are an integral part that rides on journals at each end of camshaft.

The engine is equipped with a camshaft that has a compression release mechanism (Fig. T821). Compression release mechanism parts should work freely with no binding or sticking. Parts are not serviced separately from camshaft assembly.

Renew camshaft if gear teeth are excessively worn or bearing surfaces or lobes are worn or scored. Camshaft lobe nose-to-heel diameter should be 1.3117-1.3167 inches (33.317-33.444 mm) for all models.

Camshaft journal diameter should be 0.6235-0.6240 inch (15.837-15.850 mm). Maximum allowable journal to bearing running clearance is 0.003 inch (0.08 mm).

When installing camshaft, align timing mark on camshaft gear with timing mark (chamfered tooth) on crankshaft gear.

PISTON, PIN AND RINGS. The engine is fitted with an aluminum piston that has two compression rings and an oil control ring. Piston and connecting rod are removed as an assembly from cylinder head end of engine after removing rocker arm housing, cylinder head, crankcase cover and connecting rod cap.

Measure piston skirt diameter at bottom edge of skirt at a right angle to piston pin for all models.

	Piston Diameter
OH120	3.1210-3.1230 in. (79.273-79.324 mm)
HH140, OH140	3.3080-3.3100 in. (84.023-84.074 mm)
HH150, HH160, OH150, OH160	3.4950-3.4970 in. (88.773-88.824 mm)
OH180	3.6200-3.6220 in. (91.948-91.999 mm)

Measure piston skirt-to-cylinder wall clearance at bottom edge of skirt at a right angle to piston pin for all models. Specified piston clearance is 0.002-0.005 inch (0.05-0.13 mm) for Models HH140, OH120 and OH140, and 0.003-0.006 inch (0.08-0.15 mm) for all other models.

On Models HH150, HH160, OH150 and OH160, compression ring groove width in piston should be 0.095-0.096 inch (2.41-2.44 mm) and oil ring groove width should be 0.188-0.189 inch (4.78-4.80 mm).

On Models HH140, OH120 and OH140, compression ring groove width in piston should be 0.095-0.096 inch (2.41-2.44 mm) and oil ring groove

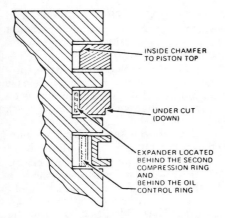

Fig. T822—Cross-sectional view showing correct installation of piston rings.

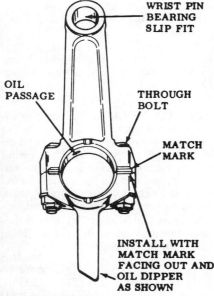

Fig. T823—Connecting rod assembly used on all models. Note oil dipper on rod cap.

width should be 0.188-0.190 inch (4.78-4.83 mm).

On Model OH180, compression ring groove width in piston should be 0.0955-0.0965 inch (2.426-2.451 mm) and oil ring groove width should be 0.1880-0.1895 inch (4.775-4.813 mm).

Side clearance of new compression piston rings in piston groove should be 0.0015-0.0035 inch (0.038-0.089 mm) for all models. Renew piston if side clearance is excessive.

Standard piston pin diameter is 0.7810-0.7812 inch (19.837-19.842 mm) for Model OH180 and 0.6876-0.6880 inch (17.465-17.475 mm) for all other models.

Piston and rings are available in standard size and oversizes.

Note location and arrangement of piston rings in Fig. T822. Piston ring

end gaps should be positioned at 90° intervals around piston.

If piston crown has an arrow, install piston on connecting rod so arrow on piston crown will point toward carburetor side of engine after installation.

Connecting rods on all models should be installed with match marks aligned and facing pto end of crankshaft (Fig. T823). Tighten connecting rod nuts to 84-108 in.-lbs. (10-12 N·m).

CONNECTING ROD. Piston and connecting rod are removed as an assembly as outlined in previous section. Connecting rod rides directly on crankpin journal of crankshaft.

Standard crankpin journal diameter is 1.3750-1.3755 inches (34.925-34.938 mm) for all models. Maximum allowable connecting rod big end diameter is 1.3765 inches (34.963 mm).

Connecting rod is available in standard size as well as undersizes.

If installing a new connecting rod, wipe off any oxidation on rod before installation.

Install connecting rod and piston as outlined in previous section.

GOVERNOR. Governor weight and gear assembly is driven by camshaft gear (Fig. T824) and rides on a renewable shaft that is pressed into engine crankcase.

If renewal of governor shaft is necessary, cut threads in shaft with a ¼-28 die so a suitable puller can be attached. Press new governor shaft in until shaft end is located as shown in Fig. T825.

If spool has an oil hole in its closed end, be sure hole is open before installation.

Adjust external linkage as outlined in MAINTENANCE section.

CRANKSHAFT AND MAIN BEARINGS. Crankshaft main journals ride in taper roller bearings at each end of crankshaft.

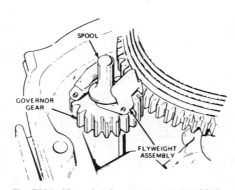

Fig. T824—View showing governor assembly installed in crankcase. Governor gear is driven by camshaft gear.

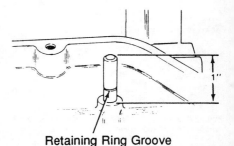

Retaining Ring Groove

Fig. T825—Press new governor shaft in cylinder block until shaft end is 1.00 inch (25.4 mm) above boss as shown.

Check crankshaft gear for wear, broken teeth or loose fit on crankshaft. If crankshaft gear is damaged, remove gear from crankshaft with an arbor press. Renew gear pin and press new gear on shaft making certain timing mark is facing pto end of shaft.

Crankshaft main bearing preload should be 0.001-0.007 inch (0.025-0.18 mm) and is controlled by varying thickness of shim gasket (17—Fig. T826).

Taper roller bearings are a press fit on crankshaft and must be renewed if removed. Heat bearings in hot oil to aid in installation.

Standard crankshaft connecting rod journal diameter is 1.3750-1.3755 inches (34.925-34.938 mm). The crankshaft should be renewed or reground if crankpin journal is tapered or worn more than 0.002 inch (0.05 mm) or is out-of-round more than 0.005 inch (0.13 mm).

Connecting rod is available in standard size as well as undersizes.

When installing crankshaft, align timing mark on camshaft gear with timing mark (chamfered tooth) on crankshaft gear.

Crankshaft oil seals should be installed flush to 0.025 inch (0.64 mm) below surface, with lips on seals facing inward.

CYLINDER. If cylinder is scored or excessively worn, or if taper or out-of-round exceeds 0.004 inch (0.10 mm), cylinder should be bored to next oversize for which piston and rings are available. Refer to following list of standard bore diameters:

	Std. Bore Diameter
OH120	3.125-3.126 in. (79.38-79.40 mm)
HH140, OH140	3.312-3.313 in. (84.12-84.15 mm)
HH150, HH160, OH150, OH160	3.500-3.501 in. (88.90-88.92 mm)
OH180	3.625-3.626 in. (92.08-92.10 mm)

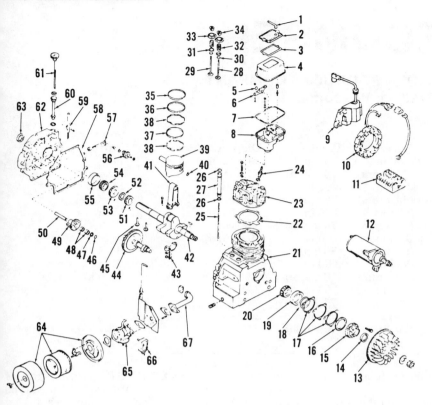

Fig. T826—Exploded view of basic engine typical of all models.

1. Breather tube	36. Second compression
2. Breather	ring
3. Gasket	37. Oil control ring
4. Valve cover	38. Ring expander
5. Snap ring	39. Piston & pin assy.
6. Rocker arm (2 used)	40. Retaining ring
7. Seal ring	41. Connecting rod
8. Rocker arm housing	42. Crankshaft
9. Ignition unit	43. Rod cap
10. Stator assy.	44. Camshaft assy.
11. Regulator-rectifier	45. Valve lifters
12. Starter motor	46. Snap ring
13. Flywheel	47. Thrust washer
14. Oil seal	48. Needle bearing
15. Bearing retainer cap	49. Dyna-Static balancer
16. Steel washer	50. Balancer shaft
17. Shim gaskets	51. Crankshaft gear
18. "O" ring	52. Spacer
19. Bearing cup	53. Balancer drive gear
20. Bearing cone	54. Bearing cone
21. Cylinder block	55. Bearing cup
22. Cylinder head	56. Governor assy.
23. Cylinder head	57. Governor arm
24. Spark plug	58. Gasket
25. Push rod	59. Oil filler
26. "O" ring	tube extension
27. Push rod tube	60. Oil filler tube
28. Intake valve	61. Dipstick
29. Exhaust valve	62. Crankcase cover
30. "O" ring	63. Oil seal
31. Lower spring cap	64. Air cleaner assy.
32. Valve spring	65. Carburetor
33. Upper valve cap	66. Fuel pump
34. Valve retainers	67. Inlet pipe
35. Top compression ring	

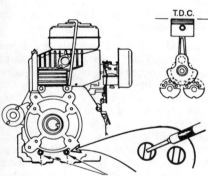

Fig. T827—View showing location of pipe plugs covering timing alignment holes on models with side-by-side Dyna-Static balancer gears. Note location of notches in balancer gears when properly installed.

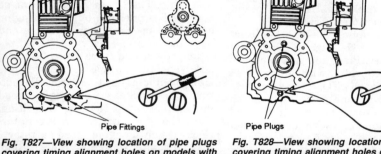

Fig. T828—View showing location of pipe plugs covering timing alignment holes on models with above and below crankshaft gear balance gears. Note location of notches in balancer gears when properly installed.

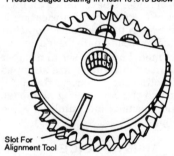

Fig. T829—Using Tecumseh tool 670210, press new needle bearing into balancer gears until bearing cage is flush to 0.015 inch (0.38 mm) below edge of bore. Note alignment notch at lower side of balancer.

DYNA-STATIC BALANCER. The Dyna-Static engine balancer consists of counterweighted gears mounted side-by-side (Fig. T827) or above and below crankshaft gear (Fig. T828) and driven by the crankshaft gear to counteract unbalance caused by the counter-weights on the crankshaft. Snap rings are used to retain balancer gears on shafts.

Renewable balancer gear shafts are pressed into crankcase cover. Press shafts into cover so height between boss on crankcase cover and outer edge of snap ring groove on shafts is 1.7135-1.7185 inches (43.523-43.650 mm).

Balancer gears are equipped with re-newable caged needle bearings (Fig. T829). Using Tecumseh tool 670210, press new bearings into gears until cage is flush to 0.015 inch (0.38 mm) below edge of bore.

When reassembling engine, balancer gears must be timed with crankshaft for correct operation. Refer to Figs. T827 and T828 and remove pipe plugs. Rotate crankshaft so piston is at top dead center on compression stroke and install cover and gear assembly so slots in weights are visible through pipe plug openings. See Figs. T827 and T828.

TECUMSEH

TECUMSEH PRODUCTS COMPANY
Grafton, Wisconsin 53204

Model	No. Cyls.	Bore	Stroke	Displacement	Power Rating
OHV14	1	3.56 in. (90.4 mm)	3.00 in. (76.2 mm)	29.9 cu. in. (490 cc)	14 hp (10.4 kW)
OHV145	1	3.56 in. (90.4 mm)	3.00 in. (76.2 mm)	29.9 cu. in. (490 cc)	14.5 hp (10.8 kW)
OHV15	1	3.56 in. (90.4 mm)	3.00 in. (76.2 mm)	29.9 cu. in. (490 cc)	15 hp (11.2 kW)
OHV155	1	3.56 in. (90.4 mm)	3.00 in. (76.2 mm)	29.9 cu. in. (490 cc)	15.5 hp (11.6 kW)
OHV16	1	3.56 in. (90.4 mm)	3.00 in. (76.2 mm)	29.9 cu. in. (490 cc)	16 hp (11.9 kW)
OHV165	1	3.56 in. (90.4 mm)	3.00 in. (76.2 mm)	29.9 cu. in. (490 cc)	16.5 hp (12.3 kW)
OHV17	1	3.56 in. (90.4 mm)	3.00 in. (76.2 mm)	29.9 cu. in. (490 cc)	17 hp (12.7 kW)

All models are four-stroke, overhead valve, single-cylinder gasoline engines equipped with a vertical crankshaft. The aluminum alloy cylinder and crankcase assembly is equipped with a cast iron cylinder sleeve that is an integral part of the cylinder. Lubrication is provided by a rotor-type oil pump that is operated by a camshaft-driven shaft.

Engine model number, serial number and specification number are stamped into the cooling shroud or on a decal. Always furnish the correct engine model, serial and specification numbers when ordering parts.

MAINTENANCE

LUBRICATION. The engine is equipped with a rotor-type oil pump that is located in the bottom of the oil pan. A driveshaft driven by the camshaft turns the rotor in the oil pump to force oil up the center of the camshaft. The pressurized oil lubricates the top main bearing and top camshaft bearing. Oil is sprayed out of a hole between the camshaft and main bearings to lubricate the connecting rod and other internal parts.

Oil level should be checked before initial start-up and at five-hour intervals. Maintain oil level at "FULL" mark on dipstick.

Recommended oil change interval is every 50 hours of normal operation. Oil should be drained when engine is warm. Manufacturer recommends using oil with API service classification SJ. Use SAE 30 oil for temperatures above 32° F (0° C) and SAE 5W-20 or 10W-30 for temperatures below 32° F (0° C).

Renew oil filter after every 100 hours of operation or more frequently if engine is operated in adverse conditions.

CRANKCASE BREATHER. The engine is equipped with a reed-valve type crankcase breather located in the side of the crankcase. Unscrew retaining screws to remove breather.

When assembling the breather, position reed valve (1—Fig. T901) against the crankcase. Place the stop plate (2) over the reed valve with notch, if so equipped, toward PTO. If the stop plate has a mark on one side, position the stop plate so mark is out. Secure reed valve and stop plate with a screw, then install the breather baffle and cover.

SPARK PLUG. Recommended spark plug is a Champion RN4C or equivalent. Recommended electrode gap is 0.030 in. (0.76 mm). Tighten spark plug to 21 ft.-lb. (28 N•m).

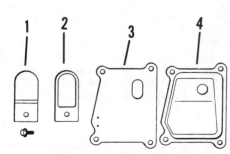

Fig. T901—Exploded view of crankcase breather.

1. Reed plate
2. Stop plate
3. Baffle
4. Cover

CARBURETOR. The engine is equipped with a Walbro LMK float type carburetor. The carburetor has a fixed main jet. Carburetors on early engines may be equipped with an adjustable idle mixture screw, while later engines have a fixed idle mixture jet.

Initial setting of idle mixture screw (12—Fig. T902), on carburetors so equipped, is one turn out. With engine at normal operating temperature and equipment control lever in "SLOW" position, adjust idle speed screw (9) to desired engine idle speed. With engine running at idle speed, turn the idle mixture screw clockwise until engine speed just starts to drop. Note screw position. Turn the idle mixture screw counterclockwise until engine speed just starts to drop again. Note the screw position, then turn screw to midpoint between the noted screw positions. If engine will not accelerate cleanly, slightly enrich the mixture by turning the idle mixture screw counterclockwise. If necessary, readjust the idle speed screw.

To disassemble the carburetor, remove the fuel bowl (18—Fig. T902), pivot pin (14) and float (16), fuel inlet valve (15) and idle mixture screw (12). Choke shaft (1) and throttle shaft (5) can be removed after removing screws from choke plate (4) and throttle plate (13).

Clean the carburetor using a commercial carburetor cleaning solvent and compressed air. Inspect components and discard any parts that are damaged or excessively worn. The fuel inlet valve (15) is available for service, but the carburetor body must be renewed if the valve seat is damaged.

The main jet is located in the side of the center fuel leg. Do not remove the main jet unless it is damaged or installation of a high altitude jet is required. To remove main jet, carefully drive jet into fuel leg; do not damage surrounding metal. Using a punch slightly larger than new jet, force jet into hole in leg so it is flush with leg surface.

When assembling carburetor, note the following: Do not deform the Welch plug (10) during installation; it should be flat. Seal outer edges of plug with nonhardening sealer. Install throttle return spring (7) so square end is up. With throttle shaft installed, both ends of spring should be to the left of center boss as viewed from throttle end of carburetor. Install choke and throttle plates so numbers are on outer face when choke or throttle plate is in closed position. Float height is not adjustable. Refer to SPEED CONTROL section to synchronize speed control mechanism and adjust governed engine speeds.

SPEED CONTROL. Use the following procedure to synchronize remote speed control and engine speed control assembly, and also adjust high and low idle speeds. Before starting procedure, be sure linkage is in good condition, including bushings in levers.

Loosen throttle control cable clamp screw (Fig. T903). Move the equipment speed control lever to "Fast" position. Align the hole in throttle lever with hole in speed control bracket by inserting a drill bit or rod through the holes. Remove the slack in the control cable and tighten cable clamp. Be sure speed control will operate through full travel from full choke to wide-open throttle. At full throttle there should be a gap of 0.040-0.070 inch (1.02-1.78 mm) as shown in Fig. T903. Bend tab to adjust gap. Start the engine and allow to reach operating temperature. Adjust governed idle speed by turning idle speed screw shown in Fig. T903. Bend high-speed adjustment tab using Tecumseh tool 670326 to adjust high speed governed no-load speed.

GOVERNOR. All models are equipped with a mechanical flyweight type governor located inside the oil pan.

To adjust external governor linkage (Fig. T904), stop engine and loosen the screw (S) securing governor lever and governor clamp. Push governor lever (L) to fully open carburetor throttle. Turn governor clamp counterclockwise as far as it will go. While holding clamp and lever in this position, tighten screw.

Refer to SPEED CONTROL section to adjust governed engine speeds.

IGNITION SYSTEM. A solid-state ignition system is used on all models. Ignition system has no moving parts and is considered satisfactory if a spark will jump a $\frac{1}{8}$ inch (3.2 mm) air gap when engine is cranked at 125 rpm.

Ignition module is mounted outside of the flywheel. Air gap setting (G—Fig. T905) between ignition module and flywheel magnets is 0.0125 inch (0.32 mm). To set air gap, loosen module mounting screws, move module as necessary and retighten screws.

VALVE ADJUSTMENT. Engine must be cold for valve adjustment. Remove rocker arm cover. Position crankshaft at TDC on compression stroke. Be sure both valves are closed. If not, rotate flywheel one revolution clockwise. Valve clearance for both valves should be 0.004 inch (0.10 mm). Loosen setscrew at center of pivot nut and turn pivot nut to obtain desired clearance (Fig. T906). Tighten setscrew to 110 in.-lb. (12.4 N•m). Rotate crankshaft two turns so it is at TDC on compression stroke and recheck adjustment.

REPAIRS

TIGHTENING TORQUE. Recommended tightening torque values are as follows:

Connecting rod bolts	210 in.-lb. (24 N•m)
Oil pan	125 in.-lb. (14 N•m)
Cylinder head bolts	230 in.-lb. (26 N•m)
Flywheel nut	58 ft.-lb. (79 N•m)
Intake pipe	95 in.-lb. (10.7 N•m)
Rocker arm studs	190 in.-lb. (21.5 N•m)
Rocker cove	55 in.-lb. (6.2 N•m)
Spark plug	21 ft.-lb. (28 N•m)

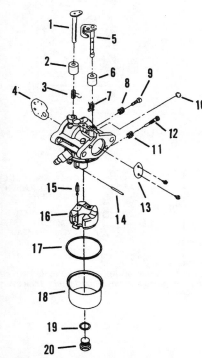

Fig. T902—Exploded view of Walbro LMK carburetor.

1. Choke shaft	11. Spring
2. Dust seal	12. Idle mixture screw
3. Spring	13. Throttle plate
4. Choke plate	14. Float pin
5. Throttle shaft	15. Fuel inlet valve
6. Dust seal	16. Float
7. Spring	17. Gasket
8. Spring	18. Fuel bowl
9. Idle speed screw	19. Washer
10. Welch plug	20. Screw

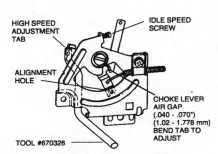

Fig. T903—Refer to text for speed control adjustment procedure.

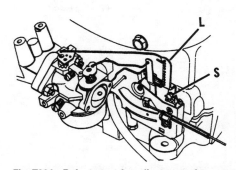

Fig. T904—Refer to text for adjustment of governor linkage.

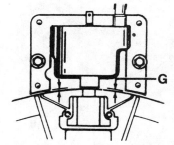

Fig. T905—Air gap (G) between coil legs and flywheel should be 0.0125 inch (0.32 mm).

CYLINDER HEAD. Always allow engine to cool completely before removing cylinder or loosening cylinder head bolts. To remove cylinder head, remove blower housing and air baffle, carburetor and intake pipe, and muffler. Turn flywheel to position the piston at top dead center of compression stroke. Remove rocker arm cover (1—Fig. T907). Loosen pivot nut setscrew (7) and unscrew pivot nuts (8). Remove the rocker arms (9). Mark pivot nuts and rocker arms so they can be installed in their original locations. Unscrew rocker arm studs (10) and remove push rod guide plate (11). Remove cylinder head retaining bolts and remove cylinder head.

Thoroughly clean cylinder head and inspect for cracks or other damage. Position cylinder head on a flat plate and use a feeler gauge to check flatness of head gasket sealing surface. Renew cylinder head if warpage exceeds 0.005 inch (0.13 mm).

Use a new head gasket when installing cylinder head. Install Belleville washer on cylinder head bolt with crown up toward bolt head, then install flat washer (Fig. T908). Tighten the head bolts following the sequence shown in Fig. T909. Tighten the bolts in 60 in.-lb. (6.7 N•m) increments to a final torque of 230 in.-lb. (26 N•m).

VALVE SYSTEM. Valve seats are machined directly in the cylinder head. Seats should be cut at a 46° angle and valve faces cut or ground at a 45° angle. Valve seat width should be ³⁄₆₄ inch (1.2 mm).

Clean all combustion deposits from valves. Renew valves that are burned, excessively pitted, warped or if valve head margin after grinding is less than ¹⁄₃₂ inch (0.8 mm). Valves should be lapped to their seats using fine lapping compound.

Valve spring free length should be 1.980 inches (50.29 mm). It is recommended that valve springs be renewed when engine is overhauled. The valve spring dampening coils are coils wound closer together at one end than the other (Fig. T910). Install spring so end with closer coils is against the cylinder head.

Valve guides can be reamed to 0.3432-0.3442 inch (8.717-8.743 mm) for use with oversize valve stems.

OIL PUMP. All engines are equipped with a rotor-type oil pump located in the oil pan (Fig. T911) and driven by the camshaft via a driveshaft. A relief valve is located in the side of the oil pan.

Remove engine from the equipment for access to oil pump cover. Remove cover and extract pump rotors. Mark rotors so they can be reinstalled in their original position. Renew any components that are damaged or excessively worn. Be sure "O" ring is installed before installing cover. Tighten oil pump cover screws to 6.2 N•m (55 in.-lb.).

BALANCER SHAFTS. The engine is equipped with two balancer shafts

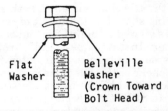

Fig. T908—Install Belleville washer on head bolt with crown toward bolt head. Install flat washer with sharp edge toward bolt head.

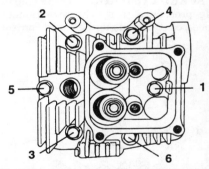

Fig. T909—Tighten cylinder head bolts in sequence shown.

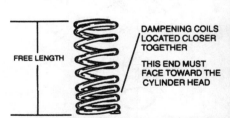

Fig. T910—Valve spring must be installed with dampening coil end positioned against the cylinder head.

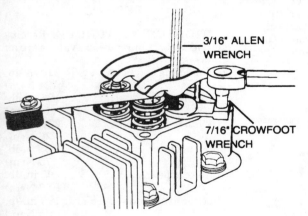

Fig. T906—Use a feeler gauge to correctly set valve clearance. Refer to text.

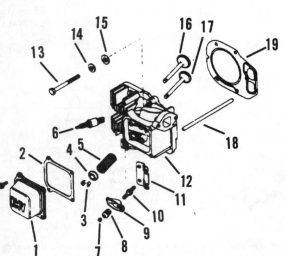

Fig. T907—Exploded view of cylinder head assembly.

1. Rocker arm cover
2. Gasket
3. Valve keepers
4. Valve spring retainer
5. Valve spring
6. Spark plug
7. Setscrew
8. Pivot nut
9. Rocker arm
10. Rocker arm stud
11. Push rod guide plate
12. Cylinder head
13. Head bolt
14. Belleville washer
15. Washer
16. Intake valve
17. Exhaust valve
18. Push rod

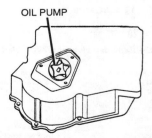

Fig. T911—Oil pump rotors are accessible after removing cover on bottom of oil pan.

(15 and 16—Fig. T912) that ride directly in the crankcase and oil pan bores. Drain oil and remove oil pan for access to the balancer shafts.

A gear (14—Fig. T912) on the crankshaft drives the balancer shaft with the thicker gear, which in turn drives the balancer shaft with the thinner gear. Note the position and configuration of the gears in Fig. T913. Thin balancer gear has one timing mark and wide balancer gear has two timing marks. Install the balancer gears so timing marks are aligned as shown in Fig. T913.

CAMSHAFT. Camshaft and camshaft gear are an integral part which can be removed from the engine after removing the cylinder head, push rods, oil pan and balancer shafts. Identify the position of the tappets as they are removed so they can be reinstalled in original position if reused.

Camshaft bearings are an integral part of crankcase and oil pan or crankcase cover. Camshaft journal diameter should be 0.6235-0.6240 inch (15.84-15.85 mm). Camshaft bearing inside diameter should be 0.6245-0.6255 inch (15.86-15.89 mm). Clearance between camshaft journal and camshaft bearing should not exceed 0.003 inch (0.08 mm). Inspect camshaft lobes for pitting, scratches or excessive wear and renew as necessary. Tappets should be renewed whenever a new camshaft is installed.

Camshaft is equipped with a compression release mechanism (Fig. T914) to aid starting. Compression release mechanism parts should work freely with no binding or sticking. Parts are not serviced separately from camshaft.

When installing camshaft, be sure that timing marks on camshaft gear and crankshaft gear are aligned as shown in Fig. T915.

PISTON, PIN AND RINGS. Piston and connecting rod are removed as an assembly. Remove cylinder head and

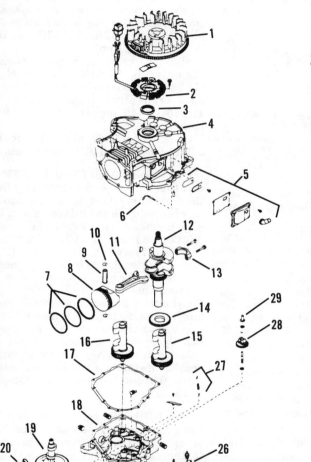

Fig. T912—Exploded view of engine internal components.

1. Flywheel
2. Alternator coil
3. Oil seal
4. Crankcase
5. Breather assy.
6. Governor lever
7. Piston rings
8. Piston
9. Piston pin
10. Retaining ring
11. Connecting rod
12. Crankshaft
13. Rod cap
14. Balancer drive gear
15. Balancer gear (wide gear)
16. Balancer gear (thin gear)
17. Gasket
18. Oil pan
19. Camshaft
20. Tappet
21. Oil seal
22. Pump shaft
23. Oil pump rotor
24. "O" ring
25. Cover
26. Oil filter adapter
27. Oil pressure relief valve
28. Governor
29. Spool

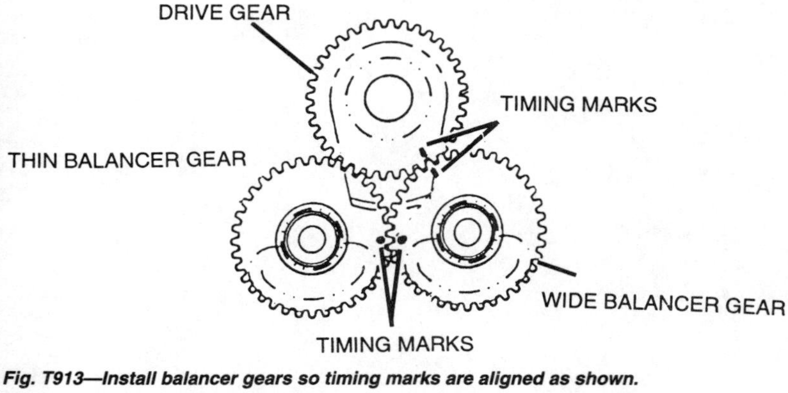

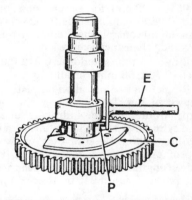

Fig. T914—Compression release pin (P) extends during starting to hold exhaust valve (E) off its seat.

DRIVE GEAR

TIMING MARKS

THIN BALANCER GEAR

WIDE BALANCER GEAR

TIMING MARKS

Fig. T913—Install balancer gears so timing marks are aligned as shown.

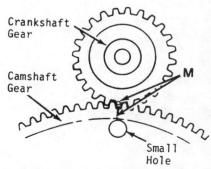

Crankshaft Gear

Camshaft Gear

M

Small Hole

Fig. T915—View of crankshaft and camshaft timing marks (M).

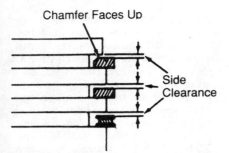

Fig. T916—Inside chamfer on top compression ring must face piston crown.

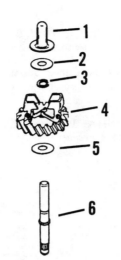

Fig. T917—Exploded view of governor flyweight assembly.

1. Thrust spool
2. Washer
3. Snap ring
4. Governor gear & weight assy.
5. Washer
6. Stud

camshaft as previously outlined. Remove connecting rod cap. Remove carbon or ring ridge (if present) from top of cylinder before removing piston. Push the connecting rod and piston out top of cylinder.

Standard piston skirt diameter, measured at bottom of skirt 90° from piston pin bore, is 3.562-3.563 inches (90.47-90.50 mm) for all models. Specified clearance between piston skirt and cylinder wall is 0.0015-0.0030 inch (0.038-0.076 mm). Oversize pistons are available. Oversize piston size should be stamped on top of piston.

To check piston ring grooves for wear, clean carbon from ring grooves and install new rings in grooves. Use a feeler gauge to measure side clearance between ring land and ring. Specified side clearance is 0.0020-0.0040 inch (0.051-0.102 mm) for compression rings and 0.0009-0.0029 inch (0.023-0.074 mm) for oil control ring. Renew piston if ring side clearance is excessive.

Ring end gap should be 0.012-0.022 inch (0.30-0.56 mm) for all rings.

Rings must be installed on piston as shown in Fig. T916. Stagger ring end gaps around piston. Lubricate piston and cylinder with engine oil prior to installing piston. Be sure that arrow on top of piston points toward push rod side of engine. Match marks on connecting rod and cap must be toward open side of crankcase after installation and must align when installing cap on rod.

CONNECTING ROD. Piston and connecting rod are removed as an assembly. Refer to previous section to remove piston and connecting rod.

Connecting rod rides directly on crankshaft crankpin. Inside diameter of connecting rod bearing bore at crankshaft end should be 1.6234-1.6240 inches (41.234-41.250 mm).

GOVERNOR. Governor weight and gear assembly is driven by camshaft gear and rides on a renewable shaft that is pressed into engine crankcase or crankcase cover.

Governor gear, flyweights and shaft (Fig. T917) are serviced only as an assembly. If governor gear shaft is renewed, press new shaft into oil pan boss so exposed shaft length is 1.350-1.365 inches (34.29-34.67 mm).

Adjust external linkage as outlined in MAINTENANCE section.

CRANKSHAFT, MAIN BEARINGS AND SEALS. To remove crankshaft, first remove all shrouds. Remove the flywheel. Remove connecting rod and piston as previously outlined, then remove crankshaft.

Main bearings are integral part of crankcase and oil pan or crankcase cover. Main bearing inside diameter should be 1.6265-1.6270 inches (41.313-41.326 mm).

Standard crankshaft main journal diameter is 1.6245-1.6250 inches (41.262-41.275 mm) for each end. Standard crankpin journal diameter is 1.3740-1.3745 inches (34.900-34.912 mm).

Crankshaft end play should be 0.0025-0.0335 inch (0.064-0.851 mm).

CYLINDER AND CRANKCASE. A cast iron liner is permanently cast into the aluminum alloy cylinder and crankcase assembly. Standard piston bore inside diameter is 3.562-3.563 inches (90.47-90.50 mm). If cylinder taper or out-of-round exceeds 0.004 inch (0.10 mm), cylinder should be bored to nearest oversize for which piston and rings are available.

Cylinder may be manufactured oversize at the factory. A cylinder bored oversize at the factory may be identified by oversize number stamped on cylinder head mating surface of cylinder. For instance, a cylinder manufactured 0.010-inch oversize is stamped ".010".

FUEL PUMP. The engine may be equipped with a diaphragm type fuel pump to transfer fuel from the fuel tank to the carburetor. A pulse line connected to the crankcase provides pressure pulses to operate the pump. A repair kit is available to rebuild the pump.

TECUMSEH
SERVICING TECUMSEH ACCESSORIES

12 VOLT STARTING AND CHARGING SYSTEMS

Some Tecumseh engines may be equipped with 12 volt electrical systems. Refer to the following paragraphs for servicing of Tecumseh electrical units and 12 volt Delco-Remy starter-generator used on some models.

12 VOLT STARTER MOTOR (BENDIX DRIVE TYPE).

Refer to Fig. TE101, TE102, TE103 or TE104 for an exploded view of 12-volt starter motor and Bendix drive unit used on some engines. To identify starter, refer to service number stamped on end cap.

To disassemble starter shown in Fig. TE101, remove nut (1) and separate drive assembly from armature shaft. Remove through-bolts (22) and separate end plates (14 and 20) and armature (16) from the frame (17).

When assembling starter motor shown in Fig. TE101, use spacers (15) of varying thickness to obtain an armature end play of 0.005-0.015 inch (0.13-0.38 mm). Note the following tightening torque specifications:

Armature nut (1):
Starters 29965,
  32468, 32468A,
  32468B, 33202 . . . . 100 in.-lbs.
                   (11.3 N•m)
Starter 32510 . . . . 130-150 in.-lbs.
               (14.7-16.9 N•m)
Starter 32817 . . . . 170-220 in.-lbs.
               (19.2-24.8 N•m)

Through-bolts (22):
Starters 29965,
  32468, 32468A,
  32468B, 33202 . . . . 30-35 in.-lbs.
                (3.4-3.9 N•m)
Starter 32510 . . . . 45-50 in.-lbs.
                (5.0-5.6 N•m)
Starter 32817 . . . . 35-44 in.-lbs.
                (3.9-5.0 N•m)

To perform no-load test for starter motors 29965, 32468 and 32468A, use a fully charged 6-volt battery. Maximum current draw should not exceed 25 amps at 6 volts. Minimum rpm is 6500.

No-load test for Models 32468B and 33202 requires a fully charged 12-volt battery. Maximum current draw should not exceed 25 amps at 11.8 volts. Minimum rpm is 8000.

No-load test for starter motors 32510 and 32817 must be performed with a 12-volt battery. Maximum current draw

should not exceed 25 amps at 11.5 volts. Minimum rpm is 8000.

To disassemble starter motors 33605, 33606 and 33835 shown in Fig. TE102. Remove end cap (1) and clip (2). Separate the drive components from the armature shaft. Remove nuts from through-bolts (14) and separate end plates (7 and 15) and armature (8) from the housing (9). Note that stops on through-bolts (14) are used to secure brush card (10) in housing (9).

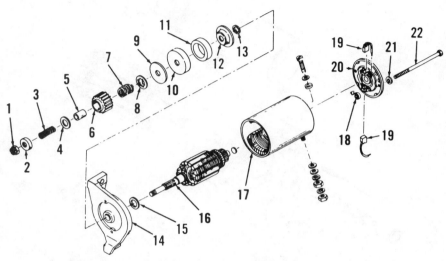

Fig. TE101—Exploded view of 12-volt electric starter used on early model engines.

1. Nut	7. Screw shaft	13. Thrust bushing
2. Pinion stop	8. Stop washer	14. Drive end cap
3. Spring	9. Thrust washer	15. Spacer washer
4. Washer	10. Cushion	16. Armature
5. Anti-drift sleeve	11. Rubber cushion	17. Frame & field
6. Pinion gear	12. Thrust washer	coil assy.

18. Brush spring	
19. Brush	
20. End cap	
21. Washer	
22. Bolt	

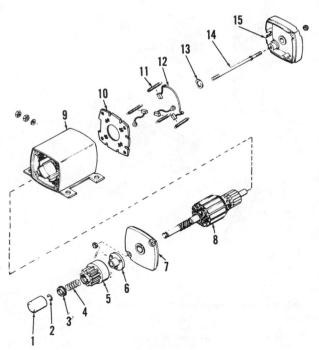

Fig. TE102—Exploded view of 12-volt starter motor used on some later models. Drive components in inset are used on opposite direction starters. Components on 110-volt starter are similar.

1. Dust cover
2. Clip
3. Spring retainer
4. Spring
5. Pinion
6. Retainer
7. Drive end cap
8. Armature
9. Housing
10. Brush card
11. Brush spring
12. Brush
13. Thrust washer
14. End cap

Through-bolts must be installed with stops toward end cover (15).

Maximum current draw with starter on engine should not exceed 55 amps at a minimum of 850 rpm for starters 33605 and 33606 or 70 amps at a minimum of 600 rpm for starter 33835. Cranking test should not exceed 10 seconds.

ALTERNATOR CHARGING SYSTEMS. The engine may be equipped with an alternator to provide battery charging direct current, or provide electricity for accessories, or both. The alternator coils may be located under the flywheel, or on some models with an external ignition module, the alternator coils are attached to the legs of the ignition coil. Rectification is accomplished either with a rectifier panel, regulator-rectifier unit, external or internal, or by an inline diode contained in the harness.

Inline Diode System. The inline diode system has a diode connected into the alternator wire leading from the engine. See Fig. TE105. The system produces approximately 3 amps direct current. The diode rectifies the alternating current produced by the alternator into direct current. A 6 amp fuse provides overload protection.

To check the system, disconnect the harness connector. Connect positive lead of a DC voltmeter to the red wire connector terminal, and ground the negative tester lead to engine. At 3600 rpm engine speed, voltmeter reading should be at least 11.5 volts. If engine speed is less, the voltmeter reading will be less.

If voltage reading is unsatisfactory, check the alternator coils by taking an AC voltage reading. Connect one tester lead between the diode and engine, and ground the other tester lead to the engine. At engine speed of 3600 rpm, voltage reading should be 26 volts, otherwise the alternator is defective. If the engine cannot attain 3600 rpm, voltage reading will be less.

Another type inline diode system provides 3 amps direct current and 5 amps alternating current. This system has a two-wire pigtail consisting of a red wire and a black or yellow wire; the diode is inline with the red wire. To test system, check voltage at pigtail connector. At engine speed of 3600 rpm (less engine speed will produce less voltage), voltage at the red wire terminal should be 11 volts DC on OHV models or 13 volts DC on all other models. Voltage at the black or yellow wire terminal should be 22 volts AC on OHV models or 13 volts AC on all other models.

If voltage reading is unsatisfactory, check alternator coils by taking an AC voltage reading. Connect one tester lead to the red wire between the diode and engine, and ground the other tester lead to the engine. At engine speed of 3600 rpm, voltage reading should be 24.5 volts on OHV models or 29 volts on all other models, otherwise alternator is defective. If the engine cannot attain 3600 rpm, voltage reading will be less.

Rectifier Panel Systems. The charging system shown in Fig. TE106 has a maximum charging output of about 3 amperes at 3600 rpm. No current regulator is used on this low output system. The rectifier panel includes two diodes (rectifiers) and a 6 ampere fuse for overload protection.

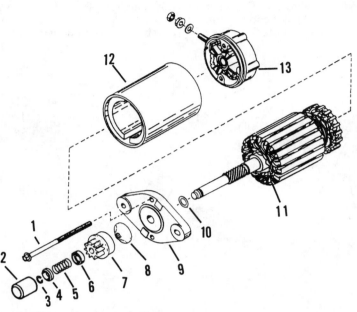

Fig. TE103—Exploded view of 12-volt starter motor used on some later models.

1. Through bolt
2. Dust cover
3. Clip
4. Spring retainer
5. Spring
6. Spring seat
7. Pinion
8. Retainer
9. Drive end cap
10. Washer
11. Armature
12. Housing
13. End cap

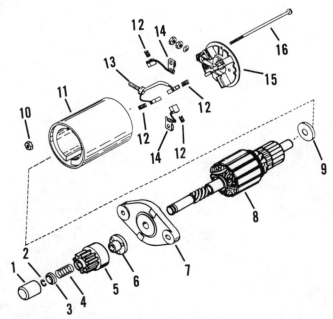

Fig. TE104—Exploded view of 12-volt starter motor used on some later models.

1. Dust cover
2. Clip
3. Spring retainer
4. Spring
5. Pinion
6. Retainer
7. Drive end cap
8. Armature
9. Washer
10. Nut
11. Housing
12. Brush spring
13. Brush
14. Brush
15. End cap
16. Through bolt

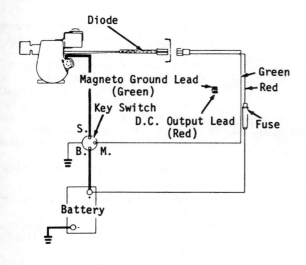

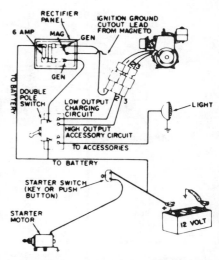

Fig. TE105—Wiring diagram of 3 amp direct current system with inline diode.

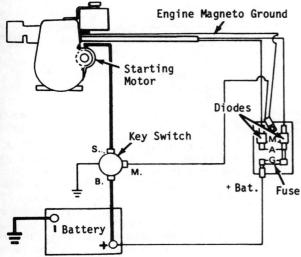

Fig. TE106—Wiring diagram of typical 3 amp alternator and rectifier panel charging system.

Fig. TE107—Wiring diagram of typical 7 amp alternator and rectifier panel charging system. The double pole switch in one position reduces output to 3 amps for charging or increases output to 7 amps in other position to operate accessories.

The system shown in Fig. TE107 has a maximum output of 7 amperes. To prevent overcharging the battery, a double pole switch is used in low output position to reduce the output to 3 amperes for charging the battery. Move the switch to high output position (7 amperes) when using accessories.

To test systems, remove rectifiers and test them with either a continuity light or an ohmmeter. Rectifiers should show current flow in one direction only. Alternator output can be checked using an induction ammeter over the positive lead wire to battery.

7, 10 and 20 Amp External Regulator-Rectifier System. The system shown in (Fig. TE108) may produce 7, 10 or 20 amperes and uses a solid state regulator-rectifier outside the flywheel that converts the generated alternating current to direct current for charging the battery. The regulator-rectifier also allows only the required amount of current flow for existing battery conditions. When the battery is fully charged, current output is decreased to prevent overcharging the battery.

To test 7 or 10 amp system, disconnect B+ lead and connect a DC voltmeter as shown in Fig. TE109. With engine running at 3000 rpm, voltage should be at least 14 volts on 7 amp system and 16 volts on 10 amp system. If reading is excessively high or low, regulator-rectifier unit may be defective. To check alternator coils, connect an AC voltmeter to the AC leads as shown in Fig. TE110. With engine running at 3000 rpm check AC voltage. Alternator is defective if voltage is less than 18 volts on 7 amp system or 19 volts on 10 amp system.

To test 20 amp system, disconnect B+ lead and connect a DC voltmeter as shown in Fig. TE109. With headlights on or another load on system so battery voltage is less than 12.5 volts, run engine from 2500 rpm to full throttle. If voltmeter indicates a voltage rise, system is good.

To check alternator coils, connect an AC voltmeter to the AC leads as shown in Fig. TE110. With engine running at 3000 rpm check AC voltage. Alternator is defective if voltage is less than 38

volts. With B+ wire connected in series with a DC ammeter as shown in Fig. TE111, alternator is defective if meter indicates less than 13 amps at 2500 rpm, 15 amps at 3000 rpm and 17 amps at 3600 rpm. Regulator-rectifier is defective if battery voltage exceeds 14.8 volts with battery fully charged.

16 Amp External Regulator System. It is not possible to perform an open-circuit DC test. To check alternator, disconnect red DC wire from regulator. See Fig. TE112. Connect AC voltmeter leads to terminals of regulator as shown in Fig. TE112. At engine speed of 3600 rpm (less engine speed will produce less voltage), voltage should be at least 31.5 volts AC. If voltage reading is less, the alternator is defective. If voltage reading is satisfactory and a known to be good battery is not charged by the system, then the regulator-rectifier unit is defective. Regulator is defective if battery voltage exceeds 15 volts with battery fully charged.

Internal Regulator-Rectifier System. The regulator-rectifier unit is epoxy covered or epoxied in an aluminum box and mounted under the blower housing. Units are not interchangeable. Three systems may be used that produce 5, 7 or 20 amps at full throttle.

It is not possible to perform an open-circuit dc test. To check the alternator, remove regulator-rectifier unit from blower housing, then reinstall blower housing. Do not run engine without the blower housing installed. Connect AC voltmeter leads to "AC" terminals of regulator-rectifier unit as shown in Fig. TE113. At engine speed of 3600 rpm (less engine speed will produce less voltage), voltage should be at

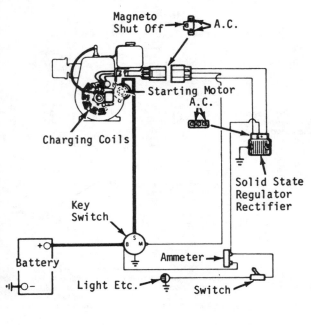

Fig. TE108—Wiring diagram of typical 7, 10 or 20 amp alternator and regulator- rectifier charging system.

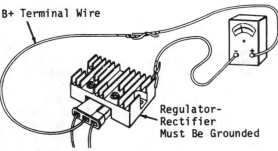

Fig. TE109—Connect DC voltmeter as shown when checking the regulator-rectifier.

least 28 volts AC for 5 amp system, 23 volts ac for 7 amp system and at least 45 volts for 20 amp system. If voltage reading is less, the alternator is defective. If voltage reading is satisfactory and a known to be good battery is not charged by the system, then the regulator-rectifier unit is defective. On 20 amp systems, regulator-rectifier is defective if battery voltage exceeds 14.8 volts with battery fully charged.

External Ignition Module Alternator. Engines with an external ignition may have an alternator coil attached to the ignition module. The alternator produces approximately 350 milliamperes for battery charging. To check alternator output, connect a dc voltmeter to battery (battery must be in normal circuit) as shown in Fig. TE114. Run engine. Voltage should be higher when engine is running, or alternator is defective.

MOTOR-GENERATOR. The combination motor-generator (Fig. TE115) functions as a cranking motor when the starting switch is closed. When the engine is operating and starting switch is open, the unit operates as a generator. Generator output and circuit voltage

for battery and various accessories are controlled by the current-voltage regulator.

To determine cause of abnormal operation, motor-generator should be given a no-load test or a generator output test. The generator output test can be performed with the motor-generator on or off the engine. The no-load test must be performed with the motor-generator off the engine.

Motor-generator test specifications are as follows:

Delco-Remy Motor-Generator 1101980

Brush spring tension . . . . 24-32 oz.
(680-900 g)

Field draw:
  Amperes 1.52-1.62
  Volts 12
Cold output:
  Amperes 12
  Volts 14
  Rpm 4950
No-load test:
  Amperes (max) 18
  Volts 11
  Rpm (min) 2500
  Rpm (max) 2900

CURRENT-VOLTAGE REGULATORS. Two types of current-voltage regulators are used with the motor-generator system. One is a low output unit that delivers a maximum of 7 amps. The high output unit delivers a maximum of 14 amps.

The low output (7 amp) unit is identified by its four connecting terminals (three on one side of unit and one on underside of regulator). The battery ignition coil has a 3 amp draw. This leaves a maximum load of 4 amps that may be used on accessory lead.

The high output (14 amp) unit has only three connecting terminals (all on side of unit). So with a 3 amp draw for battery ignition coil, a maximum of 11 amps can be used for accessories.

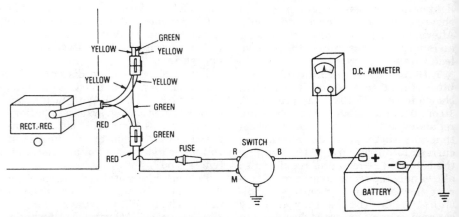

Fig. TE110—Connect AC voltmeter to AC leads as shown when checking alternator coils.

Fig. TE111—On 20 amp system, connect a DC ammeter as shown when checking regulator-rectifier as outlined in text.

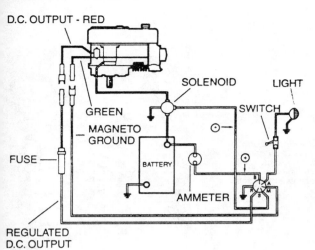

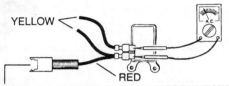

NOTE: D.C. OUTPUT MUST BE DISCONNECTED TO PERFORM A.C. OUTPUT TEST.

Fig. TE112—Wiring diagram of 16 amp alternator with external regulator.

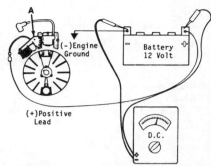

Fig. TE114—Connect a DC voltmeter to battery as shown to test output of alternator (A) on engines equipped with an external ignition system.

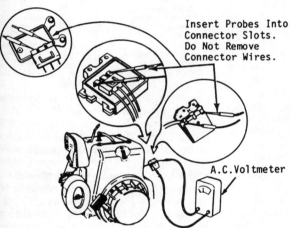

Insert Probes Into Connector Slots. Do Not Remove Connector Wires.

Fig. TE113—Connect AC voltmeter to AC leads of regulator-rectifier to check alternator output. Note that three types of internal regulator-rectifier units have been used.

110 VOLT ELECTRIC STARTER

WARNING: Exercise particular caution when testing 110-volt starter and starter circuit as damaged components may result in a dangerous short circuit.

Some models may be equipped with a 110-volt starter motor similar to 12-volt starter motor and Bendix drive shown in Fig. TE102. Note that configuration of drive assembly depends on direction of drive rotation.

Starters marked with a "CSA" label are only serviced as a unit assembly.

No electrical specifications are available. Use standard electrical testing procedures for electrical motors.

RATCHET STARTER

On models equipped with the ratchet starter, refer to Fig. TE116 and move release lever to "RELEASE" position to remove tension from the main spring. Remove starter assembly from the engine. Remove left-hand thread screw (26), retainer hub (25), brake (24), washer (23) and six starter dogs (22). Note position of starter dogs in hub (21). Remove the hub (21), washer (20), spring and housing (12), spring cover (18), release gear (17) and retaining ring (19) as an assembly. Remove retaining ring, then carefully separate these parts.

CAUTION: Do not remove main spring from housing (12). The spring and housing are serviced only as an assembly.

Remove snap rings (16), spacer washers (29), release dog (14), lock dog (15) and spring (13). Winding gear (8), clutch (4), clutch spring (5), bearing (6) and crank handle (2) can be removed after first removing the retaining screw and washers (10, 30 and 9).

Reassembly procedure is the reverse of disassembly. Centering pin (27) must

Regulator service test specifications are as follows:

Delco-Remy Regulator 1118988 (7 amp)
Ground polarity . . . . Negative
Cut-out relay:
  Air gap . . . . 0.020 in.
                     (0.5 mm)
  Point gap . . . . 0.020 in.
                     (0.5 mm)
  Closing voltage, range 11.8-14.0
  Adjust to 12.8
Voltage regulator:
  Air gap . . . . 0.075 in.
                     (1.9 mm)
  Setting volts, range 13.6-14.5
  Adjust to 14.0

Delco-Remy Regulator 1119207 (14 amp)
Ground polarity . . . . Negative

Cut-out relay:
  Air gap . . . . 0.020 in.
                     (0.5 mm)
  Point gap . . . . 0.020 in.
                     (0.5 mm)
  Closing voltage, range 11.8-13.5
  Adjust to 12.8
Voltage regulator:
  Air gap . . . . 0.075 in.
                     (1.9 mm)
Voltage setting @ °F.
        14.4-15.4 @ 65°
        14.2-15.2 @ 85°
        14.0-14.9 @ 105°
        13.8-14.7 @ 125°
        13.5-14.3 @ 145°
        13.1-13.9 @ 165°
Current regulator:
  Air gap . . . . 0.075 in.
                     (1.9 mm)
  Current setting 13-15

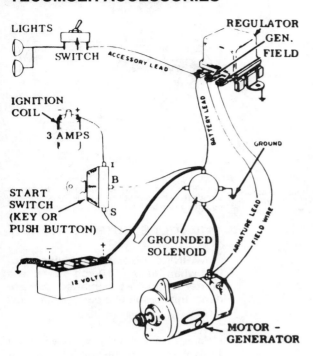

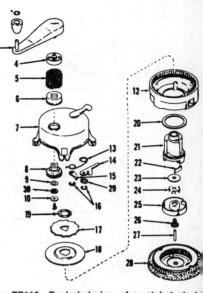

Fig. TE115—Wiring diagram of typical 14 amp output current-regulator and motor-generator system. The 7 amp output system is similar.

Fig. TE116—Exploded view of a ratchet starter assembly used on some engines.

2. Handle		18. Spring cover
4. Clutch		19. Retaining ring
5. Clutch spring		20. Hub washer
6. Bearing		21. Starter hub
7. Housing		22. Starter dog
8. Wind gear		23. Brake washer
9. Wave washer		24. Brake
10. Clutch washer		25. Retainer
12. Spring & housing		26. Screw (L.H.)
13. Release dog spring		27. Centering pin
14. Release dog		28. Hub & screen
15. Lock dog		29. Spacer washer
16. Dog pivot retainers		30. Lockwasher
17. Release gear		

align screw (26) with crankshaft center hole.

REWIND STARTERS

Friction Shoe Type

To disassemble the starter, hold starter rotor (12—Fig. TE117) securely with thumb pressure and remove the four screws securing flanges (1 and 2) to cover (15). Remove the flanges and release thumb pressure enough to allow the spring to rotate the pulley until the spring (13) is unwound. Remove retaining ring (3), washer (4), spring (5), slotted washer (6) and fiber washer (7). Lift out the friction shoe assembly (8, 9, 10 and 11), then remove second fiber washer and slotted washer. Withdraw the rotor (12) with rope from the cover and spring. Remove the rewind spring from cover and unwind the rope from rotor.

Inspect all parts for wear or damage and renew as necessary. To function properly, the ends of the friction shoes (10) must have a sharp edge. Sharpen or renew the shoes as necessary.

When reassembling, lubricate the rewind spring, cover shaft and center bore in rotor with a light coat of Lubriplate or equivalent. Install the rewind spring so windings are in same direction as removed spring. Install the rope on the rotor, then place rotor on the cover shaft. Make certain the inner and outer ends of the spring are correctly hooked on the cover and rotor. Preload the rewind spring by rotating the rotor two full turns. Hold rotor in preload po-

sition and install flanges (1 and 2). Install washers (6 and 7), friction shoe assembly, spring (5), washer (4) and retaining ring (3). Make certain friction shoe assembly is installed properly for correct starter rotation. If properly installed, sharp ends of friction shoes will extend when rope is pulled.

Remove brass centering pin (14) from cover shaft, straighten pin if necessary, then reinsert pin ⅓ of its length into cover shaft. When installing starter on engine, centering pin will align starter with center hole in end of crankshaft.

Dog Type

TEARDROP HOUSING. Note shape of starter housing in Fig. TE118, TE119 or TE121. The pulley may be secured with either a retainer screw (9—Fig. TE118 or 11—Fig. TE119) or re-

tainer pin (11—Fig. TE121). Refer to following paragraphs for service.

To disassemble the starter shown in Fig. TE118 and equipped with retainer screw (9), release preload tension of rewind spring by removing rope handle and allowing rope to wind into starter. Remove retainer screw (9), retainer (8) and spring (7). Remove dog (6) and spring (5). Remove pulley with spring. Wear appropriate safety eyewear and gloves before disengaging keeper (2) and rewind spring (3) from pulley as spring may uncoil uncontrolled.

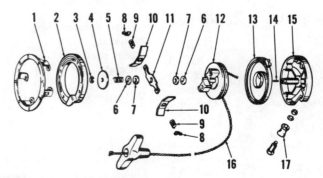

Fig. TE117—Exploded view of typical friction shoe rewind starter.

1. Mounting flange	6. Slotted washer	10. Friction shoe	14. Centering spring
2. Flange	7. Fiber washer	11. Actuating lever	15. Cover
3. Retaining ring	8. Spring retainer	12. Rotor	16. Rope
4. Washer	9. Spring	13. Rewind spring	17. Roller
5. Spring			

To reassemble, reverse the disassembly procedure. Spring (3) should be lightly greased. Assemble starter but install rope last as follows: Turn pulley counterclockwise until tight, then allow to unwind so hole in pulley aligns with rope outlet as shown in Fig. TE120. Insert rope through starter housing and pulley hole, and tie a knot in rope end. Install the rope handle and allow the rope to wind onto pulley.

Some models use centering pin (10) to align starter with starter cup. Place nylon bushing (11) on pin (10), then bottom the pin in the hole in retainer screw (9). Pin and bushing should index in end of crankshaft when installing starter on engine.

To disassemble starter shown in Fig. TE119 and equipped with retainer screw (11), pull starter rope until notch in pulley half (5) is aligned with rope hole in housing (1). Hold pulley and prevent from rotating. Engage rope in notch and allow pulley to slowly rotate so rewind spring will unwind. Remove components as shown in Fig. TE119. Note direction rewind spring is wound. Wear appropriate safety eyewear and gloves when working with rewind spring as spring may uncoil uncontrolled.

Reassemble by reversing disassembly procedure. Preload rewind spring by turning pulley two turns with rope.

To disassemble starter equipped with retainer pin (Fig. TE121), release preload tension of rewind spring by removing rope handle and allowing rope to wind into starter. Remove the retainer pin (11) by supporting pulley on a one-inch deep well socket then driving out pin using a ¼ inch punch. Remove spring (7) and retainer (8). Remove dog (6) and spring (5). Remove the pulley (4) with spring. Wear appropriate safety eyewear and gloves before disengaging keeper (2) and rewind spring (3) from pulley as spring may uncoil uncontrolled.

To reassemble, reverse the disassembly procedure. Spring (3) should be lightly greased. Assemble the starter but install rope last. Drive in retainer pin (11) until seated against shoulder of housing.

To install rope, rotate pulley counterclockwise until tight, then allow to unwind so hole in pulley aligns with rope outlet as shown in Fig. TE120. Insert rope through starter housing and pulley hole, and tie a knot in rope end. Install the rope handle and allow the rope to wind onto the pulley.

SERIES VM AND HM ENGINES. These engines may be equipped with the starter shown in Fig. TE122. To disassemble starter, release preload tension of rewind spring by removing rope handle and allowing rope to wind into starter. Remove retainer screw (11), dog cam (10), spring (9), and washer (8). Detach "E" rings (7) and remove the dogs (6) and springs (5). Remove pulley with spring. Wear appropriate safety eyewear and gloves before disengaging keeper (2) and rewind spring (3) from

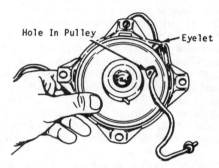

Fig. TE120—Insert rope through starter housing eyelet and hole in pulley then tie knot in rope end.

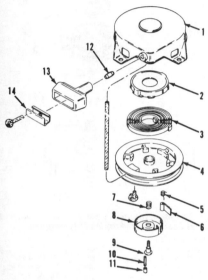

Fig. TE118—Exploded view of typical dog type rewind starter with teardrop shaped housing (1) using retainer screw (9). Some starters may have three starter dogs (6).

1. Housing
2. Spring keeper
3. Rewind spring
4. Pulley
5. Spring
6. Dog
7. Brake spring
8. Retainer
9. Screw
10. Centering pin
11. Nylon bushing
12. Rope coupler
13. Handle
14. Insert

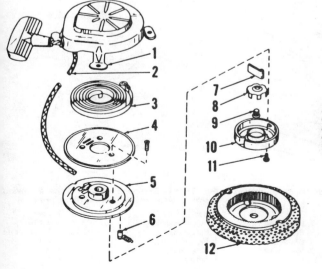

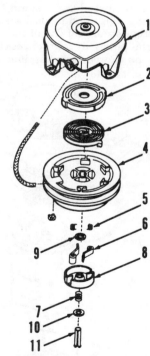

Fig. TE121—Exploded view of typical dog type rewind starter with teardrop shaped housing (1) using retainer pin (11).

1. Housing
2. Spring keeper
3. Rewind spring
4. Pulley
5. Spring
6. Dog
7. Brake spring
8. Retainer
9. Washer
10. Washer
11. Pin

Fig. TE119—Exploded view of dog type rewind starter assembly used on some models. Some units are equipped with three starter dogs (7).

1. Housing
2. Rope
3. Rewind spring
4. Pulley half
5. Pulley half & hub
6. Retainer spring
7. Starter dog
8. Brake
9. Brake screw
10. Retainer
11. Retainer screw
12. Hub & screen assy.

pulley as spring may uncoil uncontrolled.

To reassemble, reverse the disassembly procedure. Spring (3) should be lightly greased. Install springs (5) so dogs (6) are held in against pulley. Assemble the starter but install rope last as follows: Turn pulley counterclockwise until tight, then allow to unwind so hole in pulley aligns with rope outlet as shown in Fig. TE120. Insert rope through starter housing and pulley hole, and tie a knot in rope end. Install the rope handle and allow the rope to wind onto pulley.

STYLIZED STARTER. The "stylized" starter is shown in Fig. TE123. To disassemble starter, remove rope handle and allow rope to wind into starter. Position a suitable sleeve support (a ¾ inch deep socket) under retainer pawl (8). Using a ⁵⁄₁₆ inch punch, drive the pin (11) free of starter. Remove brake spring (9), retainer (8), dogs (6) and springs (5). Wear appropriate safety eyewear and gloves before disengaging pulley from starter as spring may uncoil uncontrolled. Place shop cloth around pulley and lift pulley out of housing; spring should remain with pulley.

Inspect components for damage and excessive wear. Reverse disassembly procedure to install components. Rewind spring coils wind in clockwise direction from outer end. Wind the rope around the pulley in counterclockwise direction as viewed from retainer side

of pulley. Be sure inner end of rewind spring engages spring retainer adjacent to the housing center post. Use two plastic washers (7). Install a new pin (11) so top of pin is ⅛ inch (3.2 mm) below top of starter. Driving pin in too far may damage retainer pawl.

SERIES OHV ENGINES. Two designs have been used on Series OHV engines. The Type I rewind starter is shown in Fig. TE124 and Type II rewind starter is shown in Fig. TE125. Refer to appropriate following section.

Type I. To disassemble the rewind starter, pull out the rope handle and tie a temporary knot in the rope so it cannot rewind. Remove the rope handle, untie temporary knot and allow the rope to wind into the housing. Unscrew metric nut (12—Fig. TE124) and remove components (6 through 11). Place shop cloth around the pulley (5) and lift the pulley out of the housing; spring (4) should remain with the pulley. If the spring must be removed from the pulley, position the pulley so the spring side is down and against floor, and tap the pulley to dislodge spring.

Reassemble starter by reversing the disassembly procedure while noting the

following: Apply light coating of grease to the sides of the rewind spring and pulley. Install the spring in the pulley so coil direction is counterclockwise from outer spring end.

Using a new rope of same length and diameter as the original, attach the rope handle on the rope. Install other end of rope through the guide bushing

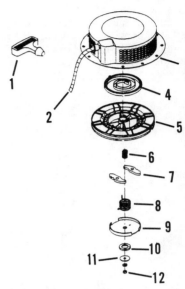

Fig. TE124—Exploded view of Type I rewind starter used on some Series OHV engines.

1. Rope handle	7. Pawl
2. Rope	8. Spring
3. Starter housing	9. Retainer
4. Rewind spring	10. Washer
5. Rope pulley	11. Washer
6. Spring	12. Nut (metric)

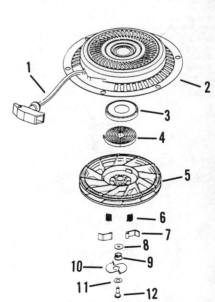

Fig. TE125—Exploded view of Type II rewind starter used on some Series OHV engines.

1. Rope	7. Pawl
2. Starter housing	8. Washer
3. Spring cup	9. Brake spring
4. Rewind spring	10. Retainer
5. Rope pulley	11. Washer
6. Spring	12. Screw

Fig. TE122—Exploded view of rewind starter used on VM and HM engines.

1. Housing	7. "E" ring
2. Spring keeper	8. Washer
3. Rewind spring	9. Spring
4. Pulley	10. Dog cam
5. Spring	11. Screw
6. Dog	

Fig. TE123—Exploded view of "stylized" rewind starter.

1. Starter housing	7. Plastic washers (2)
2. Cover	8. Retainer pawl
3. Rewind spring	9. Brake spring
4. Pulley	10. Metal washer
5. Springs (2)	11. Pin
6. Dogs (2)	

of the housing and through the hole in pulley groove (pulley is separate from housing). Pull the rope through the pulley hole and tie a knot in the end. Pull the knot into the pulley hole. Wind the rope clockwise on pulley as viewed from pawl side.

Install the pulley in starter housing. While holding the pulley in the housing, rotate pulley counterclockwise until the tang on pulley engages the hook on inner end of rewind spring. Hook a loop of rope into pulley notch and preload the rewind spring by turning the pulley four full turns counterclockwise. Remove the rope from notch and allow the pulley to slowly turn clockwise as the rope winds on the pulley and the handle returns to the guide bushing on the housing.

Refer to Fig. TE124 and install components (6 through 12). Install the return spring (8) with bent end hooked into hole of pulley hub and looped end toward outside. Then, mount the ratchet retainer so loop end of return spring extends through slot. Rotate the retainer slightly clockwise until ends of slots just begin to engage the ratchets. Press down on the retainer, install the washer and nut.

Type II. To disassemble starter, remove the rope handle and allow the rope to wind into the starter. Unscrew the center retaining screw (12—Fig. TE125) and separate starter components. To disengage the rewind spring (4) from the starter housing, rotate the pulley two turns clockwise. Wear appropriate safety eyewear and gloves to prevent injury should the rewind spring uncoil uncontrolled. The rewind spring is contained in cup (3).

Assemble starter before installing the rope. Lubricate the rewind spring before installation. Apply a small amount of grease on the brake spring (9) ends. Assemble each pawl (7) and spring (6) so spring end pushes the pawl toward the center. Apply Loctite 242 (blue) to threads of center screw (12) and tighten to 70 in.-lb. (8 N•m).

Use the following procedure to install the rope. With the starter assembled except for the rope, rotate the pulley four to five turns counterclockwise and stop when rope hole on pulley is aligned with rope outlet on starter housing. Hold the pulley so it cannot rotate and insert the rope through rope outlet in housing and hole in pulley. Tie a knot at inner end of rope, then pull rope knot against pulley. Attach rope handle and slowly release the pulley. Check starter operation.

TECUMSEH CENTRAL PARTS DISTRIBUTORS

(Arranged Alphabetically by States)
**These franchised firms carry extensive stocks of repair parts. Contact them
for name of the nearest service distributor.**

Billou's, Inc.
Phone (209) 784-4102
1343 S. Main
Porterville, California 93257

Pacific Power Equipment Company
Phone (303) 744-7891
1441 W. Bayaud Ave., Unit 4
Denver, Colorado 80223

Smith Engines Inc.
Phone (407) 855-5764
2303 Premier Row
Orlando, Florida 32807

Small Engine Clinic, Inc.
Phone (808) 841-3800
1728 Homerule Street
Honolulu, Hawaii 96819

Industrial Engine & Parts
Phone (847) 263-0500
50 Noll Street
Waukegan, Illinois 60085

Medart Engines of Kansas
Phone: (913) 422-3100
2644 S. 96th Street
Edwardsville, Kansas 66111

Engines Southwest
Phone (318) 222-3871
1255 N. Hearne, P.O. Box 67
Shreveport, Louisiana 71161

W.J. Connell Company
Phone (508) 543-3600
65 Green St., Rt. 106
Foxboro, Massachusetts 02035

Central Power Distributors, Inc.
Phone (612) 576-0901
1101 McKinley St.
Anoka, Minnesota 55303

Medart Engines of St. Louis
Phone: (314) 343-0505
100 Larkin Williams Industrial Ct.
Fenton, Missouri 63026

Gardner, Inc.
Phone: (609) 860-8060
106 Melrich Rd.
Cranbury, New Jersey 08512

Smith Engines Inc.
Phone (704) 392-3100
4250 Golf Acres Dr., P.O. Box 668985
Charlotte, North Carolina 28266

Gardner, Inc.
Phone (614) 488-7951
1150 Chesapeake Ave.
Columbus, Ohio 43212

Power Equipment Systems
Phone (503) 585-6120
1645 Salem Industrial Drive N.E., P.O.
Box 669
Salem, Oregon 97308

Pitt Auto Electric Company
Phone: (412) 766-9112
2900 Stayton Street
Pittsburgh, Pennsylvania 15212

Frank Edwards Company
Phone (801) 281-4660
3653 S. 500 West
Salt Lake City, Utah 84115

Power Equipment Systems
Phone (206) 763-8902
88 South Hudson, P.O. Box 3901
Seattle, Washington 98124

CANADIAN DISTRIBUTORS

CPT Canada Power Technology, Ltd.
Phone (403) 453-5791
13315 146th Street
Edmonton, Alberta T5L 4S8

CPT Canada Power Technology, Ltd.
Phone (416) 890-6900
161 Watline Ave.
Mississauga, Ontario L4W 2T7

WISCONSIN

Model	No. Cyls.	Bore	Stroke	Displacement	Power Rating
ADH	1	2.75 in. (69.8 mm)	3.25 in. (82.6 mm)	19.3 cu. in. (308.7 cc)	5.1 hp (3.8 kW)
AE, AEH, AEHS, AEN, AENL, AENS	1	3.0 in. (76.2 mm)	3.25 in. (82.6 mm)	23.0 cu. in. (376.5 cc)	9.2 hp (6.9 kW)
AFH	1	3.25 in. (82.6 mm)	4.0 in. (101.6 mm)	33.2 cu. in. (543.8 cc)	7.2 hp (5.4 kW)
AGH, AGND	1	3.5 in. (88.9 mm)	4.0 in. (101.6 mm)	38.5 cu. in. (630.7 cc)	12.5 hp (9.3 kW)
AHH	1	3.625 in. (92.08 mm)	4.0 in. (101.6 mm)	41.3 cu. in. (676.6 cc)	9.2 hp (6.9 kW)
AK	1	2.875 in. (73.02 mm)	2.75 in. (69.8 mm)	17.8 cu. in. (292.3 cc)	4.1 hp (3.1 kW)
AKN	1	2.875 in. (73.02 mm)	2.75 in. (69.8 mm)	17.8 cu. in. (292.3 cc)	6.2 hp (4.6 kW)
AKS	1	2.875 in. (73.02 mm)	2.75 in. (69.8 mm)	17.8 cu. in. (292.3 cc)	4.7 hp (3.5 kW)
BKN	1	2.875 in. (73.02 mm)	2.75 in. (69.8 mm)	17.8 cu. in. (292.3 cc)	7 hp (5.2 kW)

Engines in this section are four-stroke, single-cylinder, air-cooled engines with a horizontal crankshaft. Crankshaft is supported at each end by taper roller bearings.

On Model BKN, the connecting rod is equipped with insert-type bearings. On all other models, the connecting rod rides directly on crankpin journal. Pressure spray or splash lubrication is provided by a plunger-type oil pump or a dipper located on end of connecting rod cap. Pump is driven off camshaft lobe.

Ignition system consists of either a battery-type system or one of a variety of magneto systems.

Float-type carburetors from a variety of manufacturers are available. A mechanical fuel pump is available for most models.

Engine identification information is located on engine instruction plate and engine model, specification and serial number are required when ordering parts.

MAINTENANCE

LUBRICATION. A plunger-type oil pump driven off a camshaft lobe provides lubrication using one of two methods. Oil may be sprayed onto the connecting rod as shown in Fig. W1 so oil reaches internal engine components, or oil fills an oil trough as shown in Fig. W2 and the oil is splashed onto engine components.

Maintain oil level at full mark on dipstick or at top of filler plug but do not overfill. Oil should be changed after every 50 hours of operation. Change oil more frequently if engine undergoes severe operation.

Manufacturer recommends oil with an API service classification of SE, SF or SG. Use SAE 30 oil for ambient temperatures above 40° F (4° C); use SAE 20-20W oil for temperatures between 40° F (4° C) and 15° F (−9° C); use SAE 10W oil for temperatures between 15° F

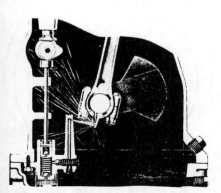

Fig. W1—View of pressure spray lubricating system used on some models.

Fig. W2—View of oil pump used to maintain correct oil level in oil trough of engines with splash lubricating system.

(−9° C) and 0° F (−18° C); below 0° F (−18° C) use SAE 5W-20.

SPARK PLUG. Recommended spark plug is Champion D16J or equivalent. Electrode gap should be 0.030 inch (0.76 mm).

CARBURETOR. A variety of float-type carburetors are used as listed. Marvel Schebler VH53 and VH70 models are replacements for older VH12 and VH14 models.

Marvel Schebler VH53 model is used on AK, AKN and AKS engines; TSX147 model is used on AHH engines and TSX676 model is used on AGND engines.

Stromberg OH 5/8 model is used on AK, AKN and AKS engines; UC 3/4 model is used on ADH, AE, AEH, AEHS and AFH engines; UC 7/8 model is used on AGH and AHH engines and UR 3/4 model is used on ADH, AE, AEH, AEHS and AENL engines.

Zenith 87B5 and 87BY6 models are used on AK, AKN and AKS engines; 161-7 model is used on AE, AEH, AEHS, AEN, AENS, AFH, AGH and AHH engines, and 68-7 model is used on some AENL and AGND engines.

For initial carburetor adjustment, open idle mixture screw 1¼ turns and main fuel mixture screw, if so equipped, 1¼ turns. Make final adjustments with

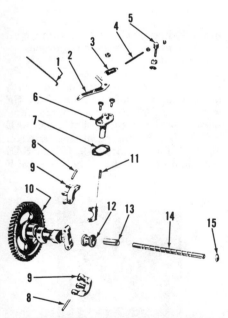

Fig. W3—Exploded view of camshaft and governor assemblies.

1. Governor control rod	9. Flyweight
2. Governor lever	10. Camshaft & gear assy.
3. Governor spring	11. Governor yoke
4. Adjusting screw	12. Thrust sleeve
5. Pin	13. Spacer
6. Support bracket	14. Support pin
7. Gasket	15. Core plug
8. Roll pin	

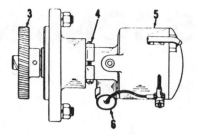
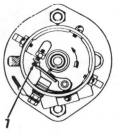

Fig. W4—Distributor used on Models AEN, AENL and AENS with battery ignition is driven by camshaft gear.

engine at normal operating temperature and running. Place engine under load and adjust main fuel mixture screw for leanest setting that will allow satisfactory acceleration and steady governor operation. Set engine at idle speed, no load and adjust idle mixture screw for smoothest idle operation.

As each adjustment affects the other, adjustment procedure may have to be repeated.

Recommended float level for Marvel Schebler VH12 and VH14 models is ½ inch (12.7 mm) and ¼ inch (6.4 mm) for VH53, VH70 and TSX models.

Recommended float level for Zenith 87B5 and 87BY6 models is $3\frac{1}{32}$ inch (24.6 mm) and $1\frac{5}{32}$ inch (29.4 mm) for 161-7 and 68.7 models.

Recommended float level for Stromberg models is ½ to 9/16 inch (12.7 to 14.3 mm).

GOVERNOR. Flyweight-type governors are used on all models.

On Models AK, AKN, AKS and BKN, flyweights are attached to camshaft and operate a sleeve and shaft arrangement (Fig. W3) to control engine speed.

Governor flyweights on remaining models are attached to a gear assembly that is driven by camshaft gear and actuates an internal and external lever arrangement to control engine speed.

Speed changes on all models are obtained by using springs of varying tension and locating spring or governor rod in alternate holes of governor control lever.

Governor-to-carburetor rod should be adjusted so it just will enter hole in governor lever when governor weights are in and carburetor throttle is wide open.

IGNITION SYSTEM. Either a battery-type ignition system with breaker points located in a distributor or a magneto-type ignition system is used according to model and application.

BATTERY IGNITION. Breaker points on battery system are located inside a distributor that is driven by the camshaft gear. Condenser is mounted externally on distributor body. Point

gap is 0.020 inch (0.51 mm) for both type Auto-Lite distributors. See Fig. W4.

To correctly time distributor to engine during installation, remove screen over flywheel air intake, make certain piston is at top dead center on compression stroke (Fig. W5) and install distributor so points are just beginning to open. Connect timing light to engine, start and run engine at rated speed and rotate distributor as necessary to set timing to specifications as follows:

ADH, AE, AEH, AEHS, AEN, AENS, AFH, AGH, AHH	25° BTDC
AK, AKN, AKS	28° BTDC
AENL, AGND	20° BTDC
BKN	17° BTDC

MAGNETO IGNITION. Eisemann and Edison magnetos were obsoleted and replaced by Fairbanks-Morse or Wico magnetos.

Breaker point gap for all models is 0.015 inch (0.38 mm).

To correctly time magneto to engine during installation, remove screen over flywheel air intake opening and timing hole plug from crankcase. Make certain piston is at top dead center on compression stroke and leading edge of flywheel vane (3—Fig. W5) marked "X" and "DC" is in register with timing mark (2) on air

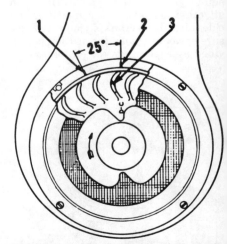

Fig. W5—View of typical ignition timing marks. Piston is at top dead center when leading edge of flywheel vane (3), marked "X" and "DC" is in register with static ignition timing mark (2).

Fig. W6—Timing gears and marks of AEN, AENL and AENS models shown in register. With marks on gears (3 and 5) aligned as shown at (4), "X" marked magneto gear tooth must show through port (2) when piston is at TDC.

1. Magneto gear
2. Timing port
3. Camshaft gear
4. Timing marks
5. Crankshaft gear

Fig. W7—Placement of timing marks on Models AK, AKN, AKS and BKN when timing magneto to piston at top dead center.

2. Crankshaft gear
3. Valve timing marks
4. Camshaft gear
5. Magneto gear
6. Magneto timing marks

shroud. Install magneto so marked tooth (Figs. W6 or W7) on magneto drive gear is visible through port in timing gear cover as shown. If timing is correct, impulse coupling will trip when crankshaft keyway is up as engine is being cranked.

Connect timing light and set timing to specifications listed for battery ignition system.

VALVE ADJUSTMENT. Valve tappet gap (cold) for intake valve is 0.008 inch (0.20 mm). Exhaust valve tappet gap is 0.014 inch (0.36 mm) for Model BKN and 0.016 inch (0.41 mm) for all other models. Gap is adjusted by turning adjusting screws on tappets, if equipped, or grinding end of valve stem if nonadjustable tappets are installed.

REPAIRS

TIGHTENING TORQUES. Recommended torque specifications are as follows:

Connecting rod:
AFH, AGH,
AGND, AHH . . . . 32 ft.-lbs.
(43 N•m)
All other models . . . . 18 ft.-lbs.
(24 N•m)
Cylinder-to-block (where applicable):
AGND . . . . 40-50 ft.-lbs.
(54-68 N•m)
All other models . . . . . 62-78 ft.-lbs.
(84-106 N•m)
Cylinder head:
AK, AKN,
AKS & BKN . . . . 14-18 ft.-lbs.
(19-24 N•m)
All other models . . . . . 26-32 ft.-lbs.
(35-43 N•m)
Main bearing plate:
AK, AKN
& AKS . . . . 14-18 ft.-lbs.
(19-24 N•m)
BKN . . . . 120-144 in.-lbs.
(13.6-16.3 N•m)
All other models . . . . . 26-32 ft.-lbs.
(35-43 N•m)

CYLINDER HEAD. When removing cylinder head, note location and lengths of cylinder head retaining screws so they can be reinstalled in their original positions.

A new cylinder head gasket should be installed to insure proper sealing. Tighten screws in a crossing pattern to a torque of 14-18 ft.-lbs. (19-24 N•m) on Models AK, AKN, AKS and BKN, and to 26-32 ft.-lbs. (35-43 N•m) on all other models.

VALVE SYSTEM. Valve seats are renewable-type inserts in cylinder block and seats should be ground to a 45° angle. Valve seat width should be $\frac{3}{32}$ inch (2.4 mm).

Valve face angle should be 45°. Stellite valves and seats, and valve rotocaps are available for some models.

Valve stem clearance in block or guide should be 0.003-0.005 inch (0.07-0.13 mm). Models AENL, AGND and BKN have renewable valve guides. Valves with oversize stems are available for models that do not have renewable guides if stem clearance exceeds 0.006 inch (0.15 mm).

PISTON, PIN AND RINGS. Piston and connecting rod are removed from cylinder head end of block as an assembly. Piston and connecting rod are accessible after removing cylinder head and engine base.

Piston may be of three or four-ring design according to model and application. Pistons and rings are available in a variety of oversizes as well as standard. Refer to following sections covering Model BKN and all other models for service information.

Model BKN. On Model BKN, top compression ring side clearance should be 0.0020-0.0035 inch (0.051-0.089 mm), second and third compression ring side clearance should be 0.0010-0.0025 inch (0.025-0.064 mm), and oil control ring side clearance should be 0.0025-0.0040 inch (0.064-0.102 mm).

On Model BKN, piston clearance should be 0.0055-0.0060 inch (0.140-0.152 mm) for engines running at less than 3000 rpm. Piston clearance should be 0.0060-0.0065 inch (0.152-0.0.165 mm) for BKN engines running in excess of 3000 rpm.

Floating-type piston pin is retained by snap rings in bore of piston. Piston pin clearance in connecting rod should be 0.0001-0.0007 inch (0.002-0.018 mm).

Install piston and rod in cylinder so oil hole in rod is toward camshaft. Install rod cap so arrows on cap and rod are aligned. Tighten rod screws to 18 ft.-lbs. (24 N•m).

All Other Models. Piston ring end gap for all models should be 0.012-0.022 inch (0.30-0.56 mm). Piston ring side clearance for all models should be 0.002-0.003 inch (0.05-0.08 mm).

Early models were equipped with a split skirt piston. Split should be toward valve side of engine after installation. Later model cam ground piston has a wide and a narrow thrust face on piston skirt. Wide side must be toward thrust side (side opposite valve) of engine after installation. Assemble piston and connecting rod so oil hole in rod or cap is toward camshaft.

On all other models, split skirt piston should have a clearance in bore of 0.0045-0.0050 inch (0.114-0.127 mm) measured 90° from piston pin at bottom edge of piston skirt. Cam ground piston should have a clearance in bore of 0.0030-0.0035 inch (0.076-0.089 mm) measured along thrust surface of skirt.

Floating-type piston pin is retained by snap rings in bore of piston. Piston pin clearance in connecting rod should be 0.0002-0.0008 inch (0.005-0.020 mm).

Tighten rod screws to 32 ft.-lbs. (43 N•m) on Models AFH, AGH, AGND and AHH, and to 18 ft.-lbs. (24 N•m) on all other models.

CONNECTING ROD. Connecting rod and piston are removed from cylinder head end of block as an assembly. Piston and connecting rod are accessible after removing cylinder head and engine base.

The connecting rod on Model BKN is equipped with renewable insert-type bearings while the connecting rod on all other models rides directly on crankpin. Undersize insert bearings or undersize connecting rod are available.

Rod-to-journal running clearance should be 0.0010-0.0018 inch (0.025-0.046 mm) for Models AEN, AENL and AENS; 0.0009-0.0032 inch (0.023-0.081 mm) for Model BKN; and 0.0007-0.0020 inch (0.018-0.051 mm) for all other models. On some models, minor adjustment is possible by varying thickness of shims between connecting rod and cap.

Connecting rod side clearance should be 0.004-0.013 inch (0.10-0.33 mm) for Models AEN, AENL and AENS; 0.009-0.016 inch (0.23-0.41 mm) for Model BKN; and 0.004-0.011 inch (0.10-0.28 mm) for all other models.

Assemble piston and rod and install as outlined in previous section.

CRANKSHAFT AND MAIN BEARINGS. The crankshaft of all models is supported at each end by taper roller bearings. Main bearings are press fit on crankshaft. Crankshaft end play when engine is cold should be 0.002-0.005 inch (0.05-0.13 mm) on Model BKN and 0.002-0.004 inch (0.05-0.10 mm) on all other models. End play is controlled by varying thickness of gaskets between crankcase and bearing plate. Gaskets are available in a variety of thicknesses.

Crankpin standard journal diameter is 1.00 inch (25.4 mm) for Models AK, AKN and AKS; 1.1255 inches (28.588 mm) for Models ADH, AE, AEH, AEHS, AEN, AENL and AENS; 1.375 inches (34.925 mm) for Models AFH, AGH and AHH; 1.750 inches (44.45 mm) for Model AGND; and 1.0003-1.0010 inches (25.408-25.425 mm) for Model BKN.

Refer to Figs. W6 or W7 for correct timing gear position for installation of crankshaft.

CAMSHAFT. The hollow camshaft turns on a stationary support pin (14—Fig. W3) and should have a running clearance of 0.0010-0.0025 inch (0.025-0.064 mm). To remove camshaft support pin, remove plug from flywheel side of crankcase, then drive pin out through pto side of crankcase (this will force out plug on pto side of crankcase). Drive in camshaft support pin from pto side of crankcase toward flywheel side. Camshaft plugs (15) should be renewed.

Governor flyweights are attached to camshaft on some models and care should be taken to avoid damaging components when camshaft is being installed.

MAGNETO DRIVE GEAR. On Models ADH, AE, AEH, AEHS, AFH, AGH and AHH, magneto drive shaft should have a running clearance of 0.0020-0.0035 inch (0.051-0.089 mm) in shaft bushing. Drive shaft end play should be 0.004-0.005 inch (0.10-0.13 mm) and is adjusted by varying thickness of gasket. Magneto drive gear is pressed on shaft so distance from coupling face of shaft to centerline of magneto mounting hole is 2.584 inches (65.64 mm).

CYLINDER. Cylinder bore section on Models ADH, AE, AEH, AEHS, AFH, AGH, AGND and AHH is separate from crankcase and may be renewed as an individual unit. Cylinder bore and crankcase for all other models are cast as a unit.

Cylinders for all models may be bored to accept an oversize piston. Cylinder bore should be bored oversize if worn or out-of-round more than 0.005 inch (0.13 mm). Pistons are available in standard size and a variety of oversizes.

OIL PUMP. A plunger-type oil pump is located in the engine base. The pump is driven by a lobe on the camshaft. See Figs. W1 or W2.

Oil pump plunger-to-bore clearance should be 0.003-0.007 inch (0.08-0.1 mm) and plunger should be renewed if clearance exceeds 0.008 inch (0.20 mm).

WISCONSIN

Model	No. Cyls.	Bore	Stroke	Displacement	Power Rating
HBKN	1	2.875 in. (73.03 mm)	2.75 in. (69.85 mm)	17.8 cu. in. (292.6 cc)	7 hp (5.2 kW)
HAENL	1	3.0 in. (76.2 mm)	3.25 in. (82.55 mm)	23.0 cu. in. (376.5 cc)	9.2 hp (6.9 kW)

Engines in this section are four-stroke, one cylinder, vertical crankshaft engines. Crankshaft is supported at each end by taper roller bearings.

Connecting rod rides directly on crankpin journal and shims between connecting rod cap and rod provide running clearance adjustment. Pressure spray lubrication is provided by a vane-type oil pump mounted to and driven by crankshaft.

All models are equipped with a magneto ignition system.

Zenith float-type carburetors are standard equipment for all models and a mechanical fuel pump is available.

Engine identification information is located on engine instruction plate and engine model, specification and serial numbers are required when ordering parts.

MAINTENANCE

SPARK PLUG. Recommended spark plug is Champion D16 or equivalent. Electrode gap should be 0.030 inch (0.76 mm).

CARBURETOR. Zenith 68-7 model (Fig. W9) carburetor is used on HAENL

engines and Zenith 87B5 model (Fig. W10) carburetor is standard equipment for HBKN engines with a variety of other carburetors used for special applications. Refer to carburetor identification number for proper carburetor identification.

For initial adjustment on all models, open idle mixture screw and main fuel mixture screw (as equipped) 1¼ turns each. Make final adjustments with engine at normal operating temperature and running. Place engine under load and adjust main fuel mixture screw (as equipped) for leanest setting that will

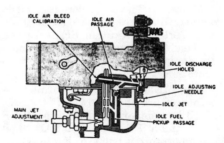

Fig. W10—Sectional view of Zenith 87B5 model carburetor showing location of idle adjusting screw and main fuel adjusting screw.

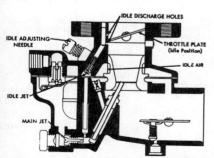

Fig. W9—Sectional view of Zenith 68-7 model carburetor showing location of idle adjusting screw and main fuel jet.

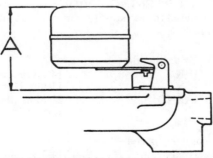

Fig. W11—Float level measurement for Zenith carburetors. On 87B5 models, dimension "A" is 31/32 inch (24.6 mm). On 68-7 models, it is 1-5/32 inch (29.36 mm).

allow satisfactory acceleration and steady governor operation. Set engine at idle speed no load and adjust idle mixture screw for smoothest idle operation.

As each adjustment affects the other, adjustment procedure may have to be repeated.

To check float level, invert carburetor throttle body and float assembly (Fig. W11) and measure distance (A) from machined surface of throttle body to highest point on float. Model 87B5 carburetor float level should be $3\frac{1}{32}$ inch (24.60 mm) and 68-7 model carburetor float level should be $1\frac{5}{32}$ inch (29.37 mm). Adjust as necessary by bending float lever tang that contacts inlet valve.

GOVERNOR. Flyweight-type governors are used on all models and flyweights are attached to camshaft and operate a sleeve and shaft arrangement (Fig. W12) to control engine speed.

Speed changes on all models is obtained by using springs (3) of varying tension, flyweights (9) of varying weights or locating spring or governor rod in alternate holes of governor control lever (2).

Governor-to-carburetor rod should be adjusted so that it just enters hole in governor lever when governor weights are "in" and carburetor throttle is wide open.

Camshaft must be removed from engine to service governor flyweights.

IGNITION SYSTEM. Fairbanks-Morse magnetos are used for all models and magneto is mounted in suspension below timing gear train. An oil drain tube is connected to magneto body to allow excess oil to drain back into engine crankcase.

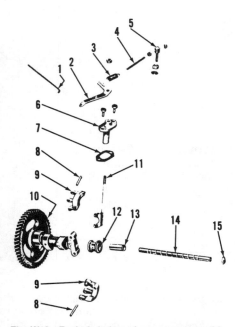

Fig. W12—Exploded view of governor assembly showing component parts and their relative positions.

1. Governor control rod
2. Governor lever
3. Governor spring
4. Adjusting screw
5. Pin
6. Support bracket
7. Gasket
8. Roll pin
9. Flyweight
10. Camshaft & gear assy.
11. Governor yoke
12. Thrust sleeve
13. Spacer
14. Support pin
15. Core plug

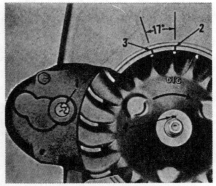

Fig. W13—Magneto timing for HBKN engines.

1. Magneto timing marks
2. Centerline mark
3. Running timing mark
4. Flywheel keyway

Magneto breaker points and condenser are accessible by removing magneto end cover. Breaker point gap should be adjusted to 0.015 inch (0.38 mm) clearance.

To correctly time magneto to HBKN engine, remove screen over flywheel air intake opening and timing hole plug from crankcase. Make certain piston is at "top dead center" on compression stroke and leading edge of flywheel vane (Fig. W13) marked "X" and "DC" is in register with timing mark (2) on air shroud. Install magneto so marked tooth (1—Fig. W14) on magneto drive

gear is visible through port in timing gear as shown. If timing is correct, impulse coupling will trip when crankshaft keyway is up as engine is being cranked.

To correctly time magneto to HAENL engine, remove screen over flywheel air intake opening and timing hole plug from crankcase. Make certain piston is at "top dead center" on compression stroke and leading edge of flywheel vane (Fig. W15) is in register with timing mark (3) on air shroud. Install magneto so marked tooth (1—Fig. W16) on magneto drive gear is visible through port in timing gear as shown.

To set running timing on either model, connect timing light, start and run engine at 1800 rpm and set timing on HBKN engines at 17° BTDC and set timing on HAENL engines at 20° BTDC.

LUBRICATION. A vane-type oil pump, mounted to and driven by the crankshaft, is used to provide pressure spray lubrication on all models. Pump is located in engine adapter base (Fig. W17).

Pump vane retainer is held in position on crankshaft by a set screw that also holds pump body in place. A strap attached to engine bearing plate keeps oil pump body stationary.

Oil pressure relief valve reed should fit firmly against oil pressure relief hole. Renew reed if it is bent or out of shape.

Maintain oil level at filler plug, but do not overfill. High-quality detergent oil, with API classification SF, is recommended. Oil change interval recommendation is every 50 hours of normal operation.

Use SAE 30 oil when operating temperatures are above 40° F (4° C), SAE 20 oil for temperatures between 40° F (4° C) and 5° F (-15° C) and SAE 10 oil if temperature is below 5° F (-15° C).

REPAIRS

TIGHTENING TORQUES. Recommended torque specifications are as follows:

Cylinder head—
　HBKN . . . . 14-18 ft.-lbs.
　　　　　　　　　　　　　　(19-24 N•m)
　HAENL . . . . 26-32 ft.-lbs.
　　　　　　　　　　　　　　(35-43 N•m)

Connecting rod—
　HBKN . . . . 14-18 ft.-lbs.
　　　　　　　　　　　　　　(19-24 N•m)
　HAENL . . . . 18 ft.-lbs.
　　　　　　　　　　　　　　(24 N•m)

Fig. W14—Model HBKN timing marks shown in register.

1. Magneto riming marks
2. Crankshaft gear
3. Camshaft timing marks
4. Camshaft gear
5. Magneto gear

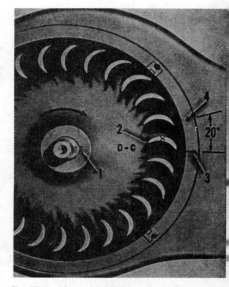

Fig. W15—View of HAENL model ignition timing marks lined up.

1. Keyway
2. Marked air vane
3. Centerline mark
4. Running timing mark

Fig. W16—Model HAENL timing marks shown in register.

1. Magneto timing mark
2. Timing port plug
3. Camshaft gear
4. Cam gear timing marks
5. Crankshaft gear timing mark

Main bearing plate—
　HBKN . . . . 14-18 ft.-lbs.
　　　　　　　　　　　　　　(19-24 N•m)
　HAENL . . . . 26-32 ft.-lbs.
　　　　　　　　　　　　　　(35-43 N•m)

Crankcase cover plate—
　HBKN . . . . 6-8 ft.-lbs.
　　　　　　　　　　　　　　(8-11 N•m)

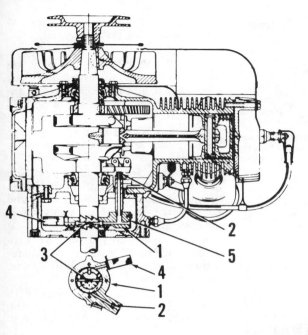

Fig. W17—Sectional view of engine oil pump as installed on vertical shaft models.

1. Pump body
2. Vertical spray jet
3. Vane assembly
4. Intake oil screen
5. Relief valve

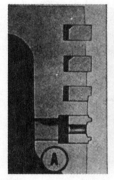

Fig. W19—Location of specification number (A) for special-type crankcase and cylinder. If number is present, add to basic part number when renewing crankcase and cylinder.

HAENL . . . . 7-9 ft.-lbs.
(10-12 N•m)

Engine adapter base—
All models . . . . 24-26 ft.-lbs.
(33-35 N•m)

Spark plug—
All models . . . . 25-30 ft.-lbs.
(34-40 N•m)

CONNECTING ROD. Connecting rod and piston assemblies can be removed from cylinder head surface end of block after removing cylinder head and side cover.

Connecting rod rides directly on crankpin journal and rods are available for 0.010, 0.020 and 0.030 inch (0.25, 0.51 and 0.76 mm) undersize crankshafts.

Rod to journal running clearance should be 0.0007-0.002 inch (0.018-0.051 mm) for all models and is controlled to some degree by varying thickness of shims between connecting rod and cap.

Connecting rod side clearance should be 0.004-0.010 inch (0.11-0.25 mm) for HBKN engines and 0.006-0.013 inch (0.15-0.33 mm) for HAENL engines.

Connecting rod on all models must be installed with oil hole in rod cap facing oil pump side of engine for proper lubrication.

Crankpin standard diameter for HBKN engines is 1.000 inch (25.4 mm) and 1.125 inches (31.75 mm) for HAENL engines.

PISTON, PIN AND RINGS. Pistons are equipped with two compression

Fig. W18—Cross section of piston rings as installed in vertical crankshaft engines. View "A" shows HBKN models and view "B" shows HAENL models.

rings, one scraper ring and one oil control ring. Install rings as shown in Fig. W18. View "A" shows ring cross section on HBKN engines and view "B" shows ring cross section on HAENL engines.

HBKN engines operated at 3000 rpm or below require a different piston than HBKN engines operating at speeds above 3000 rpm.

Ring end gap for all models should be 0.012-0.22 inch (0.31-0.56 mm) and side clearance of top ring in groove should be 0.002-0.0035 inch (0.05-0.09 mm). Side clearance of second or third ring should be 0.001-0.0025 inch (0.03-0.06 mm) and side clearance of oil control ring should be 0.0025-0.004 inch (0.06-0.11 mm). Ring gaps should be installed so they are at 90° intervals around piston.

Piston skirt clearance for HBKN engines operating at 3000 rpm or below should be 0.0055-0.006 inch (0.14-0.15 mm) and for HBKN engines operating

above 3000 rpm clearance should be 0.006-0.0065 inch (0.15-0.165 mm).

Piston skirt clearance for all HAENL engines should be 0.003-0.0035 inch (0.076-0.089 mm).

Pistons and rings are available in 0.005, 0.010, 0.020 and 0.030 inch (0.13, 0.25, 0.51 and 0.76 mm) oversizes as well as standard.

Floating-type piston pin is retained by snap rings in each end of piston and pin clearance in connecting rod for HBKN engines should be 0.0002-0.0008 inch (0.005-0.020 mm), and for HAENL engines, clearance should be 0.0005-0.001 inch (0.013-0.025 mm). Pins are available in a variety of oversizes as well as standard.

CYLINDER. Cylinder bore is an integral part of crankcase casting and, if worn or out-of-round more than 0.005 inch (0.13 mm), cylinder should be bored to nearest oversize for which piston and rings are available.

If crankcase and cylinder renewal is required, make certain number (Fig. W19) stamped as shown is added to basic part number shown in Wisconsin parts catalog when ordering new cylinder and crankcase.

CRANKSHAFT AND MAIN BEARINGS. Crankshaft on all models is supported at each end by taper roller bearings that are a press fit on crankshaft. Races are driven into bearing plate or engine block. Crankshaft end play for HBKN engines should be 0.002-0.004 inch (0.05-0.10 mm) and 0.001-0.003 inch (0.025-0.076 mm) for HAENL engines; end play is controlled on all models by varying number of gaskets between bearing plate and crankcase (Fig. W20).

Fig. W20—Crankshaft end play is controlled by number of gaskets (G) used under main bearing plate at pto end of crankcase.

HAENL engines are also equipped with a ball bearing at lower end of crankshaft that is mounted in engine adapter base below oil pump.

Install crankshaft so timing marks on crankshaft gear and camshaft gear are in register, as shown in Figs. W14 or W16.

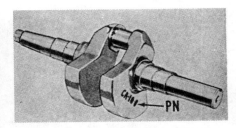

Fig. W21—When renewing crankshaft, verify part number from crankshaft being removed from engine. Number appears on counterweight as shown at PN.

If necessary to renew crankshaft, refer to Fig. W21 for location of crankshaft part number.

CAMSHAFT. The hollow camshaft turns on a stationary support pin (14—Fig. W12) and should have a running clearance of 0.001-0.0025 inch (0.025-0.063 mm). Support pin is pressed into case from flywheel end while camshaft and lifters are held in place. Camshaft plug (15) should be renewed.

Governor flyweights are attached to camshaft on all models and care should

be taken to avoid damaging them when camshaft is being installed.

VALVE SYSTEM. Valve seats are renewable-type inserts in cylinder block and seats should be ground to 45° angles. Width should be $3/32$ inch (2.38 mm).

Valve face is ground at 45° angle and stellite valves and seats, and valve rotocaps are available for some models.

Valve stem clearance in guide should be 0.003-0.005 inch (0.076-0.127 mm). All models have renewable guides and valves with oversize stems are available for some models.

Valve tappet gap (cold) for HBKN engines should be 0.008 inch (0.20 mm) for intake valve and 0.014 inch (0.35 mm) for exhaust valve.

Valve tappet gap (cold) for HAENL engines should be 0.008 inch (0.20 mm) for intake valve and 0.016 inch (0.40 mm) for exhaust valve.

Valve gap is adjusted by turning adjusting screws on tappets, if equipped, or grinding end of valve stem if nonadjustable tappets are installed.

WISCONSIN

Model	No. Cyls.	Bore	Stroke	Displacement	Power Rating
S-7D, HS-7D	1	3 in. (76.2 mm)	2.625 in. (66.68 mm)	18.6 cu. in. (304.1 cc)	7.25 hp (5.4 kW)
S-8D, HS-8D	1	3.125 in. (79.375 mm)	2.625 in. (66.68 mm)	20.2 cu. in. (330 cc)	8.25 hp (6.2 kW)
TR-10D	1	3.125 in. (79.375 mm)	2.625 in. (66.68 mm)	20.2 cu. in. (330 cc)	10 hp (7.5 kW)
TRA-10D	1	3.125 in. (79.375 mm)	2.875 in. (73.03 mm)	22.1 cu. in. (361.4 cc)	10.1 hp (7.8 kW)
S-10D	1	3.25 in. (82.55 mm)	3 in. (76.2 mm)	24.9 cu. in. (407.8 cc)	10.1 hp (7.8 kW)
TRA-12D	1	3.5 in. (88.9 mm)	2.875 in. (73.03 mm)	27.7 cu. in. (453 cc)	12 hp (9.0 kW)
S-12D	1	3.5 in. (88.9 mm)	3 in. (76.2 mm)	28.9 cu. in. (473 cc)	12.5 hp (9.3 kW)
S-14D	1	3.75 in. (95.3 mm)	3 in. (76.2 mm)	33.1 cu. in. (543.5 cc)	14.1 hp (10.5 kW)

Engines in this section are four-stroke, one cylinder engines and all models except HS-7D and HS-8D are horizontal crankshaft engines. HS-7D and HS-8D engines have an adapter base for vertical mounting. Crankshaft for all models is supported at each end in taper roller bearings.

Connecting rods used in S-10D, S-12D and S-14D engines have renewable insert-type bearings. Connecting rods on all other models ride directly on crankpin journal. All horizontal crankshaft models are splash lubricated by an oil dipper located on end of connecting rod and all vertical crankshaft models are pressure spray lubricated and have a plunger-type oil pump located on lower end of crankshaft.

Various magneto, battery or solid-state electronic ignition systems are used according to model and application.

Zenith or Walbro float-type carburetor is used and a mechanical fuel pump is available.

Engine identification information is located on engine instruction plate and engine model, specification and serial numbers are required when ordering parts.

MAINTENANCE

SPARK PLUG. Recommended spark plug is Champion D16J or equivalent. Electrode gap should be 0.030 inch (0.76 mm).

CARBURETOR. A variety of float-type carburetors are used as listed:

Zenith 72Y6 carburetor is standard on S-7D, S-8D, HS-7D and HS-8D engines. See Fig. W30.

Zenith 68-7 carburetor is standard on TR-10D and TRA-10D engines. See Fig. W31.

Walbro LME-35 carburetor is standard on TRA-12D engines. See Fig. W32.

Zenith 1408 carburetor is used on S-10D, S-12D and S-14D engines. See Fig. W33.

For initial adjustment of Zenith 72Y6 carburetor (Fig. W30), open idle mixture screw (2) ½ turn and main fuel mixture screw (10) 2 turns.

For initial adjustment of Zenith 68-7 or Walbro LME-35 carburetors, open idle mixture screw and main fuel mixture screw 1¼ turns. Refer to Figs. W31 or W32 for location of mixture screw of model being serviced.

For initial adjustment of Zenith 1408 carburetor (Fig. W33), open idle mix-

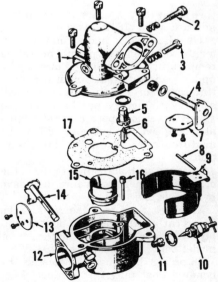

Fig. W30—Exploded view of Zenith 72Y6 carburetor used on S-7D and S-8D engines and on HS-7D and HS-8D vertical shaft engines.

1. Throttle body
2. Idle mixture needle
3. Idle speed adjusting screw
4. Throttle shaft
5. Needle valve seat
6. Needle valve
7. Throttle plate
8. Float pin
9. Float
10. Main fuel adjusting needle
11. Main jet
12. Fuel bowl
13. Choke plate
14. Choke shaft
15. Venturi
16. Idle tube
17. Gasket

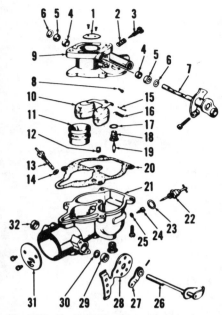

Fig. W31—Zenith 68-7 model carburetor is used on TR-10D and TRA-10D engines.

1. Throttle plate
2. Spring
3. Idle mixture needle
4. Bushing
5. Seal
6. Retainer
7. Throttle shaft
8. Idle jet
9. Throttle body
10. Float
11. Venturi
12. Well vent
13. Discharge nozzle
14. Gasket
15. Float shaft
16. Float spring
17. Gasket
18. Inlet valve seat
19. Inlet valve
20. Gasket
21. Fuel bowl
22. Main fuel needle
23. Gasket
24. Main jet
25. Gasket
26. Choke shaft
27. Choke lever
28. Bracket
29. Retainer
30. Seal
31. Choke plate
32. Plug

ture screw (5) 1½ turns and main fuel mixture screw (18) 2¼ turns.

On all models, make final adjustments with engine at normal operating temperature and running. Place engine under load and adjust main fuel mixture screw for leanest setting that will allow satisfactory acceleration and steady governor operation. Set engine at idle speed, no load and adjust idle mixture screw for smoothest idle operation.

Because each adjustment affects the other, adjustment procedure may have to be repeated.

To check float level on all models, invert carburetor body and float assembly. Refer to appropriate illustration for model being serviced (Fig. W34, W35, W36 or W37). Adjust as necessary by bending float tang that contacts inlet valve.

GOVERNOR. Flyweight-type governors driven by camshaft gear are used on all models.

Refer to Fig. W38 for S-7D, S-8D, HS-7D, HS-8D, TR-10D, TRA-10D and TRA-12D engine governor component parts, and to Fig. W39 for S-10D, S-12D

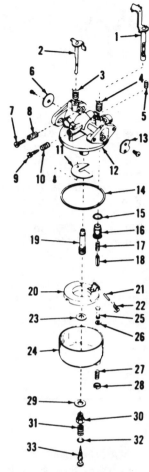

Fig. W32—Exploded view of Walbro LME-35 model carburetor used on TRA-12D engine.

1. Choke shaft
2. Throttle shaft
3. Throttle spring
4. Choke spring
5. Choke stop spring
6. Throttle plate
7. Idle speed screw
8. Spring
9. Idle mixture needle
10. Spring
11. Baffle
12. Carburetor body
13. Choke plate
14. Bowl gasket
15. Gasket
16. Inlet valve seat
17. Spring
18. Inlet valve
19. Main nozzle
20. Float
21. Float shaft
22. Spring
23. Gasket
24. Bowl
25. Drain stem
26. Gasket
27. Spring
28. Retainer
29. Gasket
30. Bowl retainer
31. Spring
32. "O" ring
33. Main fuel needle

and S-14D engine governor component parts.

Major speed changes on all models are obtained by using springs of varying tension, flyweights of varying weights or locating spring or governor rod in alternate holes of governor control lever.

To correctly set governed speeds, use a tachometer to accurately record crankshaft rpm. Refer to appropriate table (I through IV) corresponding to engine model being serviced to determine proper governor lever hole for attaching governor spring to set required speed.

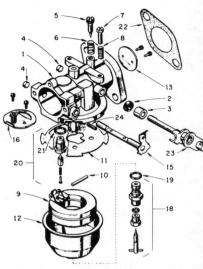

Fig. W33—Exploded view of Zenith 1408 model carburetor that is used on S-10D, S-12D and S-14D engines.

1. Carburetor body
2. Throttle shaft seal
3. Seal retainer
4. Cup plugs
5. Idle fuel needle
6. Spring
7. Idle speed stop screw
8. Spring
9. Float assy.
10. Float pin
11. Gasket
12. Fuel bowl
13. Throttle disc
15. Choke shaft
16. Choke disc
18. Main jet needle assy.
19. Washer
20. Inlet valve & seat assy.
21. Gasket
22. Gasket
23. Throttle shaft
24. Choke lever friction spring

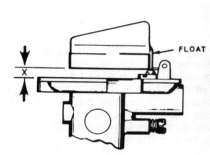

Fig. W34—Zenith 72Y6 carburetor float must be parallel to casting. Dimension "X" should be the same, measured near hinge pin and at outer end of float.

Table I—Models S-7D, S-8D

Engines to and including Serial Number 3909151

Desired Rpm Under Load	Hole Number	Adjust No-Load Rpm To
1600	3	1880
1700	3	1940
1800	3	1990
1900	3	2080
2000	4	2260
2100	4	2360
2200	4	2410
2300	4	2510
2400	4	2590
2500	4	2680
2600	5	2830

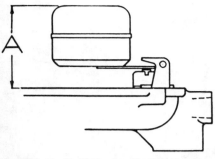

Fig. W35—Zenith 68-7 carburetor float should be adjusted so dimension "A" is 1-5/32 inch (29 mm).

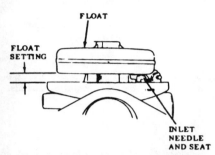

Fig. W36—Walbro LME-35 carburetor float should have 5/32-inch (4 mm) space between free end of float and gasket surface as shown.

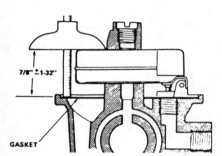

Fig. W37—Zenith 1408 carburetor float measurement should be 7/8 inch (22 mm) plus or minus 1/32 inch (0.8 mm) when measured as shown with gasket in place.

2700	5	2920
2800	5	2970
*2900	6	3040
*3000	6	3230
*3100	6	3330
*3200	6	3420
*3300	6	3510
*3400	6	3590
*3500	7	3750
*3600	7	3840

From 1600 to 2800 rpm, use 5¼-inch adjusting screw.

Above 2900 rpm (*), use 5-inch adjusting screw.

Engines beginning with Serial Number 3909152

Desired Rpm Under Load	Hole Number	Adjust No-Load Rpm To:
1800	2	2030
1900	2	2125

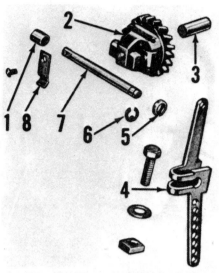

Fig. W38—Exploded view of governor assembly typical of that used on Models S-7D, HS-7D, S-8D, HS-8D, TR-10D, TRA-10D and TRA-12D.

1. Spacer		5. Oil seal
2. Gear/flyweight assy.		6. Retaining ring
3. Governor shaft		7. Fulcrum shaft
4. Governor lever		8. Vane

2000	2	2220
2100	2	2320
2200	3	2430
2300	3	2520
2400	4	2690
2500	4	2720
2600	4	2845
2700	4	2930
2800	4	3010
2900	5	3150
*3000	5	3230

*3100	5	3300
*3200	5	3350
*3300	6	3575
*3400	6	3650
*3500	6	3750
*3600	6	3800

From 1800 to 2900 rpm, use 5⅝-inch adjusting screw.

Above 3000 rpm (*), use 5¼-inch adjusting screw.

Table II—Models HS-7D, HS-8D

Desired Rpm Under Load	Hole Number	Adjust No-Load Rpm To:
1800	4	2200
1900	4	2290
2000	4	2380
2100	4	2465
2200	4	2550
2300	5	2690
2400	5	2770
2500	5	2850
2600	6	3000
2700	6	3060
2800	6	3120
2900	6	3200
*3000	6	3280
*3100	6	3340
*3200	6	3400
*3300	7	3560
*3400	7	3620
*3500	7	3685
*3600	7	3750

From 1800 to 2900 rpm, use 5⅝-inch adjusting screw.

Above 3000 rpm (*), use 5¼-inch adjusting screw.

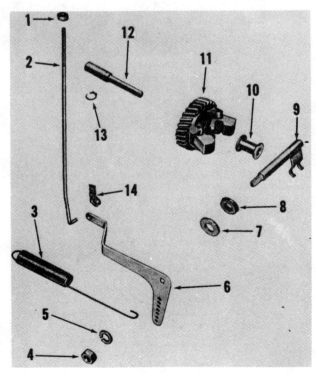

Fig. W39—Governor mechanism as used on Models S-10D, S-12D and S-14D. Refer to text for service information.

1. Locknut
2. Throttle rod
3. Governor spring
4. Nut
5. Lockwasher
6. Governor lever
7. Flat washer
8. Oil seal
9. Cross (fulcrum) shaft
10. Thrust sleeve
11. Gear weight assy.
12. Shaft
13. Snap ring
14. Clip

Table III—Models TRA-10D,
TRA-12D, TR-10D
Use Lever Spring Hole Number and
Set No Load Rpm:

Desired Rpm Under Load	TRA-10D**		TRA-12D	
2000	1	2520	3	2230
2100	1	1580	4	2430
2200	1	2610	4	2515
2300	1	2690	4	2590
2400	1	2740	4	2660
2500	1	2800	4	2750
2600	1	2890	4	2810
2700	1	2935	5	3020
2800	2	3065	5	3100
2900	2	3160	5	3180
*3000	3	3230	5	3260
*3100	3	3300	5	3325
*3200	3	3380	6	3535
*3300	3	3460	6	3620
*3400	4	3615	6	3700
*3500	4	3690	6	3790
*3600	5	3850	6	3860

**Applies to TR-10D engines Serial No. 3909152 and after.

From 2000 to 2900 rpm, TRA-10D uses 3⅝-inch adjusting screw; TRA-12D uses 5⅝-inch adjusting screw.

Above 3000 rpm (*), TRA-10D uses 5-inch adjusting screw; TRA-12D uses 5¼-inch adjusting screw.

Table IV—Models S-10D, S-12D, S-14D

Desired Rpm Under Load	Hole Number	Adjust No-Load Rpm To:
1600	1	1760
1800	2	1975
1900	2	2040
2000	2	2120
2100	3	2260
2200	3	2340
2300	3	2400
2400	4	2580
2500	4	2650
2600	4	2720
2700	4	2810
2800	5	2910
2900	5	3010
*3000	6	3150
*3100	6	3230
*3200	7	3360
*3300	7	3455
*3400	7	3520
*3500	7	3590
*3600	7	3680

From 1600 to 2900 rpm, use 3¹⁵⁄₁₆-inch adjusting screw.

Above 3000 rpm (*), use 3⅝-inch adjusting screw.

IGNITION SYSTEM. Various magneto, battery or solid-state electronic ignition systems are used according to

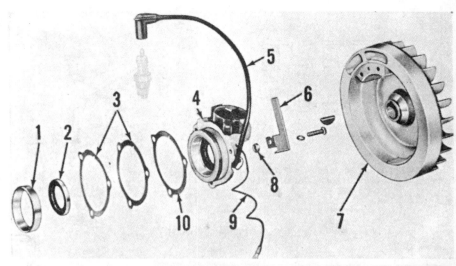

Fig. W40—Typical flywheel magneto assembly. Note crankshaft end play is adjusted by shims (3) that are offered in a variety of thicknesses. Flywheel must be removed for access to magneto stator plate.

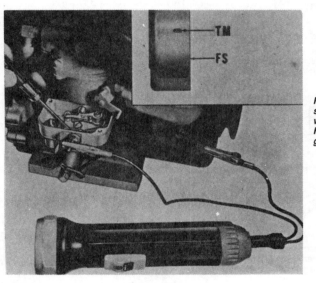

Fig. W41—Timing mark (TM) should appear in hole in flywheel shroud (FS) on S-7D and HS-7D engines as timing light goes out.

model and application. Refer to appropriate paragraph for model being service.

MAGNETO. Either Fairbanks-Morse or Wico magneto assemblies, located under the flywheel (Fig. W40), are used. Points and condenser are located in an external breaker box (Figs. W41 or W42) and are actuated by camshaft lobe via a short push rod.

Initial point gap 0.018-0.020 inch (0.46-0.51 mm) and point gap is varied slightly to obtain correct timing as outlined in **BATTERY IGNITION** section.

BATTERY IGNITION. Battery ignition system uses a conventional ignition coil, and points and condenser are the same as used for magneto system. Points and condenser location remains the same (Figs. W41 and W42). Initial point gap is 0.023 inch (0.58 mm) and

gap is varied slightly to obtain correct engine timing.

To set timing on either magneto system or battery system, position engine flywheel so timing marks appear in hole in flywheel shroud (Fig. W41) or align with timing pointer (Fig. W42), connect test light across points and adjust point gap so light just goes out.

Timing should be set at 15° BTDC on S-7D and HS-7D engines and 18° BTDC on all remaining models.

SOLID-STATE ELECTRONIC IGNITION. Breakerless capacitive-discharge (CD) ignition system is available for S-10D, S-12D and S-14D engines and is standard ignition system for TRA-12D engines.

No adjustments are possible and system has only three components: magnet (part of flywheel), stator (containing trigger coil, rectifier diode and a sili-

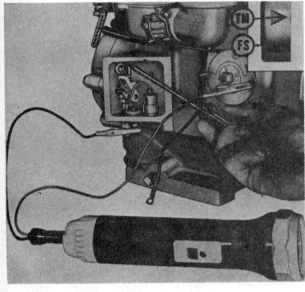

Fig. W42—Timing mark (TM) should be aligned with timing pointer on flywheel shroud (FS) on all models except S-7D and HS-7D engines as timing light just goes out. Refer to Fig. W41 for S-7D and HS-7D engines.

Fig. W43—Piston (P) is removed from top. Oil dipper (D) provides lubrication for horizontal crankshaft engines. Note placement of connecting rod index arrow at (A), location of governor shaft (GS) and that camshaft gear is fitted with a compression release (CR), typical of TR-TRA and larger models.

cone-controlled rectifier) located on bearing plate at flywheel side of engine and a special ignition coil.

If visual inspection of component parts fail to find possible cause of an ignition failure, a continuity test of ignition switch and coil should be made. If switch and coil are in working order, but ignition system still fails, renew stator.

LUBRICATION. All horizontal crankshaft models are splash lubricated by an oil dipper attached to connecting rod cap. All vertical crankshaft models are pressure spray lubricated by a plunger-type oil pump fitted to lower end of crankshaft.

Maintain oil level at full mark on dipstick or level with filler plug as equipped, but do not overfill. High-quality detergent oil, having API classification SF or SG, is recommended. Oil change interval is recommended at every 50 hours of normal operation.

Use SAE 30 oil when operating temperature is between 120° F (49° C) and 40° F (4° C), SAE 20 oil between 40° F (4° C) and 15° (–9° C), SAE 10 oil between 15° (–9° C) and 0° F (–18° C) and SAE 5W-20 oil for below 0° F (–18° C) temperature.

REPAIRS

TIGHTENING TORQUES. Recommended tightening torques are as follows:

Models S-7D, S-8D, HS-7D and HS-8D

Gear cover	8 ft.-lbs. (11 N•m)
Stator plate	8 ft.-lbs. (11 N•m)
Connecting rod	18 ft.-lbs. (24 N•m)

Spark plug	29 ft.-lbs. (39 N•m)
Cylinder head	18 ft.-lbs. (24 N•m)

Models TR-10D, TRA-10D and TRA-12D

Gear cover	8 ft.-lbs. (11 N•m)
Stator plate	8 ft.-lbs. (11 N•m)
Connecting rod	22 ft.-lbs. (30 N•m)
Spark plug	29 ft.-lbs. (39 N•m)
Flywheel nut	55 ft.-lbs. (75 N•m)
Cylinder head	18 ft.-lbs. (24 N•m)

Models S-10D, S-12D and S-14D

Gear cover	18 ft.-lbs. (24 N•m)
Stator plate	18 ft.-lbs. (24 N•m)
Connecting rod	32 ft.-lbs. (43 N•m)
Spark plug	29 ft.-lbs. (39 N•m)
Flywheel nut	55 ft.-lbs. (75 N•m)
Cylinder block nut	50 ft.-lbs. (68 N•m)
Cylinder head	32 ft.-lbs. (43 N•m)

CYLINDER HEAD. Always install a new head gasket when installing cylinder head. Note different lengths and styles of studs and cap screws for correct reinstallation and lightly lubricate threads.

Cylinder heads should be tightened in three equal steps to recommended torque using a crisscross pattern working from the center out.

Fig. W44—Open view of typical S-10D, S-12D or S-14D engine. Compare to Fig. W43. Note difference in placement of governor shaft, style of oil dipper and that cylinder and crankcase are separate castings. Flywheel should be left in place to balance crankshaft when gear cover is removed.

CONNECTING ROD. Connecting rod and piston are removed from cylinder head end of block after removing head and crankcase side cover. See Figs. W43 or W44.

Connecting rod for all models except S-10D, S-12D or S-14D ride directly on crankpin journal. Connecting rods on

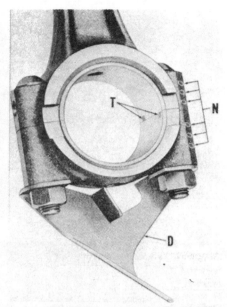

Fig. W45—Install connecting rod cap (S-10D, S-12D and S-14D) so tangs (T) of bearing inserts are on same side. Numbers (N) on rod end and cap should be aligned and installed toward gear cover side of crankcase. Oil dipper (D) open side faces outward.

should be 1.3750-1.3755 inches (34.93-34.94 mm), standard crankpin diameter for S-8D, HS-8D, TR-10D, TRA-10D and TRA-12D should be 1.3755-1.3760 inches (34.94-34.95 mm) and standard diameter for S-10D, S-12D and S-14D models should be 1.4984-1.4990 inches (38.06-38.08 mm).

Connecting rods or bearing inserts are available in a variety of sizes to fit reground crankshafts.

PISTON, PIN AND RINGS. Camground piston for all models is equipped with one chrome-faced compression ring, one scraper ring and an oil control ring (Fig. W46). Top side of rings are marked for correct installation. Ring end gap for all models should be 0.010-0.020 inch (0.25-0.50 mm) and ring end gaps should be spaced at 120° intervals around piston. A variety of oversize pistons and rings are available.

Ring side clearance in groove for S-10D, S-12D and S-14D should be: Top and second ring, 0.002-0.004 inch (0.051-0.101 mm) and for oil control ring, 0.0015-0.0035 inch (0.038-0.089 mm).

Ring side clearance in groove for all remaining models should be: Top ring, 0.002-0.0035 inch (0.051-0.089 mm), second ring, 0.001-0.0025 inch (0.025-0.063 mm) and oil control ring, 0.002-0.0035 inch (0.051-0.089 mm).

Piston to cylinder clearance should be measured at 90° angle to piston pin at lower edge of skirt. Clearance for S-7D, S-8D, HS-7D, HS-8D, TR-10D and TRA-10D models should be 0.004-0.0045 inch (0.1016-0.1143 mm), clearance for TRA-12D, S-10D and S-12D models should be 0.0025-0.003 inch (0.064-0.076 mm) and clearance for S-14D model should be 0.0025-0.004 inch (0.064-0.101 mm).

Floating-type piston pin is retained by snap rings in bore of piston and should have 0.0002-0.0008 inch (0.005-

Fig. W47—Location of specification number (A) on engines with cylinder cast as an integral part of crankcase.

0.020 mm) clearance in connecting rod of all models except S-10D, S-12D and S-14D, which use a bushing in connecting rod end and clearance in bushing should be 0.0005-0.0011 inch (0.013-0.028 mm).

Pins are available in a variety of oversizes as well as standard. Connecting rod end or bushing and piston pin bore must be reamed to fit available oversize pin.

CYLINDER. The cylinder is an integral part of crankcase casting for S-7D, S-8D, HS-7D, HS-8D, TR-10D, TRA-10D and TRA-12D models (Fig. W47), but is a separate casting bolted to crankcase for S-10D, S-12D and S-14D models (Fig. W44).

Standard cylinder bore diameter for S-7D and HS-7D models should be 3 inches (76.2 mm), standard diameter for S-8D, HS-8D, TR-10D and TRA-10D models should be 3.125 inches (79.38 mm), standard diameter for S-10D model should be 3.25 inches (82.55 mm), standard diameter for TRA-12D and S-12D models should be 3.5 inches (88.9 mm) and standard diameter for S-14D model should be 3.75 inches (95.2 mm).

Cylinder should be bored to nearest oversize for which piston and rings are available if worn or out-of-round more than 0.005 inch (0.13 mm).

Cylinder section of two-piece assembly is bolted to crankcase section and one cap screw is concealed within valve spring compartment. See Fig. W54. Tighten concealed cap screw to 32 ft.-lbs. (43 N•m) torque and all remaining stud nuts to 42-50 ft.-lbs. (57-68 N•m) torque.

the S-10D, S-12D and S-14D models have renewable insert-type bearings.

Running clearance for insert-type bearings should be 0.0005-0.0015 inch (0.013-0.038 mm). Running clearance for S-7D and HS-7D models rod should be 0.0012-0.002 inch (0.031-0.051 mm), for S-8D and HS-8D models clearance should be 0.0007-0.0015 inch (0.018-0.038 mm) and clearance for all TR and TRA models should be 0.0005-0.0015 inch (0.013-0.038 mm).

Side clearance for connecting rods with insert-type bearings should be 0.004-0.013 inch (0.10-0.33 mm). Side clearance for S-7D, HS-7D, S-8D and HS-8D models should be 0.006-0.013 inch (0.15-0.33 mm) and side clearance for all TR and TRA models should be 0.009-0.016 inch (0.23-0.40 mm).

When installing piston and connecting rod assembly on models that are not equipped with renewable bearing inserts, align index arrows (A—Fig. W43) on rod end and cap. Arrows must face toward open end of crankcase. Horizontal shaft engines that are equipped with oil dipper (D) should have dipper installed so connecting rod cap screws are accessible from open end of crankcase. Refer to Fig. W45 when assembling cap to connecting rod on S-10D, S-12D and S-14D models, and make certain fitting tangs (T) are on same side as shown. Stamped numbers (N) and oil dipper (D) should face open side of crankcase.

Standard connecting rod journal diameter for S-7D and HS-7D models

Fig. W46—Cross-sectional view showing proper arrangement of piston rings. In this typical view, top ring may not be chamfered inside as shown, but all rings are marked with "TOP" or pit mark for correct installation.

CRANKSHAFT, MAIN BEARINGS AND SEALS. Crankshaft on all models is supported at each end by ta-

Fig. W48—Locate timing mark (A) on camshaft gear between two marked teeth (B) of crankshaft gear. View is typical of S-7D, S-8D and all TR and TRA engines.

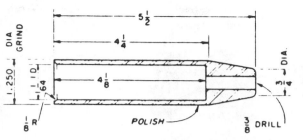

SLEEVE FOR ASSEMBLING GEAR COVER WITH OIL SEAL ON TO CRANKSHAFT

Fig. W50—Dimensions of seal protector sleeve to be used on S-7D, S-8D, HS-7D, HS-8D, TR-10D, TRA-10D and TRA-12D models.

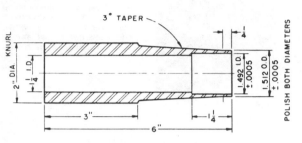

SLEEVE FOR ASSEMBLING GEAR COVER WITH OIL SEAL, ON TO CRANKSHAFT.

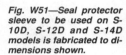

Fig. W51—Seal protector sleeve to be used on S-10D, S-12D and S-14D models is fabricated to dimensions shown.

Fig. W49—View of timing marks lined up in S-10D, S-12D and S-14D engines. In current production, camshaft gear will support a compression release mechanism as shown in Fig. W56. Camshaft thrust spring (S) and governor thrust sleeve (10) must be in place before installation of gear cover. Use heavy grease to hold camshaft thrust ball in cover hole during installation.

per roller bearings. Crankshaft end play should be 0.001-0.004 inch (0.025-0.101 mm) and is controlled by varying number of shims between crankcase and stator plate (main bearing support). See Fig. W40.

Main bearings are a press fit on crankshaft and bearing cups are pressed into stator plate and crankcase. Bearings and cups must be fully seated to correctly set crankshaft end play.

To properly time crankshaft to related engine components during installation, refer to Fig. W48 or Fig. W49 according to model being serviced.

Seals should be installed in stator plate and crankcase prior to crankshaft installation. Seal protectors (Fig. W50 or Fig. W51) should be used to prevent

seal damage during crankshaft installation.

GOVERNOR GEAR AND WEIGHT ASSEMBLY. Governor gear and weight assemblies rotate on a shaft that is a press fit in a bore of crankcase. Exploded views are shown in Figs. W38 and W39. On S-7D, S-8D, HS-7D, HS-8D and all TR and TRA models, shaft (3—Fig. W38) has had its depth in block held by a snap ring beginning with production serial number 3090152. Models S-10D, S-12D and S-14D require end play of 0.003-0.005 inch (0.076-0.127 mm) be maintained on governor gear shaft between gear and its snap ring retainer. See Fig. W52 for measurement technique to be used on these models. Press-fit shaft is driven in or out of bore to make adjustment. On models with straight governor lever and governor gear mounted above cam gear, note in Fig. W53 upper end of governor lever must tilt toward engine so governor vane will not be fouled or interfere with flyweights as gear cover is installed. On S-10D, S-12D and S-14D models, governor thrust sleeve must be in place as shown in Fig. W54 when gear cover is placed in position.

CAMSHAFT. Camshaft on all models is supported at each end in unbushed bores in crankcase and gear cover. Camshaft end play is controlled by a thrust spring (Figs. W53 and W54) fitted into shaft hub that centers upon steel ball in

Fig. W52—Make certain snap ring is correctly seated and use feeler gage to measure end play of governor gear on shaft.

a socket in gear cover. During assembly, ball is held in place by a coating of heavy grease. To remove or reinstall camshaft, place block on its side as shown in Fig. W55 to prevent tappets from falling out.

On models equipped with a compression-release-type camshaft (Fig. W56), a spoiler cam holds exhaust valve slightly open during part of compression stroke while cranking. Reduced compression pressure allows for faster cranking speed with lower effort. When crankshaft reaches 650 rpm during cranking, centrifugal force swings flyweight on front of cam gear so as to turn spoiler cam to inoperative position allowing exhaust valve to seat and restore full compression. Whenever camshaft is removed, compression release mechanism should be checked for damage to

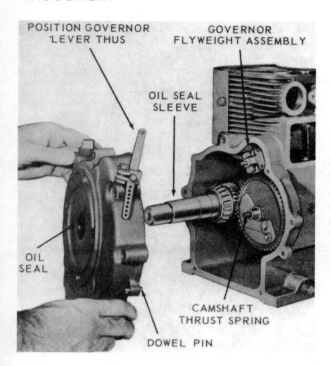

Fig. W53—To install gear cover on all models where cylinder is an integral part of crankcase, governor assembly, camshaft thrust spring and oil seal protector must be in place. Make certain governor lever is tilted as shown and governor thrust ball is held in cover with heavy grease.

Fig. W55—Place engine on its side as shown to prevent tappets dropping from block bores when camshaft is removed.

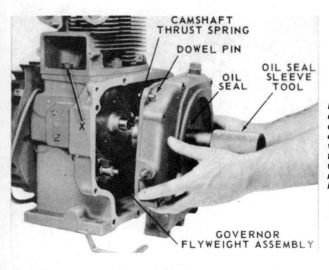

Fig. W54—Installation of gear cover on engines where cylinder is separate from crankcase. Note cap screw (X) in valve compartment, referred to in text. Protect cover oil seal with sleeve tool as shown and make certain thrust sleeve is in place on governor shaft.

Intake and exhaust valve faces are ground at 45° angles. Stellite exhaust valves and rotocaps are standard on all models.

Renewable guides are pressed in or out from top side of block. Tool DF-72 guide driver is available from Wisconsin. Internal chamfered end of guide is installed toward tappet end of valve.

Inside diameter of valve guides should be 0.312-0.313 inch (7.93-7.95 mm). Valve stem diameter should be 0.310-0.311 inch (7.87-7.90 mm) for all intake valves and 0.309-0.310 inch (7.85-7.87 mm) for all exhaust valves except for S-10D, S-12D and S-14D exhaust valves, which should be 0.308-0.309 inch (7.82-7.85 mm).

Maximum stem to guide clearance for all models except S-10D, S-12D and S-14D should be 0.006 inch (0.15 mm). Clearance for S-10D, S-12D and S-14D models should be 0.007 inch (0.18 mm).

Valve tappet gap (cold) for S-10D, S-12D and S-14D should be 0.007 inch (0.18 mm) for intake valves and 0.016 inch (0.40 mm) for exhaust valves. Ad-

spring or excessive wear on spoiler cam. Flyweight and spoiler cam must move easily with no binding.

See Figs. W48 and W49 to set timing marks in register during reassembly.

VALVE SYSTEM. Exhaust valve seats on all models are renewable insert-type. Intake seat may be machined directly into block or be of renewable insert-type according to model and application. Valve seats should be ground to a 45° angle and width should not exceed 3/32 inch (2.381 mm).

Fig. W56—View of both sides of camshaft gear to show compression release assembly installed.

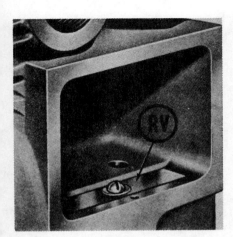

Fig. W57—Reed-type breather valve located in valve spring compartment of S-7D, S-8D, HS-7D, HS-8D, TR-10D, TRA-10D and TRA-12D models.

just by turning self-locking cap screw on tappet as required.

Valve tappet gap (cold) for all remaining models should be 0.006 inch (0.15 mm) for intake and 0.012 inch (0.30 mm) for all exhaust valves except ones used on TRA-12D models, which should be 0.015 inch (0.38 mm). Adjustment is made by carefully grinding valve stem end until required clearance is reached.

BREATHER. A reed-type breather valve (Fig. W57 or Fig. W58) is located in valve spring compartment. These reed valve assemblies should be kept clean and renewed whenever found to be inoperable.

If oil fouling occurs in ignition breaker box, condition of breather valve should be checked.

Fig. W58—Breather valve used on S-10D, S-12D and S-14D models is located in valve spring compartment cover. Drain hole (H) must be kept open.

WISCONSIN

Model	No. Cyls.	Bore	Stroke	Displacement	Power Rating
TE	2	3.0 in. (76.2 mm)	3.25 in. (82.6 mm)	45.9 cu. in. (753 cc)	11.2 hp (8.4 kW)
TF	2	3.25 in. (82.6 mm)	3.25 in. (82.6 mm)	53.9 cu. in. (883.6 cc)	14.6 hp (10.9 kW)
TH, THD	2	3.25 in. (82.6 mm)	3.25 in. (82.6 mm)	53.9 cu. in. (883.6 cc)	18 hp (13.4 kW)
TJD	2	3.25 in. (82.6 mm)	3.25 in. (82.6 mm)	53.9 cu. in. (883.6 cc)	18.2 hp (13.6 kW)
W2-880	2	3.25 in. (82.6 mm)	3.25 in. (82.6 mm)	53.9 cu. in. (883.6 cc)	20 hp (15 kW)

Engines in this section are four-stroke, two-cylinder, air-cooled engines with a horizontal crankshaft. Crankshaft is supported at each end by taper roller bearings.

Connecting rods in early models ride directly on crankpin journal and shims between rod cap and rod provide running clearance adjustment. Connecting rods in later models and replacement connecting rods for early models are equipped with renewable insert-type bearings. Pressure spray lubrication is provided by a plunger-type oil pump driven off a camshaft lobe.

Ignition system consists of a battery-type system that uses breaker points, an electronic trigger system or one of a variety of magneto systems.

A Marvel Schebler, Walbro or Zenith float-type carburetor is used. A mechanical fuel pump is available.

Engine information provided on engine identification plate may be required when ordering parts.

MAINTENANCE

LUBRICATION. Pressure spray lubrication is provided by a plunger-type oil pump that is driven off a camshaft lobe. Oil is also pumped through an external oil line and orifice to governor mechanism and timing gears.

Maintain oil level at full mark on dipstick or at top of filler plug, but do not overfill. Oil should be changed after every 50 hours of operation. Change oil more frequently if engine undergoes severe operation.

Manufacturer recommends oil with an API service classification of SE, SF or SG. Use SAE 30 oil for ambient temperatures above 40° F (4° C); use SAE 20-20W oil for temperatures between 40° F (4° C) and 15° F (–9° C); use SAE 10W oil for temperatures between 15° F (–9° C) and 0° F (–18° C); below 0° F (–18° C), use SAE 5W-20.

SPARK PLUG. Recommended spark plug is Champion D16J or equivalent. Electrode gap should be 0.030 inch (0.76 mm). Tighten spark plug to 24-26 ft.-lbs. (33-35 N•m).

CARBURETOR. A variety of float-type carburetors are used.

A Zenith 161-7 carburetor is used on Model TE and TF engines.

A Zenith 68-7 carburetor is used on Model TH, THD and TJD engines. However, some Model TJD engines are equipped with a Marvel Schebler TSX-954 or Walbro LUB carburetor.

Model W2-880 engines are equipped with a Walbro LMH-33 carburetor.

Refer to following paragraphs for service information.

Marvel Schebler TSX. Main fuel jet is fixed so no adjustment, other than replacement, is possible. Initial setting of idle mixture screw is 1 turn out. Make final adjustment with engine at normal operating temperature. Adjust idle mixture screw so engine idles smoothly and accelerates cleanly.

To check float level, invert carburetor body and measure from gasket on gasket surface to near side of float farthest away from pivot. Measurement should be 1/4 inch (6.4 mm). Bend float tang to obtain correct float level.

Zenith 68-7 and 161-7. Main fuel jet is fixed so no adjustment, other than replacement, is possible. Initial setting of idle mixture screw is 1 1/4 turns out on Zenith 68-7 carburetor and 1 turn out on Zenith 161-7 carburetor. Make final adjustment with engine at normal operating temperature. Adjust idle mixture screw so engine idles smoothly and accelerates cleanly.

To check float level, invert carburetor body and measure from machined surface of cover (no gasket) to high point of float farthest from pivot. Float level on 68-7 carburetor should be 1 5/32 inches (29.4 mm), plus or minus 1/16 inch (1.6 mm). Float level on 161-7 carburetor should be 1 5/32 inches (29.4 mm), plus or minus 3/64 inch (1.2 mm). Bend float tang to obtain correct float level.

Walbro LMH. Main fuel jet is fixed so no adjustment, other than replacement, is possible. Initial setting of idle mixture screw is 1 turn out. Make final adjustment with engine at normal operating temperature. Adjust idle mixture screw so engine idles smoothly and accelerates cleanly.

Refer to Fig. W71 for an exploded view of carburetor. Do not clean with carburetor solvent because internal passages will be damaged. Install throttle plate (10) so "W" stamped on plate is

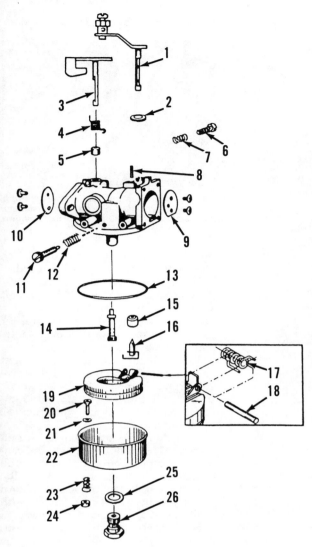

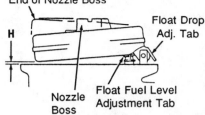

Fig. W72—Float height (H) on Walbro LMH should be 0.030-0.070 inch (0.76-1.78 mm).

Fig. W71—Exploded view of Walbro LMH.

1. Choke shaft
2. Washer
3. Throttle shaft
4. Spring
5. Seal
6. Idle speed screw
7. Spring
8. Choke stop spring
9. Choke plate
10. Throttle plate
11. Idle mixture screw
12. Spring
13. Gasket
14. Nozzle
15. Fuel inlet valve seat
16. Fuel inlet valve
17. Float spring
18. Float pin
19. Float
20. Drain pin
21. Gasket
22. Fuel bowl
23. Spring
24. Retainer
25. Gasket
26. Main jet

for attaching governor spring to set required engine speed. Note that hole numbers are counted from pivot (inner) end of lever.

Models TE, TF

Desired Rpm Under Load	Hole Number	Adjust No-Load Rpm To:
1400	2	1550
1500	3	1650
1600	3	1725
1700	4	1850
1800	4	1925
1900	5	2025
2000	6	2150
2100	6	2225
2200	7	2350
2300	7	2425
2400	8	2550
2500	9	2650
2600	9	2725

Models TH, THD, TJD

Desired Rpm Under Load	Hole Number	Adjust No-Load Rpm To:
1600	3	1725
1700	3	1800
1800	4	1925
1900	4	2000
2000	5	2140
2100	5	2210
2200	6	2365
2300	6	2420
2400	7	2540
2500	8	2675
2600*	6	2775
2700	6	2870
2800	6	2935
2900	7	3090
3000	7	3160
3100	7	3230
3200	8	3390
3300	8	3430
3400	9	3590
3500	9	3640
3600	10	3775

From 1600 to 2500 rpm, use 20-coil spring PM-75

out when plate is in closed position and opposite idle mixture screw. With carburetor body inverted, float height (H—Fig. W72) should be 0.030-0.070 inch (0.76-1.78 mm). With carburetor upright, outer end of float should be even with nozzle boss, within 0.060 inch (1.5 mm), as shown by float drop in Fig. W72.

Walbro LUB. Carburetor may be equipped with a fixed, nonadjustable main jet or an adjustable high-speed mixture screw. Initial setting of idle mixture screw is 1 turn out. Initial setting of main fuel mixture screw, if so equipped, is 1⅛ turns out. Make final adjustment with engine at normal operating temperature. Adjust idle mixture screw so engine idles smoothly. Adjust high-speed mixture screw to obtain best performance at rated speed.

Refer to Fig. W73 for an exploded view of carburetor. Do not clean with carburetor solvent. Install choke and

throttle plates so numbers are out when plate is in closed position. Round opening in gasket (12) must fit in groove on venturi (11). Notch on venturi must be toward fuel inlet valve so main nozzle in fuel body (17) will fit in notch during assembly. Measure float height (H—Fig. W74) with throttle body (7) inverted. Float height should be 1 inch (25.4 mm). Bend float arm to obtain correct float height.

GOVERNOR. A flyweight-type governor, driven by the camshaft gear, is used on all models. Major speed changes on all models are obtained by using springs of varying tension, flyweights of varying weights or locating spring or governor rod in alternate holes of governor control lever.

To correctly set governed speeds, use a tachometer to accurately record engine rpm. Refer to following tables to determine proper governor lever hole

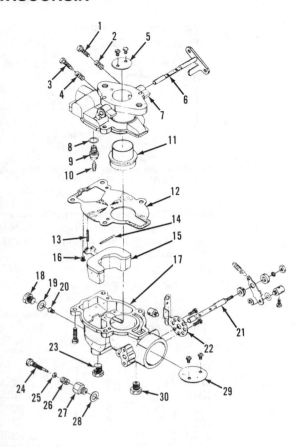

1. Idle speed screw
2. Spring
3. Idle mixture screw
4. Spring
5. Throttle plate
6. Throttle shaft
7. Throttle body
8. Gasket
9. Fuel inlet valve seat
10. Fuel inlet valve
11. Venturi
12. Gasket
13. Spring
14. Float pin
15. Float
16. Screw
17. Fuel body
18. Plug
19. Gasket
20. Main jet
21. Choke shaft
22. Plate
23. Plug
24. High-speed mixture screw
25. Gasket
26. Spring
27. Adapter
28. Gasket
29. Choke plate
30. Plug

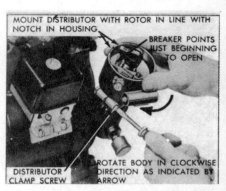

Fig. W75—View to show distributor alignment in static timing procedure. See text. Note distributor is driven through generator shift of model shown.

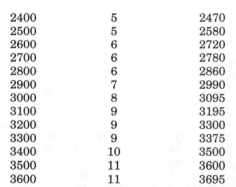

Fig. W74—Float height (H) on Walbro LUB should be 1 inch (25.4 mm).

From 2600 to 3600 rpm, use 24-coil spring PM-76

*Model TH must not exceed 2600 rpm under load.

Model W2-880

Desired Rpm Under Load	Hole Number	Adjust No-Load Rpm To:
1600	2	1700
1700	2	1800
1800	2	1890
1900	3	2000
2000	3	2075
2100	3	2160
2200	4	2270
2300	4	2370
2400	5	2470
2500	5	2580
2600	6	2720
2700	6	2780
2800	6	2860
2900	7	2990
3000	8	3095
3100	9	3195
3200	9	3300
3300	9	3375
3400	10	3500
3500	11	3600
3600	11	3695

Governor-to-carburetor rod should be adjusted so it will just enter hole in governor lever when governor weights are "in" and carburetor throttle is wide open.

IGNITION SYSTEM. The engine may be equipped with a magneto-type ignition system or a battery-type ignition system. Later battery-type ignition systems are equipped with a breakerless, solid-state trigger system.

BATTERY IGNITION. Models With Breaker Points. On models equipped with breaker points, the breaker points are located inside a distributor that may be mounted to a gear-driven generator (Fig. W75) or on an adapter attached to gear cover at magneto mounting loca-

tion. Points should be set at 0.020 inch (0.51 mm) on all models so equipped.

Distributor rotates in a counterclockwise direction at one-half crankshaft speed. Automatic advance flyweights pivot on distributor shaft below breaker point mounting plate to provide automatic timing advance.

To set timing, connect timing light and, with engine running slightly above 2000 rpm, timing should be set at 27° BTDC on TE and TF engines and 20° BTDC on TH, THD and TJD engines. Refer to Fig. W76.

To install distributor, make certain number "1" cylinder is at top dead center on compression stroke and install distributor as shown in Fig. W75. Rotate distributor counterclockwise until points just open. Set final timing with timing light as previously outlined.

Breakerless Ignition System. Models TJD and W2-880 may be equipped with a breakerless, battery ignition system. The system is identical to the battery ignition system that uses breaker points (the ignition coil is also the same), but a magnet assembly is located in the distributor to send a trigger signal to the ignition control module. Note that the red distributor wire is connected to the positive terminal of the ignition coil and the blue or black wire is connected to the negative terminal of the ignition coil.

To set timing, connect timing light and, with engine running slightly above 2000 rpm, timing should be set at 20° BTDC on TJD and W2-880 engines. Refer to Fig. W76.

To check ignition system, connect positive lead of a DC voltmeter to negative terminal of ignition coil and ground negative lead to engine. Detach high-voltage lead from distributor cap and connect to engine ground. When engine is cranked, the voltmeter should indicate voltage fluctuations from approximately 1.5 volts to 11 volts. If voltmeter indicates a constant zero voltage, pri-

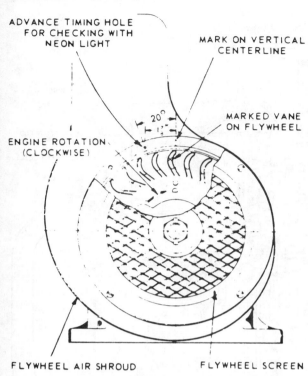

ADVANCE TIMING HOLE FOR CHECKING WITH NEON LIGHT

MARK ON VERTICAL CENTERLINE

MARKED VANE ON FLYWHEEL

ENGINE ROTATION (CLOCKWISE)

20°

FLYWHEEL AIR SHROUD

FLYWHEEL SCREEN

Fig. W76—View of flywheel timing marks for static timing of battery ignition system. Refer to text for correct running timing adjustment procedure.

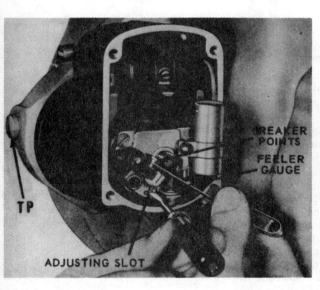

BREAKER POINTS

FEELER GAUGE

TP

ADJUSTING SLOT

Fig. W77—Adjustment procedure for magneto breaker points. Magneto shown is typical for TJD and W2-880 models. Timing plug (TP) must be removed so marked tooth is visible. See text.

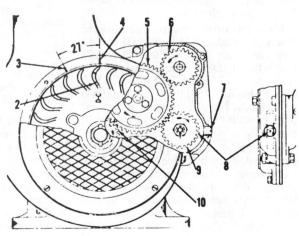

Fig. W78—Typical magneto ignition timing mark alignment. Refer to text for timing specifications.

2. Marked flywheel vane
3. Running advance mark
4. Static timing index
5. Camshaft gear
6. Governor gear
7. Timing plug
8. Marked magneto gear tooth
9. Magneto gear
10. Crankshaft gear

mary circuit is open; check connections and components. If voltmeter indicates a constant 1.0 to 3.5 volts, ignition module is shorted. If voltmeter indicates constant battery voltage, ignition module is open and must be renewed or replaced with a good unit.

MAGNETO IGNITION. Either a Fairbanks-Morse or Wico magneto may be used. However, magnetos may not be interchangeable between models due to different firing intervals.

Breaker point gap for all models should be 0.015 inch (0.38 mm). See Fig. W77.

To install magneto on engine, make certain number "1" cylinder (cylinder nearer flywheel side of engine) is at top dead center on compression stroke, remove air intake screen at flywheel and timing hole plug (7—Fig. W78). Leading edge of flywheel vane marked "X" and "DC" (2—Fig. W78) should be in register with static timing mark on air shroud. Before mounting magneto in place, turn drive gear clockwise until impulse coupling snaps, align on number one firing position. Install magneto so "X" marked tooth appears in timing port as shown (8—Fig. W78).

Set ignition timing as outlined in BATTERY IGNITION section.

VALVE ADJUSTMENT. Engine must be at ambient temperature when checking valve tappet gap. Valve tappet gap for Models TE and TF is 0.011-0.013 inch (0.28-0.33 mm) for intake and exhaust valves. On all other models, valve tappet gap for intake valve is 0.008 inch (0.20 mm) and exhaust valve tappet gap is 0.016 inch (0.41 mm).

Valve adjustment on all models is made by turning self-locking cap screw on tappet as required.

REPAIRS

TIGHTENING TORQUES. Recommended torque specifications are as follows:

Connecting rod	22-28 ft.-lbs. (30-38 N·m)
Cylinder block	32-34 ft.-lbs. (43-46 N·m)
Cylinder head	16-18 ft.-lbs. (22-24 N·m)
Engine base	22-24 ft.-lbs. (30-33 N·m)
Gear cover	16-18 ft.-lbs. (22-24 N·m)
Main bearing plate	22-24 ft.-lbs. (30-33 N·m)
Manifold	26 ft.-lbs. (35 N·m)
Spark plug	24-26 ft.-lbs. (33-35 N·m)

WISCONSIN

CYLINDER HEAD. When removing cylinder head, note location and lengths of cylinder head retaining screws so they can be reinstalled in their original positions.

A new cylinder head gasket should be installed to insure proper sealing. Tighten screws in a crossing pattern to a torque of 16-18 ft.-lbs. (22-24 N•m).

VALVE SYSTEM. Valve seats are renewable-type inserts in cylinder block and seats should be ground to a 45° angle. Valve seat width should be 3/32 inch (2.4 mm).

Valve face angle should be 45°. Stellite valves and seats, and valve rotocaps are used on some models.

Valve stem clearance in block or guide should be 0.003-0.005 inch (0.07-0.13 mm). Later models are equipped with renewable valve guides. Valves with oversize stems are available for models that do not have renewable guides. If stem clearance equals or exceeds 0.007 inch (0.18 mm), a new valve guide or valve with an oversize stem should be installed.

Wisconsin tool DF-72 guide driver is available to aid valve guide removal and installation.

PISTON, PIN AND RINGS. Piston and connecting rod are removed from cylinder head end of block as an assembly. Piston and connecting rod are accessible after removing cylinder head and engine base.

Model W2-880 is equipped with a three-ring piston and Model TJD changed to a three-ring piston effective with serial number 5219324. Pistons on all other models are equipped with four piston rings. Pistons and rings are available in standard size as well as a variety of oversizes.

Early engines were equipped with a split skirt piston and later production engines are equipped with a cam-ground piston. All replacement pistons are of the cam-ground design. Refer to following paragraphs for service specifications for type of piston being serviced.

Split Skirt Piston. Split skirt piston should have a clearance in bore of 0.0040-0.0045 inch (0.102-0.114 mm) measured 90° from piston pin at bottom edge of piston skirt. Piston ring end gap should be 0.0040-0.0045 inch (0.102-0.114 mm) for top ring, 0.0010-0.0025 inch (0.025-0.064 mm) for second and third ring, and 0.0025-0.0040 inch (0.064-0.102 mm) for oil control ring. Piston ring side clearance should be 0.002-0.003 inch (0.05-0.08 mm).

Piston pin should be 0.0000-0.0008 inch (0.000-0.020 mm) tight fit in piston and is retained at each end by a snap ring in piston bore. Pin should have

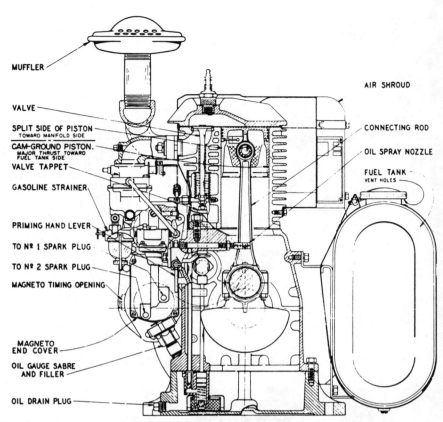

Fig. W79—Sectional view of engine components showing general location and relationship.

0.0005-0.0011 inch (0.013-0.028 mm) clearance in bushing end of connecting rod. Pins are available in a variety of oversizes as well as standard.

Install split skirt piston so split is toward manifold side of engine (see Fig. W79).

If connecting rod rides directly on crankpin, assemble piston and connecting rod so oil hole in rod cap points away from camshaft and numbers on rod and cap match and are on same side. If connecting rod has bearing inserts, disregard oil hole location, but be sure numbers on rod and cap match and are on same side. Tighten rod nuts to 22-28 ft.-lbs. (30-38 N•m).

Cam-Ground Piston. Cam-ground piston on Models TH and THD should have clearance in bore of 0.0032-0.0037 inch (0.081-0.094 mm) while piston clearance on Models TJD and W2-880 should be 0.0025-0.0030 inch (0.064-0.076 mm). Measure piston at a point perpendicular to piston pin at bottom of piston skirt.

Piston ring end gap should be 0.010-0.020 inch (0.25-0.50 mm) on all models. On pistons with four piston rings, top piston ring side clearance should be 0.002-0.004 inch (0.05-0.10 mm), second and third piston ring side clearance should be 0.001-0.003 inch (0.02-0.08

mm), and oil control piston ring side clearance should be 0.002-0.004 inch (0.05-0.10 mm). On pistons with three piston rings, top and second piston ring side clearance should be 0.002-0.004 inch (0.05-0.10 mm), and oil control piston ring side clearance should be 0.0015-0.0035 inch (0.038-0.089 mm).

Piston pin should be 0.0000-0.0008 inch (0.000-0.020 mm) tight fit in piston and is retained at each end by a snap ring in piston bore. Pin should have 0.0005-0.0011 inch (0.013-0.028 mm) clearance in bushing end of connecting rod. Pins are available in a variety of oversizes as well as standard.

When installing piston and rod, note that wide thrust face on skirt must face thrust side of engine when installed (see Fig. W79). Location of oil hole in rod may be disregarded. When installing rod cap, be sure numbers on rod and cap match and are on same side. Tighten rod nuts to 22-28 ft.-lbs. (30-38 N•m).

CONNECTING ROD. Connecting rod and piston are removed from cylinder head end of block as an assembly. Piston and connecting rod are accessible after removing cylinder head and engine base.

The connecting rod on Models TJD and W2-880 is equipped with renewable insert-type bearings and the connecting

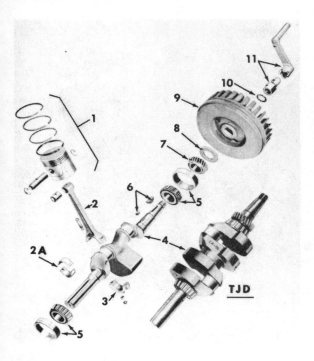

Fig. W80—Exploded view of crankshaft, piston, and connecting rod parts groups. Note differences in TJD crankshaft (4) compared with earlier style.

1. Piston & ring assy.
2. Connecting rod assy.
2A. Bearing inserts (if so equipped)
3. Connecting rod cap
4. Crankshaft (two types)
5. Main bearing
6. Woodruff keys
7. Crankshaft gear
8. Oil slinger
9. Flywheel
10. Lockwasher
11. Crank nut & crank

out-of-round more than 0.005 inch (0.13 mm). Pistons are available in standard size and a variety of oversizes.

CRANKSHAFT AND MAIN BEARINGS. The crankshaft of all models is supported at each end by taper roller bearings. Models TJD and W2-880 crankshaft connecting rod journals are 180° apart and connecting rod journals on all other models are on the same side with a counterweight opposite. See Fig. W80. Main bearings are press fit on crankshaft and bearing cups are pressed into stator plate and crankcase.

Crankshaft end play when engine is cold should be 0.001-0.005 inch (0.02-0.13 mm). End play is controlled by varying thickness of gaskets between crankcase and bearing plate. Gaskets are available in a variety of thicknesses.

Crankpin standard journal diameter is 1.750-1.751 inches (44.45-44.48 mm) for Models TE, TF, TH and THD, and 1.8756-1.8764 inches (47.640-47.661 mm) for Models TJD and W2-880.

To properly time crankshaft to related engine components during installation, refer to Fig. W81.

CAMSHAFT. The camshaft runs in unbushed bores in crankcase casting. For camshaft removal, valves must first be removed so mushroom-style tappets can be pulled clear of camshaft lobes. End play of camshaft is controlled by a three-piece plunger assembly that bears against gear cover (Fig. W82). Use care not to lose plunger, spring or wear button during reassembly.

OIL PUMP. A plunger-type oil pump is attached to the bottom of the crankcase and accessible after removing the engine base. The pump is driven by a lobe on the camshaft. See Fig. W83.

Oil pump plunger-to-bore clearance should be 0.003-0.005 inch (0.08-0.13

rod on all other models rides directly on crankpin. Replacement rods for Models TH and THD are equipped with insert bearings. Undersize insert bearings or undersize connecting rod are available.

Rod-to-journal running clearance should be 0.0007-0.0020 inch (0.018-0.051 mm) for Models TE, TF and early TH and THD engines if rod rides directly on crankpin. Rod bearing clearance on Models TH and THD with insert bearings should be 0.0012-0.0034 inch (0.030-0.086 mm). Rod bearing clearance on Models TJD and W2-880 should

be 0.0008-0.0029 inch (0.020-0.074 mm).

On models with connecting rod that rides directly on crankpin, minor bearing clearance adjustment is possible by varying thickness of shims between connecting rod and cap.

Connecting rod side clearance should be 0.004-0.010 inch (0.10-0.25 mm) for Models TE and TF, 0.014-0.023 inch (0.36-0.58 mm) for Models TH and THD, and 0.009-0.014 inch (0.23-0.36 mm) for Models TJD and W2-880.

Assemble and install piston and rod as outlined in previous section.

CYLINDER. Cylinder block section is separate from crankcase and may be renewed as an individual unit.

Cylinders for all models may be bored to accept an oversize piston. Cylinder bore should be bored oversize if worn or

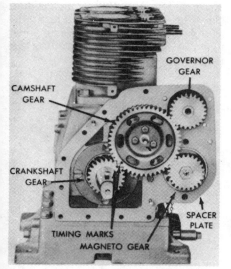

Fig. W81—View of timing gear train with gear cover removed. Note position of timing index marks on camshaft and crankshaft gears. Refer to text.

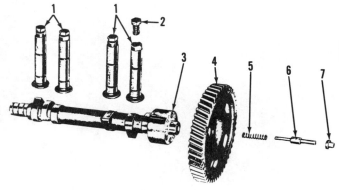

Fig. W82—Exploded view of camshaft assembly.

1. Tappets
2. Tappet adjustment cap screw
3. Camshaft
4. Camshaft gear
5. Spring
6. Plunger
7. Wear button

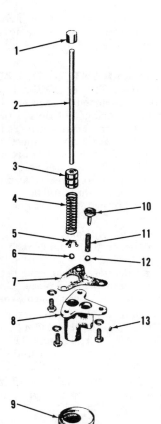

Fig. W83—Exploded view of plunger-type oil pump that is driven off a camshaft lobe. Pump body (8) may vary according to model, but basic construction is similar.

1. Cap
2. Push rod
3. Plunger
4. Pump spring
5. Retainer
6. Check ball
7. Gasket
8. Pump body
9. Sump screen
10. Retainer
11. Spring
12. Check ball
13. Core plug

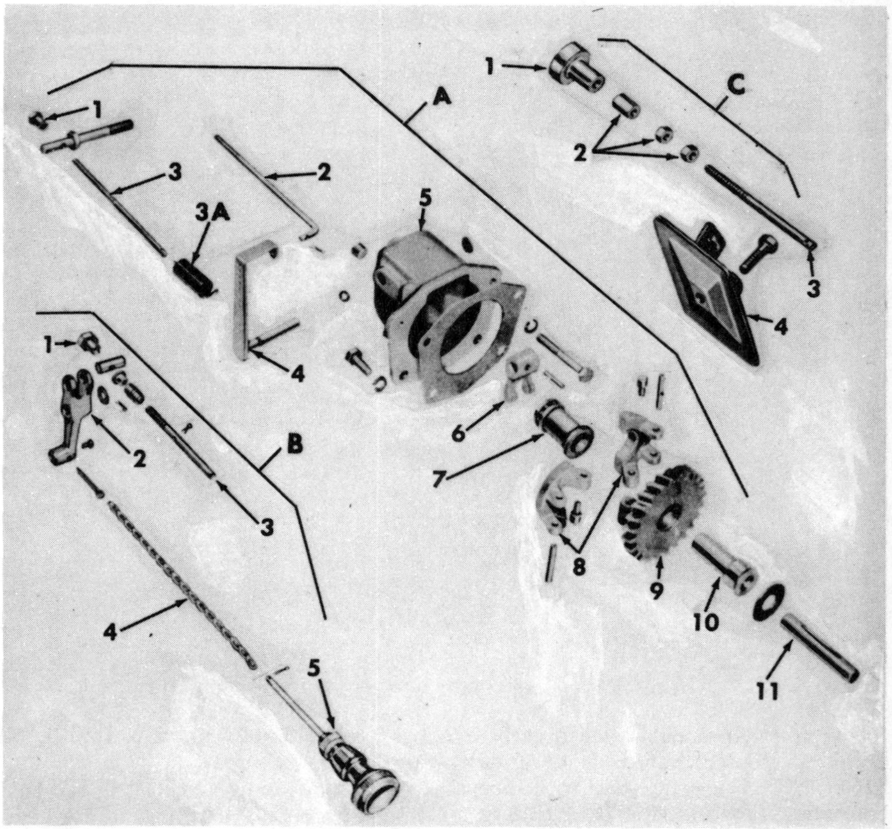

Fig. W84—Exploded view of governor assembly (A) to show general arrangement of working parts. View B is variable speed control and View C shows idle control assembly. Adjusting screw or control rod (3) connects to governor spring (3A).

A. Governor assy.
1. Adjustment nut
2. Throttle rod to governor
3. Adjustment screw
3A. Governor spring
4. Governor lever
5. Governor housing
6. Governor yoke
7. Thrust sleeve & bearing
8. Flyweights
9. Governor gear
10. Bushing
11. Shaft
B. Variable speed control
1. Locknut
2. Variable speed lever
3. Adjusting screw
4. Control chain
5. Control knob
C. Idle control
1. Control knob
2. Locknuts
3. Control rod
4. Tappet cover rod support

mm) and plunger should be renewed if clearance exceeds 0.007 inch (0.18 mm).

OIL SPRAY NOZZLES. Oil spray nozzle is installed so both metered holes can be seen when looking directly into bottom of crankcase and, when installed correctly, flats on hex body of nozzle will be parallel with top and bottom machined surfaces of crankcase. End of spray nozzle should extend 1½ inches (38.1 mm) from boss it is screwed into or be in line with the centerline of crankshaft when it is installed. See Fig. W79.

GOVERNOR. The governor unit (Fig. W84) is mounted on spacer plate shown in Fig. W81. Governor gear shaft (11—Fig. W84) is pressed into timing gear cover. Governor components must operate freely without binding for proper operation.

WISCONSIN

Model	No. Cyls.	Bore	Stroke	Displacement	Power Rating
VE4, VE4D	4	3 in. (76.2 mm)	3.25 in. (82.55 mm)	91.9 cu. in. (1505.8 cc)	21.5 hp (16 kW)
VF4, VF4D	4	3.25 in. (82.55 mm)	3.25 in. (82.55 mm)	107.7 cu. in. (1767.3 cc)	25 hp (18.6 kW)
VP4, VP4D	4	3.5 in. (88.9 mm)	4 in. (101.6 mm)	154 cu. in. (2522.6 cc)	31 hp (23.1 kW)

Engines in this section are four-stroke, four cylinder V-type with a horizontal crankshaft. Crankshaft for all models is supported at each end in taper roller bearings.

Connecting rods in early models ride directly on crankpin journal, but are replaced by renewable insert-type rods in later models and during service. Lubrication is provided by pressure spray system and gear-type oil pump is driven by an idler gear.

Magneto ignition is used except on electric start engines that are equipped with a battery-type ignition system with points located in a distributor.

Various float-type carburetors are used and a mechanical-type fuel pump with priming lever is available.

Engine identification information is located on engine instruction plate and engine model, specification and serial numbers are required when ordering parts. Suffix D engines are equipped with stellite exhaust valves and seats.

MAINTENANCE

SPARK PLUG. Recommended spark plug is Champion D16 or equivalent. Electrode gap should be 0.030 inch (0.76 mm).

CARBURETOR. A variety of float-type carburetors are used as listed:

Zenith 161-7, Stromberg UC-7/8 or Marvel-Schebler TSX-148 carburetors are used on VE4 and VE4D engines.

Zenith 161-7 or Stromberg UC-7/8 carburetors are used on VF4 and VF4D engines.

Marvel-Schebler VH-69 carburetor is used on VP4 and VP4D engines.

For initial adjustment of all models, note main fuel jet is fixed and nonadjustable, except in possible special applications.

For initial idle mixture screw adjustment for Zenith 161-7, Stromberg UC-7/8 and Marvel-Schebler TSX-148 carburetors, open idle mixture screw 1¼ turns.

For initial idle mixture adjustment of Marvel-Schebler VH-69 carburetor, open idle mixture screw 1 to 1¼ turns.

On all models, make final adjustments with engine at normal operating temperature and running. Set engine at idle speed and adjust idle mixture screw for smoothest idle operation.

To check float level on Zenith 161-7 or Stromberg UC-7/8 carburetors, invert carburetor throttle body and float assembly, and measure from furthest face of float to machined gasket surface of throttle body. Measurement should be 15/32 inch (29.37 mm) for Zenith 161-7 model and 1¼ inch (31.75 mm) for Stromberg UC-7/8 model.

To check float level on Marvel-Schebler TSX-148 or VH-69 carburetors, invert carburetor throttle body and float assembly, and measure from nearest face of float to machined gasket surface of throttle body. Measurement should be ¼ inch (6.35 mm) for TSX-148 model and 37/64 inch (14.68 mm) for VH-69 model.

Adjust float level on all models by bending float tang that contacts inlet valve.

GOVERNOR. Flyweight-type governor, driven by camshaft gear, is used on all models. Refer to Fig. W85 for exploded view of typical governor component parts.

Speed changes on all models is obtained by varying spring (12—Fig. W85) tension with adjusting screw (14) or locating spring in alternate holes of governor control lever (11).

To correctly set governed speeds, use a tachometer to accurately record crankshaft rpm. Refer to Figs. W86 or

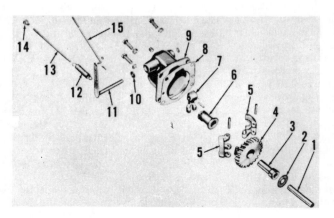

Fig. W85—Exploded view of typical governor assembly used on four-cylinder Wisconsin engines.

1. Shaft
2. Thrust washer
3. Bushing
4. Governor gear
5. Flyweights
6. Thrust sleeve & bearing
7. Yoke
8. Gasket
9. Housing
10. Oil seal
11. Governor lever & shaft
12. Governor spring
13. Control rod
14. Adjusting screw
15. Throttle rod

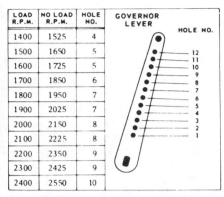

LOAD R.P.M.	NO LOAD R.P.M.	HOLE NO.
1400	1525	4
1500	1650	5
1600	1725	5
1700	1850	6
1800	1950	7
1900	2025	7
2000	2150	8
2100	2225	8
2200	2350	9
2300	2425	9
2400	2550	10

Fig. W86—Governor speed table for VE4, VE4D, VF4, VF4D models.

LOAD R.P.M.	NO LOAD R.P.M.	HOLE NO.
1400	1550	4
1500	1650	5
1600	1725	5
1700	1850	6
1800	1950	7
1900	2025	8
2000	2125	8
2100	2250	9
2200	2350	10

Fig. W87—Governor speed table for VP4 and VP4D models.

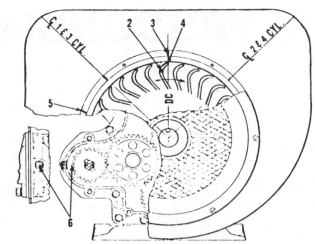

Fig. W88—Wisconsin V4 magneto timing marks.

2. "X" marked flywheel vane
3. Magneto installation timing mark
4. Leading edge of marked flywheel vane
5. Running timing mark
6. Marked tooth on magneto gear

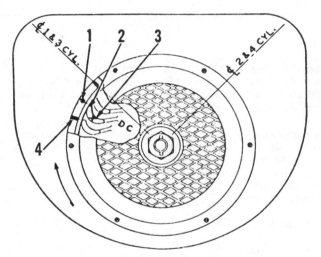

Fig. W89—Distributor timing marks used on engines equipped with early IGW-4159A engine speed distributor.

1. Distributor static timing mark
2. Leading edge of marked flywheel vane
3. "X" marked on flywheel vane
4. Running timing mark

W87 to determine correct hole in which to locate spring for desired rpm.

Governor-to-carburetor rod should be adjusted so it just will enter hole in governor lever when governor weights are "in" and carburetor throttle is wide open.

IGNITION SYSTEM. Either a battery-type ignition system with breaker points located in a distributor or a magneto-type ignition system are used according to model and application.

BATTERY IGNITION. Autolite IGW-4159A or IAD-4036D battery ignition distributor is used when engine is equipped with electric starting motor and generator. Early IGW-4159A distributor rotates at engine speed and later IAD-4036A distributor rotates at half engine speed. Breaker point gap on both distributors should be 0.018-0.022 inch (0.46-0.56 mm). Firing order is 1-3-4-2 on all models. Cylinders are numbered from flywheel end of engine and, facing flywheel, are as follows: left bank—Nos. 1 and 3; right bank—Nos. 2 and 4.

To install and time early IGW-4159A engine speed distributor, remove screen over flywheel air intake opening and make certain number 1 cylinder is at top dead center on compression stroke, and leading edge of flywheel vane marked "X" and "DC" (3—Fig. W88) is in register with distributor static timing mark (1—Fig. W89) on air shroud as shown. Install distributor so rotor is pointing toward lug (4—Fig. W90) on distributor body. Loosen clamp screw (2) and turn distributor counterclockwise until breaker points are closed. Turn distributor clockwise until breaker points just begin to open and tighten clamp screw. Positioning distributor as outlined will give a static timing of 12° BTDC for VE4, VE4D, VF4 and VF4D models, or 10° BTDC for VP4 and VP4D models.

Running timing should be 27° BTDC for VE4, VE4D, VF4 and VF4D models and 25° BTDC for VP4 and VP4D models. With engine operating at 1800 rpm, timing light should flash when leading edge of flywheel vane (3—Fig. W89) marked with an "X" is aligned with running timing mark (4) on air shroud. If not, loosen clamp screw (2—Fig. W90) and turn distributor body until correct timing is obtained. Tighten clamp screw.

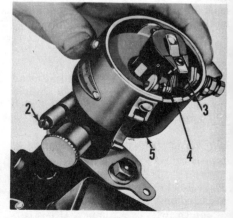

Fig. W90—Autolite IGW-4159A ignition distributor rotates at engine speed. Refer to text for timing procedure.

2. Clamp screw
3. Rotor arm
4. Lug
5. Distributor body

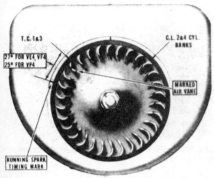

Fig. W91—Distributor timing marks in correct register for static timing. When engine is operating at 1800 rpm or above, leading edge of "X" marked vane should be in register with running timing mark when timing light flashes.

To install and time later IAD-4036A half-engine-speed distributor, remove screen over flywheel air intake opening and proceed as follows: Crank engine until No. 1 piston is coming up on compression stroke and leading edge of "X" marked flywheel vane is aligned with distributor static timing mark (T.C. 1 and 3) as shown is Fig. W91. Adjust breaker point gap to 0.018-0.022 inch (0.46-0.56 mm), then install distributor so rotor arm is centered on right hand edge of notch in distributor housing as shown in Fig. W92. Loosen distributor body clamp screw and turn distributor body counterclockwise until breaker points are closed. Then, turn distributor clockwise until breaker points are just beginning to open and tighten clamp screw. Running timing is 27° BTDC for VE4, VE4D, VF4 and VF4D models and 25° BTDC for VP4 and VP4D models. Timing marks indicating these positions are stamped on air shrouds. With engine operating at 1800 rpm, timing light should flash when leading edge of "X" marked flywheel vane is in register with running (fully advanced) timing mark on air shroud. If not, loosen distributor body clamp screw, turn distributor body until correct timing is obtained, retighten clamp screw.

MAGNETO IGNITION. Either Fairbanks-Morse FM-XV4B7, FM-ZV4B7 or Wico XH-1343 magneto is used according to model and application.

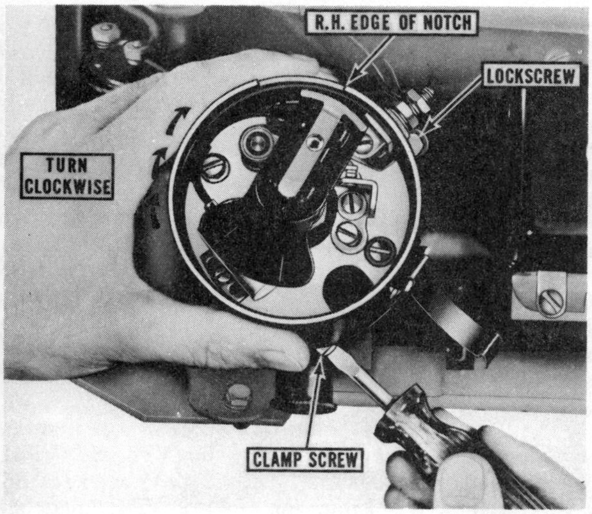

Breaker point gap for all models should be 0.015 inch (0.38 mm).

To install magneto to engine, make certain number 1 cylinder is at top dead center on compression stroke. Remove air intake screen at flywheel and timing hole plug. Leading edge of flywheel vane marked "X" and "DC" (3—Fig. W88) should be in register with static timing mark on air shroud. Install magneto so "X" marked tooth (6) on magneto drive gear is visible through port in timing gear housing as shown. To check for correct installation, slowly crank engine. Impulse coupling should snap when leading edge of marked vane on flywheel is aligned with center line of cylinders.

Procedure for setting running timing, firing order and cylinder sequence is the same as for battery ignition system.

LUBRICATION. Pressure spray lubrication is provided by a gear-type oil pump that is driven by crankshaft gear via an idler gear. Oil is pumped through an external oil line at 4-5 psi (28-35 kPa) to lubricate governor and nozzles spray connecting rods and surrounding engine components. Maximum system pressure should be 15 psi (103 kPa) and is controlled by a relief valve in pump. See Fig. W93.

To remove oil pump, remove crankcase oil pan and timing gear cover. Remove pump retaining screw (Fig. W94). Unscrew pump drive gear nut (1—Fig. W93) and use a soft brass punch to drive shaft out of gear. Oil pump assembly may now be withdrawn from crankcase. Refer to Fig. W93 for disassembly or reassembly.

Maintain oil level at full mark on dipstick, but do not overfill. High-quality detergent oil having API classification SE, SF or SG is recommended. Oil change interval recommendation is every 50 hours of normal operation and

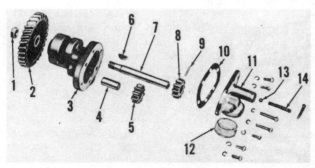

Fig. W92—Autolite IAD-4036A distributor rotates at half engine speed. When installing distributor, set rotor to body static timing position as shown.

Fig. W94—Removing oil pump retaining screw on Wisconsin V4 engine. Allen head screw is accessible after removing slotted plug (94).

Fig. W93—Exploded view of oil pump used on all models. Items 13 and 14 are the 15 psi (103 kPa) maximum pressure relief valve.

1. Nut		11. Cover
2. Drive gear	5. Idler gear	8. Pump gear	12. Screen
3. Pump body	6. Key	9. Pin	13. Relief ball
4. Idler shaft	7. Pump shaft	10. Gasket	14. Relief spring

filter should be changed every other oil change.

Crankcase capacity for VE4, VE4D, VF4 and VF4D is 4 quarts (3.8 L) and capacity for VP4 and VP4D is 5 quarts (4.7 L).

Use SAE 30 oil when operating temperature is between 120° F (49° C) and 40° F (4° C), SAE 20 oil between 40° F (4° C) and 15° F (–9° C), SAE 10 oil between 15° F (–9° C) and 0° F (–18° C), and SAE 5W-20 oil for below 0° F (–18° C).

REPAIRS

TIGHTENING TORQUES. Recommended torque specifications are as follows:

Cylinder head—
  VE4, VE4D,
  VF4, VF4D . . . . 22-24 ft.-lbs.
                              (30-33 N·m)
  VP4, VP4D . . . . 25-32 ft.-lbs.
                              (34-43 N·m)
Cylinder block—
  VE4, VE4D,
  VF4, VF4D . . . . 40-50 ft.-lbs.
                              (54-68 N·m)
  VP4, VP4D . . . . 62-78 ft.-lbs.
                              (84-106 N·m)
Connecting rod—
  VE4, VE4D,
  VF4, VF4D . . . . 22-24 ft.-lbs.
                              (30-33 N·m)
  VP4, VP4D . . . . 28-32 ft.-lbs.
                              (38-43 N·m)
Gear cover—
  All models . . . . 14-18 ft.-lbs.
                              (19-24 N·m)
Bearing plate—
  All models . . . . 25-30 ft.-lbs.
                              (34-40 N·m)
Manifold—
  VE4, VE4D,
  VF4, VF4D . . . . 14-18 ft.-lbs.
                              (19-24 N·m)
  VP4, VP4D . . . . 40-50 ft.-lbs.
                              (54-68 N·m)
Oil pan—
  All models . . . . 6-9 ft.-lbs.
                              (8-12 N·m)
Spark plug—
  All models . . . . 25-30 ft.-lbs.
                              (34-40 N·m)

CONNECTING RODS. Connecting rods and piston assemblies can be removed from above after removing cylinder head and crankcase oil pan.

Early model engines have connecting rods that ride directly on crankpin journal. Specified running clearance for these rods is 0.0007-0.002 inch (0.018-0.051 mm).

Late model engines have connecting rods with renewable insert-type bearings. Specified running clearance for

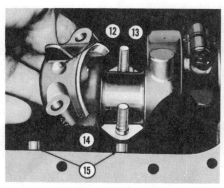

Fig. W95—Installing connecting rod and cap on Wisconsin V4 engine. Numbers on connecting rod and rod cap must face oil spray nozzle side of engine.

these connecting rod bearings is 0.0012-0.0034 inch (0.0305-0.0864 mm).

Old style rods should be replaced with insert bearing type connecting rods when they require service.

Connecting rod side clearance should be 0.009-0.018 inch (0.23-0.45 mm) for all models.

Number stamped on side of rod should correspond with number stamped on side of rod cap. Oil hole in rod cap must be toward oil spray nozzles when rods are reinstalled (Fig. W95).

Crankpin standard journal diameter for VP4 and VP4D engines with serial numbers prior to 771501 and all VE4, VE4D, VF4, VF4D should be 1.750-1.751 inches (44.45-44.48 mm). Crankpin standard diameter for VP4 and VP4D engines after serial number 771501 should be 1.875-1.876 inches (47.63-47.65 mm). Connecting rods or bearing inserts are available for a variety of undersize crankshafts.

PISTON, PIN AND RINGS Pistons are equipped with two compression rings—one scraper ring and one oil control ring—for all models (Fig. W96). Pistons and rings are available in a variety of oversizes as well as standard.

Early engines used a split skirt piston that has been replaced with a cam-ground piston in later models.

Piston-to-cylinder bore clearance when measured 90° from pin at lower edge of skirt should be 0.004-0.0045 inch (0.10-0.11 mm) for split skirt piston and 0.0035-0.004 inch (0.09-0.10 mm) for cam-ground piston.

Ring end gap for all models should be 0.010-0.020 inch (0.25-0.51 mm).

Ring side clearance in grooves for all models should be 0.002-0.0035 inch (0.05-0.09 mm) for top ring, 0.001-0.0025 inch (0.025-0.063 mm) for second and third ring and 0.0025-0.004 inch (0.06-0.10 mm) for oil control ring.

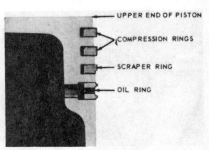

Fig. W96—Piston rings mush be installed on piston as shown.

Wide thrust face on skirt of cam ground piston must face thrust side of engine when installed. See Fig. W97.

Split skirt piston should be assembled on rod so split is on opposite side of connecting rod oil hole in connecting rod cap. See Fig. W97.

Piston pin should be 0.000-0.0008 inch (0.000-0.020 mm) tight fit in piston and is retained at each end by a snap ring in bore of piston. Pin should have 0.0005-0.0011 inch (0.013-0.028 mm) clearance in bushing in end of connecting rod. Pins are available in a variety of oversizes as well as standard.

CYLINDER HEADS. Always use new head gaskets when installing cylinder heads and make certain head bolts of varying length are in correct locations. Tighten cap screws evenly.

CYLINDER. Two cylinders are cast as a unit and bolt to the crankcase. Cylinders should be bored to nearest oversize for which pistons and rings are available if worn or out-of-round more than 0.005 inch (0.13 mm).

Standard cylinder bore is 2.998-2.999 inches (76.15-76.17 mm) for VE4 and VE4D models, 3.248-3.249 inches (82.50-82.52 mm) for VF4 and VF4D models, and 3.498-3.499 inches (88.85-88.87 mm) for VP4 and VP4D models.

CRANKSHAFT, MAIN BEARINGS AND OIL SEALS. Crankshaft is supported at each end by taper roller bearings. Crankshaft end play should be 0.002-0.004 inch (0.05-0.10 mm) for all models and is controlled by varying thickness of gaskets between main bearing plate and crankcase. Gaskets are available in a variety of thicknesses.

Main bearings are a press fit on crankshaft, rear bearing cup is pressed into bearing plate, and front bearing cup is retained in crankcase by a retainer plate and cap screws.

Timing marks should be aligned as shown in Fig. W97A during crankshaft installation.

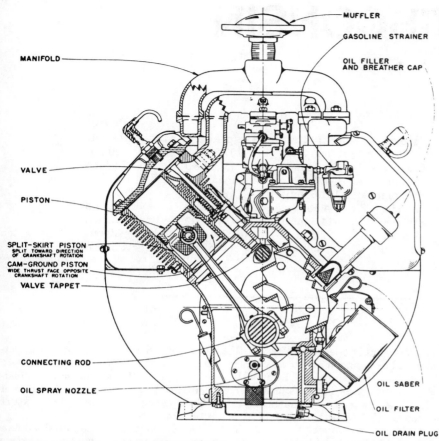

MANIFOLD

VALVE

PISTON

SPLIT–SKIRT PISTON
SPLIT TOWARD DIRECTION
OF CRANKSHAFT ROTATION

CAM-GROUND PISTON
WIDE THRUST FACE OPPOSITE
CRANKSHAFT ROTATION

VALVE TAPPET

CONNECTING ROD

OIL SPRAY NOZZLE

MUFFLER

GASOLINE STRAINER

OIL FILLER
AND BREATHER CAP

OIL SABER

OIL FILTER

OIL DRAIN PLUG

Fig. W97—Cross-sectional view of engine showing general location and relationship of component parts.

Fig. W97A—Wisconsin V4 engine with gear cover removed showing gear train and location of timing marks.

2. Magneto gear
3. Camshaft gear
4. Governor gear
5. Valve timing marks
6. Crankshaft gear
7. Idler gear
8. Oil pump drive gear

Oil seals should be installed in timing gear cover and rear bearing plate before they are bolted in place. Care should be taken to avoid seal damage during installation.

If scored or out-of-round, crankpin journals can be reground and a variety of oversize connecting rods or bearing inserts are available. See **CONNECTING ROD** section for standard crankshaft rod journal diameters.

IDLER GEAR AND SHAFT. An idler gear driven by crankshaft gear is used to drive magneto and oil pump on all models. See Fig. W97A.

To remove idler gear and shaft, remove timing gear cover, magneto or generator and distributor. Remove Allen head set screws from side of crankcase that retain idler shaft in position. Using a sleeve-type puller over end of idler shaft and against idler gear, thread a 3/8-16 cap screw into end of shaft. Pull shaft from crankcase and idler gear.

When reassembling, make certain oil slot in idler shaft is facing upward. Press or drive idler shaft into crankcase until a clearance of 0.003-0.004 inch (0.076-0.10 mm) exists between gear hub and shoulder on end of idler shaft. Lock shaft in position with Allen set screws.

CAMSHAFT. Camshaft runs in unbushed bores in crankcase casting. Camshaft gear is held on end of camshaft by three cap screws and end play is controlled by a spring-loaded plunger assembly and wear button that bears against timing gear cover. Use care not to lose plunger, spring or wear button during reassembly.

VALVE SYSTEM. Suffix "D" of engine model number indicates stellite exhaust valve and seat. All models have renewable valve seats that should be ground at a 45° angle. Seat width should not exceed 3/32 inch (2.38 mm).

Valve faces are ground at a 45° angle and valves with oversize stems are available for some models.

Early models had valve guides machined directly into cylinder casting and late models have renewable guides.

Valve stem-to-guide clearance for all models should be 0.003-0.005 inch (0.076-0.127 mm) and should be reconditioned, valves with oversize stems installed or guides renewed if clearance exceeds 0.007 inch (0.18 mm).

Valve tappet gap (cold) for VE4, VE4D, VF4, VF4D models should be 0.008 inch (0.20 mm) for intake valves and 0.015 inch (0.40 mm) for exhaust valves. Valve tappet gap (cold) for VP4 and VP4D models should be 0.012 inch (0.30 mm) for intake and 0.017 inch (0.43 mm) for exhaust valves.

Valve adjustment on all models is made by turning self-locking cap screw on tappet as required.

WISCONSIN

Model	No. Cyls.	Bore	Stroke	Displacement	Power Rating
VH4, VH4D	4	3.25 in. (82.6 mm)	3.25 in. (82.6 mm)	107.7 cu. in. (1767 cc)	30 hp (22.4 kW)
VG4D	4	3.5 in. (88.9 mm)	4.0 in. (101.6 mm)	154 cu. in. (2523 cc)	37 hp (28 kW)
VR4D	4	4.25 in. (108 mm)	4.5 in. (114.3 mm)	255 cu. in. (4184 cc)	56.5 hp (42.1 kW)
W4-1770	4	3.25 in. (82.6 mm)	3.25 in. (82.6 mm)	107.7 cu. in. (1767 cc)	30 hp (22.4 kW)

Engines in this section are four-stroke, four-cylinder V-type, air-cooled engines with a horizontal crankshaft. Crankshaft is supported at each end by taper roller bearings.

Connecting rods in early models ride directly on crankpin journal. Connecting rods in later models and replacement connecting rods for early models are equipped with renewable insert-type bearings. Pressure spray lubrication is provided by a gear-type oil pump that is driven by an idler gear.

Magneto ignition is used except on electric start engines, which are equipped with a battery-type ignition system with points located in a distributor.

Various float-type carburetors are used and a mechanical-type fuel pump with priming lever is available.

Engine information provided on engine identification plate may be required when ordering parts.

MAINTENANCE

LUBRICATION. Pressure spray lubrication is provided by a gear-type oil pump that is driven by crankshaft gear via an idler gear. Oil is pumped through an external oil line at 4-5 psi (28-35 kPa) to lubricate governor and gear train; nozzles spray connecting rods and surrounding engine components. Maximum system pressure should be 15 psi (103 kPa) and is controlled by a relief valve in pump.

Maintain oil level at full mark on dipstick or at top of filler plug, but do not overfill. Oil should be changed after every 50 hours of operation. The oil filter should be changed after every other oil change. Change oil more frequently if engine undergoes severe operation.

Crankcase capacity is 4 quarts (3.8 L) for Models VH4, VH4D and W4-1770, 5 quarts (4.7 L) for Model VG4D and 8 quarts (7.6 L) for Model VR4D.

Manufacturer recommends oil with an API service classification of SE, SF or SG. Use SAE 10W-30 oil for ambient temperatures above 0° F (−18° C) and SAE 5W-20 for temperatures below 0° F (−18° C).

SPARK PLUG. Recommended spark plug is Champion D16J or equivalent. Electrode gap should be 0.030 inch (0.76 mm). Tighten spark plug to 25-30 ft.-lbs. (34-41 N•m).

CARBURETOR. A variety of float-type carburetors are used as listed.

Zenith 68-7 or Marvel Schebler TSX-690 carburetor is used on VH4 and VH4D engines.

Marvel Schebler VH-69 carburetor is used on VG4D engines.

Zenith 12A10 carburetor is used on VR4D engines.

Zenith 87A8 carburetor is used on W4-1770 engines.

For initial adjustment of all models, note that main fuel jet is fixed and nonadjustable, except in possible special applications.

For initial idle mixture screw adjustment for Zenith 68-7 or 12A10 carburetor, open idle mixture screw 1¼ turns. Open idle mixture screw 1½ turns on Zenith 87A8 carburetor for initial setting.

For initial idle mixture screw adjustment for Marvel Schebler TSX-690 or VH-69 carburetor, open idle mixture screw ⅞ turn.

On all models, make final adjustments with engine at normal operating temperature and running. Set engine at idle speed and adjust idle mixture screw for smoothest idle operation.

To check float level of Zenith carburetors, invert throttle body and float assembly and measure from furthest face of float to machined gasket surface of throttle body. Measurement should be 1⁵⁄₃₂ inches (29.8 mm) for 68-7 carburetor and 3¹⁄₃₂ inch (24.6 mm) for 12A10 and 87A8 carburetors.

To check float level of Marvel Schebler carburetors, invert throttle body and float assembly and measure from nearest face of float to machined gasket surface of throttle. Measurement should be ¼ inch (6.4 mm) for TSX-690 carburetor or 3⁷⁄₆₄ inch (14.7 mm) for VH-69 carburetor.

Adjust float level on all carburetors by bending float tang that contacts fuel inlet valve.

GOVERNOR. A flyweight-type governor, driven by the camshaft gear, is used on all models. Major speed changes on all models are obtained by varying tension of spring (12—Fig. W98), by turning screw (14) or locating spring in alternate holes of governor control lever (11).

To correctly set governed speeds, use a tachometer to accurately record en-

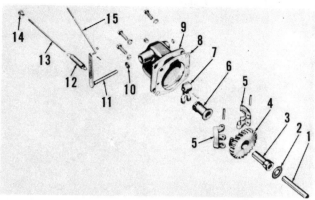

Fig. W98—Exploded view of typical governor assembly used on Wisconsin V4 engines.

1. Shaft
2. Thrust washer
3. Bushing
4. Governor gear
5. Flyweights
6. Thrust sleeve & bearing
7. Governor yoke
8. Gasket
9. Governor housing
10. Oil seal
11. Governor lever & shaft
12. Governor spring
13. Control rod
14. Adjustment screw
15. Throttle rod

LOAD R.P.M.	NO LOAD R.P.M.	HOLE NO.
1400	1525	4
1500	1650	5
1600	1725	5
1700	1850	6
1800	1950	7
1900	2025	7
2000	2150	8
2100	2225	8
2200	2350	9
2300	2425	9
2400	2550	10
2500	2625	10
2600	2750	11
2700	2850	12
2800	2925	12

Fig. W99—Governor speed table for Models VH4 and VH4D.

	VARIABLE SPEED GOVERNOR		TWO SPEED GOVERNOR	
Load R.P.M.	No Load R.P.M.	Hole No.	No Load R.P.M.	Hole No.
1400	1590	2	1580	2
1500	1650	2	1640	2
1600	1750	4	1730	3
1700	1860	5	1810	4
1800	1920	5	1930	5
1900	2000	6	2000	5
2000	2100	6	2100	6
2100	2230	8	2200	7
2200	2300	8	2300	8

Fig. W101—Governor speed table for variable and two-speed (overcenter idle control)-type governors used on Model VR4D.

LOAD R.P.M.	NO LOAD R.P.M.	HOLE NO.
1400	1550	4
1500	1650	5
1600	1725	5
1700	1850	6
1800	1950	7
1900	2025	7
2000	2125	8
2100	2250	9
2200	2350	10

Fig. W100—Governor speed table for Model VG4D.

LOAD R.P.M.	NO LOAD R.P.M.	HOLE NO.
1400	1600	4
1500	1735	5
1600	1775	5
1700	1905	6
1800	2050	7
1900	2115	7
2000	2230	8
2100	2300	8
2200	2430	9
2300	2480	9
2400	2625	10
2500	2685	10
2600	2795	11
2700	2930	12
2800	3005	12
2900	3100	12
3000	3200	12

Fig. W101A—Governor speed table for Model W4-1770.

gine rpm. Refer to Figs. W99, W100, W101 or W101A to determine correct hole in which to locate spring for desired rpm.

Governor-to-carburetor rod should be adjusted so it will just enter hole in governor lever when governor weights are "in" and carburetor throttle is wide open.

IGNITION SYSTEM. Either a battery-type ignition system with breaker points located in a distributor or a mag-neto-type ignition system is used according to model and application.

BATTERY IGNITION. Autolite IAD-6004-2F distributor is used when engine is equipped for electric starting motor and generator.

Distributor is mounted on generator (Fig. W102) on VH4, VH4D and VG4D models and on accessory drive shaft housing (Fig. W103) on VR4D and W4-1770 models.

Distributor rotates in a counterclockwise direction, as viewed from above, at one-half crankshaft speed. Breaker point gap should be 0.018-0.022 inch (0.46-0.56 mm) and firing order is 1-3-4-2. Cylinders are numbered from flywheel side of engine and (facing flywheel) are as follows: left bank—cylinders 1 and 3; right bank—cylinders 2 and 4.

To install and time distributor, remove screen over flywheel air intake opening and make certain number 1 cylinder is at top dead center on compression stroke and leading edge of flywheel vane marked "X" and "DC" is in register with distributor static timing mark (Fig. W104) on air shroud as shown. Install distributor so rotor arm is centered on notch in distributor body as shown in Figs. W102 and W103. Rotate distributor counterclockwise until breaker points are closed. Turn distributor clockwise until breaker points just begin to open and tighten clamp screw.

Running timing should be 23° BTDC on Models VH4, VH4D, VG4D and W4-1770 and 20° BTDC on VR4D models. Advance timing marks indicating these positions are ⅛-inch (3.2 mm) holes or depressions in air shroud. See Figs. W104 and W105. With engine operating at 1800 rpm, timing light should flash when leading edge of "X" marked flywheel vane is in register with running (fully advanced) timing mark on air shroud. If not, loosen distributor body clamp screw, turn distributor body clamp screw, turn distributor until correct timing is obtained, retighten clamp screw.

MAGNETO IGNITION. Either Fairbanks-Morse FM-X4B7A or Wico XHG-4 magneto is used on Models VH4, VH4D, VG4D and W4-1770. Fairbanks-Morse FM-X4A7B magneto is used on Model VR4D.

Breaker point gap for all models should be 0.015 inch (0.38 mm).

To install magneto on all models except Model VR4D, remove air intake screen at flywheel and timing hole plug. Make certain number 1 cylinder is at top dead center on compression stroke. Leading edge of flywheel vane marked "X" and "DC" (Fig. W106) should be in register with static timing mark on air shroud. Install magneto so "X" marked tooth (6) on magneto drive gear is visible through port in timing gear housing as shown. To check for correct installation, slowly crank engine. Impulse coupling

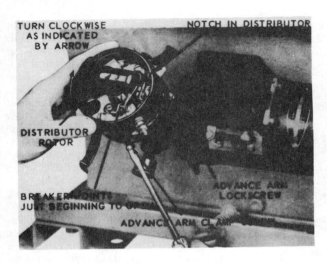

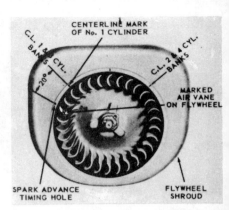

Fig. W102—When installing distributor on Models VH4, VH4D and VG4D, align rotor arm with center of notch in distributor body as shown. Notch also aligns with number 1 cylinder spark plug wire terminal in distributor cap.

Fig. W105—Running spark timing for Model VR4D model is 20° BTDC for either battery or magneto ignition.

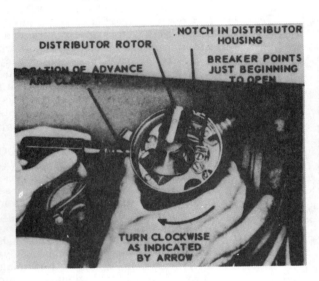

Fig. W103—On Models VR4D and W4-1770, install distributor in position shown with rotor arm aligned with center of notch in distributor body. Notch also aligns with number 1 cylinder spark plug wire terminal in distributor cap.

W105) should be in register with static timing mark on air shroud. Remove magneto end cap and turn magneto shaft in opposite direction of normal rotation until rotor is in exact alignment with timing boss on end cap as shown in Fig. W107. Lugs on magneto coupling will be horizontal at this time as shown in Fig. W108. Holding magneto in this position, install it on engine. If coupling on engine accessory shaft is not in correct position, loosen locknut and rotate coupling (Fig. W108) until slot engages lugs of impulse coupling of magneto. Tighten locknut.

Running timing should be 20° BTDC and is adjusted by resetting coupling on engine accessory drive shaft.

Procedure for setting running timing, firing order and cylinder sequence is the same as for battery ignition system.

VALVE ADJUSTMENT. Engine must be at ambient temperature when checking valve tappet gap. Valve tappet gap for Models VH4 and VH4D is 0.011-0.013 inch (0.28-0.33 mm) for intake and exhaust valves. On all other models, valve tappet gap for intake valve is 0.008 inch (0.20 mm) and exhaust valve tappet gap is 0.016 inch (0.41 mm).

Valve adjustment on all models is made by turning self-locking cap screw on tappet as required.

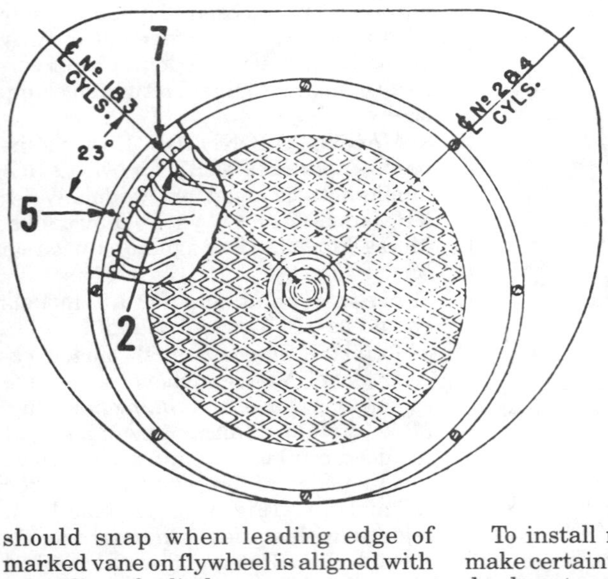

Fig. W104—Battery distributor timing marks for Models VH4, VH4D, VG4D and W4-1770 is a depression or hole (7) in air shroud.

2. "X" marked flywheel vane
5. Running spark (full advance) timing index
7. Top dead center index (centerline) for cylinders 1 and 3

REPAIRS

TIGHTENING TORQUES. Recommended torque specifications are as follows:

Connecting rod:

VH4, VH4D, W4-1770..	22-24 ft.-lbs. (30-33 N·m)
VG4D	26-32 ft.-lbs (35-43 N·m)
VR4D	40-50 ft.-lbs (54-68 N·m)

should snap when leading edge of marked vane on flywheel is aligned with centerline of cylinders.

Procedure for setting running timing, firing order and cylinder sequence is the same as for battery ignition system.

To install magneto on Model VR4D, make certain number 1 cylinder is at top dead center on compression stroke, remove air intake screen at flywheel and timing hole plug. Leading edge of flywheel vane marked "X" and "DC" (Fig.

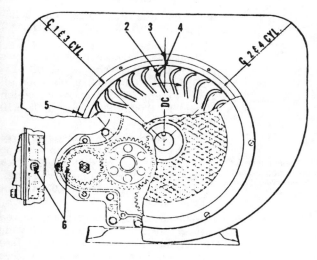

Fig. W106—Magneto ignition timing marks on Models VH4, VH4D, VG4D and W4-1770.

2. "X" marked flywheel vane
3. Magneto installation timing mark
4. Leading edge of marked flywheel vane
5. Running timing mark
6. Marked tooth on magneto gear

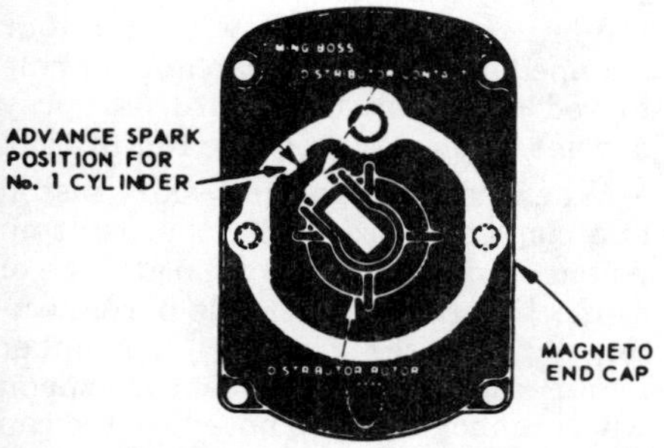

Tighten screws in sequence shown in Fig. W109 on Models VH4, VH4D and W4-1770 to 22-24 ft.-lbs. (30-33 N•m), on Model VG4D to 25-32 ft.-lbs (34-43 N•m), and on Model VR4D to 25-30 ft.-lbs (34-40 N•m).

VALVE SYSTEM. All models except Model V4D are equipped with stellite exhaust valves and seats.

Valve seats are renewable-type inserts in cylinder block and seats should be ground to a 45° angle. Valve seat width should be $3/32$ inch (2.4 mm). Valve face angle should be 45°. Valves with oversize stems are available for some models.

Valve stem clearance in block or guide on Models VH4, VH4D and W4-1770 should be 0.003-0.005 inch (0.07-0.13 mm). Later models are equipped with renewable valve guides. Valves with oversize stems are available for models that do not have renewable guides. If stem clearance equals or exceeds 0.007 inch (0.18 mm), a new valve guide or valve with an oversize stem should be installed.

Valve stem clearance in block or guide on Models VG4D should be 0.004 inch (0.10 mm). Valves with oversize stems are available for models that do not have renewable guides. If stem clearance equals or exceeds 0.006 inch (0.15 mm), a new valve guide or valve with an oversize stem should be installed.

Valve stem clearance in block or guide on Models VG4D should be 0.002-0.004 inch (0.05-0.10 mm). Valves with oversize stems are available for models that do not have renewable guides. If stem clearance equals or exceeds 0.006 inch (0.15 mm), a new valve guide or valve with an oversize stem should be installed.

On Model W4-1770, intake valve spring free length should be $2\frac{5}{16}$ inches (58.7 mm). Minimum allowable intake valve spring pressure, when compressed to 1.271 inches (32.28 mm), is 45 pounds (200 N).

On Model W4-1770, exhaust valve spring free length should be $1\frac{13}{16}$ inches (46.0 mm). Minimum allowable intake valve spring pressure, when compressed to 1.130 inches (28.70 mm), is 78 pounds (347 N).

PISTON, PIN AND RINGS. Piston and connecting rod assemblies are removed from cylinder head end of block. Piston and connecting rod are accessible after removing cylinder head and engine base.

Model W4-1770 is equipped with a three-ring piston and Model VH4D changed to a three-ring piston effective with serial number 5538322. Pistons on

ADVANCE SPARK POSITION FOR No. 1 CYLINDER

MAGNETO END CAP

Fig. W107—Align rotor with timing boss when installing magneto on Model VR4D.

Engine base:

VR4D . . . . 18-20 ft.-lbs (24-27 N•m)

All other models . . . . . 72-108 in.-lbs. (8.1-12.2 N•m)

Gear cover:

VR4D . . . . 15-20 ft.-lbs. (20-33 N•m)

All other models . . . . 14-18 ft.-lbs. (19-24 N•m)

Main bearing plate 25-30 ft.-lbs. (34-40 N•m)

Manifold:

VH4, VH4D, W4-1770 . . 18-23 ft.-lbs. (24-31 N•m)

VG4D . . . . 40-50 ft.-lbs. (54-68 N•m)

VR4D . . . . 25-30 ft.-lbs (34-40 N•m)

Spark plug . . . . 25-30 ft.-lbs (34-40 N•m)

Cylinder block:

VH4, VH4D, W4-1770 . 40-50 ft.-lbs. (54-88 N•m)

VG4D . . . . 62-78 ft.-lbs (84-106 N•m)

VR4D . . . . 95-110 ft.-lbs (129-149 N•m)

Cylinder head:

VH4, VH4D, W4-1770 . 22-24 ft.-lbs. (30-33 N•m)

VG4D . . . . 25-32 ft.-lbs (34-43 N•m)

VR4D . . . . 25-30 ft.-lbs (34-40 N•m)

CYLINDER HEADS. When removing cylinder head, note location and lengths of cylinder head retaining screws so they can be reinstalled in their original positions.

A new cylinder head gasket should be installed to insure proper sealing.

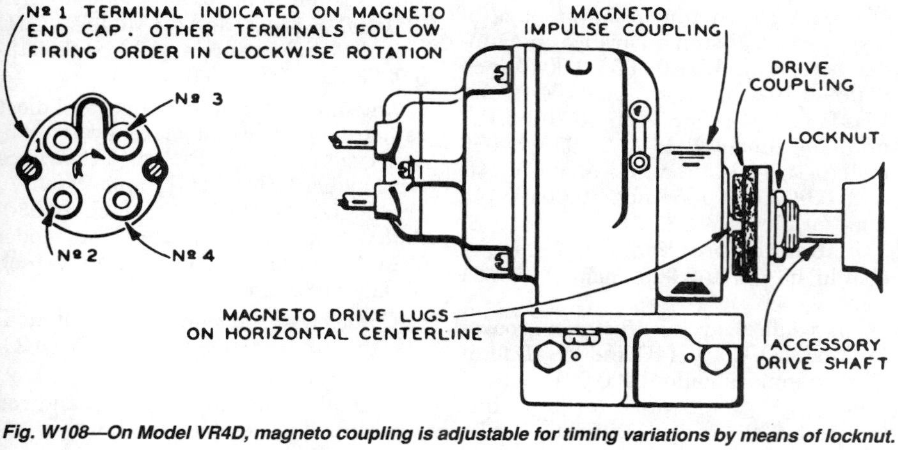

Nº 1 TERMINAL INDICATED ON MAGNETO END CAP. OTHER TERMINALS FOLLOW FIRING ORDER IN CLOCKWISE ROTATION

Nº 3

Nº 2

Nº 4

MAGNETO DRIVE LUGS ON HORIZONTAL CENTERLINE

MAGNETO IMPULSE COUPLING

DRIVE COUPLING

LOCKNUT

ACCESSORY DRIVE SHAFT

Fig. W108—On Model VR4D, magneto coupling is adjustable for timing variations by means of locknut.

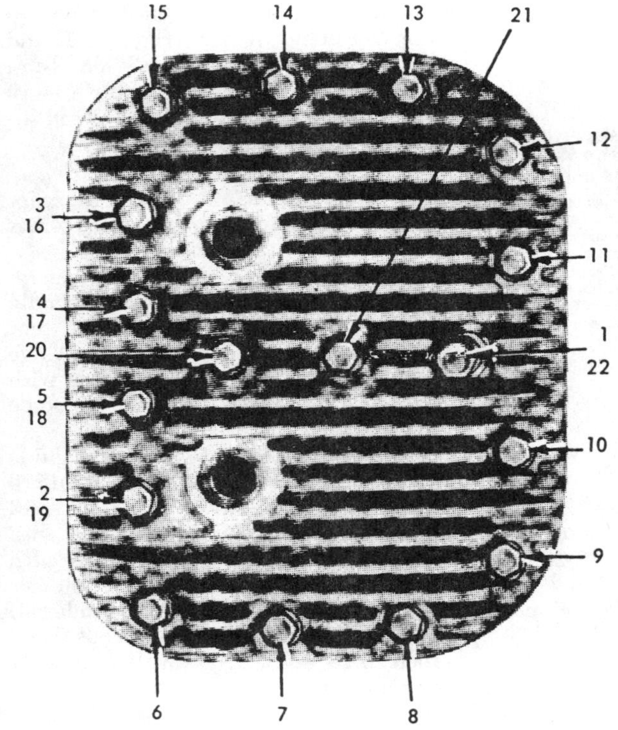

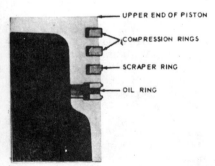

Fig. W109—Tighten cylinder head cap screws on Models VH4, VH4D and W4-1770 in sequence shown.

for second and third rings, and 0.0025-0.0040 inch (0.064-0.102 mm) for oil control ring.

Ring side clearance in piston grooves for Model VR4D should be 0.0015-0.0035 inch (0.038-0.089 mm) for all rings except oil control ring, which should be 0.002-0.004 inch (0.05-0.10 mm).

Ring side clearance in piston grooves for three-ring piston on models so equipped should be 0.002-0.004 inch (0.05-0.10 mm) for top and second rings, and 0.001-0.003 inch (0.02-0.08 mm) for oil control ring.

When assembling cam-ground piston and connecting rod, note that wide thrust face skirt of piston must face thrust side of engine when installed (see Fig. W111). Number stamped on side of rod must correspond with number stamped on side of rod cap and oil hole in rod cap must be toward oil spray nozzles when installed (see Fig. W112).

When assembling split skirt piston and connecting rod, note that split on piston skirt must be on opposite side of connecting rod from oil hole in connecting rod cap (see Fig. W111). Number stamped on side of rod must correspond with number stamped on side of rod cap and oil hole in rod cap must be toward oil spray nozzles when installed (see Fig. W112).

Tighten connecting rod nuts on Models VH4, VH4D and W4-1770 to 22-24 ft.-lbs. (30-33 N•m), on Model VG4D to 26-32 ft.-lbs (35-43 N•m), and on Model VR4D to 40-50 ft.-lbs (54-68 N•m).

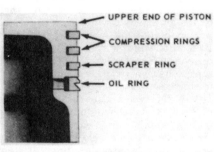

Fig. W110—On Model VG4D, piston rings for four-ring piston must be installed on piston as shown.

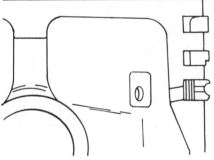

Fig. W110B—View showing piston ring arrangement of models with three-ring piston.

CONNECTING ROD. Connecting rod and piston are removed from cylinder head end of block as an assembly. Piston and connecting rod are accessible after removing cylinder head and engine base.

Early model engine connecting rods ride directly on crankpin journal. Running clearance for Models VH4 and VH4D should be 0.0007-0.0020 inch (0.018-0.051 mm) and for Models VG4D and VR4D clearance should be 0.0015-0.0028 inch (0.038-0.071 mm).

Late model connecting rods and most replacement rods have renewable insert-type bearings. Running clearance for Models VH4, VH4D and W4-1770 should be 0.0012-0.0033 inch (0.030-0.084 mm) and clearance for Model VG4D should be 0.0013-0.0035 inch (0.033-0.089 mm).

Connecting rod side play for all models should be 0.009-0.016 inch (0.23-0.41 mm).

Assemble and install piston and rod as outlined in previous section.

Fig. W110A—Correct piston ring installation on four-ring piston used on Models VH4, VH4D and VR4D.

all other models are equipped with four piston rings. Replacement pistons may be equipped with three rings. Note location and arrangement of piston rings in Figs. W110, W110A and W110B. Pistons and rings are available in standard size as well as a variety of oversizes.

Early pistons were a split skirt design and later model pistons are cam-ground. Different piston-types should not be mixed in an engine.

Measure piston diameter at a point 90° from piston pin at lower edge of piston skirt. Piston clearance in cylinder bore should be 0.0035-0.0040 inch (0.089-0.102 mm) for Models VH4 and VH4D, 0.004-0.005 inch (0.102-0.127 mm) for Model VH4D, 0.0050-0.0055 inch (0.127-0.140 mm) for Model VR4D and 0.0025-0.0045 inch (0.064-0.114 mm) for Model W4-1770.

Piston compression ring end gap should be 0.010-0.020 inch (0.25-0.51 mm).

Ring side clearance in piston grooves for Models VH4, VH4D and VG4D four-ring pistons should be 0.0020-0.0035 inch (0.051-0.089 mm) for top ring, 0.0010-0.0025 inch (0.025-0.064 mm)

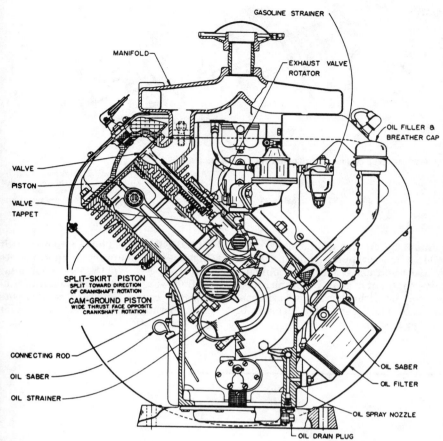

Fig. W111—Cross-sectional view of engine showing general location and relationship of component parts.

Fig. W113—View of timing gears on Wisconsin V4 engine.

2. Magneto, generator or accessory drive
3. Camshaft gear
4. Governor gear
5. Valve timing marks
6. Crankshaft gear
7. Idler gear
8. Oil pump gear

47.65 mm), for Model VG4D should be 1.317-1.322 inches (43.45-43.58 mm), and for Model VR4D should be 2.750-2.751 inches (69.85-69.88 mm).

Timing marks should be aligned as shown in Fig. W113 during crankshaft installation.

Oil seals should be installed in timing gear cover and rear bearing plate before they are bolted in place and care should be taken to avoid seal damage during installation.

CAMSHAFT. The camshaft runs in unbushed bores in crankcase casting. Camshaft gear is held on end of camshaft by three cap screws. End play is controlled by a spring-loaded plunger assembly and a wear button that bears against timing gear cover. Use care not to lose plunger, spring or wear button during disassembly and reassembly.

IDLER GEAR AND SHAFT. An idler gear, driven by the crankshaft gear, is used to drive magneto and oil pump on all models.

To remove idler gear and shaft, remove timing gear cover, magneto or generator and distributor. Remove Allen head set screws from side of crankcase that retain idler shaft in position. Use a sleeve-type puller over end of idler shaft and against idler gear, thread a 3/8-16 cap screw into end of shaft. Pull shaft from crankcase and idler gear.

When reassembling, make certain oil slot in idler shaft is facing upward. Press or drive idler shaft into crankcase until a clearance of 0.003-0.004 inch (0.08-0.10 mm) exists between gear hub

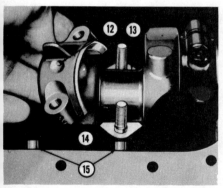

Fig. W112—Installing connecting rod and cap on Wisconsin V4 engine. Numbers on connecting rod and rod cap must face oil spray nozzle side of engine.

12. Oil hole
13. Crankshaft
14. Number on rod cap
15. Oil spray nozzles

CYLINDER. Two cylinders are cast as a unit that is attached to the crankcase. Cylinders for all models may be bored to accept an oversize piston. Cylinder bore should be bored oversize if worn or out-of-round more than 0.005 inch (0.13 mm). Pistons are available in standard size and a variety of oversizes.

Standard cylinder bore diameter is 3.248-3.249 inches (82.50-82.52 mm) for Models VH4 and VH4D, 3.498-3.499 inches (88.85-88.87 mm) for Model VG4D, 4.248-4.249 inches (107.90-107.92 mm) for Model VR4D, and 3.249-3.250 inches (82.52-82.55 mm) for Model W4-1770.

CRANKSHAFT, MAIN BEARINGS AND OIL SEALS. Crankshaft is supported at each end by taper roller bearings. Main bearings are a press fit on crankshaft. Rear bearing cup is pressed into bearing plate and front bearing cup is retained in crankcase by a retainer plate and cap screws.

Crankshaft end play should be 0.002-0.005 inch (0.05-0.13 mm) for Model W4-1770 and 0.002-0.004 inch (0.05-0.10 mm) for all other models. End play is controlled by varying thickness of gaskets between main bearing plate and crankcase. Gaskets are available in a variety of thicknesses.

Crankpin standard journal diameter for Models VH4, VH4D and W4-1770 should be 1.875-1.876 inches (47.62-

Fig. W114—Removing oil pump retaining screw on Wisconsin V4 engine. Allen head screw is accessible after removing slotted plug (94).

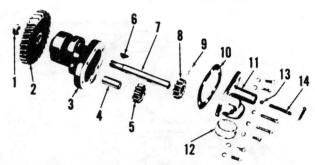

Fig. W114A—Exploded view of oil pump used on all models.

1. Nut	5. Idler gear	8. Pump gear	12. Screen
2. Drive gear	6. Key	9. Pin	13. Oil pressure relief
3. Pump body	7. Pump shaft	10. Gasket	valve ball
4. Idler shaft		11. Cover	14. Relief valve spring

and shoulder on end of idler shaft. Lock shaft in position with Allen set screws.

OIL PUMP. To remove oil pump, remove engine base and timing gear cover.

Remove pump retaining screw (Fig. W114). Unscrew pump gear nut (1—Fig. W114A) and use a soft brass punch to drive shaft out of gear. Oil pump assembly may be withdrawn from crankcase. Refer to Fig. W114A for disassembly and reassembly.

GOVERNOR. The governor unit (Fig. W98) is mounted on spacer plate shown in Fig. W113. Governor gear shaft (1—Fig. W98) is pressed into timing gear cover. Governor components must operate freely without binding for proper operation.

WISCONSIN

Model	No. Cyls.	Bore	Stroke	Displacement	Power Rating
V-460D, V-461D	4	3.5 in. (88.9 mm)	4 in. (101.6 mm)	154 cu. in. (2522.6 cc)	60.5 hp (45.1 kW)
V-465D	4	3.75 in. (92.25 mm)	4 in. (101.6 mm)	177 cu. in. (2716.3 cc)	65.9 hp (49.1 kW)

Engines in this section are four-stroke, four cylinder V-type with a horizontal crankshaft. Crankshaft for all models is supported at each end in taper roller bearings and at center journal by either a straight roller bearing with a two-piece outer race (early production) or a renewable insert-type bearing (late production).

Connecting rods for all models have renewable insert-type bearings that are lubricated by a gear-type oil pump. Oil pump provides high pressure lubrication to crankshaft bearings and rod bearings, and low pressure lubrication to camshaft bearings, tappets, valve train and governor gear train. Oil pump is driven by crankshaft gear via an idler gear.

Battery ignition, with electric starting motor and generator, is standard. However, a magneto ignition is available for manual start models.

Zenith 87 model carburetor is used for all models and a mechanical-type fuel pump is available.

Engine identification information is located on engine instruction plate. Engine model, specification and serial numbers are required when ordering parts. Special machine work on crankcase is identified by number stamped on crankcase above rear bearing plate. This number is required if crankcase is to be renewed.

MAINTENANCE

SPARK PLUG. Recommended spark plug is Champion N12Y or equivalent. Electrode gap should be 0.030 inch (0.76 mm).

CARBURETOR. Zenith 87 model carburetor, equipped with an anti-dieseling solenoid, is used on all models.

Note that main fuel jet is fixed and nonadjustable, except in possible special applications.

For initial idle mixture screw adjustment, open idle mixture screw 1¼ turns.

On all models, make final adjustments with engine at normal operating temperature and running. Set engine at idle speed and adjust idle mixture screw for smoothest idle operation.

To check float level, invert carburetor throttle body and float assembly, and measure from furthest face of float to machined gasket surface of throttle body. Measurement should be $^{31}/_{32}$ inch (24.6 mm).

Adjust float level by bending float tang that contacts inlet valve.

Anti-dieseling solenoid shuts off fuel supply in carburetor when de-energized to help assure rapid engine shut down. Engine should not run if ignition wire to solenoid is not supplied with electrical current.

GOVERNOR. Flyweight-type governor, driven by camshaft gear, is used on all models. Refer to Fig. W115 for exploded view of typical governor component parts.

On all models, speed changes are obtained by varying spring (12—Fig. W115) tension with adjusting screw (14) or locating spring in alternate holes of governor control lever (11).

To correctly set governed speeds, use a tachometer to accurately record crankshaft rpm. Refer to Fig. W116 to determine correct hole in which to locate spring for desired rpm.

Governor-to-carburetor rod should be adjusted so it just will enter hole in governor lever when governor weights are "in" and carburetor throttle is wide open.

IGNITION SYSTEM. Battery-type ignition system is standard. However, a magneto-type system is available for manual start models.

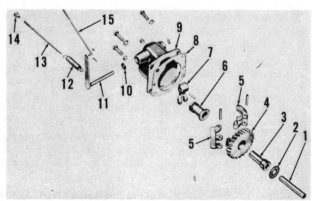

Fig. W115—Exploded view of typical governor assembly used on Wisconsin V4 engines.

1. Shaft	5. Flyweights	8. Gasket	12. Governor spring
2. Thrust washer	6. Thrust sleeve & bearing assy.	9. Housing	13. Control rod
3. Bushing	7. Yoke	10. Oil seal	14. Adjusting screw
4. Governor gear		11. Governor lever & shaft	15. Throttle rod

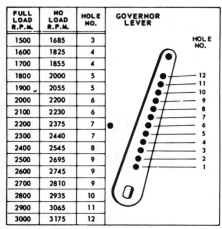

FULL LOAD R.P.M.	NO LOAD R.P.M.	HOLE NO.
1500	1685	3
1600	1825	4
1700	1855	4
1800	2000	5
1900	2055	5
2000	2200	6
2100	2230	6
2200	2375	7
2300	2440	7
2400	2545	8
2500	2695	9
2600	2745	9
2700	2810	9
2800	2935	10
2900	3065	11
3000	3175	12

Fig. W116—Governor speed table for V-460D, V-461D and V-465D models.

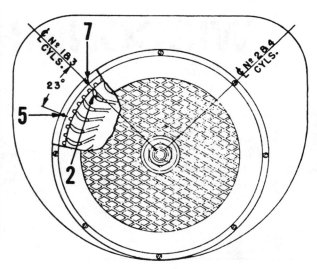

Fig. W117—Battery distributor timing marks on V-460D, V-461D and V-465D models equipped with electric starting system.

2. "X" marked flywheel vane
5. Running spark (full advance) timing mark
7. Top center index (center line) for cylinders 1 and 3

BATTERY IGNITION. Delco-Remy DR1112695 or Prestolite IAD-6004-2N distributor is used according to model and application.

Distributor is mounted on accessory drive shaft housing and turns counter-clockwise, as viewed from above, at one-half engine rpm. Breaker point gap should be 0.020 inch (0.51 mm) and firing order is 1-3-4-2. Cylinders are numbered from flywheel side of engine and (facing flywheel) are as follows: left bank—Nos. 1 and 3; right bank—Nos. 2 and 4.

To install and time distributor, remove screen over flywheel air intake opening and make certain number 1 cylinder is at top dead center on compression stroke, and leading edge of flywheel vane marked "X" is in line with centerline mark of number 1 cylinder (Fig. W117). Hold distributor so primary terminal wire (Delco-Remy) or terminal (Prestolite) is at 12 o'clock position and rotate rotor arm to 2 o'clock position (Delco-Remy) or 1 o'clock position (Prestolite) and carefully install distributor. Rotate distributor counter-clockwise until breaker points just begin to open and tighten clamp screw.

Running timing should be 23° BTDC at 2000 rpm or above for all models. Advance timing mark indicating this position is a ⅛-inch (3.16 mm) hole in air shroud (5—Fig. W117). With engine operating at 2000 rpm or above, timing light should flash when leading edge of "X" marked flywheel vane is in register with running (fully advanced) timing mark (5) on air shroud. If not, loosen distributor body clamp screw, turn distributor until correct timing is obtained and tighten clamp screw.

MAGNETO IGNITION. Fairbanks-Morse FM-X4B7D magneto is available for manual start models. Breaker point

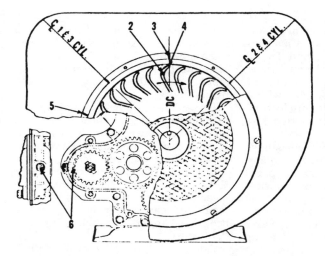

Fig. W118—Magneto ignition timing marks on manual start V-460D, V-461D and V-465D engines.

2. "X" marked flywheel vane
3. Magneto installation timing mark
4. Leading edge of marked flywheel vane
5. Running timing mark
6. Marked tooth on magneto gear

gap for all models should be 0.015 inch (0.38 mm).

To install magneto to engine, remove air intake screen at flywheel and timing hole plug. Make certain number 1 cylinder is at top dead center on compression stroke. Leading edge of flywheel vane marked "X" and "DC" (Fig. W118) should be in register with static timing mark on air shroud. Install magneto so "X" marked tooth on magneto drive gear is visible through port in timing gear housing as shown. To check for correct installation, slowly crank engine. Impulse coupling should snap when leading edge of marked vane on flywheel is aligned with center line of cylinders.

Procedure for setting running timing, firing order and cylinder sequence is the same as for battery ignition system.

LUBRICATION. Lubrication is provided by a gear-type oil pump driven by crankshaft gear via an idler gear. Oil pressure system consists of a high pressure system that provides oil at 40-45 psi (276-345 kPa) to center main and connecting rod bearings, and a low pressure system that provides oil at 3-4 psi (21-26 kPa) to camshaft bearings, tappets, valve train and governor gear train. See Fig. W119.

High pressure in the system is controlled by an adjustable pressure relief valve located beneath starter next to oil filter (Fig. W119). To adjust high pressure relief valve, remove expansion plug and lock screw from end of valve and, with engine at normal operating temperature and running at 1800 rpm, turn adjusting screw in relief valve until 40-45 psi (276-345 kPa) pressure is reached. Reinstall lock screw and expansion plug.

Low-pressure in the system is controlled by a pressure reducing valve that is nonadjustable. Low pressure should be 3-4 psi (21-26 kPa) when engine is at normal operating temperature and running at 1800 rpm. Check pressure by installing gauge in oil header (gallery) at rear of engine (Fig. W119).

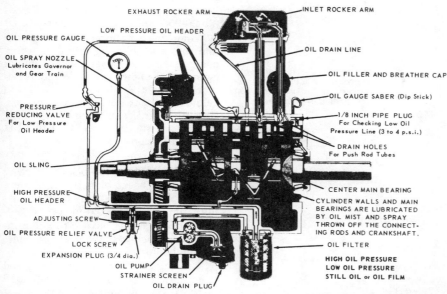

Fig. W119—Cross-sectional view of typical Wisconsin engine showing high and low pressure areas of lubrication. Note placement of gauge to check high pressure side of system and 1/8-inch pipe plug where gauge may be installed to check low pressure side.

Fig. W120—Remove slotted pipe plug and Allen head lock screw to remove oil pump.

If valve is faulty, it must be renewed as a unit.

To remove oil pump, remove crankcase oil pan and timing gear cover. Remove pump retaining screw (Fig. W120). Unscrew pump drive gear nut (1—Fig. W121) and use a soft brass punch to drive shaft out of gear. Oil pump assembly may be withdrawn from crankcase. Refer to Fig. W121 for disassembly and reassembly.

Maintain oil level at full mark on dipstick but do not overfill. High-quality detergent oil, having API classification SE, SF or SG is recommended. Oil change interval recommendation is every 50 hours of normal operation and filter should be changed every other oil change.

For all models, crankcase capacity is 6 quarts (5.7 L) without filter change and 7 quarts (6.6 L) with filter change.

Use SAE 30 oil when operating temperature is between 120° F (49° C) and 40° F (4° C), SAE 20 oil between 40° F (4° C) and 15° F (−9° C), SAE 10 oil between 15° F (−9° C) and 0° F (−18° C), and SAE 5W-20 oil for below 0° F (−18° C).

REPAIRS

TIGHTENING TORQUES. Recommended torque specifications are as follows:

Cylinder head	30 ft.-lbs. (40 N·m)
Connecting rod	32 ft.-lbs. (43 N·m)
Gear cover	18 ft.-lbs. (24 N·m)
Center main cap-to-hanger—	
Roller bearing	40 ft.-lbs. (54 N·m)
Insert bearing	32-35 ft.-lbs. (43-48 N·m)
Hanger-to-crankcase	60 ft.-lbs. (81 N·m)
Main bearing plate	32 ft.-lbs. (43 N·m)
Main bearing retainer	32 ft.-lbs. (43 N·m)
Manifold-to-head	25 ft.-lbs. (34 N·m)
Manifold-to-manifold	15 ft.-lbs. (20 N·m)
Oil pan	18 ft.-lbs. (24 N·m)
Spark plug	22 ft.-lbs. (30 N·m)

CYLINDER HEADS. To remove one cylinder head, it is not necessary to remove manifold assembly from engine. Remove rocker arm cover and manifold-to-cylinder head stud nuts, and carefully lift off cylinder head assembly, push rods and push rod tubes. Oil drain line will pull out of adapter in crankcase and will be removed with cylinder head. Rocker arms, valves and springs can now be removed from cylinder head if necessary.

If all cylinder heads are to be removed, first unbolt and remove manifold and carburetor assembly, then remove each of the four cylinder heads as outlined previously.

When installing cylinder heads, always use new head gaskets, "O" rings on push rod tubes and "O" rings on oil drain lines. Align cylinder heads by placing a parallel steel bar across exhaust and inlet ports as shown in Fig. W122. Tap heads lightly with a rubber mallet to rotate heads until port flanges are aligned with steel bar. Tighten cylinder head retaining nuts alternately in three steps: First step to 10 ft.-lbs. (13 N·m) torque, second step to 20 ft.-lbs. (27 N·m) torque and finally to 30 ft.-lbs. (40 N·m) torque.

When installing manifold assembly, align cast notches on numbers 2 and 3 inlet ports on manifold with similar cast notches on cylinder head ports. Tighten manifold-to-cylinder head nuts evenly to a torque of 25 ft.-lbs. (34 N·m).

To renew rocker arms, remove complete rocker arm bracket assembly from cylinder head. Remove set screw from

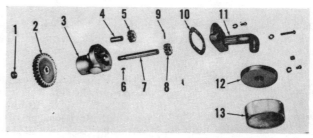

Fig. W121—Exploded view of oil pump used on V-460D, V-461D and V-465D models.

1. Nut	5. Idler gear	8. Pump gear	11. Cover
2. Drive gear	6. Key	9. Pin	12. Screen adapter
3. Pump body	7. Pump shaft	10. Gasket	13. Screen
4. Idler shaft			

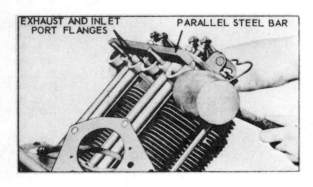

Fig. W122—View showing procedure for aligning exhaust and inlet ports when installing cylinder heads.

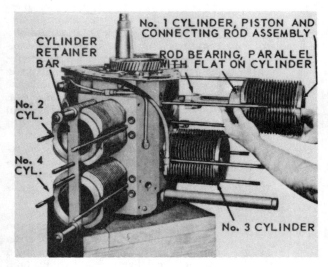

Fig. W123—View showing installation of cylinder, piston and rod assembly. Note cylinder retainer bar holding Nos. 2 and 4 cylinders in position.

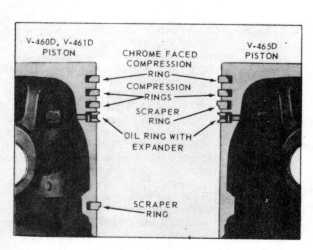

Fig. W124—View showing correct installation of piston rings on pistons.

V-461D engines, and 3.748-3.749 inches (95.20-95.25 mm) for V-465D engine.

When reassembling, install piston and rod assemblies in cylinders, then, using new cylinder base gaskets, install cylinders as shown in Fig. W123. A cylinder retainer bar should be attached to cylinder studs to hold cylinders in position on crankcase. Install cylinder heads as outlined in **CYLINDER HEADS** section.

CONNECTING RODS. Connecting rods, piston assemblies and cylinders can be removed from above after removing cylinder head and crankcase oil pan.

Connecting rods have renewable insert-type bearings and a renewable piston pin bushing.

Running clearance of connecting rod to crankpin should be 0.0005-0.0018 inch (0.013-0.045 mm).

Connecting rod side clearance should be 0.008-0.016 inch (0.20-0.40 mm).

Number stamped on side of rod should correspond with number stamped on side of rod cap when reinstalled.

Crankpin standard journal diameter should be 2.1233-2.1238 inches (53.93-53.94 mm) for all models.

Connecting rod bearings are available in a variety of sizes for undersize crankshafts.

PISTONS, PINS AND RINGS. Cam-ground aluminum pistons are equipped with two compression rings, one scraper ring and one oil control ring on V-465D, or three compression rings, one oil control ring and one scraper ring (on skirt) on V-460D and V-461D engines. Pistons and rings are available in a variety of oversizes as well as standard.

Piston-to-cylinder clearance should be measured at 90° to piston pin at lower edge of skirt. Clearance should be 0.0025-0.003 inch (0.063-0.076 mm) for all models.

Piston ring end gap should be 0.008-0.024 inch (0.20-0.61 mm) for all models. Rings must be installed on pistons as shown in Fig. W124. Stagger ring gaps 90° apart around piston.

Ring side clearance in piston grooves should be 0.002-0.004 inch (0.05-0.10 mm) for all rings.

Piston pin should be 0.000-0.0008 inch (0.000-0.020 mm) tight fit in piston and is retained at each end by a snap ring in bore of piston. Pin should have 0.0005-0.0011 inch (0.013-0.028 mm) clearance in bushing in end of connecting rod. Pins are available in a variety of oversizes as well as standard.

bottom of bracket and tap shaft out toward set screw end of bracket using a brass rod. (Beginning with engine serial number 5634850, set screw is installed with Loctite 271 and heat may be required to remove it.)

To reassemble, flat surface on shaft must align with set screw hole in bracket. Apply Loctite 271 to set screw threads and install. Lubricate shaft and rocker arms with engine oil before running engine.

Refer to **VALVE SYSTEM** section for valve tappet gap adjustment procedure.

CYLINDERS. Individually cast cylinders may be removed from crankcase after removing cylinder heads and manifold. Mark location of each cylinder so they can be reinstalled in their original positions.

Standard cylinder bore is 3.498-3.499 inches (88.85-88.87 mm) for V-460D and

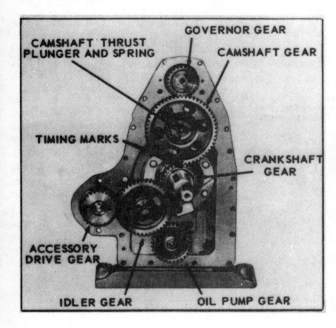

Fig. W125—Wisconsin V4 engine with timing gear cover removed showing gear train and location of timing marks.

CRANKSHAFT, MAIN BEARINGS AND OIL SEALS. Crankshaft is supported at each end in taper roller bearings and at center journal by either a straight roller bearing with a two-piece outer race (early production) or a renewable insert-type bearing (late production).

Front and rear main bearings are a press fit on crankshaft. Rear bearing cup is pressed into bearing plate and front bearing cup is retained in crankcase by a retainer plate and cap screws.

Timing marks should be aligned as shown in Fig. W125 during installation of crankshaft for all models.

SPLIT ROLLER CENTER MAIN BEARING. Center main bearing for early production engines (before serial number 4904657) was a split roller bearing type. To remove crankshaft, unbolt bearing hanger and remove oil coupling located behind crankshaft gear. Remove rear bearing plate and withdraw crankshaft with center main bearing assembly through bearing plate opening in crankcase.

To remove center bearing assembly, back bearing cap retaining screws out ¼ inch (12.7 mm) and tap cap screws lightly to separate cap from hanger. With cap and hanger removed, remove retaining ring, two-piece outer race and the 32 bearing rollers. Note crankshaft standard bearing journal diameter should be 2.300-2.3005 inches (58.42-58.43 mm) and a 0.030 inch (0.76 mm) oversize bearing is available for reground crankshafts.

For reinstallation, retain bearing rollers in split race with low-melting-point grease and install on crankshaft

securing bearing halves with retaining ring. Install cap and hanger.

Reinstall crankshaft and set end play before securing center main bearing hanger to crankcase by varying thickness of gasket between bearing plate and crankcase until 0.002-0.004 inch (0.05-0.10 mm) end play is obtained.

Tighten center main bearing cap screws to 15 ft.-lbs. (20 N•m) torque, then 30 ft.-lbs. (40 N•m) torque and finally to 40 ft.-lbs. (54 N•m) torque, then tighten bearing hanger-to-crankcase cap screws to 60 ft.-lbs. (81 N•m) torque.

NOTE: Beginning with engine serial number 4052826, cap screws for mounting bearing hanger to crankcase were lengthened to 3 inches and a spacer added under screw heads to minimize possibility of improper assembly, and there must be 0.004 inch (0.10 mm) clearance between sides of bearing hanger and crankshaft cheeks.

Crankshaft designed for insert-type bearing at center main will not interchange with crankshaft designed for split roller bearing center main without crankcase modifications.

INSERT-TYPE CENTER MAIN BEARING. Center main bearing for late model engines (serial number 4904657 or after) is an insert-type bearing. To remove crankshaft, disconnect oil line at center bearing hanger. Remove bearing cap and hanger from engine. Remove rear bearing plate and withdraw crankshaft. Note crankshaft standard bearing journal diameter

should be 2.3020-2.3025 inches (58.47-58.48 mm) and bearing inserts are available in a variety of sizes for reground crankshafts as well as standard.

For reinstallation, install crankshaft in crankcase and set end play before installing center main bearing assembly by varying thickness of gasket between bearing plate and crankcase until 0.002-0.005 inch (0.05-0.13 mm) is obtained.

Install bearing inserts in cap and hanger and install assembly on crankshaft. Tighten bearing cap screws to 32-35 ft.-lbs. (43-48 N•m), then tighten bearing hanger to crankcase cap screws to 60 ft.-lbs. (81 N•m) torque. Connect oil line.

See **CONNECTING ROD** section for standard crankshaft rod journal diameters.

On all models, oil seals should be installed in timing gear cover and rear bearing plate before they are bolted in place and care should be taken to avoid seal damage during installation.

IDLER GEAR AND SHAFT. An idler gear, driven by crankshaft gear, is used to drive magneto or accessory drive and oil pump.

To remove idler gear and shaft, remove timing gear cover, magneto or accessory drive and distributor. Remove Allen head set screws from side of crankcase that retain idler shaft in position. Using a sleeve-type puller over end of idler shaft and against idler gear, thread a ⅜-16 cap screw into end of shaft. Pull shaft from crankcase and idler gear.

When reassembling, make certain oil slot in idler shaft is facing upward. Press or drive idler shaft into crankcase until a clearance of 0.003-0.004 inch (0.08-0.10 mm) exists between gear hub and shoulder on end of idler shaft. Lock shaft in position with Allen set screws.

CAMSHAFT. Camshaft runs in unbushed bores in crankcase casting. Camshaft gear is held on end of camshaft by three cap screws and end play is controlled by a spring-loaded plunger assembly and wear button, which bears against timing gear cover. Use care not to lose plunger, spring or wear button during reassembly.

VALVE SYSTEM. All models are equipped with stellite exhaust valves and seats and rotocap on exhaust valves is standard.

Valve seats are not renewable, but may be reground at 45° angle if seat width does not exceed 3/32 inch (2.38 mm).

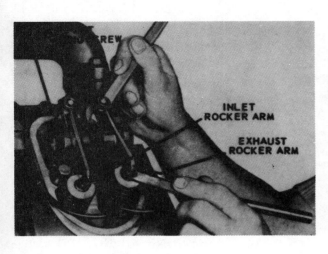

Fig. W126—Adjusting valve tappet gap in typical valve-in-head V4 Wisconsin engine.

INLET ROCKER ARM

EXHAUST ROCKER ARM

Valve faces are ground at 45° angle and valve stem clearance in guide should be 0.002-0.004 inch (0.05-0.10 mm). Valve, guide or both should be renewed if clearance exceeds 0.006 inch (0.15 mm). Press old guide out and allow 1/64- to 1/32-inch (0.40-0.79 mm) clearance between valve guide boss and valve guide shoulder. Standard inside diameter of valve guide should be 0.3440-0.3445 inch (8.738-8.750 mm).

Valve tappet gap (cold) for all models should be 0.008 inch (0.20 mm) for intake valves and 0.014 inch (0.35 mm) for exhaust valves.

Adjustment is made by turning tappet adjusting screw (Fig. W126) as required.

WISCONSIN

Model	No. Cyls.	Bore	Stroke	Displacement	Power Rating
W2-1230, W2-1235, W2-1250	2	3.75 in. (95.2 mm)	3.4 in. (86 mm)	75.0 cu. in. (1230 cc)	30 hp (22.4 kW)

Engines in this section are four-stroke, two-cylinder "V"-type, air-cooled engines with a horizontal crankshaft. Crankshaft is supported at each end by sleeve-type bearings. Connecting rods are equipped with renewable insert-type bearings.

Pressure lubrication is provided by a gear-driven, gerotor-type oil pump.

Ignition system consists of battery-type system that may use breaker points or an electronic trigger system.

The fuel system consists of a Walbro float-type carburetor and a mechanical fuel pump.

Number 1 cylinder is on the right when viewed from flywheel end of engine.

Engine information provided on engine identification plate may be required when ordering parts.

MAINTENANCE

LUBRICATION. Pressure lubrication is provided by a gear-driven, gerotor-type oil pump. Oil is pumped to bearing surfaces of crankshaft, camshaft and governor shaft. Above engine speed of 1600 rpm, system pressure should be 30-50 psi (207-345 kPa) and is controlled by a relief valve in pump. If oil pressure is less than 15 psi (104 kPa), determine cause.

Maintain oil level at full mark on dipstick but do not overfill. Oil and oil filter should be changed after every 100 hours of operation. Change oil and oil filter after every 50 hours of operation if engine undergoes severe operation.

Crankcase capacity, including filter, is 4 quarts (3.8 L).

Manufacturer recommends oil with an API service classification of SE, SF or SG. Use SAE 10W-30 oil for ambient temperatures above 0° F (–18° C) and

SAE 5W-20 for temperatures below 0° F (–18° C).

CRANKCASE BREATHER. The engine is equipped with a crankcase breather that provides a vacuum for the crankcase. A reed-type valve is located in the valve inspection covers. Remove and clean breather assembly in a suitable solvent after every 200 hours of normal operation. Be sure drain hole is down during installation of valve cover.

SPARK PLUG. Recommended spark plug for early models with 18 mm spark plug hole in cylinder head is Champion D16J or equivalent. Recommended spark plug for later models with 14 mm spark plug hole in cylinder head is Champion N6 or RN6, or equivalent. Electrode gap should be 0.030 inch (0.76 mm) on D16J and RN6 spark plugs and 0.035 inch (0.88 mm) on N6 spark plug. Tighten spark plug to 18-22 ft.-lbs. (24.5-30 N•m).

CARBURETOR. Engine may be equipped with a Walbro LMH or WHG. Main fuel jet is fixed so no adjustment other than replacement is possible. Initial setting of idle mixture screw is 1 turn out. Make final adjustment with engine at normal operating temperature. Adjust idle mixture screw so engine idles smoothly and accelerates cleanly.

Refer to Fig. W301 for an exploded view of carburetor. Do not clean with carburetor solvent as internal passages will be damaged. Install throttle plate (11) so "W" stamped on plate is out when plate is in closed position. With carburetor body inverted, float height (H—Fig. W302) should be 0.030-0.070 inch (0.76-1.78 mm). If necessary, bend float tab (T) to adjust float height. With carburetor upright, outer end of float should be even with nozzle boss, within

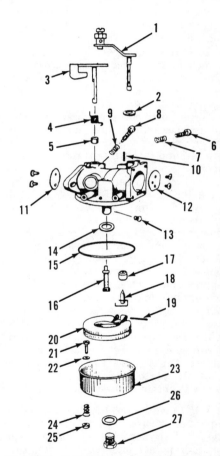

Fig. W301—Exploded view of Walbro WHG. Walbro LMH carburetor is similar except main jet (13) is part of bowl retainer screw (27).

1. Choke shaft
2. Washer
3. Throttle shaft
4. Spring
5. Seal
6. Idle speed screw
7. Spring
8. Idle mixture screw
9. Spring
10. Choke stop spring
11. Throttle plate
12. Choke plate
13. Main jet
14. Gasket
15. Gasket
16. Nozzle
17. Fuel inlet valve seat
18. Fuel inlet valve
19. Float pin
20. Float
21. Drain pin
22. Gasket
23. Fuel bowl
24. Spring
25. Retainer
26. Gasket
27. Screw

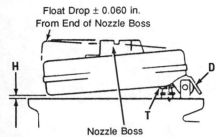

Fig. W302—Float height (H) should be 0.030-0.070 inch (0.76-1.78 mm).

Load R.P.M.	No Load R.P.M.	Hole No.	Spring	Fly-Weight
1600	1650	5		
1700	1770	5	Light	
1800	1880	6		
1900	2000	7		
2000	2420	2		Heavy
2100	2450	2		
2200	2475	2		
2300	2550	2		
2400	2620	2		
2500	2700	2		
2600	2770	2		
2700	2850	3		
2800	2925	4	Std.	
2900	3050	4		
3000	3130	5		
3100	3200	5		Std.
3200	3300	6		
3300	3410	6		
3400	3520	7		
3500	3630	9		
3600	3740	11		

Fig. W303—Governor speed table.

0.060 inch (1.5 mm), as shown by float drop in Fig. W302. Bend tab (D) to adjust float drop.

GOVERNOR. A flyweight-type governor driven by the camshaft gear is used on all models. Major speed changes on all models are obtained by varying tension of governor spring or locating spring in alternate holes of governor control lever.

To correctly set governed speeds, use a tachometer to accurately record engine rpm. Refer to Fig. W303 to determine correct hole in which to locate spring for desired rpm.

Governor-to-carburetor rod should be adjusted so it will just enter hole in governor lever when governor weights are "in" and carburetor throttle is wide open.

Additional adjustment is possible by changing flyweights (5—Fig. W304) and governor spring (25). Note differences between standard flyweight and governor spring and heavy flyweight and light tension governor spring in Fig. W305. The heavy flyweight and light tension governor spring may be used in applications such as generator sets that require minimum overrun.

Refer to Fig. W306 for adjustment of speed control devices. If equipped with a variable speed control, loosen Allen screw and relocate stop collar as required. On two-speed and fixed speed control, rotate locknut on adjusting screw to obtain desired engine speed.

IGNITION SYSTEM. The engine is equipped with a battery-type ignition system. Early models are equipped with breaker points and later models are equipped with a breakerless, solid-state trigger system. The distributor is driven by gear (11—Fig. W304) on the governor shaft. Distributor rotor rotates in a clockwise direction at one-half crankshaft speed. Automatic advance flyweights pivot on flange below breaker point or ignition module mounting plate to provide automatic timing advance.

Models With Breaker Points. Breaker point gap should be 0.020 inch (0.51 mm).

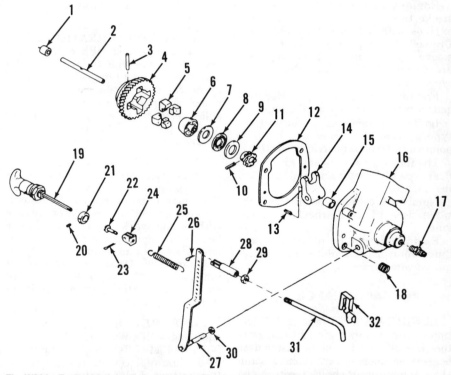

Fig. W304—Exploded view of governor unit. Bushing (1) is located in timing gear cover.

1. Bushing
2. Governor shaft
3. Roll pin
4. Gear
5. Flyweights
6. Thrust sleeve
7. Thrust bearing race
8. Thrust bearing
9. Thrust bearing race
10. Roll pin
11. Distributor drive gear
12. Gasket
13. Roll pin
14. Yoke
15. Bushing
16. Housing
17. Oil line fitting
18. Heli-coil insert
19. Speed control
20. Allen screw
21. Collar
22. Pin
23. Cotter pin
24. Link
25. Governor spring
26. Cotter pin
27. Governor lever
28. Connector
29. Locknut
30. "O" ring
31. Throttle rod
32. Clip

To check timing on variable speed engines, connect timing light and, with engine running at 3400 rpm, ignition should occur at 22° BTDC. See Fig. W307. To check timing on fixed speed engines, connect timing light and, with engine running at 1800 rpm, ignition should occur at 6° BTDC. See Fig. W307. Reach through access hole in front cover, loosen distributor clamp and rotate distributor as required to obtain desired ignition timing. Retighten clamp.

To install distributor, make certain number "1" cylinder is at top dead center on compression stroke. Position rotor on distributor shaft so center of rotor contact is about 5/8 inch (16 mm) from

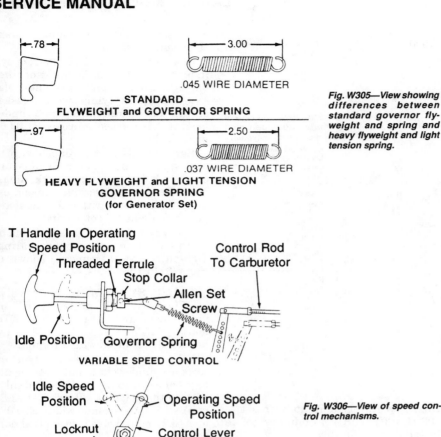

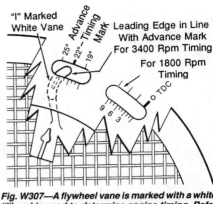

Fig. W307—A flywheel vane is marked with a white "I" and is used to determine engine timing. Refer to text.

Fig. W305—View showing differences between standard governor flyweight and spring and heavy flyweight and light tension spring.

Fig. W306—View of speed control mechanisms.

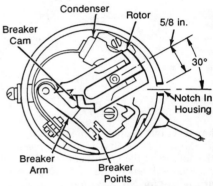

Fig. W308—Position distributor rotor as shown when installing distributor equipped with breaker points.

edge of notch in distributor housing as shown in Fig. W308. Install distributor in governor housing with rotor pointing at approximately 2 o'clock position and notch in distributor housing at 3 o'clock position as shown in Fig. W308. Rotate distributor housing counterclockwise until breaker points just begin to open. Tighten distributor clamp screw. Set final timing with timing light as previously outlined.

Breakerless Ignition System. Later models are equipped with a breakerless, battery ignition system. A magnet assembly is located in the distributor to send a trigger signal to the ignition control module.

Note that the black distributor wire is connected to the negative terminal of the ignition coil. If not equipped with a primary ballast resistor, the red or white wire is connected to the positive terminal of the ignition coil. If equipped with a primary ballast resistor and the resistor is not bypassed during starting, the red or white wire must be connected to ignition switch side of resistor. If equipped with a primary ballast resistor and the resistor is bypassed during starting, the red or white wire should be connected to ignition switch side of resistor.

Air gap between ignition module (7—Fig. W310) and magnet sleeve (6) should be 0.015-0.030 inch (0.38-0.76 mm). Loosen ignition module retaining screws and relocate module to obtain desired air gap.

To set timing, follow procedure outlined in previous section for engines equipped with breaker points.

To check ignition system, connect positive lead of a DC voltmeter to negative terminal of ignition coil and ground negative lead to engine. Detach high voltage lead from distributor cap and connect to engine ground. When engine is cranked, the voltmeter should indicate voltage fluctuations of approximately 1.5 volts to 11 volts. If voltmeter indicates a constant zero voltage, primary circuit is open; check connections and components. If voltmeter indicates a constant 1.0-3.5 volts, ignition module is shorted. If voltmeter indicates constant battery voltage, ignition module is open and must be renewed or replaced with a good unit.

Distributor shaft end play should be 0.001-0.015 inch (0.02-0.38 mm).

VALVE ADJUSTMENT. Engine must be at ambient temperature when checking valve tappet gap. Remove intake manifold and valve tappet chamber cover. Rotate crankshaft to position No. 1 piston at TDC on compression stroke. Use a feeler gauge to measure clearance between valve stem ends and tappets. Valve tappet gap for intake valve is 0.007 inch (0.18 mm) and ex-

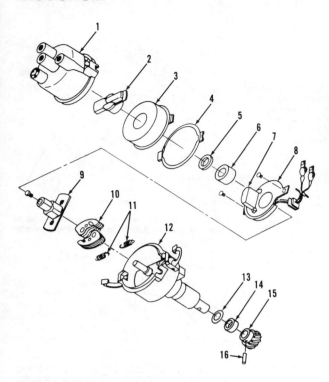

Fig. W310—Exploded view of distributor equipped with breakerless ignition system.

1. Distributor cap
2. Rotor
3. Cover
4. Gasket
5. Spacer
6. Magnet
7. Ignition module
8. Plate
9. Flange
10. Weights
11. Springs
12. Housing
13. Thrust washer
14. Spacer
15. Gear
16. Roll pin

Some screws serve as mounting stanchions for air shrouds.

Clean combustion deposits from cylinder head and check for cracks or other damage. Use a straightedge and feeler gauge to check cylinder head gasket surface for distortion. Renew cylinder head if it is warped in excess of 0.005 inch (0.13 mm).

Early models were equipped with 18 mm spark plugs. Later models are equipped with 14 mm spark plugs. Manufacturer does not recommend using cylinder heads with different spark plug hole diameters on engine.

A new cylinder head gasket should be installed to insure proper sealing. Tighten screws in sequence shown in Fig. W311 to 36 ft.-lbs. (41 N•m).

VALVE SYSTEM. Exhaust valve (6—Fig. W312) is identified by "EX" on valve head and intake valve (7) is marked "IN" on valve head. The exhaust valve is fitted with a rotator.

Valve seats are renewable-type inserts in cylinder block and seats should be ground to a 45° angle. Specified valve seat width is 0.057-0.072 inch (1.45-1.83 mm) with a maximum width of 0.087 inch (2.21 mm). Valve face angle should be 45°.

Specified intake valve stem diameter is 0.310-0.311 inch (7.87-7.90 mm). Intake valve stem clearance should be 0.001-0.003 inch (0.02-0.07 mm). Maximum allowable intake valve stem clearance is 0.005 inch (0.13 mm).

Exhaust valve stem is slightly tapered. Specified exhaust valve stem diameter is 0.308-0.309 inch (7.82-7.85 mm) at retainer end and 0.307-0.308 inch (7.80-7.82 mm) at head end. Exhaust valve stem clearance should be 0.003-0.005 inch (0.07-0.13 mm) at retainer end and 0.004-0.006 inch (0.10-0.15 mm) at head end. Maximum

---

haust valve tappet gap is 0.020 inch (0.51 mm). Note that intake valve is to the left in valve chamber opening and exhaust valve is to the right. Repeat the procedure for No. 2 cylinder.

Valve adjustment on all models is made by turning self-locking cap screw on tappet as required.

REPAIRS

TIGHTENING TORQUES. Recommended torque specifications are as follows:

Connecting rod	36 ft.-lbs. (41 N•m)
Cylinder head	36 ft.-lbs. (41 N•m)
Exhaust manifold	18 ft.-lbs. (24.5 N•m)
Flywheel	115 ft.-lbs. (156 N•m)
Gear cover	16-18 ft.-lbs. (22-24 N•m)
Intake manifold	18 ft.-lbs. (24.5 N•m)
Main bearing plate	31 ft.-lbs. (42 N•m)
Oil pan	18 ft.-lbs. (24.5 N•m)
Spark plug	18-22 ft.-lbs. (24.5-30 N•m)

FLYWHEEL. Flywheel is mounted on crankshaft taper. Use a suitable puller to remove flywheel. Flywheel should not be used if fins are damaged.

Flywheel ring gear is renewable. Carefully saw partially through ring gear, then split ring gear with a chisel.

Heat new ring gear in an oven set to 400° F (204° C) for 40 minutes before installation on flywheel.

Tighten flywheel retaining screw to 115 ft.-lbs. (156 N•m).

GOVERNOR. The governor unit (Fig. W304) is mounted on spacer plate (4—Fig. W316). Governor gear shaft (2—Fig. W304) rides in bushing (1) in timing gear cover. Governor and gear can be removed after unscrewing retaining screws. Governor components must operate freely without binding for proper operation.

Desired clearance between governor shaft and bushing is 0.0010-0.0024 inch (0.025-0.061 mm). Maximum allowable clearance is 0.0044 inch (0.112 mm). Specified governor shaft diameter is 0.4996-0.5000 inch (12.690-12.700 mm) with a wear limit of 0.4976 inch (12.640 mm). Specified governor shaft bushing inside diameter is 0.501-0.502 inch (12.72-12.75 mm) with a wear limit of 0.504 inch (12.80 mm).

Desired clearance between thrust sleeve (6—Fig. W304) and governor shaft is 0.0030-0.0054 inch (0.076-0.137 mm). Maximum allowable clearance is 0.0084 inch (0.213 mm). Specified thrust sleeve inside diameter is 0.503-0.505 inch (12.78-12.83 mm) with a wear limit of 0.508 inch (12.90 mm).

CYLINDER HEADS. When removing cylinder head, note location of cylinder head retaining screws so they can be reinstalled in their original positions.

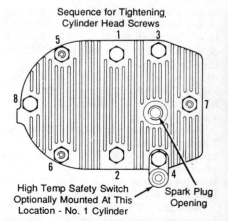

Fig. W311—Tighten cylinder head fasteners in sequence shown. Note location of high-temperature safety switch on models so equipped.

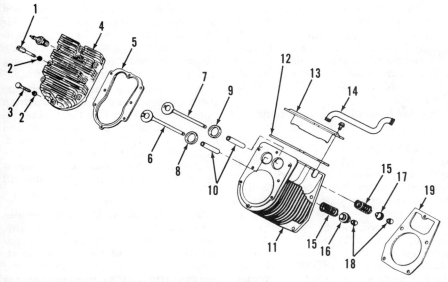

Fig. W312—Exploded view of cylinder and valve system.

1. Stud nut	6. Exhaust valve	11. Cylinder	15. Valve springs
2. Washer	7. Intake valve	12. Gasket	16. Rotator
3. Cap screw	8. Exhaust valve seat	13. Valve cover	17. Valve spring retainer
4. Cylinder head	9. Intake valve seat	& breather	18. Valve retainers
5. Gasket	10. Valve guides	14. Breather tube	19. Gasket

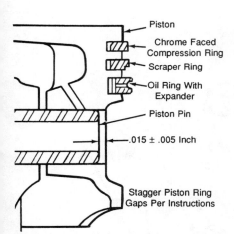

Fig. W313—View showing location and arrangement of piston rings.

3.7471-3.7475 inches (95.176-95.186 mm) for "B" piston. Measure piston diameter at a point 90° from piston pin at lower edge of piston skirt. Piston clearance in cylinder bore should be 0.0025-0.0035 inch (0.064-0.089 mm) for "A" piston and 0.0026-0.0034 inch (0.066-0.086 mm) for "B" piston.

Piston compression ring end gap should be 0.010-0.020 inch (0.25-0.51 mm). Ring side clearance in piston grooves should be 0.002-0.004 inch (0.05-0.10 mm) for top and second rings, and 0.0015-0.0035 inch (0.038-0.089 mm) for oil control ring.

Piston pin is a press fit in small end of connecting rod. Two sizes of piston pins are used as identified by a colored spot on pin boss of piston. Piston pin used in piston with green spot has a diameter of 0.8744-0.8745 inch (22.210-22.212 mm). Piston pin used in piston with red spot has a diameter of 0.8745-0.8746 inch (22.212-22.215 mm). Piston pin bore diameter in piston with green spot should be 0.87500-0.87515 inch (22.2250-22.2288 mm). Piston pin bore diameter in piston with red spot should be 0.87515-0.87530 inch (22.2288-22.2326 mm). Piston pin is not available separately from piston.

When installing piston and connecting rod, number stamped on side of rod must be toward camshaft (see Fig. W314) and number on rod must correspond with number stamped on side of rod cap. If rod is a replacement unit, refer to Fig. W315, note wide side of rod and location of bearing locating lugs and stamp appropriate cylinder number on correct side of rod and cap, then install rod. Tighten connecting rod nuts to 36 ft.-lbs. (41 N·m).

PISTON, PIN AND RINGS. Piston and connecting rod assemblies are removed from cylinder head end of block. Piston and connecting rod are accessible after removing cylinder head and oil pan.

Piston is equipped with three rings. Note location and arrangement of piston rings in Fig. W313. Pistons and rings are available in standard size as well as a variety of oversizes.

Standard pistons are marked with an "A" or "B" on piston crown. Specified piston diameter is 3.7465-3.7470 inches (95.161-95.174 mm) for "A" piston and

allowable exhaust valve stem clearance is 0.007 inch (0.18 mm).

Specified valve guide inside diameter is 0.312-0.313 inch (7.92-7.95 mm). Valves guides are renewable using Wisconsin tool DF72 or other suitable tool. If necessary, ream guide to obtain desired clearance.

Valve spring is same for both valves. Valve spring free length should be 2.040 inches (51.8 mm). Minimum allowable intake valve spring pressure, when compressed to 1.141 inches (29.0 mm), is 85 pounds (378 N).

Valve spring is a progressively wound-type (distance between coils varies end-to-end). Install valve spring so end with close-wound coils is toward spring seat.

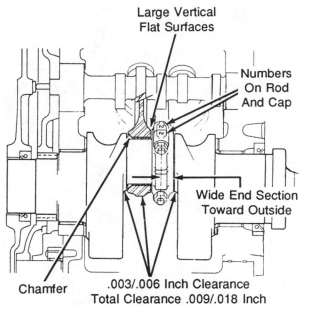

Fig. W314—Install connecting rods as shown above.

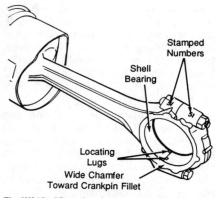

Fig. W315—View showing correct assembly of rod and cap.

CONNECTING ROD. Connecting rod and piston are removed from cylinder head end of block as an assembly. Piston and connecting rod are accessible after removing cylinder head and oil pan.

Connecting rods are equipped with renewable insert-type bearings. Rod bearing clearance should be 0.0011-0.0036 inch (0.028-0.091 mm). Undersize rod bearings are available to fit a reground crankpin. Connecting rod side play should be 0.009-0.018 inch (0.23-0.46 mm).

Assemble and install piston and rod as outlined in previous section.

CYLINDER. Cylinders are separate from crankcase and may be renewed as individual units. Note that cylinder is secured by four cylinder base retaining nuts and a cap screw located in the valve compartment.

Original equipment cylinders are marked with an "A" or "B" on top of cylinder near valve ports to match installed piston (see PISTON, PIN AND RINGS section). Specified bore diameter is 3.7495-3.7500 inches (95.237-95.250 mm) for "A" cylinder and 3.7501-3.7505 inches (95.252-95.263 mm) for "B" cylinder.

Cylinders for all models may be bored to accept an oversize piston. Cylinder bore should be resized if worn or out-of-round more than 0.005 inch (0.13 mm). Pistons are available in standard size and a variety of oversizes.

When installing cylinders, temporarily install intake manifold (handtighten manifold screws) before tightening cylinder retaining nuts so manifold and cylinders will be properly aligned. Tighten four cylinder retaining nuts to 47 ft.-lbs. (64 N•m) and retaining screw in valve compartment to 31 ft.-lbs. (42 N•m).

TIMING GEAR COVER. Besides functioning as a cover for the engine gear train, the electric starter, alternator stator and regulator-rectifier are attached to the timing gear cover. When removing timing gear cover, use care not to lose wear button (24—Fig. W316), plunger (25) or spring (26) in end of camshaft. Tighten timing gear cover screws to 16-18 ft.-lbs. (22-24 N•m).

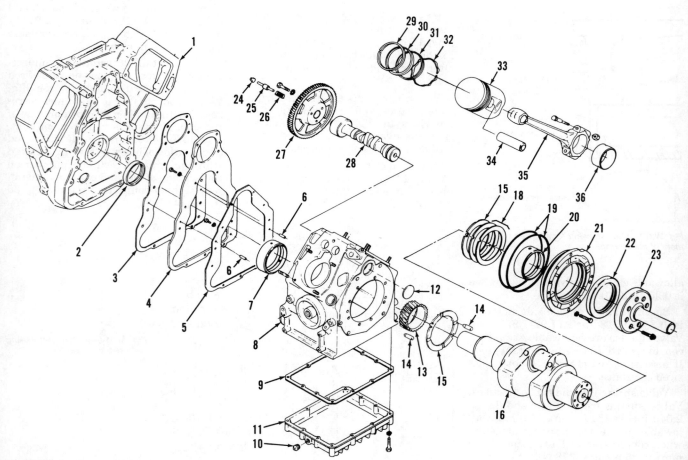

Fig. W316—Exploded view of engine.

1. Timing gear cover	13. Gear	26. Spring
2. Oil seal	14. Dowel pins	27. Gear
3. Gasket	15. Thrust washers	28. Camshaft
4. Spacer	16. Crankshaft	29. Top compression ring
5. Gasket	17. Shims	30. Second compression ring
6. Dowel pins	18. Shims	31. Oil control ring
7. Main bearing	19. "O" rings	32. Oil expander ring
8. Crankcase	20. Main bearing	33. Piston
9. Gasket	21. Main bearing plate	34. Piston pin
10. Drain plug	22. Oil seal	35. Connecting rod
11. Oil pan	23. Stub shaft	36. Bearing
12. Plug	24. Wear button	
	25. Plunger	

CAMSHAFT AND TAPPETS. The camshaft (28—Fig. W316) runs in un-bushed bores in crankcase casting. The camshaft can be removed after removing cylinders, tappets and timing gear cover. Mark tappets so they can be reinstalled in original position. Camshaft gear is held on end of camshaft by three cap screws (note that screw hole spacing is unequal). End play is controlled by a spring-loaded plunger assembly and a wear button that bears against timing gear cover. Use care not to lose wear button (24—Fig. W316), plunger (25) or spring (26) during disassembly and reassembly.

Specified tappet clearance in crankcase is 0.0003-0.0021 inch (0.008-0.053 mm) with a maximum allowable clearance of 0.003 inch (0.08 mm). Specified tappet diameter is 1.1237-1.1247 inches (28.542-28.567 mm). Specified tappet bore in crankcase is 1.1250-1.1258 inches (28.575-28.595 mm).

Camshaft bearing clearance at small end should be 0.0002-0.0036 inch (0.005-0.091 mm). Maximum allowable clearance is 0.0056 inch (0.142 mm). Specified camshaft bearing journal diameter at small end is 1.4974-1.4980 inches (38.034-38.050 mm). Specified camshaft small end bearing bore in crankcase is 1.500-1.501 inches (38.10-38.12 mm).

Camshaft bearing clearance at big end should be 0.0025-0.0044 inch (0.064-0.112 mm). Maximum allowable clearance is 0.0064 inch (0.163 mm). Specified camshaft bearing journal diameter at big end is 2.0593-2.0600 inches (52.306-52.324 mm). Specified camshaft big end bearing bore in crank-

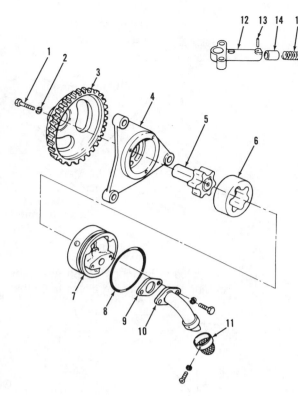

Fig. W318—Exploded view of oil pump. Relief valve body (12) is mounted on crankcase oil pan mounting flange.

1. Cap screw
2. Lockwasher
3. Gear
4. Oil pump housing
5. Inner rotor
6. Outer rotor
7. Cover
8. "O" ring
9. Gasket
10. Pickup tube
11. Screen
12. Relief valve body
13. Pin
14. Relief valve poppet
15. Spring

case is 2.0625-2.0637 inches (52.388-52.418 mm).

Be sure timing marks (1—Fig. W317) on camshaft and crankshaft gears are aligned when installing camshaft. Camshaft gear backlash should be 0.003-0.006 inch (0.08-0.15 mm).

OIL PUMP. The oil pump is mounted on the crankcase and driven by the crankshaft gear (see Fig. W317). The oil pump is accessible after removing the timing gear cover. Unscrew oil pump retaining screws to remove oil pump. The oil pressure relief valve is located on the oil pan mounting flange of the crankcase. Remove oil pan for access to relief valve.

Refer to Fig. W318 for exploded view of oil pump. Drive gear (3) is a press fit on inner rotor shaft (5).

Specified clearance between rotor tips is 0.004-0.006 inch (0.10-0.15 mm) with a maximum wear limit of 0.009 inch (0.23 mm). Specified clearance between housing bore and outer rotor is 0.0055-0.0105 inch (0.140-0.267 mm) with a wear limit of 0.0135 inch (0.343 mm). Housing bore diameter should be 2.2555-2.2575 inches (57.290-57.340 mm). Outer rotor outer diameter should be 2.2470-2.2500 inches (57.074-57.150 mm). Rotor thickness should be 0.6865-0.6875 (17.437-17.462 mm). Pump housing depth should be 0.6905-0.6925 inch (17.538-17.590 mm).

Specified clearance between oil pressure relief valve (14) and valve body (15) is 0.0015-0.0030 inch (0.038-0.076 mm) with a wear limit of 0.004 inch (0.10 mm). Relief valve diameter should be 0.4355-0.4360 inch (11.061-11.074 mm). Relief valve body inside diameter should be 0.4375-0.4385 inch (11.112-11.138 mm).

Relief valve spring free length should be 1.75 inches (44.4 mm). Relief valve spring pressure when compressed to 1.353 inches (34.37 mm) should be 5.55-6.75 pounds (24.7-30.0 N).

When assembling oil pump, press gear (3—Fig. W318) on inner rotor shaft (5) so shaft extends 0.060-0.070 inch (1.52-1.78 mm) past gear hub as shown in Fig. W319. Note arrows (see Fig. W320) on housing (4—Fig. W318) and cover (7). Arrows must point up as shown in Fig. W320 when pump is installed. Tighten cover (7—Fig. W318) retaining screws fingertight when installing cover on housing to allow alignment when installing pump on crankcase. Install oil pump on crankcase, then tighten cover retaining screws to 48 in.-lbs. (5.1 N·m). Tighten oil pump mounting screws to 108 in.-lbs. (12.2 N·m).

CRANKSHAFT. The crankshaft is supported at each end by sleeve-type bearings. Remove timing gear cover, governor, oil pump, pistons and connect-

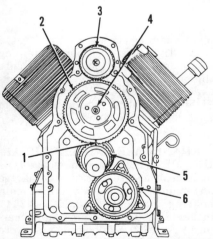

Fig. W317—View of gear train. Timing marks (1) must be aligned when assembling camshaft (4) and crankshaft (5). Governor gear (3) and oil pump gear (6) do not require timing.

1. Timing marks
2. Camshaft gear
3. Governor gear
4. Camshaft thrust plunger & spring
5. Crankshaft gear
6. Oil pump gear

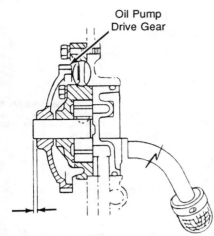

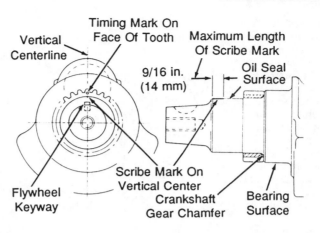

Fig. W321—Refer to text and above diagram when installing gear on crankshaft.

Fig. W319—Press gear on inner rotor shaft so shaft extends 0.060-0.070 inch (1.52-1.78 mm) past gear hub as shown above.

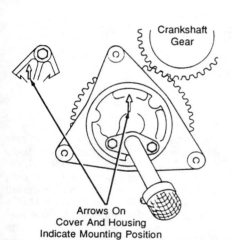

Fig. W320—Arrows on housing and cover must point up as shown when pump is installed.

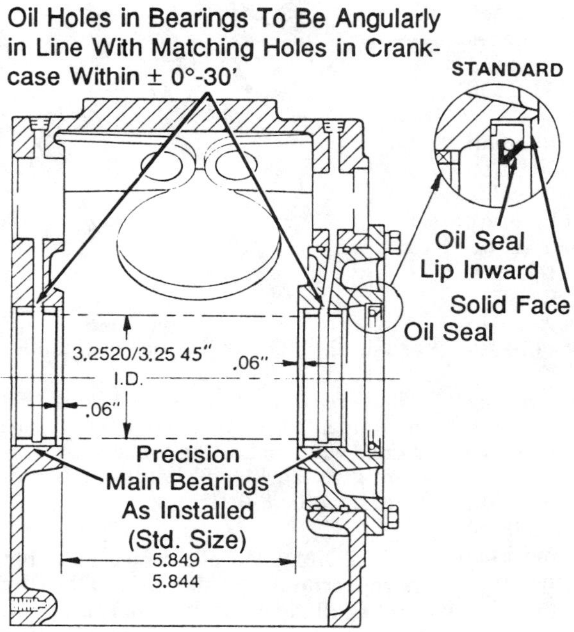

Oil Holes in Bearings To Be Angularly in Line With Matching Holes in Crankcase Within ± 0°-30'

Fig. W322—Refer to text and above diagram when installing main bearings in crankcase and main bearing plate.

ing rod, camshaft and spacer plate (4—Fig. W316). If so equipped, remove stub shaft (23)—if location of stub shaft keyway is critical for proper equipment coupling, mark stub shaft before removal. Unscrew bearing plate (21), then use threaded holes so jacking screws can be used to push bearing plate away from crankcase. Remove crankshaft.

Specified crankpin standard journal diameter is 2.099-2.100 inches (53.32-53.34 mm). Undersize rod bearings are available to fit a reground crankpin.

Specified main bearing clearance is 0.002-0.005 inch (0.05-0.13 mm) with a maximum of 0.006 inch (0.15 mm). Specified main bearing journal diameter is 3.2491-3.2500 inches (82.527-82.550 mm) with a wear limit of 3.2481 inches (82.502 mm). Main bearings that are 0.005 inch undersize are available to fit a reground crankshaft.

Thickness of thrust washers (15) should be 0.0928-0.0948 inch (2.357-2.408 mm).

Crankshaft gear can be removed by drilling holes in gear then splitting gear with a chisel. To install new gear, scribe a mark to indicate location of center of keyway as shown in Fig. W321 (mark must not extend into seal surface area). Press new gear onto crankshaft with chamfer toward crankshaft shoulder so center of one of the gear teeth is aligned with scribe mark. This should place gear tooth within 0.020 inch (0.51 mm) of centerline of crankpin. Make indentation on gear tooth to serve as timing mark.

Crankshaft end play should be 0.005-0.012 inch (0.13-0.30 mm) and is adjusted using shims (18—Fig. W316). Reverse disassembly procedure to install crankshaft. Tighten main bearing

plate retaining screws to 31 ft.-lbs. (42 N·m). Tighten spacer plate retaining screws to 18 ft.-lbs. (24.5 N·m). Be sure timing marks (1—Fig. W317) on camshaft and crankshaft gears are aligned. Tighten stub shaft retaining screws to 24 ft.-lbs. (32.6 N·m).

CRANKCASE AND MAIN BEARING PLATE. Precision sleeve-type main bearings are located in crankcase and main bearing plate. Specified main bearing diameter is 3.2520-3.2541 inches (82.600-82.654 mm). Main bearings that are 0.005 inch undersize are available to fit a reground crankshaft.

Oil holes in main bearing and oil holes in crankcase and main bearing plate must be aligned (see Fig. W322). End of main bearing should be approximately 0.06 inch (1.5 mm) from inner

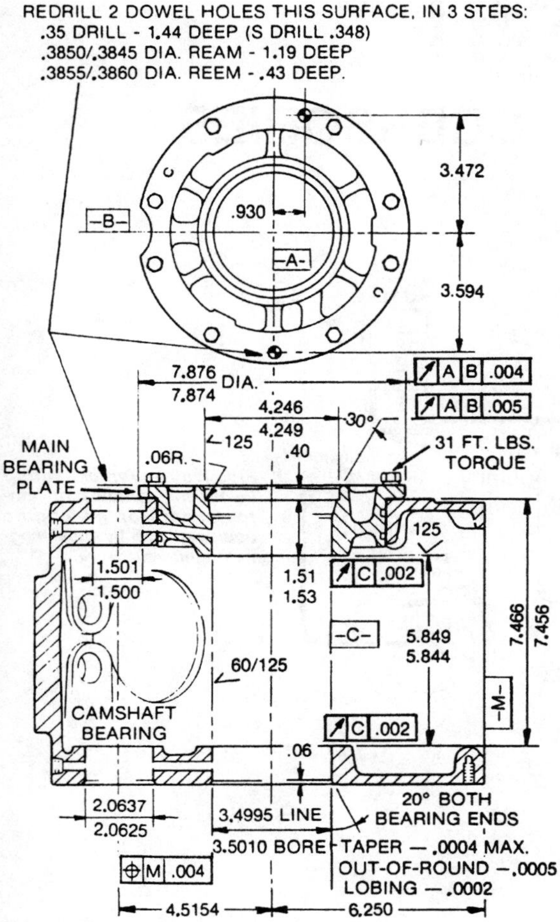

REDRILL 2 DOWEL HOLES THIS SURFACE, IN 3 STEPS:
  .35 DRILL - 1.44 DEEP (S DRILL .348)
  .3850/.3845 DIA. REAM - 1.19 DEEP
  .3855/.3860 DIA. REEM - .43 DEEP.

Fig. W323—A replacement unfinished main bearing plate must be machined to dimensions indicated in diagram. See text.

face of crankcase or main bearing plate as shown in Fig. W322

Oil seal lip of main bearing plate oil seal should face toward crankcase unless engine is equipped with an oil-operated clutch, in which case, oil seal lip should face away from engine.

Replacement main bearing plate is available only as an unfinished unit. To install replacement main bearing plate, prepare dowel holes in crankcase in three steps indicated in Fig. W323 to drill and ream for new dowel pins. Machine new main bearing plate using dimensions and specifications indicated in Fig. W 323.

FLYWHEEL ALTERNATOR. The flywheel alternator stator is attached to the inside of the timing gear cover. Refer to SERVICING WISCONSIN accessories section for service information. If alternator stator is removed, apply Loctite to screws when reinstalling alternator stator and tighten screws to 18 in.-lbs. (2.0 N•m).

WISCONSIN

SERVICING WISCONSIN ACCESSORIES

12-VOLT MOTOR-GENERATOR

A combination motor-generator, manufactured by Delco-Remy, is used on some Wisconsin engines. The motor-generator functions as a cranking motor when starting switch is closed. When engine is operating, and with starting switch open, unit operates as a generator. Generator output and circuit voltage for battery and various operating requirements are controlled by a current voltage regulator. See Figs. W501, W502 and W503.

Motor-generator belt tension should be adjusted until about 10 pounds (45 N) pressure applied midway between pulleys will deflect belt ½ inch (12.7 mm).

To determine cause of abnormal operation, motor-generator should be given a no-load test or a generator output test. Generator output test can be performed with motor-generator on or off engine. No-load test must be made with motor-generator removed from engine. Refer to Fig. W504 for exploded view of a typical motor-generator assembly. Parts are available from Wisconsin as well as Delco-Remy parts suppliers.

Motor-generator and regulator service test specifications are as follows:

Motor-Generator 1101696

Brush spring tension, oz. 22-26
Field draw:
  Amperes. 1.43-1.54
  Volts. 12
Cold output:
  Amperes. 10
  Volts. 14
  Rpm 5750
No-load test:
  Volts. 11
  Amperes, max 17
  Rpm, min 2350
  Rpm, max 2850

Motor-Generator 1101870

Brush spring tension, oz. 22-26
Field draw:
  Amperes. 1.52-1.62
  Volts. 12
Cold output:
  Amperes. 12
  Volts. 14
  Rpm 4950
No-load test:
  Volts. 11

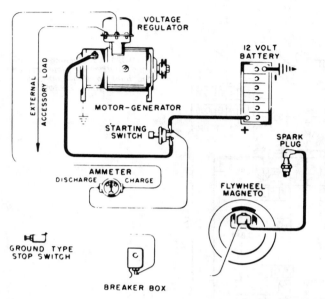

Fig. W501—Typical wiring layout for combination motor-generator on engine equipped with flywheel magneto ignition.

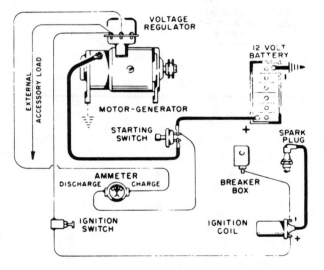

Fig. W502—Typical wiring layout for combination motor-generator on engine equipped with battery ignition.

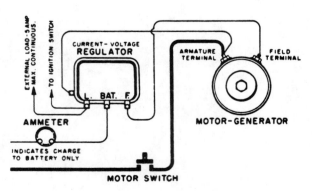

Fig. W503—Wiring connection for current voltage regulator used with motor-generator.

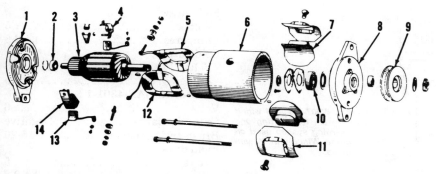

Fig. W504—Exploded view of Delco-Remy motor-generator.

1. End frame
2. Bearing
3. Armature
4. Ground brush holder
5. Field coil (L.H.)
6. Frame
7. Pole shoe
8. End frame
9. Pulley
10. Bearing
11. Field coil insulator
12. Field coil (R.H.)
13. Brush
14. Insulated brush holder

Amperes, max	18
Rpm, min	2500
Rpm, max	2900

Motor-Generators 1101871 & 1101972

Brush spring tension, oz.	24-32
Field draw:	
Amperes	1.43-1.54
Volts	12
Cold output:	
Amperes	10
Volts	14
Rpm	5450
No-load test:	
Volts	11
Amperes, max	17
Rpm, min	2500
Rpm, max	3000

Regulators 1118791 & 1118985

Ground polarity	Positive
Cut-out relay:	
Air gap	0.020 in. (0.51 mm)
Point gap	0.020 in. (0.51 mm)
Closing voltage, range	11.8-14.0
Adjust to	12.8
Voltage regulator:	
Air gap	0.075 in. (1.90 mm)
Setting voltage, range	13.6-14.5
Adjust to	14.0

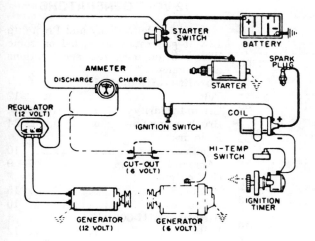

Fig. W505—Typical wiring diagram for starting and charging system used on some Wisconsin single-cylinder engines.

Regulators 1118983 & 1118984

Ground polarity	Negative
Cut-out relay:	
Air gap	0.020 in. (0.51 mm)
Point gap	0.020 in. (0.51 mm)
Closing voltage, range	11.8-14.0
Adjust to	12.8
Voltage regulator:	
Air gap	0.075 in. (1.90 mm)
Setting voltage, range	13.6-14.5
Adjust to	14.0

6-VOLT STARTER MOTORS

Autolite and Prestolite 6-volt starter motors are used on some Wisconsin engines. See Figs. W505 and W506. Test specifications are as follows:

Autolite MZ-4118, MZ-4175 & MZ-4184

Volts	6
Brush spring tension, oz.	42-53
No-load test:	
Volts	5
Amperes	68
Rpm	4000

Autolite MAK-4008

Volts	6

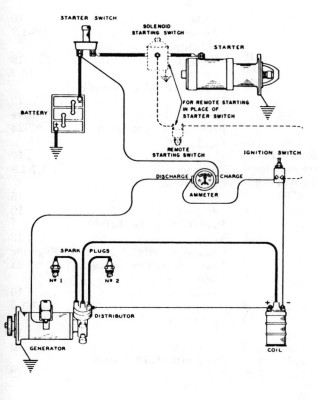

Fig. W506—Typical wiring diagram for starting and charging system used on some Wisconsin two-cylinder engines. Note distributor mounting on rear of gear-driven alternator.

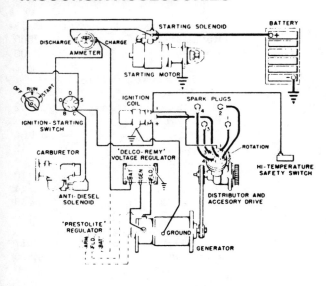

Fig. W507—Typical wiring diagram for starting and charging system used on some Wisconsin V4 engines.

Field draw:
Volts 5
Amperes 3.4-3.8
Cold output:
Volts 8
Amperes 12.5
Prestolite GAS-4301-1
Volts 6
Ground polarity . . . . Negative
Brush spring tension, oz. 15-20
Field draw:
Volts 5
Amperes 3.4-3.8
Cold output:
Volts 8
Amperes 7.1

12-VOLT GENERATORS

Autolite, Delco-Remy and Prestolite 12-volt generators are used on some Wisconsin engines. Test specifications are as follows:
Autolite GJG-4001-M
Volts 12
Ground polarity . . . . Negative
Brush spring tension, oz. 12-24
Field draw:
Volts 10
Amperes 1.7-1.9
Cold output:
Volts 15
Amperes 10
Autolite GHH-6001-F
Volts 12
Ground polarity . . . . Positive
Brush spring tension, oz. 26-46
Field draw:
Volts 10
Amperes 1.6-1.7
Cold output:
Volts 15
Amperes 14.7
Prestolite GJG-4001-MP
Volts 12
Ground polarity . . . . Positive
Brush spring tension, oz. 12-24
Field draw:
Volts 10
Amperes 1.7-1.9
Cold output:
Volts 15
Amperes 10
Prestolite GJG-4010-M
Volts 12
Ground polarity . . . . Negative
Brush spring tension, oz. 12-24
Field draw:
Volts 10
Amperes 1.7-1.9
Cold output:
Volts 15
Amperes 10
Prestolite GJY-7401-S
Volts 12

Brush spring tension, oz. 38-61
No-load test:
Volts 4
Amperes 70
Rpm 4700
Autolite MDH-4001M
Volts 6
Brush spring tension, oz. 42-66
No-load test:
Volts 5
Amperes 52
Rpm 8100
Prestolite MZ-4213
Volts 6
Brush spring tension, oz. 42-53
No-load test:
Volts 5.5
Amperes 60
Rpm 5000

12-VOLT STARTER MOTORS

Autolite, Delco-Remy and Prestolite 12-volt starters are used on some Wisconsin engines. See Fig. W507. Test specifications are as follows:
Autolite MDH-4002M
Volts 12
Brush spring tension, oz. 42-66
No-load test:
Volts 10
Amperes 38
Rpm 10,000
Autolite MDL-6001
Volts 12
Brush spring tension, oz. 52-65
No-load test:
Volts 10
Amperes 100
Rpm 4700
Autolite MDL-6011
Volts 12
Brush spring tension, oz. 31-47
No-load test:
Volts 10

Amperes 60
Rpm 3200
Delco-Remy 1107246
Volts 12
Brush spring tension, oz. 35
No-load test:
Volts 10.3
Amperes 75
Rpm 6900
Prestolite MBG-4140
Volts 12
Brush spring tension, oz 42-53
No-load test:
Volts 10
Amperes 55
Rpm 5200
Prestolite MDY-7006
Volts 12
Brush spring tension, oz. 42-53
No-load test:
Volts 10
Amperes 60
Rpm 4200

6-VOLT GENERATORS

Autolite and Prestolite 6-volt generators are used on some Wisconsin engines. Test specifications are as follows:
Autolite GAS-4301, GAS-4302, GAS-4303, GAS-4305 & GAS-4306
Volts 6
Ground polarity . . . . Positive
Brush spring tension, oz. 15-20
Field draw:
Volts 5
Amperes 3.4-3.8
Cold output:
Volts 8
Amperes 12.5
Autolite GAS-4177
Volts 6
Ground polarity . . . . Negative
Brush spring tension, oz. 15-20

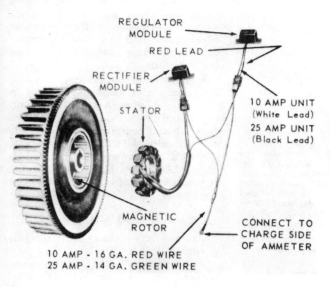

Fig. W508—View of 10-amp or 25-amp flywheel alternator charging system used on some engines. Note separate regulator and rectifier modules.

10 AMP - 16 GA. RED WIRE
25 AMP - 14 GA. GREEN WIRE

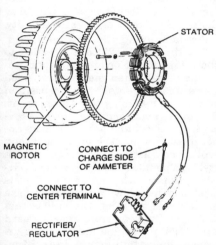

Fig. W509—View of 30-amp flywheel alternator charging system used on some engines. Note one-piece regulator-rectifier module.

Ground polarity............ Positive
Brush spring tension, oz. 35-53
Field draw:
  Volts........................ 10
  Amperes............... 1.53-1.70
Cold output:
  Volts........................ 15
  Amperes................... 17

Prestolite GJY-7401-SN
Volts........................ 12
Ground polarity.......... Negative
Brush spring tension, oz. 35-53
Field draw:
  Volts........................ 10
  Amperes............... 1.53-1.70
Cold output:
  Volts........................ 15
  Amperes................... 17

Delco-Remy 1102225
Volts........................ 12
Ground polarity.......... Positive
Brush spring tension, oz. 28

Field draw:
  Volts...................... 12
  Amperes 1.67-1.79
Cold output:
  Volts...................... 14
  Amperes 17

Delco-Remy 1102343
Volts...................... 12
Ground polarity .... Negative
Brush spring tension, oz........ 28
Field draw:
  Volts...................... 12
  Amperes 1.67-1.79
Cold output:
  Volts...................... 14
  Amperes 17

FLYWHEEL ALTERNATOR

Beginning with serial number 5188288, some Wisconsin engines may be equipped with a 10, 25 or 30-amp flywheel alternator. See Figs. W508 and

W509. To avoid possible damage to alternator system, the following precautions must be observed:

1. Negative post of battery must be connected to ground on engine.

2. Connect booster battery properly (positive to positive and negative to negative.)

3. Do not attempt to polarize alternator.

4. Do not ground any wires from stator or modules that terminate at connectors.

5. Do not operate engine with battery disconnected or disconnect alternator output lead while engine is running.

6. Disconnect battery cables when charging battery with a battery charger.

OPERATION. Alternating current (AC) produced by alternator is changed to direct current (DC) in rectifier module, or regulator-rectifier module on 30-amp system. See Figs. W510, W511 and W512. Current regulation is provided by regulator module, or regulator-rectifier module on 30-amp system, that senses countervoltage created by battery to control or limit charging rate. No adjustments are possible on alternator charging system. Faulty components must be renewed. Refer to following troubleshooting paragraph to help determine faulty component.

TROUBLESHOOTING. Malfunctions and their possible causes are as follows:

1. Full charge—no regulation. Could be caused by:
  a. Faulty regulator
  b. Defective battery
2. Low or no charge. Could be caused by:
  a. Faulty windings in stator

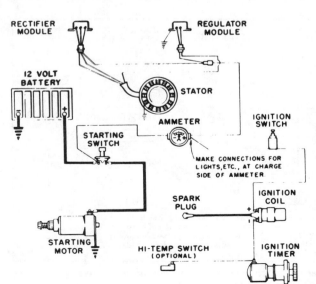

Fig. W510—Typical wiring diagram for ignition, starting and alternator charging systems used on some single-cylinder engines with 10-amp or 25-amp alternator.

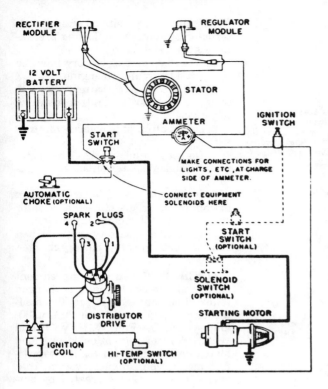

Fig. W511—Typical wiring diagram for ignition, starting and alternator charging systems used on some four-cylinder engines with 10-amp or 25-amp alternator. Wiring diagram for two-cylinder engines is similar.

either of the voltage readings is zero, or there is more than 10 percent difference between readings, stator is faulty and should be renewed.

To check stator on 30-amp systems, disconnect stator wires and connect an AC voltmeter between stator leads. Run engine and check voltmeter readings. Stator should produce (within 10 percent): 22 volts at 1600 rpm, 33 volts at 2400 rpm, 39 volts at 2800 rpm and 50 volts at 3600 rpm. If voltage readings are incorrect, stator is faulty and should be renewed.

CLUTCH

A wide variety of clutches are used on Wisconsin engines. By type, they may be wet (running in oil) or dry plate equipped and of either single or multiple disc design. Units in use are manufactured by Rockford or Twin Disc. Contact Wisconsin for parts availability.

Accompanying illustrations (Figs. W513 through W522) are intended to show adjustment points and work procedures, and when feasible, exploded views of components so relative position of parts in assembly will be apparent. Because so many engine models are covered, specific clutch parts numbers are not identified for each one, but rather, typical characteristics of each clutch style are pointed out. For practical purposes, appearance and shape of parts used is identical, with dimensions (size measurements) being the only actual difference between clutch models used with separate engine models. It is extremely important **exact identification** be taken from specification plates and tags when ordering parts.

Following are accepted principles pertaining to service for manually operated overcenter clutches:

1. Do not allow a new clutch to slip when engaged under load. Several early

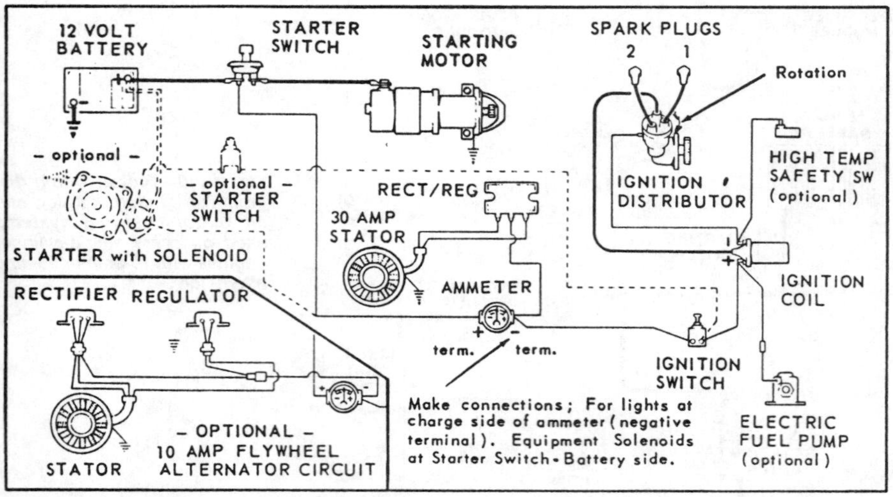

b. Faulty rectifier

c. Regulator not properly grounded or regulator defective

If "full charge—no regulation" is the problem, use a DC voltmeter and check battery voltage with engine operating at full rpm. If battery voltage is over 13.5 volts, regulator is not functioning properly. Replace regulator with a new or known good unit and recheck system.

If "low" or "no charge" is the problem, check battery voltage with engine operating at full rpm. If battery is fully charged, place a load on battery to reduce voltage. If charge rate increases, alternator system is functioning properly. If charge rate does not increase, replace regulator with a new or known good unit and recheck system. If charge rate increases on 30-amp system, regulator-rectifier was faulty. If charge rate does not increase on 10-amp or 25-amp system, replace rectifier with a new or known good unit and recheck system. If charge rate does not increase on any system when regulator, rectifier or regulator-rectifier was changed, check alternator stator.

To check stator on 10-amp and 25-amp systems, disconnect stator wires and connect an AC voltmeter to stator leads and ground. Run engine at 2400 rpm and check stator output voltage between each stator lead and ground. If

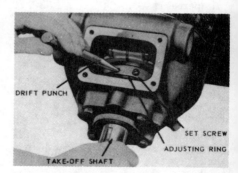

Fig. W513—Adjustment procedure for Twin Disc multiple-disc-type clutch. This clutch runs in oil of same grade as used in engine crankcase. With inspection cover removed and set screw loosened, use a punch as shown to turn adjusting ring while holding output shaft from turning. Clutch will engage with a slight snap over center when engaged if adjustment is correct. See Fig. W514.

Fig. W512—Typical wiring diagram for ignition, starting and alternator charging systems used on some two-cylinder engines with 30-amp alternator.

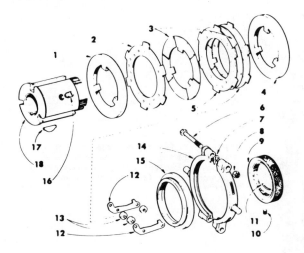

Fig. W514—Exploded view of Twin Disc clutch hub and disc assemblies. All parts are serviced. Collar assembly (14) may be bronze or die cast material. Key (17) comes in three styles. Furnish full details and order parts with care.

1. Back clamping plate
2. Sintered drive plate
3. Steel driven plates
4. Front clamp plate
5. Sintered drive plates
6. Cap screw (2)
7. Shim (2)
8. Locknut (2)
9. Adjusting ring
10. Adjuster set screw
11. Lock spring
12. Lever (6 used)
13. Lever rollers (9)
14. Collar assy.
15. Wedge sleeve
16. Hub set screw
17. Key
18. Hub

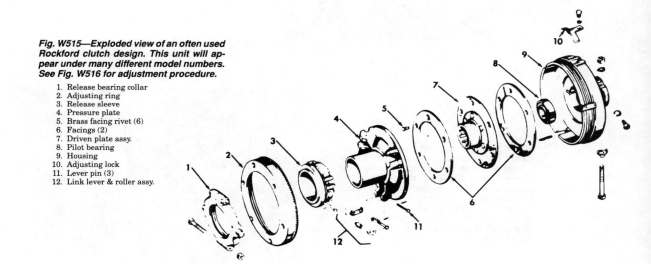

Fig. W515—Exploded view of an often used Rockford clutch design. This unit will appear under many different model numbers. See Fig. W516 for adjustment procedure.

1. Release bearing collar
2. Adjusting ring
3. Release sleeve
4. Pressure plate
5. Brass facing rivet (6)
6. Facings (2)
7. Driven plate assy.
8. Pilot bearing
9. Housing
10. Adjusting lock
11. Lever pin (3)
12. Link lever & roller assy.

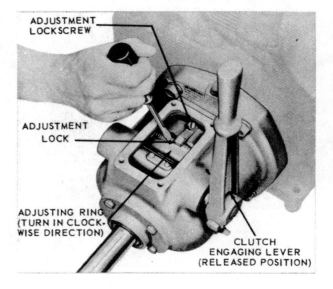

Fig. W516—Typical adjustment of clutch shown in Fig. W515. This Rockford clutch runs in oil. Oil level check plug is just below clutch lever. Loosen adjustment lock screw one turn and, while holding to prevent rotation, turn adjusting ring a notch at a time until firm pressure is required to pull lever back to engaged position with a distinct over center snap. On some models, adjustment lock is T-shaped and a pipe plug must be removed for access to its lock screw.

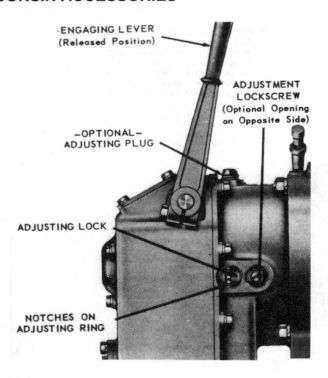

Fig. W517—View to show alternate adjustment access points when same clutch as shown in Figs. W515 and W516 is used with reduction gears. Technique for adjustment is the same.

Fig. W518—One type of Rockford dry pto clutch used on heavy-duty engines. Visible grease fitting is used to lubricate housing bearing every 50 hours. Other fitting (not shown) at left of inspection plate is for daily greasing of throwout bearing. Clutch adjusts similarly to other models: Release lock screw from adjustment lock and tighten adjusting ring until firm pressure is required to engage clutch over center.

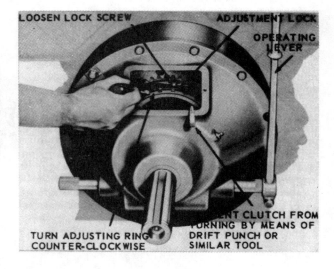

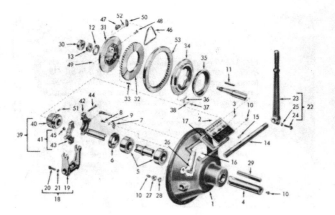

Fig. W519—Exploded view of clutch shown in Fig. W518.

1. Housing		31. Clutch body	
2. Specification plate		32. Facing	
4. Output shaft		33. Separator spring	
5. Main bearings		34. Pressure plate	
6. Bearing retainer		35. Adjusting ring	
7. Lock plate		36. Adjustment lock	
11. Key		37. Lock screw	
14. Yoke shaft		39. Release sleeve	
15. Woodruff key		41. Release bearing	
17. Gasket		46. Lever spring set	
18. Yoke assy.		47. Lever (3)	
22. Lever assy.		48. Pin (3)	
26. Grease tube		50. Lever link (6)	
29. Shaft key		53. Driving ring	
30. Pilot bearing			

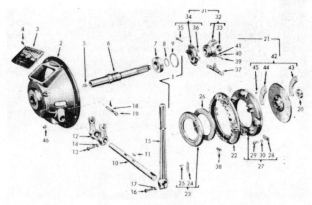

Fig. W520—Another Rockford dry pto clutch design used on some models. Note different style pressure plate (27), facings and disc (42) and sleeve and bearing (31). On this model, adjusting lock (24) must be disengaged from notches in back plate (22) so adjusting ring (23) can be turned.

2. Housing	12. Yoke
3. Instruction plate	15. Lever
6. Shaft	20. Pilot bearing
7. Bearing	21. Clutch assy. (22-45)
8. Snap ring	22. Back plate
9. Snap ring	23. Adjusting ring
10. Yoke shaft	24. Adjusting lock
11. Key	26. Adjusting ring plate

27. Pressure plate assy.
32. Sleeve assy.
34. Release bearing
37. Camshaft assy.
38. Return spring (4)
39. Lever pin (2)
42. Driven plate assy.

adjustments may be necessary if clutch begins to slip during break-in period.

2. Wet-type clutches must have oil level maintained in housing. This oil is an essential cooling medium to prevent destruction of friction surfaces. Observe service instructions printed on specification plates.

3. Dry clutches require scheduled lubrication at grease fittings mounted in clutch bell housings. One fitting is for outer bearing (output shaft) in housing and should be serviced after every 50 hours of operation. Throwout (release)

bearing should be lubricated daily. Units manufactured by Twin Disc have an external fitting for throwout bearing. Rockford clutches have an inspection plate (marked) that must be removed for access to throwout bearing grease fitting.

4. In event of poor performance, lack of power or undue vibration from power unit, do no overlook the possibility of a faulty clutch. These clutches are extremely rugged, but neglect or lack of routine maintenance may cause problems. Check for looseness or leakage at

output shaft and remove inspection plate to examine clutch body and linkage for defects or damage.

REDUCTION GEARS

Reduction gear sets in a wide choice of ratios are offered for most Wisconsin models. Some are furnished with manually operated clutches as shown in Fig. W522, and others, as in Fig. W523, are coupled to and driven directly from engine crankshaft. Some reduction gear sets are lubricated from an oil supply

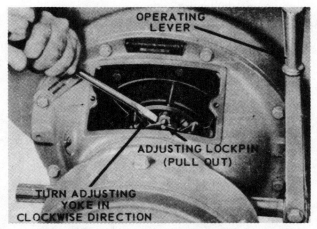

Fig. W521—Heavy-duty dry Twin Disc clutch used on some models. To adjust, pull lock pin out as shown and hold by inserting a piece of 1/16-inch (1.6 mm) wire through hole in pin. With lock pin so disengaged, turn yoke to increase pressure on operating lever as required for firm clutch action. Remove wire after adjusting and shift yoke slightly so lock pin can snap back into one of the holes in floating plate. Also see Fig. W522.

stored within their own housing and others share oil supply from engine crankcase. Units with separate oil supply call for use of high grade gear oil of SAE 90 or SAE 110 grade. Seasonal requirements for changes in engine oil viscosity determine weight of oil used for gear sets that share a common oil supply with engines. Gear oil should be

changed when warm, observing 200-hour service intervals.

Many of the reduction gear combinations offered may be mounted with output shaft at a position left, right, above or below engine crankshaft or clutch pto centerline. For this reason, several pipe plugs are fitted into outer circumference of gearcase for convenience in draining

and filling and for checking lube level in housing.

Printed specifications come with every reduction unit manufactured, usually on a metal tag or on the inspection plate. Be sure to check for lubrication instructions and for identification by number when ordering parts.

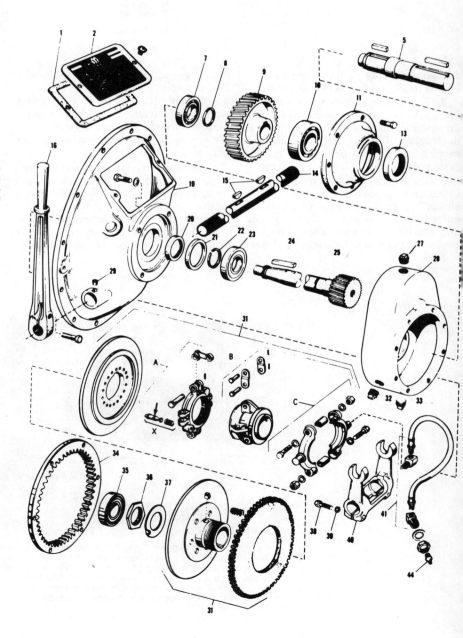

Fig. W522—Exploded view of Twin Disc dry clutch of design shown in Fig. W521 fitted with reduction gears. Note adjusting yoke (31A). Note hole (arrow) in lock pin (X) and circle of holes in floating plate for entry of lock pin.

2.	Specification plate
5.	Counter shaft
7.	Ball bearing
8.	Snap ring
9.	Reduction gear
10.	Ball bearing
11.	Cover plate
13.	Shaft seal
14.	Operating shaft
15.	Yoke keys
16.	Levers
19.	Clutch housing
20.	Shaft oil seal
21.	Bearing spacer
22.	Snap ring
23.	Shaft bearing
25.	Clutch shaft
27.	Lube plug (filler)
31.	Clutch assy.
31A.	Adjusting yoke assy.
31B.	Sleeve assy.
31C.	Split collar assy.
31X.	Adjusting lock pin
32.	Lube level plug
33.	Lube drain plug
34.	Driving ring
35.	Pilot bearing
36.	Hub nut
37.	Hub lockwasher
40.	Throwout yoke
41.	Grease tube assy.

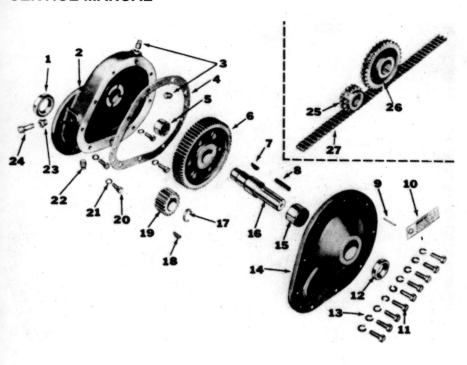

Fig. W523—Exploded view of typical reduction gear set used with some Wisconsin engines. Inset shows chain-sprocket arrangement that may be used in some cases instead of spur gears shown.

1. Oil seal
2. Main housing
3. Pipe plugs
4. Cover gasket
5. Inner bearing
6. Driven gear
7. Woodruff key
8. Square key
9. Cover pin
10. Specification tag
11. Cap screws
12. Oil seal
13. Lockwashers
14. Cover
15. Outer bearing
16. Output shaft
17. Drive gear retainer
18. Woodruff key
19. Drive gear (pinion)
20. Housing screw
21. Lockwasher
22. Drain plug
23. Reducer bushing
24. Breather (vent)
25. Drive sprocket
26. Driven sprocket
27. Drive chain

NOTES

NOTES

NOTES

NOTES

NOTES

NOTES

NOTES